The

CHELSEA HOUSE LIBRARY
of LITERARY CRITICISM

The CHELSEA HOUSE LIBRARY of LITERARY CRITICISM

TWENTIETH-CENTURY BRITISH LITERATURE

Volume 1

General Editor

HAROLD BLOOM

1985
CHELSEA HOUSE PUBLISHERS
New York

MANAGING EDITOR
Sally Stepanek
ASSOCIATE EDITORS
Brendan Bernhard
S. T. Joshi
Jack Lechner
Frank Menchaca
Julia Myer
Patrick Nielsen Hayden
James Uebbing
Anna Williams
EDITORIAL COORDINATOR
Karyn Browne
EDITORIAL STAFF
Linda Grossman
Joy Johannessen
Karin Thomsen
RESEARCH
Marena Fisher
Debbie Keates
Kevin Pask
Cornelia Pearsall
Marijke Rijsberman
DESIGN
Susan Lusk

Printed and bound in the United States of
America.

Library of Congress Cataloging in Publication
Data
Twentieth-century British literature.
    (The Chelsea House library of literary
    criticism)
    Bibliography: p.
    1. English literature—20th century—
    History and criticism—Collected works.
    2. Authors, English—20th century—
    Biography—Dictionaries. 3. Criticism—
    United States. Bloom, Harold.
    II. Series.
    PR473.T84   1985   820'.9'0091
84-27428
    ISBN 0-87754-809-9 (v. 1)

CHELSEA HOUSE PUBLISHERS
Harold Steinberg, Chairman & Publisher
Susan Lusk, Vice President
A Division of Chelsea House Educational
    Communications, Inc.
133 Christopher Street, New York, NY 10014

CONTENTS

ABBREVIATIONS

AcL	Academy and Literature		*Mot*	Motive
Am	America		MR	Minnesota Review
AR	American Review		NA	Nation and Atheneum
AS	American Scholar		*NEW*	New English Weekly
At	Atlantic Monthly		*Nwk*	Newsweek
BkmL	Bookman (London)		NR	New Republic
BUSE	Boston University Studies in English		NS	New Statesman
CJ	Conjunctions		NSN	New Statesman and Nation
CM	Cambridge Magazine			(later Statesman and Nation)
Cmty	Commentary		NY	New Yorker
CoL	Contemporary Literature		NYRB	New York Review of Books
Com	Commonweal		NYT	New York Times
CQ	Critical Quarterly		NYTBR	New York Times Book Review
Crit	Criticism		*OxM*	Oxford Magazine
Critn	Criterion		*Parn*	Parnassus: Poetry in Review
Crt	Critique		*PoR*	Poetry Review
DM	Dublin Magazine		PP	Plays and Players
EC	Essays in Criticism		PR	Partisan Review
Enc	Encounter		QQ	Queen's Quarterly
ES	Essays and Studies		*Rep*	Reporter
ESRS	Emporia State Research Studies		SFS	Science-Fiction Studies
Exp	Experiment		SLI	Studies in Literary Imagination
F&SF	Fantasy and Science Fiction		SN	Studies in the Novel
FR	Fortnightly Review		*Spec*	Spectator
FrR	French Review		SR	Saturday Review
HdR	Hudson Review		SRL	Saturday Review (London)
Hib	Hibernia		*SwR*	Sewanee Review
JML	Journal of Modern Literature		TC	Twentieth Century
LL	Life and Letters		TDR	Tulane Drama Review
LM	London Mercury			(later Drama Review)
Lon	London Magazine		*ThQ*	Theatre Quarterly
LR	Literary Review		TLS	Times Literary Supplement
LST	Listen		TSL	Tennessee Studies in Literature
LT	Listener		WG	Westminster Gazette
MD	Modern Drama		YFS	Yale French Studies
MFS	Modern Fiction Studies		YR	Yale Review
MG	Manchester Guardian			

PREFACE

The Chelsea House Library of Literary Criticism is designed to present a concise portrait of the critical heritage of every crucial British and American author. In thirty-seven volumes, the *Library* covers the entire range of British and American literature, from *Beowulf* and the earliest medieval epics to the work of such contemporary innovators as Thomas Pynchon. The five volumes of *Twentieth-Century British Literature* contain criticism of modern authors from the United Kingdom and its former colonies, the first volume covering authors from A through D.

The twentieth century has been characterized by the challenging of accepted ideas concerning the art of interpretation. To represent the growing multiplicity of critical schools and styles, consequently, is as difficult as it is necessary. In *Twentieth-Century British Literature* the editors have sought to provide the most representative essays and reviews of the modern era. In publishing critical responses to the work of each author, we have chosen material from a variety of sources—magazines, scholarly journals, and book-length studies.

As for the organization of the chapters, most are divided into two sections, extracts and essays. We have grouped the extracts into *Personal*, *General*, and *Works* categories; these sections embody material such as passages from memoirs, interviews, and biographies, short theoretical statements, and reviews of individual works. The essay sections are reserved for more extensive and in-depth studies of the authors and their works. Although most of the criticism is arranged chronologically, we have occasionally juxtaposed early and late reviews in order to highlight the critical dialogue.

Each entry contains an up-to-date, brief biography of the author. A list of additional reading on all authors covered concludes each volume, providing the reader with a thoughtful selection of material for further research. We have preserved original footnotes in the essay sections and have omitted page references within the text if the original edition has not been cited. We have also preserved the original style of each critic, retaining British spellings and punctuation. Any editorial changes appear in carets.

In determining what authors to include, the editors, in consultation with Professor Harold Bloom, have tried to balance broad representation with in-depth coverage. We have had to omit, necessarily, relatively minor figures in order to allow space for such major writers as W. H. Auden and Joseph Conrad. In making our selections, we have nevertheless given place to significant albeit lesser-known authors; in particular, we have included mystery, science fiction, fantasy, and non-fiction authors whose works have inspired substantial critical examination. Moreover, we have included certain writers who may date to the late nineteenth century but whose works have a twentieth-century relevance, as reflected in the amount and nature of modern criticism devoted to them. A similar concern for diversity has informed our selection of the criticism itself. As a result, the present work provides an informative survey of the development of literary criticism and of British literature in general in the twentieth century, while fulfilling its primary purpose of providing a range of critical views of the specific authors covered.

The Editors

MARGERY ALLINGHAM

1904–1966

Margery Allingham was born on May 20, 1904, in London. She was educated at the Perse High School for Girls in Cambridge and at the Polytechnic School of Speech Training. She intended to pursue a career in acting, but the success of her early novels—her first, *Blackerchief Dick* (1921), was published when she was 17—impelled her into full-time writing. In 1929 she introduced her celebrated detective, Albert Campion, in *The Crime at Black Dudley*, and in the succeeding decades he was featured in a score of other mystery novels.

In 1927 she married the editor and illustrator Philip Youngman Carter, and they settled into a Queen Anne house in Essex, where they remained for most of their lives. During World War II Allingham temporarily abandoned the detective novel to write two volumes of social history, and even after her return to mystery fiction she used Campion with decreasing frequency. She made her first trip to the United States in 1949. Margery Allingham died on June 30, 1966.

Allingham's detective novels are distinguished for their keen portrayal of character, taut style, and brooding atmosphere. In some of her short stories she even ventures into the macabre, the supernatural, and science fiction. Of her work she wrote: "I have no particular axe to grind and I belong to no rigid school of thought but am content to hold with the poet that the proper study of mankind is man."

General

John Strachey, in a memorable essay sixteen years ago, described Margery Allingham, Nicholas Blake and Michael Innes as "the three white hopes" of the British detective story—one of those prophecies which, as every critic ruefully knows, is apt to prove the kiss of death.

Blake and Innes have survived reasonably well; each has written a number of admirable novels, though probably none better than those early ones upon which Strachey based his judgment. Miss Allingham, I'm afraid, has progressively waned even as her reputation waxed (as a novelist, that is; her skill in the short story has increased markedly); and it would be impossible to rank her in the first category of British mystery novelists solely on the evidence of her work since Strachey's 1939 critique.

The Allingham career has been in all an interestingly patterned one. She began very young (at 19—an age comparable only to Phoebe Atwood Taylor's among professional mystery debuts) and from 1923 to 1931 wrote four foolish and often amusing high-nonsense thrillers. Then she buckled down to more frequent and more serious production, and in the years before the war wrote six novels which shifted from light-hearted melodrama to the acutely observed and characterized comedy of manners, resembling the best work of Dorothy Sayers before her and Ngaio Marsh after her—a period which reached its apogee in 1937–38 with the nearly flawless *Dancers in Mourning* and *The Fashion in Shrouds*.

By this time Miss Allingham had often been told that she was "more than a mystery novelist." Her books had been moved from the Crime Club to the plain Doubleday imprint, and were promoted and priced as "straight" novels. During the war years she wrote a non-criminous novel, a nonfiction study of England at war, and three able mysteries. In the decade since the war, she has produced (aside from her admirable short stories and less admirable novelettes) only three books—all structurally detective stories, all striving hard to be "more than just a mystery novel," and each ending by being neither an adequate piece of serious fiction nor even a competent deductive puzzle.

The Tiger in the Smoke (1952) was at least an ambitious and often wonderful failure—a novel which fell apart both as fiction and as detection but which contained some of Allingham's finest writing and characterization to date. *The Estate of the Beckoning Lady* is simply nothing in particular. As a detective story (about the not unwelcome notion of the murder of an income tax collector), it's crudely solved by the eminent Albert Campion through unfair and wholly unsubstantiated guesswork. As serious fiction, it hardly scratches the surface of any of its overnumerous characters and seems to have nothing to say beyond the thesis that taxation can create inequities. In either aspect, it is a long book full of skilled and graceful sentences which never add up to anything substantial. It's time Miss Allingham rid herself of the "more than" concept and went back to writing (as her short stories show she still can) simply one hell of a good mystery.—ANTHONY BOUCHER, "Criminals at Large," *NYTBR*, April 10, 1955, p.17

Works

DETECTIVE STORIES

Miss Allingham's progress has been particularly interesting. She began with some light-hearted and rather sentimental books in which Campion seems at times almost a figure of caricature:

> The Inspector had a vision of a lank immaculate form surmounted by a pale face half obliterated by enormous horn-rimmed spectacles. The final note of incongruity was struck by an old-fashioned deerstalker cap set jauntily upon the top of the young man's head.

That is Campion in 1931, in *Police at the Funeral*. Here he is fourteen years later, in *Coroner's Pidgin*, after some arduous war service:

> He had changed a little in the past three years; the

1

sun had bleached his fair hair to whiteness lending him a physical distinction he had never before possessed. There were new lines in his over-thin face and with their appearance some of his old misleading vacancy of expression had vanished. But nothing had altered the upward drift of his thin mouth nor the engaging astonishment which so often and so falsely appeared in his pale eyes.

Campion has not merely aged and matured; he is regarded with deeper seriousness by his creator, and so is the world in which he moves. As the years went by Miss Allingham felt herself less and less confined by the bonds of the fair play detective story, and began to write books which in effect were novels with a detective element in them.—JULIAN SYMONS, *The Detective Story in Britain*, 1962, pp. 31–32

Margery Allingham published her first crime novel in 1929. Her detective, Albert Campion, was to become famous in the course of a dozen or so subsequent mysteries. But who, as Dr Fortune might have asked, was his papa, and what his school?

> 'Campion—that is your name, I suppose?' 'Well—er no,' said the irrepressible young man. 'But,' he added, dropping his voice a tone, 'my own is rather aristocratic, and I never use it in business. . . . Listen—do you know who my mother is?' 'No,' said Abbershaw, with great curiosity. Mr Campion leaned over the side of the car . . . and murmured a name, a name so illustrious that Abbershaw started back and stared at him in astonishment.

The early Campion was an inane giggler. As a guest he was an embarrassment and Colonel Gore would have pronounced him an all-round softie. He could solve a police-baffling mystery, though: specifically, *The Crime at Black Dudley*. Exactly ten years later, on the eve of the second world war, the giggles had subsided and an altogether more dignified and cerebral detective was suggested by Miss Allingham's observation of him sitting with 'long, thin legs crossed and his pale eyes amused behind his horn-rimmed spectacles'. Furthermore, she was able to report that when urgent matters demanded his attention he would put aside *The Times* 'with regret'—a clear sign of his having outgrown the silly exuberance of youth. This Campion of 1939 lived in Bottle Street, Piccadilly, kept a manservant and was a member of the Junior Greys. One notes the matter-of-factness of the last piece of information; Miss Allingham had learned how much more effective is cool name-dropping than the girlish enthusiasm of ten years before which had set Campion

> striding jauntily down the street until, to Abbershaw's amazement, he disappeared through the portals of one of the most famous and exclusive clubs in the world.

The change in style suggested confidence that readers could safely be credited with knowing the difference between a London resort of officers and gentlemen and a brand of cigarettes.

To the very end of the Campion saga Miss Allingham's hero remained essentially a patron rather than a practitioner of criminology, even though no more was made of the business of being the son of a mother too distinguished to be named. The pattern had been set and Miss Allingham stuck to it, although there is evidence that as she developed her intelligent and experimental attitude to the writing of fiction she became impatient sometimes with the social scene to which Campion had been committed. The following passage, written in *Mr Campion and Others* (1939), has the ring not of admiration but of satire:

> Petronella was not easy to find. She was neither dancing at the Berkeley nor dining at Claridge's. He looked in at the ballet and did not see her, and it was not until he remembered the Duchess of Monewden's Charity Ball at the Fitzrupert Hotel that he found her. . . .
> —COLIN WATSON, "Gifted Amateurs," *Snobbery with Violence*, 1971, pp. 189–90

OTHER WORKS

⟨*The Galantrys*⟩ is the first non-mystery novel by the creator of that favorite of investigators, Mr. Albert Campion. As an admirer of Mr. Campion from away back, this reviewer approached *The Galantrys* with proper respect. But here Mr. Campion's creator has explored a mystery that requires far more than his suave ingenuity for its solution—a mystery that goes as deep as anything we know. This time the puzzle is the why and wherefore of a man, in his time, in his spot on earth—in application, the mystery of a whole culture.

Mrs. Carter uses James Galantry as the focus of her idea. Into her scrutiny of his character she pours her vision of past and future, of England, of society and, I think, a philosophic vision of what could be. Of course, this adds up to an attempt to write the ideal novel; it is hardly surprising that Mrs. Carter does not realize the attempt completely. But the fact that she had the courage to tackle such a theme gives her book breadth and interest.

James Galantry is the product of the century-old variety of English gentry—and the ageless, untamed gypsy. This blend of wildly incompatible racial strains, carrying the stigma of "half-breed" in early Victorian England, produces the fundamental conflict. Its effect on James' character is studied through his growing up, his courtship, loves lost and gained, his progeny, his ideals—all he cherishes and hates. The rococo background, of course, is excellent for this inner—and outer—struggle. The settings—countryside and London—are handsomely done. So are the costumes of the day, the vogues, manners and social credos.

The narrative style is, for the most part, as remote as an amused god's view of our cosmos. Occasionally it bends down gently to examine at close range some small incident which may be more enlightening than the rest. Unfortunately this method breeds a certain remoteness in the reader's feelings as well. It is evident that the author knows her people thoroughly—too thoroughly, perhaps. Too often she asks us to take her word for them and not to demand proof in the writing.

James is worked out carefully, and appealingly drawn. Sometimes he is a mirror reflecting his times and his country. Sometimes he is many-faceted. Always he is clear as a transparent jewel that shows its inner texture. . . . But the novel races too fast for its protagonist: events must be summarized, just as we would enjoy lingering over the small details and the conversation. The author, by looking both backward and forward—by reminiscing and seeing into the future at the same point—destroys our present pleasure in her scenes by striving to give them their other dimension.

Not that *The Galantrys* is metaphysical. Mrs. Carter puts down any such budding ideas in her readers—consistently, and with wit. Her style is comfortable, with no strange angles at all. Perhaps, if she had been a little more daring, both in thought and writing, her novel might have more compelling interest, more original value.—EUDORA WELTY, "Victorian Half-Breed," *NYTBR*, Oct. 31, 1943, pp. 6, 12

LeROY PANEK
From "Margery Allingham"
Watteau's Shepherds
1979, pp. 128–42

The first group of Allingham's novels[1] grows directly from her education as a thriller and adventure writer. They begin with *The Crime at Black Dudley* (1929), and include *Mystery Mile* (1929), *The Gyrth Chalice Mystery* (1931), and after an excursion into the regular detective novel, *Sweet Danger* (1933). Although these novels do have elements of the regular detective story in them, in terms of plot and characterization, these books are thrillers: if it weren't for the special Allingham ingredients they could be by Edgar Wallace. And they ignore most of the "rules" laid down by the Main Line detective story writers in the later twenties.

At the heart of each of these books beats the struggle between a titanic villain and his goons who are trying to steal or buy the birthrights of decent people (in the first two books the villains are Master Crooks and in the last two they are international financiers), and a group of good, plucky, charming, innocent people who, under the direction of the hero, triumph in the end. In each case the Foreigner, the Gangster, or the Millionaire invades the idyllic English village—Allingham's villages, containing authentic yokels, a comfortable pub, and a big house which has seen better days what with the Income tax and all, have names like Keepsake, Sweethearting, or Sanctuary—and attempts to pillage the heart of an ancient tradition which insures peace and serenity in the community. This is implicit in the attack on the family's honor and the law personified in *Black Dudley* and *Mystery Mile*, but it is explicit in the attempts on the Gyrth Chalice and on the Fitton's Earldom in the later two books. As traditional in the thriller, regular law enforcement is helpless against this sort of villain; hence the chief Scotland Yard man mentioned in Allingham's thrillers is one Inspector Deadwood, and he is only mentioned and never appears.

In thrillers, and in these books, the single menace of the villain is not enough to provide the requisite chills. There must also be a tie-in with some sort of horror, a carry-over from the gothic tale. In Allingham's books this comes from the introduction of the occult, which she learned to use as the books progressed. The first two novels have relatively mild instances of ancient and supernatural things in the legend of the Black Dudley Dagger and the legend of the Whistlers in *Mystery Mile*. In *The Gyrth Chalice*, however, Allingham introduced a subordinate plot involving witchcraft which blends with the thrill of the major good-bad struggle, and in *Sweet Danger* she brought the witchcraft sub-plot into the frame of the major action by making it genuinely confuse and threaten the heroes and provide the first crescendo which announces the climax of the novel.

But back to the heroes. Adventure stories have two basic hero patterns: there is the isolated hero who fights evil alone, unrecognized and unaided, like Richard Hannay during most of *The Thirty Nine Steps*, and there is the group comprised of the hero and his associates, like Jim Hawkins, Squire Trelawney, the Captain, and the loyal crew members in *Treasure Island*. Both patterns have their origins in the patterns of ancient myths, and each has particular advantages and disadvantages for the story teller. In all of her adventure novels, however, Allingham chose to use the hero and his associates as

the protagonist pattern. Using the group has a definite attraction for the writer trained in the serial, in that it provides more opportunity for threat, capture, and escape simply because there are more good people to be threatened, captured, and rescued, thus providing the opportunity for more incidents than in the story with the single protagonist. From the beginning, in *The Crime at Black Dudley*, Allingham uses the group with a leader who solves problems and gets folks out of tight places. In all of these early books, there is a leader accompanied by young men and women who alternately assist and naively hinder the leader's plans, young men and women who also invariably fall in love during the course of the adventures. As a plot pattern Allingham typically includes the kidnapping of one member of the group and one unconsidered act which complicates the action in the course of each of these books. . . .

When one reads, say, *Dancers in Mourning*, it is very difficult at first to believe that it was written by the author of *Mystery Mile*. This is because Allingham's writing underwent a drastic change in the early 1930's. With *Police at the Funeral* (1931) Allingham entered the world of the "regular" detective story, which she explored further in *Death of a Ghost* (1934), *Flowers for the Judge* (1936), *The Case of the Late Pig* (1937), *Dancers in Mourning* (1937), and *Fashion in Shrouds* (1938). Part of the motive for this change no doubt lies in the fact that in the thirties detective stories were more popular and acceptable than the thriller, which by then had become a lower class property and was mocked as such by the Bright Young People who wrote detective stories. Of course, Allingham had written thrillers largely to make fun of the form, but she discovered that the adventure spoof was something which needed to be done but which can only lead to stagnation if done over and over again. Part of her motive for change, moreover, came from Allingham's inclination to tinker with her own creations and to experiment with new forms. This motive can be seen in the early books in the shifts in Campion's role and his speech: he began as a secondary character and became a primary one, and he started out talking like a voluble lunatic and ended speaking pretty much like a normal person. In the early books, Allingham even experimented with the unalterable role of the villain, making the chief villain in *The Gyrth Chalice Mystery* a woman. If she could experiment within the thriller, she could also experiment with new forms, and so in 1931 she tried her hand at the detective story. And the desire to experiment did not stop here, for in each of the detective novels she tries something new, and during the thirties one can observe that the novels before and after *The Case of the Late Pig*, although they have some basic similarities, are very different kinds of books.

With *Police at the Funeral*, then, Allingham moved into the very different world of the detective story, one which has marked differences from that of the thriller. None of her new, detective novels deals with monolithic international conspiracies, but shift to the domestic murder as the central concern—almost as if she had read the "fair play" rules about the absurdity of writing a mystery story about such mythical monsters as Master Crooks and Secret Societies. Therefore much of the exotic, wild action disappears, and there are no kidnappings or extended chases in the detective books. Instead of using the whole of England as the ground for the action, the new novels concentrate on specific locales. *Police at the Funeral*, *Death of a Ghost*, and *Dancers in Mourning* are pretty much confined in terms of place with an attempt to focus on that mainstay of detective writers, the mansion. The atmosphere, sick and oppressive instead of scary, comes from the house and from an examination of the household's relationships and personalities, rather than from the suggestion of ancient and supernatural horror which colors the thrillers. Perhaps most significantly, Allingham disbands the hero-leader and his group of assistants, leaving the detective noticeably isolated in a world in which fast action, quick wits, and the other virtues of the thriller hero are of no use. . . .

A fundamental difference between the thriller and the detective story is the social and moral position of the law and its statutory enforcement. In thrillers, and Allingham's are no exception, the criminal is above or beyond statutory law and the established procedures of law enforcement which protect the community. The police are useless, and in the twenties society had not developed supra-legal police forces like MI5 or the CIA, although a few writers dreamed up comparable agencies. Thus, in the thriller the police are helpless, and the hero must 1) detect the super criminal and 2) represent self-sufficiently the force of good by either destroying the villain or bringing him into the range of the law. In the thrillers, therefore, Campion, Lugg, and the band of friends work without the assistance of Scotland Yard. The very opposite is the case of the detective story, for in it a recognized statute has been broken, and the police work to bring the offender to justice, even if they need the detective's help to do so. Allingham's move into the detective story consequently means an introduction of the police, as the title of her first regular novel, *Police at the Funeral*, indicates. Here Allingham gives the policeman, Stanislaus Oates, who had only been a voice on the phone in *Mystery Mile*, a significant role to play. One of Oates' functions, in fact, cuts the thriller down to size as he emphasizes the real nature of crime and police work. From now on the police will take charge of the body, the material evidence (especially in the bomb squad's work in *Dancers in Mourning*), and of the arrest. The hero now helps the police, instead of the police giving a limp hand to the hero as in the thriller. Consequently the hero becomes subordinate as part of a system, and his role fades when compared to the thriller hero's. Further, this new role, at least for Campion, is both humiliating (in that it involves sordid work), and alienating, for Allingham's detective hero finds that in snooping around, trying to help his friends, he is trusted neither by the police nor by the people he is investigating.

All of this happens to Albert Campion. Beginning with *Police at the Funeral* he moves into the background. He now has only moments of his old facetious role—in the opening chapters of *Police at the Funeral* and *Flowers for the Judge* he pops a few witticisms, and in the former he enters wearing a deer-stalker hat. But, in the main, Campion is pretty sober in these books, Allingham feeling that to have him behave otherwise would be inappropriate to the somber and serious tone of the books. These cases, after all, do take place in the houses of the dead, and there is no place for the cap and bells. So Campion becomes an observer and, for about three-quarters of the plot, a relatively passive one. He does not interrogate or entrap people—the other characters do most of the talking until the second catastrophe, when Campion swings into action. Symptomatic of the change in the detective books is what happens to Lugg. Largely nothing happens to him, for he appears only briefly in *Police at the Funeral* and not at all in *Death of a Ghost*. When he re-emerges in *Flowers for the Judge*, Lugg is a new man. He continues to act the comic part of the surly servant, but he has given up or forgotten his underworld connections and becomes respectable. Now he consorts with other gentlemen's valets, and looks forward to being valet of a Duke when Campion's brother dies. In the later novels of the thirties, Lugg becomes the center of the sentimental theme, as in his care for Sarah in *Dancers in Mourning*, but his role is reduced

largely to that of an ex-convict tutoring a gentleman in the ways of respectability. He becomes, and there is, no doubt, the shadow of a parallel, Falstaff who has grown old and who his master or his creator have outgrown.

Instead of depending on movement of people, as she had in the thrillers, Allingham uses the techniques of the "serious" novelist, description and analysis. Characters are not swiftly described so as to get to the main business of the book—they are the main business of the book. Therefore the key term for these books, especially *Police at the Funeral*, is "psychology." In turning to character examination and psychology, of course, Allingham was following the detective story trend of the early thirties which sought to make the regular detective story more than "a puzzle game." For Allingham at this stage, however, psychology was not synonymous with examining relationships between men and women, and in the first two regular novels she studiously avoided dealing with "the horrors of love." Even when love appears in *Flowers for the Judge*, Allingham makes Lugg speak disapprovingly of "sex rearin' its ugly 'ed," and she does not permit the agony of love to play a prominent role. Rather, in the early thirties, in *Police at the Funeral* and *Death of a Ghost*, she examines families dominated by the widow of a famous man showing not a Freudian analysis but an appreciation of the strong, vital, and valuable influence of an old woman over a group of others who understand neither her nor themselves. This also lies in the background of *Flowers for the Judge*, but there Allingham chooses to exploit the courtroom scene instead of the relationship of the heirs to the personality of Jacoby Barnabas. In each case, and in all of the subsequent books of the thirties (with the possible exception of *The Case of the Late Pig*), the action is subordinate to the passages of character description and analysis, and to the narrative voice which does the description and analysis. Naturally all of this is necessary to a detective story devoted to unmasking a hidden criminal, but it is more important than this—more important than the half-hearted fair play frame. As shown by *Death of a Ghost*, where the identity of the murderer is not in doubt for long, the important thing about Allingham's detective stories was not unmasking the criminal, which is always done with a few quick flourishes, but description of the people. It is there because Allingham wanted to be something other than a detective writer.

In the process of doing this she diminished the role of Albert Campion and radically altered his personality so that he almost functions as a neutral character. Gone are the days when she wished to make her detective hero eccentric and striking in the tradition of Sherlock Holmes. By 1937, however, she wished to resuscitate him, and she moved to do this in *The Case of the Late Pig*. Here, instead of being the unrealized Mr. Campion of the early detective novels—the narrative voice of these novels always refers to him with this formal title, and the effect in the novels of the early thirties is that he is removed from the reader—Allingham makes him the narrator of the book. *The Late Pig* is virtually Wodehousian in tone, it departs from London to take place in the pastoral village of Keepsake, and it revolves around comic characters: Lugg is more prominent, and there are Sir Leo Pursuivant, the frank parody of the military man, Campion's school chum, Whippet, and the bubbly Effie Rowlandson. The whole novel runs on a pun on the initials of a large insurance firm, and not only is psychology shoved into the background, but so is the murder mystery. In this book Allingham got back in touch with a bit of the old Campion, and this renewed attention to the hero helped her to focus the subsequent novels, *Dancers in Mourning* and *Fashion in Shrouds*.

Although in *Police at the Funeral* and other early detective books Campion stays pretty much in the background, Allingham does develop several parts of this character. The most important one for our purposes here is that of the civilized man. In the thriller Allingham had attacked the cliche hero by making Campion into a comic character, and by avoiding the rough and tumble masculinity so common to the form, but in the detective stories she uses the other technique for criticizing the bully hero by making Campion into the civilized man. One way in which she does this is by giving Campion sensitivity to art, in *Death of a Ghost*, as well as other things not commonly associated with the manly hero: in *Police at the Funeral*, for instance, Campion, "who had an eye for such things," notices that Great Aunt Catherine has a vast collection of lace and never wears the same piece twice. Much of his sensitivity shows in his understanding of other people, but it shows most prominently in his sensitivity to his own feelings. In the thirties Campion is the civilized man to whom both criminal passion and poking one's nose into others' lives are repellent. This role is most apparent at the end of *Death of a Ghost*, when Campion is both enraged by the criminal actions of another and at the same time ashamed of his own anger. The part of the civilized man, moreover, causes the hero to stay in the background, reticent of becoming involved in the ugliness of personal problems and family squabbles. After *The Case of the Late Pig*, which shows Allingham's desire to once again give the hero a prominent role, Campion as the civilized man moves toward the center of attention in the novels; he becomes more intimately involved with the action. This involvement stems from the two forces which will move the civilized man to action—love and family.

If romance was a minor current in *Flowers for the Judge*, it becomes a major factor in *Dancers in Mourning: Dancers in Mourning*, *Fashion in Shrouds*, and *Traitor's Purse* (1940) are, in effect, Allingham's romantic trilogy. *Dancers in Mourning* has, on the surface, all of the ingredients of the earlier detective novels: 1) it uses the professional world of the theater as *Death of a Ghost* uses art and *Flowers for the Judge* uses publishing, 2) it uses the oppressive atmosphere of a house and household touched by death, as in *Police at the Funeral* and *Death of a Ghost*, and 3) it uses the group of people to which Campion is attached by friendship—in fact, Uncle William in this novel is a carry-over from *Police at the Funeral*. But although all of these things are present, Allingham does not exploit them, for here she wants to focus on Campion in love, and it is the issue of love which dominates this novel. *Dancers in Mourning* is an experiment in fusing the detective story with the romance. Allingham here triangulates virtually all of the characters, and every one of the major characters, except Lugg, Uncle William, and some of the minor ones, is engaged in the agonizing process of finding and possessing their soulmates. Most are caught up in the stock romance quandary of the hopeless passion for another who has become unattainable because of circumstance. The pains of love cause personal agony, aberrant

behavior, social discomfort, and they cloud individuals' judgments and demand quantities of self-abnegation and self-discipline. And all of this can be seen most clearly in Campion who, with his hopeless love for Linda Sutane, acts out on center stage the passions of the others in the background. He is now the civilized man in love with another's wife, and the chief concern of the book is how he deals with this while helping the police solve the murder mysteries in the case. Allingham, with *Dancers in Mourning*, plunged into "the horrors of love" with a vengeance, but the result is not very satisfactory and the book is labored and unwieldy. She tried to do too much in this book (what with the persecution plot, three murders, the neglected child, presentation of the profession, depiction of the atmosphere, etc.) while making love the dominant concern of the hero's thoughts. But it taught her some lessons about character and structure.

The failure of the love business in *Dancers in Mourning* caused Allingham to rethink the combination of the compassionate man, love, and the detective story, and she tried one new combination in *Fashion in Shrouds* and another in *Traitor's Purse*, neither of which falls into the sentimental traps of *Dancers in Mourning* and both of which move her back toward some of the elements of the thriller, which she had neglected. The two later novels also show the diminution of "the horrors of love" which play such a prominent part in *Dancers in Mourning*, for in *Fashion in Shrouds*, Allingham segregates the "horrors of love" plot from the hero by using Campion's sister, Val Ferris, and in *Traitor's Purse* Amanda's infatuation with Lee Aubrey receives only miniscule attention. In fact, in *Fashion in Shrouds*, Allingham introduces a specific contrast and criticism of the love which only causes agony and soul-searching with the development of Campion's love for Amanda Fitton, the peppy, breezy, bright, and independent woman first introduced in *Sweet Danger*. All of this also changes Campion, and there is a happy blend of the old Campion and the new: he is a man who can wisecrack and quip, who can deal with danger but who can also be compassionate towards and involved with others, and be in love too. It is in these last two books that Allingham finally achieved the perfect blend of the thriller, the detective story, and the novel about people—something which she had worked toward throughout the thirties.

Notes

1. Allingham claimed that her novels fell into groups of threes, but this is not really true in the twenties and thirties. The way I see the groups is:

   Thriller: *Black Dudley, Mystery Mile, The Gyrth Chalice, Sweet Danger.*

   Regular Detective Novels: *Police at the Funeral, Death of a Ghost, Flowers for the Judge.*

   Reevaluation: *The Case of the Late Pig.*

   Romances: *Dancers in Mourning, Fashion in Shrouds, Traitor's Purse.*

A. Alvarez

1929–

Alfred Alvarez was born in London on August 5, 1929. He was educated at Corpus Christi College, Oxford, receiving a B.A. in 1952 and an M.A. in 1956. He has taught creative writing at Princeton, Brandeis, the University of New Mexico, and the State University of New York at Buffalo. At Princeton he met R. P. Blackmur, who helped him obtain a Rockefeller Foundation visiting fellowship in 1955 and 1958. Alvarez also worked as drama critic for *The New Statesman* and as poetry editor and critic for *The Observer*, to which he still contributes.

Although Alvarez has in recent years set aside his criticism for novels, poetry, and non-fiction, he is still best known as a critic, and has been a leading advocate of "Extremist" poets, such as Anne Sexton, Robert Lowell, John Berryman, and Samuel Beckett. His separation from his first wife and subsequent suicide attempt in 1961 inspired a series of poems that won the Vachel Lindsay Prize for Poetry in that year, as well as a study of suicide and literature published in 1971 entitled *The Savage God*.

Alvarez lives in London with his second wife, Anne Adams, and their two children. He also has a son by his first marriage. He is an avid rock climber, and his passion for poker led to his 1983 book *The Biggest Game in Town*, a non-fiction account of the World Series of Poker and its contestants.

Works

THE SAVAGE GOD

That Alvarez should assemble a book on the question of why suicides occur, and that he should attempt an analysis of the problem in terms of literature (and literary suicides), is surely to invite harsh criticism. For he is trying to write about a subject so very private that it arouses intense feelings of hostility, and he is doing it as a literary critic, basing his reason for this choice on the theory that the artist is "more aware of his motives than most other people and better able to express himself."

The Savage God is provocative and exceptionally well-written. Those who might object to Alvarez's assembling of criticism, near-encyclopedic fact and personal speculation, and who might reject Alvarez's basic romantic assumptions about the relationship of artists and suicide, must nevertheless admit that the book is an original enterprise, a rather fearless miscellany that achieves whatever organic form it possesses only through the consistent, eminently sane voice of the author himself.

. . . He concentrates his considerable critical ability on such figures as Plath, Hughes, Lowell and John Berryman (who did commit suicide in January, 1972), and does not consider the variety of modern and contemporary artists who have dealt with life rather than death, and society rather than the closed worlds of their own psyches. (Lowell himself has altered his poetic interests, and does not bear much resemblance to the early, self-obsessed, tortured Lowell.) But I believe that Alvarez is essentially right to relate the artist's work to his life, to believe that in contemporary times the artist's life has merged with his work, his work with his life, so that the two become invariably connected. This theory is a return to the romantic concept of the artist as Prometheus, suffering more eloquently than ordinary men and suffering in fact for the benefit of ordinary men, though Alvarez prefers to call it "existential."—JOYCE CAROL OATES, *NYTBR*, April 16, 1972, pp. 1, 28

Mr. Alvarez's first chapter is an account of the last few years in the life of his friend, the poet Sylvia Plath. I understand that her husband, Ted Hughes, thinks it inaccurate, and I am in no position to judge. It does seem clear from the facts that she intended her successful attempt to fail, as her two previous attempts had. Mr. Alvarez says, and I agree with him:

> . . . for the artist himself art is not necessarily therapeutic: he is not automatically relieved of his fantasies by expressing them. Instead, by some perverse logic of creation, the act of formal expression may simply make the dredged-up material more readily available to him. The result of handling it in his work may well be that he finds himself living it out—
> . . . when an artist holds up a mirror to nature he finds out who and what he is: but the knowledge may change him irredeemably so that he becomes that image.

The moral, surely, is that one should be very cautious in what one chooses to write about.

In our aesthetic judgments I think Mr. Alvarez and I would usually agree—one would not call good poetry what the other would call bad. But in our personal tastes, i.e., the writers we really take to our hearts, it is clear that we differ.

Reading those he calls the Extremist Poets, Plath, Hughes, Berryman, I greatly admire their craftsmanship, but I cannot sympathize fully with what they are doing. The poetry which is really my cup of tea, that, for example, to name two modern Americans, of Frost and Marianne Moore, whether tragic, comic, or satiric, is always firmly rooted in staid common sense. Mr. Alvarez's taste, whether in modern poetry or in the poetry of the past, seems to be for the extreme. For example, he obviously loves John Donne whom, great as he is, I find an insufferable prima donna; give me George Herbert every time.

Mr. Alvarez's concluding chapter is devoted to his own unsuccessful attempt at suicide. It is most moving to read but rather puzzling. For instance, he tells us that, as a child, he kept repeating endlessly to himself *Iwishiweredead*, but he cannot tell us just why this was so. The statistics, he tells us, show that:

> The incidence of successful suicide rises with age and reaches its peak between the ages of fifty-five and sixty-five. In comparison, the young are great

attempters: their peak is between twenty-five and forty-four.

Mr. Alvarez was thirty-one and already established in the literary world before he swallowed forty-four sleeping pills, but at home, so that he was found by his wife just in time to save him. To the outsider an attempted suicide has about it the aura of a sick joke. (Cowper's account, quoted in this book, of his desperate and always thwarted efforts to kill himself is pure black farce.) Mr. Alvarez's reactions to his failure are fascinating and cheer my heart.

> The truth is, in some way I had died. The over-intensity, the tiresome excess of sensitivity and self-consciousness, of arrogance and idealism, which came in adolescence and stayed on beyond their due time, like some visiting bore, had not survived the coma . . . I was disappointed. Somehow, I felt, death had let me down; I had expected more of it. I had looked for something overwhelming, an experience which would clarify all my confusions. But it turned out to be simply a denial of experience. . . . Months later I began to understand that I had had my answer after all. . . . Once I had accepted that there weren't ever going to be any answers, even in death, I found to my surprise that I didn't much care whether I was happy or unhappy; "problems" and "the problem of problems" no longer existed. And that in itself is already the beginning of happiness.

I congratulate him. That is what I mean by common sense.— W. H. Auden, "Doing Oneself In," *NYRB*, April 20, 1972, p. 3

I cannot find much in *The Savage God* which makes it worth prolonged consideration. Mr Alvarez states that he has written a "study of suicide." His publishers state that he has tried to discover why people commit suicide. But I detect—and for this I do not require to be much of a Maigret—two authors in the same Alvarez, as here exhibited; and two books. They are not easily separable.

One Alvarez ("who was educated at Oundle School, and Corpus Christi College, Oxford, where he obtained a first-class degree in English") has exploratory concerns or prime interests of a literary-sociological kind which centre upon a quartet of contemporary poets and a postulated style he calls Extremism shaped by the internal features of the present casting-mould, the present "situation." His poets, "the four leading English-language exponents of the style," are, as we know perhaps too well, the three Americans Robert Lowell, John Berryman and Sylvia Plath, and Sylvia Plath's husband and relict, Ted Hughes.

The other Alvarez is the bookman, the promoter and journaliser of his interests or concerns; and if a book is to be made—the journalist or journaliser taking over—it is likely that more readers will be attracted by the "situation" than by a close consideration of the favoured poets or their poems; and still more, if the "situation" can be subsumed and proffered in one of its morbidly fascinating elements.

The lead therefore is given to suicide. But conveniently one of the favoured poets can share the lead, since she obligingly wrote about suicide, and even committed it, and since her story has become the object of a cult ("Anything by or about Sylvia Plath goes down well on these heights"—report from Hampstead in *The Bookseller*, 25 December 1971, on "Christmas in the Bookshops"). Mr Alvarez, who has so pushed and so over-valued the poems of Sylvia Plath, can say in his prologue that they are now classics, that he and none

other introduced them to a Sunday paper, that he himself knew the poet, in life; and in death, on the kitchen floor—"The builders forced the lock and found Sylvia sprawled in the kitchen. She was still warm"—and in her coffin—"She lay stiffly, a ludicrous ruff at her neck. Only her face showed. It was grey and slightly transparent, like wax" (all of which would have been in the London Sunday paper as well had the poet's husband not protested).

The book, accordingly, begins by mixing sensationalism and concern, which it continues to do in other respects, until the reader requires a separator to divide the two, or to divide Alvarez from Alvarez. He may remember, as he turns the handle, after adjusting the disparate buckets or the bowl and the bucket, that this critic has written of his indifference to the palpability around him; and if he should have looked ahead from the prologue to the epilogue, the reader may also be remembering that Mr Alvarez confesses himself to be "a failed suicide", a fact which gives him a special personal investment, we may suppose, in his notions of external and internal violence, and Extremism.

His notions? When the last fluid ounce has passed through the machine, much of the rather small bowl of resultant cream will be found to be tinned rather than fresh, after all; to be an altered and I would say debased borrowing from Camus on the Absurd and death and suicide, and man in revolt, and creating dangerously.

Here then is the scheme of the book: in that prologue, Sylvia Plath, who must be shown to have been rather less a pathological suicide than a bold explorer of the purlieus of death into which she was tempted, always in ultimate control, always taking an explorer's risk which at last (in that London house where Yeats had once lived) proved to be too great— Sylvia Plath sensationalised beyond the business either of his readers or Mr Alvarez. Next, filling the greater part of *The Savage God*, a survey of conceptions and misconceptions of suicide and of the ways in which suicide has impressed itself on the thought and feeling and judgment of writers from Dante onwards (these are surveys of an averagely acute but secondary amateurism such as one might find in the lighter pages of *New Society*). Finally, an exposition in more detail of the Extremism of Mr Alvarez, which is the controlled exploration, through art, of "the nihilism and destructiveness of the self", reflecting accurately "the nihilism of our own violent societies." The "best modern artists" survive, if they avoid killing themselves, as "suicides of the imagination: they are scapegoats on our behalf," each "finds himself in testing out his own death and vulnerability"; and the modern art "forces its audience to recognise and accept, in their nerve-ends, not the facts of life but the facts of death and violence; absurd, random, gratuitous, unjustified and inescapably part of the society we have created."

"Not the facts of life": Mr Alvarez signs off (though still to come is his little ingratiating epilogue on how he failed to manage his own suicide) by quoting Camus in his remark "There is only one liberty, to come to terms with death. After which, everything is possible." This is neat. It will be remembered, however, that Camus, who rejected suicide (and murder), declared, "But the point is to live", in our situation of the Absurd. Camus didn't stop with the nihilism or with the liberty, he went on to what the liberty makes possible and essential. For example: "Happiness and the absurd are the two sons of the same earth. They are inseparable." Or: "We must simultaneously serve suffering and beauty."

In the heartening light of Camus, of *L'Homme Révolté* and *Le Mythe de Sisyphe*, this journalising author of *The Sav-*

age God seems to me to be indulging in the violence and the chaos: he offers a bucket mainly of skim-milk which is black and poisonous—and no wonder with the obscene carrion-Crow of the fancy of Ted Hughes perched on the rim. From the first page the writing accords; it is vulgar and execrable, half assertive, half ingratiating, if fluent.

> We sat out in the big wild garden while little Frieda,
> now aged two, teetered among the flowers.

The writing proceeds by flaccid cliché, by the language of the blind and deaf who cannot be affected by our surrounding reality; an assortment of "worlds apart", "genius", "sheer ability", "success story", "genuine article", et cetera, which makes one call Camus back once more, asking "If we are not artists in our language first of all, what kind of artists are we?", and which deprives such estimations as it may deliver of authority or plausibility.

In any case I distrust a critic who analyses a *Zeitgeist* more eagerly than he attends to a line or a cadence; whose statements are too often careless (for example, Modigliani did not kill himself, Cowper did not die in an asylum); who is so un-inventive that he cannot invent his own titles (the title of this book is purloined from Yeats, the title of the last book by Mr Alvarez was purloined from Marianne Moore, the title of his first book from Coleridge); and who is led by the carrot of his own theory to enthuse over art where art does not noticeably exist.—GEOFFREY GRIGSON, "The Extremists of Al Alvarez," *Enc*, Aug. 1972, pp. 59–60

CRITICISM

Mr Alvarez's central strength as a critic may be best introduced by one of his own remarks, from his essay on Hart Crane:

> My object here is to see what is first and worth while
> in his verse, not to show what everyone knows.

The catholicity implied in the first half of this quotation allows him to discuss poets as unlike each other as Wallace Stevens and Hart Crane with a sensitive hospitality, emphasising the 'abstraction' of one and the 'concreteness' of the other, and making out a very good case for the virtues of each. The quotation's second clause indicates that Mr Alvarez wastes no time or sentiment. He yields more than once to the temptation to produce a mildly arresting opening (as on Pound and Empson); and he indulges now and again in a briskly reductive aside (as on Dylan Thomas and Saul Bellow). But for the most part his manner is cool, alert and highly intelligent. He has a close and sensitive way of moving into the heart of a passage's effect which has something in common with the criticism of Professor R. P. Blackmur, to whom he is avowedly much indebted. As a result we are almost everywhere closely engaged whilst reading. We find ourselves in contact with an unusually perceptive mind, and though sometimes we might wish to alter an emphasis or extend the line of thought so as to make a further connection, only occasionally are we likely to be in outright disagreement.

Thus, the discussion of the American poet's need for an 'orthodoxy' and, by contrast, of the English poet's possession of a 'tradition' is very suggestive—and, incidentally, cuts right through the banalities of more parochial and one-track accounts of recent English poetic developments. The closing general essay has a similar strength, especially where Mr Alvarez discusses the different degrees to which writers of each country share a 'moral world' with their society:

> The better and more powerful their [the Americans']
> work, the nearer it draws to poetry. And this has
> nothing to do with technique with words. . . . What

matters is that the artist views his material without the intricate filters of social convention. In fact, he hardly *views*; he feels it nakedly, as though every scene and event were part of his inner life.

Mr Alvarez goes on to suggest that the American artist's sense of alienation works 'solely' towards the discovery of his own moral identity. This seems too outright a generalisation. Giving texture to much of the best American literature (particularly in the novel), whether the tone is heroic or ironic, there is surely a complex and fruitful sense of a kind of social commitment, one which does not minimise the disillusions of reality but is still deeply involved with the revivifying possibilities, with the finer affirmations, of the American dream—with what Professor R. W. B. Lewis recently called, in *The American Adam*, 'the special complexities, the buoyant assurance and the encircling doubt of the still unfolding American scene'. The note can be heard—to choose titles almost as they come to mind—in *The Great Gatsby*, *The Catcher in the Rye* and, for all its weaknesses, *The Adventures of Augie March*.—RICHARD HOGGART, "Intelligence and Insight." NS, April 12, 1958, p. 479

At last, a hopeful sign: critical books seem to be getting shorter—⟨*The School of Donne*⟩ is the fourth I have read in the past six months that does not exceed the limit of two hundred pages. Mr. Alvarez also recognizes that the critic has got to *write* for his money and not simply paste together scraps of practical criticism that we can all do for ourselves. His formulations are succinct and memorable. His scholarly information is tucked away in two appendices, surviving, as he nicely puts it, "as a silent background" for the criticism which is the main purpose of his undertaking.

The ground, of course, has been well cleared in the first place by other critics and Mr. Alvarez profits by this fact, his approval of "tough intelligence" leaning a little heavily at times on Eliot's "tough reasonableness beneath the lyric grace", his account of the post-Baconian scene deriving from L. C. Knights' paper on Bacon, which receives scant acknowledgment, and the chapter on Herbert again drawing on Knights' "well-bred ease of manner of 'the gentleman'". This last is legitimately and, I think, beautifully extended to give what must surely be one of the keenest appreciations we have of *Love bade me welcome*, Herbert's poetic being summarized as "a realism based on manners rather than dialectic".

The most substantial parts of the book are its beginning and its end. It opens with an extremely cogent account of the real nature of Donne's contribution to metaphysical poetry. One is easier here with the general drift of the piece than with some of the local formulae. Alvarez plugs rather than defines the word "intelligence": "Donne . . . was the first Englishman to write verse in a way that reflected the whole complex activity of intelligence." What of Shakespeare, one asks, and are we to withhold or re-define "intelligence" if we think of Chaucer or Langland or the author of *Sir Gawain*? Their range is, surely, immense. What is impressive about the account of Donne is the sense it gives us of his coterie affiliations and his ability to use the freedom of this coterie of witty, learned, and "unpoetical" men, to branch out away from acknowledged pieties and theory.

The end of the book is concerned with changing attitudes to the imagination, the split of poetry into the separate elements of Judgment and Fancy and the philosophical reasons for this. It is detailed, compact, and penetrating. Prior to this Cowley gets a little mauled, his role in that dissociation being insisted on rather at the expense of the poet who could write

On the Death of Mr. William Hervey, who in translating Horace could "make it new" to the tune of,

> Hence, ye profane; I hate ye all;
> Both the great vulgar, and the small;

whose paraphrase of *The Country Mouse* is one of the first magnificently Augustan poems, and whose Athaliah,

> Since he was dead who all her power sustain'd,
> Resolv'd to reign alone; resolv'd, and reign'd.

Mr. Alvarez's middle chapters are his least sustained and sustaining, but they all contain rewarding suggestions. The most graceful is that on Herbert, the most ingenious that on Crashaw which very plausibly suggests that he was the forbear not of Hopkins but of Poe; that Poe was one of the few poets who handled English rather as though it were French and that Crashaw, in short, anticipated him in so far as he was a Continental poet writing in English, using a rhetoric foreign to our own poets.

In all this one is aware of a liveliness of mind and a persuasiveness of style which argue well for the development of this critic and which, at the same time, provide the teacher with a general guide that he can confidently put into the hands of his students without blunting their appetites.—CHARLES TOMLINSON, "The Metaphysicals Revisited," *Poetry,* Jan. 1962, pp. 161–62

If there is something to be called, in a bad sense, a 'weeklies prose-style', then Alvarez possesses it. And those hardboiled clichés—'hatchet-job', 'souped-up', Donne's *Holy Sonnets* 'read like a dry run for the sermons', Sartre 'does a job on his own childhood', etc.—are really just as deadening as the clichés of board-room and pulpit, or the old jokey cricketing parlance of the Jack Squire school. They indicate nervousness. Alvarez feels he has to propitiate his reader, assuring him that he is one of a 'cool', 'hard-minded', 'totally unfooled' set. And the cost of all this irrelevant irony is to create a general atmosphere of belittlement, a sort of slope towards devaluation.

But anyway, Alvarez's values—'vitality', 'intelligence', 'coolness'—strike one as mainly social ones. He doesn't convey much sympathy for sustained imaginative artistic construction. Indeed, I don't get the feeling that he thinks of literature as an *imaginative* art at all. He regards the real business of the 'modern movement' in literature as being 'psychological realism' and goes on to say that:

> the whole story of Yeats's maturity, his change from a Rhymer to a major modern poet, is in the way he painfully brought himself to recognise the difference between his real emotions and his earlier romantic attitudes.

The *whole* story? Surely 'psychological realism', if it's a clue, is a fairly remote clue to *Sailing to Byzantium*—or *Le cimetière marin* or the work of Wallace Stevens. It leaves out so much: all that arduous and impersonal desire, through unremitting intellectual labour, to *construct* something.

How thin an idea of modernism Alvarez has can be seen from his opening paragraph about Sterne:

> Laurence Sterne is a distinctly 'modern' novelist. He has the freedom, the total originality, the sense of a man creating the form from scratch and for himself, that we now expect of any serious artist. He has, too, the modernist's apparent indifference to rules, as though aesthetic formalities were, in the final analysis, boring, and the only vindication of a work of art were the immediacy with which it expresses the personality of its creator.

And this thinness affects his judgment of the successors to 'modernism'. He is right to make propaganda for Sylvia Plath, but to speak of her work as on a level with Robert Lowell's, as he appears to do, is to praise her out of all proportion. Lowell comes to his 'confessional' material with so much larger and freer aesthetic purposes; he can make a public object out of it, whereas Sylvia Plath, conversely, makes Dachau an actor in her private drama. Her work, fine as it is, is only a private victory, a lifeline thrown out despairingly to art from a personal distress.

There are good things in Alvarez's essays. It is a serious and eye-opening remark to say that 'if there is any religious tone at all in the modern arts it is a certain Jewishness' and that the writer 'becomes, almost of necessity, either a real or an . . . imaginary Jew'. But the book leaves the impression that Alvarez is mildly fed up with literature; he is reporting on it instead of immersing himself in it, taking short views because he sees literature as only a short-time activity, of dubious worth. *Ars brevis, vita brevis,* he seems to say, and the message is rather cheerless.—P. N. FURBANK, "Cool," NS, March 22, 1968, p. 385

DANIEL F. HOWARD
"Leveling"

Partisan Review, Summer 1970, pp. 150–54

Of Alvarez one might say what he does of V. S. Pritchett: "He keeps his standards so high while performing so regularly that we tend to take him for granted." Just turned forty, Alvarez is a good generation younger than Pritchett, and these essays certify that he is, as he wants to be, more "serious" than even the best of his elders. To be "serious" includes avoiding Pritchett's "humanist fault," making "too many allowances, as though loath to hurt the feelings of some poor, dead author or deader book." And yet Alvarez isn't by any means as ruthless as he asserts; he avoids the hollow abusiveness of lesser British journalists—Muggeridge, Brigid Brophy—at worst slighting rather than insulting the old fogies of literature. His criticism has a positive force: the art that brings out the best in him is the kind that assaults the boundaries of life. Thus, he writes well on Keats, whom he sees as using poetry to fashion an understanding of and even a desire for death, and Lawrence, when "the imminence of death sharpened his life till it hurt" and Camus, living his life backwards, "consenting to his death in order to properly, knowingly, live now"; and centrally on Sylvia Plath, about whose death and last poems he writes brilliantly and with deep personal feeling.

Alvarez is in the best tradition of intellectual British journalism, and it is a mark of his quality that he is profoundly restive in it. No one is more aware than he of the danger of "relentless brightness" (for which he sympathizes with Tynan), or of "snobbishness," by which he means snuggling in with "successful young executives who still guiltily remember their university training." But he exploits the advantages of the brief, adventurous critical foray: The posture of a knowledgeable amateur contemptuous of specialized nitpicking, accepting the charge to connect literature with all other aspects of culture, and maintaining an aggressively personal voice that is, as it should be, a little outrageous or even sometimes wrong—but never sounding like *The New York Times.*

The title of one of Alvarez's earlier books, *Under Pressure: the Writer in Society* (a collection of interviews on BBC), indicates his values. He looks in literature as in life for a fundamental engagement with reality—chiefly, in the absence of believable historical events, death. What disgusts him is a talented writer like Ronald Firbank flirting with important tensions just below the level of social chatter but using his considerable artistry to obscure them. To talk about Firbank at all, he has first to discharge a splendid stream of contempt—"that coddled, wealthy *flaneur*, the darling of the Sitwells . . . the squirming, giggling shyness, the gossip, the absolute snobbery, the neurotic preciousness and drunken Catholic homosexuality . . . the most tiresome tradition of English eccentricity." Then he can consider the bare possibility of tragic implications in his work—"attenuated moods, nerves, and semi-religious languishings . . . his equivalent of a sense of tragedy." Finally, Alvarez remains unimpressed: making a gallant effort to give Firbank a fair trial in the court of seriousness, he actually announces by contrast his own admirable literary criteria.

In another fine essay he also convicts Jean-Paul Sartre. He explains Sartre's persistent unsatisfactoriness as proceeding from a childhood in the household of his adoring widowed mother and pompous grandfather, who insisted that the world reflect only himself. Though Freud runs deep in Alvarez's criticism, this is his most overtly psychological interpretation. Convincingly, he infers from Sartre's writing a guilt derived from his father's early death, the equivalent of an Oedipal impulse too easily realized. Then, forced to be a precocious child to satisfy the projections of a narcissistic and doting household, Sartre is seen as defending himself by transforming himself from the child manipulated into the child manipulating: clever, outrageous, fantastic because of the vivid, almost psychotic fantasy life that accompanied his guilty play acting, he satisfied his audience even as he stood cynically superior. So began a career in which the feelings were all wrong, misplaced, a career that succeeded by bewildering the self in a house of mirrors—not art but a "schizophrenia of brilliance."

This explanation of Sartre's bad-boyism again reveals Alvarez's insistence on the urgency of confronting "reality," one component of which is the writer's inner self—a core of honest reactions, not only liberated from coterie and chic, but also stripped of self-deception. Literature, then, is the vehicle of an expanding self moving toward extremes of being. And if one component of Alvarez's "reality" is a continuing search for the self, another is the necessity for the artist-critic to be responsible to modern culture. In this respect his acknowledged master is Matthew Arnold, and predictably, among contemporary critics, he responds to the social-cultural concerns of Lionel Trilling and Edmund Wilson. Speaking of a writer in the same tradition, Norman Podhoretz, he formulates the ideal relation between the intellectual and Culture (one in which he finds Podhoretz somewhat deficient). He proposes a special responsibility for the intellectual Jew, because "lacking a belief in an after-life, Judaism is, after all, *the* worldly religion: it centers on patriarchal authority and the intricacies of family piety; its ten commandments are a social code. At the core of it all are twin concepts of respect and responsibility. And this puts a great weight of justification on the gifted Jew, a disturbing certainty that talent, cleverness and success are not in themselves enough; one must also contribute to and maybe alter, however little, the moral climate in which one lives." Like Arnold, Alvarez sees dehumanization as the main threat to modern life, its nightmare extreme the concentration camp. The threat exists everywhere, maybe even especially in the dominant modern art form, cinema: for films are the products of a corporate, commercial, highly technological effort, heavily Jewish in personnel. They are dangerously close to

representing Jewish irresponsibility to Culture. But even poetry tends to get cut off from the human world, to become either a manufacturing of objects for a tiny group of professional connoisseurs, or worse, for the mills of academic criticism, a vicious form of "humanistic technology."

Though Alvarez constantly denies that he is nostalgic for specific moments in history when a more humane culture existed—"to be nostalgic for values and ideals wholly outside your experience is, in the end, a form of snobbery"—a nostalgia is clearly felt in most of these essays. Despising the usual ideal of pre-World War I England, its stable life and its "gentility,"—he looks back fondly to the moment of Modernism in the thirties when the great voices of Eliot and Pound and the early Leavis sounded strongly, when the Establishment writers, the "House of Lords," could be satisfyingly dismissed in favor of the major figures, who now constitute a too readily accepted orthodoxy. Alvarez's delight in imagining the thirties, and by implication his dissatisfaction with the current lack of clear causes and choices lights up his prose: "[In 1936] sensitivity and intelligence no longer seemed mutually exclusive—the great Cambridge epoch when all the intellectual disciplines were being reordered. It was the epoch of Principles: the Principles of Mathematics, of Ethics, of Literary Criticism. Its tone was analytical, quizzical, tough-minded and blandly determined—determined, that is, to explain things rationally and have done with nonsense, hostility and incomprehension." This is Alvarez projecting himself into a time when one could get, in Marianne Moore's phrase, "beyond all this fiddle."

But where to go now? Longing to offer allegiance, Alvarez finds himself culturally levitated. Yes, he is a Jew, proud of it, and proud of what he takes to be the special responsibility of Jews (in admiration of Sylvia Plath he thinks her best works come when she accepts herself as an honorary Jew); but he shares the Jew's special isolation, and in addition feels isolated from the great events that have shaped his times: he finds it hard to locate himself within events significant enough to justify the reaction he longs to give. Thus he talks eloquently about the literature of the concentration camps, about the way those who write it and those who immerse themselves in it "stir mud from the bottom" of their psyches, expose themselves to paranoia and suicide; yet beneath his talk is regret that his reaction is late and to the *literature* of the camps rather than the experience in them. In the lives of writers he admires he searches out crucial events that forge their distinction: Robert Graves's horror at World War I, Robert Lowell's acceptance of himself in a mental hospital, Sylvia Plath's confrontation with her "violent unease." But there is no detectable equivalent of these moments in Alvarez himself. Only the effort to seek them out is there; he himself feels only possible, unrealized identifications. He regrets that for him World War II was not an event but a condition: "My own generation, for instance—ten at the start of the war—grew up too late." Though he mastered Oxford (like everything else), and took a First, he never felt part of its monkishness and genteel attitudinizing. Nor is he comfortable in what he calls the "bland Metropolitan knowingness" of London and New York. A British poet, he hankers for the national urgency available to Americans; but yet he chides Auden for copping out, adopting America, and "channeling his deep neurotic disturbances into light verse." He writes a brilliant essay on New York, perhaps because it is a kind of metaphor for his excitement and unease at not belonging. Certainly he has trouble in defining his Englishness—envying the (apparently easier) West-to-East translation of T. S. Eliot and Sylvia Plath, sympathizing with R. P. Blackmur, who he says went to England at the end of his life only to be disappointed by the lack of "all those Jamesian subtleties the place no longer had."

The problem is that no nation, religion, or tradition can contain the "reality" Alvarez seeks. What is impressive about him is precisely the quest for something to be continually responsible to. He says of the Beatles: "At the Royal Command Performance or the British Embassy in Washington they still behave as though they might at any moment be held answerable to one of those unimpressed toughies they were brought up with in Liverpool." A beautiful insight into the Beatles—and into Alvarez too, who wasn't brought up with Liverpool toughies but, nevertheless, is determined to keep their faith.

Eric Ambler

1909–

Eric Ambler was born in London on June 28, 1909. After attending Colfe's Grammar School and the University of London, he became an engineering apprentice in 1928, but the next year turned to acting and then to writing advertising copy. In 1936 he wrote his first novel, *Dark Frontier*; the following year he was successful enough to abandon his copywriting job for full-time authorship. He married Louise Crombie on October 5, 1939, then left to serve in North Africa and Italy in the Royal Artillery (1940–46), where he earned the Bronze Star.

Having made army films toward the end of the war, he turned to producing and writing screenplays for many films from 1944 to 1970; his screenplay for *The Cruel Sea* (1953) was nominated for an Academy Award. Ambler later confessed, however, that he disliked screenwriting because he was never in total control of the finished product; it was, moreover, a hindrance to his own writing.

Ambler has been awarded many honors for his suspense novels, including the Crime Writers Association Award (1959), the Mystery Writers of America's "Edgar" Award (1963), and their Grand Master Award (1975). He received an OBE in 1981. In May 1958 he divorced his wife Louise, and later that year married the writer and producer Joan Harrison. They now live in Switzerland.

General

The popularity of the detective story is one of the many things which a great many people View With Alarm. The old argument that Woodrow Wilson consumed them in great numbers and that therefore they must be intellectually respectable has worn rather thin from overuse. No doubt great minds require relaxation, but even in the United States there are hardly enough great and overtaxed intellects to account for the millions of copies sold annually. There must, say some, be another explanation, and it is probably a sinister one.

Even the writers show a certain uneasy tendency to speculate about the purpose and nature of their art. Thus Eric Ambler, whose *A Coffin for Dimitrios* is usually regarded as one of the undisputed masterpieces of the genre, adds a footnote of three pages to ⟨the⟩ first American edition of *Epitaph for a Spy*, one of his earlier stories. He is concerned chiefly with the question why the sub-species called "spy story" should have been late in developing, but he reveals nevertheless the characteristic uneasiness. And just to set everybody's mind at rest the present writer would like to offer his explanation of the whole phenomenon: it is simply that detective stories are extremely popular because they, almost alone among contemporary works of fiction, do not try to do anything except please their readers.

In the beginning all novels were looked upon with disfavor as trivial production unworthy of the attention of anyone who took seriously either art or morals. Before the middle of the nineteenth century they had begun to be respectable and during the twentieth the novelist took on Social Significance as well as Art. Finally it has got to the point where almost nobody except the mystery writer will demean himself so far as to consider chiefly the innocent expectations of the reader in such elementary matters as the Happy Ending or the Triumph of Virtue.

Mr. Ambler's spy stories represent one of the more successful attempts to introduce new elements—realism, excitement and a touch of social significance—into a form which is always tending to become stereotyped. And Mr. Ambler is more successful than some others who have attempted the same thing because his modifications are not too radical. Written just before World War II, *Epitaph for a Spy* takes advantage of our sense that Nazi intrigue represents unequivocal evil on a scale grander than that of individual criminality. Its hero, a simple "common man" who blunders into an intrigue which he cannot escape from, is a personage with whom it is easy to identify ourselves because we are aware of the uneasy feeling that in a world like the present monstrous events may any moment involve us. There is, as reviewers will be sure to point out, even a suggestion of Kafkaesque anxiety in the effect which Mr. Ambler produces.

Yet at the same time he keeps us well within the limits of the novel of entertainment. Since this is a detective story and not a "serious" novel, we know that it will end well, and the tensions therefore remain pleasant, not distressing. As a concession to grim reality he does allow us a glimpse of a sub-plot in which tragedy is implicit and thus introduces a dissonance not quite appropriate to the original purposes of the detective story. Because of the extent to which it is subordinate, this sub-plot is acceptable, but it touches the limits of what is. If this sort of fiction should ever make the mistake of permitting itself to do what some would undoubtedly call "growing up" it will destroy itself. Some sort of innocent, possibly childish, optimism is of its essence.

It is certainly not necessary that our hero be quite so dependable a representative of Victorian respectability as Sherlock Holmes—except for his one shocking weakness—always was. But the detective should represent the forces of justice, and to make him as drunken, dishonest and lecherous as he frequently is today is to introduce moral ambiguity where it has no place. It is also to substitute for the simple tale of justice triumphant a usually rather smelly concoction in which the principal appeal is neither an intellectual puzzle nor a tale of right triumphant but something which looks uncomfortably like sadism and pornography. To those who scorned the detective story it used to be possible to say that at least it was an innocent escape into a simple world. I doubt that Woodrow Wilson would have relished the most popular of the current tough tales. And neither, to tell the truth, do I. A detective should be a representative of law and order. Not someone who gets bashed over the head while calling on a dangerous blonde.—JOSEPH WOOD KRUTCH, "Mr. Ambler's Spies," *NYTBR*, March 16, 1952, p. 4

Every art-form is in danger, from time to time, of being smothered by its own conventions. The classic detection novel—that blend of complex logic and pure moonshine—has succumbed to the limitations which were once its strength and is in a state of rigor mortis: its methods had been reduced to a set of formulas and one cannot live by formulas alone. The thriller, whose medium is action rather than logic, seemed to have come to an equally full stop, in Britain, at the works of John Buchan. *The Thirty-Nine Steps* and the subsequent Hannay novels, deriving chiefly from Stevenson's *Kidnapped*, set a formula which dominated the field: they were, from the literary viewpoint, dead-center middlebrow; they elevated the chase to a ritual; they transferred romance and villainy from Ruritania or Chinatown to the less exotic setting of moors, clubs, industrial streets—a background against which they took on fresh vitality: they were hearty, wholesome, antiseptic, open-air stuff—the very antithesis of everything we mean by morbid.

We saw the influence of the Buchan formula—violence against a familiar, everyday background—in such completely dissimilar books as Graham Greene's *This Gun for Hire* and Ethel Lina White's *The Wheel Spins*. Michael Innes, in *The Case of the Journeying Boy* for instance, has added to it an element of the highbrow-fantastical. But the basic ingredient remains the chase, susceptible of numerous variants: it is the common ground between thriller and detection novel. Whether we are pursuing a known villain or hero over the moors, or hunting for a mysterious X amid a labyrinth of clues, red herrings and suspects, the chase is the thing. That is why thriller and detection novel alike have so great an appeal for the white-collared worker (including the dog-collared: in Britain, the higher clergy are notorious addicts). He is a chair-borne hunter, vicariously enjoying a violence denied to him in real life: he satisfies an atavistic instinct, or rather two—the instinct of the chase and the psychological need of the guilty for punishment. He *can* run with the hare and hunt with the hounds.

In recent years the pure detection novel and the thriller have pooled their forces, producing a hybrid—the novel of suspense, it has been called. Eric Ambler's *A Coffin for Dimitrios* was a notable early product of this alliance. Mr. Ambler is not an original writer; but he gives a new twist to an old formula—a turn of the screw: indeed, he can be a master of tension. His first four books showed an unusual flair for creating alarm, if not despondency, in the gentle reader. Their atmosphere is one of disquiet, of the restive, exasperated, treacherous calm before a storm. Things, they disturbingly make us feel, are not what they seem. This ordinary little man in the hotel—what desperate secrets may he have under his derby hat. Will that innocent facade suddenly unmask a battery of menace? Whose side is X really on? *What side am I on?* We are in the twilit, illusionist world of espionage and counter-espionage, where such questions have a nightmare importance, a heart-searching urgency. It is a world to which we uneasily respond; for it is, after all, the world of our own time. . . .

We are, most of us, data-snobs, impressed by the general knowingness of a Kipling, or by the expertise of a Forester in writing an account of a cruiser action which even Royal Navy officers could not fault. Another skill Mr. Ambler commands is in the pushing of a decent, civilized, conventional man into situations where the values and conventions he has lived by do not hold good at all. George Carey has to learn the truth of what the judge had told him—that "no case, however matter-of-fact it might seem, could be considered entirely proof against the regrettable tendency of reality to assume the shape and proportions of melodrama."

This setting of ordinary individuals against abnormal circumstances is, of course, a basis of the best crime fiction too. And it raises a crucial question for the writer. We shall never return to the classic detection novel, where the characters were only ciphers in a complicated puzzle. But the genre remains a fairytale one, dependent upon the suspension of disbelief and a sort of plausible unrealism: If the characters are too solid, too well rounded, they will break through this delicate web of fantasy and ruin it. As every comedian wants to play Hamlet, so the detection or thriller novelist must resist the temptation to write another *Crime and Punishment*. It is one of Mr. Ambler's merits that he finely adjusts his characters to his medium, giving them reality enough, but never that mite too much which would destroy the airy fabric of the illusion.—C. DAY LEWIS, "With a Flair for Creating Alarm," *NYTBR*, July 26, 1953, p. 5

The much-discussed current vogue of "the anti-hero" should make Eric Ambler as much admired and respected by avant-gardists as he already is by every reader in search of intelligent entertainment. Indeed, thesis-researchers may sometime find a kind of prototype of existentialism in Ambler's long series of wholly unheroic protagonists—who become what the conditions of their existence demand of them, to the astonished delight of the reader. . . .

Eric Ambler has been writing thrillers since 1937. They have been unfalteringly brilliant; and not even Graham Greene has done more for the critical acceptance of the thriller-as-literature. But his new publishers choose to present ⟨A *Kind of Anger*⟩ as "a new and richer Ambler," and to announce, "Were it not for Eric Ambler, there would be no question of labeling it anything other than a novel."

Aside from the esthetic dubiety of the attitude implied (are books to be "labeled" by author, not by content?), this statement is fortunately inaccurate. Ambler has changed a trifle over the years, especially in this book and in last year's Edgar-winning *The Light of Day*. His anti-heroes are even more anti, and he is shifting from espionage to a more private form of international malefaction. But A *Kind of Anger* remains classic Ambler—and that is quite rich and new enough to captivate any seeker of skilled and artistic entertainment.—ANTHONY BOUCHER, "The Witness in the Bikini," *NYTBR*, Oct. 18, 1964, pp. 4, 39

Not until Eric Ambler began writing in the late thirties did any degree of sophistication about the powers of darkness enter the thriller. And even then his perspective is, from our point of view, rhetorical and simplistic. In the thirties there was still more than a touch of Buchan in Ambler's sentimental assertion that "it's not just a struggle between Fascism and Communism, it's between the free human spirit and the stupid, fumbling brutish forces of the primaeval swamp." The context of this passage is threatened torture. In fact, it is in *Background to Danger* that torture makes its delayed entrance into the spy story. Ambler's books reflect the stages of contemporary conflict, from the early days of Fascism and Nazism to the cold war.

In *Background to Danger* also Ambler displays for the first time in thriller literature a critical attitude toward capitalism. Buchan had been establishment-minded. Big Business was good, and most of its leaders were gentlemen who were deeply concerned about the future of mankind. Even the villains were gentlemen, brilliant establishment members not quite right in the head. Buchan had no use for socialism and felt that "the young entry" was not all it used to be. He would have castigated Ambler's insistence that "at some point in the business structure there is always dirty work to be done." "International business may conduct its operations with scraps of paper, but the ink it uses is human blood." Ambler himself was a little ashamed of such emotionalism. Indeed, he points out in *The Mask of Dimitrios* that "Latimer as an Englishman could never quite overcome his distaste for other people's rhetoric . . . he had recognized one or two phrases as coming from the Communist Manifesto." Nevertheless, Ambler's antipathy toward Big Business was consistently expressed in novel after novel, and he shared the view of young English intellectuals in the late thirties that "political ideologies had very little to do with the ebb and flow of international relations. It was the power of business." Consistent with this is his sympathetic treatment of the Soviet brother and sister spy team, Andreas and Tamara Zaleshoff. One would never know that the comic heavy Zaleshoff was an agent of the same country that employed Rosa Klebb and Red Grant. The writer's point of view makes all the difference. It is the voice of the writer Latimer in *The Mask of Dimitrios* and the point of view of Zaleshoff (in *Background to Danger* and *Cause for Alarm*) that pronounce so solemnly, "My curiosity about D. was that of the biographer rather than of the detective. . . . I saw him not as a corpse but as a man, not as an isolate, but as a unit in a disintegrating social system."—RALPH HARPER, *The World of the Thriller*, 1969, pp. 32–34

Works

How crooked can Communist politics be? How farcical can purge and counter-purge become? To what absurd depths of competition can man go for an opportunity to recant, to confess to Left deviationism, oppositionism, collaboration with Fascists, informing the Gestapo, and committing unmentionable obscenities involving the use of Stalin's photograph? Serious discussion of those things in literature seems to be played out. *Darkness at Noon* remains the classic, the book that revealed to the political naifs of Western Europe the authority of the dialectic, *Les Mains sales*, with its organisation, its irony, and its intellectual play, was the last comment of the country of Voltaire; *1984*, with its ice-age despair, was the last

comment of the country of Gladstone. And now, in the darkness at midnight, we are reduced to a thriller and what can best be described as a political bedroom farce.

In the position we have now reached, as the ice-age closes down on the political baboons' rock of 1951, *Judgment on Deltchev* is perhaps the only kind of book that an intelligent English writer who is not a genius could write about an East European country. The narrator, Foster, is a well-known playwright who has accepted an invitation to go as a newspaper reporter to cover the trial of Deltchev. Deltchev is a familiar figure. A pre-war minister of the second rank, he has emerged first as a Resistance leader and secondly as "Papa" Deltchev, leader of a socialist party which, in the post-war period, works with the Communists in the government. Now he is about to be tried, and he is accused, in accordance with the routine, not merely of treason, spying, and so forth, but of being a boss of a gang of reactionary assassins known as the Officer Corps Brotherhood.

What is the truth about Deltchev? The complexity of the answer is, curiously, increased by a Western simplification. There is no dialectic in this book; let Deltchev be a hero or let him be a scoundrel, Mr. Ambler's readers at least will judge him under Western eyes. It is possible—it certainly seems possible to Foster—that Deltchev is in fact a hero, a Western hero, a kind of Mittel Europa Abe Lincoln. But as things develop it becomes clear that there are too many pieces of evidence which won't fit in with this explanation, too many queer, dubious incidents. Can it be after all that the official explanation is correct—that Deltchev is, and always has been, corrupt, treacherous, and criminal?

The solution lies between these extremes, and is presented by Mr. Ambler with the smoothness, the unobtrusiveness, of a highly-skilled waiter serving a carefully chosen meal to a respected customer. Naturally it is a well-cooked meal. The best ingredients—suspense, bewilderment, irony—are served up so as to suit almost any taste. Personally, I felt sorry not to be able to swallow it steadily or to swallow it whole.—J. D. SCOTT, "New Novels," *NSN*, Aug. 25, 1951, p. 211

Like his last novel, *Judgment on Deltchev* (1952), Eric Ambler's newest is not the top-drawer product that his admirers might have hoped for. In plain language—and with the chance that we are wrong—Mr. Ambler seems to have lost the touch that made such thrillers as *Cause for Alarm* and *Journey into Fear* the very best of their kind. And this is sad news: like a good man, a good thriller writer is hard to find.

Now that Graham Greene has gone fancy for good, and Dashiell Hammett appears to have given up the pen, Ambler was in a sense the last of the master craftsmen who dealt in suspense and foul deeds. Who can forget the particular kind of devilish what's-going-to-happen-now? which Ambler produced with his deceptive straightforwardness? Is there one of his veteran readers who had the high moral courage to put an Ambler book down once he had picked it up—without reaching the last page, I mean? (As an old Ambler-addict let me say I envy such a man his cool blood; and feel fortunate that it is not in my veins.)

But all that, as the poet said, was in another country and the wench seems pretty dead. The country was Europe before the war—Ambler's perfect hunting-ground for brilliant tales of intrigue. The wench was the special kind of pre-war anxiety that lent undercurrents of Evil to every seemingly innocent situation that Ambler dangled before the reader.

Europe has changed now, and a new definition of what is wicked is needed. Ambler, apparently urged by his publishers to try and duplicate his earlier successes, is not quite in tune with the new era. He is still the meticulous artificer of the old, and where once his work had the excitement of an "inside story" from a foreign capital it now seems rather beside the point.

The Schirmer Inheritance is about the efforts of a young American lawyer to trace a German who has inherited more than a half million dollars. The search leads him through the maze of contemporary Europe—he covers more countries than a Cook's tour—and when he finally finds his quarry there is a double-twist that is as unexpected as anything in the old Ambler.

The difference between this odyssey of adventure and the English author's earlier ones is that a good deal of the *en route* business is tedious and actually padded—Ambler is marking time to carry his reader through two hundred odd pages. It is as if the author himself was a little tired of his own kind of thriller, no longer inspired, no longer savoring his own cleverness in the medium, and the result shows as it always does. This isn't to imply that isolated chapters aren't as good and exact—in characterization, detail and so forth—as anything being written by Ambler's colleagues today. They are. But in overall unity and total impact this is a bad falling-off from the high standard of his earlier books. The final and sad impression is that he has passed the crest as one of the truly first-rate thriller writers of his generation.—SEYMOUR KRIM, "Suspense," *Com*, Aug. 7, 1953, pp. 450–51

As an old hand at intrigue, violence, and Asia, Mr. Ambler kicks this tale ⟨*Passage of Arms*⟩ off with his usual skill. Girija Krishnan, an Indian employed in Malaya, is ordered, as a rubber plantation's clerk, to arrange burial for eight Chinese who have been ambushed by a British patrol in the guerrilla fighting of some years back. He gets the job done in a few pages which brilliantly evoke the countryside. Then he notices things the British have missed. From them he deduces that these Chinese, instead of being ordinary terrorists, must have formed a guard, probably for an arms cache, tucked away in some ravine. If he can only find these guns, store them safe from the weather and sell them without paying the prescribed penalty (which is death), he can gain the capital he will need to start a bus line for that part of the peninsula.

It takes Girija three years to cook up his plans. A buyer is found, the agent for Indonesian revolutionaries. Shipment, however, needs certain signatures on customs papers, and as the patsy to furnish these, an American is baited in, a middle-aged manufacturer named Olsen, on an around-the-world tour with his wife. The rest, once Olsen puts his name on the dotted line, is the disaster his naïveté leads to. He gets in deeper and deeper, winding up in a Sumatran jail, where he, the wife, and a Eurasian lady are caught in a shooting raid and mauled up by guards. Communists, insects and disillusionment.

The start, as I have said, tingles. The detail throughout is superb, especially the glimpses the author gives us into various Asian minds. And yet, for one reader at least, things began to sag, early on. I would say the trouble was too much integrity, not too little: Mr. Ambler apparently set out to master his background, and wound up with its mastering him.

Seeking a plausible antagonist, he passed up the hackneyed adventurer, and hit on the middle-aged Olsen—perhaps, I must add, with some idea of doing another Quiet American (the Greene book is mentioned once, in an oddly arresting way). If so, this American is not only quiet but dull. And the trap the background has furnished is so fiendishly perfect that not even Casanova could get out of it by his own wits alone. So Olsen is saved by others, and totes up, first to last, a straw man.

Getting back to first principles, we see once again the importance of a love story, as the armature on which all else is built. I found myself wishing, I confess, that someone, somewhere, in this book, would find a girl to seduce, or want to. No such thing happens. No love of any kind, whether sexy, noble or renunciatory, reareth its ugly head, unless Olsen's devotion to his wife, occasionally remembered, counts as such.

In short, for a picture of Southeast Asia, in all its color and the savagery of its current turmoil, this is tops, and gets down to bedrock. For poetics, it's a little skimpy.—JAMES M. CAIN, "Color of the East," *NYTBR*, March 6, 1960, p. 38

LEROY PANEK
From "Eric Ambler"
The Special Branch
1981, pp. 139–54

Ambler's particular brand of trapped men in the middle, for which he is well known, did not spring into his fiction fully formed. They developed: they grew out of the traditional romantic conventions of the spy novel going back to LeQueux, but under Ambler's hand they slowly emerge as something other than conventional even if they partake of a new sort of romanticism. As a popular writer, Ambler put in his time on the shop floor before he moved up to have an office of his own. His early novels, in fact, have much in common with the restrained, half-refined writers of the previous generation, exemplified best in the novels of Francis Beeding. Ambler uses most of the stock spy characters from the thriller tradition in his early books. Colonel Robinson, in *Background to Danger*, and General Vargas, in *Cause for Alarm*, are very much in the mold of the gentleman super villain beloved of the thriller writers of the twenties. They combine suavity with grotesqueness and have access to power, just as innumerable other villains do. Likewise, the Zaleschoffs, brother and sister, seem very much the stereotypical secret agent heroes of the popular tradition (they appear in both *Background to Danger* and *Cause for Alarm*). . . .

Instead of being action-fixated, *Epitaph for a Spy* goes back to the tradition of Conrad's *The Secret Agent* (1907), which emphasizes the mundane, seedy, sordid and pathetically inconclusive nature of espionage. Ambler, in terms of the spy novel, takes Conrad's premise to its furthest extent. Josef Vadassy is the hero of *Epitaph for a Spy*. He teaches languages, like the narrator of *Under Western Eyes* (1911), and is a stateless individual—not because of anything that he has done, but because of his father's politics and the arbitrary shifting of boundaries of states in central Europe. Although a meek and innocuous individual, the French authorities arrest Vadassy because his name has become linked to some blurred photographs of the port defenses at Toulon.

In spite of the fact that Beghin, the Naval Intelligence officer, knows full well that Vadassy did not take the photos, he forces him to return to the Hotel Reserve in order to smoke out the real spy, thereby allowing the authorities to roll up the whole espionage network. Nothing works out at the hotel. Vadassy bumbles around, making everyone suspicious, until, finally, the intelligence people make a show of arresting him, whereupon the real spy takes flight and is cornered and killed in a roof-top gun battle. The spy, whose efforts in photography are at best third class and of minimal danger to French security, is a ratty down-and-outer, whose epitaph is "He needed the money." Ironically connected to this, the sub-plot shows how Vadassy's trampling around helps Nazi agents track down an anti-Nazi agent and blackmail him into returning to Germany and his execution.

This novel is not only vital for Ambler's later development, but also for the development of the spy novel as a whole. It contains Ambler's first genuinely unwilling spy who does not choose to participate in the action but whom malign authority forces to do distasteful and dangerous things. He is the man in the middle who is battered by both sides. The only other pre-war character who approaches this is Graham in *Journey into Fear*, but his case does not have the force of Vadassy's, since Graham acts for an armaments manufacturer on the eve of war. Vadassy, in a sense, extends the situation of Conrad's secret agent, Verloc, who is also trapped by irrational demands. Ambler's character, however, deserves sympathy as Verloc does not. Another important ingredient in *Epitaph for a Spy* is the character of the agent who photographed Toulon harbor. No longer does Ambler show the villain as a dashing, bizarre character like Colonel Robinson or General Vargas. Neither do the results of his spying shake the foundations of Europe. He is merely a disagreeable, shoddy human being who works in the hope of the big pay-off, or of any pay-off. Finally, *Epitaph for a Spy* shows a different slant in its fictional organization. Ambler gives up oratorical ideology and only indirectly attacks the capitalist system through Duclos, a sanitary engineer who, in his skewed sense of reality, believes himself to be a paternalistic industrial mogul. More important than this, Ambler gives up the hunt-chase organization of his early books and centers most of *Epitaph for a Spy* around a series of interviews at the hotel, drawing technique from the detective novel. Also, in the detective novel tradition, the realistic detective novel versus the romantic one, the amateur detective is absolutely wrong about most of his observations. In his footnote to the 1951 edition of *Epitaph for a Spy*, Ambler calls the book "a mild attempt at realism." "Mild," of course, depends on what it is compared to. Compared to Horler's spy books, *Epitaph for a Spy* is *Nana*, *MacTeague* and *Sister Carrie* rolled into one, but compared to *A Gun for Sale* it is rosy hued. Still, *Epitaph for a Spy* marks an important change for Ambler and it later provided him with much to build upon.

. . . Before the war, with a few exceptions, Ambler, like other spy writers, depended a good deal upon action and its efficacy for both plot situations and characters' recognition of their real selves. After the war he dropped a good bit of the cliche action found in his pre-war books. There are, for instance, few hunt-chase scenes at the end of the post-war books. He also gives the meaning of action new scrutiny. Going as far back as Buchan, or even farther back to Stevenson and Rider Haggard for that matter, action has not only been one of the bases of the adventure-spy story, but it has also been one of its cardinal moral points. Since spy novels go back to Victorian schoolboy stories, and many really remain schoolboy stories, they preach that man's physical and mental worth are best shown in action and that action and social responsibilities, like duty, inextricably intertwine. Spy stories like this are like Carlyle for the unsophisticated. Although the twentieth century likes to pretend to have rejected Victorianism, these same schoolboy standards apply to writers like Hemingway, who operate under the loose label of existentialism. In the twentieth century, however, action may lose its association with duty, but it becomes associated with another shibboleth, knowing one's self. Just as Ambler had used this motif of the proving virtues of action before the war, he uses it after the war with a bit more examination. Thus, Colonel Jost reminds Carter in *The Intercom Conspiracy* that all the danger which he has faced

and to which he has been forced to react has had a therapeutic and liberating effect:

> You are a different man from the one I met a year ago. Then you were tired and contemptuous of the work you did. You disliked yourself. Now I detect a new confidence in you. Think. You are engaged in completing a new book for the late, respected and much lamented Mr. Latimer. Would his publishers have employed the man you were a year ago? I doubt it. You have come to terms with yourself.[1]

Along these same lines, Piet Maas in *A Kind of Anger* gets off pills and loses his sense of failure after dueling with death. Seeing life and yourself has a joyously liberating effect. After meeting danger, characters can joke. Carter's last sentence in *The Intercom Conspiracy* is "Once past the gateway to Latimer's villa I enjoyed the walk back to the inn," and George, at the close of *The Schirmer Inheritance*, laughs as he walks back to Greece. Ambler does not have the inclination to microscopically examine the psychological changes which action makes in his characters, but in the tradition of the action spy novel he notes that they do happen.

This, however, is not Ambler's only slant on the human effects of action. Like Greene, Ambler does take a critical look at the place of action in the spy-adventure book. Any rational adult who has experienced real uncertainty and danger, say, in combat, will acknowledge that it does not have a great deal to recommend it. Adults recognize the manifest potentials for pain and death in dangerous adventures, and need to be very powerfully motivated before they will willingly seek them. Adults are tender with their lives, having recognized their mortality, and having been grafted to social responsibilities in the form of professions and families. The fanatic, the imbecile or the adolescent usually becomes the street fighter or the rebel. Ambler knew all about this, and he added it to his descriptions of people involved in dangerous action. George Carey, for instance, in *The Schirmer Inheritance*, finds himself caught in situations which are not only illegal but also dangerous. He, however, dives right into them in spite of his mature instincts; he does this

> Because he loved his fellow men and was curious about them? Rubbish. More likely that the elaborate defenses of his youth, the pompous fantasies of big office chairs and panelled boardrooms, of hidden wealth and power behind the scenes, were beginning to crumble, and that the pimply adolescent was belatedly emerging into the light.[2]

Quite the same thing happens to Greg Nilsen in *Passage of Arms*:

> He regarded himself, not without reason, as a mature and level-headed man. If anyone had suggested that somewhere in the back streets of his mind another Greg Nilsen—a roistering, romantic, ten-year-old swashbuckler—had escaped from custody and was out enjoying a game of cops and robbers he would have been angrily incredulous.[3]

To drive the point hime in this novel, Ambler makes Greg's wife, Dorothy, a kindergarten teacher, and he makes Nilsen get into trouble behind her back and partly to spite her.

In all this, Ambler goes back and re-presents the double selves of Barstow/Carruthers from *The Dark Frontier*: there is a responsible, adult self which shrinks from action and an adolescent self which seeks and revels in it. By tying the action-seeking motive to adolescence rather than Providence or character molding, Ambler denigrates the value of adventure for its own sake, and the construction of his novels shows that normal people do not engage in risks unless they are trapped into it—and well and truly trapped at that.

This brings us to Ambler's man in the middle. First of all, we need to recognize that this character type has several manifestations in Ambler's post-war books. We can see Ambler's simplest use of this character in the men in the middle in *Judgment on Deltchev*, *The Schirmer Inheritance*, *State of Siege*, *Passage of Arms*, *The Intercom Conspiracy*, *The Levanter* and *Doctor Frigo*. These books turn on men (women in Ambler, when they are important to the plots, play subsidiary roles like Dorothy Nilsen in *Passage of Arms* or Lucia Bernardi in *A Kind of Anger*) coerced by forces which they definitely cannot control. Typically, intransigent and unforgiving forces, like the Palestine Action Force and the Syrian government in *The Levanter*, collide, but they also catch the heroes at the exact spot at which they collide. Thus Ambler's heroes get caught in the middle of the opposing forces because of perverse circumstances—they are in the wrong place at the wrong time—or because biases of their personalities work with circumstance to entrap them. Michael Howell in *The Levanter* happens to be engaged in trying to maintain his investments in Syria when the government goes on a nationalizing binge, and he happens to own a factory suitable for the clandestine production of arms. Further, he is a dogged and compulsive entrepreneur and engineer who believes that he can fix things with his own talents and skills. People like Howell may face dangers, but they do not make any appreciable impact on the forces which manipulate them. They become, in many cases, not so much minor participants as observers of political perversities. It is not surprising to find that in two of his post-war man in the middle novels, Ambler uses journalists (*Judgment on Deltchev* and *The Intercom Conspiracy*), in three (*State of Siege*, *Passage of Arms* and *The Levanter*) he uses engineers, and that in *The Schirmer Inheritance* and *Doctor Frigo* he uses a lawyer and a physician, respectively. All these professions for his heroes carry with them objectivity and technical know-how. Ambler's heroes, like Fraser in *State of Siege*, watch armies slug it out, and they are forced to watch from a dangerous vantage point. From watching the collisions, Ambler's simplest heroes learn something about themselves and about love—it being impossible from Ambler's view to learn anything but despair from politics. A few of them, though, get caught in the grinder and destroyed, as in *Judgment on Deltchev*. In spite of this pathetic outcome, and in spite of the fact that many of Ambler's simple heroes in the middle do not choose to be where they are or to act as they act under pressure, this sort of hero works out to be reasonably romantic, and can be seen as a logical extension of spy novel conventions since LeQueux.

Ambler, however, was not content with this, and wished to make the man in the middle into a new character. He did this first with the character of Arthur Abdel Simpson. Arthur appears in *The Light of Day* (which is not a spy novel) and *Dirty Story*. He is the only distinctive voice in all of Ambler, and in many ways he is the culmination of much of what Ambler had done both before and after the war. Unlike the romantic men in the middle who engage the reader's identification and sympathy, Arthur gains no personal knowledge or stature from the events into which he is hurled. He ends as he begins, as a crud. He does, though, learn something about living in a world of bullies by the end of the second novel, and from Arthur's discovery Ambler then built a whole other class of characters in his most recent novels. . . .

At the end of *Dirty Story* Arthur conceives a fantastic plan to place himself on a par with all the people, institutions, and states which have been doing him the dirty. Of course Arthur is a *picaro* (and Ambler does much better at this character type

than do his contemporaries, Coles and Household, who also used the *picaro* in the spy novel), but in him Ambler placed certain serious alternatives for those trapped by the powerful of the world. In him he developed a new sort of man in the middle. Now, Ambler's original victim characters may learn something from their brushes with authority and danger, but they do not substantially master them. Beginning with *The Schirmer Inheritance*, it occurred to Ambler that, although political and social entities often shift or collide so as to discomfit or crush individuals caught in the way, there exist gaps and vacuums between them which can be exploited. In *A Coffin for Dimitrios*, he demonstrated the ways in which criminals use these gaps and blind spots, and after the war he added to this the idea of the guerrilla. Both *The Schirmer Inheritance* and *The Intercom Conspiracy* use characters who have backgrounds as guerrillas. I do not want to say that Ambler advocates actual guerrilla warfare with established institutions, or considers that this sort of action might have an effect; he does not. He does, however, use it as a metaphor for the way in which his new sort of hero may prosper in a hostile world. Historically, the first of these new men in the middle is Sergeant Franz Schirmer, in *The Schirmer Inheritance*, who imitates his nineteenth century ancestor, opts out of the *Wehrmacht* which is indifferent to honor or competence, opts out of the army of the Greek communists which blackmails him, and sets up as Robin Hood along the Greek-Yugoslavian border. From his hide-out in no man's land, Schirmer can plunder institutions, like the Eurasian Credit Trust, avoid both Greek and Yugoslavian laws, and make a world for himself and his woman. Like Schirmer, Girija Krishnan in *Passage of Arms* manages to skirt legality, get the best of Mr. Tan, the Chinese capitalist, and fulfill his boyhood dream of setting up a bus company with genuine British busses. Lucia Bernardi and Piet Maas sell secret papers, not only to the Iraqi government, but also to an Italian oil company in *A Kind of Anger*. Arthur Simpson, though, does what all of these characters really want to do when at the close of *Dirty Story* he decides to set himself up as a passport-issuing country.

Before Arthur, Ambler shows these people who make and sell juice from the squeeze between powers to the likeable folks whom we should admire for their pluck and ingenuity. After Arthur, however, the position of this character becomes less simple. Arthur, *picaro* that he is, is still a pimp, a pornographer, and thief who, in spite of his whining protests of innocence, deserves all that he gets. Although they seem cleaner, the same is true of Colonels Jost and Brand in *The Intercom Conspiracy*, and Paul Firman and Mat Williamson in *The Siege of the Villa Lipp*. All these men win against the system, and have nice clothes and better accents than Arthur. But they cause far more in the way of misery and death in their milking of the system than Arthur does—misery and death, moreover, which they never see, operating as they do through cutouts, covers, and mail services, or which they stubbornly refuse to acknowledge. They come to act as states and institutions do, and they go from men in the middle to men who put others in the middle.

Just as this shift shows a more complex moral world, so do Ambler's methods of presentation become more complex in the most recent novels. Beginning with *The Intercom Conspiracy* and including *The Levanter* and *The Siege of the Villa Lipp*, Ambler has moved from the single narrative voice to presentation of collections of views which cast doubt on the truth of the main narrator. *The Siege of the Villa Lipp*, for instance, gives Firman's story as told to a writer whom he has hired, but it also contains an Afterword by Professor Krom, and this sheds new light on the whole narration: in the body of the novel, Firman shows Krom to be incompetent and weak, but the Afterword shows him to be rational, perceptive, and human. Which one do we accept? This same technique blurs the characters' moral positions and the issues of *The Intercom Conspiracy* and *The Levanter*, and becomes for Ambler another way to undercut the cliches of the spy novel.

In the thirties Ambler began writing spy novels which entertained people, but he also endeavored to make them think: think about capitalism, think about real spies, think about detectives. With sure craftsmanship Ambler changed the traditional novel of espionage. He brought to it a realistic sense of what people really are, and a new point of view toward political and economic reality. He did away with the Secret Service hero and ignored the cliches of the thirties, like secret papers. The air of distanced analysis which increasingly affects his novels may not bring him into the pale of enduring literature, but it certainly makes Ambler the superior spy writer of his generation.

Notes

1. *The Intercom Conspiracy* (New York: Bantam, 1970), pp. 207–8.
2. *The Intercom Conspiracy*, p. 209.
3. *The Schirmer Inheritance* (New York: Knopf, 1953), pp. 138–39.

KINGSLEY AMIS

1922–

Born in London on April 26, 1922, Kingsley Amis attended St. John's College, Oxford, from 1941 to 1948. He served with the Royal Signal Corps in World War II, then returned to Oxford for his B.A. and M.A. His friends there included mystery writer Edmund Crispin (Bruce Montgomery) and poets Philip Larkin, Elizabeth Jennings, and John Wain. Critics labeled Larkin, Jennings, Wain, Amis, and his collaborator Robert Conquest "The Movement" when their eloquent, anti-romantic poetry attracted notice in the mid-1950s, and singled out Amis as an "angry young man" when his first novel, *Lucky Jim*, was published in 1955. The novel, which was dedicated to Larkin and won the Somerset Maugham Award, drew on Amis' experience as English lecturer at the University College of Swansea, a position he held from 1949 to 1961. He has also taught at Princeton, Vanderbilt, and Peterhouse College, Cambridge. In 1981 he was named a Commander of the Order of the British Empire.

Amis consistently confounds the expectations of critics and readers by shifting genre, tone, and attitudes from book to book. His writing includes poetry, humorous and serious fiction, science fiction and fantasy, mystery, criticism, biography, essays, television drama, and a James Bond thriller written under the pseudonym of "Robert Markham." *The Alteration*, his science fiction novel of a Catholic Europe, won the John W. Campbell Memorial Award for 1977.

Amis lives in London. He has three children by his deceased first wife, and is divorced from his second. His son Martin is an acclaimed novelist.

General

. . . Amis is much more the novelist born. There is in the born novelist's presentation of his world and his characters a discreetness, a hesitation about final judgments, a sense of something held in reserve, which Amis has and Wain lacks; a good example is the scene in *That Uncertain Feeling* where the wealthy stick of a complaisant husband suddenly becomes toweringly formidable, not because he has been cuckolded, but because the hero's independence has reduced his wife to hysteria. The hero of *Lucky Jim* has had all kinds of topical meanings tagged on to him; in fact, he belongs to an old tradition in folk-tale, the wise simpleton or lucky blunderer. He is also a male Cinderella, for one can find in the novel bad and good magicians (Professor Welch and the rich man from London), an ogress, a thwarted witch or enchantress, and a defeated boaster. Jim Dixon is not fundamentally an angry young man but, like Wells's Kipps, a put upon young man. There is, however, very little fantasy in the sharp social and psychological observation, stylized for comedy, but never, like some of Wain's stylizations, taking wing from life. There are passages, of course, of sheer farce, the blanket-burning episode and the drunken speech (modelled, perhaps, on the similar Wodehouse oration by Gussy Fink-Nottle). But there is penetrating realism in the whole account of the relations of Jim and Margaret, the most thoroughly 'done' (in a Henry Jamesian sense) part of the book. It is a pity that where the unattractive, unhappy, and life-consuming Margaret is so wonderfully drawn, the heroine, the kindly princess, should not be much more than a sex-object, with a verbal glow around her. Of Amis's subsequent novels, the third one, *I Like It Here*, was a misfire. *That Uncertain Feeling* seemed to me a much better novel than many critics made out, but unevenly balanced between seriousness, pure farce, and high comedy; I also felt the cards were a little rigged against the unfortunate Mrs Gruffyd-Williams. The last one, *Take a Girl Like You*, seemed to me near Amis's top form; a much more subtle and comprehensive treatment of the rival claims of natural randiness and the traditional decencies than *That Uncertain Feeling*, bringing in the idea of a code of honour (Patrick ought not to have had Jenny, when she was drunk and defenceless), and working out some themes quite new to me in recent fiction: for instance, the social and sexual disadvantage at which the physically unattractive always are, and the compunction, and helpfulness, the physically attractive can sometimes show about this. The sadness, heaviness, and shame that attends Patrick's ignoble triumph at the end; Patrick's recurring fantasies of cruelty to others and death to himself; the grimly comic monologue of the aged impotent peer (he used to suck old electric batteries to see if there was any juice left in them, but there is no juice left now in his); all put the pursuit of sexual pleasure, which is Patrick's main aim in life, in moral perspective: we get a glimpse of the scholar Patrick could have been, which the gay life leaves him no time to be. Full of humour, this is nevertheless on the whole a sober rather than a funny book, like Fielding's *Amelia*: Fielding believed that good nature was the core of morals but by the time of *Amelia* had come to believe that good nature without principles was not enough. The account of the visit to Fielding's tomb in *I Like It Here* is the one really moving and memorable passage in that novel. Like Fielding's, Amis's heroes are thoroughly virile, susceptible to female charm to the point of weakness, but good-natured. Patrick, in *I Like It Here*, is made to suffer for his weakness: the friend whom he most admires rejects and despises him for his moral rape of Jenny; but about his ultimate good nature we are left in some doubt. Jenny resigns herself to the situation, but probably Patrick has no intention of marrying her. Some light has gone out for both of them; many people found this novel very coarse and nasty, but, given that some lights have gone out for Amis also, I found it a just picture of some aspects of contemporary life.

Amis, then, leaves one admiring, but with a heavy and sad feeling; in one story in his most recent publication, *My Enemy's Enemy*, he took for his hero a bachelor, the platonic admirer of a middle-aged married woman, the wife of an old friend of his. She dies, he comes to the funeral. He gets into conversation, over a meal, with the dead woman's daughter, who has married a naturalized Italian. He finds himself talking about English ways, English customs, English traditions, in an implicitly insulting and excluding way. The girl is hurt but forgiving, and asks him to come back for another meal; but she does make him realize both that her mother, whom he idealized, was not very kind about her marriage and that this patient, platonic love of his, if it involves no remorses, also runs no risks. I think Amis may in future write about superficially rather dull people, like the people in this story, but bring out with the great subtlety of moral observation which he possesses both the earnestness they can awkwardly express and the reality of moral problems one thinks of as trivial and prosaic. But I hope he still sometimes gives himself over to pure comedy, even to farce.—G. S. Fraser, "The Novel in the 1950s," *The Modern Writer and His World*, 1964, pp. 176–79

Mr. Kingsley Amis . . . began his career unluckily by being labelled an Angry Young Man and luckily by writing *Lucky Jim*. The first assured his fame, or notoriety; the second gave notice of his promise. Though it is not, I think, his best book, *Lucky Jim* is nonetheless a fine one, savaging most of the institutions and traditions still standing at the end of the Second World War and introducing a new type of classless anti- and non-hero, who manages, barely but decisively, to be more likable than his mingily pedigreed antagonists. Jim Dixon succeeds in winning our hearts and our partisanship by representing the bloody-minded id in all of us; in his wholesome hatred for teachers and for learning itself, in his honest greed for free food, free drinks, and free girls, in his innocent eye on the main chance, Jim bravely and pusillanimously takes a role a whole postwar college generation would have loved to dare to take.

Once the considerable dust of *Lucky Jim* had cleared, Amis did not immediately succumb to the sophomore jinx of the possible, nor did he immediately repeat and enlarge on his first success. The closest he came before 1960—before *Take a Girl Like You*—was *That Uncertain Feeling*, which will, and should, be remembered for its gritty, funny closeups of Welsh shabby-genteel-intellectual family life, its exegesis of the miserable politics of provincial librarianship, its measurement of the

vast canyon between classes in the Britain of 1954 or so, its convincing portrait of a man-eating piece of female county gentry, and its well-built Feydeau slapstick. But it does not begin to approach my nominee for Amis's masterpiece, *Take a Girl Like You*, in unity of theme and plot, in depth of characterization, in seriousness of play. Amis is after big game here—perhaps for the first and only time since *Lucky Jim*—and he never puts a foot wrong in his long and unrelenting stalk of the minute, particular relations between a really decent virgin and her clever, caddish, and eventually decent seducer. What makes *Take a Girl Like You* so good—and I would rank it with *A Handful of Dust* as one of the great serio-comic novels of the century—is its unrelenting intensity of observation, a word-by-word mosaic of perception that adds up to a sad, good-humored final say on the relations between men and women. Amis is especially good, like Orwell, on shabbiness and shabby gentility; on pretensions, particularly lower-middle-class ones; and on all kinds of cant and sham, for which he has an X-ray eye. But he is best and most original on the subject of sex, to which he brings the faultless eye and ear of a handsome man who has been there himself. His women possess real dimension of a kind not often seen since Fitzgerald (is it possible that only the writer who is himself attractive to women can portray them justly and affectionately, and that the others must idealize or denigrate, and in either case flatten, their female characters?); his "duds" and "smashers" of both sexes are not simply types but deep and realized personalities. Even the mysterious and marvellous Able Seaman Arthur Jackson—who is only seen "reading the news" about his failed marriage in a drunken yell under a lamppost—is as real and believable as any of the major characters.

After *Take a Girl Like You*, Amis's next two novels—*One Fat Englishman* and *The Anti-Death League*—represented dead-end forays into new milieus. The first, the story of a boorish and repulsive English publisher's rapacious visit to the United States, is nearly unreadable in its cold distaste for its characters, who to a man (or woman) are moral lepers no writer or reader would willingly identify with; the second, an experiment in futurism *cum* science fiction, gets hung up on its glittering hardware and fails to progress to a conclusion or to resolve itself as a story about human beings. *The Egyptologists*, published the year *The Anti-Death League* was, is perhaps beneath mention as a collaboration (with Robert Conquest) and as a one-joke joke that is extremely wearying. Clearly, something awful had happened to Kingsley Amis since 1960. Though this is a review of the books and not the man, it seems fair, and safe, to say that he was simply taken up: that he was made a part, perhaps involuntarily, of the mindless, circular, self-perpetuating London game called literature, with its serial TV interviews, intellectual gossip columns, and bitterly playful public controversies that never seem to end. Perhaps, like Auden's Yeats, he became his admirers; these admirers, though, were not the library-card holders of Leeds and Great Barrington or the undergraduates of Vanderbilt and Edinburgh but the tit-for-tat, *quid-pro-quo* newsmen and broadcasters and pundits and P.R.O.s and party-givers of the British (and transatlantic) metropolis.—L. E. Sissman, "Kingsley Amis at Halfway House," *NY*, April 26, 1969, pp. 163–67

Works

FICTION

A new hero has risen among us. Is he the intellectual tough, or the tough intellectual? He is consciously, even conscientiously, graceless. His face, when not dead-pan, is set in a snarl of exasperation. He has one skin too few, but his is not the sensitiveness of the young man in earlier twentieth-century fiction: it is the phoney to which his nerve-ends are tremblingly exposed, and at the least suspicion of the phoney he goes tough. He is at odds with his conventional university education, though he comes generally from a famous university: he has seen through the academic racket as he sees through all the others. A racket is phoneyness organised, and in contact with phoneyness he turns red just as litmus paper does in contact with an acid. In life he has been among us for some little time. One may speculate whence he derives. The Services, certainly, helped to make him; but George Orwell, Dr. Leavis and the Logical Positivists—or, rather, the attitudes these represent— all contributed to his genesis. In fiction I think he first arrived last year, as the central character of Mr. John Wain's novel *Hurry On Down.* He turns up again in Mr. Amis's *Lucky Jim.*

Mr. Wain's character was the picaresque hero, and the picaresque has commonly been a vehicle for satire. Mr. Amis isn't writing picaresque or even satire. He comes at times very close to farce, yet not farce as we normally think of it. His hero, Jim Dixon, is in his first term as an assistant lecturer in history in a provincial university. Everything goes wrong for him. He has the gift of precipitating the most impossible situations, situations which cannot be explained away. Thus, on his first appearance in the university, he appears to have gratuitously assaulted the Professor of English. He goes for an arty weekend at the Professor of History's, quarrels with the Professor's son, gets drunk and sets his bed on fire with a forgotten cigarette. Towards the end of the term, when he has to deliver the popular public lecture which may reinstate him in the eyes of the Faculty and save him his job, he finds himself involuntarily parodying the manner first of the principal and then of his professor, and finally embarked on a wild burlesque of all such popular lectures on his theme—"Merry England," which he is supposed to praise.

This may suggest that he is, as it were, remotely a Chaplin-figure, the *naif* who, from his very innocence, exposes the sham. Jim Dixon is far from that: he is, in his anxious way, playing the racket. If he were less anxious, he would play it better: the impossible situations arise from the fact he can never wholly kid himself that the racket is worth playing. He is not the dumb ox with the heart of gold at all; his attitude, even as he compromises, is much more that of Mr. Lewis's *Soldier of Humour.*

Lucky Jim is an extremely interesting first novel, and parts of it are very funny indeed: the episodes of the bed-burning and Jim's public lecture, for instance, mount to the complexity and tension of certain passages in the Marx Brothers' films or in the paper-hanging act one still sees from time to time in pantomime. And Mr. Amis has an unwaveringly merciless eye for the bogus: some aspects of provincial culture—the madrigals and recorders of Professor Welch, for instance—are pinned down as accurately as they have ever been; and he has, too, an eye for character—the female lecturer Margaret, who battens neurotically on Jim's pity, is quite horribly well done. Mr. Amis is a novelist of formidable and uncomfortable talent.— WALTER ALLEN, NSN, Jan. 30, 1954, pp. 136–37

Lucky Jim, the most famous work of them all, is written with enormous gusto. Mr. Amis is a very talented writer, and reveals great novelistic qualities in pursuing the mode of the farcical picaresque, set perhaps by Mr. Joyce Cary in *The Horse's Mouth,* to which he gives a new turn by imbuing it with a certain acidity. Though his situations are fantastic, he has the rare skill to make life exist on the page; he ever and again gets you "there," especially in the scenes which are nightmare fantasy, as when the hero burns his hostess's sheets (being drunk, he had let a lighted cigarette fall on them); or when he is

desperately anxious to be at the station before a certain time and the bus simply will not make haste. Our concern here, however, is with the attitude of the hero, James Dixon, a junior lecturer in history on probation at a provincial University College (Mr. Amis is a lecturer in English at such). It soon becomes apparent that he hates and despises the whole University business, especially his Professor. According to Dixon, Professor Welch is an unmitigated old fool, who certainly ought not to occupy the position that he does, though it slips out that he is a diligent enough historian who at any rate checks his references. But his great hobby is Elizabethan music, which, of course, is "phoney"; he drives a car abominably (all this is quite funny): but, we note, he is extremely kind. He goes out of his way to help Dixon in his career; he looks after a neurotic female member of the staff, Margaret, with whom Dixon conducts an inconclusive love-affair; and if his hobby is tiresome, it is at least harmless. Dixon behaves abominably; he feels— quite unnecessarily, as far as can be gathered—that he is an "outsider" socially, and takes every opportunity to be rude. His sole escape when he feels baffled is to drink too much. He plays tricks on his colleagues, writes anonymous letters, destroys documents to give people trouble, and tries to impersonate others on the telephone. Malicious and envious, he has in him no drop of the milk of human kindness. His attitude towards women isn't even that of good animal physical attraction: "the possession of the signs of sexual privilege is the important thing, not the quality nor the enjoyment of them," he concludes, exhibiting a debased *amour vanité.* When, at the end of the session, by the kindness of Professor Welch he is chosen to give a public address, he gets drunk, imitates the University officials, and finally passes out. His reward for behaving like a baboon is the post of secretary to a rich man in London, with which goes the prospect of filching somebody else's mistress. Lucky Jim! Only twice in the whole book does he show any trace of common feeling: once when he feels vaguely responsible for Margaret (he takes a mean opportunity to get out of the whole connection); and once, for a moment, when Welch forgives him about the sheets, he feels that he may have misjudged him.

It cannot be supposed that Mr. Amis likes this extremely unpleasant character to whom he has given immense vitality. He has, in an extraordinarily skilful way, made him live by making him think before us just the savage thoughts, tending to violence, that such a man, we imagine, might think: and the whole is told with such zest that we begin in an odd way to side with Dixon. But what is his function? It would appear to be to inject poison into an already diseased society, in which there is not a single individual one would like to meet, for even the well-meaning Welch is an intolerable old bore. Dixon would seem intended as the lens through which we can see a heap of crawling maggots which is what "bourgeois" society consists of, he himself being a bundle of all the vices of such a society with none of the virtues. The others, it appears, exist by means of elaborate pretence, or solemn pretentiousness. Their manners baffle Dixon. At a ball, he and Margaret and another pair are about to join another couple, one of whom is the rich man, Gore-Urquhart:

> When he saw the others coming towards them, Gore-Urquhart rose to his feet. This formality was so unfamiliar in the circles Dixon moved in that for a moment he wondered whether the other meant to oppose their approach by physical force.

It's all part of the "phoney." One might think that Dixon was the honest man—a queer sort of Alceste!—but that all the time he seems to be building up an idea of himself, as in his trick of assuming certain kinds of face, all "designed to express rage or loathing." It is a sparkling book, which some find extremely amusing: but what it is trying to do it is baffling to guess. Although Dixon's attitude and gestures are often merely schoolboy ("Dixon put out his tongue at an old woman who was staring at them"), there is too much fervor in the work for it to be meant simply as a farcical pantomime.—BONAMY DO-BRÉE, "No Man's Land," *SwR*, Spring 1957, pp. 313–15

It is a hard life being an English humorist. We all have it so firmly fixed in our minds that we are a nation of potential red-nosed comedians that any writer who shows signs of cheerfulness is instantly seized upon by critics and publicists as an opposite number in a crosstalk act. "Well, old boy, old boy," you can hear them saying, "what's going to have us in stitches to-night? No, I haven't heard the one about the young girl of Milford Haven. . . . Oh, very good, old boy, very good!" Indeed, so predictable is the reaction of a certain section of those who record their opinions that it frequently has the air of occurring in advance of the joke itself, an illusion which recalls the captive roars of laughter emitted by a studio audience. Very nice for the humorist, this, in a way. But let him beware. Should he try to make his humour that much more subtle, should he venture to introduce a serious theme into his books, then his robot readers will look at each other in dismay. "Old so-and-so getting a bit pi, eh? Off colour to-day?", and the faces will grow long and puzzled like those of men finding themselves at the Old Vic when they had expected a striptease club.

Something of this sort seems to have happened to Kingsley Amis. I find it difficult to explain in any other way the lack of understanding—the total lack of any attempt at literary analysis—shown by one or two of the notices of his new novel, *Take a Girl Like You*. For it seems to me quite evident that this is a very good book and its author's best to date (incidentally, it is also just as funny as the others). But the complexity of its view of human nature and the subtlety of its main theme have evidently been too much for reviewers all set for an Aldwych farce of the 'sixties. . . .

The setting of *Take a Girl Like You* is roughly how we live now, with the parties, the bachelor flats and the pubs, the intellectual pretensions of the inadequate and the deprecatory joking of the educated. And the ideas it suggests are contemporary too. Mr. Amis has taken human relations at a moment when "Do what you like" becomes "I don't know what to do," and there is implied in this choice a criticism of our present lack of a system of signals, where sex is concerned. The right questions can neither be asked nor answered, and people are left to hurt each other blindly. Of course, it is the romantics who do the damage. Julian who is content to take-it-or-leave-it is the corrective here, but one which implies a limitation. To the balance established in the novel between melancholy and humour corresponds an ethical balance, which leaves decency winning by a short head. And *Take a Girl Like You* strikes me as the work of a modern moralist, one who does not wish to make people good, but feels that the possibility exists of making them a little better, a very little better. This is a sad, funny, humane book, which never ignores the complexities of human nature or fails to show the narrowness of the margins involved in human decision. It is a book which demonstrates quite clearly how good and serious a novelist Mr. Amis is.— ANTHONY HARTLEY, "The Way We Live Now," *Enc*, Dec. 1960, pp. 80–82

Stanley and the Women is perhaps the most skilfully written of all Amis's novels, and for much of its length the most overtly serious. Impotence and misogyny, as in *Jake's Thing*, can be paired off for comic purposes, it may be thought, without straining the genre, madness and misogyny less easily. Amis runs them in tandem, using a narrative technique of short scenes into which the four sections of the novel are broken up to promote a feeling of pace and urgency, denying himself much of the leisurely satirical observation that made *Jake's Thing* so enjoyable a compendium of the Worst of British. In the end, the prognosis for Steve and for Stanley's marriage is not without hope, given a degree of South London stoicism. *Stanley and the Women* reveals Kingsley Amis in the full flood of his talent and should survive its ritual burning in William IV Street unscathed.—J. K. L. WALKER, "Down among the Men," *TLS*, May 25, 1984, p. 571

POETRY

Kingsley Amis writes a clever, neat sort of verse whose major visible ambition, not to be taken in, is well expressed by the cheerful vulgarity of the title, *A Case of Samples* (the literal sense being that this book is only a selection from among the author's poems). It is as though he had decided that the world exists only as literature, that he and his readers are too wise to be fooled any longer by so much literature, and that, in consequence, the remaining job for poetry (aside from cleaning up after the Grand Ball of History) is to be more or less benevolently amused at itself and its former pretensions. Here, for instance, in his "Ode to the East-North-East-by-East Wind," he shows how determined he is not to be made anyone's lyre:

> You rush to greet me at the corner like
>   A cheery chap I can't avoid,
> And blow my hair into one leaning spike
>   To show you're never unemployed.
> You sweating, empty-handed labourer,
> You bloody-rowelled, mailless courier,
>   Before you rush off somewhere new,
>   Just tell us what you do.

Notice the fine ambiguity of "mailless courier," which is good, like "mobled queen." Mr. Amis goes on about what the wind does ("Sometimes you pump up water from the ground;/Why, darling, that's just fine of you!") and finally decides as follows:

> Well now, since blowing things apart's your scheme,
>   The crying child your metaphor,
> Poetic egotists make you their theme,
>   Finding in you their hatred for
> A world that will not mirror their desire.
> Silly yourself, you flatter and inspire
>   Some of the silliest of us.
>   And is that worth the fuss?

The sense of this as I read it is that people like Shelley and Shakespeare have actually succeeded in diminishing the wind-force to a point at which it will turn no poem; because, after all, nature is only literature, one is tired of poets drawing their dreary conservative morals from nature (or literature), the wind blows in the most meaningless manner, and so on. It may be that there is no natural religion, but the belief may not be extended to say that there is no nature either; or it may, and that is Mr. Amis' own business, but why then prose along about it so, and have all one's delicate irony fetch up, as so much of this book does, in parlor verse? The ladders Mr. Amis delights in kicking over have been rungless, I suspect, these many years; and even when they're down there remains that foul rag and bone shop we have been told of.—HOWARD NEMEROV, "Younger Poets: The Lyric Difficulty" (1958), *Poetry and Fiction*, 1963, pp. 220–21

Amis the novelist, Amis the polemicist, and latterly Amis the personality on radio and television, have crowded out of attention Amis the poet; and this sufficiently illustrates the relative importance given in modern Britain to writing in verse, writing in prose, and unconsidered remarks by way of "the media." Amis's poetry, however, is much to our purpose, since far more than his novels it concerns itself quite explicitly with political issues. It does so not under Hardyesque but rather under Gravesian auspices; and so this chapter must be regarded as a digression—though a necessary one—for the understanding of the climate of political ideas in which British poets since Hardy have been working.

The political idea that Amis has been particularly concerned with is that crucial one, the concept of authority. For instance:

"THE VOICE OF AUTHORITY: A LANGUAGE GAME"

Do this. Don't move. O'Grady says do this,
You get a move on, see, do what I say.
Look lively when I say O'Grady says.

Say this. Shut up. O'Grady says say this,
You talk fast without thinking what to say.
What goes is what I say O'Grady says.

Or rather let me put the point like this:
O'Grady says what goes is what I say
O'Grady says; that's what O'Grady says.

By substituting you can shorten this,
Since any god you like will do to say
The things you like, that's what O'Grady says.

The harm lies not in that, but in that this
Progression's first and last terms are I say
O'Grady says, not just O'Grady says.

Yet it's O'Grady must be out of this
Before what we say goes, not what we say
O'Grady says. Or so O'Grady says.

This piece is what it says it is, "A language game." There is an obvious sense in which it isn't a poem. The game "O'Grady," familiar to me from my childhood, and I believe sometimes used by drill-sergeants to enforce alertness in the training squad, depends upon a simple rule: the listener obeys the orders which are prefixed by the phrase "O'Grady says," but disobeys or ignores orders given without that prefix. Sooner or later, one "jumps to it," responding to the imperative tone, though the essential prefix has not been given. Amis uses the device of this exercise to explore the nature of authority, as we know it, and its relation to power. Thus, after the first six lines we read from the poem the statement: "Authority is hollow; a thin cloak for the only naked face, power." But after the next three lines we read from the poem: "No. Authority is real; it genuinely exists to legitimize power, and not merely as rhetorical subterfuge." The next three lines say: "But since we have lost any confidence (it would have to be a religious or metaphysical confidence) that we can locate the one source of genuine authority in the world, it is as if there were no one such source but many." But, the poem goes on, this would not matter if the several sources were agreed to be objectively real. But we cannot agree or believe that this is the case, and a subjectively arrived at authority is equivalent to arbitrary power. The last three lines of the poem suggest that the answer to the conundrum is to acknowledge that the source of authority is human (some men have it, others haven't), but that this does not make it any less real. Indeed, the last four words—"Or so O'Grady says"—may be taken to mean that the location of authority in some men rather than in others may in fact have a divine or metaphysical sanction. . . .

The virtues of Amis's writing in "Autobiographical Fragment" are those of Robert Graves at his best. The dry unshadowed silhouette of the Gravesian emblematic fable is also what pleases and carries conviction in "After Goliath." But in Amis's poems since 1957 "After Goliath" stands alone; no Gravesian virtues redeem any other poem in *A Look Round the Estate*, which is subtitled "Poems 1957–1967." This collection is deplorable; and if we are still looking in our poets for the presence of Hardy, we cannot be happy to think we catch a glimpse of him in the shrill and sentimental blasphemies of a poem called "New Approach Needed":

. . . People have suffered worse
And more durable wrongs
Than you did on that cross
(I know—you won't get me
Up on one of those things),
Without sure prospect of
Ascending good as new
On the third day, without
"I die, but man shall live"
As a nice cheering thought. . .

However, it is not Hardy's remonstrances against his Creator—thin and brittle stuff as those Hardy poems are—which lie behind such an excess as this. The figure in the shadows is the more elegant blasphemer whom Amis has elsewhere honored in accomplished and frigid pastiche:

"A.E.H."

Flame the westward skies adorning
Leaves no like on holt or hill;
Sounds of battle joined at morning
Wane and wander and are still,

Past the standards rent and muddied,
Past the careless heaps of slain,
Stalks a redcoat who, unbloodied,
Weeps with fury, not from pain.

Wounded lads, when to renew them
Death and surgeons cross the shade,
Still their cries, hug darkness to them;
All at last in sleep are laid.

All save one, who nightlong curses
Wounds imagined more than seen,
Who in level tones rehearses
What the fact of wounds must mean.

Loose lips and tight lips tell the same story: the Yahoo bluster of the one, the professorial curtness of the other, provoke in us (admiringly, if all works out right) the tone which is insistently present to just the degree that it is conspicuously choked back or shouted down—the tone of whining self-pity. For Housman's Spirit of Irony easily accommodates self-pity, whereas Hardy's Spirit of Pity does not. (It is looking the other way.)

It gives me no pleasure to write of Kingsley Amis in this way. But anyone who thinks me unfair when I detect self-pity, ought to turn to other pieces in *A Look Round the Estate*, like the distressingly explicit "A Chromatic Passing-Note." And there is more to be said of the failure of *A Look Round the Estate*. For it cannot be coincidence that the only good poem in that collection, "After Goliath," is also the only poem that is political. As a polemicist Amis has been politically active of recent years—notably, and valuably, in the struggle (doubtless foredoomed, but a fight that must be fought) to maintain a modicum of authority for at least one representative figure in one situation, that is to say, for the teacher in his schoolroom. Yet this concern for authority, which was the nerve of the best of Amis's earlier poems, has of late expended itself entirely in such polemic and public action, leaving the poems to expostulate not with public servants like "aldermen" and "administrators of grants," but only with the figure of straw that atheists label "God." Of course Amis's master had gone the same way long before; Graves, once the social historian of *The Long Week-End*, withdrew forty years ago to Majorca and has since found a retreat even more securely insulated from British social and political realities—the mythological Never-Never Lands ruled over by goddesses, white and black, where lately he seems to have been joined in mumbo-jumbo by Ted Hughes. Amis is too responsible to take that way out.—DONALD DAVIE, "Lucky Jim and the Hobbits," *Thomas Hardy and British Poetry*, 1972, pp. 83–102

ESSAYS AND CRITICISM

I don't think Kingsley Amis's now famous pamphlet *Socialism and the Intellectuals* has been discussed much as literature. Yet it provides a solution of what is for writers a serious technical problem. How is the non-expert to write about a subject which is the province of specialists, professionals, and bosses?

The failure of the "intellectual" in politics is very largely his inability to solve this problem. Adopting the wrong "tone" he rules himself out of court by showing himself to be precisely, an "intellectual."

Mr. Amis's strategy is fascinating. First of all, he puts his own ignorance to the forefront. Then he writes in a style which is skilfully slovenly. "In fact this essay is a tarted-up version of a talk given to a weekend school, in which my purpose was, if nothing else, to draw as few hear-hears as possible." The epithet "tarted-up," an analytic critic might point out, is by no means ill-chosen. For the moral tone of the essay is that of reluctant, rather warm-hearted, ultimately willing (if economic interest is served) flirtation. To demonstrate this, I must change Mr. Amis's sex for a moment. The argument is that she doesn't really know much about politics, nor does she care about them, perhaps she prefers reading books, though she doesn't think much of the intellectuals either (yet she is a serious girl—reading, as it were, between the lines). She also has, somewhere, a heart of gold, and this makes her blood boil when she thinks of conservatives and critics of the Welfare State which has given girls like her a lot of treatment free. What she hates most of all, though, is all this bleedin' 'ypocrisy about "Causes," and all this sense of guilt people go on about. She prefers even the Tories to all that high-falutin talk. Self-interest is what she believes in, self-interest and a warm heart.

The effect of all this is to provoke a dramatic anxiety in the reader, especially, I suppose, if he be a Labour Party Organiser. How, oh how, get Mr. Amis to a meeting? He has only attended one so far, and left it groaning, and he has no desire to "knock at the door of the local Labour Party headquarters." He leaves socialists feeling that they are unattractive. This fascinates them.

Since contemporary criticism scarcely considers the dramatic relation of writer to reader, I shall probably be thought to be sneering at Mr. Amis. To do so would be ungrateful, if only because his remarks about the Thirties are the most just I have read by any of his generation. What I am coarsely drawing attention to is that one of the good things about the young writers is their dramatisation of the writer-reader relation. That is really the little bit of good in all the "angry young man" business. Kingsley Amis, John Osborne, and Colin Wilson (who are different in all other respects) do say "I, I, I" all the time, and in doing so, they surely represent more than themselves. With many others, I have wondered what Jimmy Porter is angry about. Perhaps it is simply that he lives in a society where he has to spend so much time insisting

on the simple fact that he is unadjustably himself. As Mr. John Osborne puts it, defending Tennessee Williams and himself against what he calls the "adjustment school"; "Every character trait is a neurosis writ small. I like my plays writ large, and that is how these are written."—STEPHEN SPENDER, "Notes from a Diary," *Enc*, May 1957, p. 69

A public image of this author as an *enfant terrible* is fairly firmly established. Indeed, such reaction to the Amis name seems almost congenital. Magnus, in his *Dictionary of European Literature*, mentions the 13th-century "Papa Amis" as a "burlesque hero of adventures of wit, cunning and horseplay," and a few pages further on censures Mrs. Aphra Behn, née Amis, for her "grossness of taste." From this a theory could perhaps be worked out, giving some Jungian excuse for common misapprehensions about the current incumbent. Some such excuse is certainly necessary: for Amis could only appear as a terrible child to a lot of old women. His real characteristic, as seen in his novels, is more the "*mâle gaieté, si triste et si profonde*" which Musset saw in Molière.

This is a temperament once common in English literature, but which seems to have rather petered out since the days of Fielding and Dickens: a robustness, an independence of mind, an imperviousness to received ideas. When such a generous and vigorous writer expresses his own thoughts and feelings, and in his own way, rather than following the patterns laid down, his first book of criticism is likely to be important. And here we have Mr. Amis saying, in effect, that our long-established tradition of fiction is grossly inadequate, that it omits a whole hemisphere of the imagination. I take this to be a major, a revolutionary assertion.

Mr. Amis is not being provocative for provocation's sake—in fact *New Maps of Hell* is written in a thoroughly unpretentious way, with amenity and humour. For, thank heaven, in spite of his imposing credentials (and the book is, moreover, based on lectures given at Princeton's Christian Gauss Seminars In Criticism, under Professor R. P. Blackmur's chairmanship), he is not a literary establishment figure slumming, patronisingly and ignorantly, among a "cultural phenomenon." Mr. Amis simply says that since the age of twelve he has been a keen reader of modern science-fiction, because he found that it filled a need not catered for by what science-fiction fans call "mainstream" literature, in which he was doubtless getting interested at about the same time. This is a feeling that many people have had: *New Maps of Hell* I take to be not a creator of change, but a sign of change, a comet flaring, as in the Bayeux Tapestry, over a community sunk in superstition.

For, whatever the reasons, we have gradually reached a position where the average cultivated man is likely to be considerably more introverted than the norm, to be attracted excessively to what others may regard as "*le spectacle ennuyeux de l'immortel péché.*" It need hardly be said that in previous cultures the literature-defining audience was not of this narrow type. Even in ours, the best have often retained an interest in the actual. If we look, for example, at the poets of the 1930s, we find that while the lesser figures were interested in Literature and the Human Soul, Auden was interested in psychology, pit-heads or the Constantinescu gear for their own sake, not primarily as book-fodder. It seems natural that he was by far the best poet. (Of course, poets have often, far more than novelists, been interested in mere science and, perhaps even more important, disinterested in mere personality: "His sense of other people's very hazy.")

Science fiction particularly strongly illustrates revulsion from the barren extremes of subjectivity. But to say that it thus fills a want, corrects an imbalance, is not to make extravagant claims for its quality, as Mr. Amis rightly points out. Though he once wrote in a review that an average issue of *Astounding* showed as much imagination and intelligence as one of *The London Magazine*, this is not the same thing as claiming *The Space Merchants* to be superior to *War and Peace*. The very modesty with which Mr. Amis actually concludes this book constitutes a powerful position: "At least a dozen current practitioners seem to me to have attained the status of the sound minor writer whose example brings into existence the figure of real standing." This is particularly so when we remember how young a *genre* modern *sf* is. It is not a rare thing for a vigorous new art form to start off at a very crude level—Latin rhymed poetry is an instance. But the improvement since the thirties is phenomenal, and might perhaps be contrasted with a certain decadence in conventional fiction, particularly the short story.

While the *genre* has attracted readership, sympathy, and comprehension from many of Amis' generation, it has left others, and particularly the most highly professionalised students and critics, baffled and ignorant. But if current methods and attitudes cannot cope with a new phenomenon, do they not stand exposed as useless *even in their fields of normal operation?* . . .

Naturally, people should read what they like, according to their temperaments. But with the man who sets himself up as a literary expert the case is different. To him I would put two propositions: if you can't tell good *sf* from bad, your expertise is exposed as worthless; and if you can't understand *sf*, you are, in some important respects, uneducated. I hope, in any case, that you will not be afraid to read this stimulating, scintillating book.—ROBERT CONQUEST, "Dragons and All Deeps," *Enc*, May 1962, pp. 77–80

EDMUND WILSON
From "Is It Possible to Pat Kingsley Amis?"
The New Yorker, March 24, 1956, pp. 140–46

"After Evelyn Waugh, what?" this reviewer asked six years ago. The answer was Angus Wilson. Mr. Wilson is still doing well. He continues to add to his album of tart and trim little pictures of the English upper middle class, shaken in its self-sufficiency and stinging itself to death. But what is to be the next phase in England, and how will it be written about? The answer, already, is Kingsley Amis, the author of two novels: *Lucky Jim*, published by Doubleday in 1954, and *That Uncertain Feeling*, which Harcourt, Brace has just brought out. These books are in the same general comic tradition as those of Wilson and Waugh. Satirical and sometimes farcical, they are derived from shrewd observation of contemporary British life, and they occasionally imply social morals. Yet between Kingsley Amis on the one hand and Wilson and Waugh on the other, a definite mutation has occurred. In the world of Angus Wilson, the pressure is already felt of the Labour-run Welfare State; a new social promiscuity has already begun. But we have here hardly more than a glimpse of the survivors of the war generation making themselves a new kind of life in an England where the class structure is breaking up and the old orientations have been partly lost. In the work of Kingsley Amis, we see everything from the point of view of such baseless unoriented young people. *The Uncertain Feeling* may be said to be the theme of *Lucky Jim* as well as of the book to which it gives its title.

The effect of these novels of Amis's on the higher level of British journalism has, therefore, been curious to watch. They have become a subject of controversy, on which people sometimes fiercely take sides. *Lucky Jim* is extremely funny. Everyone was much amused, and since it is also a kind of male Cinderella or Ugly Duckling story, it left its readers good-humored and glowing. Jim Dixon, a young instructor in a third-rate provincial college, finds himself always out of key with its middle-class gentility and academic culture, and in mischievous, embittered revolt against them. He is apparently as unlucky as possible. He commits every possible gaffe; his attempts to do what is expected of him invariably end in fiasco. The lecture on which his promotion depends turns into a comic debacle. Yet his honesty, vitality, humor, breaking through the taboos he has tried to observe, in the end win him every triumph, procure for him every prize. He knocks down his pretentious rival, obtains the devotion of a beautiful girl, is relieved providentially of a feeling of guilt in connection with another girl with whom he has gone rather far, and is rescued by a rich connoisseur from the failure of his academic career by being offered a job as his secretary. The reviewers were jolly about "Lucky Jim;" they patted him on his blond, bushy, rumpled head. But when the second Kingsley Amis book appeared, they began to become uneasy. I shall discuss this new book in a moment. In the meantime, it is enough to note that the element of loutishness here is made somewhat harder to swallow by being combined with an element of the sordid. The critics now held their noses, and in retrospect complained that Lucky Jim, waking up in the morning with a hangover and hearing someone singing Mozart in the bathroom, had murmured to himself, "Filthy Mozart." Did not Amis, it began to be asked, really share the views of his hero? Did he admire the right things himself?

. . . In noting the reception of this second book, one gets the impression that British opinion is beginning to gang up on Mr. Amis. A marked chill in the tone of the reviews has set in. The hero of the new novel does not seem to be patted on the head as Lucky Jim was. A difference in the books themselves accounts for this. In the first, the repulsive people are the opponents of the hero and his beautiful girl, and the hero and his girl score. In *That Uncertain Feeling*, all the characters are more or less unpleasant, and the hero is telling the story himself, instead of, as in the case of Lucky Jim, being told about by the author, so we are never allowed to escape from the squalors of his personality. We see only so much of the world as he knows, and this seems to make it hard for some readers to correct the illusions and distortions of his limited point of view, and to lead them more easily to attribute the character's reactions to the author, to suppose that the author is not aware how disgusting his protagonist's life is and how caddishly he and his friends are behaving. . . .

The occasionally repulsive details of this book, the indecent outbursts of the hero in his moments of lechery or fury, do suggest a certain coarseness on the part of the author as well as on that of his hero; and it contains one extremely weak episode, the one in which John Lewis, disporting himself with his mistress, is caught in the house by her returning husband and resorts to all sorts of expedients of hiding, impersonating the plumber and finally disguising himself in a female costume. All this is so clumsily implausible that it reminds us of one of those sequences of grotesque and impossible gags in a second-rate movie comedy. In other ways, American influence plays a conspicuous role in the book. The author has evidently been reading a good deal of American fiction, and the tone of his hero owes something to this, as well as the conversation of the other characters. They are full of American wisecracks and of language picked up from the movies. To an American, this is rather depressing. These young Britishers seem to have borrowed some of the worst things we have to offer, and even things that are amusing at home come to seem to us rather dreary on the lips of an Americanizing British middle class. But it is a world that, even imitating America, still carries, in an eroded and degraded form, the skeleton of its class stratification. The great problem of John Lewis and Jim Dixon both is to resist the inherited impulse to invade a superior stratum and identify their interests with it. The only things they have behind them to brace them are the victory of the Labour Government in 1945, the ideals of the Welfare State, and they hold out as best they can, at the cost of much nervous strain, much confusion of social relations, much sacrifice of individual dignity. Jim advances himself; John Lewis loses ground, but, after once having been sent sprawling, he gets up and remains on his feet. These characters are not always attractive, but they interest me more than the people, also rather unattractive though presented with better manners, in the novels of Anthony Powell. Uncertain and perplexed though they are, they have still something to build, to win.

ANTHONY POWELL
From "Kingsley's Heroes"

The Spectator, November 29, 1963, pp. 709–10

Kingsley Amis, it is hardly necessary to remark, has a notably strong public personality. This characteristic has little or nothing to do with writing as such. Some good writers possess it, others do not. However, once such a *persona* comes into existence its effects have to be taken into consideration where a critical estimate is concerned. The fact cannot be ignored. Generally speaking, one might say such an adjunct is an advantage to a writer in so much that it helps sell his books and provokes wide discussion of his work, a disadvantage in that it tends to obscure the issue as to what he is writing about and establishes him in everyone's mind as a human entity, more or less grotesque according to its form, probably far removed in any case from what the man himself is, or indeed could be like.

To define the mood with which Amis's name is associated in the popular mind is not easy. In fact, the more one looks at the supposedly 'angry' generation (no longer young), the more difficult seems any precise definition of what the whole affair is about. At the same time it might be agreed that some sort of literary adjustment has taken place during the last ten years or so, rather different from the normally ever-changing face of writing, and that the seam of guilt-ridden, class-obsessed, culturally puritanical authors and journalists, now in their forties, is possibly a shade larger than usual. Even that is uncertain. Perhaps it might be said that a body of work has come into being during that period which reflects the manner in which increased national affluence and levelling-out has confronted a (comparatively) lower middle class with a host of social, emotional and sexual problems already familiar to a (comparatively) upper middle class; a situation baffling to both sides facing each other over a small, often infinitesimal divide.

The question is whether Kingsley Amis's novels should be thought of primarily as expressing a conscious view of some such situation. At first sight, people thought that. Investigation seems to reveal little support for such a view. Like every other novelist, Amis has his own particular prejudices, but his interest is in human beings, not theories. Indeed, he might be said

to move, like Marley's ghost, burdened by a clanking chain to which is attached a formidable assortment of other writers' novels, verse, belles-lettres and newspaper articles, ponderous rusty tackle made up of items not only lacking any claim to his own originality, but also almost totally different in content. In other words, the personality conferred on Amis after the publication of *Lucky Jim* seems fated to link him through all eternity with far less talented performers writing about different things in a different manner.

With this misleading *persona* investing him, there is danger that *One Fat Englishman* may start the whole business up again. Is the new novel an attack on England? On America? On publishers? On dons? On Roman Catholics? On Jews? On drunks? On seducers? On women? There are infinite opportunities of confusing the book with every kind of extraneous matter, on the principle, dear to reviewers, that in a novel an adulterous stockbroker means an attack on the City, a homosexual ticket-collector a condemnation of the railways.

Before considering the new novel, a glance should be given at the score up to date. *Lucky Jim*, after a decade, rereads remarkably well. It is one of the funniest novels of, say, the last thirty years. The first ninety pages flow effortlessly without a drawing of breath, masterly in their manner. Return to its scenes makes it more than ever clear that, so far from being written by a man in whose life the arts play no part, they are the work of one who has thought a good deal about the arts. So far from being a protest against any given society or moral order, Dixon's relations with those amongst whom he finds himself seem natural enough, violent though they may be, at a purely human level, the characters about him drawn with extraordinary deftness.

That Uncertain Feeling made a good follow-up. The fact that the second book pointed something of a moral cannot be held against him by those who grumbled about the anarchistic strain in *Lucky Jim*. Amis was now revealed as a novelist with a world and characters of his own, writing in the way he did because—like all good novelists—he could write in no other way than his own. However, the next book, *I Like It Here*, demonstrated the dangers of having a too sizeable public personality.

I Like It Here is obviously a slight work. It is not so much a novel as a dramatised travel book with a touch of the detective story. It has its funny moments—some very funny—but it would be true to say that on the whole it aroused critical disapproval. Indeed, pages of print were devoted to expressing little or nothing but vexation. No one wishes to limit reviewers in pouring out the vials of their wrath, but there is such a thing as a sense of proportion. However, where a public figure is concerned, no proportion is possible, and it would be hard to find a better instance of how such a status can suddenly embarrass an author. The logical reply to this reception was a long 'serious' work. *Take a Girl Like You* might be held to fall within those terms of reference.

In America, it is not uncommon to find respectable critics who think *Take a Girl Like You* is Amis's best book. Certainly the novel contains much good material, but it battles all the time against a technical difficulty imposed by its form. The story is told from the point of view of a woman—always a tricky thing for a male novelist to attempt—yet deals with seduction, its main theme, from an essentially male point of view. Again and again throughout the book one feels that the comments and the laughter are men's comments, men's laughter. The same objection can be raised to some of Scott Fitzgerald's *The Last Tycoon*, though Fitzgerald's romantic approach, even when ironical, provides a certain safeguard. The scene in the masters' common-room, and elsewhere when only men are together in *Take a Girl Like You*, suggests that a great deal of good stuff could have been even better if planned as seen through the eyes of a man.

ANTHONY BURGESS
From "A Sort of Rebels"
The Novel Now
1967, pp. 141–44

The most popular anti-hero of our time has been, without doubt, Jim Dixon in Kingsley Amis's *Lucky Jim*—an astonishing best-seller of the middle nineteen-fifties. Amis caught the public mood of post-war restiveness in a book which, though socially significant, was, and still is, extremely funny. Dixon is a lower middle-class young man of no great pretensions to anything—charm, looks, learning, certainly not wealth. A stroke of luck has given him a job in a provincial university as junior lecturer in History, but a rebellious streak, which often comes out as maladroitness, qualifies his desire to conform and keep his job. Unfortunately his professor is a monumental fool much given to cultural week-ends, complete with madrigal-singing and recorder-blowing, and Dixon has other crosses to bear in high places. He asks little from life—enough money for beer and cigarettes, a nice undemanding girl-friend—but society has so organized things that he cannot have even this little. What he can have, what in fact is imposed upon him, is the great post-war sense of social purpose, hypocritical slogans about education, culture, progress. He asks for the bread of minimal comfort (along with the rest of a Britain that was sick of war and post-war austerity), but he is handed the stone of a spurious idealism.

Dixon is a radical, but radicalism is in his blood rather than his head. He detests privilege and phoney upper-class values, and he finds these wonderfully personified in Bertrand Welch, the son of his professor. To make things worse, Bertrand has a girl-friend whom Dixon hopelessly desires. One of the big themes of *Lucky Jim*—and it is a theme to be found in many English novels, as well as plays (John Osborne's *Look Back in Anger*, for instance) of the nineteen-fifties—is what anthropologists call hypergamy. This means, literally, 'marrying above oneself', and one of the great aims of the post-war rebels is to conquer a woman who belongs to a higher social class than themselves. This is an aspect of the perennial class motif which bedevils British fiction. Dixon achieves this aim, and others as well. He perpetrates enormities terrible enough to ensure his losing his university job (setting fire to Mrs. Welch's bedclothes, collapsing—after a rebellious manifesto—at a public lecture), but he gets something better—the job that Bertrand was after, as well as Bertrand's girl. He makes little dents in the smug fabric of hypocritical, humbugging, class-bound British society, but he is not big enough to portend its collapse. His is the voice of decent protest, and it is a voice that a stable society ought to listen to occasionally, though it never does.

Although we are intended to be on Dixon's side, we are also intended to laugh at him, to pity his ignorance. There is a certain ambivalence in *Lucky Jim* which is to be found also in Amis's other novels. The author, like his anti-heroes, is against culture because culture has the wrong associations—with Professor Welch and the rest of the phoneys. At the same time he cannot hide the fact of his bookishness and musicality, and the Amis protagonist always earns his living by purveying culture

(as teacher, librarian, journalist or publisher). In *I Like It Here*—Amis's least successful novel—Bowen has to apologize to himself for mentioning Elgar or Byron. The librarian hero of *That Uncertain Feeling* lives among books but reads only science fiction and cheesecake magazines. And yet the love-hate attitude to culture (it is not a matter of pure indifference) permeates the very prose-rhythms. All of Amis's novels, despite their gaiety, show up the sickness of a divided society. Lewis in *That Uncertain Feeling* is, like Dixon, drawn to an affair with a woman out of his class (a member of the Anglo-Welsh ascendancy), but he does not end by conquering her, only by scuttling back to where he belongs, with a working-class father doing the Ximenes crossword.

If Amis belongs to any tradition at all, it is to the venerable line of English nonconformism to which Defoe and Fielding belong. *Take a Girl Like You* presents a really 'good' middle-class girl whose virtue is assailed but remains impregnable. *One Fat Englishman* shows Roger Micheldene, a gluttonous, lecherous, mean-minded British publisher visiting America. Roger is the whole dance of the Seven Deadly Sins rolled into one detestable bladder of lard; Amis the novelist of detached wit is also Amis the moralist, rarely judging but always giving plenty of scope to a comic nemesis. In Amis, people do not hop into bed lightly with each other; if they do—as John Lewis does in *That Uncertain Feeling*—they always suffer for it. Micheldene can do it, as he can snub, over-eat, pontificate, because he is the villain rather than the anti-hero. Dixon, Bowen and Lewis are, being so very much against humbug, really very much for middle-class virtue.

It is not too much to ask for—that people should be good and that fags and booze should be not too expensive. Amis is even—though with a bit of a wrench—prepared to drop all claims to culture and be content with a nice read of science fiction. He has become a strong advocate of this form (which lies between highbrow literature and popular trash) and has written a critical book about it (*New Maps of Hell*) as well as, with Robert Conquest, edited several anthologies of it. One of Amis's most recent novels—a collaboration with Conquest—has shunted all pretensions to culture into little marginal jokes. The title, *The Egyptologists*, refers to a group of middle-aged men who go in for clandestine fornication under the guise of running a scholarly society (culture has found, at last, a way of making itself useful). But it is in the nature of things, as Amis sees them, that they should not get away with vice and deceit. You may play merry hell with culture, but you had better not blaspheme against orthodox morality. This is the message of the new rebels.

In 1966, Amis published a novel which, though very different from his comic-social ones, could be seen as a complement to them. Jim Dixon gave society a couple of bumbling knocks in the towser-face, but injustice and the rule of privilege would always be there. *I Like It Here*, as well as *That Uncertain Feeling*, seemed to warn about the dangers of grappling too hard with life: stay at home or you'll get hurt. Sooner or later, though, Amis had to write about getting hurt—nakedly, without playing for laughs, but under the guise of something popular, even fashionable. *The Anti-Death League* essays a masque of ultimate bitterness—not against human institutions but against God—in the form of a secret-weapon-and-spy story.

The setting is not the land of the Flemings but England now, with a cold war and a yellow peril, the chief male interest distributed among the officers of No. 6 Headquarters Administration Battalion, which is engaged on something secret. Although the apparatus of security and intrigue, with something exciting imminent, is a mere fictional means to an end bordering on the eschatological, it would be unfair to give too much of the plot away. Take it that this army unit has (as it must have) collective death in view, and that someone unknown—we find out at last, but we're expertly kept guessing—found, among these potential killers, the organization of the title. Ayscue, the chaplain, is sent an anonymous poem for the unit magazine he is starting, and this is the first shot in a war against God. God speaks in this ode *To A Baby Born Without Limbs* and promises 'plenty of other stuff up My sleeve—Such as Luekemia and polio' (the misspelling is a deliberate blind).

BERNARD BERGONZI
From "Between Nostalgia and Nightmare"
The Situation of the Novel
1970, pp. 161–70

A writer who has established a comparable reputation to Angus Wilson's in the last fifteen years is Kingsley Amis: like Wilson's, his fiction is marked by an acute comic sense, a finely responsive eye and ear for social nuance, concern about the difficulties of behaving decently, and an intermittent sense of nightmare. Admittedly these qualities, which occur in Amis's fiction in roughly the order in which I have set them down here, assume a different pattern of frequency in Wilson's work; one does not regard him primarily, as one still tends to regard Amis, as a comic novelist. Even so, to describe Amis in this way may surprise those who still think of him only as the author of *Lucky Jim* and a founding father of the Angry Young Men. But it is over fifteen years since *Lucky Jim* came out, and in that time Amis has published seven more novels, a collection of short stories and two books of peoms, together with critical studies of science fiction and the writings of Ian Fleming. One thing that this sizeable *œuvre* makes clear is that the comic spirit in Amis's work has become steadily less dominant since Jim Dixon made his carefree debut. Amis admirably refused to repeat his initial success (although a quite recent novel, *I Want it Now*, does look uncomfortably like an attempt to do just that) in a way which disconcerted readers who were eager for more of the same thing, and who were disinclined to pursue the interesting mixture of comedy and seriousness in Amis's subsequent fiction. There are also those who claim that Amis is not worth anyone's serious attention, that *Lucky Jim* is at worst a crude and childish farce, and at best no more than a faded relic of the taste of the early fifties. Nevertheless *Lucky Jim* remains, for me, a comic masterpiece, the funniest English first novel since Anthony Powell's *Afternoon Men* appeared in 1931, and a work that is surpassed only by the very best of Waugh and Powell. One would like to think that it will retain its appeal, just as their early books have, even when its sociological implications, of which so much was made in the fifties, have dwindled into a historical footnote.

On its first appearance *Lucky Jim* was assumed to inherit the comic manner of the early Waugh; but some readers also related it to famous works of Edwardian comic fiction, like Wells's *Kipps* or Arnold Bennett's *The Card*. (Jerome K. Jerome's *Three Men in a Boat* is another possible antecedent.)[1]

This critical perspective seems to me largely correct, although it needs a certain qualification. In the remarks about fiction scattered about his reviews and other critical writings—conveniently summarised in Ruben Rabinovitz's book—Amis has shown himself to be assertively anti-modern, anti-experimental, anti-cosmopolitan, to at least the same degree as

Snow or William Cooper; indeed his tastes are narrower, since he does not share Snow's admiration for Proust. Yet his way of writing fiction suggests that he has undergone, no matter how unwillingly, the influence of the Modern Movement, at least in his reliance on linguistic effect; style functions actively in Amis's comic writing, as it does in Powell's. John Gross has remarked on the way in which many of Amis's comic effects originate in his linguistic finesse rather than in the comedy of situation. Throughout his novels there is a steady preoccupation with language; we see it in characters such as Julian Ormerod in *Take a Girl Like You* or Harry Bannion in *I Like It Here*, compulsive and singular verbalisers, who are regarded by their creator with considerable affection. In *That Uncertain Feeling*, John Lewis, in the midst of his troubles, finds time to reflect on his children's speech habits: '"Yas," she said. This lowering of the *e*-phoneme is widespread, I've noticed, in childish dialect.' In *One Fat Englishman* the Danish philologist Ernest Bang keeps up a running commentary on the way the other characters talk. This concentration on verbal effects shows that Amis believes that fiction, whatever else it may be made of, is also made of words; this implicit conviction places him as a post-Joycean novelist, and distinguishes him not only from Edwardian comic writers such as Bennett or Wells or Saki, but from contemporaries such as Snow or Cooper. The stylistic dimension in Amis has been discussed at some length by David Lodge in his book *Language of Fiction*, and he gives good reasons for seeing Amis as a novelist worth serious critical attention, no matter how flawed his output might be. Although Amis writes what can be regarded as a traditional, uncomplicated narrative, he differs from the Edwardians in his degree of concentration; there are no loose, low-pressure transitional passages of the kind that one finds in Wells or Bennett, and although Jim Dixon resembles their heroes, he also exhibits an exacerbated sensitivity akin to that of Stephen Dedalus.

Even in *Lucky Jim*, which remains the most light-hearted and innocent, and certainly the funniest, of Amis's novels, there are casual references that would seem savage if it were not for the tone and the stylistic controls which preserve it: Jim dreams of stuffing Professor Welch down the lavatory, or of beating him about the head and shoulders with a bottle until he explains why he gave his sons French names; at one angry moment he is tempted to push a bead up Margaret Peel's nose. In the later novels these fantasies of hostility and aggression are more frequent and less controlled. And traces of nightmare are quite apparent in Amis's other writings. His poems, which are mostly deft, glum and *borné*, afford some relevant insights: one thinks, for instance, of 'The Box of Friends' and 'Dirty Story' from *A Case of Samples*, or 'Out-Patient' and 'Nothing to Fear' from *A Look Round the Estate*:

> it's a dead coincidence
> That sitting here, a bag of glands
> Tuned up to concert pitch, I seem to sense
> A different style of caller at my back,
> As cold as ice, but just as set on me.

The latter volume also includes 'Science Fiction', which explains Amis's own interest in that literary genre. This is one of Amis's best poems; the first stanza talks of the attraction of finding 'simpler versions of disaster', like 'a ten-clawed monster' or some other traditional horror; but the second stanza turns to contemporary apocalyptic imaginings:

> In him, perhaps, we see the general ogre
> Who rode our ancestors to nightmare,
> And in his habitat their maps of hell.
> But climates and geographies soon change,

Spawning mutations none can quell
With silver sword or necromancer's ring,
Worse than their sires, of wider range,
And much more durable.

One of Amis's own occasional ventures into science fiction, the story called 'Something Strange' is a pure exercise in nightmarish mystification.

Nostalgia, which I see as the opposite pole to nightmare, is also evident, though in a more subdued form. In *Lucky Jim* the past is regarded as a matter for suspicion: Jim Dixon has no commitment to the history he is supposed to teach, and he loathes Professor Welch's bogus attempts to revive the past by means of handicrafts and madrigal singing. Indeed, when he is forced to give a public lecture on 'Merrie England', Jim turns it into a virulent hymn of hate against all the more obvious forms of cultural nostalgia. Nevertheless Amis's attachment to a central thread of English insular nonconformism, and his distaste for cosmopolitan modernism, were sufficiently pronounced for Martin Green, in his book *A Mirror for Anglo-Saxons*, to place Amis in a select pantheon representative of the traditional English virtues, the other heroes being Lawrence, Leavis and Orwell. In so far as Amis's basic ideas about novel-writing are traditional—both as stated in his criticism and implicitly expressed in his fiction—then it is a tradition whose roots lie closer to the robustness and moral simplicity of the eighteenth century than to the high Victorian seriousness admired and to some extent imitated by Snow or Wilson. The point is made explicitly in Amis's third novel, *I Like It Here*, when Garnet Bowen, on visiting Fielding's tomb at Lisbon, falls into a vein of unexpected seriousness:

> Perhaps it was worth dying in your forties if two hundred years later you were the only non-contemporary novelist who could be read with unaffected and wholehearted interest, the only one who never had to be apologised for or excused on the grounds of changing taste. And how enviable to live in the world of his novels, where duty was plain, evil arose out of malevolence and a starving wayfarer could be invited indoors without hesitation and without fear. Did that make it a simplified world? Perhaps, but that hardly mattered beside the existence of a moral seriousness that could be made apparent without the aid of evangelical puffing and blowing.

In *Take a Girl Like You* Amis seems to have turned to Richardson rather than Fielding for his inspiration: its plot is remarkably close to *Clarissa* in outline, and offers much the same kind of interest in a long-deferred rape. Will Patrick Standish, an engaging, rakish grammar-school master of thirty succeed in laying the delectable Jenny Bunn, a virgin infant-school teacher, just down from the backward reaches of the North of England? In the end he succeeds, but not before a very long pursuit, and only when Jenny is drunk. *Take a Girl Like You* has many entertaining passages, but it is heavily padded, and it suffers from the incoherence at its centre. Patrick Standish is shown as an agreeable and gay fellow; he may be irascible and a bit promiscuous, but this is forgiven easily, just as it is with Tom Jones. Nevertheless the final rape is *not* a good thing to have done. Patrick feels badly about it, of course, but perhaps Jenny was really to blame for hanging onto her old-fashioned ideas about sex and giving him such a rotten time. The novel circles uneasily around these unresolved dilemmas, and the result is not merely ambivalence but moral and artistic incoherence. As a character Patrick is interesting, but not in focus. He is full of fears about cancer and impotence and death, which he tries to keep at bay by thinking about sex

most of the time. He regards most of the world with unrelieved hostility, particularly the ugly or the tiresome: thus when driving in the rain he gets immense satisfaction when he is 'lucky enough to send the greater part of a puddle over a sod in ragged clothes who was doing his level best to blow his nose into the gutter'. Patrick and his friend Graham concoct an elaborate fantasy directed against Jenny's landlord, Dick Thompson; they imagine that Dick is naked and they are pursuing him with syringes filled with acid or a solution of itching powder; admittedly Dick's meanness and boringness are unpleasant characteristics, yet this seems an over-compensated reaction. 'But bang's the way to get things done', writes Amis in the last line of his poem, 'Mightier than the Pen', and the lesson is applied late in *Take a Girl* when Dick is wounded by a shotgun. The world of Amis's fiction is basically Hobbesian, where mutual hostility is the normal relationship between the inhabitants. Patrick, we have to assume, is verbally aggressive, obsessed and sexually attractive; yet we never see him objectively, for the author's sympathy covers him with a protective mantle of charm. To have made him fully convincing would have required a kind of characterisation closer to Stiva Oblonsky than to Tom Jones. . . .

As I have remarked, mutual hostility is the usual relationship between the inhabitants of Amis's world. And things join in enthusiastically on the side of their owners, like Professor Welch's car, where a broken spring rips open Jim's trousers, or the terrifying geyser in Dick Thompson's bathroom which intimidates Jenny Bunn in the opening chapter of *Take a Girl Like You*. Robbe-Grillet would, no doubt, regard this as deplorably superstitious, and in a way he would be right. For there is something profoundly animistic about Amis's universe: it may not contain a God, but its characters are constantly in the toils of a powerful and malign governing force. Patrick Standish refers to this as 'Bastards' H.Q.', and this phrase seems to be a part of Amis's personal terminology. In *That Uncertain Feeling* John Lewis, swallowing a mouthful of tea-leaves after entertaining adulterous thoughts, reflects, 'Life, that resourceful technician, had administered a typical rebuke.' Dixon obtains a book he wants from a library 'with almost sinister promptitude'. A few pages later there is an elaborate example of this quasimagical attitude. Jim, riding in Welch's car, sees a fat man walking with lustful intent towards two pretty girls at a pillar-box. A little later he notices a cricket match in which the batsman, another fat man, is violently hit in the stomach by a ball. Jim is 'uncertain whether this pair of *vignettes* was designed to illustrate the swiftness of divine retribution or its tendency to mistake its target'. It would be paradoxical to call Amis a religious writer; but he is undoubtedly a superstitious one.

Notes

1. One critic who pointed out the parallel was John Holloway, in *The Charted Mirror* (1960). In an essay on Amis published in the *London Magazine* for January 1964 I dismissed any possible similarities between his work and Edwardian fiction; wrongly, as I now think.

JOHN UPDIKE
From "Jake and Lolly Opt Out"
The New Yorker, August 20, 1979, pp. 97–99

If the postwar English novel figures on the international stage as winsomely trivial, Kingsley Amis must bear part of the blame. Though he himself is a poet good enough to be generously represented in *The New Oxford Book of English*

Light Verse (which Mr. Amis edited), it is a rare sentence of his prose that surrenders to the demons of language, that abdicates a seat of fussy social judgment, that is there for its own sake, out of simple awe, gratitude, or dismay in the face of creation. His universe is claustrophobically human, and his ambition and reputation alike remain in thrall to the weary concept of the "comic novel." There was something unabashedly sophomoric about *Lucky Jim* (1953) which bespoke an eternal schoolboy; adult experience appears unremittingly oppressive to James Dixon save for the chemical holiday, the physiological crime and punishment, of drunkenness and hangover. On this one Janus-faced topic Mr. Amis could and can write with inspiration; but as farce and satire *Lucky Jim* lay uneasily between the romantic good humor of Wodehouse and the sublime hardheartedness of Waugh. Compared with a contemporaneous American study of reluctant pubescence, Salinger's *Catcher in the Rye*, it lacked not only private psychological intensity but, oddly enough, true comic edge. For there is no need to write "funny novels," when life's actual juxtapositions and convolutions, set down attentively, are comedy enough.

Amis's newest novel, *Jake's Thing*, is in fact a more ample and less artificial grab at life than *Lucky Jim*, though little in the book's reception would imply that. On the back of the jacket, the *Daily Mail* is quoted as chortling, "The funniest thing he has done since *Lucky Jim* . . . The book takes an unerring smack at our times." Well, the hilarious central subject of *Jake's Thing* is impotence and, beyond that, acedia, the deathlike condition of not caring; and the unerring smack is not at our times but at Mr. Amis's pained and isolated hero. Jake Richardson, an Oxford don who lives in London (apparently a not unusual arrangement), in an attempt to revive his libido subjects his fastidious sensibility and fifty-nine-year-old body to a series of humiliating psychiatric conferences, sex gadgets, and exhibitionistic workshops. Jake has once been a great womanizer, with over a hundred scores to his credit. He is married to his third wife, the overweight and wide-eyed Brenda. He wants, he thinks, to save his marriage. The muffled engine of the plot, the underplayed *primum mobile,* is the depth of anguish and affective embarrassment which glues this conservative, elderly man to psychologists and fellow-patients whom he despises; against the background of this poignance, nothing looms as very funny. Mr. Amis attempts to milk for a few mechanical laughs the juxtaposition of a snoopy cleaning lady with Jake's medically prescribed pornography reading and the introduction into his home of a device called "the nocturnal mensurator." No doubt some of the therapeutic language—"inceptive regrouping," "genital sensate focusing"—is meant to be droll. But the centerpiece of the satire, if satire it is—the lengthy workshop Jake and Brenda endure with the dwarfish psychologist Rosenberg, the workshop "facilitator" Ed (an American, always a bad sign), and eight sufferers from kleptomania, paranoia, inferiority complex, and assorted phobias—comes over as more horrifying than biting, more pathetic than amusing. It is by no means clear that Rosenberg and Ed are charlatans, though Jake comes to believe so, and the English reader might be disposed to expect so. To an American, conditioned to tolerance of all sorts of craziness on behalf of the soul, the extravagant exercises of group therapy seem at least a gallant attack upon virtually intractable forms of human loneliness and mental misery. Brenda, who enters this strange world in the wake of Jake's impotence, comes to argue, "Now Ed has too good an opinion of himself I quite agree, but he does help

people, or lets them help themselves which is just as good. I'm sure there are good reasons for saying he couldn't or he shouldn't or he doesn't really, but he does." The author in this debate stands a bit off to the side, giving Jake lots of space but Brenda some very good lines—better lines than her supposedly ill-educated, insecure character would warrant—and Mr. Amis's bemusement deepens as his hero, in an increasingly violent succession of verbal explosions, proceeds from wounded impotence to triumphant misogyny.

Jake, once the novel escorts him back to the predominantly male environment of Oxford, takes on some of Lucky Jim's manic recklessness, and through a drunken seduction he narrows in on the heart of his problem, which is the hatefulness of all things female. As long as he is in London, docilely busing back and forth between his sex therapist and his wife, his inklings are no more malign than the private observation, of a female anatomical part featured in a magazine called *Mezzanine,* that "in itself it had an exotic appearance, like the inside of a giraffe's ear or a tropical fruit not much prized even by the locals." But back in the university precincts, where the female minority hoots at Jake as a "wanker" and sends him a plastic phallus in the post, he is led to perceive that "they [women] don't mean what they say, they don't use language for discourse but for extending their personality." The indictment immensely widens, to include "their concern with the surface of things, with objects and appearances, with their surroundings and how they looked and sounded in them, with seeming to be better and to be right while getting everything wrong, their automatic assumption of the role of injured party in any clash of wills," etc., etc., all of which can be subsumed under the lament, in *My Fair Lady,* of Professor Henry Higgins: "Oh, why can't a woman be like us?" The ending of *Jake's Thing* is too good—too startling and too inevitable—to give away; but let it be hinted that it echoes with uncanny fidelity the notorious conclusion of Micky Spillane's *I, the Jury.*

The novel's innocent air of not having wanted to come out this way is one of its charms. Much sorrow and some wit flourish in the chinks of the shambles as marital saga, reactionary diatribe, and pilgrim's progress vainly compete to set a consistent tone. The book is made up of twenty-eight jollily titled chapters that feel like consecutive essays. As a continuously developing stream of event and revelation, *Jake's Thing* suffers from contrived jokiness and unsteady perspective; the author seems now immersed in Jake, now on the verge of disowning him, and there are curious patches where the action is summarized rather than relayed, as though the writer had to avert his eyes. As a portrait of a man, however, and the times that enclose and infuriate him, the novel is satisfyingly ambiguous, relentless, and full. Jake has more complaints than the similarly indisposed Alexander Portnoy: he can't get used to seeing Asians and blacks in the streets of London; he can't help noticing that men in dirty overalls seem to have more money to spend than he; he conducts inwardly a running criticism of the architecture, dress, manners, and cuisine he daily confronts; he suffers from moments of seeing "the world in its true light, as a place where nothing had ever been any good and nothing of significance done." He is in a rage. Yet he is also dutiful, loyal in his fashion, and beset; we accept him as a good fellow, an honest godless citizen of the late twentieth century, trying hard to cope with the heretical possibility that sex isn't everything.

John Arden

1930–

Born on October 26, 1930 in Barnsley, Yorkshire, John Arden spent the last year of World War II in the Royal Army Intelligence Corps before studying architecture at King's College, Cambridge. He went on to graduate study at the Edinburgh College of Art, where his first plays were produced. Arden won a BBC Northern Region Prize for a radioplay he wrote in 1955, and he was subsequently invited to submit his work to the Royal Court Theatre, creative home of John Osborne and Lindsay Anderson. After two years of architectural apprenticeship in London, Arden joined the staff of the Royal Court, which presented his plays for the next decade. There he met and married the actress and writer Margaretta D'Arcy, with whom he continues to collaborate professionally.

Arden's first plays were unpopular with critics and audiences until 1964, when *Armstrong's Last Goodnight* became a success. The early *Serjeant Musgrave's Dance* won a Vernon Rice Award two years later during a successful run off-Broadway. Since the late 1960s, Arden and D'Arcy have chosen to work primarily with community and experimental theater groups. Arden's "fringe" productions often evoke the *commedia dell'arte* and medieval theater that also influenced his earlier work. In Arden's works, dialogue often gives way to ballads, verse, and deliberately intrusive theatrical devices to disrupt the complacency of the audience. According to Arden, "However well acted and directed [my former plays] have been, I have become more and more aware of the difficulty of making a genuine contact with modern audiences through the traditional methods of theatre."

Arden and D'Arcy live in Ireland. They have four children.

Personal

I had a public school and university education, but the town we lived in is really the town of *Serjeant Musgrave's Dance* brought forward sixty or eighty years. It was impossible to live in such a town without being very conscious that one was a member of the minority party in the class war. To be brought up there in the 30's with the aftermath of the Depression and so forth made it clear; this was impressed on me very strongly when I was a boy. I went to the local municipal school and I suddenly became very aware of social differences in the class. I always remembered at a very early age, perhaps seven, realizing that the little boy with whom I shared a desk smelled. You know, it is very disturbing to a child to have the feeling of difference. My parents were not snobs but a number of their acquaintances were, and I did develop certain ideas as a child. I think I was a reactionary in the sense that the working classes and coal mining families and their children were the enemy. They certainly thought I was the enemy. A little boy going to school with a clean shirt and a tie and a pair of polished shoes and so forth was quite liable to get attacked in the street.— John Arden, interview with Walter Wager and Simon Trussler, *TDR*, Winter 1966, p. 42

General

Perhaps the biggest single thing to stand in the English Stage Company's favour, whenever and wherever these things finally come to be totted up, will be their continued championship of John Arden in the face of a Press dubious to hostile and of almost complete public apathy (his three plays to be performed publicly at the Royal Court achieved in all a mere seventy-three performances). And in this perseverance they have been absolutely right, as more and more people, both among the critics and among the theatregoing public, are coming to recognize. All the same, the hostility and plain indifference manifested by the vast majority of the plays' first spectators is quite easy to understand; one could even understand why many not properly attuned to Arden's work should find it downright boring. The explanation resides in one fact, simple in itself but

extremely complex in its implications: Arden permits himself, in his treatment of the characters and situations in his plays, to be less influenced by moral preconceptions than any other writer in the British theatre today.

Hence the difficulty. His work would be perfectly easy for audiences if he attacked morality; that would be shocking (even now, since conventions still rule even where convictions have flagged), it would be 'provocative', and most important of all it would imply by catagorically rejecting certain standards that these standards nevertheless existed—there would still be clear, dramatic blacks and whites, even if they did not always come in the expected places. But instead, and much more puzzlingly, he recognizes an infinitude of moral standards, all with their claims to consideration and all quite distinct from the individuals who hold them and try, more or less imperfectly, to put them into practice. Well, we can stand a little uncertainty about which are our heroes and which are our villains, but where do we stand in a situation which seems to deny the very possibility of heroism or villainy? The question may not be all that worrying on a purely personal level—one could argue that such concepts as heroism and villainy have little meaning in Pinter's work, for example—but Arden brings us face to face with it in its baldest form by writing plays which appear to be about general social, moral, and political issues: colour prejudice and prostitution, social clashes on a housing estate, pacifism, the treatment of old age. Arden the man no doubt feels strongly about all these subjects, or he would hardly choose to write about them, but his dramatist's instinct absolutely prevents him from stacking things in favour of the characters whose opinions most closely resemble his own; in an interview he has expressed 'grave objections to being presented with a character on the stage whom you know to be the author's mouthpiece'.

For behind Arden's work there seems to be brooding one basic principle: not exactly the obvious one that today there are no causes—that would be altogether too facile, and in any case just not true—but that there are too many. There are as many causes as there are people (more, since many are quite capable of espousing two or more mutually exclusive causes at the same time), and only the naïve can suppose that any two people who are, say, pacifists (to choose a nice, convenient label) will believe the same things for the same reasons. In other words, in all Arden's plays the characters we meet are first and foremost just people: not concepts cast into a vaguely human mould, with built-in labels saying 'good' or 'bad', 'hero' or 'villain', to help us into the right grooves. It follows, therefore, that the behaviour of any one person or group does not imply any general judgement. (Arden himself has said that he 'cannot see why a social play should not be so designed that we may find ourselves understanding the person's problems, but not necessarily approving his reactions to them'.) *The Waters of Babylon* is not a play in favour of prostitution and tenant-exploitation (or for that matter the reverse); *Live Like Pigs* tells us nothing about 'The Welfare State'; *Serjeant Musgrave's Dance* is not for or against pacifism *per se*; *The Happy Haven* offers no solution to the problem of old age: they are just plays about individual people affected one way or another by these issues. Hence, perhaps—until one gets used to Arden's way of seeing things at least—the confusion and irritation of his audiences: when 'parity of esteem' for all the characters is pushed so far, identification and taking sides become difficult if not impossible, and though undeniably the characters conflict—they are conflicting all the time—for many theatregoers a conflict in which they are not asked themselves to participate is in effect no conflict at all; left rudderless and all at sea, they end up lost and bored.—JOHN RUSSELL TAYLOR, "Presented at Court," *Anger and After*, 1962, pp. 83–85

"An object of art is artistic only insofar as it is not real," Orteġa y Gasset once wrote, and meant something much broader than an attack upon naturalism. Until we are able to think of drama, for all its physical contingencies and aesthetic impurities, as existing in a different realm from the "real"—the way we are mostly able to think of poetry, painting, music—we will go on disputing over everything that is peripheral and secondary in the work of a playwright like Arden, in the effort to establish its "validity," unconscious that this validity has already been established by the play's own internal processes and conquests.

There is something dispiriting about Arden's own vacillations between apology and peevish resentment. The prefaces to his plays are full of protests against his critics, but also of weakly enunciated and what can only be called supererogatory statements of his dramatic intentions. It is rather painful to hear a playwright of his stature say, as he does in the preface to *Left-Handed Liberty*, that "I am not normally an enthusiast for didactic drama" and then proceed to explicate the play's meaning, as though we had no means of discovering it for ourselves within the work. Arden has some justification insofar as a great many critics—professional and lay—do seem to have been unable to find it, just as they were stumped by the theme of *Serjeant Musgrave's Dance* or of *Live Like Pigs*. Still, however obtuse the response to the latter play was, it needn't have led Arden to such timid, ingenuous, and wholly unnecessary comments as those he made in the preface to the published text:

> When I wrote this play I intended it to be not so much a social document as a study of differing ways of life brought sharply into conflict and both losing their particular virtues under the stress of intolerance and misunderstanding. In other words, I was more concerned with the "poetic" than the "journalistic" structure of the play.

The temptation is to reply, Oh, in the manner of a *New Yorker* newsbreak. The point is that Arden, like Brecht, is much more of an artist than his *obiter dicta* might suggest. Of course, one

feels like saying to him, you're not really a didactic playwright, of course you're more interested in poetry than journalism. At the back of these strange tergiversations and pained, naïve avowals one senses a strand of the theatrical climate in England, a weather which is also beginning to take shape here: the need to be concerned (or to appear to be) in one way or another with socially and politically significant material, the fear of being seduced into too thorough-going an aesthetic stance, the embarrassment at not having, or not seeming to want to have, a clearly defined social commitment.

To describe oneself as a political or sociological playwright may very well be in this climate a ticket of admission, a way to get in out of the rain. That is to say, it seems clear from the context of Arden's remark, its surrounding clichés about man's being a social and political animal, etc., and first and foremost from the evidence of his plays, that caught between his *prédilection d'artist* and his communal sensibilities he covers himself (without guile or hope of concrete gain, it goes without saying) by pleading both. To the ideologues who would enlist his dramas in support of programs and are baffled by their resistance, he speaks wanly of poetic structure taking precedence over journalistic; to the formalists who might wish him to be less repertorial than he is, he points to the necessary basis in concrete events which all his plays exhibit.

Yet it should be obvious that the "events" of these plays are not simply dramatizations or, more subtly, aestheticized analogues of those other, historical happenings, and that the poetic interest he takes in them is not simply greater than his interest in reportage but a different kind altogether. That Arden is in some sense a thoroughly political playwright has never been at issue; every one of his works is steeped in politics and is the product of an imagination for which non-political reality—private myth, insular fortune, the discrete ego—would seem to have no independent standing as material for drama. No, what is at issue is the fate of political subject matter in his plays, the unpolitical uses to which he puts it, the transformations it undergoes under the action of his half-lyrical, half-civic and polemical sensibility, the sensibility, one might call it, of a passionate citizen, a brooding burgher.

What is the nature of political reality and how does the rest of the life of man (the title of his first play, a radio script) relate to it, or rather how does man's life come to know itself in the crucible of power, rule, and social governance? What are the prices that political necessity exacts from the moral self and the psyche? How does one celebrate life in the midst of abstractions? Such are the chief energizing questions of Arden's plays. They are what make him something extraordinarily different from a traditionally "political" or "sociological" playwright, by which, if definitions and terminology have not already descended into chaos, we mean someone for whom the immediate data of political or social organization are paramount, for whom, too, the choices involved in public existence are more or less co-terminous with the choices involved in all existence, and for whom, finally, a play is an exemplification, subtle or gross, of the virtue of making the right choices or of the cost of failing to make them.

For Arden, however, there are no clear choices—which is what pitches him above ideology; although there is a clear necessity to act publicly—which is what keeps his plays anchored in a perception of social actuality. Again and again, in one form or another, he questions, or rather raises to the dignity and ambiguous sincerity of a question, something we might call the humanness of politics, its role and function as the process and measure of our life in common. That public life *has* to be organized, and that power *has* to be exerted, are the assumptions, with their roots in a tragic awareness, of all his plays; that the private self rebels against this inexorability, in the name of its spontaneous, wayward life, of all distinct values and of the simplicities of what it considers its natural choices, is the agency which generates the "drama" of his dramas. If there is any modern book outside the literature of the theatre which provides a clue to Arden's temperament and procedures, it is surely Freud's *Civilization and Its Discontents*.

This conflict of the self, or its spontaneous element, with the organizing, abstract, equally self-interested and therefore inherently repressive action of politics is complemented and enlarged by another encounter which runs through most of Arden's work. This is the confrontation of a deadly impulse towards purity (which may be found both within the actions of power and in all fanatic attempts to do away with it) and the impure, flawed, capricious, and uncodifiable nature of reality beneath our schemes for organizing it.—RICHARD GILMAN, "Arden's Unsteady Ground," *TDR*, Winter 1966, pp. 54–56

The trouble about playwrights in our present society is that a community, even a small one like Kirbymoorside, does not speak with anything approaching a single voice. I don't know that it ever did, but I take it that *everyone* in Athens used to go and see Aristophanes' plays and even if some better-informed scholar tells me that slaves and perhaps women were excluded, I don't think it affects the argument. If they *were* excluded it was a disgrace, but their point of view was not difficult to ascertain, and Aristophanes certainly gave it expression in his work. The modern playwright is lucky if he finds himself as closely in touch with his audience as an MP does with his constituents, which is not saying much. We have too large a population, divided by too many disparities of class, income, occupation, and culture, to revert to simple dramaturgy *or* simple democracy. Any sort of community drama can at present only work, if at all, on the most modest scale. Miss D'Arcy's experiments have been modest—for anything larger I have had to make use of the professional theatre with all its remoteness, its irrelevance, and its inability to attract a "popular" audience. This is not a satisfactory situation, but it can't be cured by literature. Arnold Wesker has tried, Joan Littlewood is trying in her own different way, to find a more direct answer, and so are many others. The House of Commons has not even *begun* to try, and it needs solutions perhaps more urgently than the theatre. Until the political problem is solved, I doubt if we shall make much progress with the artistic one. Who's for a revolution?—JOHN ARDEN, interview with Walter Wager and Simon Trussler, *TDR*, Winter 1966, p. 42

Works

A soldier stands at the front of the stage. He is tall, upstanding, rigid—a dominating figure. When he speaks, his voice is powerful and commanding. He clasps his hands across his chest and begins to pray.

> God, my Lord God. Have You or have You not delivered this town into my hands? All my life a soldier I've made You prayers and made them straight, I've reared my one true axe against the timber and I've launched it true. My regiment was my duty, and I called Death honest, killing by the book—but it all got scrawled and mucked about and I could not think clear . . . Now I have my duties different. I'm in this town to change all soldiers' duties. My prayer is: Keep my mind clear so that I can weigh Judgement against the Mercy and Judgement against the Blood, and make this Dance as terrible as You

> have put it into my brain. The Word alone is terrible: the Deed must be worse. But I know it is Your logic and You will provide.

Behind the soldier stands another figure. He is in every way the soldier's opposite. Whereas the soldier's uniform is shining red and spotless, this man's rough black clothes are thick with grime. And his shape offers a contrast. When, like the soldier, he stands to attention, his body is comic and crooked, a question mark set against the straight backbone of the soldier. He imitates the soldier in everything he does. When the soldier crosses his hands to pray, this man does the same. Only in all the man's gestures there is an element of exaggeration: he takes the soldier's meaningful actions and pushes them to absurdity. When the soldier's prayer ends, the man whips off his cap. The soldier turns on his heel and leaves without seeing the man. The man remains on the stage, looking up to heaven and smirking. He murmurs, "Amen."

How are we to interpret a scene like this? There are three main possibilities.

(1) The soldier is the hero. He has all the characteristics of a hero. He is tall, handsome, eloquent and he has a good voice. Moreover, his message is clearly true. He has been shocked by a bloody incident in a colonial war and this has convinced him that war is evil. As good liberals we all know, like the soldier, that war is wicked: we are on his side. Emotionally, we identify ourselves totally with the soldier, Serjeant Musgrave. We hardly notice the crooked little figure standing behind him. If we do, he is merely an obscenity, one of the evils against which, with Musgrave, we are ready to fight.

(2) The crooked man—the bargee—is the hero. He is the little man doing down authority. Like Chaplin. Cocking a snook at pomposity. Like Harpo Marx. We identify ourselves totally with the little man. We laugh *with* him through his antics. The soldier becomes completely ridiculous.

(3) We don't identify ourselves totally with either figure. We watch, as we would watch two jugglers in a variety show. And we listen. The soldier is tall, heroic. He is clearly to be admired. But wait. Isn't there something just a bit ridiculous about the soldier's stance? When you see the crooked absurdity of the bargee standing to attention, doesn't the soldier's pose begin to look absurd, too? How ridiculous to stand with your hands clasped like that, talking to nobody!

And yet, there's something noble about the soldier. Set against him the bargee looks like a cheap clown. And the soldier's message is so obviously right—"to change all soldiers' duties."

But wait again. Isn't there something also a bit exaggerated in the soldier's language? What is all this about the Mercy and the Judgement and the Blood and the Word? As the soldier utters the words, he strains towards heaven, as if trying to catch God's ear. The bargee's gestures in imitation invite you to become aware of the soldier's self-dramatisation. Yet the soldier's sense of purpose remains admirable and there's still the element of truth in his message.

Arden presents us with two opposites which illumine each other. The opposites exist in a physical relationship on the stage. If you identify yourself with either—if, for example, the actor playing Musgrave pulls out all the emotional stops and carries you away; or if he exaggerates Musgrave's gestures to the point of caricature—the moral balance of the scene is destroyed.

The first two responses belong to what is still the accepted form of "serious" theatre—the theatre of illusion. The third belongs to a completely different tradition, in which John Arden's work belongs.—ALBERT HUNT, "Arden's Stagecraft"

(1965), *Modern British Dramatists*, ed. John Russell Brown, 1968, pp. 98–100

As a comment on political strategy *Armstrong's Last Goodnight*, by John Arden, is about a sophisticated courtier who thinks he can manipulate primitive Border chieftains by following the more advanced ideas of European statecraft. His failure is summed up in one line: 'Rationality and practicality has broke itself to pieces'. The Border clans, and notably Johnny Armstrong their archetype, don't react according to the rules. One day a chieftain will be talking of the King of Scotland as if he were a minor competitor, the next he'll be lost in delusions of grandeur at the notion of being called the King's brother. In matters of religion the clansmen are equally inconsistent. If a chieftain can try to cover a recent murder by telling the court that he and his rival are at peace, surely the same man can be relied on to resist an evangelical preacher? Not at all. When a preacher turns up, Armstrong's household change over from tribal ballads to Lutheran chants at the drop of a hat.

In his turn the preacher is infected by the violence of his new protectors, for as soon as his motives are questioned he sinks a knife through the peritoneum of the offender, who happens to be the envoy's loyal friend and secretary. The slow death involved is a good example of the legitimate use of violence on stage. It gives Lindsay a lesson about the forces he has so condescendingly manipulated and it removes the glamour which he has seen in them as a poet. 'You can never accept the gravity of another man's violence,' Lindsay has been told. Having seen his friend die, he finally does accept it, removes the last vestiges of romanticism and humanism from his diplomacy, advocates the imprisonment of the chieftains and has Armstrong hanged, after enticing him to a meeting with the King. Lindsay has learnt that the reality underlying tribal romanticism is a knife in the guts.

The action of the play is framed by the diplomat Lindsay who introduces it and signs it off. He and Armstrong are the main structural pillars, and my main criticism of the National Theatre Company's production is that both of them are weakened. In the case of Lindsay it is a matter of casting. Robert Stephens excels himself. He's unfailingly intelligent and in this part unexpectedly courtly, best of all when composing himself for an audience with the King. To say that Mr Stephens is a natural comedian does not belittle the curious dignity he arrived at in *The Royal Hunt of the Sun* and, briefly, in *Much Ado*. But it's brittle, finely drawn dignity, like that of a greyhound. It might pass for the poet in Lindsay, though not as a physical equivalent of the latter's tone in his verse as we know it. For the calculating seriousness of Lindsay the politician an actor of less agility, less mercurial temperament is needed, the more so because Armstrong is played by Albert Finney with a hypnotic presence which rivets the attention at Chichester while he's seated with his back to most of the audience, and once merely by raising his hand to grip a woman's face. I have not seen this gesture improved on since Massine's hand froze a hot whirl of action by one short movement in his Viennese ballet. Weightier opposition for Armstrong would increase the play's impact.

If one pillar of the action is frailer than seems to be necessary, the other is deliberately toppled over just before the finish by a misapplication of alienation technique. Just as *Serjeant Musgrave's Dance* refers implicitly to Cyprus, so *Armstrong* has parallels with events in the Congo and the moment chosen to hint at them is one that could equally well have been used to give us a final, barbaric taste of Armstrong's glamour. To meet the king he arrives adorned with a selection of his fabulous loot, including—and I quote from the stage directions—'a

wide-brimmed hat, turned up over the forehead', on which are pinned a number of jewelled badges after the fashion of Field-Marshal Montgomery's beret. I can't find anything in the stage directions or the surrounding dialogue to indicate that Armstrong is meant to look ridiculous in this get-up. On the contrary it makes nonsense of the primitive grandeur already claimed for him if he does. Yet the effect made by Finney, with the connivance of his directors, is of a farcical savage tricked out in European loot. This may be helpful as a comment on African politics but not as a prelude to the hanging, where Armstrong heroically improvises a Border ballad before they top him.—LAURENCE KITCHIN, "Arden," *Drama in the Sixties*, 1966, pp. 85–87

The Island of the Mighty shows an empire menaced from without and crumbling from within. Throughout the play there is the constant threat of an English invasion; we hear about the brutality of these fighters from over the water, but we never see them. Instead, we see the internal struggles of the land. Arthur exemplifies all the rectilinear Roman virtues; he has read Tacitus and Livy and fights by the book. He says his prayers; he is also autocratic, intolerant, and haunted by his own pagan past. Set against the Romanized world of Arthur is a tribal society, savage and primitive. In its purest form it is symbolized by the Picts, a group Arthur would dearly love to forget, but through neighbouring princes and their squabbles he is forced to negotiate—and eventually fight—with them. They have a secret, savage, matriarchal underlife, often repugnant in its violence, but also full of vitality and the potential for change. The Pictish values are also the old values of Arthur's world, and they are present, to some extent, in his followers and his queen, and are deeply buried in his own soul. As these two forces struggle for possession, two groups of people have to deal with the consequences—the peasants, who have to survive, and the poets, who have to make political sense of it all. . . .

The Island of the Mighty was one of the most ambitious theatre projects of the last fifty years, both in terms of its scale and of the magnitude of the themes which it handles. It makes a serious attempt to explore British and Irish myths, and to ground these myths in a real society. We are able to acknowledge them as spiritual truths, and at the same time to see their limitations. The story of the Waste Land and the Lame King, for instance, are powerful and evocative stories with considerable resonance for British and Irish readers—but here they are set in a political context. The Waste Land, in this play, is not a magical place or a spiritual state, but a real land which the peasants have to work; it has been created by the king himself, and the way to heal it is not by magic but by the hard reality of social change. Similarly the Bard, the mystic figure so profoundly discussed in *The White Goddess*, here has his work redefined; instead of a privileged and apolitical servant of the Muse, he is the servant of the people who must live through the events he sings about, challenge them and change them. He must deal in analysis as well as vision.—FRANCES GRAY, *John Arden*, 1983, pp. 135–45

MALCOLM PAGE
From *John Arden*
1984, pp. 137–45

Great claims have been made for John Arden. Jack Richardson noted that he was "considered by many close to the theater to be England's best contemporary playwright," while D. A. N. Jones described him as "the only dramatic poet in English, outside Nigeria."[1] Albert Hunt called him "one of the greatest dramatists in the English language for several centuries," and Adrian Mitchell even claimed that "he is the greatest British playwright since Shakespeare."[2] Arden, on the other hand, has never had a Broadway nor Shaftesbury Avenue production, and his reputation appears to have declined in the 1970s.

Various reasons for Arden's lack of wide popularity can be listed: he has confused commentators by his unpredictability; his interest in verse and in dignified speech has been unfashionable since the early 1950s; some productions of his plays were feeble. Many of the plays are complex, idiosyncratic, and difficult to grasp at a single hearing. He expects an alert audience willing to follow where an original mind leads. He has been reluctant to meet the requirements of the professional theater, writing for big casts at inordinate length. Other reasons are more fortuitous: accidents of geography, of political gestures, of personality conflicts around real or imagined slights, or refusal to seek worldly commercial success. Arden often seems to have been writing in the wrong era, to date somehow always out of step with audiences and their expectations.

Whatever the explanations, Arden has failed to find a substantial audience. His turning away from the London theater is mainly due to his wish to work with small communities, but is also partly due to the way in which the West End has never turned to him. The inability to find big audiences is especially sad for a man who wants to reach the people in the manner of nineteenth-century melodrama or early twentieth-century music-hall clowning.

Arden is essentially a man of the theater, though readily trying out radio and television. He has acted himself in *The Business of Good Government*, *The Royal Pardon*, "Harold Muggins," and *The Connolly Show* and likes to direct or to be involved in rehearsals. A whole play, *The Royal Pardon*, explores the balance between reality and make-believe that is the essence of theater. Ideally, he would involve his audience in an exciting neo-Dionysian ritual; instead, he seeks the participation of as many as possible of the people in Kirkbymoorside, Beaford, County Galway, or the streets around Unity Theater. Like Shaw or Brecht, Arden wants his audiences to react to serious issues, but he desires also to entertain them in as many ways as possible: with many characters, colorfully dressed; with striking visual effects, like the besieged house at the end of *Pigs* or the marketplace *coup de théâtre* in *Musgrave*; and with songs and lyrical flights of fancy. . . .

The difficulties in Arden's plays can be exaggerated. Some of the plays—notably *Musgrave*, *Armstrong*, and *The Island of the Mighty*—become more comprehensible at second seeing or reading; but on the other hand *Live Like Pigs* or *The Happy Haven* are readily accessible. Sometimes characters behave in confusing ways: Musgrave's attitudes are admirable while his actions are not; Krank and Butterthwaite are likeable people whose behavior is questioned, yet, as Arden has said, "the likeable rogue is a very old convention." At times, too, one is bewildered about what to think. Arden deliberately bewilders his audience through most of *Musgrave* because he himself is questioning the pacifist position, but at other times his subtle intelligence may have created more uncertainty than he intended. Without his statement in a letter that "Lindsay was wrong" in *Armstrong* and in an interview that Butterthwaite's corruption does a "great deal less harm" than Feng's integrity in *The Workhouse Donkey*, few would feel absolutely sure of the author's intent.

Nearly all these difficulties fall into place, however, after the recurring theme has been grasped—that of authority and the place of the rare, free, vital, spontaneous man in modern,

ordered societies. Authority rests in social institutions: kings and clergy in the past; police and mayors today. Authority is naval discipline in "The Life of Man"; Caligula, the incorruptible councillor; the housing official and policeman in *Pigs*; mayor, parson, constable, and dragoon officer in *Musgrave*; the doctor in *The Happy Haven*; Herod; the routine and regular hours of the architect's office in *Wet Fish*; police and government in *The Workhouse Donkey*; the Bishop of Bamberg and the Emperor against Ironhand; the king and Lindsay against Armstrong; King John in *Liberty*; kings and the constable in *The Royal Pardon*; soldiers, kings, and ministers in *The Bagman*; Arthur, Strathclyde, and Gododdin in *The Island*; and Grabitall and the Employers in *The Connolly Show*. Individuals without office take authority on themselves, like Henry Ginger in *Babylon*, the Bargee in *Musgrave*, and Baker-Fortescue in *The Little Gray Home in the West*. Arden knows the complexity of authority and that the police, the Labor councillors, and the Conservative businessmen somehow share it. Levels of authority are often considered: the protagonist of *Soldier, Soldier* must leave to meet his obligations; the dragoons come from outside to seize Musgrave; Doctor Copperthwaite is variously responsible to the mayor, wealthy benefactors, and the Ministry of Health; the Home Secretary in London could intervene in Butterthwaite's borough; the program for *Armstrong* contained a chart of hierarchies of responsibility. Sometimes authority figures are detestable, like the Headmaster in *Ars Longa* and the constable in *The Royal Pardon*; but Arden usually evinces understanding of the men who attempt to provide good government. He is kindly to Feng in *The Workhouse Donkey*, writes almost an apologia for Herod, and did not make clear his disapproval of Lindsay to many who saw *Armstrong*. As a result, misunderstanding exists and he is accused of amorality or of lacking a view of his own.[3]

Neither the past nor scrutiny of the present gave Arden a viable morality or a settled social philosophy,[4] and his own uncertainty explains why his earlier plays have often been found so puzzling. By 1970 he had presented much in the realm of ideas, both his wide vision about freedom, expediency, and authority and his specific comments about such subjects as Cyprus, Vietnam, pacifism, and old people. His failure to achieve a settled world view related to the varied types and contexts of his plays, for his career has been a restless search for the right kind of stage, the right company, the right community. Possibly too much of the concept of a play remains in Arden's mind and is never sufficiently on paper for others to grasp—or perhaps the failing is rather in the organization of theater, that there is never enough time to evolve an absolutely finished Arden play. His intellectuality, which can overcome theatrical qualities, may be his biggest disadvantage as a playwright. In striving to reconcile diverse influences, in seeking to reach a wide public, in exploring the use of verse, song, and music, and in trying to fit in every relevant scene, his work is too often indigestible. . . .

What are Arden's strengths? He has a flair for language, especially for the harsh, laconic, Anglo-Saxon-rooted verse line. He is endlessly curious, so that a lively and intelligent mind is always to be perceived in the plays. He has a powerful sense of the past in an age when historical drama is uncommon, re-creating the times of men like Armstrong and King Arthur and, more playfully, Nelson. The stagecraft, the gift for the theatrical moment, provides the shock of the skeleton hoisted as Musgrave dances and many more, such as the apotheosis of Butterthwaite at the end of *The Workhouse Donkey*. Arden has the ambition and audacity to keep attempting something new, trying out length and brevity, mime and masks, music and melodrama, work with and for children. And a good production of an Arden play is not only intellectually satisfying but exuberantly entertaining, promoting good feeling and high spirits, even on such unpromising topics as municipal politics and Irish oppression.

The successes are there to be read, foremost among them *Musgrave*, where mythic imagination best fuses with passionate purpose. *The Waters of Babylon*, *Live Like Pigs*, and, especially, *The Workhouse Donkey* overflow with energy and vitality. Other pieces are limited in size and scope: the spiky, abruptly episodic *Ars Longa*; the gentler, more relaxed *Royal Pardon*; the dream-nightmare meditation, *The Bagman*. In contrast *Armstrong's Last Goodnight* has a multiplicity of character and incident, and a breadth equalled only by Brecht in modern times. Arden still awaits full recognition of his great and varied achievements—and is still writing.

Notes

1. Jack Richardson, "Musgrave's Dance and Azdak's Circle," *Commentary* 41 (June 1966):75; D. A. N. Jones, "*Muggins*," *Listener* 79 (June 20, 1968):817.
2. Albert Hunt, *Arden: A Study of His Plays* (London, 1974), p. 143; Adrian Mitchell, "Priests and Prophets of the New Permissiveness," *The Permissive Society* (London: Panther, 1969), p. 38.
3. This judgment appears to originate with Tom Milne in "A Touch of the Poet," *New Left Review*, no. 7 (Jan.–Feb., 1961), and to be popularized by John Russell Taylor in *Anger and After* (London, rev. ed., 1969), pp. 83–85, and in his Introduction to *Three Plays* (Harmondsworth, 1964).
4. Cf. Simon Trussler, "Arden: An Introduction," *Encore*, no. 57 (Sept.–Oct., 1965), p. 5.

W. H. Auden

1907–1973

Wystan Hugh Auden was born in York on February 21, 1907. At Christ Church, Oxford, he was taught by Nevill Coghill, who encouraged him to explore the Old and Middle English poetry that later would inform his own. Upon graduation in 1928, Auden went to Berlin to learn German, where he was joined by his boyhood friend Christopher Isherwood. From 1930 to 1935, Auden taught at several English academies and began to attract critical notice as a poet. He was the center of a literary circle that included Isherwood, Stephen Spender, Louis MacNeice, and C. Day Lewis, all leftist and strongly influenced by Gerard Manley Hopkins. Auden co-founded the Group Theatre in 1932, and wrote for the progressive General Post Office film unit in 1935. There he began collaborating with the composer Benjamin Britten, for whom Auden wrote many librettos. Also in 1935 Auden married Erika Mann, Thomas Mann's daughter, so that she could obtain a British passport. He was an ambulance driver for the Loyalists in Spain in 1937, the year he won the King's Poetry Medal.

Auden and Isherwood came to the United States in 1939, where Auden soon met his lifelong companion Chester Kallman. Over the next seventeen years he taught poetry at various American universities, becoming a U.S. citizen in 1946. The next year he published his best-known work, *The Age of Anxiety*, which won him a Pulitzer Prize. From 1956—when *The Shield of Achilles* won a National Book Award—to 1961 Auden lectured at Oxford. Until his death, he and Kallman divided their time between Oxford, New York, and the Austrian farmhouse Auden made famous in *About the House* (1972).

Auden was extraordinarily prolific. Between 1930 and 1970 he produced many volumes of poetry, numerous plays (some with Isherwood), critical essays, scores of introductions and forewords, and translations of Brecht, Cocteau, Goethe, and Perse. Auden took pride in synthesis, asserting that "all geniune poetry is in a sense the formation of private spheres out of a public chaos." Auden's spheres grew steadily more private over the years as his poems progressed from detached commentary and analysis to celebrations of personal fulfillment. A turning point in this progression was his return to Anglicanism in the early 1940s, heralded by his 1944 Christmas oratorio, *For the Time Being*. Auden died in Austria on September 28, 1973.

Personal

There is a sense, I hope it isn't presumptuous to say, in which those of us who are a dozen or so years younger than Auden are more his contemporaries than his friends could be; for almost as soon as we began to read poetry we read his, and have gone on doing so for perhaps forty years, so that his voice is woven into our entire experience of poetry, whereas they were brought up on older poets. Then again they had a double image of the changing poems and the changing person, the blond young terror of *Lions and Shadows* matching the obscure urgency, the nightmare imperatives of the early poems: the benign somewhat self-absorbed sage speaking, in his odd quacking voice, the alert, resigned meditations of the last books. But those of us who knew him only a little, and only late, could keep separate the person and the poems. Every new book modified our idea of their authority, but that authority belonged, ultimately, to the language rather than to its virtuoso manipulator, to the dense and various world of his speech rather than to the speaker.

He resisted the grandest claims made for poetry, and called it a game, much less important than good conduct,

A. ALVAREZ

W. H. AUDEN

ERIC AMBLER

KINGSLEY AMIS

J. G. BALLARD

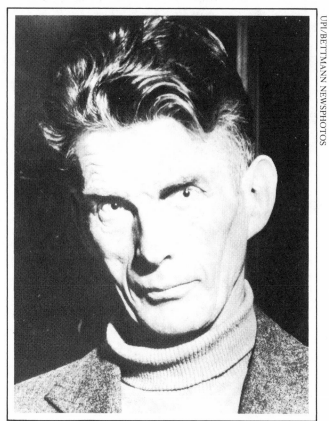

SAMUEL BECKETT

J. M. BARRIE

trivial compared with sanctity. Yet he played it as if his life depended on it—his own life, the conscience he did not wish to encumber with 'clever forgeries'—but life also in a larger sense, the life of language. For language he thought of not merely as that which differentiates man, but as what makes him the equal of the rest of creation in diversity. He alone, the lord of 'eachness', has the gift of avoiding repetition, and of naming everything. So the poet's language is the celebrant of universal presence; though, as we are told in the beautiful chill poem in memory of MacNeice called 'The Cave of Making', the celebration requires that the world be shut off; and speech itself is an absence implying presence, 'a shadow echoing/ the silent light'. It was an absorbed devotion to speech that precluded the success of the poet's prayer: 'Lord, teach me to write so well that I shall no longer want to.'—FRANK KERMODE, "W. H. Auden (1907–1973)," *NSN*, Oct. 5, 1973, p. 479

No poet's life fell more decisively in two. What was English Auden's game *about*, that tended to become like a war—was it capital and labour, communism and fascism, life and death? It hardly mattered: what rang true was that inimitable Thirties fear, the sense that something was going to fall like rain, on the other side of which, if we were lucky, we might build the Just City. English Auden was a superb, magnetic, wide-angled poet, but the poetry was in the blaming and warning.

American Auden, on the other hand, was a walking readers' digest: names—Rilke, Kierkegaard, Goethe, James—clung to him like Coney Island confetti. He spread easily into longer works, their themes our civilisation, the Christian story, the relation of life and art. Now part academic, part journalist, part international man of letters, his genius decreased in impact while maintaining, or even increasing, its productivity.

What held the two together, and us to both of them? First, his unique blend of dedication and irreverence: poetry is a fine thing, but the poet—even one of Auden's stature—mustn't give himself airs ('in the end, art is small beer'). Secondly, a love of the English language ('I believe in the OED') that was still far from subservience (he sat on Volume X at meals). Thirdly, a personal toughness and isolation that, scouting self-pity in himself and others, recalled the life-style of his Anglo-Saxon ancestors. It's hard not to read the Malebolgian 'On the Circuit' in this spirit; indeed, the last lines of his last collection have something of the same resonance, when he instructs his flesh at their moment of parting to

> . . . pay no attention
> To my piteous *Dont's*, but bugger off quickly.

It is a Stoic aspiration. It is good to know it was granted.—PHILIP LARKIN, "W. H. Auden (1907–1973)," *NSN*, Oct. 5, 1973, p. 479

I knew Wystan since the time when we were both undergraduates, and saw him at intervals until a few weeks before his death. It is impossible for me, in these surroundings, not to juxtapose two images of him, one of forty years back, and one of a year ago only.

The first is of the tow-haired undergraduate poet with the abruptly turning head, and eyes that could quickly take the measure of people or ideas. At that time, he was not altogether quite un-chic, wearing a bow-tie and on occasion wishing one to admire the suit he had on. He recited poetry by heart in an almost toneless, unemotional, quite unpoetical voice which submerged the intellectual meaning under the level horizontal line of the words. He could hold up a word or phrase like an isolated fragment or specimen chipped off the great granite cliff of language, where a tragic emotion could be compressed into a coldly joking word. . . .

The second image of Wystan is of course one with which you are all familiar: the famous poet with the face like a map of physical geography, criss-crossed and river-run and creased with lines. This was a face upon which experiences and thoughts had hammered; a face of isolated self-communing which reminded me of a phrase of Montherlant's about the artist's task of "noble self-cultivation"; a face, though, which was still somehow entertaining and which could break down into a smile of benevolence or light up with gratified recognition at some anecdote recounted or thought received. It was a face at once armored and receptive.

It is difficult to bring these two images—spaced forty years apart—together. But to do so is to find reason for our being here to praise and thank him.

His fellow undergraduates who were poets when he was also an undergraduate (Day Lewis, MacNeice, Rex Warner, and myself) saw in him a man who, instead of being, like us, romantically confused, diagnosed the condition of contemporary poetry, and of civilization, and of us—with our neuroses. He found symptoms everywhere. *Symptomatic* was his key word. But in his very strange poetry he transmogrified these symptoms into figures in a landscape of mountains, passes, streams, heroes, horses, eagles, feuds and runes of Norse sagas. He was a poet of an unanticipated kind—a different race from ourselves—and also a diagnostician of literary, social, and individual psychosomatic situations, who mixed this Iceland imagery with Freudian dream symbolism. Not in the least a leader, but, rather, a clinical-minded oracle with a voice that could sound as depersonalized as a Norn's in a Norse saga. Extremely funny, and extremely hard-working: always, as Louis MacNeice put it, "getting on with the job." He could indulge in self-caricature, and he could decidedly shock, but he did no imitations of other people's speech or mannerisms, though he could do an excellent performance of a High Mass, including the bell tinkling. His only performance was himself.—STEPHEN SPENDER, "W. H. Auden (1907–1973)," *NYRB*, Nov. 29, 1973, p.3

Rereading Auden's poems in chronological order and remembering him in the last years of his life, when misery and unhappiness had grown more and more unbearable without, however, in the least touching either the divine gift or the blessed facility of the talent, I have become surer than ever that he was "hurt into poetry" even more than Yeats ("Mad Ireland hurt you into poetry"), and that, despite his susceptibility to compassion, public political circumstances were not necessary to hurt him into poetry. What made him a poet was his extraordinary facility with and love for words, but what made him a great poet was the unprotesting willingness with which he yielded to the "curse" of vulnerability to "human *unsuccess*" on all levels of human existence—vulnerability to the crookedness of the desires, to the infidelities of the heart, to the injustices of the world.

> Follow, poet, follow right
> To the bottom of the night,
> With your unconstraining voice
> Still persuade us to rejoice;
>
> With the farming of a verse
> Make a vineyard of the curse,
> Sing of human unsuccess
> In a rapture of distress;
>
> In the deserts of the heart
> Let the healing fountain start,
> In the prison of his days
> Teach the free man how to praise.

Praise is the key word of these lines, not praise of "the best of all possible worlds"—as though it were up to the poet (or the philosopher) to justify God's creation—but praise that pitches itself against all that is most unsatisfactory in man's condition on this earth and sucks its own strength from the wound: somehow convinced, as the bards of ancient Greece were, that the gods spin unhappiness and evil things toward mortals so that they may be able to tell the tales and sing the songs.

> I could (which you cannot)
> Find reasons fast enough
> To face the sky and roar
> In anger and despair
> At what is going on,
> Demanding that it name
> Whoever is to blame:
> The sky would only wait
> Till all my breath was gone
> And then reiterate
> As if I wasn't there
> That singular command
> I do not understand,
> *Bless what there is for being,*
> Which has to be obeyed, for
> What else am I made for,
> Agreeing or disagreeing?

And the triumph of the private person was that the voice of the great poet never silenced the small but penetrating voice of sheer sound common sense whose loss has so often been the price paid for divine gifts. Auden never permitted himself to lose his mind—that is, to lose the "distress" in the "rapture" that rose out of it:

> No metaphor, remember, can express
> A real historical unhappiness;
> Your tears have value if they make us gay;
> *O Happy Grief!* is all sad verse can say.

It seems, of course, very unlikely that young Auden, when he decided that he was going to be a *great* poet, knew the price he would have to pay, and I think it entirely possible that in the end—when not the intensity of his feelings and not the gift of transforming them into praise but the sheer physical strength of the heart to bear them and live with them gradually faded away—he considered the price too high. We, in any event—his audience, readers and listeners—can only be grateful that he paid his price up to the last penny for the everlasting glory of the English language. And his friends may find some consolation in his beautiful joke beyond the grave—that for more than one reason, as Spender said, "his wise unconscious self chose a good day for dying." The wisdom to know "when to live and when to die" is not given to mortals, but Wystan, one would like to think, may have received it as the supreme reward that the cruel gods of poetry bestowed on the most obedient of their servants.—HANNAH ARENDT, "Remembering Wystan H. Auden," *NY*, Jan. 20, 1975, pp. 45–46

General

A few of the writers have appeared in the *Criterion:* two of them, W. H. Auden and Stephen Spender, have had volumes published on my recommendation by Faber & Faber. Of all the younger poets, Auden is the one who has interested me most deeply, though I feel that it is impossible to predict whether he will manifest the austerity and concentration necessary for poetry of the first rank, or whether he will dissipate his talents in wit and verbal brilliance.—T. S. ELIOT, *LT*, July 12, 1933, pp. ii–iii

Poetic justice, with its attendant ironies, must have presided over the mutually rewarding interchange that sent T. S. Eliot to England and brought W. H. Auden to this country. Eliot, whose preaching has never quite rationalized his practice, has retained a peculiarly individual talent. Auden, whose iconoclasm has merely tested his loyalties, has not broken with tradition. Craftsmanship is a surer link than manifestos and genuflections, and Auden's skill is linked with the odes of Dryden and the patter of Gilbert, with the varied masters and characteristic journeymen of English prosody. He has taught much, and can teach more, to our native poets: few of them have really mastered the technical requirements of their craft, and those who have spend most of their efforts reminding us of the fact. A book which—despite its temporizing title—takes in its stride the ballade, the villanelle, the sestina, sapphics, elegiacs and *terza rima*, while making words a vehicle for ideas instead of the contrary, is more than a current event; it is an enduring delight. When poetry is as topical and colloquial, as pregnant with issues and idioms as Auden's, it cannot be transplanted without undergoing some abstraction of matter, some intensification of manner. Imagery becomes less immediate, diction more macaronic. Gorgeous dames have Oxford accents and juke-boxes play Handel. The old familiar-exotic contrast between a concrete little England and the big abstract globe gives way to the broader antitheses of art versus nature and naturalism versus supernaturalism. But the *discordia concors*, whereby they are resolved, is still the dominant mode; Auden and Eliot can still meet, if not on the common ground of the vernacular and comtemporary, then in the rarefied atmosphere of the literary and philosophic.—HARRY LEVIN, "Through the Looking Glass," *NR*, Sept. 18, 1944, pp. 347–48

Of course, already in those opening 'thirties a Poetic Renaissance was supposed to have opened too. A number of names were current as those of promising, and even established, young poets. One reason why my book, though widely used among publicists of Modern Poetry, itself received little favour or, even, mention, was that it neither acclaimed the Renaissance nor mentioned the names, the owners of which were to exercise a predominant influence in the literary world for years to come. I naturally knew of the Renaissance and had heard of the names; but I judged that it was early yet for acclamation.

In fact, only one of these new reputations appeared to me to be supported by gifts of any promise, and that was W. H. Auden's. I did not discuss him in my book, because the promise, as I saw it, could not be asserted without a weight of qualifying and privative emphasis that, in the absence of anything to be acclaimed as *done*, might, I feared, make the introduction for such treatment seem wantonly offensive. It was the 'Charade', *Paid on Both Sides*, published in *The Criterion* in 1929, that first called attention to Auden. This curious and youthful piece might have represented the very green immaturity of a notable creative talent. But the author, it was plain, would have to work very hard, resist temptations, and achieve through discipline and maturing experience a difficult development, before anything satisfactory could come of his gifts. The childlike vividness of imagination was accompanied by the disabilities of the childish; the verbal vigour went with an obscurity of the wrong kind—that which betrays incoherence and lack of meaning; and, peculiarly ominous because of the attendant sophistication, there was, manifest in the writer's uncertainty as to the degree of seriousness he intended, a surprising radical adolescence that should have been already well outgrown. It seems to me that Auden has hardly come nearer to essential maturity since, though he made a rapid advance in sophistication.

Sophistication—that is a topic which presents itself again when we contemplate the failure to develop, or to develop satisfactorily, of the two young poets I do mention in my book, Empson and Bottrall. The diagnosis of sophistication is relevant to a great deal of the characteristic work of the early nineteen-thirties. There is that impressiveness of modish cultural equipment; that air of knowing one's way about; in short, that preoccupation with intellectuality, and the externals of profundity and subtlety; and, underneath, the correlated failure in personal development: nothing seems to happen at that depth, the established aim and bent hardly permitting it to happen. Sophistication belongs to a climate in which the natural appetite for kudos is not chastened by contact with mature standards, and in which fixed immaturity can take itself for something else.

Such a climate prevailed in the world in which Auden made his *début*—Auden whose career is worth pondering because it is the representative career of the nineteen-thirties, and has a representative significance. He entered the literary world with a reputation made at the university: as a recent critic in *The Times Literary Supplement* puts it, he was 'the Oxford intellectual with a bag of poetic squibs in his pocket'. What this critic doesn't say, or appear to realize, is that the Auden who conquered the literary world with such ease was the undergraduate intellectual. The undergraduate coterie has always had its part in the formation of talent; but the coterie in the ancient seats of learning has tended, in other days, to bring its members into touch with adult standards. That which formed Auden seems to have been able to remain utterly unaware of them. And, what was worse for him, he cannot have noticed any essential differences when he passed from undergraduate Oxford into the world where the canon of contemporary literature is established, and the currency of accepted valuations stamped. The Oxford valuation became immediately metropolitan. The undergraduate notability became a world-figure almost overnight. Auden was accepted as, beyond question, a leading intellectual and a major poet. His admirers spoke of him as having superseded T. S. Eliot.—F. R. LEAVIS, *New Bearings in English Poetry*, 1950, pp. 226–29

I began writing poetry myself because one Sunday afternoon in March 1922, a friend suggested that I should: the thought had never occurred to me. I scarcely knew any poems—*The English Hymnal*, the Psalms, *Struwwelpeter* and the mnemonic rhymes in *Kennedy's Shorter Latin Primer* are about all I remember—and I took little interest in what is called Imaginative Literature. Most of my reading had been related to a private world of Sacred Objects. Aside from a few stories like George Macdonald's *The Princess and the Goblin* and Jules Verne's *The Child of the Cavern*, the subjects of which touched upon my obsessions, my favorite books bore such titles as *Underground Life, Machinery for Metalliferous Mines, Lead and Zinc Ores of Northumberland and Alston Moor*, and my conscious purpose in reading them had been to gain information about my sacred objects. At the time, therefore, the suggestion that I write poetry seemed like a revelation from heaven for which nothing in my past could account.

Looking back, however, I now realize that I had read the technological prose of my favorite books in a peculiar way. A word like *pyrites*, for example, was for me, not simply an indicative sign; it was the Proper Name of a Sacred Being, so that, when I heard an aunt pronounce it *pirrits*, I was shocked. Her pronunciation was more than wrong, it was ugly. Ignorance was impiety. . . .

My first Master was Thomas Hardy, and I think I was very lucky in my choice. He was a good poet, perhaps a great one, but not *too* good. Much as I loved him, even I could see that his diction was often clumsy and forced and that a lot of his poems were plain bad. This gave me hope where a flawless poet might have made me despair. He was modern without being too modern. His world and sensibility were close enough to mine—curiously enough his face bore a striking resemblance to my father's—so that, in imitating him, I was being led towards not away from myself, but they were not so close as to obliterate my identity. If I looked through his spectacles, at least I was conscious of a certain eyestrain. Lastly, his metrical variety, his fondness for complicated stanza forms, were an invaluable training in the craft of making. I am also thankful that my first Master did not write in free verse or I might then have been tempted to believe that free verse is easier to write than stricter forms, whereas I now know it is infinitely more difficult.—W. H. AUDEN, "Making, Knowing, and Judging" (1956), *The Dyer's Hand*, 1968, pp. 35–38

A thinking poet poses special critical difficulties, especially when his beliefs change. Eliot's conversion was such a difficulty, and Auden's development since the thirties has raised similar problems. For like Eliot, Auden has disappointed the teleological expectations of his early admirers by failing to develop toward an end that was implicit in his beginning. This is not simply a matter of a new religious subject matter, but more fundamentally of a new view of poetry based on religious beliefs. In Auden we are faced with a major poet who in his middle years decided not to take poetry too seriously, for doctrinal reasons (which are elaborately spelled out in the Caliban section of *The Sea and the Mirror*). As an act of faith, the decision is impressive, but it has made life hard for Auden's critics and the people who teach his poems. We have all learned by now what to say about the contents of *Poems* and *Look, Stranger*, and we have polished our lectures on "Doom is dark" and "Musée des Beaux Arts"; but the work after the war is troublesome. How are we to deal with the apparent loosening of the taut, elliptical manner, the reduction of surface tension, the disappearance of anxiety as a normal tone of voice? Like his Melville, Auden has sailed into an extraordinary mildness, and mildness is not a quality that our previous experience of Auden's verse—or of modern verse in general—has prepared us for. The playing with language (and, it would seem, with the OED) in the later poems, the antipoetic, camp remarks like "ever so comfy," the chatty pastoralism and the curmudgeonly posture, all these are hard to adjust to when one has grown up on "leave for Cape Wrath tonight."

Auden has thought his way to a poetry of acceptance and celebration, and it is that arrival, I think, rather than the apparent loosening of the style, that is really at the heart of the matter. To write a poem in *praise* of limestone (or of any other substance), to bless what there is for being, to assume a stance at once calm and avuncular, is to separate oneself from the main stream of modern poetry, or what we took to be the main stream. For surely we had all agreed: poetry should be dense, difficult, allusive, and concerned with problems like Identity and Belief. But Auden seems at ease both with who he is and with what he believes and content to record his contentment in a carpet-slipper style. In his mildness he has made poetry a game, and man a comic gamesman. The early urgency has become coziness, fear has become irascibility, and all the anxieties are trivial ones. In every aspect of the work the changes have been extreme; where would one find another poet who has altered so much, and who has so completely resigned from his poetic generation?—SAMUEL HYNES, "Auden and MacNeice," *CoL*, Summer 1973, pp. 379–80

The definite article points to the recognisable if not to the already known. It recalls an actually or possibly shared experience as well as, in its 20th-century uses, reflecting the preference of modernist poetics for the particular against the general. This, as Hamilton points out, may be based on a confusion, assuming that the opposition "particular/general" is the same as the opposition "sharp/vague", which does not necessarily follow. If Eliot and Auden each show a high percentage of definite articles their reasons for doing so are fundamentally different, even though Eliot exercised a potent influence on the young Auden:

> But Eliot spoke the still unspoken word;
> For gasworks and dried tubers I forsook
> The clock at Grantchester, the English rook.
> ("Letter to Lord Byron", IV)

A line like "The simple act of the confused will" (from Poem XXVII in *Poems*, later "The Question" in *Collected Shorter Poems*, 1966), to which Hamilton draws attention, seems to be directly imitated from lines in Eliot's exactly contemporary *Ash Wednesday*, such as "The vanished power of the usual reign" or "The infirm glory of the positive hour." But this syntactical formation is rare in Auden and can be regarded as an early unassimilated influence. In Eliot the use of the definite article attempts, wistfully or urgently, to affirm the possibility of shared experiences and feelings recalled out of a fragmentary and chaotic past:

> But only in time can the moment in the rose-garden,
> The moment in the arbour where the rain beat,
> The moment in the draughty church at smokefall
> Be remembered. . . .

The experiences thus recalled are personal but not remote or esoteric, and they seek an echo in our own pasts. Auden, by contrast, can present bafflingly private experiences in a similar way, so that the attempt to participate either recoils or leads one on to speculative fiction-making:

> A choice was killed by every childish illness,
> The boiling tears among the hothouse plants,
> The rigid promise fractured in the garden,
> And the long aunts.
> (Poem XXI, *Look, Stranger!*; "A Bride in the
> 30's", *CSP*)

The effect is, as Hamilton disapprovingly remarks, "as though an entire stranger were claiming our acquaintance." More often, however, Auden's use of the definite article arises from his sense of reality as known and charted and intelligible, where all elements are potentially at least capable of classification. To quote Hamilton once more: "We have seen the fondness of Eliot and Auden for the particular image, Eliot lighting up the fragments of what is, or is supposed to be, our common experience, while Auden indicates the marks by which we may recognise this or that type of person, and diagnose his disease." Auden's classifying tendency was familiar to his friends from the beginning. In Christopher Isherwood's fictionalised autobiography, *Lions and Shadows* (1938), where the young Auden appears as "Weston", the narrator reflects on a seaside holiday:

> "Suppose Weston were here, I thought, he would
> know the names of the different species of gull—and,
> by naming them, would dismiss them to their proper
> recognised unimportant place in the background of
> the poet's consciousness. . . ."

Another stylistic feature which Auden derived from Eliot but used with a significant difference is the bizarre or unexpected simile, as in the famous opening of "Prufrock": "When the evening is spread out against the sky/Like a patient etherised upon a table." In Eliot the simile is startling but not unintelligible; the underlying idea is of the cessation of consciousness, and we are invited to recognise the strangeness of a sensibility that interprets common experience in such a clinical way. There is, too, the conviction of the early modernist poet that we should think and feel differently about such a hallowed Romantic property as "evening." In Auden this impulse is systematically taken to the point of diminishing, even trivialising, large, potent concepts or images by comparing them to something everyday or banal. As, for instance, "Desire like a police-dog is unfastened" (Poem X, *Look, Stranger!*). Or again, consider the treatment of the moon in Poem II of *Look, Stranger!*:

> Into the galleries she peers,
> And blankly as an orphan stares
> Upon the marvellous pictures.

In the revised version of this poem, "A Summer Night" (*CSP*), the comparison is made even more reductive: "And blankly as a butcher stares." This stylistic device became more frequent as Auden developed during the 'thirties; it is rare in *Poems*, moderately common in *Look, Stranger!* and a repetitive trick in *Another Time* (1940). "Brussels in Winter" from the last volume is representative, with four similes in fourteen lines: "Wandering the cold streets tangled like old string"; "The winter holds them like the Opera"; "Where isolated windows glow like farms"; "A phrase goes packed with meaning like a van." Such repetitions deaden whatever startling impact the device might have; it was, however, widely imitated, and became a major element in the collective Audenesque manner.— BERNARD BERGONZI, "Auden and the Audenesque," *Enc*, Feb. 1975, pp. 66–67

Works

PAID ON BOTH SIDES, POEMS

I must first try to outline the plot, as it is not obvious on one's first reading. There is a blood-feud, apparently in the North of England, between two mill-owning families who are tribal leaders of their workmen; it is at the present day, but there are no class distinctions and no police. John, the hero of the play, is born prematurely from shock, after the death by ambush of his father; so as to be peculiarly a child of the feud. As a young man he carries it on, though he encourages a brother who loses faith in it to emigrate. Then he falls in love with a daughter (apparently the heiress) of the enemy house; to marry her would involve ending the feud, spoiling the plans of his friends, breaking away from the world his mother takes for granted, and hurting her by refusing to revenge his father. Just before he decides about it, a spy, son of the enemy house (but apparently only her half-brother), is captured; it is the crisis of the play; he orders him to be taken out and shot. He then marries Anne; she tries to make him emigrate, but he insists on accepting his responsibility and trying to stop the feud; and is shot on the wedding day, at another mother's instigation, by a brother of the spy.

This much, though very compressed, and sometimes in obscure verse, is a straightforward play. But at the crisis, when John has just ordered the spy to be shot, a sort of surrealist technique is used to convey his motives. They could only, I think, have been conveyed in this way, and only when you have accepted them can the play be recognised as a sensible and properly motivated tragedy.

The reason for plunging below the rational world at this point is precisely that the decision to end the feud is a fundamental one; it involves so much foreknowledge of what he will feel under circumstances not yet realisable that it has to be carried through on motives (or by choosing to give himself strength from apparent motives) which do not belong to what is then the sensible world he lives in. For the point of the tragedy is that he could not know his own mind till too late, because it was just that process of making contact with reality, necessary to him before he could know his own mind, which in the event destroyed him. So that the play is 'about' the antinomies of the will, about the problems involved in the attempt to change radically a working system.

He has the spy shot partly to tie his own hands, since he will evade the decision if he can make peace impossible, partly (the other way round) because it will make peace difficult, so that the attempt, if he chooses to make it, will expose him to more risk (for this seems to make it more generous), partly from a self-contempt which, in search of relief, turns outwards, and lights on the man who seems likest to himself, for he too is half a spy in his own camp; partly because he must kill part of himself in coming to either decision about the marriage, so that it seems a first step, or a revenge, to kill by an irrelevant decision the man likest him (for whom he must at the moment, from a point of view which still excites horror in him, feel most sympathy), partly because only by making a decision on some associated matter can he string himself up to know his own mind on the matter in question, partly because what is in his mind makes him feel ashamed and guilty among his supporters, so that he mistakenly thinks it necessary for his own safety to prove to them he is whole-heartedly on their side.

In this way the spy becomes a symbol to him, both of the feud itself, of which he is part, so as to make it seem contemptible, and of his own attempt to escape from the feud, which makes him seem contemptible to his own camp; and in either case the spy is both himself and his chief enemy. And having united himself with the man he despises, he must feel some remorse and self-contempt about killing him for these accidental and neurotic reasons; at any rate it puts him in the wrong, and in part makes him deserve the consequences.

And yet it is precisely the painfulness and dangerousness of these expulsive forces that make it possible for him to give birth to a decision.

Hence we sink down, in this crucial and solvent instant of decision, into a childish scheme of judgment, centring round desire for, and fear of, the mother; jealousy of, and identity with, the brother, who is also the spy; away from the immediate situation, so that younger incidental reminiscences of the author become relevant; below the distinction between murderer and victim, so that the hero escapes from feeling his responsibility; below intelligible sexuality; and in the speech of the Man-Woman (a 'prisoner of war behind barbed wire, in the snow') we are plunged into a general exposition of the self-contempt of indecision. Then the spy is shot, and we return, with circus farce like the panting of recovery, into the real world of the play; from then on he knows his own mind, and is fated to destruction.

One reason the scheme is so impressive is that it puts psycho-analysis and surrealism and all that, all the irrationalist tendencies which are so essential a part of the machinery of present-day thought, into their proper place; they are made part of the normal and rational tragic form, and indeed what constitutes the tragic situation. One feels as if at the crisis of many, perhaps better, tragedies, it is just this machinery which has been covertly employed. Within its scale (twenty-seven pages) there is the gamut of all the ways we have of thinking about the matter; it has the sort of completeness that makes a work seem

to define the attitude of a generation.—WILLIAM EMPSON, *Exp*, Spring 1931, pp. 60–61

A recent writer has remarked that poetry, as a result of modern mechanization, has become more and more removed from the external common life of men: that its material is found more in the inner life of the individual, and its interpretation depends increasingly upon the individual's private and personal knowledge. And both these books are extreme examples of that withdrawal from the objective into the subjective world. Many passages in each of them are baffling, if not unintelligible, because they lack that measure of normality which makes communication between one individual and another possible. For mental idiosyncrasies, if they are extravagantly indulged, isolate a writer as completely as if he spoke in an unknown tongue. Thus in the first of his poems Mr. Auden invites us, so far as we understand him, to discover, amid the horrors and humiliations of a war-stricken world, the 'neutralizing peace' of indifference. But the manner of his invitation is often so peculiar to himself and so eccentric in its terminology that, instead of communicating an experience of value to us, it merely sets our minds a problem in allusions to solve. . . . ⟨A⟩lthough we can sense his general meaning, it requires a kind of effort to discover the exact relevance of his allusions which, even when we are sure of having done so, destroys the possibility of real enrichment. Such poetry, indeed, completely contradicts Keats's axiom that 'poetry should surprise by a fine excess and not by singularity': that it should 'strike the reader as a wording of his own highest thoughts, and appear almost a remembrance'; and it fails to make a living contact with us because it is the fruit of a too specialized kind of concentration. For intellectual analysis of emotional states, however sharp its focus, is poetically as barren as emotional diffuseness. And although Mr. Auden can write—

> Coming out of me living is always thinking,
> Thinking changing and changing living,

the thinking process in most of his poetry is either arbitrarily imposed upon the living or the living impulse, weakened by uncertainty and disillusion, begets a symbolism which is full of personal caprice. For a sense of chaos and defeat not only underlies but determines the very texture of his verse and particularly of the strange 'Charade', entitled 'Paid on Both Sides', with which his book begins and which, in its combination of seriousness and flippancy, presents in the form of a feud between two hostile parties, the stultifying division in his own consciousness which wrings fom him the cry—

> Could I have been some simpleton that lived
> Before disaster sent his runners here;
> Younger than worms, worms have too much to bear.
> Yes, mineral were best: could I but see
> These woods, these fields of green, this lively world
> Sterile as moon.

—F. R. LEAVIS, *TLS*, March 19, 1931, p. 221

THE ORATORS, THE DOG BENEATH THE SKIN

The Orators is an astonishing advance on Mr. Auden's first book. The first section is written in a bastard (though sometimes effective) prose too close to poetry; the second section, 'Journal of an Airman', is a scrappy blend of prose and verse and biological formulas. But the six odes and epilogue justify his being named in the same breath as Lawrence. The subject of the book is political, though it is hard to tell whether the author's sympathies are Communist or Fascist; they seem a little vaguely and sentimentally directed towards a 'strong man,' a kind of super-prefect, for the book has a slight smell of school changing-rooms, a touch of 'Stalky.' But Mr. Auden's virtuosity is amazing. He uses the whole language without self-consciousness.—GRAHAM GREENE, *OxM*, Nov. 10, 1932, p. 158

W. H. Auden has been termed the satirist of the English 'poetical renascence'. The basis of this reputation is *The Orators, an English Study*, a very perverse, obscure, somewhat exciting, and at times powerful poem. It is composed of three books: the 'Initiates', 'Journal of an Airman', and 'Six Odes'. Most of the first two books is in prose, the third entirely in verse. It has been attacked by John Sparrow in his study *Sense and Poetry* as an example of unintelligible writing. The construction is by some principle of association which, except in its broadest outline, generally defies definition. It is more difficult, perhaps more confused, than *The Waste Land*, its most likely prototype. It is more difficult because the basic symbolism of *The Waste Land* was more apparent, and the mechanism of its system of ironic reference more accessible. The system of reference and symbol in *The Orators* is a personal, if not arbitrary, matter.

In the first section of Book I, 'Address for a Prize-Day', the tone of the work is set in the speech of a visiting celebrity to the boys, a speech which moves from the clever innocence of parody to the question: 'What do you think about England, this country of ours where nobody is well?' Then for conclusion:

> Draw up a list of rotters and slackers, of proscribed persons under headings like this. Committees for municipal or racial improvement—the headmaster. Disbelievers in the occult—the school chaplain. The bogusly cheerful—the games master. The really disgusted—the teacher of modern languages. All these have got to die without issue. . . . Quick, guard that door. Stop that man. Good. Now boys hustle them, ready, steady—go.

This parable of revolution is followed by two sections of a highly personal nature which are hard to relate to the remainder of the poem except by the tone of disorder and despair pervading them. The fourth section, 'Letter to a Wound', effects a sort of ironic resolution for Book I. The victim has fallen in love with his own mortal hurt, takes a solace in its intimacy, and concocts from despair a contentment: 'Nothing will ever part us. Good-night and God bless you, my dear. Better burn this.' . . .

Auden, I am fairly confident, may be trusted to solve a good many of his stylistic problems as they arise unless he is deluded by the worship of obscurity for obscurity's sake. The graver problem that may confront him is the one of theme. His present preoccupations, if their treatment remains naïve and overt, may well result in something like a formula, a danger which both Eliot and Pound have frequently succumbed to. Satire, undertaken on his present premise, might mean a mere multiplication of instance; as a matter of incidental reference, as it occurs in much of Donne's work where it is absorbed into the tissue of the poetry, it might be a source of strength and enrichment. For the present it seems that the most constantly satisfactory poems may be pieces of that nature, for instance, II, III, XI, XV, XVI, and XXIV. But it is useless to prescribe or predict.

Auden *is* the advertised English 'poetical renascence', although Stephen Spender is claimed on the jacket of his *Poems* as its 'lyric poet'. In the short period since the publication of that volume his work has already been considerably over-rated. What is best is deeply indebted to Auden's influence; at least I assume this to be the case because of Auden's infinitely greater force and fertility. As a matter of fact, Spender is probably an inferior poet to John Pudney, whose work *Spring*

Encounter is practically unknown in this country and who seems to have profited more in a small field from some of the suggestions of Auden's poetry. Space has compelled me to be thus dogmatic about Spender. From those enthusiastic about his work I can only ask pardon for my dogmatism and a re-inspection of his performance, a re-inspection of his thoroughly conventional, 'poetical' idiom, his relaxed rhythms, and his thin, almost feminine, subject matter.

As for the 'renascence', it remains to be seen whether a swallow can make a summer.—ROBERT PENN WARREN, *AR*, May 1934, pp. 221–27

I confess to being rather disappointed by these last two books of W. H. Auden's. It looks as if the group to which he belongs—the school of young Oxford poets which includes C. Day-Lewis, Stephen Spender and Louis MacNeice—had lapsed, after their first lift of enthusiasm for the clean sweep of society promised by communism, of repudiation of the world to which they belong, into a period of relaxation into vagueness, of cooling down and marking time.

W. H. Auden has presented the curious spectacle of a poet with an original language apparently in the most robust English tradition, whose development has seemed to be arrested at the mentality of an adolescent schoolboy. His technique has seemed to mature, but he himself has not grown up. His mind has always been haunted, as the minds of boys at prep school still are, by parents and uncles and aunts. His love poems seem ambiguous and unreal like the products of adolescent flirtations and pre-school homosexuality. His talk about 'the enemy' and 'their side' and 'our side' and 'spying' and 'lying in ambush' sounds less like something conceivably to be connected with the psychology of an underground revolutionary movement than like the dissimulated resentments and snootiness of the schoolboy with advanced ideas going back to his family for the holidays. When this brilliant and engaging young student first came out so strongly for the class struggle it seemed a bold and exhilarating step; but then he simply remained under the roof of his nice family and in the classroom with his stuffy professors; and the seizure of power which he dreams of is an insurrection in the schoolroom by the students:

> I should like to see you make a beginning before I go, now, here. Draw up a list of rotters and slackers, of proscribed persons under headings like this. Committees for municipal or racial improvement—the headmaster. Disbelievers in the occult—the school chaplain. The bogusly cheerful—the games master. The really disgusted—the teacher of modern languages. All these have got to die without issue. Unless my memory fails me there's a stoke hole under the floor of this hall, the Black Hole we called it in my day. New boys were always put in it. Ah, I see I am right. Well look to it. Quick, guard that door. Stop that man. Good. Now boys hustle them, ready, steady—go.

With all this—and out of all proportion to the interest of what he has had to say—Auden's imagery and speech have had an energy, a felicity, a resource, a nerve, which have made him a conspicuous figure. He certainly has more of what it takes than anybody else of his generation in England or, as far as I can remember, in America. And in one department he is entirely successful: he has invented a new satire for the times. The most satisfactory part of his work seems to me such skits as *The Dance of Death*, with its cheap and weary rhythms; the satiric-elegiac choruses of *The Dog Beneath the Skin*; and such poems as that in this new collection in which he describes the Cambridge intellectuals,

Who show the poor by mathematics
In their defence
That wealth and poverty are merely
Mental pictures, so that clearly
Every tramp's a landlord really
In mind-events.

He is especially good at calling the roll of the lonely, the neurotic, the futile—of all the queer kinds of individuals who make up the English upper middle class. No one else has given us just this sense, at once pathetic and insipid, of the slackening of the social body and the falling apart of its cells.

But once having taken this stand, once having put themselves on record, we get the impression that Auden and his associates are at a loss as to what to do next. In some ways they appear to be retrograding. Thus the language of Auden in this new book seems to me to be actually less personal than it was in his earlier poetry. He seemed in his earlier work to have revived the traditional language of English poetry at its most vigorous, its most lively and most free, telescoping the whole tradition from the emphatic alliteration of Anglo-Saxon through the variety and ease of the Elizabethans to the irony and bizarre imagination of the generation just before his own. But in 'On This Island' it seems to me that the rhythms of the reflective and lyrical poems approach too close to the deliberate looseness of the satirical ones; and the off-rhymes begin to get on one's nerves. (Negligent rhythms and near rhymes, I suppose, are a symptom of blurred emotions. There are moments when Louis MacNeice sounds like a serious Ogden Nash.)

And it has come to be a depressing feature of the literary scene at the present time (noticeable also in this country) that writers who had hitherto seemed able to stand on their own feet have begun flopping over on one another and imitating one another's idiom—without there necessarily being any question of the normal attraction of the weaker toward the stronger. Thus Auden, whose voice we knew and liked, disconcerts us by suddenly falling into the accents of Housman or Yeats or the palest of the later Eliot. And thus MacNeice, who seems to me with Auden the most gifted of the Auden group, with a lyric impressionism quite different from the rest, appears in a recent number of 'New Verse' to have toppled over upon Auden and to have become almost indistinguishable from him. (Louis MacNeice's book, by the way, ought to be brought out in America. His north-of-Ireland accent and material make him stand out from the Oxford lushness, and in his best moments he has a combination of intensity with felicity which makes much of the work of the school sound synthetic.)

And the second of the Auden and Isherwood plays, *The Ascent of F6*, is certainly very much inferior to *The Dog Beneath the Skin*. *The Dog Beneath the Skin* had its shortcomings: a good deal of its satire was banal—it sounded as if the clever schoolboys had just discovered some of the stalest jokes of Marxism and worked them up for a school entertainment. But the first part, at any rate, was very funny; and the choruses, as I have said, were of Auden's best. *The Ascent of F6* suffers even more from the flimsiness of amateur theatricals; and here Marxism itself has been forgotten for a relapse into Freudianism. The theme is a sort of psychoanalytic version of a career like that of Colonel Lawrence. It has the peculiarly exasperating defect of appearing to be padded in a tiresome way and yet at the same time to be too short and not to exploit the possibilities of the subject.

Not, however, that Auden and his group are any worse off than other Left intellectuals. And they have given expression to their plight and their time much more brilliantly and honestly than most. The combination of communism with homo-

sexuality, of an England suburbanized and Americanized in the peculiarly dreary English way, with an English university culture as rich as the richest fruitcake, is something which has never before been seen in the history of English literature and which it took some courage and genius to get there. Besides, MacNeice and Auden are only thirty, Day-Lewis thirty-two, Spender twenty-eight. They are remarkable at that age for having been able to say so well something which had not been said before at all.—Edmund Wilson, *NR*, Feb. 24, 1937, pp. 77–78

THE DANCE OF DEATH, THE DOUBLE MAN

The poetry is thin in proportion as the irony tends to dissolve into external topical satire—e.g., *The Dance of Death*—not because it is topical, since his best poetry is often topical, but because the center is external to the poetry. In general, Auden's poetry weakens as he tries to rely upon an external framework—a doctrine or ideology.

The following passage, for instance, is an example of Auden's dominant theme and his most successful method: the satire is directed at an essential frivolousness of mind—a stodgy, comfortable, unconscious complacency which makes men disguise losses and injuries, or even accept them as a part of the natural order of things.

It is later than you think; nearer that day
Far other than that distant afternoon
Amid rustle of frocks and stamping feet
They gave the prizes to the ruined boys.
You cannot be away, then, no
Not though you pack to leave within an hour,
Escaping humming down arterial roads. . . .

The sense of grim understatement native to the tradition of Old English poetry is used to point up mercilessly the desiccation of College Quad and Cathedral Close. "It is later than you think. . . ." (An English gentleman is never late to appointments—even the ruling classes will listen to an indictment couched in these terms, the poet implies.) "Nearer that day. . . ." (The description is ominously vague. Suffice it to say that it is not all like that "distant afternoon" with its rustling of frocks and stamping of feet and the prize-giving. But the mention of the afternoon suggests what has brought to pass the day so different from it, and perhaps suggests also why the financier and his friends have lost their sense of time and do not realize the lateness of the hour.)

The phrase, "the ruined boys," is also menacingly vague. It means primarily boys ruined for living, boys moulded for other distant afternoons, not for that day, etc. But it suggests "sexually perverted," too, literally perhaps and certainly symbolically. They have been emasculated, made infertile and incapable of producing any healthy growth.

Perhaps the neatest effect of the grim humor is achieved in the last three lines where it is suggested that the descent of the whirlwind will find the gentlemen incapable of reacting even to catastrophe except in terms of their class and code. "Not though you pack . . ." (as for a weekend in the country. The gentlemen have had at least in their experience sudden invitations.)

But the final sardonic picture of the financier and his friends escaping in their saloon cars down arterial roads does not become flat and heavy-handed, for it is intimately related to the whole texture of the experience. The relationship between the elements in the passage is as intricate as in any other kind of poetry. The satire rises into a more serious mode. . . .

The satire is broader still in sections of *The Dance of Death*, where the poet relies more heavily on the external framework—and the external doctrine—to pull the poem together. The gain in clarity is immense, but the gain is at the expense of the poetry, as a comparison with some of the poetry in the more obscure *Paid on Both Sides* and *The Orators* will demonstrate.

It is some of Auden's disciples, however, whose work represents a real abuse of the use of contrasts. Mere contrast, obviously, becomes monotonous, and a continual dealing in heterogeneity soon becomes as flat as the collecting of resemblances. To fall into mere heterogeneity is the temptation of the poet who wishes to portray disintegration.

Oddly enough, it may be used with the same vagueness to portray the antithesis of disintegration, lusty growth. Whitman, for example, often uses heterogeneity for this purpose. In the catalogue passages we are given hunks of American variety:

> The mate stands braced in the whale-boat, lance and
>   harpoon are ready,
> The duck-shooter walks by silent and cautious
>   stretches,
> The deacons are ordain'd with cross'd hands at the
>   altar,
> The spinning-girl retreats and advances to the hum
>   of the big wheel,
> The farmer stops by the bars as he walks on a First-
>   day loaf and looks at the oats and rye,
> The lunatic is carried at last to the asylum a con-
>   firm'd case. . . .

The heterogeneity is used by Whitman to celebrate formlessness. The tone asks us to note how tremendous, how various the continent is, and the discords are ironical at the expense of categories of any kind. The implication is that any classifications which one possesses are made to seem shabby and inadequate when called in to take account of the enormous teeming variety of the new country.

But the game is too easy for Whitman as the proponent of nebulous bonhommie and fraternity. The poetry is thin and diluted. The game is too easy also for the celebrants of a rather vague communism—or in their negative and satiric mode, the mockers at vague confusion and disintegration.

Auden shows his superiority by his ability to assimilate the discords into a meaningful pattern. In this connection it may be well to comment on the extent to which Auden has relied constantly on a method of assimilation and synthesis. The method has resulted in charges of obscurity—some of them quite justified, many of them unjustified; but it is this method which essentially makes him a far better poet than poets often linked with him, Day Lewis and Stephen Spender. Indeed, the faults of these two poets are the result of oversimplification. Lewis, in his weaker moments, furnishes obvious cases of a flat didacticism; Spender, of sentimentality. Auden, on the contrary, even in his less tightly knit verse, works continually in a pattern of synthesis, and the ambiguity as to his attitude is a function of this pattern.—CLEANTH BROOKS, "Frost, MacLeish and Auden," *Modern Poetry and the Tradition*, 1939, pp. 18–22

In 1931 Pope's ghost said to me, "Ten years from now the leading young poet of the time will publish, in *The Atlantic Monthly*, a didactic epistle of about nine hundred tetrameter couplets." I answered absently, "You are a fool"; and who on this earth would have thought him anything else? But he was right: the decline and fall of modernist poetry—if so big a swallow, and a good deal of warm weather, make a summer—were nearer than anyone could have believed. The poetry which came to seem during the twenties the norm of all poetic performance—experimental, lyric, obscure, violent, irregular,

determinedly antagonistic to didacticism, general statement, science, the public—has lost for the young its once obsessive attraction; has evolved, in Auden's latest poem, into something that is almost its opposite. "New Year Letter" (which, with many notes and a few lyrics, forms *The Double Man*) is a happy compound of the *Essay on Man* and the *Epistle to Dr. Arbuthnot*, done in a version of Swift's most colloquial couplets. Pope might be bewildered at the ideas, and make fun of, or patronizingly commend, the couplets; but he would relish the Wit, Learning, and Sentiment—the last becoming, as it so often does, plural and Improving; and the Comprehending Generality, Love of Science, and Social Benevolence might warm him into the murmur, "Well enough for such an age." How fast the world changes! and poetry with it! What he would have said of the more characteristic glories of "Gerontion," the *Cantos*, or *The Bridge*, I leave to the reader's ingenuity.

"New Year Letter" contains Auden's ideas about everything (Life and the Good Life, Art and Society, Politics, Morals, Love, the Devil, Economic Man), organized inside a successfully concrete framework of what he has read and seen and met with. Auden's ideas once had an arbitrary *effective* quality, a personality value, almost like ideas in Lawrence or Ezra Pound. They seem today less colorful but far more correct—and they are derived from, or are conscious of, elements over most of the range of contemporary thought. Sometimes the reader exclaims delightedly, "What a queer thing for a *poet* to know!" (This replaces the resentful remark of the twenties: "What a queer thing for anybody to know!") The poets of the last generation were extremely erudite, but their erudition was of the rather specialized type that passed as currency of the realm in a somewhat literary realm. About Darwin, Marx, Freud and Co., about all characteristically "scientific" or "modern" thinkers most of them concluded regretfully: "If they had not existed, it would not have been necessary to ignore them." (Or deplore them.) In their comparison of the past and the present, the present came off, not even a poor, but a disgraceful second; "and this was not surprising," as Carroll says, since the values by which they judged—the whole climate of their judgment—were desperately and exclusively those of the past. They constituted a forlorn hope we must admire but understand. Auden's culture and doctrines are more accessible and plausible than theirs to the ordinary cultivated person, whose thought is not now essentially religious, literary, reactionary, or anti-scientific. And the manner of Auden's knowledge surprises as much as the matter; there is none of the atmosphere of stupefying scope and profoundity of information that has accompanied Pound's and Eliot's application of the methods of the industrial revolution to literature: so far as Auden's tone is concerned, London and Rome are still untouched by American hands, the great Völkerwanderung of the barbarian scholars has never occurred.

"New Year Letter" seems to me, within certain limits, a great success. It is thoroughly readable: Auden handles with easy virtuosity humorous and serious material—sometimes his method of joining them verges on simple Byronic alternation, but they tend to be swept together by the tone and verse movement, rapid, informal, and completely adaptable. The poetry, strained through so many abstractions, is occasionally a little pale; but it *is* poetry. Auden has accomplished the entirely unexpected feat of making a successful long poem out of a reasonable, objective, and comprehensive discussion. It is kept concrete or arresting by many devices: wit, rhetoric, all sorts of images (drawn from the sciences, often); surprising quotations, allusions, technical terms, points of view, shifts of tone; he treats ideas in terms of their famous advocates, expresses situations in little analogous conceits; and he specializes in un-expected coordinates, the exquisitely ridiculous term—he is remarkably sensitive to the levels and interactions of words. The poem is not quite first-rate. It lacks the necessary finality of presentation; it is at a remove; the urgency and reality have been diluted. Evil is talked about but not brought home; there is a faint sugary smell of *tout comprendre est tout pardonner*: everything is going to be all right in the end. When one remembers his earlier poetry at its best, one feels unreasonably homesick for the fleshpots of Egypt. But these are almost too many qualifications: it is a valuable, surprising poem.

In the notes there are quotations, aphorisms, exposition, verse, a few poems: if not God's plenty, at least, plenty. Some notes are valuable in themselves, some amplify or locate the poem's ideas; but these water a positive desert of Good Sense: machine-made parables, forced definitions, humorless half-truths, with which we wearily dissent or impatiently agree. (The notes specialize in neither the High nor the Low, but the Mean Sublime.) To the question, "What is the only thing that always remains work, that can never give us aesthetic satisfaction?" Auden replies, *the ethical*; the victims of his insistent raids on the Moral can ruefully agree. The lyrics called "The Quest" (conscientiously flat, abstract, and characteristic parables) seem to me rather uninterestingly unsuccessful.

I've made my review general because I wanted to emphasize, like the advertisements: "This poem's *different*"; some people who don't ordinarily read modern poetry might enjoy "New Year Letter." Since I've no space for what I should like—a careful discussion of its ideas and technique—let me finish simply by saying that it is worth buying.—RANDALL JARRELL, "New Year Letter" (1941), *Kipling, Auden, and Co.*, 1980, pp. 55–57

FOR THE TIME BEING, THE AGE OF ANXIETY

Auden's mother, who was devout and to whom he had been very close, died in 1941. *For the Time Being*, dedicated to her memory, was written in 1941–2. The subtitle is "A Christmas Oratorio"; it is of course too long to be set in its entirety, but an abridgement of it was set by the American composer, Melvin Levy, and performed in New York a few years ago. It follows the oratorio form faithfully, except that musical setting is not essential: i.e. it is an oratorio to be spoken or read. In many respects, the oratorio form enables Auden to achieve effects he sought in the plays: there is no dramatic illusion, no identification, and no dramatic characterization. There is, so to speak, a built-in alienation effect, since in the oratorio singers use only their voices to represent their roles, without acting, and the audience is aware continuously of the singers as singers as well as participants in the drama; hence the characters move in two dimensions, as, simultaneously, the unique historical characters and the moderns who are representing them. The oratorio differs from the plays in presenting a story both historical and thoroughly familiar, so that the traditional Christmas pageant or tableau can be suggested, as well as the miracle play, and the lighter elements of popular song and contemporary language can more effectively surprise the reader who expects a wholly solemn, elevated work. The verse is an equivalent for the kind of distancing produced by musical setting, and in variety of forms and meters it succeeds in producing many of the effects of music. The chorus expresses collective feelings and attitudes in a formal, often exalted manner, while the narrator, voluble, articulate, and thoroughly modern, expresses the other side of the contemporary consciousness. Together, they mediate between the audience and the action more effectively than any of Auden's previous choruses or announcers.

From the religious point of view, the form of the Christmas oratorio immediately suggests three kinds of meaning: (1) the unique Incarnation; (2) by association with Christmas and with other Christmas oratorios, plays, pageants, and the like, the annual attempt in Christendom to apprehend and experience the event as the center of the Christian year; (3) the constant attempt of Christians to understand, make viable, and in some sense repeat the Incarnation in their daily lives. *For the Time Being* generally succeeds in keeping the reader simultaneously aware of all three of these meanings. The piece is the fullest and most balanced expression of Auden's religious attitudes; the ideas and dominant images that have been seen partially and transitionally in other poems here may be seen in their final place as part of an ordered whole. Much could be said of the religious background of the piece (the respective influences of Kierkegaard, Niebuhr, Williams, Cochrane, and Eliot) and of the relation of the ideas in it to those Auden had been expounding both in prose and verse. . . .

For the Time Being has enjoyed a good deal of popularity: as we have seen, an abridged version of it was set to music by Melvin Levy and performed in New York in 1959, and it is reprinted entire in *Modern Poetry*, edited by Maynard Mack, Leonard Dean, and William Frost (New York, 1950)—a widely used textbook—and in *Religious Drama I*, edited by M. Halverson (New York, 1957); it is performed rather frequently by religious groups. Probably the fact that Eliot's *Four Quartets*, which embody many of the same themes (though in a very different way), happened to appear shortly before it has had much to do with the failure of the oratorio to impress the critics profoundly; comparison with Eliot's towering achievement is inevitable and the result is a foregone conclusion. The oratorio has also suffered from the equally inevitable comparison with the other work that originally appeared in the same volume with it, *The Sea and the Mirror*, which has seemed to most critics more brilliant, novel, and provocative, and therefore has the lion's share of their attention. Considered on its own terms, and at this distance in time, the work may be seen as a unique and remarkable success both formally and as a whole. The traditional forms of the Christmas pageant and oratorio are transformed and deepened to embody the apprehension by the modern consciousness of the central event in history, understood psychologically, emotionally, and intellectually, by constant parallels with contemporary life; the various characters represent various types and also aspects of each of us, and the different episodes represent different aspects of the religious life of the individual, as well as the historical events. There is thus a great range and variety implicit in the scope of the piece, shown most obviously in the formal variety of verse and prose. Throughout, there is a triple consciousness at three levels: first, the unique historical event of the Incarnation; second, the collective, seasonal aspect of Christmas in its place in the Christian year, with its annual attempt to make it possible for Christ to be re-born, so to speak; and finally, the moment-to-moment effort of the individual to redeem everyday life from insignificance, to manifest the Incarnation in himself, to be a Christian. There are, as always in Auden, flaws and unevenness; but the central problem of rendering these three kinds of consciousness simultaneously is solved with brilliant success, and provides an adequate unifying principle for the enormous scope and variety of the piece. The oratorio does not seem dated or topical, nor does the religious attitude expressed seem in any way eccentric or extravagant. Auden placed the oratorio last both in *For the Time Being*, 1944, and in *Collected Poetry*, 1945, presumably because he felt, with justice, that it provided a very suitable conclusion for a volume.—MONROE

K. Spears, "For the Time Being" (1963), *Auden*, 1964, 160–71

The scheme of Auden's new long poem is clear enough and rich in possibility. Four human beings meet in a Third Avenue bar, drink, discuss the seven ages of existence, get drunk, and become or discuss states of prehistoric happiness, go to the apartment of Rosetta, the one girl among them, and continue to drink until one of the men starts to make love to Rosetta just before he passes out. The poem concludes with a long passage of vague affirmation, an affirmation of Christianity which is no more convincing than Auden's rejection of Christianity twelve years back when, for example, he spoke of cathedrals as 'luxury liners for the self-absorbed.' Within this framework, which might be very dramatic, Auden inserts juke-box lyrics, parodies of the radio, and exercises in the seven or eight poetic styles of his career.

What this work comes to, at least for me (and perhaps I should say that no one else has spoken of it with anything but admiration), is the most self–indulgent book Auden has written. It is far more self-indulgent than *The Orators*. Here the seeming order is merely contrived and allows for all kinds of gratuitous excursions. In *The Orators* the seeming disorder was produced by the subliminal character of the subject matter, by the fact that very important unconscious material broke through to consciousness. It can be said that the most unique quality of modern literature is the eruption of the unconscious within areas of the conscious mind, which is not quite able to understand and control all that has forced its way up. It is significant that Auden now regards *The Orators* as a failure while in writing *The Age of Anxiety* he strives to renew communication with the subject matter which made *The Orators* one of his most exciting books.

In this new work, Auden's technical skill, which is as various as any poet's, and his easy virtuosity, which is at times too easy, show in full stength. The use of alliteration here is a beautiful addition to his enormous bag of tricks. But the result is a plethora of effects which for the most part get in each other's way. The possibility of a narrative line is muffed throughout. And the eloquent dialectic inherent in the use of dialogue comes to almost nothing because each character often speaks as if he had not heard what the previous character just said. The Third Avenue bar does not really exist in the poem, despite the juke box. There is no real anxiety in the poem, but merely the discussion of anxiety. And the characterization of the four persons is blurred or blotted out again and again when each one makes speeches which cannot be said to be out of character because they have nothing to do with character at all. Just before the end of the poem, for example, Rosetta suddenly turns out to be Jewish for the sake of a speech about the nature and the destiny of Jews; nothing whatever in Rosetta's previous remarks has prepared the reader for this revelation about Rosetta's origins and her views of them.

The poem as a whole simulates narrative, drama, and philosophical dialogue. In actuality it is hardly more than a suite of expositions, alternately discursive, allegorical, and lyrical, of Auden's thoughts and opinions. Perhaps the cause is Auden's mixed and contradictory intentions. His chief motive is now didactic. He has become a teacher, father, and prophet; he began as a subversive satirist, dissident son, and *enfant terrible*. He is now trying to write in the didactic mode while at the same time retaining the idiom of his early work, which was most successful when it was a fusion of the ominous, the flip, the colloquial, and the intuitive. In this new work, Auden attempts to use phrases such as 'You're not my dish really,' in the same kind of context as 'His Good ingressant on our gross

occasions.' The effect on one reader at least can only be compared to hearing that there's going to be a hot time in the old town tonight chortled in an extremely English accent. Perhaps it is possible to write in a style which is at once full of colloquial diction and philosophical terminology (and this work might very well be a stage in Auden's development of such a style); and perhaps it is also possible to be didactic, dialectic, lyrical, dramatic, narrative, philosophical, concrete, and abstract in the same poem. But Auden has not succeeded in doing so. There is nothing wrong with being a didactic poet, if one has a coherent set of ideas which one has lived with for a long time. But Auden is not really a didactic poet, he is something better and more important.

One also senses much that is uncertain and unclear in the ideas of which Auden now writes so fondly. It is as if he were not really sure that they were true, despite the schematism and the capitalized abstractions by means of which he presents them. Whether this be an accurate impression or not, we have from years back a good example of how easy it is to be lucid, eloquent, and utterly wrong. When Auden came to America, his coming was compared to James's and Eliot's departure for England as if it were the same kind of migration and not absolutely different: to go to Europe from America is obviously to go in the opposite direction from going to America from England. There is much to suggest that an insensitivity to this overwhelming difference may explain the quality of Auden's recent work. His genius depends upon England, upon the English scene, upon perceptions and emotions inspired by being English. It is in America that he must become a poetic teacher who versifies doctrines picked up carelessly and uncritically from a dozen heterogeneous and unexamined sources. In America too Auden has taken some of his most beautiful and serious poems and in his collected volume attached to these poems titles which are facetious and silly: 'Shut Your Eyes and Open Your Mouth,' 'Heavy Date,' 'Such Nice People,' 'Please Make Yourself At Home,' 'Do Be Careful,' 'It's So Dull Here,' 'Nobody Understands Me.' These are representative instances of the kind of tourist slanginess which has infected Auden's style as a whole and which is far from being the same thing as the colloquial actuality which gave his work of ten and fifteen years ago so much emotional force.—Delmore Schwartz, *PR*, Sept.–Oct. 1947, pp. 528–31

COLLECTED SHORTER POEMS,
THE RAKE'S PROGRESS

There is a well-known photograph in which Auden leans with Isherwood from a train-window. A cigarette droops from his friendly grin, his eyes go one better than being visionary, by being knowing: it is a latterday Childe Harold with Polidori, bidding a long farewell to perfidious Albion, because he is

> set on the idea
> Of getting to Atlantis.

Auden is the chief romantic of Freudian love, the Byron of the unconscious mind: his clubbed foot is the wound to which he once wrote a letter, his Italy is America, and he is in perpetual quest of Missolonghi. From a spiritual outpost further than Marshall-Land, from the Ibsen's glacier or Eliot's desert that make a modern poet's Cockayne, he has sent us the regular postcards of his poems: the present volume is the first of his collected correspondence.

He would hardly send us *that* unless he felt that at last, not another time, nor for the time being, but now, he has a right to our answer. And the question of questions a poet asks his readers is the one set by the dwarf in the fairy tale: we have to guess his name. Auden's critics for these twenty years have mostly preferred collecting the stamps, or cataloguing the blots, to deciphering the proud identity of the sender. But the blots, I should say, are hardly those specific to bad poets. He has borrowed from everyone he ever read? Good! His influence on his imitators has been pernicious? Splendid! He is prolific, likes assonance and private faces and horizontal man? Exc– but is it in any case relevant to look, strangers that we are, for his defects? Strictly speaking, a poet can have only one serious fault, that of not being great; and a great poet, strictly speaking, doesn't have faults, but qualities. Isn't it possible now, in the light of this collection, to call Auden great, to see that, as he once predicted they would, his features shine, and his name is Star?

As early as twenty years ago Auden invented, or rather was the first to detect under the scientific conditions of poetic imagination, that sense of guilt which has been our generation's characteristic rearward approach to eternal verities. The early

> Sir, no man's enemy, forgiving all
> But will his negative inversion

posits the same means of salvation that preoccupy his latest work: he invokes (and so, in their ways, did Pascal and Kierkegaard before him) the help of God as a supreme mental healer. Auden's task has been to retranslate the lawless language of the unconscious—with extreme caution, so that there may be no mistake about it this time—back into the sermon on the mount. For he sees Freud not only as the exposer of the shocking and true, not only as an inexhaustible suggester of knockdown poetic imagery, but as one of a line of healers and saviours.

Probably, too, his powers have been less stationary than meets the eye. While part of him remains at base, excavating for the good of us all ever deeper layers of his fissured self—

> Rummaging into his living the poet fetches
> The images out that hurt and connect—

another presses forward through the so-far endless glaciers, the ever-derelict power-houses of his universal landscape; and another undergoes new literary influences, falls in love, and ripens with age. He climbs, too, the infernal escalator on which most stand unaware they are moving:

> History
> That held one moment burns the hand—

how often has he formed and found the resolution to grip its fiery banister! The time has gone when Isherwood, with 'squat spruce body and enormous head', could

> make action urgent and its nature clear.

Mr. Leishman's great translation of Rilke helped Auden to endure and accept a journey to a war that now seems minor: now, the leading sin-eater of his age, he is masticating a greater, for which acceptance may prove neither possible nor appropriate, and all literary and personal influences powerless.

If the assemblage of his poems makes it possible, however tentatively, to call him great, it is unfortunate that their new order should conceal how he became so. Rearrangement of a poet's works in any other order than that in which they were given to him, can only doubly hide their veiled and perhaps most important subject, the life-line of a horizontal man. The time will come when

> a shilling life will give you all the facts.

It will then become of immense importance to know out on whose lawn he lay in bed, or to read

> Symondson—praise him at once!
> Our rightwing threequarter back

on 'How Auden struck me as an English master'; but of com-

paratively little to know that the poet chose to arrange his work in a punctured oval, when he had completed only two sides of an as yet unpredictable figure.—George D. Painter, *LT*, April 20, 1950, pp. 705–6

I chose Wystan Auden as librettist for my opera *The Rake's Progress* because of his special gift for versification; I have never been able to compose music to prose, even poetic prose. That he was a great poet others had assured me—I felt as much, but was too new to English to judge for myself—yet my first requisite was more modest and more specific; after all, successful collaborations between musicians and poets in dramatic works have been rare, and in fact Dryden and Purcell, Hofmannsthal and Strauss, Boito and Verdi (Boito was, rather, a great adapter, but that is almost as valuable), are the only names that come to mind. What I required was a versifier with whom I could collaborate in writing songs, an unusual starting point for an opera, I hardly need to add, as most composers begin with a search for qualities of dramatic construction and dramatic sensation. I had no knowledge of Wystan's dramatic gifts or even whether he was sensible to operatic stagecraft. I simply gave all priority to verse, hoping that we could evolve the theatrical form together and that it would inspire Wystan to dramatic poetry.

I think he *was* inspired, and in any case he inspired me. At the business level of the collaboration he wrote "words for music," and I wonder whether any poet since the Elizabethans has made a composer such a beautiful gift of them as the "Lanterloo" dance in our opera. Wystan had a genius for operatic wording, His lines were always the right length for singing and his words the right ones to sustain musical emphasis. A musical speed was generally suggested by the character and succession of the words, but it was only a useful indication, never a limitation. Best of all for a composer, the rhythmic values of the verse could be altered in singing without destroying the verse. At least, Wystan has never complained. At a different level, as soon as we began to work together I discovered that we shared the same views not only about opera, but also on the nature of the Beautiful and the Good. Thus, our opera is indeed, and in the highest sense, a collaboration.

Wystan has lived in Austria too long now, and I wish you could convince him to come back. After all, we cannot afford to give our best poet to the Germans.—Igor Stravinsky, Robert Craft, "Interviews" (1965), *Themes and Episodes*, 1966, pp. 96–97

THE SHIELD OF ACHILLES, HOMAGE TO CLIO

Mr. Auden, of course, has always been a generalizer. He has never been interested either in his own experience, or the experience of other people, for its own sake; he has been interested in it as an instance of a general case, of the sort of thing that happens. He has a classifying mind; he is at the very, very extreme opposite pole from a poet like Hopkins with his passionate concentration on *haecceitas*, thisness, "sakes," "selving" and "unselving," "inscape." The worry that critics may have had about his attitude to language in his recent books is not about this "given" element in him; it is about a painstaking frivolity, a preoccupation with ornament. He does manfully defend the baroque mode:

> Be subtle, various, ornamental, clever,
> And do not listen to those critics ever
> Whose crude provincial gullets crave in books
> Plain cooking made still plainer by plain cooks. . . .

Walter Bagehot was one of "those critics" and I agree with Bagehot that the way to make a basket of fish poetical is *not* by calling it, as Tennyson did in *Enoch Arden*,

> ... Enoch's ocean-spoil
> In the ocean-smelling osier. . . .

Or that way of handling it *does*, of course, make it "poetical": but in a soppily vulnerable way, a way for the tough and wry who hate poetry to kick at.

Let us consider, with this suspicion of "the poetical" in mind, such a passage as this of Mr. Auden's, from his recent work:

> The horn gate and the ivory gate
> Swing to, swing shut, instantaneously
> Quell the nocturnal rummage
> Of its rebellious fronde, ill-favoured,
> Ill-natured and second-rate,
> Disenfranchised, widowed and orphaned
> By an historical mistake. . . .

But for the Fall, the basic sense of that passage is, our dreams would not be Freudian dreams—would not be so shabby, guilty, and incoherent as they are (the shabbiness expressed by "nocturnal rummage," "rebellious fronde," and so on: the Fall, ironically, by "an historical mistake"). The rhetoric, the mechanisms of persuasion, in such a passage is one of expansion; the plain, underlying prose sense is "like gold to ayery thinness beat"; the lines *look* as if they were making a much more portentous and complex statement than they are making.

The title poem of *The Shield of Achilles*, a grim meditation on power politics, perhaps on the *Iliad* itself as what Simone Weil called "the Poem of Force," had a bleak impressiveness: three victims being (not exactly) crucified:

> The mass and majesty of this world, all
>   That carries weight and always weighs the same
> Lay in the hands of others; they were small
>   And could not hope for help and no help came:
> What their foes liked to do was done, their
>   shame
> Was all the worst could wish; they lost their pride
> And died as men before their bodies died.

That impresses me poetically, impresses me morally, and yet there is something about the attitude implied in it that very frighteningly raises the whole question, in the context of which in the 1930s one always, perhaps obtusely, would discuss Mr. Auden's poetry, of the power of poetic perception to influence events. An hour or so before I copied out these lines I read, in *The Manchester Guardian*, a translation of passages from M. Alleg's book, *La Question*. Mr. Alleg is the editor of a Communist newspaper, who was tortured by parachutists in Algeria. His torturers told him that they were modelling themselves on the Gestapo, that they hoped to torture Frenchmen, including liberal or radical political leaders, in France, too, and be done with the Republic. I reflected that if there is any country in Europe which men of other countries have turned to as a centre of civilization, have loved second to their own countries, it is France. I reflected also that as at least a sympathizer with Communism M. Alleg must have in his time turned a Nelson eye to the possibility that men were being tortured behind the Iron Curtain; and yet, standing up to torture himself, he seemed to speak not as a partisan but for all men. In a sense, Auden speaks also in these lines for all men— but hopelessly? In the 1930s, he seemed often ahead of events, warning us of what we might still do to dodge our fates. In a poem like *The Shield of Achilles*, he is like the chorus in a Greek tragedy, which makes all the appropriate moral comments, but knows it cannot prevent the awful thing happening. By classical standards, this should make him a more universal poet, and by revealing starkly what is worst in us, he may in

fact, in such a poem, be nerving us to pursue what is better. And yet, in a cruder way, did he not move us more when he took sides more, when he seemed to speak with even crude power, like an orator? Was "the preacher's loose, immodest tone," which he once often protested against, not part of his early power over one?—G. S. FRASER, "The Career of W. H. Auden" (1959) *Auden*, ed. Monroe K. Spears, 1964, pp. 99–101

The appearance of his latest collection, *Homage to Clio*, marks the end of the third decade of Auden's poetic life and does not alter the fact that almost all we value is still confined to its first ten years. We need not remind ourselves of his virtues—the wide-angled rhetoric, the seamless lyricism, the sudden gripping dramatisations—but to understand what succeeded it we must understand to what extent his poetry was of its time. He was, of course, the first 'modern' poet, in that he could employ modern properties unselfconsciously ('A solitary truck, the last Of shunting in the Autumn'), but he was modern also by embracing a kind of neo-Wordsworthianism which, in an effort to put poetry at the service of the working-class movement, called it 'memorable speech' and made no theoretical distinction between *Paradise Lost* and *The Young Fellow Called Dave*. This view held that if the poet were not concerned with the historic necessities of the age and akin to the healer and the explorer (typical figures!) his work would be deservedly disregarded.

Few poets since Pope have been so committed to their period. It is not only that to be at home in Auden's poetry we must recognise Bishop Barnes, Coghlan's coffin, Van der Lubbe and all the personalia of 'Last Will and Testament' (*Letters from Iceland*, with Louis MacNeice); we shall also find the depression, strikes, the hunger marchers; we shall find Spain and China; and above all we shall encounter not only the age's properties but its obsessions: feeling inferior to the working class, a sense that things needed a new impetus from somewhere, seeing out of the corner of an eye the rise of Fascism, the persecution of the Jews, the gathering dread of the next war that was half projected guilt about the last:

> The chairs are being brought in from the garden,
> The summer talk stopped on that savage coast
> Before the storms, after the guests and birds:
> In sanatoriums they laugh less and less,
> Less certain of cure; and the loud madman
> Sinks now into a more terrible calm.

It is precisely this dominant and ubiquitous unease that lay at the centre of Auden's verse and which he was so apt to express. How quickly, for example, he seized on the symbol of 'the Struggle,' 'the game . . . that tends to become like a war'; in other writers as well as Auden this concept of the 'Two Sides' was used time and again to represent the young against the old, the poor against the rich, the healthy against the diseased, the class struggle, Spain, the coming war. And whereas the conflict was originally seen as victorious (*The Orators*), as the Thirties wore on disaster became more and more likely. It was in this atmosphere that Auden's sensitivity was quickened and his perceptions heightened, perceptions not only of

> Ten thousand of the desperate marching by
>   Five feet, six feet, seven feet high,

but also how

>   in the houses
> The little pianos are closed, and a clock strikes.

I have stressed this identification not for its own sake but to make clear why Auden's outlook was completely dislocated when it ceased. As everyone knows, this came about in two ways—by the outbreak of war in 1939, and by Auden's departure for America a few months earlier. At one stroke he lost his key subject and emotion—Europe and the fear of war—and abandoned his audience together with their common dialect and concerns. For a different sort of poet this might have been less important. For Auden it seems to have been irreparable.

His immediate reaction was to take a header into literature. Previously few writers had been named in his pages—Lawrence, Owen, Katherine Mansfield—which was eloquent of his 'deep abhorrence':

> If I caught anyone preferring Art
> To Life and Love and being Pure-in-Heart.

Now there came a whole flood. One cannot but notice the shift in tone from the disrespectful reference in 1937 to 'Daunty, Gouty, Shopkeeper, the three Supreme Old Masters' to the eulogistic invocation in the *New Year Letter* of 1941:

> Great masters who have shown mankind
> An order it has yet to find . . .
> Now large, magnificent, and calm
> Your changeless presences disarm
> The sullen generations, still
> The fright and fidget of the will,
> And to the growing and the weak
> Your final transformations speak, &c., &c.

Auden no longer parries the question 'Who are the great?' with the poet's qualification

> you must ask me who
> Have written just as I'd have liked to do.

He has become a reader rather than a writer, and the Notes—eighty-one pages of James, Kierkegaard, Chekhov, Rilke, Nietzsche, Goethe, Milton, Spinoza and so on against fifty-eight pages of text—gave warning how far literature was replacing experience as material for his verse.

Some critics might think this legitimate. The likely consequences, however—loss of vividness, a tendency to rehearse themes already existing as literature, a certain abstract windiness—were very much the criticisms Auden now invited. His first three American books were long, ambitious, and stylistically variegated, yet held the reader's attention only sporadically if at all. The rambling intellectual stew of *New Year Letter* was hardly more than a vamp-till-ready; *The Sea and the Mirror*, which appeared in 1945, was an unsuccessful piece of literary inbreeding; while although in *For the Time Being*, also 1945, Auden works hard to reinvigorate the Christian myth as a poetic subject, he is too often chilly ('weave in us the freedom of The actually deficient on The justly actual') or silly ('It was visiting day at the vinegar works'). As for *The Age of Anxiety* in 1948, I never finished it, and have never met anyone who has.

Now, contrary to what has sometimes been suggested, it is no crime to write dull or even bad poetry. Even if it were, Auden has earned a reprieve many times over. Despite the bitter disappointment of the Forties for his admirers, it was really no more than they could have expected of a poet who had elected to remake his entire poetic equipment. The question was how soon he would get reorganised. His continued productivity, intermittent successes such as the speeches of Caliban and Herod (Auden has always been brilliant at prose parody—did he write 'Hetty to Nancy'?) and the sonnets in *The Quest* gave grounds for hope. If his poetry could once take root again in the life surrounding him rather than in his reading (perhaps *The Age of Anxiety* was a first struggling attempt to do this), then a new Auden might result, a 'New Yorker' Walt Whitman viewing the American scene through lenses coated with a European irony.

Ten years and three books later, one has to admit that this hope was over-optimistic. True, with *Nones* (1952), *The Shield of Achilles* (1955) and now *Homage to Clio* Auden has returned to the shorter poem as his medium: the Supreme Old Masters have retreated (though they have been replaced to some extent by the stale personages of classical mythology), and his themes have become more personal and have a greater chance of interesting. He has begun to produce a kind of long reflective poem in a stabilised tone in which every facet of his subject is exhibited at leisure, 'The Bucolics' in *The Shield of Achilles*, 'Ode to Gaea,' 'In Praise of Limestone,' and now 'Homage to Clio' and 'Goodbye to the Mezzogiorno'.

These poems are agreeable and ingenious essays, more closely directed than his earlier excursions such as 'August for the people' or 'Here on the cropped grass,' but their poetic pressure is not high—nor, indeed, is it intended to be. They read like the reflections of a practised and celebrated writer with no particular worries who is free to indulge his tastes in reading and travel, and as such we can accept them. Auden has not, in fact, gone in the direction one hoped: he has not adopted America or taken root, but has pursued an individual and cosmopolitan path which has precluded the kind of identification that seemed so much a part of his previous successes.

There would be no point in mentioning this if it did not seem to have had regrettable poetic consequences. Firstly, although he has by now recovered a dialect it is all too often an extraordinarily jarring one, a wilful jumble of Age-of-Plastic nursery rhyme, ballet folk-lore, and Hollywood Lemprière served up with a lisping archness that sets the teeth on edge.

> Romance? Not in this weather. Ovid's charmer
> > Who leads the quadrilles in Arcady, boy-lord
> Of hearts who can call their Yes and No their own.
> > Would, madcap that he is, soon die of cold or
> > > sunstroke:
> Their lives are in firmer hands: that old grim She
> > Who makes the blind dates for the hatless
> > > genera
> Creates their country matters.

Such is, explicitly, the kind of thing he likes:

> Be subtle, various, ornamental, clever.
> And do not listen to those critics ever
> Whose crude provincial gullets crave in books
> Plain cooking made still plainer by plain cooks.

This view must be what permits lines like 'Just reeling off their names is ever so comfy' or:

> She mayn't be all She might be but
> > She *is* our Mum.

Are there people who talk this dialect, or is it how Auden talks to himself?

Secondly, one cannot escape the conclusion that in some way Auden, never a pompous poet, has now become an unserious one. For some time he has insisted that poetry is a game, with the elements of a crossword puzzle: it is 'the luck of verbal playing.' One need not be a romantic to suspect that this attitude will produce poetry exactly answering to that description. Here again it seems that Auden was happier when his work had an extraneous social function, and if he feels that poetry is fundamentally unserious otherwise it is a pity he parted from it, for lack of serious intention too often means lack of serious effect.

In the end that is what our discontent comes down to: Auden no longer touches our imaginations. My guess is that the peculiar insecurity of pre-war England sharpened his talent in a way that nothing else has, or that once 'the next War' really arrived everything since has seemed to him an anticlimax. But these are only guesses. Something, after all, led him to write 'A poet's prayer' in *New Year Letter*: 'Lord, teach me to write so well that I shall no longer want to.' In any case it is our loss.—PHILIP LARKIN, "What's Become of Wystan?" *Spec*, July 15, 1960, pp. 104–5

ABOUT THE HOUSE, CITY WITHOUT WALLS

The first, and superior, half of the book is a sequence of twelve poems inspired by the rooms of his recently acquired house in Austria. Each poem carries a personal dedication, and though the anonymous reader may be charmed by intimations of custom-tailored pertinence (a husband and wife get the cellar and attic respectively, and Christopher Isherwood is awarded the toilet), he is more likely to feel merely excluded; what with the Kennedys, the Glasses, the Sinatra Clan, the friends of Norman Podhoretz, and the Pop-Camp-Hip crowd, there seem enough in-groups in the western world without a formal roll-call of Auden's acquaintanceship. Plato's vision of the Perfect City ruled by philosopher-kings seems somewhat impudently transmuted into genial snobbery:

> The houses of our City
> are real enough but they lie
> haphazardly scattered over the earth,
> and her vagabond forum
> is any space where two of us happen to meet
> who can spot a citizen
> without papers.

Technically, the sequence is marred by the erratic interruption of 'Postscripts'—short poems in another meter, often in the irksome form of haiku, tacked on wherever (however vaguely) appropriate. And it must be said that Auden, in developing each room into a cosmic instance and drawing significance from every nook, does not always avoid his besetting sin of, well, silliness. The steamy bath is extolled in an uncharacteristic non-meter which he explains as a 'mallarmesque/syllabic fog,' and the stanzas to excrement include:

> Freud did not invent the
> Constipated miser:
> Banks have letter boxes
> Built in their façade,
> Marked *For Night Deposits*,
> Stocks are firm or liquid,
> Currencies of nations
> Either soft or hard.

But in sum the twelve poems comprise an impressive essay upon Man the domestic animal; his domesticity is felt as a consecration of his animality. . . .

The house abounds in remembrances of human prehistory: the cellar 'Reminds our warm and windowed quarters upstairs that/Caves water-scooped from limestone were our first dwellings'; the archetype of the poet's workroom is 'Weland's Stithy'; like the 'prehistoric hearthstone,/round as a birthday-button/and sacred to Granny,' the modern kitchen is the center of the dwelling; and, in conclusion, 'every home should be a fortress,/equipped with all the very latest engines/for keeping Nature at bay,/versed in all ancient magic, the arts of quelling/ the Dark Lord and his hungry/animivorous chimeras.' Nor is history forgotten: the bathroom is seen as a shrunken tepidarium; the dining table is compared with 'Christ's cenacle' and 'King Arthur's rundle'; and the peace of the living-room is felt against 'History's criminal noise.' The function of each chamber is searched in such depth that a psychological portrait of man is achieved. Auden finds in defecation the prime Art, an 'ur-act of making'; in swallowing 'a sign act of reverence'; in

sleeping a 'switch from personage,/with a state number, a first and family name,/to the naked Adam or Eve.' His psychological portrait is controlled, at times playfully, by religious conceptions.

> then surely those in whose creed
> God is edible may call a fine
> omelette a Christian deed.

Biology tends toward theology; our personal and animal particulars are gounded in the divine ontology. Speech is 'a work of re-presenting/the true olamic silence.' This sequence of poems, entitled 'Thanksgiving for a habitat,' is an essay in architecture, which is to say the creation of a structure enabling the human organism to perform its supernaturally determined functions of praise and service. In a faithless age, there are

> no architects, any more
> than there are heretics or bounders: to take
> umbrage at death, to construct
> a second nature of tomb and temple, lives
> must know the meaning of *if*.

While one regrets that Auden's Christian faith is so iffy, its presence has enabled him to organize his centrifugal variety of perception into a credible humanism.

The second half, 'In and Out' (a habitat has been previously defined as 'a place/I may go both in and out of'), consists of poems, often about traveling, that are casual in tone and middling in quality. The best is the last, 'Whitsunday in Kirchstetten,' a kind of annex to the house poems, wherein the poet is discovered temporarily domiciled in church. In the author's best new style, the long lines, exotic vocabulary, and discursive sequiturs limn what was rather conspicuously absent from the house sequence—a sense of the 'public space,' the enveloping condition of the world:

> from Loipersbach
> to the Bering Sea not a living stockbroker,
> and church attendance is frowned upon
> like visiting brothels (but the chess and physics
> are still the same). . . .
> Down a Gothic nave
> comes our Pfarrer now, blessing the West with water:
> we may go.

Again 'Hammerfest,' a description of Auden's visit to Norway's northernmost township, frames within his baroque sense of lapsed time—'the glum Reptilian Empire/Or the epic journey of the Horse'—the geological innocence of a region whose 'only communities. . ./Were cenobite, mosses and lichen, sworn to/Station and reticence.' And of the many (too many) poems in haiku-stanzas, I liked best 'Et in Arcadia Ego,' a rephrasing of his habitual accusatory apostrophe to 'Dame Kind'—who 'Can imagine the screeching/Virago, the Amazon,/Earth Mother was?' The poem uses the exigencies of this Japanese form to generate lines of great energy, both polysyllabic ('Her exorbitant monsters abashed') and monosyllabic ('Geese podge home').

Auden is the supreme metrical tinkerer. Haiku, canzoni, ballades, limericks, clerihews, alliterative verse (a whole eclogue's worth)—there is nothing he will not attempt and make, to some extent, work. His ability, as in 'Tonight at Seven-Thirty,' to coin an elaborate stanza-form and to effortlessly repeat it over and over, evokes the seventeenth-century metaphysicals and Tennyson: the latter more than the former. His technical ingenuity casts doubt upon the urgency of his inspiration. It is one thing to sing in a form, whether it be Homeric hexameters or Popian couplets, until it becomes a natural voice; it is another to challenge your own verbal resources with insatiable experimentation. In any collection by

Auden there are hardly two successive poems in the same form, which gives even his most integral sequences, such as the Horae Canonicae of *The Shield of Achilles*, a restless and jagged virtuosity. As a poet, his vocation begins in the joy of fabrication rather than in an impulse of celebration: in ways it is strength, enabling him to outlive his youth, to explore, to grow, to continue to think, even—blasphemous suggestion!—to believe, in order to feed the verse-making machine. He is that anachronism, the poet as maker; but he makes expressions rather than, by mimesis, men and deeds. Compared to Eliot, he has no dramatic imagination. Despite an almost desperate metrical juggling, his plays and dialogues are the monologues of one very intellectually imaginative voice. He dramatizes all sides of an issue, but lacks the modesty, the impish and casual self-forgetfulness, that tossed off Prufrock, Cousin Harriet, Sweeney, and the curiously vigorous phantoms of *The Waste Land*. If Eliot was a dramatist, Auden is an essayist, in the root sense: he will try anything, but his adventures never take him beyond the territory of the first person singular. He is one of the few modern poets whose genius is for the long discursive poem; for all his formal invention, he has written best in two rather accommodating meters—a long, elegiac, unrhymed or loosely rhymed line less regular than pentameter, and the tetrameter quatrains or couplets associated with music hall lyrics and with light verse.

His light vein is very rich. What could be better than, say, this stanza from 'On the Circuit'?—

> Since Merit but a dunghill is,
> I mount the rostrum unafraid:
> Indeed, 'twere damnable to ask
> If I am overpaid.

or this, from *After Reading a Child's Guide to Modern Physics*?—

> Marriage is rarely bliss
> But, surely, it would be worse
> As particles to pelt
> At thousands of miles per sec
> About a universe
> In which a lover's kiss
> Would either not be felt
> Or break the loved one's neck.

In his present pleasant house, to which his dream of the City has congenially dwindled, Auden portrays his workroom, 'The Cave of Making,' with 'windows averted from plausible/videnda but admitting a light one/could mend a watch by.' By such dry clear light, a dictionary at hand, he is best read—not, as he hopes, as 'a minor atlantic Goethe' (the difference in generosity may be less between Goethe and himself than between Goethe' Europe and our America), but as a man who, with a childlike curiosity and a feminine fineness of perception, treats poetry as the exercise of wit. For almost always, in his verse, the oracular and ecstatic flights fail; what we keep are the fractional phrases that could be expressed in prose, but less pointedly. In his own anthology of light verse, he defines it as poetry written in the common language of men. Powerfully attracted by the artistocratic and the arcane, he has struggled to preserve his democratic loyalties, his sense of poetry as a mode of discourse between civilized men. *About the House*, though it contains no single poem as fine as 'Ode to Gaea' from 'The Shield of Achilles,' has nothing in it as tedious as the infatuated concept-chopping of the 'Dichtung and Wahrheit' interlude of *Homage to Clio*; and on the whole marks a new frankness and a new relaxation in tone. Auden remains, in the Spirit as well as by the Letter, alive.—JOHN UPDIKE, *Mot*, Nov. 1965, pp. 50–52

In *City Without Walls* ⟨Auden⟩ meditates on equally commonplace topics of our time—the vistas of boredom and neurosis, compulsory leisure and compelled privacy; the cult of sport and violence instead of work and war, the possibility of the Bomb and its aftermath—and in the hands of his idiom and metre (a cunning fusion of rhymeless classical measures with the stressed alliterations of Old English poetry) these ordinary fears and foretellings become a sort of magic compound delighting the eye and yet engaging the mind. Rhetoric and mediation combine—Ulysses summoning up the terrors of time and anarchy in *Troilus and Cressida*, on the one hand, and on the other Tennyson's honey-tongued flirtation in 'In Memoriam' with the gropings of Victorian science. . . . Yet another rhetorician, Langland, is played on as a mute variable in the withdrawal sequence.

> Thus I was thinking at three a.m.
> In Mid-Manhattan till interrupted,
> cut short by a sharp voice.

It tells the poet not to play 'Jeremiah-cum-Juvenal', and he retorts: 'So what, if my words are true.'

> Thereupon, bored, a third voice:
> 'Go to sleep now for God's sake!
> You both will feel better by breakfast time.'

Evading without deprecation 'the preacher's loose immodest tone', Auden secures for himself the last reward of the picking and unpicking scald—to be most simply himself when his verse is at its most entrancingly mannered. Accuracy and affection, the proper way to observe both animals and men, is present in his 'Mosaic for Marianne Moore', in which the animals she describes get a voice for their acknowledgments:

> For poems, dolphin-graceful as carts from Sweden,
> our thank-you should be a right
> good salvo of barks . . .

And in the 'Eulogy' for Professor Nevill Coghill:

> you countenanced all species,
> the alphas, the bone—
> idle, the obstreperous
> and the really rum . . .

A penetrating familiarity comprehends in its glance the animal in us all that yawns and scratches and lusts as a part of our angelic faculty and our god-like apprehension. Auden is singularly and excellently lacking in the modern dualism that is obsessed with the flesh and its mechanic achievements ('Run smoothly by Jaguar farmers') and yet cannot see itself performing the act. For him the flesh is spiritual because comic, more accurately and lyrically mimed in the copulations of the zoo than in those of the modern screen, and a *gestalt* for ever out of reach of the ludicrous *selbstlichkeit* of a Henry Miller, whose pudenda tick like parts of his typewriter.

> For a while
> we talked by the fire,
> then, carrying candles, climbed
> steep stairs. Love was made
> then and there: so halcyoned,
> soon we fell asleep
> to the sound of a river
> swabbling through a gorge.

'Love was made'—the casual passive tells us much about the poet's ability not to be himself when doing what everyone else does, and 'Song of the Devil' shows him still retaining (as in *City Without Walls*) an affection for Groddeck's theories, which have stood the test of time better than most others of their epoch.

The most remarkable *tour de force* in this collection are

the eight songs from 'Mother Courage', metrically the most subtle ballads Auden has given us. Their air of simplicity conceals a degree of technical experience and sophistication that makes the point a great deal better than does the 'war equals capitalism' insistence of their originals. 'Song of Fraternisation'—

> That May the days were bright,
> And starry every night.
> The regiment stood on parade:
> They gave their drums the usual thwack,
> They led us then behind a stack,
> Where they fraternised with us

—'Song of Unconditional Surrender', and 'Song of the Soldier before the Inn'—

> No sermon, now, Rev! It's a crime.
> The cavalry have no time,
> Dying for King and Country

—seem to me as superior to Brecht as the songs in Pushkin's 'Feast in Time of Plague' are superior to their prototypes in John Wilson's 'City of the Plague'. But then Brecht, unlike Auden or Pushkin, is undoubtedly a 'profoundly serious' writer—JOHN BAYLEY, "Halcyon Structures," *LT*, Sept. 25, 1969, pp. 413–14

SECONDARY WORLDS
EPISTLE TO A GODSON

Secondary Worlds is a bad book, and Auden's worst performance. These four lectures in memory of T. S. Eliot deal in turn with *Thomas Cranmer*, a pious verse drama by Charles Williams; Icelandic sagas; the three opera libretti by Auden and Chester Kallman; the relation between Christian belief and the writing of poetry. Since the title, *Secondary Worlds*, refers to works of art as against "the primary world of our everyday social experience," the rationale for printing these four talks as a book must be their linked relevance to what has long been Auden's overt polemic against the Romantic view of poetry. Coleridge's ill-chosen terms, Primary and Secondary Imagination, are here subverted by Auden's wit, since by secondary Auden, unlike Coleridge, does mean "inferior."

Of all Auden's writings, *Secondary Worlds* comes most directly out of the neo-Christian matrix of modern Anglo-Catholic letters: Eliot, Williams, C. S. Lewis, Tolkien. I search in vain only for references to Dorothy Sayers. Auden compensates with a quotation from *The Future of Belief*, by Leslie Dewart, a book one might not otherwise know:

> The Christian God is not *both* transcendent and immanent. He is a reality other than being Who is present to being, by which presence He makes being to be.

"To believe this," Auden modestly says, "is to call into question the art of poetry and all the arts." In *The Dyer's Hand*, an admirable performance, Auden remarked that "the imagination is a natural human faculty and therefore retains the same character whatever a man believes." In his new book, the imagination of a humane man-of-letters and talented comic poet appears to be hardening, which would be a loss.

Johnson definitively stated the difficulties of devotional verse when he observed that the good and evil of Eternity were too ponderous for the wings of wit. The mind sinks under them, and must be content with calm belief and humble adoration, attitudes admirable in themselves but perhaps not conducive to the writing of poems. One of Auden's many virtues is that, unlike Eliot and other literary Christians, he has

spared us, and mostly refrained from devotional verse. *For the Time Being*, a work dear to many churchwardenly critics, is a long and unhappy exception, but even it, unlike much Eliot, does not offer us the disciplined humility of the poet as our aesthetic experience.

It is of course one thing to deprecate the possibility of Christian poetry, or of poetry being Christian, and quite another to deprecate poetry itself, all poetry. In Auden's criticism, and particularly *Secondary Worlds*, the two are not always kept apart. When this happens, I find it is bad for my character. On a higher level the experience of reading Auden then becomes rather like reading Kilmer's *Trees*. "Poems are made by fools like me," yes, and by Dante, Milton, Blake, and Homer, but only God makes primary worlds. Or, as Auden says:

> . . . it is possible that artists may become both more modest and more self-assured, that they may develop both a sense of humour about their vocation and a respect for that most admirable of Roman deities, the god *Terminus*. No poet will then produce the kind of work which demands that a reader spend his whole life reading it and nothing else. The claim to be a "genius" will become as strange as it would have seemed to the Middle Ages.

It is possible that other artists may become more like Auden. It is likelier that other critics may become more like him for, with Arnold and Eliot, he is a poet-critic who appeals greatly to critics, little as the splendor of becoming a "poet of professors" appeals to him. Books about Auden all tend to be fairly good, just as books about, say Wallace Stevens, tend to be quite bad. This is probably not because admirers of Stevens love him less well than the lovers of Auden, but because more genuinely difficult poets do not reduce to structures of ideas and images so readily as Auden does.

Auden's poetry now maintains a general esteem among academic critics. If one's judgment of Auden's poetry is more eccentric, one needs to take up the sad burden of literary dissent. Auden has been accepted as not only a great poet but also a Christian humanist sage not because of any conspiracy among moralizing neo-Christian academicians, but because the age requires such a figure. Eliot is gone, and Auden now occupies his place, though with a difference. The difference is refreshing; Auden is wittier, gentler, much less dogmatic, and does not feel compelled to demonstrate the authenticity of his Christian humanism by a judicious anti-Semitism. He has more wisdom and more humor than Eliot, and his talent is nowhere near as sparse, as the enormous range of his lyrics show. I think it unfortunate that he should find himself in apostolic succession to Eliot, but *Secondary Worlds* seems to indicate that the succession is not unwelcome to him.

Much of *The Dyer's Hand*, despite its generosity as criticism, is darkened by Auden's obsessive doubts about the value of art in the context of Christianity. Similar doubts have maimed many writers, Tolstoi and Hopkins in particular. Insofar as Auden's uneasiness has prevented him from devotional poetry, he has gained by it, but unfortunately the effect upon him has been larger, and has resulted in a trivialization of his art. As a songwriter he remains supreme, being certainly the best in English in the century, but as a reflective poet he suffers from the continual evanescence of his subject matter. As a satirist, he may have been aided, yet the staple of his poetry is neither song nor satire but rumination on the good life, and his notion of the relation between Christianity and art has troubled that rumination. Auden is one of the massive modern sufferers from the malady of Poetic Influence, a variety of melancholy or anxiety-principle that our studies have evaded. Poetic Influence, in this sense, has little to do with the transmission of ideas and images from an earlier poet to a later one. Rather, it concerns the poet's sense of his precursors, and of his own achievement in relation to theirs. Have they left him room enough, or has their priority cost him his art? More crucially, where did they go wrong, so as to make it possible for him to go right? In this revisionary sense, in which the poet creates his own precursors by necessarily misinterpreting them, Poetic Influence forms and malforms new poets, and aids their art at the cost of increasing, finally, their already acute sense of isolation. Auden, like Byron, gives the continual impression of personal sincerity in his poetry, but again like Byron this sincerity is the consequence of a revisionary swerve away from the sincerity of the precursor. In Byron's case of Poetic Influence the great precursor was Pope, with his highly dialectical sincerity; with Auden the prime precursor is Hardy, and the poetic son's sincerity is considerably more dialectical than the father's.

Auden, in his very fine *New Year Letter* (1 January 1940, at the height of his poetic power), wrote an important poem about Poetic Influence. His precursors are invoked there as a summary tribunal sitting in perpetual session:

> Though
> Considerate and mild and low
> The voices of the questioners,
> Although they delegate to us
> Both prosecution and defence,
> Accept our rules of evidence
> And pass no sentence but our own,
> Yet, as he faces them alone,
> O who can show convincing proof
> That he is worthy of their love?

He names these fathers and judges: Dante, Blake, Rimbaud, Dryden, Catullus, Tennyson, Baudelaire, Hardy, and Rilke, connecting this somewhat miscellaneous ninefold (except for Dryden, there for his mastery of the middle style) by their common sense of isolation, fit companions "to one unsocial English boy." Of all these, Auden's most characteristic poetry is closest to Hardy's, not merely in its beginnings, and like Hardy Auden remains most convincing as a ruminator upon human incongruities, upon everything valuable that somehow will not fit together. Auden's best poems, such as the justly esteemed *In Praise of Limestone*, brood upon incongruities, swerving from Hardy's kind of poem into a more double-natured sense of ruinous circumstance and thwarted love, yet retaining their family resemblance to Hardy. But where Hardy's strenuous unbelief led him to no worse redundancies than an occasional sharp striving after too palpable an irony, Auden's self-conscious belief and attendant doubt of poetry mar even *In Praise of Limestone* with the redundancy of uneasy and misplaced wit:

> But if
> Sins can be forgiven, if bodies rise from the dead,
> These modifications of matter into
> Innocent athletes and gesticulating fountains,
> Made solely for pleasure, make a further point;
> The blessed will not care what angle they are re-
> garded from,
> Having nothing to hide.

The blessed, as Auden says so often in prose, need neither to read nor to write poems, and poems do not describe their sanctity with much success, as Auden also sadly notes, contemplating the verse of Charles Williams. Close thy Auden, open thy Stevens, and read:

> If, then, when we speak of liberation, we mean an
> exodus; if when we speak of justification, we mean a

kind of justice of which we had not known and on which we had not counted; if when we experience a sense of purification, we can think of the establishing of a self, it is certain that the experience of the poet is of no less a degree than the experience of the mystic and we may be certain that in the case of poets, the peers of saints, those experiences are of no less a degree than the experiences of the saints themselves. It is a question of the nature of the experience. It is not a question of identifying or relating dissimilar figures; that is to say, it is not a question of making saints out of poets or poets out of saints.

—HAROLD BLOOM, "Poetic Misprision" (1969),
The Ringers in the Tower, 1971, pp. 207–11

> Each year brings new problems of Form and Content
> new foes to tug with: at Twenty I tried to
> vex my elders, past Sixty it's the young whom
>   I hope to bother.

So reads the inscription on the dedicatory page of W. H. Auden's new volume, *Epistle to a Godson*, and this reader, close enough to the midway age—give or take a few annual furlongs—between Auden and his "new foes," may gropingly undertake to act as referee. In the title poem, Auden envisages a time of world crisis in the imminent future in which the survival of the race would depend on a survivor corps who

> may be called to opt for a discipline
> that out-peers the monks, a Way of obedience,
> poverty and—good grief!—perhaps chastity . . .

and Auden quite soberly sets himself the task to write works that will nourish such a hardy crop of rugged caretakers of our future. He would set an example to the young less in what he writes than in the exacting discipline of the style and form:

> Nor shoddily made: to give a stunning
> display of concinnity and elegance
> is the least we can do.

The lines hearken back to Yeats's

> Irish poets, learn your trade,
> Sing whatever is well made,
> Scorn the sort now growing up
> All out of shape from toe to top,

but Auden, adopting the posture of a much-weathered Anglo-American oldster, evidently isn't addressing young poets so much as haranguing a featureless universal new youthster. How seriously does he take his role as mentor? Indeed, fancy his striking the pose of ambassador of global politics, while adopting a tone and manner not far from light verse, despite the uniformly elegant prosody and stately—if not perhaps often statesmanlike, magisterial—syntax.

In most of Auden's recent work, his chief predilection is a flair for artlessly speaking his mind. His serio-comic tone is scrupulously well-pitched to accommodate a mode of discourse that fluctuates whimsically from clowning gossip to impassioned thought. Speaking with utmost candor in the epistle to his godson Philip Spender ("*turn your toes out as you walk, dear, / and remember who you are, a Spender*"), he negotiates gracefully from a cantankerous survey of the spoils of our illiterate political bosses ("Global Archons") to a more telling outline than is to be found elsewhere of the improbable poetics that has been gaining ascendancy in his last three volumes of poetry, starting with *About the House*:

> its dominant
> mood should be that of a Carnival.
> Let us hymn the small but journal wonders
> of Nature and of households.

In radical departure from the classical emphasis on subjects of high consequence that characterized the poems of his early and middle periods, Auden now gravitates more and more to "small but journal wonders," domestic and local occasions assuming the forefront in his gallery of common wares. But usually, the scales of the balance are tipped pronouncedly away from the avowed subjects to the unmasked dialectics of Auden's speaking voice, happily and luminously at war with itself, but inviting the reader to clandestinely eavesdrop on the self-bemused conversation; and it is no accident, surely, that the book concludes with the charming "Talking to Myself," an intellectual vaudeville act in which Auden soliloquizes jokes to his mate, his mute beloved, his own body:

> My mortal manor, the carnal territory
> allotted to my manage. . . .
> Our marriage is a drama, but no stage-play where
> what is not spoken is not thought: in our theatre . . .

Auden, confessedly, is importing into his new gabby art of the lyric "a sense of theatre" borrowed from his verse plays, as well as distilled from his decades as an erudite and shrewd entertainer on stage in the lecture circuit. His own distinctive personality, droll and caustic by turns, a favorite character from one of his plays, steps into the spotlight of the poems. He carries it off with the insouciance of a casual man shooting the breeze, but secretly ruminating in strictest prosody. Yes, for all his liberal outspokenness, the audacious and garrulous speaking out of a sagely opinionated mind, he remains a staunch formalist in his craft, and a strict rationalist in his cognitions. Hence, he dismisses the current avante-garde with gruff obstinacy:

> No, Surrealists, no! No, even the wildest of poems
> must, like prose, have a firm basis in staid
> common-sense.

His unrelenting, if obsessive, adherence to overt sanities of craft and vision exceeds all limits in a marvelous passage addressed to his body, again, in the last poem. I fancy I hear the snorts and grunts of a medieval knight bracing himself to behead a fire-breathing dragon! Auden threatens to uproot his own dream-life as, with comic arrogance, he would bully his "nocturnal manias," too, into learning the correct rules of versification:

> For dreams, I, quite irrationally, reproach You.
> All I know is that I don't choose them: if I could,
> they would conform to some prosodic discipline,
> mean just what they say. Whatever point nocturnal
> manias make, as a poet I disapprove.
> —Laurence Lieberman, *YR*, Winter
> 1973, pp. 275–76

FOREWORDS AND AFTERWORDS, THE DYER'S HAND

Forewords and Afterwords is a collection of Mr. Auden's essays and reviews, chosen from his occasional writings between 1943 and 1972. Not as formally organized as *The Dyer's Hand*, it retains many of the same themes, the nature of civilization, the hero, religion, beauty, and so forth. Most of the essays are literary, the rest are musical, mainly operatic. In prose, Mr. Auden is happiest with minor writers, because he can make the most of them: with major writers he seems to feel that only a miraculous leap of imagination would come at all close to them, and it is too late to go in for such athletics. I list his official topics: Shakespeare, Luther, Pope, Goethe, Kierkegaard, Poe, Tennyson, Mayhew, Wagner, Verdi, Trollope, Leontiev, Lewis Carroll, Van Gogh, Wilde, A. E. Housman, Cavafy, Kipling, Valéry, Max Beerbohm, Walter de la Mare,

Chesterton, Mann, Virginia Woolf, Stravinsky, Hammarskjöld, J. R. Ackerley; I may have dropped a few. Mr. Auden is splendid on Beerbohm, and on Wilde: he needs a good deal of space if he is to engage with his themes, he is cramped by the short review and can do nothing much with it except offer a few small deliberations and sign off.

Some of the essays are autobiographically revealing. We now know that among the Greek writers Mr. Auden dislikes Lucian, that among Pope's poems he could live without the *Essay on Man*, that he dislikes behaviorists, Lord Alfred Douglas, Carlyle, the *Action Française* people, the theory of random Creation, and dreams, "nocturnal manias." He particularly likes Irenaeus, Ronald Firbank's novels, Pope (on the whole), Horace, Bonhoeffer, and nearly every minor writer who has settled gracefully for minority status and therefore lives at peace with himself.

In the longer essays, as in *The Dyer's Hand*, Mr. Auden likes to set his mind working upon the distinctions between two rival forces often equally compelling: Eros and Agape, Body and Soul, Catholic and Protestant, Prospero and Ariel, Petrarch and Shakespeare (as sonneteers), humans and animals, France and England. Many of his grandest perceptions come from the practice of looking now upon this picture, now upon that: he is gifted in comparison and contrast, for the energy they release. He mentions playing a parlor game in which each player names two persons "of such different temperaments that on meeting they would dislike each other intensely, and they are condemned to live together in Purgatory until they come to understand and love each other." T. S. Eliot and Walt Whitman, he offers for a start; then Tolstoy and Wilde. I have never played the game, though I am not too old to learn, I suppose.—Denis Donoghue, "Good Grief," *NYRB*, July 19, 1973, p. 18

A teacher can render no greater service, and no rarer one, than to transmit the enthusiasm that, usually long ago, made him choose his subject for his life's work, but I don't mean to imply that Auden's criticism is enthusiasm, only, without cogency; for example, no better essays on Shakespeare have ever been written than the several that Auden includes in *The Dyer's Hand*. Though I don't accept all that he says there—I cannot agree, for one thing, that "given a few more years of Othello" Desdemona "might well . . . have taken a lover"—the general spirit of his remarks seems to me absolutely Shakespeare's own.

Almost everything W. H. Auden wrote sprang from his intense apprehension of two separate spheres of being, what we would contrast as actuality with art, or even as experience with innocence, but what he called the Natural World of the Dynamo and the Historical World of the Virgin, or, again, borrowing from J. R. R. Tolkien, the Primary World of the senses and the Secondary World of the imagination. One world is necessarily public; the other, private. The two worlds differ most significantly in their concepts of justice, always the central problem for Auden. In the World of the Dynamo, justice is "the equality of all before natural law," which means anonymity and includes suffering and death, but in the World of the Virgin, justice is "the love of my neighbor as a unique and irreplaceable being." These two worlds, and their contrastive standards of justice, Auden found in conflict in Shakespeare's *Henry IV*: "Overtly, Falstaff is a Lord of Misrule; parabolically, he is a comic symbol for the supernatural order of Charity as contrasted with the temporal order of Justice symbolized by Henry of Monmouth. . . . Falstaff's neglect of the public interest in favor of private concerns is an image for the justice of charity which treats each person, not as a cipher, but as a unique person."

It is Falstaff's sort of justice that people look for in Auden's poems and that he seeks always to establish. The haunting refrain of the first part of "In Memory of W. B. Yeats,"

> O all the instruments agree
> The day of his death was a dark cold day,

shows how unresponsive the World of the Dynamo is to the deepest needs of man, needs that Auden defines in "September 1, 1939,"

> For the error bred in the bone
> Of each woman and each man
> Craves what it cannot have,
> Not universal love
> But to be loved alone.

The Primary World is "the burrows of the Nightmare / Where Justice naked is," where "Time watches from the shadow/ And coughs when you would kiss"; it is "the midden whose odours will madden." The Primary World, ruled by law not love, will claim everyone; in *The Age of Anxiety* the Medical Intelligence officer Malin reflects on the unalterable future:

> Behold the infant, helpless in cradle and
> Righteous still, yet already there is
> Dread in his dreams at the deed of which
> He knows nothing but knows he can do,
> The gulf before him with guilt beyond,
> Whatever that is whatever why
> Forbids his bound; till that ban tempts him;
> He jumps and is judged; he joins mankind,
> The fallen families, freedom lost,
> Love become Law.

One of his most famous lines, "We must love one another or die," Auden rightly emended to "We must love one another *and* die" (he later expunged the line altogether from "September 1, 1939"), for he knew that mortality, time, and profanation cannot be denied, that they make unknown citizens of us all, finally, but that their terrors can be neutralized by secret acts of charity, the giving of love:

> Certainly, fidelity
> On the stroke of midnight pass
> Like vibrations of a bell,
> And fashionable madmen raise
> Their pedantic boring cry:
> Every farthing of the cost,
> All the dreaded cards foretell,
> Shall be paid, but from this night
> Not a whisper, not a thought,
> Not a kiss nor look be lost.

In this way Auden's poetry is poetry of affirmation and triumph.

More than anything else, Auden regretted the loss of the *sacred* in the modern world and, in both prose and verse, searched to rediscover it by asserting the incalculable value, the preciousness, of every human being. "In a society governed by the values appropriate to Labor," he wrote, thinking mainly of America, "the gratuitous is no longer regarded—most earlier cultures thought differently—as sacred, because, to Man the Laborer, leisure is not sacred but a respite from laboring, a time of relaxation and the pleasures of consumption." But the poet's commitment is perforce otherwise. "The relation of a poet, or any artist, to society and politics is . . . more difficult than it has ever been because, while he cannot but approve of the importance of *everybody* getting enough food to eat and enough leisure, this problem has nothing to do with art, which is concerned with *singular persons*, as they are alone and as they are in their personal relations." It is this understanding, I think, that explains the joy we find in his critical writings, the joy of

sharing an encounter that can never be duplicated, and explains as well the generosity and wisdom that pervade his teacher's voice.—MARK TAYLOR, "Auden's Vision of Eros," *Com*, Oct. 26, 1973, pp. 85–86

COLLECTED POEMS

For almost fifty years W. H. Auden wrote what he called 'shorts', quick chasers for the longer work, the clippings and shavings of the poetic workshop: epigram, haiku, clerihew, ballyhoo. They were an indication of the fecundity of his 'intellectual baggage', as Maritain put it, the equivalent in the literary sphere of his frugality and economy in the domestic. They were also a demonstration of what has been called 'the good crack principle' which insists that poetry should often aspire to the status of entertainment, e.g. 'Thomas Moore/ Caused a furore/Every time he bellowed his/Irish Melodies', or 'Let us honour if we can/The vertical man/Though we value none/But the horizontal one'.

Auden was also inclined to write prose in short bursts, so that the thing worked like a crazy paving or a set of stepping stones for the intelligence. When he faced the bull of reality, he was more a bandillero than a picador or matador: he made nimble dashes at the neck muscles, conspicuously rapid and skillful forays that were closer to the choreographer's than to the killer's art, closer to comedy than tragedy.

Yet in the beginning, this metaphor invoking the panache of the *corrida* would not have served. Then we would have been forced to think of the *Holmgang* (holmgang, Old Norse: 'going to the holm' or islet on which a duel was fought, hence a duel to the death). The barbarism of Northern Europe, ancient and modern, blew like a cold wind through the verse. A few lines are enough to remind us that the civility of the later verse sells the auditory imagination short: 'Doom is dark and deeper than any sea-dingle . . .' 'Who stands, the crux left of the watershed,/On the wet road between the chafing grass . . .' 'Who will endure/Heat of day and winter danger . . .'

Auden is a Norse name. His lifeline stretched into the Anglo-Saxon landscape and deposits where 'the dead howl/ Under headlands in their windy dwellings'. When he was commissioned to write a travel book, he went to Iceland, seafaring north, a wanderer in saga-land, Grendel country. That was in 1936. In 1965, in a poem called 'Amor Loci', he was still committing himself to a desolate landscape, still envisaging the desert places as the guarantee of his imagination:

> How, but with some real focus
> of desolation
> could I, by analogy,
> imagine a love
> that, however often smeared,
> shrugged at, abandoned
> by a frivolous worldling,
> does not abandon?

'A frivolous worldling'—at times he certainly was. The mighty fluency that gave us 'Letter to Lord Byron', surely the twentieth century poem that is the apotheosis of the good crack principle, more and more settled for a kind of high-table garrulousness. That original clipped and speedy utterance which was the perfect technique for flushing and bagging 'the lion griefs' in sonnet sequences, or formal lyrics, or hypnotic ballads, finally slipped into a tone somewhere between camp and costive. When public terror and private passion haunted the roots of the poems, the detachment and definition in the voice maintained the lines in high tension. When he settled into an imperious and impatient domesticity, holding the fort of a menaced bourgeois culture, the detachment occasionally mutated towards indifference and a kind of educated in-talk.

There is a story about a Ballymena listener calling the BBC one morning in 1969, after the Northern Ireland news had given a lot of coverage to speeches by civil rights leaders the previous evening. 'Tell us this,' he said, 'are yez Unionists or are yez not?' At the centre of Auden's work, an equally categorical question is implicit: 'Tell us this, are yez civilised or are yez not?' For while it is true that his feelings quickened in the presence of the desolate and worn-out and primitive, the counter-truth holds also: the human achievements of art, manners, social intercourse, just government, are all that are worth living for.

Hence the political Auden, and those poems like 'Spain' and 'September 1, 1939' which he suppressed because they stated the counter-truth too shrilly, rhetorically, 'dishonestly'. They do not appear in this edition that has been prepared by his literary executor and includes all the poems that he wished to preserve, in a text that represents his final revisions. They will be reprinted, however, in a volume due next year, to be called *The English Auden*. That book will also include a selection of other suppressed and unpublished prose and verse from the early period.

The title of the forthcoming volume is an allusion to Auden's two careers, one in England in the twenties and thirties, and the other in America after that. I think it was unfortunate for England and the native English sensibility, if perhaps fortunate for Auden himself, that he emigrated. He was the one English writer who was the heir to Lawrence as prophet and diagnostician of the country's spiritual and social ennui. By 1940 he was buoyant on the gratitude and excitement of an audience which he had created, and he chose to distance himself from them. There was nothing Joycean about the exile, distance did not lend intensity to the view. Instead it bred an eccentric gentility. Auden's later poems constitute a flourish of personality and intelligence, a prodigal play of ideas about the good life to which one's response must be delighted *Deo Gratias*. But it is work in which the self is forced to make all the running, and for the highest art, the self is best melded with the intensities and occasions of the world which produced it and surrounds it. There is something parabolic in the picture of Auden in the final year of his life, returned home to Oxford, sitting there in a coffee shop not so much unapproachable as unapproached, isolated at last in the very world where he had first discovered community.

Is it bad manners (an Auden taboo) to wonder about the relationship between the way he held experience at arm's length and his homosexuality? The climax of one of the late nostalgic love poems occurs in the phrase 'love was made'. The passive voice enters at the most active moment, grammar contrives to make passion hygienic. Had his virtuosity, his assiduous cultivation of finish, of verbal surface, anything to do with the fact that society forced him to regard his intimate nature as vicious? Certainly, in 'Three Posthumous Poems', published for the first time in this volume, the bare cry of release, the bleak satisfactions of self-knowledge suggest a mode that might have cut a deeper groove than the ones we know:

> To-night, for instance, now that
> Bert has been here, I
> listen to the piercing screams
> of palliardising cats
> without self-pity.

Auden was an epoch-making poet on public themes, the register of a new sensibility, a great sonneteer, a writer of perfect light verse, a prospector of language at its most illiterate roots and a dandy of lexicography at its most extravagant reaches. There is a Victorian bulk to this book that contains his

confident, abundant, peremptory, insouciant opus. A hundred years from now Auden's work will certainly be in permanent and outstanding profile, and for all one's niggardly withholdings, in the end one assents with a 'yes' as pleasured and whole-hearted as Molly Bloom's.—SEAMUS HEANEY, "Shorts for Auden," *Hib*, Oct. 8, 1976, p. 21

CHRISTOPHER ISHERWOOD
"Some Notes on Auden's Early Poetry"
New Verse, November 1937, pp. 4–9

If I were told to introduce a reader to the poetry of W. H. Auden, I should begin by asking him to remember three things:

First, that Auden is essentially a scientist: perhaps I should add 'a schoolboy scientist.' He has, that is to say, the scientific training and the scientific interests of a very intelligent schoolboy. He has covered the groundwork, but doesn't propose to go any further: he has no intention of specialising. Nevertheless, he has acquired the scientific outlook and technique of approach; and this is really all he needs for his writing.

Second, that Auden is a musician and a ritualist. As a child he enjoyed a high Anglican upbringing, coupled with a sound musical education. The Anglicanism has evaporated, leaving only the height: he is still much preoccupied with ritual, in all its forms. When we collaborate, I have to keep a sharp eye on him—or down flop the characters on their knees (see 'F6.' passim): another constant danger is that of choral interruptions by angel-voices. If Auden had his way, he would turn every play into a cross between grand opera and high mass.

Third, that Auden is a Scandinavian. The Auden family came originally from Iceland. Auden himself was brought up on the sagas, and their influence upon his work has been profound.

Auden began writing poetry comparatively late; when he had already been several terms at his public school. At our prep-school, he showed no literary interests whatever: his ambition was to become a mining-engineer. His first poems, unlike Stephen Spender's, were competent but entirely imitative: Hardy, Thomas and Frost were his models. . . .

The saga-world is a schoolboy world, with its feuds, its practical jokes, its dark threats conveyed in puns and riddles and understatements: 'I think this day will end unluckily for some; but chiefly for those who least expect harm.' I once remarked to Auden that the atmosphere of 'Gisli the Outlaw' very much reminded me of our schooldays. He was pleased with the idea: and, soon after this, he produced his first play: *Paid on Both Sides*, in which the two worlds are so inextricably confused that it is impossible to say whether the characters are really epic heroes or only members of a school O.T.C.

Auden is, and always has been, a most prolific writer. Problems of form and technique seem to bother him very little. You could say to him: 'Please write me a double ballade on the virtues of a certain brand of toothpaste, which also contains at least ten anagams on the names of well-known politicians, and of which the refrain is as follows. . . .' Within twenty-four hours, your ballade would be ready—and it would be good.

When Auden was younger, he was very lazy. He hated polishing and making corrections. If I didn't like a poem, he threw it away and wrote another. If I liked one line, he would keep it and work it into a new poem. In this way, whole poems were constructed which were simply anthologies of my favourite lines, entirely regardless of grammar or sense. This is the simple explanation of much of Auden's celebrated obscurity.

While Auden was up at Oxford, he read T. S. Eliot. The discovery of *The Waste Land* marked a turning-point in his work—for the better, certainly; though the earliest symptoms of Eliot-influence were most alarming. Like a patient who has received an over-powerful inoculation, Auden developed a severe attack of allusions, jargonitis and private jokes. He began to write lines like: 'Inexorable Rembrandt rays that stab . . .' or 'Love mutual has reached its first eutectic . . .' Nearly all the poems of that early Eliot period are now scrapped.

In 1928, Spender, who had a private press, printed a little orange paper volume of Auden's poems. (This booklet, limited to 'about 45 copies,' is now a bibliophile's prize: the mis-prints alone are worth about ten shillings each.) Most of the poems were reprinted two years later, when Messrs. Faber and Faber published the first edition of their Auden volume: here is one of the few which were not:

> Consider if you will how lovers stand
> In brief adherence, straining to preserve
> Too long the suction of good-bye: others,
> Less clinically-minded, will admire
> An evening like a coloured photograph,
> A music stultified across the water.
> The desert opens here, and if, though we
> Have ligatured the ends of a farewell,
> Sporadic heartburn show in evidence
> Of love uneconomically slain,
> It is for the last time, the last look back,
> The heel upon the finishing blade of grass,
> To dazzling cities of the plain where lust
> Threatened a sinister rod, and we shall turn
> To our study of stones, to split Eve's apple,
> Absorbed, content if we can say 'because';
> Unanswerable like any other pedant,
> Like Solomon and Sheba, wrong for years.

I think this poem illustrates very clearly Auden's state of mind at that period: in this respect, its weakness is its virtue. Auden was very busy trying to regard things 'clinically,' as he called it. Poetry, he said, must concern itself with shapes and volumes. Colours and smells were condemned as romantic: Form alone was significant. Auden loathed (and still rather dislikes) the Sea—for the Sea, besides being deplorably wet and sloppy, is formless. (Note 'ligatured'—a typical specimen of the 'clinical' vocabulary.)

Another, and even more powerful influence upon Auden's early work was non-literary in its origin—in 1929, during a visit to Berlin, he came into contact with the doctrines of the American psychologist, Homer Lane. (*Cf.* Auden's own account of this, in his 'Letter to Lord Byron', Part Four.) Auden was particularly interested in Lane's theories of the psychological causes of disease—if you refuse to make use of your creative powers, you grow a cancer instead, etc. References to these theories can be found in many of the early poems, and, more generally, in *The Orators*. Lane's teachings provide a key to most of the obscurities in the 'Journal of an Airman' (Mr. John Layard, one of Lane's most brilliant followers, has pointed out the psychological relationship between epilepsy and the idea of flight.)

The first collaboration between Auden and myself was in a play called *The Enemies of a Bishop*. The Bishop is the hero of the play: he represents sanity, and is an idealised portrait of Lane himself. His enemies are the pseudo-healers, the wilfully ill and the mad. The final curtain goes down on his complete victory. The play was no more than a charade, very loosely put together and full of private jokes. We revised the best parts of it and used them again, five years later, in *The Dog Beneath the Skin*.

It is typical of Auden's astonishing adaptability that, after two or three months in Berlin, he began to write poems in German. Their style can be best imagined by supposing that a German writer should attempt a sonnet-sequence in a mixture of Cockney and Tennysonian English, without being able to command either idiom. A German critic of great sensibility to whom I afterwards showed these sonnets was much intrigued. He assured me that their writer was a poet of the first rank, despite his absurd grammatical howlers. The critic himself had never heard of Auden and was certainly quite unaware of his English reputation.

The scenery of Auden's early poetry is, almost invariably, mountainous. As a boy, he visited Westmorland, the Peak District of Derbyshire, and Wales. For urban scenery, he preferred the industrial Midlands; particularly in districts where an industry is decaying. His romantic travel-wish was always towards the North. He could never understand how anybody could long for the sun, the blue sky, the palm-trees of the South. His favourite weather was autumnal; high wind and driving rain. He loved industrial ruins, a disused factory or an abandoned mill: a ruined abbey would leave him quite cold. He has always had a special feeling for caves and mines. At school, one of his favourite books was Jules Verne's *Journey to the Centre of the Earth*.

A final word about Influences—or perhaps I should say, crazes. For Auden is deeply rooted in the English tradition, and his debt to most of the great writers of the past is too obvious to need comment here. The crazes were all short-lived: they left plenty of temporary damage but few lasting traces. The earliest I remember was for Edwin Arlington Robinson. It found expression in about half a dozen poems (all scrapped) and notably in some lines about 'a Shape' in an Irish mackintosh which malice urges but friendship forbids me to quote. Then came Emily Dickinson. You will find her footprints here and there among the earlier poems: for example,

> Nor sorrow take
> His endless look.

Then Bridges published *The Testament of Beauty*, and Auden wrote the poem beginning: 'Which of you waking early and watching daybreak . . .' which appeared in the first Faber edition, but was removed from later impressions. Finally, there was Hopkins: but, by this time, Auden's literary digestive powers were stronger: he made a virtue of imitation, and produced the brilliant parody-ode to a rugger fifteen which appears at the end of *The Orators*.

MARIANNE MOORE
From "W. H. Auden"
Predilections
1952, pp. 84–102

We surely have in W. H. Auden—in his prose and verse—stature in diversity. It is instructive, moreover, to see in him the abilities he admires in others—the "capacity for drawing general conclusions," mentioned by him as "the extraordinary, perhaps unique merit" of de Tocqueville; and together with clinical attention to cause and effect, a gift for the conspectus. After speaking of de Tocqueville as a counterrevolutionary—i.e., one who has no wish to return to the condition which preceded revolution—he says, "The body knows nothing of freedom, only of necessities; these are the same for all bodies," and "insofar as we are bodies, we are revolutionaries; insofar, however, as we are also souls and minds, we are or ought to be *counter*revolutionaries." He feels that "The books of de Tocqueville belong together with Thucydides, the Seventh Epistle of Plato, and the plays of Shakespeare, in the small group of the indispensable."

Mr. Auden embodies in his work many gratitudes. His *New Year Letter*, addressed to Elizabeth Mayer—"This *aide-mémoire* . . ./This private minute to a friend"—constitutes a veritable reading list of those to whom he feels a debt, and—an even better compliment—he has adopted various of their idiosyncrasies, as in the dedication to *Another Time* he recalls Blake's

> Till I Will be overthrown
> Every eye must weep alone.

In the *New Year Letter*, he says that Blake

> . . . even as a child would pet
> The tigers Voltaire never met,

he feels that he has a debt to young Rimbaud,

> Skilful, intolerant and quick,
> Who strangled an old rhetoric,

and he says,

> There DRYDEN sits with modest smile,
> The master of the middle style.

If by the middle style he means the circumspectly audacious, he too is possessed of it.

He directs a warm glance toward Catullus,

> Conscious CATULLUS who made all
> His gutter-language musical.

Nor is Mr. Auden himself too fettered to use "who," "he," "the," or "which" as an end rhyme. He sees Voltaire facing him "like a sentinel." He says, "Yes, the fight against the false and the unfair was always worth it." He feels a debt to

> HARDY whose Dorset gave much joy
> To one unsocial English boy,

and Shakespeare? One is

> . . . warned by a great sonneteer
> Not to sell cheap what is most dear.

"Only by those who reverence it, can life be mastered." There is a suggestion of *Murder in the Cathedral* about that; as about the following reflection from A *Christmas Oratorio*, "The Temptation of St. Joseph':

> Sin fractures the Vision, not the Fact; for
> The Exceptional is always usual
> And the Usual exceptional.
> To choose what is difficult all one's days
> As if it were easy, that is faith. Joseph, praise.

Mr. Auden has a fondness for the seven-syllable-line rhythm,

> Now the ragged vagrants creep
> Into crooked holes to sleep;

the rhythm of

> Where the bee sucks, there suck I:
> In a cowslip's bell I lie . . .

and "Shame the eager with ironic praise" recalls Pope.

We infer approval of Ogden Nash in "a stranded fish to be kind to" and "had he a mind to"; again, in "Are You There?":

> Each lover has some theory of his own
> About the difference between the ache
> Of being with his love and being alone.

Appreciative of others he can afford to be. He could never

sound as much like others as others sound like him. His collected poems, moreover, constitute, as Louise Bogan says, "the most minute dissection of the spiritual illness of our day that any modern poet, not excluding T. S. Eliot, has given us." He is a notable instance of the poet whose scientific predilections do not make him less than a poet—who says to himself, I must know. In "The Walking Tour," he speaks of how

> The future shall fulfil a surer vow
> Not swooping at the surface still like gulls
> But with prolonged drowning shall develop gills.

Commenting on Maria Edgeworth's Letters, Cecilia Townsend says, "Without sorrow, the spirit dwindles."[1] "Why are people neurotic?" Mr. Auden asks. "Because they refuse to accept suffering." And in one of his *Cornelia Street Dialogues* with Howard Griffin, he says, "suffering plays a greater part than knowledge" in our acts of the will. One can say, "I *should do* this. Will I do it? A part of the mind looks on; a part decides. Also one must not discount Grace."Mr. Griffin says: "You mean supernatural intervention—the light that appeared to Saul on the road to Damascus?" Mr. Auden: "Not really supernatural. . . . It may be perfectly natural. It depends on intensification of normal powers of sensitivity and contemplation."

In an address to the Grolier Club (October 24, 1946), Mr. Auden said, "Without an exception, the characters in Henry James are concerned with moral choices. *The Beast in the Jungle* is . . . the shrinking of the subject's sovereign will from decisive choice. . . . The interest itself is in the freedom of the will. Deny this freedom . . . and your interest vanishes." We have a debt to Mr. Auden for this emphasis put on "denial of free will and moral responsibility" as "a recent feature of our novels." Why must we "see ourselves," he asks, "as a society of helpless victims, shady characters and displaced persons, . . . as heroes without honor or history—heroes who succumb so monotonously to temptation that they cannot truly be said to be tempted at all?" The thought of choice as compulsory is central to everything that he writes. "Of what happens when men refuse to accept the necessity of choosing and are terrified of or careless about their freedom, we now have only too clear a proof," he said in 1941. "The will, decision, and the consequences—there is no separating them." His "Star of the Nativity" (A *Christmas Oratorio*) says:

> Descend into the fosse of Tribulation,
> Take the cold hand of Terror for a guide;
> But, as the huge deformed head rears to kill,
> Answer its craving with a clear I Will;

"In War Time" makes emphatic

> The right to fail that is worth dying for.

Home is

> A sort of honour, not a building site,
> Wherever we are, when, if we choose, we might
> Be somewhere else, yet trust that we have chosen
> right.

And we have in the Notes to Part III of the *New Year Letter:*

> I'm only lost until I see
> I'm lost because I want to be.

We must make "free confession of our sins." Humility, alas, can border on humiliation. In the *New Year Letter*, alluding to great predecessors, he asks, "Who . . .

> Is not perpetually afraid
> That he's unworthy of his trade.
> Who ever rose to read aloud
> Before that quiet attentive crowd

And did not falter as he read,
Stammer, sit down, and hang his head?

"Cognition," he says, "is always a specific historic act, accompanied by hope and fear."

How hard it is to set aside
Terror, concupiscence and pride.

Sin, fear, lust, pride. "The basis of pride," Mr. Auden says in "Dialogue I," is to be found in "lack of security, anxiety, and defiance; . . . says pride can be defined as a form of despair." And in the *New Year Letter* he says to the Devil:

You have no positive existence,
Are only a recurrent state
Of fear and faithlessness and hate,
That takes on from becoming me
A legal personality,

We hoped; we waited for the day
The State would wither clean away,

Meanwhile at least the layman knows
That none are lost so soon as those

Afraid to be themselves, or ask
What acts are proper to their task,
And that a tiny trace of fear
Is lethal in man's atmosphere.

Aware that Aladdin has the magic lamp that "Can be a sesame to light," he says:

Poor cheated Mephistopheles,
Who think you're doing as you please
In telling us by doing ill
To prove that we possess free will.

We have this metaphor of missed logic again in *The Rake's Progress,* where Nick Shadow leads Tom astray by suggesting that he is freed by disregarding passion and reason and marrying a freak. Choice is open to us each, and in *The Sea and the Mirror,* Alonso says:

Learn from your dreams what you lack,

Believe your pain: praise the scorching rocks
For their desiccation of your lust,
Thank the bitter treatment of the tide
For its dissolution of your pride,
That the whirlwind may arrange your will
And the deluge release it to find
The spring in the desert, the fruitful
Island in the sea, where flesh and mind
Are delivered from mistrust.

Similarly, Sebastian says:

O blessed be bleak Exposure on whose sword,
Caught unawares, we prick ourselves alive!
The sword we suffer is the guarded crown.

In his preface to *The Sea and the Mirror,* Mr. Auden quotes Emily Brontë:

And am I wrong to worship where
Faith cannot doubt nor Hope despair
Since my own soul can grant my prayer?
Speak, God of Visions, plead for me
And tell why I have chosen thee.

"Happiness does not depend," he says, "on power but on love." "The person must begin by learning to be objective about his Subjectivity"; so that "love is able to take the place of hate." And in *A Christmas Oratorio:*

The choice to love is open till we die.

O Living Love replacing phantasy.

The patriot may then ("Epithalamion," *Collected Shorter Poems)*

Feel in each conative act
Such a joy as Dante felt
When, a total failure in
An inferior city, he,
Dreaming out his anger, saw
All the scattered leaves of fact
Bound by love.

"The Meditation of Simeon" (*A Christmas Oratorio*) would have us see "the tragic conflict of Virtue with Necessity" as "no longer confined to the Exceptional Hero. Every invalid is Roland defending the narrow pass against hopeless odds; every stenographer is Brunhilde refusing to renounce her lover's ring which came into existence" through the power of renunciation; and, redefining the hero, Mr. Auden's introduction to the Brothers Grimm says: "The third son who marries the princess and inherits the kingdom is not a superman with exceptional natural gifts." He "succeeds not through his own merit, but through the assistance of Divine Grace. His contribution is, first, a humility which admits that he cannot succeed without Grace; secondly, a faith which believes that Grace will help him, so that when the old beggar asks for his last penny, that is, when humanly speaking he is dooming himself to fail, he can give it away; and lastly, a willingness . . . to accept suffering. . . . From tale after tale we learn, not that wishing is a substitute for action, but that wishes for good and evil are terribly real and not to be indulged in with impunity." But, in the "Journey to Iceland," Mr. Auden asks:

"Where is the homage? When
Shall justice be done? O who is against me?
Why am I always alone?"

"Aloneness is man's real condition," he says; and as for justice, "The artist does not want to be accepted by others, he wants to accept his experience of life, which he cannot do until he has translated his welter of impressions into an order; the public approval he desires is not for himself but for his works, to reassure him that the sense he believes he has made of experience is indeed sense and not a self-delusion."[2]

"Lonely we were though never left alone," he says. We see loneliness "sniffing the herb of childhood" and finding home a place "where shops have names" and "crops grow ripe"; and in "In Praise of Limestone" (*Nones*) he reminds himself of

. . . rounded slopes
With their surface fragrance of thyme and beneath
A secret system of caves and conduits; . . .

indeed says,

. . . when I try to imagine a faultless love
Or the life to come, what I hear is the murmur
Of underground streams, what I see is a limestone
landscape.

In the essay on Henry James—already referred to—he also says, "It is sometimes necessary for sons to leave the family hearth; it may well be necessary at least for intellectuals to leave their country as it is for children to leave their homes, not to get away from them, but to re-create them"; adding, however, that "those who become expatriate out of hatred for their homeland are as bound to the past as those who hate their parents." Having, like James, left the family hearth, an exile—"to keep the silences at bay"—must "cage/His pacing manias in a worldly smile" ("Vocation," *The Double Man*). It is not, however, a case of wishing nothing to be hard.

"A problem which is too easy," Mr. Auden says, "is as unattractive as a problem which is senseless or impossible. In playing a game, the excitement lies not in winning but in just-winning, and just-losing is almost as good as winning, and the same surely is true for thinking." Alluding to superficial or hasty persons, he says in "Our Bias":

> How wrong they are in being always right.
> For they, it seems, care only for success:
> While we choose words according to their sound
> And judge a problem by its awkwardness.

"A favorite game of my youth," he says, "was building dams; the whole afternoon was spent in building up what in the end was destroyed in a few seconds."

As offsetting the tribulations of life and a sense of injustice, one recalls Wallace Stevens' emphasis on the imagination as delivering us from our "bassesse." This, poetry should do; and W. H. Auden quotes Professor R. G. Collingwood as saying, "Art is not magic, but a mirror in which others may become conscious of what their own feelings really are. It mirrors defects and it mirrors escape"—affirmed in "The Composer" (*Collected Shorter Poems*):

> You alone, alone, O imaginary song,
> Are able to say an existence is wrong
> And pour out your forgiveness like a wine.

Notes

1. *The Spectator*, October 3, 1931.
2. *Partisan Review*, April 1950, reviewing *The Paradox of Oscar Wilde* by George Woodcock. To Oscar Wilde, Mr. Auden says, "Writing was a bore because it was only a means of becoming known and invited out, a preliminary to the serious job of spellbinding."

JOHN BAYLEY
From "W. H. Auden"
The Romantic Survival
1957, pp. 127–40

Yeats's poetic statements often end, as we have seen, on a note of acceptance—acceptance of everything that life has to offer. But when we compare it with other kinds of literary expression we may feel that this attitude is one that goes well into poetry but bears little relation to the lives we actually have to lead.

> Irrational streams of blood are staining earth;
> Empedocles has thrown all things about;
> Hector is dead and there's a light in Troy;
> We that look on but laugh in tragic joy.
>
> ('The Gyres')

The effect of incantation is obvious and superb. The identity of Empedocles, and why his influence should have been so unsettling, remain unimportant. The forces that threaten to destroy us are of an august kind, Yeats seems to be saying, and we should have enough sense of style to find that consoling. None the less, it is a long way from the world of Hector to the world of Hitler; we are not Housman's 'Spartans on the sea-wet rock', and we are not the tragic heroes and heroines whom Yeats invokes as models of decorum when times are bad.

> All perform their tragic play,
> There struts Hamlet, there is Lear,
> That's Ophelia, that Cordelia;
> Yet they, should the last scene be there,
> The great stage curtain about to drop,
> If worthy their prominent part in the play,
> Do not break up their lines to weep.
> They know that Hamlet and Lear are gay.
>
> ('Lapis Lazuli')

Our individual lives, in the midst of the twentieth century, do not seem much related to this. They are complex, difficult, random, perhaps horrifying, certainly concerned with issues which appear to demand some other response than tragic gaiety. Yeats's 'acceptance' of life, in fact, often seems very much like a renunciation—where poetry is concerned—of what actually happens in life.

Whose poetry should we expect to grapple with these problems, and produce in us the attitudes which, in I. A. Richards's idiom, will be of value to us in our actual world and enable us to live effectively in it? Surely that of W. H. Auden. At the time of Yeats's final phase, Auden belonged to a group of poets whose aims were intimately connected with social and political questions; he was learned in psychology and anthropology; his approach was avowedly 'scientific'—that is to say, detailed, enquiring, impartial; he believed that an artist should be 'more than a bit of a reporting journalist'; he was in touch with all the latest ideas and the latest developments. Apparently, his whole approach to life and art could scarcely have been more different from that of Yeats. And yet as we read his poetry, and in particular the early volumes, we feel that the response we give them—and the response they appear to require—is not so different. Not that Auden renounces by implication what actually happens in most people's lives: on the contrary he is passionately interested in all the details. But the mechanism by which his poetry bites on to such material— rhetorical, self-confident to the point of arrogance, intent on securing the advantage of an immediate effect—all this is very like Yeats.

> Get there if you can and see the land you once were
>   proud to own
> Though the roads have almost vanished and the ex-
>   presses never run:
> Smokeless chimneys, damaged bridges, rotting
>   wharves and choked canals,
> Tramlines buckled, smashed trucks lying on their
>   side across the rails;
> Power-stations locked, deserted, since they drew the
>   boiler fires,
> Pylons falling or subsiding, trailing dead high-
>   tension wires;
> Head-gears gaunt on grass-grown pitbanks, seams
>   abandoned years ago;
> Drop a stone and listen for its splash in flooded dark
>   below. . . .
>
> (*Poems*, 1930. No. 22)

The gusto and sense of enjoyment here are extraordinary. As in Yeats, violence and calamity are on the way: the signs of their coming—industrial chaos, bourgeois artiness and escapism, cramped and wasted lives—are graphically described, with a pungency and detail of which Auden is already a complete master in his first 1930 volume. He has taken the metre of *Locksley Hall*, the use of which for full-blooded egotistic declamation was one of Tennyson's greatest discoveries, and he handles it with characteristic skill. He shares with Yeats an enjoyment of the situation and of the possibilities of making it *stylish*. The picture of desolation gives the reader a thrill of gratified excitement: he seems to be sharing in a vicarious *Schadenfreude*, and indulging too in the thoughtless pleasures of youth, like dropping the stone down the old working and waiting for the splash. Even the esplanade, and the hilarious precision of *sopping* and *dingy*, only give the reader that retrospective warmth which comes from remembering the boredom and glamour of childhood holidays. Staring out dully at the rain evokes at once all the rich futility of nostalgic recollection. Everything is hopeless and the country is going to the dogs, but to think this, while staring out at the rain, is somehow no inconsiderable pleasure. The attitude gives us, in some obscure way, a sense of mastery. 'Man has the refuge of his gaiety.' Or the refuge, at least, of a purely personal reaction. The tradition goes back much further. There is the silence of Don Juan in hell which Baudelaire admired—

> Mais le calme héros, courbé sur sa rapière,
> Regardait le sillage et ne daignait rien voir.

—in turn itself perhaps an echo of the more famous silence of Ajax in the *Odyssey*. What is common to all these cases is the interest of the poet and his readers in the human attitude, the sense of dramatic behaviour which human beings display in moments of crisis, disaster, or impending fear. And these attitudes are always instinctive and individual, not schooled by any intellectual process or by theories of what should be done.

Auden's variation upon this theme is to make this gesture frankly adolescent (some critics might argue that the tradition is in any case an adolescent one), and to centre the imagery and emotion of his poem in childhood experience. So far from being a call to arms, an assertion that we must get away from all this and acquire a new national identity and a new morale, the poem—as a *poem*—revels unashamedly in what we are and what we have.

> There's great delight in what we have.
> The rattle of pebbles on the shore
> Under the retreating wave.

Yeats is again an illuminating parallel. A child sees the images of disaster sharply and vividly, but irresponsibly; he does not seek to order or to understand the mess but simply adopts it as a private world, a world which gives satisfaction to his appetite and curiosity. A child might understand the silence of Ajax in hell, or rather respond in some intuitive way to its meaning, but he would not understand the causes of the Depression, the need for the elimination of the demoralised rentier class and for a change of heart that would produce a new idealism and a new dynamism in industrial relations, etc. The apparent *raison d'être* of the poem is thus in complete opposition to its effective world, 'the view from Birmingham to Wolverhampton', the private world of detailed nostalgia which haunts all Auden's earlier poetry.

These points become clearer if we compare Auden's evocations of dead nightmare landscapes and approaching doom with those of T. S. Eliot in *The Rock* and in *Burnt Norton*.

> Men and bits of paper, whirled by the cold wind
> That blows before and after time,
> Wind in and out of unwholesome lungs
> Time before and time after.
> Eructation of unhealthy souls
> Into the faded air, the torpid
> Driven on the wind that sweeps the gloomy hills of
>   London,
> Hampstead and Clerkenwell, Campden and Putney,
> Highgate, Primrose, and Ludgate. Not here
> Not here in the darkness, in this twittering world.
>   (*Burnt Norton*)

Here the nightmare is a real one, and the images, related if not to a central philosophy at least to a central *tone* of thought, are subordinate and obedient—they do not fight against the overt intention of the poem in the obstreperous delight of being themselves. The note is grave, prophetic, full of distaste; and the absence of vitality is accompanied by a curious absence of originality—the Old Testament and Blake's prophetic books, particularly the first section of Jerusalem, are visible adjuncts to

the traditional mode of writing which Eliot employs. By contrast, and in spite of the metrical debt to Tennyson, Auden's poem makes a brilliantly and strikingly individual impact. But it has the vision of a child, at once neutral and passionate, while Eliot's poem has the controlled, fatigued, but 'engaged' outlook of the middle-aged man. Nor is the difference simply one of the poet's age at the time the poem is written.

The dispossessed imagination may suffer from the lack of an intellectual tradition to set in order the experiences which impinge upon it. The adolescent imagination does not so suffer, because it is not called upon to judge what it experiences by any other standard than its own intensity. Hence the success, in a Romantic period, of the youthful talent, like that of Shelley or Keats: at a later date the boy prodigy becomes even more exaggeratedly youthful—a Rimbaud or a Raymond Radiguet. These were talents who succeeded because they grew up quickly, but their success prompted the question: why grow up at all? The cult of childhood in writing, its emotions and its private symbols, is one that is still with us today in consequence. The child was of course an important figure in early Romantic theory, as Wordsworth's *Immortality Ode* shows, but his position was a symbolic one: he was not valued for himself, but by a sort of inverted Platonist process he came to seem the possessor of truths which for the adult had faded into the light of common day. Moreover his position and function were quite overt and official—Shelley can compare himself to a tired child without giving the game away. But in Auden's poetry, as in much modern literature, the adolescent note—however strong and shaping its influence—is never admitted to be such. The closest that Auden has come to such an admission is his fondness for a Nietzsche quotation—'Maturity—to recover the seriousness one had as a child at play'—and his references to poetry as a particular sort of game.

Yeats's creation of 'Crazy Jane' gives us a clue to the importance of the adolescent outlook in modern poetry and in Auden's in particular. For Yeats, the fool figure, who in madness and simplicity has instinctive wisdom, has much deliberate meaning and is deliberately created; but two implications are of particular interest to us: Crazy Jane defies authority, and she is fully 'human' where her betters are not. Both these characteristics emerge strongly in the early poem of Auden from which we have quoted, though in an indirect way. 'Authority' is at once the industrial concerns, the wreckage of which so much fascinates the poet, and the august 'boon companions' who have betrayed us and at whom we can now cock a snook (the list of them is quite indiscriminate, as well as being chattily private, and includes at least two names who either were, or were to become, heroes of Auden). The human attitude resides in the poem's effective pleasure in the monstrous corpse of industry; in the accusation at one's betters that they don't really know what Life is; and in the complex gesture of nostalgia and self-acceptance which is made in the childhood image of watching the rain fall on the sea. An apparently denunciatory poem about industry and politics in fact makes its impact in very much the same way as one of Yeats's Crazy Jane poems, and it makes it by a use—how conscious a use one cannot say—of the attitudes and images of adolescence; for in an age of ideology and mechanisation only the child remains unmechanised and human.

Naturally the word 'human' is a question-begging one. Why, it may be objected, should one possible activity, like *Schadenfreude* or making a graceful or derisive gesture, be more 'human' than another, like setting one's ideas in order, social planning, and worrying about the future? 'Spontaneous' or what Yeats understood by 'passionate' would perhaps be better words. Keats, speaking of the 'instinctive attitudes' of the human creature as poetry's subject, was probably thinking of the same thing. If the word is given this sense, however, it is incredible that Yeats and Auden should frequently have been criticised for being 'inhuman' in their poetry. In the case of Auden especially, such an accusation seems to imply a complete failure to appreciate his poetry and to see what it essentially is.

But there are reasons for this misunderstanding. For the whole tenor of Auden's critical pronouncements on poetry has been to imply a separation between the poet as Poet, and as a responsible social being commanded to love his neighbour and behave properly, and do what he can to establish what Auden calls The Just City. The poet can indulge in all the romantic attitudes: the man must conform to the classical moral pattern. Although this dualism would have been quite intelligible to Bacon and Plato, it has never been so abruptly stated by a poet. Auden makes the distinction again and again, until we are left wondering if his obsession with it indicates some uneasiness of conscience. Why should he stress so continually that Art is one thing and Life is another, and that nothing but bad art and wrong living will come if we try to mix the two? The romantic theory of their separation is of course already well known to us: for Poe and Housman it was a necessary and comfortable one, of advantage to both sides. Housman's citing of the unpoetic phrase from the New Testament which is none the less 'the greatest discovery of the moral world', and his contention that when we say we admire poetry we are often admiring something *in* it—these are confident assertions of the romantic attitude. Auden's is more deeply considered and less confident, but in a sense no less uncompromising. He sees Art as a mirror world, complete in every detail, the only difference between it and the real world being that it does not in fact exist. In Art, as Caliban puts it in *The Sea and the Mirror*, 'all the phenomena of an empirically ordinary world are given. Extended objects appear to which events happen—old men catch dreadful coughs, little girls get their arms twisted. . . . All the voluntary movements are possible—crawling through flues and old sewers, sauntering past shopfronts, tiptoeing through quicksands and mined areas, running through derelict factories and across empty plains . . . all the modes of transport are available, but any sense of direction, any knowledge of where on earth one has come from or where on earth one is going to, is completely absent.'

Art is thus a frozen world, locked in a series of gestures which, though fascinating and arresting, remain necessarily disconnected with the continuity of living. Of course there is a clear sense in which this is true—what happens in a book, or on the stage or screen, may be 'exactly like life', but it cannot become it. But, we feel like asking, so what? Is this premise so very important? Does it lead us anywhere? Why should it need so much reiteration? The great classical writers would not have even considered it worth saying; Dante, Goethe, and Tolstoy are not disturbed by the awareness that what they write is not Life: they are preoccupied rather with the points at which Art and Life touch and interact, with the interplay of influence and resemblance, not with the initial, if basic, dissimilarity.

Why should this dissimilarity haunt Auden so much? Perhaps because he cannot really persuade himself that the way in which he likes to write, and the subject, the *ambiance* which liberate him into writing, have much to do with the part of himself that actually lives from day to day, that has come from somewhere and is going to somewhere else. Dickens, say, never appears to have been struck by such a realisation: as a novelist he seems to have complete confidence that his day-dream world and its inhabitants are as real as—perhaps more real

than—the stream of facts, decisions and problems that confronted him in the daily process of living. And Sartre, to take a very different example, seems to have complete confidence in the relevance to actual life of his imaginary hero Antoine Roquentin. But Auden seems to have no such confidence in his creations. The situations that appear and recur in his poems with such vividness are of the kind which we can imagine occurring to the poet as he closes his eyes for a liberating instant between two minutes of actual living. They are glimpses of life, brilliantly concrete, but seen from the unparticipating outside, as we see the screen when sitting in the cinema. They are 'the *voluntary* movements'—'sauntering past shopfronts, tiptoeing through quicksands and mined areas, running through derelict factories'. . . .

And so, as he says in another essay, 'there must always be two kinds of art—escape art, for man needs escape as he needs food and deep sleep, and parable art, that art which shall teach man to unlearn hatred and learn love'. The dichotomy so stated seems one of almost staggering crudity. Is there indeed no middle way between the 'altogether elsewhere' where 'the minotaur of authority is just a roly-poly ruminant and nothing is at stake', and art which is consciously connected with some ethical scheme for our betterment? Not for the poet, would seem to be Auden's reply, and indeed in his own poetic development and practice the dichotomy is very marked: his critical bluntness seems to arise from the *fait accompli* of his own work and its individual quality. Perhaps for the novelist though: Auden has always venerated this form of art, in which the phenomenology of life can be seen steadily and commented on *in extenso*. 'A higher art than poetry altogether', he calls it in one of his *Letters to Lord Byron*, and in his sonnet *The Novelist* he says that the poet, 'encased in talent like a uniform', can dash forward like a hussar or amaze us like a thunderstorm, but cannot, he implies, do very much else.

RICHARD HOGGART
From "Introduction to Auden's Poetry"
W. H. Auden
1961, pp. 14–41

Auden's technical skill, his poetic virtuosity, is indisputable; he is gifted, professional, a constant practiser. He has more than once said that he is interested in all forms of verse, from the word-of-mouth limerick to the closely designed poem of volume length. He has also said that he opposes all notions of artistic decorum and of "correct" style. So we should expect great range and flexibility in his verse; and we find it. We find also a disposition to play around, just for the fun of it. This occasionally mars the poetry, but not always. It is important not to assume that "playing around" in itself and automatically makes a poem faulty (as though "high seriousness" were indispensable). Auden thinks that the primary characteristic of a budding poet is the wish to "hang around words" and play with them—rather than the wish to reform the world or to become famous. Other professions may give such opportunities; only poetry starts by putting words into odd shapes.

As we move through Auden's poetry we notice a recurrent loyalty to a few forms, as well as a recurrent readiness to experiment. Two forms have obviously attracted him steadily: the brief lyric and the sonnet; we must look further at them later. In his first volume he wrote some curt and gnomic poems which obviously owed something to the poetry of Laura Riding and Robert Graves (*This Lunar Beauty*; *This One* are two of these). We have discussed the epigrammatic and conversational verse which followed; and in that same period Auden intermittently wrote ballads, choral songs and some poems in little-used forms such as the villanelle, the sestina and the canzone. His comic verse has been fed from several sources: army songs, music-hall and cabaret, jazz. He has from time to time, but notably in *The Age of Anxiety*, modified the alliterative line of Anglo-Saxon poetry. He has been interested in, and has written interestingly about, the challenge presented by opera libretti—the difficulty of writing a clearly running line which can be sung without confusing the singer or the hearer with a complicated interplay of suggestion, and which is yet not simply banal.

These are only typical instances from a wide range of activity by a mind deeply interested in *craft*, in the formal-play element in poetry. In suitable conditions, Auden might well have enjoyed being a court-poet. He would probably have been the court-wit at the same time, but a dry and telling wit—for his "play" usually does have, indirectly, a moral purpose.

When we think of the characteristic texture of Auden's verse we are reminded first of those impersonal and external qualities which were noted earlier. His poems are not strong in some sensory effects. He has a fine ear (as poems such as *Seascape* and *Lullaby* amply show); he responds well to patterns of colour—but seems more interested in the patterns than in the modulations of the colours themselves. There is little touch, taste or smell in his verse. He rarely lingers over his sensory effects—except when they are aural—and seems not greatly interested in them for themselves. We tend to remember his poems as shapes, as patterns of observation and analysis. He once said that he tends to see his own poems as "squares and oblongs"; that is, presumably, as structures formed out of the interplay of man's moral dilemmas. The emphasis is once again on pattern.

Similarly, his epithets do not usually carry rich sensory evocations. Lines such as these, from *Macbeth*:

> Light *thickens*; and the crow
> Makes wing to the *rooky* wood:

would hardly be likely to occur in Auden's poetry. At their most characteristic his epithets do not physically describe the objects they qualify; they are, rather, conceptual. They comment rather than describe; they set the object into a relationship with something or someone else. Often they appear in pairs so that the two adjectives set off an intellectual friction. Auden is likely to say, not "grassy slope," but "tolerant enchanted slope." He does not write:

> Lay your graceful head, my love,
> Golden on my circling arm

but

> Lay your sleeping head, my love,
> Human on my faithless arm

and the interest comes from the play of moral relations between the owners of the head and arm.

Not much need be said about Auden's favourite and recurrent technical habits; nearly all of them are clever but some clever-clever. During the Thirties in particular he made use of a type of simile in which a concrete fact was yoked to an abstract idea. This might produce an effective surprise or might seem merely smart:

> Problems like relatives standing
> Will Ferdinand be as fond of a Miranda
> Familiar as a stocking.

He has always been fond of dying falls, especially dying falls with three steps:

> That wept, and grew enormous, and cried Woe.

He has often used a sort of stylized "pointing," by means of successive definite articles:

> The boarding-house food, the boarding-house faces,
> The rain-spoilt picnics in the windswept places,
> The camera lost and the suspicion,

But many of these habits have fallen away during the last few years; today his most frequent excess is in adopting highly unusual words, dictionary-raiding and word-coining.

Auden's lyrics, as we have said, form by now a substantial group within his work and one which can claim considerable admiration. They have some striking common qualities. Most of them create a sense of stillness, the stillness of harmony and calm, or the stillness of menace. They reflect and muse. This is strange, in view of the quick and rather jackdaw-like activity of so much of Auden's poetry. Then one remembers that he quotes more than once—as though it were a reminder and corrective to his own immediate tendencies—Rilke's insistence on the need for a poet to sit still and absorb, to "bless what there is for *being*."

May with its light behaving is a typical Audenesque lyric:

> May with its light behaving
> Stirs vessel, eye and limbs;
> The singular and sad
> Are willing to recover,
> And to the swan-delighting river
> The careless picnics come,
> The living white and red.
> The dead remote and hooded
> In their enclosures rest; but we
> From the vague woods have broken,
> Forests where children meet
> And the white angel-vampires flit;
> We stand with shaded eye,
> The dangerous apple taken.
>
> The real world lies before us,
> Animal motions of the young,
> The common wish for death,
> The pleasured and the haunted;
> The dying master sinks tormented
> In the admirers' ring;
> The unjust walk the earth.
> And love that makes impatient
> The tortoise and the roe, and lays
> The blonde beside the dark,
> Urges upon our blood,
> Before the evil and the good
> How insufficient is
> The endearment and the look.
>
> (*Look, Stranger*, xvi; *Collected
> Shorter Poems*, p. 244)

In spite of the stillness Auden is not, we soon realize, simply absorbing the scene; he is quickly into moral debate again. The allegro opening recalls the pleasure of a May morning, which urges even those held in the grip of their own neuroses to relax, to be happy simply in *being*. This is a moment of simple happiness and gentleness (evoked in part by the interplay of long and short "i" sounds and by the quietly echoing pattern of predominantly off-rhymes or near-rhymes).

Thereafter the poem is sad. We respond to May much as the animals do, at first. But we also stand in the hard light of self-consciousness; we know the doubt of the double-personality, which acts and questions its actions. "Love" prompts us as it prompts "the tortoise and the roe"; but to our self-aware condition "Love" soon shows itself as inadequate.

Auden is already moving towards the more complex view of "Love" which he examines in so much of his later work.

The third stanza, with its scraps of psychology, seems far too bitty and overloaded with items; it might have been omitted without much loss. And isn't "vague" in the second stanza (Auden likes the word) so vaguely used as to become an invitation to the reader to supply what suggestions he pleases? By contrast there is an economical charge of meaning in:

> The singular and sad
> Are *willing* to recover,

and a fine conciseness in:

> To the swan-delighting river
> The careless picnics come

and in:

> We stand with *shaded* eye
> The dangerous apple taken.

Auden's sonnets are almost always compressed visual or dramatic stories, allegories of some moral problem, tightly held within the fourteen lines and the firm rhyme-scheme. Here again, Rilke is the ancestor. From him Auden learned much about the use of landscape as a symbol for abstract problems otherwise exceptionally difficult to express. "One of the constant problems of the poet," said Auden in a discussion of Rilke, "is how to express abstract ideas in concrete terms." Auden's sonnets often have in common with Rilke's an unannounced jump into the narrative, which forces the reader to pick up the legend as he goes along; a similar air of control; a similar unhurried assurance which comes partly from having firm symbols to manipulate.

Sometimes Auden seems to have become so skilled in this form that he gives the air of producing the sonnets by habit. At such times they have too glossy a finish; he over-works certain movements and phrasings and suggests that his theme has been too easily buttoned-up. Yet at their best the sonnets are good examples of memorable speech. This one shows some of the tricks, but is largely successful:

> So from the years the gifts were showered; each
> Ran off with his at once into his life:
> Bee took the politics that make a hive,
> Fish swam as fish, peach settled into peach.
>
> And were successful at the first endeavour;
> The hour of birth their only time at college,
> They were content with their precocious knowledge,
> And knew their station and were good for ever.
>
> Till finally there came a childish creature
> On whom the years could model any feature,
> And fake with ease a leopard or a dove;
>
> Who by the lightest wind was changed and shaken,
> And looked for truth and was continually mistaken,
> And envied his few friends and chose his love.
> ("In Time of War": I, *Collected Shorter Poems*,
> p. 271)

The theme—not in itself unusual— is one which, as we shall see, occurs again and again in Auden. Man is a creature who is forever *becoming*, hardly ever in a state of *being*; he is a double creature, driven by will (free-will *and* wilfulness). The animal and vegetable world (in the octave) simply *is*; without self-consciousness, these thing are what they are. Man has freedom to choose, self-consciousness. The poem muses sadly over the weight of consciousness on man but also celebrates it; for man can love, can choose to love and choose when to love. He is bound (bound to choose, even if he chooses not to choose) and free (the way his choice falls depends on him). Hence the close is far more positive than regretful.

FREDERICK BUELL
From "Idea and Voice"
Auden as a Social Poet
1973, pp. 158–72

When one wonders what Auden felt about the ideas he used, one is confronted with a number of striking facts that want explanation. Most odd is the gap between Auden's sensibility and the sensibilities of the thinkers by whom he has been most deeply influenced; to examine the nature and significance of this gap is to illuminate certain aspects of Auden's sensibility not normally examined by critics but rather seen as discrediting defects. One need only note a few of the obvious and overwhelming characteristics of the life and work of Marx and Freud to become aware of the differences between them and Auden. Both Marx and Freud were profoundly individualistic and original thinkers; with Freud, this originality had the curious side effect of making him often completely unreceptive to ideas he could not fit into his own particular frame of thought, so that, if one did not accept him as teacher, one had difficulty communicating with him. A corollary to this is that both Freud and Marx were systematic thinkers; they not only brought diverse data of experience into a comprehensive order, but also attempted to explain all experience in terms of their systems and spent their lives altering, expanding, and adapting these systems to new ends. Moreover, with Freud and Marx, system is simultaneously dogma, and the fact that their thought was meant to be applied to reality, to be put into effect, made its rigorous elaboration all the more an absolute necessity.

The contrast of such traits to what we know of Auden's sensibility is glaring. Where Freud was incapable of absorbing foreign ideas, Auden is a virtuoso of intellectual receptivity; his freedom of mind depends upon his ability to make connections between ideas in widely different realms with exuberant and spontaneous ease. Where Freud and Marx were independent and original thinkers, Auden is a marvelously adaptive spirit, able not just to be influenced by those whom he has copiously read, but also to pick up ideas nimbly, on a very fleeting acquaintance; in addition, there is an element of fashionable dilettantism present in Auden's interests, which one sees both in the fact that, in the thirties, Freud and Marx were the avant-garde rage and in the fact that Auden tends to develop his ideas in the context of small groups of like-minded thinkers. Finally, although Auden has always been primarily attracted to systematic philosophers, his own use of ideas is not strict or systematic; what is most confusing to those who try to pin down the essential Auden is the fact that he overuses these ideas, that is, he uses them in too many different and often contradictory ways; one simply cannot select any one of his formulations as central and seminal.

In terms of personality as well Auden differs radically from Freud and Marx; his freedom of spirit, his irreverence, and his hedonistic self-indulgence actually clash with the asceticism, the overwhelming earnestness and dedication to rational coherence and scientific exactitude of Freud and Marx. Whereas Freud and Marx are thinkers trying to make their ideas as responsibly faithful to reality as possible, Auden is a man whose energy is never fully bound by the content of any of his ideas. In this connection, one of Freud's descriptions of the role of nonsense in the emotional life of the child has an interesting relevance:

> And he [the child] puts words together without regard to the condition that they should make sense, in

order to obtain from them the pleasurable effect of rhythm and rhyme. Little by little he is forbidden this enjoyment, until all that remains permitted to him are significant combinations of words. But when he is older attempts still emerge at disregarding the restrictions that have been learnt on the use of words. Words are disfigured by particular little additions being made to them, their forms are altered by certain manipulations, . . . or a private language may be constructed for use among playmates. These attempts are found again and again among certain categories of mental patients.

Whatever the motive may have been which led the child to begin these games, I believe that in his later development he gives himself up to them with the consciousness that they are nonsensical, and that he finds enjoyment in the attraction of what is forbidden by reason. He now uses games in order to withdraw from the pressure of critical reason. But there is far more potency in the restrictions which must establish themselves in the course of a child's education in logical thinking and in distinguishing between what is true and false in reality; and for this reason the rebellion against the compulsion of logic and reality is deep-going and long-lasting. Even the phenomena of imaginative activity must be included in this [rebellious] category, the power of criticism has increased so greatly in the later part of childhood and in the period of learning which extends over puberty that the pleasure in "liberated nonsense" only seldom dares to show itself directly. One does not venture to be absurd.[1]

This statement is applicable to Auden in a surprisingly large number of ways. For example, the description of the nonsense in the psychology of the child corresponds closely to the nature, tone, and material of the "childish" Mortmere fantasies. The Mortmere group did have a private language; it represented an indulgence in and use of infantile modes of behavior and expression; it was based on pleasure in nonsense; and it was rebellious in this use of nonsense. Certain of these Mortmere traits endure, in analagous forms, into Auden's later work; the hint of a private language remains behind the common analytic language of the thirties, and the trait Freud ascribes to nonsense, the primacy of the "pleasurable effect of rhythm and rhyme" over sense, corresponds to our impression that throughout Auden's work poetic form is a consideration prior to sense and often functions heuristically in the creation of a poem. But what makes Freud's description especially interesting for a study of Auden is the final disparity between the assumptions behind the statement and our understanding of Auden's character. To put it simply, with Auden, the Freudian dialectic of education does not work; although Auden does "grow out" of an early indulgence in nonsense, this growth is not marked by the psychological struggle of a pleasure-seeking *Ich* struggling to evade an iron reality but finally more or less bound by it in the bands of logic and the awesome distinction between true and not-true. From what we know of Auden's education this is biographically not the case. Auden was a university prankster, and one could try to relate this fact to Freud's comment that the child's rebellious and nonsensical pursuit of pleasure reasserts itself in the student's *Bierschwefel*, a state of soul characterized by the line in *Faust*, "Mit wenig Witz and viel Behagen" ("With little wit and much pleasure"); to make this connection, however, would be wrong.[2] Auden's early fantasies can hardly be equated with the muddy dullness and banal revelry of a *Bierschwefel* and are better described as activities pursued "Mit viel Witz und viel Behagen." The crucial

difference is that education for Auden was not a repressive disciplining of energies directed toward pleasure but rather something that aided him in his pursuit of pleasure through the exercise of wit; Spender's description of Auden at Oxford is of a person who took advantage of the years of relative leisure to "fulfill his potentialities, obtain satisfaction for his desires, and maintain his attitudes, without prejudice and without accepting any authority outside his own judgement."[3]

Similarly, in Auden's work one is unable to find any trace of a subjection of fantasy to reality by means of "logical thinking" and serious use of the distinction between "what is true and false in reality"; Auden makes continual use of this distinction, for one of the staples of his poetic rhetoric is to show how an attitude, emotion, or idea is in reality false, but this is a staple of *poetic* rhetoric, something dedicated to intellectual pleasure, and as such something far different from "distinguishing between the true and false *in reality*." The sense we have of Auden during the thirties is that he lived in a quirky, willful suspension of the true and false, that for him all experience was humorously interpreted as fictional; one side of his characteristic self-parody in seeming earnestness is to reveal all his experience as partly make-believe, and his role as an "Uncle Wiz" is one of a self-made figure of myth humorously conscious of his own unreality as such.

There are a number of ways to define Auden's peculiar suspension of the "laws" of reality. One has the sense that Auden's energy is never fully bound by the content of his ideas; there is always the feeling of a Dadaistic *Nichts* behind Auden's "beliefs," for they seem to be held as if they were "answers" to life; there is always the feeling that Auden's poetic formulations are provisional to the poem he is then writing and thus played with rather than believed; and one feels that Auden is more interested in the ritual of believing than in the belief itself. To these observations we can add still others, that Auden's assertions are generally derivative from other thinkers, that they are being used experimentally (an observation also relevant to Auden's use of poetic form, even when it is an eminently traditional one, such as the sonnet or the verse essay), that the ideas are used too often and in too many different contexts to cohere finally into a body of thought, and that Auden's changes of belief are to be explained not only as changes of heart but also as exhaustion of or boredom with the ideas. Behind all of these attempts to grasp what seems most elusive in Auden, his attitude toward the ideas he asserts, lies one basic and oddly simple axiom: Auden is always conscious of his ideas as a part of literary expression, and, as such, he sees their primary end to be pleasure rather than truth. If a poet like Auden, then, does have genuine beliefs, their authenticity will be based on something wholly outside the realm of verbal expression; to be sure, faith and poetry may overlap at certain points, but, in essence, the two realms are always distinct from one another.[4] That this conviction has considerable importance for Auden's practice as a poet will become clear later; here, it will be sufficient to note that it is implicit in Auden's habit of making use of extrapoetic dogmas for his poetry, be they from psychoanalysis, politics, or theology, and that it raises a unique aesthetic problem for Auden's poetry. The success of one of Auden's poems depends not only on how well he uses the ideas he has chosen for it; it also depends on how skillfully, tactfully, and justly he manages to incorporate the sense that he is pointing beyond the poem to some ulterior truth. In essence, one could argue that the problem is unsolvable, something that is supported by readers' frequent impatience with Auden's "schoolmasterly tone." If that which is pointed to is embedded too fully in the poem, then its authority as an extrapoetic truth is vitiated; if it is simply pointed to, then it is poetically unconvincing. Or, to put it another way: how can a poem establish something as an important truth, when its validity, by definition, is not within the province of the poem and may even be undermined when exposed to poetic treatment? Even if this problem remains unsolvable, it indicates what is perhaps the most sophisticated way to consider Auden's success in individual poems and development as a poet; rather than concentrating solely on the changes in his ideas or the fact that his poems become progressively richer in number and variety of ideas, we should examine how effectively he manages to bridge the gap between an avowedly fictional voice and the various truths he so persistently seeks to refer to. From this standpoint, much of his political writing during the thirties is dissatisfying; too often Auden's parodic voice and reliance on fantasy, by means of which he tries simultaneously to exhibit the inventiveness of fiction and to assert the truth of dogma, results in a confusion or lack of control of tone rather than a bridging of the gap between word and belief.

Given, then, the extent of the gap between Auden and his sources of the thirties, Marx and Freud, we are impelled to ask a second question: just why should Auden have been attracted to these particular thinkers, who are in many ways so alien to his personality and to each other? The answer to this question is not simply that Auden, as a mobile *Zeitgeist*, was in the forefront of the fashion of his time, although this fact is indeed quite important. There is also some pattern behind Auden's preoccupation with such unlike types, something we have encountered before in a different context. The synthesis of Marx and Freud forms a structure of thought which, when viewed with an eye to its possibilities, generates a large number of poetic ideas; Freud and Marx juxtaposed are as suggestive of poetic material as was the juxtaposition of disparate sources in *Paid on Both Sides* and "Journal of an Airman." What Auden has done is to pick two systems of thought that are widely divergent but comparable and complementary in a number of interesting ways. Both Freud and Marx serve to undermine the liberal tradition, and both unmask conventional notions of reality in order to reveal the real necessity behind them; and this dialectic is the rationale for most of Auden's early rhetoric. In addition, they are admirable complementaries, for they have staked out disparate but related territories for thought: Freud deals with the individual mind and Marx with social forces; Freud is concerned with inner necessity while Marx is a student of historical law. That Freud's perspective is in many ways antagonistic to that of Marx is not damaging; it becomes a positive good, for Auden can exercise his ingenuity in working out two such perspectives simultaneously and, in doing so, have the satisfaction of reconciling two apparently opposed philosophies, each of which claims to present a comprehensive explanation of reality. In thus reconciling dogmas, Auden would achieve what is, in a certain sense, a full picture of the world; it is a full picture that is achieved by ingeniously fitting two halves together.

That Auden's mind is stimulated by this process of "working out" the disparate systems is not evidenced by his poems alone; numerous examples of it occur in the essays, examples that reveal the ingenuity of Auden's mind more baldly than the poems. The clearest summary and contrast of psychology and communism occurs in Auden's essay "The Good Life":

Psychology and Communism have certain points in common:
(1) They are both concerned with unmasking hidden conflicts.
(2) Both regard these conflicts as inevitable stages which must be made to negate themselves.
(3) Both regard thought and knowledge not as something spontaneous and self-sufficient, but as purposive and determined by the conflict between instinctive needs and a limited environment. Communism stresses hunger and the larger social mass affected by it; psychology, love and the small family unit. (Biological nutrition is anterior to reproduction, so that the Communist approach would seem from this standpoint the more basic one.) . . .
(4) Both desire and believe in the possibility of freedom of action and choice, which can only be obtained by unmasking and making conscious the hidden conflict.

The hostility of Communism to psychology is that it accuses the latter of failing to draw correct conclusions from its data. Finding the neurotic a product of society, it attempts to adjust him to that society, i. e. it ignores the fact that the neurotic has a real grievance.[5]

What Auden has done is to put one system of ideas up against another and note the similarities and antagonisms; this rather mechanical process is carried out even more methodically at another place in the essay, where Auden makes a list (u,b,x,y) of possible answers to a question posed of communism, social democracy, Christianity, and psychology, and then answers that question for each item by listing after it the relevant symbols.

To call this habit of mind simply mechanical is of course not enough; it is indeed that, but it is also related to a variety of more significant characteristics of Auden's way of thought. Such a cast of mind, especially when seen in its more complex forms, is a mark of one who enjoys playing with structures of thought for their own sakes. For example, in his book reviews, Auden enjoys creating instant frameworks of thought, be they of literary history or of structural analysis, within which the book in question may be placed; in *The Enchafed Flood*, on the other hand, Auden generates a theory of romanticism from a limited number of works of writers of different orders of seriousness and different backgrounds (Wordsworth, Melville, Baudelaire, Ibsen, Valéry, and Lewis Carroll), and the resulting theory, though capricious and unsatisfying as literary scholarship, is a source of more exciting individual ideas than many of the products of systematic scholarship. In such a poem as "Out on the lawn I lie in bed" one sees a similar process at work; a union of Freud and Marx provides a structure of ideas generative of some very beautiful and seemingly quite personal poetic language. That Auden is stimulated by playing with structures of thought, and turns especially to systematic thinkers for his ideas, is related to other predispositions; Auden's imposition of strictures on what could go into his fantasy landscape of mines and decayed industry aided him in the construction of a childhood fantasy world, and he has been consistently drawn to playing with predetermined literary forms.

A person who enjoys playing with structures of thought may have much in common with certain very recognizable types, types to which Auden has often been compared. First, there is much of the schoolboy and the scholar in someone whose ideas are generated by outside material with which he concerns himself. Both the impulse to work the material out into a lively order and the provisionality of that order to the purpose at hand are characteristic of the intellectual student, in whom the schoolboy asserts himself in an impulse toward irresponsibility and latent parody of thought and in whom the scholar is evident in the more serious ingenuity of the impulse to capture and explain as much material as possible by means of intellectual constructs. At the same time, when a variety of ideas is carried lightly, with a certain elegance, with the knowledge of the traditions behind these ideas, and with a cultivated pleasure at being able to draw so readily upon these ideas for entertaining discourse, we encounter the type of the sophisticated man; for this man, expression is peculiarly derivative from language, both from his pleasure in his command of language and literary form and from what he has encountered in the form of language, that is, all that he has read and absorbed.[6]

It is time now to turn directly to the word that has been used over and over again in this book to describe the spirit behind Auden's verse—the word "play"; we can no longer use this word without some attempt to explain exactly how it applies to Auden. In Auden's commonplace book, *A Certain World*, he notes the famous assertion made by Friedrich Schiller in his *On the Aesthetic Education of Man*: "Man only plays when, in the full meaning of the word, he is a man, and he is only completely a man when he plays." This sense of play is certainly applicable to the civilized humanism of much of Auden's verse; nevertheless, we must make distinctions between what Schiller meant by the word "play" and what we mean in applying it to Auden. Schiller's statement about play is meant to be ultimately "capable of bearing the whole edifice of the art of the beautiful, and of the still more difficult art of living."[7] We are concerned with understanding play only insofar as it helps us to speak of a particular kind of verse. One clue that shows us how we must limit our understanding of "play" is provided by the advice given to Schiller (which he did not take) to avoid the use of the word "*spielen*" (to play) because of "*unedle Nebenideen*" ("ignoble connotations"), that is, its connection with such activities as *Skatspielen* ("playing Skat," the card game); Schiller kept the word because he did not want to sever all connection between ordinary language and activities and a theory of art finally oriented toward the sublime.[8] With Auden, however, it is exactly the ordinary meaning of "play" that is crucial to defining his kind of art. Auden is a player, a gamesman, for whom art is the most difficult, various, and interesting of games, to be played at its best with a masterful skill, and a successful poem is characterized by all the delight and vividness of a game in which all of one's faculties are provisionally engaged, that is, engaged for the purpose of that game.

Notes

1. Sigmund Freud, *Jokes and Their Relation to the Unconscious,* in *The Standard Edition of the Complete Psychological Works of Sigmund Freud*, ed. James Strachey (London: The Hogarth Press, 1960), VIII, 126–127.
2. Ibid., p. 126.
3. Spender, *World within World* (London: Hamish Hamilton, 1951), p. 53.
4. One of Auden's attempts to define the areas of overlap should be quoted here; in an essay, "Writing," in *The Dyer's Hand* (New York: Random House, 1948), p. 19, he makes the following comment about poetry and belief: "What makes it difficult for a poet not to tell lies is that, in poetry, all facts and all beliefs cease to be true or false and become interesting possibilities. The reader does not have to share the beliefs expressed in a poem in order to enjoy it. Knowing this, a poet is constantly tempted to make use of an idea of a belief, not because he believes it to be true. but because he sees that it has interesting poetic possibilities. It may not, perhaps, be absolutely necessary that he *believe* it, but it is certainly necessary that his emotions be deeply involved, and this they can never be unless, as a man, he takes it more seriously than as a mere poetic contrivance."
5. *Christianity and the Social Revolution*, ed. J. Lewis, K. Polanyi, and D. Kitchin (New York: Scribner, 1936), pp. 46–47.

6. R. Roth's essay, "The Sophistication of W. H. Auden: A Sketch in Longinian Method," *Modern Philology*, 48 (1951), 193–204, illustrates well Auden's sophistication as a writer of elegies. Roth's attempt to see in Auden a sublime poet is less commendable.
7. Schiller, *On the Aesthetic Education of Man*, trans. E. M. Wilkinson and L. A. Willoughby (Oxford: Clarendon Press, 1967), pp. 107–109.
8. Ibid., pp. 331–332.

EDWARD MENDELSON
From "The Watershed"
Early Auden
1981, pp. 37–44

The guarded border between Auden and any real satisfaction is too strong to be breached by sex. In Auden's earliest poems sex often serves less as a means of achieving union than as a way to evade the risks of any "real meeting" involving more than instinct. When couples go "pairing off in twos and twos," they know the proper physical act but they resolve nothing: "Each knowing what to do / But of no use." When they separate again, they are still of no use, for they will not risk a different way of life, and end their relations with a cyclical return, "Saying good-bye but coming back, for fear / Is over there." "Over there" is not a particular place, but the hidden internal source of division, "the centre of anger" that the couples make no effort to invade or change. It is safely "out of danger."

These gnomic lines are taken from "Again in conversations," a poem written early in 1929, in which sex is as empty as repetitious talk. Auden transforms this poem's declarative mood into a highly ironic imperative in a poem written a few months later, where his voice warns against the dangerous crossing from isolation to fulfillment. The poem opens on a border, "Upon this line between adventure." Best to remain here, it says, best to "Prolong the meeting out of good nature." Here good-natured sexual relations are safe; elsewhere wait the emotional dangers of commitment or abandonment:

> Forward or back are menaces.
> On neither side let foot slip over
> Invading Always, exploring Never,
> For this is hate and this is fear . . .

Instead, "On narrowness stand," where there is "No anger, no traitor, but peace."

"Peace" is less satisfactory than it may sound. Auden used the word in two related ways: when it actually occurs, peace is an evasion of real barriers and cannot endure; when it does not occur, peace is the longed-for state of real unity that can never be achieved. A real and stable peace is unattainable, for man's ordinary condition is one of anxiety and war. An unpublished 1930 poem opens with the line: "Renewal of traditional anger in peace." Real division, inherited from the traditional past, survives the diplomats' treaties. The act of love, in "Taller to-day," may interrupt anger with a moment of "peace / No bird can contradict," peace that although "passing . . . is sufficient now." But it is sufficient only "For something fulfilled this hour, loved or endured." The poem leaves open the question whether that hour was a real fulfillment or an interval when the otherwise harrowing fact of separation was peacefully tolerated. But there is an implied emphasis in Auden's choice of *endured* as the poem's final word.

The war that peace occasionally interrupts is a civil war between the broken fragments of a whole. Its forces are the mutually opposed efforts toward wholeness made by different halves of a divided city or divided self. This civil war, as Auden wrote to Isherwood in a verse letter in April 1929, is "our study and our interest."

> Although your medium is that other, Christopher,
> The most prodigious of literary forms,
> To both this is our study and our interest:
> The fortunes and manoeuvres of this civil war,
> Man's opposite strivings for entropic peace,
> Retreat to lost homes or advance to new . . .

"Entropic peace," the peace of stasis or of dissolved distinctions, is to be found, man hopes, in "homes." Yet these homes belong either to the imaginary past or to a future yet to be achieved. The home or house (the word transcribed as "homes" is possibly "houses" in the manuscript) bears a special symbolic burden here: it is the place of an enclosed self-protective peace that is ultimately too fragile to survive. The civil war of *Paid on Both Sides* is a feud between two houses. The feud's hatred has "made a slum, / Houses at which the passer shakes his fist," while the failure of an attempted peace-making brings "the fall of an old house." The wanderer in "Doom is dark" must "leave his house," as the rider who escapes the unresolved divisions of *The Orators* rides "Out of this house." And in "Watch any day his nonchalant pauses," the repressed sophisticate who appears to be free, but is really "not that returning conqueror," stands in uneasy balance, "poised between shocking falls" which he avoids by

> Travelling by daylight on from house to house
> The longest way to the intrinsic peace.

This restates Auden's lines about "entropic peace" in his verse letter to Isherwood: the intrinsic peace is the real peace never to be attained by the divided—not through a safe daylight journey, not through any journey at all. Any deliberate movement toward satisfaction must be asymptotic and incomplete. The quest heroes of legends and fables, "The silly fool" and "The youngest son" who finally achieve their quests, are wishful fantasies, "tales in tales / Where no one fails."

Like any young man half-convinced of his superiority over the bourgeoisie from which he sprang, the young Auden tries to exempt himself from his criticism of "Man's opposite strivings." Looking down on the world around him, he sees little else than automatic processes of neurosis operating in other people. His verse letter to Isherwood details the "pity" he feels for the neurotic helplessness of his fellow man. "Our study and our interest," he tells his fellow author, is

> To trace his [man's] strategies of compensation
> "The North West Passage" to give your name to it,
> To pity his own penalties for this,
> See love transform itself to influenza
> And guilty rashes, speeding descent
> Of noble spirit, the brakes burnt out.

"The North West Passage" was Isherwood's term for the neurotic evasion of life, the elaborate compensation one makes for refusing to face one's desires and experiences directly. Auden elaborated in his 1929 journal: *Compensation is sin. The devil offers substitute pleasures for the divine will. Neurotic pain is the principle of Dante's Inferno. The North-West passage.*

Neuroses are substitute pleasures. What are the authentic ones? Auden's answer is complex and partly self-contradictory. He wrote in another 1929 journal entry:

> *Pleasure*
>   The error of Freud and most psychologists is making pleasure a negative thing, progress towards a

state of rest. This is only one half of pleasure and the least important half. Creative pleasure is, like pain, an increase in tension. What does the psychologist make of contemplation and joy?

> The essence of creation is doing things for no reason, it is pointless. Possessive pleasure is always rational. Freud you see really believes that pleasure is immoral, i.e. happiness is displeasing to God.

> If you believe this of course the death wish becomes the most important emotion, and "reinstatement of an earlier condition" [a quotation from *Beyond the Pleasure Principle*]. Entropy is another name for despair.

Man's strivings for entropic peace amount to the despair of the death wish. "Creative pleasure" has nothing to do with personal or sexual peace; it is the making of a poem, an act that increases tension and division. To enjoy life, make a poem out of it.

Freud saw a basic opposition between Eros and Thanatos, between the two great organic impulses toward sex and death. For Auden this opposition was false. Both impulses are similar movements toward entropy, and the real opposition is between these impulses and the impulse toward creative separation:

> The question is what do we mean by sex. The union or the fission of sex cells, i.e. love or hate. Freud makes sex the first and places it in opposition to the death wish. It seems to me jolly similar. . . . The real "life-wish" is the desire for separation, from family, from one's literary predecessors.

These lines attempt to realize the life-wish they describe, for the predecessor from whom Auden is separating himself in them is Freud—whose work he discovered when his father began using the new psychology in his school medical practice around 1920, when Auden was thirteen. Auden was the first imaginative writer in English to take Freud seriously—Lawrence dismissed him, Joyce derided him, everyone else ignored him—but his earliest comments on Freud take the form of arguments over psychoanalytic doctrine. "The trouble with Freud," Auden wrote in his 1929 journal, "is that he accepts conventional morality as if it were the only one." Against Freud's quietist and conservative tendencies Auden praised the activist and progressive impulses of the psyche. Later, in 1935, he would include a compendium of Freud's teachings in an essay on "Psychology and Art To-day," and in 1939 he made him the subject of a great didactic elegy. But the detailed psychological theory in Auden's poems derived less from Freud himself than from such variously heterodox psychologists as Trigant Burrow, Georg Groddeck, Eugen Bleuler, and William McDougall. In his interpretations of artists, Auden wrote in *Letter to Lord Byron*, "Freud's not quite O.K."

His argument with Freud was in part an argument with himself. As a piece of high romantic rhetoric, Auden's statement that the real life-wish is separation from the past is unexceptionable, but it contradicts everything Auden was saying elsewhere. In his verse letter to Isherwood, written during the same month as these journal entries, he refers to man's "own penalties," the penalties he inflicts on himself for his evasions of life and for his compensations. The only penalty the poem names is psychosomatic disease: he and Isherwood see repressed "love transform itself to influenza / And guilty rashes." In his journal Auden glosses these lines in a list—headed "Body and Soul"—of "hatreds" and their consequent ills:

> Hatred of the flesh. Physical Inferiority.
> Hatred of other people. Social Inferiorities.
> Hatred of physical love.

Boils. Skin diseases.
Infectious diseases.
Influenza.

On the one hand Auden is praising "separation" as the "real 'life-wish' " that opposes the death wish—which includes the wish for sex. On the other hand, he is condemning those who separate themselves by "hatred" and thereby generate disease. Separation is not precisely identical with hatred, but the two are closely similar, and Auden exalts the one while scorning the other.[1] A few months later, in the final section of "It was Easter as I walked," he will complicate matters further by writing that love *needs* death.

The edginess of Auden's early poems is partly the result of this internal contradiction. Auden at the border, Auden braving the frontier, wants to be part of a "*real* whole," to achieve a "real meeting"—but at the same time he revels in the proud creative separation that lets him look down at the world as the hawk does or the helmeted airman. Auden's indecision at the border, at the crux left of the watershed, began as indecision over how to move in space, but before long he elaborated it into the realm of time. He wanted the separation that comes with adulthood and literary maturity, "separation from family, from one's literary predecessors." But his manner was never limited to the detached laboratory stoicism that, to his first readers, offered the thrill of the absolutely up-to-date. At moments of special emotional intensity in his poems, usually moments of violent disruption or conclusive loss, a different and older note was to be heard—a faint but clear and distinct echo of Old English poems or Icelandic sagas. Auden wanted to find a language of his own, "and in our time," but he also found himself using a language of the distant past to express his experience of isolation in the present.

Just as the violence of his early poems is retained and transformed in later ones, so, correspondingly, the unbroken sense of literary tradition that informs Auden's mature work is prefigured among his modernist fragments. Auden's initial literary problem was to find independence from his literary ancestors while at the same time finding a language to write in. His reworkings of saga fragments and his echoes of Old English—both in his alliterative metres and in his direct quotations from *Beowulf*,[2] "The Wanderer," "The Battle of Maldon," "Wulf and Eadwacer"—are all elements of his solution. Since no poetic language can be entirely new, Auden deliberately sought his language outside the main line of transmission. When he spoke of the gangster-ethic of the sagas, he was not altogether disapproving, for it provided his language with an air of primitive illegality. In *The Orators* he added the more modern illegalities of underworld cant.[3]

At first, Auden's resistance to the recent literary past and his recovery of more ancient sources—both for the purpose of finding his own poetic energies—served to intensify romantic literary modes. Pound's "discovery" of Provençal and Chinese had achieved a roughly similar purpose some years before. Yet while Auden's new style severed him from the tradition favored by the immediately preceding generation, a tradition which found its ideal in the Mediterranean Renaissance, it also joined him to a very different tradition, the archaic Nordic one. Later he would recognize that his desire for a literary tradition was stronger than his wish for independence and would make his allusions and echoes more explicit. The rhymed octosyllabic couplets of *New Year Letter* in 1940, like the Horatian stanzas of many of his poems in the late 1930s, are confident of their wholeness and adequacy, as modernism's broken forms can never be, and are confident of their integration with a pre-romantic past. They learned their confidence from Auden's Old English illegalities in earlier years.

There are parallels in Auden's double sense of style— illegal yet traditional—to his double sense of history. Although he expressed vividly, in "Writing" and elsewhere, the historical nostalgia he inherited from modernism, he would constantly deny that there had ever been a past worthy of regret or that our present divisions could ever be repaired. Yet in using Old English and Icelandic literature to describe these divisions he established a literary continuity. Even when writing poetic fragments, he did not adopt the fragmentation into different national languages—bits of German, Sanskrit, Chinese— found in Eliot and Pound. His "raw provincial" taste at school for Hardy and Edward Thomas may have prepared him, when he grew more sophisticated, to make pre-Norman English the basis of his poetic language, but it did not make him insular. Its effect was to make him naturalize in his own style his exotic borrowings from Rimbaud or Hölderlin or Dante; he did not call attention to their foreignness and distance, or leave them estranged as they would have been in *The Waste Land* or *The Cantos*.[4]

Notes

1. Auden's account of the "real 'life-wish' " as separation is related to the Freudian account of the Oedipal crisis but is not derived from it. Rather, both derive from a basic and anterior romantic impulse: the urge toward self-creation, the wish to be responsible for one's being without suffering the insult of having been created by someone else.

2. The title *Paid on Both Sides*, Laurence Heyworth has discovered, is a potsherd from *Beowulf*, line 1305, possibly adapted from John R. Clark Hall's 1901 prose translation: "That was no good exchange— that they should pay on both sides with the lives of friends."

3. "Journal of an Airman" alludes to "a tan-armed *gonsil* or a *first-of-May*," meaning a homosexual boy and a young tramp. Ode IV has the line, "Youth's on the march' says *Jocker* to *Prushun*"—i.e. a pederastic tramp addressing his young companion.

4. Early in his career Auden found another poet using a similar but narrower method of naturalizing the past, and for about a year he wrote some of his poems in direct imitation of that poet's voice. Laura Riding's 1928 volume *Love as Love, Death as Death* takes over the diction of Emily Dickinson and, indirectly, the metres of John Skelton and uses them in modern style, more fragmented and syncopated than the originals. Dickinson and Skelton were among Auden's adolescent enthusiasms, but he had not yet found a way of using them in his adult work. So when Laura Riding showed how, he followed her example. Riding's "All Nothing, Nothing" begins: "The standing-stillness, / The from foot-to-foot, / Is no real illness, / Is no real fever . . ." An Auden poem of 1930 begins: "This lunar beauty / Has no history / Is complete and early . . ."— and a half-dozen other poems from 1929–30 show similar ventriloquisms. The kinds of poety he wanted to write after 1930 required a less thin-lipped style, and so he worked Emily Dickinson out of his system and began taking his Skelton, like his Old English, straight from the source.

JOHN R. BOLY
From "Auden and the Romantic Tradition in
The Age of Anxiety"
Daedalus, Summer 1982, pp. 149–53

Auden's vision of romantic origins is complex, but it is possible to get an overview of his position by using as our major texts three of his works, *The Prolific and the Devourer*, *The Enchafed Flood*, and *The Dyer's Hand*. Essentially, Auden saw romanticism as embodying the main dilemma of Western culture. In the Renaissance, a new humanism, intent upon championing the heroic individual, discarded the impediments of medieval Catholicism's authoritarian church and absolutist metaphysics. It was to be the era of rational man, distrustful of what could not be seen and touched, secure in his newfound powers of empirical method and scientific invention.

The official faith of the new humanism, Auden maintained, was the Protestant religion, which he tended to associate with a Calvinist expediency. Protestantism, in Auden's view, did not mean the nonexistence of metaphysical absolutes and spiritual reality, but it did mean their irrelevance. Accordingly, the Protestant compromise split the new humanist into an outer man governed by reason and the profit motive, and an inner man governed by sentiment and such glimpses of the divine light as grace and election vouchsafed. The outer man soon discovered that reason could justify anything, so he often became a hypocrite ruled by the genteel coercion of respectable appearances. The inner man, cast alone into the underworld of the subconscious, suffered the worse fate of perennial guilt. Without the symbols and liturgies of the discarded Catholicism—which during the post-Tridentine period was itself becoming emptily formalized—he had no mythic guide through the labyrinth of his own inwardness. Harrowing hell on his own, Protestant man discovered anew the depths of his depravity. He also discovered anew, well before Freud, the technique of ignoring that depravity through repression and its displacements.

Romanticism emerged as the new humanism's response to its own sense of discontent and failure. As would be expected in an empirical culture, romanticism began with an indisputable factual observation: the world created by a cold and calculating rationalism was a wasteland of dead mechanism and compulsive repetition, Blake's dark Satanic mills. In a double heresy, romanticism thus rejected both the Protestant split between outer and inner man and the rationalist faith in the sole privilege of reason to govern the external world. "The whole complex of ideas which we call romanticism," Auden wrote in *The Prolific and the Devourer*, "is the attempt of Protestantism to find its own brand of Catholic unity, as the evil effects of separating the private and public life become apparent."[1] Henceforth, the real man of inwardly discovered passion and energy was to turn the fallen world into the New Jerusalem. But after its always brilliant beginnings, the romantic theocracy of inwardness soon ran into serious trouble. It in effect unleashed the Protestant nightmare of a guilt-ridden, hag-ridden subconscious into the daylit, conscious world. At first, this unleashing was symbolic, an aesthetic liberation of new and exciting energies. But eventually Caliban leapt off the stage and into the audience. Rightly or wrongly, Auden saw the English and European political arena of the thirties, together with its disastrous aftermath in the following decade, as the grim proving ground of romantic kerygma. In a famous passage from "Spain 1937," he pointedly rejected romanticism's naive faith that the god of unleashed desire could build a New Jerusalem:

> What's your proposal? To build the Just City? I will,
> I agree. Or is it the suicide pact, the romantic
> Death?[2]

One could easily argue against this too simple view (as Auden himself did in *New Year Letter*), but that would be beside the point. With so radical a critic, the important thing is to find the threatening truth within his hyperboles.

Auden realized that both rationalism and romanticism were offshoots of the same Renaissance humanism, and as such, both attempted to found an absolute system on the capacities of a finite creature. But it is an ancient paradox that man, whether as mind or soul, is neither autonomous nor complete. When he tries to be, he becomes the victim either of a lifeless objectivity or an inchoate subjectivity. Romantic heretics were quick to see the limits of rational humanism, and every visionary since Blake has in one way or another resisted the "mind-forg'd" manacles that chain the imagination to a dead world of space and time. But as humanists themselves, they were slower to learn that the energies imprisoned in the subconscious, though as necessary as reason, were also incapable of delivering finite man from his plight of mortality. The romantic humanist, intent upon self-divinization, had to pretend that desire was creatively godlike and somehow eternal. Yet romantic demonologies, from Coleridge's Christabel to Eliot's Belladonna, proved the Protestant truth that desire was as readily destructive; and the notorious brevity of romantic inspiration, significantly the most obsessive theme of the new movement, proved that desire was tragically short-lived. Romantic humanism was consequently forced into a complex strategy of repression, in which its god was paradoxically denied through a truncated mythos, and its fears displaced into a compensatory poetics.

It took Auden most of the thirties to work out his objections to both rationalist and romantic versions of humanism, and as is well known, at the end of that decade he converted to Christianity. This may be seen, depending upon one's interpretive standpoint, either as a radical departure or a cowering retreat. Here I would suggest that Auden's conversion arose from his determination to regain contact with the strength of romantic origins, and that a decisive literary influence on his conversion was the mythmaking of William Blake. Auden discovered through Blake a visionary theism, closely related to the *philosophia perennis* of mystical religion, that formed within romanticism a countermovement to its humanist origins. Such theism is not involved with the moralistic and dogmatic codes of orthodox religion, for which Auden had as little regard as did Blake for Deism, or Kierkegaard for Christendom. Still less is it to be confused with such pseudomysticisms as vitalism, pantheism, or occultism, which are simply displaced projections of subconscious energies. Rather, the center of this theism is to be found in an absolute and enabling love, whose creative power is best thought of as the realizing consciousness—infinite, because containing all places, and eternal, because containing all times—that is therefore the absolute ground of the individual consciousness. This is the "I" as pure subject rather than relative object, the final perceiver presupposed by any perception, who dwells in the eternal moment and is symbolized as God. To the visionary theist, the crisis is not in finding this absolute, but in withstanding its relentless presence. And for those few who can, the perception of the jumbled fragments of space and time gives way to the discovery of eternity, the archetypal symbols and mythic patterns of involution and evolution.

Blake portrays this act of discovery in his great monomyth of creation and fall, redemption and apocalypse. Although there has been a critical tendency to set Blake apart from the other romantics, his splendidly elaborated myth traces the same recurrent passage that Geoffrey Hartman has found most crucial to all romantic and postromantic poetry, leading "from self-consciousness to imagination."[3] Within this passage, humanism as the despairing divinization of finite faculties gives way to the enabling presence discovered in visionary theism. To use Blake's virtual ideograph, natural Orc gives way to divinely empowered Los. And Blake is not alone. Shelley's Prometheus bound must give way to Prometheus unbound; Keats's Hyperion, to Apollo; Wordsworth's solitary, to the wanderer. Nor does romantic theory necessarily lag behind romantic practice. In Coleridge's brilliant deconstructive analysis of poetic inspiration in the *Biographia Literaria*, both rationally bound fancy and subconsciously bound Secondary Imagination must give way to the mystical presence dwelling in the Primary Imagination. To pursue Hartman's argument a bit further, romanticism in such apocalyptic passages betrays its humanist origins by recovering the sense of an absolute and enabling metaphysical ground, a ground beyond the subconscious psyche and its energies.

The interplay within romanticism of its theist and humanist elements is a fascinating process. But for our purposes, it suffices to note that Auden saw the tradition as gradually succumbing, in its later postromantic and modernist phases, to the humanist limitations inherent in its historical emergence. It tried to pretend that Orc or one of his relatives—Dionysus, Eros, Prometheus, or Priapus—was God. And since they were not, it was paradoxically forced to dismember and scatter the very gods it was supposed to liberate. Romantic humanism thus became a kerygma of repression, whose main liturgical acts were the inhibition and subsequent exaltation of desire, which was not deified but only displaced, and which became dangerously deformed in the process.[4]

This is an extreme claim, but Auden's reading of the romantic tradition has been recently corroborated by one of the most adventurous of romanticism's critics. In his theoretical studies since *The Anxiety of Influence*, Harold Bloom has powerfully explored the romantic humanist's, or strong poet's, retrojection of anxiety from the mortal terminus that he cannot control, to the poetic origins that he can at least pretend to. Since absolute self-sufficiency would confer immortality, Bloom argues, the strong poet is hellishly bent on apotheosizing himself through some myth of self-derivation. But unfortunately, every poet knows that poems are made, not out of nothing, but out of other poems. Hence, the poet's path to the Eden of self-derivation is blocked by some Covering Cherub of a precursor. (Derived from Ezekiel, 28: 13–16, the Covering Cherub symbolizes the repressive fears and compensating delusions that prevent man from reaching the Tree of Life.) This ancestral figure enforces the confession of derivation, the mortality implicit in a coming into, and therefore a going out of, time, which the strong poet is doomed to deny. In the melancholy logic of romantic humanism, then, poetry lapses into a sadistic cycle in which the death-dealing precursor must be repressed, slain, and then guiltily imitated. The cycle is entropic as well, charting a general deterioration in the tradition, because the slain ancestor is ultimately another Orc, a figure of the poet's own lost energies. As Bloom sums up in *Poetry and Repression*: "Poetry, revisionism, and repression verge upon a melancholy identity, an identity that is broken afresh by every new strong poem, and mended afresh by the same poem."[5] So inevitable is this logic, that Bloom, a painstaking and acute reader of texts, has convincingly shown its manifestation in a sixfold syntagm of modes and tropes that dominate post-Enlightenment poetry.

The difference between Auden's earlier deconstruction of romantic humanism and Bloom's later, more pessimistic version is the difference between the pure critic and the poet-critic. As an aspiring visionary, Auden had a personal stake in liberating poetry from the crippling consequences of romantic repression. To enable that liberation, he resorted to an adventurous misreading of Freud, a misreading he later supplanted with one of the few hopeful elements in Kierkegaard's anguished dynamic of faith. In an important article, "Psychology and Art To-Day," published in 1936, Auden acknowledged the subtle, but unvarying, disguises of displacement with which repression defends itself: conflation, inversion, reemphasis, and of course symbolization. But in noting the difference between fantasy and art, Auden insisted that art, because it emerges from a unified cultural system with a coherence of its own, is capable of forcing displacement to become self-revelatory. Analyzing the dream of a morphia addict, which

impressed him as belonging more to art than fantasy, Auden wrote: "Not only has the censor transformed the latent content of the dream into symbols but the dream itself is no longer a simple wish fulfillment, it has become constructive, and, if you like, moral." The agent of repression, the defensive censor of the imperiled ego, frantically or cleverly displaces; but then the dream itself, the means of repression, subverts the censor by revealing the truth through those displacements. Auden ends by imputing to Freud the questionably Freudian notion that *repression is not cyclical but teleological and even self-limiting:* "Not only what we recognise as sin or crime, but all illness, is purposive. It is an attempt at cure." Freud at times saw the analyst, armed with the rationally explicative devices that Jung found so inadequate, as the hero, a restorer of the mature and adult ego. But Auden's metaphor of cure finds within the very process of displacement a revelatory and potentially evolutionary force.

Notes

1. *Antaeus* no. 42 (Summer 1981): 49.
2. *The English Auden,*, edited by Edward Mendelson (New York: Random House, 1977), p. 211.
3. "Romanticism and Anti-Self-Consciousness," in *Beyond Formalism* (New Haven: Yale University Press, 1970), p. 307.
4. An excellent background study on the relation of repression to mythic tradition is Paul Diel's *Symbolism in Greek Mythology*, translated by Vincent Stuart, Micheline Stuart, and Rebecca Folkman (Boulder, Colorado: Shambhala, 1980), which applies to a body of classical myths the clinical theories of Diel's earlier *Psychologie de la Motivation* (Paris: Presses universitaires de France, 1948). Though not a theist, Diel nonetheless shows that repression originates in a fear of mortality that drives the psyche into a desperate attempt to deify itself through an exaltation of displaced desires. But such exaltation is inseparable from inhibition, because it means ignoring other desires, rather than acknowledging and integrating them. The resulting guilt, which arises from the psyche's recognition of what it has done to itself by imprisoning part of its energies in the subconscious, is what the neurotic is miserably aware of. But guilt is only an effect whose real cause lies in a preceding exaltation, of which the neurotic is typically quite proud. For Diel, the key to understanding repression is to see that its component halves of inhibition and exaltation are both consequences of the same elemental fear, and that each intensifies the other, so that repression becomes a self-perpetuating cycle, symbolized by the ouroboros, or serpent consuming itself.
5. *Poetry and Repression* (New Haven: Yale University Press, 1976), p. 27.

EDWARD CALLAN

From "The Post-Romantic Hero"

Auden: *A Carnival of Intellect*

1983, pp. 252–59

Beginning with "Sonnets from China' in 1938, and thereafter in the poetry and criticism of his middle years, Auden toned down the Byronism of his early work and began to represent the ideal heroic figure as one who is primarily a restorer and renewer; whose creativity thrives on limitations; and who might take for a motto Goethe's lines that Auden liked to quote:

> A master shows his powers in limitations
> And freedom follows from the rule of law.

One of his lecture topics as Professor of Poetry at Oxford in 1960 was "The Hero in Modern Poetry," and a subsequent essay, "The Poet and The City," defines this hero in capsule terms: "The characteristic style of 'Modern' poetry is an intimate tone of voice. . . . And its characteristic hero is neither the 'Great Man' nor the romantic rebel, both doers of extraordinary deeds, but the man or woman in any walk of life who, despite all the impersonal pressures of modern society, manages to acquire and preserve a face of his own." There are heroes of this kind in his own later poems, including, for example, the memorial poems for his housekeeper at Kirchstetten, Emma Eiermann, and for his physician in New York, David Protetch. But however much the notion of the hero in literature may differ from one age to another, Auden's definition in *The Enchafèd Flood* accords him the same characteristic marks at all times: "The exceptional individual is one who possesses authority over the average. This authority can be of three kinds, aesthetic, ethical and religious." Auden rejects the doers of extraordinary deeds as having authentic authority in our time, but he accords this authority—in its three kinds—to less flamboyant models. His 1969 poem "Moon Landing" satirizes that space-age achievement as "a phallic triumph"—"a grand gesture" by "our apparatniks,"—and he prays on history's behalf that "artists, / chefs and saints"—representing the aesthetic, ethical and religious modes—"may still appear to blithe it." Kierkegaard's triad remains his touchstone, and it is no surprise to find that his heroic ideal for our time combines in some degree qualities of imagination, reason, and belief corresponding to the three spheres of authority. Among the exemplary figures whose authority his later poems invoked are, in the aesthetic sphere, Horace and Goethe—both of whom restored Greek meters; in the ethical sphere, Dag Hammarskjöld—a man confronted with the practical task of finding more workable solutions to international problems than the "big" answers offered by nuclear stockpiles; and Isaiah, the prophet of renewal, whose image for society's malaise is fallen city walls that need rebuilding: "Look, I am laying a stone in Zion, a block of granite, a precious cornerstone for a firm foundation. . . ."

His two exemplars in the aesthetic sphere, Horace and Goethe, were skilled in the craft of verse. Horace transformed Aeolian lyric meters (especially those of Sappho and Alcaeus) into equally musical Latin rhythms; and Goethe, in turn, fitted these meters to German, as Auden did to English. For some sixteen years before he died—the period of his summer residence at Kirchstetten—Auden's work became increasingly Horatian in style and attitude. He caught the Horatian tone and spirit to greatest perfection in such poems as "The Horatians" and "Ode to Terminus" in *City Without Walls* (1969), and in many of the poems in *Epistle to a Godson* (1972).

While the example of Horace, and at times of Goethe, dominates these poems technically, their intellectual cutting edge is honed on the ideas of such modern thinkers as Karl Jaspers, Martin Buber, and Dag Hammarskjöld. Auden's later poems are commonly about man's situation in the present; and in particular about the need for an *authentic* response to life in the sense that Karl Jaspers uses the term. Jaspers defined *authenticity* as the determination to affirm life again and again; the willingness to persist in creative activity in spite of seeming futility. One could describe Dag Hammarskjöld's diary, *Markings*, as a search for such authentic existence; and Martin Buber—whose phrase "the hallowing of the everyday" to some extent summed up its essence—advocated this authentic response to life. Hammarskjöld admired Buber's thought and volunteered to translate *I and Thou* into Swedish even while burdened by his immediate duties as Secretary General of the United Nations. He was working at this translation on board the plane that carried him to his death during a mission to the Congo in 1961. Hammarskjöld left behind the private diary which Auden—with the help of Leif Sjöberg—translated into

English and published under the title *Markings*. Auden alludes to it in a stanza of "The Horatians":

> Some of you have written poems, usually
> short ones, and some kept diaries, seldom published
>   till after your deaths, but most
>   make no memorable impact . . .

Few modern lives are lived at Hammarskjöld's level of intensity. Consequently the closing lines of "The Horatians" assert that those who create in minor forms, who "hymn the small but journal wonders,"—live no less authentically than the great masters or the "authentic martyrs." This category of "authentic martyrs," which could include such dedicated men as Dag Hammarskjöld, is represented in "The Horatians" by Regulus, the Roman hostage of the Carthaginians who, sent by his captors as an emissary to Rome to arrange a truce, returned (having advised to the contrary) and submitted to their death sentence as he had promised:

> You thought well of your Odes, Flaccus, and believed they
> would live, but knew, and have taught your descendants to
>   say with you: "As makers go,
>   compared with Pindar or any
> of the great foudroyant masters who don't ever
> amend, we are, for all our polish, of little
>   stature, and, as human lives,
>   compared with authentic martyrs
> like Regulus, of no account. We can only
> do what it seems to us we were made for, look at
>   this world with a happy eye
>   but from a sober perspective."

In general, Auden's representative Horatians are busy creative spirits who heal the sick, tend libraries, or enjoy the art of cooking. (The phrase about the "happy eye" alludes to an aphorism of Wittgenstein's that Auden and Louis Kronenberger included in *The Viking Book of Aphorisms*: "Is it the essence of the artistic way of looking at things that it looks at the world with a happy eye?") Absorbed in a vocation, Horatians escape the prevailing malaise: the boredom and sense of estrangement that obsesses those for whom work is a meaningless function divorced from life. When the language of the city is infected with chronic vagueness, the Horatians heal it; when the Barbarians destroy its walls, the Horatians rebuild them. In the face of unending violence and fashionable excess, they pay their dutiful devotion to Terminus the Mentor, god of limits and boundaries, as Auden does in "Ode to Terminus," where the strict syllabic stanzas are an appropriate offering to the god of meter:

> Gods of walls, doors and reticence, nemesis
> overtakes the sacrilegious technocrat,
>   but blessed is the City that thanks you
>   for giving us games and grammar and meters.

For citizens not blessed with a capacity for "games and grammar and meters" these stanzas may serve to show that just as Horace renewed and transformed Greek lyric measures to suit contemporary Roman speech, so Auden in turn has renewed them and fitted them to twentieth-century themes. It was Marianne Moore who taught him the first step: a form of verse based on strict syllable count which he used, for example, in his ode "In Praise of Limestone." His own contribution was, in part, to endow syntax with taut muscles. Syntax thus quickened demands more vital language; and tired words must make way for livelier forms, as in these closing lines of "Old People's

Home" where Auden recounts a visit to an aged friend, Elizabeth Mayer:

> . . . we all know what to expect, but their
> generation is the first to fade like this, not at home
> but assigned
>   to a numbered frequent ward, stowed out of
> conscience as unpopular luggage.
>   As I ride the subway
>   to spend half-an-hour with one I revisage who
> she was in the pomp and sumpture of her hey-day,
>   when week-end visits were a presumptive joy,
> not a good work. Am I cold to wish for a speedy
>   painless dormition, pray, as I know she prays,
> that God or Nature will abrupt her earthly function?

These lines from "Old People's Home" have the same syllabic base as "In Praise of Limestone": that is, alternatively eleven and thirteen syllables with elision of contiguous vowels. Obviously, the demands of this pattern spurred the use of some uncommon words or forms. None of these unusual words are new coinages. They are survivals, not new arivals; and the attempt to restore their authenticity lost through misuse or neglect is linked by analogy, in the artistic context, to Horace's revitalized forms, and in the moral context to Isaiah's vision of restoring the walls of the city.

That this present age is the first in which ordinary people commonly find themselves in situations without precedent is a frequent theme in Auden's Horatian poems. Even the aged in "Old People's Home" must absorb the bewildering knowledge that their generation "is the first to fade like this." In the poem "Epistle to a Godson," addressed to young Philip Spender, who can't remember "when everyone travelled by railway," Auden reflects that only yesterday, when inherited ways, trades, and tools were still useful,

>   the old could still be helpful
>
> when they could nicely envisage the future
> as a named and settled landscape their children
>   would make the same sense of as they did, . . .

Now that change is too rapid for such accurate foresight, morbid speculation on the uncertain future may conjure up nightmare visions:

>   the Muses scuttering,
> smelly, from eutrophied Helicon,
>
>   . . .
>
>   Herod's genetic engineers commanded
> to modify the Innocents . . .

The title poem in *City Without Walls*—a brief allegorical Morality play with aspects of a divided self for characters—piles up a series of such images of a civilization in dissolution. By contrast "Epistle to a Godson" is a sane and serious vision of the unique responsibilities facing the young:

>   in elite lands your generation
>   may be called, to opt for a discipline
> that out-peers the monks, a Way of obedience,
> poverty and—good grief!—perhaps chastity . . .

Other poems in *Epistle to a Godson*, like the "Ode to the Medieval Poets" and "An Encounter" (on the meetings between Attila the Hun and Pope Leo), recall historical moments of great uncertainty which mankind endured and survived. Their general tenor is that the Horatians in any age respond creatively to the stimulus of pressures—frequently in the face of opposing bias of those who, aspiring like Faust to unfettered freedom, seek a city without walls.

Auden did not include the noisy 1960s' devotees of un-

inhibited freedom in his hopeful expectancy that the young might heal our ailing universe. His poem "Circe," on the enchantress who turned Odysseus' men into pigs, warns against the then fashionable myth of Circe's garden as a haven of universal peace, gentleness, and love:

>   Her Garden is easy to find. In no time
>   one reaches the gate over which is written
>   large: MAKE LOVE NOT WAR.

Faced by a meaningless life, Circe's children seek an unreal world to replace or destroy the old. The Horatian response to Nothingness, by contrast, is the way of affirmation in Carnival mood. Auden, paraphrasing Thoreau, once characterized the poet as "someone who having nothing to do finds something to do" and he caught the spirit of this affirmation very effectively in his "Ballad of Barnaby"—his version of the medieval story of the Jongleur of Paris, who, knowing no prayers, tumbled before the statue of the Virgin. The Jongleur, like the aged in "Old People's Home" and the young in "Epistle to a Godson," is faced with a situation without precedent. He responds—by choosing to do a technically perfect thing; and in this respect he is a Horatian too:

>   The French Vault, the Vault of Champagne,
>   The Vault of Metz and the Vault of Lorraine,
>   He did them all till he sank to the ground,
>   His body asweat and his head in a swound.
>
>   Unmarked by him, our Lady now
>   Steps down from her niche and wipes his brow.
>   "Thank you, Barnaby," She said and smiled;
>   "Well have you tumbled for me, my child."

There is a subtle implication in a number of these poems of Auden's last years that, because each life is unique, *all* human situations are, in effect, situations without precedent. And since every human perplexity provides an opportunity for creative response, this present age of rapid change is, in a special sense, the age Horatian man was made for. Auden puts it this way in "Lines to Dr. Walter Birk on His Retiring from General Practice":

>   For nothing can happen to birds that has not
>   happened before: we though are beasts with a sense of
>   real occasion, of beginnings and endings, . . .

In Auden's view, what is called for even when words fail in the face of the unprecedented is an affirmative gesture. Hence his 1962 "Whitsunday at Kirchstetten"—a serio-comic poem about the gifts of language and communication—concludes:

>   There is no Queen's English
>   in any context for *Geist* or *Esprit*: about
>   catastrophe or how to behave in one
>   what do I know, except what everyone knows—
>   if there when Grace dances, I should dance.

JOSEPH BRODSKY
From "To Please A Shadow"
Vanity Fair
October 1983, pp. 83–87

II

If a poet has any obligation toward society, it is to write well. Being in the minority, he has no other choice. Failing this duty, he sinks into oblivion. Society, on the other hand, has no obligation toward the poet. A majority by definition, society thinks of itself as having other options than reading verses, no matter how well written. Its failure to do so results in its sinking to that level of locution by which society falls easy prey to a demagogue or a tyrant. This is society's equivalent of oblivion; a tyrant, of course, may try to save his society from it by some spectacular bloodbath.

I first read Auden some twenty years ago in Russia in rather limp and listless translations that I found in an anthology of contemporary English poetry subtitled "From Browning to Our Days." "Our Days" were those of 1937, when the volume was published. Needless to say, almost the entire body of its translators along with its editor, M. Gutner, were arrested soon afterward, and many of them perished. Needless to say, for the next forty years no other anthology of contemporary English poetry was published in Russia and the said volume became something of a collector's item.

One line of Auden in that anthology, however, caught my eye. It was, as I learned later, from the last stanza of his early poem "No Change of Place," which described a somewhat claustrophobic landscape where "no one goes / Further than railhead or the ends of piers, / Will neither go nor send his son . . ." This last bit, "Will neither go nor send his son . . .", struck me with its mixture of negative extension and common sense. Having been brought up on an essentially emphatic and self-asserting diet of Russian verse, I was quick to register this recipe whose main component was self-restraint. Still, poetic lines have a knack of straying from the context into universal significance, and the threatening touch of absurdity contained in "Will neither go nor send his son" would start vibrating in the back of my mind whenever I'd set out to do something on paper.

This is, I suppose, what they call an influence, except that the sense of the absurd is never an invention of the poet but is a reflection of reality; inventions are seldom recognizable. What one may owe here to the poet is not the sentiment itself but its treatment: quiet, unemphatic, without any pedal, almost *en passant*. This treatment was especially significant to me precisely because I came across this line in the early '60s, when the Theater of the Absurd was in full swing. Against that background, Auden's handling of the subject stood out not only because he had beaten a lot of people to the punch but because of a considerably different ethical message. The way he handled the line was telling, at least to me: something like "Don't cry wolf" even though the wolf's at the door. (Even though, I would add, it looks exactly like you. Especially because of that, don't cry wolf.)

Although for a writer to mention his penal experiences— or for that matter, any kind of hardship—is like dropping names for normal folk, it so happened that my next opportunity to pay a closer look at Auden occurred while I was doing my own time in the North, in a small village lost among swamps and forests, near the polar circle. This time the anthology that I had was in English, sent to me by a friend from Moscow. It had quite a lot of Yeats, whom I then found a bit too oratorical and sloppy with meters, and Eliot, who in those days reigned supreme in Eastern Europe. I was intending to read Eliot.

But by pure chance the book opened to Auden's "In Memory of W. B. Yeats." I was young then and therefore particularly keen on elegies as a genre, having nobody around dying to write one for. So I read them perhaps more avidly than anything else, and I frequently thought that the most interesting feature of the genre was the authors' unwitting attempts at self-portrayal with which nearly every poem "in memoriam" is strewn—or soiled. Understandable though this tendency is, it often turns such a poem into the author's ruminations on the subject of death from which we learn more about him than about the deceased. The Auden poem had none of this; what's more, I soon realized that even its structure was designed to pay

tribute to the dead poet, imitating in a reverse order the great Irishman's own modes of stylistic development, all the way down to his earliest: the trimeters of the poem's third—last— part.

It's because of these trimeters, in particular because of eight lines from this third part, that I understood what kind of poet I was reading. These lines overshadowed for me that astonishing description of "the dark cold day," Yeats's last, with its shuddering

The mercury sank in the mouth of the dying day.

They overshadowed that unforgettable rendition of the stricken body as a city whose suburbs and squares are gradually emptying as if after a crushed rebellion. They overshadowed even that statement of the era

. . . poetry makes nothing happen . . .

They, those eight lines in trimeter that made this third part of the poem sound like a cross between a Salvation Army hymn, a funeral dirge, and a nursery rhyme, went like this:

> Time that is intolerant
> Of the brave and innocent,
> And indifferent in a week
> To a beautiful physique,
> Worships language and forgives
> Everyone by whom it lives;
> Pardons cowardice, conceit,
> Lays its honours at their feet.

I remember sitting there in the small wooden shack, peering through the square porthole-size window at the wet, muddy dirt road with a few stray chickens on it, half believing what I'd just read, half wondering whether my grasp of English wasn't playing tricks on me. I had there a veritable boulder of an English-Russian dictionary, and I went through its pages time and again, checking every word, every allusion, hoping that they might spare me the meaning that stared at me from the page. I guess I was simply refusing to believe that way back in 1939 an English poet had said, "Time . . . worships language," and yet the world around was still what it was.

But for once the dictionary didn't overrule me. Auden had indeed said that time (not *the* time) worships language, and the train of thought that statement set in motion in me is still trundling to this day. For "worship" is an attitude of the lesser toward the greater. If time worships language, it means that language is greater, or older, than time, which is, in its turn, older and greater than space. That was how I was taught, and I indeed felt that way. So if time—which is synonymous with, nay, even absorbs deity—worships language, where then does language come from? For the gift is always smaller than the giver. And then isn't language a repository of time? And isn't this why time worships it? And isn't a song, or a poem, or indeed a speech itself, with its caesuras, pauses, spondees, and so forth, a game language plays to restructure time? And aren't those by whom language "lives" those by whom time does too? And if time "forgives" them, does it do so out of generosity or out of necessity? And isn't generosity a necessity anyhow?

Short and horizontal as those lines were, they seemed to me incredibly vertical. They were also very much offhand, almost chatty: metaphysics disguised as common sense, common sense disguised as nursery rhyme couplets. These layers of disguise alone were telling me what language is, and I realized that I was reading a poet who spoke the truth—or through whom the truth made itself audible. At least it felt more like truth than anything else I managed to figure out in that anthology. And perhaps it felt that way precisely because of the touch of irrelevance that I sensed in the falling intonation of "forgives / Everyone by whom it lives; / Pardons cowardice, conceit, / Lays its honours at their feet." These words were there, I thought, simply to offset the upward gravity of "Time . . . worships language."

I could go on and on about these lines, but I could do so only now. Then and there I was simply stunned. Among other things, what became clear to me was that one should watch out when Auden makes his witty comments and observations, keeping an eye on civilization no matter what his immediate subject (or condition) is. I felt that I was dealing with a new kind of metaphysical poet, a man of terrific lyrical gifts, who disguised himself as an observer of public mores. And my suspicion was that this choice of mask, the choice of this idiom, had to do less with matters of style and tradition than with the personal humility imposed on him not so much by a particular creed as by his sense of the nature of language. Humility is never chosen.

I had yet to read my Auden. Still, after "In Memory of W. B. Yeats," I knew that I was facing an author more humble than Yeats or Eliot, with a soul less petulant than either, while, I was afraid, no less tragic. With the benefit of hindsight I may say now that I wasn't altogether wrong, and that if there was ever any drama in Auden's voice, it wasn't his own personal drama but a public or existential one. He'd never put himself in the center of the tragic picture; at best he'd acknowledge his presence at the scene. I had yet to hear from his very mouth that "J. S. Bach was terribly lucky. When he wanted to praise the Lord, he'd write a chorale or a cantata addressing the Almighty directly. Today, if a poet wishes to do the same thing, he has to employ indirect speech." The same, presumably, would apply to prayer.

III

Also recognizable to the point of giving one the shivers were the lines in "September 1, 1939," ostensibly explaining the origins of the war that had cradled my generation but in effect depicting our very selves as well, like a black-and-white snapshot in its own right.

> I and the public know
> What all schoolchildren learn,
> Those to whom evil is done
> Do evil in return.

This four-liner indeed was straying out of context, equating victors to victims, and I think it should be tattooed by the federal government on the chest of every newborn, not because of its message alone but because of its intonation. The only acceptable argument against such a procedure would be that there are better lines by Auden. What would you do with:

> Faces along the bar
> Cling to their average day:
> The lights must never go out,
> The music must always play,
> All the conventions conspire
> To make this fort assume
> The furniture of home;
> Lest we should see where we are,
> Lost in a haunted wood,
> Children afraid of the night
> Who have never been happy or good.

Or if you think this is too much New York, too American, then how about this couplet from "The Shield of Achilles," which, to me at least, sounds a bit like a Dantesque epitaph to a handful of East European nations:

> . . . they lost their pride
> And died as men before their bodies died.

Or if you are still against such a barbarity, if you want to spare the tender skin this hurt, there are seven other lines in the same poem that should be carved on the gates of every existing state, indeed on the gates of our whole world:

> A ragged urchin, aimless and alone,
> Loitered about that vacancy; a bird
> Flew up to safety from his well-aimed stone:
> That girls are raped, that two boys knife a third,
> Were axioms to him, who'd never heard
> Of any world where promises were kept,
> Or one could weep because another wept.

This way the new arrival won't be deceived as to this world's nature; this way the world's dweller won't take demagogues for demigods. . . .

In general, I think this man was terribly mistaken for a social commentator, or a diagnostician, or some such thing. The most frequent charge that's been leveled against him was that he didn't offer a cure. I guess in a way he asked for that by resorting to Freudian, then Marxist, then ecclesiastical terminology. The cure, though, lay precisely in his employing these terminologies, for they are simply different dialects in which one can speak about one and the same thing, which is love. It is the intonation with which one talks to the sick that cures. This poet went about the world's grave, often terminal cases not as a surgeon but as a nurse, and every patient knows that it's nurses and not incisions that eventually put one back on one's feet. It's the voice of a nurse, that is, of love, that one hears in the final speech of Alonso to Ferdinand in "The Sea and the Mirror":

> But should you fail to keep your kingdom
> And, like your father before you, come
> Where thought accuses and feeling mocks,
> Believe your pain . . .

Neither physician nor angel, nor—least of all—your beloved or relative will say this at the moment of your final defeat: only a nurse or a poet, out of experience as well as out of love.

And I marveled at that love. I knew nothing about Auden's life: neither about his being homosexual, nor about his marriage of convenience (for her) to Erika Mann, etc.—nothing. One thing I sensed quite clearly was that this love would overshoot its object. In my mind—better, in my imagination—it was love expanded or accelerated by language, by the necessity of expressing it; and language—that much I already knew—has its own dynamics and is prone, especially in poetry, to use its self-generating devices: meters and stanzas that take the poet far beyond his original destination. And the other truth about love in poetry that one gleans from reading it is that a writer's sentiments inevitably subordinate themselves to the linear and unrecoiling progression of art. This sort of thing secures, in art, a higher degree of lyricism; in life, an equivalent in isolation. If only because of his stylistic versatility, this man should have known an uncommon degree of despair, as many of his most delightful, most mesmerizing lyrics do demonstrate. For in art lightness of touch more often than not comes from the very darkness of its absence.

And yet it was love all the same, perpetuated by language, oblivious—because the language was English—to gender, furthered by the deepest agony, because agony, in the end, would have to be articulated. Language, after all, is self-conscious by definition, and it wants to get the hang of every new situation. As I looked at Rollie McKenna's picture [of Auden], I felt pleased that the face there revealed neither neurotic nor any other sort of strain, that it was pale, ordinary, not expressing but instead absorbing whatever it was that was going on in front of his eyes. How marvelous it would be, I thought, to have those features, and I tried to ape the grimace in the mirror. I obviously failed, but I knew that I would fail, because such a face was bound to be one of a kind. There was

no need to imitate it: it already existed in the world, and the world seemed somehow more palatable to me because this face was somewhere out there.

J. G. BALLARD

1930–

Born on November 15, 1930, James Graham Ballard spent the first sixteen years of his life in Shanghai. His father was a wealthy English businessman. Ballard spent World War II in an internment camp for foreigners. When he emerged, the city was a chaotic and devastated place that made a powerful impression on him. The deserted beaches, abandoned buildings, and impersonal violence of postwar Shanghai would become the landscape of his fiction.

After leaving King's College, Cambridge, Ballard worked at several odd jobs and flew in the Royal Air Force. He married Helen Matthews in 1954 and settled near London as a free-lance writer. In the early 1960s, his early short stories—later published as *The Terminal Beach*—began to appear in the British science fiction magazine *New Worlds*, which soon became the crucible of science fiction's "New Wave" movement. Writers like Ballard, *New Worlds* editor Michael Moorcock, Thomas M. Disch, and Norman Spinrad eschewed traditional SF trappings, themes, and taboos to explore what Ballard dubbed "inner space." Ballard's explorations grew denser and darker after his wife's death in 1964. His "condensed novels" were described by Brian Aldiss as "impacted visions of a timeless, dimensionless world, lacerated by anguish." These were collected as *The Atrocity Exhibition* (also titled *Love and Napalm: Export USA*); their intense violence and obsessive car-crash imagery repelled critics and attracted an ardent cult. As the New Wave was absorbed into the mainstream of science fiction, Ballard turned from *New Worlds* to the literary journal *Ambit*.

In 1984 Ballard published *Empire of the Sun*, which won the Guardian Prize. He now lives in Middlesex with his second wife, Claire. They have one child; Ballard has three by his first marriage.

General

Ballard is the author of four book-length novels to date, all of which belong to that peculiar British type which might be dubbed the one-lung catastrophe, pioneered by, of all people, Conan Doyle. In stories of this type, the world is drowned, parched, hit by a comet, smothered by volcanic gas, sterilized by the Van Allen belts, or otherwise revisited by some version of Noah's Fludde; and the rest of the story deals either with the Ark or with Adam and Eve. (In Ballard's versions, everybody gives up and nobody survives.) Ballard is not especially good at this kind of thing, partly because of the almost pathological helplessness of his characters, and partly because his rationales either make little sense or are not revealed at all (though it must be admitted that *The Crystal World* is lovely nevertheless). His real radicalism shows in his short stories.

For about ten years, Ballard has been engaged in putting together a myth. Those short stories which do not belong to an identifiable, conventional series—such as the Vermilion Sands stories—are pieces of a mosaic, the central subject of which is not yet visible, rather as though a painter were to go about making a portrait by filling in the background in minute detail and leaving a silhouetted hole where the sitter should be. The nature of this attempt has been somewhat masked by the fact that the minor characters—of which there are not very many—sometimes appear in the stories under different names; but there can be little doubt that these fragments (which are the Ballard works which most exacerbate his detractors) are going somewhere, by the most unusual method of trying to surround it, or work into it from the edges of the frame. The difficulty of seeing it whole is further compounded by the equally odd choices Ballard makes of narrative method—for example, pre-

senting one fragment in the form of the notes of a psychotic, another as articles excerpted from some mad encyclopedia. He calls these pieces "condensed novels," and has published them as a collection, but clearly the enterprise is far from being finished.

The outcome may be a failure, or it may be a seminal masterpiece. Nobody at this point in the attempt's history could possibly predict which; the plain, blunt fact is that we do not yet know what it is Ballard is talking about (and, of course, there is always the possibility that he doesn't either; we shall just have to wait and see). That Ballard is not very good as a conventional science-fiction novelist is quite beside the point, since Ballard's mosaic myth is not a conventional novel and has no antecedents. (Confronted by anything out of the ordinary in science fiction, even friendly critics like Miss Merril are all too ready to compare it to something they call *Finnegans Wake*; but in Ballard's case, as in all the others but one, there turns out to be no such relationship. Michael Moorcock has said that Ballard is the originator of his form; I think this is true.) Ballard has a most imperfect grasp of the sciences—he uses "quasars" like authors of the 1920's used "radium," as a magic word—and his discipline is dubious, but he also has a great deal of raw creativity and is a poet; and these, I take it, are the four qualities which characterize almost all the New Wave writers.—JAMES BLISH (as "William Atheling, Jr."), *More Issues at Hand*, 1970, pp. 127–28

The young English sf writer J. G. Ballard is preoccupied with time, and his novels and stories give us a new slant on it. For Ballard time assumes grotesque, dreamlike forms. Human consciousness alters the conventional notion of chronology. The paintings of Francis Bacon—whom Ballard admires—provide a visual sense of the author's preoccupation with the psychic states that may be more "real" than any objective notion of time or history.

One Ballard story, "The Day of Forever," describes a "time" when the earth ceases to rotate on its axis. In another, "Time of Passage," a man lives his life from death to birth. Throughout Ballard's work there is a constant interplay, a switching back and forth of cause and effect, between a fault in natural time and a distortion in consciousness. Time becomes subjective, frightening, something to be escaped or by which to be absorbed.

In his Vermilion Sands stories, Ballard's characters are subjected to a totally leisure-time existence—hours filled with boredom, insanity, fear of death. Time has stopped. There is nothing beyond the pointless games that are played to relieve the pressure of boredom. Whenever one seeks to obtain one's bearings, some trick is played, as though human perception were distorted, in Ballard's words, by "some faulty junction of time and space."

Ballard develops the notion of what he calls the Hubble Effect to provide a possible scientific rationale for the phenomenon he describes in *The Crystal World*. This is a process by which matter is crystallized.

> We now know that it is time . . . which is responsible for the transformation. The recent discovery of antimatter in the universe inevitably involves the conception of anti-time as the fourth side of this negatively charged continuum. Where anti-particle and particle collide they not only destroy their physical identities, but their opposing time-values eliminate each other, subtracting from the universe another quantum from its total store of time. It is random discharges of this type, set off by the creation of anti-galaxies in space, which have led to the depletion of the time-store available to the materials of our own solar system.

The process of crystallization is a means of describing not only a typically exciting sf theme, but also Ballard's subjective feelings about time:

> Just as a super-saturated solution will discharge itself into a crystalline mass, so the super-saturation of matter in our continuum [of depleted time] leads to its appearance in a parallel spatial matrix. . . . The process is theoretically without end, and it may be possible eventually for a single atom to produce an infinite number of duplicates of itself and so fill the entire universe. . . .

Is Ballard projecting onto a cosmic screen, made possible by the mathematics of physics, a sense of despair—of stopped time—reflected in such contemporary realities as cancer, the population explosion, the overcrowding of the city? Perhaps. For Ballard there is only one response to the phenomenon of crystallization: Embrace it. Thus, one of his heroes says, "There the transfiguration of all living and inanimate forms occurs before our eyes, the gift of immortality a direct consequence of the surrender by each of us of our own physical and temporal identities. However apostate we may be in this world, there perforce we become apostates of the prismatic sun." Man gains a form of immortality—endless consciousness of a world of intense crystalline beauty where *nothing ever happens*. History is not merely suspended; it is obliterated.

What *is* time? What is its relation to the three-dimensional world—to space, to nature? Can we jog ourselves back to the linear concept of time by suggesting that Ballard is merely producing in intense metaphors a child's sense of time? Imagi-

nation is supreme; there seems no end to life. But then we are jolted by the child's vision gone terribly sour. For the normal child, the sense of the moment is thoughtless and joyful. For Ballard, it seems dictated by the overwhelming fear of death.

What, then, is this life without death for which he longs? In *African Genesis*, Robert Ardrey describes it as follows:

> Pre-Cambrian life was, I suppose, a Utopia of a sort. Non-disturbance was the motto carved on its walls. Time passed, and did not pass. Separate organisms existed, and did not exist. Lacking individuality, there was little conflict. Lacking mortality, there was no fear. Peace, that supposed desideratum of the human condition, here reigned like a fat old queen. . . . Life was good. For all those who speak persuasively concerning the collective soul . . . I can only recommend the immortal slime.

Some mutation or series of mutations occurred on this planet which led to the process of reproduction rather than simple division among organisms, and an explosion of variety took place. The process of birth, life, and death entered the picture. History was born. "It would seem to me a very great question whether, had death not intervened, we should not all of us still be lost in some remote, pre-Cambrian slime. And if life is to be regarded as in its essence good, then death must be reverenced as its foremost angel."

Ballard's fear of death negates dynamic consciousness: "Looking out . . . this afternoon, I felt, not for the first time, that the whole landscape was compounded of illusion, the hulks of fabulous dreams drifting across it like derelict galleons."

Ballard seems to suggest that the modern world, like the individual paralyzed by the fear of death, lacks the will to continue. Or that, caught between the failure of past action and the inability to conceive future action, man seeks meaning in a trancelike preoccupation with timeless beauty—an escape into a form of aesthetic, eternal psychedelia: "In the evenings Beatrice and I sit among the sonic statues, listening to their voices as the fair weather clouds rise above Coral D, waiting for a man in a dark-winged glider, perhaps painted like candy now, who will come in on the wind and carve for us images of sea horses and unicorns, dwarfs and jewels and children's faces."

Ballard seems to have found his way into the depths of the great collective unconscious, only to remain stuck there, trapped among the primordial images . . . sitting, unable to take the next step. And if there is a suggestion here of escape into the ahistorical vision of an Eastern philosophy, the setting remains nevertheless unalterably Western.

In spite of our criticisms of his visions, Ballard remains for us one of the most powerful voices of contemporary science fiction. Indeed, there is real validity in symbolically stopping time so that we can momentarily cease our seemingly headlong rush into the future and take a good long look at where we are right now.—LOIS and STEPHEN ROSE, *The Shattered Ring*, 1970, pp. 101–4

The word *terminal* . . . echoes mournfully through Ballard's stories and novels. Visions of endings are everywhere: a world winding down, its inhabitants dropping off one by one into a collective final sleep; an all but abandoned earth, its oceans bleached dry, its surface a desert of sand and salt; a group of dead astronauts circling the planet like satellites, doomed to orbit for decades until their capsules cave in; Eniwetok, a cluster of disused concrete bunkers and runways and weapons ranges, littered with broken B-29s and Superfortresses, natural home of a missed apocalypse, "an ontological Garden of Eden," as one of Ballard's characters ironically says.

It is difficult, in these scenes, to separate the private terror from the public possibility, the personal nightmare from the nightmares of history. In all the stories the stress clearly falls on the mental conditions being shown, the inner spaces of psychosis and the approaches to psychosis. The historical places and imaginable historical disasters are figures; they are shapes and traces the psyche has found for the making of its own portrait. "This island is a state of mind," a character says of Eniwetok, unconsciously (or perhaps even consciously) paraphrasing Verlaine. "The psychotic never escapes from anything," a doctor says in another story. "He merely adjusts reality to suit himself. Quite a trick to learn, too." And yet another character thinks, "If primitive man felt the need to assimilate events in the external world to his own psyche, twentieth-century man had reversed this process. . . ."

But however much these stories point us toward the adjusting, projecting mind, the fact remains that our own history has provided all the adjusted material, has set the scene for every projection. It is the literal content of all these disturbed and disturbing metaphors. And indeed history skulks inside even the most insulated mind, infecting every privacy with its preferred varieties of madness; just as a number of famous private madnesses, loosed upon the world, have made up a good deal of modern history. In this context fantasy scarcely seems a mental or optional affair at all, since some of our worst dreams are identical with our worst realities.

The Best Short Stories of J. G. Ballard has a brief and handsome introduction by Anthony Burgess, and collects nineteen stories, chosen by Ballard himself, and written over a period of twenty years or so. Ballard is a master of conventional science fiction, and shares its cherished worries about crowded city life, the domination of time, the encroachments of technology, and the ravening consumer society. Concentration City, in the story of that name, is an infinite cube of streets and avenues, an endless set of Manhattans piled up on top of and alongside each other—"The Gregsons lived up in the West millions on 985th Avenue. . . ." In another story the city is so packed that there are pedestrian jams that sometimes last for days, and everyone lives cramped in tiny cubicles.

In "Chronopolis" the Time Police pursue everyone who is in possession of a watch or clock, because time was once so fiercely organized that programmers became the real rulers of the country. Three families, in "Thirteen for Centaurus," are locked in a space ship for several lifetimes. Only the fourth generation will see the end of the voyage. It then turns out that even this dim prospect is an illusion, since the space ship is still firmly planted on earth, and the whole simulated trip is a heavily funded and now regretted experiment set up by the Space Department. The families cannot be brought out because no one believes they can be trained to live in the world again. In "The Subliminal Man" a society is saturated with consumer goods it cannot want or refuse. There are four television channels, but only the commercials are different. Telephone calls are free but are interrupted by commercial breaks which get longer as the distance of the call increases—"for long distance calls the ratio of commercial to conversation was as high as 10:1."

But in spite of the skill and the invention that go into these pieces, Ballard's heart, or his head, is elsewhere. He is not primarily interested in the narrative line of his stories, or in the people caught up in the situations he has devised for them. He is interested mainly in images of the kind I have mentioned, an abandoned Eniwetok, an earth without oceans, a universe of sand or coral or salt or concrete. He hints, in two stories, at the horrors of life without sleep—operations are performed to allow men to stay awake all the time. He has characters collect, again in two different stories, what he calls "terminal documents": Beethoven's final quartets, a transcript of the Nuremberg Trials, the fusing sequences for the Hiroshima and Nagasaki bombs. In one story a man discovers he can convert the physical world and ultimately his wife into a simple set of geometrical forms, cut loose from all human meanings and associations. In another the protagonist is planning a psychic version of World War III in order to blast us all back to a lost sense of symmetry. And in still another, a mock-scientific report proposes correlations between erotic fantasies, Kennedy's death, and certain makes of automobile.

As these instances suggest, I think, this is writing which is often obsessive, and frequently in energetic bad taste. It evokes a mind, or a series of minds, haunted by dreams of emptiness and annihilation. We may not share these dreams at all—I don't—but the best of Ballard's remarkable stories—"The Voices of Time," "The Cage of Sand," "The Terminal Beach," "The Atrocity Exhibition"—confront us with landscapes we can neither disown nor forget. Even the most cheerful and least speculative of us will remember moments when this burned and ending world might have been ours.— MICHAEL WOOD, "This Is Not the End of the World," *NYRB*, Jan. 25, 1979, p. 28

In the traditional scheme Ballard could be accommodated only as the kind of cautionary writer who insists on belittling man in the cosmic perspective and enlists natural forces to overrule his presumption. But according to an interview in 1973, this is not how Ballard sees his own work. Asked why he had used the catastrophe form, he replied,

> 'I wanted to deal with a large canvas. I was interested
> in events, if you like; systems, of a very large area.
> The entire biological kingdom viewed as a single
> organism, as a single continuing vast memory. In
> fact I've never thought of them as being disaster stories, because I don't see them as having unhappy
> endings. The hero follows the logic of his own mind;
> and I feel that anyone who does this is, in a sense,
> fulfilling himself. I regard all those novels as stories
> of psychic fulfilment.'

The grand scheme, though predominant, was not paramount. Even when not 'faced with the breakup of the Universe,' Ballard's heroes tend to withdraw and dissolve. Seven of the twelve stories in *The Terminal Beach* and seven of the nine in *The Disaster Area* involve or imply the mutilation or destruction of the central character, deliberately sought if not self-inflicted. . . .

It seems that all the activities of the present are distractions from the eternal. The hero is right to renounce them and other people as blocks on his energies. 'It was almost as if the barriers between the deepest levels of the nervous system and the external world had been removed, those muffling layers of blood and bone, reflex and convention. . . .'

The reappraisal of schizophrenia is complete. The victim becomes a hero, bound on a quest through solitude and death for a reality larger than we can perceive: the true nature of the external world. Separate from it, man feels a deathwish for total immersion in it. . . .

Ballard's early catastrophe novels, *The Drowned World*, *The Drought*, and *The Crystal World*, present physical, global disasters which disrupt history and society and leave everyone alone to come to terms with an altered reality. Everyone assumes a new role as hidden factors of the disaster expose latent forces in and beyond individual personality. More often than not, these forces are destructive. The anti-social impulses that are suppressed for social living take over when society itself is destroyed. In *The Drought* Rev. Johnstone observes, '"There are too many people now living out their own failures, that's the secret appeal of this drought."' Not long after, Ransom can tell that it is not so much a 'secret appeal' as a necessity. 'After the events of the previous days, he already felt that in the new landscape around them humanitarian considerations were becoming irrelevant.'

At the same time Ballard was also writing short stories in which the disasters are private and mental. The hero-victim retreats from a fully functioning society to a point from which he sees that social life is an arbitrary and superficial pretence. It can be maintained only in denial of the true depths of mind and time, the enormities of existence. The altered reality, an ancient rather than a new arrangement, demands the mutilation or destruction of his physical identity. The catastrophe is the collapse of his own personality.

In both these kinds of story the physical catastrophe, according to Ballard, is more apparent than real. It is man's isolation which is the real disaster, and these emergencies, global or personal, offer a chance to break down the barriers, 'those muffling layers of blood and bone, reflex and convention'. The destruction of the self liberates a purer, inner being that flies straight to another plane, the reality beyond the catastrophe. Whether Ballard describes this release in terms of religion, psychology, or biological atavism, it becomes apparent that the notion is principally romantic.

With 'The Terminal Beach' Ballard came out of the allegorical distance and closed in upon the present. Traven chooses a real and very particular spot to maroon himself. 11.30°N, 162.15°E: Eniwetok, site of H-bomb tests.

> Its ruined appearance, and the associations of the island with the period of the Cold War—what Traven had christened 'The Pre-Third'—were profoundly depressing, an Auschwitz of the soul whose mausoleums contained the mass-graves of the still undead. . . .
>
> The Pre-Third: the period was characterized in Traven's mind above all by its moral and psychological inversions, by its sense of the whole of history, and in particular of the immediate future—the two decades, 1945–65—suspended from the quivering volcano's lip of World War III. Even the death of his wife and six-year-old son in a motor accident seemed only part of this immense synthesis of the historical and psychic zero, the frantic highways where each morning they met their deaths the advance causeways to the global armageddon.

Dr Osborne the biologist misunderstands Traven's resolve to stay on the island as martyrdom, but Traven is not on Eniwetok for purposes of protest or despair.

> 'For me the hydrogen bomb was a symbol of absolute *freedom*. I feel it's given me the right—the obligation, even—to do anything I want.'
>
> 'That seems strange logic,' Osborne commented. 'Aren't we at least responsible for our physical selves, if for nothing else?'
>
> 'Not now, I think,' Traven replied. 'After all, in effect we are men raised from the dead.'

Ballard's location of this story in an unambiguous present, with verifiable references and co-ordinates, gave a new immediacy to his work. The catastrophe—the development and use of a thermonuclear weapon—has already happened. A new age began on 6 August 1945. Reality is transformed since man realised his latent dreams of destruction and perfected the technology to achieve it—not only the Bomb itself, but the popular and everyday death-machines multiplying on the 'frantic highways' (of which Ballard would have much more to say later). The age is called 'The Pre-Third': that there will be a Third World War, nuclear and final, 'the global armageddon', Traven takes for granted—as if that too had already happened. In the context set up between these two fixed points—the datable past and the inescapable future—man has a terrible existential freedom. Having usurped power over his own existence as a species (the word 'genocide' was first used in 1944), he owes nothing to anyone, except perhaps to 'the still undead', to act in full consciousness of and accordance with their certain annihilation. Hence the 'moral and psychological inversions': 'in effect, we are men raised from the dead.'

Faced with Ballard's earlier disasters, sf fans had labelled him a pessimist. His preference for inhuman worlds and dissolving heroes was, they assumed, a depressive attitude. Epithets like 'melancholy' and 'maudlin' were bestowed. This new extremism seemed mere hyperbole, a sensationalism allied to the lugubrious outrage of protest poetry. But protest poets were always revisionaries, demanding that civilisation turn back from the Bomb, employing images of a Third World War as omens, premonitions that must not be allowed to come true. Traven makes it clear that he is not a protester or a martyr. Like all his predecessors in Ballard's fiction, Traven's role is to accept the disaster and acclimatise to the new environment. For him there is no appeal to considerations derived from other conditions, ideal conditions without H-bombs. Like the drowned world, the Pre-Third is another 'radically new environment, with its own internal landscape and logic, where old categories of thought would be merely an encumbrance.' Traven exemplifies his acknowledgment of that by seeking to live on the target zone, in a desolate place of sand and concrete that seems to be an advance model of 'the historical and psychic zero.'

This deliberate suppression of expected emotional response separates Ballard from the protesters, the maudlin and melancholy, setting him out on his own. He perceives clearly man's complicity with this catastrophe of his own making. While it seems a dreadful mistake and fills his conscious mind with horror, it is also the ultimate tool, the end product of his technological drive. Man now has absolute power over his own existence: the power of uncreation. The moral rectitude of the protest poets sometimes seemed curiously at odds with a certain relish for denunciation, as if they enjoyed having a Bomb to vilify. Ballard offers his psychoanalysis: destruction was what man wanted, unconsciously, all along.

Hence Traven's urge to accept it. We have seen how other writers for ⟨*New Worlds*⟩ were uncertain about the condition of man in his scientifically advanced society. They shared much the same view as Ballard, but their emotional and artistic responses were different. Their images of the sex-robots and the mad astronauts express anxiety over man's self-destructive relationship with his machines. Such images issue out of a profound alienation from the state of civilisation now and to come. The writers may not set up alternative images, of desirable states, but they commonly reject the present, even when they sense it is already too late to do so. Ballard himself had taken up these attitudes in earlier stories whose heroes hated their cities and sought to escape them, usually without success. But in his later fiction he deliberately went beyond that position, declaring acceptance of the present and breaking with the past. A new age, the Pre-Third; a new reality—just as the Surrealists determined in response to the dilemma of scientific advance. Even with the worst possible interpretation of events, Ballard insists: our artifice has become reality, nor are we out of it.—COLIN GREENLAND, "The Works of J. G. Ballard," *The Entropy Exhibition*, 1983, pp. 96–112

SF fans might not have enjoyed "The Drowned Giant" as much as mainstream readers, since Ballard slights his science, providing no explanations for the giant's appearance. And the more conventional SF story would have investigated where the giant came from, rather than what he meant. Further, the society described in "The Drowned Giant" soon lapses into its uneventful existence, a situation not generally appreciated by SF readers, who seem to appreciate apocalyptic climaxes rather than anticlimactic dissolves. The image of the face of the dead giant, moving from a dreaming tranquility to excesses of agony and shame, is poetic but not necessarily within the poetry of science fiction.

In contrast, the poetry of "The Voices of Time" should appeal directly to the SF reader, while appearing to the mainstream reader as a mass of jumbled images. Here the narrative is rich in explanations and partial explanations, while the method of composition is one of complexity rather than simplicity. The reader is bombarded with SF images, all striking and all pointing in the same direction: the universe is running down, the sun is running down, earth is running down, man is running down, and the protagonist of the story is running down most rapidly of all. The focus is on entropy. But the power of the story lies in the many ways in which its characters try to escape entropy, and in the sterility of their attempts. The hope of escaping time is held out like a brass ring, but each attempt to reach the ring leads to madness and death. Eventually the reader comes to see death as itself an escape from entropy, and the story ends in tranquility: the tranquility of exhaustion.

Although the style is usually subordinate to the subject matter, in a few places Ballard employs a bravura technique to underline certain unique situations. Generally, the chief purpose of his narrative method is to present large quantities of information without using straight exposition; Ballard includes numerous tapes, diaries, and computer read-outs as both information sources and actual "voices of time." Consequently, much of the story's background is presented elliptically, and must be reconstructed by the reader. Many writers have included such "documentation," but here the most revealing literary analogue probably would not occur to most readers: in method and content, "The Voices of Time" resembles Eliot's *Wasteland*, with a great number of images piled one on the other to form an inescapable network of arid futility. . . .

In "The Voices of Time," Ballard has used science fiction to fulfill the traditional role of the poet: to meditate on time and death. Entropy. As an SF reader, I can interpret and appreciate this story as literature because its subject matter is not alien to me. But I doubt that a mainstream reader can appreciate the subtlety and beauty of such SF works, because his own set of literary values is limited by a tradition that excludes them. It is not the writer, but the reader, that builds the distinction between science fiction and mainstream fiction into a wall. One can find the gates in that wall, as Ballard did in "The Drowned Giant," but "The Voices of Time" kept to a different path. I believe this story is literature; I'm also convinced that it is unavailable to a reader experienced only in mainstream fiction.—CHARLES NICOL, "J. G. Ballard and the Limits of Mainstream SF," *SFS*, July 1976, pp. 153–57

Works

J. G. Ballard, along with Kurt Vonnegut, Jr., and younger Americans like Thomas Disch, once seemed capable of rescuing ⟨science fiction⟩ from the mountain of fifth-rate hackwork it had become. In the earlier part of his career Ballard produced a well-written, dissonant series of novels and stories chiefly built about a single theme: the slow, terrible drift of the earth toward an apocalypse of inanition. Everything slowed and stilled and froze solid: it was a slender column to support a stack of books, but the nerviness of the language and the density of the imagination creating the disasters made the early Ballard novels readable and engrossing beyond the tight, fanatical world of the adepts. Then Ballard changed his manner and became altogether more inventive and modernist.

In *Vermilion Sands*, however, he is back in the old harness, and for all his attempts to make these nine stories widely significant, they fail even to come up to his early novels—again, he is coasting along on the strength of one idea, twisting all his material into one repetitive pattern, and the slickness and indulgence of the stories make them difficult to remember an hour after the book's been closed. The writing is creamy and precise, almost always delightful, but it cannot carry its load of inconsequential and lazy plot: in every story but one, a decadent, beautiful and exotic woman creates chaos among the futuristic, sinister trappings of Vermilion Sands, a desert resort in seedy decay, and either causes the death of a lover or blows the circuitry in the psychotropic plants, clothing, sculptures and houses which account for the book's most imaginative passages. In a preface Mr Ballard says that he is celebrating 'the neglected virtues of the glossy, lurid and bizarre'. He has kept his eyes closed for the last few years if he thinks these qualities have been neglected; and even if they were virtues, *Vermilion Sands* would do little to popularise them.

What Ballard attempts in these stories is the creation of an original and grotesque world, to be revealed in an unspectacular, off-hand way. But the conventional analogy between short stories and poetry contains a good deal of truth; any false step or slackness becomes cruelly evident. The limpness of the stories in *Vermilion Sands* is that of a poet going lax and complacent. . . .—PETER STRAUB, NS, Dec. 7, 1973, pp. 874–75

The stories collected in *Low-Flying Aircraft* are as stylish as anything ⟨J. G. Ballard⟩ has done, and told with that meticulously apocalyptic sobriety which is scarcely to be characterised as whimsical or sentimental. But Dr Ballard has kissed the Blarney Stone. He *is* whimsical—though admittedly he has a whim of iron; and he has perfected an idiosyncratic literary form which, while not precisely sentimental, might be called the Art of the Neurasthenic. He is a sick man who fondles and caresses his illness into performing the most amazing tricks—but, awkwardly, one of Dr Ballard's major symptoms is repetition compulsion. Like so many of his characters, he endlessly permutates the arid fragments of disaster in an empty gesture of making whole. Buckmaster in 'The Ultimate City,' the longest piece here, creates monuments to vanished high technology in complex pyramids of televisions or automobiles; Dr Ballard shuffles his Tarot pack of hallucinatory images into new patterns, seeking the lost *gestalt* that could reverse the fragmentation process. But this, too, is only a monument, fragments shored uselessly against our ruin; as Dr Ballard fully realises.

A more direct way of putting it is that for some years Dr Ballard has been writing the same stories over and over again. Unable or unwilling to do otherwise, he has made a minor virtue of necessity: he now tells his stories very well indeed. He knows his instrument inside out, and can plumb its every resonance as he repeats the same handful of tunes. . . . He is a synthesist—but one who never attains true synthesis, only suggestive juxtapositions of concepts he cannot fuse.— NICK TOT- TON, "Gems and Ruins," *Spec*, Dec. 4, 1976, p. 26

J. G. Ballard . . . more and more looks like a leading figure in a very rich and developing field. His earlier work was usually cast as science fiction, but he has long since worked loose from that pocket. Like many excellent contemporary writers, from Italo Calvino to Thomas Pynchon, he draws on science-fiction methods to create a magical modern fantasy. A writer of enormous inventive powers, an explorer of the displacements produced in modern consciousness by the blank ecology of stark architecture, bare high-rises, dead superhighways and featureless technology, he has, like Calvino, a remarkable gift for filling the empty, deprived spaces of modern life with the invisible cities and the wonder worlds of the imagination.

The Unlimited Dream Company is a book of this kind, a remarkable piece of invention, a flight from the world of the familiar and the real into the exotic universe of dream and desire. Indeed, the image of flight dominates the book. Blake, a young man who has failed at being a medical student, Jesuit novice and pornographic writer, becomes obsessed with the idea of flying. He takes a job at London Airport, steals a light aircraft and crashes it into the Thames at Shepperton. This is an ideally luminous landscape for J. G. Ballard, rich in suburban detail, webbed in by rivers, locked in by a motorway, and the home of a film studio. Miraculously and mysteriously,

Blake survives the crash and steps out of the water into a world that is like a surrealist painting, populated by posed figures—a doctor-mistress, a madwoman-mother and a priest-father—who start to struggle for possession of him. He tries to leave Shepperton, but the town holds him; the citizens seem strangely to have been expecting him, as a messiah or a bearer of strange powers. And these he proves to have. The crashed plane shimmers in the water with a dead body in it, perhaps his own. For the citizens of Shepperton, Blake performs strange wonders, spinning abundance and exuding sexual energy, drawing them away from their work and into a new world of polymorphous perversity.

Blake's name, presumably, is no accident. He opens the doors of alternative perception and evokes apocalyptic mirages of heaven and hell. Mr. Ballard invents a superabundant world for him to perform in. He dreams of birds, animals and fishes, and becomes them, moving through air, earth and water. When he spills his semen, exotic trees and flowers grow and wild animals and birds join him, along with the children, the old, the mothers, all of whom he manages to incorporate into his physical body and project into flight. It is heady stuff, a dreamy pastoral, but Mr. Ballard sustains it from a well-funded imagination, a prolix style and a great mythical sense. At times, but only at times, the metaphors grow a little too thick, and the pastoral too innocent. But this is above all a book about the fertility of the imagination. It is dense and erotic and magical, a pleasure to read. And it leaves me with no doubt that Mr. Ballard is a very important fantasist.—MALCOLM BRADBURY, "Fly Away," *NYTBR*, Dec. 9, 1979, pp. 14–16

GEORGE BARKER

1913–

George Granville Barker was born in Essex on February 26, 1913. He graduated from Regents Street Polytechnic in 1930, and published his first book of poetry three years later. From 1939 to 1941 he taught English literature in Japan. He has since taught at the State University of New York at Buffalo, the University of Wisconsin, Florida International University, and York University. Barker's poems have won a Guinness Prize, a Borestone Mountain Poetry Award, and a Levinson Prize from *Poetry* magazine.

A contemporary of Dylan Thomas, Barker often speaks of writing as a physiological need, a compulsion, "an unpardonable occupation for a grown man, unless he's got to do it." This aspect of Barker's work is most evident in his long poem of 1950, *The True Confession of George Barker*, an indictment of his world, his friends, and himself. Barker's poetry often addresses Catholic issues, such as guilt and original sin: "God is dead," writes Barker, "but his death can wrestle." In addition to his poems, he has written two short plays and three novels.

Barker has been married twice, and has four children. He lives in Norfolk, England.

Personal

I was born near Epping Forest. My father was a policeman and my mother was a lady who was born in an Irish village. She was the daughter of a pilot of Cork Harbour. They moved from where I was born when I was about two, and we went to a huge tenement in Chelsea. I went to the local school, which was an enormous place. It had fifteen hundred boys and girls; they were all horrid—they were marvellous, tremendous. I got a scholarship from there when I was about thirteen, and I met

some Jesuit priests. I started writing poems—I think the first poem I wrote I wrote when I was seven. These priests knew that I wrote verses, you see, which was really quite extraordinary in this place. . . . Well, it was. You get a lot of chaps, you know, whose fathers were coalmen, and things like that, but not many who write verses. These priests came to my mother's . . . and so I used to go to the office of these two priests, who shouldn't have been there, but they were there, for their own reasons; I used to go there about three evenings a week. It was where I was really educated—these two Jesuits would tell me to read this and read that and read the other.

I was very physically precocious, and I was terribly in love. I was supposed to go to this school I'd got a scholarship at, and I went there for a year, but I got fed up with it. And I left school and got a job. I used to wear a long blue cloak down to my ankles, and an enormous Spanish sombrero, so I got the sack after about three days. I was supposed to have been an office boy. I used to take Milton with me—a few massive books—and I was called in by this very milk-soppy fellow, horrible little man, who said to me, "I refuse to employ someone who looks like an utter nihilist here, you're sacked." And so I had about twenty jobs between the time I was fifteen and the time I was eighteen, at least twenty. And when I was eighteen I got married. (My present wife I married in Italy, about six years ago.) And when I was eighteen too I sent this poem which I had written called "Daedalus" to Walter de la Mare, and that's how it all began. De la Mare in turn sent it to Eliot, as I told you. Then, I had no money, so Eliot did the most extraordinary thing: I never knew who they were, but he got five people to put ten shillings a week each into a bank and he gave me two pounds ten a week for years; that was what we lived on. I was given a cottage by a lady who was a friend of David Archer's, a cottage in Dorset, and my wife and I went down there. . . . And that's all.—GEORGE BARKER, interview with Cyrena N. Pondrom, *CoL*, Autumn 1971, pp. 400–401

General

There seems to be considerable disagreement among critics regarding the virtues of George Barker's poetry. The majority, without bothering to qualify their verdict, treat him as a minor adjunct to the Auden-Spender-Day Lewis triumvirate; others as an interesting freak who altogether defies placement; others yet—I daresay a tiny minority—see in him a poet of superb and very personal gifts but of startling unevenness of execution. There is no denying that Barker is harder to place than either Auden or Dylan Thomas, for a number of reasons. His poetic antecedents are not only more various but also more obscure; the tenor of his verse is strangely and unfashionably affirmative (the affirmations being forthright, anagogic and prophetic rather than paradoxical in the manner of Kierkegaard); and his writing abounds in dazzling and unclassifiable conceits that make Gongora or Crashaw look prim by comparison. Though, as Clement Greenberg has remarked, Barker "owns the past of English poetry congenitally," he does not quite belong in the mainstream; though clearly not a sectarian in matters of technique—of the order of, say, W. C. Williams or Marianne Moore—he is nevertheless sufficiently heterodox to pass for a heretic.

Barker's main heresies are his frequent abuse of hyperbole and pathetic fallacy, and there are several minor ones besides. He has been severely trounced on many of these scores, even by critics who are ordinarily charitable and mild-mannered. Rolfe Humphries speaks of Barker's language as "pretentious, emulous, nervous, excited, compulsive—*vain*. Where does it get you?" Yes, where does it get you? The answer is, Certainly not to quiet excellence; possibly nowhere; possibly to grandeur. Eliot's well-known remark about Hardy: "At times his style touches sublimity without ever having passed through the stage of being good" seems to apply even more accurately to Barker. True, it resolves nothing; it simply states a paradox; besides, Eliot intended it to be a stricture. But is occasional sublimity really so contemptible a thing? I am inclined to think that it is a triumph within the reach of very few writers and that it should be acknowledged no matter by what questionable leaps or shortcuts the poet has managed to attain it. . . .

George Barker belongs clearly in the same category as Ronsard and Victor Hugo—I can imagine much worse company—because of his fundamental dependence on eloquence. His virtues are those of the rhetorician or, to avoid certain pejorative connotations attaching to that term, those of the enthusiastic devotee of language *qua* language. The intellectual substratum of his verse is either thin or confused; the sentiment often exquisite but never sharply focused. His individual tropes and symbols do not bear close examination; they would be ludicrous were it not for the magnificent rhetoric that carries them along and, finally, welds them together. But the fact remains that again and again Barker manages to weld his linguistic oddities or incongruities into complete wholes and that in each successful instance the result is not only a *rapture* but sheer verbal magic. . . .

George Barker has been a victim of one of the current fashions in criticism: that of judging a poet not by his best but by his worst work. Try Wordsworth or Tennyson—let alone Swinburne or Hart Crane—by that standard and you will arrive at an equally preposterous estimate. But critics nowadays are prone to detect absurdity everywhere except in their own procedures.—F. C. GOLFFING, "Mr. Barker and His Critics," *Poetry*, April 1948, pp. 34–38

In *The Oxford Book of Modern Verse*, Yeats had noticed another break with the dominant style of the time, and had prophesied that here was very likely a forerunner of a future literary revolution. I refer of course to George Barker. If the work of the previous generation was rhetorical, if the self was hidden behind panaceas for the world ill, in Barker, rhetoric is pushed to the critical point where it turns into its opposite. The world ill is taken into the self. Barker seems to swallow the sick public soul, neutralize it with his own spiritual intoxications, and then cast it forth, and his own occult inwardness along with it. This may not be the most lucid description of what is actually an impressive and exciting artistic process to observe, but it is obviously far removed from the ambulatory, jaded eye of Louis MacNeice. Barker's verse is not just exhortative, like a political speech, it really is excited, its dynamism does not come from a rhetorical formula, but from a disturbed and disturbing internal vortex. Barker has often been compared to Blake. He is rather like Blake, but like Blake in reverse, a mirror image. Blake objectified his internal conflicts, not the absurd "conflicts" of the Freudian clinic but the actual struggle that always goes on in the awakened soul of man. He made mythological dramatis personae out of the elements of the self, and set them at war with each other. In many ways his method was not unlike that later developed by Carl Jung. Barker, on the other hand, has taken the figures of the collective unconscious which have assumed a terrible reality in our time, shorn them of their hypostatization, and set them at war within his own self. If this were the end of the matter, the situation would be uncontrollable, and unendurable, and would soon degenerate into madness or total irresponsibility. Barker's earliest work did, often, seem to stop here, but in later work the savior, the harrier of this interior hell, becomes more and more manifest. He is, as one might guess, the Divine Eros fleshed, the simple abandon and finding of the self in the act of love. In style too, Barker resembles a reversed Blake. Where Blake hunted for the particulars, the inescapable objectivity to garb his subjective vision, Barker pushes the subjective hallucination to the point where it takes body for others. This is what some Surrealists say, programmatically, that they attempt. Barker does not try to reach a predetermined goal in the reader's consciousness by the use of psychiatric devices. He is, with great passion, a kind of person.—KENNETH REXROTH, "Introduction" to *The New British Poets*, 1949, pp. xvi–xvii

Works

We may find it useful here to examine another poem, a sonnet by George Barker, which owes something to Hopkins in its diction: the subject is an actual experience of the poet's—the sight of two men swept overboard in the Mediterranean.

> The seagull, spreadeagled, splayed on the wind,
> Span backwards shrieking, belly facing upward,
> Fled backward with a gimlet in its heart
> To see the two youths swimming hand in hand
> Through green eternity. O swept overboard
> Not could the thirty-foot jaws them part,
> Or the flouncing skirts that swept them over
> Separate what death pronounced was love.
>
> I saw them, the hand flapping like a flag,
> And another like a dolphin with a child
> Supporting him. Was I the shape of Jesus
> When to me hopeward their eyeballs swivelled,
> Saw I was standing in the stance of vague
> Horror; paralysed with mere pity's peace?

The seagull image with which this sonnet opens is extremely brilliant, both symbolic and evocative; the words pick their punches very coolly; the rhythms, which are excellently contrived throughout the whole poem, convey first a resistance to the wind and in the next two lines a surrender to it. Our initial impression is a purely physical one—the picture of a seagull swept backwards over the wake of a ship. It is a sight so familiar to us all that the poet is able to take great imaginative liberties with it, yet remain intelligible. When the first impression is peeled off, we become aware of another meaning beneath it: the seagull, which 'Span backwards shrieking, belly facing upward', prepares us emotionally for the two men whirled away in the ship's wake. At this point, the phrase 'Fled backward with a gimlet in its heart' introduces a third motif. It contains not only the previous suggestion of a remorseless force skewering the bird and pushing it backwards, but also the idea of anguish—the anguish of one who sees 'the two youths swimming hand in hand through green eternity', and is helpless—the anguish, in fact, of the poet himself 'standing in the stance of vague horror; paralysed with mere pity's peace'. The sharp, precise word 'gimlet' admirably points this double significance.

But after this the poem is not, perhaps, altogether satisfactory. Our attention begins to wander a little, distracted by images which do not tie in so closely to the theme. We admire the way the smooth rhythm of the seagull's recession changes into the choppy rhythms of

> O swept overboard
> Not could the thirty-foot jaws them part,
> Or the flouncing skirts that swept them over
> Separate what death pronounced was love.

But the images for the waves—jaws and flouncing skirts—are gravely dissonant, and they make no contact with the seagull image. And then, in the sestet, we have two more images, equally centrifugal—the 'hand flapping like a flag' and the 'dolphin with a child supporting him'. Now the cause of our dissatisfaction lies, I fancy, in the poet's failure to maintain the ambivalence so beautifully created by the opening lines. He is trying to be in two places at once, in the consciousness of the drowning men who see him as 'the shape of Jesus', and at the core of his own experience as a witness of their fate. The poem, attempting thus to look outwards and inwards at the same time, becomes emotionally unfocused: we do not doubt the intensity of the poet's experience; but we find that the pure, subjective images rising from the inwardness of this experience do not perfectly fuse with the images which are intended to convey its external cause. Mr. Barker's poem is somewhere half-way between the purer kind of poetry we have been discussing and the impure kind. It is at least sufficiently impure to admit one direct statement or piece of poetic argument—that the waves could not 'Separate what death pronounced was love'.— C. DAY LEWIS, *The Poetic Image*, 1947, pp. 128–30

The True Confession has had a rough passage. After it had been broadcast in the Home Service of the B.B.C., the Director-General apologized for this lapse of taste—and very properly so: those with ears attuned to the delicacy of music-hall comedians and minds purified by the ritual of parlour-games on television cannot be expected to stomach a poem whose pages exude so rank a smell of the Old Adam. *The True Confession* bristles with coarse words and lewd thoughts, for Barker describes in brutal and gross detail aspects of sexuality which almost all poets have shunned or tried to transcend. He depicts himself as a dirty small boy and as a grubby adolescent, tormented and fascinated by the power of sex, and it is a mark of his rare honesty that he has omitted none of the warts on this unprepossessing self-portrait. Scatological and distasteful as the poem is in places, it remains essential to any understanding of Barker's work; a few vigorous Rabelaisian passages and some finely-sustained lyrical stanzas are among the best things that he has written; and nowhere does it sink to the incoherent ranting of the *Collected Poems* at their most delirious.—JOHN PRESS, *Rule and Energy*, 1963, p. 70

Although geographical allusions establish a setting in space, others back up the basically dynamic concept of time which dominates *Calamiterror*. When at the beginning of Book IV the growing poet asks his muse to "bring/The evening vivid with mythologies," he refers to an important constituent of the poem, itself vivid with mythology. The mythological references and symbols strengthen the cyclical pattern and indicate that the central consciousness sees himself related to the archetypal patterns of the collective unconscious.

The myths most pervasive are those of ascent. The Phaeton story is implied in Book II where the celestial aspect of the newborn babe aspires to return from whence it came, only to be forced by a fall into the chaos of the human condition: "Then the heavenly curvetting through heaven,/The bird, the butterfly the aeronaut,/The final bone falls like the Indian boy." The simile probably refers to Phaeton who went to India, region of sunrise, where he began his calamitous trip through the heavens in an effort to assert his divine parentage. Images of attempts at flight suggest Phaeton, Icarus, and any number of rebellious heroes. The myths describe the eternal aspirations of youth "Seeking a place and time he does not know." The recurring symbol of the salamander is related to Phaeton, who would inherit from Apollo the eternal element of fire, the soul. Barker's persona wants to be "Runaway rainbow," although, in words appropriate for Barker's "Daedalus," he says, "at my feet falls the burnt out fragment/The finger or the face sheered off clean."

Polar to the myth of ascent is the narcissus archetype of descent into the waters of self; for much of *Calamiterror* explores the implications of narcissism. In Book VI (Stanza 3), when the speaker begins to realize that his world has been distorted, he exhorts others who wander in nature to "Throw up no mountain featured with self's face. If "you" admire "the bright mask/Suspended through the depths . . . down/Internally and eternally drowned you go. I know." References to Narcissus, Hylas, Apollo, and Ixion people the poem.

When the individual's history records the struggle for release from the body, when the individual is self-contained, a world unto himself, references to myth underlie the imagery. As the speaker comes to think of himself less as a hermaphroditic god, he uses fewer references to Greek legend. Throughout the poem, however, allusions to Christianity establish correspondence between the sacred and the profane to enunciate the central tension between spiritual aspirations and the claims of the body and physical life.

The mythopoeic technique extends and universalizes the individual experience of *Calamiterror*. Direct or implied allusions to poets and poetry are equally important: they produce the sense of the continuity of the poet's experience. In Book V, for example, the aspiring mystic has a preliminary vision, brief and less significant than the one of Blake in Book VI; the first vision reminds him of death by water, like Shelley's, and "instructs me in ambition." In Book VIII, this ambition becomes "Milton nibbling like a mouse" (Stanza 5). Although Milton is only an allegorical synonym for ambition, Blake is the symbol for the mystic and a focal point for the whole poem.

The turning point in the persona's dark night of spirit acknowledges the debt. Stanzas 9 through 12 of Book VI present Blake as the central vision in the apocalyptic experience of the calamiterror: "I saw/The figure of William Blake bright and large/Hung over the Thames at Sonning. I had not had this." The vision is almost like a Blake engraving. The poet explains that he had thus far apprehended the external universe as a materialist, "Acknowledging the element of matter," and not wholly as a mystic. He had not discovered his archetype: "I had not acknowledged this,/I had not encountered prototype." The speaker realizes that Blake too had "worlds and worlds in his abdomen,/And his bosom innumerably enpeopled with all birds." The vision implies Blake's debt to Swedenborg, "labouring like a dream in his stomach," and Barker's debt to Blake, "myself the minor bird on the bough." Significantly, however, this image suggests that Yeats was the major and Barker a minor disciple of Blake. The speaker admits that he has been the apostle of Blake, who is "Absolute, glittering, actual and gold,"—the pattern of the visionary of apocalyptic literature and the speaker's Ideal.

Through Blake, then, the poet comes upon revelation; the apocalypse is paradoxical in that he apprehends not eternity but the real world. He realizes that objective reality will make of subjective chaos an ordered universe. When he recognizes the importance of "external fact," his vision of Blake falls (Stanza 12). This catastrophe for subjectivism comes about as "Fragments of his torso breaking past me" is juxtaposed to "It was/The object of the physical world breaking on me." The fall of introverted mysticism makes the young man into a poet-prophet who is, ironically, like Blake. . . .

Barker espouses the Blakean idea that action in itself is good and that "Sin is not to act." Even his treatment of man as a dualistic combination of warring opposites—the superhuman and the subhuman, energy and reason, spirit and flesh—may be traced to Blake, who believed, as Barker does at the start of *Calamiterror*, in the god-man. Barker's opposed forces and the whole conception of his poem are related to Blake's contraries, without which there is "no progression" and to the reiteration of Blake's ideas as Barker found them in Yeats. Barker's babe is itself a marriage of heaven and hell. Blake's theory that "one portion of being is the Prolific; the other the Devouring" is part of the total fabric of *Calamiterror*.

The poem progresses from Blakean monism, which insists upon dualities within one entity, to Wordsworthian dualism, which accepts the separation and interplay, rather than the identification of subject and object. The development and certain ideas and experiences explored are surely influenced by Wordsworth. Although *Calamiterror* makes no specific reference to the author of *The Prelude*, *The Recluse*, and *Tintern Abbey*, he is present in the background. Barker's subject is, like Wordsworth's, the growth of the poet's mind.—MARTHA FODASKI, "*Calamiterror*: The Mind of Man My Haunt," *George Barker*, 1969, pp. 60–63

GEORGE BARKER
From "Poetry and Reality" (1937)
Essays
1970, pp. 79–90

The law of possibility which Aristotle defines in the sixth book of the Poetics is an internal and not an external law. The logic of possibility should proceed not necessarily from the external laws of reality, although these supply us with our judgement, but from the internal logic of possibility which proceeds from the postulates of the poem. Thus the law of the real governing the actions of the poem is internal; the violation of the poem's own laws is the violation against which the critic must protest, and not principally against any apparent or supposed violation of external law. It is for this reason that the cluster of violent death with which Hamlet closes affects the spectator as horrible and catastrophic and not as hideous and ludicrous. For the same reason, that obvious violation of natural law which frequently achieves the effect of poetry passes into and through the intelligence of the reader without dislocating it: its ravage is the ravage of the inexplicably poetic, not the dislocation of the inexplicably illogical. . . .

In default of any more adequate explanation of the relationship between the Real and the Imaginative as it occurs in the process of poetry, I propose to adopt the preceding theory and in its light to examine the principles of selection and rejection which govern the imagination of the poet. It is obvious that various principles of selection may at one time concur within the imagination of the poet; the physical brilliance of an image, the verbal euphony of certain words, the associations of certain combinations of words, and the entire paraphernalia of technical apparatus, all these modify in some degree or other the figure that has arisen in the imagination. But when, as in major poets, this figure appears to have been born with the habiliment of its proper euphony and its perfect articulation clothing it, a principle of selection which I have not yet contemplated enters and governs the poet's imagination. I mean the reference of this figure of the imagination to the real world, the inverted metaphor which is not only illustrative in the text of the poem, but which returns again like a reflection to the world from which its components were drawn. The lines:

When I perceiue that men as plants increafe,
Cheared and checkt euen by the selfe-same skie:

exhibit the consummation of all principles of selection; the image, the sound, the entire paraphernalia of technical apparatus, elucidate the original figure of the imagination: and this figure of the imagination presents an intuitive judgement of the real world. In this manner the imagination, by exploiting the real so as to reveal its condition, performs a judgement upon it; and in this manner it is possible to describe poetry as a criticism of life. The highest exploitation of the real occurs when through this exploitation the imagination of the poet reveals the conditions of the real. The great phrase, which I had hoped not to quote,

Ripeness is all

reveals this. What I am concerned with here is that the reversal of flight performed by the imagination of the poet, the return to the world of the real, usually illuminates the real world with the extraordinary light of that region of the imagination from which it has flown. The subject of poetry is the actions of men, according to the definition of Aristotle; and it is to be assumed that under this definition may be classed those actions which fail to achieve the outer world, and remain within the man to precipitate, later, action of a sort differing from that which might have immediately resulted. It may be taken, in other words, to embrace the subjective processes as well as the objective processes. The actions of men necessarily involve not only the real world, but all ascending spheres of the real. Not only is the physical body of the human immediately caught up in the processes of the most minor action, but so to some degree or other is the entire human sphere. The poet, in dealing with the actions of men, deals with all degrees and all removes of reality. It is from this world, it is from this series of worlds, that the poet derives his material and the mechanics of his work. The language of the poet achieves its effects mainly by reason of its being not the language of common men, which the language of the poet can never solely be, but by having as its heart the terms of the common.

What is beauty?
. . .
saith my sufferings then.

Because I claim that the imagination of the poet illuminates and at its best apotheosizes the real or scientific world, and because this illumination or apotheosis performs an analysis of its subject, I claim that the poet suffers an obligation to the real or scientific world, which should in no sense be confused, as it is frequently confused, with the obligation of the scientist to the real world. Accurate ascertainments about matter and time and space properly constitute the obligation of the scientist, and these ascertainments are only in a strictly limited sense more 'true' than the ascertainments of the poet about the phenomena which transcend the real. I am referring to Dr Richards' theory of the 'pseudo-statement'. Regarded as scientific statement the ascertainments of poetry (e.g. Beauty is Truth, Truth Beauty) may appear as pseudo; but, conversely, regarded as imaginative or poetic statement the ascertainments of science may often be regarded as pseudo. Obviously the statements of poetry are not to be regarded as scientific statements, which is the only condition under which they become pseudo, for then it would appear that not only is science Truth, but it is also Beauty. It appears that the cause of this confusion is the inveterate propensity of the human to accept as absolute, statements which cannot be more than eminently relative. The accurate ascertainments of science are acceptable as accurate only in the sphere of the actually real or scientific. The antithesis to Poetry is Science or Matter-of-Fact, wrote Wordsworth. The 'pseudo-statements' of poetry become pseudo-statements only when considered as scientific statements.

This is by no means to suggest that the statements of poetry cannot apply or refer to the real or scientific world, for this suggestion would at the same time be the suggestion that none of the ascertainments of poetry were ascertainments, but 'fictions'. I do not suggest this because the ascertainments of poetry are ascertainments about the sphere of the transcendental, and in the same degree that the transcendental affects the

real, so does the statement of poetry refer to the real. Because it is not susceptible to scientific analysis it is transcendental; *because* the statements of poetry are such as not to be susceptible to scientific categories they are poetry. The antithesis is that of Wordsworth. And in the same manner that the antithesis of passion and of will evolves metre, and the antithesis of the imagination and the intellect evolves the poem, so the antithesis of the scientific and the transcendental evolves poetry.

It is perhaps permissible, if the terms are used pretty broadly, to say that the scientist investigates *how* men behave, and the poet investigates *why* they behave. And allowing for what is commonly called the human element and what I have hitherto termed the inherent transcendent, it will be seen that these two problems are by no means the same. It is also stultifying to consider one as Truth and the other as Fiction. This is no more the legitimate antithesis than that of Poetry and Prose. Both contribute, in fact, to the Truth in the first instance and Poetry in the second instance. (Incidentally, I should like to remark that in the composition of prose the antithesis of the will and the passion may again but to a lesser degree be present; in the words of Ezra Pound, 'Poetry ought to be as well written as Prose.') The function of the poet and the function of the scientist complement each other in the work of expediting that consummation of human development which may or may not flower into perfection of self-knowledge.

The past has witnessed the exploitation of the scientifically real by the poet; the future should witness the exploitation of the poetically transcendent by the scientist; and it may be the end of poetry. But until such times as this, poetry will presumably continue to be written, and science continue to consider this remarkable. This is precisely as it should be, for the reason, firstly, that it emphasizes the real or scientific, and secondly, that it confirms the poet in his position as imaginative exploiter of the real: and both of these conditions contribute to the writing of poetry. Eventually this very antagonism becomes that 'balanced antagonism' which Coleridge detected in the process of poetry.

Finally it is to be remembered that the legitimate and indigenous region of the intellect is anything and anywhere; and that the legitimate and indigenous region of the imagination is anything and anywhere: and that in the extraordinary event of a meeting what occurs is poetry. The intellect reverts to feminine, receiving the impregnation of the imagination, which it gestates and feeds and eventually delivers into words.

The gender of imagination is masculine. The act of writing the poem corresponds to the act of generation; the materials of poetry are feminine; the element of poetry is masculine. It appears then that the sum ascertainment in scientific terms of this paper is that the element of poetry, the inherent transcendent, is Imagination.

JOHN PRESS
From "The Fourfold Vision"
Rule and Energy
1963, pp. 72–81

Barker is unequivocally committed to the belief that poetry is a Dionysian activity and that 'the function of the poem as a poem is to glorify'.[1] Although he is a prolific writer, he constantly recurs to a few obsessive themes and he tends to compose in sequences or groups or cycles of poems: 'Pacific Sonnets', 'Personal Sonnets', 'Sacred Elegies', 'Secular Ele-

gies', 'Four Cycles of Love Poems', 'Cycle of Six Lyrics', and
'Nine Beatitudes to Denver' are characteristic titles. One leading motif in his work is poverty, not the ideal of Christian
poverty as a vocation, but the sour fact of being poor in the
chilly, drab English slums of the years between the wars. It is
not fanciful to attribute much of the wildness, the resentment,
the savage incoherence of Barker's verse to his understandable
hatred of the world which bred him, or to see in the fantastic
opulence of his imagery an attempt to find compensation for
the dinginess of his early years:

> It was hard cash I needed at my root.
> I now know that how I grew was due
> To echoing guts and the empty bag—
> My song was out of tune for a few notes.[2]

> For half a dozen simple years
>   We lived happily, so to speak,
> On twenty-seven shillings a week;
>   And, when worried and in tears,
> My mercenary wife complained
>   That we could not afford our marriage,
> 'It's twice as much', I explained,
>   'As MacNeice pays for his garage'.[3]

This personal discontent spills over into a more general hatred
of the English social order as it was before the war. In the long,
dull 'Vision of England '38', the poet talks with such worthies
as St. George and William Blake, who denounce capitalist
oppression, and the poem ends with an unconvincing invocation to a Political Prince who shall liberate England.

In his later verse, Barker occasionally reverts to this theme
of English society, but the note of personal grievance and deprivation is no longer dominant. We find instead an impersonal
survey of England's plight in the post-war world, an utterance
tinged with a prophetic grandeur:

> I thought of Britain in its cloud
> Chained to the economic rocks
> Dying behind me. I saw the flocks
> Of great and grieving omens crowd
> About the lion on the stone.
> And I heard Milton's eagle mewing
> Her desolation in the ruin
> Of a great nation alone.[4]

"Stanzas on a Visit to Longleat House in Wiltshire, October
1953' expresses a Yeatsian contempt for 'the hog of multitude'
tramping through a noble house now reduced to a 'fouled
public nest'. Yeats, it was said, became so aristocratic that he
started to evict imaginary tenants, and Barker assumes here the
role of the Victorian squire, as he watches

> The ragged-arsed mechanics squat
> Owning what they haven't got . . .

> In car-park, garden and urinal
> The free and ignorant, almost
> As easy as at a Cup Final
> Gawk through the stone-transparent ghost
> Of this once noble house, now lost
> In the gross error of survival.

>   . . .

We find in Barker's avowal of his metaphysical beliefs the
same lack of steadiness and of wholeness which is so disturbing
in his religious poetry. Again, we are in a world of tension and
of frenzied ambivalence, where everything threatens to spin
out of control and to involve the poet in the general ruin. The
nearest approach to an explicit statement of his philosophy

occurs towards the end of 'Goodman Jacksin and the Angel',
where he envisages the cosmic process as dialectical:

> The law of dialectics is
> How Love evolves. There are no
> Two ones of any kind but must
> Bring forth a firstborn third to prove
> That the arithmetic of love
> Transcends our lonely dust.

> Thus Love and Death together got
> Under a dark constellation . . .
> Then from their open-eyed embrace
> Rose the first god that ever was,
> With doom in his face.

The nature and the significance of this primeval god remain an
enigma, nor is Barker's concept of morality free of the mystery-
mongering, the flirtation with chaos, which seem to be the
mainsprings of his poetry:

>   Underneath
> The human heart, I believe,
> Lives a god who cannot grieve
> No matter how disastrous
> The crimes our passion brings on us
> Because this ungrieving god
> Knows that either bad or good
> Might look, from a better angle,
> Like a double-headed angel.[5]

A poet obsessed by this kind of paradox, which hovers
above an abyss of nihilism, will find it hard to formulate any
coherent imaginative vision of the world, and may be tempted
to strike a variety of effective theatrical attitudes, to sound a
note of grandiloquent despair or of hollow triumph. Barker has
not escaped these perils. The worst vices of his poetry—a fondness for such excruciating puns as 'I see phallic: you,
cephalic';[6] an addiction to spattering his pages with rhodomon-
tade and verbiage; a lack of self-criticism that permits him to
reprint in his *Collected Poems* a poem as gristly as 'Calamiterror', in which for over thirty pages he works himself into an
epileptic lather about blood, loins, and bowels—are symptoms
of this radical uncertainty and instability rather than a product
of technical clumsiness. . . .

What is missing all too often in his work is the power to
shape his brilliant but erratic perceptions into a coherent design, to staunch the verbal haemorrhage that gushes over his
poems, to subdue the frenetic waywardness of his temperament, and to bring poetic order into a universe which, for him
as for his triple-headed Manichee,[7] appears to be incurably
dualistic and anarchical. His nearest approach to a wholly satisfying poem is 'Channel Crossing', where he is in full command
of his talents and where the rich profusion of imagery develops,
instead of blurring, the intricate poetic argument. Barker meditates on the destiny of Europe, scarred by war, and on the fate
of England, protected by the bulwark of the Channel against
the worst ravages of continental fanaticism, yet facing an imminent decline. He hears 'the old lip of the sea' ask the question 'What can a dead nation say?' and gives us a melancholy
answer. The lines about the fishes evoke a precise image of the
deep-sea creatures' aimless dartings here and there, but they do
more than convey an accurate picture of the swift movement.
They remind us that we live in a world of displaced persons and
that the freedom of the amoral natural world differs from that
liberty which is the proper element of man.

Notes
1. 'The Miracle of Images'.
2. 'Epistle I'.
3. *The True Confession*, Book IV.

4. 'Channel Crossing'.
5. 'To my Son', Part II.
6. *The True Confession*, Book II.
7. See 'Sonnets of the Triple-headed Manichee'.

J. M. BARRIE

1860–1937

James Matthew Barrie was born in Kirriemuir, Farfarshire, on May 9, 1860. When he was six his brother David died in an accident; Barrie did not remember his brother well, but his mother was overwhelmed by the loss and turned to young James as a replacement for her son. It is claimed that this early influence was important in Barrie's later image of himself as a perennial young boy.

Barrie was educated at the Glasgow Academy, the Dumfries Academy, and Edinburgh University; he matriculated from there in 1878, and earned the M.A. in 1882. While at college he contributed to the *Edinburgh Courant* (1879–82), then joined the staff of the *Nottingham Journal* (1883–85). Barrie then moved to London and engaged in much journalistic activity in Grub Street. His first novel was *Better Dead* (1887)—a title he later used to describe the novel's quality—and his first play was *Richard Savage* (1891).

In 1894 he married the actress Mary Ansell, but from all accounts the marriage was very unhappy. Barrie divorced her in 1909 when he discovered her in an affair with another man, and he did not remarry. Meanwhile Barrie began a vigorous career in playwriting and producing. In 1896 he travelled to the United States to confer with the Broadway producer Charles Frohman; this, plus his friendship with the children of many of his friends—especially those of Arthur and Sylvia Llewelyn Jones—was an important factor in the creation of *Peter Pan* (1904).

Barrie's earlier work, *Auld Licht Idylls* (1888), was the source of inspiration for the Kailyard School—a group of writers, including "Ian Maclaren", Neil Munro, and J. J. Bell, which celebrated the virtues of Scottish provincial life. Barrie also wrote several acclaimed novels. He received honorary degrees from St. Andrew's, Edinburgh University, Oxford, and Cambridge. He was knighted by George V in 1913, and received the Order of Merit in 1922. In that year he became Rector of St. Andrew's, and from 1930 to his death on June 19, 1937, he served as Chancellor of Edinburgh University.

Personal

It is apparent that Barrie existed in a hyper-personal, highly charged atmosphere of charm and pain, and that with every year of his life the temperature round him rose; that to inspire him was to become his victim, and, at the same time, to be unwilling assistant at his tortuous victimization of himself. For actors in Barrie's personal drama there was only one possible exit: death. The drama had the mysterious compulsions, the subjectivity, and, to an extent, the pathology of a dream.

. . . Barrie was spared the final ironic tragedy: he never ceased to believe in the worth of his own work. But he continued through his life to be subject to devastating silences, melancholies. His emotional make-up was so odd that if he could manage to live at all (as he did), one feels that he could have sustained almost any conditions. With people he seems to have avoided any relationship that his imagination, under the rule of symbols, could not in its turn rule, mould and inform. The failure of his marriage—as to which Mr. Mackail's reticence is to be respected—went in deep: this was something worse than a death. I am convinced there was not a trick in his art: not only did technical hard work go to the output of it, but he was innocent of, at least, the *wish* to exploit. He wrote of his own nostrums. Children, big dogs, beautiful mothers, strong hearts, weak wills, great wishes, mild realizations—he wrote

for an age to which these were dear. From an urbane London his imagination turned back to float Kirriemuir and its pious ones in a world-illusion. But to that shrine of illusion he himself rendered his yearly pilgrimage North. Barrie's art was art of the kind that is overflow, superfluity from a man's person; an affectable man's art for an affectable age. Minor art, if you like, for minor men. But it has a strength out of one kind of suffering. And who shall say any suffering is unreal?—ELIZABETH BOWEN, "Barrie" (1941), *Collected Impressions*, 1950, pp. 149–51

He's a queer mixture—an extraordinarily plural personality. For all that apparent haphazardness, there seems plenty of shrewdness, almost 'canniness'. As for the legend of his being himself 'The Boy Who Wouldn't Grow Up', I see no evidence whatsoever of this. On the contrary, he strikes me as more than old. In fact, I doubt whether he ever *was* a boy. But then, for the matter of that, Peter Pan isn't a boy, is he? He's a wish-fulfillment projection in fable form of the kind of mother—Barrie's an expert at her—who doesn't want her son to grow up. Talking of sons and mothers, Barrie is an immense admirer of D. H. Lawrence and speaks much of him. I remember Lawrence telling me Barrie had been one of the first people to write to him in praise of *Sons and Lovers*.

I find one important part of my job is to prevent Barrie

saying 'yes' to invitations, whose acceptance he would afterwards regret. He says he can never do any work at all with an engagement hanging over him. Which invitations should be accepted, which refused, I have to know by instinct, for when the time comes and he finds himself confronted with a blank evening—possibly one of several in succession—he may well regret having refused. I suspect the truth is that he is leading the cloistered, jealously-guarded life of a writer working, as for so many years has been his habit, some eight hours a day; whereas in point of fact he isn't at present, so far as I can see, really writing at all. Were he in the grip of an inspiration, surely he wouldn't spend so much time reading *The Times*? Probably he courts solitude, but like quite a few others, occasionally feels lonely when it's too successfully secured. Long notice is what he hates. He likes some friend to ring up and say 'Can I come to dinner tonight?' An invitation to dinner three weeks off produces a nerve storm. Some hostesses show remarkable persistence.

I love his burry voice, with its subtle Scottish lilt. He pronounces certain words strangely. 'I had a haddock this morning,' he declares now and again. At first, I thought he meant he'd had fish for breakfast, and I didn't know how to look suitably interested. Not until the third time, did it dawn on me he was telling me he'd had a headache!

Last night I dined with him. He was in one of his garrulous moods—in snatches even autobiographical, talking with some pride of his early poverty, which I rather suspect he romanticises. (I notice most people tend to exaggerate their own poverty and other people's wealth.) He told me the greatest shock of his childhood had been when he saw someone drop a penny and not bother to pick it up. (I nearly told him the greatest shock of my life had been finding someone hadn't bothered to cash seventeen hundred pounds worth of cheques!)

He declared that, while at Edinburgh University, he had subsisted almost entirely on potatoes which he kept in a sack in his bedroom, and that when he first came to London—a step taken on the strength of having had a few articles accepted by *The Pall Mall Gazette*—he ate very little except buns, and had often felt very lonely; also, that once when a tooth came out he hammered it into position again with the wooden back of his hair-brush.

When he confessed he'd never consulted an oculist, but had just adopted someone else's spectacles, I gave him no peace until he authorised me to make an appointment for him. I'd already forced him to go to an osteopath for what I'm sure is incipient writer's cramp, but he was very sceptical about this treatment. The aim is to make a certain bone in the patient's neck crack. So, to spare the osteopath disappointment, Barrie snaps his fingers from time to time. This hoax has taken in the osteopath so successfully that he has become intolerably complacent, and Barrie, having worked so hard to make things seem a success, now declines to undergo any further treatment.

Yesterday I plucked up courage to ask about that St. Bernard dog, whose soulful expression has been getting more and more on my nerves. It's a portrait of Barrie's dog Porthos, who came into *The Little White Bird*, and was, also, the inspiration for the character of Nana in *Peter Pan*. Barrie told me some children who had been to *Peter Pan* refused to go to sleep until their dignified nurse consented to bark at them. (I didn't, and I trust no one ever will, tell *him* that one child had been killed because, after seeing *Peter Pan*, he 'thought beautiful thoughts', and confident that these thoughts would enable him to fly, jumped out of the nursery window!)—Cynthia As-quith, *Portrait of Barrie*, 1954, pp. 18–20

Works

DRAMA

"Peter Pan; or," adds Mr. Barrie, "The Boy Who Wouldn't Grow Up". And he himself is that boy. That child, rather; for he halted earlier than most of the men who never come to maturity—halted before the age when soldiers and steam-engines begin to dominate the soul. To remain, like Mr. Kipling, a boy, is not at all uncommon. But I know not anyone who remains, like Mr. Barrie, a child. It is this unparalleled achievement that informs so much of Mr. Barrie's later work, making it unique. This, too, surely, it is that makes Mr. Barrie the most fashionable playwright of his time.

Undoubtedly, *Peter Pan* is the best thing he has done—the thing most directly from within himself. Here, at last, we see his talent in its full maturity; for here he has stripped off from himself the last flimsy remnants of a pretence to maturity. Time was when a tiny pair of trousers peeped from under his "shortcoats," and his sunny curls were parted and plastered down, and he jauntily affected the absence of a lisp, and spelt out the novels of Mr. Meredith and said he liked them very much, and even used a pipe for another purpose than that of blowing soap-bubbles. But all this while, bless his little heart, he was suffering. It would have been pleasant enough to play at being grown-up among children of his own age. It was a fearful strain to play at being grown-up among grown-up persons. But he was forced to do this, because the managers of theatres, and the publishers of books, would have been utterly dumfounded if he had asked them to take him as he was. The public, for all its child-worship, was not yet ripe for things not written ostensibly by adults. The managers, the publishers, the public, had to be educated gradually. A stray curl or two, now and again, an infrequent soap-bubble between the fumes—that was as much as could be adventured just at first. Time passed, and mankind was lured, little by little, to the point when it could fondly accept Mr. Barrie on his own terms. The tiny trousers were slipped off, and under the toy-heap were thrust the works of Mr. Meredith. And everyone sat around, nodding and smiling to one another rather fatuously, and blessing the little heart of Mr. Barrie. All was not yet well, though—not perfectly well. By force of habit, the child occasionally gave itself the airs of an adult. There were such moments even in *Little Mary*. Now, at last, we see at the Duke of York's Theatre Mr. Barrie in his quiddity undiluted—the child in a state of nature, unabashed—the child, as it were, in its bath, splashing, and crowing as it splashes. . . .

Our dreams are nearer to us than our childhood, and it is natural that *Peter Pan* should remind us more instantly of our dreams than of our childish fancies. One English dramatist, a man of genius, realised a dream for us; but the logic in him prevented him from indulging in that wildness and incoherence which are typical of all but the finest dreams. Credible and orderly are the doings of Puck in comparison with the doings of Peter Pan. Was ever, out of dreamland, such a riot of inconsequence and of exquisite futility? Things happen in such wise that presently one can conceive nothing that might not conceivably happen, nor anything that one would not, as in a dream, accept unhesitatingly. Even as in a dream, there is no reason why the things should ever cease to happen. What possible conclusion can inhere in them? The only possible conclusion is from without. The sun shines through the bedroom window, or there is a tapping at the bedroom door, or—some playgoers must catch trains, others must sup. Even as you, awakened, turn on your pillow, wishing to pursue the dream, so, as you leave the Duke of York's, will you rebel at the dream's rude and arbitrary ending, and will try vainly to imagine what other unimaginable things were in store for you. For me to describe to you now in black and white the happenings in *Peter Pan* would be a thankless task. One cannot communicate the magic of a dream. People who insist on telling their dreams are among the terrors of the breakfast table. You must go to the Duke of York's, there to dream the dream for yourselves.—MAX BEERBOHM, "The Child Barrie," *SRL*, Jan. 7, 1905, pp. 13–14

J. M. Barrie is the foremost English-writing dramatist of our time, and his plays, taken together, make the most important contribution to the English drama since Sheridan. He unites the chief qualities of his contemporaries, and yet the last word to describe his work would be the word eclectic. For he is the most original of them all. He has the intellectual grasp of Galsworthy, the moral earnestness of Jones, the ironical mirth of Synge, the unearthly fantasy of Dunsany, the consistent logic of Ervine, the wit of Shaw, the technical excellence of Pinero. In addition to these qualities, he has a combination of charm and tenderness possessed by no other man. I am aware that the last two sentences will seem to many readers mere hyperbole. I will refer such doubters to the published plays.

. . . Mr. Barrie is a great playwright because he understands human nature, knows how to represent it in conversation and in action, has enormous sympathy with his characters, and what is equally important, has enormous sympathy with the audience. His plays are full of action; and yet the story of each play can usually be given in a few sentences. What is it then, keeps the audience at strained attention? If some character ask a question, we would not miss the answer for all the world. His people capture us almost instantly, because, while composing the play, their creator himself felt their reality. They were right there, in the room with him. He saw their faces and heard their voices. In a conversation with Mr. John D. Williams, he said, "It is my contemptible weakness, that if I say a character smiled vacuously, I must smile vacuously; if he frowns or leers, I frown or leer; if he is a coward and given to contortions, I cringe, or twist my legs until I have to stop writing to undo the knot. I bow with him, eat with him, and gnaw my mustache with him. If the character be a lady with an exquisite laugh, I suddenly terrify you by laughing exquisitely. One reads of the astounding versatility of an actor who is stout and lean on the same evening, but what is he to the novelist who is a dozen persons within the hour? Morally, I fear, we must deteriorate; but that is a subject I may wisely edge away from." . . .

Barrie is not a self-appointed prophet; he does not assume intellectual leadership; he is neither cynic nor schoolmaster; he never scolds; but he has done more to elevate the English stage than any other man of our time. And he has accomplished this simply by writing plays that are built on the permanent foundations of human nature, that are full of action, shining with brilliant dialogue, sparkling with wit and humour, heart-shaking with tragedy, and clean as the west wind. His is the drama of ideas, as distinguished from the drama of opinions.

Barrie's plays are the shows of this world. He gives us pictures of all humanity—our follies, our impossible and futile dreams, our sordidness, our nobility, our vanity; and he accomplishes this without a trace of venom or of scorn, without a flavour of superiority; he loves men, women, and children. But in him Love is never blind.—WILLIAM LYON PHELPS, "J. M. Barrie," *Essays on Modern Dramatists*, 1921, pp. 2–66

FICTION

It is twelve years since the publication of A *Window in Thrums*, and in the meantime Mr Barrie has issued only three novels. When a favourite of the public asserts himself only once in four years he takes the risk of being forgotten, or at least of receiving polite interest in exchange for enthusiastic admiration; but Mr Barrie's fame is as authentic, as actual, to-day as it was in 1889. Although *Auld Licht Idylls* preceded A *Window in Thrums*, it was the latter which, at a single stroke, established its author's position. A *Window in Thrums* secured for Mr Barrie more than the warm regard of his readers; it secured their unchangeable affection; so that everyone is incurably prejudiced in his favour, everyone is jealous for his reputation, everyone is ready to make excuses for him. And it may be said that he has needed excuses; for in these twelve years only his ambition has developed. He has industriously tried to write a great novel, but he has failed; we loyally cover up his failure, pointing to this and that excellence of his books, and assuring one another that none but a man with a touch of genius could have written them; nevertheless we cannot entirely hide our disappointment, and occasionally we hint to him that he might return to short stories. We still confidently believe that he will repeat the success of A *Window in Thrums*, and we shall continue to believe: it is an article of faith; in order not to forget it we constantly remind ourselves of it.

Now, after twelve years, it is permissible and proper to examine the foundation of a man's fame, to test, if we can, its ultimate security. We shall always love A *Window in Thrums*, but that need not prevent us from attempting to find out whether or not it quite deserves all our passionate worship. Our chief boast concerning A *Window in Thrums* has ever been that it makes us both laugh and cry, and we have said this in a tone to imply that to cause laughter and tears is the first and noblest aim of imaginative literature. But the first and noblest aim of imaginative literature is not either to tickle or to stab the sensibilities, but to render a coherent view of life's apparent incoherence, to give shape to the amorphous, to discover beauty which was hidden, to reveal essential truth. The great artist may force you to laugh or to wipe away a tear, but he accomplishes these minor feats by the way. What he mainly does is to *see* for you. If, in presenting a scene, he does not disclose aspects of it which you would not have observed for yourself, then he falls short of success. In a physical and a psychical sense his power is visual, the power of an eye seeing things always afresh, virginally, as though on the very morn of creation itself.

This supreme visual power, this virtue of the eye which creates by seeing, Mr Barrie does not possess. No trace of it is discoverable in any of his work. He can select his facts with exquisite skill, but he sees them as a plain man. Take one of the most famous pieces in A *Window in Thrums*—a piece which the author thought sufficiently good to use again in the stage version of *The Little Minister*—"Preparing to receive company." There is nothing in it that the average reader would not have learnt for himself had he been fortunate enough to witness the scene recorded. The humour of it wants no revealing, and it is neither subtilised nor intensified. The incident is intrinsically and obviously amusing, and the author's phrases are happy—and that is all. It is the unconscious conviction of this lack of visual—that is, creative—power which drives Mr Barrie to be always, at any cost, either humorous or pathetic, and to divert by nimbleness of fancy and jugglery of phrase. When he is neither humorous nor pathetic he is nothing. A

Window in Thrums is one long oscillation between making a certain class of people ridiculous by reason of their manners, and making them dignified by reason of their extraordinary trials and fortitude. There is no "setting" to the pictures, no landscape, no verbal beauty, no feeling for anything except the figures; the figures might be against a background of brown paper; they are posed like models in a studio; you will find no Egdon Heath in Mr Barrie, no sense of nature's large inclusiveness; with Mr Barrie man is man, and nature is something different, something negligible. As regards the humour and pathos, which alone constitute the book (imagine a diet of sugar and salt, a literature consisting solely of humour and pathos!), the humour is more spontaneous than the pathos. The pathos is too much insisted upon, even forced—as in "Waiting for the Doctor" and "Jamie's Homecoming." One cannot but observe how again and again the author saddens one with the fact that it all happened long ago, "in the dear dead days beyond recall," that everyone is dead and buried now, and the old house in ruins. This, to be frank, is not playing the game. From the beginning Mr Barrie has had a tendency to sentimentalise, by which I mean to affect or exaggerate sentiment; the tendency was distinctly to be felt in *A Window in Thrums*; in *The Little Minister* it became more marked, more noticeably saccharine; and in the stage version of *The Little Minister*, that excessively profitable lump of sweetstuff, it amounted to a confirmed habit of mind.—Arnold Bennett, "Mr J. M. Barrie," *Fame and Fiction*, 1901, pp. 37–41

Barrie's most ambitious venture into fiction took the form of two closely linked novels in which he set out to expose the fundamental weaknesses of the artistic temperament. Usually known as the "Tommy" novels, these books achieved a notable success in disarming critical reaction. Hammerton, who was unsettled by Barrie's unpredictable flights into mawkishness and cynicism, prefers not to discuss these aberrations; and he actually asserts that "No good purpose would be served . . . by entering into an exposition of those points in which *Sentimental Tommy* fails as a novel. . . ." Darton goes even further in rejecting criticism by insisting that "Such novels—and there have been few at all like *Sentimental Tommy* and *Tommy and Grizel*—are to be felt, not dissected." Even Moult, who sometimes remembers that he is supposed to be writing a critical study of Barrie, rhapsodizes about the *Tommy* books as the work of "an English Gogol." Certainly *Sentimental Tommy* is an entertaining tale, and it is, arguably, Barrie's best work of fiction; but there is nothing sublime about it, nothing that puts it beyond criticism. It reveals Barrie's tongue-in-cheek whimsy and puckishness at their most engaging; but it does not reveal a profound thinker exploring and illuminating the artistic temperament. The only temperament enlightened is Barrie's, and it is therefore absurd to over praise the novel as a kind of universal *kunstlerroman*, like Joyce's *Portrait of the Artist* or Mann's "Tonio Kröger." Tommy Sandys is an alter ego of Barrie but of no other literary artist. And the fundamental weakness of the two novels in which he appears is that, except for Tommy himself, the only character Barrie really understands, the characters are, for the most part superficial or implausible, or both. . . .

Barrie is so frequently dismissed as a sentimentalist, according to the conventional usage of the word, that it is bound to surprise readers of the "Tommy" novels that he uses the word "sentimental" in a special sense. Tommy's sentimentality is his belief in the masks that he creates at the expense of his own personality. Sentimentality, which makes him as a writer, destroys him as a man. He starts out as a hero

and becomes an object lesson, a late Victorian equivalent of Walter Mitty or Billy Liar. Like these more recent characters, he believes the parts he plays more than he believes in himself. Ironically, Barrie's representation of himself in the character of Tommy Sandys is a mask additional to those assumed by Tommy and torn away by his creator. Barrie's own involvement with the novels made it impossible for him to see this objectively. But, in laughing bitterly at and with Tommy, the adult-boy, he was laughing at himself, the adult writer unable to escape from the childhood experience that provided his creative material. He was also trapped, like Tommy, by the glamor of popular success. The irony of his position, represented in Tommy's relations with Grizel, is that the masks which brought him success as a writer acted as barriers to love. The fictions he created in his psychological rivalry with David became progressively more elaborate, but we know from *Margaret Ogilvy* that Barrie's mother saw through them just as Grizel eventually saw through Tommy.—Harry M. Geduld, *Sir James Barrie*, 1971, pp. 45–52

LOUIS WILKINSON
"Sir James Barrie:
Confectioner and Parlour-Magician"
The Dial, August 1923, pp. 167–69

Sir James Barrie is related, with peculiar intimacy, to the mind and the emotions, to the naïveties and idealisms of the American and British public. He loves easy pretty illusions, and so does the average Anglo-Saxon. As an anodyne for those modern discontents that are the besetting virtues of our introspective serious writers and readers he has been found invaluable. From the "unpleasant truths" of Shaw and Galsworthy and Wells the patron of the circulating library turns in relief to warm and cheer his heart with the agreeable fantasies, the dainty make-believes, the harmless friendly humour of this Scotch sentimentalist.

Barrie is never disquieting, he is never bitter. Though he may indulge us and himself in sarcasm, the sarcasm is always genial. To most readers he is seldom anything but charming and companionable. He is the most "taking" of playwrights or novelists, and he never offends the normal proprieties. Like Mr A. S. M. Hutchinson, whom he praises so highly and so significantly, Barrie can be read aloud in any drawing-room to any lady. His humour is very like the humour of Punch; middle-class drawing-room humour, reassuringly undistinguished, always wholesome, always safe. When we think of the husband who declared that "his first two wives were angels; and so is the third, in many respects"—of the other husband who "clapped his hands when his wife died, and exclaimed: 'Hip, hip, hurrah!' adding only as an afterthought: 'The Lord's will be done!'"—of the dour Auld Lichts who "always looked as though they were returning from burying a near relative"—of the minister who believed that "no other denomination could be saved, and not so many of his own"—we realize at once how well and how shrewdly such jests avoid the danger of giving any real offence. They are just daring enough; they are on the right side of the line: there is not implicit in them, as there is in the jests of Hardy or Shaw, any vital discontent with or any serious attack upon either orthodoxy or marriage. You may laugh and yet moult no feather of your respectability. But when we remember, in contrast, the individual and revealing, the philosophic humour of writers of genius—such as Sterne or Ben Jonson—we may react somewhat from our enjoyment of Barrie's little jokes.

A writer may be judged by his humour: he may also be judged by his view of women and by his feeling for romance. Now to many there is no doubt something very attractive in Barrie's chivalry; something very charming in his tender self-deceptions about maids and wives and mothers and domestic felicities. He appears, in this regard, as a susceptible and high-minded adolescent to whom the more advanced volumes of feminine psychology are fast sealed. But many women enjoy adolescent devotion, many women like being idealized. They accept with ironical enjoyment—most profoundly concealed!—the tributes of the sentimental male; and they read Barrie novels or witness Barrie plays with an enjoyment of precisely the same kind. None the less most of them know well enough in their hearts that Barrie and his kin are not really their best friends. "How like you in the plan is woman, Knew you her as we!" wrote that true feminist, George Meredith. Barrie does not agree. "Oh, man!" he cries, in an orgy of abasement before the glimpses of those vistas of spiritual beauty which the name Woman discloses to him: "Oh, man! selfish, indelicate, coarse-grained at the best!" He would cherish, at all costs, in women, that "purity infinite, spotless bloom," in the male demand for which Meredith detected an "infinite grossness."

Is there, perhaps—the disconcerting reflection must sometimes have occurred to some of his admirers—is there not perhaps, after all, a certain element of grossness, of vulgarity, even, in Barrie's treatment of sex—a sort of obscene decency, one might call it? Though he never offends "nice" susceptibilities, does he not offend other susceptibilities which are characterized by a delicacy of a different kind? Witness the emphasis—the particular sort of emphasis—that he gives to certain passages in the conversation of the children in *Peter Pan*; witness the particular quality of his comments on certain innocent observations that occur in *The Young Visiters*.

There is, in relation to sex, a special sort of respectable and discreet facetiousness that is altogether alien to great writers. It is, to finer taste, infinitely more offensive than sheer ribaldry, of which, indeed, numerous men of the highest literary genius, including notably Shakespeare himself, are abundantly capable. When Barrie refers to the beating of a lover's heart as a "palp," or when he talks with a smirk of "Little Mary," he is perhaps not more coarse in the usual sense than is Mercutio when telling Juliet's nurse the time of day, but he is certainly more coarse-grained. It is this same coarseness of grain that makes Barrie incapable of depicting true passion. The poetic intensities of love are outside his scope, and he therefore takes refuge in sentimentalism, though somewhat more subtly, no doubt, than his own Sentimental Tommy. The lover whose romance has poetic quality transmutes by a sovereign alchemy the baser metal of fleshly desire to pure gold; but the desire is not destroyed: it never can be. The sentimentalist, with his thinner and weaker emotions, is ashamed of that element of desire which his lesser love lacks strength to interfuse. So he tries hard to pretend it is not there; he lies to himself about it, and the whole tissue of his feeling is tainted by the morbid blight of this pretence. Lack of poetic strength is the original cause.

Nor is this lack, in Barrie, any the less evident when we turn from the "love-interest" in his work to those more fantastic and whimsical excursions which some regard as providing his chief claim to recognition. How little of the glamour of Celtic fairyland has the sugar-sweet magic of this Lowland Scot! Peter Pan is no Ariel: he can wake not even the most distant echo of that fairy music that sounds from the yellow sands of an island veritably enchanted. "Pretty touches," it is true, abound in *Peter Pan*, and children will probably always like the play be-

cause of the pirates, but of beauty it has no single touch, no single thrill. Poetry and prettiness—a gulf lies in between; and think of Mary Rose—Mary Rose, not for remembrance! Only the poet can be fantastic without being absurd. Contrast, with Barrie, Walter de la Mare.

But the author of *Mary Rose* and *Peter Pan* is not a negligible figure. He serves a purpose. In a rather curious and quite illuminating way he shows what comes of that kind of fancy that does not strike deep roots in heart or head. He shows us make-believe and whimsy falling just short of imagination, sentiment just missing romance, humour ranging just outside the arena of laughing philosophy. He has never felt passion, nor poetry's "wand-like touch," and so, for all his success, he fails; fails, in all his pleasantness and prettiness, in all his sterile charm.

DAVID DAICHES
From "The Sexless Sentimentalist"
The Listener, May 12, 1960, pp. 841–43

I have recently read through nearly all of Barrie's plays and most of his stories and sketches. It was an unnerving experience. I had not realized before with what steady and skilful perversity Barrie exploited his public's emotional concern with human relationships or with what disturbing cunning he gave his own strangely distorted rendering of the human situation. He dealt in the elemental things of life, in the relations between mother and son, brother and sister, husband and wife, reality and dream. In his characteristic work he is out from the beginning to implicate the reader or the audience, to play on their emotional responses. The appeal to the audience in *Peter Pan* to indicate that they believe in fairies and so save the life of Tinker Bell, is symbolic of Barrie's whole relation with his audience. He wants to get it uncomfortably involved, embarrassingly and desperately involved in that cruelly sentimental world of boy-men and sexless marriages and corrupting feeling which he portrays in so many of his plays and stories.

I call it 'cruelly sentimental' because it is impossible not to be struck by a streak of real cruelty in Barrie: he takes a positively masochistic pleasure in frustrating all normal expectations about the proper satisfaction of adult human relationships. Tommy marries Grizel only after she has gone out of her mind, in order to act as nurse, and when she recovers she knows that he is only pretending to love her and so—though Barrie does not put it as bluntly as this—she decides that they must not sleep together. *Mary Rose* is a play about the frustration of the marriage relationship and in so far as the ending is happy it is because each partner has learned to be happier without it. In *A Window in Thrums* a whole family's emotions are concentrated on the son. He reciprocates this passion but he is led astray by a London hussy so that he repudiates his aged parents and loving sister, to return home only after they are all dead. At the end of *The Admirable Crichton* we sense exactly the same masochistic pleasure. Crichton, the butler and the best man among them all, voluntarily restores his earlier position of servitude and confirms the social prejudices of his stupid employers. Time and again Barrie builds up all his sentimental resources to picture a relationship on which the whole emotional centre of the play or story rests and then he destroys it before our faces; there is the brave laugh which says that after all life is like that or there is the whimsical shrug which tells us that, like the character of Margaret in *Dear Brutus*, it was but a 'might-have-been' after all.

At the bottom of all this lies a fierce resistance to the

implications of any mature human relationship. The clue can be found in his early prose sketches and stories. Here children grow up in the streets of a London slum or of a poverty stricken Scottish village, totally ignorant of the so-called 'facts of life' and believing—sometimes, we feel, believing until the end of their days—all the sugary Victorian monstrosities about where babies came from and how and why people got married. The account of Tommy's reactions to the birth of his sister, in *Sentimental Tommy*, and his relations with the little rich girl Reddy (who, of course, dies in childhood)—all set in a context of a swarming London street life—is positively grotesque in its calculated whimsy. Again and again in these stories the love of brother and sister is treated as the same in kind but greater in quality than the love of a man and his sweetheart. All love, in fact, is sexless. Barrie even goes so far as to have his teen-age brothers and sisters sleep together—which is more than most of his husbands and wives do. In *Auld Licht Idylls* Jamie, courting Janet, wants to draw back and have his sister instead. ('I'm thinking', Jamie said at last a little wistfully, 'that I micht hae been as well wi' Christy'. Christy was Jamie's sister. It is a revealing remark.)

But isn't *Peter Pan*, at least, a great children's classic? One may grant that many children see and enjoy it every year—though largely, I suspect, because it is a stage play, it is live theatre, which children see all too rarely and which nearly all children love. For many children it is the first play they see, and of course they adore it—one always adores one's first experience of the live theatre in action. But surely it is a thoroughly embarrassing play. From the opening domestic scene, which is neither truly imagined domestic comedy nor genuine farce nor pure fantasy but an uncomfortable mixture of satire, whimsy, music-hall, and emotionalism—from this opening scene through all the varied action with its deliberately shifting levels of probability and its studied playing up to the traditional prop-

erties of childhood imagination, right up to the final confrontation of Wendy's affection and Peter's egotism, there is that same distortion of human relationships, that sexless confounding of different kinds of love and concern, that same delicate cruelty, that Barrie has always dealt with. We may accept it here because it is a play largely about and for children. But I don't know. I saw *Peter Pan* only once as a child, and it made me acutely uncomfortable; now I read it with squirming embarrassment. It is not only the degeneration of the classical Pan into a whimsical symbol of permanent pre-puberty that is intolerable; again, one might accept that in a play for children.

Perhaps I can explain my discomfort by a comparison. Peter Pan remarks defiantly 'I don't want to go to school and learn solemn things. No one is going to catch me, lady, and make me a man'. Put this beside Huckleberry Finn's similar remark: 'The Widow Douglas she took me for her son, and allowed she would civilize me; but it was rough living in the house all the time, considering how dismal regular and decent the widow was in her ways; so when I couldn't stand it no longer I lit out'. Put these two together and Peter Pan is exposed. Huckleberry Finn's refusal to grow up and be respectable is a profoundly ironic critical gesture, whereas Peter Pan's behaviour represents a contrived adult escapism.

For Barrie, literature was an escape from life and at the same time a revenge taken on life for daring to pose adult problems involving real human relationships. The cloying sweetness belongs to the escape, and the cruelty to the revenge. Perhaps we may conclude from this that at bottom he was impelled less by unscrupulousness than by an inwardly tortured and divided personality. Perhaps I have overstressed the calculating side of Barrie. Clearly, something within him helped to twist his view of human relations into the pattern I have been describing. For those who want to explain rather than evaluate his work there is much more to say.

Samuel Beckett

1906–

Samuel Barclay Beckett was born in Dublin on April 13, 1906. He attended the University of Dublin's Trinity College, where he excelled in French and cricket. Beckett earned a B.A. in 1927, taught English in Paris from 1928 to 1930, then returned to Trinity to teach French, receiving an M.A. in 1931. During this period, his idol James Joyce dictated parts of *Finnegans Wake* to Beckett, who translated a section into French with Alfred Peron. Beckett also published a study of Proust. In 1932 he left Trinity to travel through Europe. He spent most of the decade in a black depression, suffering several nervous breakdowns, and undergoing years of psychoanalysis. He settled in Paris in 1937; his spirits picked up the following year when his first novel, *Murphy*, was finally published—after 41 rejections. Also in 1938 Beckett met pianist Suzanne Deschevaux-Demesnil, with whom he has lived ever since.

From 1940 to 1942 Beckett was active in the French Resistance. Sought by the Nazis, he and Suzanne escaped to a farm in Free France, where Beckett lay low and wrote for three years. After the war, he spent a year working at a Red Cross hospital, then resumed his life in Paris. Beckett concentrated on a trilogy of novels (*Malone Dies* and *Molloy*, 1951; *The Unnamable*, 1953), but turned to drama as a "diversion" when he became blocked. His first play, the long and elaborate *Eleutheria*, went unproduced; his second was the epochal *Waiting for Godot*, written in French. This seminal work of Absurdism was an immediate success in Paris in 1953, and Beckett's 1954 English translation a triumph in London. On Broadway, however, *Godot* mystified audiences and critics, who caught up with it years later in revival. Beckett continued to write novels, but his dramatic diversions became more frequent: *Endgame* in 1958, *Krapp's Last Tape* in 1960, *Happy*

Days in 1962, and *Play* in 1964 all won Obie awards off-Broadway. Other awards for Beckett include an honorary doctorate from Trinity in 1959, an International Publisher's Prize in 1961, and the Nobel Prize for Literature in 1969. Beckett often directs his plays, which grow ever shorter. He scoffs at most critical interpretations of his work: "My work is a matter of fundamental sounds made as fully as possible, and I accept responsibility for nothing else." Besides his novels and plays, Beckett has written poetry and translated Rimbaud and Apollinaire.

He lives in Paris with Suzanne, whom he married in 1961.

Personal

Beckett was addicted to silences, and so was Joyce; they engaged in conversations which consisted often of silences directed towards each other, both suffused with sadness, Beckett mostly for the world, Joyce mostly for himself. Joyce sat in his habitual posture, legs crossed, toe of the upper leg under the instep of the lower; Beckett, also tall and slender, fell into the same gesture. Joyce suddenly asked some such question as, 'How could the idealist Hume write a history?' Beckett replied, 'A history of representations.' Joyce said nothing, but some time afterwards he informed the young man, 'The only amateur philosopher of any value I know is Carducci.' Later, 'For me,' he said, 'there is only one alternative to scholasticism, scepticism.'

Though he liked having Beckett with him, Joyce at the same time kept him at a distance. Once he said directly, 'I don't love anyone except my family,' in a tone which suggested, 'I don't like anyone except my family either.' But Beckett's mind had a subtlety and strangeness that attracted Joyce as it attracted, in another way, his daughter. So he would ask the young man to read to him passages from Mauthner's *Beiträge zu Einer Kritik der Sprache*, in which the nominalistic view of language seemed something Joyce was looking for. Once or twice he dictated a bit of *Finnegans Wake* to Beckett, though dictation did not work very well for him; in the middle of one such session there was a knock at the door which Beckett didn't hear. Joyce said, 'Come in,' and Beckett wrote it down. Afterwards he read back what he had written and Joyce said, 'What's that "Come in"?' 'Yes, you said that,' said Beckett. Joyce thought for a moment, then said, 'Let it stand.' He was quite willing to accept coincidence as his collaborator. Beckett was fascinated and thwarted by Joyce's singular method.— Richard Ellmann, *James Joyce*, 1959, pp. 661–62

I waited for the author of *Waiting for Godot* in the Paris office allocated him by his publisher. But I wondered if he was going to show up: through timidity, unsociability, or possibly just as part of his system, until today, he had energetically refused to be interviewed.

This writer, so often described as being fierce, is now in his fifties. He's an Irishman, like James Joyce, and it's said that Joyce preferred Beckett to many of his other translators. Beckett taught English for three years at our Ecole Normale and later taught French at Dublin's Trinity College. In London, he published several books of poems, a study of Proust, and a novel, *Murphy*, but before its release a German bomb destroyed the entire edition.

Never despair. In 1938, Samuel Beckett came to France to stay, and thenceforth wrote in French; his trilogy, *Molloy*, *Malone Dies*, and *The Unnamable* drew rave notices from those critics partial to difficult literature. Nevertheless, even the most fervent among them are disappointed by his latest work, *Comment c'est* (How things are). As for his play, *Waiting for Godot*, more generally accessible although nothing happens in it, it was put on two hundred times at the Théâtre de Babylone and was triumphantly received in several European countries, notably in Germany.

The question remained: Was the disconcerting Samuel Beckett going to show up? Yes, there he was!

Both of Molloy's legs are paralyzed, Malone is in death throes, and the Unnamable is a paraplegic living in a sort of coffin. But the man who infused life into these monsters is handsome and healthy-looking, tall, blond, and well-tanned, with regular and noble features. He looks closely at you from behind thick spectacles; often his thin lips curl with a touch of irony and wiliness.

He had just arrived from a village in the Département of Seine-et-Marne, where he has bought a small piece of property, thanks to a modest inheritance.

Knowing how he can't stomach the farce of a professional literary life, I told him how I envied him for being able to work in peace there, and he agreed heartily: 'You're quite right. The country's a lovely place to write in.'

'So you've done a lot of writing lately?'

'Not a thing. A little gardening. Odd jobs. No writing though.'

'Is that the truth?'

'Only some very short pieces, sort of short stories.'

He glanced at the door. To clear the air, I told him that in the past I'd been slightly acquainted with the children of his master James Joyce when the latter had lived near the Champs-de-Mars.

Beckett scrutinized me amiably: 'Oh, so you knew George and poor little Lucia?'

'Why "poor"?'

He gestured vaguely.

'Joyce considered you one of his best translators. Can it be claimed you are also his disciple? Your long interior monologues . . . '

'Oh! well you know, I only translated personally—I mean all by myself—Anna Livia Plurabelle. But here in Paris, I've done numerous anonymous translations to earn my living. Do you mind?'

He sat at his desk and began to sign title pages. So, like everyone else, Samuel Beckett dedicates his books! I eased down on the edge of his desk.

'Your novels are rather difficult reading. Were they hard to write?'

'Oh, yes, but they came in one great spurt of enthusiasm.'

'Enthusiasm?'

'*Malone* grew out of *Molloy*, *The Unnamable* out of *Malone*, but afterwards—and for a long time—I wasn't at all sure what I had left to say. I'd hemmed myself in. To try to break loose, I wrote those short texts, those little stories if you wish, that I call "écrits pour rien."' (Translator's note: double sense, either 'pointless writings' or 'written pointlessly'; he is referring to *Nouvelles et Textes pour rien*.)

'Have contemporary philosophers had any influence on your thought?'

'I never read philosophers.'

'Why not?'

'I never understand anything they write.'

'All the same, people have wondered if the existentialists' problem of being may afford a key to your works.'

'There's no key or problem. I wouldn't have had any reason to write my novels if I could have expressed their subject in philosophic terms.'

'What was your reason then?'

'I haven't the slightest idea. I'm no intellectual. All I am is feeling. *Molloy* and the others came to me the day I became aware of my own folly. Only then did I begin to write the things I feel.'—GABRIEL D'AUBARÈDE, "Waiting for Beckett," tr. Christopher Waters, *Trace*, Summer 1961, pp. 156–58

About five years ago, we met by chance on Rue Guynemer; as he asked if I were working, I told him that I had lost my taste for work, that I didn't see the necessity of bestirring myself, or 'producing,' that writing was an ordeal for me. . . . He seemed astonished by this, and I was even more astonished when, precisely in reference to writing, he spoke of *joy*. Did he really use that word? Yes, I am sure of it. At the same moment I recalled that at our first meeting, some ten years earlier at the Closerie des Lilas, he had confessed to me his great weariness, the feeling he had that nothing could be squeezed out of words any more. . . .

With writers who have nothing to say, who do not possess a world of their own, one speaks only of literature. With him, very rarely, in fact almost never. Any everyday topic (material difficulties, annoyances of all kinds) interests him more—in a conversation, of course. What he cannot tolerate, at any rate, are questions like: do you think this or that work is destined to last? That this or that one deserves its reputation? Of X and Y, which one will survive, which is the greatest. All evaluations of this sort tax his patience and depress him. 'What's the point of all that?' he said to me after a particularly unpleasant evening, when the discussion at dinner had resembled a grotesque version of the Last Judgment. He himself avoids expressing opinions about his books and plays: what's important to him are not obstacles that have been overcome, but obstacles yet to be faced. He merges totally with whatever he is working on. If one asks him about a play, he will not linger over the content or the meaning, but over the interpretation, whose most insignificant details he visualizes minute by minute—I was about to say second by second. I will not soon forget his spirited explanation of the requirements to be satisfied by an actress wishing to play *Not I*, in which a single breathless voice dominates space and substitutes itself for it. How his eyes gleamed as he *saw* that mouth, insignificant and yet invading, omnipresent! One would have thought he was witnessing the ultimate metamorphosis, the supreme downfall of Pythia!

Having been fond of cemeteries all my life, and knowing that Beckett liked them too (*First Love*, one may recall, begins with the description of a cemetery, which is, by way of parenthesis, the one in Hamburg), I was telling him last winter, on the Avenue de l'Observatoire, about a recent visit to the Père-Lachaise Cemetery, and about my indignation at not finding Proust on the list of 'celebrities' buried there. (I first discovered Beckett's name, by the way, thirty years ago in the American library, when I came across his little book on Proust one day.) I don't know how we ended up with Swift, though now that I think about it, there was nothing unusual about the transition, given the funereal nature of his mockery. Beckett told me he was re-reading the *Travels*, and that he had a predilection for the 'Country of the Houyhnhnms,' especially for the scene in which Gulliver is mad with terror and disgust at the approach of a Yahoo female. He informed me—and this was a great surprise to me, above all a great disappointment— that Joyce didn't care for Swift. Moreover, he added, Joyce, contrary to what people think, had no inclination whatever for satire. 'He never rebelled, he was detached, he accepted every

thing. For him, *there was absolutely no difference between a bomb falling and a leaf falling.*' . . .

I am not particularly attracted to Wittgenstein's philosophy, but I have a passion for the man. Everything I read about him has the power to move me. More than once I have found common traits in him and in Beckett. Two mysterious apparitions, two phenomena that please one by being so baffling, so inscrutable. In both, one and the other, the same distance from beings and things, the same inflexibility, the same temptation to silence, to a final repudiation of words, the same desire to collide with boundaries never sensed before. In another time, they would have been drawn to the Desert. We now know that Wittgenstein had, at one time, considered entering a monastery. As for Beckett, one can very easily imagine him, a few centuries back, in a bare cell unsullied by any decoration, not even a crucifix. You think I am rambling? Consider, then, the faraway, enigmatic, 'inhuman' look he has in certain photographs.

Our beginnings count, that goes without saying, but we only take the decisive step toward ourselves when we no longer have an *origin*, and when we offer just as little subject-matter for a biography as God does. It is important, and it is not important at all, that Beckett is Irish. What is certainly false is to claim that he is the 'perfect example of an Anglo-Saxon.' At any rate, nothing displeases him more. Is this because of the unpleasant memories he still has of his pre-war stay in London? I suspect him of accusing the English of 'commonness.' That verdict, which he has not expressed but which I am expressing in his place like a summary of his reservations, if not of his resentments, I cannot personally subscribe to, and this all the more so because, doubtless due to a Balkan illusion, the English seem to me to be the most devitalized and most menaced, and therefore the most refined and civilized of peoples.

Beckett, who curiously enough feels completely at home in France, has actually no affinity whatever with a certain hardness, a trait that is eminently French, Parisian to be precise. Is it not significant that he has put Chamfort into verse? Not all of Chamfort, true, but only a few maxims. The enterprise, remarkable in itself and moreover almost inconceivable (if one considers the absence of lyric spirit that characterizes the skeletal prose of the Moralists), is equivalent to an avowal, I dare not say a proclamation. It is always in spite of themselves that restrained minds betray the depth of their natures. Beckett's is so impregnated with poetry that it becomes indistinguishable from it.

I believe him to be as deliberate as a fanatic. Even if the world were to collapse, he would neither abandon work in progress nor change his subject. As far as essentials are concerned, he certainly cannot be swayed. As for everything else, as for inessentials, he is defenseless, probably weaker than any of us, weaker even than his characters. Before writing these few notes, I proposed to reread what Meister Eckhart and Nietzsche had written, from different perspectives, about 'the noble man.' I did not carry out my project, but I have not forgotten for a moment that I thought of doing it.—E. M. CIORAN, "Encounters with Beckett," trs. Raymond Federman, Jean A. Sommermeyer, *PR*, 1976, pp. 281–85

I must have gone to Paris expecting something to occur but I never dreamed for an instant what was in store for me. In spite of the fact that I took every consolation which crossed my path, I was entirely obsessed for over a year by the strange creature, Samuel Beckett. He came into my life the day after Christmas, 1937. I had known him slightly. He had been to our house on the Avenue Reille. I knew that he was a friend of James Joyce, that he had been engaged to his daughter and had caused her great unhappiness. Beckett was not Joyce's secretary, as everyone has since claimed, though he was perpetually doing errands for him. Joyce had a Russian Jewish intellectual for secretary, called Paul Léon, who was later killed by the Germans.

Beckett was a tall, lanky Irishman of about thirty with enormous green eyes that never looked at you. He wore spectacles, and always seemed to be far away solving some intellectual problem; he spoke very seldom and never said anything stupid. He was excessively polite, but rather awkward. He dressed badly in tight-fitting French clothes and had no vanity about his appearance. Beckett accepted life fatalistically, as he never seemed to think he could alter anything. He was a frustrated writer, a pure intellectual. I met him again at Helen Joyce's. . . .

The thing I liked best about our life together was that I never knew at what hour of the night or day he might return to me. His comings and goings were completely unpredictable, and I found that exciting. He was drunk all of the time and seemed to wander around in a dream. I had a lot of work to do because of my gallery and often I had to get up in the afternoon to see Cocteau, who was to have the opening show. Beckett objected to this; he wanted me to remain in bed with him.

It seemed ironic that I should create a new existence for myself because I had no personal life, and now that I had a personal life, it had to be sacrificed. On the tenth day of our amours Beckett was untrue to me. He allowed a friend of his from Dublin to creep into his bed. I don't know how I found it out, but he admitted it saying that he simply had not put her out when she came to him, and that making love without being in love was like taking coffee without brandy. From this I inferred I was the brandy in his life, but nevertheless I was furious, and said that I was finished with him. The next night he phoned me, but I was so angry that I refused to speak to him. A few minutes later he was stabbed in the ribs by an unknown maniac on the Avenue d'Orléans and taken to a hospital. I had no idea of this and as I was leaving for London I wanted to say goodbye to him. When I called his hotel the proprietor told me what had happened. I nearly went mad. I rushed to all the hospitals in Paris but could not find him. Finally I phoned Nora Joyce, who told me where he was. I went to him at once, and left some flowers and a note telling him how much I loved him and that I forgave him everything. The next day James Joyce went to see Beckett in the hospital and I went with him. As he was semi-blind, it took Joyce a long time to be conducted by his secretary to the right ward. But by a sort of instinct I rushed in and without any help found Beckett. He was surprised to see me, as he thought I had left for London. He was very happy. I said goodbye to him. I knew he was in good hands because Joyce was looking after him, and that he would be laid up for a long time. I had to go back to London to open my gallery, but I meant to return to Paris as soon as I could.—Peggy Guggenheim, *Out of This Century*, 1979, pp. 162–65

General

Why is Beckett interesting as a writer? As a contemporary phenomenon, he is one more negative protest against the world going to the slaughterhouse, one more protest on behalf of privacy, a voice for myopia. He is a modern Oblomov, fretful and apathetic, enclosed in private fantasy, dropping off into words instead of sleep. They are eloquent, cunning, unremitting words.

He is far from feeble, for there is a devil-like slyness in the half grin on the faces of his old men who can hit out with their crutches. What tedium! They exclaim—speaking not only of existence and human solitude—but, we suspect, of ourselves. His imagination has the Irish cruelty and self-destructiveness that Yeats once spoke of. Beckett's anti-novels, like all anti-novels, have to deal with small areas of experience because their pretension is to evoke the whole of life, *i.e.* life unfixed by art; the result is that these verbose books are like long ironical, stinging footnotes in small print to some theme not formulated. But there is a flash of deep insight in the madness he evokes: it is strange that in a generation which has put all its stress on youth and achievement, he alone should have written about old age, loneliness and decrepitude, a subject which arouses perhaps our deepest repressed guilt and fears. He is the product of a civilisation which has become suddenly old. He is a considerable, muttering, comic writer, and although he conveys unbearable pain, he also conveys the element of sardonic tenacity that lies at the heart of the comic gift.—V. S. Pritchett, "An Irish Oblomov," *NS*, April 2, 1960, p. 489

If the novel is defined as a pleasant tale, spun for the amusement of the reader by craftsmen of narrative technique, adept in the invention of interesting characters and the construction of intricately patterned plots, then Samuel Beckett could not be called a novelist at all, at least as far as the books he has written in French are concerned. But if, on the other hand, it were permissible to define the novel as a work in prose in which an imaginative artist may explore, with uncompromising honesty, ruthless integrity, and utter frankness, the human condition in all its naked absurdity, then prose poets like Franz Kafka or James Joyce can be called great novelists. Then too Samuel Beckett can take his place among them as one of the most profound and most significant novelists of our time. For Beckett, like Kafka, does not write for the amusement of readers. It is doubtful if, in writing his books, he ever even thinks of readers. Beckett writes because he has to write, because he is under a compulsion to search for the nature of his own self, and thus to explore the depths of being, the nature of the predicament of man and his existence. . . .

Because among his earliest published writings there are essays on Proust and Joyce, and because he belonged to Joyce's circle, it has become one of the endlessly repeated clichés of literary reviewers that Beckett is a follower of Joyce, or has been influenced by Proust. In fact, even a fairly casual examination of his work must show that he owes little to either of these writers. As Beckett himself once pointed out in conversation, Proust is an analyser, Joyce a synthesizer. But if Proust dissects reality by examining it minutely, if Joyce builds a new reality by the creative use of language, Beckett does neither of these things: he is searching for the nature of reality itself by eliminating and discarding layer after layer of accidental qualities, by peeling off skin after skin of the onion to reach the innermost core, the nothingness at the centre of being. For Beckett, as he says in his essay on Proust, 'the artistic tendency is not expansive but a contraction. And art is the apotheosis of solitude. There is no communication because there are no vehicles of communication.' To Beckett, therefore, the novel is not an act of communication or storytelling, it is a lonely and dedicated exploration, a shaft driven deep down into the core of the self. It is a self-contradictory, Quixotic, but because of this an infinitely heroic and noble attempt at expressing the inexpressible, saying the unsayable, distilling the essence of being and making visible the still centre of reality. Demokritos the Abderite, in one of Beckett's favourite apophthegms, said: 'Nothing is more real than nothing.'

This exploration has nothing to do with mere description,

it rejects 'the grotesque fallacy of realistic art—"that miserable statement of line and surface", and the penny-a-line vulgarity of a literature of notations' (*Proust*), the efforts of 'realists and naturalists worshipping the offals of experience, prostrate before the epidermis and the swift epilepsy, and content to transcribe the surface, the façade, behind which the Idea is prisoner' (ibid.).

Yet how is the unsayable to be said, the uncommunicable to be communicated? As Beckett himself put it in describing the difficulties of one of his earlier heroes, Watt:

> . . . the only way one can speak of nothing is to speak of it as though it were something, just as the only way one can speak of God is to speak of him as though he were a man, which to be sure he was, in a sense, for a time, and as the only way one can speak of man, even our anthropologists have realized that, is to speak of him as though he were a termite.

Having left the surface of reality, Beckett's later novels deal with archetypes, they take place in a *'présent mythologique'* as Molloy puts it. Beckett's later novels have no story, no beginning and no end because they examine archetypal situations that are ever-present attributes of the human condition. . . .

What Beckett has in common with Swift is the combination of the deepest moral earnestness and artistic integrity with what in its essence is a comic talent. However much he may appear to be exploring the depths of human squalor and degradation, Beckett always remains a master of sardonic humour. Those critics who accuse him of unrelieved gloom and pessimism merely reveal that they lack the sense organs required to see how hilariously funny much of Beckett's vision can be: the audiences who rocked with laughter at *Waiting for Godot* had a very much clearer perception of the true nature of Beckett's genius—which lies precisely in his ability to produce the liberating catharsis of laughter by confronting his public not only with the sordidness of the human condition but also with a vision of its utter pettiness and inanity: that is why Beckett calls Demokritos' saying about the reality of nothingness a guffaw. When we see that all is vanity we can laugh even at the horrors of existence. . . .

Beckett's work is entirely *sui generis*, unclassifiable, disturbing, funny, cruel, and inspiring. It defies all attempts at interpretation—like the world of atomic particles where the introduction of an observer itself changes that which is to be observed. Like Michelangelo, who chipped away the rock to reveal the delicate beauty that had always been imprisoned within it, Beckett works by discarding layer upon layer of conventional narrative material: description, character, psychology, incident, plot, to lay bare the secret workings of the human mind. But here too he can only work, as it were, by measuring out the limits of the sayable so that the unsayable may be guessed, hidden behind the last, impenetrable barrier.

Beckett's novels and plays are not easily accessible. They must be approached with due humility, read more than once, wrestled with and fought for. Beckett is a poet working for his own salvation. Public relations and an easy urbanity in the presentation of his work are not included in his basic brief.

And yet, although he has made no effort at achieving fame or creating a following, he has become famous and has won relatively wide support. Perhaps the most difficult writer of his generation, he has reached his public as a dramatist, as a writer of the most poetic radio plays of his time, and as a novelist. This is a fact that goes a long way towards restoring one's faith in the power of the dedicated pursuit of truth and beauty.—MARTIN ESSLIN, "Samuel Beckett," *The Novelist as Philosopher*, ed. John Cruickshank, 1962, pp. 128–45

The number of contemplatives is always small, for of all strenuous lives the contemplative life is most strenuous. The strain and the joy of climbing Mount Everest, though doubtless extreme in their kind, are little enough by comparison with the strain and the joy of achieving some vision, in however dark a glass, of that universal order in which all opposites, contrarieties and contradictions are reconciled, that subtle harmony we call truth or love or God. The achievement is especially difficult for those who, like Samuel Beckett, are atheists and antitheists: for Beckett has reconciled the atheist and antitheist positions by making God a figment of the misanthropic and masochistic side of our nature, in whose service is perfect misery. This, I think, may be a key to the meaning of Beckett's works; it is given to us, or seems to be given to us, in *The Unnamable* and its second part, *Comment c'est*; for in all the previous novels God seems to be a malevolent imbecile, but in these two he speaks directly at last, and we learn that his words are *logoi spermatikoi*: with him, to utter is to create, and to be is to utter. He has no wish to utter anything, he says, no wish to manifest himself in any way, no wish to be; he longs for silence and nonentity; he is sick of creation; he would gladly end the whole sorry game if only "they" would let him; and we gradually realize that by "they" he means us.

All Beckett's other central characters wreck their lives pursuing the Unnamable. Their pursuit is vain, because they do not recognize five cardinal facts about him: (1) that they have created him in their own image; (2) that he therefore is also seeking the Unnamable, whom he calls his master; (3) that they are his master, since by being himself, such as he is, he does their will, such as it is; (4) that whatever mutual need there may be, the notion that man can find peace in God is on a par with the notion that God can find peace in man; and (5) that since individually and collectively men have a very imperfect understanding of God, he has a very imperfect understanding of himself. He conforms willy-nilly to their conceptions of him, caricatures though he knows them to be; like theirs, his own conception of himself is continuously evolving; his story is never finished, his being never complete or determined, though he includes all things and is all things. Certainly the Unnamable is Satan as well as God: he refers to Christ as "the other," which is Satan's traditional way of avoiding the name; he calls himself a "protégé" of the master, which Satan certainly is; he is a prisoner, he is damned, he is full of ill will toward the human race and toward himself, and from his eyes forever flow tears such as martyrs weep. All this we learn fairly early in his egocentric monologue, which seems to ramble but turns out to be beautifully organized; at the same time, however, he tells us frankly that everything he says is a lie—as we might expect; that even if he could fall asleep the lies would go on dribbling from his mouth; and it follows logically that this statement also is a lie. So that we know nothing about him except that, being unfinished, being involved in endless flux, being himself the flux, he is obviously unhappy. The depth of his unhappiness, his dissatisfaction with himself, is indicated by the fact that in *Comment c'est* he divides himself into three persons and tries triads of names on himself; and the three persons, following the best of models, differ only as three torches burning with one fire. The schizophrenic's misery lies in the fact that, though split, he remains *one*. Beckett's God is lonely.

Thus, though similar in many ways, he differs essentially from the God of the Neo-Platonists and the more sophisticated

Jewish and Christian mystics. Their God, like Einstein's, is subtle but not malicious. He is perfect and serene; his happiness is himself; and since his creatures are partial manifestations of himself, all is well with them whether they realize it or not; everything is for their good, even though, since it is a limited good apportioned to their limited natures, it may seem evil. Thus Job on his dunghill praised God; thus the Hassidim in their ghettos, ragged, hungry and subject to pogroms, danced for joy; thus the whole line of Christian mystics, from Saint Paul onward, have found that the way to their deepest satisfaction lay through the acceptance of suffering, physical and mental, voluntary or involuntary, their own or others'. The next best thing to being poor, like Antoinette Bourignon, is visiting the poor, like Evelyn Underhill. It is this point of view that Beckett opposes: starting with the undeniable fact of human suffering, he concludes that not all is right with the world and asks what kind of God could have created it or even permitted it.

To this old question he offers two different answers: in the plays God is if not all-powerful at least all-stupid, which for purposes of domination is perhaps even better, and infinitely malicious—nothing is too low or mean for him to do, no practical joke is too banal; but in the novels God becomes man repeatedly, incarnating himself in a series of weary neurotics whom he delights in frustrating, tormenting, mutilating and driving mad. Only when he speaks in his own proper Neo-Platonic person—an absurd contradiction for which he says he is not responsible—do we realize that his creatures have created him—or are creating him—and that he is merely carrying out the assignment they have given him—or are in process of giving him.—J. MITCHELL MORSE, "The Contemplative Life according to Samuel Beckett," *HdR*, Winter 1962–63, pp. 512–14

I link Beckett with Genet because the plays of both are modern works of metatheatre. Beckett's metatheatre is very special. His plays almost never present a play-within-a-play sequence. And his characters, although imaginative creations, have a kind of sad naturalness. Their physical oddities, inflictions, and illnesses are exhibited; they wheeze, they whine, they groan or sigh unguardedly, as people do in real life. James Joyce, who in his writings never overlooked human infirmities, no doubt influenced Beckett to describe people naturalistically. All the same, Beckett's plays are very far from realism. How does he get his strange effects?

Every one of Beckett's plays suggests that some decisive action has gone on before the characters have come into our view. Take Beckett's two principal works, *Waiting for Godot* and *Endgame*. The characters in these plays, Estragon and Vladimir, Pozzo and Lucky, Hamm and Clov, Nagg and Nell, are made dramatic, not so much by what they do as by what has already happened to them. They show us the results of dramatic action, but not that action itself. Their drama consists in having been capable of drama at some time, and in their remembrance of that time. On the stage, they remember that once they had a stage for their thoughts, feelings, and better bodies.

All of Beckett's plays are epilogues and hence contracted. His people are people who have dwindled, as a result of what they did or what was done to them. Moreover, all that is left for them to do, as we catch sight of them, is to play. And the action, insofar as there is action in any play of Beckett's, consists precisely in playing. Estragon's life with Vladimir is a series of scenes they put on to while away the time. Certainly

Pozzo and Lucky have nothing particular to do; Pozzo's only possible action is to exhibit Lucky's tricks as a theatre manager might put on those of an acrobat or a freak. In *Endgame*, all that is left for Hamm and Clov is to play, but without joy. Here is one of Beckett's strongest dramatic effects. In *Krapp's Last Tape*, the protagonist, who is also the only person on the stage, plays with himself. If this sounds masturbatory, then I have not been misunderstood. As a matter of fact, Krapp's eating of a banana is done in such a way—and Beckett's stage directions are very precise—as to give just this suggestion. Moreover, Krapp plays with his tapes, on which his memories are transcribed. He plays with his memories, too—all writers do that—but Krapp does it without any aim or purpose. What has happened to him? This we are not told. Perhaps nothing much more than that time has passed. But the passage of time, however slow it may seem, however gently said our farewells to each particular moment, is drastic in the extreme. Time brings infirmity and death closer; it effaces the thrill of past enjoyment. As an individual's past time increases, the future time left him dwindles. It is at this moment that an individual becomes interesting to Beckett, and worth setting on the stage.

In *All That Fall* there is a definite and simple action. An infirm, old woman, weary and wheezing, struggles to the station to meet her blind husband and take him home with her. But the real event is not in the action presented; rather, through this action the real event is indicated: what time has done to both the woman and her husband. We see their different infirmities, caused by the same enemy of both—time. Weakness, tiredness, blindness, lameness, deafness, oldness—these are its effects.

In Beckett's most recent play, *Happy Days*, he presents a woman buried in the ground to her waist. Just as much of her is gone as is present when the curtain rises. The action of the play consists in her sinking deeper into the ground, so that when the curtain falls, only her head is visible. In the meantime, there is nothing for her to do but to recall what is absent from the stage and to play with her husband, who circles about her on all fours. Is he like a dog on the scent, trying to find the trail of all that is gone?

Why are time and its effects so important to Beckett? Because, I suspect, of his nostalgia for eternity. Should we not be, at the very least, the playthings of eternity and not merely the playthings of time? Such is the question Beckett poses in his plays, thus suggesting that the actual characters are themselves the scenes of an invisible action: the action of time, which might be eternal itself, or the surrogate, although we cannot be sure of this, for eternity.

But these plays cannot be understood or appreciated fully unless we recognize that for all their special content, oddity, and purely personal lyricism, they conform to the kind of dramatic work I have designated as metatheatre: what makes them so special is that life in these plays has been theatricalized, not by any attitudes taken by the characters, not by any tricks of dramaturgy, and not by the author's intent to demonstrate any propositions about the world, but by the mere passage of time, that drastic fact of ordinary life.

But we should expect in metatheatrical works some element of metaphysical wonder; and there is that in Beckett's plays. Who is the real enemy of Vladimir, Estragon, Lucky, Pozzo? Of the characters of *Endgame*, *All That Fall*, *Krapp's Last Tape*, and *Happy Days*? Who is their enemy? If the author knew for sure, he would have told us in works of didactic character; he would not have played with his doubts and fancies, nor would he have presented characters who do little other than play. He would have written works with a thesis, not pieces of metatheatre.—LIONEL ABEL, "Beckett and Metatheatre," *Metatheatre*, 1963, pp. 83–85

Since life is no more than the comedy of life, no more than an attempt to play at living, no more than an embryonic farce, the often childish or capricious "games" that represent life onstage must necessarily be borrowed from genres in which the spectacle consists of failure, stumbling, and the resistance of objects—that is, circus and vaudeville sketches and their outgrowth, the motion-picture farce. Among others, the hat business in *Godot*, Mrs. Rooney's difficulties with Mr. Slocum's car in *All That Fall*, and Winnie's struggle to decipher the trademark on her toothbrush in *Happy Days* clearly establish the equivalence between daily life, made up of obstacles, repetitions, and failures, and the most elementary and crudest forms of theatrical comedy. Farce of this kind is grating, precisely because the equivalence is made so obvious and because the spectator's life is directly concerned. Beckett's characters are constantly caught between their own clumsiness and the resistance of objects (shoes that are too narrow, hats too small, car doors too low, windows too high), including their own bodies (prostate conditions, hemorrhages, itching). Moreover, they forget necessary objects or misplace them, especially in *Fin de partie* and *Krapp's Last Tape.*

In fact, Beckett's universe is one of perpetual irritation, in which nothing works—a universe of imperfections, in which things would seem to have been created not for man, nor actually against him, but merely in order to exist in a state of passive resistance to his efforts. In *Actes sans paroles, Happy Days*, and *Play* Beckett is more explicit. Objects literally slip away from the character in the pantomime *Actes sans paroles*, while the noticeable atmosphere of concrete uneasiness that pervades his spoken plays is replaced by an abstract notion of frustration. Winnie is prisoner of a sandpile into which she is gradually sinking, and the three characters of *Play* are reduced to immobile heads and invisible bodies compressed into urns: here the physical world is not only irritating but altogether paralyzing.

In the plays in which the characters enjoy a relative freedom of movement, all the small obstacles of daily life cause men to make a series of efforts that represents, in a way, the more general attempt to give a structure and meaning to life. The various attempts made are given a theatrical quality by means of techniques borrowed from the art of clowns and which result in pure theatricalism. In *Godot* Beckett uses a twentieth-century myth—that which best expresses man's attempt to live decently in a world of hostile objects and social groups: Charlie Chaplin's Tramp. In Act II of *Godot* the curtain rises on Estragon's boots placed "front center, heels together, toes splayed," and Lucky's bowler hat thrown somewhere in the background. Chaplin's cane is missing, as if the tramps, relatives of Chaplin's Little Man, had not managed to achieve his elegance.

Chaplin's Little Man is a modern myth and, apart from Hitler, the only modern myth sufficiently distant and individualized. Hollywood, the Party, the middle-class American and Frenchman, and the capitalist are all institutions, collectivities, or abstractions raised to the level of myth. Chaplin's Little Man emerged directly as a myth, with his own individuality and his own past. His universality is guaranteed in part by his generality. He is known, recognized, and loved by about everyone. In suggesting Charlie Chaplin, Beckett is using a contemporary tradition to give a visible sign of the play's universality, as well as to show that the universal is in the present.

In *Godot* Beckett multiplied the Little Man's family. The character closest to the source is Vladimir, with his attempts at playing a certain worldly game: "Never neglect the little things in life," he says as he buttons his fly, and when he is asked his opinion on Lucky's dance, "There's something about it . . . ," he says, "squirming like an esthete." On the other hand, Estragon's shoes most clearly recall the Little Man's classic attributes, and it is Estragon who kicks like him in order to have his revenge. All the characters, however, wear bowler hats as a sign of their participation in the myth, for Chaplin's Tramp is the myth of man who, despite everything, *plays* at being a man.

Although Beckett's other dramatic works are not concerned with the myth itself, the idea of life as a game and of man's attempt to play it remains a central theme. The titles *Fin de partie* and *Play* are themselves indicative of it. On the other hand, the physical agitation and narratives that represent those attempts to play are constantly countered by images of release through annihilation. Just as in *Godot* there are the motifs of Estragon's Oblomovitis, the characters' supine positions, and suicide as a possible solution, so in *Fin de partie* the characters waver between play and a desire for annihilation, in *All That Fall* Mrs. Rooney wants to be transformed into a "big fat jelly" or disappear into her comfortable bed, and in *Happy Days* Winnie's gradual sinking into the sand, while apparently not her fondest wish, is nevertheless representative of the theme of fusion with inert matter, of a final repose that has already been accepted by her body.

The struggle between an attempt to play and the wish for self-destruction is always accompanied by an awareness of life's absurdity and brevity: "The same day, the same second . . . ," as Pozzo says; or Mrs. Rooney's "Just one great squeak and then . . . peace. They would have slit her weasand in any case," after Mr. Slocum had squashed a hen with his car; or Hamm's "Moments for nothing, now as always, time was never and time is over, reckoning closed and story ended," which concludes *Fin de partie*. *Krapp's Last Tape* ends in a kind of stupor, with the tape recorder turning silently after Krapp's last words on the best years of his life: "I wouldn't want them back." Beckett's great feat is to make the spectator experience simultaneously the interminable series of minutes that make up his life—a game that never stops ending and in which he exists in a state of permanent tension, perpetually headed for defeat—and the somewhat objective awareness of life's brevity. "The end is in the beginning and yet you go on," says Hamm parodying T. S. Eliot. Life is a bad play performed for nothing, yet it is the only one we have. Mrs. Rooney dreams of annihilation but continues nonetheless to appreciate the landscape and makes every effort to walk without falling. Hamm and Clov call out for the end to come but continue to play the hateful game of the man who cannot sit down and the man who cannot get up.—JACQUES GUICHARNAUD, "Existence Onstage: Samuel Beckett," *Modern French Theatre from Giraudoux to Genet*, 1967, pp. 253–56

In the disciplined process of writing dramatic texts, in the experience of seeing them performed by highly skilful actors, and in the work of directing significant productions of his own plays, Beckett has developed a profound understanding of the communicative value of the dramatic images he uses. While his plays have become briefer and more cryptic through the years, this brevity and intensification do not reveal an increasingly esoteric and private theatrical imagination. On the contrary, they demonstrate Beckett's increasing faith in the communicative resources of the theatre. His specific images have become briefer and more compressed as he replaces his already limited exposition with single images and brief statements that convey the sense, if not the detail, of some extended experience. When I use the term cryptic, I do not mean symbolic in the sense that these images need to be translated or decoded. On the contrary, the spectator needs only to read them sensitively, carefully constructing models from the data they project. Because Beckett returns again and again to the same images, I could discuss them as self-referential. While his writing is self-conscious in that sense, it is more useful to look at specific images as formal schemes, organisational strategies with which he works as he consistently distils his material, aiming at the simplest version that can communicate the process dramatised. Each unit of time represented in the action is metonymic of a succession of temporal segments—the two days of *Godot*, for example; and each specific image is a metonym of a larger image as it signals, but does not reproduce, a unit of narrative information. These images do not signify something other than what they are; they are neither allegorical nor iconographic. These brief, condensed signifying units replace narrative exposition, and the process of reading or attending a Beckett play demands a careful consideration of each unit in terms of its individual substance and its relationship to each other unit.

The discussion of the absence of narrative in Beckett has become a critical commonplace, and my insistence on the presence of an implied or embedded narrative in Beckett's plays has been an attempt to counter that common argument. When I use that term, however, I also intend to emphasise the gap between the present consciousness and the specific image that occupies it. That distance between consciousness and image represents an irredeemable gulf between past and present. The sense of time which that distance implies forms the framework of an attenuated and equivocal narrative.—CHARLES R. LYONS, *Samuel Beckett*, 1983, pp. 170–72

Works

WHOROSCOPE

The question now arises, since he is present in every line of the poem: Why Descartes? What did the great seventeenth-century philosopher mean to the avant-garde twentieth-century poet? Which of the many possible Descartes did Samuel Beckett choose—or did he invent a new Descartes? . . .

There is no doubt some analogy between the late-scholastic speculations on the life to come, which represented a tendency opposed to the empirical and scientific side of Descartes' mind, and on another plane the divination of the future by means of horoscopes. At any rate, a generally antimetaphysical or antiabstractive bias coupled with a disposition favoring the present and the concrete is what Beckett found in Descartes—and, though more poet than scientist, in himself as well. It may seem strange to find the author of the *Metaphysical Meditations* opposed to metaphysics, but Descartes in his *Principles of Philosophy* drastically reduced the part traditionally assigned to metaphysics and gave it an ancillary position in the order of presentation, which amounted to "nothing less than a revolution." Metaphysics is no longer the servant of theology; "it is oriented almost solely and exclusively toward natural science, and its chief aim is to furnish the principles needed by natural science, and its chief aim is to furnish the principles needed by natural science." *Whoroscope* opens with the oath "By the brothers Boot." With this the narrator aligns himself with the physicians who refuted the Aristotle of primal matter and substantial forms—and beyond him the contemporary Peripatetics—in a book published in Dublin, as Beckett (for once proud of his native city) points out in the note. Soon we find the narrator making disparaging remarks about syllo-

gisms and Jesuitasters and throwing these practitioners of the scholastic method "out of the skylight." "[Descartes] took alarm and from then on considered the Society as a formidable army coming at him. He was not at all disconcerted, but calling up all his courage, he resolved to march out alone against them all . . . ." Later, in another tone, he deplores the downfall of Anne Marie de Schurmans, become through scholastic disputations "a pale abusive parakeet." But most important are the two references to the critical period Descartes spent in the "hot-cupboard," where the great plans for destruction and recreation germinated. "He spent the rest of the winter and Lent on the Bavarian frontier in a state of indecision, thinking himself well rid of the prejudices of his education and his reading, and continuing to meditate upon his plan to rebuild everything from the bottom up." And elsewhere, "The following nine years were spent by Descartes in an attempt to rid himself of his prejudices . . . . But at the same time as this work of destruction, he pursued another task, with a view to reconstructing a truly scientific doctrine."

In the poem, Beckett suggests this more creative urge by linking Descartes to others associated in one way or another with the new science, or with innovations in mathematics and philosophy: Galileo, Bacon, Harvey, Faulhaber, Beeckman, Roten, Gassendi, and even the Rosicrucians. "In the name of Bacon," swears the narrator, who also invokes as a cherished colleague the discoverer of the circulation of the blood. At the same time, the fictional Descartes is no more a believer in "creation by committee" than his real prototype, who tells us at some length in the second part of the *Discours de la méthode* of his preference for individual achievement. Hence, the above relationships are generally critical and even on occasion contemptuous: "if he was of one mind with the innovators in the design of toppling Aristotle, he hardly agreed with them on a new doctrine to replace the old one." Descartes' confidence in his own ability to erect the city of the future is great—and the narrator's is even greater in the first part of the poem. Beckett conveys the latter's proud self-assurance through excessive abuse of Galileo, which, significantly, is based on an error in identification, and through the arrogance of such expressions as "I'll pebble you all your hen-and-a-half ones." . . .

When Beckett, like Descartes, attacks abstract speculation, he chooses a different way, the way of the poet. (Paradoxically, several times it is the abstract speculation of Descartes himself that he attacks. If not a scholastic, Descartes was, after all, a philosopher and not immune to the temptations of theological debate.) One example among many of the poetizing of the abstract occurs in the passage on the Eucharist. The technical, philosophical atmosphere disappears. Aristotle, for example, becomes "the master," and the movement of air and molecules the specific and humanized movements of the zigzag and the jig, both at the same time onomatopoetic and unifying on the level of sound. Similarly, contact becomes "kiss." The role of the senses and sense impressions is greatly increased and made much more concrete. The "olfactory sense," for example, becomes simply "nose," while bread and wine are specified as "the watery Beaune and the stale cubes of Hovis." The conventional formulas of language are broken, and Beckett attempts, as every poet must, to revitalize his instrument. We no longer "partake of the bread and wine, which is the body and blood of Christ" but, in a reversal of order that cracks the cliché "breadandwine" and a telescoping that strips dogma of its linguistic veils, we "drink Him and eat Him." Perhaps even more striking, however, is the shift from the engaged, serious, confident tone of someone convinced he has made a discovery that will lead a step further on the road to truth, to the half-amused, half-nostalgic skepticism of the disengaged poet, who would perhaps like to share such a commitment but cannot, for whom all this is a game, a "sophistry" that at best furnishes material for poetry. There is no revolt here and hardly any bitterness, only a gentle and suffering irony that hovers between sympathy and satire. In "what the master of them that do did" the deliberate use of incorrect English and the comical alliterative juxtaposition of *th*'s and *d*'s are, basically, reductive. "Watery" and "stale" and "How's that, Antonio?" undermine in a similar way the seriousness of the Cartesian enterprise, the first two by stressing the imperfection of things human, the last by the flippant familiarity of the question and the implication that the whole demonstration is no more than clever casuistry.

While in this passage Beckett has drawn a Descartes who in comparison with his model is considerably less sanguine, the tone of the passage remains quite ambivalent, although tending certainly toward the pessimistic. The association of "throne" and "faecal," "foul and sweet," and "sad or lively" is indicative of the survival in the narrator of positive attachments. In the final analysis, nevertheless, this is a case in which the fictional Descartes, who occupies a kind of middle ground between the real philosopher, René Descartes, and the poet, Samuel Beckett—shifting now closer to the one, now to the other—moves decidedly in the direction of the poet-author and away from the philosopher-source. The language become poetic—concrete, imaged, emotive. The tone, more subjective, suggests in its ambivalence both human idealism and human misery. While abandoning the abstractness of philosophical language, Beckett keeps the universal implications of Descartes' discussion, so that each detail, woven into the sensuous fabric of a particular human existence, at the same time opens out onto a perspective of the condition and fate of man. It is this expansive force of Beckett's writing, perceptible as occasional flashes in *Whoroscope* and in his later work gaining in intensity and especially in the power to sustain itself unbroken almost indefinitely, that makes him one of the most poetic and moving of modern writers.

Descartes and the narrator diverge (or Beckett and the narrator converge) again in the phrase "in one sun's drowning," which permits another glimpse of the part of the poet. In the context, "(Jesuitasters please copy)," the implications for Descartes are scientific, and the phrase suggests the Ptolemaic view that the sun moves around the earth. For Beckett, the somewhat timeworn image has the triple advantage of referring to the astronomical debates that involved Descartes, of evoking the night of visions in the *poêle*, and of serving his own purpose as a poet by reinforcing the poem's general movement from life to death. It is not a Cartesian expression. In its fidelity to a real world of the senses that maintains itself and its value as sensuous experience, while at the same time, and with discreet persistence, speaking of man's fate—in its love and its sorrow—it is typical of Beckett. In its lack of originality and in the relative weakness of the message that comes through, it is not yet the mature Beckett. . . .

A final non-Cartesian theme is the revolt against this human plight, against a destiny that keeps us, like the embryonic chick of the poem, in darkness and then kills us before we have really begun to live. Beckett's characters can be situated at different points on a scale ranging from revolt to apathetic acceptance, as his art can be said to vary in the proportion of satire and poetry it contains. He is always to some degree the ironist who criticizes, even if only implicitly, as well as the poet who recreates experience. The obscene puns in *Whoroscope* and elsewhere, which have been too often criticized as hollow

preciosity or "Irishism," in reality function, often quite effectively, as an expression of that revolt.

If the part of the poet is to be found in the selection of particular Cartesian characteristics, as well as in the choice of components that can hardly be ascribed to the seventeenth-century philosopher, it is also evident in the exaggeration or distortion of other traits, and, finally, in the absence of certain qualities one might expect to find present. Descartes defended himself against the implication that he had said nothing with his "cogito, ergo sum" that Augustine had not said before him. While we can see here the germ of the narrator's derisive remarks about the "coy old frôleur" (74), the poet has turned self-defense into aggression, a happy circumstance for those in search of Beckett behind the mask of Descartes. As Baillet writes, "Of all the instances in which Descartes' thought coincided with that of the ancients, none surprised him more agreeably than his meeting of minds with Saint Augustine. . . . It was not only that this saint rejected the judgment of the senses, and that he admitted still other opinions which they seemed to hold in common with the disciples of Plato. It was principally in the matter of the distinction between mind and body, and his great principle of *thought*, from which he concluded in favor of our existence."

In *Whoroscope* the Cartesian "cogito, ergo sum" fuses with the Augustinian "si fallor, sum" to become "Fallor, ergo sum!" (73), and, typically, thinking becomes erring. Although he admitted the fallibility of human reason, Augustine claimed knowledge of man's condition and destiny. The poem denies the possibility of such knowledge. At the time of his conversion, Augustine left a life that in some ways—in its submersion in elemental physical existence, in its chaos and meaninglessness, but also in its suffering and anguished need to know—makes contact with the existence of Beckett's characters. The narrator, when he rejects the *cogito* but keeps the *sum*, refuses to renounce such elemental existence. In the scorn implicit in the Anglicizing of the Latin ("He tolle'd and legge'd" [75]) and in the reduction of spiritual conversion to a superficial change of clothes ("he buttoned on his redemptorist waistcoat" [76]), we can see Beckett's attack on such "escapism" in the face of the disagreeable, but for him real, human condition of ignorance and abandonment.—LAWRENCE E. HARVEY, *Samuel Beckett: Poet and Critic*, 1970, pp. 33–42

MURPHY

It is easy, flippant, and correct to say that Mr. Samuel Beckett—whose first, very imitative novel, *More Pricks than Kicks*, I remember more by Joyce than chance—has not yet thrown off the influence of those writers who have made *Transition* their permanent resting-place. But Mr. Beckett, who is a great legpuller and an enemy of obviousness, would hate to be reviewed by the cash-register system that deals in the currency of petty facts and penny praises, so if I do not straight-forwardly praise his new book *Murphy*, for its obvious qualities—of energy, hilarity, irony, and comic invention—then it is his fault: he should never try to sell his bluffs over the double counter. I must say that *Murphy* is difficult, serious, and wrong.

It is difficult because it is written in a style that attempts to make up for its general verbosity by the difficulty of the words and phrases it uses for the sake of particular economy, and because the story never quite knows whether it is being told objectively from the inside of its characters or subjectively from the outside. It is serious because it is, mainly, the study of a complex and oddly tragic character who cannot reconcile the unreality of the seen world with the reality of the unseen, and who, through scorn and neglect of 'normal' society, drifts into the society of the certified abnormal in his search for 'a little world.' Murphy is the individual ostrich in the mass-produced desert.

I call the book wrong for many reasons. It is not rightly what it should be, that is what Mr. Beckett intended it to be: a story about the conflict between the inside and the outsides of certain curious people. It fails in its purpose because the minds and the bodies of these characters are almost utterly without relations to each other. The Dublin Professor, whose mental adventures and adventurous conversations are loud and lively and boisterous, is a slap-stick, a stuffed guy, when he moves; his mind is Mr. Beckett's mind, and is full of surprises, but his figure is that of the taped and typed 'eccentric professor' of music-hall and cartoon. The Dublin tart talks furiously and excessively, with a vocabulary like a drunken don's; the street bookie can speak like this in a pub, 'The syndrome known as life is too diffuse to admit of palliation. For every symptom that is eased, another is made worse. The horse leech's daughter is a closed system. Her quantum of wantum cannot vary;' but tart and bookie are no more than walking, gesticulating brains, and the story fails because no-one can care at all what happens to their bodies. And much of the book is loosely written; 'The imperturbable negligence of Providence to provide money goaded them to such transports as West Brompton had not known since the Earl's Court Exhibition,' for instance.

The story begins in London, and progresses through a conventional Dublin, where every tart is a crank and every pub-bore a self-starter, to a series of obscure events in lunatic-asylums and lodging-houses that might have been created by P. G. Wodehouse, Dickens, and Eugene Jolas working in be-wildered collaboration. Mr. Beckett supposes that he writes about the lowest strata of society, about the dispossessed and the regardless-of-possession, but he takes a most romantic view of it; he looks generously at the dregs, and makes every dirty, empty tankard wink at the brim; romantically he searches in the gutter for splendour and, in every fool and villain he finds, substitutes the gunpowder brain for the heart of gold.

And, lastly, Mr. Beckett's humour, for the book is packed with it even in the most serious sections and the most pathological discussions. Sometimes the humour is like that of an Irish comic journalist forced to write in an advanced Paris-American quarterly, sometimes like that of an old-fashioned music-hall character-comedian attempting to alter his act for a pornographers' club. And always it is Freudian blarney: Sodom and Begorrah.—DYLAN THOMAS, *NEW*, March 17, 1938, pp. 454–55

WATT

Beckett's first step, in the mature phase of his career which began in France during the war, was to commence where *Ulysses* left off, with the comedy of the inventory. He does this in *Watt*, his last novel in English, and *Watt's* point of de-parture is the Ithaca episode of *Ulysses*. In the Ithaca episode Joyce produces the great scientific catechism, in which all the empirical data of the book get revolved before the reader "in the barest and coldest way." It is a particularly sensitive spot in the tissue of *Ulysses*, since it is the point of growth where Joyce explicitly tackles and develops the encyclopaedism of Flaubert, which Flaubert had brought to a dead end. Here is what the catechism tells us about Bloom's entry into the house:

> Resting his feet on the dwarf wall, he climbed over the area railings, compressed his hat on his head, grasped two points at the lower union of rails and stiles, lowered his body gradually by its length of five feet nine inches and a half to within two feet ten

inches of the area pavement, and allowed his body to move freely in space by separating himself from the railings and crouching in preparation for the impact of the fall.

For this passage Joyce is known to have undertaken special research; he despatched his Aunt Josephine to Number 7 Ec-cles Street to verify whether a man of medium height would be capable of negotiating this leap without injury. So fiction (Bloom's size) becomes fact, and fact (the areaway at 7 Eccles St.) is incorporated into fiction, and both meet in the inventory of facts, two more items in the encyclopaedia of Dublin. Now here is Beckett:

> Watt's way of advancing due east, for example, was to turn his bust as far as possible towards the north and at the same time to fling out his right leg as far as possible towards the south, and then to turn his bust as far as possible towards the south and at the same time to fling out his left leg as far as possible towards the north, and then again to turn his bust as far as possible towards the north and to fling out his right leg as far as possible towards the south, and then again to turn his bust as far as possible towards the south and to fling out his left leg as far as possible towards the north, and so on, over and over again, many many times, until he reached his destination, and could sit down. So, standing first on one leg, and then on the other, he moved forward, a headlong tardigrade, in a straight line. The knees, on these occasions, did not bend. They could have, but they did not. No knees could better bend than Watt's, when they chose, there was nothing the matter with Watt's knees, as may appear. But when out walking they did not bend, for some obscure reason. Notwithstanding this, the feet fell, heel and sole together, flat upon the ground, and left it, for the air's uncharted ways, with manifest repugnancy. The arms were content to dangle, in perfect equipen-dency.

If this, in the abstractness of its language and the gravity of its cadence, evidently resembles the Ithaca section of *Ulysses*, it differs still more markedly. It is more general; it tells us about Watt's way of advancing due east, for example, not of how Watt went to a particular place; there is nothing for an Aunt Josephine to go and verify. Yet strangely enough it is at the same time more particular, since Bloom jumps as any man would have jumped, but Watt's way of advancing due east, for example, is so far as we can tell peculiar to Watt. It is as though Watt were the legitimate object of sober curiosity, scientific observation, and minute recording, in order to augment man-kind's small stock of reliable knowledge. And we note too a certain mimetic fullness, for not one complete pair of steps is fully described, but two, to make sure they are alike, before the generalization is risked that all the others are similar, until Watt gets to his destination, and can sit down. But here an-other force is frankly at play, namely the writer's pen setting down words, and then setting down more words, and then setting down the same words over again, so that we have before us a piece of writing, and a piece of writing with little of great importance to communicate, indeed a fiction which is at the same time an exercise in symmetry and ritual.

The more we read of *Watt*, indeed, the more does the grave determination to recover and record all that is knowable of this eerie character compromise and contradict itself; for more and more palpably the book is a composition, ritualistic, repetitious, compulsive: and the detached, encyclopaedic style more and more evidently rehearses not facts but possibilities, not evidences but speculation. Thus for half a page we pursue the minutiae of Watt's indecision, whether to shut the door, from which he feels a draught, and set down his bags, and sit down, or to shut the door, and set down his bags, without sitting down, or to shut the door, and sit down, without setting down his bags, and so on, for eight possibilities, including the possibility of leaving things as they are. A technique of inventory very like Joyce's is handling less and less real material; and the closed system indispensable to inventory is no longer, as it tended to become for Joyce, the closed system of the transacted past, but the closed system of possibilities arrived at, amid given presupposed data, by logical analysis. And logical analysis pertains to a mental world; what Beckett is doing is subtracting from the methods of *Ulysses* all the irreducible realities of Joyce's Dublin, and so transposing the novel to a plane of empty but oddly gripping construction.—Hugh Kenner, "Samuel Beckett: Comedian of the Impasse," *Flaubert, Joyce and Beckett: The Stoic Comedians,* 1962, pp. 77–81

Watt is one of the most difficult, and at the same time one of the most brilliant novels that Beckett has written. It is difficult, but not in the sense that *The Unnamable* or *Comment c'est* are difficult—plotless novels, vast tapestries of words fitfully illuminating featureless "Selves" problematically existing in a fourth or fifth dimension. Watt lives and moves in *our* dimension, his life is the banal life of common Dublin folk. His background is made up of ordinary things: trams, local trains, canals, the Leopardstown racecourse, sunsets, houses, gardens, stairs, and stars. He has an unmistakable reality—a sordid, down-at-heel reality not unlike that of Murphy, who, aeons ago, he was; he still remembers those ancient constellations "which he had once known familiarly by name, when dying in London." He is "a very fair linguist" (all Beckett's people are). His past contains "two well-defined romances"; he is one of those "big bony shabby seedy haggard knock-kneed men, with rotten teeth and big red noses," and when first espied by Mr Hackett, propped up motionless in the twilight against a wall, he seems so perfectly integrated into the familiar world of Things, that he might have been "a parcel, a carpet for example, or a roll of tarpaulin, wrapped up in dark paper and tied about the middle with a cord." Yet somehow, wherever Watt exists, reality shifts oddly out of focus. Upon the friendly three dimensions of our lives, he imposes carefully his own, compounded out of words and numerals. And the numerals plunge headlong into the infinite, while the words lead straight to Mr Knott. Or Not. Or Knot. Or Naught. Or Néant-Nichts-Nirvana, what you will.

Words are names for Things. The Thing, the *Ding-an-sich,* may well exist, or equally well may not, but while we have a word to name it, it exists for us, and we are safe. So also with people. Give Mr X—that indefinable Other, that alien Self—a name, and we can enclose him in our orbit, assimilate him, make him ours, familiar, harmless, three-dimensional. Our world begins with names:

> "My name is Spiro," said the gentleman.
> Here then was a sensible man at last. He began with the essential . . .

—or, failing "proper" names, we can at least define the Thing as "Man":

> . . . a big fat yellow bun
> for Mr Man and a bun
> for Mrs Man and a bun
> for Master Man and a bun
> for Miss Man . . .

—Man with a capital, M for Man, and M for Murphy, Micks, Molloy, Moran, Malone, Mahood, Macmann. . . . All Beckett's names have meanings, sometimes just Dickensian and ironic (Miss Fitt, Miss Carridge or Miss Rosie Dew), occasionally archetypal-clownish (Bim, Pim or Bom), more often names so dense with hypothetical suggestiveness, that we may choose and guess and argue as we please, and still come nowhere near reality. Godot, for instance. Or Hamm: Hamm, the ham-actor; the Hamlet, whose life is bounded in a nutshell—skull or cell—and yet might count himself king of infinite space, were it not that he had bad dreams; Hamm the Hammer, bearing down on Clov (Engl.: "clown" or "cloven." Fr.: *clou,* "a nail"), and Nell (another "nail") and Nagg (Germ.: *Nagel,* yet another "nail"). Or Mr Knott (Germ.: *Not,* "need": what can Naught need?). Or Watt—or What? The answer—Not, or Knot, or Naught. A jungle of hypotheses, each leading, quite literally, nowhere. For if the reality of man can be so much as guessed at, it can only be as a negative, or at best a question. Behind the name, the man; behind the man, the Void.

Murphy knew what his mind was; it had a form, or at least it admitted of description. Not so Watt. Watt's journey is a pilgrimage in search of meaning, and when first we meet him, he is outward bound. Driven by that obscure compulsion which all Beckett's people experience and accept, but which none can explain, he journeys to the house of Mr Knott, there to become a servant. In Mr Knott's house there are always two domestics: the newcomer, who serves the ground floor, and the old-established resident, who serves the upper floor which Mr Knott himself inhabits. When Watt arrives, Erskine, who previously has served the lower floor, moves up the stairs, while Arsène, who has earlier served the upper floor, moves out. And so Watt serves the lower floor. After a passage of time, however, a new servant arrives—Arthur. Relentlessly, the wheels of cause-and-effect revolve: Watt moves up the stairs, and Erskine vanishes. And then, one day, after yet another passage of time, Watt finds "in the kitchen a strange man sitting in the gloaming of the expiring range, on a chair"—as Watt himself had once sat. This man is called Micks. And so Watt's period as a servant in the house of Mr Knott comes to an end. Bag in hand and hat on head, he makes his slow way to the station, and takes the train, to nowhere in particular . . . to "the further end of the line." And when we meet him again (not later, but earlier, for time plays curious tricks) he is in an asylum, walking backwards, talking backwards, and in this devious manner trying to explain what happened when he lived with Mr Knott—his God, his ultimate, his *Nichts:*

> Abandoned my little to find him. My little to learn
> him forgot. My little rejected to have. To love him
> my little reviled. This body homeless. This mind
> ignoring. These emptied hands. This emptied heart.
> To him I brought. To the temple. To the teacher. To
> the source. Of nought.

The novel, however, is not about Watt's actions. Its true subject is Watt's mind, and the peculiarity of Watt's mind is that it makes no intrinsic distinction between words and objects. In short, Watt is a logical positivist, a living incarnation of the theories of Fritz Mauthner and of Ludwig Wittgenstein. And the "tragic flaw in his armour of logic and language" appears when, in the house of Mr Knott, he encounters a silence which is more real and more significant than speech.

Wittgenstein's argument, reduced to its simplest terms, is this: it is the human mind alone which divides up the formless continuum of the universe into distinguishable objects. The first characteristic of man is his ability to *identify*, and in order to identify, he must have language. To the child, all flowers are "flower" until it learns the words for "buttercup" and "daisy." Where there is no language, continues Wittgenstein, there is no thought; and where there is no thought, there is nothing but the massive, unidentified Totality of existence: there is All and Nothing. There are words or . . . silence. "Wovon man nicht sprechen kann," concludes the *Tractatus logico-philosophicus*, "darüber muss man schweigen."

In other words, we can never hope to know anything about phenomena; we can only know something about the *words* relating to phenomena. Moreover, since language is the product of our own minds, it can never be anything but arbitrary; on the other hand, it lies within our power to make it at least as logical and as positive as possible. Then at least we shall know precisely what our words mean in relation to each other, even if we may never know what they mean in relation to an ultimate reality.

If this is a scientific approach to language, then Watt is the supreme scientist of literature. His sensory evidence provides him with an awareness of phenomena; and once he has identified the phenomenon, found a word or words for it, and further, if the phenomenon is puzzling, shuffled around in the electronic computer of his mind all possible combinations of words which appear to relate to that phenomenon, then his knowledge is complete. The "meaning" of the phenomenon is exclusively the meaning of the words which "explain" the phenomenon; to seek for "meanings" in some mysterious or metaphysical domain beyond language is absurd. Beyond the word is Nothing.

For Watt, then, meaning and language are identical; and provided that he can formulate a statement in words about an event, he can dismiss it. It is "explained," and therefore harmless. What he cannot explain, he ignores—and must ignore—as literally meaningless. For Watt, there are material phenomena, and there is a linguistic mechanism called "mind" which manufactures "meaning." The notion that the meaning could actually reside in, or be involved with, the phenomena themselves, is inconceivable. And this is "comforting" to Watt. Nothing is mysterious, or frightening, or hostile, provided that the words are there to "explain."

But words are not absolute values in themselves. An explanation may be good and comforting, but another explanation may be equally good and equally comforting, and which of them is right? Since the mechanism of Watt's mind deals exclusively with linguistic logic—where one word is as good as another, and all are arbitrary—any one combination is as good as any other also; and if there are a dozen explanations, then the only resort is to give them all, knowing for certain, in consequence, that the "correct" one must be somewhere there among them. Another thing: the word-computer can only hope to function on condition that Watt gives it *all* the data, not merely a selection. This is the factor that accounts for the most extraordinary feature of *Watt*—the lists, the sequences, the merciless enumerations, the grotesque and exhaustive series of permutations and combinations of word-data which distinguish it from any other novel in the language. To Watt it seems perfectly clear that, given the *totality* of the relevant data, and given the leisure in his mind to reshuffle that data into every logically conceivable combination, there *must* emerge a verbally, and therefore logically, satisfying explanation. Not, of course, that this final explanation will ever actually "explain" anything—as is evident from the fantastic episode of Mr Knott's dog and Mr Knott's unfinished dinner. Watt's method is guaranteed to produce results which are flawlessly logical; at the same time, however, these results are wholly divorced, not merely from ultimate reality (whatever that may be), but also from common sense. By the end of the novel, Watt, with all his postulates and calculations, has said *nothing whatsoever* that is of the slightest relevance, either to himself or to Mr Knott. The "meaning" of each situation eludes him just as surely as it did before he started; none the less, by reducing the imponderables to language, he has contrived an exorcising explanation in a secondary dimension—and is thereby comforted:

> He had turned, little by little, a disturbance into words, he had made a pillow of old words, for a head.

Watt is the first incarnation of what is to be one of the primary themes of Beckett's later work: the failure of man, in his search for the significance either of himself or of the cosmos, to penetrate the barrier of language.—RICHARD N. COE, "Words and Numbers," *Samuel Beckett*, 1964, pp. 36–41

MOLLOY

Molloy is divided into two parts: the first is Molloy's own narrative; the second is the narrative of Jacques Moran, who receives a message through one Gaber from an undefined Youdi to go and find Molloy. The echoes of Gabriel and Yahweh make it obvious by analogy that the name "Godot" is intended to sound like "God." Youdi, or someone similar to him, is once referred to as "the Obidil," which is an anagram of libido. The associations of Molloy are Irish, pagan, and a Caliban-like intelligence rooted in a disillusioned sensitivity. Moran is French, nominally Christian, and a harsher and more aggressive type of sterility. Molloy, like many of Beckett's characters, is so crippled as to resemble the experiments on mutilated and beheaded animals that try to establish how much life is consistent with death. He is also under a wandering curse, like the Wandering Jew, and is trying to find his mother. There are echoes of the wandering figure in Chaucer's *Pardoner's Tale*, who keeps knocking on the ground with his staff and begging his mother to let him in. But Molloy does not exactly long for death, because for him the universe is also a vast auto-erotic ring, a serpent with its tail in its mouth, and it knows no real difference between life and death. Overtones of Ulysses appear in his sojourn with Lousse (Circe), and the mention of "moly" suggests an association with his name. He is also, more Biblically, "in an Egypt without bounds, without infant, without mother," and a dim memory of Faust appears in his account of various sciences studied and abandoned, of which magic alone remained. Like the contemporary beats (in *Murphy*, incidentally, the padded cells are called "pads"), he finds around him a world of confident and adjusted squares, who sometimes take the form of police and bully him. "They wake up, hale and hearty, their tongues hanging out for order, beauty and justice, baying for their due." The landscape around him, described in terms similar to Dante's Inferno, changes, but he is unable to go out of his "region," and realizes that he is not moving at all. The only real change is a progressive physical deterioration and a growing loss of such social contact as he has. The landscape finally changes to a forest and Molloy, too exhausted to walk and unable, like Beckett's other servants, to sit, crawls on his belly like a serpent until he finally stops. He arrives at his mother's house, but characteristically we learn this not from the last sentence but from the first one, as the narrative goes around in a Viconian circle.

Just before the end of his account, Molloy, who hears voices of "prompters" in his mind, is told that help is coming. Moran sets off to find Molloy, aware that his real quest is to find Molloy inside himself, as a kind of Hyde to his Jekyll. He starts out with his son, whom he is trying to nag into becoming a faithful replica of himself, and he ties his son to him with a rope, as Pozzo does Lucky. The son breaks away, Moran sees Molloy but does not realize who he is, and gets another order to go back home. He confesses: "I was not made for the great light that devours, a dim lamp was all I had been given, and patience without end, to shine it on the empty shadows." This ignominious quest for self-knowledge does not find Molloy as a separate entity, but it does turn Moran into a double of Molloy, in ironic contrast to his attitude to his son. Various details in the imagery, the bicycle that they both start with, the stiffening leg, and others, emphasize the growing identity. Moran's narrative, which starts out in clear prose, soon breaks down into the same associative paragraphless monologue that Molloy uses. The quest is a dismal failure as far as Moran and Molloy are concerned, but how far are they concerned? Moran can still say: "What I was doing I was doing neither for Molloy, who mattered nothing to me, nor for myself, of whom I despaired, but on behalf of a cause which, while having need of us to be accomplished, was in its essence anonymous, and would subsist, haunting the minds of men, when its miserable artisans should be no more."

The forest vanishes and we find ourselves in an asylum cell with a figure named Malone, who is waiting to die. Here there is a more definite expectation of the event of death, and an awareness of a specific quantity of time before it occurs. Malone decides to fill in the interval by telling himself stories, and the stories gradually converge on a figure named Macmann, to whom Malone seems related somewhat as Proust is to the "Marcel" of his book, or Joyce to Stephen and Shem. Here an ego is projecting himself into a more typical figure (I suppose Malone and Macmann have echoes of "man alone" and "son of man," respectively, as most of the echoes in Beckett's names appear to be English), and Macmann gradually moves into the cell and takes over the identity of Malone. Malone dreams of his own death, which is simultaneously occurring, in a vision of a group of madmen going for a picnic in a boat on the Saturday morning between Good Friday and Easter, a ghastly parody of the beginning of the *Purgatorio*. Dante's angelic pilot is replaced by a brutal attendant named Lemuel, a destroying angel who murders most of the passengers.— NORTHROP FRYE, "The Nightmare Life in Death," *HdR*, Autumn 1960, pp. 445–47

THE UNNAMABLE

The *Unnamable* is one of the most painful of Beckett's books, and it imposes its pain on the reader. It would be dishonest to pretend that its anguish did not cause discomfort in us, that its hatred, grief and misery did not make it somewhat unbearable to read. More dishonest still, however, would be to wish to ignore this novel, which is considered by some as its author's best work and which has already made an impression on younger writers, such as Harold Pinter. . . .

The netherworld inhabited by the Unnamable is hardly an actual place, merely a zone of grey half-light, although even this is not certain. 'I have been here, ever since I began to be, my appearances elsewhere having been put in by other parties . . . this place was made for me, and I for it, at the same instant.' He seems, in any case, to be at the centre of it; he occasionally sees lights and once hears 'a little cry, stifled outright', a sound as inexplicable as Molloy's gong. His body is 'incapable of the smallest movement' and his 'eyes can no longer close as they once could', when, that is, he was Malone. 'They must be as red as live coals,' and certainly weep contin-

ual tears, 'which flow all over my face, and even down along the neck'. He knows little about his body, except that it occupies a seated position, although he cannot say what he is sitting on. If he is clothed, it is only lightly; his head, though covered like other heroes' with pustules,

> is a great smooth ball I carry on my shoulders, featureless, but for the eyes, of which only the sockets remain. And were it not for the distant testimony of my palms, my soles, which I have not yet been able to quash, I would gladly give myself the shape, if not the consistency, of an egg . . . for the consistency is more like that of mucilage.

Malone had said 'I do not expect to see my sex again' and the natural consequence of this is that the Unnamable lacks such a member altogether: 'why should I have a sex, who have no longer a nose? All those things have fallen, all the things that stick out, with my eyes, my hair . . . I am a big talking ball'. Beckett thus strips his heroes of their organs and members until by the *Textes pour rien* they have no body left whatsoever. Mahood, for instance, still possesses a leg at first, but he soon loses it when he enters the jar; even there, however, he still has a sex, whereas his successor Worm has nothing left at all.

The Unnamable 'seems to remember' birds, such as the cockatoo, but his knowledge of the world of men is, he insists, limited either to what his delegates have told him ('years is one of Basil's ideas') or to what he has learnt from his fictions, from 'my appearances elsewhere . . . put in by other parties'. His delegates have told him 'what I know about men and the ways they have of putting up with it' and have given him 'courses on love, on intelligence, most precious, most precious'. They also have taught him 'to count, and even to reason. Some of this rubbish has come in handy on occasions, I don't deny it', so much so that 'sometimes it seems to me I am there, among the incriminated scenes, tottering under the attributes peculiar to the lords of creation, dumb with howling to be put out of my misery'. In fact the Unnamable knows quite a lot about men, enough, anyway, to hate and despise them: 'love, there's a carrot never fails' he chuckles, before laughing at 'their capacity for work and aptitude for happiness'. He tells himself a depressing tale of human inconstancy in order, he says ironically, to know 'what love can do, well well, so that's emotion, that's love':

> They love each other, marry, in order to love each other better, more conveniently, he goes to the wars, he dies at the wars, she weeps, with emotion, at having loved him, at having lost him, yep, marries again, in order to love again . . . you love as many times as necessary, as necessary in order to be happy. . . .

The similarly sardonic account of Mahood's family culminates in a paroxysm of intense loathing of life, especially of women: 'the one for ever accursed [who] ejected me into this world and the other . . . in [whom], pumping my likes, I tried to take my revenge'. 'I like to fancy,' he adds, 'that it was in mother's entrails I spent the last days of my long voyage,' wallowing in her remains.

He tells himself that the world of men 'must be terrible' because it is never dark there and never deserted, and although he compares his fate to that of Prometheus, he hastens to add that 'between me and that miscreant who mocked the gods, invented fire, denatured clay, and domesticated the horse, in a word obliged humanity, I trust there is nothing in common'. He nevertheless remembers the earth quite well, or rather two places on it, Ireland ('my island home') and Paris, for both of which he feels something akin to nostalgia. It is interesting to remark in this connection that the restaurant where Mahood was a 'jar-man' actually existed. Following up a shrewd surmise made by Rayner Heppenstall, I discovered that there was formerly an eating-house called the 'Ali-Baba' with, appropriately enough, a 'thief' outside it, fixed in a jar, supporting the menu. Beckett places it in the novel (without naming it) in the rue Brancion, facing the bust of the propagator of horse-meat, Emile Decroix; this bust is set over the eastern entrance of the Vaugirard abattoirs in the fifteenth *arrondissement*. The real Ali-Baba stood, however, in the rue de Dantzig, on the western side of the abattoirs, near a dilapidated round wooden building inhabited by artists (*La Ruche*) which may well have suggested the windowless rotunda in which Mahood's family live. The restaurant, run by an old woman, fell on hard times and had to close about ten years ago. Beckett would have known it since he lived at one time in the rue des Favorites, not far away.— JOHN FLETCHER, *The Novels of Samuel Beckett*, 1964, pp. 179–85

WAITING FOR GODOT

No new play on the London stage has had a more unexpected and exciting success in recent years than Mr. Samuel Beckett's *Waiting for Godot*. Audiences and critics have, in this country, immediately apprehended its appeal, but there has been no serious attempt to define its theme. Any discussion about what *Waiting for Godot* 'means' soon loses itself in a tangle of cross-purposes. Nor do Mr. Beckett's novels, such as *Molloy* and *Watt*, throw much light on the appeal of the play. In one sense, indeed, they do not share that appeal. In his narrative prose, Mr. Beckett presents the paradoxical picture of a man of very great talent, and possibly even of genius, using all his gifts with enormous skill for the purpose of reducing his readers to a state of tired disgust and exasperated boredom. But *Waiting for Godot* is not, except to the most squeamishly fastidious of playgoers, in the least disgusting. It is anything but boring, it instead extracts from the *idea* of boredom the most genuine pathos and enchanting comedy. Again, the message of Mr. Beckett as a novelist is perhaps a message of blank despair. The message of *Waiting for Godot* is perhaps something nearer a message of religious consolation. Audiences do not leave the theatre, after seeing his play, feeling that life has been deprived of meaning. They feel rather that a new light has been cast on life's meaning, at several deep levels.

What sort of light, however? That is what so far eluded critics of the play as performed. Mr. Beckett is rumoured to have instructed his English producer not, by any manner of means, to tell the actors what the theme of the play was. Yet unless Mr. Beckett whispered his central secret in the producer's ear, the warning was probably unnecessary. The elusiveness of the core has, indeed, led some critics to contend that there is no core; that the whole startling effect of the play on the stage depended on excellent production and acting and on Mr. Beckett's own mastery of the mechanics of stagecraft. The play, on this theory, would resemble the machine recently invented by an ingenious Californian, which works perfectly, with the minimum of friction, but does no 'work,' performs no function. Or, to put this with more dignity, the theory might be that Mr. Beckett in *Waiting for Godot* dramatizes the notion of emptiness. This, or something like this, was the reaction of the French dramatist Jean Anouilh to the first performance of *En Attendant Godot* in Paris. 'Nothing happens. Nobody comes, nobody goes, it's awful! But,' M. Anouilh added, 'I think the evening at the Babylone is as important as the première of Pirandello, put on in Paris by Pitoeff in 1923.' And from what we know of Mr. Beckett's other work, we might assume that to

dramatize emptiness, to have his much ado literally about nothing, may have been his conscious intention. Yet, with a play even more than a poem, we have to consider not the author's conscious intention—not what the author, in a conversation, might say he believed about 'life'—but the whole complex significance, the valid levels of meaning, of a coherent structure. What *Waiting for Godot* essentially is is a prolonged and sustained metaphor about the nature of human life. It is a metaphor also which makes a particular appeal to the mood of liberal uncertainty which is the prevailing mood of modern Western Europe; and which makes (to judge by the play's failure in Miami) much less appeal to the strenuous and pragmatic temper of the contemporary American mind. It is also a play by an Irishman, by a friend and disciple of James Joyce; a play, therefore, by a man whose imagination (in the sense in which Mr. Eliot used this phrase of Joyce himself) is orthodox. In other words, we should consider where Mr. Beckett springs from and what he is reacting against in his roots. Even at his most nihilistic he will come under Mr. Eliot's category of the Christian blasphemer.

The fundamental imagery of *Waiting for Godot* is Christian; for, at the depth of experience into which Mr. Beckett is probing, there is no other source of imagery for him to draw on. His heroes are two tramps, who have come from nowhere in particular and have nowhere in particular to go. Their life is a state of apparently fruitless expectation. They receive messages, through a little boy, from the local landowner, Godot, who is always going to come in person to-morrow, but never does come. Their attitude towards Godot is one partly of hope, partly of fear. The orthodoxy of this symbolism, from a Christian point of view, is obvious. The tramps with their rags and their misery, represent the fallen state of man. The squalor of their surroundings, their lack of a 'stake in the world,' represents the idea that here in this world we can build no abiding city. The ambiguity of their attitude towards Godot, their mingled hope and fear, the doubtful tone of the boy's messages, represents the state of tension and uncertainty in which the average Christian must live in this world, avoiding presumption, and also avoiding despair. Yet the two tramps, Didi and Gogo, as they call each other, represent something far higher than the other two characters in the play, the masterful and ridiculous Pozzo and his terrifying slave, Lucky. Didi and Gogo stand for the contemplative life. Pozzo and Lucky stand for the life of practical action taken, mistakenly, as an end in itself. Pozzo's blindness and Lucky's dumbness in the second act rub this point in. The so-called practical man, the man of action, has to be set on his feet and put on his way by the contemplative man. He depends—as becomes clear, in the first act, from Pozzo's genuine though absurd gratitude for the chance of a little conversation—on the contemplative man for such moments of insight, of spiritual communication, as occur in his life. The mere and pure man of action, the comic caricature of the Nietzschean superman, Pozzo, is like an actor who does not properly exist without his audience; but his audience are also, in a sense, his judges. Pozzo and Lucky, in fact, have the same sort of function in *Waiting for Godot* as Vanity Fair in *The Pilgrim's Progress*. But they are, as it were, a perambulating Vanity Fair; Didi and Gogo are static pilgrims. It is worth noting, also, that Didi and Gogo are bound to each other by something that it is not absurd to call charity. They treat each other with consideration and compunction (their odd relationship, always tugging away from each other, but always drawn together again, is among other things an emblem of marriage). Pozzo and Lucky are drawn together by hate and fear. Their lot is increasing misery; but if Didi and Gogo are not obviously any better off at the end of the play than they were at the beginning, neither are they obviously any worse off. Their state remains one of expectation.—G. S. FRASER, "They Also Serve," *TLS*, Feb. 10, 1956, p. 84

Samuel Beckett's point of view seems pretty close to that of Anouilh or Sartre. *Waiting for Godot* is, so to speak, a play that one of them ought to have written. It is the quintessence of 'existentialism' in the popular, and most relevant, sense of the term—a philosophy which underscores the incomprehensibility, and therefore the meaninglessness, of the universe, the nausea which man feels upon being confronted with the fact of existence, the praiseworthiness of the acts of defiance man may perform—acts which are taken, on faith, as self-justifying, while, rationally speaking, they have no justification because they have no possibility of success.

Like many modern plays, *Waiting for Godot* is undramatic but highly theatrical. Essential to drama, surely, is not merely situation but situation in movement, even in beautifully shaped movement. A *curve* is the most natural symbol for a dramatic action, while, as Aristotle said, beginning, middle, and end are three of its necessary features. Deliberately anti-dramatic, Beckett's play has a shape of a non-dramatic sort; two strips of action are laid side by side like railway tracks. These strips are One Day and the Following Day in the lives of a couple of bums. There *cannot* be any drama because the author's conclusion is that the two days are the same. That there are also things that change is indicated by a play-within-this-play which also has two parts. The first time that the characters of the inner play come on they are a brutal Master and his pitiful Man; the second time they are both equally pitiful because the Master has gone blind.

What has brought the play before audiences in so many countries—aside from snobberies and phony publicity—is its theatricality. Highbrow writers have been enthusiastic about clowns and vaudeville for decades, but this impresses me as the first time that anything has successfully been done about the matter. Mr. Kerr gave Bert Lahr all the credit for a traditional yet rich characterization, which, however, had been skillfully put together by Mr. Beckett. The author, to recapitulate, has not only been able to define the 'existentialist' point of view more sharply than those who are more famously associated with it, he has also found for its expression a vehicle of a sort that people have been recommending without following their own recommendation.

It is, therefore, an important play. Whether it is more important than these two achievements suggest is the question. To me, the play did not come over with the force of revelation, nor with that of sheer greatness. Mr. Beckett's voice is interesting, but one does not quite find it individual, because it does not quite seem new. One is surely not exploiting an external fact unfairly in saying that Mr. Beckett is excessively—if quite inevitably—over-influenced by Joyce. If Russian literature is cut from Gogol's *Overcoat*, Irish literature is cut from those coats of many colors, *Ulysses* and *Finnegans Wake*.

I do not think the play is obscure except as any rich piece of writing is obscure. No doubt there are meanings that will disengage themselves in time as one lives with such a work, yet enough is clear from the first not only to arouse interest but to communicate a sense of a unified and intelligible image of life. I take it that Beckett belongs to that extensive group of modern writers who have had a religious upbringing, retain religious impulses and longings, but have lost all religious belief. I should differentiate him from, say, Sartre, in that he does not write from the standpoint of atheism but, theologically speaking, from that of skepticism. People who have seen *Godot* are

able to suggest this or that solution—Christian, anti-Christian, etc.—precisely because Beckett has left the door open for them to do so. They are wrong only if they intimate that the author himself passed through the door and closed it behind him. Rough words have been spoken about the allegedly excessive symbolism of the play. This is unjust. Beckett's finest achievement is to have made the chief relationships, which are many, so concrete that abstract interpretations are wholly relegated to the theater lobby. He gives us, not tenets, but alternatives seen as human relationships (between bum and bum, master and man); also as ordinary human attitudes to God, Nature, and Death on the one hand, and, on the other, to the 'trivialties,' such as clothes, defecation, smells.—ERIC BENTLEY, "The Talent of Samuel Beckett," *NR*, May 14, 1956, pp. 20–21

Godot is God. Don't you see that the word is the diminutive of the root-word *God* which the author has borrowed from his mother tongue? After all, why not? Godot—why not, just as well?—is the earthly ideal of a better social order. Do we not aspire to a better life, better food, better clothes, as well as to the possibility of no longer being beaten? And this Pozzo, who is precisely *not* Godot—is he not the man who keeps thought enslaved? Or else Godot is death: tomorrow we will hang ourselves, if it does not come all by itself. Godot is silence; we must speak *while waiting for it*: in order to have the right, ultimately, to keep still. Godot is that inaccessible *self* Beckett pursues through his entire *oeuvre*, with this constant hope: "This time, perhaps it will be me, at last."

But these images, even the most ridiculous ones, which thus try as best they can to limit the damages, do not obliterate from anyone's mind the reality of the drama itself, that part which is both the most profound and quite superficial, about which there is nothing else to say: Godot is that character for whom two tramps are waiting at the edge of a road, and who does not come.

As for Gogo and Didi, they refuse even more stubbornly any other signification than the most banal, the most immediate one: they are men. And their situation is summed up in this simple observation, beyond which it does not seem possible to advance: they are *there*, they are on the stage.

Attempts doubtless already existed, for some time, which rejected the stage movement of the bourgeois theater. *Godot*, however, marks in this realm a kind of finality. Nowhere had the risk been so great, for what is involved this time, without ambiguity, is what is essential; nowhere, moreover, have the means employed been so *poor*; yet never, ultimately, has the margin of misunderstanding been so negligible. To such a degree that we must turn back in order to measure this risk and this poverty.

It seemed reasonable to suppose, until recent years, that although the novel for example could free itself of many of its rules and traditional accessories, the theater at least had to show more discretion. The dramatic work, as a matter of fact, accedes to its true life only on condition of an understanding with a public of some kind or other; hence the latter must be surrounded with attentions: it must be offered unusual characters, it must be interested by piquant situations, it must be caught up in the complications of a plot, or else it must be violently taken out of itself by a continuous verbal invention, deriving more or less from delirium or from poetic lyricism.

What does *Waiting for Godot* offer us? It is hardly enough to say that nothing happens in it. That there should be neither complications nor plot of any kind has already been the case on other stages. Here, it is *less than nothing*, we should say: as if we were watching a kind of regression *beyond* nothing. As always in Samuel Beckett, what little had been given to us at the start—and which seemed to be nothing—is soon corrupted before our eyes, degraded further, like Pozzo who returns deprived of sight, dragged on by Lucky deprived of speech—and like, too, that carrot which in the second act is no longer anything but a radish. . . .

"This is becoming really insignificant," one of the vagabonds says at this point. "Not enough," says the other. And a long silence punctuates his answer.

It will be evident, from these two lines, what distance we have come from the verbal delirium mentioned above. From start to finish, the dialogue of *Godot* is *moribund*, extenuated, constantly located at those frontiers of agony where all of Beckett's "heroes" move, concerning whom we often cannot even be certain that they are still on this side of their death. In the middle of these silences, these repetitions, these ready-made phrases (typical: "One is what one is. The inside doesn't change."), one tramp or the other proposes, now and then, in order to pass the time, that they make conversation, "repent," hang themselves, tell stories, insult each other, play "Pozzo and Lucky," but each time the attempt breaks down and peters out, after a few uncertain exchanges, into suspension points, renunciations, failures.

As for the argument, it is summarized in four words: "We're waiting for Godot"—which continually recur, like a refrain. But like a stupid and tiresome refrain, for such waiting interests no one; it does not possess, as waiting, the slightest stage value. It is neither a hope, nor an anguish, nor even a despair. It is barely an alibi.

In this general dilapidation, there is a kind of culminating point—that is to say, under the circumstances, the reverse of a culminating point: a nadir, an oubliette. Lucky and Pozzo, feeble now, have collapsed on top of each other in the middle of the road; they cannot get back up. After a long argument, Didi comes to their aid, but he stumbles and falls on top of *them*; he must call for help in his turn. Gogo holds out his hand, loses his balance, and falls. There is no longer a single character standing up. There is nothing left on stage but this wriggling, whining heap, in which we then observe Didi's face light up as he says, in a voice almost calm again, "We are men!"

We all know what the "theater of ideas" was: a healthy exercise of the intelligence, which had its public (though it sometimes treated situations and dramatic development in a rather cavalier way). We were somewhat bored in this theater, but we "thought" hard there, out front as well as on stage. Thought, even subversive thought, always has something reassuring about it. Speech—beautiful language—is reassuring too. How many misunderstandings a noble and harmonious discourse has created, serving as a mask either for ideas or for their absence!

Here, no misunderstanding: in *Godot* there is no more thought than there is beautiful language; neither one nor the other figures in the text except in the form of parody, of *inside out* once again, or of corpse.

Language is that "twilight" described by Pozzo; announced as a set-piece by a great deal of throat-clearing and whip-cracking, crammed with sounding phrases and dramatic gestures, but sabotaged at the same time by sudden interruptions, familiar exclamations, grotesque lapses in inspiration:

(*Lyrical.*) An hour ago (*he looks at his watch, prosaic*) roughly (*lyrical*) after having poured forth ever since (*he hesitates, prosaic*) say ten o'clock in the morning (*lyrical*) tirelessly torrents of red and white light it begins to lose its effulgence, to grow pale (*gesture of the two hands lapsing by stages*) pale, ever a little paler, a little paler until (*dramatic pause, ample gesture of the two hands flung wide apart*) pppfff! finished! it comes to rest. But—(*hand raised in admonition*)—but behind this veil of gentleness and peace night is charging (*vibrantly*) and will burst upon us (*snaps his fingers*) pop! like that! (*his inspiration leaves him*) just when we least expect it. (*Silence. Gloomily.*) That's how it is on this bitch of an earth. (*Long silence.*)

And then comes the thought. The two tramps have asked Pozzo a question, but no one can recall what it was. All three simultaneously take off their hats, raise their hands to their foreheads, concentrate intensely. Long silence. Suddenly Gogo makes an exclamation, he has remembered: "Why doesn't he put down his bags?"

He is referring to Lucky. This is, as a matter of fact, the question which had been asked some moments before, but in the interval the servant has put down the bags; hence Didi convinces everyone by concluding: "Since he has put down his bags it is impossible we should have asked why he does not do so." Which is logic itself. In this universe where time does not pass, the words *before* and *after* have no meaning; only the present situation counts: the bags *are* down, as if forever.

Such reasoning was already to be found in Lewis Carroll or in Jarry. Beckett does better: he gives us a specialized thinker, Lucky; on the command of his master ("Think, pig!"), he begins:

Given the existence as uttered forth in the public works of Puncher and Wattmann of a personal God quaquaquaqua with white beard quaquaquaqua outside time without extension who from the heights of divine apathia divine athambia, divine aphasia loves us dearly with some exceptions for reasons unknown but time will tell and suffers . . . [etc.]

In order to shut him up, the others are forced to knock him over, beat him up, trample on him, and—the only really effective method—to take off his hat. As one of the two vagabonds says: "Thinking isn't the worst."

We cannot overemphasize the seriousness of such reflections. Over seventy centuries of analysis and metaphysics have a tendency, instead of making us modest, to conceal from us the weakness of our resources when it comes to essentials. As a matter of fact, everything happens as if the real importance of a question was measured, precisely, by our incapacity to apply honest thinking to it, unless to make it retrogress.—ALAIN ROBBE-GRILLET, "Samuel Beckett, or Presence on the Stage" (1953/1957), *For a New Novel*, tr. Richard Howard, 1965, pp. 114–20

Certain critics have described *Godot* as an "allegorical play," whereas it is in fact altogether symbolic without being traditionally allegorical. Allegory implies analysis, exteriorization, and a concrete representation of the elements of the analysis. In *Godot* the elements of waiting (psychological, symbolic, or metaphysical), which remain *within* the characters, are not even individually conceptualized but are continuously and synthetically experienced by the characters. Moreover, there are no personifications of the abstract or the imaginary: Vladimir is not the personification of the soul or of the thirst for God; Estragon is not the personification of material hunger. Although the subject of *Godot* is the waiting for what never comes, and although the play, from beginning to end, evokes that gaping emptiness within man which, according to the play, is his very condition, it does not contain the intermediary that is characteristic of allegory: the reduction to abstract elements.

The play also avoids the traps of expressionism and the dangers of the "play of ideas," since there is no question of abstract qualities or intellectual analyses. Although Vladimir and Estragon sometimes "philosophize," they are in no way like those profound and lucid tramps occasionally found in theatre or films. *Godot* does not imply that out of the mouths of tramps comes wisdom. What they say is not explicit and is immediately transposed into poetry; it is chiefly an effort in the direction of ideas, memories, and a crude intellectualization of feelings or impressions—so that the interest lies not in their reasoning but in the effort they make to reason. The vague ideas they express are not given for themselves, but have a purely dramatic function: they are one of the poles toward which the characters desperately strain. There is neither debate nor confrontation, as in Giraudoux, Anouilh, or Sartre, but merely a representation of the vacuum that separates the characters from what they want to attain.

The absence of any intellectual debate and the spectacle of a constant state of tension sets *Godot* radically apart from the "play of ideas" and recalls symbolist drama, in which intellectual content is not given a logical and discursive form of expression—a form unsuitable for treating a reality that in itself is experienced. The late nineteenth-century symbolist playwrights were concerned with reaffirming the reality of the Idea as against ideas—that is, the totality of an Essence grasped by intuition in contrast to analytic categories. By the same token, Mood (*Etat d'âme*) was opposed to Discourse. Whereas Discourse gradually develops in time, advancing through the moments of an action, Mood is immobilized in order to evoke an eternity. To the naturalistic discourse, to the sequence of events linked together by the relation of cause and effect, moving ahead in time which is comparable to that of an office worker, a physicist, or even Darwin, symbolist drama opposed "moments, minutes that are eternal." Almost Bergsonian in intention, it became "static drama"—a drama that does not move forward and in which nothing happens, similar to a "ball that seems inert" but is "charged with electricity." In extreme cases it has been reduced to the presentation of a painting onstage.

Rémy de Gourmont's description of symbolist drama would seem to anticipate *Godot*:

> Hidden in mist somewhere there is an island, and on that island there is a castle, and in that castle there is a great room lit by a little lamp. And in that room people are waiting. Waiting for what? They don't know! They're waiting for somebody to knock at their door, waiting for their lamp to go out, waiting for Fear and Death. They talk. Yes, they speak words that shatter the silence of the moment. And then they listen again, leaving their sentences unfinished, their gesture uncompleted. They are listening. They are waiting. Will she come perhaps, or won't she? Yes, she will come; she always comes. But it is late, and she will not come perhaps until the morrow. The people collected under that little lamp in that great room have, nevertheless, begun to smile; they still have hope. Then there is a knock—a *knock*, and that is all there is: And it is Life Complete, All of Life.

The play itself must flow; its time is that of the performance. But within the play, time is neither that of the scientist nor that of the watch-wearing spectator: it is a synthesis of the time of the performed anecdote and the time of "All of Life." Since waiting contains both of these dimensions at every moment, it

is the same whether it lasts for one hour or for fifty years. Here the similarity with *Godot* is obvious. In each act there is an anecdote that takes place in the evening and continues for a few hours. The two evenings are consecutive, yet they are situated in different seasons, and "one day we are born, one day we die, the same day, the same second" (Act II). Moreover, the inaction characteristic of static drama is closely related to that of *Godot*. Gestures or words lose their inherent finality when considered in the light of eternity: they are leveled off by the waiting, by the consciousness of a missing transcendency. Experiencing great love or eating a carrot are two "adventures" that dissolve in the same grayness, the same hollow.

A transcendency can color the world in two contrary ways: it can enrich it (two pieces of wood become the Cross; a red rag embodies the liberation of man) or it can make it appear insignificant, as in Rémy de Gourmont's description or in *Godot*. The transcendency that strips the meaning or ordinary value from an action and substitutes no glorification on any other level took a different form in Shakespeare: the sound and fury of Macbeth's adventures dissolve into a final nothingness, and life becomes no more than a tumultuous story "told by an idiot." Didi's and Gogo's clownish tricks and screams, like Macbeth's machinations, would not be insignificant were they given for themselves, but their meanings are reduced to zero by the waiting for Godot. While in *Macbeth* zero is reached at the end of a long trajectory, a long evolution, in *Godot* it is given in advance and is thus responsible for the play's apparent inaction (despite all the activity), for the fact that it marks time, and for the impeccable constancy with which the basic tension is maintained.—Jacques Guicharnaud, "Existence Onstage: Samuel Beckett," *Modern French Theatre from Giraudoux to Genet*, 1967, pp. 230–34

First, let us consider Beckett as a dramatist of the absurd. Camus, in *The Myth of Sisyphus*, delimited the concept of absurdity for us. Establish that 'divorce between the mind that desires and the world that disappoints' and the sense of absurdity comes flooding in, leading the modern mind to despair or to rebellion or, in extreme cases, to a kind of religious rehabilitation. Now the work of art that is born out of a conviction of the absurdity of the human condition may not get so far as the full philosophical statement of *The Myth of Sisyphus*. It may merely show men (not so often women) face to face with the absurd, stuck in a void which cannot breed the choice so necessary to the existentialist. It may, if it is an ambitious work of art, try to convey to the reader or auditor the whole *quidditas* of absurdity. This will entail a non-naturalistic approach to the subject-matter, the use of impressionistic or symbolic devices, the creation of a crepuscular time-space continuum. Once history throws up the concept, we are already waiting for Beckett. What makes *Waiting for Godot* a popular play (and it is that, despite the ritual of the lowbrow sneer) is that in it the Camusian and the demotic denotations of absurdity conjoin. In Beckett we see the absurdity of absurdity.

Vladimir and Estragon wait, no more. They pass through the forms of despair and rebellion, but, not being Camus heroes, they do not act; they only wait. If in Camus we catch echoes of the stoicism of Seneca, in Beckett we smell the leavings of Christian hope. This is not to say that *Waiting for Godot*, with its allusions to the thieves who were crucified with Christ, with its property tree by which the tramps have been told to wait, is to be regarded as a Christian morality: very far from it. But the symbols of Christianity are drenched with suggestive richness, and any Western artist who rejects them is a fool: the rite is the poet's rest. And so Beckett's enduring Saturday is the one that comes between Good Friday and Easter Day, except that time has a stop after Christ's crucifixion. Saturday refuses to become Sunday, and we are stuck with 'a large measure of despair and a small measure of hope'. The thing to do is to wait, even though we can be quite sure that the waiting will not be rewarded. Life is a wretched grey Saturday, but it has to be lived through.—ANTHONY BURGESS, "Enduring Saturday," *Urgent Copy*, 1968, pp. 85–86

ENDGAME

In the enterprise of contemporary unconventional theatre Samuel Beckett's *Endgame* reveals a singleness of tone and a tenacity of purpose that commands respect as well as bafflement. It is a more concentrated work than *Waiting for Godot*, and, for all its negativism and existentialist nausea, a vigorously imaginative one. Though allusive it has no self-conscious artiness. The movements of *Endgame* are musical rather than plotty; the familiar Aristotelian dramatic movement of a clearly defined beginning, middle, and end would be less expressive in this ostensibly unregretful account of the dissolution of the world and the hopelessness of the human condition.

In the Cherry Lane Theatre production of the 1957–58 season, as well as in subsequent reading of the text published by the Grove Press, *Endgame* recalled the relentless artistry of Joyce, Beckett's countryman and fellow-exile. First written like *Waiting for Godot* in French for the French avante-garde stage, *Fin de Partie* was translated by the author into English under the Joycean title of *Endgame*. The texture of the work in English was therefore entirely authentic, and it is the *texture* rather than the transparent structure (of which there is little) that provides the meaning of the work. Hardly anything happens in the play; nearly everything that might have happened has already transpired: the world has been mysteriously destroyed, perhaps by a nuclear explosion and fallout. What concerns Beckett is the end-of-the-party *feeling* or endgame—not the story nor even the poem, but the poem's musical suggestiveness and imaginative reverberation. The author's feat lay in his ability to make these elusive qualities almost continuously arresting. *Endgame* may go down in the history of the modern theatre as a masterpiece of dramatic decadence. I intend no slur in this designation, for I prefer well-expressed decadence to ill-expressed health. . . .

The yardsticks of dialectical materialism and moralism are equally out of order in appraising the play. Dialectical materialism could only say that *Endgame* is decadent. Moralism and theology would say that the play is sinful, since nothing damns the soul so much as despair of salvation. Neither yardstick could tell us that this hauntingly powerful work of the imagination is art. . . .

There is little point in trying to unriddle *Endgame* for you unless you have already responded to its essence without an explanation. How far must we go as playgoers in finding specific and consistent definitions for the two symbolic main characters? Hamm is a tyrannical old despot who sits paralyzed in his wheelchair; his youngest servant, Clov, wheels him around in a curious room with two windows, one affording a view of the land and the other of the ocean. The specific allegorical identity of these two protagonists doesn't really matter. We care more about the immediate stage reality, the end-of-the-world, end-of-the-party reality that they evoke. The *sense* of the work, the sense of impasse, doomsday, and existentialist absurdity is far more real than any discourse can make the play. That is why the good symbolist poem transcends explanation; it is greater than its symbols. If a symbol could be exhausted by definition it would not really be poetic, for it would then have only one fixed or frozen meaning.

There is no formula for ultimate despair, any more than there is for ultimate ecstasy. In this transcendence of formulistic statement *Endgame* is beyond allegory. Any explanation, as in the case of all true poetry, is bound to be only a vague and broken shadow of the thing itself. Coleridge said, "Poetry gives most pleasure when only generally and not perfectly understood." Nothing happens in *Endgame* and that nothing is what matters. The author's *feeling* about nothing also matters, not because it is true or right but because it is a strongly formed attitude, a felt and expressed viewpoint. The *bitterness* matters, as, for example, in the fear expressed by Hamm that mankind, now virtually extinct, might be revived, that evolution might start all over again because of the flea in Clov's trousers (for which reason it must be extirpated at once with insecticide). The *sense of entrapment* matters, as when Hamm says violently, "Use your head, can't you, use your head, you're on earth, there's no cure for that!" The intensity of Hamm's *contempt* matters, as when he shouts sarcastically, "Get out of here" [the shelter, outside of which everything is dead or dying] "and love one another! Lick your neighbor as yourself." The elegiac *mood* matters when Hamm, giving up all resistance to imminent death, sums up his (and mankind's?) situation: "You cried for night; it falls, now cry in darkness." And he reflects, "Moments for nothing, now as always, time was never and time is over, reckoning closed and story ended."—JOHN GASSNER, "Beckett's *Endgame* and Symbolism," *Theatre at the Crossroads*, 1960, pp. 256–59

In *Endgame* the physical situation on stage is instantly grimmer than that of *Godot*. From the country road suggesting far-off space, and the tree connoting growth, we move to a dim room whose two high, tiny windows, facing earth and sea, respectively, are curtained; the lone picture has its face to the wall. Egress from the room is possible only to Clov—and not to Hamm in his armchair on castors, not to Nagg and Nell in their respective ash bins. Much of the comic stage business revolves around this circumscribed physical situation: Clov covers and uncovers the ash bin dwellers, and they themselves pop into sight and disappear. Clov climbs on a ladder to see out of the two windows; he wheels Hamm around the room and returns him to place; Hamm insists upon being first "right in" and then "more or less in" the center.

The plot of *Endgame*, like that of *Godot*, can be more easily summarized than can Beckett's later fiction. But relationships are ambiguous, and interpretation complex. Nagg and Nell are Hamm's parents, but Clov is variously called his son, menial, creature, and dog. An offstage Mother Pegg is never revealed as the mother of anybody, and like the rest of the offstage world, she is presumably dead when the play begins. After Clov sights a small boy on the beach, he prepares to leave Hamm. The small boy, however, does not appear on scene, and Hamm, covering his face with the bloody handkerchief of the opening tableau, seems resigned to the death that has already overtaken—perhaps at his instigation—the remaining world.

The plot is nakedly built on cruelty, suffering, and death. Beckett himself describes *Endgame*: "Rather difficult and elliptic, mostly depending on the power of the text to claw, more inhuman than *Godot*. One analysis of *Endgame* reads it as a tragedy, but a tragedy that vacillates between terror and farce. In *Godot*, Vladimir complains that it hurts to laugh, but in *Endgame* Hamm and Clov reiterate that they no longer feel like laughing. Nevertheless, Clov's five brief laughs are the first sounds in *Endgame*, and the play may be interpreted as a bitterly ironic version of creation and resurrection, making incidental use of comic devices, above all repetition. . . .

With characteristic irony, Beckett accents the cruel inhumanity of *Endgame* by frequent evocation of the Bible in the light of its delineation of man's role, particularly with respect to the superhuman. Thus, Hamm, son of Nagg, instantly recalls Ham, son of Noah. Nagg, like Noah, has fathered the remnant of humanity, but rather than make a covenant with God, he tells a joke at God's expense. Biblical Noah faithfully follows God's command to perpetuate all species by thriftily introducing couples into the ark; but Beckett's Nagg is indifferent to, or unaware of, the universal death outside the shelter.

Although Noah's animals are absent from *Endgame*, the play abounds in animal association: Hamm is an edible part of pig, and Clov either its spice accompaniment, or perhaps a reference to the cloven-hoofed animals which, pigs excepted, were the only permissible meat for biblical Jews. A nag is a small horse, and Nell a common name for a horse; Nagg-nag and Nell-knell are puns as well. Hamm refers to Clov as his dog, and Clov makes a toy dog for Hamm. Clov feeds Nagg Spratt's medium animal biscuits. An off-stage rat and an on-stage flea are objects of Clov's murderous intent, for rather than propagate all species, Nagg's progeny, Hamm and (perhaps) Clov, seek to extinguish them. The flea in Clov's trousers is fiercely and farcically destroyed lest a new evolutionary line lead to humanity again. Even a punning sex joke is made to serve the theme of universal destruction. After applying insecticide freely, with exaggerated, slapstick gestures, Clov adjusts his trousers. He has killed the flea "unless he's laying doggo."

Hamm: Laying! Lying, you mean. Unless he's *lying* doggo.
Clov: Ah? One says lying? One doesn't say laying?
Hamm: Use your head, can't you. If he was laying we'd be bitched.

In Genesis, "Ham, the father of Canaan, saw the nakedness of his father, and told his two brethren without" (9:22). Beckett's Hamm, by ironic contrast, has no brethren and cannot see; his Canaan is circumscribed to the "bare interior" of the room on the stage, and his father is relegated to an ash bin in that room. Biblical Noah curses his son for seeing him naked, and Beckett's Hamm curses his father for conceiving him. The biblical curse of Noah to Ham is: "a servant of servants shall he be unto his brethren" (9:25). Nagg also curses his son, but not with a prophecy of servitude, for Hamm is master of his domain, which is reduced to the stage room.

Hamm refers to his kingdom—an ironic name for the room before our eyes. In production, his armchair looks like a mock-throne, his toque like a mock-crown. He utters high-handed orders to Clov, a servant who is intermittently good and faithful. Both Hamm and Clov suggest that the world off stage perished by Hamm's will. Even more cruel than Hamm's own lust for destruction is that of the "I" of Hamm's story, which, like the play proper, is full of biblical reminders.

Hamm sets his chronicle on Christmas Eve, that time of birth rather than death, of peace on earth, and good will towards men. But Hamm, ironically, fills the narrator-protagonist of his tale with ill will in a desolate world, which Hamm describes in terms of numbers on thermometer, heliometer, anemometer, and hygrometer. Just as Hamm is lord of a lifeless earth, and sole custodian of its dwindling supplies, so Hamm's narrator-hero rules a similar domain. The father of a starving child crawls before him, begging for food. With charity towards none, but cruelly recalling a divine charity towards a people in exile, Hamm's "I" screams at the groveling father, "But what in God's name do you imagine? . . . That there's manna in heaven still for imbeciles like you?"

Similarly the blindness, darkness, suffering, and above all

death that fill *Endgame* comment ironically on a biblical context. The most frequently repeated line of the play is Hamm's "Is it not time for my pain-killer?" Although Hamm is literally asking Clov for a pill, it becomes increasingly evident that the only true pain-killer is death. When Clov asks Hamm whether he believes in the life to come, the sardonic answer is, "Mine was always that." The ring of the alarm clock is "Fit to wake the dead!"

On two separate occasions, Hamm cries out in anguish, "Father, Father!" and, as Jean-Jacques Mayoux has suggested, "How can we not think of the 'Eli Eli' of that other supreme moment?" Towards the end of the play, Hamm utters several phrases which derisively twist Scripture: "Get out of here and love one another! Lick your neighbor as your self! . . . The end is in the beginning. . . . Good. . . .Good. . . .Peace to our—arses." In the French text Hamm compares the small boy outside the shelter to a dying Moses gazing at the Promised Land.

Since *Endgame* is unmistakably a play about an end of a world, there are many recollections of the Book of Revelations. In the vision of St. John the Divine, Christ says he has "the keys of hell and of death," in ironic contrast to Hamm, who knows the combination of a cupboard that presumably contains the wherewithal to keep them *alive* in their hell in the shelter.

Revelations is full of phrases about light and darkness, sea and earth, beginning and end, life and death. After the destruction of Babylon, a great voice from heaven utters the words, "It is done." In the New Jerusalem, "The length and the breadth and the height of it are equal," even as the length, breadth, and height of Clov's kitchen, whose thousand cubic feet might be a caricature reminder of the millennium of Revelations.

Within the tight text of *Endgame*, the frequency and mockery of the biblical echoes cannot be ignored in any interpretation of the play, and the fourth Gospel is crucial for such interpretation. Not only does the English *Endgame* contain the fugal variations upon Christ's last words, "It is finished," but in this gospel particularly, Christ affirms that He is the light; He speaks of "my Father" and "my Father's house." Beckett's Hamm has dispensed and extinguished light; he calls upon his father and insists that his house is the only asylum.

St. John tells the story of Lazarus, resurrected by Christ, and we learn both from that account and the Passion that in biblical times corpses were wrapped in linen clothes, a napkin around the head, and anointed with oil and spices. In *Endgame*, Clov may be a spice anointing corpses; it is he who lifts the sheets from near-corpses, but it is Hamm who focuses attention on the napkin that covers his head when the play opens and closes—even as a napkin covered the head of Lazarus and of Christ.—RUBY COHN, *Samuel Beckett: The Comic Gamut*, 1962, pp. 226–32

The dialogue of *Endgame* is a brilliantly contrived exercise in the art of repartee. Unfortunately, discussion of a single passage, one of the best, will have to stand for analysis of a quality of conscious formal elegance which pervades the whole:

Hamm: Nature has forgotten us.
Clov: There's no more nature.
Hamm: No more nature! You exaggerate.
Clov: In the vicinity.
Hamm: But we breathe, we change! We lose our hair, our teeth! Our bloom! Our ideals!
Clov: Then she hasn't forgotten us.
Hamm: But you say there is none.
Clov (sadly): No one that ever lived ever thought so crooked as we.
Hamm: We do what we can.
Clov: We shouldn't.

The issue behind this exchange is clear enough—whether Nature and Nature's God have temporarily withdrawn themselves from man or have actually ceased to exist. But serious concern with this question is submerged in this sharp, witty, paradoxical dialogue, often dependent on the interplay of verbal connection and logical non-sequitur, which is of a kind that has fascinated the Irish from Swift to Shaw. Hamm's straight-man assertion provokes Clov's stock response, "There's no more Nature." His denial is categorical in form, an either/or, but Hamm impossibly calls it an exaggeration, at the same time employing a rhetorical exclamation made familiar by the rest of the play. Hamm's response, instead of collapsing the conversation, elicits an equally impossible concession from Clov, "In the vincinity," as though Nature, if it existed, could exist locally but not universally. This Hamm ignores, launching into the vigorous if paradoxical proof that universal decay is evidence for Nature's continued existence. Instead of replying to this in terms consistent with his previous denial, Clov counters wittily by accepting the existence of human decay as evidence of Nature's benevolence, "Then she hasn't forgotten us." Hamm takes this to be Clov's admission that he was wrong, a move which Clov tries to thwart with a sententious aphorism, "No one that ever lived thought so crooked as we." Hamm pounces on this by implying that crooked thinking is all to the good. But his words are ambiguous, for "can" here means both "the best we can" and "what we have to do." Thus the Parthian shaft comes from Clov, who outwits Hamm by repeating his disapproval of crooked thinking in a way which supposes that people do by choice what Hamm has unintentionally said they do by necessity. After a pause, this vigorous little canter earns Clov his master's praise, "You're a bit of all right, aren't you?" This adapts the vulgar British phrase as admiration for Clov's high technical proficiency in playing games with a concept whose varying definitions have worried thinkers of our civilization for over two thousand years. It is because of a similar delight in technical expertise that Hamm on a later occasion cannot resist self-congratulation:

Clov: Do you believe in the life to come?
Hamm: Mine was always that. (Exit Clov.) Got him that time!

Once again, a serious subject, the fate of man's external soul, is used mainly as an occasion for repartee, and this juxtaposition of a formal surface with serious, often terrifying depths accounts for much of what Beckett in his correspondence with Alan Schneider referred to as "the power of the text to claw."

A word frequently applied to Beckett's work is "poetic." What the adjective really points to in Beckett's plays (a context in which it is pejorative if it replaces the honorific qualification "dramatic") is the extra-ordinary ability of the language and stage-craft to imply, suggest, connote, evoke, and set off expressive nuances. In this respect *Endgame* fulfils expectations which derive to us from our experience of the Symbolist tradition in poetry and drama, for it was Mallarmé's principle that "to name is to destroy; to suggest is to create." It is this, and the traditional assumption that drama imitates a reality beyond itself, which Beckett has chosen to exploit. And he exploits it by providing the play with a level of action, which ignores its own significant implications. The surface of *Endgame* insists upon itself as a meaningless technical exercise of the medium in its own right and refuses to acknowledge anything beyond its own expertise. Beckett stresses this in his own comment on the play, again in a letter to Alan Schneider:

> My work is a matter of fundamental sounds (no joke intended) made as fully as possible, and I accept responsibility for nothing else. If people want to have headaches among the overtones, let them. And pro-

vide their own aspirin. Hamm as stated, and Clov as stated, together as stated, nec tecum nec sine te, in such a place, and in such a world, that's all I can manage, more than I could.

The life of *Endgame* is in the tension it creates by the harsh juxtaposition of the depths and the surface, the "overtones" and what is stated, a doubleness which is apparent in the frequent pauses in the play. On the one hand these are hushed silences in which the resonances of the text may vibrate and amplify in the mind of the audience—"God," "light," "Nature," "ended." At the same time these pauses are merely technical requirements, rests between moves in the last game which is *Endgame*, no more, no less. Thus the dramatic structure of the play enacts a dialectic which Beckett has stated elsewhere—in *Watt*, his second novel—as, "this pursuit of meaning, in this indifference to meaning." In so far as we recognise this as an insight into the conditions of human existence we will be able to respond to the full effect of *Endgame*.—ANTONY EAST-HOPE, "Hamm, Clov, and Dramatic Method in *Endgame*," *MD*, Feb. 1968, pp. 431–33

HOW IT IS

It seemed that after *L'Innommable*, Samuel Beckett had led the novel into some kind of impasse from which it could never emerge, unless by a repetition of what had already been done. And so one could expect a long silence on Beckett's part. Having reduced the essential elements of the novel-plot, characters, action, language—to their bare minimum, how could any writer push the experiment further? Yet with the recent publication of *Comment c'est*, Beckett once more manages to carry the form of the novel into a completely new and original no man's land.

This time we are in a world completely stripped of all norms of life. And yet, somehow, we are able to identify, if not a place, or characters, or a story, at least the human anguish, the pathos of a semi-existence. The novel is divided into three distinct parts: Before Pim, With Pim, and After Pim. A vague notion of a human being is crawling in the mud towards a certain destination, towards another wretched being: Pim, whom he meets in part two and with whom he establishes a strange and painful relationship. The first person narrator having reached his victim in part two, after a slow journey in part one: 'jambe droite bras droit pousse tire dix mètres quinze mètres reste là dans le noir la boue tranquille. . . .' stretches in the mud next to Pim. Now he covers parts of Pim's body with his own, stabs him in the posterior with a can opener, inscribes bloody words on Pim's back by scratching him with his nails, hits him on the head to make him sing, to make him talk, or to force him to stop talking. Then he leaves Pim, or is it Pam, or Krem or Kram (for as usual in a Beckett novel, names are constantly shifting) for a new destination. At this time begins the journey (of part three) towards a certain Bem—or Bim, or someone else. It is not quite certain whom the new victim will be. For that matter we are not even sure whether it is the narrator or Pim who now proceeds towards Bem in part three (they seem interchangeable). Nothing is certain in this Beckett world. The only certainty is this vicious circle within an infinite and yet limited limbo. This going to and coming from, in an infinite time at an excruciatingly slow pace, and always face down in the mud.

The remarkable achievement of Beckett in this novel is the simplicity and economy with which he manages to create the situation. The whole book is built on a series of simple sentences repeated at various stages in a fragmentary rhythm. The syntax itself within the punctuationless sentences is broken and distorted. Only a few identifiable objects appear in the novel: a can opener, a bag full of sardine and tuna fish cans which the characters drag along on their journey, and a few broken memories of a world which seems to lie above in the light, a kind of lost reality. And yet, in spite of the disconnected appearance of the language and of the narration, the whole construction of the novel is mathematically arranged. The whole situation is so well thought out, that one feels caught up within the strange world of the novel. There is no way out for the reader, nor is there any escape from the limbo for Pim, Pem, Pam, Bem. . . .They are all in motion, in rotation, becoming alternately: tormentors or victims.

Why then three parts to this novel? One, or at most two would seem to suffice. Or for that matter why not four, or ten, or twenty? Beckett himself points out this possibility in the novel, and again as in *Waiting for Godot*, where a third act could have easily followed in the same pattern as the first or the second act, one could also expect other parts to continue this novel almost to infinity. But this time Beckett manages, in the last few pages of the novel, to destroy the whole construction by having the narrator pretend that everything described was an illusion, a creation of the mind, a useless mumbling of the mouth, thus destroying the whole fiction of the novel.

Beckett, once again, places himself in a most unusual position among the modern novelists. And even though he may again be attacked for his pessimism and for his nihilistic view on life, still he seems to redeem himself through the artistic creation. Only silence could reduce Beckett's vision to complete 'darkness.' Yet, his insistence on creating more novels, on having his characters—however distorted—express themselves even in the most clumsy manner, defeats his nihilism and places the artistic creation above dark reality.—RAYMOND FEDERMAN, *FrR*, May 1961, pp. 594–95

Of all Beckett's fiction . . . it is *Comment c'est* that offers the extremest instance of his impatience with literature and of his determination to produce a fiction that will be against the very idea of fiction itself. Here we encounter a novel that is not only stripped of every vestige of plot and action and character but one in which even the last remaining props of syntax have collapsed and in which therefore the narrator simply "says it as he hears it"—

> my life last state last version ill said ill heard ill recaptured when the panting stops ill murmured to the mud brief movements of the lower face losses everywhere.

It is Pim, whoever he is, who gives the book something like a fixed centre, and that this is Beckett's intention is announced in the opening lines, in which the narrator says: "how it was I quote before Pim with Pim after Pim how it is three parts I say it as I hear it." Pim's role here is very much like that of the Absent One in *Godot*: it is, presumably, in his image that the narrator dimly describes (as do Gogo and Didi in *Godot*) a presence and a power to be united with which is to be no longer wholly under the dominance of meaninglessness and despair: so his diary begins with the record of his journey towards Pim—through a "vast stretch of time," in the dark, and by way of his crawling naked over terrains of mud and slime: "ten yards fifteen yards half on my left side right foot right hand push pull flat on my belly mute cries half on my right side left foot left hand push pull flat on my belly mute cries not a syllable to be changed in this description."

But, after the narrator does finally reach Pim, their "vie en commun" in no wise proves to be the radiant blessing that one might have expected it to be. Indeed, after crawling eastward through great stretches of mud, this naked pilgrim with a sack tied round his neck finds Pim's condition to be identical with

his own: he, too, lies prone in the mud with his sack. And it may well be the rage of disappointment that leads the narrator to take up with respect to him a relation very much like that of Pozzo to Lucky in *Godot*: in any event, he becomes Pim's scourge and torturer, varying his blows to the head with sharp jabs of a can opener into Pim's anus. But the fist and the can opener are instruments of instruction as well as of anger, for it is through a carefully administered ritual of beatings and stabbings that the mute narrator teaches Pim when to sing and when to speak, himself responding by tracing out his replies on Pim's back, letter by letter.

Part I of the book is devoted to the journey in search of Pim, and Part II to the encounter; then, in Part III, we gather that a radical reversal of things is under way, for Pim is now crawling across the muddy wastes of the world in search of one whom he in turn shall torment—while the narrator is waiting for still another personage called Bom, to whom he will be apprenticed in much the same way that Pim was apprenticed to him. And it is suggested that these reversals are periodic, so that the narrator may look forward to still another time when he will again be the torturer, as Pim may again be destined to be the tortured. The moral judgment, in other words, behind which the book lines itself up is as clear as it is bleak: Beckett's intention would seem to be to say that, though life in the human city is comprised of manifold relations, they all move within the single polarity involving torturer and victim, both roles being enacted in turn by all men in the various relations with one another into which they are brought by the adventures of life. As it is put by the narrator: each of us is at the same time Bom and Pim executioner victim schoolmaster dunce plaintiff defendant dumb and theatre of a word found again in the dark the mud there nothing to correct.—NATHAN A. SCOTT, *Samuel Beckett*, 1965, pp. 76–79

HAPPY DAYS

Beckett's *Happy Days* attempts that almost impossible task of transferring to the stage the bodilessness and utter isolation of his novelistic characters. The characters of *Waiting for Godot* still were able to move about, even if they mainly preferred to sit and wait like Vladimir and Estragon or wandered around in circles as did Pozzo and Lucky. In *Endgame* two of his characters, the old parents of Ham, were completely stationary, with only their heads occasionally protruding from the ashcans they inhabited. Ham himself was sedentary and almost motionless—though talking incessantly. But Clov at least moved about restlessly from room to room and climbed up and down his ladder. Physically he was entirely free even to leave. The only protagonist and character of *Krapp's Last Tape* was sedentary and only from time to time crept and puttered around his tape recorder. But in *Happy Days* the bodilessness and motionlessness of the two characters is carried to the extreme. . . .

Beckett's *Happy Days* is, to an even greater extent than his *Waiting for Godot*, drama stripped for inaction. Nothing happens, nothing moves—nothing even sprouts or grows as did the tree in the earlier play. The liveliest event that takes place on the stage and brings about happiness and laughter among the characters is the sudden appearance of an emmet that crosses Winnie's mound, carrying what appears to be an egg and provoking Willie to exclaim "formication." Like other Beckett characters, Winnie is engaged in dreaming that she is happy. It helps her pass the time, as it helped Estragon and Vladimir. But Winnie doesn't even wait for Godot to come. Passing the time is her main concern: "Ah yes, so little to say, so little to do, and the fear so great, certain days, of finding oneself . . . left, with hours still to run, before the bell for sleep, and nothing more to say, nothing more to do, that the days go by, certain days go by, quite by, the bell goes, and little or nothing said, little or nothing done." Since no further pains are possible, Winnie simply wishes to "wait for the day to come—the happy day to come when flesh melts at so many degrees and the night of the moon has so many hundred hours."

There is in this play no longer a trace left of traditional theatre concerned with character, action and episodes that have a beginning, a middle, and an end. It represents human existence in its nakedness, the drama of man is *Dasein* in the Heideggerian sense of the word. Heidegger saw this drama contained in the very word itself, though in everyday language *Dasein* means simply "existence." For divided into its linguistic components, the word means "being here" or "being there," which Heidegger has understood to imply the "here and now," *hic et nunc* of Being. Man as *Dasein* is a sort of *lumen naturale* that sheds the light of understanding on the world around him (including himself) and lends to that-which-is-there individuality and actuality, providing it with spatial and temporal relationship. In this way man gives meaning to the world. He neither creates this world nor observes it as an outsider; for he is anchored in it and receives his horizon from it. But he is the small, ephemeral intelligence without whom the vastness of Being would remain unindifferentiated.

Amid the "unbroken plain and sky receding to meet in far distance," the background on which *Happy Days* opens, Winnie imbedded in her mound seems a stage-rendering of Heidegger's "here and now" of Being. It is not clear whether the sun is glaring down upon her or whether she is that light of intelligence through which a world becomes visible to man. In the midst of the wasteland, her mound is the world of man. She is mankind: a part of Being, rooted in Being which, at the same time reveals man's world or rather: through whom man's world reveals itself. Thus the drama that unfolds upon the stage is the very drama of man, inescapably caught in the paradoxical union of mind and matter, word and flesh. Like Heideggerian *Dasein*, Winnie appears, helplessly *geworfen*, "thrown" into time and place and humanness, and surrounded by the implements that belong to the every-day existence of man. Beckett has again proved his mastery by presenting the tragedy of this forlornness in the light of comedy.—EDITH KERN, "Beckett's Knight of Infinite Indignation," *YFS*, Spring-Summer 1962, pp. 49–51

FILM

. . . Beckett's *Film* can be considered an allegory about autobiography, for it is concerned with the creation and definition of the relationship between the self and the world. That relationship is bounded by the I or the self (of "auto"), the He or Other of "bio," and the re-presentation of primary feelings of these parts of the self and other into a mediated form, a "graphy." The "graphy" of Beckett's *Film* incorporates a number of autobiographical impulses: it is a narrative about narration, about telling and being told. It is a discourse on the nature of presence and absence, on the function of memory, and on the rhetorical modes of self-presentation.

It is no accident that these impulses are similar to the strategies of the cinematic process. Beckett has always created a meta-world, using the rhetorical premises of an artistic medium to describe his own peculiar universe of the contingent self. As with all of Beckett's works, the allegorical level solicits our attention more than the literal one. We recognize quickly that O's flight from perceivedness is really a flight from being entrapped by cinema, specifically, the system of looks

and responses on which the cinema is based: the nature of looking and being looked at; the shifting points of view between subject, viewer, and omniscient narrator; the constituency of the cinematic image with its *aura* of presence (what Barthes calls the "reality of the having-been-there").

In its movements towards and away from self-definition, *Film* presents the central dualities in art and reality. Non-Being is locked in a love/hate embrace with Being, and both are enfolded in a mediated form. The character's attempt to blot out his past, to flee all allusions and connotations of the self, results in a confrontation with the projected reconstituted self. In cinema, as in reality, there is only representation and self-reflection. Both the duplicated images of the self in film and photography and the images involuntarily evoked by memory and thought are received through limited partial views which are framed by the seeing eye, the inner eye, and the camera eye. Reference to other systems of representations (the drawing, the photos, the mirror) underline cinema's codic differentiation from these systems of representations. The fact that O cannot escape the gaze of the camera and us, in other words, cannot escape being reproduced, underlines as well cinema's own specificity as a particular means of representation. What is posited is that all our forms of consciousness are allusive and referential systems of signification.

The epistemological implications of the O's frenzied flight from perceivedness is that perception "invests" humans with presence, but a presence which always excludes, from which we are forever outside. O will not accept this contingent partial angle of all viewing. He will not offer his self to be looked at, fixed, appropriated. His search, then, is the pursuit of what is excluded from the views of characters, things, the camera, and us. He seeks what lies beyond the frame, beyond the world contained within view. It is here that O is hoisted on his own double movement, towards and away from absence or non-being. His search for the Other, for Absence, for an unmediated non-being, is a paradoxical dead end. What is not cannot be perceived and, therefore, cannot be assimilated or validated. What is present, however, is only a segment of the unattainable complete view of the world as a whole. This explains why O looks in horror at his double. His search for the other led back to the self, but the self that is always the other because it represents the self at the particular moment of apprehension, stripped of the accretions of the past and, therefore, stripped of its accumulated significance.

O's activities raise epistemological issues which are congruent with critical notions about cinema, especially in regard to the impossible dream of total cinema. Stanley Cavell has stated that "what we are shown on the screen is always only one of an endless number of equally possible views . . . nothing the camera does can break out of its circle of viewing." The essence of film is its "absence of what it causes to appear to us." Inversely, we are absent from it. Thus, we are absent from something present to us, which is both present (in that it bears physical connections to real persons and things) and absent (in that it is an illusionistic and reduced semblance of real persons and things). In this double role of the cinematic image reality is and is not represented, is and is not present to us.

No matter how much he rejects perceivedness, O is always present to us as we watch him try to be absent—from the camera, from God, and from us. Yet O is absent to us, the time of his presence only recorded and projected. We as his pursuers (along with the camera) are terrifyingly present to him, although absent from "the circle of viewing."

The involuted regressions of the apparent polarities of presence and absence communicate the major emotion in

Film, terror: the terror that lurks in the recognition that the unattainable other is the unconsoling mirror image of the self; the terror implied in the self-negating flight; and the equal discomfort with self-love or self-approbation. Furthermore, both metaphysical and Oedipal fears are implicit in the recoil from the fixed "severe" stare of the mother and of an illusory God. *Film* subverts the Proustian autobiographical method where Oedipal sensations are revived in order to achieve a unification of self and art-making. There is no Nietzschean joy in the emptied and dispossessed O, whether sundered or finally united with his counterpart.

The real terror at the root of *Film*'s cinematic allegory is, finally, the absent "presence" that exists outside the frame, a reminder that there is always something outside the self. The whole extraneous world (whether called God, Godot, the unknown, the Unnamable, or the Not-I, to use Beckett's own galaxy) is represented by the absent field that lies in some menacing nebulous space between the screen and the spectator, between the self and all Others. Indeed, *Film* is continually circling around the central phenomenological notion at the heart of both cinema and reality: absence. *Film* is about absence—the absence of the subject from the viewer and the means of production (God or any external authority that produces meaning; the technical processes of the cinematic apparatus; direct experience) and, obversely, the absence of the viewer from the means of production and the subject.—RUTH PERLMUTTER, "Beckett's *Film* and Beckett and Film" *JML*, 1977, pp. 86–88

MAURICE BLANCHOT
"Where Now? Who Now?" (1953), tr. Richard Howard
On Contemporary Literature, ed. Richard Kostelanetz
1964, pp. 249–54

W̲ho is doing the talking in Samuel Beckett's novels, who is this tireless "I" constantly repeating what seems to be always the same thing? What is he trying to say? What is the author looking for—who must be somewhere in the books? What are we looking for—who read them? Or is he merely going round in circles, obscurely revolving, carried along by the momentum of a wandering voice, lacking not so much sense as center, producing an utterance without proper beginning or end, yet greedy, exacting, a language that will never stop, that finds it intolerable to stop, for then would come the moment of the terrible discovery: when the talking stops, there is still talking; when the language pauses, it perseveres; there is no silence, for within that voice the silence eternally speaks.

An experiment without results, yet continuing with increasing purity from book to book by rejecting the very resources, meager as they are, that might permit it to continue.

It is this treadmill movement that strikes us first. This is not someone writing for beauty's sake (honorable though that pleasure may be), not someone driven by the noble compulsion many feel entitled to call inspiration (expressing what is new and important out of duty or desire to steal a march on the unknown). Well, why *is* he writing then? Because he is trying to escape the treadmill by convincing himself that he is still its master, that, at the moment he raises his voice, he might stop talking. But is he talking? What is this void that becomes the voice of the man disappearing into it? Where has he fallen? "Where now? Who now? When now?"

He is struggling—that is apparent; sometimes he struggles secretly, as if he were concealing something from us, and from himself too, cunningly at first, then with that deeper cunning which reveals its own hand. The first stratagem is to interpose between himself and language certain masks, certain faces: *Molloy* is a book in which characters still appear, where what is said attempts to assume the reassuring form of a story, and of course it is not a successful story, not only because of what it has to tell, which is infinitely wretched, but because it does not succeed in telling it, because it will not and cannot tell it. We are convinced that this wanderer who already lacks the means to wander (but at least he still has legs, though they function badly—he even has a bicycle), who eternally circles around a goal that is obscure, concealed, avowed, concealed again, a goal that has something to do with his dead mother who is still dying, something that cannot be grasped, something that, precisely because he has achieved it the moment the book begins ("I am in my mother's room. It's I who live there now."), obliges him to wander ceaselessly around it, in the empty strangeness of what is hidden and disinclined to be revealed— we are convinced that this vagabond is subject to a still deeper error and that his halting, jerky movements occur in a space which is the space of impersonal obsession, the obsession that eternally leads him on; but no matter how ragged our sense of him, Molloy nevertheless does not relinquish himself, remains a name, a site within bounds that guard against a more disturbing danger. There is certainly a troublesome principle of disintegration in the story of *Molloy*, a principle not confined to the instability of the wanderer, but further requiring that Molloy be mirrored, doubled, that he become *another*, the detective Moran, who pursues Molloy without ever catching him and who in that pursuit sets out (he too) on the path of endless error, a path such that anyone who takes it cannot remain himself, but slowly falls to pieces. Moran, without knowing it, becomes Molloy, that is, becomes an entirely different character, a metamorphosis which undermines the security of the narrative element and simultaneously introduces an allegorical sense, perhaps a disappointing one, for we do not feel it is adequate to the depths concealed here.

Malone Dies evidently goes further still: here the *vagabond* is nothing more than a *moribund*, and the space accessible to him no longer offers the resources of a city with its thousand streets, nor the open air with its horizon of forests and sea which *Molloy* still conceded us; it is nothing more than the room, the bed, the stick with which the dying man pulls things toward him and pushes them away, thereby enlarging the circle of his immobility, and above all the pencil that further enlarges it into the infinite space of words and stories. Malone, like Molloy, is a name and a face, and also a series of narratives, but these narratives are not self-sufficient, are not told to win the reader's belief; on the contrary, their artifice is immediately exposed—the stories are *invented*. Malone tells himself: "This time I know where I am going . . . it is a game, I am going to play . . . I think I shall be able to tell myself four stories, each one on a different theme." With what purpose? To fill the void into which Malone feels he is falling; to silence that empty time (which will become the infinite time of death), and the only way to silence it is to say something at any cost, to tell a story. Hence the narrative element is nothing more than a means of public fraud and constitutes a grating compromise that overbalances the book, a conflict of artifices that spoils the experiment, for the stories remain stories to an excessive degree: their brilliance, their skillful irony, everything that gives them form and interest also detaches them from Malone, the dying man, detaches them from the time of his death in order to reinstate the customary narrative time in which we do not believe and which, here, means nothing to us, for we are expecting something much more important.

It is true that in *The Unnamable* the stories are still trying to survive: the moribund Malone had a bed, a room—Mahood is only a human scrap kept in a jar festooned with Chinese lanterns; and there is also Worm, the unborn, whose existence is nothing but the oppression of his impotence to exist. Several other familiar faces pass, phantoms without substance, empty images mechanically revolving around an empty center occupied by a nameless *I*. But now everything has changed, and the experiment resumed from book to book, achieves its real profundity. There is no longer any question of characters under the reassuring protection of a personal name, no longer any question of a narrative, even in the formless present of an interior monologue; what was narrative has become conflict, what assumed a face, even a face in fragments, is now discountenanced. Who is doing the talking here? Who is this *I* condemned to speak without respite, the being who says: "I am obliged to speak. I shall never be silent. Never." By a reassuring convention, we answer: it is Samuel Beckett. Thereby we seem to draw closer to what is of concern in a situation that is not fictional, that refers to the real torment of a real existence. The word experiment is another name for what has actually been experienced—and here too we try to recover the security of a name, to situate the book's "content" at the stable level of a person, at a personal level, where everything that happens happens with the guarantee of a consciousness, in a world that spares us the worst degradation, that of losing the power to say *I*. But *The Unnamable* is precisely an experiment conducted, an experience lived under the threat of the impersonal, the approach of a neutral voice that is raised of its own accord, that penetrates the man who hears it, that is without intimacy, that excludes all intimacy, that cannot be made to stop, that is the incessant, *the interminable*.

Who is doing the talking here then? We might try to say it was the "author" if this name did not evoke capacity and control, but in any case the man who writes is already no longer Samuel Beckett but the necessity which has displaced him, dispossessed and disseized him, which has surrendered him to whatever is outside himself, which has made him a nameless being, The Unnamable, a being without being, who can neither live nor die, neither begin nor leave off, the empty site in which an empty voice is raised without effect, masked for better or worse by a porous and agonizing *I*.

It is this metamorphosis that betrays its symptoms here, and it is deep within its process that a verbal survival, an obscure, tenacious relic persists in its immobile vagabondage, continues to struggle with a perseverance that does not even signify a form of power, merely the curse of not being able to stop talking.

Perhaps there is something admirable about a book which deliberately deprives itself of all resources, which accepts starting at the very point from which there can be no continuation, yet which obstinately proceeds without sophistry and without subterfuge for 179 pages, exhibiting the same jerky movement, the same tireless, stationary tread. But this is still the point of view of the *external* reader, contemplating what he regards as only a tour de force. There is nothing admirable in inescapable torment when you are its victim, nothing admirable in being condemned to a treadmill that not even death can free you from, for in order to get on that treadmill in the first place, you must already have abandoned life. Esthetic sentiments are not called for here. Perhaps we are not dealing with a book at all, but with something more than a book: perhaps we are approaching that movement from which all books derive, that

point of origin where, doubtless, the work is lost, the point which always ruins the work, the point of perpetual unworkableness with which the work must maintain an increasingly *initial* relation or risk becoming nothing at all. One might say that The Unnamable is condemned to exhausting the infinite. "I have nothing to do, that is to say, nothing in particular. I have to speak, whatever that means. Having nothing to say, no words but the words of others, I have to speak. No one compels me to, there is no one, it's an accident, a fact. Nothing can ever exempt me from it, there is nothing, nothing to discover, nothing to recover, nothing that can lessen what remains to say, I have the ocean to drink, so there is the ocean then."

It is this approach to *origin* which makes the experience of the work still more dangerous, dangerous for the man who bears it, dangerous for the work itself. But it is also this approach which assures the experiment its authenticity, which alone makes of art an essential research, and it is by having rendered this approach evident in the nakedest, most abrupt manner that *The Unnamable* has more importance for literature than most "successful" works in its canon. Try listening to "this voice that speaks, knowing that it lies, indifferent to what it says, too old perhaps and too humiliated ever to be able to say at last the words that might make it stop." And try descending into that neutral region where the self surrenders in order to speak, henceforth subject to words, fallen into the absence of time where it must die an endless death: ". . . *the words are everywhere, inside me, ouside me, well well, a minute ago I had no thickness, I hear them, no need to hear them, no need of a head, impossible to stop them, impossible to stop, I'm in words, made of words, others' words, what others, the place too, the air, the walls, the floor, the ceiling, all words, the whole world is here with me, I'm the air, the walls, the walled-in one, everything yields, opens, ebbs, flows, like flakes, I'm all these flakes, meeting, mingling, falling asunder, wherever I go I find me, leave me, go toward me, come from me, nothing ever but me, a particle of me, retrieved, lost, gone astray, I'm all these words, all these strangers, this dust of words, with no ground for their settling, no sky for their dispersing, coming together to say, fleeing one another to say, that I am they, all of them, those that merge, those that part, those that never meet, and nothing else, yet something else, that I'm quite different, a quite different thing, a wordless thing in an empty place, a hard shut dry cold black place where nothing stirs, nothing speaks, and that I listen, and that I seek, like a caged beast born of caged beasts born of caged beasts born of caged beasts . . .*"

GERMAINE BRÉE
From
"The Strange World of Beckett's 'grands articulés'"
tr. Margaret Guiton
Samuel Beckett Now, ed. Melvin J. Friedman
1970, pp. 73–85

In one of his rare press interviews Beckett made a somewhat surprising statement, perhaps for the benefit of his commentators.[1] He never, he declared, reads philosophers and does not understand them. The key to his novels must be sought in his own sensibility. It is here, and here alone, that his characters, in some mysterious manner, are born. And yet the fact remains that Descartes is the narrator of *Whoroscope*; that Democritus and Schopenhauer appear in the poems of *Echo's*

Bones; that the Pythagoreans and Geulincx, quoted in *Murphy* and the respective favorites of Neary and Murphy, have never ceased to haunt his world;[2] that his early studies of Joyce (1929) and Proust (1931) reveal a considerable facility for methodical, abstract discussions; and finally that, from a certain point of view, Beckett's work has an affinity with that of the most metaphysical of French critics, Maurice Blanchot.

Indeed Samuel Beckett's fictional world, especially *Watt*, contains a quasi-Rabelaisian parody of all the rhetorical and logical devices that have permitted Western man, like Beckett's Ubu-esque creation, the "man-pot" Mahood, to hold a "partially waterproof tarpaulin" over his skull. Describing, reasoning, discussing, examining—Beckett's characters never tire of these activities, though no two of them proceed in exactly the same way. They share our "deplorable mania" not only for "when something happens wanting to know what" but furthermore for wanting, like Watt, to know why. Beckett is thus something of a contemporary Faust who, through the agency of his characters, indiscriminately, and with ferocious humor, undermines all our past and present attempts to give reality an intelligible structure, to "think out" our human situation.

We can thus readily understand that Beckett should find philosophy unintelligible—as regards its proposed aims, not its intellectual procedures. These he tirelessly ridicules. Not without reason did he invent Macmann, that character Malone talks to himself about, who, while believing that "he had done as any man of good will would have done in his place and with very much the same results, in spite of his lack of experience," nonetheless acknowledges that, in gardening, he is "incapable of weeding a bed of pansies or marigolds and [of] leaving one standing." Beckett's verbal clowning produces a similar devastation, as do certain Jarry-like inventions which allow him to reduce our relations with the physical world to the status of a simple diagram: two pots for nourishment and evacuation; a bag of canned foods; a pebble or, in prosperous times, sixteen pebbles to suck; and so forth.

Like Joyce, perhaps still more than Joyce, Beckett seems marked by the scholasticism of his philosophy classes at Trinity College. We can find many traces of it in his imaginary world. Descartes and Geulincx are perhaps given an important role in his early novels because they broke with the great intellectual tradition which from Plato to Thomas Aquinas, via Aristotle, conceived creation as a moving hierarchy of creatures oriented toward a perfect and definitive form, a final cause, God. Descartes thus unintentionally prepared the way for Beckett's "great articulates"—creatures whose special articulation, in body, thought or speech, even though sadly defective, makes them forget that they are really "frightened vagabonds," willy-nilly dragging aimlessly along, dying by degrees, while words and images spin round and round inside their bony white skulls. Skulls, jars, rooms, or other habitations, and the monotonous surrounding "country" form the two inseparable and rhythmically alternating settings for the adventures of Beckett's great articulates: beings who travel, or rather wander, toward some illusory "home" or "refuge," telling each other their adventures, while their dual disarticulation proceeds insidiously, "by direct route."

Beckett's characters seem to parody the pre-Copernican theory that all incomplete and abortive forms move toward that which perfects them by completing them. They are strangely intent on travel if only in spirit, even when bedridden or "in jars," or on relating their travels; they seek one another and form unstable couples when, for a few brief moments, one seems to appear in order to complete the other: Celia and Murphy; Watt and Sam; Molloy and Moran; Malone and Macmann; Mahood and Worm; Pim and Bem—to name a few. Identified with each in turn, yet each time reemerging, modified by the contact, just as the different characters emerge from one another, there always finally remains he who is known only by his voice, a voice which, as a matter of fact, is not his own, the nameless one who is "alone here, the first and last" and nonetheless is never there, the animator of this verbal cosmos and source of its Logos, like the God of Genesis.

Murphy, tied to his rocking-chair by seven scarfs, attempting to attain perfect repose through an increasingly frenetic rocking can hardly fail to remind us, however vaguely, of certain Thomistic categories: that, for example, of celestial beings halfway between God and terrestrial beings who, since they are endowed with essential forms, know no other kind of movement than that of movement in repose. Murphy's ignominious fall, hindside foremost—which does not in the least discourage Murphy himself—is but the first of a whole series of falls precipitating Beckett's characters, one after the other, into any and every muddy ditch. Beckett thus brings out both the pathos and absurdity of our mental postures by grossly simplifying them and turning them into concrete situations which his characters act out physically: Pim (whose identity merges with that of the narrator of *How It Is*), his shoulders firmly encircled by an arm whose hand plunges into his bag, crawling in the mud with a can opener, his main educational tool, between his buttocks, is the latest, and strangest, of Beckett's fantastic inventions.

It is significant that Beckett should devote so much space to descriptions of his characters' physical bearing—their gaits and means of locomotion, from bicycling to crawling.[3] Strange to us, though completely natural to them, these are both comic and puzzling: Murphy, as perceived by Celia, standing motionless in the middle of a London thoroughfare, staring up at the sky; Watt's curious gyrating movement; Molloy perched on his bicycle with his crutches and game leg; the absurd, Ubu-esque structure formed by the Morans, father and son, as they proceed on their single bicycle, along the roads that will not lead to Molloy; and finally, "the trip by direct route" "in darkness mud" of the voiceless protagonist of *How It Is*, doing the "right leg right arm push pull flat on your stomach silent curses left leg left arm push pull flat on your stomach silent curses fifteen meters stop waddle." A Beckett character's means of locomotion is a piece of factual evidence, a *donnée* such as might be discerned by an inhuman eye observing the successive variations each infinitesimal character brings to the continuous, irresistible movement carrying it along into the interior of an unchanging countryside.

Beckett's cosmos retains a few traces of the medieval sky, "a world up there" occasionally glimpsed "in the blue," far from the mud and excrements. Although the episodes in *Murphy* are located, with Joycean precision, in London and Beckett's early environment near Dublin, where *Watt* also begins and ends, the scenes of the succeeding novels become progressively vague. Hill, swamp, shore, sea, forest, open country, city are eventually reduced to a single flat stretch of mud. This too, however, is related to medieval metaphysics: the universe of concentric zones, the symbolism of the circle and the center, of the elements and seasons, of light and movement. Beckett's man, like medieval man, is "molded from all the kingdoms." "There somewhere man is too," Moran solemnly remarks as he reflects on his mission to find Molloy, a "vast conglomerate of all of nature's kingdoms, as lonely and as bound." When Beckett's characters refer to birth, wombs, expulsion, copulation, excrements—Beckett seems particularly obsessed with fecal matter and urine[4]—in short, to human existence, the situations and images have Freudian overtones. But, after *Watt*, Beckett's characters evolve in a setting which is, on the whole, more in the tradition of Dante or of Milton;[5] we sense a familiar metaphysical vision beyond the imaginary structure.

This world, with its primeval slime, its expulsions, falls, and painful progressions, its halts and temporary refuges, its play of light and shade, its creatures sinking into or emerging from the mud, is now and then strikingly reminiscent of Dante's *Divine Comedy*—particularly, perhaps, as seen through Gustave Doré's illustrations. "Nights without Night" and "Days without Day," to borrow Michel Leiris's title—everything unfolds in the "imperfect shade" and "doubtful light" of an engraving, each character evolving in what Malone calls "my personal light," or else in that indirect lunar light in which this dim world is sometimes rather gently bathed.

Dante, to be sure, as many critics have pointed out, made a deep impression on Beckett's imagination. The lazy Belacqua, whom Dante places in the indecisive zone of Antepurgatory, is one of his special favorites, as also, though to a lesser extent, Sordello, his companion—the poet who at first is silent.[6] And Beckett, as he constructs his "mental country," occasionally alludes to Dante. The narrator of *The Unnamable*, "stuck like a sheaf of flowers in a deep jar, its neck flush with my mouth," his head held up by an iron collar; the narrator of *How It Is*, crawling on his stomach with his face in the mud; the crippled Moran, painfully proceeding through a forest during an entire winter; Macmann, lying under the open sky during a violent rain storm—how Dante-like these situations and places are! They recall the glacial rain in the third circle of the inferno; the forest of suicides in the seventh; and, persistently, the memory of Malebolge's domain, the eighth circle, where the perjurors, or falsifiers in words, drag themselves through the mud throughout eternity.

All Beckett's characters, including Murphy, are victimized by words, and all, beginning with Watt, must contend with that voice, "qua-qua," presiding over the birth of characters and scenery which accompanies the reader as faithfully as Virgil accompanied Dante. Unlike Virgil, however, it has a wide range of tones, according to whether or not it asks, or answers, all the questions.

These characters are "entrusted with missions" and inhabited by voices. At the beginning of *Molloy* a vaguely defined character, who is seated on a protuberance in the shadow of a rock, is ordered to go and find his mother—a mission that is imposed on him, an obligation he cannot evade. Later another more clearly defined character named Moran receives another order, from somewhere else, to set out in search of Molloy. Both will afterwards be obliged to make a report on their adventures. The narrator of *The Unnamable* is surrounded by numerous emissaries who force him to speak and who must be "satisfied." The entire adventure of the voiceless character in *How It Is* consists in obliging another person, Pim, to emit a few words, by "extorting" his voice from him. Malone seems to have chosen freely to write, but it is a form of defence against an "old debtor." And Watt, one of the "old members" of the gang and the first victim of the word, loses the faculty of common speech at Mr Knott's house; he nonetheless continues to repeat exactly the same broken phrases, in increasingly complex combinations, for the benefit of another character, Sam, who then interprets them.

These missions and obligations are apparently futile since none of the designated envoys reaches his goal. Watt begins his visit at Mr Knott's, the other characters begin their stories, calmly and reasonably, intent only on accurately observing and reporting existing events; but they gradually find themselves impelled into difficult zones where other voices mingle with their own, where other characters appear before them, so that Pim-Bem of *How It Is*, himself apparently a derivative of Mahood's abortive Worm, thinks for a moment that perhaps a "not one of us" exists whose "anonymous voice" is heard in the blurred but nonetheless communicable words extracted from, murmured by, the infinite series of Bem, Pim, Bom that he glimpses moving very slowly in closed ranks from west to east. In the same way, after *Watt*, one, then several omnipresent narrators, all using the first person, emerge from the omniscient narrator of the traditional novel form. They meet, converse, collide, sometimes in the same sentence, and replace each other without warning. The same device was already used by Laforgue; with Beckett it is of more than purely literary significance: the passage from the author's "I" to that of a character creates a third, and unknown, "I." To close in on the language of everyday discourse, to track it down and find—and never find—a voice which is one's own, is the task of a poet or a metaphysician.

Speech is the animating principle of Beckett's comedy which, as such, is very far removed from that of Dante. Unlike Dante's tortured victims, Beckett's characters discuss their miserable and repugnant situation very calmly; they find it not only tolerable but, on the whole, fairly good and, primarily concerned over the possibility of eviction, accept its inevitable deterioration in good spirit. When it comes to describing this situation, enumerating its advantages, discussing its resources, effecting certain improvements, hanging on, they could hardly be excelled. Inventing "begging boards" adapted to the almsgiver's psychology; fixing up a row boat so that it is waterproof on top with a hole in the bottom for immersion purposes, finding the best way to suck sixteen stones one after the other in perfect order; finding the perfect solution to the difficult problem of locomotion if you happen to have two stiff legs of unequal length; making the continually deferred inventory of one's possessions—Beckett's characters undertake these "little diversions" with happy zeal. They throw themselves into the game *à mots perdus* as it were, sometimes enjoying it for several pages at a time. Beckett's fantasy and humor are here strangely mingled both with ferocity and with compassion.

If, however, these characters are commanded to tell a story or relate their own adventures, panic inevitably ensues. Molloy, Moran, Mahood, and others assume voices and forms as best they may, appear and disappear without ever being completely born; they die piecemeal, departing this life feet first as all must do, but without ever ceasing to disappear; meanwhile "the other," the nameless narrator who, after *Watt*, always begins the story in the first person, speaks on and on. This is the "I" heard in *The Unnamable* before Mahood appears with his complement, Worm—that recalcitrant larva who lends an ear even though he refuses to be born:

> This voice that speaks, knowing that it lies, indifferent to what it says, too old perhaps and too abased ever to succeed in saying the words that would be its last, knowing itself useless and its uselessness in vain, not listening to itself but to the silence that it breaks. . . . It is not mine, I have none, I have no voice and must speak, that is all I know. . . .

A sort of anguish hovers over the human comedy, the drama of a creation continually menaced by abortion, an unsuccessful enterprise, situated somewhere between darkness and light, which must always be re-begun. Beckett himself advanced the theory in his essay on Bram van Velde.[7]

Beckett's fiction, committed to failure, thus apparently stems from a very personal experience: this onerous obligation to speak—an activity of vital importance, inspired by a force than comes from "elsewhere," and frightens him because it threatens to plunge him down into the eighth circle of hell with the falsifiers in words—he who would have been so well satisfied with Belacqua's rock. In order to name "the unnamable," say "the unspeakable," he must resort to the "jokes," "fairy tales," and "lies" that will enable these specters to make their way toward light. At the same time Beckett is also faced with the cruel necessity of destroying his fable in order to protect himself, as best he can, against the possibility of being alienated (depredated, expropriated, dispossessed, dislodged, displaced) by "the other" that he has created. He is thus obliged to flout the forms emerging from his story by every possible means. He must annihilate everything susceptible of being annihilated; everything, in other words, that is part of himself. Beckett is not inclined to "upholster" the truth. He does not wish to add anything to reality, he does not wish to transform anything. This is why he has so little patience with those who attempt to reduce his "fables" to a system of clear ideas. As the narrator of *The Unnamable* remarks, with somewhat exaggerated eloquence: "Perhaps I shall be obliged, in order not to peter out, to invent another fairy-tale, yet another, with heads, trunks, arms, legs, and all that follows, let loose in the changeless round of imperfect shadow and dubious light." The "others" who "pass by" the narrator are thus able, by dispossessing him, to "pass for" him, abandoning him, nameless, before an empty, "immeasurable" stretch of time which—sand, mud, water or whatever—insidiously suffocates him. These confrontations of narrator and character; the substitutions, during the course of the story, of one protagonist for another; the emergence, from nothingness, of one or several characters—sometimes an infinite series of new and *sans imprévu* "representatives," "agents," "surrogates," or "avatars" of "the unnamable"—these all give rise to considerable confusion, agitation, and also anguish. At such times Beckett's style begins to pant, take on incantatory overtones, produce a sense of uneasiness, while, both in contrast and in defiance, countering and neutralizing the incantation, irony, parody, and occasionally coarseness intervene, and the author begins to multiply his admonitions to himself: That's enough, no, not that; something went wrong here. During the whole course of the story the narrator comments on its developments: "Well, well, I wasn't expecting that"; "This will all have to be rewritten in the pluperfect"; "Now that we know where we're heading, let's go"; "What a bore"; "I'm fed up with all this make believe." He also occasionally addresses the reader: "I'm using the present tense, it's so easy to use the present tense when you're dealing with past events. It's the mythological present, don't pay any attention to it." It is up to us to decide which of the various "I"s is presently speaking, to keep up with the various verbal tricks and traps which often fit into existing patterns of rhetoric. Beckett here turns Joyce's devices to his own ends: puns, subtly dislocated quotations of prose or poetry, unexplained allusions, unfamiliar words taken from the technical language of philosophy, medicine, or natural history. In this respect he is nearer to Queneau than to any other contemporary writer. Since Beckett is extremely learned, no existing lexicon or encyclopedia would be adequate for those seeking a precise definition of every term or explanation of each allusion. These are all undoubtedly procedures characteristic of the epic form—negative, as it were anti-heroic, epics unfolding in an "immeasurable time"; "badly" told, taken up over and over again by the voice that animates the characters—characters vaguely aware that they are yet once again about to make gestures they have already made several times before. The evolving presence in Beckett's world is not so much the scenery and characters, "conveniences" that can easily be renewed, as the quality and behavior of this voice. Beckett sometimes indulges in surprisingly facile effects, lingers over puerile jokes; the voice idles along, fading into an interminable plashing sound; the same ironic dialogue monotonously recurs; the reader yawns. But the writer never abandons his hand-to-hand combat with language, his unceasing struggle to subject it to an "unnamable" truth resuscitated by this very combat and by-passed as soon as it is named, his own past-present.

Beckett's often brutal descriptive realism, which links him with the expressionists, should not obscure the specifically "fabulous" character of his novels. *Murphy*, despite the strangeness of its hero, is, from this point of view, still close to the familiar adventure story genre, solidly anchored in everyday reality. But beginning with *Watt* and the visit to Mr Knott, the strange and monstrous depths of Beckett's universe increasingly tend to absorb the characters who are part of himself. One is reminded of Odilon Redon's disturbing creatures, of the bizarre, although innocent, monsters Dubuffet seems to mold out of mud; or of Michaux's "properties." Vivian Mercier, who is also Irish, considers Beckett's combination of the grotesque and the macabre a form of Irish humor that is also found in native legends and fairy tales.[8] Beckett's characters remind him of "sheela-na-gig"—figurines with bald heads, emaciated bodies, crooked legs, and enormous mouths and genitals. According to Mercier they reflect primitive man's anguished reaction to the process of sexual reproduction, a form of death, and expulsion from the maternal womb, a prefiguration of his expulsion from life. It would indeed appear that Beckett's characters stand, as it were, between himself and the "murmur" of a voice situated in nothingness, forming a sort of barricade against dread.

The stories told are, moreover, strikingly similar, unfolding according to a cyclical epic pattern, frequently pointed out by Beckett, which becomes increasingly simplified: voyage, quest of encounter, combat, separation, return; sometimes, especially in the early novels, the patterns are complicated by secondary episodes, pauses in sheltered spots and love affairs in deceptive refuges, for example—that are "seen" retrospectively and seem to parody certain types of fiction. The characters, no less than the stories that they tell, have a certain air of family resemblance, and a whole network of reminiscences—encounters, objects, words—are carried over from one novel to the next. Everyone wears the clownlike Beckett uniform, or what remains thereof: for the hats, long, stiff coats, odd shoes, and ill-fitting, cast-off garments of the "human envelope" may vanish one after the other; there still remains the long white hair, dirty and matted, the accumulated filth of centuries. As a matter of fact we soon begin to realize that, from *Murphy* to *How It Is*, it is doubtless the same adventurer that goes his way and gives birth, from book to book, to the unpredictable and inevitable book that follows. Beckett thus follows his own adventure on the trail of "that little creature in numerous disguises" who haunts him. Each stopping place along the way appears to be the last but always turns out to be "next to last" or the "penultimate." He too, like his own characters, must set out again, proceeding from west to east, against all natural forces and the underlying order of the cosmos. His own adventure thus rejoins that long, monotonous human enterprise that is based on written language, as old as man himself and never finished. And so the annihilation of Samuel Beckett proceeds along its course.

Notes

1. Gabriel d'Aubarède, *Nouvelles Littéraires* (16 February 1961).
2. Hugh Kenner in *Samuel Beckett: A Critical Study* (New York: Grove Press, 1961); Frederick J. Hoffmann in *Samuel Beckett: The Language of Self* (Carbondale: Southern Illinois University Press, 1962); Samuel Mintz in "Beckett's *Murphy*: A Cartesian Novel," *Perspective* II (Autumn 1959): 156–59; and Jacqueline Hoefer in "Watt," *Perspective* II (Autumn 1959): 166–82 have all shown the extent to which Beckett's work demands of the reader a solid philosophic background. Professor Julius Weinberg of the University of Wisconsin has shown me a very pertinent parody of Leibnitz in *Watt* (132–35). Mr Endon, the mad chess player with the vacant eye, in *Murphy*, Mr Knott, Watt's master, who creates an infinite number of starving dogs in order to dispose of his left-overs, and other persistent "Godots" emphasize this particular aspect of Beckett's work.
3. See Kenner: "The Cartesian Centaur," in *Samuel Beckett: A Critical Study*.
4. Despite a few grotesque descriptions of copulation and some allusions to masturbation, Beckett does not give much prominence to sexual functions, the genital organs of his protagonists being for the most part in pitiable condition. On the other hand, Beckett himself seems to have become aware of the often pointless monotony of his recurring scatological jokes and allusions: the protagonist of *The Unnamable* at one point decides to eliminate them.
5. In "From an Abandoned Work" performed over the BBC on 14 December 1957, the elderly protagonist and narrator, like Krapp, dictates his autobiography, seeing himself again as a young man studying Milton's cosmology with his father.
6. Belacqua is the protagonist of Beckett's first stories, *More Pricks Than Kicks* (London: Chatto & Windus, 1934); he reappears, directly or indirectly, in all the novels, and is mentioned again in *How It Is*.
7. See the third dialogue in Samuel Beckett, "Three Dialogues," *Samuel Beckett: A Collection of Critical Essays*, ed. Martin Esslin (Englewood Cliffs, N.J.: Prentice-Hall, 1965).
8. Samuel Beckett and the Sheela-na-gig," *Kenyon Review* 23 (Spring 1961) p. 299.

A. ALVAREZ
From *Beckett*
1974, pp. 12–17

In the first days of his fame Beckett was usually bracketed with Ionesco as a dramatist of the Absurd. This was understandable but misleading. *The Bald Prima Donna*, which was first produced in Paris in 1950, three years before *Godot*, was not only a smash-hit—still running twenty years later, like *The Mousetrap* in London—it was also a turning-point, the first genuinely anti-theatre theatre. Ionesco took the successful formula for light comedy and stood it on its head. He used the conventional middle-class drawing-room setting and conventional clichés for dialogue—culled, in fact, from a language primer. The result was both put-on and discovery. The platitudes, so remorselessly swapped by two model British families, were subtly doctored into madness, so that what began as a joke finished as the poetry of banality, absurdity in the most literal sense of the then fashionable term. When Camus talked of the Absurd in *The Myth of Sisyphus* he meant a life lived solely for its own sake in a universe which no longer made sense because there was no God to resolve the contradictions. In other words, what Camus called Absurd, Kierkegaard—more Christian, more precise and even less optimistic—had called Despair. But for Ionesco, Grand Master of the Theatre of the Absurd, absurdity was what it usually is: raging, hilarious farce.

Beckett, however, is an Absurdist in the strict, appalled sense that Camus intended. He has created a world in which Godot never comes and Mr Knott lives up to his name, in which it seems perfectly natural to pass one's time in an urn or a dustbin, up to the neck in sand or face down in the mud, a world which, seen from the skull-like room of *Endgame*, is devastated, post-atomic and so empty that a solitary human being seems like a monstrous intrusion. Absurdity in Ionesco's more obvious sense appears only on the side: as the obsessional calculations by which his characters plot and predict and so make safe every eventuality, as the vaudeville patter with which they ritualise their relationships, and as the occasional vaudeville calamities—the pratfalls and collapsing trousers—which they stoically endure. Absurdity in this sense is a by-product of their metaphysically absurd condition; it is the best they can hope for, the worst they always expect.

No doubt the superficial resemblances between Beckett and Ionesco made it easier for the public, already softened up by the latter's more taking brand of Absurdity, to accept Beckett's stringent vision. Yet the final difference between the two writers is radical and profound. Unlike Beckett, who maintains a mollusc-like taciturnity in the face of all criticism, Ionesco has always been a controversialist, unable to resist the temptation to justify and explain himself in interviews, articles and tetchy letters to the editor. In recent years he has even published his notebooks in which he comes on unconvincingly as a deep thinker. Yet in practice his genius lies not in his profundity but in his ability to create dramatic images which are as immediate, as affecting and as irredeemably strange as dreams, and then to let them work themselves out with a dream's irrational but compulsive logic. He makes it seem perfectly normal for there to be rhinoceroses in the street or a corpse growing in the bedroom. Everything makes sense yet is beyond reason. He once remarked to an interviewer:

> The dream is pure drama. In a dream, one is always in mid-situation . . . I think that the dream is a lucid thought, more lucid than any one has when awake, a thought expressed in images, and that at the same time its form is always dramatic.[1]

At his best, Ionesco has been true to his dreams. He almost never creates characters of any depth or substance; the people in his plays are sudden and two-dimensional, like the figures in a dream. And, as in a dream, the complexity is all in their immediate situation. He has put his nightmares on stage, unadulterated and with an uncanny sense of what works in that tight space framed by the proscenium arch. The result is pure nihilism. After all, what can survive when the placid façade of middle-class life splits open and the submerged fantasies come pulsing through? There is a curious intensity in Ionesco's best plays: the tone may be farcical yet the effect is single and unhesitating, like that of a lyric poem.

Ionesco's dream-world is unpredictable, irrational and abrupt. Beckett's is the opposite of all that: it is the world of chess, meticulous and utterly rational. Appropriately, one of his finest plays is called *Endgame* and the hero prefaces each stage of its development by announcing, 'Me to play.' Precision above all else, even though the game he is ending is his own life. It is also a world of such acute self-consciousness that the created characters are continually puncturing the illusion of art: 'This,' says Clov, 'is what is called making an exit'; after a particularly tedious interchange Hamm appropriates the audience's response by remarking, 'This is deadly'; Malone writing in bed becomes indistinguishable from Beckett writing in his study, for ever breaking off to ensure that the reader is aware that the words he is reading are those that Malone is writing.

And so on. When Ionesco is unable to think of an ending he relapses into whimsy; his characters float away giggling into the heavens, like Babar the Elephant. Beckett's, on the other hand, lapse into arithmetic. *Watt* is particularly prone to this counting mania: page after page is devoted to the possible combinations of notes produced by three frogs croaking 'Krak! Krek! Krik!' respectively; to the various ways in which someone might move about a room or dispose of a key; to the family tree of the disastrous Lynches, whose unfulfilled amibition is to achieve a combined age of one thousand years and whose combined ailments would fill a hospital. Similarly, Molloy plots like a computer how to dispose of his sixteen sucking stones in four pockets in such a way that he will never suck the same stone twice in succession. Finally, exacerbated by reason beyond reason, he throws them all away except one, which he promptly loses. Mathematics, as Molloy explains, is the one assured consolation in an unpredictable and literary universe:

> In winter, under my greatcoat, I wrapped myself in
> swathes of newspaper. . . . The *Times Literary Sup-*
> *plement* was admirably adapted to this purpose, of a
> never failing toughness and impermeability. Even
> farts made no impression on it. I can't help it, gas
> escapes from my fundament on the least pretext, it's
> hard not to mention it now and then, however great
> my distaste. One day I counted them. Three hun-
> dred and fifteen farts in nineteen hours, or an average
> of over sixteen farts an hour. After all it's not ex-
> cessive. Four farts every fifteen minutes. It's nothing.
> Not even one fart every four minutes. It's unbeliev-
> able. Damn it, I hardly fart at all, I should never
> have mentioned it. Extraordinary how mathematics
> help you to know yourself.

It is a point well and plangently made, although, surprisingly, he has miscalculated: 'four farts every fifteen minutes' is more, not less, than 'one fart every four minutes'. I know of only one other place in Beckett's works where his arithmetic lets him down.[2]

Over the years Beckett's mathematical obsessions have become a little less obtrusive but they still remain. In an extraordinary late piece of prose, *Imagination Dead Imagine*, the precise positions of two immobile bodies in a sphere are plotted by geometrical coordinates. These bleak notations are all that remains of an experimental programme which began around 1930 as a kind of homage to James Joyce and ended as nothing less than the assassination of both the novel and the play in their received, conventional forms.

Of course, Beckett's experiments, like Ionesco's, are finally a matter of temperament. Ionesco developed his special form of anti-theatre because, like many intellectuals, he was contemptuous of the stage: 'I started writing for the theatre,' he once remarked, 'because I hated it.' Beckett's peculiar revolution seems rooted even deeper: 'You would do better,' says Molloy, 'at least no worse, to obliterate texts than to blacken margins, to fill in the holes of words till all is blank and flat and the whole ghastly business looks like what it is, senseless, speechless, issueless misery.' It is as though the whole of Beckett's writing career were a search for an adequate artistic expression for his depression and his distaste for art, a slow but inevitable progress from manic high style through obsessionality to the latest minimal works, which are as close to silence as a man can decently get while still remaining a practising author. He himself summed it up in a 1949 dialogue with Georges Duthuit, when he described the fate of the artist as being resigned to 'the expression that there is nothing to express, nothing with which to express, nothing from which to express, no power to express, no desire to express, together with the obligation to express'. It is like the last words of *The Unnamable*: 'you must go on, I can't go on, I'll go on.'

Notes

1. Claude Bonnefoy, *Conversations with Eugene Ionesco*, New York, 1971, p. 10.
2. At the beginning of *Murphy* the hero is described as being lashed naked to his rocking chair by seven scarves; only six are accounted for.

BRIAN FINNEY
From *"Assumption* to *Lessness*
Beckett's Shorter Fiction"
Beckett the Shape Changer, ed. Katharine Worth
1975, pp. 64–81

Beckett's shorter fiction has inevitably received less attention than the longer works owing to its early inferiority and its later difficulty. Yet it has its own distinctive contribution to make to our knowledge of his world. It is a form uniquely suited to Beckett's stark and deliberately simplified vision of man's predicament. For over a decade now it has constituted his only fictional output. Even where it fails artistically, it can throw fascinating light on subsequent works. All the uncollected shorter fiction up to *More Pricks Than Kicks* comes into this category.[1] There are the two early stories 'Assumption' (1929) and 'A Case in a Thousand' (1934), besides two self-contained extracts from his suppressed first novel 'Dream of Fair to Middling Women' published as 'Sedendo et Quiescendo' and 'Text' in 1932.[2] Despite their obscurity in both language and meaning they contain nuggets Beckett was to mine later.

In 'Assumption' the male protagonist is locked in an unnatural 'humanity of silence'. Contact with a woman leads to nightly crucifixion ('each night he died and was God') from which he longs to be released into 'the light of eternity'. Finally love breaks down his dam of silence and with 'a great storm of sound' he dies. Beckett still had to discover the imprisoning effects of time-bound speech on those desiring dissolution into a timeless void. But the story is potent with themes that continue to obsess him. The collapse of a lifetime's silence that leaves the suffering victim 'fused with the cosmic discord' is a situation he has recently reverted to with great effect in *Not I*. The concept of man as a suffering God, crucified by the world and sexuality in particular, anticipates numerous parallels between successive heroes and Christ: the stoning of the hero of 'The End'; Molloy making his entry to his Jerusalem on a bicycle; Macmann and 'Bom' stretched out on the ground in the attitude of the cross: the list is endless.

In particular the association Beckett makes between women and death in 'Assumption' is developed more fully in his subsequent fiction. In 'Assumption' the woman contemplates the hero's 'face that she had overlaid with death'. In the chapter 'Love and Lethe' from *More Pricks Than Kicks* Belacqua sets out on a suicide pact with his latest girl, Ruby, only to end up making love instead. Beckett claims sardonically that 'at least on this occasion, if never before nor since, he achieved what he set out to do'. Love means exile from the self; for Beckett this is a little death in a less playful sense than that punned on by his Elizabethan predecessors. It constantly distracts Belacqua in both 'Dream of Fair to Middling Women' and *More Pricks Than Kicks* from seeking refuge in his mind, which both he and Murphy saw 'as the last ditch when all was said and done'. Murphy goes one better than Belacqua in managing to turn his back on Celia, the first of many prostitutes that feature as the heroines of his subsequent fiction.

Behind Beckett's paradoxical attitude to love and sexuality lies his vision of man's suffering condition. The illusory joys of sex lead to the all-too-real suffering of a new life. His opening remark to John Gruen in 1970 was: 'The major sin is the sin of being born.' He went on to claim that he has a clear memory of his own foetal existence, one of agony and darkness. This could well explain the enigma inherent in Beckett's other early short story, 'A Case in a Thousand', where Dr Nye, the protagonist, refuses to accept man's universal sadness as anything but a personal disorder. Only after his nurse has related to him 'a matter connected with his earliest years' too trivial to 'be enlarged on here' can one make any sense of his earlier proposition: 'Myself I cannot save.' He has already undergone the trauma of birth, but can at least avoid bequeathing it to a further generation. To Beckett midwife and gravedigger are indistinguishable.

Dr. Nye anticipates Belacqua's wish 'to be back in the caul, on (his) back in the dark for ever', which would at least avoid the 'night-sweats' of his sexuality. *More Pricks Than Kicks* (1934) has been given more attention than Beckett would have liked (to judge from the blurb on the Calder & Boyars reissue of 1970), primarily because Belacqua stands first in his long line of fictional derelicts. He shares with them many of the distinctive features which instantly set Beckett's protagonists apart from so-called normal experience. His physical disabilities and his associated love for bicycles, his sloth, his abhorrence of clocks and other reminders of his temporal condition, his distinction between mind and body, his 'faculty for acting with insufficient motivation', and his penchant for lunatic asylums all find parallels in the heroes of the subsequent novels.

What is distinctive about this first book of short stories is its concentration on Belacqua's sexual misadventures. During the course of the book Belacqua is paired off in turn with Winnie Coates, Alba Perdue, Ruby Tough, Lucy, Thelma *née* bboggs, and the Smeraldina. In each relationship Belacqua's conduct reverses the norms of gallantry. A moment of tenderness for him on Winnie's part strikes Belacqua as 'a drink of water to drink in a dungeon'. Love at the least is an imprisonment—with minor privileges for good conduct. Belacqua appears to be seeking a wife or mistress who is so uninterested in him sexually that he is freed of his bodily compulsions, able to seek slothful peace in an extended 'Beethoven pause' of the mind. Only that bluestocking, the Alba, seems capable of such selflessness; yet their platonic night together ends with the comment in German 'Not possible . . .'.Ruby lets him down badly, depriving him of his 'temporarily sane' determination to commit suicide with the 'ignis fatuus' of her sex appeal. Much to his disappointment Lucy stubbornly refuses 'to establish their married life on [the] solid basis of a cuckoldry'. Belacqua's idea of marital happiness is only achieved when she has been 'crippled for life and her beauty dreadfully marred'.

Belacqua seeks to escape from the bondage of his sexuality by playing the peeping Tom. It is an inadequate solution to a problem which is solved in more solipsist style by his successors in the *Nouvelles* and the trilogy (*Molloy*, *Malone Dies*, and *The Unnamable*), who resort to onanism. But at least it detaches him one remove from the evil of procreation, besides saving him the physical effort in the spirit of Dante's original, 'sloth's own brother'. Lucy does not survive her accident long, and only after his own death is Belacqua finally able to enjoy the

prospect of his third wife, the Smeraldina, taking Hairy as her cicisbeo because 'this is what darling Bel would wish'. Simultaneous detachment from, and satisfaction in, the sexual act is only permissible to the dead. The living are already in Purgatory. Belacqua's lifelong endeavour to attain a god-like omniscience from sex ('I am what I am' he claims, like St. Paul, to whom the title also refers) is doomed to failure in a godless world. There are more pricks that kicks to life in every sense.

Belacqua's fictional successors learn faster the bitter connection between their sexuality and the curse of their own conception. Molloy even admits to sometimes confusing his mother's image with that of his old lover, Ruth, an experience that he finds 'unendurable, like being crucified'. Rather than inflict the pain of existence on another generation, the French heroes set out to reverse the pattern of growth, to return to the tomb of the womb, to spend their last days, like Mahood, in their mother's entrails. Their efforts to effect the impossible are comic, their failure tragic. Conception is irreversible and these heroes are constantly being ejected from their womb-like refuges and thrown back violently on to the stage of life, like the Player in *Act Without Words*.

This image of repeated expulsion first surfaces as a dominant motif in the four *Nouvelles* (*Premier amour*, 'L'Expulsé', 'La Fin', and 'Le Calmant' respectively translated as *First Love*, 'The Expelled', 'The End', and 'The Calmative'), Beckett's earliest French fiction, written in 1945 before both *Mercier and Camier* and the trilogy. In all but one story ('The Calmative') the hero makes his fictional entrée on being expelled from a womb-like room, which in the case of *First Love* has been bequeathed him by his father. In all three stories the exiled anti-hero spends his time wandering in search of a substitute refuge, which when found proves hopelessly inadequate. In the initial room the hero, like the foetus, was at least fed and evacuated regularly. But the coffin-shaped cab of 'The Expelled' (the title speaks for itself), the sitting room emptied of its furniture in *First Love*, the hut in 'The Calmative', and the basement room, cave and shed in 'The End' all fail to reproduce even the substitute convenience of the initial room. In 'The End', for example, the hero is only saved from starvation by the chance arrival of a cow; and where previously he had had his chamber pot emptied daily, in his shed he dirties his own nest. As he sardonically says of his tragi-comic predicament: 'To contrive a little kingdom, in the midst of the universal muck, then shit on it, ah that was me all over.' Interestingly, there is less comic detachment in the earlier version of this story which reads in place of the last phrase 'ah the pity of it'.

Far the most interesting of the *Nouvelles* in this context is *Premier amour* (*First Love*), which Beckett withheld from publication until 1970 and which only appeared in English translation in 1973. Beckett wrote to me saying he withheld *Premier amour* because he found it 'even less satisfactory than the others', and now regrets having released it for publication. I must confess that I still find it the most fascinating of the four *Nouvelles*. From the beginning the first-person narrator links marriage with death, his own marriage to Anna with the death of his father. Marriage can only bring mortality to the child born from it into sorrow. Considering that the narrator remembers the trauma of his own birth, the date of which lies graven in his memory 'in figures that life will not easily erase', it is surprising—even to him—that he should so quickly be involved in inflicting the same agony on another. What emerges from his account of his first love affair is that yet again he is only seeking in this woman a return to the womb. Expelled from the room in his father's house, his clothes dumped outside it like an afterbirth, he re-creates the image of his initial room in the house of Anna, the prostitute he meets and goes to live with. Although she undertakes all the maternal functions of feeding him and emptying his pot, he is driven to desert her by the birth-cries of what she alleges is his child, cries which continue to haunt his memory for the rest of his life.

Crudely summarised in this way, the story sounds like the neurotic outpourings of a sick mind. What above all saves it from this charge is Beckett's comic detachment. As Nell says in *Endgame*, 'nothing is funnier than unhappiness'. The narrator is life's victim, doing his best to avoid the gross errors of his fellow creatures, but finally and hilariously proving just as vulnerable. Fleeing from Anna, his first love, he takes refuge in an abandoned cow-shed. There

> for the first time in my life, and I would not hesitate
> to say the last if I had not to husband my cyanide, I
> had to contend with a feeling which gradually
> assumed, to my dismay, the dread name of love.

Above all what convinces him that he must be in love is finding himself tracing the word 'Anna' on 'time's forgotten cowplats'. By this Augustinian juxtaposition of love and excrement, as of sublime language and banal action, Beckett induces us to laugh at the essential tragedy of existence. For existence is not all suffering. As the narrator has come to realise: 'Catch-cony life! To be nothing but pain, how that would simplify matters! Omnidolent! Impious dream!' Such temporary wisdom and detachment fails to prevent him being ricocheted between the extremes of love's tortures and relative happiness. He even finds himself pulling up nettles under the evil influence of love, instead of manuring them as was his usual custom, Beckett informs us, tongue in cheek, with all malevolent weeds. Weeds remind him of the reality of things which is only concealed by the ephemeral beauty of flowers. Repeatedly the hero of the *Nouvelles* obtains hyacinths or crocuses as *memento mori* over whose decay and promise of oblivion he perversely rejoices.

Apart from the unforgivable association between love and birth, the narrator also finds love a distraction from what he sees as his only hope in life, 'supineness in the mind, the dulling of the self and of that residue of execrable frippery known as the non-self and even the world, for short'. This search for the oblivion of womb or grave that obsesses the heroes of all his subsequent fiction can only be conducted by being oneself: 'For when one is [oneself] one knows what to do to be less so', he claims, little appreciating the epistemological complications awaiting his fictional successors pursuing this programme. Whereas love on the other hand means exile from the self, 'and it is painful to be no longer oneself, even more painful if possible than when one is'. Paradoxically true as this may be, the narrator of *First Love* is unable to use this theoretical insight to extricate himself from Anna. His expulsion from her refuge is ironically forced on him by the unforgivable reproduction of life, in which he may have played an unwilling part.

First Love contains so many of the major themes of the French fiction in embryonic form that it deserves greater attention than it has received to date. The narrator experiences all the problems of perception that are to torture his successors. The outside world, other people, even his own memory are not to be trusted, since, as Beckett said in *Proust*, 'the individual is a succession of individuals, the world being a projection of the individual's consciousness'. Words like 'love' and 'beauty' remain enigmas to this lover, qualities he has read about but is liable to apply to the wrong situations, owing to the subjective nature of his perception. Despite her age and permanent squint, Anna could well be beautiful, he claims, if he had some data on beauty—which none of us has, Beckett implies. Constantly the certainties of daily living are being undermined by the narrator's painfully honest scepticism. For example, he returns to the bench for the fourth or fifth time, 'at roughly the same hour, I mean roughly the same sky, no, I don't mean that either, for it's always the same sky and never the same sky, what words are there for that, none I know, period'. The incomprehensible nothingness of reality can only be approximated to by the writer's use of such mutually annihilating antitheses.

In fact the entire story is constructed in this manner. The narrator loves death and hates love, that death of the self. He seeks out the self to escape it. He tells his story so as to reach 'là où le verbe s'arrête', as Beckett wrote in the French version but omitted from his English translation ('the point where speech ceases'). For, like the heroes of the other *Nouvelles* and the trilogy, he is a writer whose writings 'are no sooner dry than they revolt me'. As a writer he is particularly aware of the vulnerability of language: 'I heard the word fibrome, or brone, I don't know which, never knew, never knew what it meant and never had the curiosity to find out. The things one recalls! And records!' Words are as arbitrary as life and as meaningless. How can one person ever be sure that the meaning of what he says is not understood wholly differently by the recipient? How can we ever get outside our own heads? If we can't, then all life becomes a fiction, and, like the narrator of *First Love*, we can decide to alter someone else's name from Lulu to Anna without more than our usual inconsistency.

Like his contemporaries, Nabokov and Barth, Beckett never lets his reader forget the deceptive nature of the form he is using. He plays linguistic games throughout the *Nouvelles*. The narrator of 'The Expelled' ends up unable to explain why he told this story rather than another: 'Perhaps some other time I'll be able to tell another. Living souls, you will see how alike they are'—alike because they emanate from the same brain. In all the *Nouvelles*, as the narrator of 'The Calmative' explains, 'we are needless to say in a skull'. Like his successors in the trilogy he tells himself 'this story which aspires to be the last' to calm himself in the terrifying face of death. Repeatedly Beckett reminds us that life is a fiction of our own invention: 'So much for that description' he will make his hero exclaim with satisfaction, or 'No reason for this to end or go on. Then let it end.' In parodying fictional conventions he is mocking the artificiality of the life we have invented for ourselves: aesthetic and metaphysical considerations become indistinguishable in his work.

The remaining three *Nouvelles* anticipate the structure and major themes of the trilogy quite closely at times. Both sets of works present the same protagonist, exiled from the oblivion of the womb in a world of his own invention, seeking to end his suffering existence by coming to know his unknowable self. Like Belacqua, Murphy and Watt before him, and Molloy, Moran, Macmann and Mahood after him, the hero of 'The Expelled' finds his body a very imperfect instrument of locomotion. Whenever he attempts mentally to correct the clumsiness of his gait he 'managed a few steps of creditable execution and then fell'. Mind and body are related to each other too precariously to withstand any conscious interference by mind alone. It is appropriate that the dualist philosopher Geulincz's *Ethics* should be mentioned by name in the same story. The hero of the *Nouvelles*, like those of the trilogy, wears his father's hat and greatcoat, suffers from similar sores of the scalp, and tramps across the same landscape with its fortified town, hill, bogs and coastline.

The links between the two trilogies of stories and novels are of two kinds: similarities in situation, and references in the novels to events in the stories. There are a number of striking parallels between 'The Expelled' and *Molloy*, 'The End' and *Malone Dies*, and 'The Calmative' and *The Unnamable*. In the first pair both heroes begin their wanderings in the prime of life, have a contretemps with policemen, knock down old women or their dogs and confess to being the author of their own stories. In the second pair both heroes seek to create their own fictional death; both seek out rooms in which their food is fetched and their pot emptied regularly, only to lose these conveniences; both slowly degenerate into tramps, now sitting on the bench by the river first introduced in *First Love*, now exposed to the elements; both end drifting out to the open sea in a boat to meet their imagined end. The final pair, 'The Calmative' and *The Unnamable*, both imagine the continuation of mind and voice after the body has died. Both heroes are tortured by fictional assassins or tyrants of their own invention in a place of terror that both identify with the inside of their distant skulls. Both attempt to escape into the silence of their true self by telling their own story rather than one about a fictional counterpart, and both in effect conclude: 'All I say cancels out, I'll have said nothing'—and go on.

If these parallels suggest repetition, the way in which each subsequent work demolishes its predecessors suggests progression of a kind. Not only does each of the four *Nouvelles* trace the roughly chronological career of the same protagonist (twenty-five years old in *First Love*, ninety years old when he died according to 'The Calmative'), but all three novels that follow draw on the *Nouvelles* for incidents in their characters' past history. Molloy remembers his past incarnation as the hero of 'The End' who put out to sea in a boat and wonders if he ever returned from that journey. This memory of his is promptly undermined by speculating whether any relationship is possible between past and present selves, the one setting out and the one returning. Likewise Malone has a photograph of the ass by the shore that carried him to his cave in 'The End', a cave that Malone now remembers with pleasure, where in the earlier story he had felt compelled to abandon it. Once again memory is playing tricks on its victim. Even the Unnamable acknowledges his past origins in the *Nouvelles* by quoting the opening sentence of 'The End', 'They clothed me and gave me money.' He sees all his predecessors from Belacqua to Malone in orbit around him and disowns them all as fabrications of a self that still remains inaccessible, because unnamable. Each protagonist acknowledges his fictional predecessors in order to demolish them, another example of Beckett's use of mutually destructive antitheses. . . .

Beckett has travelled a great distance from the verbal exuberance of his early short fiction. Linguistic acrobatics have given way to the conscious dislocation of language. The puns and scholarly wit of *More Pricks Than Kicks* have no place in his latest work, where a sparse vocabulary is ranged against itself in a series of mutually annihilating paradoxes. Thwarted by the relativity of perception, Beckett has concentrated, increasingly as time has passed, on inventing literary forms that can overcome the subjective limitations of traditional fiction, obsessed as it is with 'figments' like love, beauty, time and memory. In the last phase of his writing he has sought literary structures that admit the chaos of man's meaningless existence while not excluding man's hopeless search for an order and a meaning to life. The result has been a series of prose texts whose difficulty is matched by their originality. The little population of lost ones, the pastoral idyll of *Enough*, and the body face to ⟨face with⟩ endlessness join their predecessors in a gall-

ery of unique and compelling images that reflect Beckett's life-long search for that impossible shape that will capture in its own destruction life's ultimate shapelessness.

Notes

1. See R. Federman and J. Fletcher, *Samuel Beckett: His Works and His Critics*, University of California Press, 1970, for full bibliographical sources of these stories.
2. A further extract, 'Jem Higgins' Love-Letter to the Alba', was published in the Durham University magazine, *New Durham*, in June 1965.

WOLFGANG ISER
From
"The Pattern of Negativity in Beckett's Prose"
The Georgia Review, 1975, pp. 706–19

I

Negativity and construction—this is Sartre's definition of the principle underlying literature. He uses this definition in order to try to establish the function of literature in the context of human society. Negativity is to be regarded as one aspect of freedom, because it is not, as Sartre says in *What Is Literature?*, a matter merely of "the abstract ability to say no, but of a concrete negativity that retains for itself that which it rejects, and is completely colored by it." As such, it gives a degree of free play to the reader of the literary text it colors, for his task is to discover that which the work suppresses. One might say, in this respect, that negativity transforms the work into a kind of suction effect: because the reader seems to be relentlessly drawn into the world, the text opens up for him.

This particular effect distinguishes negativity from simple negation, for as Kenneth Burke has shown, negation contains the imperative demand to seek the positive elsewhere than in what is negated, and this demand is nearly always accompanied by a number of signposts to point the way: what the reader has to find can be taken to be the opposite of what has been negated, and so contrasts and contradistinctions form a frame of reference within which the intention of the negation can be discovered. In this way negations enable literary texts to stimulate specific attitudes to specific social situations. However, when such frames of reference are dismantled or even deliberately suppressed, negation changes into negativity, and instead of a demand we have what I have called a suction effect.

Negativity is the hallmark of the typical Beckett text. It is produced by a relentless process of negation, which in the novels applies even on the level of the individual sentences themselves, which follow one another as a ceaseless rejection and denial of what has just been said. The negation may relate either to a statement, or to something preceding that statement. If a statement is negated, this does not mean that nothing is left of it. A poster stamped "performance cancelled" is still a poster, and is all the more striking if, as in this case, there are no other posters to tell you what *is* on. The fewer orientations there are, the more oppressive will be the cancellation of what we *have* been given. The Beckett reader is continually being confronted by statements that are no longer valid. But as the negated statements remain present in his mind, so the indeterminacy of the text increases, thus increasing the pressure on the reader to find out what is being withheld from him. At the same time the cancellation of statements teaches him that he is not to be given any specific orientation, and this evokes in him an even greater need for finding out what the negated orientation actually drives at. Thus negativity turns out to be a basic constituent of communication. If we look at the process of negativity in this light, we will see that Beckett's work is by no means so negative or destructive as many critics would have us believe—especially those who, like Lukács, feel obliged to view his writings as the "most profound pathological debasement of man." Indeed negativity can be regarded here as a structure of bringing forth—at least potentially—infinite possibilities. This becomes clearer if we take a closer look at the other type of negation, the one that is related to what precedes a statement. If a negation can no longer be viewed in terms of any given frame of reference, it explodes into a multiplicity of possibilities. This process is as old as human society. The Ten Commandments contain a typical example: "Thou shalt not make thee *any* graven image, *or* any likeness *of any thing* that *is* in heaven above, or that *is* in the earth beneath, or that *is* in the waters beneath the earth" (Deuteronomy 5:8). The history of Christian art shows the extent to which this negative commandment has "exploded" into an endless variety of graven images and likenesses. The same applies to Beckett. The continual negation of the ideas evoked by the texts—the self and its history, the end and its ending, the demand (in *Imagination Dead Imagine*) that imagination itself be negated as the origin of such images— constitutes the massively productive force that releases all these possibilities, a force to which the very existence of Beckett's own works bears eloquent testimony.

Negativity brings into being an endless potentiality, and it is this potentiality that forms the infrastructure of Beckett's writings. By negativity we mean the hidden motive for the many negations and deformations that condition the characters we meet in these works. It stimulates communicative and constitutive activities within us by showing us that something is being withheld and by challenging us to discover what it is. If we take the term negativity to cover the deformations of Beckett's characters and also their own negative aspects which in turn lead to so many negativized situations, we may begin to understand what is actually conveyed by negativity. Merleau-Ponty has said, with reference to pictorial art, that "it is peculiar to the visible . . . that it is duplicated by something invisible which is, to a certain extent, absent and which the visible makes present." If we apply this to Beckett's works, we will find that our own imaginations are concerned not with concretizing the deformations of the characters or their constant failures, so much as with the duplication of the "invisible," for the concretizing of deformations and failures can only come about if we can discover their cause, and this is never given to us. We are compelled to try to fulfill a hidden potential, as we seek to conceive the conditions which alone can lead us to the sense of what we are reading. Thus negativity mediates between presentation and reception: it initiates those processes of imagination that are necessary to bring out the virtuality of those conditions, which—though linguistically not stated—are responsible for all the deformations of the characters and their constant failures. It is an important agent of the interaction between text and reader, and at the same time it constitutes the point at which Beckett's texts sink their roots into life itself.

Tavistock School's psychoanalytical research into communication takes as its starting-point the fact that negativity is the basic regulator of human communication. As R. D. Laing remarks, it is characteristic of human relations that we have no real knowledge of how we experience one another. This fundamental gap in our knowledge leads us first to a productive process through which we build up our own conceptions of how our partner experiences us; we base our reactions upon these projections. Our imaginary picture, then, is a product

that enables us to cover the unbridgeable gap in human relations. However, we then find that this product is only the image of a reality which certainly exists—for our partner must experience us in some way or other— but which we can never know. Consequently such images can also distort human relations and even destroy them, as they tend to become reified, i.e., come to be taken for realities in themselves and not just as substitutes that we need in order to bridge the gaps of the unknowable in interpersonal relations. Herein lies the ambivalence of negativity: the interaction might be a triumph of social creativity in which each is enriched by the other, or it might be a spiralling débâcle of increasing mutual hostility from which neither benefits.

In Beckett's dramas there is an almost total breakdown in communication. Perhaps this is because the characters spring from a consciousness of the extent to which communication can only take place by way of projected ideas, and from an awareness of the fact that these can only be revealed as projections if they are constantly made to disappear in the dialogue of the characters. Therefore these characters appear to be constantly on their guard to prevent a communicative interaction from happening. Built into their behavior is the knowledge that dialogue as a means of partners "tuning in" to each other can only produce projections; these may provide the bridge between people, but at the same time they undermine that bridge, because they are subjective ideas which can slide all too easily into psychopathological conditions. Beckett's art of negativity consists in the fact that this situation, which prevails throughout human society, is not simply conveyed to us as such; instead we are made to feel the impact of this situation for ourselves by the deliberate omission of the basic features of dialogue in the conversation of these characters.

This impression is all the more remarkable in that the titles of the plays always open up horizons of human endings—*Waiting for Godot, Endgame, Happy Days, All That Fall*—as a background against which we are to see the characters. We expect them to come to some kind of understanding in the face of such situations. However, as we are deprived of their projections, we begin to project ourselves, only to realize again and again that our conceptions fall short or lead nowhere—i.e., that they *are* projections. And yet in our everyday lives we are always guided by the conviction that our conceptions can grasp realities; we are not aware that they may represent mere fictions formulated because we find ourselves confronted by realities of whose existence we are conscious but which we can never actually know. In our human relationships we act as if we knew what our partner was experiencing from our presence. But in Beckett's dramas, we can only provide motives for the continual negation of the dialogue by realizing that our explanatory conceptions are in fact nothing more than fictions. This realization, however, does not help us in any way to solve the social or historical problems we are faced with. On the contrary, the fact that we have seen through our fictions brings forth a new and almost insoluble dilemma: we know that they are false, but at the same time we know that they are useful. The seem to provide us with knowledge wherever we are temporarily or permanently ignorant. Now if we know that, as Vaihinger puts it, they are "deliberately false," do we sacrifice their usefulness? Or do we hold onto them precisely because they are useful, and so close our eyes to what we know about them? . . .

IV

Beckett's novels turn upon two basic elements of human existence: the identity of the self, and the end. We have not discussed the "end" in any detail here, but suffice it to say that these are two topics one of which can only be experienced by means of self-evidence, while the other, a reality that effects us all, cannot be experienced (except, of course, in a way that is incommunicable). This "inexperienceability" and "unknowability" is profoundly disturbing for us. The extent of the disturbance can be gauged from the plethora of pictures and images produced by it, ranging from the apocalypse to the new political millennium.

Now as such pictures constitute our response to "inexperienceability" and "unknowability," they are by their very nature fictional. And yet their lack of reality does not disturb us, because they give us the illusion of access to those areas of life that are inaccessible. Beckett's novels certainly show us that fiction acts as a compensation for what our mental processes and physical actions cannot supply, but the process does not stop at revealing to us why we stand in need of fiction. Although we become aware of it, this insight does not make us act on what we know. Thus Beckett's first person narrators go on. Even though they cancel out the possible meanings of their utterances with every succeeding sentence, they still go on, so that they are clearly fascinated by the process of cancellation itself and cannot tear themselves away from it. If the unmasking of fiction as deliberate falsehood were the sole object of these novels, the time and energy spent on the unmasking would be out of all proportion. The same purpose would have been more convincingly served by a pointed satire. The fact that these narrators cannot stop is an indication of the degree to which they are caught up in the process of fiction building and destroying. This may seem like an end in itself, but it is in fact conditioned by a self-generating structure that *cannot* be halted. The characters know that all access to the world and to themselves is subject to the restrictions of their perspective. Perspective, however, is as Merleau-Ponty says, "the invention of a controlled world, which one possesses totally in a momentary synthesis." The characters are continually frowning upon such syntheses as pragmatically oriented fictions. But as they are inescapably caught up in the midst of ever-changing situations, this mode of comprehension is the only one possible, even though real comprehension is *not* possible. Their knowledge of this fact can only retain its validity through a ceaseless production and rejection of perspective-oriented meanings.

Such an unremitting process of rejection might be expected to bore both character and reader to death, but this is not the case because the rejections never remain static. A perspective can only come into being through a situation, and the fiction can only be useful in terms of a situation. The fiction takes on its form through its reference to concrete problems which it has to solve, and that is why there can be no such thing as an abstract fiction, for without this concrete function, it would really be nothing. And so Beckett's characters reject ever-changing fictional "gestalten," each of which they have themselves invented in order to solve ever-changing, concrete problems.

Every cancellation involves a negation, but negations take longer to work out than affirmations, and as this process again can only take place through the mode of perspectives, the characters find themselves with more and more to do. As we have already observed, the negations cancel out previous fictional "gestalten," but these are not removed from the scene altogether; they remain as cancelled "gestalten," and so inevitably give rise to conjectures as to the cause and motivation of the cancellation. Thus negation leads to an unending and ever-increasing activity on the part of the characters.

This activity is by no means welcome, for it constitutes the growing compulsion to get away from something to which they are in fact permanently fixed. The perpetual effort to retract

what has been stated has its counterpart in their physical existence as well: it is to be seen in the paradoxical cheerfulness that overcomes them in their increasing deformity and paralysis. For the body is the first and last hold that man has on the world; reliance on the body means recognition of an irrevocable factor to which we owe our presence in the world. And so as the body (like the language) progressively loses its function, Beckett's characters formulate new hopes. Stanley Cavell, with reference to *Endgame*, gives the following description of these hopes: " . . . salvation lies in the ending of endgames, the final renunciation of all final solutions. The greatest endgame is Eschatology, the idea that the last things of earth will have an order and a justification, a sense. That is what we hoped for, against hope, that was what salvation would look like. Now we are to know that salvation lies in reversing the story, in ending the story of the end, dismantling Eschatology, ending this world of order in order to reverse the curse of the world laid on it in its Judeo-Christian end. Only a life without hope, meaning, justification, waiting, solution—as we have been shaped for these things—is free from the curse of God."

A rejection of hope, meaning, justification, and a simultaneous repudiation of our being caught up in the ever-changing situations of life leaves us, in fact, like nowhere men in a nowhere land. And this is precisely the position of Beckett's characters, who have rejected all the alternatives and so leave themselves without alternatives, thus revealing the insurmountable finiteness of man to be an endless or in-finite going on. They know that all connections and relations are fictional in that these are the means by which we delude ourselves that we have brought order into chaos. The only escape from this naïveté is to reject fiction, but such a rejection can then be as meaningful (and so as suspect) as the meaning we gain from establishing connections, and so on. Any meaning, any interpretation automatically carries with it the seeds of its own invalidity, for it must exclude everything that runs counter to it. Beckett's characters know this, and so with every interpretation they present the weaknesses of that interpretation, thereby invalidating it. This process is extremely ambivalent: on the one hand it shows that the indeterminacy of human existence cannot be resolved by pragmatic definitions; on the other, it does away with the coagulating demand for validity posed by all forms of interpretation.

Fiction, then, is both a symptom and a product of man's finiteness. It permits those pragmatic extensions necessitated by his entanglement in an indeterminate and undefinable life. The rejection of fiction, however, prevents us from arbitrarily following our inclinations to reify what we should so like to regard as realities—those explanations that clarify the inexplicable. But the rejection of fiction does not lead to a Utopian enlightenment of man, for what would be the use of merely fixing ourselves in the knowledge of our unknowability? What Beckett's rejection of fiction reveals is the nature of man's inescapable limitations: it is an infinite retention of the self within this insurmountable finiteness. Herein lies the true significance of Beckett's negativity, for finiteness means being without alternatives, and this intolerable condition explodes into an endless productivity, of which both the origin and the product are fictions. The game with fictions can never stop, and it is this fact that endows man's finiteness with its infinitude. Such a situation can only be conveyed through the rejection of fiction if finiteness is to be seen as itself and not as the expression of something else. The perpetuity of the process springs from the fact that a denial must be preceded by a statement, but in turn the denial itself become a statement, and this bring forth the next denial, and so on *ad infinitum*. Thus the rejection of fiction becomes a structure of communication; it conveys the ceaseless activity of man as the irremovability of his finiteness.

If finiteness is to be experienced as itself, it must be without meaning, because otherwise it would be experienced in terms of a frame of reference greater than itself from which it would receive its meaning. Beckett's novels are an attempt to show up all references as pragmatic fictions, so that ultimately we may see finiteness as the basic condition of our productivity. But the novels themselves are fiction. And herein lies both the fascination and the oppressiveness of Beckett's work, for this fiction does not help us to forget our finiteness by virtue of orderly myths and explanations; it makes us *feel* what we are inescapably caught up in. We can no longer retreat to a safe distance through such explanations, because the experience communicated here continually brings us back to their pragmatic conditionality, which in turn invalidates them. Explanations are not possible—the most we can do is experience the unknowable, and herein lies the greatness of Beckett's achievement. He has fulfilled to the letter a saying attributed to him "that art, an arrangement of the inexplicable, never explains."

JOHN PILLING
"Writings on Literature and Art"
Samuel Beckett
1976, pp. 13–24

A testimony to the intimate and ineffable nature of an art that is perfectly intelligible and perfectly inexplicable.

(*Proust*)[1]

The most important neglected part of Beckett's total *oeuvre* to date is undoubtedly his criticism, which he himself repeatedly disparages and which remains uncollected. It is no part of my intention to examine it as criticism, though it is only fair to point out that the *Proust* book (1931) and the *Our Examgmination* essay (1929), especially the former, are both a good deal more than Beckett prophetically outlining the course he in fact followed for the next forty years. These essays, and his other scattered writings, are, in fact, an essential prerequisite to a full understanding of Beckett, and if at times they are difficult to understand—Beckett's range of reference is very large and his style bizarre—he is rarely less than stimulating and always exciting. Behind the erudition is an intense interest in the theory and practice of art in general and his own art in particular.

Tracing the development of Beckett's aesthetic thinking involves extracting from his scattered reviews those passages where Beckett is unmistakably speaking in his own voice. The task is complicated by the fact that Beckett's *literary* criticism is actually quite sparse, most of his critical corpus consisting of art criticism, 'best forgotten' in Beckett's opinion.[2] Furthermore, it is almost entirely called forth by the fact that the painter under discussion is one of Beckett's personal friends, who has either been unjustly neglected or unjustly criticized. This is the case with his article on Henri Hayden and his frequent essays on the van Velde brothers; it is also the case in his reviews of poems by Thomas MacGreevy and Denis Devlin. Beckett has remained constant in his interests: he wrote five separate pieces on the van Velde brothers between 1938 and 1961, and three on Jack B. Yeats between 1936 and 1954. Appropriately enough, the

three paintings hanging in his Paris flat are by Bram van Velde, Henri Hayden and Jack B. Yeats.

Joyce was also a personal friend, and it was to defend his 'Work in Progress' that he wrote *Dante . . . Bruno. Vico . . . Joyce* at the age of 23. Among the more interesting contents of this earliest performance are a warning: 'The danger is in the neatness of identifications. . . .Literary criticism is not book-keeping',[3] and a surprisingly violent attack on such book-keepers:

if you don't understand it, Ladies and Gentlemen, it is because you are too decadent to receive it. You are not satisfied unless form is so strictly divorced from content that you can comprehend the one almost without bothering to read the other. This instinctive skimming and absorption of the scant cream of sense is made possible by what I may call a continuous process of copious intellectual salivation. The form that is an independent and arbitrary phenomenon can fulfil no higher function than that of a stimulus for a tertiary or quaternary conditioned reflex of dribbling comprehension. . . .Here form *is* content, content *is* form.[4]

The conclusion is less impressive than what builds up to it; the crude wrath was an indulgence Beckett did not allow himself when he came to write *Proust*—though he described it to me as an 'angry book'—written largely in a café near the École Normale Supérieure where he taught between 1928 and 1930. This brief essay, commissioned by Richard Aldington, is easily the high-water-mark of his criticism, though he refuses to translate it into French. Although he gave over his university long vacation to reading the 'abominable sixteen-volume edition' twice, and still regards it as more about Proust than himself,[5] the aesthetic beliefs behind it strike one immediately as having great relevance to Beckett's own practice as a writer. From behind a pseudo-metaphysic of time—split into its component parts of habit and memory—comments on technique occupy the centre of the discussion, notably in the surreptitious introduction of his basic premise in the second paragraph: 'He is aware of the many concessions required of the literary artist by the shortcomings of the literary convention. As a writer he is not altogether at liberty to detach effect from cause.'[6] Only much later does he reiterate and expand this anti-logical stance, praising Proust for his 'fine Dostoyevskian contempt for the vulgarity of a plausible concatenation'[7] and for the way he has grasped the implications of such an alogical procedure: 'he understands the meaning of Baudelaire's definition of reality as "the adequate union of subject and object" and more clearly than ever the grotesque fallacy of a realistic art—"the miserable statement of line and surface", and the penny-a-line-vulgarity of a literature of notations.'[8] The book-keepers are again taken to task; Beckett never names names but he seems to be thinking of the naturalists, Wells, Bennett, Zola, *et al.* What is clear is that a complete way of looking at the world—and the concomitant way of reproducing it as art—is being outlined; the reality of the 'realists' is no more real than that of the 'impressionists', among whom he numbers Proust. He is careful to define precisely what he means by this term: 'By his impressionism I mean his non-logical statement of phenomena, in the order and exactitude of their perception, before they have been distorted into intelligibility in order to be forced into a chain of cause and effect.'[9] Once again logical form is attacked, and the method of this impressionism is revealed: 'The copiable he does not see. He searches for a relation, a common factor, substrata. Thus he is less interested in what is said than in the way in which it is said.'[10] Leaving on one side for a moment the concern with style, it is clear that this assertion of substrata, of an internal form, has been necessitated by the removal of external form, 'the chain of cause and effect'. Beckett harks back to Baudelaire again to explain the double form of the creative process, the perception of reality by the artistic mind and the reproduction of it in art by the workman:

> The work of art [is] neither created nor chosen, but discovered, uncovered, excavated, pre-existing within the artist, a law of his nature. The only reality is provided by the hieroglyphs traced by inspired perception [identification of subject and object] . . . for the artist, the only possible hierarchy in the world of objective phenomena is represented by a table of their respective coefficients of penetration, that is to say, in terms of the subject. (Another sneer at the realists.) The artist has acquired his text: the artisan translates it. 'The duty and task of a writer (not an artist, a writer) are those of a translator.'[11]

The double process described here in oblique terms is only made clearer when he returns to the implications for style, left on one side after his assertion that Proust is more interested in manner than matter. When he turns to discuss Proust's style, Beckett repeats the indivisibility of form and content that he had earlier found in Joyce:

> style is more a question of vision than of technique . . . he makes no attempt to dissociate form and content. The one is a concretion of the other, the revelation of a world. The Proustian world is expressed metaphorically by the artisan because it is apprehended metaphorically by the artist: the indirect and comparative expression of indirect and comparative perception.[12]

Proust's double 'impressionism' is here clearly stated and placed alongside the non-logical statement of 'substrata'. Although the 'substrata' are very much part of Proust's project, related to the excavation mentioned earlier, on two occasions Beckett seems to read rather more into *A la Recherche du temps perdu* than is actually there, giving us the tantalizing glimpse of a writer unknowingly prophesying his own course:

> The only possible spiritual development is in the sense of depth. The artistic tendency is not expansive, but a contraction. And art is the apotheosis of solitude. There is no communication because there are no vehicles of communication. . . .The only fertile research is excavatory, immersive, a contraction of the spirit, a descent. The artist is active, but negatively, shrinking from the nullity of extracircumferential phenomena, drawn into the core of the eddy.[13]

The disappearance of the artist by total immersion is not an original idea—Flaubert's *style indirecte libre* and Joyce's God behind the handiwork had already propounded this notion—but these two passages are nevertheless original in their suggestion of a sinking circular structure at the centre of which the artist may be found, solitary, uncommunicating. The 'core of the eddy' recalls 'the ideal core of the onion'; both are symbols of Beckett's idea that 'the only world that has value and significance' is 'the world of our own latent consciousness.'[14] This is to be Beckett's own territory; he will go on excavating and contracting, only to find the centre of the circle does not exist. And if the ideas on communication are not new—Eliot and Hulme, to name only two, had anticipated these—the horrifyingly logical pronouncement that 'There is no communication because there are no vehicles of communication'[15] is an astonishingly accurate forecast of the struggles he will later

wage, and indicate how near we are to the nihilism of the surrealists Beckett knew. Unconsciously perhaps—he admitted to me: 'Perhaps I overstated Proust's pessimism a little'— Beckett has placed his Proust just where Edmund Wilson (in the same year, 1931, in *Axel's Castle*) places him, on the main thoroughfare from symbolism to surrealism.

The implications of this final necessity—we move from premise to process to product to audience—are not elaborated in *Proust*. But in 1932 he wrote his first full-length novel 'Dream of Fair to Middling Women', and certain implications become very much clearer. It is cast in so loose a mould that there is ample space for Beckett to develop his opinions on every conceivable matter, but uppermost among his aims is a desire to formulate for himself (in the uncannily prophetic manner of the *Proust* monograph) an aesthetic in which he can put his faith. It contains a passionately mandarin account of the mechanics of creation:

> The night firmament is abstract density of music, symphony without end, illumination without end, yet emptier, more sparsely lit, than the most succinct constellations of genius. . . . The ecstatic mind achieving creation . . . rises to the shaft-heads of its statement, its recondite relations of emergal, from a labour and a weariness of deep castings that brook no schema. The mind suddenly entombed, then active in an anger and a rhapsody of energy . . . such is the ultimate mode and factor of the creative integrity, its proton, incommunicable; but there, insistent, invisible rat, fidgeting behind the astral incoherence of the art surface.[16]

Beckett's desire is that we should 'school ourselves . . . from the desire to bind for ever in imperishable relation the object to its representation'[17] and he is concerned enough to hypothesize an ideal response: 'The experience of my reader shall be between the phrases, in the silence, communicated by the intervals, not the terms.'[18] He has accepted that the absolute absence of absolutes commits one to a median position: 'for me the one real thing is to be found in the relation.'[19]

Even more importantly, it commits one to passivity in relation to one's material; only in this way can one avoid falsifying the relationship. The right kind of passivity is hedged round with a number of courses masquerading as ideal. There is the studied randomness, reminiscent of Surrealism: 'one can always organise a collision. . . . But how . . . could it be anything but the fruit of a congruence of enormous improbability?'[20] There is the consolation of the undifferentiated picaresque: but 'fake *blasé* . . . is a vulgarity that I cannot tolerate'.[21] Nothing merely auto-destructive will do: 'How could the will be abolished in its own tension? . . . The will and nill cannot suicide.'[22] Two solutions offer themselves: the first is the 'incoherent continuum' that he associates with Rimbaud (and, rather more eccentrically, with Beethoven),[23] the second is the 'perpendicular, *diamanté* styleless writing of Racine and Malherbe, writing of great clarity that is not ashamed to show the materials, 'the flints and pebbles . . . humble tags and commonplaces' of which it is composed.[24] As yet Beckett can see no way to bring these two together and collapse them into one another, but a considerable amount of dead wood has been cleared away. And the subject-matter, at least, is situated. The 'dark gulf', with the 'glare' of the will expunged, has been seen, and seen clearly. Now only the means to reproduce a place 'where there was no conflict of flight and flow . . . without axis or contour' are lacking.[25]

In the next six years he wrote several reviews, but none of

them reveals a significant development in his thinking. Much of his most profound thinking was obviously done in private, and in a letter to a German friend, Axel Kaun, in 1937, he revealed how difficult a solution would be: 'Grammar and style. They appear to me to have become . . . obsolete. . . . A mask.'[26] His area of concern is much more obviously technique than in the earlier published works and the very basis of literary expression, language, comes in for a startling attack. Beckett's aim is a 'literature of the Unword' where language is eroded 'until that which lurks behind it . . . begins to trickle through.'[27] What he later (in 1962) called a 'syntax of weakness'[28] is even outlined in detail in the letter: 'Is there any reason why that terribly arbitrary materiality of the word's surface should not be dissolved . . . so that for pages at a time we cannot perceive [the tonal surface] other than . . . as a vertiginous path of sounds connecting unfathomable abysses of silence.'[29] This desire for an erosion of language is a natural step from the assumption in *Proust* that there are no vehicles for communication, but in a contemporaneous essay on the poet Denis Devlin, Beckett develops one of the more important implications of this as far as the audience of art is concerned:

> Art has always been this—pure interrogation, rhetorical question less the rhetoric. . . . The time is not perhaps altogether too green for the vile suggestion that art has nothing to do with clarity, does not dabble in the clear, and does not make clear, any more than the light of day (or night) make the subsolar,— lunar and —stellar excrement.[30]

Here he states bluntly that the task of art is to contemplate and not to solve problems. The laboratory novel of the naturalists, the social novel of the 1930s, the *engagé* work of any period, all this, Beckett would claim, manifests a 'morbid dread of sphinxes, solution clapped on problem like a snuffer on a candle.'[31] There is a respectable ancestry for this theory that art does not explain, but only contemplates. Chekhov for example wrote: 'you confuse two conceptions: the solution of a question and the correct setting of a question. The latter alone is obligatory for the artist.'[32] Flaubert also said: 'The stupidity consists in wanting to arrive at conclusions.'[33] Less respectable, and rather more verbose, is the similar claim of the surrealistically orientated 1932 manifesto *Poetry is Vertical*, among whose signatures Beckett's name appears, and among whose ideas is the idea of loss of self developed in the *Proust* essay:

> The final disintegration of the 'I' in the creative act is made possible by the use of language which is a mantic instrument, and which does not hesitate to adopt a revolutionary attitude towards word and syntax, going even so far as to invent a hermetic language, if necessary.[34]

The 1938 distaste for clarity is clearly an extension of this but, for all Beckett's despair about the possibilities of words, he is not yet in anything like an extreme position with regard to expression.

It is in his first major article on the van Veldes, of 1945, that the insufficiency of the word becomes critical: 'each time that one wishes to make words do a true work of transference, each time one wishes to make them express something other than words, they align themselves in such a way as to cancel each other out.'[35] The crucially important idea of 'cancelling out' is new, even if the sneers at the realists' 'stories of objectivity and things seen'[36] are not. The idea of translation first propounded in connection with Proust's 'impressionism' is retained, but in a slightly modified, slightly vaguer form:

> There is no painting. There is only pictures. These, not being sausages, are neither good nor bad. All that one can say about them is that they translate, with more or less loss, absurd and mysterious compulsions towards the image, that they are more or less adequate oppositions of obscure internal tensions.[37]

The procedure is no longer so clear-cut: the compulsions are 'mysterious', the tension 'obscure', the results only approximate. The need to reflect ordinary phenomenal reality has effectively been removed altogether, and the practice of art has been made more difficult:

> To force the deep-seated invisibility of exterior things, to the point where invisibility itself becomes a thing . . . that is a labour of diabolic complexity, which requires a framework of suppleness and extreme lightness, a framework which insinuates more than it asserts.[38]

While this outline of internal form is an elaboration of elements that can be found in *Proust*, artistic composition is now seen as inherently much more problematic, in fact 'a labour of diabolic complexity.' Beckett briefly toys with the idea of impossibility which figures so importantly in the *Three Dialogues* four years later: 'For the painter, the thing is impossible. It is moreover, in representing this impossibility that modern painting has extracted its greatest effects.'[39] With this state of affairs now prevailing, it is hardly surprising to find criticism dismissed as 'hysterectomies with a trowel'[40] and to learn that 'the work considered as pure creation, whose function stops with its genesis, is consecrated to the void.'[41]

His second major article on the van Veldes, of 1948, is largely a repetition and consolidation of already stated views. Having decided in the first article, that 'the static thing in the void' is 'finally . . . the visible thing, the pure object',[42] he again praises these painters for a totally new approach to the old question of subject and object, reality and representation. They are the trail-blazers in what he calls 'the first assault on the object grasped independently of its qualities, in its indifference, its inertia, its latency',[43] and their particular brillance lies in 'glimpsing in the absence of relation and in the absence of object the new relation and the new object.'[44] Form, it must be stressed, is still retained, but it will be a form unlike anything ever seen before, and the content which it shapes, and which shapes it, will be equally new, since the process of perception and representation has been fundamentally altered. The artist's aim and the realization of that aim stand now in an essentially problematic relation to one another.

On the thesis that the problematic and impossible are the essence of modern art, no more subtle analysis than the *Three Dialogues with Georges Duthuit* exists. These highly stylized arguments were born from actual conversations Beckett had with the then editor of *transition*, and were re-worked and published on Duthuit's suggestion that Beckett make his views more generally known. As an introduction to the three painters dealth with they are perhaps only marginally enlightening, but as brief, brilliantly constructed vignettes (full of incidental Beckettian humour) clearly outlining Beckett's theories, they are of extreme interest and importance to the reader. In the first, on Tal Coat, Beckett replies to Duthuit's description of pure abstraction as the liberation all artists have longed for by questioning whether a real revolution has taken place on even the most basic level. For him, Matisse and Tal Coat have only 'enlarge[d] the statement of a compromise' by remaining 'on the plane of the feasible.'[45] Tal Coat is only doing what has always been done; 'thrusting towards a more adequate expression of natural experience.'[46] Duthuit common-sensibly asks, 'What other plane can there be for the maker?' Beckett's reply is that logically there can be none, but accepted ideas of logic are something he had been combating since 1931. This does not prevent the final development of that 1931 position being a massive paradox: 'The expression that there is nothing to express, nothing with which to express, nothing from which to express, no power to express, no desire to express, together with the obligation to express.'[47] But what other conclusion can there be to a situation in which there is no communication and no vehicles of communication? Most important of all perhaps is Beckett's emphasis, no doubt due to the experience of the trilogy, on the fact that the artist is no longer in control:[48] he is, by an ambiguous force of whose origin he is ignorant, somehow compelled to express despite the total obstacles to expression. Logic has been replaced by conditions of paradox and impossibility which, in the second dialogue, Beckett admits may only be a dream: 'my dream of an art unresentful of its insuperable indigence and too proud for the farce of giving and receiving.'[49] And yet to anyone who finds remaining 'on the plane of the feasible' a good thing, Beckett asks: 'What is the good of passing from one untenable position to another, of seeking justification always on the same plane?'[50] The dialogue on Bram van Velde is designed to show precisely how his friend has gone one step further than anyone else: 'Others have felt that art is not necessarily expression . . . van Velde is the first whose painting is bereft . . . of occasion in every shape and form . . . and the first whose hands have not been tied by the certitude that expression is an impossible act.'[51] The 'impossibility' is dramatically formulated in Beckett's parallel statements concerning van Velde's situation and what he does with it: 'The situation is that of him who is helpless, cannot act, in the event cannot paint, since he is obliged to paint. The act is of him who, helpless, unable to act, acts, in the event paints, since he is obliged to paint.'[52] When Duthuit squarely faces for the first time the 'obligation' Beckett spoke of in the first dialogue, his question, 'Why is he obliged to paint?' only receives the reply, 'I don't know.' His second query, 'Why is he helpless to paint?', prompts Beckett to a simpler statement of his idea in the first dialogue: 'Because there is nothing to paint and nothing to paint with.'[53] Thus, with the logic he affects to despise, Beckett demonstrates that if it is an art of the impossible, it must also necessarily be an art of failure. In Beckett's own words: 'To be an artist is to fail, as no other dare fail.'[54] This accounts for the 'impasse' he encountered to the writing of the trilogy,[55] the subject and object united by Baudelaire are now always threatening to cease to exist. He has moved from the position of language being problematic to that of the whole of existence being problematic. Everything becomes a paradox. As Beckett said to Roger Blin, 'I have nothing to say but I can only say to what extent I have nothing to say.'[56]

In these scattered essays Beckett is demonstrably more concerned with the genesis of a work of art and the conditions in which and out of which it comes to exist; only occasionally is he concerned with formal categories. And yet as well as a gradual erosion of language in the ever-contracting excavation inwards, which gives a general direction to Beckett's work as a whole, there is also the necessity from Beckett's point of view, for pattern in the separate works that make up the corpus, works with a form much like that he found in Bram van Velde's paintings: 'a framework of suppleness and extreme lightness, a framework which insinuates more than it asserts.'[57] The question of form dominates the 1961 interview with Tom F. Driver. Beckett first of all distinguished his work from Kafka's, in

one of his most brilliant and accurate self-analyses: 'Kafka's form is classic, it goes on like a steam-roller, almost serene. It seems to be threatened all the time—but the consternation is in the form. In my work there is consternation behind the form, not in the form.'[58] The new, 'un-classic' form is elaborated in detail, when Beckett talks, as he often does, of 'the mess':

> The confusion is not my invention. . . . It is all around us and our only chance now is to let it in. The only chance of renovation is to open our eyes and see the mess . . . there will be new form, and . . . this form will be of such a type that it admits the chaos and does not try to say that the chaos is really something else.[59]

In a 1962 conversation with Lawrence E. Harvey, Beckett made quite clear what it is that causes 'consternation'—it is the artist's self: 'Being is constantly putting form in danger. . . . I know of no form that does not violate the nature of Being in the most unbearable manner.'[60] But he went on to say, using almost the same terms as those of the Driver interview, 'If anything new and exciting is going on today, it is the attempt to let Being into art.'[61] The implicit equation, Being = Chaos, is, of course, felt everywhere in Beckett's fiction, and it is the equation of a man who can say, 'I'm not interested in any system . . . I can't see any trace of any system anywhere'[62] and who can nevertheless write prose fiction with as fine a sense of form as anyone now writing.

Since there has been a 'rupture of the lines of communication between subject and object'[63] ('Recent Irish Poetry', 1934), both the artist and the occasion have become unstable terms of relation. 'All that should concern us', therefore, 'is the acute and increasing anxiety of the relation itself.'[64] By 1945 Beckett was convinced that this was what would constitute the new relation, but in 1949, talking to Duthuit, he was unable to prove it to his own satisfaction. In the *Three Dialogues*, his most severe formulation, he reasserts the absence of occasion, and yet postulates a kind of imprisoned freedom for the painter Bram van Velde, less free than Masson's and more dearly bought, but more impressive in so far as it is operating in an entirely different set of conditions, beyond 'the plane of the feasible.'

Van Velde is 'free' because of his helplessness; he does not know what he wants to do, and he is incapable of achieving it anyway: desire and potency are dead. Yet he is only paradoxically free, for certain areas have inevitably been ruled out altogether in moving beyond the plane of the feasible. His freedom is so limited that it is quite remarkable that he paints at all. Van Velde's struggle is, consequently, of a much higher order than Masson's 'wriggling',[65] or the 'fidgets' of Rilke he had complained of fifteen years before.[66] Leonardo's *disfazione* (destruction) (which fascinated Beckett as early as the *Proust* volume)[67] masks a basic possessiveness inherent in him;[68] van Velde's *disfazione* is genuinely contingent, unwilled and uncontrollable. Van Velde is an artist who remains in the domain of the particular, with his eye on the object but who nevertheless achieves, by some magic that Beckett does not discuss, a form that can be generally appreciated. Beckett's analysis of his own work in 1961 is strikingly similar and, incidentally, a model of lucidity: 'The form and the chaos remain separate. The latter is not reduced to the former. That is why the form itself becomes a preoccupation, because it exists as a problem separate from the material it accommodates.'[69] A formulation like this helps to explain his difficulty in coming to terms with Surrealism. He knew many of the leading surrealists and praised it in 1934 as 'celebrat[ing] the cold comforts of apperception'[70] but by 1945 he found its 'dérèglement . . . de tous les sens' too rationally (and hence wilfully) based, describing it (via Lautréamont, whom the surrealists revered) as 'a sewing-machine on an operating table.'[71] The phrase nicely catches the mechanical qualities he finds in Surrealism at the same time as summoning up a fantastic surreal image. Beckett admits that such painting can produce masterpieces, but temperamentally he prefers work like Jack B. Yeats's who 'brings light, as only the great dare bring light, to the issueless predicament of existence',[72] or that of the van Veldes' that 'state[s] the space that intervenes'[73] as a result of the sundering of subject and object. In a text written to accompany the catalogue for an exhibition of Avigdor Arikha's work (1966) Beckett both describes and embodies his predicament. Through an imagery of battle ('siege', 'wound', 'truce') Beckett develops the idea that the 'without' is 'impregnable', 'unseeable', 'unmakeable.' Expressing oneself is still possible, but expression is severely reduced in scope. The painter's job, like the writer's, is to record the 'marks of what it is to be and be in face of', the latter part of which phrase emphasizes once again that a symbiosis is unavoidable, and that the object cannot simply be ignored.[74] We have travelled from Baudelaire, whose aesthetic formed the basis of the *Proust* volume, and who turned the book of nature into a 'dictionnaire hiéroglyphique'[75] through Joyce, whose 'Work in Progress' had the 'savage economy of hieroglyphics';[76] to Bram van Velde, who intuits hieroglyphs without the wherewithal or the desire to translate them into more accepted language-codes. Van Velde—and, more importantly, Beckett—achieves a generalized particularity which becomes an ebony tower rather than the more familiar ivory variety.

Despite this last sleight-of-hand—this recommendation of the 'tour de'ébène'[77]—it is sometimes difficult not to feel that Beckett's criticism reveals an acutely enervated aestheticism peering from behind a somewhat quixotic rationalism. Judged by his own high standards of excellence, he is clearly no Valéry. But there is a very genuine honesty (bred of helplessness) in the confusions and evasions, and a manifest intelligence (residue of the failure of the Faustian intellect) at work in these writings. Furthermore, by post-dating the practice, the theory helps to make it more accessible, without having to enter the work (as Joyce's did) to do so. He rejects unequivocally symbolism, satire, Prometheanism, misanthropy, sensationalism and pot-boiling, and rests his case on a qualified humanism. This humanism has been variously described as 'defensive', 'quietist' and 'graveyard' and should at all times be distinguished from the tragic variety exemplified by Camus.[78] It is, nevertheless, determinedly humanistic because Beckett's aim is a literature that is 'the passive receptacle for a self entirely independent of literary inventiveness.'[79] He realizes it is impossible of attainment. 'You realise the absurdity of what you advance?' says Duthuit. To which Beckett replies, 'I hope I do.'[80]

Notes

1. *Proust*, p. 92. The *Proust* volume was among the first serious considerations of Proust's work in England. Beckett describes Mozart in the same terms at the end of the unpublished lecture 'Le Concentrisme' (R.U.L.).
2. John Fletcher, *Samuel Beckett's Art*, London, 1967, p. 20.
3. *Our Exag.*, pp. 3–4. Cp. 'You simplify and dramatize the whole thing with your literary mathematics' ('Dream', p. 91).
4. Ibid., p. 13.
5. That he genuinely wished to make Proust clearer is shown by his distaste for those critics who prized above all Proust's incomprehensibility ('Proust in Pieces', *Spectator*, no. 5530, 23 June 1934, pp. 975–6).
6. *Proust*, p. 11.

7. Ibid., p. 81. Cp. Jacques Rivière, 'Dostoevsky and the Creation of Character', *The Ideal Reader*, London, 1962, pp. 218–22; and Marcel Proust, *By Way of Sainte-Beuve*, London, 1958, p. 287.
8. *Proust*, p. 76. The Baudelaire quotation may be found in 'Philosophic Art', *Baudelaire as a Literary Critic*, ed. L. and F. Hyslop, Pennsylvania, 1964, p. 187. The Proust quotation may be found in *Time Regained*, trans. Stephen Hudson, p. 239.
9. *Proust*, p. 86.
10. Ibid., p. 83.
11. Ibid., p. 84. Cp. Baudelaire on the artist as translator in his 1861 essay on Victor Hugo. Both Rivière (*The Ideal Reader*, p. 120) and E. R. Curtius (*Marcel Proust*, tr. A. Pierhal, Paris, 1928, p. 24) stress this aspect. Cp. Breton's antagonism to the 'style of pure information' in the 1924 Surrealist Manifesto.
12. *Proust*, pp. 87–8. See *Time Regained*, p. 247, and Proust's letter to Antoine Bibesco in *Letters*, tr. Mina Curtis, London, 1950, pp. 189–90. 'Dream', p. 42, makes this clearer: 'You couldn't experience a margarita in d'Annunzio because he denies you the pebbles and flint that reveal it. The uniform, horizontal writing, flowing without accidence, of the man with a style, never gives you the margarita.'
13. *Proust*, pp. 64, 65–6.
14. Ibid., p. 13.
15. Ibid., p. 64.
16. 'Dream', pp. 14–15.
17. Ibid., p. 142.
18. Ibid., p. 123.
19. Ibid., p. 24.
20. Ibid., p. 104.
21. Ibid., p. 154.
22. Ibid., p. 109.
23. Ibid., p. 91.
24. Ibid., p. 42.
25. Ibid., p. 107–8.
26. Harvey, p. 434.
27. Ibid., pp. 433–4.
28. Ibid., p. 435. Beckett told Herbert Blau that French had 'the right weakening effect' (M. Esslin, *The Theatre of the Absurd*, Harmondsworth, 1968, p. 29).
29. Ibid., p. 434 and footnote. Cp. Balzac, *The Magic Skin*, Caxton edition, London, n.d., p. 90.
30. 'Denis Devlin', *transition*, no. 27, April–May 1938, pp. 289, 293 (hereafter cited as 'Denis Devlin').
31. Ibid., p. 290.
32. Letter of 27 October 1888 to A. S. Souvorin, quoted by Miriam Allott, *Novelists on the Novel*, London, 1959, p. 99.
33. Quoted in *The Novelist as Philosopher*, ed. J. Cruickshank, London, 1962, p. 98.
34. *transition*, no. 21, p. 148.
35. 'Le Monde', etc., p. 352 (my translation).
36. Ibid., p. 352.
37. Ibid., p. 350–1.
38. Ibid., p. 354.
39. Ibid., p. 354.
40. Ibid., p. 349.
41. Ibid., p. 349.
42. Ibid., p. 352. Cp. Joyce's Aquinas-based aesthetic in *Stephen Hero* and *Portrait* (criticized by H.-J. Schulz, *This Hell of Stories*, The Hague, 1973, p. 82ff) and 'Dream', p. 31: 'There is only category, that furnished by your stases.'
43. 'Peintres', etc., p. 4.
44. Ibid., p. 7. Cp. 'Dream', p. 112 (quoted earlier).
45. *Proust*, pp. 102–3.
46. Ibid., p. 101.
47. Ibid., p. 103.
48. Cp. Beckett's remark to Driver: 'The kind of work I do is one in which I'm not master of my material.' The interview with Driver is in *Columbia University Forum*, IV, Summer 1961, pp. 21–5.
49. *Proust*, p. 112.
50. Ibid., p. 110.
51. Ibid., p. 121.
52. Ibid., p. 119.

53. Ibid., p. 120.
54. Ibid., p. 125. In the view of Hegel (*Aesthetics*, tr. F. P. B. Osmanton, London, 1920, vol. 2, pp. 53–4) Romanticism was necessarily an art of failure.
55. See interview with Shenker (*New York Times*, 6 May 1956, section 2, pp. x, 1, 3).
56. P. Mélèse, *Beckett*, Paris, 1969, p. 10 (my translation).
57. 'Le Monde', etc., p. 354.
58. See interview with Driver. Cp. 'Dream', p. 159: 'We were once upon a time inclined to fancy ourself as the Cézanne, shall we say, of the printed page, very strong on architecture.'
59. See interview with Driver.
60. Harvey, p. 435.
61. Ibid., p. 435.
62. See interview with Shenker.
63. 'Recent Irish Poetry', *Lace Curtain*, no. 4, Summer 1971, p. 58.
64. Ibid., p. 58.
65. *Proust*, p. 110.
66. *Criterion*, vol. 13, July 1934, p. 706.
67. *Proust*, p. 31.
68. Ibid., p. 112. Cp. Leonardo da Vinci, *Treatise on Painting*, London, 1877, p. 142.
69. See interview with Driver.
70. 'Recent Irish Poetry', p. 58.
71. 'Le Monde', etc., p. 353. Lautréamont wrote: 'He is beautiful, like the chance meeting of a sewing-machine and an umbrella on an operating table' (*Les Chants de Maldoror*, canto 6, section 1).
72. 'MacGreevy on Yeats', *Irish Times*, 4 August 1945, p. 2 (hereafter cited as 'MacGreevy on Yeats').
73. 'Recent Irish Poetry', p. 58.
74. Beckett liked cubist painting, perhaps because 'the emphasis . . . is not placed on the problem of *space* itself but on the problem of the subjective dynamism existing between objects in space and the observer' (Christopher Gray, *Cubist Aesthetic Theories*, Baltimore, 1953, p. 85). Cp. Beckett on Proust's autosymbolism (*Proust*, p. 80).
75. *Baudelaire as a Literary Critic*, ed. E. and F. L. Hyslop, p. 88.
76. *Our Exag*, p. 15.
77. 'Denis Devlin', p. 289.
78. Beckett indirectly criticizes Camus in *T.N.*, p. 133.
79. Leo Bersani, *Balzac to Beckett: Centre and Circumference in French Literature*, Oxford, 1970, p. 323. Cp. 'Dream', p. 10: 'The only perspective worth stating is the site of the unknotting that could be, landscape of a dream of integration.'
80. *Proust*, pp. 120–1.

IHAB HASSAN
From "Beckett: Imagination Ending"
The Dismemberment of Orpheus
1982, pp. 210–22

I

Samuel Beckett pursues the vanishing form till it nearly vanishes. He is an apocalyptic by reduction, possessed by the idea that the universe must evacuate itself; a visionary comedian who knows that human consciousness cracks into a bitter joke; and a supreme example of the postmodern artist, turning the malice of language against itself. "My work," he says, "is a matter of fundamental sounds made as fully as possible, and I accept responsibility for nothing else!"[1] The sounds and the silences dramatize, in Cartesian parody, the very laws of thought; in bits and pieces, they summon universal man, *quidam*, "somebody; one unknown."

Beckett inherits the verbal deviltry of Ireland and shares the black humor of Swift. He learns from Joyce, learns enough to trust his own voice. He begins by parodying the inventories of *Ulysses* and the puns of *Finnegans Wake* and ends by devising a system of combinations and permutations more pure than Joyce ever invents. It is as Kenner observes: art becomes a "closed field" and the total verbal competence of Joyce yields to the thorough "incompetence" of Beckett.[2] The Dadaists by comparison seem lax. More than Hemingway, Kafka, or Genet, Beckett gives himself to Pythagorean stringency and truth. He reaches beyond Existentialism, beyond Aliterature, into a silence that sings. . .

III

Certain motifs emerge from Beckett's earliest efforts and return to give his major work shape. In his essay on *Finnegans Wake*, *Dante . . . Bruno. Vico . . . Joyce*, he admonishes the readers of Joyce: "This writing that you find so obscure is a quintessential extraction of language and painting and gesture, with all the inevitable clarity of the old inarticulation. Here is the savage economy of hieroglyphics."[3] It is as if Beckett speaks of himself. Even in the matter of hieroglyphs, both Joyce and Beckett believe that things with common numerical characteristics—the four Gospels, the four seasons, etc.—tend toward significant relations.

Joyce may be Beckett's transubstantial father and Kafka closer to his secret self, but it is Proust who helps to define his artistic conscience. Like Proust, Beckett confronts in every work that "double-headed monster of damnation and salvation," Time, with its twin attributes of Habit and Memory.[4] "The individual is the seat of a constant process of decantation," Beckett notes in his *Proust*, "decantation from the vessel containing the fluid of future time, sluggish, pale, and monochrome, to the vessel containing fluid of past time, agitated and multicolored by the phenomena of its hours."[5] The art of time, of entropy, is really a comic routine. If music is the formal analogy to Proust's art, vaudeville is the analogy to Beckett's. With uncanny foresight, Beckett defines vaudeville as "the comedy of an exhaustive enumeration."[6] We are prepared for the bitter hilarity of numbers.

Beckett continues his dour reflections on Time in *Whoroscope* which puns obscenely on celestial knowledge and degrades the movement of the spheres. If life is abortive—"How rich she smells,/this abortion of a fledgling!"—the history of the Western mind that Descartes began and Beckett must continue is no less so.[7] Decartes's voice prays: "grant me my second / starless inscrutable hour."[8] This is also Beckett's prayer. Crowded with scientific details and sexual allusions, the poem presents an embryology of Time. But it is also, in its puns and biographical references, an ironic tribute to Descartes, Seigneur du Perron, the one figure in intellectual history whom Beckett can neither accept nor ignore.

In the poems of *Echo's Bones* and the stories of *More Pricks than Kicks*, Beckett tests out his comic devices: garbled quotation, twisted cliché, jargon, pun, incongruity, etc. Belacqua appears as the hero of a vanishing consciousness, and his inactions evoke the mysterious banality of Beckett's world. Bicycles and clocks, madness and suicide, objects and abstractions, mingle in satiric or macaronic patterns of verbal dexterity. On the surface, Beckett seems to question the social and moral reality of middle-class Dublin. Beneath, he struggles toward a metaphysical question: man's sordid awareness, alienation, in the universe.

This leads us to the background of his thought. The patterns wherein his learning and imagination mesh, his metaphors of the human condition, derive from poets and philosophers of the past. Beckett adapts these patterns and metaphors to the postmodern world with consummate irony; his work seems a parodic reflection on Western history.

Once again, we return to Descartes. For Beckett, the universe of reason has withered, and the great philosopher who predicted the unity of all sciences in a rational method has become a glorious scarecrow in the fields of thought. Cartesian certainties, which depend on the uniformity of the mental process and of mathematical analysis, now yield to universal doubts. And as metaphysics once yielded to the scientific method, so the latter must give way, Beckett believes, to epistemological mysteries. The starting point of meditation is no longer the Cartesian "Je pense, donc je suis," but rather, "Je me doute"; and the point is quickly reached where the facts of inquiry dissolve into the reality of the inquirer, casting further doubt on both. Moreover, by making the reflexive act of consciousness the seat of reality, Descartes ushered dualism into Western thought while admitting solipsism by the back door. For the French thinker saw clearly the essence of the material world as extension and motion in space; the problem remained for him to explain how, in a dualistic universe, mind and matter could ever touch. His ruse was to assume that the pineal gland, the *conarium* on which Beckett puns obscenely, brought together the invisible world of the mind and the divisible world of matter. But Descartes's hapless disciple, Geulincx—Beckett refers to him in *Murphy* and again in *The Unnamable*—denied his master's ruse. Like the later Occasionalist Malebranche, Geulincx did not agree that mind and matter need be united; both were separate and real, though only mind could be known directly to man. Beckett adopts this absurd dualism with a vengeance. In his recurrent figures of men riding on bicycles, "Cartesian Centaurs," he gives us an image of bodies whirring in space like machines and of an intelligence superimposed on it grotesquely; the mind discards the body as a man discards his bicycle.[9]

Matter, then, in Beckett's world is alien, obdurate, and even threatening; nothing functions well; some metaphysical rust clogs all mechanism. His characters seek peace in entropy, in silence. Beckett writes: "To restore silence is the role of objects."[10] Meantime, however, mind is set free from decaying matter; it turns endlessly upon itself, droning words, dribbling numbers.

The fate of consciousness in a closed system may be glimpsed in the works of Ludwig Wittgenstein whose *Tractatus Logico-Philosophicus* and *Philosophical Investigations* also envisage the possibilities of solipsism in word and number. Wittgenstein finally prefers to conceive of language as a game, a concept that Beckett's work puts to constant practice. Wittgenstein says:

> Systems of communication . . . we shall call "language games." They are more or less akin to what in ordinary language we call games. Children are taught their native language by means of such games. . . .We are not, however, regarding the language games which we describe as incomplete parts of language, but as languages complete in themselves, as complete systems of human communication. To keep this point of view in mind, it very often is useful to imagine such a simple language to be the entire system of communication of a tribe in a primitive state of society. Think of primitive arithmetics of such tribes.[11]

Much of Beckett's prose seems like the arithmetic of a primitive tribe, struggling to convey in numbers its dim sense of reality. His anonymous heroes solemnly perform combinations and permutations; they repeat their words and vary their gestures *ad nauseam*; they add and tabulate all the trivia of existence. They are what happens to the mind when the mind has nothing to contemplate but its own symmetry, when language, caught in the paradox of its own self-denial, aspires to ratio. What began as Cartesian science ends as fiction, and fiction, Geulincx once argued, is intelligence demonstrating its sole freedom. Thus the tabulators of Beckett are also narrators. Their story, like a surd, tends toward silent infinity.

The heroes of Beckett, we see, are metaphysical clowns, *jongleurs* of solipsism. They are also morbid quietists, cripples, impotents. They suffer from radical acedia. Thus Dante's Belacqua, reclining in Purgatory, becomes the archetype of all Beckett's heroes who delay their salvation through spiritual indifference. Beckett, of course, knows his Dante exhaustively, identifying him with the coherence of faith, as he identifies Descartes with the coherence of reason. The shadow of Belacqua, tinged by more self-parody than we suspect, falls on all the heroes of Beckett—from Belacqua Shua to Murphy strapped in his rocking chair to Pim crawling through the mud—in testimony to the vanity of all human effort.

Yet human effort, in Beckett's view, appears not only vain; it is also blighted from the start. His pessimism frequently sends him to Calvin, Augustine, and Paul, to the Gospels and the Eucharist, in search of images of man's ambiguous fate. He echoes the famous statement of Augustine, "Do not despair: one of the thieves was saved; do not presume: one of the thieves was damned," in various works. The image of the Crucifixion, agony in geometric form, the two thieves proposing the final alternatives of salvation and damnation, fascinates Beckett. At times, he seems to accept Descartes's postulate of a malevolent deity; at all times, he identifies man's sin as the sin of birth. "Beckett's characters," Hoffman says, "suspecting or knowing themselves as defective creatures, are deeply suspicious of their creator."[12] Beckett's own suspicion is deeper. If God is dead, then nothing is permitted, and man is superfluous.

The intellectual tradition that Beckett finds most congenial appears melancholy indeed, though there are other writers, like Bruno or Vico, who seem to have aroused his interest. John Fletcher also traces the ideas of the Pre-Socratics in Beckett's early fiction: Pythagoras and Empedocles, Heraclitus, "the lachrymose philosopher," and Democritus, "the laughing philosopher," who appear in *More Pricks than Kicks* and *Murphy*.[13] To Democritus, called the Abderite, Beckett makes a number of allusions of which the most Beckettian occurs in *Malone Dies*: "Nothing is more real than nothing," quotes Malone.[14] This intuition, a source of cheerfulness to Democritus, becomes a source of epistemological despair to Beckett who feels closer, no doubt, to the ideal of the Nonent propounded by a Sicilian sophist, Gorgias of Lentini. The Nonent, in the terse paraphrase of A. J. Leventhal, assumes:

1. Nothing is.
2. If anything is, it cannot be known.
3. If anything is, and can be known, it cannot be expressed in speech.[15]

In Beckett's world, then, epistemology reveals only ambiguity. It is as if persons, objects, and events were observed hazily from a distance, and the act of observation itself, as in his *Film* (1967), invalidated both subject and object. The senses are seldom offered data sufficient for judgment, and when they are, the time lag between perception and expression condemns the latter to eternal obsolescence. The senses thus end by refusing to distinguish between illusion and reality, and consciousness, far from directing action or controlling matter, ends by displaying its infinite mutations. The principle of causality seldom operates. As a result, no logical relation obtains between particulars (objects) and universals (concepts). When definitions are attempted, they are usually made in the negative, by a process of elimination, a protocol of reduction, as if to define the world were to empty it. In the game that the mind plays with itself, language, of course, is the original flaw. As Molloy says:

> There could be no things but nameless things, no names but thingless names . . . the world dies too, foully named. All I know is what the words know, and the dead things, and that makes a handsome little sum, with a beginning, a middle, and an end as in the well built phrase and the long sonata of the dead.[16]

If habits, of which language is the deadliest, deaden, only the "suffering of being" awakens all the faculties of man. Against the silence of the dead, there is the silence of the agonized living. The latter may be the highest value in Beckett's world, this side of apocalypse. Thus from *The Unnamable*, who is Molloy eons later:

> . . . it's to go silent that you need courage, for you'll be punished, for having gone silent, and yet you can't do otherwise than go silent, than be punished for having gone silent.[17]

On this foundation, the impossible art of Beckett rests.

Comedy restores that art to the realm of possibility. The comedy is clownish, cruel, absurd. It recalls some ideas of Henri Bergson on laughter. Bergson identifies the cause for laughter as everything rigid, mechanical, or eccentric, everything that threatens the elasticity that social life requires. His main insight which applies closely to Beckett's work, is that automatism and repetition are of the essence of comedy. "We laugh," Bergson says, "every time a person gives us the impression of being a thing."[18] Thus the fundamental processes of comedy are "Repetition," "Inversion," and "Reciprocal Interference of Series." Comedy is after all akin to number; its variations are a product of lucidity become automatic. Absurd comedy, however, introduces another element: it combines number and dream, drawing on images and obsessions that only dreams contain. This is the comedy of Beckett par excellence, and its laughter is never benevolent. Though laughter may finally serve to redress social evils, its immediate impulse is darker. In the laugher, Bergson discerns "a degree of egoism and, behind this latter, something less spontaneous and more bitter, the beginnings of a curious pessimism which becomes the more pronounced as the laugher more closely analyses his laughter."[19]

Vaudevillian and grotesque, Beckett's humor is essentially metaphysical; it assumes the absurdity of the universe and eludes conventional tragedy or comedy by confronting the automatism of number with the cruelty of nightmare. His satire is neither social nor even moral. It is the satire of a man who tries to bear his own company. Swift, Kafka, and Alfred Jarry, more than Rabelais or Joyce, define the tradition of the sadistic jest that Beckett exploits. The jest, as comedy often requires, calls attention to the carnal nature of man; and it transposes moral into physical concerns. Because the humor is reductive and sadistic, it tends to focus on scatological rather than erotic functions. Waste is the sole process of nature in a wasting universe from which Eros must be banished. Copulation, therefore, thrives but feebly, usually among cripples or octogenarians, as further proof of the mind's disgust with life. Beckett's three "modes of ululation," described in *Watt*, are the bitter laugh in the face of evil, the hollow laugh in the face of falsehood, and the mirthless laugh in the face of human wretchedness. All three laughs do not restore man to nature or society; they howl his alienation.

Beckett's concept of contractive comedy is implicit in his general view of art. In his essay on the Dutch painter, Bram Van Velde, Beckett is explicit. To him, art is a fidelity to failure, and also "a kind of Pythagorean terror, as though the irrationality of pi were an offense against the deity, not to mention his creature."[20] Art, then, is failure and frozen outrage. "I know," he says, "that all that is required now . . . is to make . . . this fidelity to failure, a new occasion, a new term of relation, and of the act which, unable to act, obliged to act, he [the artist] makes an expressive act, even if only of itself, of its impossibility, of its obligation."[21] Obligation, we see, wrestles with impossibility, and the result is always pyrrhic. The artist, like so many heroes of Beckett, can neither continue nor desist.

Since Beckett believes that the world "is expressed metaphorically by the artisan because it is apprehended metaphorically by the artist . . . ," it is not surprising to discover that his contractive tendency affects all aspects of his technique.[22] But contraction and even negation sustain a fierce life in Beckett's art, and silence implies an apocalyptic project for the transformation of consciousness. Though he comes closer than any other writer to piercing the heart of the Muses, there is far less love in him for "easeful death" than there is in Keats, Kafka, Genet, or Céline. "There are many ways in which the thing I am trying in vain to say may be tried in vain to be said," he confesses.[23] Beckett does not put aside the obligations of his vanishing forms.

Notes

1. Samuel Beckett, "Letters on *Endgame*," *Village Voice*, March 19, 1958.
2. Hugh Kenner, *Flaubert, Joyce, and Beckett: The Stoic Comedians* (Boston: Beacon Press, 1962), pp. 72–78.
3. *Our Exagmination round His Factification for Incamination of Work in Progress* (New York: Grove Press, 1962), p. 15.
4. Samuel Beckett, *Proust* (New York: Grove Press, 1931), pp. 1, 7.
5. Ibid., pp. 4f.
6. Ibid., p. 20.
7. Samuel Beckett, "Whoroscope," in *Poems in English* (New York: Grove Press, 1963), p. 4.
8. Ibid., p. 4.
9. This term is coined and subtly defined by Kenner, *Samuel Beckett*, pp. 119f.
10. Samuel Beckett, *Molloy* (New York: Grove Press, 1955), p. 16.
11. Ludwig Wittgenstein, *The Blue and Brown Books* (Oxford: Basil Blackwell and Mott, 1958), p. 81.
12. Frederick J. Hoffman, *Samuel Beckett* (Carbondale, Illinois: Southern Illinois University Press, 1962), p. 63.
13. John Fletcher, "Samuel Beckett and the Philosophers," *Comparative Literature*, vol. 17 (Winter 1965), pp. 43f.
14. Samuel Beckett, *Malone Dies* (New York: Grove Press, 1956), p. 16.
15. A. J. Leventhal, "The Beckett Hero," *Critique*, vol. 7 (Winter 1964–65), p. 29.
16. *Molloy*, p. 41.
17. Samuel Beckett, *The Unnamable* (New York: Grove Press, 1958), p. 151.
18. Henri Bergson, "Laughter," in *Comedy*, ed. Wylie Sypher (Garden City, New York: Doubleday, 1956), p. 97.
19. Ibid., p. 189.
20. Samuel Beckett, Georges Duthuit, and Jacques Putnam, *Bram Van Velde* (New York: Grove Press, 1958), p. 10.
21. Ibid., p. 13.
22. *Proust*, p. 67.
23. Samuel Beckett, "Three Dialogues," *transition* (1949), p. 102.

MAX BEERBOHM

1872–1956

Henry Maximilian Beerbohm was born in London on August 24, 1872. While still at Merton College, Oxford, he began contributing caricatures and essays to London periodicals. In 1895 he left Oxford to act as secretary to his half-brother, actor-manager Herbert Beerbohm Tree, but soon settled in London as a professional wit. Elegant and good-natured, Beerbohm at once achieved extraordinary popularity. He was a member of the literary circle of Oscar Wilde and Aubrey Beardsley, but it often seemed that "Max" knew everyone and drew everyone, including Henry James, Algernon Swinburne, G. K. Chesterton, and legions of London socialites. Later friends included Gordon Craig, Ezra Pound, and Dante Gabriel Rossetti.

Beerbohm impudently named his first book *The Works of Max Beerbohm*. In 1898, he replaced George Bernard Shaw as drama critic for the *Saturday Review*. Shaw, who dubbed Beerbohm "the incomparable Max," recommended him for the post after reading a Beerbohm essay—attacking Shaw. Beerbohm left the magazine and London for Rapallo, Italy, in 1910 after marrying actress Florence Kahn. In Rapallo he wrote his three most enduring works: the outrageous satire *Zuleika Dobson* in 1911, the well–executed parodies of *A Christmas Garland* in 1912, and the short stories of *Seven Men* in 1919. "My gifts are small," Beerbohm said. "I've used them very well and discreetly, never straining them."

Beerbohm returned to England for World War I, and again for World War II. During the latter, he made for the BBC what John Updike called "those famous radio broadcasts whose impeccably enunciated nostalgia borrows gallantly from the context of blitzed London." Beerbohm was knighted in 1939, and granted honorary doctorates by Oxford and Edinburgh in the 1940s. His wife died in 1951; Beerbohm married again only weeks before he died on May 20, 1956.

Personal

Because of his early precocity and his open old-fashioned scorn of the new royal circle, of the new, popular writers of the Edwardian era, of Arnold Bennett and of H. G. Wells, because of his antiquated elegance in dress, Max Beerbohm came to be regarded as a man of the 1890s. In fact his full flowering was in the 1920s. He wrote little then, but it is the decade of his best collections of essays, of his most brilliant drawings, exhibited at the Leicester Galleries, of the publication of *A Survey* (1921), *Rossetti and His Circle* (1922), *Things New and Old* (1923), *Observations* (1925).

He lived abroad, and from being a ubiquitous man about town he had become a secluded and exclusive celebrity. On his rare visits to London everyone strove to meet him. I was not one of the young men to whom invitation cards came in great profusion—I was the author of one light novel and a heavy biography—but on one of these later visits I managed to find myself in his company.

To say that I was invited to dine with him by my solicitor gives a wrong impression. I had no solicitor in those happy days. There were no japanned deed cases painted with my name in E. S. P. Haynes's office. He had acted for me, it is true, in a single disagreeable piece of legal business, but he gave me far more in oysters and hock during its transaction than he charged me in fees. He was the most remarkable of solicitors, a man who actually enjoyed the company of literary men of all ages and reputations. A second Watts-Dunton? the reader will ask. Not a second Watts-Dunton. Haynes did not seek to restrain the pleasures of his clients; however extravagant, he applauded and promoted them.

I kept no diary then. I think it must have been in the spring of 1929 that I received the invitation to dine *en famille* in St. John's Wood to meet Max Beerbohm. I came with joy, for Max Beerbohm was an idol of my adolescence to whom

every year had deepened my devotion. It was my first visit to Mrs. Haynes. Hitherto my meetings with Haynes had been in a subterranean bar in Chancery Lane. Now I saw him at home, in a home that might have come straight from the pages of du Maurier's *Punch*; Mr. Vandyke Brown, A. R. A. at home.

As soon as I entered the drawing room I realized why I had been asked: I was by far the youngest man present and I was there to provide a lively partner for the youngest Miss Haynes. Everyone else was illustrious, each an idol of mine. It was my first sight of Hilaire Belloc and of Maurice Baring. Either of these on any other night would have been a prodigious treat, but my eyes and ears were for Max. He was very polite and quiet. I stood far off with the youngest Miss Haynes, who had been dandled on the knees of these resplendent beings and regarded them as jolly old buffers. Preposterous to record, she seemed genuinely more interested in me and my friends than in them.

In the dining room the separation persisted. Max sat far away, and between us hung the barrier of elderly intimacy and allusion. How well everyone talked and how loudly! All save Max. How they laughed and chaffed! What robust vocabularies, what rare knowledge, what exuberant fancies vollied and thundered between me and the object of my devotion! How spendidly lacking they were in any sort of side! What capital good fellows they were! And how Max enjoyed them, and they him! Every now and then with perfect timing, but quite inaudibly to us at the end of the table, the gentle exquisite inserted his contribution. How joyously Belloc and Baring acclaimed him! Admirable wine circulated. I spoke freely to Miss Haynes about Robert Byron and Harold Acton. Then the ladies left us, and chairs were about to be drawn up when there irrupted two or three youngish men who (with their women folk, now in the drawing room) had been "asked in later." Chairs drew apart again. More glasses were brought. The decanter went from hand to hand. It was a memorable evening, but through it all thrilled the faint Panpipe of disappointment. When at length I left I had nothing to remember of Max Beerbohm; a "Good evening" and a "Good night." I returned to the club where I lived, slightly drunk but slightly crestfallen.

It was there that I was vouchsafed a second chance. I found that club a convenient place to sleep, but already my then fast, smart preferences were alienating me from it. It was the genial resort of respectable men of letters, where the spirit of Edmund Gosse still reigned in the morning room and the younger members seemed mostly to be employed by the B. B. C. The truth must be told, I felt rather superior to the place. And there in the hall next day at one o'clock, watch in hand, a host evidently expecting a guest, stood Max Beerbohm. He did not wear the tall hat and tubular coat of the Nicholson portrait; he was military rather than aesthetic in his dandyism. But he was smart as paint.

I sidled forward wondering whether to accost him or not. He observed my movement, smiled and held out his hand. I remarked that the previous evening had been very pleasant. He agreed and added that he greatly looked forward to seeing the portrait on which he understood I was at work. He had heard Tonks speak of it with unusual warmth. In that awful moment his friend arrived. I slipped away broken. No luncheon for me that day; rather the Hamam Baths, which in that happy epoch existed for just this purpose—to soothe the wounded heart.

Under that exotic cupola I sprawled and sweated; I plunged into the raftered hall where the bust of "Sligger's" father gazed down on mobled mankind. I dozed through the afternoon and at sundown had hot buttered toast and whisky and soda. Then, a better man, I returned to the scene of my disaster to dress for the evening.

I was greeted by the porter with a letter addressed—could it be?—in the fine little handwriting which fills the spaces of the famous drawings. How I wish I had kept it! Part of the anarchy which I then professed, was a disdain for personal records. I remember the gist but not the inimitable diction. It was an apology. Max Beerbohm was growing old, he said, and his memory played tricks with him. Once in his own youth he had been mistaken by an elder for someone else and the smart troubled him still. He reminded me that he knew my father well and had seconded him in days before I was born for this very club. He said he had read my novel with pleasure. He was on his way back to Italy. Only that prevented him from seeking a further meeting with me.

It was an enchanting document. More exciting still was the thought that, seeing my distress, he had taken the trouble to identify me and make amends.

Good manners were not much respected in the late twenties; not at any rate in the particular rowdy little set which I mainly frequented. They were regarded as the low tricks of the ingratiating underdog, of the climber. The test of a young man's worth was the insolence which he could carry off without mishap. Social outrages were the substance of our anecdotes. And here from a remote and much better world came the voice of courtesy. The lesson of the master.—EVELYN WAUGH, "Max Beerbohm: A Lesson in Manners," *At*, Sept. 1956, pp. 75–76

He had just had an attack of flu and received us sitting in a chair in front of a little fire. He was eighty-two—it was two years before his death—and he was suffering from an inflammation which had encircled his round blue eyes with red rings. But his appearance surprised me by a kind of impressiveness which I had not expected to find. He always liked to represent himself in his caricatures with an almost cherubic head and a frail and wispy figure, the extremities also di-

minishing; but he was actually rather taller than he looks in these, and his head was larger and stronger than I had imagined even from his photographs. There was something rather Germanic about his nose and jaw and his blond mustache. He struck me as both very Edwardian and as rather continental than English. He was a good deal more positive, also, than his writing would have led me to believe, even a little contentious—though it may be that I stimulated this tendency. His hands were quite astonishing—they seemed unlike any others I had ever seen. Instead of being slender with tapering fingers, the fingers were long and of uniform thickness, almost like the legs of a spider crab, and they were sharpened at the ends like pencils. It was as if they were very large engraver's tools, the instruments of a formidable craftsman. He wore one ring with a green scarab.—EDMUND WILSON, "A Miscellany of Max Beerbohm" (1963), *The Bit between My Teeth*, 1965, pp. 42–43.

As a man he was engaging but odd: after his early precocious impact as caricaturist and essayist he remained, in a fairly literal sense, a dandiacal ornament of the London literary scene for several years. He succeeded Shaw as theater critic of the *Saturday Review*; he wrote some memorable reviews though he never really enjoyed the theater and was horribly tormented by the need to produce copy to a weekly deadline. When, at length, he resigned he was never to take up a regular paid job again. It was part of Beerbohm's life-style that he preferred to live with his parents on a small private income supplemented, when he chose, with the proceeds of drawing and writing, to any serious thoughts of a career.

Despite this deliberate standing-back from life Beerbohm was a man of ready feelings, and he liked girls, particularly actresses. In the early nineties he fell in love from across the foot-lights with Cissy Loftus, a celebrated fifteen-year-old comedienne: he wrote elaborately whimsical letters to his friends proclaiming his passion, which appears to have been genuine enough while it lasted. Subsequently he was engaged to another actress for a very long time; the engagement seems to have been more sustained by Beerbohm's sense of duty than by any profound devotion on his part, and eventually it was broken off.

Finally, at the age of 38, Beerbohm married Florence Kahn, a beautiful but rather forbidding American actress; this marked his farewell to London, and for the next forty-five years, apart from the periods of the First and Second World Wars, Beerbohm lived in quiet retirement in Italy. The decision to retreat there with his wife was the solution to a problem that had gnawed at Beerbohm for years—how to find enough money to support a wife without taking a regular job. Italy, where the cost of living was so much lower than in London, was to provide an ideal answer.—BERNARD BERGONZI, "Max," *Com*, June 25, 1965, p. 452

General

For the caricatures and the writings are not manifestations of two arts, but of one. There are a number of proverbs, which may or may not be generally true, about shoe-makers sticking to their lasts and Jacks-of-all-trades being masters of none. But these do not apply to Max Beerbohm who has but one trade. He is a satirist: so that it is less odd than at first glance it might appear that he should have succeeded equally well both as author and as artist. Other writers have been known to play with pencil and with paint-box: some of them have become quite distinguished amateurs of the game. And some painters have used a pen, as did Whistler, with such effect as to inspire

Max Beerbohm to write an essay about his writing. But in each case the alternative task has been no more than a hobby, or a pleasant change of occupation. It seldom happens that the dual impulse is found in one man. The explanation in Mr. Beerbohm's case is merely that the impulse is not dual, but single. His two means lead him to the same end. There is hardly a turn of thought in his writings which does not find its counterpart in his caricatures. To and fro we may go from one to the other, backwards and forwards and back again, and we find each time the same wit, the same sense of what is ludicrous, the same intelligence behind the sense.—BOHUN LYNCH, *Max Beerbohm in Perspective*, 1922, pp. 7–8

If he had been less modest, he could have affected this era profoundly, for there is much similarity in some aspects of our own day with similar aspects of the day in which Max Beerbohm found life at the Café Royal. But he is so far a dilettante that he has written only what it amused him to write, and solemner talents than his strut their little hour upon a stage he might have occupied. It is to his elegance that all refer, as if he were no more than a survival from a gracious period; and not to that deep laughter which is the source of his quality as a writer. How unjust that is to Beerbohm! From the early nonsensical essays (which are so wise, as well as so fastidiously-written) to the incomparable parodies brought together in *A Christmas Garland*, the extravagance of *Zuleika Dobson* (that delicious supplement to the novels of his adored Ouida), and the fantastic literary anecdotes to which he gives the title *Seven Men*, he has been laughing pointedly and without cruelty at the foibles of men. According to the analyses of humour prepared by the humourless, Max Beerbohm is impossible. He could not exist. He laughs where he loves; and loves where he laughs; but he neither beams nor sniggers. By the annotated laws of laughter, no man could behave so anomalously. The question arises whether Max Beerbohm is a man or a fairy.—FRANK SWINNERTON, *The Georgian Scene*, 1934, p. 247

Edmund Wilson has recently remarked that, with the exception of Bernard Shaw, he "reads and rereads Max" as he does not any other British prose writer of his youth. Certainly something of this kind must be behind the Beerbohm revival of recent years. Perhaps this is because Max Beerbohm, more than anyone else, provides fortification against the careerism, humorlessness and raw self-assertion that make up so much of the content of current intellectual life. . . .

"My gifts are small," Beerbohm once wrote to Bohun Lynch, another of his biographers. "I've used them very well and discreetly, never straining them; and the result is I've made a charming little reputation. But that reputation is a frail plant. Don't over attend to it, gardener, Lynch." Yet, despite his disclaimers, the plant has proved not nearly so frail, for Beerbohm's achievement was quite considerable. In *Zuleika Dobson* he wrote one of the few unrelievedly comic novels in the English language. He was the leading drama critic of his day. No finer parodist lived. Over the years he built up a formidable stock of essays, portraits, stories and memoirs, almost all of which have upon them the stamp of agelessness. And as a caricaturist he was second only to the great French draftsman Sem, and even this seems open to argument.

Max Beerbohm's greatest work, without doubt, was his own life. Orderly, elegant, sympathetic and generous, in all its aspects governed by an effortless command of style—it was one of the truly superb creations of Edwardian England (that he was able to keep it flawlessly intact while living in his villa in Rapallo till his death in 1952 is all the more remarkable). In such a life the anecdote naturally looms large, and Beerbohm

seemed to have had an inexhaustible supply. The story of his meeting with Henry James could perhaps stand one more retelling.

Beerbohm was en route to the Savile Club to read a newly published James story when he came upon the American novelist in the street. James, who talked as he wrote—that is, with great, maddening circumlocution—was in top form. He was, as Beerbohm said, "a great hesitater, you know, the greatest of hesitaters." After a bit James invited Beerbohm to join him in viewing a new Augustus John at the Grafton Galleries, but Beerbohm claimed a previous appointment. "Henry James," he reports, "walked on alone, and I made my way to the Savile to read his story. I preferred, somehow, to be with the Master's work rather than with the Master himself."

A perfect judgment, and one in which anyone who has looked through Leon Edel's masterful biography will concur. Beerbohm's judgments were not always so. He seemed, for one thing, incapable of appreciating larger, bulkier talents. Goethe he abhorred. Dostoyevsky was the occasion for "Kolniyatsch," his wickedly funny travesty on the Garnetts' find ("Their promised biography of the murdered grandmother is eagerly awaited. . . ."). And on the subject of Shaw he was close to pathological. He went so far, in a conversation with Edmund Wilson, to describe how ridiculous Shaw appeared from behind: " . . . the back of his head came straight down and made a line with his neck. At first nights in his early days, he wasn't true to his principles—he wore evening clothes to the theater, but a suit so shiny that, if you went behind him, you could see your face in it like a mirror." It may have been not so much Shaw as success—large, glowing success—that Beerbohm despised. This sort of treatment appears all the more shabby for the fact that it was Shaw who chose Beerbohm as his successor as drama critic on the old *Saturday Review* and who tagged him with the word "incomparable."

Elsewhere, Beerbohm comes off as nothing if not immensely likeable. He was, indeed, charm incarnate, and his great trick was to be simply, indubitably, himself.

Beerbohm described himself as a prosist. It is a fit word, at once conferring professional status and implying that all the discipline and care that go into the best poetry ought also to go into the best prose. In his hands prose took on lucidity, power and perhaps most of all, grace. For one who so frequently wrote on autobiographical subjects, it is astonishing how he always managed to avoid massaging his own ego.—JOSEPH EPSTEIN, "The Beerbohm Revival," NR, June 27, 1964, pp. 32–33

To say that a man wears a mask is to say that the person as he appears to be to others, perhaps even to himself, differs from the person he really is. He may wear one for various reasons. He may simply be a crook, like the man who professes love to lonely spinsters in order to swindle them out of their savings. He may be someone who is afraid or ashamed of certain aspects of his nature, which he therefore tries to hide from others and himself. Young people, who are still uncertain of their identity, often try on a succession of masks in the hope of finding the one which suits them—the one, in fact, which is not a mask. Another possibility is described in Beerbohm's story "The Happy Hypocrite": in order to win the heart of a nice girl, a rake assumes a mask of virtue, but ends up by becoming in reality what at first he had only pretended to be. Lastly, among artists of all kinds—though here the use of the word "mask" is questionable—it is not uncommon for their artistic *persona* to express but a limited area of their total experience.

Max Beerbohm falls into none of these categories. He was

certainly no crook. At an astonishingly early age he knew exactly the sort of person he was, and he never showed the slightest desire to be anyone else. Lucky enough to be equally gifted in two artistic media, and without any ambition to transcend his limitations, he made his caricatures and his writings between them say everything that was in him to say. The behavior and conversation of most people vary a little according to the company they happen to be in, but Max's were the same wherever he was. Indeed, if there does seem something not quite human about him, something elfish, it is because, as an adult, he retained the transparency of a child. Intentionally or unintentionally, Oscar Wilde's wisecrack about him is acute: "Tell me, when you are alone with Max, does he take off his face and reveal his mask?". . .

As a literary critic, Max was wise to confine himself for the most part to literary parodies of the few writers he knew well. Of poetry, as of music, he had no understanding—Henley's "Invictus" was one of his favorite pieces—and both his taste and his reading in fiction were too limited to make him a critic of note. His table-talk criticism is sound enough as far as it goes: he is never mean—though he should have spotted the difference between Virginia Woolf's handling of "the stream of consciousness" and Joyce's—and even in writers whom he finds antipathetic he is always ready to admit their virtues. If his admiration for "Eminent Victorians" now seems excessive, one can understand it: he recognized that Strachey's literary ideal was akin to his own. In noting the authors whom he singles out for praise, I am puzzled by one thing. Had I been Max, there would have been two persons, both living, of whom I should have felt wildly envious—Ronald Firbank and James Thurber. I have searched through the Turner *Letters*, *Max*, and *Portrait of Max* and have found but one slight reference to Thurber and none to Firbank. Can it have been that he was?

As a parodist, he is probably the finest in English. His only rivals are James and Horace Smith, the authors of *Rejected Addresses*. Unfortunately, literary parodies can never appeal to more than a limited and highly sophisticated public, for they can be appreciated only by a reader who is intimately acquainted with the authors parodied. Caricature, or visual parody, is much more accessible, since to "get" a caricature it is not necessary to have seen the subject oneself. Thus, while Max's caricatures should delight almost everybody, the only writings of his which are likely to reach a wide public are the stories—*Zuleika Dobson*, *Seven Men*, *A Variety of Things*.

Greatly as I admire both the man and his work, I consider Max Beerbohm a dangerous influence—just how dangerous one must perhaps have been brought up in England to know. His attitude both to life and to art, charming enough in him, when taken up by others as a general cultural ideal becomes something deadly, especially for the English, an intelligent but very lazy people, far too easily bored, and persuaded beyond argument that they are the *Herrenvolk*. One may be amused—though not very—that after living in Italy for forty-five years Max still could not speak Italian, but such insularity is not to be imitated. "Good sense about trivialities," he once wrote, "is better than nonsense about things that matter." True enough, but how easily this can lead to the conclusion that anyone who attempts to deal with things that matter must be a bore, that rather than run the risk of talking nonsense one should play it safe and stick to charming trifles.

How many charming talents have been spoiled by the instilled desire to do "important" work! Some people are born to lift heavy weights. Some are born to juggle with golden balls.

True enough again, one thinks at a first reading; at a second, one notices the insidiousness of the metaphor. In the circus, the juggler is superior to the weight lifter, for juggling is an art and lifting heavy weights primarily a matter of brute strength. Had Max written that some are jugglers, some (shall we say?) lion-tamers, the comparison might have been just. As it is, he slyly suggests that minor artists may look down their noses at major ones and that "important" work may be left to persons of an inferior kennel, like the Russians, the Germans, the Americans, who, poor dears, know no better. The great cultural danger for the English is, to my mind, their tendency to judge the arts by the values appropriate to the conduct of family life. Among brothers and sisters it is becoming to entertain each other with witty remarks, hoaxes, family games and jokes, unbecoming to be solemn, to monopolize the conversation, to talk shop, to create emotional scenes. But no art, major or minor, can be governed by the rules of social amenity. The English have a greater talent than any other people for creating an agreeable family life; that is why it is such a threat to their artistic and intellectual life. If the atmosphere were not so charming, it would be less of a temptation. In postwar Britain, the clothes, accents, and diction of the siblings may have changed, but, so far as I can judge, the suffocating insular coziness is just the same. Suffocating for nine artists out of ten; it so happened that Max was the exceptional tenth man, whose talents were fostered by family life and exactly tailored to its tastes.—W. H. AUDEN, "One of the Family" (1965), *Forewords and Afterwords*, 1973, pp. 368–82

Works

FICTION

The Happy Hypocrite is a wonderful and beautiful story, though I do not like the cynical directness of the name. The name one gives to one's work, poem or picture—and all works of art are either poems or pictures, and the best both at once—is the last survival of the Greek Chorus. It is the only part of one's work in which the artist speaks directly in his own person, and I don't like you wilfully taking the name given by the common spectators, though I know what a joy there is in picking up a brickbat and wearing it as a buttonhole. It is the origin of the name of all schools of art. Not to like anything you have done is such a new experience to me that, not even for a silver dressing-case full of objects of exquisite inutility such as dear Reggie in his practical thoughtfulness provided for me on my release, shall I surrender my views. But in years to come, when you are a very young man, you will remember what I have said, and recognise its truth, and in the final edition of the work, leave the title unchanged. Of that I feel certain. The gift of prophecy is given to all who do not know what is going to happen to themselves.

The implied and accepted recognition of *Dorian Gray* in the story cheers me. I had always been disappointed that my story had suggested no other work of art in others. For whenever a beautiful flower grows in a meadow or lawn, some other flower, so like it that it is differently beautiful, is sure to grow up beside it, all flowers and all works of art having a curious sympathy for each other. I feel also on reading your surprising and to me quite novel story how useless it is for gaolers to deprive an artist of pen and ink. One's work goes on just the same, with entrancing variations.—OSCAR WILDE, Letter to Max Beerbohm, c. May 28, 1897, *The Letters of Oscar Wilde*, ed. Rupert Hart-Davis, 1962, p. 576

The student of English prose will of course find in *Zuleika Dobson* many curious echoes of the *Yellow Book* mode. He will note such cadences as "It was made of ivory, and of fluted ivory were the slim columns it swung between." And he will delight in such a sentence as an exhibit of the manner of the 'nineties. He will observe also, as an illustration of period, the author's somewhat belated pre-occupation with the names of hardstones and jewels. And he will delight in Sir Max Beerbohm's more personal pastime of introducing into his paragraphs words which are recorded in the dictionary (if recorded at all) under the sub-heading *Obs.* Lovely, and perhaps useful words, such as ebon, gallimaufry, opetide, disseizin, deliquium, jacamar, peripety, and octoradiant star. I like that sort of thing: I do it (but not quite so much) myself. These are but baubles which it amused, and has always amused, Max Beerbohm to attach to the damask of his style. Only a man devoid of all sense of tone or movement, devoid of all sense of the flux and reflux of our English tongue, could fail to observe the ingenuity, the assiduity—nay the utter hard work—which has gone to the perfecting of Sir Max Beerbohm's lovely cadenced style.—HAROLD NICOLSON, *"Zuleika Dobson—A Revaluation," LT,* Sept. 25, 1947, p. 522

In the title of *Zuleika Dobson* there is a simple juxtaposition of the exotic and the British; but in the novel itself the two are entangled in a curious way. I agree with Mr. Kronenberger—though I know we are in a minority—that there is something unsatisfactory and, as he says, "unpalatable" about this book. The trouble, I believe, is due to the fact that in this case the two sets of colors, instead of being blended in a fabric, have got into a kind of snarl. What is the pattern or the point of *Zuleika?* Is it a satire or parody or nonsense or what? It is full of amusing things and patches of clever writing, but it has also tiresome stretches of the thought and conversations of characters who do not even have the two-dimensional kind of life—like that of the people of Congreve or Firbank—that is possible within a comic convention. Max Beerbohm may be trying to satirize the admiration of Oxford for a duke, but, just as he frankly himself adores Oxford, so he seems fascinated, less frankly, by his duke, who sets the fashion for all the other undergraduates. (One remembers Max's eulogy of Ouida; and his attitude toward the Duke is closely related to his attitude toward royalty, a subject with which he was preoccupied in his first two collections of essays and to which, in both his writings and his drawings, he has constantly returned. Though he has made a good deal of fun of English monarchs and their households, one feels that he has been somewhat beglamored by them. The waspishness he sometimes displayed at the expense of George V and his family—whom he saluted with satirical verses at the time of the coronation and later caricatured so sharply that a protest from an official source compelled Max to remove certain drawings from one of his exhibitions—seems largely to have been prompted by resentment at their failure to be glamorous enough.) But though it is English to love a duke, the Duke of Dorset projected by Beerbohm is Byzantine and apocalyptic. The hyperbole of magnificence here has its effectiveness, poetic and comic, but it is surely not of Oxford. The wholesale suicide at the end of the book is also apocalyptic, but it seems to me completely unreal, completely unamusing. An exotic imagination has lost touch with an English subject.—EDMUND WILSON, "An Analysis of Max Beerbohm" (1948), *Classics and Commercials,* 1950, pp. 435–36

An ambiguity of the sixth type occurs when a statement says nothing, by tautology, by contradiction, or by irrelevant statements; so that the reader is forced to invent statements of his own and they are liable to conflict with one another. We have already considered examples of contradiction which yield a

direct meaning, and these might be regarded as in this class; thus Moses, according to the Authorised Version, told the Lord that 'Thou hast not delivered thy people at all,' but 'Delivering thou hast not delivered' is the more direct translation in the margin. 'Though you said you would,' or 'No doubt from your point of view you are delivering us all the time, but it does not seem much to us,' or 'I do not presume to say you are not delivering your people, but I find myself puzzled and unable to say that you are.' In Hebrew this, presumably, is a polite idiom, and cannot fairly be put into the sixth type because its meaning is not in any doubt; the device is in a sense real and active, but it is not conceived as a contradiction.

Contradictions of the same kind, however, when they are used as jokes, fall more definitely into this type, because the reader is meant to be conscious of them as such. The paragraph which describes the appearance of Zuleika Dobson is a pretty example.

> Zuleika was not strictly beautiful.

'Do not suppose that she was anything so commonplace; do not suppose that you can easily imagine what she was like, or that she was not, probably, the rather out-of-the-way type that you particularly admire'; in this way (or rather, in the gambit of which this is a parody) jealousy is placated, imagination is set free, and nothing has been said (what *is* this strict type of beauty, anyway?) which can be used against the author afterwards.

> Her eyes were a trifle large, and the lashes longer than they need have been.

Not knowing how *large* the *trifle* may be, the reader has no means of being certain whether he would be charmed or appalled. 'To me, from an academic point of view, this face is all wrong; but never mind me, boys; don't let me spoil your fun.' Her *brow was not discreditable;* her hair, we are positively told, was curly. 'I must say I find something very excessive about all this; but you, of course, would have been impressed.'

> The mouth was a mere replica of Cupid's bow.

He is becoming petulant; after *not strictly beautiful* it is no kindness to construct her out of *familiar models;* the *flashy-looking creature* had the same face as every one else, only twice as much of it. The eulogy now rises out of apparent understatement into warm but ambiguous praise:

> No apple-tree, no wall of peaches, had not been robbed, nor any Tyrian rose-garden, for the glory of Miss Dobson's cheeks. Her neck was imitation-marble. Her hands and feet were of very mean proportions. She had no waist to speak of.

The negatives in the first sentence throw a prim pattern over its lush fullness, force one to think 'no, the tree had not,' and give it, as a doubt in the background, exactly the opposite meaning, as by an Italian or vulgar-English double negative. In the second, of course, her *neck* could only *imitate* marble, but was it imitating *imitation-marble?* the doubt reminds us of the appalling possibilities in imitating many perfectly genuine marbles, and perhaps of the *imitation-marble* environment of her early struggles. And then, since *mean* may be medium, small or without quality; since a waist is at once flesh and the absence of flesh; we are left in doubt whether the last two sentences mean that her beauty was unique and did not depend on the conventional details, or that these parts of her body were, in fact, not good enough to be worth mentioning, or that they were intensely and fashionably small.

This contradiction as to the apparent subject of the statement seems very complete; it is not obvious what we are meant to believe at the end of it. But it cannot be said to represent a conflict in the author's mind; the contradiction removes the reader from the apparent subject to the real one, and the chief 'meaning' of the paragraph, apart from the criticism in its parody, is 'please believe in my story; we have got to take it sufficiently seriously to keep it going.' I hope I need not apologise, after this example, for including Mr. Beerbohm among the poets.—WILLIAM EMPSON, *Seven Types of Ambiguity*, 1953, pp. 176–77

ESSAYS

But, however much they differ individually, the Victorian essayists yet had something in common. They wrote at greater length than is now usual, and they wrote for a public which had not only time to sit down to its magazine seriously, but a high, if peculiarly Victorian, standard of culture by which to judge it. It was worth while to speak out upon serious matters in an essay; and there was nothing absurd in writing as well as one possibly could when, in a month or two, the same public which had welcomed the essay in a magazine would carefully read it once more in a book. But a change came from a small audience of cultivated people to a larger audience of people who were not quite so cultivated. The change was not altogether for the worse. In volume III of ⟨*Modern English*⟩ *Essays* we find Mr. Birrell and Mr. Beerbohm. It might even be said that there was a reversion to the classic type, and that the essay by losing its size and something of its sonority was approaching more nearly the essay of Addison and Lamb. At any rate, there is a great gulf between Mr. Birrell on Carlyle and the essay which one may suppose that Carlyle would have written upon Mr. Birrell. There is little similarity between *A Cloud of Pinafores*, by Max Beerbohm, and *A Cynic's Apology*, by Leslie Stephen. But the essay is alive; there is no reason to despair. As the conditions change so the essayist, most sensitive of all plants to public opinion, adapts himself, and if he is good makes the best of the change, and if he is bad the worst. Mr. Birrell is certainly good; and so we find that, though he has dropped a considerable amount of weight, his attack is much more direct and his movement more supple. But what did Mr. Beerbohm give to the essay and what did he take from it? That is a much more complicated question, for here we have an essayist who has concentrated on the work and is without doubt the prince of his profession.

What Mr. Beerbohm gave was, of course, himself. This presence, which has haunted the essay fitfully from the time of Montaigne, had been in exile since the death of Charles Lamb. Matthew Arnold was never to his readers Matt, nor Walter Pater affectionately abbreviated in a thousand homes to Wat. They gave us much, but that they did not give. Thus, some time in the 'nineties, it must have surprised readers accustomed to exhortation, information, and denunciation to find themselves familarly addressed by a voice which seemed to belong to a man no larger than themselves. He was affected by private joys and sorrows, and had no gospel to preach and no learning to impart. He was himself, simply and directly, and himself he has remained. Once again we have an essayist capable of using the essayist's most proper but most dangerous and delicate tool. He has brought personality into literature, not unconsciously and impurely, but so consciously and purely that we do not know whether there is any relation between Max the essayist and Mr. Beerbohm the man. We only know that the spirit of personality permeates every word that he writes. The triumph is the triumph of style. For it is only by knowing how to write that you can make use in literature of your self; that self which,

while it is essential to literature, is also its most dangerous antagonist. Never to be yourself and yet always—that is the problem. Some of the essayists in Mr. Rhys' collection, to be frank, have not altogether succeeded in solving it. We are nauseated by the sight of trivial personalities decomposing in the eternity of print. As talk, no doubt, it was charming, and certainly the writer is a good fellow to meet over a bottle of beer. But literature is stern; it is no use being charming, virtuous, or even learned and brilliant into the bargain, unless, she seems to reiterate, you fulfil her first condition—to know how to write.

This art is possessed to perfection by Mr. Beerbohm. But he has not searched the dictionary for polysyllables. He has not moulded firm periods or seduced our ears with intricate cadences and strange melodies. Some of his companions—Henley and Stevenson, for example—are momentarily more impressive. But *A Cloud of Pinafores* had in it that indescribable inequality, stir, and final expressiveness which belong to life and to life alone. You have not finished with it because you have read it, any more than friendship is ended because it is time to part. Life wells up and alters and adds. Even things in a book-case change if they are alive; we find ourselves wanting to meet them again; we find them altered. So we look back upon essay after essay by Mr. Beerbohm, knowing that, come September or May, we shall sit down with them and talk. Yet it is true that the essayist is the most sensitive of all writers to public opinion. The drawing-room is the place where a great deal of reading is done nowadays, and the essays of Mr. Beerbohm lie, with an exquisite appreciation of all that the position exacts, upon the drawing-room table. There is no gin about; no strong tobacco; no puns, drunkenness, or insanity. Ladies and gentlemen talk together, and some things, of course, are not said.—VIRGINIA WOOLF, "The Modern Essay," *The Common Reader*, 1925, pp. 221–23

Beerbohm's second collection of essays took its title from the stated intention in "Diminuendo" to write "no more." In 1899 Beerbohm had been for a year dramatic critic for *The Saturday Review*. At twenty-seven, he was well established as critic and essayist. *More* includes twenty essays, though the volume is little larger than *Works*, which contained only seven. Six of the essays were reprinted from issues of *The Saturday Review* before he joined its staff; six were drawn from the 1897 series in *The Daily Mail*.

Most of the essays are close to the ephemeral journalism in which the writer takes the easy road to interest by expressing a taste for something unpopular or a distaste for something popular. The subjects themselves are often shallow, but the essays are usually interesting for turns of phrase and for some individuality in point of view. The amalgam of rebellion and conservatism was beginning to form; he rejected convention when it was stupid and valued tradition when it was interesting. Among his tastes are fires (for their beauty); the seaside, when deserted in the off-season; sign boards (instead of the crowded display windows); old-time music halls (for their vulgarity); Ouida, the popular novelist (for her vitality in lieu of "art"). Among Beerbohm's distastes are Madame Tussaud's waxworks (ingenious but abortive and depressing), the crowded Strand (so full of pretense), serious music (though for other reasons Covent Garden is amusing), *Punch* (its quality has declined), sculpture (a lost art), overzealous planning to "beautify" London, the overaffectionate attitude toward children, bicycles (especially for women), knighthood (it is too common now), and even royalty itself (an absurd institution).—BRUCE R. MCELDERRY, JR., *Max Beerbohm*, 1972, p. 48

CARICATURES

One sunny morning in May, many years ago, one of our most eminent politicians was strolling from the office in Whitehall, where he had been transacting Imperial affairs with a philosophic calm, into Leicester Square.

He was a tall, handsome man of extreme distinction, he was very well known, and people stared at him and whispered his name to each other, pleased and a little excited to have seen the great man. As he passed the door of a certain picture gallery, he saw advertised, as being within, an exhibition of caricatures by Mr. Max Beerbohm, of whom he had never heard. He was of very Athenian mind, seldom neglecting the opportunity of seeing some new thing, though he often found himself sadly disappointed, and he entered. Being instantly recognized he was admitted without payment, and a catalogue was obsequiously handed to him. He saw his own name on the page, and naturally made a bee-line for No. 21. A strange, misshapen object, scarcely human but more like a long, languid worm, met his eye, and he referred again to his catalogue, for he felt sure he must have made some mistake. But it was correct, and he looked more closely. Evidently Mr. Max Beerbohm—whoever he was—could not draw at all, and he passed on with a slightly pained expression. He found several of his friends framed in neighbouring pillories, and his pain abated. A faint smile irradiated his classical features as he read the captions which accompanied these outrages. Before leaving the gallery, he returned to No. 21, and his pain came back, like the stabbing of some inflamed nerve.

He lunched with a most distinguished hostess, and mentioned his experience. She had been there, too, and hastened to say that the caricature of him was most objectionable, and not in the least like him, but they both thought that some of the others were very amusing. When luncheon was over they went back to the exhibition together, and in an absent-minded manner surveyed No. 21. Quite suddenly he gave a shout of laughter in which she joined. "I must instantly buy it," he said.

This long story is probably *trovato*, but it is certainly *ben*. Mr. Beerbohm's victims may possibly wince when they first observe what he sees in them, but the pain passes off, and they cannot help laughing. Their friends feel no pain, but laugh at once. Blandly corrosive, but with a suave and positively Chesterfieldian politeness Mr. Beerbohm makes fools of them. He is not kind, for a kind caricature is a contradiction in terms, and you must not go to him if you are in need of self-esteem. But, as regards him, the French proverb that ridicule kills is not applicable. Malicious ridicule may be fatal, but there is also a tonic ridicule, which is wholly beneficial. I regard Mr. Beerbohm as one of our greatest moral reformers of character, for to be able to make people see their ridiculous points is surely the first step towards their regeneration. In time, if he caricatures them sufficiently often, they may become splendid fellows.— E. F. BENSON, "'Max,'" *Spec*, Jan. 31, 1931, p. 144

The series called "Tales of Three Nations," done in 1923, in which Max cartoons the shifting relations, between Napoleon's time and our twenties, of Germany, France and England, shows a point of view quite free from nationalism and a consistent sympathy with the underdog. He was frightened, however, by the Russian Revolution, and it provoked some of his bitterest pictures. He seems always to have been biassed against Russia and one suspects that here a British provincialism combined with some Baltic inheritance to produce an unreasonable prejudice. But, aside from the vagaries of the Russians, the turn that things were taking dismayed him. In *A Survey* (1921), he explained, in an epistle to Britannia, that he "used to laugh at the Court and at the persons around it; and this distressed you rather. I never laughed with you at Labour. Labour didn't seem to me quite important enough yet. But Labour is very important now, very strong indeed; as you have found. And I gathered, this year . . . that you thought me guilty of not the very best of taste in failing to bow my knee to your new Baal." In *Observations* (1925), his last volume of topical caricatures, he has a drawing of Civilization wedded to the hideous Industrial System: "You took me for better or wuss in younger and 'appier days, and there'll be no getting away for you from me, ever"; and another, of the Governing Classes booted, bewigged, epauletted and equipped with a silk hat and an umbrella, assailed by a demon-eared Communism brandishing a knife and a torch. It is really the whole modern world that Max Beerbohm despises and dreads; but he has never worked out a consistent line for dealing with contemporary problems. His point of view is instinctively that of the cultivated merchant class. He may admire the feudal mobility, but he is not necessarily sympathetic with them. He prizes the security and freedom of the old-fashioned middle-class gentleman, but he hates all the horrors and rigors, on the masters' side as well as the workers', which have eventually resulted from the system upon which these advantages were based. The difficulties of his position are disarmingly exposed in his essay on servants in *And Even Now*—it appears that he does not like to be waited on and would be glad to see domestic service abolished—in which he calls himself a Tory anarchist.—EDMUND WILSON, "An Analysis of Max Beerbohm" (1948), *Classics and Commercials*, 1950, pp. 438–39

In its transformations, caricature often works by creating a visual metaphor—Gladstone a shark, Chesterton a stomach—and it entails unlikeness as well as likeness, as a metaphor does. The classic example is Charles Philipon's gross, pear-shaped face of Louis Philippe (*poire* is slang for "fat-head"). Philipon was accused of treason for it, but defended himself by showing how he had arrived at a pear. He drew four versions of the King, starting with a likeness and reducing him step by step to a bulging pear. Each transformation being plausible, Philipon was acquitted. This story, which appears in, among other places, Thackeray's *Paris Sketch Book*, interested Beerbohm enough to form the basis for two caricatures. One refers directly to the French incident. The other is a drawing in four stages, turning Whistler into a snuffed-out bedtime candle. Like Philipon's *poire*, it is a visual pun or metaphor.

The *poire* and the candle are explicit, schematic examples. Typically, Beerbohm's caricature transforms from within. Exaggerate what is salient: this formula enabled him to show men both to their own satisfaction and to our detached view, whence the mixture of reverence and ridicule in his caricatures. "H.R.H. The Duke of Cambridge," from *Caricatures of Twenty-Five Gentlemen*, is a good example. The man was a cousin of the Queen's, and commander in chief of the Army until forced to resign in 1895 because he was an obstacle to reform. Beerbohm drew him as a heavy oval form settled in a theater box, with closed eyes and jowls sunk in his collar. The honorific title and public setting create the outside point of view the world has. At the same time, the Duke's complacence expresses his own view of himself. Depending on how we feel, we can see him as uselessly pompous or as august, and his own outlook can be either bloated or full of dignity. Years later, Beerbohm drew the figure over again to make its torso even heavier and more immovable, thus removing the ambivalence—he can only seem pompous—and proving the power of caricature to release a moral through a visual perception.

"The whole man must be melted down, as in a crucible," Beerbohm's 1901 recipe has it, "and then, as from the solution, be fashioned anew. He must emerge with not one particle of himself lost, yet with not a particle of himself as it was before. . . . And he will stand there wholly transformed." The violent, reductive image of melting a man down counters a popular notion, which Beerbohm occasionally followed, that caricature merely pulls one feature out of shape. The key phrase in his recipe is "wholly transformed," for caricature can be a radical and integrating process. In his finest portraits, Beerbohm manages to shape an entire person—his appearance and role in the world—as a metaphor for his essential nature. By being unjournalistic, he gets a longer span into his critique of men, a truer drift and a figure that will hold. The first drawing he did of Arthur Balfour, in 1894, is a single long curve connecting hat and shins, and he held to that afterwards, emphasizing stooped shoulders and adding a drooping moustache and sad eyes. Balfour's sloping body is a visual figure for patrician uncertainty, and combines with his height (twice too tall for the proportions, in a 1907 drawing) to exaggerate the man's uneasy Olympian attitudes. Beerbohm also drew Edward Carson, the Irish statesman and lawyer who prosecuted Wilde, in a long curve, but Carson's has the tenseness of a whip, Balfour's the looseness of a question mark.

Some of the other truly caricatural figures that come to mind are Frank Harris preened and inflated like a fighting cock, as if to signify his sexual activity and self-confidence, and the bluntness of Balfour's rival, Bonar Law. Nothing demonstrates the metaphoric vision more clearly than the brief emendations and notes Beerbohm made in 1920 on his 1896 drawings of Rudyard Kipling and Pinero. He took care to correct the back of Kipling's neck and make it "more brutal," because that detail bore out his opinion of the man. It was equivalent to the overmuscular language and the actual brutality in Beerbohm's *Christmas Garland* parody of Kipling. Of course Kipling's jaw bore the brunt of distortion in all the caricatures Beerbohm drew of him, and if we look at the jaw and the neck in paintings or photographs of Kipling, we can see that Beerbohm's judgment of the man determined his technique before the technique conveyed a judgment. For changing the 1896 Pinero, Beerbohm had similar cause. As a critic he had persistently exposed the playwright's intellectual weaknesses, so the "dome-like brow" seemed "all wrong" and he redrew Pinero leaving "no top to his head." This technique is far subtler than the common journalistic habit of drawing verbal clichés—something Beerbohm did once, for example, by putting William Archer's head in clouds because he hoped for a national theater. The drawings of Balfour and Harris undergo the same transition from physical to moral terms as words like "devious," "upright," "overblown," "eccentric," or "supercilious." This identity between the process in words and the process in pictures lies at the heart of the language of caricature.

Sometimes in relying on a salient feature to express the whole man, Beerbohm developed signs for the people he drew: Pinero's eyebrows, "like skins of some small mammal," Beerbohm said, "just not large enough to be used as mats." Making preliminary sketches, he could draw a face three or four times and keep to an identical configuration. Also, after many years of not having done a man, particularly one toward whom his attitude had not changed, he would produce precisely the kind of distortion he had originally made. He kept the sign in his mind's eye, partly as a matter of technique and partly because his own example led him to expect that men essentially settle in themselves. If they do not, if men can change from mean to

generous, arrogant to humble, sloppy to scrupulous, then the art of caricature may lose its attaching power. Beerbohm did an elaborate drawing illustrating this possibility, "One fine morning, or How they might undo me." In it he stands at the side, recoiling from a file of thirty men winding past him. Each of them has altered in some point from the way Beerbohm habitually drew him: Balfour has a goatee, Pinero's eyebrows are shaved off, Moore's upper lip is clean, Rothenstein smiles instead of scowling, Kipling's jaw does not jut out, Shaw sports a high collar, buttonhole, tiepin, cufflinks, and spats, Rosebery wears a walrus moustache, and Hall Caine without his moustache is passing closest to Beerbohm and glaring in panicky anger. They all look wrong, distressed, and seem to want to revert to the way Beerbohm drew them. Besides pointing out the economy he relied on in grasping men by their salient features, "How they might undo me" contains a reverse wisdom—namely, that these eminent men themselves rely on outer props and costume to realize a personality.—JOHN FELSTINER, *The Lies of Art*, 1972, pp. 113–16

MAX BEERBOHM
"Why I Ought Not to Have Become
a Dramatic Critic" (1898)
Around Theatres
1930, pp. 3–7

Every one delighted in G. B. S. Even they who were his targets snatched an awful joy in the illicit study of his writings, and will have heaved a sigh, not wholly of relief, at the news of his resignation. I am disappointed by that stroke of fate which has eclipsed the gaiety of green-rooms. Of all his readers none mourns G. B. S. more inconsolably than I, his pious successor. For, with all his faults—grave though they are and not to be counted on the fingers of one hand—he is, I think, by far the most brilliant and remarkable journalist in London, and, in succeeding him, I labour not merely under my own modesty, but also under the impatience of the public before me. I am in the predicament of the minor music-hall artiste sent on as an "extra-turn," tremulously facing the prolonged thunder of calls for the "star" who has just sung. A pathetic smile, a little gesture of appeal—and the thunder, still rumbling round the distant gallery, gradually subsides. My voice is audible at length. But it is not much of a voice. My song, also, is not much of a song.

I will not raise in my readers hopes which I cannot realise for them. It is best to be quite frank. Frankly, I have none of that instinctive love for the theatre which is the first step towards good criticism of drama. I am not fond of the theatre. Dramatic art interests and moves me less than any of the other arts. I am happy among pictures, and, being a constant intruder into studios, have learnt enough to know that I know nothing whatever about painting—knowledge which, had I taken to what is called "art-criticism," would have set me head-and-shoulders above the great majority of my colleagues. Of music I have a genuine, though quite unenlightened, love. Literature I love best of all, and I have some knowledge of its technicalities. I can talk intelligently about it. I have my little theories about it. But in drama I take, unfortunately, neither emotional nor intellectual pleasure. I am innocent of any theories on the subject. I shall have to vamp up my first principles as I go along, and they will probably be all wrong and all dull. For I have never even acquired any lore in this kind of criticism. I could not test a theory nor quote a line of Hazlitt,

Lamb, Lewes and the rest, whose essays in dramatic criticism I have never read. I have, however, a fragmentary recollection of Aristotle's fragment on the drama, which I read for "Mods." The examiners, if I remember rightly, marked my paper "gamma-minus-query"—a clear proof that even in my adolescence I was not stage-struck. Ignorance of the ideas expressed by previous critics is not, I admit, in itself a grave defect. It may even be an advantage, as making cerebration compulsory, and so giving freshness to one's style. Likewise, I can imagine that a man who had never been in a theatre might, were he suddenly sent forth as a dramatic critic, be able to write really charming and surprising and instructive things about the stage. But my readers must not look for any freshness or cerebration from me. I could find my way blindfold about every theatre in the metropolis, and could recite backwards most of the successful plays that have been produced in the last ten years. Though I have no theoretic knowledge of the drama, I am a rich mine of theatrical gossip, and I know (and do not dispute) all the current judgments on actor Tom, playwright Dick, and stage-manager Harry. Out of my very cradle I stepped upon the fringe of the theatrical world, and my familiarity with the theatre has been a matter of circumstance rather than of choice. I remember being really bored by a play on the evening of my tenth birthday. That a visit to the theatre can be regarded, as it is regarded by some men to their dying day, as a treat, has always bewildered and baffled my imagination. In the whole world, no phenomenon is so inexplicable to me as a queue of men and women at a pit-door. I am not, fortunately, a person of expensive habits, but I confess that I have never regarded any theatre as much more than the conclusion to a dinner or the prelude to a supper. It appals me to think that in future I shall be obliged to keep my attention fixed, never taking my eyes from the stage except to make a note upon my cuff. I, who have never left a theatre with any definite impression of pleasure or displeasure, am curious to know how on earth I am going to fill so much as half a column of this paper, week by week, with my impressions. My self-respect and my ignorance of bygone formulae of drama will prevent me from the otherwise easy task of being an academic critic. I shall not be able to branch off, like G. B. S., into discussions of ethical, theological or political questions, for on such questions I am singularly ill-informed. I have not that well-considered attitude towards life which gave a kind of unity to G. B. S.'s worst inconsistencies about art. In a word, I don't quite know what to do with the torch that G. B. S. has handed to me.

Of the literary quality in any play, I shall perhaps be able to say something, but I shall be hopelessly out of my depth in criticising the play itself. The mere notion of criticising the players simply terrifies me, not because I know (as, indeed, I do) nothing about the art of acting, but because I have the pleasure of personal acquaintance with so many players. One well-known player and manager is my near relative. Who will not smile if I praise him? How could I possibly disparage him? Will it not be hard for me to praise his rivals? If I do anything but praise them, what will become of the purity of the Press? Most of the elder actors have patted me on the head and given me sixpence when I was "only *so* high." Even if, with an air of incorruptibility, I now return them their sixpences, they will yet expect me to pat *them* on the head in the *Saturday Review*. Many of the younger actors were at school with me. They will expect me to criticise them as an old playmate should. With most of the others I have, at least, a nodding acquaintance. To one of them I had nodded so often that, only the other day, we wrote a play together—a play which, by the way, no manager will now be able to accept, lest he be thought venal. How can I

criticise the acting of a collaborator? If I do not care for one of his impersonations, how can I do aught but write an eulogy in these columns and put my true opinion into a sealed envelope to be opened after my decease and immediately destroyed? My whole position is unfortunate. I have the satiric temperament: when I am laughing at any one I am generally rather amusing, but when I am praising any one, I am always deadly dull. Now, such is the weakness of my character that I cannot say in print anything against a personal acquaintance. I think I have met all the habitual playwrights in my time. Therefore, in criticising an average production, I shall be obliged to confine myself to slating such members of the cast as I have never met. If they have acted well, this will undoubtedly be hard on them. Even if they have not acted well—and I for one shall not know whether they have or not—their punishment will be out of all due proportion. The only advice I can offer them, meanwhile, is that they should make haste and meet me.

It has struck me, in reading this article, that I have not given my readers much hope of edification. Let them console themselves with the reflection that they are less to be pitied than I am. I shall miss G. B. S. quite as much as they will, and they will not be compelled to read the articles which I *shall* be compelled to write. This absurd post which I have accepted will interfere with my freedom in life, and is quite likely to spoil and exhaust such talent as I might otherwise be exercising in literary art. However, I will not complain. The Editor of this paper has come to me as Romeo came to the apothecary, and what he wants I give him for the apothecary's reason. I daresay that there are many callings more uncomfortable and dispiriting than that of dramatic critic. To be a porter on the Underground Railway must, I have often thought, be very terrible. Whenever I feel myself sinking under the stress of my labours, I shall say to myself, "I am not a porter on the Underground Railway."

J. G. RIEWALD
From "Max Beerbohm and Oscar Wilde"
Sir Max Beerbohm, Man and Writer
1953, pp. 129–41

*T*he Picture of Dorian Gray was published in 1891, five years before *The Happy Hypocrite*. It is the story of the young, handsome, and wealthy Dorian Gray, whose magnetic personality enables his friend Basil Hallward to create his masterpiece—a life-size portrait of Dorian. The latter, however, gradually falls under the sway of the decadent, cynical mocker Lord Henry Wotton, who gives him a book of the *A Rebours* type to read, and finally brings about his moral ruin. But, as the sinister result of a wish once passionately expressed, Dorian's face, in spite of his debauchery, preserves its innocence and youth, while his crimes and the advance of the years are duly registered on the carefully hidden portrait. Regardless of conventional morality Dorian, like another Faustus, now plunges into a life of mere pleasure. He begins his career by repudiating his first pure love, Sibyl Vane, a little East End actress, and ends it by murdering his friend Basil Hallward. But, though his cunning, combined with the mask of his eternal youth, shields him from discovery, he does not escape his Nemesis. At last he also wants to make away with the only remaining witness of his shameful double life—the life-size portrait, which the corruption of his soul has now changed into the picture of a horrible old monster; and with the knife that had once stabbed the painter he now stabs his work. But he has reckoned without his host, for the portrait which, as his visible conscience, might have been a positive factor in his life, now assumes the role of avenger, and destroys him. And, Wilde concludes, when the footmen entered the room, "they found, hanging upon the wall, a spendid portrait of their master as they had last seen him, in all the wonder of his exquisite youth and beauty. Lying on the floor was a dead man, in evening dress, with a knife in his heart. He was withered, wrinkled, and loathsome of visage."

Beerbohm's fantastic parable is a subtle variation on this theme. For the background of his *Happy Hypocrite* he took his beloved Regency period—which must have fascinated him in the years 1894–96—and for its hero Lord George Hell, one of the Regent's boon companions, who spends his evenings with La Gambogi, an Italian dancer. Lord George is wicked, and he is proud of his wickedness, until, all of a sudden, he falls in love with the ingenuous Jenny Mere, a *débutante* in a new operette. But Jenny spurns his love, because she can never be the wife of a man whose face is not saintly. In the desperate hours that follow this rebuff, the buck conceives the means of winning Jenny Mere. A fashionable mask-maker in Old Bond Street supplies him with the mask of a saint, which will forever hide his evil countenance. When he leaves the shop, La Gambogi stands watching her lost lover with sinister eye, and orders a spy to track him down. But Lord George does not heed her and, with his heart all sunshine, hurries on to his Jenny, who now accepts him on the strength of his saintly face. He at once marries her under the name of "George Heaven," and brings her to a woodman's cottage, where they have a wonderful honeymoon. And as the days go by he truly repents the evil he has done in the past, and the spectre of the *femme fatale* gradually recedes into the background. However, on the "mensiversary" of their wedding the jealous Signora discovers them in their cottage. Like a panther she springs upon her old lover and tears away the mask, but to her immense dismay she sees that the face under it is as saintly as the mask has been. To Lord George bewailing the imposture he has wrought upon her Jenny says: "Surely, your face is even dearer to me, even fairer, than the semblance that hid it and deceived me. I am not angry." After that she "put her arms round his neck; and he was happier than he had ever been."

The analogy with *Dorian Gray* is obvious. The leading motive of both stories is the Good and the Evil, set off by the mask of hypocrisy. In Wilde's novel this motive is expressed in the following telltale sentences: "Each of us has Heaven and Hell in him" and "In hypocrisy he had worn the mask of goodness." This more or less "decadent" theme must have appealed to Beerbohm's impish imagination, for his story of Lord Hell, alias Lord Heaven, may be interpreted as a delicate, though unintended, parody of it. The fact that Max never allows the parody to interfere with his independence of treatment would seem to strengthen this supposition, and may have been the reason why the unconscious parody has never been recognized as such. But in spite of the difference in treatment the parallelism is unmistakable. In the case of Dorian the "mask of goodness" is the mask of his own radiant youth; in the case of Lord George it is the mask of a saint. This detail is symbolic of their attitudes. While Dorian's life is spent in the pursuit of worldly pleasures, Lord George aims at a higher and more spiritual bliss. The function of their masks varies accordingly. Dorian's fleshly mask of youth not only hides the moral degeneration which reveals itself in the portrait; it also precipitates it. Lord Hell's mask of wax, on the other hand, is a triumphant earnest of the moral regeneration which, owing to

a momentary glimpse of uncorrupted virtue granted him in the person of Jenny Mere, has begun to manifest itself under it. Dorian as well as Lord George know that the life they are leading is insincere, and, though their ends differ, they both accept hypocrisy as a means of multiplying their personalities. Furthermore, both Wilde and Beerbohm (who once called his story *a fable with a moral*) acknowledge the regenerating power of pure love and a good intention. "Love makes people good," Sibyl Vane is heard to remark in Wilde's novel. But these words, which are in fact the theme of Beerbohm's story, do not get a chance of realizing themselves in Dorian Gray, because his intentions are evil. At the end of his life, it is true, he tries to remove the traces of vice from the portrait by being good; but even then he remains the typical hypocrite. It is at this point that the story is taken up by Beerbohm. His tale begins where Wilde's novel leaves off. Beerbohm's hero, Lord Hell, is of good will, which is enough to make a Lord Heaven of him. He, whom pure love forced to assume the mask of hypocrisy, becomes the *Happy* Hypocrite, whereas the pleasure-seeking Dorian, whose mask has turned into an instrument of crime, is the typical *Unhappy* Hypocrite.

The parallelism between the novel and the fairy-tale is not restricted to the leading ideas; it also shows itself in the structure. The heroes are both wealthy men, who fall under the spell of a disastrous influence. Both get a chance of redeeming themselves by loving a pure girl. In both cases this girl is an actress, whom they "discover" in the playhouse. Both conceal their surnames from their sweethearts who, not unnaturally, consider themselves unworthy of their lovers. The revenge motive, too, runs parallel. Dorian and Lord George are both persecuted; the former by Sibyl's brother, who seeks to avenge his sister's suicide; the latter, after his metamorphosis, by a spy of the vindictive Signora. Furthermore, Mr. Isaacs, the manager of Sibyl's little theatre, appears in Beerbohm's story as Mr. Garble who, like his prototype, insists on the girls addressing their lovers as "My Lord", while Mr. Aeneas, "the fashionable mask-maker" of Old Bond Street, takes the place of Mr. Hubbard, "the celebrated frame-maker" of South Audley Street. In the same way Basil Hallward's sudden disappearance, which caused so much excitement, finds its logical, and even verbal counterpart in the sensational disappearance of Lord George Hell. The likeness also appears in the scene between James Vane and the prostitute and that between the Signora and the Dwarf. It even seems to affect the names. For while Sibyl's lover is known to her as "Prince Charming", it is as "King Bogey" that Lord Hell acquires a doubtful reputation in nurseries. But it becomes especially striking towards the end when Dorian's dead body on the floor finds its serene counterpart in Lord George's mask lying upon the lawn, upturned to the sky.

The parallelism even shows itself in such minor details as Dorian's nightly ramble through London after he has left Sibyl Vane, and Lord George's nocturnal peregrination through the same city after Jenny Mere has rejected him. In almost the same words we learn that, at the ensuing dawn, Dorian found himself close to Covent Garden, while Beerbohm's hero, at that hour, was treading the outskirts of a little wood in Kensington. Wilde as well as Beerbohm then go on to describe the morning air, heavy with the scent of flowers, and dwell on the sinister aspect of the sleeping city. Another possible parallel is the description of Dorian's home-coming in the morning ("The bright dawn flooded the room, and swept the fantastic shadows into dusky corners, where they lay shuddering") and that of Lord George's similar *rentree*: "Shadows lay like memories in every corner of the dim hall." The account of the light slanting through the window is equally suggestive.

Analogous structural and stylistic parallelisms exist between Beerbohm's fantastic story and some of Wilde's other writings. Thus the theme of *The Happy Hypocrite*—a saint converting a sinner—is generally reminiscent of Wilde's *La Sainte Courtisane*, while two of its leading motives—a belief that love is stronger than evil, and the idea of the soul being able to metamorphose the face—occur in Wilde's stories. To take one instance only, in "The Fisherman and his Soul" the hero's love proves stronger than the evil with which he is tempted, while the Star-Child, in the story of that name, changes face twice in accordance with the state of his soul. His second metamorphosis, which, in fact, resembles the one related in *The Happy Hypocrite*, even finds its stylistic counterpart in Beerbohm's story. "And lo! his face was even as it had been," Wilde exclaims; and Beerbohm echoes: "But lo! his face was even as his mask had been." The cadences of the writing, too, are definitely Oscarish.

These, and similar parallelisms bring out the affinity between *The Happy Hypocrite* and *Dorian Gray* on the one hand, and that between *The Happy Hypocrite* and Wilde's fairy-stories on the other. But it should be insisted that these affinities are of an entirely different nature. While, as to form, *The Happy Hypocrite* is an imitation of the Wildean fairy-story, it can be shown that, in substance, it is an unconscious parody of the "decadent" atmosphere suggested in *Dorian Gray*—a parody, therefore, done in the fairy-tale technique of which Beerbohm's victim was a master. This enables us to connect it with a definite and important stage in the history of Max's artistic relations with Oscar Wilde—the transition between the parodical and the imitative stage. It need hardly be stressed that this subtle blend of parody and pastiche is far more characteristic of the real Beerbohm than the two or three attempts at pure imitation that followed.

That *The Happy Hypocrite* may be looked upon as an unconscious parody of Wilde's novel is proved by many significant touches. I only select a few. When Dorian, at the end of his criminal double life, persuades himself that he is mending his ways, there appears in the mouth of the portrait "the curved wrinkle of the hypocrite." Beerbohm raises this scene to the level of parody. When Lord George stigmatizes the saint's mask he has just tried on as too "contemplative", Mr. Aeneas promptly makes it into the mask of a saint who loves dearly by putting "a fuller curve" upon the lips. On one occasion, Wilde tells us, two gentlemen left the smoking-room of the Churchill, because Dorian Gray came in. Beerbohm improves upon this as follows: " . . . whenever he [i.e., Lord Hell] entered a room . . . they would make straight for the door and watch him very severely through the key-hole." This "through the key-hole" is conclusive. Furthermore Lord Henry's statement "I adore simple pleasures. . . . They are the last refuge of the complex" finds its caricatural illustration in the incident of the once famous *gourmet* eating buns with Jenny Mere—a "pagoda" of buns, to match Lord Henry's "pyramid" of seeded strawberries. Finally there is parody in the way in which Max describes the tearing away of the mask. In *Dorian Gray* the *denouement* is accompanied by a "horrible cry" and a "crash", while the unmasking scene in *The Happy Hypocrite* is enlivened by a "wild cry" and a "loud pop, as though some great cork had been withdrawn." Even the name Jenny Mere seems to contain an allusion to Wilde's predilection for that word in his novel: Sibyl Vane, for Dorian, is "*mere* beauty"; she has, according to him, "not *merely* art", but personality also, while on the fatal evening she is for him "*merely* a commonplace, mediocre actress".

Though there are certain indications that would seem to point to such a conclusion, it is difficult to prove that Beerbohm, in the person of Lord Hell, intended to give us a caricature of Oscar Wilde, the *man*. Of course, it cannot be gainsaid that the latter has drawn his own portrait in the character of Lord Henry Wotton. Considering the close parallelism that I have shown to exist between *Dorian Gray* and *The Happy Hypocrite*, it is, therefore, not impossible that Beerbohm, in his turn, should present us with a picture of Oscar in the person of Lord George Hell. The fact that he makes his hero exactly as old as Wilde was reputed to be when he published his *Dorian Gray*, may be a mere coincidence; for in the play he is "about 45."[1] But there are other clues. A recent biographer described Wilde's figure as inclining to corpulence, and his face as fleshy, humorous, "proconsular," and, at first, repellent.[2] Beerbohm's Lord George is a "vast and fearful gentleman," and "rather like Caligula, with a dash of Sir John Falstaff." Whenever this personage enters a room many people get up and leave. The same thing had happened to Wilde himself, who, moreover, retaliated in much the same way as Lord Hell;[3] for, when the ladies gathered up their skirts as they passed the wicked Lord, "he would lightly appraise their ankles." And then there is Lord George's fondness for fine clothes, and his "sudden disappearance" from the social sphere. Beerbohm's explicit statement that his Lordship was a non-smoker—his only virtue, and that a negative one—only heightens the poignancy of the jest, since everybody knew that Wilde was a tremendous smoker. Finally, the saintly mask capable of transforming the features of a George Hell into those of a George Heaven, may symbolize contemporary hopes about the purifying influence of the punishment Wilde was undergoing. Beerbohm himself refers to this sentiment in his review of *De Profundis*, written in 1905: "Nothing seemed more likely than that Oscar Wilde, smitten down from his rosy-clouded pinnacle, and dragged through the mire, and cast among the flints, would be *diablement changé en route*."[4] It is certainly remarkable that all these indications concern the "decadent" side of Wilde's life and character. In view of my thesis that Beerbohm's fantastic story may be looked upon as a parody of the "decadent" *contents* of *Dorian Gray*, this circumstance would seem to strengthen the conjecture that at least some of the mockery in *The Happy Hypocrite* is directed against the *person* of Oscar Wilde.

Notes

1. Cf. "Vague Hints from the Author to the Company," in George Arliss, *Up the Years from Bloomsbury* (Boston: Little, Brown, 1927), pp. 185 ff.
2. Hesketh Pearson, op. cit., pp. 162–163.
3. Cf. ibid., p. 266.
4. "A Lord of Language," *A Peep into the Past and Other Prose Pieces by Max Beerbohm* (London: William Heinemann, 1972), p. 38.

LORD DAVID CECIL
From "Introduction" to
Max Beerbohm: Selected Prose
1970, pp. 7–17

'The incomparable Max', Shaw called him. The phrase has stuck. Indeed it is apt; from the first Max's work was too individual profitably to be compared with that of anyone else. Not that it was always the same. Max the impertinent exquisite of the 1890s changed gradually into Max the mature and subtle humorist of the 1920s. His style altered along with his spirit: the florid Rococo of the essay on 'Dandies and Dandies' sobered and refined itself into the classic Chippendale of the essay on 'Going Out for a Walk'. All the same the difference between the two is far less than their likeness. From the beginning to the end of his career Max's work is homogeneous; an expression of the same personality and the same attitude towards his art.

This is that of the entertainer. From the start of his career Max thought it the first duty of an artist to be true to the nature of his talent and to refrain from writing on subjects that did not inspire it. 'It is curious', he writes, 'how often an artist is ignorant of his own true bent. How many charming talents have been spoiled by the desire to do "important" work. Some are born to juggle with golden balls, some are born to lift heavy weights.' He was not ignorant of his own bent. He knew he was a juggler and he devised his work accordingly. Though as capable as anyone of serious views and deep feelings he recognised that these did not stir his artistic impulse: so that very rarely does he allow them to appear openly in his work. Deliberately he writes not to disturb or to instruct but to please: and more particularly to amuse.

For—and this is the second distinguishing characteristic of his work—his genius was a comic genius. The aspects of experience that stimulated him to create were the aspects that made him smile or laugh: the balls he juggled with were jokes: the Max Beerbohm entertainment is a comic entertainment. But it is one of a special and superior kind, for it is the expression of a special and superior man. Max was very intelligent, with a sharp, searching intelligence, continually at work noticing and concluding. Half his jokes are also penetrating comments on human nature. Well-informed comments too! Max liked to make out that he was imperfectly educated. In fact every page he wrote reveals him as the heir to an ancient culture which has furnished his mind, enriched his imagination and refined his taste, disclosing itself in his every casual allusion and in the unobtrusive, graceful confidence of his tone of voice. Finally culture and intelligence alike are strengthened by the fact that they are under the direction of a shrewd judgment. Unlike some intelligent people Max was extremely sensible. He surveyed the world with a realistic gaze that made him as impervious to nonsense as Dr Johnson himself, however much it was accepted by respectable or fashionable opinion. . . .

Sceptical about 'messages', Max never questioned the value of art. Indeed the impulse behind the work, in so far as it was not comic, was aesthetic. The Beerbohm entertainment set out to entertain by its beauty as well as by its fun. Max grew up during the period of the Aesthetic Movement; and though he laughed at it—as at most things—he shared its views. For him, art was the most important and most precious of human activities: and the distinguishing mark of a work of art was its beauty. Even a caricature, he thought, should aim at beauty—'beauty to be achieved by the perfect adjustment of means to ends'. Max's feeling for beauty, apparent in his unsleeping sense of form, also showed itself in his taste. This was in keeping with the general character of his genius. Though he could recognise grand or primitive types of beauty, he preferred it light, delicate, elegant; beauty in its humbler, gayer manifestation as prettiness. Mingled with his sense of fun, this sense of beauty often incarnated itself in the form of graceful extravagant fantasy, the fantasy of wicked 'Lord George Hell' converted to a saintly life by wearing a saintly wax mask, of the busts of the Roman Emperors outside the Sheldonian Theatre at Oxford

bursting out in sweat at the sight of beautiful, fatal Zuleika Dobson. Yet—and this is one of the things that gives Max's work its unique flavour—his fantasy is always disciplined by his intelligence and his good sense. It is never silly: its charm comes largely from the fact that it is seen against an unwavering standard of realism and reason. The behaviour of the busts may be fantastic, but not the Oxford scene in which it takes place: Lord George Hell's conversion is described with a conscious, self-mocking affectation of manner which makes it quite clear that the reader must not take it too solemnly. Whatever clouds of fantasy may encircle Max's head his feet were always firmly on the ground.

The effect of this contrast running through his work is ironical. Irony is its most continuous and consistent characteristic; an irony at once delicate and ruthless, from which nothing is altogether protected, not even the author himself. Ruthless but not savage: Max could be made angry—by brutality or vulgarity—but very seldom does he reveal this in his creative works. His artistic sense told him that ill-temper was out of place in an entertainment, especially in an entertainment that aspired to be pretty as well as comic. His ruthlessness gains its particular flavour from the fact that it is also good-tempered. On the other hand it is not so good-tempered as to lose its edge. Max's irony is never that sort of 'kindly' irony that softens and sentimentalises. His artistic sense tells him that softness, as much as savagery, would destroy the clear bright atmosphere needed for his entertainment to make its effect.

The Max Beerbohm entertainment takes various forms. First of all there are the parodies. Here Max is a supreme master. He manages to parody his victim's sense as much as he does his style. Henry James, once questioned about his next work, replied, pointing to Max Beerbohm: 'Ask that young man. He knows me better than I know myself.' Reading the James parody in this selection, one sees what he means. If Henry James had chosen to write about two children waking up to find their stockings on Christmas morning this is what he would have said. And this almost is how he would have said it. The exaggeration of style needed to make parody amusing is all the more effective because it is so very slight. Sometimes Max hardly seems to exaggerate at all. 'If Euclid was alive to-day (and I daresay he is) . . . ' Is this a phrase of Chesterton's or a phrase from Max's parody of Chesterton? Once again the likeness is of sense as well as of style. The sentence is an illuminating critical comment on Chesterton's whole mode of thought. So is the parody on James a profound and friendly criticism of James, so is the parody of Kipling a profound but devastating criticism of Kipling.

Max's entertainment took two other forms. The first is the occasional essay. Of these there are four volumes: *The Works of Max Beerbohm*, *More*, *Yet Again* and the last and best, *And Even Now*. Max's essays are what may be called 'pure' essays; that is to say they are vehicles not for instruction or confession but designed simply to fulfil his creative impulse, which is to amuse. If he does make a serious point in them, it is in a playful tone; any imaginative moment takes the form of a playful flight of fancy. For the rest they are deliberate exhibitions of personality. This personality is not a self-portrait. Max the essayist is not the same as Max the man, but rather a fictitious figure made up of those particular elements in his composition that he judged would enhance his entertainment. He isolates some of his own qualities—his humour, his fancy, his wit, his taste in style—and uses them as material from which by means of an elaborate process of arrangement and staging he creates the protagonist in his one-man show.

Such a type of essay is hard to write successfully, as can be realised by reading the essays of Max's imitators. On the one hand to keep the tone so consistently light is to run the risk of making the whole thing seem flimsy; on the other hand the writer who consciously exploits his personality easily appears an exhibitionist all too obviously anxious to show off his charm. Max walks the tightrope between these dangers with confidence and ease. His essays do not seem flimsy because they are not built of flimsy materials; they are the product of too lively an intelligence, too observant an eye. Such pieces as those on 'The Naming of Streets' or 'Hosts and Guests' are packed with enough fresh ideas and insights into human nature to furnish forth fifty average 'serious' writers. If the reader fails to notice this, it is only because Max's tone is so carefree and throw-away.

Intelligence saves his essays from flimsiness; good sense saves them from self-admiring exhibitionism. No doubt Max is showing off; it is the function of the entertainer to show off. But he is far too sensible to be unaware of this fact and far too humorous not to be amused by it. In the essay entitled 'Going Out for a Walk' he describes vividly how bored he has been by a fellow walker; but the climax of the piece is his unexpected revelation that he knows the fellow walker is likely to have found him equally boring. It is a secret of his strength that he is one of the very few writers whose irony is so impartial as to include himself.

Along with his 'pure' essays we may consider Max's critical pieces, mostly drawn from his work as the dramatic critic of the *Saturday Review*. He wrote these reluctantly as a means of livelihood; and they do show his limitations. One cannot call them failures; they are too clever and too accomplished. But the critical mode, except in the form of parody, did not stimulate him. Criticism is not primarily a comedian's mode. Max knew it. 'My whole position is uncomfortable,' he remarked. 'I have a satiric temperament; when I am laughing at anyone I am generally rather amusing but when I am praising anyone I am always dull.' Here he goes too far; he did not know how to be dull. It is true, however, that only now and again in these criticisms does he seem vitally and unmistakably himself, and that is when he leaves off talking about a play to follow some comic or whimsical train of thought suggested by it, or to re-create with affectionate amusement some personality which has appealed to his fancy, like Irving or Dan Leno; when in fact he stops being a critic and reverts to being an entertainer.

The last category in his entertainment consists of his stories. These in their turn subdivide into two types. First come his two fables, *The Dreadful Dragon of Hay Hill* and *The Happy Hypocrite*. *The Dreadful Dragon of Hay Hill* is not included in this book; even more than his play reviews it exposes Max's limitations. Written after the First World War, it is designed to illustrate his conviction, taught him by the war, that mankind is incurably, congenitally quarrelsome. This is a bleak conviction and, for all that Max writes in his usual playful tone, it is a bleak tale. As such it does not suit his talent, for bleakness involves the eclipse of that good-humour which is an essential condition of his inspiration. At the same time he lacks the harsh force to drive his story's harsh moral home. Max cannot divest himself of his usual easy urbanity. This blunts the cutting edge of his attack on humanity. *The Happy Hypocrite* also points a moral, namely that by wearing a mask of goodness you may become good; for, as Max said: 'I hold that Candour is good only when it reveals good actions or good sentiments, and that when it reveals evil, itself is evil.' Here for once he is talking seriously. And wisely too; these principles, put into practice, are a good deal more likely to lead a man to live a satisfactory life than are all the hot gospels preached by

the prophets of romanticism, from Shelley down to D. H. Lawrence. *The Happy Hypocrite* is charming as well as wise; with a fresh youthful charm that makes it impossible to omit it from any selection of its author's best work. Its only fault is that its charm and its wisdom do not completely harmonise. The mock-nursery-tale mode in which Max has chosen to tell his story is a little too childish to carry the weight of its mature moral.

There is no such fault in the second group of his stories, *Zuleika Dobson* and *Seven Men and Two Others*. These, along with his best parodies, are his masterpieces. They are best described as satiric fantasies and owe their peculiar flavour, even more than his other works, to the fact that they are a blend; on the one hand of humour and prettiness, on the other of fact and fancy. Most of them involve extravagant flights of fancy; yet each is founded on Max's personal experience of the real world and each derives substantial interest from the fact that it is sedulously true to it. Fantasy is at its prettiest and boldest in *Zuleika Dobson*. This tells how the most beautiful woman in the world arrived in what was then the exclusively male world of Oxford; how all the undergraduates fell in love with her and how they drowned themselves for her sake at the close of the boat races. This preposterous idea is exploited to its full preposterousness. No note of serious feeling checks the foaming flood of high spirits on which the tale sweeps along. It is consistently and audaciously heartless. Yet the fun is not 'sick'; there is no question of the author taking an equivocal pleasure in pain. Our pleasure in it is unqualified by the smallest hint of horror or perversity. With all this, it is truthful too; the truest picture of Oxford in fiction. Dons and students and Rhodes scholars, Eights Week, Balliol concerts, exclusive dining clubs—every characteristic phase and fact of University life is described with an extraordinary, perceptive insight. Finally it is written in a style which is a masterpiece of sustained virtuosity, a parody of aesthetic fine writing which is even finer than the manner which it mocks. As a blend of comedy and prettiness *Zuleika Dobson* has no equal in English literature but *The Rape of the Lock*.

Seven Men and Two Others, written in the full maturity of its author's spirit and manner, is an even subtler triumph. It is the most autobiographical of his works in that he appears himself in each piece and also in that each relates to a phase of his own experience. Of the stories from it selected here, 'Enoch Soames' is about the London of the Decadent Nineties, 'Argallo and Ledgett' is set in the literary world of the Edwardian age, '"Savonarola" Brown' recalls Max's life as a dramatic critic, 'James Pethel' is set in the Dieppe where he spent his youthful holidays. I have chosen these pieces for this collection partly because they are my favourites and partly because they are the most variously representative of his genius. 'Enoch Soames' shows Max the satirist at his keenest. It is at once the truest and most amusing portrait that we have of the world of *The Yellow Book*. Equally true, equally comic, is the portrait of the Edwardian literary world in 'Argallo and Ledgett'. In '"Savonarola" Brown' we get Max's gift for exuberant fun at its most infectious. Like Buckingham's *Rehearsal* and Sheridan's *Critic* it is a skit on pseudo-poetic tragedy. It is more laughable than either; and it rises at moments to be a parody not just of pseudo-tragedy but of Shakespeare himself.

. . . For in the end it is to Max's comedy one returns when attempting to analyse his achievement. It is its central pervading characteristic and that which gives him his place in literature. A distinguished place: Max is not a giant of the art of letters but still less is he one of its dwarfs—except to those who rate the comic element in human existence as of minor importance. For me, his work is the finest, richest expression of the spirit of comedy in all twentieth-century English literature, and the most varied, ranging, as it does, from the subtle satire of 'Enoch Soames' to the extravagant fantasy of *Zuleika Dobson*, from the ironic moralising of *The Happy Hypocrite* to the ironic pathos of 'William and Mary', from the psychological comedy of 'James Pethel' to the sheer rollicking fun of '"How Shall I Word It?"' It shines equally in a sustained passage of comic eloquence like the Duke of Dorset's proposal to Zuleika and in a concentrated epigrammatic phrase, as when Max says of the fashionable sages of his period: 'It distresses me, this failure to keep pace with the leaders of thought, as they pass into oblivion.'

BRENDAN BEHAN

1923–1964

Brendan Behan was born in Dublin on February 9, 1923. His father, a member of the Irish Republican Army, was in an English prison at the time. At age nine Behan joined the IRA's youth organization, Fianna Eireann; at thirteen, he wrote a series of anti-Fascist articles for an IRA newspaper; at fourteen, he was expelled from Catholic school and apprenticed to a house painter. Behan entered the ranks of the IRA in 1939, but was arrested in Liverpool while delivering a suitcase of explosives for his first mission. After two months in prison, he was sent to a borstal, an English reform school. Released in 1942, Behan was soon arrested for shooting at police and served three years in an Irish prison.

Over the next few years Behan worked as a house painter, a seaman, a pimp, a singer, and a journalist. He wrote his first play, *The Quare Fellow*, in 1954, drawing on his prison experience. A production at the tiny Pike Theatre in Dublin impressed the director-producer Joan Littlewood, who brought Behan to London to revise the play for her experimental company, The Theatre Workshop. At this time Behan met and married Beatrice ffrench-Salkeld, a painter. They later had one daughter. The new version of *The Quare Fellow* was extremely successful in England and America in 1956. Behan wrote his next play in Gaelic, then translated and adapted it for Littlewood. The result, *The Hostage*, was a satirical collage of dialogue, songs, dances, and jokes, which poked fun at the IRA as well as the English. It proved as successful as its predecessor. Behan's 1959 autobiography, *Borstal Boy*, was banned in Ireland; it was later adapted for the stage.

As Behan's drinking grew heavier, he turned to the tape recorder, dictating several rambling travel books and a sequel to *Borstal Boy*. He died of alcoholic complications on March 20, 1964.

Personal

Brendan's whole life had been conditioned by a hatred of England. His period in Borstal and his acquaintanceship with both Joyce and the boys with whom he became friends there, gave him a new image to grapple with, that of the decent Englishman, which he gradually began to blend with his political beliefs. At Borstal, in fact, he learned to play up to the English. In the British Isles, none of the four nationalities is more popular with the English than the Irish. The Irishman seems to embody all that the Englishman seems to have exorcised from his life in the pursuit of duty. He is the anti-self of the Saxon. With his wealth of colourful phrases, his songs, and wit, his quaint proverbs, his laughing, joyful personality, Brendan was the most popular boy at Hollesley Bay.

'He's a comical bastard, ain't he?' his mates used to boast when a new prisoner met Brendan. Phrases like 'He'd say Mass if he knew Latin', or 'He'd mind mice at a cross-roads', had a sharpness which appealed to the working-class ear, and an imagery which at the same time they found impossible to duplicate. He learned quickly what the English demanded of the Irish in order to enjoy them. He found the formula and played up to it. He wanted to please, to be liked. All his life this was to plague him—the desire to shine: the fatal formula he found in Borstal of how to play Paddy to the Saxon was to contribute to his downfall when he set out to conquer the world of letters and drama in London twenty years later.—ULICK O'CONNOR, *Brendan Behan*, 1970, p. 59

General

The Behan story, in a way, begins with the Playboy riots of 1907. Irish nationalism, the Establishment-to-be, had fuelled (and, of course, was fuelled by) the new drama but Synge had dared to call a spade a shovel, and so rose the hullabaloo-clamorous reminder that, it there was to be theatre in Ireland, it must be theatre according to the rules. The O'Casey riots emphasised the point, and O'Casey's departure—granted his quarrel was more with The Abbey than the mob—was, in its consequences, an Establishment victory. Denis Johnston, through the '30s, was too hot for The Abbey to handle—The Gate Theatre gave him refuge. By the '40s, respectability had won: the writers had been driven from theatre to the comparative safety of the short-story and the lyric poem. Do you dare to write a play? Behan dared but, by now, the venue had to be London. Truth might flourish in Stratford E.15, but, in Dublin the blinds were down.

This then—the manner in which the stifling of a theatre is illustrated—is an important part of the story. There is, however, something more to be said: it may well be that Behan, with all his naked vitality, ultimately won. Censors cannot provide for everything. Even if he had to campaign from abroad, such was the brio of his gift that polite and politic Ireland shuddered—and in the shudder was undone: the spasm was irrevocable, charted. No Vance Packard is needed to detect that the island can never be the same again.—Tom Mac-Intyre, "This Dying Lark" (1965), *The Art of Brendan Behan*, ed. E. H. Mikhail, 1974, p. 63

The fact that Behan's work was never very well understood must have caused him considerable pain and must also have affirmed his suspicions of his deficiencies. Most of what has been written about Behan, either during his own lifetime or since, deals with the real issues of Behan's work only in the most cursory way. Augustine Martin's *Threshold* article on Behan is an excellent case in point, but it must be added that Martin is not any more guilty of distortion than most of the others who have written about Behan. The "quare fellow" who gives Behan's first full-length play its title is, as Behan wrote the script, condemned to death for the murder of his brother; but Martin identifies the "quare fellow's" crime as that of murdering his wife. The hangman in *The Quare Fellow* is a boisterous sort who is very much bothered by taking the life of another human being. As a consequence of the guilt he feels, the hangman can do his job only if he is drunk. To insure that he is not too drunk to perform, the hangman brings a keeper with him to each job. Martin, apparently remembering the hangman's keeper, identifies the hangman as "a cheerful, innocuous little man who sees the execution simply as a job to be done." Martin correctly identifies the effectiveness of the humor in Behan's play, but his failure to correctly identify either the crime of the "quare fellow" or the identity of the hangman must ultimately lead to an inaccurate interpretation. It seems the journalists and critics expected very little of Behan's work, and therefore did not think it worth their while to examine it too closely.

Behan undoubtedly deserved more serious critical attention than he received, but he was not sure enough of his writing to demand such attention. As it was, he drew the gaze of the critics and the public alike away from his work by building a public image which gave the world exactly what it expected from him. He was too gentle and amiable, too weak and unsure, to do otherwise.

The shame is that Behan believed that only sensationalism—in his work and in his life—was required of him. Perhaps, if the critics had required more of him, he would have demanded more of himself. Certainly he would not have been satisfied to remain a house painter, for the audience he would have found as a painter who also sang and told clever stories simply would not have satiated him. He needed a larger audience; and, though he indeed gained it, he gained it perhaps a bit too easily. His talent and his need to be heard were so great that he surely could have raised the quality of his writing to meet the more objective critical standards which should have been applied to his work from the start. However imperceptive the criticism of Behan's work was, it surely acted only as a catalyst. Behan's suicidal insecurity would in any case have eventually killed him and his work.

The stage personality of the Irish drunk which Behan had before used as a tool to call attention to his writing became in the last five or six years of his life his reason for being, his substitute for work. This sensitive, intelligent, and perceptive man, this writer who could make an obscure "quare" fellow universally interesting, was at the last frantically attempting to make his false personality interesting by dropping names which had associated with it. In that sad and almost totally insignificant book, *Brendan Behan's New York*, Behan is forced

to fill his pages, or more accurately his tape, with reminiscences of the famous. At a *bar mizvah* service for Leonard Lyons' son, he meets Frank Loesser, Ethel Merman, and Paddy Chayevsky. Tallulah Bankhead tells him a tired joke. In Greenwich Village he meets Allen Ginsberg, Jack Kerouac, Thornton Wilder, and the late James Thurber. Behan simply thought none of his own work worth talking about. He drank more and more to hide this horrible fact from himself, and finally his liver died, his brain and creativity having preceded it by about three years.

Certainly few have had as many reasons to drink as did Brendan Behan. He was indeed a kind and sensitive person; in fact, too sensitive, says brother Brian: "Underneath his ebullience he was a quivering mass of too much feeling. Feelings deep, raw and violent that were liable to explode at the slightest provocation. Then like a mad stallion he couldn't bear to be bridled by anyone." Brendan cared too much for his family, for his church, and for Ireland. His family, because of its poverty and Behan's years in jail could not, unfortunately, equip him with much stability. The church excommunicated him. English cruelty and Irish stupidity destroyed the Ireland he worked for. He cared; he was frustrated; and he attempted to hide this frustration behind enormous waterfalls of booze. He was a romantic, and he laughed and he drank largely because he was sensitive enough to discern the absurdity of his idealistic commitment in a world and nation where the rewards seemed to be greatest for the cynics and the non-committed.—Ted E. Boyle, "Life and Influences," *Brendan Behan*, 1969, pp. 29–30

Works

It is a curious fact that Behan's plays, which are much more daring and outrageous than O'Casey's and Synge's, have scarcely caused a murmur of protest when they were presented in Dublin. Perhaps Irish audiences have seen their essential seriousness, perhaps they have recognised the essential tho' carefully disguised innocence . . . perhaps they feel more kinship with the inherent Catholic consciousness that informs them. It must be remembered that all our great playwrights, Yeats, Synge, O'Casey, Wilde, Goldsmith, Beckett, have been in the Protestant tradition. In any case Mr. Gabriel Fallon has had this to say of Behan's work:

> He has merely taken life as he found it and constructed in his own terms with a facility, which at its highest point, amounts to genius. That he has done so to the annoyance of self-appointed moralists and professional patriots is, perhaps inevitable in this country which still cherishes a skin-deep supersensitiveness as its greatest virtue. Behan is not asking us for our laughter. Properly understood, he demands our understanding, our pity, our sympathy and—should we possess such a quality—our Christian charity.

This, to me, seems to get to the heart of Behan's elaborately concealed preoccupation. He wished us to see with the spirit of charity that whole region of agony, anguish and tragic absurdity that lurks at the darker frontiers of our world. (If there is an existentialist ring about these terms it is deliberate. Behan is more of a European than his Irishy act might suggest and it may be significant that Gabriel Marcel found *The Hostage* "deeply impressive".)

Hitherto we have seen this world imperfectly, thro' the distorting lenses of conventional cliché. Behan, especially in *The Hostage*, makes war on the cliché views of things, the theatrical half-truths that surround death, patriotism, religion, love. Here again a man is sentenced to death. In this case he is not guilty of any particular offence. He is a young English soldier called Leslie, and the I.R.A. have captured him as a hostage and intend to shoot him if one of their own men who has been sentenced to death is executed. He is imprisoned in a Dublin brothel where Behan has assembled a company of prostitutes, fanatics, perverts, and eccentrics. Here Leslie is forced to wait and listen to the songs, jokes, sententious posturings, religious and patriotic platitudes that Behan puts in the mouths of his characters and which he deploys in brilliant and hilarious juxtaposition. An innocent young servant girl called Teresa befriends him and these are really the only two characters on the stage. Everyone else is in varying degree the mouthpiece for some petrified and lifeless platitude. The mad Monsewer with his kilt and bag-pipes who thinks the "Troubles" are still going on; he is given that old song "The captains and the Kings" which he sings at a most incongruous moment, nostalgically recalling gracious Georgian days:

> By the moon that shines above us
> In the misty morn and night,
> Let us cease to run ourselves down
> And thank God that we are white,
> And better still are English
> Tea and toast and muffin rings
> Old ladies with stern faces
> And the captains and the kings.

There is the enigmatic Mulleady: "I'm a secret policeman and I don't care who knows it!" Miss Gilchrist the badly damaged religious fanatic, Pat the wounded veteran of the old I.R.A., the perverts Princess Grace and Rio Rita. This mad meaningless swirl of figures revolves round the bewildered Leslie who can scarcely grasp or believe the reality of his salvation. Eventually he is killed and the whirl momentarily stops, and Teresa is given one brief poignant speech over his body:

> . . . I will never forget him. He died in a strange
> land and at home he has no one. I will never forget
> you, Leslie. Never till the end of time.

It looks for a moment as if the play is going to dissolve in pathos, but this is the one thing Behan cannot allow. Instead he has Leslie jump up and lead the company in a final song. This ending has offended many critics. Mr. Sam Hynes in an interesting article in the American periodical *Commonweal* states the case thus:

> In the end the hostage dies a meaningless accidental
> death, and then hops up again to sing a comic song.
> The whole play oscillates between irony and pity:
> irony without purpose and pity without focus. But
> purposeless irony is a final denial of values and un-
> focussed pity is sentimentality.

This is clear and trenchant reasoning, if the premises are correct. But supposing Behan has a purpose beyond those gestured towards by Mr. Hynes! I suggest that Behan wants to demonstrate that there is essentially something meaningless and accidental about all political assassinations. That he refuses to treat death with the reverence of traditional drama precisely because modern man does not treat it with the reverence and pathos of traditional man. In other words he is not recoiling from or dismissing the fundamental significance of death but underlining and satirising a whole modern attitude, and his ending is really his master-stroke, the ironical twist that throws the whole play back into perspective. And finally the song Leslie sings is not so very comic really. It is an old song that goes:

> The bells of hell
> Go ting-a-ling-a-ling
> For you and not for me.
> Oh death where is thy sting-a-ling-a-ling
> Or grave thy victory?

The song, sung by the dead man, refuses to let the audience comfort itself with any sort of phoney pathos. It points out to us our fundamental indifference, the "I'm alright Jackery" exhibited by the world as represented on the stage. And ironically as the song ends the world goes on doing just that:

> If you meet the undertaker
> Or the young man from the Pru
> Get a pint with what is over
> Now I'll say goodbye to you.

In fact Behan thinks that death is important enough not to be clothed in clichés. Mr. Hynes claims that this is all "the tough con's refusal to expose himself to emotion!" I believe that is true, but it is by no means the whole truth.

I would therefore suggest that *The Hostage* is primarily a satire. It is not delicate nor indeed always successful satire. But it is not without reverence. It is not patriotism, religion or sex that he is attacking but rather the false attitudes we adopt towards them, the clichés in which we express these attitudes and in which all their falsehood is petrified and perpetuated. This is the purpose of all the songs and set speeches. These songs and speeches, couched in their appropriate clichés, are set against a background and a moment that exposes their fundamental falsehood and absurdity, the half-truths and the mushy sedatives that they dispense. This is Behan's method of shaking people out of their mechanised narcotic stupor. It is basically the method of Shaw and Swift and all the great satirists.

I am not claiming that Behan has already proven himself a great dramatist. His faults are all too obvious. He is often obscure, inclined to substitute vulgarity for wit, given at times to dreadful stage-Irishy both in dialogue and sentiment. He obviously finds great difficulty with construction and no one knows how great his debt is to Joan Littlewood in this respect. However, it cannot be denied that with her he has pioneered a new dramatic form in the modern theatre. His *Hostage* has been a great blast of fresh air blowing thro' contemporary drama, it has really been a cleansing influence, for Behan's sensibility is essentially robust and healthy. He has restored the belly-laugh to its proper place in serious theatre; it had been absent since the days of the great Elizabethans. This in itself is a very considerable achievement.—AUGUSTINE MARTIN, "Brendan Behan" (1963), *The Art of Brendan Behan*, 1974, pp. 59–62

The Quare Fellow, set in an Irish prison on the eve of an execution, is a direct result of Behan's experiences during his prison years. In *Confessions of an Irish Rebel*, he in fact relates the exact incident which inspired the play:

> "Being summer, I had come in late from the exercis-
> ing yard after a game of hand-ball with a young fel-
> low from Limerick called Hickey. . . . On this day as
> Hickey and I came in together, Bernard Kirwan was
> with his visitors and two warders, and shoving aside
> the two warders who stood aghast at the idea of a
> condemned man having contact with anybody, he
> dashed out from the cell and he embraced us
> both. . . . Years later I based my play 'The Quare
> Fellow' on the last few weeks of this man's life."

The Quare Fellow is not, however, simply a reportorial account of Bernard Kirwan's last weeks and execution. It is

Behan's unique, tragi-comic observation of man's schizoid nature—his capacity for evil, and his bent for kindness. As Kenneth Tynan noted in his review of *The Quare Fellow*, "Behan's convicts behave with hair-raising jocularity, exchanging obscene insults even while they are digging the murderer's grave. . . . With superb dramatic tact, the tragedy is concealed beneath layer after layer of rough comedy." Tynan was not alone in sensing the unorthodox tone of the play. John Russell Taylor, in *Anger and After*, states that "In *The Quare Fellow* the tragic undertones are always present, and though they are seldom insisted on we are conscious throughout of a sensation in the comedy akin to that of dancing on a coffin-lid." Such dancing may be exactly what Behan had in mind in *The Quare Fellow*, and Behan comes by this propensity naturally, for this sort of behavior is an integral part of the time-honored Irish wake. Says Vivian Mercier, in *The Irish Comic Tradition*,

> The Irish propensity for macabre humour may easily be traced to the world-renowned Irish wakes, at which merriment alternates with or triumphs over mourning, in the very presence of the corpse. Convivial drinking and cheerful conversation are the best-known features of modern wakes, but it is generally accepted that dancing, singing, and horse-play formed an essential part of the wakes in earlier times. Few people nowadays, even in Ireland, are aware that the old horse-play included some quite elaborate mimed dramas, reminiscent of fertility ritual. Lady Wilde went so far as to write "The Wake Orgies," while Henry Morris believed that the wake games "came down in unbroken descent through all the centuries from the Cluichthe Caointe, or 'Games of Lamentation,' mentioned so frequently in our pagan Irish literature." The similarity between the ancient Irish games and the funeral games so familiar in Homer has often been pointed out. In *A Handbook of Irish Folklore* Mr. Seán Ó Súlleabháin lists 130 specific wake games, besides a number of more informal wake amusements; among the latter we find "performing tricks on the corpse," a practice which might be the cause or effect of a macabre sense of humour but clearly has ritual status also.

Obviously, however, many critics do not understand this comic-macabre aspect of *The Quare Fellow*. Judith Crist sees the play as a rather shallow bit of propaganda directed largely toward the evils of capital punishment: "No one says anything that has not been said in dozens of other prison dramas . . . there is little comedy and less drama on the stage." In his objection to *The Quare Fellow* Richard Hayes asserts that "Capital punishment . . . is at once too proximate and too remote to provoke us to responses other than luxurious indignation or sadistic curiosity."

The Quare Fellow is, however, much more than a humorous diatribe against capital punishment. Certainly, by the time the curtain drops on this "comedy-drama," the viewer is aware that Behan is against the death penalty—as what ex-prisoner might not be. But *The Quare Fellow* is only incidentally an indictment of capital punishment. The play transcends any specific human cruelty. It is essentially a satire and a celebration—a satire on man's stupidity and a celebration of man's irrepressible vitality.—TED E. BOYLE, "The Quare Fellow," *Brendan Behan*, 1969, pp. 69–71

Borstal Boy reflects Behan's true mental state. . . . This is not a hero's book. From the moment he is arrested, his main concern is to save his skin. He would never dream of assaulting an officer for two reasons: one is that he has "no wish to commit suicide", and the other that

from a mixture of cowardice and laziness—two parts cowardice to one part laziness—and the fear of not being sure of winning, I don't like tangling with anyone. . . .

Behan often feels desperate, particularly in Walton Jail. The change from freedom to captivity must be worse for a boy of sixteen than for an experienced political fanatic. The first Sunday in Walton brings this situation home to Behan:

> I could not even walk, but sat huddled on the bed in my blankets, with tears in my mind and in my heart, and wishing I could wake up and find out that I had only been dreaming this. . . .

And misery is to stay with him continuously in Walton but, and this is important, he never feels completely downcast. His hope remains unbroken:

> The outside gate closed on us. As it swung to, I saw the bit of road outside. There was an old man going past, shoving a handcart before him, his breath steaming on the cold air. As he looked in, I suppose he said to himself, "You're never bad but you could be worse," and pushed on in better heart.

Behan's own attitude is reflected in the old man's words. When he is brought back from the Assizes he notes how "it was great for a minute to stand there and hear the traffic . . . and feel thousands of free people about us." Such a passage makes the book so different from what other prison writers said before Behan: he is not preoccupied with the hatred of his gaolers but tries to enjoy the moment whenever possible. If he finds a good-natured warder he has a good word for him, and when he finds an opportunity to turn "a bad time . . . into a grand one", he takes it, which is all the more easy for him since he has "a sense of humour that would nearly cause me to burst out laughing at a funeral, providing it was not my own." While Behan rests content with little in Walton, he enjoys thoroughly his time in Hollesley, where he rejects any suggestion of escape.

When reading Irish prison literature, the only answer to James Stephens' question "can one's mind go to prison as well as one's body?" is "Yes". The minds of most Irish prison writers were affected by the walls that cut them off from their normal social environment. Behan kept his normal reactions. He was fortunate enough to be of strong mental health and to be gifted with an exceptional memory; both features together helped him to overcome the dull and desperate moments. In view of his almost unresisting acceptance of prison, *Borstal Boy* almost parodies the autobiographical cliché of the unknown artistic talent suffering in a public school, misunderstood by the world that surrounds him.

Behan brings humour and sometimes even an atmosphere of relaxation into his narration. These bright moments are necessarily less frequent in the dull atmosphere of Walton than in the friendlier surroundings of Feltham and Hollesley. To make the best of his internment, he conforms to the rules imposed on him; like Rossa he goes "in for being civil to those who can help myself or my country." This, together with his self-confidence and friendliness, makes him a personality respected by warders and prisoners alike. He is always looking for contact and is quickly accepted by others. Once he has become the "china" of one of the other fellows, this relationship is respected by all. Not everyone qualifies as a friend, but once such a relation is established, it is "a double diabolical bloody liberty" to interfere with it. Harty, for instance, gets a considerable shock when he realizes that Behan has not accepted him as a friend. Yet of all the people Behan meets during his stay in three various institutions only one boy is looked upon and treated as an outsider. Even the few women in Hollesley were accepted by the boys unconditionally. Not so Ken, for whom Behan's liking grows the more desperate Ken's situation becomes. The reason for Ken's loneliness lies in his different social background and Behan is the only one to understand this. Although he himself was much more of an exception in Borstal since he had not been sentenced for a crime, he felt nearer to the other boys than Ken because

> I had the same rearing as most of them. . . . All our mothers had all done the pawn-pledging on Monday, releasing on Saturday. We all knew the chip shop and the picture house and the fourpenny rush of a Saturday afternoon. . . .

. . . Behan's humour draws strength from a lively sense of disproportion. Johnston and Mooney, two warders in Walton, "were in charge of the Young Prisoners because they had special qualifications in Y.P. training." Whether Behan speaks the truth or not when he adds that "Johnston had been twelve years in the Scots Guards and Mooney had been middle-weight champion of India" does not matter—the ironic characterisation criticizes the jail's staff policy. He bears his isolation with dignity. When he gets Number One treatment, he suddenly realizes that he should give up humming a carol of Thomas Hardy's because "it does not look the thing not to look unhappy in the nick, especially and they going to the trouble of putting you on Number One."

Sometimes irony is mixed with sarcasm, particularly when he feels attacked by opportunistic countrymen, or when the discrepancy between a writer's impression and reality goes too far for him. He comments on Bernard Shaw's saying that no man was ever the same after having seen the Irish Sea at dawn or sunset:

> You could sing that if there was an air to it. I know a good many . . . that are not the same after seeing it, and some of them hung or shot, or gone mad, or otherwise unable to tell the difference.

Yet he does not exclude himself from ironic criticism. When he realizes that he missed the chance to help another boy he adds, self-mockingly, "there's a fearless rebel for you."

. . . Behan's ability for exact observation enables him to describe a character in few words. In *Borstal Boy* a great number of officials and prisoners are described, and Behan is able to give each of them his characteristic life. He draws his figures by setting them off against the dull and tedious background; the photographer, whom he saw only once for a few minutes

> was a young man with a pin head and a little moustache. He was wearing a sports coat and flannels. I could not imagine him laughing or being excited but at a cricket match.

His descriptions of prison officers are particularly colourful. The doctor in Walton Jail is

> a dark man, not very old, and very hard in an English way that tries to be dignified and a member of the master race that would burn a black man alive or put a pregnant woman out the side of the road in the interests of stern duty . . . the doctor set his lips and spoke through them, like an English officer in a film about the Khyber Pass.

The Governor comes off somewhat better:

> a desiccated old man, in tweed clothes and wearing a cap, as befitted his rank of Englishman, and looking as if he would ride a horse if he had one.

If Behan uses clichés he tries to modify them. When he says of Inspector Sullivan that he had "the thin lips of an Englishman", he adds at once: "and that was all right, too—wasn't it his country, to have any kind of lips he liked?"

. . . *Borstal Boy* contains a number of thoughts on the I.R.A. though it is not a political confession. The two official statements he makes, one after his arrest, the other in the dock, are part of a formality. When he says to the inspector, "the I.R.A. does not let me into all its secrets" and "I know something, of course, of the I.R.A. in Dublin, but . . . I'm not a G.H.Q. man", he speaks the truth. His part in the organisation was indeed of minor importance. For all that he keeps up the Republican ideal, but is careful to distinguish himself from the "crawthumpers" in the I.R.A., from those

> wrap-the-green-flag-round-me junior Civil Servants that came into the I.R.A. from the Irish League, and well ready to die for their country any day of the week, purity in their hearts, truth on their lips, for the glory of God and the honour of Ireland.

If he is sometimes attacked verbally by warders and boys about his I.R.A. activities, he is careful not to get excited about it and to reply merely in his mind. We note that he never defends the I.R.A.'s policies but only the individuals who, out of conviction, fight for their country. He shows a keen sense of justice.—PETER RENÉ GERDES, *"Borstal Boy," The Major Works of Brendan Behan,* 1973, pp. 112–19

The Quare Fellow is set in an Irish prison, and its three acts cover approximately twenty-four hours. What distinguishes these hours from all the others of prison routine is that they precede an execution, carried out at the end of the final act, and what the play presents is the manner in which both prisoners and wardens live out those twenty-four hours in the shadow of death. Although there is a great deal said about hanging and although the play is strongly opposed to legalized execution, *The Quare Fellow* is not merely a diatribe against capital punishment. It is a study of human nature which irreverently but compassionately confronts man with a reflection of himself, his society, and the facile distinctions he makes about his own behavior and that of his fellow creatures. Not only are the penal system and government-sanctioned executions subjected to close scrutiny, but so are public attitudes toward such matters as sex, politics, and religion.

Although it deals with a number of serious themes, *The Quare Fellow* is filled with humor, much of it hilarious. However, within almost every humorous line and scene there is a bite. Spontaneously one laughs at the deftly delivered witticisms, only to sense, in the midst of laughing, the presence of pain. This occurs time after time, and the viewer, while enjoying the gaiety of the proceedings, sees his prejudices, pretensions, and preconceptions, and those of his society, exposed for what they are. Viewing the play is a bittersweet experience out of which emerges an energetic affirmation of life.— RAYMOND J. PORTER, *Brendan Behan,* 1973, pp. 20–21

HILAIRE BELLOC

1870–1953

Joseph Hilaire Peter René Belloc was born on July 27, 1870 in St. Cloud, France. He grew up there and in Sussex, England, to which he returned in his late thirties. His sister later achieved fame as thriller writer Marie Belloc Lowndes. Belloc left school at seventeen to travel through England, France, and the United States. After a year as a French soldier, he entered Balliol College, Oxford, from which he graduated in 1895. Belloc married in 1896, the year he published his first two books. In 1899 he moved from Oxford to London and plunged into journalism and politics, working with G. K. Chesterton against the Boer War. The two grew so close that George Bernard Shaw referred to them as "the Chesterbelloc."

Belloc became a British citizen in 1902, and wrote his most successful book, *The Path to Rome*, the same year. From 1906 to 1910 he sat with the Liberals in Parliament and edited a Conservative newspaper. He lost both posts after decrying Jews, Protestants, and political corruption on the floor of the House of Commons. Belloc then founded his own newspaper, *The Eye-witness*, which he edited in 1911. The death of his wife in 1914 shook him badly—Belloc wore only black for the rest of his life. During World War I he wrote and edited a hugely popular weekly war journal, and lectured on military history at Trinity College, Cambridge. After the war he continued to write profusely; he eventually produced more than 150 books, including novels, histories, political tracts (increasingly conservative as he aged), travelogues, children's verse, poetry, and essays. He was fiercely Catholic and determinedly anti-socialist, and had little patience with anyone who wasn't. His wit was renowned, although his most famous epigram is often misattributed to Oscar Wilde: "When I am dead / I hope it may be said / 'His sins were scarlet, but his books were read.'"

Belloc had five children; his eldest son died in World War I, his youngest in World War II, after which he ceased to write. He died on July 17, 1953.

Personal

I still have very clearly in memory the appearance of Belloc as I first saw him. He must have been slightly over thirty, not very tall but very broad-shouldered and with that fine head cocked at its usual considering angle. He bent over a small table, smiling, his big white shirtfront bulging; and he surveyed the congregated Fabians as if they were simple-minded children to whom he was unfolding the wonders of the universe. In fact he was explaining, among other things, with much salt, a few of the fallacies which lay fatally behind the principles of their own movement. He was confident, gay, rich in lively asides or extravagant alternative phrases. He made everybody laugh— that was intended—as his tongue played with the words of triumphant ridicule; and having made them laugh he slew them. Never was there such a Fabian slaughter.

I recall him at another time, also at a Fabian meeting (and a public one, for I was never a Fabian), speaking rather quietly, and somehow less confidently, at the Memorial Hall in Farringdon Street. I think he had been severely attacked at a previous meeting: at any rate he had papers with him, and may have been reading or carefully speaking from notes. And so low did he hold his head that somebody, hoping to disconcert him, called from the back of the hall: "Speak up!" There was a hush at the interrupter's cheek; but Belloc, lifting his head, only smiled, and like lightning answered the affront. The fluty French voice, rather high-pitched but never otherwise than pure and fluent; the French "r" that is very nearly a "w"; the arrogance which his former modest demeanour had concealed—all rose. He called out: "It's all wight: I'm only talking to myself." The interrupter's brief advantage was destroyed; and the lecture proceeded with increased animation on the speaker's part.

Belloc is no longer the same young and triumphant man of those early days. He is stouter, more preoccupied. The keenness of his face has roughened, and his colour is deeper. Having grown small side-whiskers, he would look like John Bull if he did not look like a French parish priest. His black cloak and low-crowned black felt hat increase the priestly effect, and I do not think that Belloc has ever lost pride in the fact that he was born a Frenchman; but there is none the less a good English look to him which also, I hope, he would not disclaim. He is more considerate of fools than he used to be. He reads Trollope at nights, and spends much time at his home in Sussex, where he writes more histories and biographies in praise of the Catholic Church, and more satirical tales for Chesterton to illustrate, but no more accounts of his journeys in France or North Africa or of the Four Men who made such songs of good wine and good ale and the Sussex inns. Alas that it should be so!—FRANK SWINNERTON, "Catholic Liberalism," *The Georgian Scene*, 1934, pp. 90–91

In the days when Belloc was known to Bentley and Oldershaw, but not to me, when they were all together in the Radical group at Oxford, Belloc himself chiefly frequented a much smaller group which called itself the Republican Club. So far as I can make out, the Republican Club never consisted of more than four members, and generally of less; one or more of them having been solemnly expelled either for Toryism or for Socialism. This was the club which Belloc celebrated in the fine dedication of his first book; of which two lines have passed into some popular celebrity: "There's nothing worth the wear of winning but laughter and the love of friends;" but in the course of which he also described in more detail the ideals of this fastidious fellowship.

HILAIRE BELLOC

BRENDAN BEHAN

MAX BEERBOHM

E. F. BENSON

JOHN BETJEMAN

ARNOLD BENNETT

EDMUND BLUNDEN

We kept the Rabelaisian plan
We dignified the dainty cloisters
With Natural Law, the Rights of Man,
Song, Stoicism, Wine and Oysters.

We taught the art of writing things
On men we still would like to throttle,
And where to get the blood of kings
At only half-a-crown a bottle.

Of the three other corners of this very Four-Square Gospel of Citizenship, that is of Belloc's three constant colleagues in the old Republican Club, one is still, I believe, a distinguished exile and official in Burma; or as his old friends loved to say with sour smiles of affectionate resignation, "a Satrap"; as if he had somehow Medised, or condescended to the oriental barbarism which we call Imperialism. I have no doubt that as a fact he was a happy and highly satisfactory Satrap; but he was the one member of the group whom I never met. The other two Republicans, who were Belloc's most intimate friends at Oxford, have both in different ways played a considerable part in my own life. One was John Swinnerton Phillimore, son of the old Admiral whose name made a sort of background for the Kensington of my boyhood, afterwards Latin Professor at Glasgow University and one of the first classical authorities of his time; now, alas, only an ever-deepening memory. The other was Francis Yvon Eccles, the distinguished French scholar, whom I now meet all too seldom through his gravitation towards living in France. . . .

The chief fact relevant to this chapter, however, is that Belloc's career began with the ideals of the Republican Club. To those who talk about ideals, but do not think about ideas, it may seem odd that both he and Eccles have ended as strong Monarchists. But there is a thin difference between good despotism and good democracy; both imply equality, with authority; whether the authority be impersonal or personal. What both detest is oligarchy; even in its more human form of aristocracy, let alone its present repulsive form of plutocracy. Belloc's first faith was in the impersonal authority of the Republic, and he concentrated on its return in the eighteenth century, but rather specially touching its military aspect. His first two books were the very fine monographs on the two most famous of the French Revolutionists; and he was, in that sense, very heartily revolutionary. But I mention the matter here for a special reason, in connection with something in which he was and is rather unique in this country; native and rooted as is his real relation to this country. I have already remarked that to know him well is to know that, as a man, he is English and not French. But there is another aspect in his curious case. In so far as he is a traditionalist, he is an English traditionalist. But when he was specially a revolutionist, he was in the very exact sense a French Revolutionist. And it might be roughly symbolised by saying that he was an English poet but a French soldier.—G. K. CHESTERTON, "Portrait of a Friend," *The Autobiography of G. K. Chesterton,* 1936, pp. 298–302

No one among the generation of our fathers and grandfathers can excite in enlightened liberals such a pleasurable glow of self-righteous indignation as Hilaire Belloc: a notorious and impenitent antisemite; the most militant of all Catholics in an age of intense proselytizing, an ultramontanist who despised Jesus as a milksop but worshipped him as God because the Church told him to do so; a self-styled Republican who preferred the company of aristocrats, a radical in politics who turned against Lloyd George's radical measures because he put before his political principles his hatred of the man as an adulterer and a trickster; an admirer of Napoleon and Mussolini who, he persuaded himself, favoured the common man

despite the enormities against the poor which their military ambition led them to commit; a controversialist who did not even pretend to have a regard for common accuracy, let alone truth, a shameless plagiarizer of his own books (in 1928 and 1929 he wrote twelve and by the end his publications numbered 150)—books which he dictated, leaving the editing of the text and the correction of the proofs to his secretary; a journalist who took jobs as an editor without the faintest intention of appearing in the office and who then fell into a fury when his employers did not recognize that they owed him a living; a fabulous talker and prodigious drinker, a satirist and wit yet with strong claims to go in second wicket down for England as a bore forever repeating the same tales, a man whose ideas were formed by the time he was twenty and who never changed them, who laid down the law on any subject that took his fancy, military affairs being a favourite on which his prognostications were usually wrong; a husband so chaste that he was at a loss for some months how to consummate his marriage satisfactorily, worshipping his wife and yet so indifferent to her feelings that he rarely stayed with her longer than a couple of months before he was off on another tour abroad on his own, a husband who would never come home to dine with her if he could find the company of other roisterers; an absentee father who saw his children for the most part flee his company when they grew up, having known very little of it in their childhood except in the form of his imperious temper; a man of filthy habits, his clothes covered with soup, candle-grease and dandruff, the coat pockets stuffed with a bottle of white port, bread and fishbones; a poet whose light verse alone is read today and whose best-known rhythmic feat, "Do you remember an inn, Miranda?", which inspired a generation of unmarried Fabian ramblers to wander over Europe revelling in the joys of the simple life, now turns out to be addressed, not to a woman (for that would have been to condone fornication), but to echo the family name of the Duke of Miranda who happened once to be the Spanish ambassador in London.— NOEL ANNAN, "The Joys of Bigotry," *TLS,* April 27, 1984, p. 467

General

It may seem irrelevant to touch upon sociology in a sketch primarily devoted to letters; but a living body of writing cannot be divided into watertight compartments, and it is essential to indicate the structure of thought implicit in all its activities. Belloc's sociological beliefs may briefly be outlined thus. That 'widely distributed property as a condition of freedom is necessary to the normal satisfaction of human nature'. That in the high Middle Ages, by the time that peasants had come to own and farm their land, and manufacture and trade were organized by self-governing guilds dedicated to God, an approach to such a life existed. That it could only continue and flourish under a strong centralized monarchy holding and using its power to protect the small man. That the acquisition of monastery lands by a number of powerful families after the Reformation began to sap the royal power, which subsequently dwindled, struggling, until its temporary extinction during the Great Rebellion of the seventeenth century. That it flared up again for two more reigns, but was finally crushed out by the Glorious Revolution of 1688, when rich men got rid of the last King to exert real power, and installed a foreign puppet who would carry out their desires. That because the industrial revolution, a process in itself morally neutral, occurred first in a country governed by an oligarchy concerned with the acquisition of abstract wealth and power rather than with the production and use of concrete objects, it brought about an evil and inhuman oppression of the poor, already cheated out of the lands they held by traditional tenure, through the passage of

Acts of Parliament confiscating all holdings of whose owner-ship no written proof existed. That the event known as 'the glorious palladium of our liberties' was in fact the glorious palladium of the liberty of the powerful to exploit the weak; and that, in order to restore a fully human life to the vast majority of Britain's twentieth century population it was necessary first to realize with humility in what miserable helplessness and frustration they lived, and then to take strong measures com-pletely to alter the structure of society.

The historical justification of these beliefs is put forward in a number of narratives and biographies. A statement of the current situation, and of alternatives for the future is made in *The Servile State* (1912), a remarkable prophecy of economic totalitarianism. Plans for the restoration of that individual eco-nomic independence which is the only solid basis for in-dividual political liberty are outlined in a number of pamphlets and articles and in several books. *Economics for Helen* (1924) sets the claims of freedom and responsibility against those advantages of personal security and general stability which the Servile State may give. *An Essay on the Restoration of Property* (1936) distinguishes between the Distributist and the Social Credit proposals (remarking that the ultimate end of the former is economic freedom, and of the latter increased purchasing power), advocates various means of distributing ownership in land, shops, and collective enterprises, and postulates that there will be no middle way for the future between general small ownership and general (unlabelled) industrial slavery.

Some of these theories were already distastefully familiar in the peaceful, safe, comfortable educated England of forty years ago, as formulated and iterated from the Marxist point of view; notably those concerned with the exploitation of the weak, the meaninglessness of political liberty without eco-nomic power, and the complete inadequacy of the liberal tradi-tion to handle industrial problems. That they should be put forward from a fresh angle, by a man bred up in the Christian tradition and indeed appealing to it, outraged all those who had quietly accepted the belief that their country, 'broadening down from precedent to precedent', was the leader of mankind in its inevitable progress towards perfection. The theories and the proposals were received with that thick, muffling, stifling silence which is the most potent and most infuriating of all defences against unwelcome argument.

Belloc, whose English mother, descended from that un-compromising Unitarian Joseph Priestley, had spent her youth in the unpopular nineteenth century struggle for the emancipa-tion of women, Belloc whose French forefathers had fought in the Revolutionary wars, continued to reiterate his convictions; but there became apparent a note of strain and exasperation, as of one who shouts perpetually at those who are deaf because they will not hear.—RENÉE HAYNES, *Hilaire Belloc*, 1953, pp. 12–14

Works

The essays are so many and various that it is almost impossible to discuss them *en bloc*. They consider with wit, ferocity, learn-ing, personal reminiscence, prejudice, compassion, in-tolerance, common sense, a wide experience of the outer world and a most noble prose style almost every aspect of individual human life; but they do not touch upon science, technics, or any sort of statistical generalization. To read them is like dining at ease with a really great conversationalist; in them the rich-ness and depth of the written word amply replace that air of golden geniality—say the spiritual equivalent of candle-lit cigar-smoke and the lingering vibration of wine—which gives to its spoken counterpart a quality evaporated by print. Some—

products of his years in Parliament, of his unsuccessful struggle for the public auditing of Party funds, and of the libel action in which his paper ⟨the Eye Witness⟩, was involved just before the first world war—are political and polemical. Others discuss incidental aspects of those main themes with which his large-scale books are concerned: religion, history, social patterns, places, buildings, people. Scattered through them all come remarks on the critical assessment of literature and the close consideration of style, and it is evident that these have been his preoccupation on and off throughout his life as a writer. Enor-mous though his own output has been, it becomes clear that its form has never been allowed simply to determine itself like lava cooling into shape after a volcanic eruption. Setting verse aside for the moment, innumerable scattered sentences show that he has been perpetually aware of the various methods and skills and techniques inherent in the writing of good prose. Witness for instance his remarks in praise of Dr. Johnson, that he 'puts all there is to say of a considered judgement . . . into the anti-thetical form, than which no better medium has ever been discovered for condensing and preserving a conclusion'; his pointing out that where Voltaire's verbal 'economy is like a sphere, the maximum content for its surface, Johnson's is like strong soup, a concentration of nourishment'; his condemna-tion of Milton's 'haggis-prose of controversy' and his summary 'there are some men who think that concision is a matter of short words and short sentences. It is not so. Concision is a matter of giving what you have to give in the last compass compatible with lucidity'. His reflections on the rhythms of Tyndale and of Cranmer, those great Scripture translators, show his recognition of the power of prose to shape channels of feeling. They show also a nice discrimination between the kind of prose which is, as it were, a natural phenomenon, a growing thing that needs only pruning and training to bring it to per-fection; and the kind that is deliberately willed, made, carefully and slowly, painfully chiselled by the conscious mind from unwieldy boulders of hard, compressed, unformulated thought. Cranmer's exquisite style was, he contends, of the latter sort. The 'utility-diction', so to speak, of his letters, was as clumsy and tautologous as that of most sixteenth century En-glish correspondence. It was only when he set himself down to his great work, the Prayer Book liturgy, whose cadences were to evoke and to echo Anglican devotion for hundreds of years, that he became 'a jeweller in prose'.

Belloc's own magnificent English should be less read about than read; and preferably read aloud. It is not only a flexible and sensitive and precise instrument for conveying meaning. It can give to the listener a shock of auditory pleasure like that shock of visual delight with which unerring draughts-manship is seen.

A group of admirers have, indeed, modelled their own writings upon its clarity, its muscular rhythm, and its gusto. Few of them, however, have been sustained by an impulse of such strength as Belloc's 'spouting well of joy within that never yet was dried'; and occasionally, as happens with all 'schools', the followers have tended to exaggerate even to caricaturing point the characteristics of their chosen master. In serious writ-ing they have been apt to enlarge and over-simplify outline and emotion, and to overwork and make hackneyed such adjectives as 'great' as a numinous equivalent for 'large' or even 'big'; and in loose-limbed comedy or knockabout satire to force high spirits to such a pitch that one at least of them has been very properly reproached with talking through Mr. Belloc's hat. *Le style c'est l'homme*; but *l'homme* is in the singular.—RENÉE HAYNES, *Hilaire Belloc*, 1953, pp. 20–22

The subject of fame bothered Belloc; he has written of it, and in those later days, when his mind was apt to chew the cud of earlier meditations, it recurred in his talk continually. What was this curious illusion which the human mind can neither analyse nor renounce? I think if he had been offered the choice whether he would rather be remembered by his prose or by his verse, he would have chosen the latter. He used to say that of all his books only four really satisfied him—I am not sure which, but *Belinda* would certainly have been named among them. It was his affectation to talk, sometimes, as if he wrote only for money; poverty and the publishers never allowed him to 'linger in his rightful garden'—that of verse.

Verse he called it, not out of modesty, I think, but because he was old-fashioned enough to think of poetry as something which must be polished and repolished until it was perfect in form. This does him no good with the moderns; our critics, in every kind of art, will only let us admire what is flung at us as a smudge, supposedly representing some impression in the artist's mind, all the better for being shapeless. To smell of the midnight oil damns you. Of such contemporary movements Belloc showed little consciousness, although *The Missing Masterpiece* gives us a hint of what he thought about them. His, in any case, was the classical tradition, deeply rooted in him as in Maurice Baring, though in either case it was difficult to see whence it had sprung. He always talked as if they had taught him precious little Latin and Greek at the Oratory, but his letters written at the time make us hesitate to accept his estimate. I have a copy of *Caliban* in which he inscribed two very mournful lines from the *Iliad*, with four wrong (but quite plausible) accents to show that he did not copy the quotation out of a book. He belonged to that period, that culture, in which a receptive mind refreshed itself, almost unconsciously, at the spring of the Classics.

The same influence penetrated into his style, derivatively, through his admiration of French poetry, and especially that of the Augustan period. When he wanted an instance of superlatively good literature, he referred you to *Le Misanthrope*. Of our own poets I think his favourite, in spite of a profound divergence of temperament, was Milton. In architecture he proclaimed, tirelessly, the Gothic; in literature, it seems to me, all his feeling was for the baroque, its marble simplicity, its dignified restraint. If you want to place him among English poets, you must not put him side by side with his contemporaries, or even with the Victorians. He belongs to the classical period which began with Milton, and ended (for most of us) with Gray.

He belongs to the classical period in his mastery of cadence. By which I mean, not a mere manipulation of sounds, with a musical effect, quite divorced from the sense of what you are saying, and sometimes compelling you to say it unconvincingly—you get it *ad nauseam* in Swinburne. I mean that perfect marriage of sound and sense which now and again, especially in the rounding-off of a poem, creates a kind of stillness in the mind. Such lines, I mean, as:

> They also serve, who only stand and wait,

or:

> And universal darkness buries all.

It is not unknown, to be sure, in recent poetry—Housman knew the magic of it—but Belloc is continually achieving it. In such lines, I mean, as:

> . . . and having seen that stone
> (Which was your image), ride more slowly on,

or:

> And her lips virginal,
> Her virginal white feet,

or (with a devastatingly conversational effect):

> On with my coat and out into the night.

There may be those who are unmoved by such effects; who think them artificial, thought up. Certainly the moderns have no use for them. I only note that they were dear to the Augustans, and to Belloc.—RONALD KNOX, "Introduction" to *Collected Verse*, 1958, pp. 13–15

The fact that a number of Belloc's novels make interesting reading today is a testament to his native talent, for with only a few exceptions he took little interest in them, either during or after their composition. Almost all of the twenty-odd works of fiction were written quickly; most took no more than a couple of weeks. Had he chosen, he could surely have improved the quality of his novels, yet he probably would have left their content and strategy the same. Belloc was an aesthetic conservative; the novel was for him an established genre, like the sonnet, and he never thought in terms of modifying or expanding it. Except for the topicality of his subject matter, his fiction might have been written any time in the nineteenth or even the eighteenth century. Although he lived in a period that could be called the age of the novel, he ignored the more ambitious writers such as Joseph Conrad, Virginia Woolf, and James Joyce.

Belloc's attitude toward most of his fiction derived from his belief that the novel was the least demanding and least exalted of the genres. For a classicist like Belloc, epic poetry was the most noble kind of literary expression. The novel, which emerged as a popular genre as recently as the eighteenth century, was appropriate for writers who were unable to summon the time, intelligence, and magic to create poetry, and for those who needed money quickly. All that Belloc thought necessary for a novel was a thin story line and a talkative narrator. He had plenty of stories, and few writers have been able to talk as easily on so many topics. He simply paced back and forth in his study, dictating his novels.

As a result, the typical Belloc novel has an intrusive narrator and simple characterization. Unlike contemporaries such as Conrad, who often built their novels around the narrator's personality and perception, Belloc almost always used the omniscient narrator—the all-knowing teller of the tale who, more often than not, is indistinguishable from the author. And like Belloc himself, the narrator strays from the story when the mood strikes.

The characters other than the narrator usually remain two-dimensional. Whereas the modern novelists were exploring the inner recesses of their characters' sensibilities, Belloc believed that most people are essentially simple, and therefore that fictional characters could be defined adequately in a few pages. And although the characters do not always fully understand themselves, Belloc never withholds any crucial information from his readers.

Because of his approach to characterization, most of the novels follow a standard pattern. The narrator introduces a character by describing his lineage, social status, profession, physical appearance, and, finally, central personality trait. Often, Belloc presents in this way three or four characters, none of whom seems to have anything to do with any of the others. As the novel progresses, however, relationships entangle them. Eventually, all of the characters are drawn together for the climax and then the resolution of the novel.

Those who pick up a Belloc novel never forget they are reading a book. The prominent narrator prevents them from becoming too involved with any of the characters. In the more successful of the novels the characters are skillfully constructed embodiments of their primary traits, just as are the characters in a comedy of humors from the late Renaissance. In the less successful of the novels the characters are simple marionettes. Either way, Belloc was able to achieve his basic goal: to teach or amuse his readers by telling them a good story. . . .

One of Belloc's favorite books was Samuel Johnson's *Rasselas*, the eighteenth-century philosophical fable about the title character's search for happiness. Whereas the purpose of a novel is usually to convey a complex vision of reality through the interplay of several developed characters, the philosophical fable develops a simple, unified vision of life. De-emphasizing the traditional techniques of fiction—characterization, dialogue, description—the writer of the philosophical fable concentrates on articulating and demonstrating a thesis. A novel is descriptive, a philosophical fable is didactic.

All of Belloc's novels are, to a degree, philosophical fables, for they all quite consciously and deliberately make a point. In addition, Belloc rarely succeeded in creating a fully developed character. A final characteristic of the philosophical fable that is evident in all of his fiction is a heavy reliance on coincidence. In a well-crafted novel the incidents seem to flow naturally and inevitably from the personalities of the characters. Belloc, however, had no interest in realistic motivations. In *A Change in the Cabinet*, for example, when he wants to introduce the comic scene in which the protagonist suffers from the attack of veracititus, Belloc simply arranges for him to receive a crack on the back of the head. The accident happens when the headrest falls off the barber's chair in which the character is sitting; the scene is otherwise unconnected to the story. Once the character receives the blow, Belloc is free to get to his comic scene quickly. . . .

The evolution of Belloc's outlook on life is reflected in his fiction. After his first real novel, *Emmanuel Burden*, he could rarely sustain a sympathetic identification with his subject. Except for *Belinda* and *The Girondin*, the novels show Belloc's increasing sense of aloofness. In the political novels this distancing increases the sharpness of the satire while weakening the other aspects of the fiction. But in the farces Belloc's distancing adds a disturbingly clinical coldness. When he realized that his political novels had no more practical effect on the establishment than any of his other writing did, he tried to transform his satiric vision into a comic one. Yet Belloc could emulate P. G. Wodehouse—whom he called the greatest living writer in English—no more successfully than he could have emulated James Joyce. He could mimic the technique, but the result was all wrong. Fiction was not Belloc's natural medium; only when he was totally engaged by his subject—the French Revolution, idealized romance, and a financier who he hoped would maintain his integrity—could he engage his readers.—MICHAEL H. MARKEL, *Hilaire Belloc*, 1982, pp. 77–98

H. G. WELLS
From "Mr. Belloc's Art of Controversy"
Mr. Belloc Objects to the Outline of History
1926, pp. 1–9

I am responsible for an *Outline of History* which has had a certain vogue. I will assume that it is known by name to the reader. It is a careful summary of man's knowledge of past time. It has recently been reissued with considerable additions in an illustrated form, and Mr. Belloc has made a great attack upon it. He declares that I am violently antagonistic to the Catholic Church, an accusation I deny very earnestly, and he has produced a "Companion" to this *Outline* of mine, following up the periodical issue, part by part, in the *Universe* of

London, in the *Catholic Bulletin* of St. Paul, Minnesota, in the *Southern Cross* of Cape Colony, and possibly elsewhere, in which my alleged errors are exposed and confuted.

Reflections upon the Real Mr. Belloc

Mr. Belloc is a man four years my junior, and his academic career was briefer and not more brilliant than mine. Since he came down from Oxford to the world of London thirty years ago, he has done no original historical work of any distinction. He has been a popular writer as I have been a popular writer, and he is no more if no less a scholar than I am. There has been much incidental and inconsequent brightness in his discursive career—funny verses and stories, an amusing rather than a serious period in Parliament, much pamphleteering, lecturing and speaking; he has been active and erratic; now he would be urging on an anti-Semitic campaign; now, in association with Horatio Bottomley, attempting to hound Masterman, his old friend and rival, out of politics; the war made him the most confident of military "experts," and he has done quite a number of clever revivifications of this or that historical event. That is his record. It gives him a respectable position in the republic of letters, in which also my position is respectable. No doubt he has every right and very considerable qualifications for the criticism of such a popular work as my *Outline*. But there is nothing in his career and nothing in his quality to justify this pose of erudition and insolent superiority he assumes towards me, and which he has made an integral part of his attack. He has assumed it entirely in relation to this controversy. He has thrown ordinary courtesy and good manners to the winds because only in that way can he hope for a controversial advantage over me.

The Clue to Mr. Belloc's Disconcerting Pose

This disconcerting pose is part of his attack. That is why I am obliged to discuss it here. Upon many points the attack is almost pure pose; there is no tangible argument at all. It is very important to note that and bear that in mind. It has to be borne in mind when Mr. Belloc is accused of inordinate vanity or of not knowing his place in the world. I doubt even if he is really very vain. I realised long ago that his apparent arrogance is largely the self-protection of a fundamentally fearful man. He is a stout fellow in a funk. He is the sort of man who talks loud and fast for fear of hearing the other side. There is a frightened thing at the heart of all this burly insolence. He has a faith to defend, and he is not sure of his defence. That mitigates much of his offence, even if it mitigates little of his offensiveness.

Let me say a word or so more of excuse and explanation for him. These personalities of his are, so to speak, not a personal matter. There is more in them than that. Mr. Belloc's attack upon my *Outline* does not stand alone among his activities; it is part of a larger controversy he wages against the modern, the non-Catholic vision of the world. He has carried on that controversy since his Balliol days. The exigencies that oblige him to pretend, against his better knowledge and common civility, that I am petty and provincial and patriotic and wilfully ignorant and pitifully out-of-date, oblige him to pretend as much about most of those who stand for modern science and a modern interpretation of history. He would pretend as hard about Sir Ray Lankester, for example, or about Professor Gilbert Murray or Sir Harry Johnston or Professor Barker, as he does about me. It is a general system of pretence. It is a necessary part of—I will not say of *the* Catholic attitude, but of *his* Catholic attitude towards modern knowledge.

The necessity for a pose involving this pretence is not very difficult to understand. Long before Mr. Belloc embarked upon the present dispute he had become the slave of a tactical fiction, which reiteration had made a reality for him. He evoked the fiction as early, I believe, as his Oxford days. It may have been very effective at Oxford—among the undergraduates. Then perhaps it was consciously a defensive bluff, but certainly it is no longer that. He has come at last to believe absolutely in this creature of his imagination. He has come to believe this: that there is a vast "modern European" culture of which the English-speaking world knows nothing, of which the non-Catholic world knows nothing, and with which he is familiar. It is on his side. It is always on his side. It is simply and purely Belloccian. He certainly believes it is there. It sustains his faith. It assuages the gnawing attacks of self-criticism that must come to him in the night. Throughout these papers he is constantly referring to this imaginary stuff—without ever coming to precisions. Again and again and again and again—and again and again and again, he alludes to this marvellous "European" science and literature, beyond our ken.

He does not quote it; it does not exist for him to quote; but he believes that it exists. He waves his hand impressively in the direction in which it is supposed to be. It is his stand-by, his refuge, his abiding fortress. But, in order to believe in it, it is necessary for him to believe that no other English-speaking men can even read French, and that their scepticism about it is based on some "provincial" prejudice or some hatred of Catholics, or southern people, or "Dagoes," or "foreigners," or what you will. That is why *Nature* wilfully ignores the wonderful science of this "Europe"; and why our Royal Society has no correspondence with it. But he has to imagine it is there and make his readers imagine it is there, and that there is this conspiracy of prejudice to ignore it, before he can even begin to put up any appearance of a case against such a résumé of current knowledge as the *Outline of History*.

BERNARD BERGONZI
From "Chesterton and/or Belloc" (1959)
The Turn of a Century
1973, pp. 130–33

If Chesterton was at his best when writing about books, Belloc was certainly at his best away from them. One need only glance at the brief essay on Jane Austen in these *Selected Essays* to see how little of a critic he was, for his essential egotism prevented him from removing his attention from himself to the work in front of him for very long. But on the other hand he was very much more of an artist than Chesterton. Re-reading his poems for the first time in several years, I was agreeably surprised, for Belloc appears in them as a good minor poet who deserves at least the same reputation as that now enjoyed by Housman: his wish to be remembered primarily as a poet seems eminently reasonable. The epigrams, of course, are deservedly famous, and one wishes we had now a political satirist who could achieve the lethal compression of 'Epitaph on the Politician':

> Here richly, with ridiculous display,
> The Politician's corpse was laid away.
> While all of his acquaintance sneered and slanged
> I wept: for I had longed to see him hanged.

There are few places outside Pope where precisely this note has been struck, and struck so well. Belloc's sonnets suggest that he was one of that remarkably small company of English poets who could genuinely think and feel and write—without apparent effort—in sonnet form. The language is almost as derivative and literary as Chesterton's, but the best of Belloc's

poetry does give one the traditional romantic pleasure of hearing the voice of a vigorous and authentic personality coming through the somewhat threadbare diction and conventional rhythms. To this extent, Belloc is not merely bookish. And a similar quality redeems quite a lot of his bellelettrist prose, which is written according to prescriptions not very likely to recommend it to the modern reader, for Belloc came to literary maturity when the classically-inspired canons of 'beautiful English' and the 'fine style', largely divorced from content, were still the norm. Nowadays we see prose style as much more intimately a function of content, feeling and attitude, and are readily reminded of Max Beerbohm's comment on Pater—'that sedulous ritual wherewith he laid out every sentence as in a shroud'. But the strange thing is that though Belloc wrote prose according to these somewhat external prescriptions, much of it is still good when judged by other standards. One might mention, for instance, the set-piece called 'The Relic' in the present book of essays, which conveys extremely well the intensely personal quality of Belloc's experience in a Spanish church.

In fact, Belloc's apprehension of the world seems to have needed the measured and calculated quality of his prose, or the formality of his verse, in order to be coherently conveyed at all. For despite his aggressively dogmatic and assertive manner, I feel that his inner life often existed on the edge of chaos and near-despair. The tension is certainly apparent in his writing. Though, like Chesterton, he whole-heartedly accepted the Catholic world-picture, Belloc did so as an act of disciplined intellectual assent, whereas Chesterton believed because the whole nature of his mind was constituted to do so. It is, perhaps, these sustaining tensions that give the sense that Belloc was both a greater artist and, for all his disagreeable attitudes, a great man. One sees, for instance, the inner isolation and unhappiness appearing for a moment beneath the rigid mask in the conclusion of his essay, 'On Unknown People':

> How often have I not come upon a corbel of stone carved into the shape of a face, and that face had upon it either horror or laughter or great sweetness or vision, and I have looked at it as I might have looked upon a living face, save that it was more wonderful than most living faces. It carried in it the soul and the mind of the man who made it. But he has been dead these hundreds of years. That corbel cannot be in communion with me, for it is of stone; it is dumb and will not speak to me, though it compels me continually to ask it questions. Its author also is dumb, for he has been dead so long, and I can know nothing about him whatsoever.
>
> Now so it is with any two human minds, not only when they are separated by centuries and by silence, but when they have their being side by side under one roof and are companions all their years.

In fact, Belloc was a good deal closer to the characteristic masters of modern literature than we may at first imagine. He, too, was a *déraciné* figure with a bewildering variety of *personae*: ex-scholar of Balliol, ex-French artilleryman, Sussex farmer, Liberal politician, anti-Dreyfusard, London man of letters, sailor. All these figures in turn inspired different aspects of his writing but never gave him anything like the conviction that a genuine set of cultural roots would have done. It is certainly true that the English connection, and in particular his friendship with Chesterton, were beneficial to him as a man, and modified the potentially sinister elements on his Gallic side. Had he remained wholly a Frenchman it is only too easy to imagine him as a supporter of Maurras, professing a purely 'political' Catholicism, and subsequently a man of Vichy. As it happens, Belloc's devotion to the culture of Western Europe as a whole, and to Catholicism as the incarnation and guardian of that culture, were clearly a form of compensation for his lack of more intimate roots. This devotion, too, was not without its unfortunate side, for it could lead him into such dangerous half-truths as the pronouncement that 'the Faith is Europe, and Europe is the Faith'. Yet it is impossible not to be moved by the extent of Belloc's knowledge and love of England and France and Italy and Spain and the Catholic parts of Germany. He knew these countries and their people and buildings intimately because he had been over most of them on foot. *The Path to Rome* is as much the record of a love-affair as a travel-book. Belloc's concept of 'Western culture' was something much more personal and existential than the purely literary and eclectic kind of 'tradition' compiled by Pound or Eliot, in their rather Adam Verver-ish fashion.

But in a final judgement it is Belloc's lack of interest in a specific literary tradition, and his tendency to oppose flatly the deeper tendencies of his age rather than to interpret and explore them, which makes him remote and inaccessible to present-day criticism. And much the same is true of Chesterton. Together with their non-Christian contemporaries they lived and argued in a world that seems almost as strange and distant as the Paris of Aquinas. Nowadays we tend to agree with Russell that 'it is better to doubt than to believe', and the conceptual apparatus of our literary criticism is made up of hints from Arnold and Richards about the 'free play of ideas' and the 'organisation of impulses'. So we go in fear of the stock response and the pre-existing *Weltanschauung*: thus far has criticism become itself ideological, with its own built-in 'deflections'. Yet this is clearly another and larger matter. Where Chesterton and Belloc are concerned, the Christian humanist is as likely as the agnostic to find them fallen idols rather than living gods in the heaven of literature. But their sleeping features deserve, at the very least, a long and respectful stare, before they are finally eroded by the winds of time.

ARNOLD BENNETT

1867–1931

Enoch Arnold Bennett was born on May 25, 1867, in Staffordshire. As a youth, Bennett worked in his father's law office, then as a law clerk in London. In 1893 he became assistant editor of the weekly magazine *Woman*, moving up to editor in 1896. His first short story had appeared the previous year in *The Yellow Book*; his first novel, *A Man from the North*, was published in 1898. Bennett achieved fame, however, by writing several breathless adventure serials for a newspaper syndicate.

In 1900 Bennett left *Woman*, and in 1901 began writing a series of novels set in the "Five Towns" of Staffordshire. In 1902 he moved to Paris, where five years later he married Marie Soulie. 1908 brought the Five Towns novel *The Old Wives' Tale*, an immediate success with readers; critics generally consider it his best novel. Bennett became a critic himself the same year, penning a book review column for *New Age* as "Jacob Tonson." The column ended in 1911; Bennett would revive it under his own name for the *Evening Standard* in 1926. Also in 1911 he conducted a well-received lecture tour of the United States, despite the handicap of a lifelong speech impediment.

Bennett moved to Essex in 1912, but returned to Paris near the end of World War I to act as minister of propaganda for France. After the war he settled in London, where he entertained lavishly. To maintain his standard of living, Bennett wrote constantly—stories, essays, plays, and thirty-three novels. Critics lamented his inconsistency, but his sales were steady. In 1921 Bennett and his wife separated; in 1922 he met Dorothy Cheston, with whom he had a daughter. The following year his novel *Riceyman Steps* won a James Tait Black Memorial Prize. He died in London on March 27, 1931. His journals were published posthumously in three volumes.

Personal

Consider, to begin with, his astounding appearance. Though he was not actually obese, his outlines had the swelling quality of a balloon. He moved his limbs with a curious stiffness, as if they were thick like a pachyderm's. His head was habitually retracted, as if some one was flourishing a fist in his face and he was dealing with the situation by cool rigidity of bearing. His hair proved that its grayness was not a sign of any serious slackening of vitality by rising in a cockatoo crest. Among the stammerers who have cashed in on their disability he ranked very high, his trick of closing his eyes and holding his mouth open for a moment before he said the important word in the sentence had been developed to the pitch of perfection. His style of dressing had quieted down in later years, and he no longer went to the opera in a shirt front embroidered with green fleur-de-lys, but it was still cumbrous and ornate, rather like English Empire furniture. See him steering this portentous personality through the crowd on a first night, halting to drop the sage and pontifical witticism in the right ears, and ask oneself if Edwin Clayhanger ever for one moment attained to such positive existence.

Yet this figure, though it was certainly Arnold Bennett, though it answered to his name and wrote his books with his hands, was not quite the real Arnold Bennett. It was a creation of the real Arnold Bennett, just as Edwin Clayhanger was. It was a baroque exterior into which a shy man had converted all the oddities of which he was most sensitive, so that he could have somewhere to hide. It was a piece of acting.

What was the character he impersonated? One might call it the perfect Londoner. If one wanted to see Arnold Bennett and the occasion was not urgent, one had no need to make an appointment with him, provided one was going to any important public function during the next few days. He was sure to be there. I can think of no figure in New York which dominates the social scene as he did in London. For he was not only ubiquitous, he was always the most conspicuous person present. His bearing advertised that he was reveling in these circumstances. He seemed to be saying that of course he had assisted at so many of these occasions, and his intensity of being had enabled him to extract so much more from them than ordinary people could, that he could now no longer be stirred to excitement by anything of the sort, though he still enjoyed his special privilege of perception. And that, of course, amounted to staking out his claim to be the ideal metropolitan which the provincial longs to be. But the whole attitude was faintly burlesqued. It was freely admitted that the claim was absurd.—Rebecca West, *Arnold Bennett Himself*, 1931, pp. 5–7

Arnold lived in Montmartre, I think in the rue des Dames, and he had a small dark apartment filled with Empire furniture. He was exceedingly proud of it. It was very tidy. Everything was in its place. It was not very comfortable, and you could not imagine anyone making himself at home in it. It gave you the impression of a man who saw himself in a certain rôle, which he was playing carefully, but into the skin of which he had not quite got. As everyone knows, Arnold had then given up the editing of a magazine called *Woman*, and had settled in Paris to train himself for the profession of literature. He was reading Stendhal and Flaubert, but chiefly Balzac, and I think he told me that in a year he had read through the whole of the *Comédie Humaine*. He was just beginning on the Russians, and talked with enthusiasm of *Anna Karenina*. He thought it, at that time, the greatest novel ever written. I am under the impression that he did not discover Tchekov till much later. When he did he began to admire Tolstoy less. Like everyone else who lives in Paris, he had come across a particular little restaurant where you could get a better meal for less money than anywhere else. This one was on the first floor, somewhere in Montmartre, and now and then I used to go over to dine, Dutch Treat, with him. After dinner we went back to his apartment and he would play Beethoven on a cottage piano. Arnold's plan of campaign was cut and dried. He proposed to make his annual income by writing novels, and by writing plays to make provision for his old age. Because I had lately had my first play produced he gave me one of his to read. I criticised it with vigour. He had made up his mind to write two or three books to get his hand in, and then write a masterpiece. I listened to him, but attached no importance to what he said. I did not think him capable of writing anything of consequence. When I asked him what sort of book his masterpiece was going to be, he said, something on the lines of *A Great Man*; but this, he added, had brought him in nothing at all, and he couldn't afford to go on in that style till he was properly established.

Arnold was good company, and I always enjoyed spending an evening with him, but I did not much like him. He was very cocksure and bumptious, and he was rather common. I do not say this of him depreciatingly, but as I might say of someone else that he was short or fat. I left Paris, and it was many years before I saw much of him again. . . .

The criticism to which he devoted much time during his later years came in for a good deal of adverse comment. He loved his position on the *Evening Standard*. He liked the pow-

er it gave him and enjoyed the interest his articles aroused. The immediate response, like the applause an actor receives after an effective scene, gratified his appetite for actuality. It gave him the illusion, peculiarly pleasant to the author whose avocation necessarily entails a sense of apartness, that he was in the midst of things. He read as a man of letters, and whatever he thought, he said without fear or favour. He had no patience with the precious, the affected, or the pompous. If he thought little of certain writers who are now more praised than read, it is not certain that he thought wrong. He was more interested in life than in art. In criticism he was an amateur. The professional critic is probably somewhat shy of life, for otherwise it is unlikely that he would devote himself to the reading and judging of books rather than to the stress and turmoil of living. He is more at ease with it when the sweat has dried and the acrid odour of humanity has ceased to offend the nostrils. He can be sympathetic enough to the realism of Defoe, and the tumultuous vitality of Balzac, but when it comes to the productions of his own day he feels more comfortable with works in which a deliberately literary attitude has softened the asperities of reality. That is why, I suppose, the praise that was accorded to Arnold Bennett for *The Old Wives' Tale* after his death was cooler than one would have suspected. Some of the critics said that, notwithstanding everything, he had a sense of beauty, and they quoted passages to show his poetic power and his feeling for the mystery of existence. I do not see the point of making out that he had something of what you would like him to have had a great deal more of and ignoring that in which his power and value was. He was neither mystic nor poet. He was interested in material things and in the passions common to all men. He described life, as every writer does, in the terms of his own temperament. He was more concerned with the man in the street than with the exceptional person. Everyone knows that Arnold was afflicted with a very bad stammer: it was painful to watch the struggle he had sometimes to get the words out. It was torture to him. Few realized the exhaustion it caused him to speak. What to most men was as easy as breathing, to him was a constant strain. It tore his nerves to pieces. Few knew the humiliations it exposed him to, the ridicule it excited in many, the impatience it aroused, the awkwardness of feeling that it made people find him tiresome, and the minor exasperation of thinking of a good, amusing or apt remark and not venturing to say it in case the stammer ruined it. Few knew the distressing sense it gave rise to of a bar to complete contact with other men. It may be that, except for the stammer, which forced him to introspection, Arnold would never have become a writer. But I think it is not the least proof of his strong and sane character that, notwithstanding this impediment, he was able to retain his splendid balance and regard the normal life of man from a normal point of view.—W. Somerset Maugham, "Arnold Bennett," *LL*, June 1931, pp. 414–21

Never have I known anyone else so cheerfully objective as Bennett. His world was as bright and hard surfaced as crockery—his *persona* was, as it were, a hard, definite china figurine. What was not precise, factual and contemporary, could not enter into his consciousness. He was friendly and self assured; he knew quite clearly that we were both on our way to social distinction and incomes of several thousands a year. I had not thought of it like that. I was still only getting something between one and two thousand a year, and I did not feel at all secure about getting more. But Bennett knew we couldn't stop there. He had a through ticket and a timetable—and he proved to be right. . . .

We were both about of an age; to be exact he was six months younger than I; we were both hard workers, both pushing up by way of writing from lower middle-class surroundings, where we had little prospect of anything but a restricted salaried life, and we found we were pushing with quite surprising ease; we were learning much the same business, tackling much the same obstacles, encountering similar prejudices and antagonisms and facing similar social occasions. We both had a natural zest for life and we both came out of a good old English radical tradition. We were liberal, sceptical and republican. But beyond this we were very different animals indeed. While I was becoming more and more set upon changing my world and making it something entirely different and while Conrad was equally set upon wringing an unprecedented intensity of phrasing out of his, Bennett was taking the thing that is, for what it was, with a naïve and eager zest. He saw it brighter than it was; he did not see into it and he did not see beyond it. He was like a child at a fair. His only trouble was how to get everything in in the time at his disposal, music, pictures, books, shows, eating, drinking, display, the remarkable clothes one could wear, the remarkable stunts one could do, the unexpected persons, the incessant fresh oddities of people; the whole adorable, incessant, multitudinous lark of it.

There it was. What more could you want?

Since I have just been writing about educated and uneducated types I perceive I am exposed to the question whether Bennett was an educated type. I would say that in my sense of the word he was absolutely immune to education and that he did not need it. He was impermeable. He learnt with extraordinary rapidity and precision. He was full of skills and information. The bright clear mosaic of impressions was continually being added to and all the pieces stayed in their places. He did not feel the need for a philosophy or for a faith or for anything to hold them together. One of the most characteristic, if not the best of his books, is *Imperial Palace*, a most competent assemblage of facts, but told with an exultation, a slight magnification. His self-explanation—explanation rather than analysis—is the *Card*. In that book he shows that he could see himself as plainly and directly as he saw anything else. It is not a self dramatization; it is pleased recognition, even of his own absurdities. *A Great Man* again is delighted self-caricature—even to his youthful bilious attacks. If there was any element of self-deception in his *persona* it was a belief in the luck that comes to men who are "Cards"—Regular Cards. His investments for example were too hopeful. When he died—and he died a well spent man—he left a holding of Russian securities, which he had bought for a rise that never came. . . .

It was perhaps a part of his competent autonomy that Bennett was so remarkably free from the normal infantilism of the human male. He was not so dependent upon women for his comfort and self-respect as most of us are; he was not very deeply interested in them from that point of view. And he had not that capacity for illusion about them which is proper to our sex. The women in his books are for the most part good hard Staffordshire ware, capable, sisterly persons with a tang to their tongues. He seemed always to regard them as curious, wilful creatures—to be treated with a kind of humorous wariness. There were pleasures in love but they had their place among other pleasures. To have a mistress in France was, he felt, part of the *ensemble* of a literary artist, and afterwards it seemed to him right that the household of a rapidly rising novelist should have a smart, attractive wife, a really well-dressed wife. So that he set about marrying rather as he set about house-hunting. For him it was as objective a business as everything else. Marriage wasn't by any means that organic life association at once accidental and inevitable, that ingrowing intimacy, that it is for less lucidly constituted minds.

Yet he was not cold-hearted; he was a very affectionate man. Indeed he radiated and evoked affection to an unusual degree, but in some way that I find obscure and perplexing his sexual life did not flood into his general life. His personality never, so to speak, fused with a woman's. He never gave the effect of being welded, even temporarily, with the woman he was with. They did not seem really to have got together.

I think there was some obscure hitch in his make-up here, some early scar that robbed him of the easy self-forgetfulness, that "egoism expanded out of sight," of a real lover. I associate that hitch with the stammer that ran through his life. Very far back in his early years something may have happened, something that has escaped any record, which robbed him of normal confidence and set up a lifelong awkwardness.—H. G. WELLS, *Experiment in Autobiography*, 1934, pp. 534–39

General

The meaning of life to Bennett, in so far as the word "meaning" can be applied to so diffused an impression as he leaves, seems to be simply that, though life never fails to cheat the individual, and though the onlooker cannot fail to be filled with an overwhelming sense of the ironic hopelessness of it all, life is nevertheless worth living, simply because each individual instinctively and tenaciously holds it to be so. There is no need to realize desires, it is enough for average human nature to believe that they may be realized—round the next corner: no life is dull unless the liver of that life feels it to be purposeless—a frame of mind very rare among simple people. Arnold Bennett's genius is original in the double vision which he brings to his creation of human consciousness, in his power to combine the sense of ironic detachment from the lives he presents, with, at the same time, a complete identification with them. On the one hand we are made keenly conscious of how environment has warped and prejudiced these minds, how imperfectly they are exercised and trained, how inadequate and superficial and impoverished they are, how much they miss of the potentialities of existence. This is just the impression which Wells also gives us, but Wells leaves us with that impression and nothing more: we never get away from that one point of view. But Bennett goes further. Having shown us these lives as they appear in the light of a sophisticated, cultivated experience, he proceeds to identify himself with his creations, to show how these lives appear to themselves, and how, viewed from that standpoint, nothing is lost to them, because the whole perspective is entirely altered.—ELIZABETH A. DREW, "Arnold Bennett," *The Modern Novel*, 1926, pp. 205–6

The explanation of the apparent vagaries of Mr. Bennett appears to be that he does not write potboilers, but that he conscientiously produces three grades of work—writing good novels for those who like literature, novels for those who read fiction, and books like *The Strange Vanguard* for those who read anything. Certainly, no one can expect Mr. Bennett to go on producing *The Old Wives' Tale*, but there ought to be some sub-title—diversions of a novelist—recreations of a man of letters—which should enable the reader to classify these later works with the corresponding frolics of leisured headmasters, journalising clerics, or poetical gaolbirds. Imagine Mr. Yeats producing three grades of poetry, or Mr. John three qualities of painting, and the absurdity of the apologia for Mr. Bennett becomes apparent. For Mr. Bennett is in a responsible position. He is one of the very few famous novelists of the last generation who have not entirely lost the respect of youth. This is partly because he has resisted the sclerosis of the imagination which drives elderly novelists into the last Tory refuges of English society, so that while Mr. Galsworthy and Mr. Walpole are borne down the stream of time, humped anxiously on slabs of property like Eskimo dogs marooned by the thaw on crumbling pack-ice, Mr. Bennett is appreciating Proust and Joyce, and even inducing other people to do so too. Again, Mr. Bennett does not write about himself. His novels are not self-dramatisations; they are not axe-grinders, and do not date like the propaganda of Wells or the satire of Galsworthy. Lastly, Mr. Bennett has an aesthetic sense; his books are for those—or could be—who like writing as much as those who like reading, and the praise of authors is ultimately more gratifying than a vast popularity with scientists, stockbrokers, or American culture fans. With all these advantages, Mr. Bennett might become a very powerful influence in contemporary literature. A drastic critical operation could curtail his Siamese liaison with Mr. Galsworthy if only he could write for a public as intelligent as himself. Mr. Wells and Mr. Shaw, the remaining evangelists, have always been pamphleteers rather than literary artists; Mr. George Moore is an artist and nothing else. The new generation, suspicious of mere technique, is equally unmoved by mere propaganda; it finds in writers like Proust a blend of style with a personal philosophy of life which other generations discovered in Flaubert or Dr. Johnson. Mr. Bennett has—if he left off telling the man in the street what he calls 'the difference between a book and a bath bun'—the profound experience of life and the capacity to generalise from it in artistic form which nearly all his theorising contemporaries lack; but, instead of being a pilot, he is a populariser, and when he might show a tragic and intelligent perception of the beauty of life and the value of art, he writes *Accident* instead.

It is also urged that Mr. Bennett's excessive love of life is the explanation of his often mediocre comments on it. But just as the love of wit is no justification for a profusion of bad puns, so there is something peculiarly irritating about Mr. Bennett's gourmand affection for existence in general. To love life is to have the curiosity to search for the occasions when life is lovable, and the enterprise to create them. Human life is, after all, a picture-puzzle with half the pieces missing: to love it is to love it where it makes sense, and to make sense of it is the selective principle of all art. Mr. Bennett does not select in his carefully graded C3 novels; he gives full rein to his own preoccupation with male vanity and material success, and to his reader's desire for a happy ending.—CYRIL CONNOLLY, *NS*, Jan. 19, 1929, p. 470

His novels, short stories, sketches, book reviews, plays, "trifles," and "pocket philosophies" have been in perpetual flow for a full quarter century. By 1903, he was writing a half million words a year, which is rather more than the total number in the English language. All told, he should now have to his credit fifteen millions of words. He has been able, he says, to "tear the entrails" out of "a pile of new books" and write "a fifteen-hundred-word *causerie* on them, passably stylistic, all inside sixty minutes." When the literary essay was an art it took Sainte-Beuve a week to write a *Causerie du Lundi*, with one morning off on the day of publication. Bennett, coming later, has outdone even Trollope, who trained himself, with his watch on the table before him, to turn off two hundred and fifty words every fifteen minutes for three hours on a stretch. In the light of Bennett's achievement, Trollope's three thousand words from five to eight o'clock in the morning seem paltry, though in the old days it was thought to be a marvellous feat. Composed under high pressure, Bennett's miscellaneous books and essays may still amuse by their flippancy or mock seriousness, but it would never occur to anyone to re-read them. They are too thin for any language or any public except the English. Likewise the account with his early plays, written single-handed or in collaboration to increase the sale of his novels, is long since closed.

Other novelists have earned their bread largely as hack-writers. But at their worst, Thackeray and Fielding were never able to keep their minds moving, day in and day out, along a plane a degree or two beneath the intellectual. Their fugitive pieces are still being collected and read for the ideas, the wit, and the humor that are always there in some measure. It was left for Bennett to carry professionalism in literature to the point where it becomes sheer commercialism. The question with him, frankly confessed in *The Truth about an Author*, has been how much he could get for a certain number of words in an apt and pleasing arrangement. Stop at this point with Arnold Bennett and one is confronted with a writer whose other characteristics, whatever they may be, are submerged in commercialism.—WILBUR L. CROSS, "Arnold Bennett," *Four Contemporary Novelists*, 1930, pp. 64–66

In the divided self there must always be conqueror and conquered, and in Arnold Bennett the fundamental succumbed to the comparatively superficial. His once deep feeling for humanity became humanitarianism, and his "charity" an amiable benevolence. Once he could write that one must be able to "look upon the drunkard in his drunkenness, and upon the wife-beater in his brutality, with pure and calm compassion," and there was in the words themselves a compelling force which revealed the soul behind them. Later in life he phrased it: "To think kind thoughts of others, and never to think unkind thoughts is, for me, the summit of righteousness, the secret of happiness, and the only gateway to any success worth calling success." There is perhaps not so much difference in what is said, but how different is the way of saying it! It is, like the difference between *The Old Wives' Tale* and *Riceyman Steps*, just a measure of the failure of Arnold Bennett as novelist and artist, a failure which led the author of the former work to leave behind him as his last unfinished novel the polished vacuity of *Dream of Destiny*, and as his last short story the entirely commercial efficiency of *Venus Rising from the Sea*.—GEOFFREY WEST, *The Problem of Arnold Bennett*, 1932, pp. 83–84

Arnold Bennett belongs with Moore among superior products of France. During the nineties Bennett read the French realists, learned of cause and effect from Taine and Herbert Spencer, and with Moore and James came to share Flaubert's idea of the novel, not as so much material, but as art, selective, impersonal, final. He made elaborate technical studies of form and development; and he counted verbs. Of English realists Moore, whose *Mummer's Wife* Bennett read three times, seemed most admirable. Like Moore and Zola, Bennett recorded what he observed in notebooks and in the *Journals* he kept after the fashion of the Goncourts. Priding himself, like Moore, upon knowledge of women, whom he observed with and without his notebook, Bennett arrived at the point of being astonished at nothing. By his own devices this provincial man had freed himself from the puritanism of his youth to arrive at a moral disinterestedness unusual among Englishmen. He freed himself, that is, to a point; for like his heroes he remained in part the creation of his lower middle-class commercial and religious environment. He was all the French can do to a Wesleyan Methodist.—WILLIAM YORK TINDALL, *Forces in Modern British Literature: 1885–1946*, 1947, p. 160

At the outset of his career, Bennett wrote, "The day of my enthusiasm for 'realism,' for 'naturalism,' has passed." He has been shown to be a psychological portraitist of considerable penetration; he has been shown to be a sophisticated and systematic symbolist. Later in his career he wrote, "No novelist has yet, or ever will come within a hundred million miles of life itself. . . . The convention chosen by an artist is his illusion of the truth." He has been shown to be an allegorist, creating illusions—perhaps they should be called heterocosms—that bear not a one-to-one but a distant relationship to reality. Again at mid-career he wrote, "in the sense meant by the average critic, I am not photographic," and elsewhere he described his art in Wordsworthian terms: "all literature is the expression of feeling, of passion, of emotion . . ."; "the book is nothing but the man trying to talk to you, trying to impart to you some of his feelings." His basic feelings, it has been shown, are those of amusement and compassion in response to the human situation; his tone of voice is manifest in his prose style. At no time beyond the first couple of years of his career did he concede to realism anything more than technical usefulness in attaining his romantic end: "My desire," he said, "is to depict the deeper beauty while abiding by the envelope of facts." He has been shown in his creation of mournful, grave, sensuous images—"variations on the theme of beauty."

This display of his art offers problems for the literary historian. It is not only the problem of a close connection with the romantics but also the problem of an immediate connection with the French, Russian, and English novelists from whom he learned his craft and alongside of whom he practiced it. The nature of the so-called realist tradition, the elements of its heritage from the past, and the relationships among the writers who figure in it are problems that will vex the historian for years to come. And the answers will affect and be affected by another problem: that of the relationship of the realists to the novelists since the first World War, those who seemingly dispossessed the realists and those who appear to be their legitimate heirs. As was pointed out in the Introduction, the first group owes an unquestionable debt. The debt of the second group is questionable, since such writers as John Wain and John Braine have many more books to write. The problem that besets the definition of realism may be the same as that which besets the definition of romanticism: the boundaries of its influence have not yet been measured. It is an interesting fact that John Wain comes from the Five Towns.

When all is said and done, Bennett remains a realist in the most serious sense. The epitaph that he wanted for his grave was not "he tried to create illusions," but "he tried to destroy illusions." Although he thought that he was a million miles from life, he did not turn his back on it. "The notion that art is first and the rest of the universe nowhere," he wrote in *The Author's Craft*, "is bound to lead to preciosity and futility in art." Art for art's sake, which is one of the bases for the modern conception of the art work as a heterocosm, was attractive to Bennett, as some comments in his *Journal* make clear; but he kept the rest of the universe in mind. No one would argue that the less dedicated the artist, the better his art. There is, as Bennett knew as well as Yeats or Joyce, a choice that the artist must make for art over life; and Bennett's life was dedicated mainly to art. But he did believe that devotion could lead to a dead end. In the early sixties it does not seem as philistinic as it once did to ask how sharply the artist ought to turn away from life, to ask whether he can afford to devote himself almost entirely to a wonderful heterocosm ingeniously sustained in mid-air. Not many people, scholars or not, read *The Old Wives' Tale* today. Still fewer, it would appear, read *Finnegans Wake*.

The most serious sense in which Bennett remains a realist is the most ordinary sense. His art is a vulgar art; it is intended for ordinary people; it aims to speak of life in a manner comprehensible to them. The title of Book Four of *The Old Wives' Tale* need not be perplexing. For all the necessary ingenuity of construction, for all the sophistication of characterization and theme that lies hidden from casual eyes, the book speaks directly to the ordinary intelligence. So does that touching moment in *Clayhanger*, when Big James, upon learning that Darius has had a stroke and may die, says to Edwin, "But for over twenty years I've worked for him, and now he's gone, never will I lift my voice in song again!" The moment is prepared for three hundred pages in advance when Big James sings proudly and powerfully at the "Free and Easy"; it has ironies that are worth exploring; and it is bound intricately to the basic image of the novel. But it is most impressive in an immediate ordinary way.—JAMES G. HEPBURN, *The Art of Arnold Bennett*, 1963, pp. 177–79

Arnold Bennett had nothing of the high moral tone, the vague but real distress about the injustice and unkindness of the world, that make Galsworthy such an attractive and dignified figure in spite of his limitations. But Bennett was a writer of far more genuine natural talent. He was born an artist, but he crippled himself by accepting the standards of vulgar success. His best novel, *The Old Wives' Tale*, is in the tradition of Flaubertian realism, and handles, with extraordinary skill, the ageing of the two heroines and the passing of time. He delighted in the commonplace, described with exactness. The life that he understood most intimately was the life of the English provincial lower middle classes in the pottery towns of the Midlands, where he had grown up. This is the background of his best novels and of collections of humorous short stories, such as *The Card*. Unfortunately, though this was the world he both knew and wrote about best, the world that attracted him most was one of vulgar metropolitan luxury; and he found that he could make as much money, which freed him from the provincial world, by popular farcical or romantic novels as by serious work. As a book-reviewer in the popular press, he could make or break reputations, and he lowered the standards of criticism. He became famous and wealthy, and enjoyed the trappings of success, his yacht, his cigars, the deference of head waiters. But the cost of becoming a lion in London society— and writers so different as Osbert Sitwell and H. G. Wells have borne witness to Bennett's social charm—was loss of touch with his roots and squandering of his gifts. Sadly, in his inner life he never appeared very happy. Friendly and charming though he was, he seems to have lacked the gift of intimacy, and his very ebullience as a social personage was that of a provincial not quite able to take his success or position for granted, never wholly at his ease. He was a natural artist making his first great successes in a period when few were discussing literature from a purely aesthetic point of view; the literary journalism of Wells and Shaw and Chesterton was all about 'ideas'. Bennett had no 'ideas' in that sense, and therefore never got any very intelligent criticism from his contemporaries. Mrs Woolf, alone, pointed out something lacking in him in a pamphlet called *Mr Bennett and Mrs Brown*, in which she went tooth and nail for his dogged interest in externals, his lack of feeling for mood or soul or inwardness. Yet it is that feeling for externals, exact and solid, which gives his best books their weight and truth.—G. S. FRASER, *The Modern Writer and His World*, 1964, pp. 84–85

Ultimately the beauty of a work of fiction for Bennett was inseparable from the author's imaginative compassion. There was beauty in tragic happenings only if the author had a feeling for the gentle sweetness of the suffering mortals whose mistakes and misfortunes he was depicting. In 1896, virtually at the outset of his career, Bennett set down in his *Journal* the dictum: "Essential characteristic of the really great novelist: a Christ-like, all-embracing compassion" (October 15). He found this, of course, in Hardy, who, to be sure, would not have characterized himself as being Christlike. He found it especially in Dostoevsky. Of the two early scenes in *Crime and*

Punishment where the drunken Marmeladov laments his daughter's prostitution Bennett wrote, "They reach the highest and most terrible pathos that the novelist's art has ever reached." Unlike Conrad, who could not endure Dostoevsky's "prehistoric mouthings," Bennett was willing to immerse himself in the emotion with no reservation—no fear lest what was naïve might also be sentimental.

In *The Author's Craft* Bennett reiterated his belief that to be great a novelist must have nobility of soul, and this time it was Fielding, "unequalled among English novelists," who was his supreme example. To be sure, the argument may somewhat beg the question, for Bennett certainly did not approve of all the motives which in their private lives had impelled his favorite authors. He was speaking of them only as artists capable of escaping from their personal identities to live intensely in the sorrows and yearnings of imaginary beings. If many others besides Hardy, Dostoevsky, and Fielding could qualify, the antithesis for Bennett was James Joyce. Though Bennett granted him flashes of genius, he climaxed a devastating attack upon him in "James Joyce's *Ulysses*" with a most uncompassionate pronouncement: "His vision of the world and its inhabitants is mean, hostile, and uncharitable. He has a colossal 'down' on humanity. Now Christ, in his all-embracing charity, might have written a supreme novel. Beelzebub could not."

A corollary, perhaps, to his need for greatness of spirit was the fact that a novelist must, above all, love his principal character. In *Point Counter Point* the essential defect was that Huxley "hates and despises his characters." Returning to Zola in *The Savour of Life*, Bennett balanced praise with the complaint that Zola "lacked sympathy," that he had a "chill, disillusioned hostility towards human nature." And one of several complaints against Galsworthy was that he insisted on drawing his characters from the middle class, against which he had a "fierce animosity." In "The Progress of the Novel," where he tried to sum up the impressions of a lifetime, Bennett came back to his initial belief: "As a rule, but not always, the greatest novelists have been the greatest sympathisers."

Even in 1929 the notion that creation of great literature required nobility of mind as well as mastery of the craft was becoming a little quaint. In some circles during the 1950's and 1960's it was to be dismissed as naïve. Indeed, with all his alertness to new ways, Bennett remained in a tradition that included Fielding, Scott, Meredith, and Hardy. However pertinent to man as a social being, literature, for Bennett, was not a device for political or social renovation; still less was it a means for publicly exhibiting whatever violent feelings might be at war in an author's soul. Bennett's concern was human nature, not the peculiarity of a unique nature; and he expected an author to meditate the overwhelming passions, the irresistible impulses toward violent action, until he had acquired some confidence that he comprehended them and could depict them in an orderly way. He also believed that, however sordid his subject matter, an author should focus on its inherent aspects of beauty.—WALTER F. WRIGHT, *Arnold Bennett: Romantic Realist*, 1971, pp. 107–9

Works

NOVELS

The reading of the *Man from the North* has inspired me with the greatest respect for your artistic conscience. I am profoundly impressed with the achievement of style. The root of the matter—which is expression—is there, and the sacred fire too. I hope you will give me the credit for understanding what you have tried for there. My dear Sir, I do envy you the power of coming so near your desire.

The thing as written is undeniable. To read it was to me quite a new experience of the language; and the delight was great enough to make me completely disregard the subject.

This at first; but as you may suppose I've read the book more than once. Unfortunately, I don't know how to criticize; to discuss, however, I am ready. Now the book (as a novel, not as a piece of writing) *is* disputable.

Generally, however, I may say that the die has not been struck hard enough. Here's a piece of pure metal scrupulously shaped, with a true—and more—a beautiful ring: but the die has not been struck hard enough. I admit that the outlines of the design are sharp enough. What it wants is a more emphatic modelling; more relief. And one could even quarrel with the design itself.

Nothing would give me greater pleasure than to have it out with you, the book there on the table, to be thumped and caressed. I would quarrel not with the truth of your conception but with the realism thereof. You stop just short of being absolutely real because you are faithful to your dogmas of realism. Now realism in art will never approach reality. And your art, your gift, should be put to the service of a larger and freer faith.—JOSEPH CONRAD, Letter to Arnold Bennett, March 10, 1902, *Joseph Conrad: Life and Letters*, Volume I, ed. G. Jean-Aubry, 1927, pp. 302–3

The Old Wives' Tale is the history of two sisters, daughters of a prosperous draper in a Staffordshire town, who, separating early in life, through the flight of one of them to Paris with an ill-chosen husband and the confirmed and prolonged local pitch of the career of the other, are reunited late in life by the return of the fugitive after much Parisian experience and by her pacified acceptance of the conditions of her birthplace. The divided current flows together again, and the chronicle closes with the simple drying up determined by the death of the sisters. That is all; the canvas is covered, ever so closely and vividly covered, by the exhibition of innumerable small facts and aspects, at which we assist with the most comfortable sense of their substantial truth. The sisters, and more particularly the less adventurous, are at home in their author's mind, they sit and move at their ease in the square chamber of his attention, to a degree beyond which the production of that ideal harmony between creature and creator could scarcely go, and all by an art of demonstration so familiar and so "quiet" that the truth and the poetry, to use Goethe's distinction, melt utterly together and we see no difference between the subject of the show and the showman's feeling, let alone the showman's manner, about it. This felt identity of the elements—because we at least consciously feel—becomes in the novel we refer to, and not less in *Clayhanger*, which our words equally describe, a source for us of abject confidence, confidence truly *so* abject in the solidity of every appearance that it may be said to represent our whole relation to the work and completely to exhaust our reaction upon it. *Clayhanger*, of the two fictions even the more densely loaded with all the evidence in what we should call the case presented did we but learn meanwhile for what case, or for a case of what, to take it, inscribes the annals, the private more particularly, of a provincial printer in a considerable way of business, beginning with his early boyhood and going on to the complications of his maturity—these not exhausted with our present possession of the record, inasmuch as by the author's announcement there is more of the catalogue to come. This most monumental of Mr. Arnold Bennett's recitals, taking it with its supplement of *Hilda Lessways*, already before us, is so describable through its being a monument exactly not to an idea, a pursued and captured meaning, or in short *to* anything whatever, but just simply *of* the quarried and gathered material it happens to contain, the stones and bricks and rubble and cement and promiscuous constituents of every sort that have been heaped in it and thanks to which it quite massively piles itself up. Our perusal and our enjoyment are our watching of the growth of the pile and of the capacity, industry, energy with which the operation is directed. A huge and in its way a varied aggregation, without traceable lines, divinable direction, effect of composition, the mere number of its pieces, the great dump of its material, together with the fact that here and there in the miscellany, as with the value of bits of marble or porphyry, fine elements shine out, it keeps us standing and waiting to the end—and largely just because it keeps us wondering. We surely wonder more what it may all propose to mean than any equal appearance of preparation to relieve us of that strain, any so founded and grounded a postponement of the disclosure of a sense in store, has for a long time called upon us to do in a like connection. A great thing it is assuredly that *while* we wait and wonder we are amused—were it not for that, truly, our situation would be thankless enough; we may ask ourselves, as has already been noted, why on such ambiguous terms we should consent to be, and why the practice doesn't at a given moment break down; and our answer brings us back to that many-fingered grasp of the orange that the author squeezes. This particular orange is of the largest and most rotund, and his trust in the consequent flow is of its nature communicative. Such is the case always, and most naturally, with that air in a person who has something, who at the very least has much to tell us: we *like* so to be affected by it, we meet it half way and lend ourselves, sinking in up to the chin. Up to the chin only indeed, beyond doubt; we even then feel our head emerge, for judgment and articulate question, and it is from that position that we remind ourselves how the real reward of our patience is still to come—the reward attending not at all the immediate sense of immersion, but reserved for the after-sense, which is a very different matter, whether in the form of a glow or of a chill.—HENRY JAMES, "The New Novel," *Notes on Novelists*, 1914, pp. 329–32

The Five Towns present in a staggeringly simple way the whole riddle of industrialism. It is deplorable and indispensable; you cannot get along without it, and you cannot endure the results of it. If the industry were less homely, like the manufacture of silks, or if it were more primitive, like the cultivation of the soil, the case would gain something in dignity and lose something in force. As it is, the case stands midway between the luxuries and the necessities. Crockery is necessary enough to call the whole county into existence without a direct affront to the reason; it is luxurious enough to cause one some disturbance when it defaces the whole county. And it is totally and irrevocably lacking in human dignity. The whole affair is pathetically ludicrous and grimly droll. It is not futile, like the making of trinkets; it is not physiologically ghastly, like the mining of coal. Nothing about it is either tragic or splendid. It is merely dull, in a large complacent way.

Nothing but crockery could have served the purpose half so well. It raises the whole unified problem of industrial organization without any of the special issues, such as unsanitary conditions, extreme poverty, exploitation of one class at the will of another, or actual danger to life and health. The only question one asks is, Can it all be worth while? And that is a question, as Mr. Bennett means it to be, without an answer. This spectacle of industrialism is simply part, a focal part, of the larger spectacle called modern life; and the question insists on translating itself into, Is modern life worth living?

From such great blocks and lumps of reality Mr. Bennett fashions the frame and a good deal of the substance of his typical books. He treats the Five Towns with a prolonged and tremendous series of appeals to the physical senses; he conveys subtly an impression of their effect on the masses of people who dwell in them, and of their importance to other masses of people throughout England. How familiar the author is with his material, even the most trifling details that go to make up his atmosphere, only he can prove. Literature has probably never known a more exhaustive degree of "saturation" with one kind of data, or a more consistent example of "hugging the shore of the real." . . .

And when Mr. Bennett deals with the Five Towns historically, as he often does, he is still dealing with people. As he traces the manufactures from the era of private and random enterprise down to the period of corporate monopoly, he is really tracing the different products of two generations of men, and hence the differences in the men themselves. Not the spectacle of industrialism alone, then, is the object of his interest and the source of his material, but the definable results of that spectacle on individual and collective life. If his people seem more and more smothered and muffled in things, that is how the author wishes them to seem. He is trying to show character with all the material wrappings round it. On one hand the conditions, on the other hand the human results of the conditions—the conditions illuminate the people, and the two merge and fuse. The folk are almost a translation into compendious form of their environment and history; and in that fact alone is enough justification of the Five Towns novels as pieces of "art." The author has chosen to take people among the massed conditions where souls remain most solitary; and, having taken them, he shows what it is that makes them solitary.—HELEN THOMAS FOLLETT, WILSON FOLLETT, "Arnold Bennett," *Some Modern Novelists*, 1918, pp. 213–18

Time can be celebrated consciously also, and we shall find an example of this in a very different sort of book, a memorable book: Arnold Bennett's *The Old Wives' Tale*. Time is the real hero of *The Old Wives' Tale*. He is installed as the lord of creation—excepting indeed of Mr. Critchlow, whose bizarre exemption only gives added force. Sophia and Constance are the children of Time from the instant we see them romping with their mother's dresses; they are doomed to decay with a completeness that is very rare in literature. They are girls, Sophia runs away and marries, the mother dies, Constance marries, her husband dies, Sophia's husband dies, Sophia dies, Constance dies, their old rheumatic dog lumbers up to see whether anything remains in the saucer. Our daily life in time is exactly this business of getting old which clogs the arteries of Sophia and Constance, and the story that is a story and sounded so healthy and stood no nonsense cannot sincerely lead to any conclusion but the grave. It is an unsatisfactory conclusion. Of course we grow old. But a great book must rest on something more than an "of course," and *The Old Wives' Tale* is very strong, sincere and sad,—it misses greatness.—E. M. FORSTER, *Aspects of the Novel*, 1927, pp. 62–63

In his "good" novels, which were good enough to figure in Henry James' dissection of the "new novel" a decade or so ago, Mr. Bennett has given us some pretty nearly first-rate fiction of the naturalistic school. One can subscribe somewhat to the objection of James, that in such novels as these we have all the circumstances of interest but not the "working out" of it—the saturation in the *donnée*, but no kind of evocation of its center. It is the slice of life for its own sake, and would no doubt have given the utmost satisfaction to the brothers Goncourt. And if one asks no more of the novel than that, then one must admit that Mr. Bennett is an admirable novelist and often a deeply moving one. He is solid and unsparing; he is an expert crafts-man; he can be penetrating without being sentimental, and in his complete knowledge of English middle-class life he is the legitimate successor of Gissing, and rivaled, among his contemporaries, only by Mr. Maugham in his *Of Human Bondage.*

One does not go to Mr. Bennett, as one goes to the greater novelists, for the personality behind the book—there is no grandeur in Mr. Bennett, no nobility, no richness, no poetry. One does not bring away from him a spiritual fragrance, as one does from James or Turgenev, nor a tragic sense of life's great-ness, as one does from Tolstoi or Hardy or Melville. Nor does one expect that from him. One expects, and one gets, a sober and meticulous and extremely convincing narrative, which deals with rather somber and dreary people, who, though in-trinsically uninteresting, become interesting through Mr. Ben-nett's patient and level skill in portraiture.

The other Mr. Bennett is a different horse of another color. He is the most conscienceless of potboilers. In *The Pretty Lady,* it is true, there were indeed traces of skill; Mr. Bennett could not entirely forget that there was a good novelist some-where in him, and the book had its flashes of brilliance. In *The Vanguard,* alas, Mr. Bennett seems to have succeeded wholly in his task of forgetfulness. Surely never has a novelist of Mr. Bennett's reputation and ability produced so appalling a piece of trash. The whole story is utterly unreal. One never for a minute believes in this millionaire and his yacht and his wife and his financial machinations. The thing is as hollow as a cream puff and not half so sustaining.

Nor, on the other hand, does Mr. Bennett succeed, as Mr. Huxley might have done in similar circumstances, in making an extravaganza of it. He leans a little in that direction, but he leans timidly; and the result is a novel which is neither the one thing nor the other. The humor is forced and vapid, the satire is machine-made, the action is incredibly thin and unconvincing. One reads it only with the greatest difficulty; and one gets from it only a renewal of one's astonishment that a man who can, when he wants, write so well should stoop to the production of a literary sham so shameless.—CONRAD AIKEN, "Bennett, Arnold" (1928), *A Reviewer's ABC,* 1958, pp. 132–33

In the work of no other English novelist, perhaps of no other European novelist apart from Balzac, do property and money play so large a part, and it is not beside the point to note that in Bennett's delineation of this singularly graceless community the characters who are aware of civilisation, who are not exclu-sively concerned with property and money, tend to find them-selves involved in the end in financial disaster; one remembers the Orgreaves in *The Clayhanger Family.* The concern for property and money sets the limits, then, of Bennett's picture of Five Towns life. Within those limits his favourite themes are indicated in the following sentence from *Sacred and Profane Love:* "There are only two fundamental differences in the world—the difference between sex and sex, and the difference between youth and age." To these must be added a preoccupa-tion with illness and death; the whole seen and felt in the light of an intense awareness of the passage of time, the passage of time in the most purely chronological sense. There is, of course, an obvious relationship between an obsession with money and an obsession with time.

It is significant that for the only major work he produced when he went outside the area of the Five Towns, *Riceyman Steps,* he chose a district of London, Clerkenwell, as grimy and unsplendid almost as the Potteries themselves and found there

the same quality of miserliness and its undoing by illness and physical decay that had been so deeply impressed upon him in his native environment.

All the same, Bennett is a regional novelist with a differ-ence. In this connection we may think of a much greater novelist, Hardy. Hardy was of Wessex, and remained of Wes-sex, in a way Bennett was never of the Five Towns. For Hardy, Wessex was the universe and we accept it as a microcosm of the universe. It does not enter our heads to think of it as provincial or limited in time to the period of the 1840s any more than our first thought of *Lear* is that it has its action in pre-Saxon Brit-ain. But for Bennett the Five Towns were always provincial; he left them when he was twenty-one, and never lived in them again as a native or for more than a few days at a time. Steeped as he was in them, in their atmosphere, history and traditions, as a writer he was completely outside them, and as a writer his attitude towards them is always expository; he is explaining them, exhibiting them, to the outside world which is not pro-vincial. Perhaps he had to go outside them to become con-scious of them, for all the time they exist implicitly in relation to a larger world which Bennett accepts as a norm, whereas for Hardy the norm was Wessex itself. The Five Towns are seen, therefore, as strictly eccentric to the main centres of culture. Mr. Pritchett has noted that one of Bennett's favourite words was "detracting," and in some ways Bennett's attitude to the Five Towns is detracting. The result is, though *The Old Wives' Tale* transcends the Five Towns, what we get in the Five Towns novels is a picture of the provinces. The picture is true just because it is of the provinces, while in Hardy the picture of life is true not simply because it is of Wessex. At his best Bennett does achieve a universality of a kind, but it is not Hardy's kind. It is a limited universality. We can say: Yes, this is a picture of life not only in the Five Towns, but in any provincial industrial community of England and America dur-ing the last three decades of the nineteenth century; but we cannot say more than this. We are given, with great skill and with great accuracy, a picture true for a certain kind of commu-nity at a certain point in time. It is a great achievement, but one not in the category of the greatest. It is only in a few passages in *The Old Wives' Tale* and *The Clayhanger Family* that we are brought face to face not merely with the human situation at a given date in a given place in North Staffordshire but with the eternal human situation. And this means that though in two or three books Bennett is a master he is neverthe-less not more than a minor master.—WALTER ALLEN, *Arnold Bennett,* 1948, pp. 41–43

ESSAYS AND CRITICISM

As a journalist he is always topical, always in touch with the latest movement but one, and conversant with very nearly the newest idea. And he has mastered words so thoroughly that he can make them express almost anything he pleases. As a rule, his pleasure consists in punching his readers hard, in a not too vulnerable spot; and he rarely fails to achieve his end. If the notes in some weekly review strike you so forcibly that you are startled out of your post-prandial nap at your club, ten to one they were dashed off by Mr. Bennett in his bath. (Every mo-ment in the life of a business author must be made productive.) Mr. Bennett's fountain pen is a fountain which never runs dry, and all his literary products are "good selling lines," certain to please a "high-class public," guaranteed to be of superior quali-ty. With what emotion must the world of publishers regard this man, who never lets them down, who during long years has proved himself the acme of reliability! If some American Dol-lar Combine had occasion to commission, say, an epic in twelve cantos on "Liberty" or a concise cyclopædia of literature, to be delivered in a fortnight, to whom could it address itself with more confidence than to Mr. Bennett? If he agreed to their proposal, and accepted their terms, there would not be the smallest doubt that (*force majeure* excepted) the epic or the cyclopædia would be delivered on the appointed day, and would be found a sound and serviceable piece of work.—Douglas Goldring, "The Gordon Selfridge of English Letters," *Reputations*, 1920, pp. 149–50

. . . ⟨If⟩ we judged his literary personality by the lay sermons christened by him "Pocket Philosophies," his vision of life, though full of sound common sense and honesty of outlook, is nothing but a restatement of maxims and aphorisms already better expressed by the sayings of Christ, Epictetus, and Marcus Aurelius. There are nine Pocket Philosophies and they may be distinguished—by their titles. Otherwise they are a triumph of saying the same thing, very often, at considerable length, in a variety of different ways. Their message is an excellent one. He tells us to cultivate our human, physical, and mental mechanism to its utmost perfection, and gives sound advice as to the best way of doing it; on the mental plane, how to stir the mind from the sloth of custom and polish it from the tarnish of years of disuse; on the moral plane how the biggest things in life depend on the perfect adjustment of the smallest, how supremely important is kindliness of heart and the avoidance of moral indignation, with many valuable maxims against grumbling and bad temper and worry, becoming the slaves of habit, judging harshly and running away from life. He is the Walter Camp of the mental and moral organs, illustrating a Daily Dozen for the heart and mind, full of healthy common sense, seeing life in proportion, and anxious that the plain man and woman should realize how through cowardice, conceit, hypocrisy, stupidity, intolerance, and self-pity they get so very much less out of their ordinary existence than they might. But again, the "Pocket Philosophies" are journalism. What they say is true, but what literature does and what journalism does not is to give the truths of life *adequate and memorable expression* in artistic form. The "Pocket Philosophies" stand in the same relation to literature as the Daily Dozen to the Russian Ballet.—Elizabeth A. Drew, "Arnold Bennett," *The Modern Novel*, 1926, pp. 200–201

Perhaps my first reluctance to treat of his series of exhortatory essays arises from a distrust of didacticism—the natural recoil of the old-time victim of the Nonconformist birch. Perhaps my secondary hesitation proceeds from knowledge that what Bennett is telling me is largely right, and that because I haven't the industry, pluck, resolution to carry out his admonitions as to the husbandry of time I shall lose self-respect. Admonitions! Strange it is that the British, who appreciate in their great poets, essayists, politicians, the didactic as a chastening flavour in the fervour of appeal, resent the deliberate use of the ecclesiastical perch by the novelist. The sybaritism of the true literary acolyte, however, will lead him to kiss the rod of the Bennett treatises because of the aptness of the truncheon's use and the grace of its wielding.

Though the tenor of these works is "improving", their matter is attractive. Graces lure the reader on; stepping stones are placed for his feet. The literary lucubrations domesticate the classics or unmew them: what was dragon is now pet and the bird on the perch is seen in eagle flight. His accuracy and completeness of statement, his symmetrical building up of a forceful summit of conclusion, are faultlessly adept. The clear mind never relaxes guidance; that alert brain recalls all relevant detail. His construction is as simple as the building up of army

units from battalions to brigade, brigades to division, divisions to corps, and corps to army—or vice versa. Thus he shepherds his minutiae of fact and observation, groups them in generalisations, gathers the arguments to a climax; without raggedness, without strain to the reader, continuity, cohesion are achieved.

Of course it is only the fine art of common sense, or the fight for truth, he is preaching. But with what verve, what rhythm! In the philosophic introduction to *Our Women*, on the subject of the artist and the woman, form and inspiration, sex criticism and persiflage, the unerring note is struck again and again. . . .

Many of the principles enunciated in the Pocket Philosophies are suitably expounded in action (but usually without the slightest propagandist warp) in the novels and plays, as: the lesson-giving on women's duty to preserve her charm and run an efficient household which is, not too subtly, one of the pivots of *The Love Match*; the onus of making the right choice between political fanaticism and the gamble of marriage in *The Lion's Share*; Rachel Fleckring's confession that the "price of love" was to cherish weakness and bravado as well as strength; the tragic career of Lilian; the reconcilement of Clayhanger to the prevalence of injustice in life, as typified and embodied in the person of his wife, Hilda Lessways, in *These Twain*; and even the monstrous ravish by time that is the poignant theme of *The Old Wives' Tale*.—Oswald H. Davis, *The Master*, 1966, pp. 55–57

OTHER WORKS

Mr. Arnold Bennett's book about America does not make us see Stars and Stripes: that is its charm. The States it describes are states of mind, *états d'âme*, oftener than the seven-and-forty parallelograms—and nobody properly appreciative of Mr. Bennett's idiosyncrasy, of the way his egotism works, will take that to mean it is but an account, an Anatole Frenchified account, of his own soul's adventures among those forty-seven masterpieces. It is other people's souls he is interested in: instead of putting the Paternal poser "*What is this engaging personality to me?*" his instinct is always to ask "*What sort of time would I be having if I were this engaging personality?*"—and in this account of a seven weeks' (less one day) trip we find him trying on successively, eagerly, as no other literary traveller ever has done, the shoes of lift-boys, millionaires, railway captains, kindergartners, telephone-girls, baseball players, hotel managers, newly married couples, professional murderers, and others. . . .

"*What do you do with yourself in the evenings?*" asked Mr. Arnold Bennett. It is exactly what we all want to know, of course; what *do* these strange creatures, these monsters of legend, in their incredible world of sky-scrapers and gloating trusts—what *do* they do behind the façade? What happens at home, when there is no longer any audience, and the seven-leagued shoes are off and the feet on the fender? But it is a question nobody has hitherto had the courage, lacked the sentimentality, to let drive straight into their skins. In this particular instance, as it happens, it does not get all the way home. "A little disconcerted by this perhaps unaccustomed bluntness," the giant seems to have shuffled rather sheepishly. "Oh," said he absurdly, "I read insurance literature." Perhaps Jack ought to have had at him again, beaten down that clumsy guard—but, indeed, the confession is fairly full. The evasion avows even more than honesty, gives us more of the man: it is easy to translate that "insurance literature" into terms of domesticity; a pretty poor sort of giant, after all. And in other cases the disclosures are of the completest. Very effective, for instance, was Mr. Bennett's raid on the seraglio of the New York Telephone Exchange; and good, increasingly good, is the long last chapter, called "Human Citizens." The former reduced the fantastic curse of the telephone ("millions and millions of live filaments uniting all the privacies of the organism and destroying them in order to make one immense publicity") to a human "convent of girls requiring sugar and couches and thirsting for love." And in the second there is a tale of a domestic squabble, a squabble that ends with a poached egg spinning across a breakfast-table, flung by an over-strung small wife, that positively humanizes the whole of New York. The flight of that egg is like a metaphor reversed. It is the flight of the American eagle stated in homelier terms.

But perhaps the finest effect of this faculty for reducing all things to the personal equation is the neat way it packs up and makes portable the whole of the physical side of the great American scene. In an old land like Italy, say, where so much that is essential to the onlooker lies outside the private life of the citizen, it probably would not work very well; but in America, the Land of Performance, where everything visible is a piece of apparatus, and the whole structure is indeed a house of Cards, this valuation of all things in terms of their net human value, their power for effectual "functioning," does shrink down the whole place, keeping it perfectly proportioned, and at the same time passes it over to us in a condition that requires only the addition of our own daily experience to swell it back to its full size, firm and vivid. Mr. Wells and Mr. James, the best packers we have had hitherto, employed a much less reliable process. They strove to vaporize what they saw, turned it into generalizations, and sent us over consignments of the spirit of the place, which we had to recondense in accordance with accompanying directions. They sent diagrams too, but in the main they followed the Franco-Paternal plan. Mr. Bennett delivers the goods. From generalizations of any sort, with immense self-denial, he steadily refrains. In the whole book there are only three: "It seems to me that the brains and the imagination of America shine superlatively in the conception and ordering of vast organizations of human beings and of machinery, and of the two combined." "The rough broad difference between the American and the European business man is that the latter is anxious to leave his work, while the former is anxious to get to it." "The American citizen unquestionably has the most comfortable home in the world." These are all—and even these are reflectors to throw the light more sharply back upon the details.—Dixon Scott, "The Commonsense of Mr. Arnold Bennett," *Men of Letters*, 1916, pp. 127–31

The Journals have an aggressive, glowing, spending vitality. The rapid and immediate giving out of excitement, eschewing cold perfection of presentment, in response to each and every impact of event or flit of inner stirring, is the natural issue of the aim of *The Journals*—the depiction, in spirit and imprint through daily jottings of hour-by-hour factuality of the instantaneity of life.

Life is touched at all points—travel, reverie, conviviality: and rarely is missing, side by side with Bennett's gusto in helping himself with both hands to experience, the analytical bent, the unflagging urge of the critical impulse. Half the extracts one marks in *The Journal* deal with criticism in varied forms, and not least with criticism of his own character. He cannot go to a museum without rating the exhibits; measure a nostrum out without analysing it and the entertaining sanguineness of himself and human nature. (Towards the subject of quack remedies, Bennett, though he relied on physician friends, kept a curiously open mind, and he experimented with quick-cures and records their effects in his diaries.) Even if he comments

on his neuralgia, insomnia, deterioration of eyesight or addiction to smoking, the universe and himself are often entertainingly indicted. . . .

Amid the heterogeneity of interest and sensation we have tried to sum up in discussing *The Journals*—his versatility of flair, his wide assimilations of experience, his incredibly patient feats of missal-writing, his trotting off to do a water-colour or see a picture-gallery or attend a first night or a violinist's début—we find, as I have said, that Arnold Bennett's observations are as much prompted by the critical and analytical bent as by his tremendous response to the general interest of things. But the differentiated tendencies do not annul each other; they mutually enrich. The more we are involved in this pervasion and immanence of active criticism—comment on the phenomena of existence, on the wave-like lapping against him of events and people, on thoughts that continually strike him like missiles, on art in general—the more we feel that from such contacts emerges the essential Bennett, pugnacious, virile, straightforward, whose zest, whose sophistication, whose wide and vigorous interplay with past and contemporary interests, was an outstanding wonder of our time. Penetration into Arnold Bennett's tissue of critical work but augments our sense of knitting up with life. If we carry his central fastnesses of criticism of himself, and of philosophies he discards or accepts; if from ambushed vigil as diary-readers we regard the repeated sallies, the sweeping yet just verdicts on people and the arts; fully aware, all the time, of the foraging, recording, retentive instincts of the novelist: we are, I repeat, exhilaratingly conscious—as perhaps learning the final seal of his greatness—of contact with a diligent and dilated spirit that not only creates, not only illuminates life widely and fearlessly, but also kindles in us desire to seek, assess, enjoy and establish in the sight and grasp of men—as if it was a bridge we had built or a fountain unstopped—the discovery of the majesty and miracle of living.

Yes, in a sense, in *The Journals*, this omnivorous, ubiquitous vitality, appreciative or depreciatory, has reached its highest efficiency. Springing primarily from the critical instinct, passing across a whole world of facts, of created art, like a breeze through a forest, disseminating from that forest its strong fragrance, shaking off rotten accretions, reinvigorating for us the air, enriching us with perception of volatile magic, Arnold Bennett's spirit in *The Journals* gradually intoxicates us with its own power, until we come, too, to be happily at home in the forest, and find ourselves undergoing the metamorphosis of the artist, aspiring to change—nay, changing—our grossness into the questing of the spirit. Arnold Bennett the artist has stooped, and into that which was dead has breathed life.—Oswald H. Davis, *The Master*, 1966, pp. 84–89

WILLIAM DEAN HOWELLS
From "Editor's Easy Chair"

Harper's Magazine, March 1911, pp. 633–36

One of the slighter trials of the adventurer in the uncharted seas of literature is to have tardier navigators hailing him under their laggard sails, or the smoke-stacks of their twin-screw, turbine, separate-tabled, thirty-thousand tonner, and bellowing through their trumpets, so that all the waste may hear, the insulting question whether he has ever sighted such and such islands or sojourned on the shores of such and such continents: islands where he has loitered whole summers away, continents where he has already founded colonies of enthusiastic settlers. Probably the most vexing thing in the whole experi-

ence of Columbus was having Vespucius ask him whether he
had happened to notice a new hemisphere on his way to India;
though it could have been no such trial as having people come
to you with books of Mr. Arnold Bennett, and urging you to
read *The Old Wives' Tale*, as if the places and persons of it were
entirely novel to you half a dozen years after you had read *The
Grim Smile of the Five Towns*. Still, it shall not spoil our
pleasure in speaking of Mr. Bennett, now, when everybody else
knows him or knows about him.

Perhaps they do not know all about him. Perhaps they do
not know, even if they know that he began writing fiction in
partnership with Mr. Eden Phillpotts, that he united his own
with that other uncommonly sincere and original talent in
writing romances as ungenuine as any we happen to think of at
the moment. Yet one ought to distinguish, one ought to say
that the joint output of the firm was brilliantly ungenuine,
though perhaps it was the worse for being so. It may have
deceived them as to its real nature so, and kept them the later
from finding their true selves.

'Lights that do mislead the morn'

are fires more fatally ineffectual for good than none. But Mr.
Bennett seems to have trusted longer to their will-o'-the-wisps
than Mr. Phillpotts. The generation of his real and true work is
partially *A Man from the North*, 1898; *Anna of the Five Towns*,
1902; *Whom God Hath Joined*, 1906; *The Grim Smile of the
Five Towns*, 1907; *The Old Wives' Tale*, 1908; *Clayhanger*,
1910. The generation of his romantic novels, since he left
writing them together with Mr. Phillpotts, is partially *The
Grand Babylon Hotel*, 1902; *Buried Alive*, 1904; *The Gates of
Wrath*, 1908; *Hugo, The Glimpse, The Ghost*, fantasticalities of
dates not precisely ascertainable by us, but evidently coeval
with the contrasting realities cited. There are two or three of his
books which we have not read, and which we cannot classify,
but apparently he has found a comfort, or a relaxation, or an
indemnification in writing a bad book after writing a good one.
It is very curious; it cannot be from a wavering ideal; for no
man could have seen the truth about life so clearly as Mr.
Bennett, with any after doubt of its unique value; and yet we
have him from time to time indulging himself in the pleasure
of painting it falsely.

As far as we have noted, his former partner, since their
dissolution, has not yielded to the same sort of temptation.
Alike in their truer work they have preferred the spacious limit;
they have tended to the gigantic, the one in height, the other in
breadth; and they have tended alike to the epical in motive, to
the massive in form. The mass of Mr. Bennett is wrought over
with close detail, which detracts nothing from its largeness,
though in his latest work he has carried largeness to the verge of
immensity, without apparently reflecting that immensity may
be carrying largeness too far. If he does not break under it
himself, his reader may; though it is only honest to say that we
are not that sort of reader. In fact, *Clayhanger* has left us
wishing that there were more of it, and eager, or at least impatient, for the two other parts which are to complete the
trilogy promised; an enemy might say threatened; but we are no
enemy, and we rather admire the naïve courage of the author
in giving so brave a warning, especially at a moment when the
reader may be doubting whether he can stand any more of
Hilda. For ourselves we will say that we can stand a great deal
more of Hilda, and that we should like very much to know how
or why, having just engaged herself to Clayhanger, she should
immediately marry another man. We should like to have the
author's explanation. We are sure that it will be interesting,
that it will be convincing, even if it is not satisfactory. That is
his peculiar property: to be convincing if not satisfactory, and

always to be interesting. We would not spare the least of his
details, and as we have suggested, his mass is a mass of details,
not only superficially but integrally.

If it shall be demanded how, since he is a mass of details,
his work can also be epical, we will say that the central motive
of his fiction—that is, his good fiction—is the collective life of
those Five Towns and that his fiction revolves round this,
falling back into it by a force as of gravitation, when it seems
finally thrown off from it. It is epical, not with the epicality of
the *Odyssey*, but of the *Iliad*, and its hero is a population of
Achaian homogeneity; yet it is not Homeric so much as it is
Tolstoyan, and its form, its symmetry, its beauty is spiritual
rather than plastic. For this sort of epical grandeur, which we
find in high degree in Mr. Bennett's true fiction, the supreme
Russian gave once for all the formula when he said, 'The truth
shall be my hero,' and it was not necessary for the Englishman,
when he took the Five Towns for his theme, to declare that he
was going to act upon it; you could not read a dozen paragraphs
of his book without seeing what he meant to do, what he was
already about. Tolstoy's inspiration was his sense of the essential value of every human being, who in any scheme of art
must be as distinctly recognized as every other, whether prominently shown or not. Something must be said or done to let
you into the meaning of every soul in the story; none could be
passed over as insignificant; each presence contributed to the
collective effect, and must be proportionately recognized. Life
may seem to consist of a few vast figures, of a few dramatic
actions; and the representation of life may reflect this appearance; but for the artist there can be no seeming except as
the result of being, and his design, in fiction at least, must be so
Pre-Raphaelite that the reader can always see the being within
the seeming. The nakedness of humanity under its clothes
must be sensible to the painter or he will not be able to render
the figure, even if apparently it is no more part of the drama
than a table or a chair; really, it can never help being part of the
drama.

We do not say that the perception of this is always evident
in what Mr. Bennett does, or the consciousness of it; but we do
say that without it, latent or patent, his work would lack mastery, the mastery which we feel in it. He has by means of it
made his Five Towns, just wherever or whatever they are, as
actually facts of the English map as if their names could be
found in the gazetteer. The towns are so actual, in fact, that we
have found their like in our own country, and when reading
the *Grim Smile* of them, we were always thinking of certain
American places. Of course one always does something of this
sort in reading a book that convinces, but here was a book that
studied unexpected traits of English life and commended them
so strongly to our credence that we accepted them for American, for New England, for Connecticut. Afterward in reading
more of the author's work, say *The Old Wives' Tale* and
Clayhanger, we were aware of psychical differences in those
manufacturing-town, middle-class English people from our
own, which we wish we could define better than we shall
probably be able to do. Like our own they are mostly conscientious, whether still sunk in their original Dissent, or
emancipated by the Agnostic motions of modern science; they
are of a like Puritan conscience with our own New-Englanders;
they feel, beyond the help of priest or parson, their personal
responsibility for wrong-doing. But it appears that they accept
Nature rather more on her own terms and realize that human
nature is a part of her. They do not prize respectability less;
they prize it rather more; but they do not stretch accountability
so far as our Puritanized wrong-doers; they know when to stop
atoning, when to submit, and, without any such obsolete
phrasing, leave the rest to God. Those conscientious, manu-

facturing-town, middle-class English outlive their expiation; they serve their terms; but with our corresponding penitents the punishment seems a life sentence.

Of the sort of vital detail in which the author abounds it would be only too easy to multiply instances, but we will take only one, one so luminous, so comprehensive, that it seems to us the most dramatic incident, like, say, a murder, or an elopement, or a failure in business, could not be more so, or so much so, in so little space. When Sophia, in *The Old Wives' Tale*, after her long sojourn in Paris, had come back to her sister in one of the Five Towns, and they were both elderly, ailing women, they were sitting one night waiting for supper. 'The door opened and the servant came in to lay the supper. Her nose was high, her gaze cruel, radiant, and conquering. She was a pretty and an impudent girl of about twenty-three. She knew she was torturing her old and infirm mistresses. She did not care. She did it purposely. . . . Her gestures as she laid the table were very graceful, in the pert style. She dropped forks into their appointed places with disdain; she made slightly too much noise; when she turned she manoeuvred her swelling hips as though for the benefit of a soldier in a handsome uniform.'

Here is not only a wonderful bit of detail, a pinch of mother earth precious beyond rubies, but a cosmical implication in which a universe of circumstance and condition and character is conveyed. Here is not only a lesson in art beyond the learning of any but the few honest men and women presently writing fiction, but an illustration of the truth which commonplace detail alone can give. It is at once intensely realistic and insurpassably imaginative, as the realistic always and alone is; but more than anything, it is interesting and poignantly pertinent to the affair in hand, which is not to ascertain or establish the excellence of Mr. Arnold Bennett's work, but to put the reader upon the train of a psychological inquiry often, not to say constantly, engaging the curiosity of the Easy Chair, and moving it to speculation which it has had no great difficulty in keeping trivial, at least in appearance. We mean the question of that several self, which each of us is sensible of in his own entity, without much blushing, or, in fact, anything but a pleasing amaze, but which he perceives in others with stern reprobation as involving a measure of moral turpitude.

We have already noted not only the wide disparity, but the absolute difference of nature in the two varieties of Mr. Arnold Bennett's fiction, parallel in time and apparently of like deliberate intention. So far as our knowledge of it goes, and we do not say it goes the whole way or quite inclusively, every alternate book of his is ungenuine in material, false in make, and valueless in result, so far as any staying power with the reader is concerned. We can think of but one such story which seems to summon a measure of reality to the help of its structural hollowness; in *A Great Man* there is something like human comedy in the unhuman farce; a good deal of living detail in the persons and situations from time to time forces your faith in the general scheme of make-believe. It is an amusing book; it is good farce; but it is essentially farce, and things do not happen in it, but are made to happen. For the rest, we may safely say, the author's different books are as unlike as so many peas: peas out of the pod, and peas out of the can; you have but to taste, and you know instantly which is which.

It is not less than wonderful, the difference in the product which is apparently always green peas; we use the figure respectfully and for its convenience, and not in any slight of a writer whose serious performance no one can pass us in prizing and praising. Since Tolstoy is gone, and Björnson is gone, and Flaubert, and Zola, and the Goncourts, and Frank Norris, and all the early naturalists are gone, and we have no more books from Perez Galdós or Palacio Valdés, there is no writer living in whose reality we can promise ourselves greater joy than Mr. Bennett. For one thing, we can instantly know it from his unreality; we lose no time in doubt; the note of truth or the note of untruth is struck with the first word; in one case we can securely lend our whole soul to listening to the end; in the other, we can shut the book, quite safe from losing anything.

But again the question is not so much aesthetical or ethical (the one always involves the other) as psychological. Apparently there are two selves of the one novelist who are simultaneously writing fiction entirely opposed in theory and practice. Can there, outside of the haunts of the Advertising Muse, be any possible comparison between *The Gates of Wrath*, say, and *The Old Wives' Tale*, say? If we are right in holding that there can be none, then is not it within the force of hypnotic suggestion to constrain the self of Mr. Bennett writing such books as *The Gates of Wrath* to write such books as *The Old Wives' Tale*, and to do this invariably? The self which we here propose to constrain may reply that it addresses an entirely different public which does not care for *Old Wives' Tale*, but wants *Gates of Wrath*, and continually more of them. To any such argument we should return that a public of this sort is profitably negligible; and in our contention we believe we shall have the earnest and eager support of that self of Mr. Bennett's which writes only, and can write only, *The Old Wives' Tale*, and the like, and to which we are now looking impatiently for the two remaining parts of the *Clayhanger* trilogy.

Of course there is always the chance that there may be two Mr. Arnold Bennetts, rather than two selves of one. Or it may be that there is a pseudo-Mr. Arnold Bennett who is abusing the name of a master to foist his prentice inventions upon the public. In this case we hardly know what to suggest in the way of remedy. It would be difficult to bring such a matter into court, or if it could be got there it might result in giving an undesirable extension to the publicity of the prentice work. Otherwise, we should hope that something in the nature of an injunction might be made to apply to the practices of the pseudo-Mr. Arnold Bennett, which are clearly *contra bonos mores*. After all, however, it may be best simply to let the genuine author write the ungenuine down. He is unquestionably competent to do so, or at least there is no author now living who is more competent. It is scarcely the moment, here at the foot of our fourth page, to state his qualifications in full, but we may say that the genuine Mr. Arnold Bennett writes with a directness which is full of admirable consciousness. Slowly, carefully, distinctly, he accumulates the evidence of situation and character, and then sets them forth so steadily, so clearly, that your mind never misgives you as to their credibility. In the long stretches of time covered by the action, the persons of the drama grow up from childhood to youth, from youth to age, and when they die it is no more theatrically than when the immense majority of the race daily attests its mortality. More important than all this, it is shown how each seed of character bringeth forth fruit of its kind, and does not turn into some other kind because of the weather, the drought, the frost, the tempest; no nature is changed in a single night from black to white, or the reverse. We do not allege instances because the books are all instance, but what is certain, without any such trouble, is that here once more, and in the years that we might have feared would be years of famine, we have a harvest of fiction, such as has not been surpassed in any former season, and the field of it is so wide that no one of wholesome appetite need hunger. Whether the reaper shall finally stand out against the sky as vast as the reapers of other days, does not matter.

Probably he will not. Along with other kinds of heroes, the author-hero has probably gone forever. At least, in the interest of literature, we hope so.

J. B. PRIESTLEY
From "Mr. Arnold Bennett"
London Mercury, February 1924, pp. 394–406

There are more than fifty volumes now in the 'List of Works to date,' that faces the title page of every book by Mr. Bennett, and at the very sight of this monstrous bibliography, a kind of despair falls upon the critic who would try to estimate such an author. Nor is there any way out of it; the list must be faced resolutely, manfully, or the criticism will suffer. It will not do to treat Mr. Bennett as the author of only three books instead of fifty-three; we cannot write at length about *The Old Wives' Tale*, *Clayhanger* and, let us say, *Riceyman Steps*, and then condemn all our author's other works, his fantasias, short stories, plays, pocket philosophies and books of travel and chit-chat, to the pulping machines with one wave of the hand. Many of these works may cut a better figure in their author's ledger accounts than they ever will in the literary histories of our time, but they are there and cannot be rightly ignored, for the real Mr. Bennett is not the writer of this or that book but is to be found somewhere behind all these books, perhaps buried beneath them but buried alive. Moreover, it is dangerous to dismiss whole rows of these less important volumes, because Mr. Bennett, being amazingly unequal, can suddenly fall to writing well in unexpected places just as he can fall to writing badly. As examples of the craft of writing, the actual business of setting down a number of facts and impressions in words, as distinct from the wider art of creation in literature, he has probably given us nothing better than the first few sketches in *Paris Nights*, which was called a 'bold, brilliant, exciting book' when it first came out but has not, I imagine, attracted much attention recently; so that, to take only this one example, Mr. Bennett cannot be fairly judged without his *Paris Nights*. It is clear that to be seen distinctly he must be seen against the background of his complete works, good, bad and indifferent; many people only know the author of *The Human Machine* or *How to Make the Best of Life*, some others only know the author of *The Old Wives' Tale* or *Clayhanger*, but both authors must be the subjects of any critical estimate of Mr. Arnold Bennett. The only danger there is in such a thorough examination, when space is limited, is that the mere bulk of work prevents close detailed criticism, with its eye on the individual book, its insistence upon chapter and verse, and inevitably encourages that loose easy generalising mode of criticism of which Mr. Bennett so far has had, perhaps, more than his fair share. This danger, however, is the least of many, and if Mr. Bennett has to suffer yet a few more easy generalisations, he must remember that he himself has been generalising no less easily and loosely throughout some half a hundred volumes.

These volumes are the work of a trinity of authors. The first, the most prolific and easily the best known, is the omniscient Mr. Bennett, the connoisseur, the tipster of life and the arts, the man who can put you wise, who can tell you a thing or two, who has made a stir in the big city and is now 'in the swim,' 'in the movement' (his favourite phrases—see works *passim*), a terrible fellow who knows more about life than even the head waiter of the Grand Babylon Hotel. He has been

everywhere and knows everything; he is curious and knowledgeable about cities, books, railway trains, soup, water-colours, frocks and skirts, and the Parisian Theatre; he is a lover of experts and probably wishes to become the expert of experts. In all this intense curiosity about every side of the life of his own time there is a zest, gusto, infectious enthusiasm, that is entirely admirable. At a time when so many clever persons are trying, in one way or another, to escape from life, to pretend that the real world is not there, we have here a very clever man who cannot have too much of it, a realist who discovers as much delight in a fact as some of his fellow authors do in an idea, and has the power to communicate something of that delight. Whatever else he may be, this Mr. Bennett is certainly a great journalist. Yet the result of this intense curiosity, this unflagging zest for things, is an attitude that is knowing rather than wise. There are too many limitations. Whole sides of life and states of mind, and these by no means the least important, some of them perhaps the most important, seem to mean nothing to him; he knows his world like the great journalist he is, but it is still the journalist's world, the world of the evening papers and not that of the poets, the saints and mystics, the great philosophers and historians; the voice is always that of an oracle, brimmed with certainties, but it is too often the oracle of the smoke-room. The section of his work which, with something like blasphemy, he cheerfully labels Belles-Lettres is nothing less than an epic of the cocksure. In his so-called Pocket Philosophies, or at least in some of them, he combines the vulgarity of the early Utilitarians (whose detachment perhaps modified it) with the equal vulgarity of a typical smart young materialist of the Eighties, whose dying whispers can be caught in Mr. Bennett's favourite metaphors, his talk about the Human Machine and so forth. Many sensitive readers, after learning from our author how to make the best of life, must have come to the conclusion that life was not worth making the best of, so sadly had it been vulgarised. So, too, his criticism, though there are delightful elements in it, is too often merely the cheerful impudence of a clever man who is not making a critical effort and is too interested either in attacking or following literary fashions to be capable of such an effort. It is this Mr. Bennett who is responsible for the miscellaneous books, who contributes a paragraph on every other page in the lighter novels, does his share of the dialogue in the plays, and even finds his way into the more serious novels. Unfortunately for him and fortunately for us, however, his work, except that in the pocket philosophies, is usually brought to nothing because there is someone at hand to give the game away, to reveal the fact that the writer is not really a bored encyclopaedic guide to the life of wealth and taste but is really a dazed enthusiast, a kind of wondering poet from the provinces, staggered at the way he is 'getting on.' You have only to open the first book to hand of Mr. Bennett's to see how frankly the game is given away: 'Then it suddenly occurred to me that if I had gambled with louis instead of five-franc pieces I should have made 200 francs—200 francs in rather over an hour! Oh, luxury! Oh, being-in-the swim! Oh, smartness! Oh, gilded and delicious sin!' That is not the first Mr. Bennett at all; it is the second, chanting his happy litany.

This second Mr. Bennett is simpler, more naive and enthusiastic, and altogether more engaging than the first; and he is nearer by a thousand leagues to the soul of literature, for he has one quality that is an essential ingredient of great romance—a sense of wonder. True, it is very limited; not only is the past closed to it, that living past which has been woven into the fabric of tradition and has secured for our delight the fragrance, colour and bloom of centuries, but much else that does not glitter on the surface of things is hidden from it too; and yet even this limitation is our gain, for it means that our author is lost in wonder at things that most other authors have ceased to wonder at, so that in his own fashion he has created a new kind of poetry. He is Wonder in a billycock, Romance with an excursion ticket to London, as mazed and dizzy at the sight of Harrods or the Savoy Hotel as Mr. de la Mare is with his dream of Arabia or Mr. Turner with his vision of the Andes; he comes to a metropolitan hotel as Childe Harold came to the Dark Tower. The advantages of being a provincial, one who has long been acquainted with the solid realities of life as they are to be discovered in small industrial towns, where the solid realities are most starkly displayed, and who is now zestful and ripe for the magnificent frivolities, the splendid mummeries, of London, these advantages were never better illustrated. In novel after novel, particularly those of the lighter kind, it is this Mr. Bennett, with his fresh vision, his humour and high spirits, who carries off the situation; he has only to take us all into a big hotel or restaurant or the Turkish Baths, and the trick is done and we are all excited, interested or amused again, all stepping out of King's Cross or St. Pancras still grasping the return half of our tickets, trying to look like persons who know what is what and are not to be trifled with, great city or no great city, but inwardly out-gasping and -gaping stout Cortez himself. He does it time after time; Denry's whole existence, as we know him in *The Card* and *The Regent*, is one long excited climb; Priam Farll and his lady go trotting about the town and we are thrilled anew with them; Mr. Prohack quits his office to be one of the idle rich and has some wonderful sensations in the West End; and so on and so forth; the situation never palls on the writer and we catch something of his zest. He is the rhapsodist of gigantic hotels and restaurants, White Cities, fashionable theatres and clubs, Turkish Baths, two thousand pound motor cars, pianolas, exclusive tailors, labour-saving devices, everything that is modern, expensive, luxurious, and not to be found in the Five Towns, or at least, in the Five Towns when Mr. Bennett lived there. Practically all his lighter stories, most of which he certainly enjoyed writing, are stories of wealth and luxury; they are crowded with millionaires who live in suites at colossal hotels, and are, in reality, a kind of fairy story that Mr. Bennett, seeing relaxation after the austerities of naturalistic fiction, is telling to himself, an old dream that comes back to his mind every time he sits down to write an easy idle tale. There is a fairy tale somewhere in every creative artist, and Mr. Bennett's is an up-to-date medley of millionaires whose hotel bills are twenty-five to fifty pounds a day, magnificently expensive and charming women of the world, experts, from medical to sartorial, ready at any moment to dance attendance and charge astounding fees, a full chorus of chefs, waiters, chauffeurs and flunkeys; and in the midst of it all some half-sophisticated, half-simple soul, busy fulfilling old dreams and pinching himself to discover if he is yet awake; while in the background, the symbol of the luxurious life, the heaven of all climbers and Cards and Human Machines and men who live on twenty-four hours a day, there looms and blazes against the night sky—the Grand Babylon Hotel. If Mr. Bennett should ever become a legend and his work come to be regarded as a number of folk tales (and stranger things have happened), about one-third of his works will be grouped together as the Grand Babylon Hotel Cycle and attempts will no doubt be made to determine its religious significance. Meanwhile, the significance for us of these comedies of high life and high jinks that are played, without regard to expense, on carpets five inches thick, lies in the fact that in them the dreams and aspirations, the romantic possibilities of what had hitherto appeared to be the least promising class in the kingdom, the middle-aged members of the middle-class, have been seized upon and pressed into service as they never have before, for the possible instruction of a few sociologists and the delight of all good novel readers. Finally, the secret of these romantic comedies of middle-age by a middle-aged novelist, the secret of their somewhat naive charm, is that at heart they are simply boyish; this second Mr. Bennett is nothing more (nor less) than a brilliant and delightful youth, not quite out of his teens, who has outgrown his tin soldiers and treasure islands only to make the Grand Babylon Hotel, golden, shining, the centre of his dreams and summit of his aspirations.

But even though another ten stories should be added to it, the Grand Babylon Hotel cannot entirely blot out the night sky and the strange stars, and not all the hosts of porters and page boys can prevent Change and Death from forcing their way into its velvet, gilded lounge; in short, there is a great deal more in life, and in the art that would pretend to grapple with life, than was ever dreamed of in the philosophy of the second Mr. Bennett. But there is yet another Mr. Bennett, the third and last, who has made the largest contribution to the major works but who is yet less distinct than the others and can hardly be described, without grave injustice, in a few lines. He does not glide over the surface of things as the other two do; he has not their almost metallic optimism; indeed, all his brave epicurean gestures cannot prevent us from noticing that he is at heart troubled and somewhat pitiful, sceptical, but, despite his fine show of indifference, not coolly sceptical, but disturbed, leaning ever towards pessimism. He it is who has written so many passages like the following, which comes from that little encounter between Carlotta and old Lord Alcar in *Sacred and Profane Love*:

> ' . . . Only the fool and the very young expect happiness. The wise merely hope to be interested, at least not to be bored, in their passage through the world. Nothing is so interesting as love and grief and the one involves the other. Ah! would I not do the same again!'
>
> He spoke gravely, wistfully, and vehemently, as if employing the last spark of divine fire that was left in his decrepit frame. This undaunted confession of faith which had survived twenty years of inactive meditation, this banner waved by an expiring arm in the face of the eternity that mocks at the transience of human things, filled me with admiration. . . .

He it was—to go from an early book to one of the most recent—who wrote the title (but nothing else) of the last volume of philosophy for the million that the first, omniscient, Mr. Bennett gave us; the title is *How to Make the Best of Life*, which has a strange ring, suggesting that the writer, so apparently cheerful, so cocksure, believes in his heart of hearts that life is a bad business—but (and we can see him yawning and shrugging) he can give the young readers a few tips that might ease their gradual descent into the grave. He it was, too, who devised that fine melancholy thing, *The Old Wives' Tale*, which has two suffering heroines, Constance and Sophia Baines, and three conquering heroes, Time, Mutability and Death. The shadows of these three are over *Clayhanger* too, and here again we cannot fail to notice how, in selecting and arranging his material, he has chosen to emphasize the passing of the old, the coming of the new, change and decay. Here, we feel life, which may be something more than sound and fury, may be coloured with passion, shot through with beauty, brought into harmony for an hour or so by love, is still a tale told by an idiot, the silliest, saddest old wife. Many critics have seen in this Mr. Bennett a sociologist, mainly because sociology in the guise of fiction has been fashionable and Mr. Bennett happens to have worked closely over large canvasses and has been inspired more by the character of a whole region than by a few individuals; but actually, though he has sometimes taken over a few sociological tricks from his friend, Mr. Wells, he is no sociologist.

. . . If we turn back to the fifty-odd volumes, the Bennett canon, we may choose to see them not as the work of three different authors but as the work of one author who has been played upon by three different sets of influences corresponding to the three divisions into which his life, during its most formative period, very easily falls. There is, first, his childhood, education and early manhood in the Five Towns. From 1867 to the beginning of the Nineties, young E. A. Bennett, brisk as a bee, was unconsciously hiving facts and impressions, scenes and characters for the day when Arnold Bennett, already a smart journalist with a story or two to his credit, should seek a new element for his fiction and suddenly pluck out these fat golden honeycombs. Mr. Bennett created the Five Towns but only after they had created him. It must not be thought, though, that he owes his success to the interest and appeal of his chosen 'locality'—as some smaller writers do—for the result would have been just the same had he been born and bred in Lancashire or the West Riding, on the Tyne or the Clyde. He was made by the Five Towns only because they stuffed his head with material to which he had only (it is a big 'only') to apply his later dexterity and craft to transform into magnificent fiction; and this material was so plentiful, his early memories crowded so thick and fast upon him, that his work, willy-nilly, took on that fullness and richness which is one of the glories of English fiction. There was a time when Mr. Bennett, under French influences, was probably all in favour of thin, rigid, brittle narratives, of the kind that are quite wrongly regarded as masterpieces of technique, and so was all against such fullness and richness, such lively and crowded canvasses, but fortunately there was a divinity that shaped his ends and that divinity was the Five Towns, 'smouldering and glittering' in his memory. His real mastery and his real popularity began with the Five Towns stories, and, with the exception of his latest novel, *Riceyman Steps*, all his best work is linked up with his birthplace. It must not be forgotten, too, that his early popularity was due in part to the fact that he had what we might call a 'locality' reference that helped the ordinary reader to remember his name and work; he was the Arnold Bennett who wrote amusing stories about the Five Towns. At first, in his volumes of short tales, like the *Grim Smile of the Five Towns*, and such things as *Helen with the High Hand*, he had a tendency to act the showman instead of the plain chronicler; in the middle of a story he would beat a big drum and invite the reader to walk up, walk up, to see the strange characteristics of the Five Towns. This trick, however, in its most aggressive form, he soon dropped and there is little of it after 1908. He shares with his sturdy fellow-townsmen, whom he has described with such gusto, many leading traits, not the least of which is a robust sense of humour that, if it lacks subtlety, has at least few blind spots. Like them, too, he is always steadily aware of the grim realities, the unpleasant facts of existence; he knows the provincial and industrial tragi-comedy.

The second period is that of his early years in London, when he was engaged in journalism and ingenious pot-boiling of various kinds. He became a very successful journalist, and has remained one ever since; most of his lighter novels, whatever else they may be, are certainly good journalism, and so too are many of his plays; their style and manner are often those of the short articles on the leader page of a newspaper, and their topics are frequently the topics of the moment, though not so ephemeral in interest that the novels cannot be read or the plays performed after the lapse of a few years. Such a novel as *Mr. Prohack*, for example, has only a slight story, but is such excellent journalism that it could have been split into fragments, with only a few changes, and published in this periodical and that magazine as sketches of the times. During this period he edited a popular paper for women, and it is often claimed that this experience, obviously a very valuable one, initiated him into all the secrets of feminine psychology; he was admitted behind the scenes and has stayed there ever since. Certainly no modern novelist (if we may believe women themselves) can touch in the details of a woman's life so lightly and surely; but a good deal more than a few years' acquaintance with popular journalism for women is needed to make a man the father of great daughters in literature, and if there is an advantage in knowing some feminine characteristics, as it were, off by heart, such easy knowledge is also not without danger to a creative artist, as we shall presently see. What such popular journalism did do was to give him a thorough understanding and appreciation of the topics, the situations, incidents and characters that have the firmest hold upon the popular imaginations; and this understanding enabled him to lead the monster gently by the nose, and taught him not to fly in its face. His journalism gave him ideas, not purely literary ideas, but ideas of every description, and no novelist of our time has had more; with him, as the late Dixon Scott once pointed out, there is no deception; he not only tells us exactly what his characters can do, but he actually shows us how they do it; when he introduces into a novel a new kind of house or an ideal theatre he gives us an exact description of the labour-saving devices in the house and the interior arrangements of the theatre; when he tells us how Denry made a fortune and a reputation as a wit and joker, a Card, we see exactly how it was done, we are given the schemes, the wit and jokes, until we realise that the writer himself is a Card too, and that we might all set up as Cards if we studied the life of Denry with sufficient care. Further, it taught him that the great sin in writing is to be dull, and since then he has been many things, exasperating, irritating, intolerable, but never dull; even when he was working under the influence of the bleakest naturalistic theory of the art of fiction, he was never dull, but always bright, alert, efficient, if nothing else. But while he learned to see the dramatic situation, and the equally dramatic 'problem' in his miscellaneous writing, and to make his style snappy and perky and button-holing, in all but his very best pieces of work we see the trail of the newspaper and the bright weekly all over his situations and his style, and in the latter we too often hear the click and rattle of efficient mechanism that is functioning freely (the metaphor and the several words that compose it are all favourites of Mr. Bennett's) rather than the music of an instrument, finely tuned and delicately handled. Even in his best things he never achieves a really fine style. He has written a good deal about prose style, but it is very doubtful if he realises what is involved in a great prose style. He, in common with many other writers on the subject, appears to think that style is simply the accurate expression of the writer's matter or thought. But style, in the purely literary sense of the term, has a three-fold function: it expresses the thought by a logical arrangement of symbols; it contrives to intensify emotion by its undertones and overtones, suggestion and association of all kinds; and further it gives pleasure of itself merely as an arrangement, a pattern, a decoration. Most of us think ourselves fortunate if we succeed in making our style fulfil the first part of its function, and Mr. Bennett, like Mr. Wells, but unlike Mr. Hardy or Mr. Conrad, is no more successful. He sometimes comes near to a personal style by making use of certain tricks, the chief of which is a succession of short exclamatory sentences that begin with a panting conjunction and end with a gasping mark of exclamation; but such tricks are far from being pleasant. Indeed, had there not been another set of influences at work, Mr. Bennett might have declined altogether into a writer of bright melodramas and amusing clap-trap articles. 'When one looks back,' he has written, 'one sees that certain threads run through one's life, making a sort of pattern in it. These threads and the nature of the pattern are not perceived until long after the events constituting them. I now see that there has been a French thread through my life.' This last set of influences, in short is the result of his early interest in French, chiefly modern French, literature (at a time when his acquaintance with our own literature was only slight), and of an equal interest in French life that finally led to his living in France for nearly ten years.

It is obvious that an impressionable man of letters cannot prefer a foreign literature (and one entirely alien in its outlook and manner) and suffer a voluntary exile for so long without some considerable change taking place in his point of view and his methods of work. Only a long and close study, based on something more than an outside knowledge of Mr. Bennett's work, could assess the value of such influences, but we may reasonably permit ourselves a few guesses. In the first place, France developed and sustained his literary conscience; Mr. Bennett may have boiled the pot but he has at least boiled it properly and not taken money for leaving it luke-warm; never at his worst has he fallen into the disgraceful slovenliness that spoils so much of Mr. Wells's later work; and at his best, though he may not reach the last subtleties of construction or the ultimate felicities of style, he has shown a fine conscientious craftsmanship and has done all that a man can consciously do to bring his work near to perfection. Further, contact with French life and thought has, I imagine, sharpened his sense of the dramatic and given to his handling of any dramatic situation a certain lightness and crispness. He is not by nature a dramatist at all because his finest work demands that background to the action which only a novelist can touch in; and the people of his plays are not so solid as the persons in his novels mainly because he sees them as a novelist sees them; but nevertheless he has contrived to write a number of successful and entertaining plays simply because he has good ideas, original but not too original (think of *Milestones*, *What the Public Wants* and *The Title*), and because he has, too, this light but sure dramatic touch. So far, this literary apostasy has brought nothing but gain; but actually there have been serious losses. Mr. Bennett, who, unlike many novelists, has always been something of a literary theorist, began writing novels at a time when he was a fervent admirer of Mr. George Moore, Maupassant and the French naturalistic school. He was a great advocate of 'technique,' which really meant nothing more than a suppression of the narrator and a deliberate simplicity in the narrative, the action, the background. Later, in *The Author's Craft*, which is easily the best of the short talks and is really a very sensible and lucid discussion of some very difficult subjects, he admitted that his earlier attitude towards the novel was mistaken:

> With the single exception of Turgenev, the great novelists of the world, according to my own standards, have either ignored technique or have failed to understand it. What an error to suppose that the finest foreign novels show a better sense of form than the finest English novels!

What an error, indeed! The fact is, of course, that the art of fiction as practised by the great novelists *is* technique, and any other 'technique' is either some inferior method or a mere catch-phrase of the pontifical critic. But Mr. Bennett began with such admirations, and in following the wrong masters did violence to his own genius. He himself is essentially a Romantic with certain ironical, sceptical twists in his mind; and his early ideas of what a serious novel should be seem to me to have been definitely harmful because they have made him divide his work in a fashion that has hindered his development as a great novelist. To put it shortly, the second Mr. Bennett has never settled down to work in harmony with the third Mr. Bennett; we have had all the rich comedy, the fantastic romance of the commonplace, the high spirits on one side, and the writer's magnificent sense of a social background, his wide sweep, his feeling for obscure and only half-articulate tragedy, his grave pity, on the other side; *the Card* is a fine tale and *Clayhanger* is a finer, but we might have had, and might still have, a story that was both the Card and Clayhanger and therefore something more, which would have been unquestionably one of the greatest works of our time. The naturalistic and realistic elements in his work have always been sadly overemphasized by critics. He is essentially one of our English Romantics, whose feeling for romance is so strong that he can find it where most persons would never even dream of looking for it; indeed, this may be said to be his great contribution to the English Novel. Practically all his more serious novels are simply romantic obstacle races, almost romantic conjuring tricks; for he carefully puts away all the usual trappings, shows us the most commonplace people in the dingiest and dreariest setting, takes off his coat and rolls up his sleeves, and proceeds to evolve romance. One of his first serious novels, *Leonora*, shows us that it is possible for a woman verging on middle-age, the mother of grown-up daughters, suddenly to become the victim of a consuming romantic passion. Mr. Bennett himself, I imagine, must be surprised when he learns that he is regarded, as he so often is regarded, as one of the enemies of romance, only anxious to destroy the illusion by holding out for his readers' inspection the wigs and grease-paint and pasteboard castles of this life, a writer who stands chuckling with Time himself over the crumbling ruin of so many little lives. It is true, as we have seen, that he is aware, and by no means blithely aware, of the ironies of existence in such a world, and that behind his superficial convictions, his downright opinions on art and Bollinger 1911 and barbers, there lurks a mournful scepticism, but actually this only makes him more passionately attached to the romance, the dumb poetry, the hidden agonies and exultations of commonplace persons. He has made full use of the simple fact that however dull and prosaic a man may appear to others, however tedious his life may seem, to himself his life is always exciting, amazing, and he himself a daily miracle; and in three out of every four of Mr. Bennett's stories, it will be found that the most piquant effects have been obtained simply by a continual contrast of what he might call the 'the outside' and the 'inside' views of a person's motives, actions, character. If, as I imagine, his readers so often mistake his intentions, no doubt the fault is largely his and is the result of some flaw in his art; but it is easy to see what has happened, for while the reader (of the more important novels) has naturally seen the story progressing in a forward direction, as it travels from the first chapter to the last, Mr. Bennett himself has seen the story backward, as it were, has first conceived the final situation and then worked out the rest of the tale in the light of that. The difference is important. Thus, in *The Old Wives' Tale* the reader sees the history of one of Time's innumerable conquests, the decline and fall of feminine grace and beauty, the eternal cruel process by which two exquisite girls, things of wonder, are slowly transformed into two helpless old women; but the author, while he sees all this too, really begins with a vision of two lonely old women, harmless creatures in a provincial town who would excite no comment beyond perhaps a pitying remark, and then realises that behind them, even them, there is an epic, the play of gigantic instincts, a series of strange tragi-comedies that have been secretly enacted in commonplace shops, houses and hotels. We see the two old women and 'nothing more'; but he sees the whole story, typical and yet marvellous, and that is his triumph. That he conceived the story in *The Old Wives' Tale* backwards is made plain in his preface to the later edition, and there can be little doubt that the same thing happened with the later tales. In the Clayhanger trilogy, he probably began with a mental picture of a seemingly commonplace married couple, middle-aged, middle-class, prosperous, contented, apparently prosaic. But behind them he saw, reeling back into the middle years of last century, the histories of Edwin Clayhanger and Hilda Lessways, and he knew that the middle-aged ease of *These Twain* was nothing less than a port in some Fortunate Isles that the pair had only reached after incredible adventures on the high seas of youthful life. Again, he probably saw that magnificent novel, *Riceyman Steps*, from the angle of those contents-bills noted in the last chapter, Mysterious Death of a Miser in Clerkenwell, Midnight Tragedy in King's Cross Road and the rest, and actually we ought to have such newspaper summaries of the story somewhere at the back of our minds when we are reading it, so that we are conscious of the piquant, or, rather, in this instance, moving contrast already noticed, the contrast here between 'a sordid affair in Clerkenwell' involving one of the seediest parts of London, two misers, a simple charwoman who steals scraps of bacon, and her semi-idiotic lover, the contrast between this and the actual story as we come to know it from within, a story that has in it humanity and the world, love and death, strange loyalties and fantastic bravery, and that odd nobility and even beauty, which a ruling passion, no matter how ignoble it may appear, (which was reviewed at length in these pages two months ago), though it lacks the epic fullness of the two great Five Towns stories and is more limited in its scope, is undoubtedly Mr. Bennett's greatest achievement as a pure craftsman, and is perhaps the best example of his disguised romantic method, of the romance that fights its way through reality when all the gates of easy appeal have been barred.

But in none of these works has the complete Mr. Bennett appeared; something that crackles and blazes so delightfully in the lighter novels has been rigidly excluded from them, and for this exclusion, this deliberate limitation, we may perhaps thank those early views of the novel, largely learned under French influence, that have already been noticed. That influence, too, is partly responsible for a certain characteristic that is at once a virtue and a great fault in Mr. Bennett as a novelist. This is a generalising tendency which can be seen in everything he touches but which is most easily observed in his treatment of love. He is, above all our other novelists, the novelist of middle-aged love; time after time, he has, for example, shown us with much humour, dramatic effect, and truth, the way in which apparently bored, condescending or amused husbands, who pride themselves on a lack of sentiment, conceal in their bosoms an immense admiration, genuine passion and solid respect for their wives; no living novelist is better able to handle the general realities of sexual relations. But—and here he seems to me very French—the relations always remain too general; it is always, or nearly always (for Hilda Lessways and Clayhanger perhaps provide an exception) a man and The Sex; we are not shown the peculiar, the unique relation between two individuals, a certain man and a certain woman, but we are simply shown 'an affair' in progress; the situation is touched off very cleverly, but it is merely typical, an approximation, excellent indeed for brisk articles on married life or light comedies but beneath the level, the highly individualised level, of great fiction; everywhere the emphasis is laid on what might be called the constant factors in sexual life, love and marriage as they appear to a psychologist and not as they should appear to an artist; his men may be finely individualised but they are not individualised in their sexual relations, and as for his women, they are too often simply *La Femme*, and no sooner do they make their appearance than we hear, coming faintly down the wind, the vast and endless generalisations of the Boulevards. This is not the least but it is the last of the many limitations that must be noticed, however ungrateful it may seem, in any account of one of the most prolific, entertaining and (within certain limits) conscientious writers of our time. When Denry the Card was chosen as Mayor, one of his rivals, with the solemnity of a literary critic, asked what Denry had done, 'what cause was he identified with,' and this devil's advocate was crushed by the reply that Denry was identified 'with the great cause of cheering us all up.' Mr. Bennett, in his lighter work, in which he has sketched so inimitably the urban comedy of the twentieth century, is identified with the same great cause and is, indeed, a Denry of letters. In his more ambitious novels, he has done something more worth while than even playing the Card, for he has taken ugly places in ugly epochs and by dint of rare understanding and noble labour has transformed their chronicles into art; has set a whole host of seemingly commonplace persons, the people of well nigh a whole countryside, marching down the years in that great procession which is headed by Hamlet and Falstaff, Uncle Toby and Cleopatra, Becky Sharp and Squire Western, Mr. Pickwick and the Wife of Bath.

VIRGINIA WOOLF
From "Character in Fiction"
The Criterion, July 1924, pp. 409–30

M y belief that men and women write novels because they are lured on to create some character which has thus imposed itself upon them has the sanction of Mr. Arnold Bennett. In an article from which I will quote he says: 'The foundation of good fiction is character-creating and nothing else. . . . Style counts; originality of outlook counts. But none of these counts anything like so much as the convincingness of the characters. If the characters are real the novel will have a chance; if they are not, oblivion will be its portion. . . .' And he goes on to draw the conclusion that we have no young novelists of first-rate importance at the present moment, because they are unable to create characters that are real, true, and convincing.

These are the questions that I want with greater boldness than discretion to discuss to-night. I want to make out what we mean when we talk about 'characters' in fiction; to say something about the question of reality which Mr. Bennett raises; and to suggest some reasons why the younger novelists fail to create characters, if, as Mr. Bennett asserts, it is true that fail they do. This will lead me, I am well aware, to make some very sweeping and some very vague assertions. For the question is an extremely difficult one. Think how little we know about character—think how little we know about art. But to make a clearance before I begin, I will suggest that we range Edwardians and Georgians into two camps: Mr. Wells, Mr. Bennett, and Mr. Galsworthy I will call the Edwardians; Mr. Forster, Mr. Lawrence, Mr. Strachey, Mr. Joyce, and Mr. Eliot I will call the Georgians. And if I speak in the first person, with intolerable egotism, I will ask you to excuse me. I do not want to attribute to the world at large the opinions of one solitary, ill-informed, and misguided individual.

My first assertion is one that I think you will grant—that every one in this room is a judge of character. Indeed it would be impossible to live for a year without disaster unless one practised character-reading and had some skill in the art. Our marriages, our friendships depend on it; our business largely depends on it; every day questions arise which can only be solved by its help. And now I will hazard a second assertion, which is more disputable perhaps, to the effect that on or about December 1910 human character changed.

I am not saying that one went out, as one might into a garden, and there saw that a rose had flowered, or that a hen had laid an egg. The change was not sudden and definite like that. But a change there was, nevertheless; and, since one must be arbitrary, let us date it about the year 1910. The first signs of it are recorded in the books of Samuel Butler, in *The Way of All Flesh* in particular; the plays of Bernard Shaw continue to record it. In life one can see the change, if I may use a homely illustration, in the character of one's cook. The Victorian cook lived like a leviathan in the lower depths, formidable, silent, obscure, inscrutable; the Georgian cook is a creature of sunshine and fresh air; in and out of the drawing-room, now to borrow the *Daily Herald*, now to ask advice about a hat. Do you ask for more solemn instances of the power of the human race to change? Read the *Agamemnon*, and see whether, in process of time, your sympathies are not almost entirely with Clytemnestra. Or consider the married life of the Carlyles, and bewail the waste, the futility, for him and for her, of the horrible domestic tradition which made it seemly for a woman of genius to spend her time chasing beetles, scouring saucepans, instead of writing books. All human relations have shifted—those between masters and servants, husbands and wives, parents and children. And when human relations change there is at the same time a change in religion, conduct, politics, and literature. Let us agree to place one of these changes about the year 1910. . . .

But now I must recall what Mr. Arnold Bennett says. He says that it is only if the characters are real that the novel has any chance of surviving. Otherwise, die it must. But I ask myself, what is reality? And who are the judges of reality? A character may be real to Mr. Bennett and quite unreal to me. For instance, in this article he says that Dr. Watson in *Sherlock Holmes* is real to him: to me Dr. Watson is a sack, stuffed with straw, a dummy, a figure of fun. And so it is with character after character—in book after book. There is nothing that people differ about more than the reality of characters, especially in contemporary books. But if you take a larger view I think that Mr. Bennett is perfectly right. If, that is, you think of the novels which seem to you great novels—*War and Peace, Vanity Fair, Tristram Shandy, Madame Bovary, Pride and Prejudice, The Mayor of Casterbridge, Villette*—if you think of these books, you do at once think of some character who has seemed to you so real (I do not by that mean so lifelike) that it has the power to make you think not merely of it itself, but of all sorts of things through its eyes—of religion, of love, of war, of peace, of family life, of balls in country towns, of sunsets, moonrises, the immortality of the soul. There is hardly any subject of human experience that is left out of *War and Peace*, it seems to me. And in all these novels all these great novelists have brought us to see whatever they wish us to see through

some character. Otherwise, they would not be novelists; but poets, historians, or pamphleteers.

But now let us examine what Mr. Bennett went on to say—he said that there was no great novelist among the Georgian writers because they cannot create characters who are real, true, and convincing. And there I cannot agree. There are reasons, excuses, possibilities which I think put a different colour upon the case. It seems so to me at least, but I am well aware that this is a matter about which I am likely to be prejudiced, sanguine, and nearsighted. I will put my view before you in the hope that you will make it impartial, judicial, and broad-minded. Why, then, is it so hard for novelists at present to create characters which seem real, not only to Mr. Bennett, but to the world at large? Why, when October comes round, do the publishers always fail to supply us with a masterpiece?

Surely one reason is that the men and women who began writing novels in 1910 or thereabouts had this great difficulty to face—that there was no English novelist living from whom they could learn their business. Mr. Conrad is a Pole; which sets him apart, and makes him, however admirable, not very helpful. Mr. Hardy has written no novel since 1895. The most prominent and successful novelists in the year 1910 were, I suppose, Mr. Wells, Mr. Bennett, and Mr. Galsworthy. Now it seems to me that to go to these men and ask them to teach you how to write a novel—how to create characters that are real—is precisely like going to a bootmaker and asking him to teach you how to make a watch. Do not let me give you the impression that I do not admire and enjoy their books. They seem to me of great value, and indeed of great necessity. There are seasons when it is more important to have books than to have watches. To drop metaphor, I think that after the creative activity of the Victorian age it was quite necessary not only for literature but for life, that someone should write the books that Mr. Wells, Mr. Bennett, and Mr. Galsworthy have written. Yet what odd books they are! Sometimes I wonder if we are right to call them books at all. For they leave one with so strange a feeling of incompleteness and dissatisfaction. In order to complete them it seems necessary to do something—to join a society, or, more desperately, to write a cheque. That done, the restlessness is laid, the book finished; it can be put upon the shelf, and need never be read again. But with the work of other novelists it is different. *Tristram Shandy* or *Pride and Prejudice* is complete in itself: it is self-contained; it leaves one with no desire to do anything, except indeed to read the book again, and to understand it better. The difference perhaps is that both Sterne and Jane Austen were interested in things in themselves; in character in itself; in the book in itself. Therefore everything was inside the book, nothing outside. But the Edwardians were never interested in character in itself; or in the book in itself. They were interested in something outside. Their books, then, were incomplete as books, and required that the reader should finish them, actively and practically, for himself.

. . . I will open the first book that chance puts in my way—*Hilda Lessways*. Let us see how he makes us feel that Hilda is real, true, and convincing, as a novelist should. She shut the door in a soft, controlled way, which showed the constraint of her relations with her mother. She was fond of reading *Maud*, she was endowed with the power to feel intensely. So far, so good; in his leisurely, surefooted way Mr. Bennett is trying in these first pages, where every touch is important, to show us the kind of girl she was.

But then he begins to describe, not Hilda Lessways, but the view from her bedroom window, the excuse being that Mr. Skellorn, the man who collects rents, is coming along that way. Mr. Bennett proceeds:

The bailiwick of Turnhill lay behind her; and all the murky district of the Five Towns, of which Turnhill is the northern outpost, lay to the south. At the foot of Chatterley Wood the canal wound in large curves on its way towards the undefiled plains of Cheshire and the sea. On the canal-side, exactly opposite to Hilda's window, was a flour-mill, that sometimes made nearly as much smoke as the kilns and the chimneys closing the prospect on either hand. From the flour mill a bricked path, which separated a considerable row of new cottages from their appurtenant gardens, led straight into Lessways Street, in front of Mrs. Lessways' house. By that path Mr. Skellorn should have arrived, for he inhabited the farthest of the cottages.

One line of insight would have done more than all thos lines of description; but let them pass as the necessary drudgery of the novelist. And now—where is Hilda? Alas. Hilda is still looking out of the window. Passionate and dissatisfied as she was, she was a girl with an eye for houses. She often compared this old Mr. Skellorn with the villas she saw from her bedroom window. Therefore the villas must be described. Mr. Bennett proceeds:

> The row was called Freehold Villas: a consciously proud name in a district where much of the land was copyhold and could only change owners subject to the payment of 'fines,' and to the feudal consent of a 'court' presided over by the agent of a lord of the manor. Most of the dwellings were owned by their occupiers, who, each an absolute monarch of the soil, niggled in his sooty garden of an evening amid the litter of drying shirts and towels. Freehold Villas symbolised the final triumph of Victorian economics, the apotheosis of the prudent and industrious artisan. It corresponded with a Building

Society Secretary's dream of paradise. And indeed it was a very real achievement. Nevertheless, Hilda's irrational contempt would not admit this.

Heaven be praised, we cry! At last we are coming to Hilda herself. But not so fast. Hilda may have been this, that, or the other; but Hilda not only looked at houses, and thought of houses; Hilda lived in a house. And what sort of a house did Hilda live in? Mr. Bennett proceeds:

> It was one of the two middle houses of a detached terrace of four houses built by her grandfather Lessways, the teapot manufacturer; it was the chief of the four, obviously the habitation of the proprietor of the terrace. One of the corner houses comprised a grocer's shop, and this house had been robbed of its just proportion of garden so that the seigneurial garden-plot might be triflingly larger than the other. The terrace was not a terrace of cottages, but of houses rated at from twenty-six to thirty-six pounds a year; beyond the means of artisans and petty insurance agents and rent-collectors. And further, it was well built, generously built; and its architecture, though debased, showed some faint traces of Georgian amenity. It was admittedly the best row of houses in that newly settled quarter of the town. In coming to it out of Freehold Villas Mr. Skellorn obviously came to something superior, wider, more liberal. Suddenly Hilda heard her mother's voice. . . .

But we cannot hear her mother's voice, or Hilda's voice: we can only hear Mr. Bennett's voice telling us facts about rents and freeholds and copyholds and fines. What can Mr. Bennett be about? I have formed my own opinion of what Mr. Bennett is about—he is trying to make us imagine for him; he is trying to hypnotise us into the belief that, because he has made a house, there must be a person living there.

E. F. BENSON

1867–1940

Edward Francis Benson was born on July 24, 1867, at Wellington College, where his father was headmaster. His childhood home was an early inspiration. Benson and his two brothers were expected to contribute regularly to a family magazine, and they all went on to become professional writers. Benson became interested in archeology at King's College, Cambridge, and after graduating in 1892 he joined the staff of the British School of Archeology in Athens. In 1893 he published his first novel, *Dodo*. This *roman à clef* satirizing an English society woman was a scandalous success, not least because Benson's father had become Archbishop of Canterbury.

Benson returned to England in 1895 to write full time. This he did for the rest of his life, eventually producing more than ninety books. Most were extremely popular novels of bourgeois foibles, including the "Lucia" series, which began with *Queen Lucia* in 1920. Benson also wrote biographies, plays (notably a successful adaptation of *Dodo* in 1905), and several volumes of memoirs, the best-known being *As We Were: A Victorian Peepshow*. From 1934 to 1937 he served as Mayor of Rye, where he lived in the former home of his close friend, Henry James. In 1938 he received an OBE, and an honorary fellowship from Magdalen College, Cambridge. Benson died in London on February 29, 1940.

Personal

It was in this epoch, for which "the nineties" is a convenient expression, that the long retarded spring burst into fullest summer and never has there been a more diverse flowering. Reac-

tion against the old conventions had already done its work, and out of it there came the new force which reaction generates. It had its fakes and its hoaxes, ever so many of them, but spurious reputations are won in every decade and quietly lost in the next, and time has dealt with them as it will no doubt deal with those of today, whose possessors now broadcast each other's praises through groves of loud-speakers. Many volumes of prose and poetry held by the nineties to be pearls of great price have long ago crumbled into dust, and certain critics now point derision at the nineties because they thought that such were real. Such a method is unsound, for no age has ever been able to judge of its own output, since fashion and the whim of the moment invariably selects much that takes its fancy and ascribes to it immortality, but now we are far enough off from the nineties to be able to judge with some approach to true perspective, and those authors, whom I have named, seem to me to be just as admirable today as they did when with the enthusiasm of youth I hailed each new volume as containing some supreme and ultimate revelation of art. I confess that I was then tipsy with the joy of life and the horns of Elfland were continually blowing, but the ferment still stirs in me and the horns still blow with undiminished magic when I read *Tess of the D'Urbervilles* or the *Jungle Book*.

It was not only because in those years I was of an age ripe but still fresh to enjoy the flowering of fine literature, that I account myself fortunate, but because these same years saw, glimmering from the darkness of the unknown, such manifestations of scientific marvels as no other short period can point to. Motor-cars and moving pictures, telephones and electric lighting, X-rays and other ultra-spectrum potencies, flying and submarines and the beginnings of wireless were all then in process of discovery and adaption to human uses. Today these have passed into the categories of conveniences which we take for granted, but then they were amazing and scarcely credible. Motoring was an adventure: well do I remember staying at a country house some ten miles from the nearest station, whose owner had one of those newfangled spit-fires, a hoarse tremulous monster of most uncertain gait. Some half dozen guests of whom I was one were leaving at the end of our stay, and the ritual was as follows. A cart with our luggage started an hour and a half before the time of our train. Twenty minutes later the motor set off with those who were daring enough to trust themselves to it, and, a quarter of an hour after the motor had gone, a brake with a pair of fast horses, so that if the motor had broken down or become intractable it would pick up the derelicts and convey them to the station. On this occasion the motor behaved surprisingly well. In spite of its having to stop whenever a horse-drawn vehicle appeared on the road, while the terrified animal was led past it, it came within sight of the luggage-cart half a mile from the station, and arrived there a quarter of an hour before the brake. So those great strong horses had not gained on us at all!—E. F. BENSON, "The Movement of the Nineties," *As We Were*, 1930, pp. 284–86

Works

MAKE WAY FOR LUCIA

One of the characteristics common to Edwardian comedy is that it is a fairy tale for adults—indeed in the double meaning of the word. Its characters are seen as sexless. We can put this down to convention rather than to Puritanism, but the artifice does not mean that the novelist does not know or cannot insinuate what is going on under the surface of manners. It may be the point in the *Lucia* comedies of E. F. Benson that his people are neutered and that they are exhilarated and liberated by taking part in a useful psychological fraud. His enormously popular *Lucia* novels, now published in one fat volume, may even be a comically insinuating diagnosis.

What does Lucia, his self-appointed Queen of Riseholme, want as she sits in her fake medieval house or her garden where

only Shakespearean flowers are allowed to grow? Certainly not sex. Not even connubial sex; her ruling passions are for power and publicity; she wants the gossip columns to mention her. She wants to dish her rivals. What about her husband, Peppino, writing his privately printed and artily bound little poems? No sex there or, we can guess, elsewhere. The pair have sublimated in dozens of little arty affectations, their happy marriage consolidated by the lies of baby talk and in snobbish snatches of Italian they have picked up from waiters in Italy. When an Italian singer comes to stay they can't understand a word he says.

And what about Georgie, Lucia's devoted *cicisbeo*, always on the go socially when she commands, playing his bits of Mozart to her, listening to her playing the first movement of "dear Beethoven's" *Moonlight* Sonata—the second is too fast. Georgie keeps changing his clothes, sits in his doll's house, doing his embroidery, painting a little picture or two, and being "busy at home" one day a week when he is having his toupee fixed and his hair dyed. Homosexual probably, but no boys in sight; certainly a Narcissus. There is no need to tell us: he gives himself away in his frenzied cult of youth, his fuss about his bibelots, his malicious pleasure in seeing through "*cara*" Lucia's snobbery, her frauds, and her lies instantly, enjoying his horror of her as a sister figure he cannot do without. And then there are the various loud masculine ladies of the clique in Riseholme: hearty butches in combat with Lucia's bitcheries; even the surrounding overweight wives with their sulking or choleric husbands are without children and exist in stertorous comic relief. The servants are faithful. The monstrous Lady Ambermere calls hers "my people," as if she were an empress. The obsequious tradesmen of the town seem to be the only people engaged—but off the scene—in the vulgar task of begetting their kind.

Since it is not sex that makes this world go round, what does? Gossip above all, spying from windows, plotting about teas and dinner parties, a genteel greed for money and news, and above all matching wits against Lucia's ruthless gifts. Our culture hound, who poses at her window, swots up in the Encyclopedia before distinguished guests arrive, pretending to have read Nietzsche or Theophrastus, can't distinguish between Schumann and Schubert. She steals a guru from Daisy Quantock, hooks a medium—a fake Russian princess—and although these things lead to farcical disaster, she rises above it and is on to the next fad like a hawk. Her dishonesty is spectacular, her vitality endless; and if Riseholme tears her to pieces and is deeply hurt when she inherits a small fortune and takes a house in London to conquer Society there with the same assurance, they long for her to return and, when she does, welcome her with joy. After all, Lucia may have made herself ridiculous but she has come back: she is Life.

Lucia's bids for power in London lead to disasters far beyond the mishaps of Riseholme; but her resilience in intrigue grips us. At the center of the novels is Georgie—"*Georgino mio*"—and their close relationship is based on fascination—she needs his spite, he needs her deceits. Each is the other's mirror. At one point a delightful opera singer almost snatches him because she can see Lucia as a joke; but this infidelity is nominal. When she shows signs of wanting to be cuddled in Le Touquet, he sheers off in terror and returns to Lucia, forgiven. . . .

The period is surprisingly the post-1918 one, but that beastly war is not mentioned. Pockets of Edwardian manners survived long after that war, for inherited money is the great preserver of dead cultures. Many of his characters—notably minor ones like Lady Ambermere, a woman of slowly enunciated and grandiose rudeness—were in action fifty years ago. I can remember their accents and their syntax. And here lies part of Benson's absurd spell: his ear for the dialogue of cliques is quick and devastating, for he understands the baby talk of fairyland which, of course, sex and our four-letter words have destroyed. (Unless mass society's own nonstop chatter about "fucking," "screwing," and the boys "having it off" is itself a new fairy tale jargon.) The minor catch phrases preserve their cracked notes. "How tarsome!" exclaims Georgie. "Au reservoir" spreads like measles in place of "*au revoir.*" There is a key to Benson's wicked mind in the following passage between Lucia and "*Georgino mio*":

> "*I domestichi* are making *salone* ready."
> "*Molto bene*" [she said.]
> "Everybody's tummin'," said Georgie, varying the cipher.
> "Me so *nervosa!*" said Lucia. "Fancy me doing Brunnhilde before singing Brunnhilde. Me can't bear it."

The key word is "cipher." Benson knew the cipher of all his characters. His pleasure was in the idiotic gabble of life. Is he too tepid for export? Years ago Gilbert Seldes compared Benson with the Sinclair Lewis of *Main Street* but pointed out that Lewis spoiled his book by his violent fury. Benson was never furious when he killed an age. He believed that love lasts longest when it is unkind.—V. S. PRITCHETT, "Pleasures of Malice," *NYRB*, June 23, 1977, pp. 8–10

"The art of these books lies in their simplicity," wrote Nancy Mitford, whose devotion to the Lucia saga was shared by W. H. Auden and Noel Coward. "The jokes seem quite obvious and are often repeated: we can never have enough of them." Benson created a small-scale world that is a pleasure to enter. Unemphasized details, no part of his comic intent, have taken on a period glow in the half-century since these novels first appeared. On her morning shopping tours, the main purpose of which is collecting thrilling gossip, Lucia stops at the poulterer's and wavers between pheasant, partridge, wild duck and hare for dinner.

But Nancy Mitford was mistaken, I think, in suggesting that the books show their age by the fact that "in Lucia words, 'that horrid thing which Freud calls sex' is utterly ignored." Nothing could be franker than Benson's tracing Lucia's motives for taking a "lover" in London: "The idea of having a real lover was, of course, absolutely abhorrent to her whole nature, and besides, she did not know whom she could get. But the reputation of having a lover was a wholly different matter . . . and most decidedly it gave a woman a certain *cachet.* . . . It would be quite dreadful if he misunderstood and unexpectedly imprinted on her lips or even her hand a hot lascivious kiss." When Georgie and the widowed Lucia decide to convert their bloodless idyll into marriage, there is a finely gauged scene in which they sound each other out about a union without unwelcome "connubialities." Sex in these books is evaded by the characters, not ignored by the author.—WALTER CLEMENS, "Importance of Being Lucia," *Nwk*, July 4, 1977, p. 73

Edward Frederic Benson died in 1940 at the age of 72, having published some 80 books—light fiction and historical biographies—nearly all of which are now out of print. He came from a highly literary family, son of an Archbishop of Canterbury and brother of A. C. Benson, the essayist, and Robert Hugh Benson, who is chiefly remembered for *Come Rack! Come Rope!*, a bloodcurdling account of Catholic martyrdom after the Reformation in England.

Throughout the 1920's and 30's his *Lucia* novels attracted an enthusiastic cult, rather similar—although larger and less self-consciously literary—to the present one for Anthony Powell's *A Dance to the Music of Time*. There are, indeed, many comparisons to be made between the two, and Powell is just old enough to have greeted the *Lucia* novels on their first appearance; but I should be surprised if any reissue of *Dance* 35 years after its author's death will cause half the excitement or pleasure of *Lucia*. Like most of my generation, I had only dimly heard of E. F. Benson, while taking P. G. Wodehouse and Saki with my mother's milk. He comes now as an entirely delightful surprise. . . .

It is seldom one can read through 913 pages with unflagging delight. Without this reissue I might have gone to my grave without ever knowing about Lucia or Miss Mapp. It is not a risk anyone should take lightly.—AUBERON WAUGH, "913 Pages of Delight," *NYTBR*, Aug. 7, 1977, pp. 1, 27

There is an underground in this country; an underground bound together by an ideology more compelling than the Weather Underground's apocalyptic paranoia. There is an international band of happy followers more devoted to one another than any college fraternity during the estrus of rush week and in comparison to which sisterhood is powerless. There is a secret society whose center may or may not be London, a religion whose home is Rye in Sussex, whose adherents may be among your most respected friends, neighbors and business associates. You may never know it. For these people do not seek converts. They are more jealous of their membership than any Mafia or Mensa. There are no special assemblies either en masse or in secret session: Two can be a quorum. Indeed, these people do not necessarily recognize one another until, like the shaking of the sacred urn among Bacchantes when the slopes of Mount Cithaeron trembled in joyous expectation at the cries of "Euhoe Bacche!" that special name is uttered: Lucia.

Who is this Lucia who inspires such a following? She is Mrs. Emmeline Lucas, wife of Philip Lucas, alias Peppino; arbiter of taste, fashion and fad among her neighbors; hated, feared, loved, admired, but always deferred to by them; implacable enemy yet prime analogate of fraud; vacillating but always victorious; matrona potens of the bridge table; semi-bucolic Boadicea; and only incidentally the main character in a series of novels by E. F. Benson collected here under the general title *Make Way for Lucia*.

In these novels, written between 1920 and 1939, Benson has created a small world consisting of two British villages and populated that world with characters so idiosyncratic and so improbable that they must have been based on real people. In the first novel we are introduced to the village of Riseholme, which "might perhaps, according to the crude materialism of maps, be included in the kingdom of Great Britain, but in a more real and inward sense . . . formed a complete kingdom of its own," and to the "queen" of that kingdom, Mrs. Lucas, known to her friends simply as Lucia. Though Lucia is "essentially autocratic," her subjects are allowed and even encouraged to develop their own minds or their own lives, provided always that those lives met at the junction where she was stationmaster." As a final note in introducing her, Benson adds that "she believed in God in much the same way that she believed in Australia. . . ." We are also introduced to Lucia's somewhat epicene sidekick, Georgie Pillson, whose main occupations when not plotting with Lucia seem to be watercolors, embroidery and the careful dusting of his "bibelots."

The third novel introduces an entirely new cast of characters and centers around Miss Elizabeth Mapp, a malevolent counterpart to Lucia, in a village named Tilling. Tilling is clearly identifiable as Rye in Sussex, and it was here that Benson wrote the novels using his own home (Lamb House, where Henry James had also lived and written) as the residence of the main character. It should be mentioned at this point that Georgie also has his counterpart in Tilling: the flamboyant Irene Coles, a young artist whose main occupations seem to be insulting and/or embarrassing Miss Mapp, and painting slightly lurid canvasses of wrestling women.

The stage is set for the rest of the novels. Lucia moves to Tilling, the fiefdom of Miss Mapp, and there ensues a struggle for power that Milton would have despaired of describing. Yet for all this mighty conflict there is no identifiable plot, just a series of delicious episodes enharmonically modulating into one another.

The result is compulsive reading, though I am not altogether certain why. Even on fourth reading I found the books difficult to lay aside. There is no doubt that Benson's style helps carry them. He uses structures and cadences redolent of those which make Thackeray and Trollope such great fun to read aloud, but without a hint of those excesses which make Dickens such a paralyzing bore.

Perhaps that is the key. It is as if Benson has accomplished with a chamber group what Trollope created for full orchestra in, say, the Barset Chronicles. The two have created individual worlds whose inhabitants should not really exact much of our interest and whose problems ought not interest us at all. Before we know it we have been snared; we develop a passionate interest in the characters, their activities and even their gossip.

Trollope's world of Barsetshire, though closed, is nonetheless real. Benson's villages, though artfully executed, do not stand close scrutiny. There are, for instance, no children in these novels. Marriages exist, but more as partnerships in intrigue than as personal or (heaven forfend!) physical relationships. If Georgie Pillson had a sexual dimension to his character, he would be as gay as a garden party and a very unfair stereotype. But this dimension is missing in Georgie, in Irene Coles, as redoubtable a daughter of Bilitis as ever rode a motorcycle, and in the other characters as well. Benson's world is one in which everyone is middle-aged and living on an income for which he no longer toils. Death intrudes three times: twice between novels for the convenience of the story in the next book and only once in the course of the narration—and even that takes place offstage in a humorous way.—PETER MATTHEWS, "The Giddy, the Grim and the Gay," *Am*, Feb. 18, 1978, pp. 125–26

OTHER WORKS

Think of meeting Dodo again, after all these years, and finding her quite unspoiled, quite as gay and irresponsible, capable of the same variety of amazing chatter, and just as good a companion as ever she was in the old days. To be sure, ⟨*Dodo's Daughter*⟩ is ostensibly about Dodo's daughter, but where Dodo is Dodo dominates. The selfish and epigrammatic Nadine is well done, extremely so, and her love story is engaging, but it's Dodo we are really glad to see and hear—especially hear!

For no one ever wrote chatter as Mr. Benson writes it. Brilliant, inconsequent, nonsensical chatter, such as persons might actually talk, if they were clever enough. You are never sure where any one in this book will end, whatever the subject may be that has started him or, usually, her. Be it Seymour, with his passion for jades (not the female, but the Chinese sort), or Berts without a brain, or Esther or Nadine or even John the Prig, they none of them make a set speech—they talk,

and it's wonderful. It's a revelation of how little talk there is in most books, in spite of all the quotation marks running down the pages. . . .

You have to be in a certain mood to read the Dodo books, young or old. But then if you begin to read one you are sure to get into that required mood without the least loss of time. Beginning this sequel took courage. We had loved the old Dodo, and it seemed such a pity to have resurrected her, perfect in her day, and to bring her, somewhat stiff and forced to a galvanic effort at life, back among a world of readers who had no further use for her. But that is an idea doomed to be killed early. . . .

It doesn't seem to matter particularly that the thread of the story is an entertaining one to unravel, with a villain in it no other than the drunken and yet elegant old Prince, once Dodo's husband; lots of love, a jilt, a great storm and heroic rescue, with minor matters. Of course it is jolly having a well-told and amusing story thrown in, but it is the characters that delight you most. What a group they are! And how exquisitely Mr. Benson draws in the scenic background, the sweet country, the town, the sea. When he writes of the storm it is truly a storm he brings into the page, until you feel its mighty buffetings and hear its shriek and roar and watch the wild motion of it, sea and wind.

But always and above all it is the people who count. Seymour, "who ought to have been drowned, when he was a girl, like a kitten," and to whom Nadine engages herself because she doesn't love him nor he her, and so as to prove to Hugh, who does love her, that there is no use going on proposing. And Berts, who might be engaged to Esther, for "they often used to talk about getting engaged to each other some day, in a mild and sexless fashion, but they were neither of them in a hurry." Berts is big, idiotic, likeable, and a good tennis player, "nine feet high, but somehow ladylike," as Edith says, and can also talk amazingly, particularly on the subject of his mother. Next to Dodo the greatest joy in the book is Edith, Mrs. Arbuthnot, who has become racier with the passage of time. She, her music, her costumes—at one moment we meet her in one of Dodo's most magnificent dinner gowns, with her golf boots on, for she is always losing her luggage—and her opinions, expressed quite as wonderfully as Dodo's. As Dodo says:

> Oh, Edith, at last the "Hunting of the Snark" has come true. I see now that we are Boojums. People softly and silently vanish away while we are talking, dear. They can't stand it, and I've noticed it before. Dear old Chesterford used to vanish sometimes like that, and I never knew until I saw he wasn't there.

Nadine is not the only one who has a love story. Dodo has hers, too, and at last it is a real love story, not like the ones she used to have in the first book. Dodo and Jack are married at last, quite early in the story, and a most enchanting couple they make. There is much more womanly tenderness in Dodo nowadays than there was. She has deepened and sweetened, and she is happy, as well as clever and gay. It is an achievement, this ripened Dodo, completely in character, who has taken Fate's unkinder gifts with the sporting spirit which was always her fetish, and loves life as eagerly as ever she did.

One could go back and forth through these pages, and quote something from each one to bring a laugh or start a thought. It all glitters, but not with the glare of paste. The rays are many colored, rich, glowing. The life portrayed is one of careless ease and the habit of play, but it is not wasted. Not a bit of it. No more than the perfume of those flowers born to blush unseen. To be sure, Dodo and her set do not blush unseen, nor seen either, for that matter. But the mere fact that they exist is delightful and amusing, as much to the rest of the world as to themselves.

Dodo's Daughter is a kind of glorified nonsense, but it has the juice of life in it, and it has the power of making you feel entirely content as you read. One would like a new Dodo every year. Lacking that, this new Dodo will probably be read and reread as often as was the earlier volume. The lovers of Dodo may be a selected class, but they are not inconsiderable in number, and they will grow in bulk considerably during the ensuing months.

As a closing bit of advice, we want to warn readers not to read this book while alone. The desire to share its best little bits is too overpowering. If you haven't some one near to whom you can quote these fragments hot from the page you are likely to begin talking to yourself, or to try to recollect certain special gems next day for the benefit of the first person you encounter. And as you are sure to get them wrong, for they all hang together in a kind of spontaneous mosaic that won't stick verbatim in any mind, this is criminal. It might turn a prospective Dodo fan away without a trial—and to deprive any one who would enjoy Dodo from doing so is cruel and unusual punishment.—HILDEGARDE HAWTHORNE, "Mr. Benson's Dodo as Charming as Ever," *NYTBR*, March 22, 1914, pp. 130–31

In life and in literature E. F. Benson was a master of discrimination. A sense of humour, a sense of quality—these are the flavours that permeate every page of ⟨*Final Edition*⟩; they are as unmistakable as the savoury smell that hangs about a good kitchen. Everything that comes out of that kitchen is treated with the same care and skill; there is no browning, no tin-opener, no sauce out of the bottle. The prose style of E. F. Benson's final works (the trilogy of reminiscences and the best of the biographies) does not seem to me to have received enough praise, though it is surely the perfection of melodious courtesy. Beguiling, perfectly mannered, his sentences slip past unnoticed, precisely fulfilling their author's principle.

> I demand that prose should have a certain intrinsic beauty of its own quite apart from the meaning it conveys. This beauty is quite consistent with the utmost lucidity and does not depend at all on decoration.

He finished *Final Edition* just before his death, and a publisher's note tells us that he devoted exceptional pains to its revision. It would therefore have been a kindness to clean up the few sentences which illness obliged him to leave untidy or ill-punctuated; they show like a dandelion on the centre court at Wimbledon.

Apart from its immense readability and ceaseless flow of appropriate and amusing anecdote, *Final Edition* has the interest of containing remarkably candid disquisitions on the literary personalities (they were all literary to the bone) of the author and his famous brothers. Those who knew A. C. Benson were aware of far more in that acute intelligence than the armchair piety of his popular essays; and E. F.'s discussion of A. C.'s dual nature makes one long for the uncensored publication of the voluminous and highly inflammatory diaries of the Master of Magdalene.

> The evangelist of a placid reflective life told him that his university work was a very second-rate affair, while the busy effective don looked with scorn on the cheap facility of the writing which so large a circle of readers found inspirational. Below his ceaseless in-

dustry he recognised that his mind was essentially lazy, he did not take the trouble to think out these problems for which he prescribed faith and tranquillity, as if these could be procured at a chemist's, like a bottle of opodeldoc to be well rubbed in and for external application only.

That is admirable, and on Hugh's Catholicism the light, though kinder, is scarcely less penetrating. Penetrating it remained, even when turned inwards upon the amusing, successful novelist which was all that, by middle age, E. F. Benson had made of himself. The gaiety of his novels was threadbare, they did not bear re-reading; and this worried him as it would not have worried his brothers. Alone of the brilliant Bensons, of whom he appeared the least distinguished, E. F. had the discrimination and self-criticism to see what was petty in his busy intellectual life and what was trivial in his productions. In the middle of a prosperous and admired career he deliberately set himself to make a clean sweep and do better. Among the books that resulted, *Charlotte Brontë* is a capital biography; but it is the three volumes of reminiscence—*As We Were*, *As We Are* and the present volume—which constitute his real achievement. Pretending only to sketch in the surface traits of his time, and relying upon that highly developed instinct of discrimination and that impeccable style, E. F. Benson produced something small but durable, an agreeable footnote to history which many future readers will prefer to the solemn text itself.—DESMOND SHAWE-TAYLOR, "Discrimination," *NSN*, Jan. 11, 1941, pp. 42–44

E. F. Benson's numerous ghostly tales fall into two categories: visionary outdoor stories that attempt to communicate a romantic sense of place, and grim, claustrophobic stories that frequently involve supernatural revenge in haunted-house settings. In both categories he is a master of imagery and a consummate craftsman, although his stories have a curious tendency to fall apart at the end ("And No Bird Sings," "The Face," "The Room in the Tower"). His celebrated skill in characterization and social commentary, especially praised by critics in his revived Lucia novels, is always brought to bear in his ghost stories, making them some of the most sophisticated in the genre.

The outdoor stories are in the mystical tradition of Blackwood and Machen: nature, which is both dazzling and sinister, has animistic qualities that suggest supernatural forces. "The Man Who Went Too Far," Benson's most famous tale in this category, unleashed a Pan-like deity similar to Machen's "The Great God Pan." "A Tale of a Deserted House," a more obscure work, has a vast sense of space that recalls Blackwood. Although Benson is less magical and surreal than Machen and less original in his elemental imagery than Blackwood, he has a deft sense of contrast: his stories have a healthy out-of-doors quality, a relentless prettiness, that suddenly becomes stained with the onslaught of vampires ("Mrs. Amworth"), mummies ("Monkeys"), or giant slugs ("Caterpillars," "Negotium Perambulans," "And No Bird Sings"). Although Benson stocks his forests and landscapes with all manner of demons and ghosts, he has a special, charmingly perverse fetish for monstrous slugs and wormlike creatures.

His claustrophobic haunted-house tales are as gray and grim as any in the genre. Especially powerful is "The Bath-Chair," the story of a man haunted by the ghost of a crippled, vengeful father. Others include "Naboth's Vineyard," "The Corner House," and "James Lamp." Even the stories that do not quite come off have a strong sense of cumulative buildup and invariably contain memorable apparition scenes. The control and understatement in Benson give him an affinity with M. R. James, as does his flair for sardonic humor. His collections are uniformly high in quality, despite the critical carpings of August Derleth and Edmund Wilson. The stories have also appeared in *Weird Tales* and in numerous anthologies, notably Lady Cynthia Asquith's collections.—JACK SULLIVAN, "Psychological, Antiquarian, and Cosmic Horror: 1872–1919," *Horror Literature*, ed. Marshall B. Tymn, 1981, pp. 233–34.

JOHN BERGER

1926–

John Peter Berger was born on November 5, 1926, in London. He studied at the Central School of Art and the Chelsea School of Art, for a time supporting himself by teaching drawing. During the years of 1944–46 he served in the Buckinghamshire and Oxford Light Infantry.

Despite Berger's many and varied interests (as painter, art critic, novelist, essayist, translator, film and television writer), it has been Art (shaped by his Marxist viewpoint) that has been the mainstay of his career. Vision itself, what he calls "ways of seeing," is his central theme. He was art critic for the *New Statesman* for ten years, and his books *The Success and Failure of Picasso* (1965), and *Art and Revolution* (1969) contain some of the most challenging views on the role of art today that we have.

Berger has written four novels to date, the latest of which, *G.* (1972), won the Booker Prize and the James Tait Black Memorial Prize. In his acceptance speech for the Booker Prize, Berger attacked its sponsors for their imperialist activities.

In 1975 he published *A Seventh Man*, a portrait of migrant workers in Europe. During the 1970s his collaboration with Swiss film director Alain Tanner resulted in several films, one of which (*Jonah Who Will Be 25 in the Year 2000*) won the New York Critics' Prize for the best scenario of 1976. He also created a series of television programs on art and the way we look at the world, called *Ways of Seeing*.

Berger has been married twice and has three children. He has lived in London, Paris, and Switzerland. He now lives in the French Jura, the setting for his trilogy *Into Their Labors*, of which the first part, *Pig Earth*, was published in 1980. His latest book is *Another Way of Telling*, a collaboration with the photographer Jean Mohr. John Berger now lives in the French peasant community he portrayed in *Pig Earth*.

Works

FICTION

A Painter of Our Time purports to be the story of one Janos Lavin, Hungarian painter of genius, as told by his friend, an English art critic named John. Since John Berger is a well-known English art critic and painter, it is safe to assume that the views of the hero are those of the author. In fact, there would be little point to the work if this were not so.

Janos Lavin had fled Hungary in 1919 to escape the anti-Communist terror. Settled in London, he paints on in an obscurity relieved only by the short-lived success of his anti-Nazi etchings during the war, and pieces out a livelihood by holding a precarious teaching job. Eventually, in 1956 when Janos is sixty, recognition and prosperity overtake him. Unaccountably irritated by success, he disappears, apparently in order to participate in the Budapest uprising—though on which side it is hard to say. "I myself," John writes, "would like to believe that Janos, if he is now alive, supports Kadar."

The bulk of *A Painter of Our Time* consists of a journal intermittently kept by the hero during his last four years in London, in which he records his reflections on politics, society and art—and particularly on the problems and progress of his own paintings.

Much of John Berger's—or Janos Lavin's—comment on

art in general and on the problems of the artist in society is interesting and sound, though it would be more at home in an essay than in such a novel as this. Tolstoy said that the function of the novelist's art is "to make that understood which in the form of argument would be incomprehensible." Mr. Berger seems rather to use fiction to obscure ideas that would be clear in the form of argument and as an excuse for not organizing and developing ideas as they deserve.

To the end of the book, Janos' convictions and motivations remain obscure. He is a Marxist, though more than a little of a deviationist at his moments. At one point he maintains that the artist can serve the Communist cause as well by producing works "under his own volition" exempt from any editing as by being an immediate propagandist. Yet at practically the same time he says, "You can't work for anything under the cover of art. I can't even work for Socialism under the cover of my art." Judging by his appreciation of Poussin and his statement that "Cubism is to us what Anatomy was to Michelangelo," his own work is not touched by the kind of "social realism" that Moscow decrees. Also it is doubtful that his dictum that "all great drawing . . . drawing to discover . . . is drawing from memory" would find much favor in neo-Marxist criticism. His assertion that all artists "work for different ends; a few of them personal, most of them social and historical" definitely straddles the party line.

One of the chief weaknesses of the book is that it is almost impossible to visualize Janos' paintings. To create as a character in a novel a painter who is at once an authentic genius, living in his own right, and a composite of several other painters is quite possible. Proust's Elstir is a compound of Manet, Renoir, Monet, Whistler and other impressionist painters; yet he is a convincing character and the reader has a clear conception of what his work looks like.

Janos' masterpiece, except that it is of monumental dimensions and contains human figures, never comes into focus. It seems to be such an incongruous scramble of Picasso's *Guernica*, Léger's *Les Constructeurs* and the Douanier Rousseau's *Match de Rugby* that all his comments on it as a work in progress flutter off into nothingness.

According to the dust jacket, the book proposes to answer the question: "How does the artist function in this fragmented world of the twentieth century?" If the question means what it seems to mean, the inevitable answer must be that he functions in as many different ways as there are individual artists and differing environments for them. Like the fictional Janos, both Léger (whom Janos calls "the greatest artist of our time") and Picasso are Marxists, but it is hard to find any significant common ground in the way they function in the modern world.— RAMON GUTHRIE, "Creed for an Artist," *Nation*, April 1959, p. 346

Always a didactic, Mr. Berger believes that no convincing portrait of a painter has ever been done in fiction and, in this novel, attempts to give us one. We have only to compare the journal of Delacroix or the letters of Van Gogh with novels like Zola's *L'Oeuvre*, Maugham's portrait of Gauguin, or Joyce Cary's very funny sub-Turnerian rapscallion, to see Mr. Berger's case. Gulley Jimpson's methods as a painter were sploshing and literary; he convinces merely as a picturesque Bohemian of his period, never as a serious artist. There is a fundamental hostility between the literary and the pictorial media. One can see this very plainly in Zola's novel—to my mind, by far the most conscientious attempt at the subject. Zola drew partly from close observation of Cézanne, but was unable to resist blending 'my own intimate life as a creative artist. . . . I shall also give him the wish to execute huge modern decorative works, frescoes giving a complete survey of our day and age', *i.e.*, novels by Zola, not pictures. The other difficulty is the romanticisation of the lives of painters; this was justified for a time in the nineteenth century when the belief that 'the artist' and 'the bourgeois' were two different people was an article of faith. It was later debased. Here Mr. Berger is no less romantic than his predecessors, though in another way. His title, with its echo of Lermontov, is one clue. Another is his belief that the good artist now is not so much at odds with the bourgeois, as he is married to the Future, at present identified with the class struggle. Mr. Berger is well-equipped as a painter and as an earnest, provocative and puritanic critic. As a satirical impression of the art world and an account of a painter's real technical preoccupations, the novel comes very close to the painter at work.

The work consists of the diaries of Janos Lavin, a Hungarian refugee Communist of the Bela Kun period, who fled to Berlin and, later, on to London in 1938. His marriage to an upper-class girl with a small private income gives him the conventional sacrificial victim from the bourgeoisie. We read a portion of his London diaries helped out by occasional comments from Mr. Berger. Lavin is now 60, an intense, dedicated and prosaic man who looks earthy like a potato. He has the true painter's obsession. He has the ageing man's sadness and stoicism. He has the émigré's guilt; the Communist's agonies of conscience. His lifelong friend in Hungary has just been executed. (The moral issue is jesuitically evaded by the argument that the British 'commit murder'—Cyprus, Malaya, etc.—and that the Communists, belonging to a higher morality, 'execute'.) Lavin, a killer himself, is torn between faith and doubt. Faith—if that is what it is—wins and Lavin disappears to Hungary and is probably shot—it hardly seems to matter on which side for the important thing is to be immersed and implicated. We must compare Lavin's disappearance with the death of Claude Lantier in front of his masterpiece in Zola's *L'Oeuvre*; both are stage suicides. Lavin speaks of petit bourgeois irrationalism; the charge rebounds. We may go on to think of Dr Zhivago's comment on his friend who gloried in having been re-educated in gaol. 'It was like listening to a circus horse describing how it broke itself in.'

It would be a nice point to decide whether Lavin went to Hungary because he was passionately a Hungarian, a refugee, as a Communist, as a painter losing faith in his art, as an impulsive human being living blindly in the present. He is really less interesting as 'a painter' than as 'a refugee', a lay figure who is in a state of anguished dialogue with his socialism. Here we meet Mr. Berger debating intensely and often brilliantly with himself, often also in self-contradiction. Lavin, for example, mistrusts the view of Sir Gerald Banks, the civilised connoisseur, that the essence of the act of the artist is risk; but appears later to believe in the artist's mysterious autonomy. The account of Lavin's visit to Sir Gerald's house is a pleasant piece of comedy. This very well-written scene and the final one describing Lavin's successful show, indicate that Mr. Berger has a gift for light satire, which the solemnity of the diary of Lavin has concealed. A diarist has the privilege of being God Almighty, but *did* the different visions of Delacroix, Cézanne, Van Gogh, etc., spring 'from the conviction that they each knew that life could be better, richer, juster, truer than it was'? *Is* it true that 'Every modern attempt to create a work of art is based on the desire (usually undeclared) to increase the value of the experience that gave rise to the work. In the nineteenth and twentieth centuries such an increase in *value* must inevitably be counted in terms of human pleasure, truth or justice'? Always justice? A little later, Lavin makes a sharper self-judgment. 'Sentimental works are ones which have never really been begun, which embody only the hope instead of the discovery'. Still later in the struggle, Lavin argues with his old Marxist teachers and says 'we have made a profound mistake whenever we have used our Marxism to make an arbitrary division between art that is for us (progressive art) and art which is against us (decadent art)'. There is only good or bad—but 'we' understand the difference better than the 'bourgeois'(!). Do not ask for Socialist art to be judged by Socialist standards. 'The standards will be untrue and opportunist. Instead, turn artists into Communists'. All the same: 'I cannot, as an artist, work by the light of an historical principle. I must work by the light of my senses—here and now. For an artist there is no such thing as a period of transition. *He faces his subject as if it were timeless*. How much has been lost by this simple fact not being understood? Even in a period of transition men grow old and die and children are born. The politician can sometimes forget this. I, never'. All this is at Mr. Berger's infuriating best. It is an encumbered, pugnacious, one-track best, ingeniously argued; full of sound, simple things as well as the well-known dogmatisings which, since *Dr. Zhivago*, have finally lost their spell.

By presenting Lavin to us mainly through his diaries, Mr. Berger protects Lavin and enhances his sincerity. The fidelity to the painter's temperament is perhaps glum but unmistakable and loving. If Lavin's arguments are often crude, his dilemma as an émigré is perfectly understood and felt. But the true task of the novelist is to expose and the weakness of the portrait springs from the excessive convenience of the diaries: they induce an uncritical, incurious and unimaginative view of character and deny Lavin life as a figure in the round. It is a judgment on the method that one comes with relief on Mr. Berger's own brief interventions in the book.—V. S. PRITCHETT, "From the Horse's Mouth," *NSN*, Nov. 15, 1958, pp. 701–2

Of all the discarded masks in the steamer trunk of cultural history, none seems less promising to wear or to meditate on than that of Don Juan. Every popular psychology book for years has minutely explained that under the Don's omnivorous sexuality lurks impotence and death, the objectification of human relations, and a childish ego forcing the world to make up for not being an extension of himself. Especially in 1972, when no one wants to be treated as an object, Don Juan would seem to be the arch-villain, his sexual pride an index of his emptiness.

But in John Berger's excellent and fascinating new novel *G.*, "a novel on the theme of Don Juan," dedicated to "Anya and her sisters in Women's Liberation," there appears not the sexual coup-counter of the Freudians, but the Don Juan who captured the European imagination for more than 200 years— Tiro de Molina's Don Juan, Molière's Don Juan, Mozart's Don Giovanni, Byron's Don Juan—the symbol of personal freedom, the eternal rebel against God, against nature, against society, against culture, in the name of a world in which the only complex and authentic elaborations of identity and relation are made sexually.

In the thick mulch at the roots of the English novel, the Don Juan figure, the libertine, played a central part. He was a self-justifying, self-contained character as pure in his way as the moral and spiritual woman who so often opposed him, each attempting to assert a personal definition of the self-sufficient personality. But Berger, who has been the art critic of the *New Statesman*, and most recently the author of *The Success and Failure of Picasso* and *Art and Revolution*, makes his Don Juan more similar to Byron's—the boyish and fallible voyager after sexual adventure who sardonically but compassionately observes the shams and deceits of the societies he moves through.

The hero of Berger's novel is G. (for Giovanni), the illegitimate son of an English mother and an Italian father. Rich and privileged, he is free to travel. He was conceived four years after the death of Garibaldi in 1886, born in Paris, raised by an aunt and uncle in England—and he was dead in Trieste on the day war was declared by Italy and Austro-Hungary. The events of European history swirl around G., counterpointing our view of his personal destiny. History in this book is often a matter of crowds, of Garibaldi's ragged army entering Naples in 1860, or the rioting workers in the streets of Milan in 1898, or the crowds of Bosnian nationalists, Italian Irredentists and Hapsburg soldiers in the streets of Trieste in 1915.

Part of the power and fascination of G. comes from this extraordinary mixture of historical detail and sexual meditation—for at the intersection of G. and history is Berger's attitude toward heroism. G. is neither the public romantic Garibaldi, who galvanizes an entire people, nor is he a private romantic like his friend Chavez, who in 1910 won a prize for being the first man to fly over the Alps. Garibaldi is already dead before G. is born. But, while Chavez, the aviator, that image of the modern hero so mocked and mourned from the Cubists to Renoir's movie *The Rules of the Game*, attempts his great action (to the awe of crowds of peasants), G. seduces a chambermaid in a nearby hotel. And, while Chavez lies dying for no apparent reason, G. is superficially wounded by the

Peugeot representative at the competition, who has become irate at G.'s attentions to his wife. My crude parallels here convey little of the rich elaborations Berger makes of these events, which take up a large part of the center of the novel.

G. is not a hero like Chavez or Garibaldi. We never see him conquering women in hordes, although that may be perfectly consistent with his character. Berger focuses instead on a very few of his relationships with women. G. is not a victimizer but a willing victim whose nature is a release for the nature of others. He has the ability to evoke more reaction in others than he feels in himself, but always on the sexual basis of a one-to-one encounter, not on the grandiose scale of previous standards of heroism.

"The stranger who desires you and convinces you that it is truly you in all your particularity whom he desires, brings a message from all that you might be, to you as you actually are." Through what in *The Success and Failure of Picasso* Berger calls "the shared subjectivity of sex," G. establishes a perspective apart from the subject-object and object-object relations of public history. He is a vessel into which others may pour themselves to learn their shapes.

Sexuality is central to *G.*, but in this book the timeless moment of sex must always be considered within the context of history. When Berger is not writing novels, he is a painter and Marxist art critic with a keen sensitivity to the unique psychological and esthetic moment of a painting as well as to the historical, social and cultural setting that conditions its creation. In *Picasso*, he says "Only in fiction can we share another person's specific experiences. Outside fiction we have to generalize." Berger's decision to write fiction is dictated by a choice of subject matter, a desire to express himself in a way criticism might not allow. The urge of the critic to explain becomes transmuted into the urge of the novelist to be baffled. As Berger remarks in *G.*, "All generalizations are opposed to sexuality."

Of the novels written since World War II, those I have been most moved by have been concerned with character, and in the last 10 or 15 years, with character amid the opaque rhythms of history. Who would have predicted, watching the flood of Frank Yerbys, Kathleen Windsors, and Taylor Caldwells pouring from the book clubs of the 1940's and 1950's, that a good proportion of the great imaginative works of the 1960's could be called, without too much stretching, "historical novels": *Catch-22*, *The Sotweed Factor*, *LittleBig Man*, *V*, *The Tin Drum*, *The Armies of The Night*, *One Hundred Years of Solitude*. In these novels, unlike the earlier historical novels, history is an arena for understanding the relative values of the self and what lies outside and tries to determine it, rather than refuge for a passion and jollity the modern age denies, a primitivist playground or a Joycean nightmare from which we wake relieved in the present.

Because G. is also self-conscious about the act of its own creation, some readers might think it superficially resembles *The French Lieutenant's Woman*—i.e., historical novel, intrusive author, passion in the twilight of Victoria. But *G.*—in addition to its vividly portrayed characters and the crashing immediacy of its historical setting—is a complex novel of ideas that sets off in the reader meditations about sex, history and the nature of the novel that could never have been excited by the flaccid ironies and self-important complacencies of John Fowles's work.

Literary self-consciousness, for Berger, is a metaphor for human self-consciousness, the necessary partialities and deceits involved when one person tells you about a third, even when that third is himself. Time and again, Berger intervenes to allow his characters to escape from a control he never meant to wield. Oddly enough, for all such intervention, G. is less loose (almost less personal) than his critical works. But the coldness, the detachment in the prose gradually reveals itself as an unwillingness to control, and the insistence of his voice becomes more and more hypnotic, until the reader is increasingly guided by its perceptions, its stories, its asides, even its reticence.

Part of my pleasure in reading G. arises from just such a growing feeling for the intricate relations between its characters, settings, ideas and form—a kind of interdependency that great novels always exhibit. G. puts the reader in contact with a writer for whom the novel *is* a special way of writing, a special way to think about the problems that most vitally concern us. The hermetic lure of the Nabokovian novel, with its equal attack against history and character, is the quintessence of the modernist lure: the novel that finishes novels, literature telling us that literature is basically worth nothing; fans, it's all parlor games, and now back to the *real* business.

G. belongs to that other tradition of the novel, the tradition of George Eliot, Tolstoy, D. H. Lawrence and Norman Mailer, the tradition of fallible wisdom, rich, nagging and unfinished. To read G. is to find again the rich commitment to the resources and possibilities of the genre—and a writer one demands to know more about. Not to sit at the feet of his aphorisms or unravel the tangles of his allusions, but to explore more fully an intriguing and powerful mind and talent.—LEO BRAUDY, "Don Juan as a Blend of Sex and History," *NYTBR*, Sept. 10, 1972, pp. 19–20

First, let me express my sense that this ⟨G⟩ is the most interesting novel in English I have read for a good many years (since *Catch-22* to be precise, which one ought to be). Second, let me acknowledge doubt about how to treat it: to be content with expressing a sense of its "importance," or to say what it's about and then risk an interpretation that may be a misinterpretation. I'll try to be risky.

What's it about? Well, G's for Giovanni, among other things, and Don G is certainly a major presence in the book. He has been acclaimed, paradoxically, as an unlikely saint of women's lib, because he sees women as a kind of sexual Sinn Feinner, for themselves alone, which can be very liberating for them. G (1887–1915) is endowed—not the right word perhaps, yet an element of magic is implied—with what you might call a seeing prick. This penetrating wand has been achieved—not the right word again, but not so wrong as you might think—through an unusual combination of circumstances. He is, as the men he cuckolds don't hesitate to say, an Italian bastard; he is rich, but not too (*i.e.* he has the advantages without the responsibilities of being a capitalist); more or less abandoned by his American mum—in favor of Fabianism—to upper-class (declined feudal) English cousins; wafted to Milan in 1898 to meet his dad and there, through the agency of a young Roman girl with a budding moustache, given a view of the class struggle at close quarters; seduced at 15 by his already incestuous aunt who, by seeing the world cockeyed on account of imperialism and the Boer War, begins to see herself straight.

Note, please, it is I, not John Berger, producing this *seductio ad absurdam*. But it illustrates my dilemma: how to talk about this fine, serious, stimulating book without making it seem what it isn't, absurdly schematized, ridiculously abstract.

G is in fact about as schematized as a Cubist painting or a Fielding novel. And though Berger's not as relaxed or funny as Fielding, there can't be many novelists who plunge as readily into graveyards full of abstract nouns, and there's a moral there too, though I haven't the space for it.

The latter two-thirds of G is chiefly devoted to two epi-

sodes (the first superb, the second not yet completely taken in by this reader) in which the "principal protagonist" is able to reveal simultaneously the simple potency of his magic weapon and the complex vulnerability of the bourgeois world. The first is set around the Simplon Pass in 1910 where a Peruvian aviator is flying over the Alps; the second in Trieste in 1915 where it is still hard to know who is at war with whom but where a phase of history (and G himself) is staggering brutally to a close with a combination of bang and whimper. Here at last women's and national liberation begin to link up and we get a whiff of the third world which will emerge from the two coming wars. G comes as near to dying on the barricades as so unillusioned a realist could well do.

G seems to me a fascinating work which, for all my admiration, I may well still be underestimating. It is one of the few serious attempts of our time to do for the novel what Brecht did for drama: to reshape it in the light of 20th-century experience and theory other than the purely subjective or self-analytical. Since most of us have become more or less incapable of responding to any art which is *not* so based, G isn't an easy book to deal with. To get on to the right track Thomas Mann is no doubt a help, but one might also profitably go back to the early Dos Passos novels.

Dos Passos, like almost all 20th-century American novelists, seems to have been ruined by a demon of sentimentality which I suppose is linked, culturally, with a long standing Anglo-Saxon contempt for any kind of systematized thinking. But in *USA* he was trying to tackle some of the problems Berger is faced with in G, though the latter is an intensely European book. Dos Passos managed to achieve what perhaps Berger doesn't, an immediate impact at once appreciable by an audience reared in a quite different tradition. But he achieved it at the expense of undermining the very aims of objectivity and demystification which one part of him was seeking. Berger is infinitely more conscious of what he is up to and what it implies in terms of art. It is possible, perhaps, to feel that he is *too* self-conscious and that this costs him an element not so much of human complexity (he gets that all right) as of human warmth. But maybe such a reaction is itself part of the imprecision of feeling he is fighting. Fifteen years ago I'd have suppressed the doubt: now it seems important not to. But, emphatically, within the context of saluting a fine, humane and challenging book.—ARNOLD KETTLE, "Trying to Reshape the Novel," *NR*, Oct. 7, 1972, pp. 29–30

OTHER WORKS

⟨A *Fortunate Man*⟩ is a beautiful book, beautifully written, and illustrated with striking, movingly apt photographs. Its beauty should occasion no surprise because it is a long, thoughtful essay on man, written by a brilliant art critic and social commentator.

The fortunate man is Dr. John Sassall, a country doctor by choice, in a depressed English country setting. The place may not matter, in the ordinary sense, since the relativity of human experience is accentuated. However, the evocative prose and the pictures do not so much complement the scenes and episodes as give pure visual expression to the heard and spoken words:

> English autumn mornings are often like mornings nowhere else in the world. The air is cold. The floorboards are cold. It is perhaps this coldness which sharpens the tang of the hot cup of tea. Outside, steps on the gravel crunch a little more loudly than a month ago because of the very slight frost.

Berger has undertaken to evoke two levels of humanity in his long, somewhat rambling essay: *the* country doctor, and *a* country doctor. Sassall, *a* country doctor, comes through more strongly than the genus, particularly since the photographs of the grim parish he serves and its moody parishioners command our attention even when the essayist is generalizing on man, the role of the doctor or eschatology. One parishioner:

> With the warm water and cotton wool he cleaned away the little droplet of blood from her worn, large arm, the colour of stone or bread, as though it had acquired the colour through its scrubbing and baking.

And another:

> She wore a very worn black lace petticoat. The room was as little furnished as the kitchen. There was a large bed in one corner with some blankets on it and some more blankets on the floor. There was also a chest of drawers with a clock on it and a transistor radio. The windows were overgrown with thick ivy and since there was no plaster ceiling and holes in the rafters, the room scarcely seemed geometric and was more like a hide in a wood.

It is refreshing, and necessary for an objective writer to undertake to describe the other world of medicine, the one of care and cure. Some potboiling novelists have managed to earn several livelihoods from romanticizing medicine just as others have done rather well by grim surgery on the profession and professionals. Somehow the view of the doctor-patient cosmos isolated from economics and politics has not had a fair exposure. Berger compensates for this:

> We can now return to our original question. How is it that Sassall is acknowledged as a good doctor? By his cures? This would seem to be the answer. But I doubt it. You have to be a startlingly bad doctor and make many mistakes before the results tell against you. In the eyes of the layman the results always tend to favour the doctor. No, he is acknowledged as a good doctor because he meets the deep but unformulated expectation of the sick for a sense of fraternity. He recognizes them. Sometimes he fails—often because he has missed a critical opportunity and the patient's suppressed resentment becomes too hard to break through—but there is about him the constant will of a man trying to recognize.

An image emerges of what the golden-age doctor might have been—or should have been. Berger touches on the pity and pain and fear which has been the traditional role of the doctor to allay. In the few vignettes of the doctor's patients he introduces the sensitivity and selflessness a doctor is expected to have and the vast relief it can bring.

About to leave a desperately sick woman's side, recognizing the unvoiced despair of her husband, Dr. Sassall stays, asks for a cup of tea, chats, taking the time for reassurance in response to a mute plea. Gravely treating a young girl, in symptoms that might have been dismissed as adolescence or egocentricity, sympathetically he finds a need for self-expression:

> "I sometimes wonder," he says, "how much of me is the last of the old traditional country doctor and how much of me is a doctor of the future. Can you be both?"

Our health planning and budgeting today, necessary as it may be, comprehends the loss of the human relationship, but seems unable to replace or sustain it. Family doctors are disappearing, relatively and absolutely, in numbers. Perhaps compassionate support was never really there to the degree we would like to think it ought to be now. It certainly cannot ever be without the Sassalls. In looking to a future in which better medical care is brought to all of our people, we need better organization, more specialists, a wider distribution of all types of physicians, and new types of health workers. But without the deep insights and sympathy and understanding of a figure like the family doctor, interposed between the mechanical marvels of modern scientific medicine and suffering men, it will be hopeless.

Within the struggling pilot programs of community health services and neighborhood health centers, there will need to be Sassalls—questioning, listening, hastening to serve and soothe. Peabody said: "The secret of the care of the patient is caring for the patient." And Berger makes a similar point:

> Some of the young who decide to become doctors are at first influenced by this ideal. But I would suggest that one of the fundamental reasons why so many doctors become cynical and disillusioned is precisely because, when the abstract idealism has worn thin, they are uncertain about the value of the actual lives of the patients they are treating. This is not because they are callous or personally inhuman: it is because they live in and accept a society which is incapable of knowing what a human life is worth.

Before we simply sigh and put Berger's book away, responsible medical educators might consider using it as a text in medicine and perhaps as the best examination for admission to medical school. Anyone who reads it unmoved should not become a doctor:

> We give the doctor access to our bodies. Apart from the doctor, we only grant such access voluntarily to lovers—and many are frightened to do even this. Yet the doctor is a comparative stranger.

There is another aspect to Berger's deep, thoughtful commentary. He correlates the dilemma of the doctor's questioning to humanity's quest, and here he makes equally striking observations. In a not unlikely analogy he sees Sassall as a creation of Conrad's—an ex-navy officer, living a shipboard life, whose interim existence is of the same questing nature of Conrad's heroes:

> The rooms remind one of a ship's officer's cabin. There is the same cosiness, the same ingenuity in fitting many things into a small space, the same odd juxtaposition of domestic furniture and personal effects with instruments and appliances.
>
> It is as though time became the equivalent of Conrad's sea: the sickness the equivalent of the weather. It is time which can promise "the peace of God" and which can lash and destroy with "unimaginable" fury. Again, I am forced to use what may be a clumsy metaphor in the attempt to define a hidden, subjective experience—the generalized impact on a doctor's imagination of the suffering which he meets almost daily and which cannot be settled by writing prescriptions.

Not merely the analogue of Sassall to Conrad heroes but the stuff of which we ourselves, every day, doctor or patient, search for and seek—the roots of life and its meanings:

> It is impossible to say now whether this period of crisis was induced by his decision to examine within himself the basis of what up to now he had projected outwards as "the unimaginable," or whether he entered a period of crisis and therefore decided to look more closely at himself. Either way it bears some resemblance to the period of isolation and crisis which precedes in Siberian and African medicine the

professional emergence of the shaman or the inyanga. The Zulus have a name for this process. The
inyanga, they say, suffers because the spirits will give
him no peace and he becomes "a house of dreams."

A beautiful book. Sociologists have said all this about
doctors and the doctor-patient relationship and the divergence
of expectation of the two. But there is a world of difference
between Berger's creative presentation and a sociological document: the difference between Oscar Lewis and Zola, for example, on the culture of poverty.—GEORGE A. SILVER, "Story
of a Country Doctor," *Nation*, Sept. 4, 1967, pp. 181–82

Reading the social criticism of John Berger, one is continually
reminded of his parallel careers as a painter, art critic, and
novelist. Over the past 20 years he has applied these various
talents to develop a Marxism that is not just a social theory, but
an integrated way of perceiving reality: a way that incorporates
the lessons of modern art about proportion, perspective and the
creative interaction between the eye and the object of its attention. So, though any traditional economist could measure the
contribution of migrant workers to Western Europe's prosperity, Berger in *A Seventh Man* goes beyond straightforward analysis of their function as producers. With the aid of Jean Mohr's
eloquent photographs, he shows us both what the migrants'
world of factories and barracks looks like and how the world of
the privileged local inhabitants appears to them. In the manner
of a novelist, he reconstructs in several dimensions the migrants' experience of working and living in exile. His book thus
creates a close identification with the migrant workers' unhappy conditions and becomes a moral meditation on the relations between rich and poor individuals, classes and nations.

In its advocacy of Western Europe's "invisible men," and
its linking of text and photographic image, *A Seventh Man*
invites comparison with *Let Us Now Praise Famous Men*, that
minor American classic of the 1930's by James Agee and the
photographer Walker Evans. But Berger's study implies that
Agee's concept of marginality—a way of life with its own laws
and customs, apart from the mainstream—has now been made
obsolete by the scale of modern social organization. The excitement a few years ago at the discovery of an unknown
"Stone-Age" tribe in the Philippines only reinforces the general
truth that our culture has become one of total interconnection
where no one is left alone, or left out.

As their biblical title implied, Agee and Evans were inton-
ing a pastoral lament for a vanishing man: the Southern tenant
farmer or "sharecropper" who had been made superfluous by
mechanization and big business. Despite his classic American
virtues, he was being forced either to leave the land, or to
become a different, and lesser, man on it.

But Berger's tone is polemical rather elegiac, and rightly
so, since he speaks for men who come from marginal peasant
cultures, but are not at all marginal in their function for the
countries where they work. "The country would close down in
a week without the foreigners," a West German businessman
recently said of them. "Who would collect the garbage, clean
the streets, wash the windows, construct the buildings, and do
the dirtiest jobs in the plants? These are jobs Germans won't
do." To fill such jobs the affluent countries of Northwestern
Europe have imported, from their poorer neighbors to the
South and East, some 11 million workers—one-seventh of the
manual workers in Germany, one-quarter in France and
Switzerland.

Though some are eventually able to settle in the country
where they work, most are imported for a set term, which may
be as short as nine months, after which they are sent home. In
exhange for a chance of escape from the poverty and stagnation
of rural life, the migrant worker becomes a displaced person.
Leaving his family, culture and language, he is taken to a
country where he has no claim to citizenship, and where he
must submit to the unfamiliar discipline of factory labor. He is
thus uprooted and transformed; his experience recapitulates
that of an entire class in the Industrial Revolution—except that
he must adjust in a few months to changes that occurred over
generations in the host country.

Though Berger by no means overlooks the strictly economic disabilities of the migrant worker situation, he is most
concerned to reveal the less obvious inner wounds inflicted by
wrenching a man from a peasant society into one based on
advanced industry, while giving him little to cushion the shock
except the company of those who share his ordeal. Deprived of
a present identity, he lives entirely in the future hope that by
his savings he may improve his position when he goes back to
his native village. He has no effective intellectual or organiza-
tional weapons against a system that permits his labor to miti-
gate the internal conflicts of Europe's wealthiest societies and
thus sustains their continued dominance of the weaker countries on the periphery. For when business booms, the availability of migrant workers makes it possible to keep wage demands
under control and preserve differentials between manual and
intellectual work; when there is a slump, the main burden of
unemployment can be shifted onto them by mass repatriations.
Though the average West European feels that he has discharged his obligation to the migrant by paying him a wage that
is higher than he could get at home, it is evident that the
migrant's journey to the metropolis does not diminish the inequality between rich and poor, but actually reinforces the
already privileged position of Western Europe.

In reality, Berger argues, the world has now become a
single, interdependent community and our ideas about individual morality and personal choice must be revised accordingly. This was the theme of his remarkable counterpart to
A Seventh Man, *A Fortunate Man* (1967), which examines
the life of an English country doctor. Dr. John Sassall suffers
none of the obvious hardships of the migrant worker: he lives in
unspoiled country where he is widely known and respected,
and he does work that is vital, highly skilled and intellectually
satisfying. Yet his happiness and usefulness, says Berger, can
only be considered relative; for in the affluent West even such
men of good will are implicated in a general condition of
"exemption and deferment," which is the product of their privileged isolation from the life and death issues that the other
three-quarters of mankind must confront. "Unaccustomed to
choosing, unaccustomed to witnessing the choices of others,
we find ourselves without a scale of standards for judging or
assessing one another. The only standard which remains is that
of personal liking—or its commercial variant, which is Personality." For even a doctor to know the worth of his work, he
must know "the value of the actual lives of his patients," which
under present conditions remains unknowable.

Berger himself does not claim to possess any ready-made
formula that would determine this value. Though he was
aligned with the British Communist Party early in his career,
he has since exiled himself from his native country; in France
and Switzerland he has lived as a writer rather than a Party
militant, and he has been sharply critical of the Soviet government on Czechoslovakia and other issues. He believes that we
are now passing through an "interregnum": a basic re-
examination of Marxist tenets, brought about by our age's
justified skepticism of the "so-called historical laws" that 19th-
century intellectuals were so fond of proclaiming. A socialist

thinker must still reject the ethic of possessive individualism that rules in the capitalist world, but he should base his critique on his direct perceptions of how the society works, rather than on a canonical theory that may easily hide reality while purporting to explain it. Nor should he expect his commitment to revolution to absolve him from a duty to bear "faithful testimony" to the actual experience of those caught up in the turbulence of history; Berger has pointed to the quixotic revolutionary Victor Serge as an exemplary figure of this kind.

Though Berger accepts the need for classical Marxism to be revised in the light of modern experience, he remains optimistic about the global prospects of the Left, since he believes the revolutionary impulse to be a vital and intrinsic part of human nature itself, rather than just an occasional outburst of enthusiasm at times of crisis. The history of art, he argues, shows that man has always created ideal images of human possibility that express the radicalism of his desires and his dissatisfaction with what is. Even the nude, says the hero of Berger's first novel, *A Painter of Our Time* (1958), is "a revolutionary subject. The body suggests, on a sensuous level, all that man is capable of becoming on every level when he has at last created that society which will be worthy of himself." Conversely, the most limited of outlooks is the petit-bourgeois one that "refuses to speculate on how the world could be changed"—against the evidence that man lives in a perpetually unstable state of tension between the actual, the possible and the ideal.

In the past few years Berger has rounded out his vision of modernity in the Western world: with *G.* (1972), his most ambitious and penetrating novel, with the pictorial essay *Ways of Seeing* (1973), with the documentaries on *A Fortunate Man* and *A Seventh Man*, and with his script for Alain Tanner's film *The Middle of the World* (1974), yet he has never reached an audience on the scale of that commanded by more flamboyant and superficial radical intellectuals of the 1960's. In his commitment to a dialectic view of reality he involves the reader in a scrupulous working out of interlocking contradictions, rather than in ritual affirmations of dissent. His views on art, his original field and the one in which he is most expert, run so much against the grain of current dogma that they are more often sneered at than confronted; his novels are too densely cerebral and schematic to be easily digested; his social criticism is too idiosyncratic to offer much comfort to orthodox Marxists, while at the same time it offends the dominant mood of liberal expediency in the West. Yet, fashionable or not, his 11 books make a strong claim to represent, for the post-war period, the broadest and most cogent expression in English of the socialist imagination.—PAUL DELANY, "John Berger's Socialist Imagination," *NYTBR*, Jan. 11, 1976, pp. 19–20

To write convincingly of peasants, not least if you once produced a book on Picasso, would seem as doomed a literary enterprise as creating Trotskyite love-lyrics. For no social figure has surely been glamourised and debunked in such fine proportion; the word can suggest the moral beefiness of an Adam Bede just as easily as it can evoke a surly cretin smeared in cow-shit. *Pig Earth* is a set of stories, poems and essays about French peasant life by a well-known English intellectual; and it's therefore obvious even before opening it that its chief problem will be that of the stance it assumes towards its own subject-matter.

It's a relief to learn as early as page 7 that John Berger does actually live in a peasant community and to some extent shares its working life; but the real evidence that the book isn't the fruit of research in the British Library emerges in its doggedly scrupulous detail, its sheer unshowy knowledgeability about, say, slaughtering a cow:

> The son pushes a spring through a hole in the skull into the cow's brain. It goes in nearly 20 centimetres. He agitates it to be sure that all the animal's muscles will relax, and pulls it out. The mother holds the uppermost foreleg by the fetlock in her two hands. The son cuts by the throat and blood floods out on to the floor. For the moment it takes the form of an enormous velvet skirt, whose tiny waist band is the lip of the wound. Then it flows on and resembles nothing.

This is the kind of reverent, self-obvious passion for material life which makes Berger such a fine art-critic; yet it's a reverence which thrives upon notable limits. *Pig Earth* is a relentlessly realist work, silently dedicated to smashing the demeaning stereotypes of its subject in the interests of telling it like it is. But how is it, exactly? For a socio-political account of the plight of the world peasantry we have to wait for the finely analytic 'Historical Afterword', in which Berger reflects upon the peasantry's economic infrastructure, its cultural conditions, the possibility of its impending extinction as a class. That Berger is one of the few English writers who can interleave poems and political essays of equivalent intricacy is a gloomy symptom of the ideologically convenient division of labour which paralyses our culture: poetry for private emotions, politics for more abstract affairs. It's a fact/fiction dichotomy which Berger's writing has consistently subverted: indeed, when he argues here that every peasant village lives by a kind of adjustable self-image, constructs through its circuits of gossip and storytelling a continuous portrait of itself, he shrewdly implies that village life is itself a sort of fiction.

Yet there's a rift between the complex speculations of the 'Afterword' and the graphic immediacies of the tales themselves, which tend to buy their descriptive fidelity at the cost of emotional complexity and political awareness. Most of the pieces centre, predictably, on work; and while there's no denying that work is pivotal to peasant existence, a purely realist presentation of it is bound to edge out less brutally palpable issues of class, politics, exploitation.

Not that these are wholly lacking: a story entitled 'The Value of Money' dramatises starkly enough the conflict between peasant and state bureaucracy. Yet when Marcel, the peasant protagonist, finally lands in gaol for turning his rifle on the tax inspector, his response is to contemplate his idle hands and mourn for the 'habit of working' of which he's bereft. No doubt a realist portrayal of a peasant's reaction; yet as long as Berger's fictions remain in such simple 'reflective' relation to their subject-matter, they too stay imprisoned within an inevitably partial consciousness. There's no way in which the Berger who writes the 'Afterword' can 'be' the Marcel of whom he writes; and it won't do, either, just to recount the occasional peasant narrative in the first person. In the end, *Pig Earth* could press its politics only by breaking beyond its realist forms—patronising though it may seem to hand down such advice to the author of *The Moment of Cubism*.—TERRY EAGLETON, "A Sort of Fiction," *NSN*, Jan. 15, 1980, p. 876

The standard objection to John Berger's criticism of the visual arts is that it is too sentimental, too earnest. Leftist critics in particular tend to find Berger mushy and vague, despite his obviously rigorous position on the social functions of art in capitalist (or socialist) society. Such objections, however, seem to me both inaccurate and uninteresting, given Berger's deliberate style of commentary and its remarkably suggestive, as well as original, accomplishments.

Nevertheless, Berger is not easy to digest, partly because he has a great deal to say in his stream of essays, books of criticism, film scripts and novels, and partly because he says it in unusual ways. He relies on no single method, although he takes from various semiologists and iconographers the better things they have to offer. He is that rare being, an unorthodox Marxist who doesn't feel the need to construct a massive new theoretical framework to account for the unforeseen complexities of late capitalism. His knowledge of art history, philosophy and literature, like his acute political sense, is sophisticated without being heavy or obtrusive. The best thing about him, though, is his relentless striving for accessible truths about the visual arts—their ambiguity, memorial enchainments, half-conscious projections and irreducibly subjective force.

Berger has been typecast as an English eccentric who has chosen to live among peasants in a particularly rough and mountainous area of France. A closer look at his recent work, however, reveals a more systematic, philosophical and political project than the rather empirical cast of his prose suggests. His interest in the peasant life he discusses in *Pig Earth*, for example, is intensified by the fact that such life is now threatened with extinction. Similarly, his studies of Picasso, photography and "ways of seeing" attempt to rescue the valuable in art from the false reputations, advertising clichés and routine judgments that might otherwise triumph. Berger's project is to distinguish the authentic from the merely successful, and to save the former from the ravages of the latter.

Another Way of Telling is perhaps his most ambitious work along these lines: for the first time he offers an explicit and sustained account of art's positive uses in a setting hostile to art as felt experience. Berger's co-author is the great Swiss photographer Jean Mohr, with whom he produced such classics as *A Fortunate Man* and *A Seventh Man*. *Another Way of Telling* begins with a series of personal reflections by Mohr on his art; next is Berger's extended essay, "Appearances," on the meaning of photographs and photo-sequences; followed by "If each time . . . ", a section containing 150 photographs by Mohr, carefully arranged and centered around the life of an elderly French peasant woman. Berger returns with "Stories," a few pages on the relationship between prose narratives and the order of visual succession. The book ends with an absolute masterpiece of a photograph by Mohr opposite a short poem by Berger: photograph and poem together produce another way of telling about the reality of an old peasant, this one a man, facing a day's chores at an ungodly morning hour. Narrative has been replaced by constellations of experience (what Gerard Manley Hopkins would have called bursts of meaning) that convey the privacy as well as the context of the old man's life.

This rather schematic account cannot do this rich book justice. The photographs that accompany Mohr's ruminations on his artistic practice are extraordinary both as pictures and as accompaniment to the text. This is especially true of two sets of photographs. One consists of pictures of a blind Indian girl who, while listening to Mohr make animal sounds, breaks out into a shatteringly beautiful smile; a moment later we see her lapsing back into lonely repose. The second set is of hungry Indonesian children running alongside Mohr's train, hands outstretched yet receiving nothing. He says that they became an obsession with him, a feeling echoed by the children's fugitive grace, despite their emaciated bodies and unnaturally bright eyes.

But at the heart of the book is, I think, an argument *against* linear sequence—that is, sequence construed by Berger as the symbol of dehumanizing political processes. For Mohr and Berger, the contemporary world is dominated by monopolistic systems of order, all engaged in the extinction of privacy, subjectivity, free choice. According to Berger, this state of affairs is a consequence of the violent conflation of time with History—objective, official, real—that occurred as part of industrialization in the nineteenth century. "Public photography" reduces a man weeping or "a door or a volcano" to a statistic, a recordable fact, a commodity. Subjectivity, whose last social function is "the individual consumer's dream," is forcibly attenuated:

> From this primary suppression of the social function of subjectivity, other suppressions follow: of meaningful democracy (replaced by opinion polls and market-research techniques), of social conscience (replaced by self-interest), of history (replaced by racism and other myths), of hope—the most subjective and social of all energies (replaced by the sacralization of Progress as Comfort).

In control systems and in scientific investigations, photographs supply identity and information respectively. In advertising or journalism, photographs are used *as if* they belonged to the same order of truth as science or control systems; the communications industry would like to press viewers into accepting the photograph as evidence either of buyable goods or of immutable reality. Buy this product because it will make you happy; the poor are sick and hungry, and that's the way it is.

In fact, because of its peculiar status as a quotation from reality containing traces of the historic world, the photograph bears an ambiguity within itself that is not so easily co-opted. As a "way of telling," the historical mode not only objectifies the world; it also forces on it "the principle of historical progress." This, Berger says, does "a deep violence" to subjective experience by coercing reality into linear forms that narrate progress—thus eliminating the timeless, the dead, superstition, embedded conservatism, eternal laws, fatalism and the like. Private photographs, however, those "fragile images, often carried next to the heart or placed by the side of the bed, are used to refer to that which historical time has no right to destroy." Every photograph, therefore, is the result of a choice (of the instant to be photographed) although its meanings depend on the viewer's ability to lend it a past and a future, to reinsert the discontinuous instant into a durational continuum. The photograph's ambiguity can thus either be acknowledged—at which point interpretive words supplied for the photograph lift it from the level of fact to the level of suggestion and ideas—or denied, in which case it is subject to "the opportunism of corporate capitalism."

To read or interpret photographs, then, is to unite the human expectation of coherence with the language of appearances. The richer the photograph in quotation, the broader the scope for creative interpretation and the more the photographic instant achieves "another kind of meaning." This new kind of meaning is born when "confronting the event [the subject of the photograph] extends and joins it to other events, thus widening [the photograph's] diameter." All this, like a stone in water, breaks the one-directional flow of sequential narratives decreeing that what journalists, government discourse and scientific experts say is History, whereas the private subjective experience is not. Photographs are therefore potentially insurrectionary, so long as the language interpreting them does not, like most semiological discourse, become "reductive and disapproving."

Berger's language is neither. No one can more ably turn frozen surfaces into tractable worlds, "appropriated by reflection, permeated by feelings." And no one has so persuasively made it possible to read a sequence of photographs—in this particular case, the set of 150 that radiate out from one humble peasant life—as a "field of coexistence like the field of memory." In destroying the notion of sequence, Berger allows one to see mutual "energies of attraction" between photographs, so that, as he says, the ambiguity of photographs "at last becomes true." And this ambiguity, of course, is another way of telling about human life.

Berger and Mohr answer directly and eloquently to the need for some leftist alternative to an almost incredibly successful capitalist culture, whose inhuman sequences of order—the newspaper columns, TV news narratives, official expertise—assume a silently complacent constituency. Their work derives from Walter Benjamin in some ways (Benjamin also preferred the episodic, deliberately un-booklike collection of pieces, seeing such "inconspicuous forms" as better suited to influence "active communities" than "the pretentious, universal gesture of the book") and from Marcuse in others. The frankly libertarian and optimistic bias of Berger's style, however, is his alone.

And yet, for all its brilliance, *Another Way of Telling* leaves me with a certain skepticism. True, the media, advertising and the "experts" have cornered the market on "objective truth." Even truer, the oppositional culture has in the main been co-opted almost beyond redemption; impotence is the leftist intellectual's common lot today. But the rediscovery of subjectivity as a social value, and of time and timelessness as embodied in a photograph, are feeble bulwarks against the encroaching sea of cement. As passionately as Ruskin, Berger seems to believe that a proper schooling of the visual faculties will make for a more effective counter-hegemonic cultural practice

Two questions are left unanswered by Berger's work. First, can one really undertake esthetic/intellectual projects in the private sector, so to speak, and then launch out from there directly into politics? Unlike Lukacs and Gramsci, Berger fails to deal with the power of ideology to saturate culture. There can be no unilateral withdrawal from ideology. Surely it is quixotic to expect photographic interpretation to serve some such purpose.

The second question is the central one of oppositional politics—what to do? Photography, Berger says, deals with memory and the past. What of the future? Even if he wishes to deal only with cultural politics, *Another Way of Telling* demands a further step which Berger does not take: connecting his esthetics with action. It is a measure of Berger's achievement as a writer that for him that step wouldn't be hard to take.—Edward Said, "Bursts of Meaning," *Nation*, Dec. 4, 1982, pp. 595–97

UNSIGNED

"John Berger and the Artist's
Duty to Transcend Despair"

Times Literary Supplement, January 9, 1972, pp. 644–45

The hero of John Berger's new novel, G, is an Anglo-Italian Don Juan whose short but dedicated life between the sheets spans the turn of the century. The bastard son of an Anglo-American heiress and an ugly Italian merchant of Livorno, he becomes as an adult a self-absorbed and self-possessed sexual "devil" with a recurrent leer. G neither demands nor repels our sympathy; although presented as a radically alienated product of bourgeois hypocrisy, he also emerges as a type of existential hero completely devoid of bad faith.

When the heiress Laura announces her pregnancy, the obese purveyor of candied fruits, Umberto, pleads with her to settle in a neighbouring Italian city so that he may love his only son as a father should and, more important, so that his only son may love him as a son should. But Umberto is married to a barren woman; refusing to play second fiddle or kept mistress, Laura haughtily returns to England resolved to devote her life to her child. Yet the society to which she belongs—mother, nurse, and maid—intervenes. In a nicely ironical twist, Mr Berger causes the mother simultaneously to embrace Fabianism and to discard her son. The boy, who is given no name for 127 pages, then called G, is reared on a farm by a brother and sister, Jocelyn and Beatrice, whose relationship he only later discovers to be incestuous. Thus he becomes a privileged orphan whose expensive upbringing can never atone for the stigma, the offence, of the primal parental abandonment.

His character develops accordingly. At the age of five he falls sexually in love with his governess, Miss Helen, without expecting any return. Otherwise he accommodates to superior force, to the tutor who beats him by rota, to the ragged strangers who one day lead him into the woods and enact an obscure passion play over the bodies of two dray horses, to the public school-boys who in later years bait the Italian side of him with the jibe that his mother must have been Garibaldi's mistress. G learns to isolate and immunize himself, to achieve self-sufficiency; conscious of no resentments as a child, he will devote his adult life to an unremitting saga of vengeance.

So much for the first half of Mr Berger's novel, which is fluent, touching, convincing and often brilliantly expressed. But already there are signs that the author intends to baffle and frustrate the clients of a conventional narrative. Declining to be God, he disclaims omniscience at crucial moments. After the dray horse episode, obviously formative because later recalled, we read: "His fear is overcome, both his fear for himself and (for it is different) his fear of the unknown . . . overcome by another, stronger revulsion. It is beyond me to create a name for this revulsion: the ones I can think up all simplify." A comparable termination occurs when, at the age of eleven, G is abruptly taken to Milan to meet his father. It is 1898, and the boy not only witnesses but becomes swept up in the ferocious revolutionary fighting and the savage repression which stabilized the bourgeois-parliamentary system of Giolitti. At the height of the battle, when G is being cradled by an unknown and ugly Roman girl, who pretends that he is her fiancé, Mr Berger brings down the curtain: "I cannot continue this account. . . . From this point on everything I write will either converge on a full stop or else disperse so widely that it will become incoherent."

Three years later a new twist occurs. Beatrice, having married an officer and been promptly widowed in the course of the Boer War, returns to the farm and seduces the fourteen-year-old boy. A trauma? Hardly. Assured yet gentle, G takes her almost as an inheritance, a right. When we next meet him he is already an adult, a wealthy young man for whom aviation is a peripheral hobby, now staying in Domodossola to witness the first airborne crossing of the Alps. But the purpose proves to be as contingent as the hobby is peripheral. While the intrepid Peruvian flyer, Geo Chavaz, heroically braves the meteorological hazards of the Alpine peaks and valleys, G sets his mind to seducing a hotel maid. The existential paradox of the man becomes clear: a cynical and ephemeral frivolity masks the most serious and human of drives:

> His desire, his only aim, was to be alone with a woman. No more than that. But they had to be deliberately not fortuitously alone. . . . In the company of others women always appeared to him as

more or less out of focus . . . because they were continuously changing in their own regard as they adapted themselves to the coercions and expectations of the others around them.

Thus the orphan abandoned by his mother chooses in order to be chosen, and the seducer who apparently treats females as objects in reality invests them with self-determination. In one of his many discursive passages, Mr Berger further explains, "The stranger who desires you and convinces you that it is truly you in all your particularity whom he desires, brings a message from all that you might be, to you as you actually are."

After the maid, and in rapid succession, G seduces the wife of a wealthy Parisian motor-manufacturer who puts three bullets in his shoulder and despatches him to hospital just at the time when the hero, Chavaz, who has crashed inexplicably on landing, is dying amidst universal admiration and mourning. But Chavaz's death moves G no more than the thought of his own; so thoroughly has he been lagged by life that he is insulated against his own mortality. He is without a sense of history, either past or future.

The final act takes place in Trieste in 1915, on the eve of Italy's declaration of war, in an imperial city populated by haughty Austrian officials, opportunistic Italian merchants, irredentist Italian nationalists and, providing the immediate context of G's own tortuous dénouement, by violent Bosnian separatists. By this time G's permanent rebellion has transcended the flesh which is still its vehicle, its occasion. Aspiring to seduce the wife of an Austrian banker, and completely assured of success, he prefers in the event to penetrate the society rather than the woman by bringing to a posh ball a simple Bosnian working girl, Nusa. In this city of smouldering animosities and proud causes, G's isolation and indifference achieves its final, fatal political translation: because he is distrusted as a spy, as a clandestine foreigner, by every faction, the ultimate agents of his death emerge at random from the last roulette.

When G was still a work in progress, Mr Berger remarked of it: "I do not know whether it will be eventually categorized as an essay, a novel, a treatise, or the description of a dream." Which reminds us that Mr Berger himself is not so much a star as a galaxy of talents in search of a centre of gravity and a literary form which can synthesize his gifts as art critic, essayist and novelist. At a time when the traditional boundaries of fact and fiction, of imagination and intellect, are in a state of flux, no one is better equipped than he to lay minefields across the borders, to cancel the poet's proverbial licence and to pluck the authorial eye (and "I") from a privileged anonymity. G is a work which raises questions of great critical interest. It does not, however, always succeed in fashioning convincing connexions, whether causal or structural.

In *Permanent Red* (1960), Mr Berger remarked that every painter must discover his own personal point of departure, whether it be geometry, the density of pigment or whatever, and then push his creativity beyond it. But Mr Berger himself, arriving at the stadium burdened by an abundance of talents, found himself entering simultaneously for the sprint, the mile, the shot, and the pole-vault. Performing extremely well at all but winning none, he finally reached a solution: G is the pentathlon. Put in a more realistic idiom, Mr Berger's dilemma, rather rarer in this country than in France, is that of the *intellectual* who is *also* an artist. One thinks of a Jean Cassou, an André Chamson, a Simone de Beauvoir. And although the painter's eye might seem to be Mr Berger's most distinctive characteristic as a writer, it would probably be more useful to

regard the intellectual's fierce analytical intelligence and seriousness of moral purpose as his true point of departure. Certainly G, which is almost totally devoid of humour, is fundamentally an exploration of morality.

In *Permanent Red*, Mr Berger defined the critic's task, but it must also apply to the artist: "First, you must answer the question: What can art serve here and now? Then you criticize according to whether the works in question serve that purpose or not." As a humanistic Marxist who believes that the artist's proper duty is to overcome the fragmentation, alienation, and despair endemic to a decadent bourgeois culture, he has argued that the nature of all art is an attempt to define and render unnatural the distinction between the actual and the possible, to express the inadequacy of the given state of things, sometimes with horror, sometimes by presenting the desirable ideal. (It is possible to quarrel with his denial of art as ever being a mimetic celebration of nature.) One recalls Mr Berger's biting descriptions, in *A Painter of Our Time* (1958), of the commercial acolytes of art, and his portrayal of a talented Hungarian émigré painter who lives in poverty for years because his work lacks the bright trendiness necessary for success. In a later book, *The Success and Failure of Picasso* (1965), Mr Berger does not spare the great artist during his two phases of relative flippancy: his period after the First World War, when he entered the *beau monde* and imitated Ingres, and the years after 1944 when he relapsed into an easy, sentimental invitation to Arcadia.

In G, the serious moral purpose underlying the hero's promiscuity is frequently made explicit. For example: while plotting to seduce Monsieur Hennequin's wife, G directs the following thoughts at the husband:

> You chose this woman as you made her your own. At any moment the degree of conviction in your choice depended on your estimate of how exclusively she belonged to you. . . . You chose Camille's innocence, delicacy, maternal feeling, spirituality. She emphasized these for you. She suppressed the aspects of herself which contradicted them. She became your myth. The only myth which was entirely your own.

In other words, she became your property. Mr Berger's hostility towards private property, particularly as it affects works of art, quite legitimately extends to woman-as-property. The role of woman in G's society merely exemplifies the general social structure, so that G himself can be regarded as an anarchist revolutionary (propaganda by deed), or, to use a phrase that Mr Berger, borrowing from Ortega y Gasset, applies to Picasso, as a "vertical invader" (even if his occupation is mainly horizontal).

Determined to situate G in his social and historical context, Mr Berger frequently resorts to an alternative narrative, describing in considerable detail the significance of Garibaldi, life in the trenches during the early months of the First World War, or the political intrigues of Trieste. Part montage, part "living-newspaper", these excursions too often represent a failure of tact and discrimination. So obvious are the social juxtapositions that the reader may feel himself taken for a fool incapable of making connexions; at the same time Mr Berger robs his own narrative of homogeneity. In the event it is never quite clear whether G-as-Don Juan is being presented as an alienated product of a specific society, or whether his fundamental existential rebellion merely acquires its specific form, its particular life-style, from the age in which he lives.

Such an ambiguity is the more surprising in that Mr Berger here gives himself full rein as a didactic essayist, shifting without a blush from the implicit to the explicit. His high talents as an essayist are confirmed in his new collection, *Selected Essays and Articles*, which contains, apart from "The Moment of Cubism", pieces of Guevara, Jack Yeats, Le Corbusier, Victor Serge, and Walter Benjamin. The volume closes with three connected reports on the Czechoslovak crisis in the wake of the Soviet invasion, which are models of acute political observation and compassionate understanding. As an essayist, however, Mr Berger does not always resolve connexions to the extent he achieved in his brilliant analysis of a dedicated country doctor, *A Fortunate Man* (1967). One notices in his *Picasso* a hiatus between the painter and the backcloth, between a genius the nature and source of whose inspiration is wonderfully captured on the one hand and the existence of Lenin, monopoly capitalism and exploitation of the Third World on the other. Aimé Césaire is introduced—because he is quite different from Picasso. Of course Marxist historians and essayists, more than most, are tormented by the difficulty of explaining the precise links between the artist and his environment, between the "base" and the "superstructure". In "The Moment of Cubism" Mr Berger again wrestles with the problem, promotes heuristic enthusiam above discretion, and then, retreating, admits that the Cubists were not interested in politics, "were not aware of all that we are now reading into their art", and were joined to their time by a route which "remains unknown".

The main connexion which Mr Berger as an essayist has to make in *G* is between sex and history. One must say here that his skill and subtlety in matters of sex is by no means anticipated in his earlier work, although both *A Painter of Our Time* and *The Foot of Clive* (1962) display, as subsidiary themes, an ironic understanding of the brash and banal ad man's image of female allure. Yet *G* treats sex quite differently. Indeed not only is *G* himself physically unprepossessing, but not one of his conquests is described in a way likely to arouse the reader's erotic interest. But the main dilemma is this: that having offered himself full didactic scope to discuss as well as describe sex-within-history, to approach the matter both analytically and imaginatively, Mr Berger seems to recoil from these possibilities: "All generalizations", he writes, "are opposed to sexuality." He then adds: "That is the only poem to be written about sex—here, here, here, here now." And why? Because, he argues, "extreme single-mindedness . . . accompanies sexual desire . . . the conviction that what is desired is the most desirable possible. An erection is the process of total idealization." (Presumably Sartre never said this, but one often senses his shadow hovering over Mr Berger's search for essences; nevertheless, fortunate is the writer whose occasional ghost is Sartre.) The odd thing about this generalization (apart from the preceding statement that all generalizations are hostile to sexuality) is that it seems to turn truth inside out.

Imagine the sailor's angry penis hurrying from the ship for a one-night stand, and the whole edifice collapses. Mr Berger's assertion that the true equation of sex is "the experience = I + life", and is therefore "inexpressible in the third person and in the narrative form", flies in the face of all experience except those privileged encounters which are so rare. And if sex is really as he says it is, then surely he is wasting his energy writing about it. In fact he is not wasting his energy or ours, because he writes so well, but one must admit that this book's commentary on itself is often marred by a distrust of the written word so radical as to be, in a stubbornly professional writer, downright perverse.

Yet this perversity is the child of a genuine creative tension and of a spirit of experimentation which rejects easy solutions. The painter's eye confronts the dialectician, the naturalist recognizes that the illusion of mimesis is a sham, and the disciple of Cubism searches for a literary equivalent of Fernand Léger's geometrical optimism. These remarks can be developed less elliptically by once again returning to the early Berger. Take, first of all, the writer-as-painter.

Mr Berger was once a student at the Central and Chelsea Art Schools. The early chapters of *A Fortunate Man* are essentially inspired by visual factors, by the shifting appearances and surprising angles of small men trapped within a larger nature. In the first short sketches of *Selected Essays*, he once again indulges his delight in watching and seeing: no obvious dramatic content is required. But these are doodles: in *G* he must paint, he must integrate the shape of things with human causality, with feeling and knowing (as Alain Robbe-Grillet did in *La Jalousie*). How? Clearly aspiring to the stark, unsentimental precision of Cubism, he must suppress the naturalistic-documentary impulses so apparent in *The Foot of Clive, Corker's Freedom* (1964) and *A Fortunate Man*. In the first two of these books, both novels, Mr Berger married naturalism to its second cousin impressionism by juxtaposing and overlaying sharply recorded images of humdrum behaviour, associating inner landscapes with physical objects and allowing consciousness a free flow. More than a literary style was involved here; the obligation to life carried a moral weight—as with Zola. Consider only the years of steady observation which supported the portrait of the country doctor, or the exacting compilation of data about card indexes, filing systems, and styles of deference which brought the thwarted Corker's little employment agency to life.

Why does Mr Berger feel constrained to suppress this heritage? Naturalism encourages empathy by suggesting a direct congruity between life and art. In *Art and Revolution* (1969), a study of the Soviet artist Ernst Neizvestny, he voiced a critical estrangement from naturalism which was bound to exact its price in his creative writing. Art, he said, must be transformation. While disapproving of the spineless decadence which infects modern art, he has nevertheless accepted the tacit modernist premise that the old Renaissance-Enlightenment certainties about reality and perspective are dead. The work of art ceases to be nature and becomes artifact; the spectator becomes nature. Searching within the modernist school for an affirmation of optimism and human solidarity compatible with his own ideology, his admiration settled on the post-revolutionary Russian avant-garde and on the prewar Cubists. In these circles a faith in the social relevance of art was reconciled with an honest approach to the medium itself, to the *process* of art. Here is the launching-pad for *G* as a literary structure.

About Cubism Mr Berger has written extensively. The real subject of Cubism, he argues, is sight itself. The two-dimensional surface of the picture serves as the constant by which we approach the variables, the hidden surfaces and dimensions. Claiming that the Cubists were the first to paint totalities rather than agglomerations, and tracing the movement back to the confident materialism of Courbet and the reluctant scepticism of Cézanne, he made bold to describe Cubism as the only example of dialectical materialism in painting. Mr Berger is too sensible a writer to reduce *G* to a single stylistic label, but the emphasis clearly emerges:

> I isolate parts in order to follow my eyes, instant by instant, faithfully. . . . The fresh evidence of each part, of each new sight of her, contributes to my perception of her as a whole, and makes this whole continually move and pulsate like a heart, like my own heart.

Or consider this:

> Whom were we walking?/I was a knee which wanted the thigh on the other leg./The sounds of my most tender words were in your arse./Your heels were my thumbs./I was hiding in one corner of your mouth.

The resemblance to Braque or Picasso in the years 1907–14 is certainly very striking. Elsewhere the author offers a fuller explanation of his literary philosophy:

> But I have little sense of unfolding time. The relations which I perceive between things . . . tend to form in my mind a complex synchronic pattern. I see fields where others see chapters . . . I write in the spirit of a geometrician. . . . One of the ways in which I establish coordinates extensively is by likening aspect with aspect, by way of metaphor.

The confession about "unfolding time" is a revealing one: probably it accounts for the lack in all of Mr Berger's novels of a certain dramatic urgency. But in so far as we are concerned with the overall style or structure of *G*, one notices that Mr Berger attempts to translate Cubism into literary terms by employing and rather over-taxing many of the devices used in recent years by Sarraute, Sollers, Butor and the other novelists who have said farewell to naturalistic certainty and divinely certified mimesis. Mr Berger's entire narrative is broken up into hundreds of double-spaced sections, some of them constituting only a single line or phrase, thus deliberately exposing the hiatus between conception and achievement. The gear shift in which he moves from "he" to "I" to "you" is so well greased as to be virtually automatic. This is alienation with a vengeance.

With increasing frequency Mr Berger imposes himself on his own story. Turning the page, one may suddenly come across a personal dream having no direct bearing on the action, or an account of a recent visit to a Paris laundry. The message is twofold: work in progress; torment. As the confessions of difficulty multiply, the reader may begin to wish books were sold with a guarantee: "The way my imagination forces me to write this story is determined by its intimations about those aspects of time which I have touched but never identified. I am writing this book in the same dark." There are also passages which stretch the reader's credibility:

> Armed with the entire language of literature we are still denied access to her experience. There is only one possible way of, briefly, entering that experience: to make love to her. Then why do I want to describe her exhaustively, definitely, when I fully recognise the impossibility of doing so? Because I love her. I love you Leonie. . . . It was he who said this.

Was it? The paradox here is that in *G* Mr Berger once again displays a high talent for set-scenes and dialogue of a conventional kind. One remembers the impact, in *A Painter of Our Time*, of the episode in which Janos Lavin and his friend the narrator John visit the private art collection of Sir Gerald Banks. Perhaps Mr Berger now regards such victories as Pyrrhic ones.

He may be right. But the modern writer must either yield some territory to the *dramatic* heritage of fiction or risk alienating his readers in the wrong way. To emphasize that the failings of *G* are the result of a rich endowment of talents and of a bold, experimental intelligence which distrusts the safe, mediocre and provincial, is not to explain these failings away. One comes away from *G* as from many modern paintings: provoked and stimulated, yet baffled and faintly resentful.

JOHN BETJEMAN

1906–1984

John Betjeman was born in London on August 28, 1906. He attended Magdalen College, Oxford, where he caroused with classmate Evelyn Waugh to the disapproval of their tutor, C. S. Lewis. Betjeman was expected to join his father's business after he left Oxford, but he had long since decided to become a poet, and his first volume appeared in 1931. To support himself during the 1930s he sold insurance, edited guidebooks, taught cricket and English, wrote film criticism for the *Evening Standard*, and worked for *Architectural Review*. Betjeman's passion for Victorian Gothic architecture led him to campaign tirelessly for its preservation and to write a number of books on the subject, the first of which was *Ghastly Good Taste*, published in 1933. Also that year he married the writer Penelope Chetwode, with whom he had two children.

After World War II Betjeman began appearing regularly on television, as both poet and architectural enthusiast. His sales rose steadily, approaching bestseller status with 1959's *Collected Poems*. Awards poured in, including several doctorates, a Heinemann Award in 1948, Foyle Poetry Prizes in 1955 and 1959, the Queen's Poetry Medal in 1960, a Royal Society of Literature Award in 1968, and knighthood in 1969. Three years later Betjeman succeeded C. Day Lewis as Poet Laureate. Betjeman continued to write carefully rhymed and metered verse throughout his career. "However light his means," commented Louise Bogan, "his purpose is never trivial."

Sir John Betjeman died on May 19, 1984, in Cornwall, where he lived for many years with Lady Elizabeth Cavendish and with his beloved teddy bear, Archibald Ormsby-Gore.

Personal

"May I half change?" This question, to the house prefect in charge of games, was how a junior boy would ask if he could change his school jacket for a blazer, be excused the compulsory games which he hated, and go off to the Marlborough Downs to play golf. He was the only boy in the house who brought his golf clubs to school. Others had sets at home, but they either enjoyed games, tolerated them or lacked the moral courage to do the same as John Betjeman. John's request was seldom refused.

That is but one example of the many ways in which John

differed from us all in his days at Marlborough, and differ he did. That may have contributed to his being bullied more than other boys. This made him hate the school, as is clearly shown in *Summoned by Bells,* but he was by no means the only junior boy to dread each new term. Physically he was smaller than average but his most striking feature was his long, straight, jet black hair, almost Chinese in effect. The rule in the early 1920s was of course short back and sides, but somehow John always managed to have a long straight wisp of hair hanging across his face, an effect greatly accentuated by its very blackness.

He was not exactly the neatest of boys. He cared nothing about his clothes—or was that his way of protesting about the standard black school suit? One felt that had we been allowed to smoke, his lapels would always have been covered in ash. . . .

There was something about this small boy which made him stand out from all the others. When not in class, most boys would amble out in groups and talk, but John tended to be solitary. What was very noticeable was that he always carried books. He was an avaricious reader and I personally was eternally grateful to him for introducing me to Aldous Huxley (among other writers).

Apart from always carrying books—above all, books which were not the usual range of schoolboy reading—John read poetry, which few people did unless it was part of their work—and he also wrote it. He was always writing something, and no one could mistake that large round script with few lines to a page, very unlike the usual juvenile handwriting.

There was a strong philistine element in most public schools at that time, and Marlborough suffered from it like the others. It was the prelude to the bitter conflict between Hearties and Aesthetes, particularly at Oxford, in the mid-1920s. To counteract this hearty trend, a group of about seven or eight intellectuals from different houses, including John, got together and produced a magazine called *The Heretic.* . . .

One's first year at Marlborough was usually spent in a junior house. The solitary small boy from the junior house became the quaint shy boy in his senior house, and by his very individuality John did much to make us realize that conformity was not everything. Term after term, this became more and more appreciated. The higher in the school he got the more popular he became, and the more he influenced all those around him with his humour, his droll wit and his idiosyncrasies. The odd little boy had already become a likeable eccentric.—Arthur Byron, "Betjeman at School," *LT*, May 22, 1984, p. 22

General

That it is possible to convey something of the physical appearance and varied life of post-war England, the poetry of John Betjeman is sufficient proof. I am not referring to his attacks on the Welfare State with its nasty bureaucrats and its idle workers and its superficial courses in progressive citizenship; for there creep into his verse on these occasions a certain thinness and half-hearted petulance never found in his other poems, however much he may laugh at the quirks and snobbishness of his characters. Where Betjeman succeeds is in showing us, with such skilled precision, how his beloved Victorian and Edwardian England has been almost swept away by the new England of coffee bars, television masts, mass-produced goods, and miles of sodium-lit suburbia, a world in which, as one of his friends remarked, regular attendance at the cinema is the ideal preparation for a funeral service at the crematorium.—John Press, "A Neutral Tone," *Rule and Energy*, 1963, pp. 7–8

Two other poets of the 1930s who had not such a wide public, who were thought of mainly as clever writers of light verse, but who tend today to be taken much more seriously than that, were William Plomer and John Betjeman. When I wrote the first version of this book Betjeman was the special taste of a minority who hugged their appreciation to themselves; he was very much of a clique highbrow taste; he has now, with his *Collected Poems*, become a best-seller and in liking him as I still do, one is likely to be thought of as a sentimental middlebrow. However, Betjeman appealed to the most notable younger poet of the 1930s, Auden, and still appeals to a poet who might be claimed as the leading younger poet of the 1950s, Philip Larkin. One is not in such bad company after all. One element in Betjeman's popularity in the 1950s was probably that he expressed the mood and sentiment of a recrudescent conservatism that went far wider than politics; a tendency for many people to look sentimentally and narrowly back towards older elements of the English life, because it seemed uncomfortable to look realistically forward. Betjeman is certainly not very likely ever to have a wide international or even American reputation. He is too local. He requires his readers to carry in their heads a map of London, so that 'the curious Anglo-Norman parish church of Kentish Town' or the now vanished trolley-buses diminishing towards Highbury, or the polychromatic wall of a Victorian church, St. Saviour's, Aberdeen Park, at once ring a bell; it is period flavour, not intrinsic beauty he is looking for, so that it might be said that not only in his attitude to English architecture, but also to English life, he has become something he once denounced in a prose essay, a 'sentimental antiquarian'. Yet no perception of the world so exact and specialized as Betjeman's can finally be dismissed as merely sentimental. In their Cornish seaside bungalow, the children of Mrs Hanks (sometime in the late 1920s or early 1930s) are preparing for a dance:

> Norman and Gordon in their dancing pumps
> Slide up and down, but can't make concrete smooth.
> 'My Sweet Hortense. . . .'
> Sings louder down the garden than the sea.
> 'A practice record, Phoebe, Mummykins,
> Gordon and I will do the washing-up.'
> 'We picnic here! we scrounge and help ourselves,'
> Says Mrs Hanks, and visitors will smile
> To see them all turn to it.

For an expert in popular music 'My Sweet Hortense' probably dates this episode precisely. So the Christian names Norman, Gordon, and Phoebe, the expression 'mummykins', and Mrs Hanks's perhaps faintly forced cheerfulness about doing without servants and the family lending a hand, are enough for a sufficiently informed English reader to place the Hanks family in their exact social stratum. There is a wealth of implication, of digested and implicit knowledge, behind Betjeman's deceptively simple surfaces, and the feelings he arouses in us are often not simple. At a first glance this passage might appear almost cloyingly sympathetic; at a second glance, we see that the Hanks *ménage* is 'placed' as coolly and distantly as a satirical novelist might place it. We are left with a complicated feeling of recognizing both an element of comic pretence and one of human grit and decency in a milieu we might have been tempted to feel merely cheaply superior about. Such a complicated feeling cannot be dismissed as 'sentimental'; though a readiness to be unembarrassed by natural sentiment, whether his own or that of his characters, is one of Betjeman's strengths.

Betjeman's appeal is probably, in spite of his very wide public, predominantly a class and age-group appeal: to the lower-upper middle classes, especially those living on pensions or fixed incomes in a time of rising prices and notable social mobility, up and down. It is also an appeal to latent and inarticulate Christian and conservative sentiments, which are often particularly strong in those, like some of his more intellectual admirers, who call themselves agnostics and regularly vote Labour. Any reader of Betjeman, who wants to enjoy him, must at least provisionally accept this profound conservatism of his, even when it is concerned with what is no longer there to conserve. . . .

Betjeman is also, of course, an acknowledged master of humorous light verse, but it is on his more serious side, his poetry of personal attachment, that I have preferred to dwell. The seriousness does, of course, also express itself through humour and the humour even in a piece like *The Arrest of Oscar Wilde at the Cadogan Hotel* intended for mock-melodramatic recitation is never wholly shallow. John Sparrow, in his excellent essay on Betjeman, speaks of that poem as 'an attempt to create an atmosphere of "period" by wheeling on the old stage properties—the astrakhan coat, the hock and seltzer, *The Yellow Book*—all too conscientiously into place': he might have added that the third and second last stanzas (entry of the police) are pure burlesque; but the very last stanza, even while we are laughing our heads off, does suddenly remind us with the lines,

He staggered—and terrible-eyed,
He brushed past the palms on the staircase . . .

that poor Wilde's farce was after all a tragic one. We are suddenly a little ashamed of ourselves for having been so heartlessly amused. Betjeman can be facile and his blank-verse autobiography, *Summoned by Bells*, seems to me to have very little poetry in it and to be primarily a bit of overripe character-acting, for an over-indulgent audience. But at his best Betjeman is a subtly sincere writer, light in hand but true in feeling, in the tradition of Prior, Praed, Thackeray, and in the tradition indeed of the more intimate and domestic side of greater poets than Praed or Thackeray, Tennyson, Browning, even Hardy. He is, at his best, too skilful a poet ever to have been effectively parodied or to have found an effective imitator or competitor.—G. S. FRASER, "The 1930's and the Second World War," *The Modern Writer and His World*, 1964, pp. 306–10

Works

John Betjeman's *Slick But Not Streamlined* brings the reader up against some unexpectedly weighty considerations. Modern poetry, although filled with nostalgia of various kinds and degrees, is notably lacking in pathos. Pathos, it might be said, is an emotion derived from contemporary objects or contemporary experiences; it is not a yearning for the past. Modern poets have so firmly eliminated pathos from their work that the suspicion sometimes arises that they are incapable of experiencing it, that the modern sensibility has become so hardened and abstract that entire areas of emotional response are outside its range. We would not wish, certainly, for a return to the sentimental repining of early and middle Romanticism. Yet this lack of true pathos deprives modern verse of a whole set of emotional effects and reverberations. Betjeman has nevertheless made a serious and emotional contribution to the modern lyric, all the more surprising since every effort has been made by his American publishers to emphasize his lighter side. Even W. H. Auden, who has written an introduction to Betjeman's book, dwells lengthily on the poet's skill as a satirist and on his "theatrical" manner of presenting things. Satirist and wit Betjeman surely is, but a special kind of gravity underlies a good deal of his work. Nothing is farther from pathos than parody, which is Betjeman's manner of projection, and it is an unexpected

experience to find him now and again pushing parody over into the region of pure feeling. (Gide observes somewhere in his *Journal* that aesthetic problems that will not yield to a frontal attack may sometimes be solved by oblique or outflanking methods.) Betjeman brings off his effects with the greatest deftness. He is capable of writing in the most glittering way about British middle-class mores; he is capable, too, of abruptly stepping into another dimension, where sensibility is all. Suddenly, we are in the midst of pathos before we realize what response is being demanded of us. Because Betjeman's interests are basically topographical and architectural, he goes directly toward visible and concrete symbols of middle-class pretensions and yearnings: churches and chapels, parsonages, suburbs, provincial gaslit towns and seaside lodgings, railways, viaducts, factories, tearooms, and hotels. He involves these various locales and structures in perfect replicas of nineteenth-century verse forms, not forgetting the hymn. But he matches form to feeling, rather than the other way around. So, instead of getting a stream of sly jokes and satirical cuts, we get poems whose high spirits and sharp observation are continually breaking off to admit the spirit of place and of character, the sadness of human beings and of things. The dangers in Betjeman's method are obvious. Some of his poems hang in a hair's-breadth balance between the success of sincerity and the failure of smartness. The tone of "The Arrest of Oscar Wilde at the Cadogan Hotel" is not quite a success. On the other hand, "Parliament Hill Fields" (a note of nostalgia, it must be admitted), "Death in Leamington," "Sudden Illness at the Bus-Stop," and the exquisitely satirical "Bristol and Clifton" are perfect examples of how emotion may be smuggled into the modern lyric without restricting its freedom or dulling its finish and point.—LOUISE BOGAN, "John Betjeman," *Selected Criticism*, 1947, pp. 343–45

What exactly *is* Betjeman? Surely one of the rare figures on whom the aesthetic appetites of an age pivot and swing round to face an entirely new direction. It is hard to tell whether such figures govern or are governed by the tendencies they focus so sharply; individually they may not rank as major talents—Morris, Langley—but for a time they have the curious power to alter people's idea of what is beautiful. Throughout the work of the writer, broadcaster, propagandist and poet John Betjeman can be traced the same insistent pattern, a rejection of modernism. If the spirit of the first third of our century was onwards, upwards and outwards, the spirit of Betjeman was backwards, downwards, and inwards. If the architecture of the age was Nuremburg, its heroes the working class, its concrete by-passes lit with sodium, Betjeman exalted Comper interiors, clergymen's widows, and gaslight. This opposition was not confined to aesthetics. If the age had no religious beliefs and thought everyone was a socialist nowadays, Betjeman professed Christianity and proclaimed a benevolent class system the best of all possible worlds. In a time of global concepts, Betjeman insisted on the little, the forgotten, the obscure: the privately-printed book of poems, the chapel behind the Corn Exchange, the local landscapes in the Museum (open weekdays 2 p.m.—4 p.m.). And slowly our tastes have begun to turn his way. We have stopped laughing at the Victorians. Local history is a recognised syllabus subject in schools and universities. The glamour of left-wing politics has unaccountably dulled.

His *Collected Poems*, whose astonishing success (over 30,000 in two months) by now need not be underlined, show clearly that his position in literature is analogous. He is against the kind of poetry this century has made its own. He has written and created a taste for comprehensible poems in regular metre, and his themes have earned him every vituperative adjective in criticism—cosy, nostalgic, bogus, adolescent, snobbish, corrupt. This has not hindered the growth of his reputation. The three most noteworthy talents in post-Eliot English poetry, said Edmund Wilson last year, are Auden, Dylan Thomas and John Betjeman, and though an American is not likely to be the best judge of Betjeman's quality, at least Mr Wilson cannot be associated with the Princess Margaret /Top People/U- and Non-U *blague* that hangs obscuringly round Betjeman's name. Auden dedicated *The Age of Anxiety* to him. And he must have the largest public of any living poet. 'There has been nothing like it since *Don Juan*,' said his publishers, who of course also published *Don Juan*.

The chief significance of Betjeman as a poet is that he is a writer of talent and intelligence for whom the modern poetic revolution has simply not taken place. For him there has been no symbolism, no objective correlative, no T. S. Eliot or Ezra Pound, no rediscovery of myth or language as gesture, no *Seven Types* or *Some Versions*, no works of criticism with titles like *Communication as Discipline* or *Implicit and Explicit Image-Obliquity in Sir Lewis Morris*. He has been carried through by properties and techniques common to all but his immediate predecessors: a belief that poetry is an emotional business, rather than an intellectual or a moral one, a belief in metre and rhyme as a means of enhancing emotion, a belief that a poem's meaning should be communicated directly and not by symbol. These were characteristics of poetry in the days when it was deemed a kind of supernatural possession. (How much today requires the hypothesis of divine inspiration?) And the result is that Betjeman's poems, however trivial or light-hearted their subject, always carry a kind of primitive vivacity that sets them apart from those of his contemporaries, and captures the reader's attention without his intellectual consent:

> In among the silver birches winding ways of tarmac
> wander
>   And the signs to Bussock Bottom, Tussock
> Wood and Windy Brake,
> Gabled lodges, tile-hung churches, catch the lights
> of our Lagonda
>   As we drive to Wendy's party, lemon curd and
> Christmas cake.
>   Rich the makes of motor whirring,
>   Past the pine-plantation purring. . . .

There is in Betjeman someone who weeps at Victorian ballads ('My heart finds rest, my heart finds rest in Thee') and roars out Edwardian comic songs ('There's something about a 'varsity man that distinguishes him from a cad'), someone to whom every Betjeman poem seems to *matter* in a rare refreshing way. For Betjeman's poetry is nothing if not personal: it is exclusively about things that impress, amuse, excite, anger or attract him, and—and this is most important—once a subject has established its claim on his attention, he never questions the legitimacy of his interest. Energy most modern poets spend on screening their impulses for security Betjeman puts into the poem. If this had not been so, he would have never been able to celebrate Pont Street and the doctor's intellectual wife in the decade of the Left Book Club, Miss Joan Hunter Dunn during the blitz, or *Sunday Afternoon Service* in the year of Labour's post-war victory:

> Even the villas have a Sunday look.
> The Ransom mower's locked into the shed.
> 'I have a splitting headache from the sun,'
> And bedroom windows flutter cheerful chintz
> Where, double-aspirined, a mother sleeps;
> While father in the loggia reads a book,
> Large, desultory, birthday-present size. . . .

The public has been a long time taking him seriously partly because of this, but a much larger reason is of course that many of his poems are funny. Readers find it exceedingly difficult to combine the notions of being serious and being funny. Yet Betjeman is a particularly good example of this ambiguity, because the things that oftenest make him giggle—sex and class—clearly matter to him tremendously, and indeed they do to most of us. It may be that some of Betjeman's appeal springs from his preparedness to release feelings we are not entirely unashamed of, and are therefore inclined to make fun of. . . .

This Peter-Simplified view of England, perhaps not more unjust than views from the opposite side from 'Wystan, Rex, all of you who have not fled' in the 'thirties, shows the political colour of Betjeman's adherences. But broad political generalisation of any shade robs Betjeman of one of his style's chief weapons—the precise name, the unique instance ('Oh! Fuller's angel-cake, Robertson's marmalade' etc.), and this lack of particularity lessens his power to convince. His villainous Town Clerk is just a bogy, his Welfare State education a very distant prospect. The real explanation may be that Betjeman is too much of his age—he is after all a TV star, not a hermit—to attack it convincingly.—PHILIP LARKIN, "Betjeman en Bloc," *LST*, Spring 1959, pp. 14–17

In 1958 a literary event took place which is still talked about with astonishment and incredulity. The *Collected Poems* of John Betjeman were published and, within a few weeks of publication, thousands of copies had been sold. The publishers, John Murray, have declared that nothing like this had occurred in their experience since Byron's *Childe Harold* took London by storm. John Betjeman, whose very personal and original lyrics about love, religion and architecture had hitherto appealed only to a comparatively small group of devotees, had, in fact, the sort of literary success which is much more commonly found among novelists than among poets.

Much surprise has been expressed at this unprecedented event in contemporary English poetry. The reasons for Betjeman's success are, however, not really so hard to find. Even if one discounts the fame the poet had himself achieved as a television personality of great warmth and charm, one can still find a number of purely *literary* reasons why his poems found such a large public. In the first place, Betjeman writes in the sort of literary forms (many of them Romantic or Victorian in origin) which most people have become familiar with at school. His language is entirely contemporary, certainly, but his forms and cadences are profoundly traditional; in this matter, indeed, he writes as if Ezra Pound, Eliot and Auden had never existed. The second reason for the success of Betjeman's poems is the fact that they deal largely with subjects which are peculiarly sympathetic even to unliterary readers; they are much concerned with love, lust, religion and religious doubt. But they also have an edge of humour and satire so that however serious the poet himself may be, and often is, his readers never need feel too involved or too anxious about the sort of demands that are being made upon them. It would, of course, be facile to say that the English are a race of Philistines, but they are undoubtedly a people who are a little afraid of seeming to take themselves too seriously. Betjeman is a poet who (and this is not a pejorative statement) seldom asks them to do this.

It would be a pity if Betjeman's genuine gifts both as a serious minor poet and as a brilliant light verse writer were forgotten in the general controversy about the popular success of his *Collected Poems*. He is a poet who achieves his effects first, by a rare honesty about himself and his motives and feelings, and second, by the extreme skill of his versification.—ELIZABETH JENNINGS, *Poetry To-day*, 1961, pp. 29–30

Mr. Betjeman also, but by more subtle methods, prevents the question which is art and which is piffle. He busies himself in concealing the difference. In the same poem he puts tremendous-statement lines about God and the Faith, and obsolete-gesture lines like '*Deeply I loved thee, 31 West Hill!*' and '*I'll fight you, Betjeman, you swine, for that*'. Within limits he knows he may depend upon us—upon our sense of humour, or what Miller would call our 'cultivated feeble-mindedness'—for the correct response. For example, there is a solidarity of class and education about our amused affection for the bad lines in certain poems of Crabbe, of Wordsworth, of Arnold. They take their place with other objects and habits as part of the defence of a way of life threatened by the defection of the servant class. It is a way of life that permits nonconformity in inessentials; there are words you cannot say and clothes you must not wear, but you may be miserable at school, stupid with a gun, and eccentric about architecture. What you may never be, in spite of Orwell's example, is proletarian in the manner of Miller; you will always think of the world as populated by 'the chain-smoking millions *and me*'. '*That topic all-absorbing as it was, Is now and ever shall be to us*—CLASS.'

Here, in this autobiography, Mr. Betjeman speaks of the experiences of childhood ('before the dark of reason grows') but the past he longs for is not his own. His great merit is archæological—his power to construct cultural patterns from discrete objects. He is happiest with the late Victorian-Edwardian objects, suggesting that he is really one of them and has somehow strayed on to the wrong level among the modern trash, mantelpieces, doilies, etc. Some of his best poems present the two epochs in significant contrast: 'The Old Liberals', the poem on the death of George V. Mr. Betjeman gets many of his effects by sabotaging the present with the past. (This book is got up, not very attractively, to look as if it came out fifty years ago.) Not long ago I saw him give a brilliant performance in a television programme about Marylebone Station. He pointed out the telltale juxtapositions: big, craftsman-like carving defaced by British Railways signs, the solidity and size of the hotel that reflected the public standing of the Midland manufacturers who used it; then a glass of sherry as he sat, pretending to be a respected manufacturer, in a vast sofa; finally the wry smile, the comic-archaic shrug of resignation. Mr. Betjeman's is an art of obsolete gesture. This allows him to say what he likes about the great subjects—lust, death, bereavement—in his own way, and yet to exploit the advantages of modern self-irony. '*Deeply I loved thee, 31 West Hill!*' would not be a tolerable line in a local newspaper poet. All depends upon the reconstruction of a dead epoch; Mr. Betjeman travels back into the past, but need not go far to find what he needs, certainly not to Poros or Delphi.

His autobiographical poem disappoints; blank verse lends itself less well than archaic stanza-forms to his purposes, as one can see from the examples in *Collected Poems*. It is simply too easy; the sense of effort, of positive archaism, is essential. One sees this clearly wherever the new poem goes over old ground. The sadistic nurse who plagued him about death and hell counts for little here after the excellent 'N.W. 5 & 6'. The insult remembered through life—when somebody called him 'a common little boy'—is much less impressive here than in 'False Security'. The richest pages are about Oxford, the 'dear private giggles' and the Kolkhorst Sunday-morning routs; but even there the best writing is in the long 'irregular ode' to Oxford.

Mr. Betjeman, inevitably, also brings Wordsworth to mind; they both deal with the disciplines of love and fear. The understanding of these led Wordsworth not to the loving reconstruction of a dead culture but, much more in Miller's

manner, to a visionary dreariness, to the remoter sources of humanity: '*Oh mystery of man, from what a depth Proceed thy honours?*' There are different ways of being a sage, but they all seem to require a journey to the past: to the bric-à-brac of Highgate, or the tomb of Agamemnon.

Anywhere but here, any time but now. As to the means of getting away, there seem to be many, some involving *mesure* and some not; and however you travel you will find, it seems, that a lot of people want to go with you.—FRANK KERMODE, "Henry Miller and John Betjeman," *Puzzles and Epiphanies*, 1962, pp. 150–52.

W. H. AUDEN
"Introduction"
Slick But Not Streamlined
1947, pp. 9–16

It is difficult to write seriously about a man one has sung hymns with or judiciously about a poet whose work makes one violently jealous. Normally when I read good poetry, for example Mr. Eliot's line

    The place of solitude where three dreams cross

my reaction is one of delighted admiration; a standard of excellence has been set in one way which I must try to live up to in mine: but when I read such lines of Mr. Betjeman as

    And that mauve hat three cherries decorate
    Next week shall topple from its trembling perch
    While wet fields reek like some long empty church

I am, frankly, rather annoyed because they are not by me. My feeling is similar to that one has when, on arriving at some long-favorite picnic spot in the woods, one finds that another trespasser has discovered it too.

Indeed, like a character in a tale by Hoffman, I can never make up my mind whether Mr. Betjeman was born after the flesh or whether he was magically begotten by myself in a punt on the Cherwell one summer evening in 1926. I have no memory of company on the outward journey on that occasion; I only know that *two* of us returned. Since that day Mr. Betjeman has indubitably existed, looking, to the outward eye, like anyone else, as an editor of the *Architectural Review*, an editor of the Shell-Mex guidebooks to the English counties, a husband, a father, a churchwarden, a secretary to a local of the Agricultural Laborers' Union, etc., but I *wonder*. Even if there was a real Betjeman once, I am afraid that he has been evicted and his place taken by the obstinate spirit of my favorite aunt Daisy. She was said to be what is called "mentally retarded" and was looked after in a convent (from which she occasionally ran away), and used to come to us for the Christmas holidays, when her brilliant skill at Happy Families belied her reputation for not being "quite all there." She had one obsession; being totally deaf in one ear, she would implore us to promise that, when she died, we would not bury her too deep, for then she might never hear the last trumpet. Sure enough, at her funeral, when the coffin was being lowered into the grave, it stuck halfway down and refused to budge. It is my secret conviction that she fooled us all about being buried and that it is her dear chilblained mittened hand which now prompts Mr. Betjeman's pen. How else could he have entered so intimately into my childhood? How else could he be so at home with the provincial gaslit towns, the seaside lodgings, the bicycles, the harmonium, above all, the atmosphere of ritualistic controversy? By the time I could walk, I had learned to look down with distaste on "Prots"—they were said never to kneel properly but only to squat—to detest the modernism of our bishop, and mildly deplore the spikyness of Aunt Mill, who attended a church where they had the Silent Canon and Benediction. How else could he know—apart from church organists and myself nobody else does—what hymns are sung to Melcomb, Eudoxia, Redhead 76, Nicaea, Irby, Stockport, University College, etc., or which composer enunciated that curious and original doctrine:—"As it was, it was in the beginning"—?

Because of all this, it is quite impossible for me to bore the reader with a serious critical introduction to Mr. Betjeman's work. I shall not spoil the field for potential Ph.D.s by discussing the influence on the poet's development of Ebenezer Elliott or C. S. Lewis, or by counting the number of his references to the bicycle. Besides, Mr. Betjeman has said for himself all that needs to be said in the extract which follows this introduction. A few general remarks about topophilia may, however, be in order here since, so far as I know, it rarely attacks professional poets in this country.

Topophilia differs from the farmer's love of his home soil and the litterateur's fussy regional patriotism in that it is not possessive or limited to any one locality; the practised topophil can operate in a district he has never visited before. On the other hand, it has little in common with nature love. Wild or unhumanised nature holds no charms for the average topophil because it is lacking in history (the exception which proves the rule is the geological topophil). At the same time, though history manifested by objects is essential, the quantity of the history and the quality of the object are irrelevant; a branch railroad is as valuable as a Roman wall, a neo-Tudor teashop as interesting as a Gothic cathedral. America is so big, the countryside not actually under cultivation so wild, that the automobile is essential to movement. Topophilia, however, cannot survive at velocities greater than that of a somewhat rusty bicycle. (Hence, Betjeman's obsession with that vehicle.) The American landscape, therefore, must probably be left to the farmers and the nature lovers, and topophilia will flourish chiefly in the cities where it is possible to walk; moreover it is more likely to be found among ward bosses than among literary men.

For example, that well-known poem by the late Stephen Vincent Benét, "I've fallen in love with American names," is not a topophiliac poem. When the poet enjoins the reader

> Bury my heart at Wounded Knee

the latter is not convinced that the poet had ever been there or would have like it if he had. It remains a pretty name on a historical map, like the names in Milton.

A topophil would probably have written something like

> Bury my heart at the corner of West 4th and 6th
> Avenue:

But topophiliac poetry does get written here and appears from time to time in local newspapers. As I write, the current issue of the New Yorker contains a specimen from the Carlisle (Pa.) Valley Planter, celebrating the last trolley from Carlisle to Holly.

> The line was on North Pine Street, just opposite old
> Hotel Argone. Charles Lenhart was the conductor,
> and
> Norman Leidigh motored it along. Bong! Bong! went
> the gong
> when Norman tramped on it. Along went the car
> with few people
> in it, and groaned and creaked as it went
> out the street and, by golly, on reaching Mt. Holly,
> for

it would run nevermore, stopped of itself for medicine right in front
of Doc Snyder's drugstore.

Much as I admire the New Yorker, it disturbs me that this poem should appear in small type under the patronising heading Poesy Department. Its technique may not be very distinguished, but the reader who does not recognise that this is poetry (and poetry a great deal better than much which appears in the more favored and well-paid positions in the New Yorker) has very poor taste. He will never appreciate one of my favorite stanzas in English poetry:

> Here's success to this foreign station
>   Where American ships without horses ride,
> And Portugueses from every nation
>   Comes in rotation upon the tide.
> But not forgetting Haulbowline Island
>   That was constructed by Mrs. Deane:
> Herself's the lady that has stored the water
>   To supply the vessels upon the main.

Nor will he like Mr. Betjeman.

> The sun was low on the railway line
>   And over the bricks and stacks
> And in at the upstairs windows
>   Of the Dawley houses' backs,
> When we saw the ghost of Captain Webb,
>   Webb in a water skeeting,
> Come dripping along in a bathing dress
>   To the Saturday evening meeting.
>   Dripping along—
>   Dripping along—
>   To the Congregational Hall;
> Dripping and still he rose over the sill and faded away
>   in a wall.

This is technically brilliant where the Carlisle poem is inept, but it belongs to the same poetic genre, and I would like to hope that the publication of this volume will inspire American topophils to take poetry seriously and American poets to take topophilia seriously.

It is one of my constant regrets that I am too shortsighted, too much of a Thinking Type, to attempt this sort of poetry, which requires a strongly visual imagination. I have seen what was the most beautiful building in New York, the El station at Sands Street, vanish unsung. Had I only Mr. Betjeman's talent, what a lovely poem I should have written about it. What lovely poems would I be writing now about Schrafft's's Blue Plate Special, Stouffer's teashop, the Brighton Beach Line, the General Theological Seminary on Ninth Avenue at Twenty-first Street, the Shakespeare garden in Central Park, the Portuguese Jewish cemetery on West Eleventh Street, Italian opera in Brooklyn, the Garibaldi house on Staten Island, Welfare Island, the Hotel Seville on Twenty-ninth Street, Sam's Umbrella Shop, the Museum of American Indian Art, etc., etc.

I am tempted at this point to try to forestall any idiotic critic who may think—whether with approval or disapproval is all one, for both are equally wrongheaded—that Mr. Betjeman's poems are trivial, that, because he does not write earnestly about religion, love, and death, he is lacking in real faith and sincere emotion, but I realise that the blind cannot be argued into vision. If the reader cannot see for himself that when Mr. Betjeman writes

> Oh! then what a pleasure to see the ground floor
> With two tables for two laid as tables for four,
> And bottles of sauce and Kia-Ora and squash

Awaiting their owners who'd gone up to wash. . . .
And I think, as these fancy-lit sights I recall,
It is these we are fighting for, foremost of all.

he means exactly what he says, nothing I could say will make
him. I will content myself with asserting dogmatically that, this
season, the man of good will will wear his heart up his sleeve,
not on it. For better or worse, we who live in this age not only
feel but are critically conscious of our emotions—there is no
difference in this respect between the highest of highbrows and
the most farouche of soda jerkers—and, in consequence, again
for better or worse, a naïve rhetoric, one that is not confessedly
"theatrical," is now impossible in poetry. The honest manly
style is today only suited to Iago.

Let me end as I began, on a personal note. Were it possible to escape from our duties to God and our neighbor into our
private islands of schizophrenic bliss, very few of us, I fancy,
would take with us any of the great works of world literature.
Our libraries would consist, for the most part, of those books
which, read in childhood, formed our personal vision of the
public world. To these tattered, dog-eared volumes, however,
most of us have in the course of our lives added one or two
extra treasures. In my case Mr. Betjeman's work belongs—so
do the novels of Ronald Firbank and the Li'l Abner cartoons—
to this tiny group of later additions to my original nursery
library: he is privileged to stand beside *Icelandic Legends,
Machinery for Metalliferous Mines, Eric or Little by Little,
Lead and Zinc Ores of Northumberland and Alston Moor*
(Stanley Smith, M.A., D.Sc. H. M. Stationery Office. 3s6d
net), *Struwelpeter, Mrs. Beeton's Book of Household Manage-
ment* (the 1869 edition), *The Edinburgh School of Surgery,
Hymns Ancient and Modern* (with tunes), and *Dangers to
Health*, a Victorian treatise on plumbing with colored plates
which, incidentally, I lent to Mr. Betjeman twelve years ago
and he has not yet returned. I see I shall have to pray Aunt
Daisy to speak to him most severely about it.

DONALD DAVIE
From "The Hawk's Eye"
Thomas Hardy and British Poetry
1972, pp. 105–11.

I f we were right to think that the unusual rigidity and intricacy of Hardy's meters and stanza patterns had something
to do with the phase of Victorian culture which he lived
through, that of heavy engineering, we shall not expect to find
this characteristic transmitted to any of his successors. For we
need not subscribe to the comically confident assertions of
some authorities, who would have it that because our technology is now electronic, there is a sort of necessity for the poet to
compose "by field"; but we may feel that indeed the way in
which Hardy rivets one verse line to another by clanging exact
rhymes and builds up in this way a finely tooled metrical machine is inappropriate to our sense of what really conditions
and keeps running the world in which we live now.

However, there is the exceptional case of John Betjeman.
For in Betjeman's poetry we do find, in the decades since
Hardy died, something approaching the rigidity and intricacy
of Hardy's metrical procedures. If the particular model in some
of Betjeman's poems is Kipling rather than Hardy, this does not
alter our sense that in any case the forms are inappropriate to
the historical circumstances in which the poet is using them,

and indeed that Betjeman is in many instances attracted to
them for just this reason; in other words, that there is an air of
antiquarianism and connoisseurship which hangs heavily
around many of Betjeman's poems which are most expert and
intricate as metrical constructions.

Thus, I find Betjeman most successful and most moving
when his writing least reminds me of anything one might find
in Hardy or Kipling or another poet of their generation. This
holds true even when the master that we hear Betjeman's poem
allude to is a poet of an earlier generation yet, for instance
Tennyson. The effect is more valuable still when Betjeman has
asserted his independence of Hardy not just in his verse forms
but also in what he chooses to say; for instance, when he is as
straightforwardly and unaffectedly Christian as Hardy is atheist.
One of Betjeman's most touching and valuable poems is one
that qualifies on both these counts, "Sunday Afternoon Service
in St. Enodoc's Church, Cornwall." This poem, in skillful but
unobtrusive and unambitious blank verse, is too long to quote
in full; this is a pity, because a great deal of the impressiveness
of the poem depends upon the way in which it sustains itself
through easy modulations of tone and feeling. . . .

When W. H. Auden was introducing Betjeman to an
American audience, in 1947, he faced the matter of this compulsion in Betjeman always to quiz his readers:

> I will content myself with asserting dogmatically that,
> this season, the man of good will will wear his heart
> up his sleeve, not on it. For better or worse, we who
> live in this age not only feel but are critically con-
> scious of our emotions . . . and, in consequence,
> again for better or worse, a naïve rhetoric, one that is
> not confessedly "theatrical," is now impossible in
> poetry. The honest manly style is today only suited to
> Iago. [1]

But this prophecy was no sooner uttered than events disproved
it. In the years since 1947, on both sides of the Atlantic, naïve
rhetorics and manly tones have been very much in evidence.
The quizzical and evasive ironies which are favored by both
Auden and Betjeman now seem to be a peculiarity of their age
group, not a condition of "this age." In any case, in "Sunday
Afternoon Service in St. Enodoc's Church, Cornwall," the
reader is quizzed by the poet only from time to time, and then
gently and with tact; the poet's eye (and therefore the reader's) is
elsewhere—on the matter being contemplated, not on the relations of the poet-performer with his audience.

As much cannot be said, however, of poems in which
Betjeman draws nearer to the Hardyesque. There is, to take a
blatant example, a poem called "Dorset," which is an imitation
of Hardy's "Friends Beyond":

> Light's abode, celestial Salem! Lamps of evening,
>   smelling strong,
> Gleaming on the pitch-pine, waiting, almost empty
>   evensong:
> From the aisles each window smiles on grave and
>   grass and yew-tree bough—
> While Tranter Reuben, Gordon Selfridge, Edna Best
>   and Thomas Hardy lie in Mellstock Churchyard
>   now. [2]

And a coy and maddening footnote by the author tells us that
the names in the last line of this stanza and in the corresponding lines of the two earlier stanzas—T. S. Eliot, H. G. Wells,
Edith Sitwell, Mary Borden, Brian Howard, Harold Acton—
are "put in not out of malice or satire but merely for their
euphony." The self-conscious "tease" of performing the parody

at all, compounded by the double-take to which this disingenuous footnote invites us, puffs such a dense vapor of self-consciousness about the poet's relationship to his readers that behind it the lineaments of the poem as in any way a considered utterance entirely disappear.

A much less obvious case, but one which in the end we have to regret more bitterly, is a poem called "The Heart of Thomas Hardy":

The heart of Thomas Hardy flew out of Stinsford
churchyard
A little thumping fig, it rocketed over the elm trees.
Lighter than air it flew straight to where its Creator
Waited in golden nimbus, just as in eighteen sixty,
Hardman and son of Brum had depicted Him in the
chancel.
Slowly out of the grass, slitting the mounds in the
centre
Riving apart the roots, rose the new covered corpses
Tess and Jude and His Worship, various unmarried
mothers,
Woodmen, cutters of turf, adulterers, church re-
storers,
Turning aside the stones thump on the upturned
churchyard.
Soaring over the elm trees slower than Thomas
Hardy,
Weighted down with a Conscience, now for the first
time fleshly
Taking form as a growth hung from the feet like a
sponge-bag.
There, in the heart of the nimbus, twittered the heart
of Hardy
There, on the edge of the nimbus, slowly revolved
the corpses
Radiating around the twittering heart of Hardy,
Slowly started to turn in the light of their own
Creator
Died away in the night as frost will blacken a dahlia. [3]

The extremely difficult verse line, one sort of English hexameter, is handled here with something approaching Hardy's inventiveness and finesse in similarly ringing the changes upon rare and difficult metrical arrangements. One notes admiringly how fast the poem gathers speed, to take off with "rocketed" in the second line; and how Betjeman uses the rapidity of spoken rather than written syntax, in a touch like the adverbial "thump" of line 10. And the grotesque literalness of the image created, a myth rendered with the effect of hallucination, can without self-evident foolishness, and appropriately enough considering the subject, be described as Dantesque. If for the first and even the second reading the direction of the poem, and the intention behind it, remain equivocal—is the poem a tribute to Hardy, or an attack on him?—we are ready to believe that the ambiguity faithfully reflects the struggle of emotions in

a reverently believing poet when regarding the spectacle of his loved and admired master who is infidel and blasphemer. In fact I take the poem to be a hyperbolical compliment to Hardy, in that his fictional creations at least *start* to turn around him, as the souls of God's creations turn around Him continually in eternal adoration and love. Indeed we should have to say that the admiration for Hardy and the pity for him are in this poem adjusted one to the other most memorably, were it not for a single betraying phrase—"various unmarried mothers." Everything else in the poem, certainly including the makers of the Brummagem sacred furniture, if it is appropriate to the character or the *persona* of John Betjeman, is appropriate no less to the character and the historical circumstances of Thomas Hardy. The image of the conscience made physically present, "hung from the feet like a sponge-bag," is magnificent. But . . . "various unmarried mothers"! At that point in the poem, quite needlessly and ruinously, there intrudes a flippantly knowing and heartless voice out of some shallowly competitive conversation at a college high table. The failure of nerve is lamentable and irredeemable: and the chance of a more splendid compliment to Hardy than anyone else is likely to pay has been irretrievably muffed and missed. This is what happens when the cosmic irony with which, in Hardy or Housman, the universe confronts man, becomes the evasive and defensive irony with which the poet confronts the universe, including that part of the human universe which he envisages as his readers.

If I propose that this sort of evasive obliquity in the poet's stance toward his audience was forced upon Betjeman by the inappropriately rigid forms which he adopted from Hardy, rather than from some psychological or social maladjustment in himself, I am giving him the benefit of the doubt. I am happy to do so, however; it is a sort of giving to which critics are not much prone. The point to be made is in any case one that does not depend upon this particular illustration, though this may enforce it. The rigidly intricate metrical and stanzaic arrangements of Hardy could be used, in the years after his death, only by poets who were willing or eager to stand obliquely to their audience. This is not the same as saying (what I do not believe) that the traditional accentual-syllabic meters of English have been self-evidently superseded by *vers libre*; it is a quality of curious tenacity in the handling and elaboration of those meters which seems to be appropriate to the generation of Hardy and Hopkins, Patmore and Kipling, but inappropriate to every generation since.

Notes

1. W. H. Auden, Introduction to *Slick But Not Streamlined. Selected Writings of John Betjeman* (New York, 1947).
2. Betjeman, "Dorset," from the *Collected Poems.*
3. Betjeman, "The Heart of Thomas Hardy," from *Collected Poems.*

EDMUND BLUNDEN

1896–1974

Edmund Charles Blunden was born on November 1, 1896, in Yalding, Kent. He was educated at Christ's Hospital in London, which he would later celebrate with plays, poems, and a history. His first poetry, published in 1914, was exclusively pastoral; after he left the Royal Army in 1919 with a Military Cross, he would write of war as well as nature. Blunden worked briefly for the *Athenaeum* in London before entering Queen's College, Oxford. There he wrote the long poems *The Waggoner* and *The Shepherd*, the latter of which won a Hawthornden Prize in 1922.

In 1924 Blunden earned his Oxford M.A. and became Professor of English Literature at the University of Tokyo. He left in 1927, then had his greatest success the following year with *Undertones of War*. From 1931 to 1943 he taught at Merton College, Oxford, and in 1932 he delivered the Clark Lectures at Cambridge. During World War II he was a staff member of the Oxford Senior Training Corps; after the war he returned to Tokyo with the United Kingdom Liaison Mission. He remained in the Far East through much of the next two decades, teaching at the University of Hong Kong.

Blunden was a scholar and a prolific critic, whose many "rediscoveries" included 19th-century poet John Clare. He edited numerous anthologies, and wrote acclaimed biographies of Percy Bysshe Shelley and Thomas Hardy, both of whom were important influences on Blunden's poetry. His awards include the Benson Medal in 1932, the CBE in 1951, the Queen's Gold Medal for Poetry in 1956, and the Order of the Rising Sun, Third Class, from the Japanese government in 1963. He was married three times, and had six children. Edmund Blunden died on January 20, 1974.

Personal

B. is amazingly industrious. And he lives in an atmosphere of intense devotion to the art of poetry. I came away feeling that he is one of the very few men for whom my friendship will never lessen. He is, in fact, almost the ideal friend and fellow-craftsman. My visit has consolidated our friendliness, and I feel that I now understand him completely, and admire him more than ever.

I wish I could describe him clearly, but he is difficult to recapture in writing. He has a good deal in common with old Hardy. A simplicity and honesty beyond praise, and a quality of being one with his work to which he has such a noble devotion.

Of course he continually reverts to the John Clare theme, which is almost an obsession with him. He speaks of J.C. with a passion of love and pity and admiration. And it is thus that B. himself will live in our hearts when he too is gone, if he should anticipate our journey to the Elysian places where poets go, when their literary careers are accomplished.—SIEGFRIED SASSOON, *Diaries 1920–1922* (entry for June 16, 1922), ed. Rupert Hart-Davis, 1981, pp. 174–75

Your fiftieth birthday. What shall we give you?
    An illuminated address
Would be hard on one who was never at home with
    Pomp or pretentiousness.
Here is a loving-cup made from verse,
    For verse is your favourite of metals:
Imagine its stem like a tulip stalk,
    Its bowl a tulip's petals
And the whole as gracefully formed and charactered
    As a poem of your own.
What shall the toast be? Fifty years more?
    A century? Let it be known
That a true poet's age is truthfully reckoned
    Not in years but in song:

So we drink instead to that happy girl
    Your Muse—may she live long!
But we pledge our love, our love for one
    Who never has burned or bowed
To popular gods, and when fame beckons
    Modestly melts in the crowd.
Into the crowd of your haunting fancies—
    The streams, the airs, the dews,
The soldier shades and the solacing heartbeams—
    You melt, and fame pursues;
And our good wishes follow you, even
    To the fortunate meadows where
Tonight your loving-cup is raised
    By Shelley, Hunt and Clare.
      —C. DAY LEWIS, "Lines for Edmund Blunden
        on His Fiftieth Birthday" (1946), *Collected
        Poems 1954*, 1954, p. 282

As a tutor at Oxford, anxious to help undergraduates to love literature, and indifferent to examination results, he encouraged young poets like Keith Douglas. In Japan, in two visits, in the 1920s and the 1940s, he laid a foundation of goodwill that was able to bridge the second world war. It is surprising how many English poets have been in Japan: Binyon, Hodgson, Blunden, Plomer, Empson, Barker, Quennell, myself, Enright, Thwaite, Kirkup. Of all that set, Blunden, without setting himself up as a professional Japanologist, fitted in most completely with the traditional Japanese idea of the *sensei*. I well remember, at a party two or three weeks after I had landed, a Japanese novelist telling me: 'The difference between you and Mr Blunden is that Mr Blunden knows and loves the Japanese people!' Three weeks, to be sure, was a short time in which to have learned to know and love them . . . ! But another difference, of course, was that Blunden is a very fine poet, with a permanent place in the English tradition; and that would have been my real reason, deeper than reasons of gratitude, sentiment, or traditionalism, for voting for him (for Professor of

Poetry at Oxford). I would not, as I say, have been meaning that I do not think Lowell a very grand poet, too. I would not, finally, have been voting for what is called 'the Establishment', or for the controllers of literary fashion: these, all through, have been unequivocally on Robert Lowell's side. Since about 1930 Blunden, partly because he has written and published rather too many poems in his later years, poems of uneven quality, but more because of shifts in poetic fashion, has had less critical attention, not more, than he deserved.—G. S. FRASER, "Edmund Blunden," *Lon*, April 1966, pp. 79–80

General

Criticism of contemporaries must always be limited and superficial, since growing organisms cannot be definitely measured. But, in comparing the output of 1922 with that of 1911, I have to confess that I see little evidence of evolution, or progress. Perhaps it is an error to expect from poetry, which is eminently a perfection of early youth, any sign of growth. Most of our lyric poets have written their best pieces, and have exhibited the fullness of their powers, before they were thirty. But it was my hope that the new writers, now admitted to the sacred ranks from which expulsion is impossible and where fame becomes mechanical, would go a little further than their forbears, and strike out in new directions.

Of this I see but one example, Mr. Edmund Blunden, whose future will be watched with the most eager anticipation. He displays all the characteristics of a mind inspired by the close and independent contemplation of nature exercised in imagination. That he is under the spell of John Clare is evident; and is curious, since Clare never boasted a disciple before. Mr. Blunden will grow out of this, when he perceives that why Clare was not a poet of the first rank was that his attention was hampered by incessant beauties, and that he lacked the gift of selective apprehension. Already, in the very remarkable piece in which "The Giant Puffball" speaks, Mr. Blunden has got beyond Clare, and I have no doubt that he will rise much further yet. No more interesting star has appeared of late in our poetical heavens.—EDMUND GOSSE, "Georgian Poetry," *More Books on the Table*, 1923, p. 232

Great as is the power of country life over me, and of that stately march of the seasons above, around, below it, yet I have always suspected myself of some inclination to explore other subjects. Indeed, I might have replied more than once from my actual state of mind, to some who conceived me to be a pastoral archaism, in the lines of my beloved Charles Churchill:—

> Secure, for me,
> Let ——— smuggle nonsense, duty free:
> Secure for me, ye lambs, ye lambkins bound,
> And frisk, and frolic, o'er the fairy ground:
> Secure for me, thou pretty little fawn,
> Lick Sylvia's hand, and crop the flow'ry lawn. . . .

I notice this, not ungratefully—for to be read as a picturesque interpreter of the English countryside, when so rich a literature stands and grows already in that field, is remarkably good luck—but with the desire that those who take up this book will not altogether skip those pages which are non-rural. They were derived from unstrained, general feelings.

It should be remarked here too, by way of preliminary, that War became part of the author's experience at a date so early (that is, in comparison with ordinary times) as to mould and colour the poetry almost throughout this book. The fact may be of use to explain or excuse metaphors and turns of thought which would now be foreign and elusive to the reader of a young poet.—EDMUND BLUNDEN, "Preface" to *The Poems of Edmund Blunden*, 1930, pp. vi–vii

Blunden's valuation of nature and rustic life is neither simple nor simple-minded. He has often in prose, besides arguing the merits of the old rural order, frankly granted its shortcomings— the sometimes degraded condition of the farm labourer, the brutishness of the untutored man, the lack of hygiene—and such things have their place in his realistic poems. But his positive claims for the old rural life as *he knew it* (a necessary emphasis) should not, any more than those of Leavis's 'discovery', George Sturt, be lightly brushed aside. They derive from the full and firmly based experience of his early years in the Kent village of Yalding, where he found 'a relationship of various talents and masteries, and courteous differences, which composed a serene, just kind of life'. What, above all, has been lost is the highly articulated life of a local community: 'The loss is not only one of a picturesque spectacle, but of a social idea', what in his recollections of Yalding in *English Villages* he calls 'a compact commonwealth of the most charming variety and possibility'. 'It is not to Kent', he maintains—perhaps guarding himself against those who can cite Hardy or the Hammonds— 'that we look in the days of Charles Dickens . . . for instances of oppression and want, or the cold separation of class from class.' Economic progress has left man 'less locally capable' and less locally conscious—'local patriotism' is a creative virtue. He had, like Sassoon, his squirearchical Kentish counterpart (Blunden himself was the village schoolmaster's son), the good fortune to have been reared in one of those fruitful pockets of rural England where a creative community life survived till near our own time. It stands for him as no fanciful ideal against which to measure what succeeded it. Inevitably, he well knows, it has become 'the lifetime in the picture' ('A Family Discourse'), but looking back to recall its values is not escapism; in reply to those who assert it is, one might well vary the admonition of the closing couplet of his sonnet 'Victorians':

> Devise some (life), and live it, beyond theirs,
> Or I shall think you but their spendthrift heirs.

Those younger 'heirs' today for whom, as a student said to me recently as Romantically as one could wish, 'the city is evil' again, may find in Blunden a congenial voice. They are concerned, more desperately than he—now the war between man and nature has reached a critical stage—'to see whether man can ever set his scientific novelties in a balance with the possibilities of simplicity'.

Blunden is an honest poet; he is clear-sighted enough to look upon that former landscape with an artists's eye, as a country of the mind now. An obliterating shadow was cast over that dead Arcadia by the terrible struggles of our century—first and most deeply by the Great War, 'the difficult dumb-show of my generation', which exploded not only humanitarian visions but also 'the pastoral fairy-tale'. In his war poems, as in 'The Dynasts', the fair face of nature is ravaged and scarred.— MICHAEL THORPE, *The Poetry of Edmund Blunden*, 1971, pp. 20–21

Edmund Blunden, like Graves, has every claim to be regarded as a Georgian. He, too, was absorbed in country scenes and folk-lore, into which the reality of war made a brutal intrusion; and, like Graves, he precipitated his experience in a memorable prose work, *Undertones of War*. Yet if there is one quality which distinguishes Blunden from the other Georgians it has always been the intensity of his absorption in the countryside. When dealing with Blunden it is hardly appropriate to talk of the 'rural scene' with all that that implies of a background or mere setting: he knows the country with a deep knowledge and a deep love and it pervades the whole structure of his mind and feelings. Reading Blunden, one is reminded of a number of literary antecedents: Richard Jefferies, John Clare and, inevitably, Wordsworth; but one is equally aware, I think, of the eighteenth-century proto-Romantics, notably Thomas Gray. Blunden's world of nature is not particularly wild or wayward in a Romantc fashion: it is ordered and in harmony with man, and it offers, above all, an image of civilization, the pattern of a pastoral, pre-industrial society. It goes a good deal deeper than the weekend-cottage view of nature of the typical Georgian. That this was an anachronistic, even primitivistic view to hold in the opening decades of the twentieth century goes without saying: Blunden's poetry, traditional in themes, language and feeling, is entirely naked to any attacks that the embattled modern sensibility cares to make upon it. But I am not now concerned with defending all of Blunden's poetic procedures, merely with pointing out that it was his particular cast of mind and feeling that enabled him to stand up to the experiences of the Front with remarkable firmness. . . .

Unlike Graves, Blunden continued to write poems about the war once it was over: he returned thankfully to the contemplation and celebration of the countryside, its creatures and its lore, but his feelings were played upon, though not distorted, by the memory of war—as, for instance, in '1916 Seen From 1921':

> Tired with dull grief, grown old before my day,
> I sit in solitude and only hear
> Long silent laughters, murmurings of dismay,
> The lost intensities of hope and fear;
> In those old marshes yet the rifles lie,
> On the thin breastwork flutter the grey rags,
> The very books I read are there—and I
> Dead as the men I loved, wait while life drags
> Its wounded length from those sad streets of war
> Into green places here, that were my own. . . .

Undertones of War contains a sizeable 'Supplement of Poetical Interpretations and Variations': one of these poems, 'Third Ypres', had previously been published in a collection called *The Shepherd* in 1922: Blunden described it as one of his most comprehensive and particular attempts to render war experience poetically. In it Blunden makes the direct confrontation of violent experience that characterized Rosenberg, Owen and Sassoon; it is, without a doubt, his finest war poem. . . . Blunden's major contribution to the literature of the Great War was in prose. Yet his war poems contain the same qualities of mind and feeling that were displayed so brilliantly in *Undertones of War*—above all, the concrete presence of physical environment and awareness of detail. If they are neither traditionally heroic nor radically anti-heroic, they are the products of a gentle mind intent upon preserving its defences; not, in such conditions, an ignoble aim.—BERNARD BERGONZI, "Graves, Blunden, Read," *Heroes' Twilight*, 1980, pp. 68–72

Works

POETRY

To say that the distinguishing mark of Mr. Blunden's Muse is that she tires with us would be to offer him a doubtful phrase; so would the suggestion that he has made this dullness interesting. But, obliquely, such a dullness does seem to be his subject—not the lack of intellect, but the lack of interest. And before pursuing this inquiry it should be noted that in fact Mr. Blunden *has* written one of the few compressed and greatly poetic lines of contemporary verse. Few reviewers can have done a greater service to literature than Mr. J. C. Squire when, in a review of Mr. Blunden's *The Waggoner*, he quoted from the poem *Almswomen* 'All things they have in common, being so poor'. The line leapt to the eye as being at once in the grand

style. Beyond the mere fact that it told, it had in itself a sense of depth and significance. It established itself permanently in the memory, and could be quoted, without indecency, in the presence of Shakespeare himself.

So high a triumph cannot often befall a poet unless he be one of the greater ones, which perhaps Mr. Blunden is; he has time and space before him to show. But having admired with all possible worship the achievement of such a line we may admit that it is exactly the largeness and the intensity of it which are lacking in many of our poets, and even (comparably anyhow) in Mr. Blunden himself. But he has one great advantage—he does not stress and accentuate his own personality. The 'I's of his poems are subdued; he is not his own centre. *He* is not dull, for he is so little there to be dull. His very style is as impersonal as can be, and perhaps this is what distinguishes it. There is in it a perpetual quiet, but it is a quiet which flows towards such profundities as are heard in the line already quoted. That line has in its particularity the general sense that Mr. Blunden's poems are in movement. They are not the contained wayside pools of much modern verse; they proceed towards infinity.

. . . There is communicated in these poems no ecstasy and little joy; the steady, slow, universal life which they record discovers no such raptures. There is an occasional—and very beautiful—poem of fantasy, but Mr. Blunden's verse hardly ever moves rapidly. His thunderstorms are equable and his north winds restrained. Extreme freshness and extreme roughness are alien to his mind; they dwell in a world of more immediate apprehension than Mr. Blunden normally inhabits, in the world (perhaps) of childhood. There are poems about childhood, but it is childhood at a distance. Distance is in this poetry, and a knowledge of the grave weariness that came in traversing that distance. Such weariness has certainly not affected the stanzas, nor does it affect the reader, but it is in many places their unacknowledged subject. The mere mass of details accentuates it; they are all comments on the single Shakespearian line 'A long while ago the world began'. The rustics are old, the shepherd, the molecatcher, the almswomen, the matmender, the gipsy wives, and others—they have travelled far in time. And other experiences which are the subjects of poems are such as in themselves cause memories of the passage of many years—war and death.—CHARLES WILLIAMS, "Edmund Blunden," *Poetry at Present*, 1930, pp. 208–11

The volume of his *Poems* (1914–1930) is a collection which does full justice to the work which made him known to the British public as a "nature poet" and it is in much of the verse of these "English Scenes" that he is at his worst. You feel that he is at times "acting nature" as much as any poet could "act mystic". One consequence of this weakening of his grasp on reality while playing with details which he does not make significant is that the longer pieces are dull and monotonous. The metrical skill which distinguishes his best poetry seems to fail, and often an easy sentimentality takes its place. And his language then is wordy and weak, too, for the use of metre and rhyme without sufficient depth of experience in the words is deadly to expression. Always a mild reflection on old scenes or a merely pleasant description of rural sights is more readable in prose. Instead of selecting a few specially weak lines here and there, I will quote the final section of "Old Homes", which is a series of nostalgic recollections of the poet's native village:

> Vision on vision blooms; long may they bloom,
> Through years that bring the philosophic gloom,
> Sweetening sleep with its strange agonies racked,
> And shedding dew on every parching tract,

In every pleasant place a virtue adding,
A herb of grace to keep the will from madding:
And, happiest village, still I turn to you,
The alabaster box of spikenard you:
To your knoll trees, your slow canal return
In your kind farms or cottages sojourn;
Enjoy the whim that on your church tower set
The lead cowl like a Turkish minaret;
Beat all your bounds, record each kiln and shed,
And watch the blue mists on each calm close spread.
My day still breaks beyond your poplared East
And in your pastoral still my life has rest.

The root of the trouble with this appears to be that the poet is stuffing out with familiar imagery a sentiment that he has failed to express. The above is only about a tenth of the piece, and the recollections just ramble on like a pleasant little prose essay up to this painfully forced conclusion, in which there is no indication of a true poet's mind. Words with tremendous associational value, like "vision", are misused, and the reference to "philosphic gloom" is a representative example of the poet "acting simple", for a reading of his poetry shows him as a poet who absolutely *must* think about experience. In his mind there may have been a passionate feeling, but it was overwhelmed by all this pretty stock scenery. The third line of the above quotation refers to the mental agonies of the poet turned soldier in the War, and what those agonies were no reader of his book *Undertones of War* needs to be reminded.—R. L. Mégroz, "Nature Poetry," *Modern English Poetry 1882–1932,* 1933, pp. 223–25

In *Shells by a Stream* there is a poem called "Thomasine". It is of extraordinary merit, and has great value as an example of the poetry of the unperceived. Though it is built upon what might be hastily spoken of as a Wordsworthian fable, it is not in the least Wordsworthian, and the distinction is important to an understanding of it.

The fable is of a girl named Thomasine. One evening after sundown she is sent by her father with a message to the miller whose house in on the bounds of the parish. While she is on her way in the clear afterglow, a moorcock calls, and the call enters into her. It is repeated.

            . . . again the cry
      Climbing the miles and miles of sky.

She comes to the miller's house.

      She had him thenceforth in her hand;
      She knocked, he came; it might have been planned;
      But her thought was up the stream—
      That call in the reeds was all her theme.

He goes aside to consider her father's message and to write his reply, taking little account of the messenger; "his plain business waits not", and soon she is gone, carrying home his answer; yet here, unrecognized by either, is the origin of a love that grows until "Life's many-roomed Mansion has but one room for them. . . ."

The poem's significance depends, in the first place, on its communication of the nature of their love. Seen in this aspect, it is that thing rare in poetry and, indeed, in literature: a celebration of the happy and enduring marriage of true minds.

      The primrose here I'd happily bring
      To peep with grace, the wren to sing;
      The thrush's egg I'd borrow to deck
      This chronicle with a hue as pure
      As it should have; the royal swan's white neck
      Should not the shining whiteness there one whit
         obscure.

      "Love, I was nothing till you made Me."
      "And I was here alone, and here are We."
      Thence in its strength their epithalamy. . . .

The last three lines have their ancestry in Herbert, and the whole of the passage quoted, in the sureness of its feeling, its lovely boldness in taking the great risks of poetry, its faultless use of a measure lengthening to the hexameter, reads with honour in the memory of that other poet who hearkened "to the birds' love-learnèd song". Read again to the word "epithalamy", and, continuing, hear how Blunden establishes the blessing upon the love of these two:

      The mirror gleams in the shades, the ancient house
      Whispers of something known to the apple-boughs
      Just by the window; she, a thought alone,
      Listens to all the night, comes, claims her own.
      All the hosts of fear are nothing here,
      Grudge and bad cheer
      Overthrown.
      He does her no wrong; she wins him, she the flood
      That bears him childlike, while he thinks his voyage
         good.

      Day, and life ahead;
      Would it were mine to utter more
      Than from some broken knowledge now was said,
      And trace them in Time's wonder, shore on shore
      Achieving . . .

There leave them in their peace. The poem is so radiant with blessing that it appears in the reader's mind, after he has read it again and again with increasing gratitude and has taken it in to himself, almost as an answer to that prayer of love spoken nearly four centuries ago:

      Spread thy broad wing over my love and me,
      That no man may us see;
      And in thy sable mantle us enwrap,
      From feare of perrill and foule horror free.
      Let no false treason seeke us to entrap,
      Nor any dread disquiet once annoy
      The safety of our joy.

Criticism may be wisely hesitant to quote new verses side by side with the greatest Epithalamion in English, and it would be at once foolish, and irrelevant to Blunden's intention, to suggest that Spenser's elaborately sustained masterpiece is now challenged; but if it is true that Blunden's lines, summoning that supreme memory of his namesake, are illumined, not dulled, by it, shall we not say so? And is it not true?—Charles Morgan, "Edmund Blunden's 'Thomasine,'" *Reflections in a Mirror,* 1947, pp. 133–36

The English countryside, of course, still needs but little transfiguration to become poetry's province, when 'the bees of Dalham' are 'in the bramble-flowers' or big-woolled sheep at the 'plain green work of eating', or a village or market town affirm their stubborn antiquity and harmony of detail.

In his rendering of all these experiences there is the same quality. They have been taken up into that immemorial Now which is the realm of the loving imagination; a realm in which the distinctions of past and present are maintained but reconciled in a timeless instant. Often the Then, in Mr. Blunden's verse, may be poignantly contrasted with Now. Yet, if ever he deplores the present, it is for lacking the integrity, not the picturesque trappings, of the past.

Yet is is admittedly in his response to a larger convulsed present that his imagination is least adequate. The charge brought against him that he has failed to come to grips with contemporary reality and is for that reason inevitably only a minor poet has some truth in it. His very virtues are here his defects. His rootedness in the past and the soil make him impervious to the distractions, the mechanized tensions, the life-and-death struggle of the modern world. He does not stand between two worlds, one dead, one struggling to be born, but in a world of his own, secure and at peace, though tempests rage without or its tranquil air quivers now and then at the thud of distant explosions.

Probably Mr. Blunden recognizes clearly enough that civilization is at a major crisis of death or rebirth. But as a poet he does not identify himself with that crisis. If he felt it intimately in himself, he would be compelled to do so. But manifestly he does not. He would seem, to a great extent, to be immune from the conflict which tests and torments so many of his contemporaries. Not so completely as Robert Bridges, but relative to the acuter sickness of his age with something of a like aesthetic detachment, he cultivates the virtues of an unwounded sensibility and a quiet mind. So far as he seeks to heal the wounds of his time, it is by reaffirming the peace which has been the quality of happier times and which survives, both by the good fortune of his birth and upbringing as a countryman and by faithful cherishing, in himself.

In the realm of poetry integrity is the one essential quality. It alone gives creative order and permanence. But its content, its degree of intensity by which the strife of opposites is resolved in a harmony that includes them, varies from the high-strung to the low, from the large to the small. In the great poet there is the greatest intensity and comprehensiveness. He has adventured most, has challenged most discord and conquered it imaginatively. No poet can be great without such spiritual adventure, such suffering of extremes.

Many of Mr. Blunden's younger contemporaries have so ventured and suffered, but they have not conquered, not yet. Their verse at best reflects the stress and anguish of the battle as it sways now this way and now that. Mr. Blunden has not plunged deeply into the fight, thought he has passed through it. He has accepted only so much of the discord as he can master and subdue without endangering his poise. And so, much of his verse is bathed in the pastoral or even bookish placidity of a gracious backwater.

In maintaining the continuity of human tradition he has mostly turned a blind eye to what is involved in the shattering of that tradition. His poetry is neither burdened nor intensified by any acute sense of crisis or of crumbling walls. And when momentarily his vision turns, as in the poem *Exorcized*, from the near and known and loved to a large but emptier world in which perverted forces grapple, he can be unrealistically innocent. Yet he is wise in this, that he seldom treads ground which his imagination has not intimately worked, circumscribed as that ground may be. Consequently the tradition which he maintains, he also renews.—HUGH I'ANSON FAUSSET, "Edmund Blunden's Later Poetry," *Poets and Pundits*, 1947, pp. 195–97

UNDERTONES OF WAR

We have also had Edmund Blunden's *Undertones of War*. It must be confessed there is something more than odd in Blunden's story. As you read deeply into it your uneasiness grows. This poet's eye is not in a fine frenzy rolling. There is a steely glitter in it. It appears to be amused by drolleries not obvious to us. It is as though, in the midst of a pleasing and animated conversation after dinner, you fancied you heard distant and indeterminate music not altogether unfamiliar. What was that? You withdraw your attention a little from the talk to get a clue

to those disturbing strains; you become absent in mind from the lamp-light and the cosy talk, and see an outer world of dubious reflections and ominous shapes, a region vast and dark and as cold to human hope and aspiration as a polar solitude. What, at dinner? Yes, there the heads of those happy talkers remain between you and that foreboding night, still animated and unaware, and they continue to say nothing while making foolishly eager movements. You have to pull yourself together—come out of that disturbing dream—begin to chatter again with the others.

Blunden's book, in fact, is by a ghost for other ghosts; some readers will not know what it is all about; they will say so, not being ghosts, and seeing none. Yet it is a humorous book, though its fun is wan; through its pale fun you can see the tangibilities of to-day solid in their appropriate places. You soon have more than a suspicion that Blunden is not addressing you at all, you the reader, but presences not visible. His cheerful voice is addressed over your shoulder, and your amusement fades when that fancy chills it. You turned round; and nothing is there! This ghostly play, once you are aware of it, disturbs your confidence in the tangibilities of your own hearty day with a hint that there are tidings withheld. What is it the shades know and laugh over?

Blunden says nothing about that. Why should he? The shades would know it, and so need not be told. Yet the uneasy reader persists in trying to find it out. He suspects that this is a rare book in which much is secreted in the blank spaces; the best of it maybe. He might be overhearing, by chance, allusive but exciting reminiscences by men out of sight. At first he supposes their shattering adventures were by the body and of the sword; then becomes awed by more than a suspicion that these reminiscences are of something worse than the blood, mire, and the shocks of war's explosions. Somebody was shot through the heart, we gather, yet continued to smoke and laugh. Something was worse than the fury of the enemy. What was it? The listener wonders whether it might have been the old folk at home; for the soldier appears to have been lonelier in spirit when in London and more antagonistic to what was current there than when guessing on his belly at night behind the German wire whether he would get what was meant for him. He had a better understanding of Fritz than of us. We were the aliens. There was understanding through common adversity in France; in London there was but a revival of the old horrible hue-and-cry, and to the soldier home 'on leave' that was dismaying. Yet no. It is not that. Though that may have been so, it will not account for all we find in Blunden's book—or rather, for what falls across it like a shadow, sounds through it as an elfish laugh. Is it any good trying to understand the ghost of a child who has played knuckle-bones in Hell for shocking forfeits? As a haunting presence it has some upsetting ways, especially when it would play with us by the study fire, after midnight. You find yourself hoping that nobody else in the house heard that laugh. Somehow, though, its spectral merriment is more to us than all the starry host.

There is loveliness in this narrative of Blunden's. Let no man read it who fears the magic of names—Mesnil, Beaumont, Hamel, Givenchy, Festubert, Mazingarbe, Zillebeke, Thiepval, Richebourg–St. Vaast. And Ypres! The jags of that city's pallid ruin, with imprisoned echoes jibbering at the hurrying wayfarer, rise again in Blunden's story. The fellows who went through the Menin Gate of Ypres, and vanished, they live again, and glints and suggestions of the night which swallowed them; the face of a pal seen for a moment by the light of a star-shell; the friends in a dug-out eyeing each other while waiting to be buried ('we do not exist'); the elder chum who ignored the worst of it, whose complexion was always rosy, whose solidity could not be moved by any sudden frightfulness, and who jollied his weaker brethren then with steadying advice; the boozy sergeant-major, good-humoured and soft, who became a centre of gravity when things went wrong. After all, the men are the best of Blunden's book; and that is right. That at least we were sure to get from a poet. This story of war stirs and proceeds with living figures, and its scenes are authentic with trifles forgotten till Blunden reminds us of them. The old front line comes back. It is solid. You can hear the mud of the Salient when the duckboards squelch under the feet of unseen men 'going up' at night. You can smell the Somme. You may potter around Mesnil, and shudder again in the silence of its ghastly sunlight. And if to stir those apprehensions does not mean we are reading good prose, then there is no other way of proving it, that I know. Yet there is more in the book than that. Something æolian breathes through its lines. You may hear echoing, as one used to hear desolation murmuring when the night was suspect and the flares above the trenches were few before dawn, the wonder and awe of the sacrificed who did not know why this had come to them; for Blunden's is a tribute to the unknown soldier more lasting than the pomps about a cenotaph.—H. M. TOMLINSON, "War Books," *Critn*, April 1930, pp. 414–17

Blunden's great long poem, though it is written in prose, is *Undertones of War*. The books with which one naturally compares it are Sassoon's *Memoirs of an Infantry Officer* and Graves's *Good-Bye to All That*. Blunden is not a natural story-teller, as Graves is; nor has he, like Sassoon, that compulsive recall of total social situations which makes for the great memoir. He has something of that incuriosity about other people, as distinguished from the impact which they make on him at a particular moment, that separates the poet from the novelist. The 'place' of *Undertones of War* is not really Flanders or the trenches, but the poet's mind; and that mind shrinks from displaying in detail the whole brutality of war, it has what a good young critic, Mr Michael Thorpe, in a still unpublished dissertation on Sassoon and his contemporaries, has called 'a selective realism'. Blunden can be harsh, horrifying and definite enough:

. . . the shell had burst all wrong. Its butting impression was black and stinking in the parados where three minutes ago the lance-corporal's mess-tin was bubbling over a little flame. For him, how could the gobbets of blackening flesh, the eye under the duckboard, the pulpy bone be the only answer?

More typical are meditative passages in which outer nature is seen as the vulnerable companion of the soldier. I shall take one of these passages and break it up, according to its natural pauses and cadences, into free verse, using the devices of visual prosody:

> Still I hear
>   their slouching feet
> at last on the footbridge
>   over the Ancre
>   by Avelny
> where a sad guard
>   of trees dripping
>   with the
>   dankness of autumn
> had nothing to say
>   but sempiternal
>   syllables, of which
> we had our own
>   interpretation.
> The shadows on the
>   water
> were so profound
>   and unnavigable
> that one felt them as
>   the environment of
>   a grief of gods
> silent and bowed,
>   unvisitable
>   by breeze or star. . . .

Print the carefully cadenced, the compulsively pausing prose that way and Blunden can be seen as an English equivalent of the Pound of the *Cantos* or the Williams of *Paterson*, as the forerunner of the David Jones of *In Parenthesis*.—G. S. FRASER, "Edmund Blunden," *Lon*, April 1966, pp. 82–83

EDWARD BOND

1934–

Edward Bond was born in London on July 18, 1934. He left school at fifteen, worked at a number of odd jobs, and served for a time in the army. In the early 1960s Bond joined the Royal Court Theatre, which presented *The Pope's Wedding* in 1962. Three years later, the Royal Court production of his play *Saved* sparked a furious controversy that make Bond famous—or infamous, according to critics who were outraged by the play's violence, particularly the stoning of an infant by a mob. *Early Morning*, produced in 1968, was equally violent and equally controversial; it was the last play to be censored by the Lord Chamberlain's office. Bond observed, "People who do not want writers to write about violence want to stop them writing about us and our time. It would be immoral not to write about violence." Both *Saved* and *Early Morning* were revived in 1969 to belated acclaim.

   Lear, Bond's adaptation of *King Lear*, was a substantial British and American success in 1971. His subsequent plays have been less accessible and less popular, but critics' estimation of his importance continues to rise. He has translated Chekov's *The Three Sisters* and Wedekind's *Spring*

Awakening, and has written librettos for the ballet *Orpheus* and for two Hans Werner Henze operas. His screenplays include *Blow-Up* in 1967 and *Walkabout* in 1971. Bond has won a George Devine Award, a John Whiting Award, and a D.Lit. from Yale in 1977.

Edward Bond lives in London with his wife, Elizabeth, whom he married in 1971.

General

Living involves failure. Evolution is the record of failure at the same time as it's the record of success. So is history. So is moral action. No action is wholly pure. No action except death is final. So there are no supernatural guarantees for the strength and endurance of moral actions, and no actions that protect our sanity except our own. This idea depressed the nineteenth century. They called it God being dead. They thought of human beings as dwarfs isolated in an empty world, and human action as morally meaningless and fundamentally irrational. They saw the universe as a coffin. In our time that becomes the commonplace idea that life is absurd, that we can't prevent suffering except of the most elementary sort—and then only if the economics of charity don't disrupt our own security. In ⟨*The Sea*⟩ Evens argues against this pessimism. The universe spontaneously produces life. It's said there are many other inhabited worlds. We may never contact them, but at least we're not biological freaks cowering in the corner of a vast and otherwise empty lunatic asylum. It suggests we're not the only world in which moral problems arise. The universe produces minds with moral consciousness. When we look at the night sky there are other moral beings, an infinity of space and time away, looking at the night sky in our direction and asking the questions we ask.

Moral actions have meaning because we give them meaning. We act morally because we're concerned for others' happiness. Or if that's too ambitious for our society, at least for their freedom from obvious pain and need. What gives living a meaning and stops it being absurd?: our happiness and pain, the happiness we feel when others are happy, the pain we feel when others despair. It's a natural human reflex to smile when others smile. It's also naturally human to shudder when they suffer—only we're taught not to, it costs too much. Happiness and pain are the things that give social life meaning, and it's an uncivilized crime to ignore this and say: No, life is absurd. We can't avoid our moral element. People who live by the sea never get away from its sound. It murmurs, roars, soothes, threatens, and shifts like an unanswered question. And we, who live with other men and women, never get away from moral involvement with them. Some try. But you deny the humanity of others only by destroying your own. And when you destroy your humanity you destroy the most characteristic mark of your species. You cripple yourself. And then—because when you subvert moral concern you subvert your own intelligence—you end by asking why your life is empty and trivial, and why you've created a society threatened by political gangsters.

. . . Evolution proceeds by solving problems. You could almost say moral evolution proceeds by making mistakes. Without problems our species would stagnate and probably regress. The act of solving is almost as important as the solution itself—because it means we keep the ability to grow. In a scientific age we should remember that we may reach a time when science will make more problems than it solves. I'm not denying the value of science and technology. But scientists work in a society which includes politicians, sick people, rabid militarists, and commercial imperatives. These impose their own characteristics on the social use of science. And because our institutions were evolved by pastoral communities, there are no democratic institutions for the control of science and technology—even though they change our lives more than anything else. There is no pure science because all science takes place in a social context, no such thing as the abstract search for knowledge because knowledge becomes technology and so changes our lives. When scientists talk of pure science, or knowledge for its own sake, they're asking to be allowed to act like apes. Apes make H-bombs. Being human is a matter of choosing to be human.—Edward Bond, "Author's Program Note on *The Sea*" (1974), *Bingo and The Sea*, 1975, pp. 122–24

Because of his historical, evolutionary view of society, the child and the old man are key figures in Bond's social philosophy and plays. The old tend to destroy or corrupt the young, but aggression and violence can be supplanted by pity. The victimizing of the young is a minor theme in *The Pope's Wedding*, but is dominant in *Saved*, *Early Morning*, *Narrow Road*, and *Lear*. The children may be as uncomprehending as the drugged "doormat" of *Saved* or as selfconsciously positive as Arthur of *Early Morning*. They may be killed as sacrifices to jealousy, boredom, ambition, and other adult feelings (*Saved*, *Narrow Road*) or they may be threatened by a cancerous social corruption (*The Pope's Wedding*, *Early Morning*, *Lear*.) Through suffering or insight, the young may become figuratively old (Scopey, Arthur, the boy's ghost). Old men, like Disraeli, Gladstone, Basho (Bond's worst character), and Lear at the beginning tend to perpetuate a fall of which they are products. However, old men can indicate a "*method* of change" for the better. Alen, the most consistently victimized of the old men, has simply withdrawn. Harry offers Len a constructive peace. Lear, beginning as the oppressor, ends as Bond's most powerful illustration of genuine change—"the Oedipus, atavistic fury" transformed into insight and enlightenment.—Joseph E. Duncan, "The Child and the Old Man in the Plays of Edward Bond," *MD*, March 1976, pp. 8–9

Edward Bond does not write about violence: he writes about the effects upon the human spirit of a violent environment. Only very occasionally is effect out of proportion to cause, and even then the surgical precision of the scrutiny, visual and verbal, prevents the violence from titillating, however much it may shock. Bond's plays yearn to explore the gentleness and compassion of which humankind is capable, and many of his characters display natural goodness under acutely difficult circumstances. But he is too honest an artist, and too scrupulous a craftsman, to dwell upon the tranquil moments in his plays—though when they do occur they thus work to deeper and truer effect. He believes himself an optimist that they occur at all.

In truth, one should not write about violence and Bond in the same breath. Yet not to do so would be to ignore the climate of critical opinion in which his work is too often discussed—whereas that climate, if it is to be changed, must first be defined. Why has Bond's work prompted so wilfully obtuse a response from otherwise intelligent critics? How does its 'cruelty' differ from that advocated by Artaud, the French visionary, whose latter-day apologists too often conceive violence as an end in itself? Bond has his own, persuasive answers, and increasingly has felt it necessary to provide them by way of prefaces to his printed plays: but should not the plays themselves be less open to misunderstanding, if such special authorial pleading is necessary?

It has to be remembered that when Bond began writing, little more than a decade ago, humanity was still wreaking havoc, unchecked and unthinking, upon the world's material resources. There was no 'energy crisis', little recognition that raw materials were not inexhaustible, and no real understanding of the long-term effects of blind technological advance. Neither had these matters much preoccupied the generation of playwrights immediately preceding Bond's. John Arden, Arnold Wesker, and (at least in his early work) John Osborne were all socially conscious writers, but essentially in an older tradition, of commitment to political solutions. Bond's early plays were thus prophetic—indeed, they remain so, in that the problems of which he writes are very far from solved, although they are now more widely recognized. The Victorian condemnation of Ibsen's *Ghosts* as a play 'about' venereal disease is closely analogous to the enduring misconception that Bond's *Saved* is 'about' stoning a baby to death.

Bond's plays probe causes, and display effects. Sometimes, in his more naturalistic pieces, he extends awareness by a direct representation of a perhaps unfamiliar way of life: more recently, he has tended to work by universalizing rather than particularizing the human condition. Always, it is that condition with which he is concerned—a condition which is desperate, because of the damage mankind persists in inflicting upon itself. Yet he exhibits, despite his avowed atheism, an unquenchable faith in humanity's divine spark, and in the slender but real possibilities for redemption.—SIMON TRUSSLER, *Edward Bond*, 1976, pp. 3–4

What I want now to explore is how Bond's own theatrical practice makes use of the particular brand of Brechtianism with which he undoubtedly came into contact through Gaskill, as well as through the tradition of English attitudes to Brecht that I have sketched. Bond himself is unsure about the influence of Brecht on his work. He agrees that *Narrow Road to the Deep North* is 'somewhat Brechtian in shape and so on', but, he continues, '*Saved* for instance uses the same technique, it just happens to be set in a different age. There's a Brechtian tie-up there, but that's purely because the original on which it was based happened to be that. So I don't think I'm influenced by Brecht at all'. Certainly my analysis of the theatrical interconnections between Bond and Gaskill, Gaskill and Brecht, are not designed to be read as anything like 'influence' in its traditional sense. Instead I am attempting to see the emergence of Bond's work as the result of the specific nature of the theatrical culture at a particular juncture in time.

Even apart from questions of influence, Bond is unclear about Brecht. In another interview he complains about Brecht that 'his plays are so naïve, it's not true', but also admits 'I rather admire Brecht actually. I think his naïvety covers painful knowledge'. Naïvety is of course the charge that Bond's critics most often use against his plays. Most revealing is Bond's condemnation, in a lecture at Cambridge University in 1975, of Brecht's slogan 'Food first, morals later'. Bond objects because he fails to see the irony in Brecht's use of the phrase in *The Threepenny Opera*. The slogan comes as part of a song by Jenny and Macheath, designed by them as an extenuation of their actions. But the song continues,

What keeps a man alive if not the hours
He spends devouring, tearing, killing all that he can?
That's how man lives his life, he has the power
To make himself forget that he's a man.

What Bond lacks here, as the English attitude to Brecht has always lacked, is a comprehension of Brecht's irony. As Brecht said in that final notice to the Berliner Ensemble, 'There is in

England a long-standing fear that German art . . . must be terribly heavy, slow, laborious and pedestrian', and Brecht advised the company, 'we must keep the tempo of a run-through and infect it with quiet strength, with our own fun'.

Clearly what Bond has 'taken from' Brecht is not based on an accurate reading; it seems to have been mediated through Gaskill. Through his attitudes to stage objects, Bond, as I shall show, achieves a dramatic structure based on the *gestus* that Brecht analyzed as at least potentially social in its presentation. Through the objects, the unit of the scene becomes in Bond the basis for the analysis of the social existence of the individual. For Brecht, this basic principle, the concept of the *gestus*, is the key to the entire theory of epic theatre and its particular manner of theatrical narrative.

In the prefatory note to *The Pope's Wedding*, Bond defines the mode of staging that is his practice for nearly all his plays:

> In these sixteen scenes the stage is dark and bare to the wings and the back. Places are indicated by a few objects and these objects are described in the text. The objects are very real, but there must be no attempt to create the illusion of a 'real scene'.

The emphases are precisely where the tradition of British Brecht productions would lead one to expect them: the objects are real, the set is not. From the beginning of his work, Bond focuses our concentration on the objects and their use. They are all 'those which show usage' in Brecht's phrase; if they did not they would not be 'very real' as Bond demands. . . .

Let me sum up the nature of Bond's plays in a few phrases: Bond's plays turn the spectator into an observer and force him to take decisions; they are a picture of the world, the presentation of the world as object through objects, presented in argument, in the conflict that they lay bare between the human and the objects that manifest reality; they demand attention not on the end of the play, but on its course, because each scene stands for itself; they explore rationally the social determinism of the individual.

Most of these phrases are not mine at all. They come from the essay that Brecht appended to *The Rise and Fall of the City of Mahagonny*, the essay which is of course the *locus classicus* for Brecht's exposition of the principles of his epic theatre; they come from the list of characteristics of epic theatre that Brecht opposed to the dramatic theatre.

The accuracy of Brecht's phrases as a description of Bond's work is immediately striking. In a roundabout way, through concentrating on the socio-political nature of Bond's plays we have returned to the connection between Brecht and Bond. Bond's perception of his society has led him to develop a theatrical method that is extremely close to the aims of Brecht's epic theatre. The social analysis has produced a theatrical mode that is profoundly Brechtian.

Oddly, this connection has been implicitly noted before. In *Confessions of a Counterfeit Critic*, Charles Marowitz, one of the principal writers in *Encore*, commented of Bond that 'his work demands the kind of epic approach that continental theatres can provide'. The 'epic approach' of the plays is Brecht's, yet it would be wrong to search for detailed echoes; what Bond has achieved is primarily rooted in the Royal Court and the work of William Gaskill. That is the reason why his work fails to use significant parts of Brecht's theory of a Marxist drama; Bond does not make full use of alienation effects in the acting since such effects have never been a part of the English acting tradition, nor have they been particularly well understood in England. In spite of such omissions, Bond is achieving the recreation, in the context of British theatre, of the theatrical practice that Brecht outlined. His political analysis has led him to Brecht's conclusion for, as his writings show, Bond knows that the practice of theatre is not simply a theatrical art but necessarily a political one.—PETER HOLLAND, "Brecht, Bond, Gaskill, and the Practice of Political Theatre," *ThQ*, Summer 1978, pp. 27–33

Works

At the risk of appearing to hoist myself on to a bandwagon that is going very nicely without my help, may I be allowed a word concerning the much-fought-over play *Saved*, by Edward Bond, at the Royal Court? . . .

In his play of marvellously observed dialogue and first-rate dramatic form, Edward Bond places his act of violence in the first half, as is done in *Macbeth*, *Julius Caesar*, etc. Unfortunately the extreme horror of this scene, though no more lurid than many an accustomed fact to which English railway toilets give testimony, has run away with most dramatic criticism and blinded it to the rare qualities shown in the rest of the play, which from time to time achieves astonishing heights of dramatic prowess and containing a last scene of which Chekhov himself would have purred his approval, a scene lasting how many minutes? (time stood still for me) with its one singular utterance of three words. . . .

By all means let us protect our children from such evils— and incidentally *Saved* is a club performance, which is the nearest approximation we in the theatre can make to the X certificate. But as facts of life they are as indigenous to our natures, and to be as capably apprehended and understood, as the accepted stot—and for the same reasons, because the non-apprehension or non-understanding of our natures is going to make a mess of things, and cause appalling horrors to be perpetrated under the name of justice or even sanctimony. . . .

As I have said, *Saved* is not for children but it is for grown-ups, and the grown-ups of this country should have the courage to look at it; and if we do not find precisely the mirror held up to nature in which we can see ourselves, then at least we can experience the sacramental catharsis of a very chastening look at the sort of ground we have prepared for the next lot.—LAURENCE OLIVIER, "The Tragic Theme," *PP*, Jan. 1966, p. 28

Except for some Victorians, who saw it as the face of self-help rewarded, everyone has been appalled by the stolid, pompous figure that juts out of the wall just above Shakespeare's tomb. Could this 'self-satisfied pork butcher', as Dover Wilson dubbed the monument, really be the earthly likeness of the Immortal Bard? Surely not—and yet there was a Shakespeare who, so far from conforming with the common image of poets as tousled, unworldly spendthrifts, was embarrassingly interested in acquiring property, securing his investments, pursuing debtors and their sureties in the courts, and generally achieving prosperity and status in the cabbage-patch of Stratford. The apparent dichotomy between this acquisitive burgher and the anguished author of *Timon* clearly fascinates Edward Bond; and in the bizarrely titled *Bingo*, or 'scenes of money and death', he uses it to illustrate his belief that good men must be contaminated, and may be corrupted, by a vicious economic system. Or, to put it another way: if Shakespeare was capable of cooperating in the rise of capitalism, what hope of resistance from lesser beings, like you and me?

It goes without saying that this Shakespeare won't be very easily reconciled with the one who rounded off *The Winter's Tale* so serenely, or, for that matter, the one who appears to rejoice at the prospect of Iago being exquisitely and endlessly tortured to death. A despairing, disgusted suicide seems scarcely less historically credible than a lesbian love-affair between Queen Victoria and Florence Nightingale. And yet, whether he's writing of the treatment of vagrants in 17th-century England or the details of Shakespeare's own dealings in Stratford, Bond consistently aims at an authenticity he never contemplates in that mad fantasy, *Early Morning*. Even the saloon-bar binge with Jonson has a basis in tradition, though Shakespeare's fatal acquisition is supposed to have been a fever, not a phial. Indeed, his account of the enclosure controversy seems rather more accurate than that of the redoubtable Rowse, who misreads a vital document in order to be able to claim that Shakespeare was opposed to the landgrabbers. Bond isn't interested in offering us a fictional archetype of suffering mankind, like his own (or Shakespeare's) Lear: he wants our attention for a specific period, an actual person. How is it (we're to ask) that a man whom we worship for his humanity could bear to live in a society we know to have been so cruel? How can we, his descendants, bear to live in a society directly derived from it?

This is the sort of question that Bond asks again and again, in play after play. All, from *Saved* to *The Sea*, may be seen as the dramatic equivalents of those insistent Oxfam ads which thrust children with sparrow-legs and pigeon-bellies under our well-nourished noses. Each insists that we face the kind of realities that make us instinctively drop our eyes and change the conversation; each consciously, perhaps presumptuously, attempts to make us more sensitive and responsible to the world's suffering.

But several things distinguish Bond's *Bingo* from, say, his *Lear*. First, the cruelties, being better documented and more unsensationally presented, are less easy to dismiss as the feverish symptoms of his pathological imagination. That is a strength. Second, the emphasis on economic and social conditions seems to suggest that they alone are responsible for human suffering, and leaves us unclear whether or not Bond still thinks that mankind is also afflicted with an innate and immutable sadism, as certainly seemed the case in *Lear*. That seems to me a weakness, or at least a limitation. Third, the ending is Bond's bleakest to date, implying, as it does, that it may be less painful and more honourable to die than to live in a bad world. That is not a strength, nor a weakness, but a bald statement of disaffection and disgust, as hard to subject to impersonal criticism as someone's suicide note.

The play's language ranges from the engagingly mundane ('you just sit there and brood all day,' the dreadful Judith tells her father, 'you must learn that people have feelings') to the self-consciously 'poetic'—but what dramatist would not become a trifle strained when called upon to write death-knell speeches for his greatest precursor? Most of the time, the dialogue is simply and unpretentiously eloquent, Jane Howell's production equally modest and straightforward—though I don't think much is gained by setting the play within what appears to be a forest of violin-strings or the beginning of some massive game of cat's cradle. Sue Cox's prim, cold Judith is a good dry run for Regan; Rhys McConnochie's Jonson, smiling venomously over his cups, might be developed into an admirably sinister Edmund; but I can, I fear, find no such grand comparison for Peck's dour angst in the main part. I wish he'd dare to be a little more like Lear, or Gloucester, or *someone* with a soul as well as a frown. But it's a fascinating play; and I'm as impressed to find it first performed in a nutshell on the Exeter campus as I was sorry to share the experience with an audience scattered into desultory twos and threes, as if to pray. When it reaches London, as it surely must, the problem will be how to prevent overcrowding in stalls and gods alike— BENEDICT NIGHTINGALE, "The Bourgeois Bard," NS, Nov. 23, 1973, p. 783

JOHN RUSSELL TAYLOR
From "Edward Bond"
The Second Wave
1971, pp. 84–91

In retrospect one might guess that *Saved* represents a transitional phase in Bond's work, one in which he is, more or less consciously, striving to free himself from the naturalistic style of *The Pope's Wedding*, with its meticulous notation of local country speech and recreation of a recognizably real world for its characters to live in, and reaching out towards the overtly non-realistic manner of *Early Morning* (1968). *Saved* could have made a thoroughly effective play in Bond's entirely naturalistic manner, or, seen in a different light, if he had managed to divorce it entirely from naturalism. But the text as it stands seems to me an interesting but finally unsatisfactory compromise. No question of compromise with *Early Morning*, though. Here naturalism is thrown right out of the window, and Bond is able to get straight down to what he has to say, without the necessary periphrases of superficially naturalistic drama.

Which is just as well, seeing that what he has to say is quite complex enough without the superimposition of purely technical subterfuges as well. If *The Pope's Wedding* and *Saved* can be seen as about—among other things—the corruption of man's natural innocence by 'upbringing and environment', which is to say by the forces exerted on him by abstractions like society, Christian morality, the repressive rule of order, *Early Morning* moves a stage further, or if you like starts at the other end. The two earlier plays are about the suffering classes; *Early Morning* is about those who impose the suffering, exert the pressures. The play is a nightmare comic fantasy in which characters with historical labels—Queen Victoria, Florence Nightingale, Gladstone, Disraeli—mingle with modern characters and talk with complete equanimity about people and events which came long after their deaths. They live in a world of arbitrary, institutionalized cruelty, where cannibalism, metaphorical and later literal, is the order of the day, and the great discovery of the play's martyr-figure, Prince Arthur, is that people 'don't just hate their own life—they hate life itself. It's a matter of conscience, like duty in the blood: they stay alive to kill.' Hence it follows that, 'What we need now is the great traitor: who kills both sides, his and theirs.'

The themes are completely consistent from *The Pope's Wedding* to *Saved* and from *Saved* to *Early Morning*. Each has an innocent (or relatively innocent) martyr-figure who with saintly or perhaps merely masochistic devotion opens himself to the worst that life has to offer. Each assumes some pervasive Oedipal situation in which humanity is seen as divided into put-upon, ill-used children and cruel, arbitrary, inscrutable parents who mete out punishments and occasional rewards with the savagery and unassailable authority of Old Testament gods. And each allows us to suppose that something may remain uncorrupted, some shred of natural goodness may survive; there is always a straw, if no more than a straw, to clutch at. It is no doubt in these terms that we should understand the indestructibility of Prince Arthur in *Early Morning*. Though his Siamese-twin brother, George, dies and is resurrected and dies again, still stubbornly attached to him; though he himself dies but cannot lose his living ability to feel pain; though he is dissected and eaten by his family in heaven, so that nothing but a neat pile of bones remains; yet, at the last, unremarked by those participating in the final cannibal feast, he comes again from his coffin, silent but undestroyed. . . .

Early Morning, of course, had even more trouble with censors and the censorious than *Saved*. And yet somehow, as has so often happened in the new drama in Britain, things were subterraneously working in Bond's favour, so that what started as incomprehensible, shocking, inducive of immediate, unthinking fury gradually came, without anyone's knowing quite how, to be accepted as, at the very least, an inescapable fact of theatrical life, so that even those who did not like Bond's plays very much found themselves agreeing to his importance. Though he had, meanwhile, written or collaborated on a number of film scripts (Volker Schloendorff's *Michael Kohlhaas*, based on a story by Kleist, Tony Richardson's *Laughter in the Dark*, based on the novel by Nabokov, and most notable, Antonioni's *Blow Up*, elaborated by Bond, in collaboration, from an original story idea by Antonioni), it could hardly be said that they had aided his acceptance, since even the relatively few filmgoers on whom the technical credits impinge would find it very difficult to isolate anything specifically and unmistakably Bond's from the films as a whole. More important, obviously, was the Royal Court's dedicated espousal of his cause, culminating in their 1969 season of his plays, which even on the level of a PR operation was an undoubted triumph. But most important of all, it seems to me, is the appearance of his fourth play, *Narrow Road to the Deep North* (1968), first at Coventry, then in London, since there at last he seems to have found a form completely adapted to his content, and to have written a play which works perfectly on many levels, one at least of which almost anybody can understand and appreciate.

The principal reason for this is that in *Narrow Road to the Deep North* Bond achieves precisely the right degree of abstraction from everyday reality for his play to work as a parable without raising a lot of essentially irrelevant objections in his audience's minds. It is short, sharp, and determinedly to the point; it is also far enough removed in time and space (Japan some time vaguely in the Meiji period) not to bother us about whether it is realistic or not. Instead we are left free to respond to the play simply as a tale that is told, a succession of happenings which may, if we wish it, be interpreted in some particular sense but which do not absolutely require interpretation as a necessary means of appreciation. . . .

As one would expect, *Narrow Road to the Deep North* contains themes and ideas carried over from earlier plays, notably in those parts which concern the Western barbarians Basho brings in to vanquish Shogo. The evangelizing Georgina, with her cynical manipulation of the forms of Christianity as an instrument of government, a way of keeping the masses subservient, has many overtones of Bond's Queen Victoria in her speech and behaviour, and the denunciation of Christian morality in general is familiar from earlier plays, though here more pointedly and economically expressed. (It is worth noting, however, that Georgina is to some extent humanized by contradictory traits like sympathy for the murdered children, and that it is these contradictions which ultimately drive her mad.) Familiar too is the character of Kiro, another innocent seeking contact with the worst of the world; and if he finally despairs and kills himself, the naked swimmer who at that very moment emerges from the river carries with him unmistakable overtones of innocence new-born. Basho too fits in, as the inhuman dweller in the ivory tower, who fails in humanity at the crucial moment (if he had saved the child in the prologue presumably the rest of the play would never happen) and then temporizes, accommodates, reacts when he does—to preserve his own peace of mind—too hastily and wrong, all in the cause of some deluding abstract ideal of the dedicated life of poetry. If anyone is the villain of the play, he is.

But the play also marks a new stage in Bond's mastery of his material and his ability to display it to best advantage. The dialogue is pared to the bone, and placed with a poetic wit and economy which shows the hand of a master stage craftsman— something which before one would hardly have put in the forefront of Bond's qualifications as a dramatist. And above all, the play bears the mark on every page of Bond's maturing as a dramatic thinker, his increasing awareness of the complexities of life and moral decision. He has remarked of this play that 'There are good things and bad things in almost everybody in the play, and it is the incidents which speak for me.' He has said much the same of earlier plays, but this time the intention is really carried through to complete achievement.

BENEDICT NIGHTINGALE
From "Edward Bond"
A Reader's Guide to Fifty Modern British Plays
1982, pp. 101–4
Lear

Shakespeare's *King Lear* is a play Bond enormously admires, but one he thinks crucially flawed. In particular, he dislikes its stoicism. 'To endure till in time the world will be made right' is, he says, a dangerous moral, especially for a world whose time may be running out. Indeed, the play is a little comfortable: 'You don't have to question yourself or change your society'. His job, therefore, was to rewrite it 'for ourselves, for our own society, for our time, for our problems'.

The execution turned out to be as bold as the intention. We are shown a semi-mythic, semi-modern Britain ruled by Lear, a paternalist tyrant using slave labour to build a great wall which will keep his enemies out and guarantee eventual 'peace' and 'freedom' inside. His daughters, Bodice and Fontanelle, at first sound sensible, like their prototypes, Goneril and Regan. They will marry Lear's hereditary enemies, the Dukes of Cornwall and North, and raze the wall. Before long, however, they have overthrown their father and instituted a régime even more vicious than his. In time, they too are overthrown, by a revolutionary army led by one Cordelia, whose husband has been murdered for harbouring the fugitive Lear. But this, it appears, is only to substitute Stalinism for arbitrary Tsarism. Means are subordinated to ends; 'political officers' interrogate the prisoners of the old régime, and 'undesirables' are shot; Fontanelle and Bodice are killed without trial; a petty swindler is hanged because 'certain economic offences have been made capital with retrospective effect' and he is a 'social liability'; and people are once again press-ganged to build the selfsame wall. Many of the old atrocities are perpetrated, but this time more calculatedly and coldly. Lear himself is blinded in an attempt to make him politically ineffective, with what the horribly considerate doctor performing the operation calls 'not an instrument of torture, but a scientific device'. In 1971, when the play was first performed, Bond manifestly took a more sceptical view of violent revolution than now and, as we'll see, tended to regard the winning of hearts and minds as the prime way of achieving social change.

Shakespeare's Lear makes a spiritual journey, Bond's a more political one. In defeat, he's at first maddish, self-pitying, vindictive: he has been 'too trusting, too lenient'. But when he is captured by his daughters' soldiers, he shows a genuine altruism by trying, unsuccessfully, to protect those who have protected him. In captivity he begins to elaborate what's to become the play's central metaphor, that of an animal in a cage, clawing to escape. Like Shakespeare's Lear, he achieves sanity in apparent madness, and, like Gloucester, he sees clearly only

when he is blind. He denounces evil, especially that done in the name of order, justice and good. He learns compassion, and eventually he learns that compassion is not enough.

Here's the relevance of one of the play's odder inventions, the ghost of the character who originally offered Lear sanctuary, the 'gravedigger's boy'. He attaches himself to the deposed king, and at first serves a similar function to Shakespeare's disguised Edgar. His presence helps instruct the old man in pity. But Bond, the first dramatist since the Jacobeans to make widespread use of them, has said that ghosts are 'always nasty and corrupt'; and this one becomes hardly less so than the spectral cannibals of *Early Morning*. He wants Lear to return to his old farm and withdraw with him into an essentially private world. As the play proceeds, he becomes more and more importunate, and also thinner, more wasted, more obviously representative of a kind of living death. Lear, explains Bond, 'has a clear vision of a golden age which his political activities have helped to destroy, but he has to recognize that its loss is irrecoverable, and there are great dangers in romanticizing and clinging to the impossible'. 'Some things are dead, but they die with difficulty,' he says, and adds elsewhere, 'When Lear tries to hug this image of the past, it becomes evil. . . . So that if you have aspirations and do nothing to make them real, then you aren't really thinking of utopia, you're just wasting your time in some sort of daydream.'

So Lear learns he must act, and act now. At first he delivers social parables to pilgrims visiting the Tolstoyan homestead where he lives with his disciples. But the government finds his enthusiasm for disarmament dangerous, and prepares to execute him, whereupon he comes to a decision that coincides with the second and final death of the gravedigger's boy, who (significantly) is savaged by the pigs he wanted Lear to spend his old age serenely tending. He travels to the wall and is shot as he begins to dismantle it: his belief, his exemplary commitment, will presumably survive.

In his author's words, he 'makes a gesture in which he accepts responsibility for his life and commits himself to action'; and 'responsibility', as often in Bond's work, seems a key concept. We must learn to take our share of responsibility for the future, for the present that will determine it, and, hardly less importantly, for the past that has fashioned the present. There is a curious scene in which Lear rhapsodizes over Fontanelle's body, which is undergoing an autopsy: the point, as he recognizes, is that he himself irreparably damaged what might have been the outer expression of that inner order and beauty. He 'destroyed' her. One of the things that worries Bond about Shakespeare's original is its failure to recognize that Lear helped cause Goneril and Regan; and he attempts to fill this supposed gap both here, and by bringing on Bodice and Fontanelle as they were as children, to offer an impressionistic memory of dead soldiers and a 'terrible bell'. No wonder they turned into loveless, destructive adults.

Bond's less attractive characters are always corrupted rather than corrupt. Cordelia, too, is what she is because her father was a 'priest' who 'taught her everything'. At first, she strikes us as withdrawn, unfriendly, neurotic; later, she sacrifices all to an arrogant vision of what's right. For Bond, she is 'a moralized person, and moralized people are not good people . . . She always has the words "good" and "justice" on her lips. And she is an absolute disaster for any society. So I very much wanted to convey through that figure that the people who have manipulated and taken over the language of ethics in our society are in fact very violent and destructive people.' Indeed, the play is substantially about upbringing and education. Many have been irrevocably twisted by their backgrounds, and some go on to try to indoctrinate others. Suffering and the ability to identify with others' suffering enables Lear to break the cycle. 'I must become a child . . . I must open my eyes and see,' he declares over Fontanelle's entrails: he ditches his old intellectual luggage, re-educates himself, and becomes a seer, instructing eager acolytes in Bond's view of the world.

Of course, not everyone will endorse that view, and even those who do may feel the gap between our own world and the one shown here is too wide for his purposes. We can hardly disclaim the play's atrocities, which include, not only Lear's blinding, but a scene in which Bodice destroys the eardrums of a tongueless captive with her knitting needle while Fontanelle screeches, 'Kill his hands! Kill his feet. . . . I want to sit on his lungs.' More sadistic things have been done on and off the world's battlefields in our own era. But it seems that Bond wants us to identify his overt violence with the more covert violence he believes to be institutionalized in a society in which, as Lear says, we 'send our children to school in the graveyard', 'jackals and wolves' rend the poor and hungry, and 'good, decent, honest, upright, lawful men who believe in order . . . devour the earth'. Indeed, he would specifically compare Cordelia with Mary Whitehouse, the celebrated

propagandist for moral cleanliness. But doesn't it take an exorbitant effort of imagination and will to witness the play's savageries and detachedly extrapolate truths about our own predicament from them?

Still, the play remains an impressive achievement. Some bardophiles may feel that Bond unjustly patronizes Shakespeare for the crime of having lived before Marx; and they may reasonably attack him in turn for the relative thinness of those passages in which his chopped, exact style becomes metaphoric, 'poetic'. Compare, for instance, his Lear's 'Who shut that animal in a glass cage? O God, there's no pity in this world. You let it lick the blood from its hair in the corner of a cage with nowhere to hide from its tormentors' with 'Poor naked wretches, wheresoe'er you are, that bide the pelting of this pitiless storm . . . '. Yet the very fact we make such comparisons shows that Bond is writing with an audacity, ambition and scope too rare in the contemporary theatre. How many modern plays contain seventy speaking parts, involve the clash and collapse of civilizations, and force us to ask ourselves such large questions as how we should hope to be governed, how rightly to live in an unjust world? Very few and most of them are by Edward Bond.

ELIZABETH BOWEN

1899–1973

Elizabeth Bowen was born in Dublin on June 7, 1899. Her father entered a mental hospital when she was seven, and her mother died six years later. Bowen was left in the care of "a committee of aunts," shuttling back and forth from Ireland to England. Near the end of World War I she worked in a Dublin hospital for shell-shocked soldiers, an experience which deeply affected the young Bowen. She began to write seriously, supported by her recovered and remarried father. Her first stories appeared in 1923, the year she married Alan Cameron. In 1926 he took a teaching position at Oxford, where Bowen wrote her first novels, strongly influenced by Henry James and her friend Virginia Woolf. *The Death of the Heart*, published in 1938, is often cited by critics as one of the greatest novels of the century.

Bowen served during World War II in the Ministry of Information and as an air-raid warden. After the war she contributed frequent reviews to the *Tatler* and other publications; she also wrote for the BBC. In 1948 she was made a CBE. She later received honorary doctorates from Trinity College in 1949 and Oxford in 1956; a Royal Society of Literature Award in 1965; and the James Tait Black Memorial Prize in 1970 for her last novel, *Eva Trout*.

After Alan Cameron died in 1952, Bowen returned to her childhood home in Kildorrery, Bowen's Court, which she celebrated in a volume of memoirs. She later moved to Kent, where she died on February 22, 1973.

Personal

We are meeting an enchanting little girl, the Elizabeth Bowen of age 7 recently transplanted from Ireland to England, in her prophetic relationship to the woman and the writer she was to become. We find it possible everywhere and time after time to make the jump.

The schools she was sent to nourished what was to become her life-long love affair with other people's houses, for, she says, "Never had I the misfortune to be educated in any building erected for that purpose." Digging, the leader of her schoolgirl companions, through walls and into foundations of some former rectory on speculation of secret passages quite naturally turned into writing stories about houses a little later. "For all that," she says, "it was the foreground I stood upon

that possessed me. Underfoot, it lost nothing by being *terra firma*: actual and tangible, it remained magic."

One is made aware in these pages of the scattering of seeds due for later flowering into *The Death of the Heart*, *The Little Girls*, *Eva Trout* and other fiction. And well does one recognize this child. There is the same sense of expectation, the eagerness to join in, take part, that gives its special strength and delight to her writing. She was a prime responder to this world. It was almost as if she'd been *invited* here. Some great pleasure lay deep inside her great sophistication—and here she was, at the top of her form, arrived to do it honor: a romantic, of course—self-described. A romantic with a particularly penetrating power of observation, and a joyous sense of the absurd.

What she says about the Irish is as wonderful as what she

has made dramatically clear in stories. All share in inborn traits: belligerence ("poles apart from aggressiveness," "your belligerent person tends to sail through life in excellent spirits"). The passion for virtuosity of all kinds. The ability to strike root wherever set down, a peculiarity of the Anglo-Irish—which of course she is. And there is writing: "To *that* we have taken like ducks to water." But, she goes on to say, "Possibly, it was England made me a novelist," because with the move, there was to be "a cleft between my heredity and my environment—the former remaining, in my case, the more powerful." "If you began in Ireland, Ireland remains the norm: like it or not." "What had to be bitten on was that two entities so opposed, so irreconcilable in climate, character and intention, as Folkestone and Dublin should exist simultaneously, and be operative, in the same life-time, particularly my own."

"I am not a 'regional' writer in the outright sense"—but she is in another: "Since I started writing, I have been welding together an inner landscape, assembled anything but at random." Not people and places in their own identities, but people and places that experience called up in her became her stories and novels. They represent her reactions to experience, her "beholding afresh."

Her understanding of a wide range of relationships might easily have been rooted in what she describes in her childhood nature as "outgoing." Later on, her grown-up generosity might have been a form of concentration almost psychic, and in her writing this may have become the novelist's gift of quick perception, and a working tool. Fascination with the outside world, in retrospect, and through the intensity of writing fiction, becomes sharp scrutiny. A highly conscious ability to imagine herself in another's place is a writer's power too—in her case, to precipitate a highly complex plot and a full house of vivacious characters.—EUDORA WELTY, "As if she had been invited into this world," *NYTBR*, Jan. 5, 1975, p. 4

General

The subject of Elizabeth Bowen's stories is poetry. This statement requires some explanation. What I mean by it, is that there are moments in the experience of all of us when our lives enter into a world of poetry. Poetry is, for poets, a specialized world, but this world has moments when it literally impinges on the real world; moments when we are in love, when a disappointment suddenly becomes a symbol of everything that we are striving for and that we have lost, which has a significance far greater than the disappointment itself. Such moments of 'literal poetry' are a very proper subject for prose, because they are, in fact, prosaic and real; the real and the literal suddenly become one with the genuine poetry at the heart of existence.

On the other hand it would be untrue to say that 'literal poetry' was the whole subject of prose fiction. A short story writer like V. S. Pritchett is not writing about poetry, he is using his realistic approach to impress us with the scale of reality and the variety of character which goes up to make the world. His stories make one feel that one knows too little about the kind of life outside one's own room and circle of acquaintance. They are like a geography lesson which gives one a sense of the size of and the unknownness of the world. This sense of scale is something in which Miss Bowen is rather lacking; although she shows a sympathetic understanding of the life of people living in new houses at the edge of arterial roads in her story 'Attractive Modern Homes,' this understanding is of the kind which makes someone write a poem rather than produce a measured and really convincingly objectified picture of a way of life outside her own.—STEPHEN SPENDER, "Books and the

War," *The Penguin New Writing #5*, ed. John Lehmann, 1941, pp. 140–41

Plot must further the novel towards its object. What object? The non-poetic statement of a poetic truth.

Have not all poetic truths been already stated? The essence of a poetic truth is that no statement of it can be final.

Plot, story, is in itself un-poetic. At best it can only be not anti-poetic. It cannot claim a single poetic licence. It must be reasoned—onward from the moment when its none-otherness, its only-possibleness has become apparent. Novelist must always have one foot, sheer circumstantiality, to stand on, whatever the other foot may be doing. (N.B.—Much to be learnt from story-telling to children. Much to be learnt from the detective story—especially non-irrelevance.)

Flaubert's *'Il faut intéresser.'* Stress on manner of telling: keep in mind, 'I will a tale *unfold.*' Interest of watching silk handkerchief drawn from conjuror's watch.

Plot must not cease to move forward. The *actual* speed of the movement must be even. *Apparent* variations in speed are good, necessary, but there must be no actual variations in speed. To obtain those apparent variations is part of the illusion-task of the novel. Variations in texture can be made to give the effect of variations in speed. Why are *apparent* variations in speed necessary? (a) For emphasis. (b) For non-resistance, or 'give,' to the nervous time-variations of the reader. Why is *actual* evenness, non-variation, of speed necessary? For the sake of internal evenness for its own sake. Perfection of evenness = perfection of control. The evenness of the speed should be the evenness inseparable from tautness. The tautness of the taut string is equal (or even) all along and at any part of the string's length.—ELIZABETH BOWEN, "Notes on Writing a Novel" (1945), *Collected Impressions*, 1950, p. 250

To his enormous credit the modern English novelist—writers like Isherwood, Elizabeth Bowen, and Graham Greene—have conserved the human fragments in an iron age when human lives, what I feel and you feel, are considered to be shameful. Human beings are simply archaic, ivy-covered ruins, preserved by the connoisseur, and they stand out oddly in the new world of the masses. They are seen in a twilight.—V. S. PRITCHETT, "The Future of English Fiction," *PR*, Oct. 1948, p. 1067

When Elizabeth Bowen's name is mentioned, other women novelists are mentioned too—often ineptly: Mr. Pritchett's comparison with Virginia Woolf won't really work. To fit Miss Bowen into a group is one thing, to find her origins quite another. Having subscribed above to the big male-female opposition, I am not really reneging if I bring in Henry James as her true progenitor. James is the unique example of a writer who (and there is no Western substitute for these terms) allowed the *yin* principle to overcome his *yang* when he settled in Europe. Those endlessly qualified sentences with their spinsterish scruples were a bequest not only to Edith Wharton, but to a whole line of woman novelists, of whom Miss Bowen is one:

> He more than looked, he continued to look, he stared at this person, so disingenuous, of a so impassioning wish to be in the right. So strong had become his habit of mind that he saw no behaviour as being apart from motive, and any motive as worth examining twice.
> Deep and beautiful on this her smile came back, and with the effect of making him hear what he had said just as she had heard it. He easily enough felt that it gave him away, but what in truth had everything done but that? It had been all very well to think at moments that he was holding her nose down

and that he had coerced her: what had he by this time done but let her practically see that he accepted their relation?

One of these passages is from *The Ambassadors*, the other from *The Heat of the Day*.

The involutions of James's prose, the torturings of natural syntax to avoid the cliché, the enthroning of the cliché where the cliché is not even enlightening—all this was James's substitute for poetry. But, paradoxically, if there had been more poetry in him there would have been a less massive image of a civilisation. In Miss Bowen there is a great deal of poetry: it is what lightens her involutions, and if it sometimes drops to mere fancy (the French clock 'busy . . . on the chimneypiece, amid idling china'), that is appropriate—it serves her concern with 'atmosphere.' Where James articulates a whole culture, Miss Bowen conserves a particular place at a particular time; this is a feminine gift. The theme of *The Death of the Heart* is the massacre of innocence, but what we remember best is the scenery through which young, betrayed Portia passes—frosty Regent's Park, dingy hotel furniture. *The House in Paris* is really about its eponym; *A World of Love*, in which the real protagonist is the sensibility of the author, seems to be nearly all 'atmosphere.'

It is the 'atmosphere' of war-time London, encapsulated so miraculously in *The Heat of the Day*, that survives the strange story of Stella Rodney and her lover. I've always found him hard to take—the man who, discharged wounded from the services, becomes a traitor; Stella can't swallow the treason either, but her incredulity is of a different order from the reader's. There's a parallelism in *The Heat of the Day* which is perhaps typical of all Miss Bowen's work—a world of intense and highly credible detail which conjures one's own sensuous and emotional memories, though so heightened that it feels like a re-living (remember Louie, who 'had, with regard to time, an infant lack of stereoscopic vision; she saw then and now on the same plane; they were the same'); a world of people who are never quite real and often unmemorable. A miracle makes the parallels meet: while the weaving of atmosphere and the accumulation of detail proceed, the illusion of solid existence holds. But, behind the whirl of phenomena, there doesn't seem to be much of a thing-in-itself.

The Little Girls is Miss Bowen's first novel for nine years. She hasn't, apparently, been using those nine years to plot new departures, though her observation of the contemporary world is, as we expect, very sharp: 'atmosphere' is still her business. But the contemporary world is only part of it. Three women of sixty—Dinah, Clare and Sheila—were schoolgirls together in 1914 (Dicey, Mumbo and Sheikie). Dinah, an ageless beauty, summons her friends from the past by means of newspaper advertisements. A great burier-for-posterity, she wants to know what's happened to a box the three of them buried at St. Agatha's all those years ago ('We are dead, and all our fathers and mothers. You who find this, Take Care. These are our valuable treasures, and our fetters . . . Here are Bones, too . . .'). This gives Miss Bowen an opportunity for a delicious recall and a fine scenic set-piece on what's become of the school's site now:

> . . . The revenants stood back, backs to the balustrade—above them, ten or a dozen nice-looking houses, spaced out over the hill's face, harmlessly contemplated the Channel; garages, their doors painted pastel colours, sat on ledges surrounded by landscape gardening. . . . In general, the gardens were veiled in the thinly dusky yellows and coppers and bronzy purples of mid-autumn. . . .

And so on. This, I think, is authentic flavoursome Bowen.

The box, when they find it, is empty. The warning comes too late for the three, but not for the reader; the story is, in fact, an easy morality: 'Gently dip, but not too deep.' The intensities of a childhood relationship are invoked in middle age at one's own peril. Never choose to call back past time: choice, anyway, is dangerous. 'We were entrusted to one another, in the days which mattered, Clare thought. Entrusted to one another by chance, not choice. Chance, and its agents time and place. Chance is better than choice; it is more lordly. In its carelessness it is more lordly. Chance is God, choice is man.' Moral profundities swirl about, among the aubergine jerseys and the coloured scenery-motifs on cups and bowls. They are of much the same order as the discrete elements of the sensuous world that Miss Bowen proves, so lavishly, to exist. What James made terrifying is here rather charming.

Confronted by so much technical brilliance, even when not awed by reputation, the reader may well blame himself for being, as he thinks, insufficiently moved. But what Miss Bowen has achieved is less the peopling of time and place with entities which, like Emma Bovary or Charlus or Bloom, have a human validity which bursts their literary bonds, than the furnishing of time and place with the conditions which might enable such beings to exist—and this means not only 'atmosphere' but the texture of skin and hair and bags under the eyes. There are times when, seduced by the miraculously caught cadences of feminine speech, one wakes to the shock of thinking it all a contrivance—a device for moving spheres (if one may use the old metaphysical imagery) which in themselves have no intelligence. Perhaps all this is going too far: the book is, after all, a comedy, a pleasant warning against the dangers of nostalgia, a demonstration of the allure which informs a sensuous world uncoloured by nostalgia. It is a wonderful artefact, a triumphant Female Novel by one whose gifts release her from the more male duty of being just among the Just, among the Filthy filthy too, and of suffering dully all the wrongs of Man.—ANTHONY BURGESS, "Treasures and Fetters," *Spec*, Feb. 12, 1964, p. 254

As a writer, Bowen must be evaluated on the basis of about a dozen stories and five novels—*The Last September*, *To the North*, *The House in Paris*, *The Death of the Heart*, and *The Heat of the Day*. (A case could be made, too, for *The Little Girls*.) Her nonfiction and autobiographical writings, though they have wit and sometimes genius to recommend them, aren't under consideration here. On the basis of her fiction alone, Bowen is as good as Evelyn Waugh, better than Ivy Compton-Burnett, Graham Greene or Henry Green. Her novels yield to Woolf's in visionary intensity but are superior to them in formal construction, variety of subject, and moral force. Bowen said she liked the work of her younger contemporaries Iris Murdoch and Muriel Spark, and she shares some characteristics with them, but there is really no reason to bring their names together (as Glendinning does in the introduction to the biography).

Bowen is below the greatest novelists—Flaubert, George Eliot, Tolstoy, James, Proust—but like them she reflected constantly and profoundly on the nature of fiction. So much so, that the "laws" of fiction came to constitute a metaphorical system for her, used in the novels themselves sometimes to help present the action, as in this passage from *The Heat of the Day*:

> His concentration on her was made more oppressive by his failure to have or let her give him any possible place in the human scene. By the rules of fiction, with which life to be credible must comply, he was as a character 'impossible'—each time they met, for in-

stance, he showed no shred or trace of having been continuous since they last met.

Conversely, Bowen's brilliant "Notes on Writing a Novel" have a poetic, almost an allegorical quality. She can say, for example, "Characters must *materialize—i.e.*, must have a palpable, physical reality. . . . Physical personality belongs to action. . . . Eyes, hands, stature, etc., must appear, and only appear, *in play*." Discussing dialogue, she says, "Speech is what the characters *do to each other*." And, in general, "The presence, and action of the poetic truth is the motive (or motor) morality of the novel."

It would be wrong, however, to regard Bowen as a rule-book novelist. The rule she most often waives is the one proscribing authorial comment. Rather like one of the "innocents" in her own novels, Bowen can't keep quiet about what she sees and knows. The proportion of comment to narrative is much higher than Flaubert, say, would have tolerated. Yet Proust commented even more freely than Bowen, and her rushes of insight are often as good as his. In both cases you feel that some principle of genius is at work, so that the propensity must be indulged, and the rules broken—all the more since the results are so startling. As much by their weaknesses as by their strengths do artists come into their own.

Much of the moral energy of Bowen's novels resides in just these passages of authorial comment. In them, she renews for English fiction the tradition of the French *moralistes*—La Rochefoucauld, La Bruyère, and the great women diarists and letter-writers of the eighteenth century. But she is still squarely within the precincts of fiction: these passages arise directly from the action presented, and they illuminate what comes after them. Moreover, Bowen isn't deficient in the way many moralists are, so intent on the meaning, purely, of human action they lack sensory awareness. Bowen is all perception. Reading her you realize you have never paid close enough attention to places or persons, the mosaic of detail that composes the first, or the voices and gestures that reveal the second. Her novels invariably take the point of view of an omniscient narrator; and, if omniscience means all-seeing as well as all-knowing, the term is especially apt for Bowen. Of course, this very knowingness can be a fault: the reader may feel as though Bowen is always too far ahead, running circles around reader consciousness. This is an unpleasant sensation if only because it gives, inevitably, an impression of unreality: no one feels that life is told by an omniscient narrator; and that point of view in novels is most effective when least obtrusive. For the most part, however, Bowen strikes the right balance between the transparence and opaqueness of reality.

As a prose stylist Bowen is elegant but quirky. She casts for the short sentence, the clipped epigram. We don't normally associate delicacy of observation with a percussive syntax like Bowen's, but that is her compound. Reading her is like being pelted with feathers, occasionally the quill end. Critics have sometimes complained about her inversions. Habitually she puts the most important word of a sentence in attack position at the beginning or tonic position at the end. By turns, the sentences can seem mannered or forceful. Certainly they contribute to the Anglo-Irish flavor of her writing. Sentences like hers can only be written by someone who has grown up with a special speech-music in the ear.

R. P. Blackmur noted that in Henry James's last novels there was always "a plot which does truly constitute the soul of the action, which does truly imitate the conditions and aspirations of human life as seen in the actions of men and women of more than usual worth and risk." Bowen would certainly have acknowledged these ideals as her own; and she realized them well—except for the last phrase, "more than usual worth and

risk." Consistently she made it a part of novelistic plausibility not to invent larger-than-life characters. The figure, so common in her novels, of the innocent young girl forging toward experience leaves an impression less of "worth and risk" than of the destructiveness of innocence, to self and others. Other kinds of characters in Bowen tend to be all too human; we always look a little down at them. Yet if we are in fact experiencing an "ironic" phase in literature, as understood by Northrop Frye, in which fictional characters are typically marginal, hindered, or "low," Bowen can't be called to special account—she is only doing as other moderns do. Larger-than-life characters in modern fiction? There are none; but their absence is felt more keenly in Bowen's novels because in all other ways they exhibit the characteristic strengths of the nineteenth-century classics. The brilliant, humane analysis, the patient, even heroic notation of physical detail remind us of the older books, and, so conditioned, we scan Bowen's pages with an unconscious expectation of finding heroes there. Their failure to appear, then, disappoints. On the other hand, Bowen has created many magnetic and memorable characters—Stella in *The Heat of the Day*, Emmeline in *To the North*, and (perhaps the nearest Bowen came to inventing an heroic character) the housemaid Matchett in *The Death of the Heart*. All of these go readily into that stock everyone keeps of fictional persons—Mr. Casaubon, Pierre Bezhukov, Mrs. Dalloway, and so forth—characters that have caught special human qualities or attitudes toward experience and come to stand for them. In a fictional world made actual and palpable, Bowen's characters move and make their discoveries, comic or tragic or both together. These novels themselves will soon be rediscovered; new biographical and critical studies would help clarify Bowen's place among English novelists. Weighing real issues, and with a small readjustment of the sights, readers ought to reach a fair view of Elizabeth Bowen—as one of the few masters of modern fiction.—ALFRED CORN, "An Anglo-Irish Novelist," *YR*, Summer 1978, pp. 619–22

Works

> He felt that most profound concern possible for another human being, when it becomes a question no longer of the extent of one's own possession of them, but, transcending this, of what in their untouchable selves they *are*.

This, one of the very many wise and sensitive observations in Elizabeth Bowen's novel *The Hotel*, I feel inclined to apply to the book itself and my relation to it as a reviewer. Because, by one of those simperings of occasion (as Sir Kenelm called them) that do sometimes happen, here is a creation of most delicate and difficult texture which is going to come into the hands of a great many more readers than would usually encounter a book of that sort. It has been chosen by the Book-of-the-Month Club, and it will be extraordinarily interesting to observe how it fares with so large a subscription list. I believe (since reviewers have to use their trade argot now and then) that its triumphant naturalism will carry it through.

Rose Macaulay is quoted as having said of this book that "it is hard to describe its quality without seeming over-enthusiastic." True indeed. The material of the story is casual enough: merely a few weeks' episodes in the lives of a few people in a hotel on the Italian Riviera. Of course as soon as one says Riviera, you imagine a certain crystallized type of novel; but how different this is. Elizabeth Bowen's triumph is that never in her exquisite comedy of the mirths and acids of social observation does she rely for an instant on cheapened effects, easy tricks, or meretricious glamors. The word "sophisticated," which has undergone queer diversions in recent years (it has become customary to use it when what is really meant is "sophomoric") may here be genuinely applied. Here is the subtle pourri of real sophistication, a wit that is not harsh or bawdy or mean.

Elizabeth Bowen—or Mrs. Cameron, if you insist—is a young writer; as is so characteristic of an Irish woman she is still under thirty—in fact, under twenty-nine. But this is not a young book, it is frugal and keen, rich with the rather desperate wisdom of maturity. It is social comedy of the most intricate merit, malicious and tender, the neat elixir of observation. Its people are dreadfully alive, so much so that you carry them on in your mind after finishing the story, wondering what will become of them. The hotel itself, the lounge with its grove of chairs, the drawing room where an unbroken front of matronhood warmed its knees at the fire, the lift, even the Honorable Mrs. Pinkerton's private bathroom (with the "Shetlands" on the radiator), all these are a décor that every traveled reader knows by heart. Americans, great connoisseurs of lavatory detail, will have their small private merriments over the so characteristically British toilet appointments of the visitors—the sponge-bags and loofahs and wash-stands and slop-pails; and the solid dressing-table ware of the Honorable Mrs. Pinkerton.

This is a book that two readers particularly would have been excited by—Jane Austen, Henry James. And I think I should add a third, our well-loved "Elizabeth." For it is much more than what the term "social comedy" suggests: it conveys genuine tragedy and pity, and even a sense of the sinister in the enigmatic (yet how recognizable) person of Mrs. Kerr. If you insist on character study of the Younger Generation, I believe both Sydney and Veronica are considerably more authentic than a good many more melodramatically romanticized young questioneers.

Elizabeth Bowen has the rare and the difficult gift: she can impart character in a flash. Her crisp dialogue makes one hanker for a stage to hear it on. It is a brilliant and triumphant book, and I pay it the greatest compliment I know, by believing that there will be some (oh lucky, lucky people!) who will imagine it a little dull.—CHRISTOPHER MORLEY, "Their Untouchable Selves," *SR*, April 7, 1928, p. 740

Miss Bowen certainly does not let *her* inability to describe the passage of time dictate the theme. Her novel, *The House in Paris*, covers a period from before the birth of an illegitimate child until he has reached the age of nine. The popular novelist would have described every one of these years, however dull to the reader the accumulation of trivialities. Miss Bowen has simply left them out with the merest glance backward; we may believe that she has been forced to omit, but she has made of her omissions a completely individual method, she has dramatized ignorance. How with so little known of the 'backward and abysm' can she convey her characters with any clearness? It is impossible, but her consciousness of that impossibility proves her great value as a novelist. She makes it the virtue of her characters that they are three parts mystery; the darkness which hides their past makes the cerebrations which we are allowed to follow the more vivid, as vivid as the exchanges of people overheard talking on a platform before a train goes out. It is an exquisite sleight of hand: the egg was in the hat, now it is being removed from the tip of a robust woman's nose. We must fill in for ourselves what happened between; the burden of that problem is passed to the reader. To the author remains the task of making the characters understand each other without our losing the sense of mystery: they must be able to tell all from a gesture, a whisper, a written sentence: they have to be endowed with an inhuman intuition as James's characters were endowed

with an inhuman intelligence, and no writer since James has proved capable of a more cunning evasion. Unable to convey the passage of time, she has made capital out of the gap in the records; how can we doubt the existence of a past which these characters can so easily convey to each other?—GRAHAM GREENE, "The Dark Backward: A Footnote" (1935), *Collected Essays*, 1969, p. 72

In *The Death of the Heart* a novelist of extraordinary gifts has confronted the generations, so that they gaze across a sort of No Man's Land with reciprocated dismay. Yet this is to state the theme too baldly, for age depends on temperament no less than on actual years; we have all known old people unspotted by the world, and children with already wizened hearts. The conflict in the book is really between the innocent and the fallen, Miss Bowen's view of innocence being very different from the ordinary:

> Innocence so constantly finds itself in a false position that inwardly innocent people learn to be disingenuous. Finding no language in which to speak in their own terms, they resign themselves to being translated imperfectly. They exist alone; when they try to enter into relations they compromise falsifyingly—through anxiety, through desire to impart and feel warmth. The system of our affections is too corrupt for them. They are bound to blunder, then to be told they cheat. In love, the sweetness and violence they have to offer involves a thousand betrayals for the less innocent. Incurable strangers to the world, they never cease to exact a heroic happiness. Their singleness, their ruthlessness, their one continuous wish makes them bound to be cruel, and to suffer cruelty. The innocent are so few that two of them seldom meet—when they do meet, their victims lie strewn around.

This long quotation is necessary because you miss the whole point of the book, I think, if you take it for the tragedy of a child appalled by the corruption of her elders, and heartbroken by a young scoundrel. It is the story, comic as well as pitiful, of two unworldly creatures at sea in our intricate society, where only elasticity usually survives, and of the damage they inflict no less than of the damage they endure. . . .

External violence has been avoided throughout, no crockery has been smashed, no marriage-vow broken, no virginity lost—we can think, if we like, that Time will enable the single-minded Portia to desert to the enemy and settle into their prudent, adaptable ways. But the sheet has been smirched, the canker has attacked the rose, the middle-aged have stared into a looking-glass, the earth has made one more revolution towards its destined disintegration. Fuss about nothing? Well, this is not an epic or a saga, it is more an ironic comedy than a tragedy. Miss Bowen writes with sustained detachment. Living is like this, she seems to say, the exaltations and despairs of youth give way to the more qualified pleasures and more bearable distempers of maturity. In our several ways we make the best of a not very good job, and those of us who do this most incompetently are in a sense the pick of the bunch. The inability to compromise has great beauty—look at the perfection of swans on water, inseparable from their ungainliness on land—but "if one didn't let oneself swallow some few lies, I don't know how one could carry the past. . . . What makes you think us wicked is simply our little way of keeping ourselves going. We must live, though you may not see the necessity. In the long run, we may not work out well. We attempt, however, to be more civil and kindly than we feel." Innocents like Portia make life impossible—"nobody can afford to have a girl as thorough as that about." Finally, "we can't afford to suffer; we must live how we can."

It would be possible to treat this disillusioned book as a devastating impeachment of bourgeois corruption and futility. "I suppose there's nothing so disintegrating as competitiveness and funk, and that's what we all feel." But the deep distresses and conflicts exposed in this novel seem to me to belong less to a class than to the condition of man. In Regent's Park they become articulate, but you do not escape from them in Rotherhithe or even Rostov-on-Don.—RAYMOND MORTIMER, "The Death of the Heart," NSN, Oct. 8, 1938, p. 534

Modern fiction of the subtler kind when written by women is likely to depict at length the trouble resulting from unsuitable and complicated people falling in love. The stays and obstacles once provided by difference in social position, family feuds, missent letters, and trumped-up misunderstandings have narrowed into drama arising from the fact that the lovers have neuroses that do not match, are in love for the wrong reasons, in love too late or too soon, or are incapable of love at all. Elizabeth Bowen in her previous novels has described such combinations, and Madame Colette has worked with them for years. Miss Bowen has also probed with great thoroughness into the reaction of sensitive children, sometimes the offspring of mismatings, thrown into situations of which they hold only one or two clues. *The House in Paris* successfully brought off an atmosphere of emotional tension, resulting when the past, present, and future converged on such a child, who was caught, between journeys, in rooms full of the tragedy to which he owed his being. *The Death of the Heart* turns on a girl of sixteen, the product of a misalliance, who, when introduced into the "edited life" of her half-brother's smart London household, throws upon it the full glare of her innocence, breaks through its surface, and shows the lack of human feeling on which it is based. . . .

Miss Bowen has elsewhere spoken of "the limitations of English narrative prose, with its *longueurs* and conventions dangerous to truth." In her novels she has taken every precaution to reduce these conventions to a minimum. The strokes come close, and every stroke tells. Miss Bowen is particularly good at reflecting one character in another, always making it clear that some people see things partially while others take in every detail. Matchett, the self-contained upper servant, with her toughened sympathy and snobbery and her pride of the good artisan, sees everything. Eddie sees everything—in his way—and himself, "at once coy and insolent," only too well. Matchett can sum people up. Of the "sacrificing" first Mrs. Quayne she says: "I couldn't care for her; she had no nature"; of Anna: "Oh, she has her taste and dearly loves to use it. Past that she'll never go." Eddie says of Anna: "She loves to make a tart out of another person. She'd never dare to be a proper tart herself." Thomas has an occasional moment of insight into the society about him: "self-interest, given a pretty gloss." But Portia, not yet absorbed into "the guilty plausibility of the world," sees more than everything. She detects the impossibility of a natural human relationship between these people who write letters, go to dinner parties, talk at tea—always "stalking each other." She watches "thoroughly"; she tries to shake some human response out of Eddie; she importunes; she nags with the implacable fury of first love. At the end she gives the show away to simple, kind Major Brutt. "Anna's always laughing at you. She says you are quite pathetic. . . . And Thomas thinks you must be after something. They groan at each other when you have gone away. You and I are the same."

Miss Bowen's talent is so rich and so searching, and this novel stands so far outside the class of novels which resemble packaged goods put up for the trade, that one is tempted to give her nothing but praise. She sees deeply, but not widely enough. Corruption has not lately entered the class of which she writes; the heart is not dying in these people; it never lived in them. And her tone, too keyed up, never lets down for a moment; the *longueurs* are deleted to such an extent that they are missed. Beautifully-done descriptions of times of day and the weather edge the action—to a tiresome degree. The backgrounds for emotions are chosen with care; one, an empty seaside boarding-house on a Sunday morning, is almost unbearably appropriate. Miss Bowen can cook the vulgar English to the same crispness to which she treats their betters. But *The Death of the Heart* is too packed, too brilliant, for its own good. What Miss Bowen lacks is a kind of humility. She has forgotton more than many novelists ever knew, but what Turgenev, for example, knew, and was chary of expressing, she cannot quite deal with. Once in a while the reader hears the accent of self-satisfaction, if not display, in the novelist. But for all that, *The Death of the Heart* deepens our view of the horrors experienced by open innocence up against a closed world.—LOUISE BOGAN, "The Pure in Heart" (1939), *Selected Criticism*, 1955, pp. 125–28

In her latest novel, *The Heat of the Day*, Miss Bowen achieves by subtlety what a male novelist, treating a similar subject, would have tried to achieve by power. For the first time since *The Last September* she has chosen a theme which takes her outside the bounds of private life. Yet she avoids, with extraordinary adroitness, the threats to her scope offered by an international plot to sabotage the Allied war effort during the autumn of 1942. In creating the figures of the traitor, Robert Kelway, and the counter-spy, Harrison, the temptation to strain her imagination beyond bearing must have been considerable. For the world in which these men move, when they are off the stage—the world behind the life, public and private, of Stella Rodney—is that which writers like Simenon and V. S. Pritchett and Graham Greene do not have to invent because they know it. Miss Bowen does not attempt to invent it: as Jane Austen would have done, she takes it for granted, but without losing sight of its effect on character and behaviour. She loads her three central figures with the heaviest possible responsibility: the fate of nations is assumed to depend, at least to some extent, on the good faith and intelligence required by the work in which they are engaged; and their 'reality', as characters of fiction, is to be measured by our awareness of the ways in which their humanity is modified by what they are compelled to do.

This bringing of public to the bar of private life gives weight and solidity to a story which is painfully dramatic, but never merely sad. Finer and subtler in the analysis of complex feeling than *The House in Paris*, wider in range than *The Death of the Heart*, *The Heat of the Day* is cunningly built up in scenes each of which concentrates the light upon a portion of the displayed canvas. Time plays—is meant to play—little part in the drama, which is superficially laid out in the first few chapters. All that is left is for us to discover, through Stella's eyes, what is really there. The characters do not change: what changes is our attitude towards them. In the process of gradually stripping her people Miss Bowen shows a control that only occasionally falters—though when it does falter, in the case of Robert Kelway, the result is nearly disastrous. Her portrait of the counter-spy, Harrison, is her most brilliant feat. We end by feeling something like affection for this unbearable creature whose unlovability is the clue to his comfortless self. (Incidentally, this figure is an ironic comment on the possible results of a complete victory of character over personality.) It was clever of Miss Bowen to have seen Harrison, not as sub-, or super-, but as pseudo-human—provisional—mechanical—sinister and rigid as a being invoked by a sorcerer's spell.

His concentration on her was made more oppressive by his failure to have or let her give him any possible place in the human scene. By the rules of fiction, with which life to be credible must comply, he was as a character 'impossible'—each time they met, for instance, he showed no shred or trace of having been continuous since they last met. His civilian clothes, though one could be remotely conscious of alternation in suit or shirt or tie, *seemed* to vary much less than Robert's uniform; the uninterestingly right state of what he wore seemed less to argue care—brushing, pressing, change of linen—than a physical going into abeyance, just as he was, with everything he had on him, between appearances.

Perceived with the acuteness of extreme distaste, but not entirely without sympathy, Harrison is much more convincing than Robert Kelway, who suffers from Miss Bowen's inability to invest him with any charm. Apart from the fact that he is alleged to be good-looking, tall, and lame in one leg, it is difficult to see why Stella (whose attractiveness we never for a moment doubt) should have been drawn to so null a man. There are signs of fumbling here: astonishment that Robert should be capable of treachery somehow gets confused with a more general wonder that men should be the odd creatures they are.

This one failure is not enough to spoil the book, though it does rob the climax of intensity—and even, perhaps, of plausibility. But if the positive aspects of Robert go by default, the author manages, in brilliant fashion, to account for the flaw in his character which has produced the spiritual vacuum. Readers of Miss Rebecca West's *The Meaning of Treason* will recognise a similar method of putting two and two together. Both have a characteristically feminine eye for the details of an ambience, but Miss Bowen, although writing a novel, is the less emphatic. 'Holme Dene', the house (it is not a home) of the Kelways, is the counterpart of 'Waikiki' in *The Death of the Heart*, and of the London house of Mark Linkwater and his sister in *To the North*: all of them suggestions that Miss Bowen is unceasingly concerned with the opposition between poetry and that which is foreign or hostile to it. These houses, and their inhabitants, are outside the world of poetry because they are emotionally sterile and have no spring of being save the will to survive. For those to whom the poetic is an absolute value there is moral evil in the resistance to it. Even Harrison, we are made to feel, is preferable to the Kelways, because he aspires to poetry through the possession of Stella. His angry refusal to take her, when she at last offers him the shell of herself, gives him a pathos of which the Kelways and their kind are wholly incapable. 'Holme Dene'—"the abode of The Thing", as Charles Addams would call it—is a triumph of Miss Bowen's satirical vein. It is better done than 'Waikiki', because the author enjoys it less; the issues being graver, the fun is less hyperbolic.

Everything that *implies* the character of Robert Kelway is more successfully rendered than the man himself. These implications include an opponent who is essentially more formidable even than Harrison: Stella's son, Roderick, who has—and is—everything that Robert lacks. The human excellence of Roderick, and his very evident charm, are enhanced by a tinge of pathos inherent in his exposed condition—exposed, I mean, by the fact of being shovelled, straight from school, into the army, in war-time. This portrait is a wholly admirable one,

partly because it is drawn so delicately, and without explanatory emphasis. Roderick's dry humour, and his respectful love for his mother, win the reader's affection at once. His *raison d'être*, where the plot of the novel is concerned, depends on our comprehension of his implicit standards. Before his unexpected inheritance of Mount Morris he is presented simply as a nice boy waiting to see what life may have to offer. Then, the quiet resolve with which he accepts the inheritance (Miss Bowen is careful to deprive this of the more obvious attractions, as well as saddling it with a grave drawback in the form of a supposedly mad female cousin) shows us the quality of his character. In no other kind of person—certainly not in Robert Kelway—should we accept as plausible the same blind grasp of the offered responsibility, the same unhesitating rejection in advance of all other chances, including those of special talents yet undiscovered. To Roderick, a dilapidated 'place' in Ireland, which he has not even seen and which he has every reason to fear may be a white elephant, is the first of all claims on his allegiance, just because to make such a choice is part of a gentleman's heritage.

Roderick is necessary to Miss Bowen's design because he alone aspires, by the nature of his choice, to rescue certain values from a world in dissolution. I wish I could feel equally certain about the propriety of letting Louie Lewis, and her friend Connie, into the story. In herself Louie is, of course, a gloriously amusing figure, but she is *necessary* only if the novel is intended to give an inclusive picture of war-time London—an assumption which, I feel, the author would be the last to sanction. As if aware that Louie's position in the book could be thought anomalous, Miss Bowen defiantly entrusts her with the final chapter—an act of unwisdom aggravated by a certain sentimentality inherent in the scene itself.

Nevertheless, *The Heat of the Day* is literature: as a whole it will stand up to serious criticism of detail because its effect, as a work of art, is homogeneous and impressive. Miss Bowen has gone to school with Henry James, but in order to learn how best to express an original vision. The result is an analytical prose continually enlivened by deft allusion and clever imagery. And her idiom is poetic because it is sustained—like that of James and Conrad—at the level of drama.—Edward Sackville-West, "Ladies Whose Bright Pens," *Inclinations*, 1949, pp. 95–99

Elizabeth Bowen is a novelist who has much in common with Miss Lehmann. The world they are both at home in is one with traditions of assurance, of elbow-room—perhaps, if one is making fine distinctions, an 'upper-class world' in Miss Bowen's novels, an 'upper-middle-class' one in Miss Lehmann's—and they both have gripping stories to tell, which they tell, on the whole, in what strikes the ordinary reader as a 'sound, old-fashioned way': the interest in experiment showing itself more in the shaping of paragraphs and sentences, the freshening up of the novelist's language, than in the structure of the book as a whole. Towards the end of the 1940s Miss Bowen published a novel about London life during the war, *The Heat of the Day*. It vividly evokes the tense, exalted atmosphere of the black-out and the air-raids. A woman, Stella Rodney, discovers that her lover, Robert Kelway, is a traitor and is blackmailed by a secret agent, Harrison, who offers to spare the lover if, as a reward, the lady will 'yield herself' to him. On this harsh and what might seem rather melodramatic framework, Miss Bowen has erected a structure of words which allows us to grasp, not only a particular scene at a particular time, but a general pattern running through English life. Robert's terrible family, living at a house called Holm Dene, 1900 mock-Tudor, placed 'in the middle of nothing', explain, if they do not excuse, the mood of disgust with the dregs of middle-class English life that has turned Robert into a traitor; with the Kelways, natural conversation, spontaneous intercourse, freezes dead. Behind Stella's own poise and charm there is the failure of her first marriage; the husband, broken by the First World War, who turned from her wit and charm to a commonplace kindly nurse who could give him the protection he needed. We feel sorry even for Harrison, who, like the first husband, is a wounded soul; a man without background, living in a world of intrigue and subterfuge, without friendship and without love. Robert, the unfortunate hero, saves the situation by committing suicide. Stella herself, one of the most attractive heroines in English fiction, generous and direct, is bewildered by the inner twistedness of the males she has to deal with, but has magnanimity and generosity enough to reach out and try to understand even Harrison. But there is one untwisted male in the book: Stella's son, Roderick, who represents the persistence of hope, as Stella represents the persistence of warmth and courage. Miss Bowen's heroines tend to be women with a capacity for fullness of living and loving, to which life offers only imperfect or dangerous satisfaction.—G. S. FRASER, "Looking Back and Forward in the 1940s," *The Modern Writer and His World*, pp. 150–51

During the war era Miss Bowen, like some of her contemporaries, found it impossible to write novels. The daily events were too immediate to be material for artistic presentation, and too momentous to permit of their being ignored in favor of other topics. She brought out two volumes of admirable short stories, but it was eleven years after *The Death of the Heart* before she gained the perspective needful for a novel about the cataclysm. In *The Heat of the Day*, against a background of London blackouts and bombings, she presents (unexpectedly) a spy story: the divorced heroine's lover is under suspicion of being an enemy agent, and a counter-intelligence officer tries to blackmail her into becoming his mistress. As it would have been outside of Miss Bowen's scope to write a spy-thriller in the style of John Buchan or Graham Greene, she leaves the intrigue totally vague—as it would be in the mind of the distraught woman—and thus enhances the mood of helpless terror. The persecutor, never fully individualized, lurks as an emanation of evil, a symbol of the inhuman destructiveness of the war; and the unexplained, fragmentary nature of the action, in which the spy-plot is not clearly co-ordinated with the love story, reproduces the dislocation of normal social patterns and ethical values. The heroine's confidential work in a government office is not defined, and for a long time she has no idea as to whether or not her lover is guilty of the treason imputed to him. The crux of her dilemma is that both her actual and her would-be lover prove to be equally and totally devoid of moral principle; at some points the two men seem almost to be complementary manifestations of a single identity.

The melodramatic potential of the situation is all the more diminished by an elaboration of style that approaches the elusiveness of Henry James. Even the dialogue lacks the naturalness of the conversation in Miss Bowen's other novels— a further device for conveying the nightmarish feeling of the Blitz years. These effects help to make the book seem to be an allegory of current history. The improbable traitor is an embodiment of the English Philistinism that blindly carried the country into war, and his guilt-stricken suicide stands for the elimination of his class's self-deluding complacency. In this aspect, the novel ends on a note of hope, conveyed through two youthful survivors: the heroine's adolescent son has inherited an estate in Ireland, and presumably the aristocratic

standards that go with it; and the last paragraph symbolically depicts a working-girl, a secondary character in the story, holding her bastard infant up to look at a flight of swans winging westward.

Having presented her testament of war-time London, the gist of which is that no intelligible connection between personal feeling and external reality could subsist under such chaotic conditions, Miss Bowen returned in her next novel, *A World of Love*, to Ireland, where the destructive crises of a generation previous have been succeeded by inertia. Hence the effect of hallucination, already disturbingly perceptible in *The Heat of the Day*, becomes more conspicuous. The title of the book is derived from the mystical meditations of Thomas Traherne: "So is there in us a world of Love to somewhat, though we know not what in the world that should be." This combination of emotional yearning with intellectual uncertainty is the theme of the whole novel. The setting is a crumbling, isolated country-house that seems to be totally detached from the living world; and the landscapes, while described with all Miss Bowen's customary poetic vividness, are suffused with an unearthly light. As in her preceding novel, the preciosity of style enhances the effect of illusion: a reader will scarcely accept occurrences as objectively real when they are suspended in an opalescent medium of metaphors, alliteration, double negatives, inversions, and literary echoes.

As in *The House in Paris*, an ingenious device is employed to convey a complex relationship of past and present. The events of the novel occur in a span of three days, but their motivating impulses date back a full generation. The heroine, typical of Miss Bowen's romantic young rebels against tedious conformity, discovers a package of love letters written by a former owner of the house, who was killed in the First World War, long before she was born. She falls in love with her image of the seductive young man, and when her secret is discovered it infects the two older women of the household, who both loved him and whose dormant passion and antagonism are thus revivified. The spell of the past is not exorcised until the end of the story, when the two women begin to find themselves purged of their unresolved tensions and the young girl abruptly transfers her romantic ardor from her dream of the long-dead letter-writer to a normally alive man whom she has never seen until he steps off an aeroplane in the last paragraph of the book.

In *The Little Girls*, published nine years later, the study of obsessive fantasy is carried much further and the past which is spectrally resuscitated is not thirty but fifty years gone by. Though the theme is still the disparity between the romantic will and the harsh realities, the protagonist is now not a self-centered girl but a widow past sixty, whose comfortable life has enabled her to remain emotionally an adolescent. The imminence of old age impels her to sentimental nostalgia and a compulsion to construct some sort of objective memorial of her existence. She fills a cave in her garden with assorted odds and ends that she has accumulated, and then decides to seek out two school friends who shared with her a similar escapade half a century before. The gradual disclosure of their intervening lives combines the fascination of a detective story with the morbid interest of psychiatric case-histories. The author's technical skill is undiminished in the handling of the evidence, but the total effect is not wholly satisfactory in its precarious balance between whimsy, sentiment, and serious psychology. In reviving juvenile nicknames and games, Mrs. Delacroix is more silly than charming, and the reader remains uncertain as to whether the picture of the three women is sly satire or sympathetic insight. The reunion, in which the three display jealousy, suspicion, and all uncharitableness, is contrasted with the gaiety of their childhood pranks, presumably to indicate time's malevolent deforming of branches that should have grown full straight; but the contrast is almost too violent to be credible. The conclusion, when the long-buried chest is found to be empty and the instigator of the quest suffers an inexplicable trance and bruising, seems pointlessly mystifying. The whole story, indeed, is crammed with details which may possibly have symbolic import but which are more likely to appear merely grotesque; and the author's involution of style sometimes approaches unintelligibility.

Elizabeth Bowen's fiction has always been strangely hard to classify. An expert craftswoman, she tends to bedazzle readers with her verbal virtuosity and opulence to the point of obscuring other qualities. While her novels are deceptively simple—even trivial—in incidents, they must be considered as something more than domestic comedy. She is frequently ironic but seldom quite satiric, since satire requires a more specific target than she seems to aim at. The persistent implications of symbolism and the poetic exquisiteness of style set her work apart from realism, yet no metaphysical significance can be confidently recognized. Somewhere close to the surface of the everyday life that she depicts there is an elusive vein of fantasy, and the fantasy is apt to be redolent of evil. She is perhaps the most representative novelist of the hypercivilized modern intelligence, aesthetically sensitive and morally concerned, but inadequate for coping with the blind forces and mechanisms of twentieth-century existence.—LIONEL STEVENS, "A Group of Able Dames," *The History of the English Novel*, Vol. 11, 1967, pp. 293–96

Perhaps it is wrong to attempt to place authors too carefully—wrong, as Francis Hope recently said, to try to sort them into first, second, third and fourth divisions. But even if wrong it is a natural desire, and I can think of few novelists who more arouse the desire and more successfully frustrate it than Elizabeth Bowen. What, after all, is she up to? Is she merely the highly elegant, dazzlingly intelligent star of the psychological thriller class, or is she a serious contender for a place in the great tradition? And what, anyway, would be the distinctions—of genre, of talent, of purpose?

Her new novel, *Eva Trout*, is certainly a most impressive book. It creates a world so engrossing, so fully imagined in its own terms, that when interrupted while in the middle of reading it I would look up, vaguely, no longer quite sure where I was. This kind of creation is in itself a rare gift: one shared by Iris Murdoch, who also shares some of Miss Bowen's other eccentricities. Their worlds, in fact, are not dissimilar: the background of *Eva Trout* is one of gothic castles, vicarage gardens, expensive hotels and restaurants, feminine institutions, suicidal homosexual passions. Eva herself is an heiress, large, orphaned, feeling herself unloved, yet capable of inspiring strong passions in others—passions almost invariably disastrous. . . .

And the questions that the book raises are, also, profound. They are serious matters, not to be negated by the frivolity of Miss Bowen's predilection for names like Constantine and Iseult—both of these being, in fact, most carefully drawn villains, whose conversation over oysters about the future of Eva is a joy to read. The theme—corruption, wealth and innocence—is worthy of Henry James, whose name is indeed invoked by the writer herself, and there is one scene, where Eva tracks down the vicar's son at Cambridge and asks him what she can do with her money (realising, as she speaks, that she wants him with it, but that if she buys him she will never have him), that has the authentic Jamesian frisson of moral anguish. As

well as the theme, as an additional benefit, there are those marvellous passages of description, for which Elizabeth Bowen is so justly famous: the prose, always elegant even when—or perhaps most when—tortuous, achieves a number of effects that are almost breathtaking, as in a description of Hereford Square, for instance, which enables the writer to display her excellent way with flower pieces. She is also witty: several of her puns are really most satisfying.

With all these qualities, it would seem grudging to complain. And yet finally one must, because there is something about the book that cheats the very seriousness with which the reader wishes to take it. The ending is symptomatic. It is crude, melodramatic, improbable—despite the careful plotting of the revolver and the constant premonitions of violent death—and it is at once facile and contrived. Worst of all, it makes one look back through the book at things which had seemed solid, and question their substance. I must confess, in fairness, to a strong dislike of melodrama and of the supernatural, both often used by Miss Bowen, and I can see that others may not share this dislike at all. But even so the ending of this book seemed to me summary, and simply not fair to what had gone before.

Also, it is a pity that some of the characters should be so insubstantial—particularly Iseult's husband, who must be meant to represent some kind of physical presence. To me, he was simply not there. Miss Bowen is magnificent when she writes about conspiracy, duplicity and ambiguity, and her achievement—despite her final cutting of the Gordian knot—is extremely impressive. But with the simple, with the world of common sense, she does not cope. Though perhaps in that (for good or for ill, see it as one may) she is merely the closer to Henry James.—MARGARET DRABBLE, "Fixed Star?," *LT*, Feb. 1969, pp. 214, 216

ELIZABETH BOWEN
"Out of a Book" (1946)
Collected Impressions
1950, pp. 264–69

I know that I have in my make-up layers of synthetic experience, and that the most powerful of my memories are only half true.

Reduced to the minimum, to the what did happen, my life would be unrecognizable by me. Those layers of fictitious memory densify as they go deeper down. And this surely must be the case with everyone else who reads deeply, ravenously, unthinkingly, sensuously, as a child. The overlapping and haunting of life by fiction began, of course, before there was anything to be got from the printed page; it began from the day one was old enough to be told a story or shown a picture book. It went on up to the age when a bookish attitude towards books began to be inculcated by education. The young person is then thrown out of Eden; for evermore his brain is to stand posted between his self and the story. Appreciation of literature is the end of magic: in place of the virgin susceptibility to what is written he is given taste, something to be refined and trained.

Happily, the Eden, like a natal climate, can be unconsciously remembered, and the magic stored up in those years goes on secreting under to-day's chosen sensations and calculated thoughts. What entered the system during childhood remains; and remains indistinguishable from the life of those years because it *was* the greater part of the life. Probably children, if they said what they thought, would be much franker about the insufficiency of so-called real life to the requirements of those who demand to be really alive. Nothing but the story can meet the untried nature's need and capacity for the whole. Of course one cannot narrow down children to the reading child; but I could not as a child, and I cannot now, conceive what the non-reading child must be like inside. Outdoor children were incomprehensible to me when I was their age, and I still find them dull; I could not, and cannot, find out what makes them do what they do, or why they like what they like; and of such children now they are grown up I can only say that I cannot conceive what they remember, if they do remember—for how can even the senses carry imprints when there was no story? The non-reading active children were not stupid; they had their senses. Nor was it the clever children who read most, or who were at any rate the ones who inhaled fiction—quite apart there were always the horrible little students, future grown-ups, who pursued knowledge. The light-headed reading child and the outdoor child had more in common (in fact, the life of sensation) than either had with the student. Readers of my kind were the heady ones, the sensationalists—recognizing one another at sight we were banded together inside a climate of our own. Landscapes or insides of houses or streets or gardens, outings or even fatigue duties all took the cast of the book we were circulating at the time; and the reading made of us an electric ring. Books were story or story-poetry books: we were unaware that there could be any others.

Some of the heady group remained wonderfully proof against education: having never graduated these are the disreputable grown-ups who snap up shiny magazines and garner and carry home from libraries fiction that the critics ignore. They read as we all once read—because they must: without fiction, either life would be insufficient or the winds from the north would blow too cold. They read as we all read when we were twelve; but unfortunately the magic has been adulterated; the dependence has become ignominious—it becomes an enormity, inside the full-sized body, to read without the brain. Now the stories they seek go on being children's stories, only with sex added to the formula; and somehow the addition queers everything. These readers, all the same, are the great malleable bulk, the majority, the greater public—hence best-sellers, with their partly artful, partly unconscious play on a magic that has gone stale. The only above-board grown-up children's stories are detective stories.

No, it is not only our fate but our business to lose innocence, and once we have lost that it is futile to attempt a picnic in Eden. One kind of power to read, or power that reading had over us, is gone. And not only that: it is a mistake to as much as re-open the books of childhood—they are bare ruined choirs. Everything has evaporated from those words, leaving them meaningless on the page. This is the case, for me, even with Dickens—I cannot read him now because I read him exhaustively as a child. Though I did not in those years read all his books, I cannot now read any that I did not read then— there is no more oxygen left, for me, anywhere in the atmosphere of his writing. The boredom I seem to feel as I pursue the plots is, really, a flagging of my intellect in this (by me) forever used up and devitalized air. I came to an end with Dickens when I had absorbed him into myself.

Yes, one stripped bare the books of one's childhood to make oneself—it is inevitable that there should be nothing left when one goes back to them. The fickleness of children and very young persons shocks their elders—children abandon people, for instance, without a flicker, with a simplicity that really ought not to be hurting: the abandoned one has been either a 'best' friend or an object of hero-worship, and the more emotionally fruitful and fanciful the relationship, the more com-

plete the break. 'Where is So-and-so these days? I don't seem to have heard anything about him (or her) for a long time. Haven't you two got any more plans?'— 'Oh, I can't be bothered.' What applies to people applies to books, and for the same reason: everything that was wanted has been taken; only the husk or, still worse, mortifying repetition remains. The child is on the make—rapacious, mobile and single-minded. If the exhausted book survives physical abandonment—being given away or left out in the garden in the rain—it languishes on in its owner's indifferent keeping; however, once memory and sentiment have had time to set in and gather about it, it is safe. I still keep a row of books I loved as a child—but I neither wish nor dare to touch them.

What do I mean by those books making myself? In the first place, they were power-testing athletics for my imagination— cross-country runs into strange country, sprints, long and high jumps. It was exhilarating to discover what one could feel: the discovery itself was an advance. Then, by successively 'being' a character in every book I read, I doubled the meaning of everything that happened in my otherwise constricted life. Books introduced me to, and magnified, desire and danger. They represented life, with a conclusiveness I had no reason to challenge, as an affair of mysteries and attractions, in which each object or place or face was in itself a volume of promises and deceptions, and in which nothing was impossible. Books made me see everything that I saw either as a symbol or as having its place in a mythology—in fact, reading gave bias to my observations of everything in the between-times when I was not reading. And obviously, the characters in the books gave prototypes under which, for evermore, to assemble all living people. This did not by any means simplify people for me; it had the reverse effect, and I was glad that it should—the characters who came out of my childish reading to obsess me were the incalculable ones, who always moved in a blur of potentialities. It appeared that nobody who mattered was capable of being explained. Thus was inculcated a feeling for the dark horse. I can trace in all people whom I have loved a succession from book characters—not from one only, from a fusion of many. 'Millions of strange shadows on you tend.'

Also the expectation, the search, was geographic. I was and I am still on the look out for places where something happened: the quivering needle swings in turn to a prospect of country, a town unwrapping itself from folds of landscape or seen across water, or a significant house. Such places are haunted—scenes of acute sensation for someone, vicariously me. My identity, so far as I can pin it down at all, resides among these implacable likes or dislikes, these subjections to magnetism spaced out between ever-widening lacunæ of indifference. I feel certain that if I *could* read my way back, analytically, through the books of my childhood, the clues to everything could be found.

The child lives in the book; but just as much the book lives in the child. I mean that, admittedly, the process of reading is reciprocal; the book is no more than a formula, to be furnished out with images out of the reader's mind. At any age, the reader must come across: the child reader is the most eager and quick to do so; he not only lends to the story, he flings into the story the whole of his sensuous experience which from being limited is the more intense. Book dishes draw saliva to the mouth; book fears raise gooseflesh and make the palms clammy; book suspense make the cheeks burn and the heart thump. Still more, at the very touch of a phrase there is a surge of brilliant visual images: the child rushes up the scenery for the story. When the story, as so often happens, demands what has not yet come into stock, indefatigable makeshifts are arrived at—as when a play that calls for elaborate staging is performed by an enterprising little company with scanty equipment and few drop-scenes. Extension (to draw an iceberg out of a fishmonger's ice-block) or multiplication (to make a thin, known wood into a trackless forest) goes on. For castles, gorges, or anything else spectacular out of art or nature, recollections of picture postcards, posters or travel albums are drawn on; and, of course, the child to-day has amassed a whole further scenic stock from the cinema. This provision of a convincing *where* for the story is a reflex.

For the child, any real-life scene that has once been sucked into the ambience of the story is affected, or infected, forever. The road, cross-roads, corner of a wood, cliff, flight of steps, town square, quayside or door in a wall keeps a transmuted existence: it has not only given body to fiction, it has partaken of fiction's body. Such a thing, place or scene cannot again be walked past indifferently; it exerts a pull and sets up a tremor; and it is to indent the memory for life. It is at these points, indeed, that what I have called synthetic experience has its sources. Into that experience come relationships, involving valid emotion, between the child reader and book characters; a residuum of the book will be in all other emotions that are to follow.

In reverse, there are the real-life places—towns, seaports, suburbs of London—unknown to the child, though heard of, which become 'real' through being also in books. For instance, after *David Copperfield* I could not hear either Dover or Yarmouth mentioned, in the most ordinary context, without excitement: I had a line on them. Towns that were in books, and the routes between them travelled by characters, stood out in relief on the neutral map of England. Not a Londoner, I was continuously filling in and starring my map of the environs—at Richmond lived Sir Percy, the Scarlet Pimpernel, and his wife Marguerite, who fainted into a bed of heliotrope in her riverside garden; at Highgate, the Steerforths and Rosa Dartle; at Blackheath and Lewisham, the E. Nesbit children. When I came to read *Kipps*, I was made dizzy by the discovery that I had, for years, been living in two places, Hythe and Folkestone, that were in a book. Historic places one was taken to see meant no more and no less to me than this; history was fiction—it took me a long time to be able to see that it gained anything further from being 'true.'

Though not all reading children grow up to be writers, I take it that most creative writers must in their day have been reading children. All through creative writing there must run a sense of dishonesty and of debt. In fact, is there such a thing, any more, as creative writing? The imagination, which may appear to bear such individual fruit, is rooted in a compost of forgotten books. The apparent choices of art are nothing but addictions, pre-dispositions: where did these come from, how were they formed? The æsthetic is nothing but a return to images that will allow nothing to take their place; the æsthetic is nothing but an attempt to disguise and glorify the enforced return. All susceptibility belongs to the age of magic, the Eden where fact and fiction were the same; the imaginative writer was the imaginative child, who relied for life upon being lied to—and how, now, is he to separate the lies from his consciousness of life? If he be a novelist, all his psychology is merely a new parade of the old mythology. We have relied on our childhoods, on the sensations of childhood, because we mistake vividness for purity; actually, the story was there first—one is forced to see that it was the story that apparelled everything in celestial light. It could lead to madness to look back and back for the true primary impression or sensation; those we did ever experience we have forgotten—we only remember that to which something was added. Almost no experience, however much simplified by the distance of time, is to be vouched

for as being wholly my own—*did* I live through that, or was I told that it happened, or did I read it? When I write, I am re-creating what was created for me. The gladness of vision, in writing, is my own gladness, but not at my own vision. I may see, for instance, a road running uphill, a skyline, a figure coming slowly over the hill—the approach of the figure is momentous, accompanied by fear or rapture or fear of rapture or a rapture of fear. But who and how is this? Am I sure this is not a figure out of a book?

ELIZABETH HARDWICK
"Elizabeth Bowen's Fiction"

Partisan Review, November 1949,
pp. 1114–21

The mere thought of criticizing Elizabeth Bowen's work makes one feel like one of the disaffected scoundrels in her novels who induce the death of the heart. The temptation to think of this author as she thinks of her heroines is almost irresistible. Her sunny reputation invites the cheerful, impressionistic remark; disinclination is rude; the air here is mild, polite, congratulatory. (She's not so perfect as Jane Austen, nor so original as Virginia Woolf, but how glad we are, etc.) Miss Bowen inspires confidence: the popular novelist, recently elected a Companion of the British Empire, with a London home in Regent's Park and a family house in County Cork, a sensitive, careful writer whose fineness of feeling is neatly ruffled with wit and laced with snobbery. E. Sackville-West speaks of her cleverness, her fresh and startling style; V. S. Pritchett thinks of her as a poet.

To go on from there is much more difficult. First, there is the well-bred woman of sensibility, moderately elegant, sensitive to differences in class, moralistic about taste, courtesy and fidelity; but there is another Elizabeth Bowen, a sturdy, determined writer, a romantic feminist who serves up a perennial dish: the tragedy of the Fine Girl and the Impossible Man. These are obviously women's books. The surface is urbane and complex, but unusually evasive, as though it were in some kind of secret struggle with the franker soul which has devised these stories of an innocent woman's maltreatment by the reprobate, the mysterious man, the weak or unfaithful lover. This theme, this bold heart throb, perhaps contributes to the popularity of the novels, and no doubt the decorative writing, the slow, oblique presentation of character are peculiarly necessary—without the latter adornments the sophisticated reader might reasonably question the whole matter. The style—Henry James, Virginia Woolf and Katherine Mansfield—is extraordinarily fluent and diverting; one hardly notices, under its spell, the bias of the content, the oppressive tidiness of the values. In these novels, love's prerogatives are real; ambivalence is wicked, a moral and also a social failure, for the conflicts are somehow a part of the class struggle and the author appears to be a conservative of nostalgic temperament.

The opinion, or sentiment, that occurs again and again in Elizabeth Bowen's fiction and which seems to have commanded the labors on her ancestral chronicle, *Bowen's Court*, is that to know *who* you are, to be close to your past, to feel the pride and obligations of family and place, are, if not the most exquisite and difficult attainments, a great source of personal and national virtue. These warm, sustaining emotions are found most frequently in the gentry and upper class; the disloyal, the insincere and unreliable are the homeless, the shapeless nobodys, the complacent, vapid middle class, the mysterious foreigner, the restless, self-loving *arriviste*. In the case of very young girls, such as Lois in *The Last September* and Portia in *The Death of the Heart*, the pattern is reversed and the family betrays. However, here the reversal is necessary for pathos, the thundershowers of pity that are the main weather of these two novels. By whom can a young girl be more miserably misunderstood, since she has little freedom of movement, than by her family? To be sure, Portia in *The Death of the Heart* has a more democratic fate: she is victimized impartially by all classes and with such supererogatory heartlessness that one yawns, occasionally, and suspects Portia really may be the nuisance her selfish betrayers believe. Even in this book, with its villainous cast, the real sewer of corruption is a young man, Eddie, who has overdrawn himself socially. . . .

As a sort of subhead to hereditary class, there occurs the abstract notion of Home, representing familiarities, allegiances, duties and affections; under Home there is a particularity, the actual house in which the character lives. From the Home or lack of it, one's house, enriching or blighting the senses and manners, Elizabeth Bowen creates a fantastic environmental psychology, as implacable, materialistic and mortifying as the verdict of a property assessor. For those who pass the test, and it is character that is at stake, the images are loving and generous. In *Bowen's Court* she writes:

> Yes, here is the picture of peace in the house, in the country round. Like all pictures, it does not quite correspond with any reality. Or, you may call the country a magic mirror, reflecting something that could not really exist. . . . I suppose that everyone, fighting or just enduring, now carries one private image—one peaceful scene—in his heart. Mine is Bowen's Court. War has made me this image out of a house built of anxious history.

And about Karen Michaelis in *The House in Paris*:

> The Michaelis lived like a family in a pre-war novel in one of the tall, cream houses in Chester Terrace, Regent's Park. Their relatives and old friends, as nice as they were themselves, were rooted in the same soil. . . . That unconscious sereneness behind their living and letting live was what Karen's hungry or angry friends could not tolerate.

Frequently, the environmental ethic slips down a peg or two to include not only the family and the house but the very furnishings. By a complicated theology of objects the noble and the lost soul are defined. This is the moral intransigence of the interior decorator, the wrath of the goddess of the drapery and table setting. Peace is a well-lit drawing room, purity is light, airy, spacious, and in its presence the glasses shine and the flowers are forever fresh. The guilty lead an uneasy existence among the thick, dark, impersonal objects in a furnished room (Eddie in *The Death of the Heart*); or communicate rudely with family members by means of a speaking tube (Markie in *To the North*); or bear upon their souls the terrible scar of one of those boy's dens, in which the coins, birds' eggs, trophies and snapshots of youth are kept intact by a vulgar family (Robert Kelway in *The Heat of the Day*).

In *The Heat of the Day*, Miss Bowen's recent novel, the limitations of these sentiments are most painful. This is the story of a personable man of reasonably typical experience who betrays his country to the Nazis. No doubt such a decision for a man like Robert Kelway is incomprehensible—insanity, depravity, or misplaced cupidity, something hard and hardening that refuses to melt into its origins must be the only answer. Only a handful of Englishmen out of millions actively sup-

ported the Nazis, but Miss Bowen hardly seems to realize the peculiarity of her situation. She looks at the inscrutable with a cheerful, disparaging glance, confident that it too is a matter of bad breeding.

Robert Kelway seems both unfamiliar with and embarrassed by Nazi ideology; he is "English," as thoroughly discomfited by an extreme position as the author herself. His manner has the dream-like, humbled and baffled quality of an actor badly miscast in a role and when he says, ". . . look at your 'free' suckers, your democracy—kidded along from the cradle to the grave," we feel him wince, wink and shrug; this is clearly not his line. But these few dogmatic utterances are mere fillers and the real motives for his treason are found back home, nestling behind the shrubbery and bird baths. Look for Robert Kelway, the traitor, in the fact that his bumptious middle-class family thinks of its home only as a poor investment, a galling swindle to which they are doomed because it would be a "slight" not to sell for more than they gave. Stella Rodney, the heroine, meeting her lover's family for the first time and hearing their conversation about selling the house, thinks, "How can they live, anyone live, in a place that has for years been asking to be brought to an end?" Stella is gentry by extraction and, though uprooted by the war and private circumstance, has retained her identity and pride. "A handsome derelict gateway opening on to grass and repeated memorials round the walls of a church still gave some sort of locale, however distant, to what had been her unmarried name." She is appalled by the Kelways and they are an unappetizing lot, bulky, clumsy people, though the historical significance of their watch-dog snappishness is not apparent to me. The author seems to feel that for all its overweening middle-class vanity this family (and the middle class too?) is socially and humanly menacing; it is a dangerous weight, "suspended in the middle of nothing." Robert Kelway, then, has nothing to defend, neither his own kind nor his country; his indifference to the fate of England is symbolized by his willingness to sell (sell out?) his family house.

It is impossible, I think, to exaggerate the stubborn inadequacy of this motivation for treason. You feel as if you'd witnessed a fascinating crime and then heard the neighbors, rocking in their porch chairs, explaining, "I'm not surprised. That boy never appreciated his home!" Aside from the amount of "bad taste," vulgarity, discomfort, nothingness, useless property and vexing poverty vigorously defended by both sides in every war, Miss Bowen is too cautious to mention the one thing that *might* have motivated Robert Kelway, anti-Semitism, since it is hard to see what else the Nazis had to export to England and America. (Nobody took the body building exercises seriously.) *The Heat of the Day* is a curiously sentimental and confused reflection on a deplorable family with a stunted sense of the emotional value of property; and that this is the true theme is elaborately and tediously acknowledged by the subplot, which has to do with an estate in Ireland inherited by Stella Rodney's son. As a political novel, or a commentary on the English middle class, or a character novel, except for the engaging treatment of Stella Rodney, it is too impalpable to be held in the mind.

The House in Paris is widely esteemed, or at least I *believe* that to be the case. (Nothing is more difficult to track down than Miss Bowen's true reputation. Praise, so far as I have read, is indefinite and generally brief, a quick smile from Connolly, Pritchett or E. Sackville-West. Animadversion is equally curt. I have the feeling the *Scrutiny* people lump Miss Bowen with such writers as Rose Macauley and Rosamund Lehmann.) The mystery and witchery in *The House in Paris*, the sinister French boarding house, the unfathomable Mme. Fisher, and the farouche, precocious children are somewhat spurious and overwrought, in contrast to the love affair in the center of the novel which is a shy and incomplete Jamesian international episode. Karen Michaelis, wealthy, family-loving, rooted English girl, falls in love with Max Ebhart, a French Jew of highly conventionalized conception: neurotic, homeless, intelligent, nervous, ambitious. ("I cannot live in a love affair, I am busy and grasping. I am not English; you know I have no humor to cushion myself with; I am nervous all the time.") Max is literally and symbolically homeless; Karen feels with him "more cut off from her own country than if they had been in Peru." Max commits suicide and Karen bears his child illegitimately. Max is the most sympathetically treated of Miss Bowen's major male characters, though not the most interesting. He is spared the contempt usually heaped upon the men, perhaps because he is not a person at all but a captivated spirit, enchained by the wicked Mme. Fisher. Of course Karen will not marry him; he is neither free nor real enough to marry anyone; he is an appealing, romantic threat, an *image* that excites and haunts a young girl's mind on the eve of her marriage to the Right Man. The book has the suggestiveness and improbability of a dream.

The most striking thing about Miss Bowen's novels is that the attitudes and generalities which establish the tone, the more weighty reflections on status and character, either contradict or have nothing to do with the action. This author, as Mme. de Sévigné said of herself, is often very far from being entirely of her own opinion. Her typical heroines (Karen in *The House in Paris*, Emmeline in *To the North*, Stella in *The Heat of the Day*) are described as well-bred, calm, honest and attractive; they represent class and family virtue, and yet we can understand their actions only in terms of bohemia, that land no parent, relative or property owner ever enters. The girls are unconventional and daring, not in the manner of artists or intellectuals, but in the more starchy, unprogrammatic way of independent, competent business women. In love they lack caution and, to some degree, conscience; with fanatical doggedness they deceive their parents and friends, have illegitimate children, open affairs with men they know little about, and even commit murder, or at least that is the way I interpret the ending of *To the North*. All of the neat, loving domestic purity of the heroine's background does not keep her away from the sordid scenery of weekend cottages and hotel rooms. And it is almost always the heroine who passes beyond the expected and discreet in love; indeed, the man's "betrayal" is simply his embarrassment, his disabling reasonableness, his unwillingness to "live on the top of the Alps."

The main characteristic of the heroines is incuriosity. We can sympathize with the traitor Robert Kelway when he tells Stella he thought she knew of his secret activities. "How could she not have suspected *something*?" he and the reader wonder. Markie in *To the North* tells Emmeline, as they take off for a weekend in Paris, that he doesn't wish to marry her, but for some reason she discounts his frank admission; Eddie in *The Death of the Heart* is understandably astonished that Portia should have imagined he loved her. The heroines are bemused, credulous, and humorless; their high-mindedness is often only a fantastic, unrelenting literalness; we can seem to hear their desperate pleading going on long after the disaster, "But I thought you said—" and "How could you when—?" or "But you promised—."

The men are complex, ambiguous, dissatisfied—qualities Miss Bowen looks upon with finicky contempt. At the best, this contempt gives a structure to the story and a resolution to the plot. Elizabeth Bowen's novels *end*, usually in the death of the man (*The House in Paris*, *The Last September*, *The Heat of the*

Day, To the North). One cannot help but see these concluding immolations as the "woman's revenge," condign punishment for male weakness, hesitation and disingenuousness. And if there is something chilling and merciless in these finales, no one can doubt they give prodigal relief to both feminine sentiment and womanly outrage.

Since Miss Bowen's purest talent is for the simple love story, she seems to me at her best in *To the North*, a harsh, terrifying and unaffected book. Even the title avoids the sentimental disguise of the other novels and candidly indicates the zero temperature at which these love affairs end. Emmeline, the heroine, has the charm of an admission; she is in the flesh what you have felt the other heroines really were, no matter what the author pretended. Fresh, competent (a business of her own), myopic, always reaching for her glasses or seeing the world through a pleasant, deceptive haze, exorbitantly insensitive to the true character of her lover, unwilling to countenance his frantic warnings, idealistic, cruel when disabused, she hounds the fleeing man, and finally, when she can no longer avoid facing the truth, gets him into a car and drives so fast they are both killed. This book has the finished, clean and moving success the others merely hope to achieve by considerable cant about taste and manners.

I cannot share E. Sackville-West's statement in *Horizon* that "Elizabeth Bowen is already assured of a superior place in any civilization capable of appreciating, say, *Middlemarch*." This critic might have gone through the whole of *The Cambridge History* without finding a comparison more unflattering to Miss Bowen. But I wonder if these comparisons are meant to be taken seriously. They are apparently an accepted form of discourse and whenever the subject under discussion is a woman writer we can always expect to pass the time of day with chatter about Jane Austen, Charlotte Bronte and George Eliot.

Just where Elizabeth Bowen "belongs" I cannot say. Readable, gifted, the very equanimity of her work makes criticism difficult. In a relaxed mood, she offers one the satisfaction of unabashed tears, an emotional evening in which love retains all its old sovereign rights, and the final pleasure of witnessing the bad end to which the inconstant come. As in an opera libretto you must take the roles on faith—a grunt of satire or a shiver of commonsense on the spectator's part would be enough to disrupt the performance and bring the pretty scenery down upon the soprano's head.

HARRIET BLODGETT
From "Gain in Paradise Lost"
Patterns of Reality
1975, pp. 26–37

Miss Bowen's young heroines must learn to be adults of emotional vitality and moral integrity. Twenty-two-year-old Sydney of Miss Bowen's first novel *The Hotel* (1927) masters the proper nature of woman, as do the comparable heroines of *The Last September* (1929) and the much later *A World of Love* (1955). Sydney will eventually become the six-tyish heroines of *The Little Girls* (1964), but whatever her age, "Sydney" will sustain Miss Bowen's central myth of the Fall: growth into higher consciousness with gain in Paradise lost. In a pointed clue to the myth which is the embodiment of her cherished moral and spiritual values, Miss Bowen chooses "A Rev. J. D. L. Milton—*John*?"—the Protestant clergyman James Milton—as lover of the first Sydney. A tempter's role goes to Sydney's adored Mrs. Kerr, a serpent of regressive attraction to the unconscious. Since psychic integration and redemption through trial, or maturation and moral crisis, presage all the Bowen novels, *The Hotel* is an important harbinger.

Sydney's maturational problems are not singular, and like all Bowen heroines she lives in a sorry place. The unnamed genteel Riviera hostelry[1] of *The Hotel* is a "doll's house" refuge for the unwilling in body, heart, and spirit. The hotel's clientele are emotional misfits, as much culturally disturbed as psychologically warped in this first Bowen indictment of the moral, spiritual, and emotional aridity of modern life. Miss Bowen's accusee is to range from sterile modernism to eroded traditionalism. *The Last September*, set in the County Cork of 1920, varies *The Hotel*'s charges. Its more complex symbol and setting, the Ascendancy estate Danielstown, is both a stifling environment and an unhealthy personality. Projecting its inhabitants' psychic lag, Danielstown is a denial and a stasis: captive to an etiolated past, attitudinized, sensuously parochial. (*The Heat of the Day*, 1949, conversely will use an equivalent estate, Mount Morris, as a positive symbol for a structured way of life that relates, rather than alienates.) The heroine Lois is given an extended (expository) vision of Danielstown's apprehensive existence in alienation and darkness. With its dubious, unenlightened reality, this "reservoir of obscurity"—where trees are "spread like a rug to dull some keenness, break some contact between self and senses perilous to the routine of living,"—is sundered from natural and supernatural alike, from whatever is vitally emotional and irrationally energetic, from whatever offers insight into truth and conviction in God. Only outside its demesne can the cattle move "like saints, with a mindless certainty." The Ascendancy, as such, is not the villain; the English Michaelises in *The House in Paris* (1935) are later Danielstowners, sharing an equally futile life because the best, in Yeats's phrase, "lack all conviction" in anything but their narrowly secure group-routine. Danielstowners draw "up closer to one another" and are 'Compassed about . . . by so great a cloud of witnesses' to their spiritual death.

Whereas Lois feels constricted at Danielstown, *The Hotel*'s young moderns are only too free in their lax, muddled post-war society. Feckless Victor (a sub-plot character) has been unable to find employment since the war and is "said to be suffering from nervous depression in consequence"; "enforced inactivity must come very hard on poor Mr. Ammering, who played tennis all day long with a set face and went out at nights with the Lawrences to dances at other hotels, where he talked to his partners most beautifully about the war." Although the young, bored by their freedom, find nothing to live for and are willing merely to drift along, Miss Bowen—whose acerbity perhaps reflects her own youth—is vastly impatient of them. Shallow Veronica, a girl of Sydney's age, helps define the problem of modernism as an issue of the reluctant, vocationless spirit. Blasé Veronica casually decides to marry lazy Victor because she might as well marry and generate; after all, 'What am *I* to do? I don't want to be anything. I'm not modern.' The personality is far less modern than the attitude since Veronica is a healthy animal with strong biological instincts but very meagerly developed consciousness. Neither will Veronica make much of a wife or a mother, nor does she care to. Her antipathy to a professional career includes Miss Bowen's appraisal of her reluctance to exercise her capacity to *be* a person. The human vocation, Miss Bowen assumes, is a career which persists, whatever the times. *The Hotel* bridges the themes of modern career and personal spiritual vocation as skeptical Sydney, for whom the Church is dead, questions Milton's professional vocation: 'Though it may have been an

Idea in the first place that made churches to be built, it was the churches already existing, with rows for people to sit in, and a pulpit and things all ready that had to be filled, that made you into a parson.' Milton, who "in the assured retreat of office . . . had had no need to ask what he was," renews his human calling at the hotel.

Sydney, meanwhile, finds her vocation. She matures into full consciousness and becomes the real "woman" who participates more truly in God's image because she is freed from the compulsions of morally blind instinct and because her developed consciousness centers in her soul, not her intellect. Her soul knows what Evelyn Underhill has called "the metaphysical object". Even if, like Sydney, one would prefer to disavow supra-mundane realities—and even if the word *God* is never mentioned—one may find himself subject to experiences of transcendental affirmation. *Vocation*, properly speaking, includes man's acknowledgment of God as his Creator, his act of faith or *credo*. Miss Bowen prefers to be circumspect; her characters do not explicitly say, "I believe in my Lord God and His purposes." All of her books do, however, assume the Christian ethos with its diminution of ego-centricity, including the ultimate egocentricity of assuming oneself to be autonomous. Her characters have a need to acknowledge their divine source and more or less tacitly do acknowledge it: whether morally they are brought to give of themselves for others, or spiritually they are brought to the act of faith whereby they relinquish sovereignty, or psychologically they are brought to the *Self* which is the psychic equivalent of a Christian soul. One must heed what her characters see and do, not what they pronounce.

Though she never questions pulpits or has a transcendent vision, nineteen-year-old Lois has also like Sydney to find her vocation. Schooldays over, the future is a blur, except that she should be "womanly." Danielstown may smother her; meanwhile it is a cozy place for one unwilling to 'think':

'But why do you stay here?'
'I can't think,' said Lois, startled.
'You like to be the pleasant young person?'
'I like to be in a pattern.' She traced a pink frond [in the carpet] with her finger. 'I like to be related; to have to be what *I* am. Just to *be* is so intransitive, so lonely.'
'Then you will like to be a wife and mother.' Marda got off the writing table and began to change her stockings. 'Jacob's ladder,' she explained. 'It's a good thing we can always be women.'
'I hate women. But I can't think how to begin to be anything else.'

With its progression from staying at Danielstown to denying womanhood, the brief passage defines Lois's problem by skillfully juxtaposing gesture (Lois's tracing a Jamesian figure; Marda's getting off the writing table), statement (Lois's desire to be herself yet related in a pattern; Marda's proposing marriage and motherhood), and image (Jacob's ladder). Lois's ladder to fulfillment will have to incorporate and surpass her social and sexual roles. Her psychic energies must feed her moral being and her creative nature; her meaningful pattern must transcend her and reach from earth to heaven. Marda suggests an easy womanhood, not womanliness: the free yet responsible personality, energetic to feel and act and relate whole. Marda gets *off* the *writing table* as she proposes backsliding, yet Lois's individual pattern of meaningful identification (unlike Sydney's) includes becoming a writer. But Lois as yet cannot contemplate writing, which is 'so embarrassing', 'so personal.' In addition to her human nature, Lois needs to accept her special nature and talents as a source of volition and vocation.

Hymning love rather than urging vocation, the late *A World of Love* strikes a less duteous note than the earlier novels. It had taken Miss Bowen some time to realize in fictive translation the large role love played in her philosophy: how tragic was the death of the heart among men when so generous was the gift of God's love to them. The major social consciousness now is concern for the civilization which, having brought itself through error to war, must restore itself through love, assimilating its losses of persons and of faith better than it did after World War I. The book is quietly recalling the disturbed past from its very first sentence in which the sun rises "on a landscape still pale with the heat of the day before." *The Heat of the Day* is Miss Bowen's wartime novel. Two world wars with their unnatural deaths lie behind this novel's action so that now two generations of "unlived lives" crowd "the living's senses"; and Jane Danby, its twenty-year-old heroine seeking the attachments of maturity, has "grown up amid extreme situations and frantic statements" while "altogether the world was in a crying state of exasperation." But Jane, auguring "a new world," discovers a world of love accessible to all. Miss Bowen's aptly chosen epigraph from Traherne reminds us that "There is in us a world of Love to somewhat, though we know not what in the world that should be . . . Do you not feel yourself drawn by the expectation and desire of some Great Thing?" (*Centuries of Meditations*, I.2). For Traherne, as for Miss Bowen, man's desire for Truth derives from the soul's memory of Paradise; the world of love, stemming from the same divine memory, is an expression of *amor dei*.[2]

Miss Bowen saw this book as being "of Ireland, but not specifically Irish"[3] perhaps because it is really a universal legend of a house in decay ever since the young lord of the manor died in war, but now to be renewed through faith in love. Mysteriously summoned Jane becomes a mythic quester who not only matures into perfected womanhood and love, but also within three days conducts the stifled souls at Montefort farm back from the land of the dead. Jane's pursuit of love, renewing memory and desire, is a sanctified quest; the book, a modern grail legend. Begun in a period of near-drought, it culminates with rain falling as Jane, her Montefort mission completed, meets the youth Richard Priam, a rain god descended at Shannon Airport, and (in the novel's last sentence) "they no sooner looked but they loved." Even Shakespeare's Rosalind, who scoffed at Celia and Oliver's precipitousness, fell in love, and love remains the fructifying ascensional force that defines the truest self.

The young heroine of *A World of Love* is assigned a redeemer's role. This narrative translation of the Christ aspect of the myth of the Fall is a concentrating of theme which Miss Bowen develops only after *The Hotel* and *The Last September*.[4] The more simply conceived early books are concerned rather with what the heroine can make of herself. *The Hotel*'s Sydney Warren, resting on the Riviera after having overworked herself at a university, becomes overly attached to elegant Mrs. Kerr, who drops her abruptly when son Ronald comes to visit; whereupon Sydney in despair agrees to marry James Milton, more than twenty years her senior. Her subsequent release of him and repudiation of Mrs. Kerr attest her growth in emotional and moral awareness and self-integration.

At the outset, Sydney is so self-involved that few people have independent reality for her. Her tendency to visualize herself from outside, playing roles before others—objectification in which she will habitually "fall back on an outside consciousness" of appearances—is a defense against the painfulness of personally responding. Not only does Sydney still need to learn to confront emotional reality directly; there is

an unacknowledged split in her temperament between mind and feeling, a very apparent conflict between her actual sensibility and her assumed attitude of aloof, disillusioned rationality. While she misconstrues herself "a Realist" who believes only in present, unidealized actualities, and deals "austerely" with her "imagination," she is far less rational than her philosophy allows for and thus has yet to resolve her feelings about deity. Even if she is proud not to be 'encumbered' like James, she has not quite succeeded in reasoning God away, and in place of traditional credence has merely substituted something like superstitious dread.

Up to a point, Miss Bowen values Sydney's stubborn skepticism. As Sydney insists, man cannot live for a tradition or, mechanically, through it. Sydney envisions opening the front of the hotel as one unhinges a doll's house and seeing all the 'propped' 'dolls' therein 'doing appropriate things in appropriate attitudes as though they had been put there to represent something and had never moved in their lives'. . . . There must be interior volition and a sense of freedom. Sydney feels obscurely that man really has no free will—whether one looks at him in terms of his conventional responses, his physical compulsions, or some metaphysical determining fate. Sydney has yet to feel actively that man (as Miss Bowen believes) has creative freedom, for Fate may place him in situations, but he makes his personal and moral being.

Since this means that man must free his psychic energies for the use of his higher, conscious system, Sydney's captivating Mrs. Kerr is extremely important. A character in whom, to use an apt phrase from *Bowen's Court*, the "untoward work of the soul"[5] appears, Mrs. Kerr fuses the Christian and psychological themes in the book. In her orbit are dimness and gloom, like lapsing back into unconsciousness; her minions belong to the devil, their free will inoperative since their psychic energies are trapped in the dark, primitive self. Mrs. Kerr confirms a speculation of Sydney's that 'the whole Past . . . may be one enormous abeyance' and makes her impression that Mrs. Kerr 'isn't at all modern' a heavy irony. A symbolic projection of an archetypal image, the primordial, transpersonal *Anima*, this "attractive" female who smiles "like a priestess" is the numinously potent Magna Mater or Great Moon Goddess of myth. The Great Mother (whom Sydney unknowingly worships) is a collective vestige of man's psychic condition before individual differentiation enabled him to love and be responsible as a person in intimate relationships; she is a pre-spiritual tie to the chthonic or female earth world stage before the emergence of a "heavenly" masculine deity. A claim of depth psychology is acknowledged in a double-entendre passage about the "state of mind" which is individual responsibility—a state which belongs to the more recent stage of man's psychic development after the most ancient chthonic-feminine has married, or become transformed into, the heavenly or paternal-masculine. . . .

The transformation has not succeeded: Mrs. Kerr has neither higher spirit nor God; she still corresponds to a stage of blind instinctive drive. Her threat is evidenced by Ronald, whose emotional life his unloving mother (who is also the transpersonal mother) menaces. Ronald, who sees her in the guise of "the Beata Beatrix", is captive to her mysterious power—"this feeling of being burnt in upon that left no room for desire." Rendering him incapable of normal love, Mrs. Kerr is destroying him just as the primitive Great Godesses of myth destroyed their son-lovers. The "realistic" character, with her wholly self-referring emotions, meshes with the symbolic character. Mrs. Kerr is always a crudely immoral manipulator of other persons.

In confronting Mrs. Kerr, one is confronting regressive or unmatured and unregenerate aspects of oneself. Thus Milton's crucial interview with Mrs. Kerr is his descent or relapse into the dimness of an unconscious world. . . . Equating Mrs. Kerr with the devil, Miss Bowen also makes the interview a temptation scene from the myth of Fall in which Mrs. Kerr proclaims the triumph of those who have "fallen away" from good—equivalent to saying, never made their way up to it. Her purpose in summoning him to the eerie tête-à-tête (the scene is laboriously mysterious) is to advise him that Sydney is devoted to him while insinuating deftly that Sydney's motives are to be suspected. Not wanting to give the girl up, Mrs. Kerr plays the Tempter who adapts truth to serve private ends. While it is not love that impelled Sydney to accept Milton's proposal, neither is it quite the opportunism, retaliation, or gesture which Mrs. Kerr proposes, but rather despair and a yearning for comfort. The temptation finally fails since Milton is too sound to be corrupted by such machinations; he has already shown himself capable of love as the relationship between individual beings it should be: "He felt that most profound concern possible for another human being, when it becomes a question no longer of the extent of one's own possession of them, but, transcending this, of what in their untouchable selves they *are*."

The opening portion of the scene is concentrated enough to reproduce here as an example of how Miss Bowen from the start was presenting symbolic scenes in naturalistic guise:

. . . Mrs. Kerr said thoughtfully: 'Religion, I suppose, is an immense outlet for gratitude.'

'One would be sorry to make use of one's religion as an outlet for anything.'[6]

She retracted. 'The psychologists have led one so astray.'

'The fallacy's older than they are.'

'I suppose so,' agreed Mrs. Kerr . . . 'You have felt, I dare say, that force of—of religion in Sydney. I've had to draw back there, because I don't, as you see, understand. One never would hold her, lacking that.'

'I don't see her ever as a person to be absolutely held.'

She was moved by a deep-down amazement . . . 'Not held? You forget,' she said, 'I've been her friend.' She reflected: 'Does new power bring with it, perhaps, its own disabilities? You are, aren't you, quite newly her lover? You mayn't see yet, may not admit intellectually, but you must surely *feel* that.'

'You don't think I quite understand what I've got.'

'I don't think you can trust yourself yet to look down very deep. But you ought—she is yours absolutely. We have all of us fallen away.' There was not a note in her voice of anything but triumph; she smiled at him like a priestess.

'You feel I need to be told this?' he said . . .

'There is no need,' she said with a penetrating, long look. 'You do know.'

Mrs. Kerr properly declares her inability and reluctance to 'understand' the force of (higher) religion and her inability plus desire to *hold* Sydney. She urges Milton to exert control over Sydney as if he were an absolute power, to assume godhead in the way of the sinner. Since down very deep he would like to do so, there is 'no need' to tell him. Nonetheless, by the end of the scene, Milton realizes that he has had a terrible new shock, though its "meaning" eludes him. The real evil and omnipresence of the power drive become meaningful to him when he proves their truth on himself by finally releasing his adored

Sydney at her request. When he acknowledges that, since Sydney does not love him, she 'is right' to break the engagement and he cannot hold her back, the moon is synchronously divested of its force; it rises "opaque and lustreless."

Sydney's initial absorption in Mrs. Kerr is so extreme that she can find "the possibility of not being kept in mind . . . a kind of extinction." Her auto-erotic attachment is incipient homosexuality[7] which could develop perniciously, but the sexual immaturity is only part of a broader emotional immaturity: her attempt to deny a fully matured femininity. Another hotel guest makes a pointed observation that Sydney is "curiously dammed up: there was certainly something *in* the girl." Mrs. Kerr is an aspect of Sydney herself. Because Sydney is attracted to or in the clutches of the lesser woman in herself, the first time she and Mrs. Kerr appear onstage together, Miss Bowen deftly insinuates into the text Sydney's need to escape from the aegis of the chthonic moon goddess. . . .

The process begins "with the knife-edge of a first realization" that Mrs. Kerr, who has rushed by her on the stairs, is preferring Ronald to Sydney, a deprivation to Sydney's sense of importance which is like death. With unfortunate obviousness, Sydney feels the knife as she approaches a cemetery, where she is "not proof against the ordinary reflections on mortality". Dejected because her wasted life but moves towards pointless death—"the last and most humiliating of those deprivations she had begun to experience"—Sydney begins to reconsider James's proposal. His future "spun itself off into infinity. He did not acknowledge finality anywhere"; for him death has "in a cognizant mind its order". She contemplates "with a faint inclination" what it might be like to share a life with a person for whom events have "this overtone of significance". Sydney yearns for at least vicarious participation in meaningful life and death. But she still wants most of all to matter to Mrs. Kerr, and thus does not accept Milton until after Mrs. Kerr ruptures all ties by an ugly accusation that Sydney expected more from her than she decently ought to give. Too blurred by her pain as yet to see Mrs. Kerr's nature clearly, Sydney instead counters her rejection with the solace of Milton's love.

When Milton analogizes their coming marriage to the Irish fairy tale of Curdie, who opened a door into heaven, Sydney objects 'I've no faculty of wonder.' Yet events disprove her. Traveling down a steep mountainside with Milton and Mrs. Kerr and a cousin, Sydney, deeply depressed, longs for an accident at 'the next corner . . . the next corner.' Suddenly a roadblock appears—out of nowhere. As Milton says, it is 'Funny we shouldn't have seen it ahead of us . . . or underneath us.' The (apparently) fortuitous intervention which stops the car culminates in Sydney's passage through rebirth into a life of meaning. After the others leave the Fiat, Sydney, her background illuminated, looks down on the unreal hotel in the shadows during a powerful experience of perception. . . . She has felt, as she shortly afterwards tells James when she breaks her engagement, 'the shock of being alive . . . I had had no idea we were as real as this. I'd never realized it mattered so much.' "She seemed protected [he thought] by some kind of exaltation."

Reborn Sydney's vision after her "downward" journey completes a transformational experience in which she accepts herself as a unity of flesh (hands, body, hills) and spirit that prolongs the light. Transforming his natural corporeality into spirit—creating "isolation above the regular approach of night" or "unnatural endless prolongation of the daylight"—is man's way to conquer death. The knife blade of this saving realization cuts even keener than the "knife edge" of that deadly first rejection of Mrs. Kerr's; and Sydney no longer needs James's infinity, for she has found her own. The unnatural "isolation . . . above night" has "connected itself in her mind with her present shocked sense of having been flung back on to living"—she was "defeated" when she tried to will her death because she cannot control Fate. The only death she can will is willing acceptance of death to her ego: that creative death of accepting limitation to her autonomy which is an acceptance of God and a rebirth into light. Sydney accepts. She is carefully placed in the *Fiat* to recall the hymn to creation in Genesis, the affirmations starting with the Divine "Fiat lux" (i.3) acknowledging God as creator with man as climax of His creation through whom His purposes are to be fulfilled. In terms of Campbell's monomyth, the hero has encountered the most important fabulous forces; in Jungian terms she has found access to her *Self.* Has Sydney had an experience of illuminating grace? The novel says only that from her own depths, through that fusing "imagination" which being a "Realist" she was wont to belittle, Sydney has achieved a new apprehension of reality.

Notes

1. It derives from a locale. Miss Bowen (as quoted in *Twentieth-Century Authors*, eds. Stanley J. Kunitz and Howard Haycroft [New York, 1942], 169) drew on her stay 'one rather awful winter' in a resort hotel at Bordighera to which she had gone as a companion-tutor to some young cousins. The 1951 preface to ES explains, "I increasingly wished to write a novel—the ideality of hotel life as a stage for one came to me, one afternoon, in a flash. The Italian Riviera, on which I had spent one winter in a hotel, offered—with its social futility, pretty backdrop, and dramatic changes of weather—propitious climate for a first novel of mine" (xvii–xviii).

2. William Heath cautions the reader not "to equate the simplicity of the epigraph with Miss Bowen's position"—she is merely "relying on Traherne's vocabulary". Traherne, "regarded from a secular point of view", also talks about "escape" from "finite limitations" through illusion and "by using religious terms . . . solves the dilemma of the romantic will by defining for it an ideal illusory goal" (*Elizabeth Bowen*, 130–131). This contorting is surely unnecessary. Miss Bowen chose an epigraph which is a definition of Christian love and therefore a suitable epigraph for her book. Heath, who finds an "odd discrepancy" between the "manner" of HD and that of WL (p. 20), has much trouble with WL because it is the novel least amenable to his thesis.

3. John K. Hutchins, "On an Author", interview in *New York Herald Tribune Books*, March 26, 1950, p. 3.

4. Jane's role is modelled on Portia's in the earlier DH but is distinctively different since Jane has little interrelationship with her family: her responses are concentrated upon an imaginary lover, Guy. Whereas Portia's very nature elicits family changes, only Jane's absorption in love and her chance discovery of important love letters constitute her more superficial agency. WL has imaginative brilliance but suffers from a lack of sustained interplay between characters and from an over-wrought prose. L. P. Hartley reviewed this "verbally difficult" book appreciatively (*Spectator*, CXCIV [March 11, 1955], 294); most other critics were less approbatory.

5. BC, 248. Miss Brown uses the phrase when discussing her ancestors' shortcomings. Her description of the founder of Bowen's Court is interesting both for the values revealed and for the use of psychological terms to discuss moral and spiritual problems: "Henry's weakness . . . had lain in a sort of infantilism. Nothing shows him to have been without religion, but I see his religion as that of the lonely night-nursery—dreads quickly followed by solace, contrition by exaltation. It was a religion that, as a grown man, he might feel but could no longer apply. It was a religion inefficacious for the grown man, and most of all for the father. He built his children a house, but he gave them no principle. . . . Spiritually tongue-tied, he let his sons make little gods of themselves for want of any idea of God, and their characters went weak from the vital lack" (BC, 248–249).

6. Miss Bowen apparently does not share Milton's certainty about religious outlets. The reader will be interested in an analogous early short story, "All Saints" (1923), in which another smug clergyman's ideas are challenged by a mysterious lady in black, whose 'real name is Mrs. Barrows' (*i.e.*, primitive burial barrows) and who is "not elderly" but "perennial" (ES : E, 65, 64). She offers the vicar a new window for the Lady Chapel and very disturbing ideas about the powers of unsanctified saints.

7. Miss Bowen considers the relationship between unmatured sexuality and cruelty in a contemporaneous (1929) story "The Dancing Mistress". Miss Joyce James (!), the mistress with "dreamy and cold eyes in which personality never awakened" (DD, 182) who relates only to her mannish pianist, has an "unrealized self" (DD, 185) desirous of killing the pupil she regularly torments.

HERMIONE LEE
From "The Life Room"
Elizabeth Bowen
1981, pp. 129–40

Although the first two volumes of short stories preceded *The Hotel*, and although Elizabeth Bowen was writing stories throughout the Twenties and Thirties which overlapped in themes and atmosphere with the novels, it seems useful to consider this part of her work as a whole, at this point, before going on to her war-time and post-war writing. Inevitably, the appraisal must be limited. Not every story out of almost eighty can be given its due; several which are excellent—'The Dancing Mistress', 'Joining Charles', 'The Last Night in the Old Home', 'Look at All Those Roses', 'A Love Story', 'The Tommy Crans'—I have only been able to mention briefly. And Elizabeth Bowen deserves consideration as a short story writer alone. It's here that her careful effects, her mannered emphases, her exact detailing of atmosphere, and the disconcerting suggestiveness produced by these techniques are most immaculately and resonantly employed.

It is not, I think, necessary to look at the stories in a chronological order. Elizabeth Bowen herself, retrospectively, dismisses the importance of chronology. '"Development" may appear in any one writer's successive novels; in successive short stories I hold it to be a myth.[1] In the same Preface, though, she remarks on some changes in her techniques—'At the beginning, I over-wrote'—and adds that she has moved from a liking for impressionism and 'free form' to a preference for narratives with 'a beginning, a crisis, and an end'. And she later points to the extreme shortness of the sketches in the first two books, *Encounters* (1923) and *Ann Lee's* (1926), as evidence of her being essentially 'a visual writer, with no taste for analysis'.[2] Character came later.

Of course chronology does matter to some extent. There is a great difference between the brief impressionistic early sketches, and the major stories of the three central collections, *The Cat Jumps* (1934), *Look at All Those Roses* (1941), and *The Demon Lover* (1945). (*Joining Charles* (1929) is an interesting transitional volume.) Some of the best of these central stories— 'The Disinherited', 'Summer Night', 'Ivy Gripped the Steps'— are long and structurally complex enough to merit the title of *nouvelle.* . . .

Attempts, however, to locate other chronological groupings—perhaps more satires on social affectations, more stories about children away from home, in the earlier volumes—will be fraught with exceptions. Elizabeth Bowen's own disregard for chronology is broadly justified. Her stories are remarkably coherent: what she calls 'Bowen terrain', which is a spiritual as well as a geographical locality, haas a recognisable atmosphere, a consistency of theme, in stories written forty years apart, although the emphasis noticeably gathers to a head in the war-time stories: 'Where shall we be when nobody has a view of life?' asks a wartime visitor to Ireland of a girl who is eager to leave it, in 'Sunday Afternoon'. 'How are we to live without natures?' the woman exclaims at the end of 'The Happy Autumn Fields'. 'They are too rare—visions of where we are', the narrator comments in 'Summer Night'. Many of the stories chart an ominous vacancy, a lack in people or in places of a proper sense of themselves. But in so doing, the stories themselves sustain a responsible self-consciousness: they are not merely atmospheric, comical or macabre, but embody a distinct 'view of life.'

Elizabeth Bowen is clear about the responsibility of the short story. It must be '*necessary*', it must have a 'valid central emotion', as with a lyric poem.

> However plain or lively or unpretentious be the manner of the story, the central emotion—emotion however remotely involved or hinted at—should be austere, major. The subject must have implicit dignity.[3]

Writing about Irish and American short stories in the Introduction to her own 1936 selection, she praises the 'semi-poetic' art of enforcing 'amazement' through understatement. This she calls the 'extraverted' short story, 'bare of analysis, sparse in emotional statement', which provides 'general significance' through the particular. For the short story to justify itself, it must mean seriously or, as she puts it, 'must raise some issue'. It's a severe rubric, resting as it does on words like 'necessary' and 'austere', and recommending 'exact and impassive' narration.[4] It leads her to criticise those of her own early stories which exhibit or betray 'sentiments' too unguardedly.[5]

Paradoxically, though, she feels that the short story allows for extremes that the novel cannot admit: hallucination, dreams, fantasy, the unfamiliar. The short story is in some senses 'a free zone':

> More than half of my life is under the steadying influence of the novel, with its calmer, stricter, more orthodox demands: into the novel goes such taste as I have for rational behaviour and social portraiture. The short story, as I see it to be, allows for what is crazy about humanity: obstinacies, inordinate heroisms, 'immortal longings'. At no time, even in the novel, do I consider realism to be my forte.[6]

The point is reiterated in the later preface to *A Day in the Dark*, where she says she has felt it 'unethical' to include the supernatural in her novels. 'Unethical': Elizabeth Bowen is always at pains to stress the writer's moral responsibility in choosing what will do for the different *genres*. This is a Jamesian attitude to the writing of fiction, particularly in its admission of the fantastic into the short story (or *nouvelle*) but not into the novel. Like Elizabeth Bowen, James characterizes the peculiar value of the *nouvelle* as the paradoxical confluence of 'free' subject and 'controlled' procedure:

> The thing was [in *The Turn of the Screw*] to aim at absolute singleness, clearness and roundness, and yet to depend on an imagination working freely, working (call it) with extravagance; by which law it wouldn't be thinkable except as free and wouldn't be amusing except as controlled.[7]

The control and the focus of her stories arises initially, she says, from their settings. This is true of the novels too, of course, and she is scathing about the 'negative apathy' which she repeatedly encountered in thesis writers and interviewers about 'Bowen terrain'. 'Am I not manifestly a writer for whom places loom large?'[8] It is places, far more often than faces, which have 'sparked off' stories; some 'arose out of an intensified, all but spellbound beholding on my part, of the scene in question.'[9]

There are obvious examples of this, like the story set in a garden blazing with roses, first seen from a car by a bored couple driving back to London; the story set in suburban woods full of families out for the day, providing no shelter for a pair of lovers; or the story set on a bleak new housing estate which drives a middle-aged woman to the point of madness. As their title suggests ('Look at All Those Roses', 'A Walk in the Woods', 'Attractive Modern Homes') the effect of these places *is* the story. But that interrelationship between place and plot is almost always discernible, even when the stories are less obviously about a particular location. It is a moral interrelationship in the tradition of Jane Austen, Henry James and E. M. Forster, and 'raises the issue' of inheritance and continuity. 'Bowen terrain' is not a wild uninhabited countryside. She is not interested in the aesthetic effects of landscape nor in a Wordsworthian contemplative solitude. The characteristic position of her people in relation to the sea is, like Gavin in 'Ivy Gripped the Steps', to stand with their back to its 'heaving mackerel vacancy', longing to be with the crowd on the promenade. The tendency of her settings is towards a social diagnosis, and she likes nothing so much, in the stories as in the novels, as to put groups of people into the place they deserve. The moral interrelationship between places and people, already seen to be crucial in the Anglo-Irish work, is very acute in the short stories.

Places are used repeatedly to expose a deficiency in the people who inhabit them, either because they have been built or landscaped for a diminished quality of life, or because their decline presents a challenge that can't be met by the occupants. Many of them, therefore, are not fulfilling their intended function. There are family houses which have fallen into disuse, seaside hotels and esplanades which have become scenes of desolation. The moral scheme of the places quickly becomes recognisable. Certain locales are always bad for the soul, and recur in the stories, which chart an opposition between experience and innocence, or a withdrawal from a pointless surplus of experience, or a social group so anaesthetised that it's not aware it has lost anything.

New estates on the outskirts of towns, used as a central image for the death of the heart in 'Attractive Modern Homes', are always felt to impose a baleful separateness and sameness on their inhabitants. The girl narrator of 'Songs My Father Sang Me'—a story which laments for a lost England—grew up in a wilderness of bungalows near Staines. 'The only point about that region is that it has no point and that it goes on and on.' 'The Disinherited', Elizabeth Bowen's major critique of middle-class life in the Thirties, begins on an 'exclusive estate' outside a University city: a locale carefully established to provide inadequate opposition against the violent rootlessness and dislocation that the story describes:

> You undertook not to keep chickens, put up a frame garage or hang out clothes . . . Few houses had gone up so far; those there were stood apart, like Englishmen not yet acquainted, washed by clear upland air and each in its acre of wiry grass that had lost its nature, being no longer meadow and not yet lawn. Half-made roads, like the first knowing cuts of a scalpel, mapped the flank of the hill out, up to the concrete water-tower upon its crest. No buses approached, and there were and would be no shops.
> ('The Disinherited', *CJ*)

Elizabeth Bowen's prejudices are disclosed by the loaded opposition between the desirable, absent 'meadow' and 'lawn', and the reality of 'concrete water-tower', and by that cunningly sinister use of the knowing scalpel. But what is lamented is not only rural or aristocratic seclusion: it is also the absence of houses and shops, a tradition of ordinary life.

By contrast, she allows more feeling to provincial suburbs, which can at least be ambiguous.

> This was one of those roads outside growing provincial cities that still keep their rural mystery. They seem to lead into something still not known. Traffic roars past one end, but the other end is in silence: you see a wood, a spire, a haughty manor gate, or your view ends with the turn of an old wall . . . And, each standing back in half an acre of ground, there were two or three stucco houses with dark windows, sombre but at the same time ornate, built years ago in this then retired spot. Dead lime leaves showered over their grass plots and evergreens.
>
> ('A Queer Heart', *LAR*)

Anything might happen in those retired, provincial, neo-Gothic houses, which fascinated Elizabeth Bowen all her life. The same ingredients—dead lime leaves, stucco gate-posts, sundials, laurels, church-like windows—recur in story after story.[10] Such places arouse expectations of the uncanny which they do not always fulfil. A slight but interesting story called 'Reduced', about a woman with a mysterious past (she has been cleared of murdering her last employer) who is hired by a thrifty unpleasant man as a cheap governess for his two daughters, makes use of this kind of dubious setting:

> Pendlethwaite was not a loveable house. Built about 1880 of unpleasing maroon brick, it creaked inside with pitch-pine; its church-like windows peered narrowly at the smiling landscape round; its grounds darkened a valley with belts of laurel and stiff, damp-looking lumps of unindigenous firs. The house looked dedicated to a perpetual January: sunnier seasons beat back from its walls.
>
> ('Reduced', *LAR*)

The perfect setting, it would seem, for untoward events: those ominous verbs suggest that something horrid is imminent. But a rather more unexpected effect ensues. The governess has created a secret world shared by herself and the children, alienated (like Portia's and Matchett's world) from the rest of the house. The chill, ugly house doesn't lend itself to any scene of ugliness or violence, but there is a quiet ominousness about the children's incipient mutiny.

That sort of large, chilly house is repeatedly used for a falling apart in family life. In 'The Needlecase', a too-large house in dismal countryside is kept on for the sake of a prodigal absentee elder son. Another errant son necessitates the auctioning of the family house in 'The Last Night in the Old Home'. In 'The Disinherited', the feckless, impoverished Davina takes the innocent Marianne away from her house on the new estate for a night out. They track down a seedy collection of bored bohemians who have taken over 'Lord Thingummy's' stately home. The language for this incongruous scene is carefully charged, at once elegiac and sinister:

> One door stood open, and light peered in at the glacial sheeted outlines of furniture and a chandelier that hung in a bag like a cheese and glittered inside the muslin. A chill came from the hearthstones: the house was masterless. Alnog a pathway of drugget over the marble, at a quick muffled shuffle as though conducting a funeral secretly, the revellers passed down the hall to a door at the far end. They shot

through with a rush, each unwilling to be the last, and shut the door defiantly on the echoing house.

> ('The Disinherited', *CJ*)

The relationship between the house and its transient inhabitants—they camp out, lie around, make love, leave some litter—bleakly illustrates the impoverishment of the present. Cutting against that scene is the sinister bungalow ('the papers call it a love nest') which features in the journal of Davina's aunt's chauffeur, from whom Davina is borrowing money in return for favours, and who reveals in his journal that he has murdered his upper-class mistress. Though the chauffeur's soliloquies have to work too melodramatically for an overall sense of tawdry dispossession, the 'terrain' of the story—the stifling bungalow, the soulless estate, the decaying Big House—is brilliantly managed.

In the Irish stories, the 'Big House' is rarely described in its hey-day. Instead there is a struggle to sustain the tradition, involving personal sacrifice (as in 'The Tommy Crans') or a sad stoicism (as in 'Sunday Afternoon'). The castle in 'Her Table Spread' is an absurd futureless place of desperate hopes and wild sallies into the wet bat-haunted night. Only in 'The Happy Autumn Fields' is there a vision of the Big House in all its glory, brimming with a ritualised, traditional family life and of objects which partake of that life.[11]

> There was a look like velvet in the darker parts of the air; sombre window draperies let out gushes of lace; the music on the pianoforte bore tender titles, and the harp though unplayed gleamed in a corner, . . . The towering vases upon the consoles, the albums piled on the tables, the shells and figurines on the flights of brackets, all had, like the alabaster Leaning Tower of Pisa, an equilibrium of their own. Nothing would fall or change.
>
> ('The Happy Autumn Fields', *DL*)

But this, the only idyllic account in the stories of an enduring house, is a lost world, painfully glimpsed in the imagination of a wartime Londoner who is searching for relics in a bombed house. The opposition in this very fine story between a place where 'nothing would fall or change' and the destruction of the war is central to Elizabeth Bowen's use of place.

The eschatology of her desolate locales is quite explicit. An early story, 'The Dancing Mistress', begins with a November sea fog coming up 'over the edge of the cliff, and mounting the plate-glass windows', filling 'the Metropole ballroom with premature twilight'. The girl of the title is jaded, professional, with 'cold eyes in which personality never awakened'. Her only passion is a vindictive spite directed at her clumsiest pupil. The story works because the idea of a lost soul is so firmly expressed by the setting: 'the fog was lifting, but the taxi went slowly through spectral streets like a blind snorting animal.' The empty road house in 'The Disinherited', where Davina's friends fail to show up, with its 'horrid light' and 'ashtrays' sending up 'a cold fume', is hell: 'A glittering Neon sign like wolves' eyes read: OPEN ALL NIGHT, at which thought a dry weariness pervaded the brain.'

It is in the ghost stories, or stories in which the supernatural is just held at bay, that the atmosphere most matters, and her talent for what Sean O'Faolain calls 'compression of suggestion'[12] is most inventively used. Elizabeth Bowen's attraction towards the short story as a 'free zone', a narrative area where fantastical extremes are possible, is most evident in the ghost stories. Kipling and M. R. James have evidently influenced the creation of 'charged' settings (Kipling's 'The House Surgeon' and 'They' come to mind), but *The Turn of the Screw* is important too. Writing of James's *nouvelle*, Elizabeth

Bowen takes its main 'terror-ingredient' to be 'moral dread'. 'I need not point out that it is the stench of evil, not the mere fact of the supernatural, which is the genuine horror of *The Turn of the Screw*.'[13]

Like Henry James, Elizabeth Bowen relies in her ghost stories on accumulative suspense and sharp moments of shock; and she also relies on uncertainty about what is happening, a kind of creeping malaise. These factors are emphasised in her own account of Le Fanu's *Uncle Silas* (itself expanded from a short story), a book which in its Gothic setting, its psychological intensity and its very peculiar tone, had a strong influence on her writing. (The setting is not Irish, but it has all the feeling of 'the hermetic solitude and the autocracy of the great county house'.[14]) Elizabeth Bowen makes a fine analysis of Le Fanu's 'oblique, suggestive art' (both here and in her introduction to *The House by the Churchyard*), and in doing so singles out characteristics all of which can be applied to her own writing: Le Fanu's 'voluptuousness' as a terror-writer, his cunning in playing on the reader's childhood 'helplessness and apprehension', the ambiguity of all the characters (which infects the reader with Maud Ruthyn's 'fatalistic mistrust' of everyone she meets), and the important relationship between outdoor weather and 'psychological weather'. She is also impressed by the claustrophobia of the book, which is the keynote of her own horror stories.

Her interest in *Uncle Silas* centres on Maud Ruthyn's character, whose responses she calls those of a 'highly intelligent, still more highly sensitive, child of twelve'. The novel, she says, is characteristically Irish in its sexlessness and its 'subliminated infantilism'. 'Maud is, by nature, a bride of Death.' This very acute comment on Le Fanu's novel points towards some of her own characters in the short stories: the 'child-wife' of 'The Apple Tree', locked in the nightmare of a schoolfriend's suicide; Pepita, in 'Mysterious Kôr', not properly grown up and consoling herself with a fantasy life; Marianne in 'The Disinherited', rapt in a kind of angelic, ungrown innocence. Elizabeth Bowen's account of Maud Ruthyn's psychological peculiarities explains her own preference for pre-adolescent characters or for girls who have not quite grown up:

> She is an uncertain keyboard, on which some notes sound clearly, deeply and truly, others not at all. There is no question, here, of Victorian censorship, with its suggestive gaps: Maud, on the subject of anything she does feel, is uninhibited, sometimes disconcerting. And equally, in the feeling of people round her we are to take it that, child-like, she misses nothing.[15]

This, of course, has as much bearing on the novels as on the short stories: Portia and Emmeline are called to mind, and it's interesting, in this context, that Elizabeth Bowen has censored the supernatural from her novels.[16] Emmeline is *almost* a 'bride of Death', the house in Paris is *almost* a haunted house.

Even in the short stories, the supernatural is often a psychological suggestion rather than an actuality, and she is always careful to root the possibility in ordinariness. This again is a Jamesian technique:

> We want it clear, goodness knows, but we also want it thick, and we get the thickness in the human consciousness that entertains and records, that amplifies and interprets it . . . Prodigies, when they come straight, come with an effect imperilled; they keep all their character, on the other hand, by looming through some other history—the indispensable history of somebody's *normal* relation to something.[17]

The normality, in the Elizabeth Bowen stories, is often comi-cal. In 'Green Holly' a bored group of experts secluded in war-time secrecy in 'Mopsam Grange' (one of those sinister pseudo-Gothic houses) find their tired relationships livened up by a pair of romantic ghosts. In 'The Cheery Soul', a visitor who's come to sponge on a rich Midlands couple for Christmas (again in a large chilly house) finds the couple mysteriously vanished, and a rude, but definitely spectral, cook in possession. There's a less affable comic note to 'The Inherited Clock', in which the girl who's inherited a 'skeleton' clock can't remember any of the violent episodes in her past which are connected with it.

The playfulness of these stories is not very successful, largely because they necessitate genuine, unmistakeable 'prodigies'. When Elizabeth Bowen moves into the realm of uncertainty, on the lines of *Uncle Silas*, the effects improve greatly. 'Pink May', one of her rare first person narratives, is told by a silly sort of girl whose marriage and love-affair have fallen apart during the war, and who blames it all onto a 'ghost' who is, as it turns out, the girl's suppressed conscience. By far the best of the stories to make play with a 'possible' haunting is 'The Cat Jumps', which bristles with the implied violence for which Elizabeth Bowen admires Le Fanu:

> In so far as *Uncle Silas* uses physical horror, the use is extremely sophisticated: Maud's quick and almost voluptuous reactions to sound, sight, touch and smell make her the perfect reagent. The actual sound of a murder, a messy butchery, has probably never, in any gangster story, been registered as it is here.[18]

In 'The Cat Jumps', Rose Hill, the scene of a Mr Harold Bentley's indescribably horrible murder of his wife, has stayed empty for two years until it's bought by a no-nonsense family, the Harold Wrights, and their three rationally brought-up children. 'They had light, bright, shadowless, thoroughly disinfected minds'; they are uninhibited and up-to-date. They take the *New Statesman*, and read Krafft-Ebing and Havelock Ellis (the story dates from 1934), and plan to 'lay' the Bentleys with no trouble at all. In spite of their busy efforts, though, a peculiar aroma seems to linger round the house, 'a smell of unsavoury habitation, of rich cigarette-smoke, stale in the folds of unaired curtains, of scent spilled on unbrushed carpets, an alcoholic smell.' Their first week-end house-party, with a collection of like-minded guests, isn't as clear-headed an occasion as they had intended. One of the female guests turns out to have an unfortunate passion for the subject of the Rose Hill murder: Muriel knows where in the house each bit of Mrs Bentley was dismembered, and with just what relish Mr Bentley took his time. The weather turns oppressively dank and dark. By the end of the evening, an unnerving dissolution has taken effect on these bright modern personalities:

> On the intelligent sharp-featured faces all round the table something—perhaps simply a clearness— seemed to be lacking, as though these were wax faces for one fatal instant exposed to a furnace. Voices came out from some dark interiority; in each conversational interchange a mutual vote of no confidence was implicit. You would have said that each personality had been attacked by some kind of decomposition.
>
> ('The Cat Jumps', *CJ*)

Bed-time is a moment of horror: to all the women in the house, it seems as though the spirit of Harold Bentley has taken over their husbands. And, indeed, as the story ends on a strained peak, part farce, part nightmare, it looks as if that might well be so. Elizabeth Bowen has perhaps rather too easy fun with the Harold Wrights' up-to-dateness, but no summary can do justice to the nice obliqueness with which the 'terror-ingredients'—the encroaching history of the house, the dissolution of the personalities—are achieved.

The real subject of this farcical horror-story, as that central quotation about 'decomposition' makes plain, is Elizabeth Bowen's characteristic subject: the relative lack of intensity and passion in the inheritors of this horrid place.

Notes

1. Preface to *A Day in the Dark* (1965), p. 7.
2. 'Pictures and Conversations', *PC*, p. 60.
3. Introduction to *The Faber Book of Modern Stories*, ed. Elizabeth Bowen (Faber, 1937), p. 14.
4. Ibid, p. 11.
5. Preface to *Stories by Elizabeth Bowen* (New York, 1959), A, p. 77.
6. Ibid, A, p. 80.
7. Henry James, Preface to *The Aspern Papers*, *The Art of the Novel*; *Critical Prefaces by Henry James*, ed. R. P. Blackmur (New York, Scribners, 1934), p. 172.
8. 'Pictures and Conversations', *PC*, p. 34.
9. Preface to *Stories by Elizabeth Bowen*, A, pp. 78–9.
10. Eg. 'The Cassowary', *Joining Charles*; 'The Cheery Soul', *Demon Lover*; 'The Inherited Clock', *Demon Lover*; 'Green Holly', *Demon Lover*.
11. 'The locale of the Victorian family house in "The Happy Autumn Fields" is, though not stated, to me unshakeably County Cork.' Preface to *A Day in the Dark* (1965), p. 9.
12. Sean O'Faolain, *The Short Story* (Dublin, Mercier Press, 1972), p. 240.
13. An Introduction in *Uncle Silas: A Tale of Bartram-Haugh* by J. S. Le Fanu (London, The Cresset Press, 1947). *Collected Impressions*, p. 16.
14. Ibid, *Collected Impressions*, p. 4.
15. Ibid, *Collected Impressions*, p. 5.
16. Preface to *A Day in the Dark* (1965), p. 9.
17. Henry James, Preface to *The Altar of the Dead and Other Stories*, 1909, *The Art of the Novel*, p. 256.
18. An Introduction in *Uncle Silas*, *Collected Impressions*, p. 17.

JOHN BRAINE

1922–

John Gerard Braine was born in Bradford, Yorkshire, on April 13, 1922. His mother was a librarian, an occupation Braine himself chose in 1940. He was an assistant librarian in Bingley, Yorkshire until 1951—except for a year as a telegraph operator in World War II—and received his ALA from the Leeds School of Librarianship in 1949. Braine went to London in 1951 to make his fortune as a journalist, but could sell only a few articles. When his mother died at the end of the year, Braine returned to Yorkshire, frustrated and depressed. He soon contracted tuberculosis, and spent 1952 and much of 1953 in a sanatorium, where he began to write *Room at the Top*. Published in 1957, the novel was an immediate hit, and a rallying point for young intellectuals. A 1959 film version was equally popular; Braine's 1962 sequel *Life at the Top*, filmed in 1966, somewhat less so. He continued the story of the ambitious Joe Lampton in a television series of the early 1970s, *Man at the Top*.

Braine's subsequent novels have seldom pleased critics, who persist in comparing them with *Room at the Top*. *The Jealous God* (1964) won praise from some, as did *The Queen of a Distant Country* (1972). Braine has also written a biography of J. B. Priestley, published in 1979. In 1976 he was Writer in Residence at Purdue University.

John Braine lives in Surrey with his wife, Helen, whom he married in 1955, shortly after completing *Room at the Top*. They have four children.

General

When *Room at the Top* appeared five years ago, John Braine, like the unfortunate Colin Wilson just before him, was given the full treatment. The talent-spotters spotted him, the trend-mongers classified him and eventually, by a stroke of good fortune, an intelligent director got hold of the book and transformed it into an adult film, using a French actress to do justice to a classic French theme.

That was in 1957, when the craze for literary fashions was acute. And Braine was, distinctly, on the right side—not of the angels but angries. His hero was one of the new meritocracy. It was easier to identify with him than with the reigning idols: he was not as disconcertingly funny as Lucky Jim, nor as passionately verbal as Jimmy Porter. Joe Lampton was a grimmer, more single-minded, less imaginative figure. His sole concern was success, and success meant the gratification of his appetites—for things, for cash, for women. Amis's and Osborne's heroes were sympathetically bad gamblers, liable to throw the whole game for some idiosyncratic gesture.

Joe Lampton played his cards remorselessly close to his chest. And won every hand. If the happy endings of *Lucky Jim* and *Look Back in Anger* were out of tune with everything which went before them, that of *Room at the Top* was inevitable. When it came to the crunch, Our Joe could do no wrong. The book was convincing because Braine himself seemed convinced. He had created a moral crook who had the courage of his crookedness. And although, like a thriller writer, he often seemed to congratulate his hero on his ruthlessness, as if it were somehow endearing to be a swine—well, that was in character. The whole attempt to cross *Le Diable au Corps* with *The Road to Wigan Pier* was as ambitious as Joe Lampton himself. A touch of megalomania was in order.

It was also right for the time at which it appeared, the day of the shopping locusts. 'I wanted an Aston-Martin,' Joe announces early in the book, 'I wanted a three-guinea linen shirt, I wanted a girl with a Riviera suntan.' What with top people reading *The Times* on every billboard, the title of Braine's novel became a campaign slogan like 'You've never had it so good.' The plot was a kind of Tory fairy tale. And the transformation scene took place, significantly, in the local Conservative Club.

'This the first time you've been to this club?'

'This or any Conservative club,' I said. 'My father'd turn in his grave if he could see me.'

'So would mine,' he said, and winked. 'So would mine, lad. But we're not bound by our fathers.'

I looked at him coldly. . . .

That mixture of coy old-chappery and rather chill self-righteousness was typical of the novel. Yet it explains some of its appeal. Joe passionately lusts after riches and success ('lust' is a word Braine uses continually and in an oddly old-fashioned, disapproving way), but he hates himself for doing so. And this split in his feelings can produce a corresponding tension in the writing. There is, at his best, a loving but slightly touchy accuracy in Braine's descriptions of the paraphernalia of High Life, as though he were trying to extricate himself from his moral dilemma by his skill as a writer.

It was this quirky, more artistic impulse which controlled his second novel, *The Vodi*. Its hero was a failure, chronically tubercular and spiritless, who excused his weakness by paranoid fantasies about evil little Vodi who exist simply to do dirt on the harmless. It was a more complex, imaginative work than *Room at the Top*. In it Braine risked allusiveness, swerved a little from the obvious story-line, sorted out his effects with some subtlety and, above all, took as his theme a flop confirmed in his floppiness. Despite the last, unconvincing couple of pages, Dick Corvey doesn't get the girl he wants. Unfortunately, the book, like its hero, was a relative failure. Braine had been pigeon-holed. In his novels, local boys were not supposed to make bad—even if, in the process, the author had taken a step forward as a writer. And perhaps Braine thought the same way: *The Vodi* lacked the absorbed assurance of his first novel.

He has tried to recoup with *Life at the Top*, a book with few artistic pretensions and a heavy dose of the mixture as before: success and consumer goods. Yet, in theory, *Life at the Top* is far more of a moral tale than the earlier books. . . .

The mechanical plot would scarcely matter if there were life and substance elsewhere. But there isn't. Instead of firmly created characters, like Alice Aisgill or Dick Corvey's father, there are generalized types. Even at his best, Braine has rarely been at ease with dialogue; his people always talked self-consciously, in inverted commas. Now they chatter indistinguishably. It is as if Joe, having put Dufton behind him once and for all, had woken to find himself in a ghost town. And the writing has become as vague and blank as the people. In his first book Braine fixed that Conservative Club vividly in a sentence. But here it has become a drawn-out, rather maudlin fantasy of a 'green and buff country' from which Joe, club member and Tory town councillor, will never escape. The buoyancy and sharp-eyed precision of the young man on the make have gone. In their place oozes a drunken self-pity, occasionally lapsing into violence: poor little *nouveau riche* boy. . . .

It strikes me that it is not the situation but the morality which is false. Braine's heroes have always been as obsessively preoccupied with trademarks as is Fleming's James Bond. The books bristle with brand names of drinks, food, furniture, cars and cosmetics. In *Room at the Top* the roll-call of things Joe wanted was positively fierce. In *The Vodi* it was nostalgic, almost tender. But in *Life at the Top* these names and things are the only form of discrimination. You know that the boyfriend of Joe's future mistress doesn't stand a chance since he drives a Ford Popular. It is as though everything and everyone wore a tag on which was meticulously detailed price, horsepower and performance. At times, it reads less like a novel than a fictionalized consumers' report.

. . . The spectacle of John Braine indulging his weaknesses on a pot-boiler like *Life at the Top* is no less poignant than that of Joe Lampton contemplating, in a trance of gratified boredom, his Zephyr, his Maple's suite, his crammed cocktail cabinet, his children, his wife—in that order.—A. ALVAREZ, "Braine at the Top," NS, Oct. 5, 1962, p. 458

Mr. Braine is not a peculiarly gifted writer. He has many virtues, he is a good competent novelist, he shows an engaging urge toward honesty of vision, he has a clear and workmanlike style; but he does not display the quality of understanding, either of individual motivations, or the way the social world is put together, or of the nature of creative language that would place him in any first class. He is a good craftsman, among many equals. What we have to ask is why *Room at the Top* should have enjoyed such signal success; and whether its sequel is likely to do the same.

In the first place, the *theme* of *Room at the Top* was exactly right for its moment—bestsellerwise, that is to say. England is full of Joe Lamptons, Jimmy Porters, Lucky Jims. "Angry young men" is not really the best name for them or for their creators: they are uprooted young men, they are lost, before they are angry. The Welfare State now confers what used to be "a gentleman's education" upon all of the sons and daughters of the poorer classes who show more intelligence than quite a dimmish average—not, as formerly, only upon the most brilliant. These young people emerge into the world with moderate learning, moderate intelligence and immoderate ambition. What they need, in addition, to satisfy the last is, of course, *connections*. Children of the richer classes, no brighter or better educated, have uncles, wealthy schoolfriends, father's business pals. They get ahead.

The Lamptons, on the other hand, have to *make* their connections; and that is one of the first things that John Braine's books are about. They are the narrative equivalents of the current sociological treatises upon "the meritocracy" or "organization man." This is timely. It is also timely that they appear (though it *is* only an appearance) to cut through one of the standard English hypocrisies—the hypocrisy over money. Before the war no English novelist ever did anything so vulgar as to mention a sum of pounds shillings and pence. He took refuge in evasions of the type of "a very large sum," "of moderate means," "a miserable pittance." Now we know that Joe's house cost £4,500 and that the inventory of its contents amounted to £2,700. And, most important of all, Braine states quite clearly Lampton's belief—which is, to every appearance, his own—that money and efficient plumbing and motorcars are good in their own right, quite irrespective of the quality of mind and sensitivity of experience that one brought to them. Quite a large factor in Joe's determination to leave his new mistress is the antiquity of her geyser and dilapidation of her bath. His whole attitude, in fact, toward the appurtenances for which he sacrifices his love and freedom is that naïve one of the typical poor, who always prefer to give £40 for a new and shoddy plywood chest-of-drawers, rather than £20 for a piece of solid Georgian mahogany.

The whole dynamic of the books indeed rests upon two "truths" and their opposition—which we may call "matinee truths" and "matinee false opposition," because they are just the sort of thing that keeps the phony drama alive. One, that it really is, actually, better to be rich than poor. Two, that one can pay too big a price for it. These revelations absolutely knock them in the teacupped aisles. The impact is clinched by scare after scare that is purest cliché—the stern forbidding father-figure (Mr. Brown) who offers you money to leave his daughter alone, then slaps you on the back when you refuse to take it—unsurprise after unsurprise that keeps the whole house hushed. A million copies sold.

One must add, for it largely undermines the whole "social-theory" structure of the two books, that Mr. Braine has a remarkably unreal and immature conception of what really constitutes "the top." Business-success in a small northern town, apparently. Or, if one likes, simply business-success: the bigger your salary, the more "top" you have got. But, even on the most materialistic lines, there are other and "better" tops than that. There is power as well as money, and the two don't anywhere near wholly overlap. There are the professions, which in the Braine world appear simply not to exist. A bishop, we must suppose, or a Vice Chancellor or a Harley Street surgeon, are also at the top. And, even financially, there is better money than business-money. There is money from inheritance and land. (I speak, naturally, in terms not my own. And I have also no space in which to argue how far the Braine and Lampton views of the world are to be identified or not.)

But, when all the easy demolition is done, there still remains something solid and human at the core. It may not be very distinguished, but at least it is felt and real. The plentiful "strong" sex passages are not so much created as day-dreamt, but at least they are roughly the right dreams and remind one, in more ways than in their setting, of the early D. H. Lawrence—in both cases, too, the forceful and compulsive nature of the man-woman relationships is founded on a deep basis of pure prudery (see the key scene in *Room at the Top* when Joe learns that Alice once posed nude). The social morality may be naïve and crude, but at least it is memorably presented and comes down on the right side. And *Room at the Top* was also a first novel, with all and more than all the freshness that implies. It was a bright and early morning book, and its author was obviously a very nice young man.

Now, it is noon and the dew is off. *Life at the Top* is very much "the mixture as before," perhaps a little better, perhaps a little worse. But, necessarily, it is not news. That is quite enough about Joe Lampton now.—HILARY CORKE, "Getting to the Bottom of the Top," NR, Nov. 3, 1962, pp. 23–24

Works

Room at the Top, the first novel of a young English writer named John Braine, is a brilliantly sustained tragi-comedy. Most first novels are hot-faced attempts to kick off the clodhoppers of adolescence, which is the sort of struggle best finished within the bosom of the family. But Mr. Braine already knows just how much prodding the priceless luck of his own creativity can take. There is no rheumy poetic prose in his book. There is very little sound from the ropes and pulleys that get characters into rooms, seated, their knees crossed, and their cigarettes lit. His flashbacks and descriptions do not intrude like misplaced whales. Mr. Braine is also at home with a knowledge that most novelists never even dream of—the indispensable lubricating powers of humor. His subject matter—a young, lowborn English accountant, Joe Lampton, who gains the world and loses his soul—is squarely in the line of the great English social novels. Although Mr. Braine deals largely with his own generation, he unfailingly regards it with a buoyant detachment that would be remarkable in a writer three times his age. Where Dickens, for one, often tended, because of personal difficulties, to view the social struggles around him with a myopic and nervous sentimentality, Mr. Braine, like E. M. Forster, calmly dons corrective bifocals on the first page and never takes them off. He is fully aware that the slow, tangled process of a lower class pushing upward, like bubbles in a swamp, is in reality a series of shamelessly materialistic ma-

neuvers. At the same time, he is aware that all oneupmanship, no matter how cruel, is inevitably funny and, as a result, deserving of mercy. When the angles of his vision are miraculously brought together in the last chapter, the effect is of classical tragedy, inside out: Joe Lampton, whose only nobility is honesty, is destroyed by self-knowledge.—WHITNEY BALLIETT, "The Successful Zombie and the Grade Two Girl," NY, Nov. 2, 1957, p. 186

John Braine has been called one of England's angry young men, but *Room at the Top* is not an angry book. Rather it is a novel of recognition—that the cramping system of class distinction in England has had it, and can, will and must be beaten by such as Joe Lampton. It is a sardonic work by a writer whose hero knows the price of everything. The novel is saturated with prices—the price of furnishings, clothes, automobiles and girls. Joe is always measuring everything and everybody with whom he comes in contact—the height, muscle and finances of his rivals, the horsepower of cars, the dimension of houses and rooms, the youth of a woman's bosom, and particularly the social grades of people—which are actually worked out from grade one down to grade twelve. It is a novel of sadness and regret that a young man should be forced to such extremes of maneuvering in order to rise out of his class. Another Yorkshire writer, Eric Knight, had his hero, Sam Small, literally take flight. There are no flights in *Room at the Top*. Joe Lampton crowds and elbows his way, and finally arrives after an agonizing expense of spirit to become, as he brutally calls himself, a Successful Zombie.

Room at the Top is a novel by an honest writer who concedes Joe Lampton nothing and still makes us want to put an arm around his shoulder and say to him: "Nobody blames you." And in the book Joe Lampton replies: "Oh my God, that's the trouble."—ALAN HARRINGTON, "A Question of Price," *Nation*, Dec. 7, 1957, p. 439

Room at the Top has its faults. There is an implausible manufacturer father, a prop-cupboard blunt, crude money-maker who respects blunt, crude money-makers, and who, when he finds Joe has got Susan with child, 'tests' his character and then ushers him into the opulent world of the Top. Susan, I personally find not so much implausible as unbearable. Perhaps such a portrait of a shallow, arch, spoilt little sugar mouse is accurate. Yet I find it difficult to believe that even Joe, with his steel-tipped ambition, but who is neither stupid nor illiterate, could stomach a girl who chirps like a sexy tom-tit: "Oo, *wicked!* Susan tingle. Susan tingle up and down. Do it again." There are occasions, too, when the writing side-slips into woman's magazine serialese—"The pillow smelled faintly of lavender; it reminded me of something. It was her scent, cool as clean linen, friendly as beer"—and evocative and fresh though much of his description is, it is tinged with a copywriter's gushy cleverness. The book's most distinctive flavour, both its strength and weakness, is its sensuality, a voluptuous sensitivity to colours, shapes, textures—and price-tabs. (Bernard Wall did a witty parody in *The Twentieth Century* of a young man checking on his mistress's social status by doing a quick mental inventory of the value of her bedroom contents.) Momentarily this slithers into a rather curious new kind of romantic slushiness; but most of the time his eye maintains a cool accuracy and, rather in the manner of the short stories in the *New Yorker*, Braine knows precisely how to pinpoint a particular salary level by the use of the correct brand-name (Coty, Riley Pathfinder, Earl Grey, Gold Rolex Oyster), a trick not much employed by British writers. *Room at the Top* is not a novel adventure story, for Joe Lamptons have been purposefully bed-hopping to success ever since society arranged itself in layers. But few books have revealed so explicitly the actual shape and shimmer of the fantasy-life longings of a Joe Lampton, and certainly no one until John Braine had described the exact kind of urges operating within the postwar specimen. Looking back at Jim Dixon you realise that, in this respect, you know nothing of his inner life, that the Wain men are personifications of a set of circumstances, and Jimmy Porter of course hates and rejects the very things that Joe so obsessively wants.

"You're the most un-neurotic person I know," Alice tells him, and it is true that he has a single-mindedness, a beautifully brutal simplicity of purpose, that is not a characteristic of the heroes of other contemporary novels. Yet even Joe retains a small buried kernel of dissentience. Although he feels a complacent contempt for the young men of the class he has deserted (he watches one boarding a bus: ". . . navy-blue overcoat, gloves and scarf . . . solid mass of brilliantined hair and mass-produced face, bony, awkward, mousy, the face behind the request on Forces Favourites, the face enjoying itself at Blackpool with an open-necked shirt spread out over its jacket, the face which Wilfred Pickles might love but which depressed me intensely—Len or Sid or Cliff or Ron. . . .") he has not entirely lost his conscience about them. He explains: "I'm like a brand-new Cadillac in a poor industrial area, insulated by steel and glass and air-conditioning from the people outside, from the rain and the cold and the shivering ailing bodies. I don't wish to be like the people outside, I don't even wish that I had some weakness, some foolishness to immobilise me among the envious coolie faces, to let in the rain and the smell of defeat. *But I sometimes wish that I wished it.*" (My italics.)

Despite his ruthlessness, his vulgarity and his calculated lechery (although he remarks "I may be obsessed by sex but there are worse things to be obsessed by", he isn't really obsessed by it—he uses it) Joe is not an unsympathetic character. He is human, and warm impulses flicker like summer lightning through his success campaign. And the part of him that he has deliberately stifled is still sufficiently alive for him to acknowledge to himself, in the shock of Alice's death, that he is a cheapskate and that what he wants is comparatively not worth a farthing.

John Braine once told me what set the plot of *Room at the Top* in motion. "I saw a man sitting in a big shiny car. He'd driven up to the edge of some waste ground, near some houses and factories, and was just sitting there looking across at them. It seemed to me there must have been a lot that led up to that moment."—KENNETH ALLSOP, "The Neutralists," *The Angry Decade*, 1958, pp. 88–90

We have grown accustomed to think of America as the country of the one-book writer, instant reputations and critical hyperbole, but the truth is that in recent years there's been at least as much literary mischief done in London. Inflationary show-biz rise and falls (yesterday Ivor Novello, today Arnold Wesker) have always been with us, but, traditionally, lit. crit. was supposed to be less windy, more circumspect. It's not so. The current vogue, unnecessarily cruel, seems to be to overpraise a first book to the point of blurbiness, retire to reflect, and then do a self-redeeming carve-up on the man if he's fool enough to risk another.

So one day Colin Wilson went into the British Museum, saw everything, and behold it was very good. And he spake unto Gollancz face to face, as a man speaketh to his friend; and there came forth many editions. And another day John Braine came down from the mountain-top and all of Fleet Street rose up and worshipped, every man at his purple typewriter. And

none saw or suspected that Theodore Dreiser and many, many more had already staked claim to the same mountain. Now both these latter-day prophets have been sent out to wander in the wilderness. They shall commit *Daily Express* reviews, suffer surtax, but they shall not be praised again by those who anointed them in the first place.

There never was any question of John Braine being an original writer. *Room at the Top* was a carbon cousin of the traditional American immigrant novel. Ambitious boy embarrassed by parents' bad accent quits tenement for golden city, marries boss's daughter, discovers too late . . . money isn't everything. The virtues of the novel did not rest with its intelligence or style, but in the writer's assurance that it had not been done before. The novel, rather old-fashioned, nevertheless had drive, power. It was very readable. Published in 1957, it was also timely—a not unimportant consideration.

In *Life at the Top*, Braine continues with Joe Lampton's argosy. With a hop, skip and a jump, the author has graduated from the poor-boy-makes-good-at-a-price story to a sort of dubbed version of a more contemporary American morality tale, the novel of suburban disenchantment. As such, unfortunately, it is more reminiscent of Sloan Wilson than, say, Richard Yates. Like John O'Hara, the master of this genre, Braine is obsessed by brand names, detailed lists of possessions acquired by our hero on his ride to empty success, and seemingly forthright sex. (Braine and O'Hara heroes, future scholars please note, are generally the *only* horny chaps in town, they are very big on love in the afternoon, the devils, and always find the girls breathlessly grateful. 'It's never been like this for me before.' 'A man with some real zing in him at last.' Etc. etc. etc.) In fact, it has occurred to me that *Life at the Top* could be more profitably reviewed by a sociologist or, come to think of it, Leslie Adrian. He could draw up a comparative list of salaries, status-symbols, Johnnie Walker intake, and the availability of mortgages and adulteresses, in the suburbias of O'Hara and Braine. This, I suppose, would give us a kind of opportunist's *Which?*

Life at the Top picks up Joe ten years later. He is uneasy with his rich-bitch wife, two cars, a house that contains all mod. cons., and in-laws who are for ever putting him down, but, on the credit side, he adores the younger of his two children, a girl. Returning home from London early one day he discovers his wife, Susan, in bed with a top person, who, it turns out, is the real father of the child Joe loves so much. . . . Outside, it's raining. Joe leaves Susan for a mature left-wing lady journalist, has his fling, then returns because the children need him—and it's the right thing to do. This, I admit, is putting it very baldly, but the architecture of Braine's melodramatic plot is badly exposed, the beams creak so much from over-use, that it is only the most naïve book-club reader who will not always be at least one step and a chocolate ahead of the writer.

The most serious failure in the novel is Joe Lampton. He's never a character—he's an attitude, a cipher. Surely nobody's psyche—top, bottom, or middle—is compounded entirely of class problems. It's too simple, isn't it? Braine may have chosen to write about a straw man, but I'd like some assurance that, if called upon, he could fill a character with flesh and blood, as Sillitoe does. The dialogue in the book is never more than plausible. If she says that, he might, conceivably, say this. It works. So does automation. The prose throughout is clean, but has no distinctive tang. Open at any page of a new novel by, say, Bellow, Amis or Muriel Spark, and you immediately know who wrote it. It's not so with Braine. The best that can be said of his book is that it's very readable, it's fast and somewhat sexy. Braine also supplies an abundance of realistic documentary detail. That, however, is the stuff we praise films for. We expect it from a serious novelist. Like correct grammar.—MORDECAI RICHLER, "Tougher at the Bottom," *Spec*, Oct. 19, 1962, p. 602

Room at the Top was taken by many to be a straight account of achieved ambition. Young man puts boss's daughter in family way and then has it made. But there was much more to the book than that—there was guilt, betrayal of love for the sake of hypergamy (a word much bandied by critics in the fifties: it means bedding and perhaps wedding a woman of superior class to oneself), the sense that the price of success can be too high and that this, alas, is usually only discovered when success is attained.

The hero of *The Crying Game*, young Frank Batcombe, knows all about the roots of human guilt, since, like Mr. Braine himself, he is a Catholic. Indeed, many of his fellow-denizens of swinging London are Catholics, and none of your once-fashionable Greene-Waugh-type converts, either; thus, the object of Frank's hypergamous aspiration, though as permissive as any mini-agnostic dollybird, is of an old recusant family that told Henry VIII to go and get stuffed. Everybody knows the right but follows the wrong, meaning promiscuous bed-hopping. The right is reserved for their politics. . . .

There is a certain engaging innocence about the zest with which Frank engages permissive London. One can only hope that Mr. Braine has achieved an act of astonishing empathy here, and that the delighted full reporting of booze and fornication is not expected to elicit the reader's sympathy. For it all becomes very boring (though it might not be so to Braine's provincial readers) and one wants the parties to end and the story to develop. But there is virtually no story.

The sensuality is matched by the fashionable spirit of reaction that, as one knows from his television and journalistic dicta, Mr. Braine has bidden supervene, with no decent liberal intermission on his former radicalism. There is contempt for the Progs, or progressives, and an oft-repeated slogan "Down with Oxfam!" Frank doesn't repent of his ultra-conservatism (in which even Pope John is a raving Prog). And his curious ability and that of his friends to reconcile nightly fornication with pre-ecumenical orthodoxy goes unrebuked by any fictional nemesis.

A strange book altogether and a very disappointing one. Occasionally one is reminded that Mr. Braine can write well when he wants to. Some of the descriptions of London are tautly lyrical. Sometimes a young man's gusto for metropolitan life finds words and rhythms that lift the heart. Occasionally Mr. Braine shocks in the Greene way—Frank washing down the "meaty" aftertaste of the eucharist with draft Guinness, the terse scene in which a reefer-smoking queer is beaten up. But the hedonism is too often as self-conscious as the papistry, and the narrative style gives off the stale apple smell of old popular magazines. Mr. Braine can do better than this: I hope he knows it.—ANTHONY BURGESS, "At Home in London," *NYTBR*, Oct. 27, 1968, pp. 5, 70

I was lucky enough to get an advance copy of Mr Braine's *Writing a Novel* ('. . . not a treatise . . . but a practical manual'), and with business so slack at the Catford shop where I sell personal products that I was wandering around in a daze not knowing whether to scratch my watch or wind my bum, I thought I'd try my hand at it. I mean, at writing a novel. Agewise I was jake: 'A first novel shouldn't be written much before the age of 30.' And, before I even started, I seemed to fit Mr Braine's definition of a writer: 'A writer is a person who writes, a writer is a person who counts words'—which is exactly what I do every time I send a cable to the warehouse.

When I read, 'You mustn't even think about acceptance or rejection, but only about writing a novel which will satisfy yourself,' I got this idea of writing an experimental novel in the third person. I turn the page and Mr Braine says, 'it's absolutely imperative that you put out of your mind any notion of experiment'. The reason, apparently (but not to me: I like smut and confusion in lower case letters) was 'brutally simple: experimental novels aren't accepted'. Out the window goes *The J. G. Ballard of Peckham Rye* and *Naked Wimpy*, and a hundred pages later I scrapped my third person idea when I came across the teacher's nag, 'I strongly recommend that your first novel should be in the first person'.

Then I was all set. My first person novel was about a year ('A year should be your limit') in the life of a personal products salesman ('Always write from experience. Your experience is absolutely unique') who's kind of strung out and not getting any flashes ('A straightforward passage in time with no flashbacks is best') and doesn't give a fish's tit whether he lives or dies ('Never put down your thoughts about life and death and time in the novel'). He's got this chick. She knows what it means to be a woman. Her brain's all tangled up in her fallopian tubes and vice-versa ('it makes sense to do anything that you can to set your novel apart'), the gizmo that gives it the title ('I needn't stress the importance of a good title'), *Womb at the Top*.

After that I was off like a bride's nightdress. I got my characters' names ('Go through the gazetteer, preferably the *Times Gazetteer of the World*, and pick out 30 or so plausible-sounding names') and started in writing three times a week ('three two-hourly sessions a week are quite enough'), just scratching away like mad ('Don't stop writing in order to think'), remembering that 'brand names should be capitalised' and stopping every now and then to 'check the names of fictitious firms against the directories like Kelly's *Manufacturers and Merchants Directory*,' which wasn't easy since the public library refused to let me take it home, meaning a 5p bus-ride every time I invented a company. That was awful. I used to sit on the top deck wondering if the man who wrote 'No person, no place, no object, no event is dull or boring or commonplace' could ever have taken a bus ride through Catford.

Following the rules very carefully—after all, Mr Braine promised that his 'book's function is to instruct you how to write a novel which will be published'—I put a lot of stuff in about the personal products centre ('devote at least a third of your space to your characters at work'). I never forgot that 'one setting you should be careful about is the bedroom,' and painstakingly 'avoided . . . too explicit a description of the sexual act'. But I think I went wrong there, because Mr Braine says the sexual act 'is much the same for everybody, unless they're double-jointed and extremely inventive' (which shows how little he knows about the personal products market) and my salesman and his chick were both or why else would I write about them?

It was a headache, but I finished the damned thing late one night, writing *The End* after Chapter 19 and then I flicked through *Writing a Novel* one last time to find (oh crap, I thought) staring out at me, 'You must have at least 20 chapters'. I dashed off another one. It was fairly bad writing, but my novel was the right size and I was beginning to agree with Mr Braine's saying, 'It's incredibly stupid to reduce your chances of publication simply to play the role of dedicated artist.'

> As soon as you've finished the novel, give yourself one working week off, then spend the next three weeks planning your second novel.

I sat back and read *Enemies of Promise* and several other titles recommended in Mr Braine's book, a dreadful one by Lionel

Trilling, a preposterous one by Graham Greene about a miracle in Clapham, and another one by the Russian martyr and millionaire whose picture was in the papers a few weeks ago when he went to live in Switzerland and open a bank account.

You know the rest of the story. *Womb* was a smash, the film made me as rich as Tom Metfield in *The Queen of a Distant Country* and people say it put Linda Lovelace on the map. I've quit my job in Catford and now live in a thatched cottage in Blackheath where I am, like Mr Braine, a full-time writer and limited company. I'm currently writing a book about

Writing a Book and plan to gang up with my publisher and advertise it as a manual for hopeful scribblers in the provinces. Mr Braine is right:

> success isn't an empty shell, it's sweet and succulent
> all the way through. Apart from the money, there is
> the satisfaction of having your name mean some-
> thing.

I just wish I was as certain as Mr Braine that my name means what I think it does.—PAUL THEROUX, "Personal Products," *NS*, May 3, 1974, pp. 631–32

ROBERT BRIDGES

1844–1930

Robert Seymour Bridges was born on October 23, 1844, in Walmer, Kent. He attended Corpus Christi College, Oxford, where he befriended Balliol student Gerard Manley Hopkins. After graduating, Bridges wandered about Europe until 1871, when he began to study medicine at St. Bartholomew's Hospital in London. Having written poetry in secret for years, Bridges surprised his friends by publishing a collection in 1873—which he subsequently rounded up and destroyed, as he would later destroy most of his personal papers and letters.

From 1875 to 1882, Bridges was a hospital physician in London, shouldering a massive workload and writing several books of sonnets, published anonymously. After a bout with pneumonia in 1882, he retired to Yattendon in Berkshire. In 1884 he married his next-door neighbor, Monica Waterhouse, with whom he would have three children. For the next twenty years, Bridges worked on numerous verse dramas, an influential critical essay on Milton, and his poetry. He often experimented with exotic meters, notably the "stress prosody" he had developed with Hopkins. In 1907 he moved to Oxford, where he invented new phonetic spellings for English. This endeavor led him to co-found the Society for Pure English, which he led until his death.

In 1913, Bridges succeeded the infamous Alfred Austin as Poet Laureate. He soon became known as "the silent Laureate" for the infrequency of his official poems. He edited a popular anthology of wartime uplift, *The Spirit of Man*, in 1916, and the first collection of poems by Hopkins in 1918. At the end of World War I, Bridges led a controversial movement to resume relations between English and German universities. The death of his daughter Margaret in 1926 was the sad inspiration for what is often considered his masterpiece, the long philosophical poem *The Testament of Beauty*, published in 1929. Bridges died in Oxford on April 21 of the following year.

Personal

Of his frankness and incisiveness, qualities in which I never met his equal, many stories were told. He was the only man I ever met who seemed to say exactly what came into his mind the moment it came into his mind. His conversation was like that of Dr. Johnson thinking aloud—if one adds to that great man the gift of imagination and critical subtlety, as well as often essential justice. The effect was heightened by a slight stutter, not enough to impede what he said, but enough to give a sudden rushing as of wings to its emphatic conclusion. 'I *detested* his philosophy; his religion I *despised*: and I didn't think much of his poetry. *But*—he was a very nice fellow.' This placed the poet in question and made everything satisfactorily clear. 'Some people say he's a Jew. But I say—he's only a Welshman.'

No one ever minded in the least what Mr. Nowell Smith has styled 'his childlike delight in his own powers and special advantages, his boyish love of brusque personal encounters'. On the contrary, incidents when he had clubbed some unwary friend were gleefully told over Oxford, and nearly always by the victim himself first. I never met any one to whom his frankness was not a cause of added zest in his company.

He himself was roughly treated in 1920, when he was responsible for a letter which he got signed by as many prominent members of the academic world as possible, and sent to the heads of German universities, expressing a wish that intellectual co-operation might be resumed. *The Times* handled him with extraordinary severity, in repeated magisterial castigations which now make very amusing reading.

Bridges's sense of decency makes him willing to try to help forward better relations with a people whose responsibility for the drawn-out tragedy of the War he felt deeply. But those who jumped to the belief that he had gone wickedly radical and pacifist were mistaken. In the General Strike, 1926, the Archbishop of Canterbury issued a far from revolutionary appeal for the restoration of peaceful discussion. Yet, as the *Letters of George Gordon* (published 1943) have reminded us, even this temperate expression of desire struck Oxford (and other places) as an outrage. I was asked to get signatures to the manifesto and, aware that on Boar's Hill I was *in partibus infidelium*, set out doggedly to tour my very sticky parish. Its two stickiest inhabitants proved to be two celebrated poets. 'No', was all that Bridges would say (and·he said it often). 'The old ship's—going down! And I'm—going down—with it!' 'Ah!' said G. N. Clark of Oriel when I told of my experiences. 'He's thinking of the fellows on the quarterdeck! Not the poor devils down in the engine-room!'

As true conservatism should, Bridges's conservatism ranged over the past as well as the present. He met Gilbert Murray shortly after a book had been published which pleased and impressed him. 'You ought to read it, Murray! It's a grand book. It says—just what *I've* always said about the French Revolution.' 'What is that?' 'Why, that it was all—damned nonsense.' 'In what way damned nonsense?' 'Why, all a put-up job! You read the book and you'll see!' Which perhaps did not mean much more than that Bridges regarded the French Revolution as, quite definitely, a bad thing.

In 1924 I became his neighbour, and presently a very near neighbour. Bridges would appear in my study, which was outside the house; drop into a low chair, talk for a few minutes, and then go. His absorbing interest was words, their origin and shades of meaning. He possessed of course all of Murray's lordly *Oxford English Dictionary*, but not the handy one-volume edition, which was all I had. This he would borrow therefore, to find the commonest and most current usage of some word. 'You were out when I called yesterday,' he told me once. 'When did you call?' He stated the time. 'I was in,' I said. 'No, you weren't. I came into your study and you were out. And' (his voice rose reprovingly) 'you've been messing your books about again! Your *Dictionary* wasn't in the right place and I had to hunt for it. See that it is kept where it should be!'

Sometimes I had a book which he wanted to read—perhaps a book which he suspected I did not intend him to read. He would appear in our drawing-room, which had a long low window: demand the book, and, throwing himself down in a chair which had runners, propel himself swiftly up to the window, and sit there, hat shading his eyes and feet flung up to the sill, reading until he finished, when he would wander out again. He read in this fashion my *Other Side of the Medal*, a book which I suppressed from his notice as unlikely to give him much joy. But he heard of it somehow or other and insisted on my digging it out.

The value of his service to our tongue, in his S.P.E. tracts, has never been adequately recognized. Yet this interest sometimes gave rise to individuality which found trifling expression. A story is told of his being asked by a group of reformers to lunch with them, and to address them afterwards. Bridges told them that he had come to an important decision. They had no doubt often wondered whether *neither* should be pronounced *neether* or *nyther*. After long thought he had come to announce that the word should be rejected altogether, for a new brief form, *nith*.

One day he met Gilbert Murray and H. A. L. Fisher in the Broad, outside Blackwell's. They chatted a while, and Bridges asked Fisher what he thought of a certain Victorian poet. 'I don't much care for him', Fisher replied. 'He uses such low mean words—words like *cab* and *tram*.' Bridges considered this carefully. '*Cab?*' he remarked at last. 'A *bad* word! But *tram?* A *beautiful* word!' . . .

'He was not, I think,' writes Oliver Elton, 'a man to argue with.' Perhaps not. But you got on famously if you ventured curtly to disagree with him, he took this generously. Once, on my way across the fields to my lecture in Oxford, having time to spare I called for a few minutes of conversation. He was in one of his extremely infrequent moods of depression, and begged me to stay. I stayed (and my class later forgave me), and we talked all morning. Yet all I remember is three trivial matters. As he sat there disconsolately, sometimes reaching forward to throw another log on the fire (his fires were always wood fires), he began to praise, as I thought excessively, a lyric

by a living writer. I made no comment, and he suddenly flashed at me, 'It's better than Andrew Marvell, anyway!' (he knew my delight in Marvell). I neither agreed nor disagreed, but continued our general conversation, across which from time to time the same challenge was flung, 'It's better than Marvell!' Finally Bridges paused, looked at me hard, and asked, 'Don't you think so?' 'No, I do *not*.' Immediately the talk passed into smooth water, and the whole morning remains as a sunny ecperience.

The second of the three things I remember was merely personal. In 1915 I had sent him a book of mine which he never acknowledged. Now, ten years later, he growled irrelevantly, 'I didn't like that book you sent me!' I had known this all along, of course; and, though he did not name the book, understood perfectly that he was plucking out this tiny thorn of memory which had been vexing him. We laughed simultaneously, and that was that. We made no further reference to it.

The third matter was the prose work which Coventry Patmore considered his greatest work, destroyed because Hopkins told him, 'That's telling secrets!' Bridges too read it in manuscript and discussed it with Hopkins. They both thought it worthless and in bad taste, as Rabindranath Tagore considered Bengali Vaishnava erotic mystical verse. 'Hopkins did not want to hurt Patmore's feelings, so all he said was, "That's telling secrets!" ' . . .

Life he regarded as far too precious to waste in being bored, by men or by books. One day I found on his table a verse play which the author, a distinguished poet of my own generation, had just sent him. I showed some interest, and when I left I borrowed it. I was well on my way to the gate when the door opened, and Bridges, anxiety in every feature, called after me. 'I shouldn't read *much* of that if I were you, or you'll become—a most *frightful* bore!'—EDWARD THOMPSON, *Robert Bridges 1844–1930*, 1944, pp. 92–96

It was difficult to believe, on meeting Mr Bridges, so easily did he breathe our biting modern air, that he was born in the first decade of the reign of Queen Victoria, and learned his letters in the Laureateship of Wordsworth. He was so frankly and vitally there before you, with such challenge in voice and eye, and in the whole splendid length of him, shaggy-crowned, such lounging and half-arrogant power. Even that atmosphere which lay about him as of some ampler, more leisured, and now vanished age, hardly prepared one for the discovery that he had been familiar as a child with the sight of the Great Duke (a valued memory), and had watched, as a boy of ten, from a Walmer garden, the departure of Napier's fleet for the Baltic under the new power of steam—in those days when first was seen

> low and black
> Beside the full-rigg'd mast the strange smoke-stack.

There must have been much that he could tell about the great Victorians and their ways, but somehow one did not think to ask him. There was never a man less built for the part of mumbling ancestor. His talk was not of bygones, but of present, future, or eternal things: his work or yours, what the scientists or psychologists were doing, or the younger poets, what wireless *will* do, or if the sun shone and nature luxuriated, the life of birds and flowers, perhaps, or the principles of beauty and rightness in the conduct and the arts of man. . . .

I am still left with the feeling of our loss, however due to nature, of the great Englishman he was. No man was more steadily true to himself. His physical and mental beauty matched each other, and equipped him superbly for the life he chose. He was of noble and even heroic presence, and his careless outdoor strength and grace, growing more picturesque with age, expressed the colour and delicacy as well as the masculine humour and outspoken freedom of his mind. He was poet, scientist, philosopher, naturalist, musician, philologist, typographer, and country gentleman—a mixture of qualities that would have been surprising in another man, and probably ineffectual, but that in him achieved their harmony. He grew up, through the kindness of fortune, unwarped by the struggle of living, with none of the inevitable vices of a profession. He used the gifts of fortune responsibly, setting an example of high-minded devotion to all the arts of Beauty and to the spiritual advancement of mankind. Before he died he delivered in the *Testament of Beauty* his message of belief in the goodness of the human heart, and of faith in the religious foundation of human life.—G. S. GORDON, *Robert Bridges*, 1946, pp. 8–9, 38

General

'The crowd, incapable of perfectness', is not likely ever to be much attracted by such verses as those of Mr. Robert Bridges, of which the chief merit is a quiet unpretentious perfectness, which has the air of coming not from laboured finish, but from finished habits of thought, feeling, and life, combined with and aided by a scholar's attainments. Though differing from Mr. William Barnes in almost every other quality, Mr. Bridges resembles the Dorsetshire poet more than any other modern writer in this character of perfectness which bears little or no sign of work: a character the opposite to that of the best poems of Tennyson, in which the manifestation of finish and fully accomplished labour constitutes of itself no small grace. Another probable obstacle in the way of Mr. Bridges's acceptance by the public is his singular though entirely unostentatious independence of any other poet or school. He seems to have read and felt with fullness, but with such impartiality that people will never begin by admiring his verses because they are like those of some one else whom they may happen to admire; nor is the absence of this great and almost universal first cause of popular favour balanced by anything that most readers would think 'striking' or 'original'. We feel quite sure that Mr. Bridges would be absolutely distressed if any reader whom he respected should be detained by any line or passage of his to say or think 'That's fine!' He aims at and attains a style so equable, and the eminently beautiful lines or passages are so proportioned to and arise so naturally out of eminent occasions, that nothing is 'striking' until it is made to stand alone, and then most of the beauty vanishes because it is relative. In what he writes Mr. Bridges is thoroughly 'masterly', because he knows exactly the powers he is master of, and never attempts to strain them. In this, too, he resembles Mr. Barnes, who never fancies that, because he is a writer of matchless idylls and eclogues, he ought to try his hand at epics or odes. No extracts could give any idea of that equable and steady poetic flight, of which the main charm consists, not in its altitude, but its sweet and unlaboured evenness. There is no passage fit for isolation to compare with the sixteen or twenty lines in praise of Athens in Mr. Swinburne's *Erechtheus*, or with two or three of the love-passages in *Maud*; but we question whether posterity—if there should be any posterity capable of classic art—will not finally judge *Prometheus the Firegiver* to be the most valuable work of the three.—COVENTRY PATMORE, "'Prometheus the Firegiver'" (1885), *Courage in Politics*, 1921, pp. 143–45

The Victorian spirit commissioned a number of men of genius to remain on the chaotic scene, and still the scene of new promise, which terminated the main effects of Victorianism; to remain there, reserved yet influential, modest yet exalted, blessing at once and tantalizing the tentative regeneration. One more of them is gone, and has surprised us by going even at the age of eighty-six. The youthfulness, even the boyishness of Robert Bridges had become so perennially clear a picture that one never opened a newspaper with the apprehension of finding his name in the obituary. Since he was so exactly and happily an Englishman, it may not be inappropriate to say that the man himself was, as seen in his old age, a triumph of the English race. Whoever set eyes on him and his easy, fearless, spirited movements, or heard his fresh, decisive conversation, must have felt that a country which produces such a veteran is fortunate. Had Shelley lived into his eightieth year, there could hardly have been a surer union of strength and beauty in his presence.

The unconquered nimbleness of body in the Laureate was not more remarkable than that spiritual and intellectual alacrity which resulted in his splendid philosophical poem and final metrical innovation. Hardy, with *The Dynasts* long established among the grandeurs, ended his work with nothing indeed of anticlimax, but with a diminuendo; Bridges, with all his variety of lyric and essay in existence, had nevertheless a late oportunity to crown his labour with an invention of ampler sway and profounder speculation. He took that opportunity. Normally those who awake to find themselves famous are young in years. Bridges changed all that.

Perhaps the Victorian spirit already suspected of irony would smile faintly at the suggestion that a Poet Laureate can be other than a famous man. Nor would one overstate the case of Robert Bridges. Yet *The Testament of Beauty* was 'the turning-point in his career', as they say; nothing like that revelation's popularity had happened to him before. His earlier writings (beginning, to the best of my knowledge, with a book of verse in 1873) had won him something like the reputation of Landor, but still more secluded and unhurried. A faithful audience purchased the *Shorter Poems* (the third edition of the collection, dated 1891, now before me, shows that they did their best). About twenty years later there appeared what might be called a 'popular edition' of his poetical works at the Oxford University Press; among those who acquired this, I proudly remember, was the present writer. Clearly the Bridges public was growing; and the observation on the anthology lettered 'Bridges to Kipling', 'What do we want bridges to Kipling for?' seemed to belong to the Dark Ages. Mr. Asquith in a moment of inspiration chose the poet for the mantle of Tennyson, transmitted as it was through forgotten Alfred Austin. Obscurity still prevailed, and the new Laureate 'reigned a private man'. Occasionally, disapproval of the situation was expressed by a journalist; the eminence but hardly the importance of Robert Bridges began to be observed and accepted; his poetry continued to be published and esteemed. Then, *The Testament of Beauty* lit up the academic sculpture with which the name of the Laureate was tastefully embellished, and all eyes turned with sudden wonder towards the now significant Robert Bridges.

The office of Poet Laureate has been ridiculed, and its abolition urged, by many men who should have known better, even some Victorians. Whether the last holder left any explicit statement of his view of Laureateship, I do not know; I venture to think that none of his predecessors ever exhibited in practice a fuller or finer comprehension of the functions proper to the national poet. In the first place, Bridges displayed the dignity of poetry. Servility or opportunism, that have not one of the many mansions in that palace, found no approach to him. He continued to be the same sensitive melodist and interpreter of scene and thought as before. He was not unwilling to write on a national theme—but then, it would be also his own by nature, as, the tercentenary of Shakespeare. Then, since poetry is only one of the instruments by which the character of a nation is to be cultivated, enlightened, and directed, Bridges continually brought into action his other auxiliary gifts and studies. Those were numerous. He was intent upon (to catalogue these ideals crudely) the speech of England, how he should pronounce it, and how write it down; upon the music of England, and the improvement of voice and verse in religious services; upon the general realization of poetry, in its total influence and its minor construction; upon typography, which plays for better or worse on our daily life; upon the illumining of poetical achievements not generally known; and upon the worth, cheerfulness, aspiration, and endurance of the English people. 'The Spirit of Man' was a Laureate work, although not what a narrow conception of the Laureateship would term so; its making was poetical, and its effect in companioning us at a terrible period with a rich, distilled perfume of culture was Miltonic, 'compleat, and generous'.

But these words are not in the nature of a panegyric; for Bridges remains still with the reader as he personally regards him, a private man, to whose music each is invited without strain or demand. The *Shorter Poems*, maybe, are securest in our capricious memories; their fluting was of so silvery a touch, so charming a juncture. It is nearly the hour again to repeat his,

> 'Wanton with long delay the gay spring leaping cometh;
>   The blackthorn starreth now his bough on the eve of May:
> All day in the sweet box-tree the bee for pleasure hummeth,
>   The cuckoo sends afloat his note on the air all day,'

and to seek what fancy vows to be his especial 'bower beside the silver Thames'.—EDMUND BLUNDEN, "The Ideal Laureate" (1930), *The Mind's Eye*, 1934, pp. 216–20

The death of Robert Bridges at the ripe age of eighty-six gives us pause, on this side of the ocean, chiefly as a reminder of differences between Britain's poetry of this period and our own. For Bridges was rightfully the Laureate, in that he was typically British, and British of the upper class accustomed to titles and honors; a poet of the more decorous and gentlemanly English tradition, deriving not from Chaucer and Shakespeare, not from the ballad-vendors of King Henry or the swashbuckling player-playwrights of Queen Elizabeth, but from that *preux chevalier* Sir Philip Sidney, from the mannerly Robert Herrick, with Wordsworth and Tennyson, two other laureates, for more immediate ancestors.

Hardy, almost his exact contemporary, was also English, but he was something more; rooted in Wessex, he yet looked beyond the traditions and aristocratic prejudices of his little island, and took the world for his province, with all its heavy load of common people. But Bridges remained in a walled garden discreetly planted among classic colonnades. He had followed the regulation courses at Eton and Oxford; indeed, the frock-coated classicism of Oxford suited him so well that he passed his whole long life in the quiet countryside shadowed by its towers.—HARRIET MONROE, "Bridges as a Lyrist," *Poetry*, June 1930, p. 146

In the London *Mercury* for August, 1920, Bridges published a review of the book called *Little Essays*, made up of selections from Santayana's writings. In it he described the latter's phi-

losophy very discerningly as "a building-up of idealism—that is, the supremacy of the imagination—on a naturalistic or materialistic basis . . . taking its most persuasive support from the idea of beauty." Bridges then added this most significant statement: "The philosophy (Santayana's), as I understand it, *is very consonant with my own thought*: there is no pretence of hiding the unsolved riddle of life. The Sphinx lurks in all systems; different schools only hustle her from pillar to post, and if she is to be driven into any corner where her presence is obvious, her best refuge is in the unsearchable atom . . . for whatever immaterial agency there may be, or even should we come to be convinced that all ultimate agency was immaterial, our minds would be unable to conceive of its mode of action except in material terms."

In the same review there is a possibly somewhat prophetic discussion by Bridges of Santayana's opinion "that it is the function of poetry to emotionalize philosophy; that the great poem must be the æsthetical exposition of a complete theory of human life, so far as that is understood; and that there is therefore at present a finer opportunity for a great poet than the world has hitherto offered." Bridges concludes that ". . . poetry will use philosophy rather than be used by it. But such a poem as Mr. Santayana desires and foretells, if ever it should be written, will necessarily be written by a great poet, and he will write good poetry." These lines were written about six years before the *Testament* was begun, and it would be interesting to know whether Bridges was led to undertake the writing of the poem as a fulfilment of his friend's prediction and wish.

Bridges, then, like Santayana whom he resembles in many intellectual and emotional particulars, is (if labels must be affixed) a naturalist intent upon vindicating the primacy of the ideal in the cosmic scheme of things that our arts and sciences reveal. His philosophic formula (if, again, we must resort to tags and slogans) is close to Santayana's famous "No ideal without a natural basis; nothing in nature without an ideal fulfilment." Both men, that is, see no valid human ideal that is super-natural in the sense of "not rooted in the natural basis of the physical world." And both hold, on the other hand, that it is only the possible "ideal fulfilments" of the physical world which give it the slightest abiding significance for mankind. Both, while under strong Platonic influences, have departed from Plato in the direction of Aristotle.—HAROLD A. LARRABEE, "Robert Bridges and George Santayana," *AS*, Jan. 1932, pp. 176–77

It is interesting to reconsider this late Victorian bard of Boar's Hill, scholar and muscular metrical Christian, from our disadvantage point in 1953, surrounded by

> the scanty dwarf'd intelligence
> of a new race of beings, the unhallow'd offspring
> of them who shall have quite dismember'd and destroy'd
> our temple of Christian faith and fair Hellenic art.

The defect is obvious: lack of inspiration. No poet seems so consistently without it; and yet, unblessed by any heavenly visitation, he worked bravely on, steeping himself in the true and beautiful—Plato, Dante, Wordsworth, and, above all, Milton—studiously observing the minutiae of the countryside, dryly doing his best as our official poet during a momentous war, sitting on Hopkins's manuscript and pondering problems of prosody: until suddenly, in his eighties, the Muse took pity on him and changed his Martha into Mary. Grace flowed, inspiration descended, and the long and difficult but also intelligent and beautiful *Testament of Beauty* appeared, dedicated to the King and running into fourteen editions, a modern miracle, a swansong of Victorian integrity, Edwardian learning and Georgian questioning, where Christian platonism

> passionat soul and sense
> blend in a rich reverie with the dying year.

The five volumes of shorter poems which appeared between 1873 and 1893 contain, however, some lovely things in which nicety of observation and felicity of rhythm compensate for a certain monotony of diction and feeling: a gardener-poet, a walker and a boatman quietly develops, growing familiar with the moods of the countryside and constituting himself the poet of winterspring, the season when January bequeaths to February and March its faltering authority:

> Hale Winter, half resigning ere he go,
> Doth to his heiress shew
> His kingdom fair.
> In patient russet is his forest spread,
> All bright with bramble red,
> With beechen moss
> And holly sheen: the oak silver and stark
> Sunneth his aged bark
> And wrinkled boss.

'January,' 'November,' 'The Palm Willow,' 'London Snow,' 'A Robin,' 'The Upper Skies,' 'Screaming Tarn'—these and many other slight but haunting and graceful poems end by producing a quiet intoxication in the reader, an aquatinted calendar of the English scene.—CYRIL CONNOLLY, "The Bard of Boar's Hill" (1953), *Robert Bridges: Prose and Poetry*, ed. John Sparrow, 1955, pp. xliii–xliv

Works

POETRY

The deliberate act by which Mr. Bridges laid aside the profession of medicine for (what to him must have seemed) the equally arduous profession of poetry was a symbol of his general approach to poetry in all its ways. The deliberate and learned interest which he has taken in the manners and habits of prosody, in the Society for Pure English, in handwriting and phonetics, continue to express that approach. His mind seems to know all the time what it is doing; it judges seriously, if lightly; it is aware of its rejections as well as of its acceptances, even when those rejections appear so natural that almost any other poet would have forgotten them altogether, or perhaps been hardly aware that they existed. Joy, for example, which, in so many poets, seems but an accident of their mood, is here a conscious choice, almost a duty, and even, sometimes, an effort. That some of the finest of his lyrics rise into an attitude of pure delight is no contradiction of this; rather, it is its reward. 'Man's duty is to be happy,' said Dr. Johnson; Mr. Bridges's verse might almost be said to have fulfilled that duty after many a conflict and in spite of many an adversary. That it had an original leaning that way is to say no more than that Mr. Hardy's has had a leaning towards a thwarted happiness or Mr. Kipling's towards a fatalistic morality. But Mr. Bridges omits the consideration of evil fortune less than Hardy omits the consideration of good fortune. 'The master Reason' rides always on the right hand of his Muse when she goes through the cruel habitations of the earth, and directs her attentive glance not only to them but also to the satisfying stars. That the stars have been by now a little touched by the literary taint makes the metaphor only the more just. For a great deal of the happiness in this poetry arises from the recollection of great art.

> Days that the thought of grief refuse,
> Days that are one with human art,

> Worthy of the Virgilian muse,
> Fit for the gaiety of Mozart—

these are the terms in which he praises the 'brighter days' of the sea in one poem; and in another (*Dejection*) he warns his soul, 'revolving hopeless strife,

> Pointing at hindrance, and the bare
> Painful escapes of fitful life . . .

> O soul, be patient: thou shalt find
> A little matter mend all this;
> Some strain of music to thy mind,
> Some praise for skill not spent amiss.'

But this too, since literature nowadays is never unselfconscious, accentuates the inward and retired deliberation of this admirable verse. However frequent, however exact, the delight in external things may be, it is within that such delight justifies itself by reason and virtue.

This deliberation accentuates the momentary nature of Joy which is in certain of the lyrics so intensely expressed.

> Haste on, my joys! your treasure lies
> In swift, unceasing flight.
> O haste, for while your beauty flies
> I seize your full delight.

Poets enough have lamented a fugitive joy; not many have realized, as Mr. Bridges has done, that such a flight is indeed (in our present mode of being) of its very nature—that, without it, Joy apparently could not be at all. To such a dogma speculation can offer objections enough; it is, beyond all speculation, confirmed by experience. And it is from profound experience that this verse arises. . . .

Love, diligence, wit, justice, courage, temperance, reason—these are the qualities Mr. Bridges praises and recommends to the young adventurer. They are, transmuted into poetry, the qualities of his verse; they are the analysed elements of its beauty as it praises Beauty. They are the method of his experience, and the things his genius chooses to experience are selected by them. Besides great art, a few things are preeminent in his poetic knowledge—the English landscape, man in society, Hellenism, solitude, piety. These things, communicated by those virtuous Pleiades named above, cause a profound and still delight. But it is a delight which may require a certain similarity of temperament or a certain prolonged discipline before it can be accepted, especially from a reader used to more violent effects. Violence attends on the steps of a number of our poets, and, so long as it is only allowed to act at its master's bidding, even violence may have its work to do. But it is an uncertain slave, and one whom Mr. Bridges would never spend a farthing to buy or shelter.—CHARLES WILLIAMS, "Robert Bridges," *Poetry at Present*, 1930, pp. 20–26

I do not know how old Homer was when he wrote the Odyssey. Longinus' comment upon it is well known. "I speak of old age," he says, "but it is none the less the old age of Homer." The Odyssey, he means, is not so great a poem as the Iliad: as an old man's work tends to be, it is in parts a little garrulous. But it is still Homer. Mr. Robert Bridges published his *Testament of Beauty* on the day on which he entered his eighty-sixth year. Yet a good critic, whose name I think I can guess, has said of it already that it is not only his greatest poem, but his youngest. If that be true, or if anything like it be true, then the history of literature can scarcely afford a parallel; but, for a like achievement, we shall have to go to the sister art of music, to the old age of Verdi. That from that art we should have to seek our analogue would, I think, especially please Mr. Bridges; who, like Milton, it may be suspected, has sometimes not known, of that "blest pair of Sirens," Music and Poetry, which the more truly held his heart; and who perhaps laboured no lines of this, his last poem, more lovingly than those in which he speaks of the violin:

> even as those well-toned viols, matured by time, which once,
> when the Muse visited Italy to prepare
> a voice of beauty for the joy of her children,
> wer fashioned by Amati and Stradivari and still,
> treasured in their mellow shapeliness, fulfil
> the genius of her omnipotent destiny,—
> speaking with incantation of strange magic to charm
> the dreams that yet undreamt lurk in the unfathom'd deep
> of mind, unfeatured hopes and dim desires,
> uttermost forms of all things that shall be.

For my own part, I feel not too much disposed to ask whether, in *The Testament of Beauty*, Mr. Bridges is in fact greater than himself, nor whether the poem has all that abundant youth that is alleged. In our first surprise, we are likely to exaggerate its youthfulness; and I do not know that to do so is to pay Mr. Bridges a compliment. After all, what does life mean if, at eighty-five, a man has still the heart, or the want of it, not to be as old as he is? We must not allow some of the modernities of the poem too much to engage our judgment. Airplanes, wireless, the latest discoveries in Mesopotamia, the newest types of agricultural machinery, the post-war undergraduate, Freudism and a whole book upon the subject of sex—all these things remind us that Mr. Bridges knows in what order of world he has grown old. And certainly we may felicitate him that he should retain into extreme age all that lively interest which he has in the modern world, its inventions and curiosities, and that he should bring to all these things a free speculative spirit. Nor will anybody grudge him what I may call his occasional youthful clevernesses—as when, speaking of the assimilation of European science by the Oriental peoples, their magi, he says, their wise men, "hav seen the electric light in the West"; or when, commenting on the displacement of the scythe by the reaping-machine, and speculating what the small creatures in the corn make of it, surely, he says, "the grasshopper wondering knoweth his god." These pleasant sophomorisms no one would wish away. Again, when he touches questions of politics, I do not know how young Mr. Bridges is not prepared to be. In his contempt for the mob he is as young as Shakespeare—and as delightfully unreasonable. Indeed, this poem would not be Mr. Bridges' if whim and prejudice nowhere shewed their forehead—or even their teeth.—H. W. GARROD, *"The Testament of Beauty," Poetry and the Criticism of Life*, 1931, pp. 129–31

Bridges' narrative *Eros and Psyche* and the four mythological dramas are perhaps generally regarded, like Tennyson's *Idylls*, as the sometimes beautiful mistakes of a born lyrist, and the multitude who bought but did not read *The Testament of Beauty* are not likely to discover the long poems written a generation and more ago. Yet these everywhere reveal the poet's special quality, and their defects as well as their virtues illustrate his attitude toward art and life. The scholarly traditionalist, the technical experimenter and contriver of subtle rhythms, the singer of love and joy and beauty, they are all here.

Eros and Psyche, first published in 1885, was revised in 1894; the original twelve "measures," containing three hundred and sixty-five stanzas, were named after the months of the year. Apart from countless verbal improvements, a number of the changes indicate somewhat less concern with mere nar-

rative and more with philosophic interpolations. The first version lacked the faults, and the unforgettable felicities, of *Endymion*, because Bridges' artistry and taste were mature, and because his gospel of beauty was a quiet familiar possession rather than a new revelation. Keats thought, wisely enough, that further work on *Endymion* would be unprofitable; the minute revision of *Eros and Psyche* would not have been carried out by a less scrupulous artist than Bridges, or by a more inspired poet.

He described the work as "in all essentials a faithful translation of Apuleius' story," but there are modifications on almost every page; since this section is not a thesis I can only indicate something of their general character. The Hellenizing of the story hardly goes beyond the substitution of Greek names for Latin ones. Bridges' choice of Crete instead of Apuleius' unlocalized setting permits allusions to Cretan places and myths, such as the unnecessary bronze giant Talos, and a gorgeous sunset is composed of "the phenomena which followed the great eruption of Krakatoa." As we should expect, the poet frequently and beautifully works in the natural background, sometimes for its own sake, sometimes, as in the account of the sacrificial procession, to heighten the pictorial vividness of the action. More obtrusive, though not often disagreeably so, are the incidental allusions to mythology. Spenser may have been the chief model, but Bridges' usual brevity is more Ovidian than Spenserian. The paintings on the walls of Psyche's room, which show "Love's victories over the gods renown'd," recall the more luscious pictures of "Cupids warres" in the house of Busyrane. The descriptions of Eros, Pan, Hera, Aphrodite's chariot, and Hermes are elaborately pictorial passsages for which Apuleius gives only hints. The catalogue of the melodious names for the sea-nymphs, which comes from Homer, attracted Bridges as much as Spenser. Such ornamentations, if mostly pleasant in themselves, do not help to preserve the serious import of the story.

A number of elements contribute to the effect of sophisticated unsophistication. There is, as in William Morris, the general process of idealizing and refining, the softening of some harsh motives and circumstances of the original, the "gentler characterization of Psyche." Bridges does not rationalize the supernatural—the speaking tower remains a speaking tower—and he even introduces marvels on his own account. A bit of science is less in harmony with the spirit of a fairy-tale; the younger sister's fall from the cliff inspires a definition of the law of gravity and accelerated motion. In addition to mythological lists in the Elizabethan fashion we have a series of half-Elizabethan "sentences" on the power of love, and even an arcrostic on Purcell. Such things, along with the archaisms of diction, carry the suspicion of preciousness, of studied quaintness. *Eros and Psyche* has been called "if not the best, . . . the most beautiful narrative poem in the language," and Bridges' coolness, restraint, human feeling and delicate purity of style wear better than the dreamy sweetness and sensuousness of Morris. Yet, as the stanzas glide by in their ordered beauty, we may wish here also for the robust, racy spontaneity of Adlington's prose or Marmion's slipshod verse.

For a modern poet, however perfect his structure and style, cannot afford to be content with story-telling of deliberate simplicity. As Hopkins wrote to Bridges: "The story you have not elevated but confined yourself to making it please. Eros is little more than a winged Masher, but Psyche is a success, a sweet little 'body,' rather than 'soul.'" We go back again and again to *Endymion* mainly because Keats was struggling to utter the faith that was in him. Bridges, to be sure, has his faith also, and it has been said that he devised his framework of months and days because he wished the symbolic implications of the story to be deeply pondered. Although a formal scheme which invites, and rather often necessitates, padding may appear a dubious means to that end, still the symbolic implications are at times made explicit, in a manner highly characteristic of the poet. Beauty is the native food of man's desire "And doth to good our varying world control." Psyche's beauty purges passion of its earthly soil. She is more beautiful than Aphrodite because—here speaks the nineteenth-century romantic—she carries the immortal question in a mortal face, "The vague desire whereunto man is born." And that Hedonè or Joy, the daughter of Eros and Psyche, means more in Bridges than the *Voluptas* of Apuleius we know, but we know it less from this poem than from his others. Thus while the few hints of a parable, including the grave benediction of the "envoy," add something to the story, they do not make a compelling reinterpretation of it. Hence the tenth reading of the poem yields no deeper pleasure than the first.—DOUGLAS BUSH, "From the Nineties to the Present," *Mythology and the Romantic Tradition in English*, 1937, pp. 433–36

Philosophical argument—and *The Testament of Beauty* is full of argument—is not, in general, suitable material of poetry. In so far as philosophy is simply 'love of wisdom', a passionate striving of the human spirit for answers to its inevitable questions, almost all great poets are philosophers; and the answers which they get and pass on to others, however fragmentary, do more in fact to encourage and fortify the human spirit than the completest theories of philosophers who are not poets. But poets proceed mainly by intuition, by imagination, by the expression of concrete momentary experience, not by systematic reasoning and the excogitation and correlation of abstract principles. Dante, Shakespeare, and Goethe have probably taught more wisdom to mankind than all the philosophers since Plato: but neither they nor the innumerable other true poets, whose 'love of wisdom' has been the most elevating influence in the world, have expressed themselves in ostensibly philosophical or didactic poems. Lucretius, and perhaps Pope, are the only obvious exceptions in western literature. There have been many other versified treatises on the nature of things, on God, on Man, on the Soul, on the Universe. But nobody reads them either for their poetry or for their philosophy, the reason being not that their authors were feeble philosophers, which they often were not, but that they were not real poets. Pope was not a real philosopher, but he was a real poet: Lucretius was both. Robert Bridges was both, as the general character of his writings before the *Testament of Beauty* indicated. Whether he has succeeded in expressing his philosophy in a didactic poem (which, as we have seen, he familiarly called his *De Hominum Natura*) which will live in the hearts and minds of poets and lovers of poetry, as the didactic poem of Lucretius lives, time alone will show. Lucretius has the great advantage of having secured a niche in the spacious temple of the ancient Muses. Bridges has to take his chance in the incessant output of the modern printing-press. Lucretius again is the poet of one of the outstanding scientific theories of the universe. Will the same be said of Bridges centuries hence? Some will smile at the mere question: but here again it is time alone which, as Pindar says, 'proves by trial the very truth'.

It is, however, certain that *The Testament of Beauty* is a philosophical poem which bases itself upon the theory of Evolution popularly associated mainly with the name of Darwin, as definitely as the *De Rerum Natura* based itself upon the atomic theory of Democritus as developed by Epicurus. It is also true that *The Testament of Beauty* is the first attempt of a poet to express a definitely reasoned aesthetic theory of life. Aesthetic has always been the Cinderella of philosophic studies. The pure intellectual curiosity of philosophy has always

been liable to be coloured by the pragmatic aim of achieving peace of mind. It has tended to study the feelings quite as much in order to control as to understand them. While truth and goodness beckon the philosopher to the 'pure serene' in which he hopes to breathe at ease, beauty awakes those disturbing emotions which, at least if he is more philosopher than poet, he prefers to forget. Christian morality, on the whole, has reinforced, with an emphasis quite alien to the apparent temper of its founder, that hostility to sensuous beauty which the experience of his frailty has constantly engendered in struggling man. Beauty is suspect because of its companionship with pleasure. There has been an age-long antagonism between morals and religion on the one hand and art and poetry on the other. The earlier phase of the Renaissance was an attempted harmony; but it was soon broken up. The High Renaissance stands over against the Reformation as Art without conscience against Morality without taste. It is only as a result of the liberating force of the scientific spirit that Beauty has begun to vindicate its place in the trinity of the absolute values. Thus it has come about that *The Testament of Beauty* is the first great didactic poem of aesthetic philosophy, and as such it seems likely to have an historic advantage over other long poems in the ever-increasing stream of literature.—NOWELL CHARLES SMITH, "Introduction" to *Notes on* The Testament of Beauty, 1940, pp. xii–xiv

There is perhaps a closer affinity between the artistic aims of Milton and Bridges than between those of any other English poets. Both regarded lyric poetry as an art rather than as a vehicle for the expression of personality, and both were consequently stylists in the best sense. The same individualism and imaginative autonomy combines in both poets with a traditionalism seeking its inspiration in very diverse and apparently irreconcilable sources. Both knew classical literature, and wrote poems in Latin; both were keen students of music and wrote on music. Unlike Keats, Bridges never tried to escape Miltonic influence, for he knew Milton to be at the very center of English poetry: the centripetal force which drew together the various strands of English poetry from Chaucer to his own day, the centrifugal force which made that early poetry accessible to later poets. Yet Bridges was conscious of one dangerous aspect of Milton's influence, and his "Neo-Miltonic syllabics" represent an effort to open new fields for experiment, to rebuild the bridges Milton had burned behind him by the absolute, and in a sense devastating, perfection of his style: ". . . Milton's blank verse practically ended as an original form with Milton."

Milton's marked influence on Bridges' prosody and on the style of the masques *Prometheus the Firegiver* and *Demeter* will be considered in later chapters. His influence on the lyric poetry is seen primarily in *The Growth of Love*. There is no sonnet in which some Miltonic characteristic, such as grammatical inversion or suspension of narrative verb, does not occur. Some of Bridges' inversions recall particular lines in Milton, as in

Until at length your feeble steps and slow,

but the full extent of Milton's influence can be observed only through more ample quotation. The sonnet "To the President of Magdalen College, Oxford," for instance, only too patently announces its parentage in Milton's sonnet "To Mr. Lawrence":

Since now from woodland mist and flooded clay
I am fled beside the deep Devonian shore,
Nor stand for welcome at your gothic door,
'Neath the fair tower of Magdalen and May,
Such tribute, Warren, as fond poets pay

For generous esteem, I write, not more
Enhearten'd than my need is, reckoning o'er
My life-long wanderings on the heavenly way. . . .

The closest emotional affinities are with the Milton of the earliest period, the Milton of "Arcades" as well as "Il Penseroso." In both poets a joy in nature alternates with a placid and not uncherished literary melancholy. Bridges' two Spring Odes owe their structure to "L'Allegro" and "Il Penseroso," while the diction of "On a Lady Whom Grief for the Death of her Betrothed Killed," though Spenserian on the whole, shows the influence of the Nativity Ode. "May Morning" and other short poems by Milton show the generalized treatment of nature found in Bridges' poems, and achieve their verbal music by the same means. The first stanza of "There is a hill beside the silver Thames," for instance, has the very tone of Sabrina's song.—ALBERT GUÉRARD, JR., *Robert Bridges*, 1942, pp. 45–47

February, 1877, was a significant date in the two poets' lives. Had Bridges not decided to send his poems to his friend and ask for his appreciation, Hopkins might have remained silent about his own work. As it is, Bridges's confidence led him to ask for his fellow-poet's frank opinion of his experiments; this meant a constant interchange of manuscripts or books of poems, and a painstaking consideration of little details. For greater convenience we shall study Hopkins's criticism before we turn to Bridges's. Although they reacted upon each other, and alternately took precedence of all other topics or receded in the background, a separate examination will help us to understand better what Bridges asked and obtained, what he gave in his turn, and the benefit Hopkins himself derived from it. . . .

Because Bridges obviously seeks originality in being composed, graceful and classical, Hopkins is most strict in his criticism. He insists that 'the meaning shd. be felt at once' and hunts down ambiguous expressions. Of one sonnet, he writes,

I cannot make out, do what I will, who is that conqueror? It might be Love, it might be Death, it might be Time, but there are reasons against each. 'Yet has no secret with the soul pourtrayed' means, I suppose, 'Yet has no secret in common with the there pourtrayed soul', but it is a very ambiguous phrase. It reads as if it meant something it cannot mean.

Even the real value of a demonstrative adjective is carefully looked into:

I will say that I think it wd. be better to write 'one irrevocable day'. 'That . . . day' is ambiguous: you mean *ille dies*, the particular day which in fact did, etc.; I took it for *is dies*, a day such that, whenever it shall come, it is doomed to etc.

More than anything else, he warns Bridges against 'echoes'. In the 'Hymn of Nature' he finds 'lines that distinctly echo Milton, I mean distinct passages; and Tennyson too'. In the same letter he says that the 'Elegy' is unequal,

because, as I told you and I now maintain my past judgment, there are two lines in it echoing Gray's: *they do it, they will do it to every ear, it is a great fault to do it, and they do it.* They are not at all the best lines and they can be easily changed and yet they echo lines which are held to be of faultless and canonical beauty. The subject and measure shd. of themselves have put you on your guard. Gray's poem may be outdone but, if you understand, it cannot be equalled.

The underlined words, the repetition of 'they do it', and the judicious remark at the end of the passage stress the stong opposition of the critic to anything that savours either of plagiarism or of conscious transposition. In his considered opinion the great masters of the past can be admired but they cannot be imitated and it is useless to try to equal them; one must do otherwise or else the only way out of the difficulty is to outdo them, and that is not an easy task. Had Hopkins lived, what would have been his criticism of the poems of T. S. Eliot or Ezra Pound which deliberately use 'echoes' as a literary and poetical device? He might have repeated what he said about Bridges's historical play, *Nero*: 'The echos [*sic*] are a disease of education, literature is full of them; but they remain a disease, an evil'.

Obviously the writer of those words cared for originality above all things and was irritated by the burden of literary memories. Bridges on the other hand enjoyed the company of the classics, and had learnt his art at their feet. All the plays he wrote between 1883 and 1890 were either translated from the Greek or imitated from Greek or Latin authors. *Prometheus the Firegiver* is a mask in the Greek manner. *The Feast of Bacchus* is partly translated from Terence, who had borrowed the plot from Menander. *The Return of Ulysses* dramatizes the chief scenes in Homer's *Odyssey*. A passage in *Achilles in Scyros* is copied from Calderon's *El Principe Constante*, a play from which Bridges borrowed the subject of his *Christian Captives*. No one borrowed more consistently or more freely. Quite naturally he also tried his hand at translating sonnets of Michelangelo into English verse, and Hopkins was attracted in spite of an ingrained aversion for that exercise.

I should be very glad to see your prose of Michelangelo's sonnets and also your verse, for though I do not like verse-renderings of verse (according to the saying, *Traduttore traditore*) yet I think you could do them if anyone can.

A guarded compliment! But Bridges may have smiled when reading the passage, for Hopkins himself had his try at verse-renderings of verse, translating Horace and Latin hymns into English and Shakespeare's songs into Latin and Greek.—JEAN G. RITZ, *Robert Bridges and Gerard Manley Hopkins, 1863–1889: A Literary Friendship*, 1960, pp. 76–84

DRAMA

M. Maeterlinck, in his beautiful "Treasure of the Humble," compares the dramas of our stage to the paintings of an obsolete taste; and the dramas of the stage, for which he hopes, to the paintings of a taste that cannot become obsolete. "The true artist," he says, "no longer chooses Marius triumphing over the Cimbrians, or the assassination of the Duke of Guise, as fit subjects for his art; for he is well aware that the psychology of victory or murder is but elementary and exceptional, and that the solemn voice of men and things, the voice that issues forth so timidly and hesitatingly, cannot be heard amidst the idle uproar of acts of violence. And therefore will he place on his canvas a house lost in the heart of the country, a door open at the end of a passage, a face or hands at rest." I do not understand him to mean that our dramas should have no victories or murders, for he quotes for our example plays that have both, but only that their victories and murders shall not be to excite our nerves, but to illustrate the reveries of a wisdom which shall be as much a part of the daily life of the wise as a face or hands at rest[.] And certainly the greater plays of the past ages have been built after such a fashion. If this fashion is about to become our fashion also, and there are signs that it is, plays like the plays of Mr. Robert Bridges will come suddenly out of that obscurity into which all poetry, that is not lyrical poetry, has fallen, and even popular criticism will begin to know something about them. Some day the few among us, who care for poetry more than any temporal thing, and who believe that its delights cannot be perfect when we read it alone in our rooms and long for one to share in its delights, but that they might be perfect in the theatre, when we share them friend with friend, lover with beloved, will persuade a few idealists to seek out the lost art of speaking, and seek out ourselves the lost art, that is perhaps nearest of all arts to eternity, the subtle art of listening. When that day comes we will talk much of Mr. Bridges; for did he not write scrupulous, passionate poetry to be sung and to be spoken, when there were few to sing and as yet none to speak? There is one play especially, *The Return of Ulysses*, which we will praise for perfect after its kind, the kind of our new drama of wisdom, for it moulds into dramatic shape, and with as much as possible of literal translation, those closing books of the Odyssey which are perhaps the most perfect poetry of the world, and compels that great tide of song to flow through delicate dramatic verse, with little abatement of its own leaping and clamorous speed. As I read, the gathering passion overwhelms me, as it did when Homer himself was the singer, and when I read at last the lines in which the maid describes to Penelope the battle with the suitors, at which she looks through the open door, I tremble with excitement.

> "*Penelope:* Alas! what cries! Say, is the prince still safe?
> *The Maid:* He shieldeth himself well, and striketh surely;
> His foes fall down before him. Ah! now what can I see?
> Who cometh? Lo! a dazzling helm, a spear
> Of silver or electron; sharp and swift
> The piercings. How they fall! Ha! shields are raised
> In vain. I am blinded, or the beggar-man
> Hath waxed in strength. He is changed, he is young, O strange!
> He is all in golden armour. These are gods
> That slay the suitors. (*Runs to Penelope.*) O lady, forgive me.
> 'Tis Ares' self. I saw his crispèd beard;
> I saw beneath his helm his curlèd locks."

The coming of Athene helmed "in silver or electron" and her transformation of Ulysses are not, as the way is with the only modern dramas that popular criticism holds to be dramatic, the climax of an excitement of the nerves, but of that unearthly excitement whose fruit is wisdom, and which is of like kind with the ecstasy of the seers, an altar flame, unshaken by the winds of the world, and burning every moment with whiter and purer brilliance. . . .

The poet who writes best in the Shakesperean manner is a poet with a circumstantial and instinctive mind, who delights to speak with strange voices and to see his mind in the mirror of Nature; while Mr. Bridges, like most of us to-day, has a lyrical and meditative mind, and delights to speak with his own voice and to see Nature in the mirror of his mind. In reading his plays in a Shakesperean manner, I find that he is constantly arranging his story in such and such a way because he has read that the persons he is writing of did such and such things, and not because his soul has passed into the soul of their world and understood its unchangeable destinies. His *Return of Ulysses* is a triumph of beauty, because its classical gravity of speech, which does not, like Shakespeare's verse, desire the vivacity of common life, purifies and subdues all passion into lyrical and meditative ecstasies, and because the unity of place and time in the late acts compels a logical rather than instinctive procession of incidents; and if the Shakesperean *Nero: Second Part*

approaches it in beauty and in dramatic power, it is because it eddies about Nero and Seneca, who had both, to a great extent, lyrical and meditative minds. Had Mr. Bridges been a true Shakesperean, the pomp and glory of the world would have drowned that subtle voice that speaks amid our heterogeneous lives of a life lived in obedience to a lonely and distinguished ideal. . . .

The more a poet rids his verses of heterogeneous knowledge and irrelevant analysis, the more he purifies his mind with elaborate art, the more does the little ritual of his verse resemble the great ritual of nature, and become mysterious and inscrutable. He becomes, as all the great mystics have believed, a vessel of the creative power of God; and whether he be a great poet or a small poet, we can praise the poems, which but seem to be his, with the extremity of praise that we give this great ritual which is but copied from the same eternal model. There is poetry that is like the white light of noon, and poetry that has the heaviness of woods, and poetry that has the golden light of dawn or of sunset; and I find in the poetry of Mr. Bridges the pale colours, the delicate silence, the low murmurs of cloudy country days, when the plough is in the earth, and the clouds darkening towards sunset; and had I the great gift of praising, I would praise it as I would praise these things.—W. B. YEATS, "Mr. Robert Bridges" (1897), *The Correspondence of Robert Bridges and W. B. Yeats*, ed. Richard J. Finneran, 1977, pp. 51–58

The eight published plays of Robert Bridges are more than equal in bulk to the rest of his work. It has often been said that Lyrical Poetry is typically a by-product from the crucible of Drama, and, for this reason, I suppose we must be glad that they have been written. I do not know what was the size of the original editions, but one, at any rate, the first part of *Nero*, is out of print; and however great or small a vogue they may have had in their own day, it is certain that they have given rise to a good deal of unintelligent criticism in ours. Certainly it is unfair to judge them as they have been judged, by the standards which a Renaissance of Poetic Drama has created. They are only another illustration of that impatient return to ancient methods which sprung, as I have already suggested, from the poet's discontent with the outworn creeds of his time. They are frankly derivative. *The Feast of Bacchus* is "in a Latin manner"; *The Christian Captives, Achilles in Scyros* and *The Return of Ulysses* are "in a mixed manner"; while *Palicio* is labelled Elizabethan. In the appendices to these plays Bridges has acknowledged his indebtedness to other dramatists from Menander to Calderon; and for this reason it is only by the conventions of these "manners" that he can be fairly judged.

In the majority of the Bridges' plays drama resolves itself into a string of situations, passionate, intellectual, or fantastic, in which puppets, entangled almost beyond hope in the dramatist's own elaborate snares, gradually shake themselves free— by the dramatist's permission. It implies a convention that holds dramatic dignity inconsistent with an everyday setting; so that every drama is in spirit, if not in fact, a costume play. I suppose the idea of Drama as a thing transcending everyday experience, or at least as only symbolical of such experience, was adopted with the intention of keeping its poetry unfettered, and in this tradition Bridges has only followed the lead of such writers as Byron, Tennyson, Browning, Swinburne and Morris. Indeed, it is strange that Drama should have gained so little from the concentration of these poetical intelligences upon it, and that we should have needed to wait till the twentieth century for the poetical drama which Synge found, not among their stately abstractions, but among the peasantry of the Arans.

The secret of a living drama is to strike a just balance between the action and the idea. The poets in their disgust with the wooden materialism of drama as they found it tried to coax it into life by imaginative flights, and failed because the other essential was neglected. Bridges, elaborately scheming to cover the old stage carpentry with a gloss of poetic richness, has failed for a slightly different reason: because his plays have been a loose mixture of the two elements, lacking that intense heat of conception which fuses both into the imperishable alloy.—F. E. Brett Young, *Robert Bridges: A Critical Study*, 1914, pp. 145–47

YVOR WINTERS
From "Traditional Mastery"

Hound and Horn, January–March 1932, pp. 321–27

Dr. Bridges' meters have been so often and so fruitlessly discussed that I shall omit entirely to analyze them, though his importance as a subtle and learned renovator of English meters is sufficiently great. It is my belief that he has been long enough patronized as a sugar-coated pill for those who wish to brush up on their metrics, as a minor manipulator of outworn graces, and that he should be recognized once and for all as the sole English rival of Hardy in nineteenth-century poetry, as, in all likelihood, considering his formal versatility, the range of his feeling, and the purity of his diction, a diction so free from any trace of personal idiosyncrasy that a successful imitator of it could never be detected as an imitator but would appear only as that most unlikely of phenomena, a rival, that he should, I say, in all likelihood be recognized as the most valuable model of poetic style to appear in the language since Dryden. . . .

Dr. Bridges possessed much more curiosity about the possibilities of various forms than has been shown by most of our modern experimenters. Mr. Pound, Dr. Williams, and Miss Moore, for example, have all worked in a straight line, as if impelled by some more or less fanatical dogma, toward a certain form or tempo, and, having once perfected it, have become slaves to it. Miss Moore, indeed, seems to have exhausted the possibilities of her style and to have abandoned writing; even Mr. Stevens writes, or at least publishes, less and less; and Mr. Pound appears to have entered upon "the old age of a watery realist," indulging in looser and looser repetitions of cadences and mannerisms in Canto after Canto. In fact, some of his recent Cantos are scarcely more coherent than his correspondence. Dr. Bridges seems to have been fully aware that a change of tempo involves a complete or nearly complete change in the range of feeling perceived, that it opens up, in other words, a fresh field of subject matter; if one follows his career step by step one finds him taking up one tempo after another, exhausting its possibilities (for himself), and dropping each, once he has thoroughly mastered it and before it has mastered him.

The longer and slower lyrics should be approached only after the shorter have been studied, since in the shorter pieces the diction is more concentrated, less consciously toned down, and the quality of the style is more immediately apparent. I quote three stanzas from a fairly early poem entitled Dejection:

> Wherefore tonight so full of care,
> My soul, revolving hopeless strife,
> Pointing at hindrance, and the bare

> Painful escapes of fitful life?
> Shaping the doom that may befall
> By precedent of terror past:
> By love dishonoured, and the call
> Of friendship slighted at the last?

> By treasured names, the little store
> That memory out of wreck could save
> Of loving hearts that gone before
> Call their old comrade to the grave?

Compare the above lines to the following, from one of the latest lyrics, *Low Barometer*:

> The south-wind strengthens to a gale,
> Across the moon the clouds fly fast,
> The house is smitten as with a flail,
> The chimney shudders to the blast.

> On such a night, when air has loosed
> Its guardian grasp on blood and brain,
> Old terrors then of god or ghost
> Creep from their caves to life again. . . .

> Unbodied presences, the packed
> Pollution and remorse of Time,
> Slipp'd from oblivion, reënact
> The horrors of unhoused crime.

The quality of language over the gap of time is constant. In restraint, economy, richness of feeling, in what I should call an extreme generality or universality of import accomplished with no loss in the specification of the perception, these poems and a few others in the volume will stand the most scrutinizing comparison, I believe, with any of Shakespeare's sonnets. No living poet is capable of such masterly writing, and the number of poets dead is very small.

In his longer and more meditative lyrics, Dr. Bridges achieved a poetry, the norm of which is scarcely more intense than the norm of distinguished prose, but which, thanks to the quality of its diction, syntax and cadence, never falls short of extreme distinction, and which rises at need and without shock from distinction to extraordinary beauty. Poetry of this sort is not inferior to poetry of the shorter and more lyrical sort, though it may be harder to appreciate and is certainly less popular at the present time. It can handle material impossible in the more specialized lyric: what it loses in concentration, it can regain in subtlety of detail, completeness of description, range of material, and structural elaboration. . . .

In Elegy among the Tombs (*Sad sombre place*) and *Joy, sweetest life-born joy* a longer stanza is employed at a comparably slow tempo, the material being dictated by a somewhat more logical intention. To quote from these poems is even more unfair than to quote from the preceding one; so much depends on the structure, musical and logical, of the entire piece. Lines that may seem insignificant in a quoted fragment, take on significance in relation to the whole, take on a significance of a sort that can be established only by the greatest stylists, in fact, since it depends upon the subtlest and most minutely controlled of stylistic relationships. These poems, like so many others by their author, may even appear insignificant when read complete for the first or even the fifth time, only to become profoundly moving on the fifteenth or twentieth. Most readers, unfortunately, are nearly always ready to judge as dull that which surpasses them in technical knowledge or in human wisdom to any very great extent; what is not understood seems bad. And Dr. Bridges so far surpasses nearly any of his readers in these respects, is so utterly free of any impure attraction, any undisciplined "personality", that his genius has been ignored more unjustly than that of any other writer since Landor.

In the last two poems mentioned, in Dejection, and in a good many others, one encounters an attitude that may seem at first glance mere Victorian optimism, and which in a very few pieces (Fortunatus Nimium, for example) comes near to verging on Victorian optimism, but which is, in reality, something far more sombre and intelligent, a more or less classical resignation, with frequently, as in the professedly optimistic close of Dejection and Elegy among the Tombs, an undercurrent of calm and carefully restrained bitterness.

Dr. Bridges has been so often and so angrily compared to his friend Gerard Hopkins that I may perhaps be pardoned for a word on this subject. Hopkins seems to me to have been a truly great poet, though I cannot carry my enthusiasm as far as do his most violent admirers. The qualities that have won Hopkins almost immediate recognition during the past few years are, I fear, the very reasons for his limitations and his definite inferiority to Bridges. The mere fact that a man is a radical technical innovator does not render him a greater poet than the man who is less an innovator; extreme originality of method almost always involves exreme departure from the norm of experience, involves specialization and limitation of feeling. The greatest technical experimenter in English literature is, I suppose, Milton, and he is muscle-bound by his magnificence and the intricacy of his syntax. When he is not grand, he is grandiloquent; there is no transition between the two in Miltonic blank verse; and he killed English blank verse for two centuries. So with Hopkins: he can express with his violent rhythms an extremely special kind of excitement arising from religious experience, but he can express little else, and even the religious experience is incomplete, for if he does not deal wholly with the resultant excitement, he certainly throws his emphasis very heavily upon it. We are told, for instance, in superbly impassioned verses that the mind has mountains, but the nature of those mountains is never wholly clear. In Bridges the nature of the mountains is absolutely clear—that is, the experience is rendered whole—and the terror of the mountains is not isolated from all other experience but is seen in firm proportion. There is in the metrical experimentation in the present volume of Bridges quite as much originality of thought as in the experiments of Hopkins, coupled with a much more thorough knowledge of English meters and the complexities of feeling involved in their history. Bridges' technique, if the less obviously original of the two, is the more sensitive and the more widely applicable instrument of perception. In saying this, I do not wish it to be thought, let me repeat, that I am blind to the sensitivity or the power of Hopkins, a poet who moves me very deeply.

This limiting effect of the elaborately original may be one reason for the extreme shortness of so many of the most brilliant of contemporary careers: a narrow vein of feeling only can be explored, and once it is finished, the author has got himself so far from a fresh starting point that he lacks either the courage or the vigor to do anything about it; he has systematically deadened himself through specialization. If there is any truth in this supposition, extreme originality of style would appear to be one of the shortest cuts to that condition of atrophy, from which its most fanatical devotees seek, by its means, to escape. On the other hand, traditionalism is not equivalent to dullness; the diction of Dr. Bridges is as fresh and living as that of Dr. Williams; his meters allow him greater freedom, or rather greater range; he is in general a more civilized man. It is to be hoped, for the sake of twentieth-century poetry, that he will receive the study which his own poetry merits.

LIONEL STEVENSON
From *Darwin among the Poets*
1932, pp. 335–43

Although chronologically of the generation of Thomas Hardy, Robert Bridges requires consideration among the living poets, and as the last of them, because his poetic discussion of science and faith did not come until after the younger men had their say and because its widespread acceptance suggests that it accords with the current interest. Having been a physician by profession, Bridges must have been fully acquainted with modern scientific tenets, but most of his poetry was of classic or lyric or pastoral types in which philosophizing did not enter. . . .

The bulk of Bridges' poetry shows no tendency to analyze the relationship of religion and science. The references to God sounds orthodox enough, and the general outlook is optimistic, as in *January*:

> And God the Maker doth my heart grow bold
>> To praise for wintry works not understood,
> Who all the worlds and ages doth behold,
>> Evil and good as one, and all as good.

This does not mean, however, that modern scientific concepts are ignored. The first epistle in classical prosody, entitled *Winter Delights* and published in 1903, gives a detailed and enthusiastic survey of the whole scope of science. Although declaring himself to "lack the wizard Darwin's scientific insight," he shows intimate familiarity with his theme. First comes geology:

> Time's rich hieroglyph, with vast elemental pencil
> Scor'd upon Earth's rocky crust,—minute shells slowly collecting
> Press'd to a stone, uprais'd to a mountain, again to a fine sand
> Worn, burying the remains of an alien organic epoch,
> In the flat accretions of new sedimentary strata;
> All to be crush'd, crumpled, confused, contorted, abandon'd,
> Broke, as a child's puzzle is, to be recompos'd with attention.

These "very vestiges of creation," he says, are "the only commandments by God's finger of old inscribed on table of earthstone."

Next comes astronomy, with the contrast of all human ambition for conquest with the "utter wilderness of unlimited space," and yet the power of the human mind to measure and map the universe, the triumph of Bessel in discovering Procyon and of Adams and Leverrier in discovering Neptune. Equally vivid pictures are given of the achievements of physics in computing the speed of light, using the spectroscope, and reducing to mathematical formulas "all force and all motion of all matter." Anyone who neglects these sciences, says Bridges, "is but a boor as truly ridiculous as the village clown" who thinks that the sun moves around the earth. The poet does not expect to comprehend first-causes through scientific research, but he insists that the fullest possible study of physical phenomena is the duty as well as the pleasure of self-respecting minds.

For a moment he confesses a sense of futility in face of Nature's vastitude, wastefulness, and unconcern toward the human race; but soon he decides that, since man is the highest work of Nature, "he wrongs himself to imagine his soul foe to her aim, or from her sanction an outlaw." The greatest achievement of the modern era, to Bridges, is the "new science of Man, from dreamy scholastic imprisoning set free," and based solely on physical law. He sketches the field of anthropology, remarking the paradox that we should turn to our most primitive ancestors in order to comprehend modern civilized beings. Then he goes on to surgery with its discovery of antiseptics and to medicine with its epochal strides in bacteriology.

Admitting that his generation has overstressed Nature at the expense of other human interests, he refuses to believe that spiritual Grace is doomed. Science has merely "exposed the rotten foundation of old superstition," and all the theologians "are thrown to the limbo of antediluvian idols,"

> Only because we learn mankind's true history, and know
> That not at all from a high perfection sinfully man fell,
> But from baseness arose: We have with sympathy enter'd
> Those dark caves, his joyless abodes, where with ravening brutes,
> Bear or filthy hyena, he once disputed a shelter:—
> That was his Paradise, his garden of Eden,—abandon'd
> Ages since to the drift and drip, the cementing accretions
> Whence we now separate his bones buried in the stalagma.

Bridges declares that he finds the highest inspiration in the evolutionary record,

> this tale primæval of unsung,
> Unwritten, ancestral fate and adversity, this siege
> Of courage and happiness protracted so many thousand
> Thousand years in a slow persistent victory of brain
> And right hand o'er all the venom'd stings, sharpnesses of fang
> And dread fury whate'er Nature, tirelessly devising,
> Could develop with tooth, claw, tusk, or horn to oppose them.

Touching upon the development of religion, he begins to suggest that it is a manifestation of man's aesthetic sense, but breaks off with "'tis an unsolved mystery." We cannot judge Nature by our standards of good and bad, beauty and ugliness; human achievements in the arts seem so superior to the confusions and abominations of Nature that she might feel ashamed, were she not able to retort, "Fool, and who made thee?" Thus ends what may be called the first real poem of modern science, since it is the first by a man equally trained as a scientist and a poet.

The companion epistle, *To a Socialist in London*, applies the same evolutionary principles to the social sciences. Bridges has no faith in the utopian vision of social equality because it violates the law of the survival of the fittest. He assumes that our mental limitations prevent us from being able to formulate absolute ethical laws, and furthermore sees logical fallacies in communism. He cites first the Malthusian doctrine that the world would become overpopulated, and then goes on to portray vividly the "merciless outrage" of destruction throughout the whole range of living creatures. . . . To the argument that this view would produce "mere horror and despair" unless one believes that the human being is exempt from this principle by virtue of his moral ideals, Bridges retorts that the love of sport and of warfare reveals the principle still at work. The remainder of the poem insists on the permanence and value of the human love for pleasure and luxury and rank, without which life would be miserable and hopeless. . . .

More than a quarter of a century later, Bridges expanded the ideas of these three epistles into *The Testament of Beauty*, and picked up the broken thread of the first one with regard to the aesthetic basis of faith. Many of the selfsame arguments appear, such as the praise of wine, the justification of war as inherent in progress, and the parable of the bees as proof of the stultifying effects of communism. Fundamentally, however, it resembles the earlier poems in being based solidly on the whole cycle of modern science. Bridges draws his ideas and examples, not only from astronomy, chemistry, and physics, but from the latest theories of embryology, eugenics, and psychology. He refers to Coué and Freud, is glib regarding the "mutual inexhaustible interchange of transmitted genes," and devotes most of his third book to the analysis of sex.

In particular, *The Testament of Beauty* elaborates the idea of the epistle *To Robert Burns*, that all human existence depends on the primeval instincts, which are now reduced to two, selfhood and breed, otherwise self-preservation and reproduction. The whole poem is devoted to showing how these instincts instigated evolution and still control all conduct, though now somewhat sublimated into less material forms. He shows in detail how the instinct of reproduction has the same relationship to the race as that of self-preservation has to the individual, and how it grew out of the other by means of the pack-organization for offense and defense. He insists that human reason is the direct outcome of these instincts, and that now the next step is the development of spiritual perceptions under the influence of the love of beauty. There is nothing of Masefield's mysticism involved here; spiritual beauty is, to Bridges, identical with that which causes attraction between the sexes.

He does not, however, counsel surrender to the brute impulses. They all can be degraded into mere self-indulgence, but the result of it is bound to be destruction, while the austerer type survives. Thus a severely practical and utterly evolutionary code of ethics is created: good conduct is that which betters the species, and duty and conscience are equivalent to the law of nature, the necessity of survival. The key-word of the poem is "reason," and reason is nowise disparate from the "animal senses," since it grew directly from them; specifically, reason is the sublimation of the elder instinct, selfhood, while the sense of beauty is the sublimation of the younger, breed. He sees all nature as consistent, through the four stages "atomic, organic, sensuous, and self-conscient," and man therefore as an integral part, shaped by heredity and environment, akin to all the prior stages.

Permeated though the poem is with scientific thought, it is equally permeated with religious feeling. All natural processes are referred back to the will of God, and all the moral doctrines are supported by the teachings of Christ. Bridges repeatedly declares that science does not reveal first-causes, and that lack of faith induces a despair which is inimical to evolution. He dismisses the evidences of cruelty in nature as examples of the folly of applying our human standards beyond their scope. Reason and spiritual perception, he insists, ought to co-operate; and invisible influences, something like Plato's Ideas, are the most potent forces in existence.

Thus Bridges accomplished at last what the poets had been striving for during almost a century. He wrote a poem in which all the tenets of evolutionary science, including its very latest applications, were fully and authoritatively accepted, and yet he harmonized them with idealistic and spiritual faith such as poets seem determined to retain.

ALBERT GUÉRARD, JR.
From *Robert Bridges*
1942, pp. 257–66

Odell Shepard has written that during "a period in which the most representative poet has been Walt Whitman, the apostle of shuffle and sprawl and warm wet wallowing, the Laureate has maintained according to his abilities the standards of the poet who was born in Mantua just two thousand years ago."[1] It would perhaps be more accurate to say that he had maintained these standards during a period in which the most representative poet has been Jules Laforgue, the apostle of romantic irony in feeling and eccentricity in style. But against either background—the primitivism which runs from Whitman to William Carlos Williams, or the self-conscious, penitent and ironic art of the Symbolists and T. S. Eliot—Bridges has remained, in company with the later Yeats and Robert Frost and a few others, an isolated figure with some of the naïve sweetness of Sainte-Beuve's "classic." By so doing he has, it seems to me, showed us the strength or weakness of the genuinely traditional poet in any age.

Two temptations await the consciously and speciously traditional poet. He may consider the tradition as something exotic,[2] and regard the poetry of his predecessors merely as the source for recondite allusions or startling echoes. Surely the Cantos of Ezra Pound resemble nothing so much as a graduate student's Midsummer Night's Dream! On the other hand, he may be slavishly obedient to the tradition, or more often to a particular master, and merely copy the forms, meters and language of an earlier day, without recognizing the perceptual value of those forms and meters or the true meaning of that language. From the many imitators of T. S. Eliot during the last decade two or three really important poets have emerged—and a much larger number who repeated only the familiar formulae: the broken rhythms and the esoteric learning, the inhibited characters and the startling juxtapositions of mood. Robert Bridges either escaped or conquered both these temptations—self-conscious traditionalism and slavish imitation—with remarkable success. . . .

The distinguishing characteristic of Bridges' traditionalism is its critical and selective quality. In his lyrics, Bridges studied Milton and Heine and Herbert as a painter or composer studies an earlier master, analyzing and mastering their technical experiments and valuable innovations; trying, above all, to understand the emotions and mental attitudes which their styles conveyed. It was necessary, perhaps, for him to understand the cynicism which Heine had failed to overcome or the skepticism which Arnold had failed to overcome before he could master these emotions in himself. Similarly, a study of Milton and Herbert may have aided him to achieve that reconciliation of divergent claims, of two contradictory goods, which the fully civilized man must achieve. Bridges' emotional and moral experience was enriched by every poet he studied; or, to be more exact, by every poet of whom he became a part. That some of his early sonnets should have represented *pastiche* rather than imitation was perhaps inevitable. But eventually the mannerisms and particular voice of Milton, for instance, were left behind, and there remained only a valuable and now wholly personal element of style. The reader who wishes to see various stages through which Bridges' education, in a particular case, passed, has only to compare the unmistakably Miltonic blank verse of the opening of *Prometheus the Firegiver* with the pure and unmannered blank verse of *Achilles in Scyros*. The individuality as well as the richness of this later blank verse could

have been achieved, however, only after the study of Milton, Shakespeare and other great masters in the form.

In the plays this critical and selective traditionalism is even more marked. None of the plays is wholly original; each is based on mythology, history, or an earlier story or play. Bridges' significant contribution, however, lies not so much in his transmutation of old material, as in his skillful exploitation, in a single play, of various dramatic traditions and forms. That is, he makes use of good dramatic conventions found in Elizabethan tragedy, for instance, while ignoring stage conventions of Elizabethan tragedy which no longer have any value; in the same play he makes similar use of dramatic conventions from Greek and Spanish Renaissance drama, again rejecting those which had a purely transitory significance. In the best of his plays—*The Christian Captives, Achilles in Scyros* and the two plays on *Nero*—he thus mediated between various dramatic traditions, and achieved a form combining valuable elements from each. Whether or not his own experiments in this direction were successful, they point an interesting alternative road to the modern contemporary dramatist who feels that a dramatic convention, once it has become obsolete, can never be used again.

In *The Testament of Beauty*, this critical and selective traditionalism appears in the diversity of philosophical sources rather than in the structure of the verse. In contrast to modern professional philosophers, with their desperate cleaving to one or another particular and narrow school, Bridges formulated a philosophy which could embrace the ethical dualism of Aristotle and the naturalism of Spinoza, Darwin's theory of evolution and the best ideals of historical Christianity, a Neo-Humanist insistence on self control and a Bergsonian contempt for purely conventional morality. The poem is not, however, the product of an unthinking eclecticism. Its only serious obscurities result from a theory of essences which is never clearly defined.

Like every genuinely traditional poet, Bridges was a conscious experimentalist. The cautious nature of his metrical experimentation has a particular force today, when poetry has not yet recovered from the excesses of free verse. He recognized that the possibilities for variation in certain meters had been exhausted, and that new rhythms would have to be found. But he also knew that a subtle extension of the rules of blank verse, for instance, would in the end be more rewarding than the abolition of all formal meters. The difference between radical experiment divorced from all past attainment and cautious experiment to enrich old rhythms is illustrated by a comparison of sprung-rhythm or sprung-meter as used by Gerard Manley Hopkins and Bridges. By introducing sprung feet into every line, Hopkins arrived at a fevered rhythm capable of conveying only intense excitement. Bridges, on the other hand, used sprung meter as an occasional resource for variation or counterpoint in standard accentual and accentual-syllabic poems. In his hands, it became a particularly valuable means of introducing momentary excitement, of calling sharp attention to a particular word or phrase. As a result of Bridges' experiments, many poets are today able to use sprung-meter occasionally with rewarding effect. But a successful imitator of Hopkins has yet to appear.

The first important characteristic which appears in all of Bridges' poetry, its traditionalism, is not unrelated to the second, its wide moral pertinence, its concern with universal human problems. At a time when nearly all serious poets seem dedicated to the proposition that life cannot be understood, the conception of poetry as a means of establishing order in the emotional life of man seems to have fallen into fairly complete abeyance. To the reader of *The Waste Land* and the latest psychological textbook, the generalizations of *The Testament of Beauty* and the rounded character studies of Bridges' plays must seem as quaint and factitious as the subjects of his lyrics—scenes of the English countryside, clearly defined conflicts between reason and desire, ordinary grief and joy, simple and unfrustrated love. Many poets, indeed, seem bent on outdoing the psychologists in their systematic reduction of the soul to a bundle of reflexes; of an hour's living to a congeries of unrelated sensations. The Shandean conception of human character is of course much older than Jung, Adler and Freud—certainly as old as the medieval interpreters of dreams—but it has penetrated poetry only in recent years. Since much of human experience is fragmentary, automatic and little understood, poets regard any lucid record of an experience and any shaped and patterned emotion as fictions of the truant intellect. Perhaps the strongest prohibition of contemporary criticism of poetry is the one it has posted against any appearance of the rational intellect, with its ancient tendency to use simple exposition and abstract language.

The critic who regards with alarm this submergence of the intellect, this surrender of the poet to the raw material of his poetry, runs the danger of blinding himself to the enormous value of recent psychological discoveries and to the very real value of recent poetic experiments. Had Irving Babbitt been successful in forbidding the poet and novelist to explore the subconscious and the abnormal, he would have rendered impossible some of the chief masterpieces of our day. He should rather have complained of poets and novelists who were not philosophers as well as psychologists; who refused to understand (and therefore control) experience in the way that an ordinary civilized man understands and to a certain extent controls his experience.

The lucid, exact and complete evaluation of human experience in Bridges' lyrics is the ultimate reason for their greatness, as it is the ultimate reason for the greatness of Milton's and Shakespeare's. The best of the *Shorter Poems* define and give life to a series of attitudes toward some of the central difficulties of man: the struggles of faith and skepticism, of reason and instinct, of individual happiness and the laws of a mechanistic civilization. They define and vivify these attitudes not by precept or disinterested description, but by the actual presentation and molding of experience. The completeness of the definition is indissociable from the problem of poetic form. Poetic perception—the act of willing, seeing, or understanding something—is also the act of giving shape to something; of defining it through all the resources at the artist's command: meter and total structure as well as image and abstract language. The poet who succumbs to the more extreme types of organic form, and allows his subject-matter to dictate its own embodiment, sacrifices the best parts of his inherited language. He becomes, as Bridges never became, the meek stenographer of half-understood sensations and impressions. In the last analysis, Bridges' greatness as a stylist cannot be separated from his "masterly control of the material" with which he deals. And it should not be forgotten that this material is, in the best lyrics, the normal experience of the civilized human being.

If the lyrics represent successful attempts to understand the poet's own experience through the definition of impulses and attitudes, the plays represent the more detached studies of a philosopher. Not since the Elizabethans, perhaps, has English drama concentrated so successfully on the study of human character as in Bridges' two plays on Nero. Whether these plays can ever be acted is a matter of small importance beside the richness of their psychology. As Charles Lamb observed, the

qualities which we most admire in Shakespeare's tragedies can seldom be transferred to the stage. Particularly today, with the professional theater so utterly devoid of serious content or intellectual interest, the actability of a profound psychological tragedy can hardly be used as a standard by which to measure its value. It seems to me that the characterizations of Nero and Seneca in Bridges' two Nero plays are among the most impressive in English dramatic literature. In Seneca we have a rich and living study of the decay of the power of judgment as a result of a life of continual moral compromise; in Nero we have a pendant study of the disintegration of personality as a result of self-indulgence and an uncontrolled lust for power. The other plays are less interesting psychologically, but nearly all of them contain passages of great lyric beauty. The reader interested only in Bridges' style cannot afford to ignore the masques *Achilles in Scyros*, *Prometheus the Firegiver* and *Demeter*, for in them he will find some of the firmest and richest blank verse in English poetry. The indifference in which Bridges' plays are held can be explained only by the fact that almost no one has read them.

The active effort to understand and illumine human experience is most easily seen, of course, in *The Testament of Beauty*. The fact that Bridges' philosophy—an idealism erected on naturalistic foundations—closely resembles that of George Santayana in no way impairs its value. Although its occasional pedestrian and amateurish explorations of minor epistemological problems contribute little, the poem represents a courageous attempt to reconcile the truth of naturalism with a necessary respect for reason and the ethical heritage of dualistic philosophies. How can man control and refine his animal nature without sterilizing the emotions which make for his happiness? How can he preserve freedom of will in a world he never made? How can he assert and maintain the autonomy of reason without setting up consciousness and rational control as objects of worship, as ends rather than means? *The Testament of Beauty* attempts to solve these problems. That they were the problems which chiefly concerned the most thoughtful Victorians, and that they are now largely ignored, does not alter the fact that they are our problems, problems which have to be answered. "The army of unalterable law" has indeed marched in a way which Meredith could scarcely have predicted, and a ruthless imperialism and theory of the state has been rightly described as "organic." The central subject of *The Testament of Beauty* is the possibility of directing and controlling, rather than passively accepting, the organic and dynamic forces of life.

In all these ways, but especially in his insistence on the autonomy of human imagination and reason, on their power to understand and control experience, Bridges is a truly traditional poet; in Sainte-Beuve's words, "a true classic." Like many traditional poets with the same ideals, he has been accused of two serious faults: limitation of range and poverty of emotion. Although it belongs to the jargon of contemporary criticism, the term *range* is seldom defined. If range is measured by the varieties of human action with which an artist deals, Bridges' range is small. One could likewise say that the range of Flaubert is smaller than that of Zola, or, to make an extreme case, that the range of Wordsworth is smaller than that of Southey. But this kind of range—this diversity of physical experience—is unimportant beside the range of a Thomas Mann or a Henry James. Mann and James show little or none of James Farrell's familiarity with the *mores* of the lowest classes, yet they explore far more deeply the mind and heart of man. The concern of the great artist is with depth rather than breadth of experience. If range is measured by this depth, the novels of Jane Austen exhibit as wide a range as those of Scott. In this sense, the range of Bridges is also very wide. If he was isolated from the realms of experience which a full social documentation of his time would have required, and if he largely ignored the criminal or abnormal mind, he more than compensated for these limitations by his full understanding of the experience of the civilized man. And this understanding was, as I have said, at every point lucid, sound, complete.

Only the critic who demands incoherence could accuse Bridges of poverty of emotion. He effected, in fact, an unusually successful compromise between the extreme romantic's unformed and incoherent emotionalism and the sterile restraint of the Neo-Classic. The fresh and honest joy of the *Shorter Poems*, their uninhibited acceptance of beauty and love, would indeed have seemed shamefully "romantic" to the emotionally starved creatures of Eliot's *Waste Land*. In the love poems, we have the calm purity of Jonson's songs rather than the meaningless intensity of Shelley's "Indian Serenade"; in the more sombre lyrics, the tragic accent of Donne's "A Hymn to God the Father" rather than the violent hysteria of Thompson's "The Hound of Heaven." More than any poetry of the last century, Bridges' lyrics are the product of a sensibility which has been enriched and civilized without being crippled or destroyed.

Notes

1. Odell Shepard, "Robert Bridges," *Bookman*, LXXI (1930), 154.
2. Cp. Winters, *Primitivism and Decadence*, p. 74.

DONALD E. STANFORD
From "Preface" to *In the Classic Mode:
The Achievement of Robert Bridges*
1978, pp. 9–12

When Robert Bridges's *Testament of Beauty* appeared in 1929 the day after the poet's eighty-fifth birthday, it was enthusiastically received by the critics and achieved a popular success unusual for serious poetry in any age. Several years later, few people were reading Bridges, and fewer still were writing about him. A glance at any standard bibliography from 1935 to 1975 tells the story. The accumulation of articles and books—scholarly, critical, and popular—on Ezra Pound and T. S. Eliot, for example, is enormous and appears to be endless. The entries for Robert Bridges are relatively very few. The Pound-Eliot star was in the ascendancy, and those young intellectuals in the depression years who went for *The Waste Land* and *The Cantos* and for the early poetry of Auden were impatient with the remote and cool classicism of Bridges. It was one of those periodic changes in taste which seem to occur about every half century in the history of literature. *The Waste Land*, published in 1922 (seven years before *The Testament of Beauty*), had, by the mid-thirties, carried all before it. There was a continuing revolution in the arts as well as in society, and the kind of poetry that Bridges wrote—finished, quiet, meditative, beautiful, powerful, and profound—was buried in the libraries in spite of the attempts of a few American critics like Yvor Winters and later Albert Guérard to keep it alive. But tastes change, and almost fifty years after Bridges's death, there are a few signs that there may be a revival of interest in the work of this distinguished poet and in what he stood for.

The terms *classic*, *classical*, and *classicism* have been frequently used with reference to Bridges's poetry in the text of this book and in the title. Some defense of their use may be needed, particularly in view of the fact that the distinguished scholar Douglas Bush has called Bridges's work romantic, and also in view of the fact that Eliot, who wrote a very different kind of poetry from Bridges, called himself a classicist. Furthermore, Bridges himself praised highly certain romantic poets. He liked some of Keats and he had an embarrassing enthusiasm for Shelley, and he thought that the two most famous neoclassical poets, Dryden and Pope, were very dull dogs indeed. Can the argument that Bridges's verse was predominantly classical be maintained? And what are the virtues, if any, of classicism?

Bridges as a practicing poet (and not merely as a theoretician) rarely departed from the notion that a successful poem should make its appeal *as a whole* and not as a series of disjunctive brilliant parts. The poem should have unity, coherence, and a logically demonstrable structure and be expressed in a language that had beauty without sentimentality and power without sensationalism or vulgarity. Furthermore, he believed that serious poetry should have a rational content that could be discussed intelligently even with those who might disagree with it. For example, he carried on a comprehensible dialogue with George Santayana concerning the philosophical ideas of *The Testament of Beauty* even though the two seemed to be in disagreement about such fundamental terms as *essence* and *influence*. He was, on the other hand, very impatient with William Butler Yeats's irrational occultism, a fact that may have prevented a close friendship between them, for Bridges was fascinated by Yeats as a person and admired his early poetry. But the occultism bored Bridges, if not to tears at least to irritation. As a man of reason, Bridges could discuss his differences with Santayana. He could not do so with the romantic Yeats.

As a technician and as a theoretician Bridges believed that all successful poetry should have a prosody, and he believed that the prosody could be formulated—which he proceeded to do. His various treatises on the subject are not easy reading, but they are an important and necessary part of the total picture. For everything he did in the metrics of his poems—and he experimented with many different rhythms and meters—Bridges had his reasons. His views on the conventional meters of English verse that he himself employed so brilliantly are to be found in his studies on Milton's prosody. The theory behind his early experiments in accentual verse (in collaboration with Hopkins) are set forth in his essay on stress prosody published together in one volume in the final edition of his study of Milton. The extensive experiments in quantitative verse are explained in his 1916 edition of *Ibant Obscuri* and elsewhere. His invention of *neo-Miltonic syllabics*, which led to the "loose Alexandrines" of *The Testament of Beauty*, is analyzed in his "Note on New Verse" reprinted in the *Collected Essays*.

It is this combination of rationally intelligible subject matter and expert craftsmanship that I call *classical*. And there are some further considerations. In his Memoir of Digby Dolben, Bridges said:

> . . . when he [Dolben] began to write poetry he would never have written on any subject that did not deeply move him, nor would he attend to poetry unless it expressed his own emotions. . . . What had led me to poetry was the inexhaustible satisfaction of form, the magic of speech, lying as it seemed to me in the masterly control of the material. . . . Dolben imagined poetic form to be the naive outcome of peculiar personal emotion. [1]

Mastery of form is what we expect in classical verse. Self-expression of one's "peculiar personal emotion" is the hallmark of the romantic school. *The Waste Land*, for instance, is really a romantic poem expressing peculiar personal emotions, in spite of many opinions to the contrary. It is a piece of "rhythmical grumbling" as Eliot himself called it in later years. Now Bridges and his friend Hopkins also had *their* religious problems, and of these three poets, it was Bridges who defined his religious difficulties in verse that comes closest to the classical standards of mastery of form and of clarity, simplicity, and disciplined control of the emotions. In "The Affliction of Richard" he addresses God:

> Though thou, I know not why,
> Didst kill my childish trust,
> That breach with toil did I
> Repair, because I must:
>   And spite of frighting schemes,
> With which the fiends of Hell
> Blaspheme thee in my dreams,
> So far I have hoped well.

And it was the Jesuit priest who was indulging in romantic self-expression of his "peculiar personal emotion" when he complained to Christ in "Carrion Comfort":

> But ah, but O thou terrible, why wouldst thou rude
>   on me
> Thy wring-world right foot rock? lay a lionlimb
>   against me? scan

> With darksome devouring eyes my bruise'd bones?
>   and fan,
> O in turns of tempest, me heaped there; me frantic to
>   avoid thee and flee?[2]

Now the fact that in these two poems Bridges had mastered a conventional metrical form while Hopkins was attempting an unconventional one does not necessarily make Bridges's poem inferior. Hopkins, like most writers of romantic temperament, was excessive in his approach to any subject, and when it came to prosody he was obsessed with the notion of *make it new*. He developed a prosody with a unique system of scansion of unnecessary complexity that no one could follow in its entirety except, perhaps, himself.

Finally, it should be noted that Bridges, more than any other poet of the period, had what one vaguely calls the "Greek spirit." He was, of course, thoroughly familiar with the literature and the philosophy of Greece, and, in his life as well as in his work, he seems to have developed that harmony of mind and heart which one thinks of as the principal attainment of the Greek ideal.

Notes

1. *The Poems of Digby Mackworth Dolben*, ed. with a Memoir by Robert Bridges (London, 1911), pp. xviii–xix.
2. *The Poems of Gerard Manley Hopkins*, eds. W. H. Gardner and N. H. Mackenzie (London, New York, Toronto, 1967), p. 99.

RUPERT BROOKE

1887–1915

Rupert Chawner Brooke was born on August 3, 1887, at Rugby. He attended school there (where his father taught) and then went to King's College, Cambridge, where he studied classics with F. M. Cornford and philosophy with G. E. Moore from 1906 to 1909. Brooke joined the Cambridge Fabian Society and wrote many critical articles for the *Cambridge Review*. He did not, however, receive first-class honors in classics, and, stunned by this failure, turned his attention to poetry and the study of English literature. His *Poems* appeared in 1911 to a warm reception, and his thesis, *John Webster and the Elizabethan Drama*, helped him to become a Fellow of King's College in 1913. During this time he traveled extensively—to Germany and Italy in 1911, to the United States in 1913 and 1914, and to Tahiti in 1914. He became simultaneously associated with the Cambridge circle of Moore and Goeffrey Keynes and the Bloomsbury group of Virginia Woolf and Lady Ottoline Morrell; he and Bertrand Russell shared a mutual dislike and disapproval. His interest in the Georgian movement in poetry led to his co-editing of the first anthology of *Georgian Poetry* in 1912.

At the outbreak of the war he joined the Navy. His sudden death aboard ship in the Aegean on St. George's Day, April 23, 1915, conjoined with the posthumous publication of his famous war sonnets, *1914*, helped to foster a legend of Brooke as a symbol of the tragic waste of war.

Among his other works are a series of *Letters from America* (1913) and a one-act play, *Lithuania* (1912).

Personal

I thank you ever so kindly for this advance copy of Rupert's volume, which you were right (and blest!) in feeling that I should intensely prize. I have been spending unspeakable hours over it—heart-breaking ones, under the sense of the stupid extinction of so exquisite an instrument and so exquisite a being. Immense the generosity of his response to life and the beauty and variety of the forms in which it broke out, and of which these further things are such an enriching exhibition.

His place is now very high and very safe—even though one walks round and round it with the aching soreness of having to take the monument for the man. It's so wretched talking, really, of any "place" but his place *with* us, and in our eyes and affection most of all, the other being such as could wait, and grow with all confidence and power *while* waiting. He has something, at any rate, one feels in this volume, that puts him singularly apart even in his eminence—the fact that, member of the true high company as he is and poet of the strong wings (for he seems to me extraordinarily strong,) he has *charm* in a way of a kind that belong to none of the others, who have their beauty and abundance, their distinction and force and grace, whatever it may be, but haven't that particular thing as he has it and as he was going to keep on having it, since it was of his very nature—by which I mean that of his genius. The point is that I think he would still have had it even if he had grown bigger and bigger, and stronger and stronger (for this is what he *would* have done,) and thereby been almost alone in this idiosyncrasy. Even of Keats I don't feel myself saying that he had charm—it's all lost in the degree of beauty, which somehow allows it no chance. But in Rupert (not that I match them!) there is the beauty, so great, and then the charm, different and playing beside it and savouring of the very quality of the man. What it comes to, I suppose, is that he touches me most when he is whimsical and personal, even at the poetic pitch, or in the poetic purity, as he perpetually is. And he penetrates me most when he is most hauntingly (or hauntedly) English—he draws such a real magic from his conscious reference to it. He is extraordinarily so even in the War sonnets—not that that isn't highly natural too; and the reading of these higher things over now, which one had first read while he was still there to be exquisitely at stake in them, so to speak, is a sort of refinement both of admiration and of anguish. The present gives them such sincerity—as if they had wanted it! I adore the ironic and familiar things, the most intimately English—the Chilterns and the Great Lover (towards the close of which I recognise the misprint you speak of, but fortunately so obvious a one—the more flagrant the better—that you needn't worry:) and the Funeral of Youth, awfully charming; and of course Grantchester, which is booked for immortality. I revel in Grantchester—and how it would have made one love him if one hadn't known him. As it is it wrings the heart! And yet after all what do they do, all of them together, but again express how life had been wonderful and crowded and fortunate and exquisite for him?—with his sensibilities all so exposed, really exposed, and yet never taking the least real harm. He seems to me to have had in his short life so much that one may almost call it everything. And he isn't tragic now—he has only stopped. It's we who are tragic—you and his mother especially, and whatever others; for we can't stop, and we wish we could.—HENRY JAMES, Letter to Edward Marsh (June 6, 1915), *The Letters of Henry James*, Vol. 2, 1920, pp. 472–74

He confronted his fellow-creatures like the sensitive, serious, scrutinizing boy he was, ready to face what and who might come without flinching; smiling lip and steady eye. One was conscious of occasional shynesses and silences, of even a little awkwardness at times that was in itself a grace. One was still more conscious of an insatiable interest and speculation. His quiet gaze took you in; yours couldn't so easily take him in, in either sense. These are my own remembrances; few, alas, however vivid and unfading: and even at that they are merely those of one of the less responsive sex.

In spite of life's little disillusionments (which, it is prudent to remember, we may cause as well as endure), in spite of passing moods of blackness and revulsion, nothing could be clearer in his poems, in his letters, and in himself, than his zest and happiness. Looking back on his school-days he said that he had been happier then than he could find words to say. How many born *children* would echo that sentiment. What wonder, then, that at twenty he describes himself as in the depths of despondency 'because of my age'? And a little later: 'I am just too old for romance.' What does this mean but that he found life so full and so arresting that he was afraid he might not be able to keep pace with it? It was a needless apprehension. The sea was deep beneath the waves and the foam. If he had lived to

be, let us say, forty, he would have come to much the same conclusion, though, perhaps, with more emphasis and with more philosophy. He was never to experience *that* little misfortune! He flung himself into the world—of men, of books, of thought and affairs—as a wasp pounces into a cake-shop, Hotspur into the fighting. When his soul flourished on Walter Pater and Aubrey Beardsley, he thought it a waste of time to walk and swim. When, together with meat and 'alcohol', he gave up these rarified but in their own fashion admirable dainties, and lived, as it is fabulously reported, on milk and honey, it seemed a waste of time to do anything else. He could not be half-hearted. Indeed, in that 'tearing hunger to do things'—working, playing, reading, writing, publishing, travelling, talking, socialism, politics—any one thing seemed a waste of time, because meanwhile the rest of life's feast was kept waiting.—WALTER DE LA MARE, "Rupert Brooke and the Intellectual Imagination" (1919), *Pleasures and Speculations*, 1940, pp. 194–95

Rupert Brooke—yes! Glancing once more into his poems, I detect a note of breezy obviousness. There is a good deal of *le geste* here. For all those travels in America and the Pacific his outlook was circumscribed, and I should not call his emotional stock of that period a rich one. He was a dear, transparent, social creature, whose attitude towards everyday things reminded me of a Newfoundland puppy entering a strange room, and sniffing at all those unfamiliar objects with delighted tail-waggings. Another Brooke might have emerged in course of time, had the chance been given.

A college view of life may be both keen and just, but is unavoidably narrow. Happy the man who can absorb what such a training has to give him, and then excrete the rest. Some never succeed in doing either the one or the other: Brooke had already passed the first stage. I think there was that germinating in him which Fate hindered from coming forth, and this cannot be said of all mortals of promise who die young. It was with Brooke not a question of intellectual clarification, but of readjustment and appraisement of experience. Likely enough he would have realized the dream of his friends and admirers, for he possessed what is lacking in many, in too many, in far too many, of his craft: a spinal column. Brooke was vertebrate. His was a positive gift, a yea-saying to life—the poet's first requisite. The animal in him was not atrophied, as in so many of us. He was assimilative and zestful, unafraid of realities, responsive to phenomena. The spoilt-darling phase was nearing its end when he died in Tris Boukes Bay.—NORMAN DOUGLAS, *Looking Back*, 1933, p. 327

Soon afterwards Davies departed, and I was alone with Rupert Brooke for about half an hour. Some way removed from me, he sat by a window serenely observing the trees of Gray's Inn gardens. From time to time his eyes met mine, but it was with a clouded though direct regard. I was conscious that his even-toned voice was tolerant rather than communicative, and that his manner had become gravely submissive to the continuing presence of a stranger. He may have been shy, but I am afraid he was also a little bored with me. We agreed that Davies was an excellent poet and a most likeable man. I then asked him a few clumsy questions about his travels. His replies were reserved and unilluminating. One fragment of our talk which I remember clearly was—as such recoveries often are—wholly to my disadvantage.

"What were the white people like in the places you stayed at in the tropics?" I had asked. ("The tropics" sounded somehow inept, but it was too late to correct myself now!)

"Some of them," he said, "were rather like composite characters out of Conrad and Kipling."

Hoping that it would go down well, I made a disparaging remark about Kipling's poetry being terribly tub-thumping stuff.

"But not always, surely," he answered; and then let me off easily by adding, "I used to think rather the same myself until Eddie made me read *Cities and Thrones and Powers*. There aren't many better modern poems than that, you know."

I could only admit that I had never read it. And yet, if I'd been more at my ease, I might have saved my credit by telling him that I knew by heart the first eight lines, which I really loved, of Kipling's "Neither the harps nor the crowns amused, nor the cherubs' dove-winged races."

After that it seemed safer not to mention poetry any more. It would be comforting if I could record that I expressed some admiration for his work—if I had said, for instance, how delightful I thought his Grantchester poem. But I didn't. I was, indeed, reduced to informing him of the uninspiring fact that we'd been at Cambridge together for a term—the autumn one of 1906. Yes, that was his first term there, he replied, and he'd acted in the Greek play—the *Eumenides* it was—as the Herald. This was something I'd entirely forgotten, though it came back to me vividly now. For the Herald had been such a striking figure that everybody in Cambridge had talked about him. But I didn't mystify him by exclaiming "So I *had* seen you before!" I merely thought how odd it was that I had never connected the Herald in his gorgeous red and gold with the young poet whose work had since then startled and attracted me.—SIEGFRIED SASSOON, *The Wealth of Youth*, 1942, pp. 214–15

General

I had read, I think, practically all the poems published in this book while Rupert Brooke was still living, and I still think, as I thought then, that the double sonnet, *Menelaus and Helen*, and the five sonnets, including the now famous one which serves as his epitaph, represent his finest achievement. Much of Rupert Brooke's work expresses the exuberance of youth; it represents the will to love or the will to die, and the straining desire towards the "white flame" of poetry, characteristic of young poets, rather than definite achievement. Brooke was in love with death long before the war came; his poems are full of this hunger and desire for death as the consummation and preserver of beauty; and this in itself is characteristic of the adolescent poet before life has been fully realized. Brooke ran toward death as toward the consummation which life had not given, perhaps could not have given to one of his temperament. He went toward death as the "great lover"—not of life as he thought, but of death itself. There are men of whom this is true. Brooke was one of them. This in no sense belittles his heroic sacrifice, for he had everything to live for.

The greater part of Brooke's work is fluent, exuberant, rhapsodic, and often reminiscent—now of Yeats, now of John Masefield (as in *The Great Lover*, which reflects the spirit and cadences of *Biography*), now of Swinburne, and often of the seventeenth century poets in his use of the rhymed couplet. He had an individual turn, nevertheless, which made one sure that he would become more self-expressive in form as well as in content. The war, or the anticipation of death, gave Brooke an intensity, clarity, and a greater degree of precision, than he had attained before except in one or two instances. In many of the earlier poems the feeling for words and for the sound of them rather embalmed and obscured the sense and the image. Had he survived the war he would certainly have gained in depth and richness of experience and in austerity of expression.

Much of his work is frankly playful in intent; this is part of its charm for many people, and for others a serious defect. This was probably temperamental. Some poets conceal sensitiveness in this way, others by satire. Whether Brooke was content that his work should remain so, we may not know. He was only twenty-eight when he died.

His death is a symbol of the waste of war.—ALICE C. HENDERSON, *Poetry*, Feb. 1916, pp. 262–64

Nothing in Brooke's work is more conspicuous than its preoccupation with actual experience, its adventurousness, its daring, its keen curiosity and interest in ideas, its life-giving *youth*fulness. Nothing in his work is more conspicuous by its comparative absence than reverie, a deep still broodingness. The children in his poems are few. They are all seen objectively, from without; though a wistful childlike longing for peace and home and mother dwells in such a poem as 'Retrospect' or 'A Memory'. I am not sure that the word 'dream' occurs in them at all.

'Don't give away one of the first poets in England,' he says in one of his letters, 'but there is in him still a very, very small portion that's just a little childish.' Surely it was the *boy* in him that boasted in that easy go-ahead fashion, the boy in him that was a little shamefaced to confess to that faint vestige of childishness. Imagine William Blake or Traherne being apologetic about it! The general theme of his poems is the life of the mind, the senses, the feelings, life here and now, knocking with the knocker, slamming the door, however impatient he may be with life's limitations. Their longing is for a state of consciousness wherein this kind of life shall be possible without exhaustion, disillusionment, or acute reaction; especially the reactions physical and otherwise of growing old—and that of a second childhood.

His words, too, are for the most part absolute symbols; they mean precisely what they say and only what they say. Whereas the words of the mystics and the poets of a childlike imagination seem chiefly to mean what is left hinted at, rather than expressed. His world stands out sharp and distinct, like the towers and pinnacles of a city under the light of a cloudless sky. Their world, old as Eden and remoter than the Euphrates, lies like the fabric of a vision, bathed in an unearthly atmosphere. He desired, idolized, delighted in, and praised things-in-themselves, for their energy, vividness and naturalness; they do so for some disturbing yet solacing inward and spiritual significance, and for the reality of which things are the painted veil. *They* live or at least desire to live in the quietude of their own spirit, in a region of which a certain order of dream seems to be a reminiscence, in a faraway listening, and they are most happy when at peace, if not passive. He is all questing activity, apprehensiveness.

Nothing pleases him so much as doing things, although, fretted that both body and mind so rapidly weary, he may pine for sleep. His writing, whether in his poems, his study of Webster, or in his letters, is itself a kind of action; and he delights in things touched, smelt and tasted. He delights in them, that is, not merely for their beauty or for any remoter original they may only represent, but for their own sharp sake. He is restless, enquiring, and veers in the wind like a golden weathercock. He is impatient of every vague idealism, as wary as a fox of the faintest sniff of sentimentality. To avoid both (not always quite successfully) he flies to the opposite extreme, and to elude the 'rosy mists of poets' experience he lays emphasis on the unpleasant and sordid aspects of life. At any cost he intends to record fully and concisely the chosen salient instant's actual content—even if that instant was spent in being sea-sick. How appalling to be old *and* amorous! Say so then in a pungent sonnet. It is a poetic duty, and it will be also something of a lark. Truth at all costs: ecstatic, sober, sane or sour; let beauty take care of itself. So he came to write and to defend poems that in his friend's witty and conciliatory phrase one finds it disquieting to read at meals. A child alone, a visionary, lives in eternity; a man in time; a boy in the passing moment. It is the moments that flower for Brooke. What is his poem 'Dining-room Tea' but the lovely cage of an instant when in an ecstasy intellectually observed and analysed time and the world and even the tea streaming out of the teapot stood still?—WALTER DE LA MARE, "Rupert Brooke and the Intellectual Imagination" (1919), *Pleasures and Speculations*, 1940, pp. 181–83

There can be no question that his brain was both a fine instrument and a strong one; but there are other questions, for is it not true that the intellectual poet, unlike the visionary poet, improves and develops with age? Though Keats died younger, and Shelley only a year or two older, than Rupert Brooke, both left behind them unmistakable proof not merely that they were great poets, but that their greatness was of a particular character. If we cannot call Rupert Brooke a great poet, that is to some extent the result of feeling that, compared with the others, he has left us only sketches and premonitions of what was to come. He was of the type that reacts sharply to experience, and life would have taught him much, perhaps changed him greatly. Like Dryden, like Meredith, like Donne himself, as Mr Pearsall Smith has lately shown us, it might have been in prose and not in poetry that he achieved his best. It might have been in scholarship; it might have been in action. But if we seem to disparage what he left, there again we trace the effect of friendship. We do not want our friend rapt away into the circle of the good and the great. We want still to cherish the illusion that the poems will be bettered, the adjectives discussed, the arguments resumed, the convictions altered. The actual achievement must always have for those who knew him a ghostly rival in the greatness which he did not live to achieve. But he was of the few who seem to exist in themselves, apart from what they accomplish, apart from length of life.—VIRGINIA WOOLF, "The Intellectual Imagination" (1919), *Books and Portraits*, 1977, p. 91

Rupert Brooke left the world in a chariot of fire. He was something more than either a man or a poet; he was and is a Personality. It was as a Personality that he dazzled his friends. He was overflowing with tremendous, contagious vitality. He was the incarnation of the spirit of youth, wearing the glamour and glory of youth like a shining garment. Despite our loss, it almost seems fitting that he did not live to that old age which he never understood, for which he had such little sympathy, and which he seems to have hated more than death. For he had the splendid insolence of youth. Youth commonly feels high-spirited in an unconscious, instinctive fashion, like a kitten or a puppy; but Rupert Brooke was as self-consciously young as a decrepit pensioner is self-consciously old. He rejoiced in the strength of his youth, and rolled it as a sweet morsel under his tongue. He was so glad to be young, and to know every morning on rising from sleep that he was still young! His passionate love of beauty made him see in old age only ugliness; he could not foresee the joys of the mellow years. All he saw consisted of grey hairs, wrinkles, double chins, paunches. To him all old people were Struldbrugs. We smile at the insolence of youth, because we know it will pass with the beauty and strength that support it.—WILLIAM LYON PHELPS, "Brooke, Flecker, de la Mare, and Others," *The Advance of English Poetry in the Twentieth Century*, 1925, pp. 124–25

Works

Someone remarked the other day that Rupert Brooke's one volume was nothing more than an amazing collection of intellectual jokes. Maliciousness was not intended: it is plain what he meant. Poems like "The Voice," or "Menelaus and Helen," or "A Channel Passage," or others that might be named, are *jokes*. But English people attach levity to the word. A good joke is after all more stimulating than the best Piece of Advice: it is the most necessary thing for a poet to be able to laugh well. Consciousness, that most unhappy burden of intellectual man, Rupert Brooke bore with a smile always, sometimes with a jeer: sometimes he laughed outright. It was impossible to him to restrain what he felt. He had to be plain. He preferred to be amused, and he would laugh because undue seriousness was obnoxious to him. His principal failing was a fear of being taken seriously. When he had loved too much, or if he thought he had felt too deeply, in clearer moments afterwards he would laugh his feelings away in a poem. He was often stimulated to write by the queerness or incongruity of some emotion or situation, rather than by its actual intensity. He would push situations impulsively away from him, to see how they looked at a distance. Imaginative representation of life was often baulked by keenness of participation: the event would burn itself out in occurrence. Thus his love-sonnets are seldom successful. His imagination, taken up with the idea of poetry in general, and the sonnet-form in particular, fails to cast itself back and link itself up with events. It is in poems purely of the imagination, and more particularly when uncurtailed by the sonnet-form, that his range and accuracy of visualisation are most conspicuous. . . .

The influences which appear to have moulded his style belong chiefly to the Elizabethan and Jacobean periods in English poetry. To these must be added the strong impress of classical scholarship and of university training. Intensely English by disposition as in the quality of his tastes, he showed in his poetry a white joyful ardour for beauty, together with that cool-headed sincerity which is characteristic of our most typically English poets. It is important to emphasize that the so-called indiscretions were in reality wise and happy children brought to birth in the full legitimacy of all natural offspring. To him it was like hypocrisy to restrain or reserve the direct expression of himself out of consideration for others. The language of some of his verse is almost uncannily direct: the image to be conveyed seems to anticipate (as it will sometimes in excited speech) the words designed to convey it. He is in the rare but fortunate position of having almost escaped the influences of later English poetry. Thus we find little in him of the intricate verbosity or the psychological subtleties of some of the poets of the twentieth century. Also the methods, manners, and free rhythms of the new style in poetry, which have harassed so many, and brought not a few to disaster, left him almost untouched. He contented himself with the simple and definite forms of the older tradition, the quatrain, rhymed couplets (usually octosyllabic) and the sonnet. Blank verse, however, he did not use: I cannot find that he wrote a single poem in it, nor indeed any poem without rhyme—"The sweet lad Rhyme," as he calls it. . . .

It is interesting, and not invidious, to compare him with his contemporaries. There is no one the least like him—though he had several imitators. No one has his frankness, no one has his ingenuity, his incisiveness, or his humour—no one will pretend to have: no one will be ashamed to confess that he has not. It is intensely difficult to write about him. It is almost impossible to forget him as a friend and remember him, as one would wish for purposes of comment and criticism, solely as a poet. I am at the same time glad to have the opportunity of writing something about his poetry, yet sorry to have fallen into the snare of consenting to do so. At present my most instinctive comment would be nothing more than "Damned Good"—for my mind is too full of the man.—HAROLD MUNRO, "Some Thoughts on the Poetry of Rupert Brooke," *CM*, May 22, 1915, pp. 424–27

Viewed in the light of what we now know about Brooke, his war sonnets can no longer be read as a simple clarion call to arms: they are a desperate attempt by a tormented man to find emotional relief from a morbid self-disgust. His outburst against intellectuals—'dehumanized, disgusting people. They are mostly pacific and pro-Germans. I quarrel with them twice a day'—is symptomatic of his irritability, and of his refusal to consider the possibility that the war was not an heroic endeavour. A letter to Raverat towards the end of 1914 sounds an hysterical note: 'I really think that large numbers of male people don't want to die. Which is odd. I've been praying for a German raid.' His natural humanity and good sense reasserted themselves when he saw for himself the miseries inflicted by the war on the refugees pouring out of Antwerp. And a letter written soon after the outbreak of war rings truer than the heroics of the war sonnets, the efforts to convince himself that there was a meaning in his life: 'I'm so uneasy—subconsciously. All the vague perils of the time—the world seems so dark—and I'm vaguely frightened.'— JOHN PRESS, "The Georgians," A *Map of Modern English Verse*, 1969, p. 113

Brooke's '1914' sonnets were written during November and December of that year, and were published in a miscellany called *New Numbers*; they were not widely read at first, but on Easter Sunday 1915, Dean Inge, preaching in St. Paul's, quoted 'The Soldier' from the pulpit; the poem was reprinted in *The Times* and aroused immense interest. And in a week or so there came the news of Brooke's death in the Aegean (unglamorously, from blood poisoning, but on active service): the juxtaposition of the poem in which Brooke had reflected on the possibility of his death—'If I should die . . . '—and the news of his actual death was sufficient to promote him to the status of a hero and martyr. The sonnets themselves are not very amenable to critical discussion. They are works of very great mythic power, since they formed a unique focus for what the English felt, or wanted to feel, in 1914–15: they crystallize the powerful archetype of Brooke, the young Apollo, in his sacrificial role of the hero-as-victim. Considered, too, as historical documents, they are of interest as an index to the popular state of mind in the early months of the war. But considered more narrowly and exactly as poems, their inadequacy is very patent. Such a judgment needs qualification. It is, for instance, a commonplace to compare Brooke's sonnets with the work of later war poets, notably Wilfred Owen. This seems to me to prove very little, except, in a purely descriptive way, that poets' attitudes changed profoundly as they learned more about the war. Beyond this one might as well attempt to compare the year 1914 and the year 1918. A more useful comparison is with Brooke's own earlier poetry, and with contemporary works that express a broadly similar state of mind. Brooke's poetic gifts were never robust, and he was very far from being the most talented of the Georgian group, but at his best he had a certain saving irony and detachment of mind, which, very naturally, were absent from the 1914 sonnets. At the same time, the negative aspects of his poetry, a dangerous facility of language and feeling, are embarrassingly in evidence. To compare like with like, the sonnets seem to me inferior to Kipling's 'For All We Have and Are' and to Julian Grenfell's 'Into Battle', both products of the

opening phase of the war.—BERNARD BERGONZI, "Brooke, Grenfell, Sorley," *Heroes' Twilight*, 1980, pp. 41–42

Brooke's poetry gives the impression of great ease and fluency; but we know from a number of witnesses, intimate friends who were with him when he was at work, and fellow writers, that he worked with great care, often re-wrote a number of times, and would leave gaps in his lines until he could find what he judged to be the exactly right word or phrase.

The chief weakness of his poetry—and it is a weakness markedly in contrast to the mastery in this particular sphere shown by Donne and by his almost equally admired Webster— was a preference for vague grandiloquence and high-sounding generalities in preference to the concrete word and the freshly illuminating image, the poetical cliché instead of the original imaginative discovery. It may be partly due to a lingering fondness for the affected romanticism of the nineties he had felt in his youthful phase; it continued to slip into his more mature poetry all too often when his mind was not working at top pressure.

Phrases such as 'in wise majestic melancholy train', 'some low sweet alley between wind and wind', 'dark scents whisper', 'the grey tumult of these after-years', 'song's nobility and wisdom holy', 'the heart of bravery swift and clean', which have a fine exalted ring but when examined mean nothing precise at all, from time to time pad out his verses throughout his adult career and not merely his beginnings when he was searching for a style; in fact they become his style as soon as he forgets his wit and light-heartedness and abandons those realistic touches that so shocked the critics of his first book. With what relief, then, one comes across the precise and vivid images with which in *The Great Lover* he enumerates the concrete things that evoke his love in recollection: 'wet roofs, beneath the lamplight', 'the rough male kiss of blankets', 'the good smell of old clothes', 'brown horse-chestnuts, glossy new'; though even in this attractive and original, though imperfect, poem he cannot resist the glib poetical rhetoric of phrases such as 'the inenarrable godhead of delight' and 'out on the wind of Time, shining and streaming'.—JOHN LEHMANN, *The Strange Destiny of Rupert Brooke*, 1981, pp. 134–35

JOHN H. JOHNSTON
From "The Early Poets"
English Poetry of the First World War
1964, pp. 28–36

The charges against the "adolescence" of Brooke's prewar verse are comprehensible in terms of the new social consciousness that poetry assumed in the twenties, after the publication of T. S. Eliot's *The Waste Land*. The effete pastoralism that was the characteristic element of Georgian poetry represented an attempt to escape from the realities of modern urban and industrial life. Brooke himself, the most talented of the Georgians, seems to have realized that his ruminations among the "haunts of ancient peace," his melodious Platonic speculations on life and death, and his witty "metaphysical" conceits (after the manner of Donne and Marvell) were far from constituting the whole substance of poetic reality; his occasional "ugly" verse is an unsuccessful attempt to break out of the daydream of an artificial and self-conscious "poetic" attitude. Brooke admitted, in a letter to his publisher, that there was much "unimportant prettiness" in his 1911 volume, which his "new and serious" verse was intended to offset.[1] The "new and serious" verse, however, instead of reflecting a maturing sensibility or even the slightest social comprehension, merely presents unpleasant and even disgusting minor effects, as in "A Channel Passage":

> Retchings twist and tie me,
> Old meat, good meals, brown gobbets, up I throw.

These were the effects at which Brooke would "grasp relievedly" after he had "beaten vain hands in the rosy mists of poets' experiences." In this casual explanation we have a glimpse of the meaningless dichotomy upon which Georgian values were based: the "poetic" or unreal on the one hand, and the unpoetic or "real" on the other. Most Georgian verse eschewed the real—the broad reality of contemporary life—and subsisted on rosy poetic mists; Brooke, its most admired exponent, hardly manifested any genuine inclination to escape from the attitudes and practices that have come to be identified with it. . . .

Elegant, melodious, rich in texture, decorous and dignified in tone, the 1914 sonnets do not deal with war; they reveal a sophisticated sensibility contemplating itself on the verge of war. Like Wordsworth's impassioned sonnets of 1802, Brooke's *1914* was inspired by a great moral and social crisis; but instead of defining that crisis, as Wordsworth does, in national and historical terms, Brooke merely presents its effects on his own rather specialized range of responses. Though the poet refers to himself only in Sonnets II and V (this fact has been adduced to disprove the charge of egocentricity), he could hardly have done otherwise without appearing ludicrously immodest and affected. Actually, the earnest, fervid, self-revelatory nature of the sequence and its progression to the eloquent intimacy of Sonnet V leave no doubt about the highly personal nature of the sentiments expressed therein. . . .

At least one of the educated young Englishmen for whom Brooke was ostensibly speaking refused to join in the public acclaim granted *1914*. In a letter written a few days after Brooke's death, Charles Sorley, a soldier and a poet himself, recorded a few penetrating observations: "That last sonnet-sequence of his . . . which has been so praised, I find (with the exception of that beginning 'These hearts were woven of human joys and cares, Washed marvellously with sorrow' which is not about himself) overpraised. He is far too obsessed with his own sacrifice, regarding the going to war of himself (and others) as a highly intense, remarkable and sacrificial exploit,

whereas it is merely the conduct demanded of him (and others) by the turn of circumstances, where non-compliance with this demand would have made life intolerable. It was not that 'they' gave up anything of that list he gives in one sonnet: but that the essence of these things had been endangered by circumstances over which he had no control, and he must fight to recapture them. He has clothed his attitude in fine words: but he has taken the sentimental attitude."[2]

Sorley's criticism is acute and essentially correct. It touches the heart of the situation for the volunteers of 1914, whereas Brooke's sonnets convey only a limited—and even distorted—aspect of that situation. The tenor of Sorley's remarks suggests that he, at least, did not regard Brooke as the spokesman for any general mood; the passage is a criticism of both Brooke's lack of maturity and his artistic culpability in taking "the sentimental attitude"—an effect, as Sorley implies, of choice. But Brooke was not really free to choose; his commitment to the attitudes and techniques of Georgian lyricism was such that he could hardly deal with the war in any other way. To have admitted fact or necessity or expedience among his spiritualized motivations would have been to destroy a semi-private fantasy of heroic self-sacrifice and moral regeneration. A hint of what may have been his real feelings emerges unexpectedly, considering the positive sentiments of *1914*, in an early account of his reaction to the first news of the war. "I'm so uneasy—subconsciously," he wrote. "All the vague perils of the time—the world seems so dark—and I'm vaguely frightened."[3] Perils, darkness, subconscious fears—these physical and emotional realities find no expression in *1914*, though they surely menace the very values upon which the poet bases his appeal. It was Brooke's misfortune to be the originator of sentiments that were soon to be swallowed by a vast tide of uncompromising fact and fully materialized perils. After the idealistic mood had evaporated, the suspicion grew that the appearance of the innocent enthusiast of 1914, while possible in terms of "Poetry," was something of a reproach and an embarrassment in the harsher terms of history.

Notes

1. See the passage quoted by Marsh, *Rupert Brooke*, p. 81.
2. Marsh, *Rupert Brooke*, p. 146.
3. *The Letters of Charles Sorley* (Cambridge, 1919), p. 263.

John Buchan

1875–1940

John Buchan was born in Perth, Scotland, on August 26, 1875. He attended Hutcheson's Grammar School and the University of Glasgow, where he studied classics with the young Gilbert Murray. Buchan neglected to gain a degree, however (much later, in 1919, the university granted him an honorary degree), and went instead to Brasenose College, Oxford, on a scholarship in 1895. There he won the prestigious Stanhope Prize for his essay *Sir Walter Raleigh* (1897).

In 1901 Buchan passed the Bar exam and became a barrister. Very shortly thereafter, however, he went to South Africa as private secretary to Lord Milner during the Boer War. Returning to England, Buchan settled into a law practice in which he was never entirely happy or comfortable, but in 1907 he joined the staff of the publisher Thomas Nelson in London. In that same year he married Susan Charlotte Grosvenor, with whom he had three sons and a daughter. During the early part of World War I he suffered ill-health (it was at this time that he wrote *The Thirty-Nine Steps*,

ELIZABETH BOWEN

ROBERT BRIDGES

JOHN BUCHAN

JOHN BRAINE

JOYCE CARY

ROY CAMPBELL

BASIL BUNTING

ANTHONY BURGESS

published in 1915), but soon became a war correspondent and later worked with Intelligence for the Foreign Office.

After the war he settled down with his family at Elsfield Manor near Oxford, where he wrote the majority of his books. After having served as Deputy Chairman of Reuter's, he sought political office and won a seat in Parliament in 1927, representing the Scottish universities. From there his political stature grew. In 1932 Buchan became Lord High Commissioner to the General Assembly of the Church of Scotland. In 1935 he was appointed Governor-General of Canada by George V, and spent the remainder of his life there. His Canadian odyssey is recorded in the posthumously published autobiography, *Sick Heart River* (1941). Buchan became a Companion of Honour in 1932, and was made Baron Tweedsmuir in 1935. Some months before his death on February 11, 1940, he signed Canada's declaration of war against Germany.

Buchan was a hugely prolific author. Although he is now known for his adventure novels involving Richard Hannay, he himself felt that his most serious work was in history and biography, including *Augustus* (1937) and a history of World War I. His output spanned virtually every branch of literature with the notable exception of poetry.

Personal

At John Lane's I met John Buchan, just now principal 'reader' to the Bodley Head. A very young, fair man; charmingly shy; 'varsity' in every tone and gesture. He talks quietly in a feminine, exiguous voice, with the accent of Kensington tempered perhaps by a shadow of a shade of Scotch (or was that my imagination?). Already—he cannot be more than 23—he is a favourite of publishers, who actually seek after him, and has published one book. He told me that his second novel, a long Scotch romance, was just finished, and that he had practically sold the serial rights. . . . A most modest, retiring man, yet obviously sane and shrewd. Well-disposed, too, and anxious to be just; a man to compel respect; one who 'counts'.—ARNOLD BENNETT, *The Journals of Arnold Bennett: 1896–1910* (entry for June 23, 1896), 1932, pp. 10–11

I suppose I was a natural story-teller, the kind of man who for the sake of his yarns would in prehistoric days have been given a seat by the fire and a special chunk of mammoth. I was always telling myself stories when I had nothing else to do—or rather, being told stories, for they seemed to work themselves out independently. I generally thought of a character or two, and then of a set of incidents, and the question was how my people would behave. They had the knack of just squeezing out of unpleasant places and of bringing their doings to a rousing climax.

I was especially fascinated by the notion of hurried journeys. In the great romances of literature they provide some of the chief dramatic moments, and since the theme is common to Homer and the penny reciter it must appeal to a very ancient instinct in human nature. We live our lives under the twin categories of time and space, and when the two come into conflict we get the great moment. Whether failure or success is the result, life is sharpened, intensified, idealised. A long journey, even with the most lofty purpose, may be a dull thing to read of if it is made at leisure; but a hundred yards may be a breathless business if only a few seconds are granted to complete it. For then it becomes a sporting event, a race; and the interest which makes millions read of the Derby is the same, in a grosser form, as when we follow an expedition straining to relieve a beleagured fort, or a man fleeing to a sanctuary with the avenger behind him.

. . . I never consciously invented with a pen in my hand; I waited until the story had told itself and then wrote it down, and, since it was already a finished thing, I wrote it fast. The books had a wide sale, both in English and in translations, and I always felt a little ashamed that profit should accrue from what had given me so much amusement. I had no purpose in such writing except to please myself, and even if my books had not found a single reader I should have felt amply repaid.

. . . Being equally sensitive to the spells of time and of space, to a tract of years and a tract of landscape, I tried to discover the historical moment which best interpreted the *ethos* of a particular countryside, and to devise the appropriate legend. Just as certain old houses, like the inns at Burford and Queensferry, cried out to Robert Louis Stevenson to tell their tales, so I felt the clamour of certain scenes for an interpreter.

The best, I think, is *Witch Wood*, in which I wrote of the Tweedside parish of my youth at the time when the old Wood of Caledon had not wholly disappeared, and when the rigours of the new Calvinism were contending with the ancient secret rites of Diana. I believe that my picture is historically true, and I could have documented almost every sentence from my researches on Montrose. In *The Free Fishers* I tried to catch the flavour of the windy shores of Fife at a time when smuggling and vagabondage were still rife. I had always felt keenly the romance of the Jacobite venture, but less in its familiar Scottish episodes than in the dreary ebb of the march to Derby, so I took that period for my attempt in *Midwinter* to catch the spell of the great midland forests and the Old England which lay everywhere just beyond the highroads and the ploughlands. Finally, in *The Blanket of the Dark* I chose the time when the monasteries fell and the enclosures began, and I brought all the valleys of Cotswold into the picture.

These were serious books, and they must have puzzled many of the readers who were eager to follow the doings of Richard Hannay or Dickson McCunn. That is the trouble with an author who only writes to please himself; his product is not standardised, and the purchaser is often disappointed. I once had a letter from an Eton boy who, having a taste for a bustling yarn, was indignant at anything of mine which did not conform to that pattern. He earnestly begged me to 'pull myself together.' . . .

In my book on Sir Walter Scott, published in the centenary year of his death, I tried not only to pay tribute to the best-loved of Borderers, but to repeat my literary *credo*. All these four books were, indeed, in a sense a confession of faith, for they enabled me to define my own creed on many matters of doctrine and practice, and thereby cleared my mind. They were a kind of diary, too, a chronicle of my successive interests and occupations. They were laborious affairs compared to my facile novels, but they were also a relaxation, for they gave me a background into which I could escape from contemporary futilities, a watch-tower from which I had a long prospect and could see modern problems in juster proportions. That is the supreme value of history. The study of it is the best guaranty against repeating it.—JOHN BUCHAN, "An Ivory Tower and Its Prospect," *Pilgrim's Way*, 1940, pp. 194–99

In 1924, John and Susan Buchan paid a visit to the States. I drove them around New Hampshire, which reminded them of the Highlands of Scotland. We climbed Chocorua, and John, a member of the Alpine Club, proved a testing companion of the trail. Talking continuously, even on the steepest stretches, he accomplished the ascent in fifty minutes. Muttering "Non sum qualis eram," foaming at the mouth but trying to look pleasant, I just managed to keep within sound of the one-sided conversation.

We went to Washington, where I sat in the outer office of the White House talking with C. Bascom Slemp, while John went in to see President Coolidge. He came out after an hour, twice his allotted time, flushed and smiling. Asked what they had been talking about, he replied, "Latin poetry." The President, he said, had shown a surprising knowledge of Virgil and Horace, and had spoken eloquently of what the language and literature of Rome had meant to him all his life.

I inquired, rather skeptically, "Wasn't it you who did most of the talking?"

"No," he said, "it was the President himself." . . .

My last visit with him was in Ottawa in 1939. I came away gravely anxious. The malady that for a quarter of a century had beset the slight body that housed that valiant spirit had grown worse. The Governor-General went through the exhausting routine of his work, but at what cost of dogged nervous effort. Then came the war. He wrote, "We are entering a long, dark tunnel, but I believe there is light at the end." He carried on the Vice-Regal round more splendidly than ever. Some of his best speeches were made in the open air to troops, in sleet or snow, on cold winter mornings. As usual he was writing three books at the same time: his "Essay in Recollection," *Pilgrim's Way*; his perhaps even more autobiographic last adventure story, *Mountain Meadow*, first entitled and still called, in England, *Sick Heart River*; his book of Canadian legends for young readers. The completed manuscript of the first reached me late in January, 1940. Two weeks later came the report of his sudden illness. The news was better, worse, better again. Then came the voice of Elmer Davis at the close of his evening communiqué: "Lord Tweedsmuir died tonight at 7.30."

At Ottawa, a few days later, I was given the autograph manuscript of two unfinished chapters of *Pilgrim's Rest*, the fishing book he had begun immediately upon finishing *Pilgrim's Way*. Deciphering with difficulty the cursive script, I read the last words that came from that tireless pen. It was the conclusion of an excursus on the prose of mortality: "There is Lockhart on the death of Scott, and Colonel Henderson on the death of Stonewall Jackson. There is the last paragraph of Thomas Hardy's *Woodlanders*. And not least there is Emily Brontë: 'I lingered round them under that benign sky; watched the moths fluttering among the heath and the harebells, listened to the soft wind breathing through the grass, and wondered how anyone could ever imagine unquiet slumbers for the sleepers in that quiet earth.'"

Surely it was of himself, as well as of Sir Edward Leithen, that he was speaking in the last sentence of *Mountain Meadow*, written a month before: "He knew that he would die; but he knew also that he would live."—FERRIS GREENSLET, "John Buchan," *At*, Sept. 1943, pp. 62–64

Works

For the last weeks I have been reading, inch by inch, your *Montrose*: keeping it in the Wireless Cabin, which lies between our barracks & our offices, and from which I have to collect 'in' signals several times a day. I used to take ten minutes off each time, for *Montrose*, which came as a revelation to me.

I had not suspected, from my desultory reading of the Civil War, that such a man then existed. The *style* of his last words on the gallows! and those profound memoranda on political science. I've tried to think back for other military commanders who could write like that, and I'm bothered if I can think of one: Xenophon was only a Walter Long kind of a sportsman, beside him, & J. Caesar too abstract. Your man stands out, head and shoulders.

He has been unlucky in waiting three hundred years for a real biographer: but he must be warmly happy, now, if anything of his personality can still feel. You unwrap him so skilfully, without ever getting, yourself, in our way. The long careful setting of the scene—first-rate history, incidentally, and tingling with life, as if you'd seen it—& on top of that the swift and beautifully-balanced course of action. Oh, it's a very fine thing.

I'm glad you allow common-sense to interpret the documents. A fetish of the last-school-but-one was to believe every document. As one who has had the making of original historical records I know how weak & partial and fallible they are. Fortunately you have been a man of affairs, and so are not to be taken in, like a scholar pure.

There is great labour behind the book, which yet reads easily, for your digestion has been able to cope with all the stony facts. Your small characters (often only a word long) brighten the whole thing. Incidentally, you have been honest to see the fineness of Cromwell, under the homespun. Argyll is unforgettable: Huntly, too: and Hurry. Alasdair less so. He didn't Colkitto enough to live in my reading. I wonder why? Didn't you want him to clash with Montrose, in prowess? Also you left out Rupert—I mean, you mention him, well enough, but you do not make him walk & talk, whereas you bring to life Elizabeth & the Palatine circle. I suppose you were concentrating your high lights. Charles, the king, is finely drawn, as a shadow on the wall of his contemporaries. I suppose you know the fineness of your writing? The way you line in the execution of the King is marvellous. Montrose would have envied you those two or three sentences, & the full-stop and paragraph, after them.—T. E. LAWRENCE, Letter to John Buchan (Dec. 26, 1928), *The Letters of T. E. Lawrence*, ed. David Garnett, 1938, pp. 627–28

More than a quarter of a century has passed since Richard Hannay found the dead man in his flat and started that long flight and pursuit—across the Yorkshire and the Scottish moors, down Mayfair streets, along the passages of Government buildings, in and out of Cabinet rooms and country houses, towards the cold Essex jetty with the thirty-nine steps, that were to be a pattern for adventure-writers ever since. John Buchan was the first to realize the enormous dramatic value of adventure in familiar surroundings happening to unadventurous men, members of Parliament and members of the Athenaeum, lawyers and barristers, business men and minor peers: murder in 'the atmosphere of breeding and simplicity and stability.' Richard Hannay, Sir Edward Leithen, Mr. Blenkiron, Archie Roylance and Lord Lamancha; these were his adventurers, not Dr. Nikola or the Master of Ballantrae, and who will forget that first thrill in 1916 as the hunted Leithen—the future Solicitor-General—ran 'like a thief in a London thoroughfare on a June afternoon'.

Now I saw how thin is the protection of civilization. An accident and a bogus ambulance—a false charge and a bogus arrest—there were a dozen ways of spiriting one out of this gay and bustling world.

Now Leithen, who survived the perils of the Green Park and the mews near Belgrave Square, has died in what must

seem to those who remember *The Power House* a rather humdrum way, doing good to depressed and starving Indians in
Northern Canada, anticipating by only a few months his
creator's death.

What is remarkable about these adventure-stories is the
completeness of the world they describe. The backgrounds to
many of us may not be sympathetic, but they are elaborately
worked in: each character carries round with him his school,
his regiment, his religious beliefs, often touched with Calvinism: memories of grouse-shooting and deer-stalking, of sport at
Eton, debates in the House. For men who live so dangerously
they are oddly conventional—or perhaps, remembering men
like Scott and Oates, we can regard that, too, as a realistic
touch. They judge men by their war-record: even the priest in
Sick Heart River, fighting in the desolate northern waste for the
Indians' salvation, is accepted by Leithen because 'he had
served in a French battalion which had been on the right of the
Guards at Loos'. Toc H and the British Legion lurk in the
background.

In the early books, fascinated by the new imaginative
form, the hair-breadth escapes in a real world, participating
whole-heartedly in the struggle between a member of the Athenaeum and the man who could hood his eyes like a hawk, we
didn't notice the curious personal ideals, the vast importance
Buchan attributed to success, the materialism . . . *Sick Heart
River*, the last adventure of the dying Leithen seeking—at
Blenkiron's request— the missing business man, Francis Galliard, who had left his wife and returned to his ancestral North,
has all the old admirable dry ease of style—it is the intellectual
content which repels us now, the Scotch admiration of success.
'Harold has a hard life. He's head of the Fremont Banking
Corporation and a St. Sebastian for everyone to shoot arrows
at.' Even a nation is judged by the same standard: 'They ought
to have made a rather bigger show in the world, than they
have.' Individuals are of enormous importance. Just as the
sinister Mr. Andrew Lumley in *The Power House* was capable
of crumbling the whole Western world into anarchy, so Francis Galliard—'one of Simon Ravelston's partners'—must be
found for the sake of America. 'He's too valuable a man to lose,
and in our present state of precarious balance we just can't
afford it.'

But though *Sick Heart River* appears at the moment least
favourable to these ideas (for it is not, after all, the great men—
the bankers and the divisional commanders and the
Ambassadors—who have been holding our world together this
winter, and if we survive, it is by 'the wandering, wavering
grace of humble men' in Bow and Coventry, Bristol and Birmingham), let us gratefully admit that, in one way at any rate,
Buchan prepared us in his thrillers better than he knew for the
death that may come to any of us, as it nearly came to Leithen,
by the railings of the Park or the doorway of the mews. For
certainly we can all see now 'how thin is the protection of
civilization'.—GRAHAM GREENE, "The Last Buchan" (1940),
The Lost Childhood and Other Essays, 1952, pp. 104–5

GERTRUDE HIMMELFARB
From "John Buchan: An Untimely Appreciation"
Encounter, September 1960, pp. 46–53

John Buchan—popular novelist, biographer, historian,
Member of Parliament, and finally Governor-General of
Canada—died in 1940, one of the last articulate representatives
of the old England. He is the paradigm—the parody, some

would have it—of a species of English gentleman now very
nearly extinct. The manners and morals celebrated in his
books, the social prejudices unwittingly disclosed in them, and
the attitudes and philosophy suggested by them have already
acquired the faded tint of a period-piece. Before they vanish
altogether, it may be interesting to take pause, to enquire into
an ethos that for some is an embarrassing memory, for others a
remembrance of lost grandeur.

There is indeed matter for embarrassment in Buchan's
novels. There is the clean, good life which comes with early
rising, cold baths, and long immersion in fog and damp, in
contrast to the red-eyed, liverish, sluggish, and demoralised life
of the town. There is the casual bravery, classically un-
derstated, of his heroes. ("There's nothing much wrong with
me. . . . A shell dropped beside me and damaged my foot.
They say they'll have to cut it off.") There is the blithe provincialism and amateurishness of his spy-adventurer who complains that the natives in a Kurdish bazaar do not understand
any "civilised tongue," of his Member of Parliament who cannot pronounce "Boche" names and confuses Poincaré with
Mussolini, of the Cabinet Minister who will not be bothered to
read the newspapers while on vacation. There is the penchant
for sports that requires every hero (and every respectable villain)
to be a first-class shot, and looks upon politics, espionage, and
war alike as an opportunity to practise good English sportsman-
ship: Richard Hannay, his principal hero, is much distressed at
not "playing the game" when he abuses the hospitality of a
particularly heinous villain; elsewhere he permits a German
agent, plotting to spread anthrax germs through the British
army, to escape rather than ignobly shoot him in the back; and
another hero, Sandy Arbuthnot, during a tremendous cavalry
attack involving Cossack, Turkish, German, and British
troops, can be heard crying, "Oh, well done our side!"

Even more reminiscent of the English public-schoolboy is
the curious blurring of sexual lines. All Buchan's heroes turn
out to have "something girlish" about them: a husky mountain
guide has hair "as flaxen as a girl's;" Peter Pienaar, the uncouth
Boer adventurer, has a face "as gentle as a girl's," as does a
general in the same novel; Sandy Arbuthnot has "a pair of
brown eyes like a pretty girl's;" and a six-and-a-half-foot Negro
chieftain has hands "more like a high-bred woman's than a
man's." Even some of his historical heroes have the same
ambiguous sexuality: Augustus is portrayed with "features so
delicately modelled as to be almost girlish." Similarly, his
heroines have more than a little of the young boy in them:
boyish hips, boyish stride, wholesome boyish manners and
interests. Even these endearing qualities, however, cannot entirely allay the unease of the hero. When Hannay, then well in
his forties, meets the bewitching Greenmantle, he is thrown
into panic at the thought of sitting beside her: "Never having
been in a motor-car with a lady before, I felt like a fish on a dry
sandbank." His friend, Archie Roylance, had also been "as shy
as a woodcock" of those "mysterious and unintelligible" creatures. "Fresh and unstaled by disillusion," he finally falls in
love with Janet, but he succumbs, the author proudly reports,
not to the vulgar charms of "swelling bosoms and pouting lips
and soft curves and languishing eyes;" the fresh and unstaled
phrases that come to his lips are "jolly," "clean-run," "a regular sportswoman," and, as an after-thought, "amazingly good-
looking." Occasionally, Buchan might be found to poke fun at
this priggishness. Of Walter Scott he once said: "For women he
had an old-fashioned reverence, and . . . regarded them very
much as a toast to be drunk after King and Constitution."
Nevertheless, he respected Scott's diffidence: "I do not suggest
the severe doctrine that no man can write intimately of sex
without forfeiting his title to gentility, but I do say that for

Scott's type of gentleman to do so would have been impossible without a dereliction of standards."

So far the Buchan ethos amuses more than it offends. It becomes displeasing when private foibles begin to impinge upon public morality. The most serious item in Richard Usborne's indictment of Buchan (in his *Clubland Heroes*) is Buchan's preoccupation with success, his top-of-the-form ethic. A dinner-party in a Buchan novel assembles a typical assortment of guests: Bonson Jane "had been a noted sportsman and was still a fine polo player; his name was a household word in Europe for his work in international finance . . . it was rumoured that in the same week he had been offered the Secretaryship of State, the Presidency of an ancient University, and the control of a great industrial corporation;" Simon Ravelstone is president of "one of the chief banking houses in the world;" his son is "making a big name for himself in lung surgery;" and another guest is "about our foremost pundit . . . there were few men alive who were his equals in classical scholarship." So closed is the universe inhabited by these Calvinist-minded characters that they can agree to the precise rank and order of their success. Thus Sandy Arbuthnot is "one of the two or three most intelligent people in the world," Julius Victor is the "richest man in the world," Medina is the "best shot in England after His Majesty," Castor is the "greatest *agent-provocateur* in history," and there is one of whom it is said, with a fine conjunction of precision and vagueness, that "there aren't five men in the United States whose repute stands higher."

Yet closer attention to the novels suggests that these marks of success are not the ends towards which his heroes—or villains—strive. They are the preconditions of their being heroes or villains at all, much as the characters in fairy tales are always the most beautiful, the most exalted, the most wicked of their kind. They are the starting points for romance, not the termination. Indeed the theme of the more interesting of the novels is the *ennui* or *tædium vitæ*, which afflicts precisely those who have attained the highest state—and because they have attained that state. In *John Macnab*, three of the most eminent men in England, dispirited by a surfeit of success, deliberately engage in an adventure of illegality in order to court exposure and disgrace. And in *Sick Heart River*, a famous American financier and an equally famous English barrister leave their comfortable establishments to suffer pain and death in the far north. All Buchan's heroes are periodically beset by fatigue and lassitude, a "death-wish" that is overcome by divesting themselves of their urban identities—success being an urban condition—and donning the shabby, anonymous clothes of the countryman. Only when the perils of nature and of the chase have roughened up the smooth patina of success, leaving the body scarred and the mind tormented, can they resume their normal lives and identities. . . .

There is no denying that Buchan is as remote as can be from the modern writer-intellectual in his tastes and judgments. Any "right-thinking" intellectual would be offended by his description of the "advanced" community of Biggleswick in *Mr. Standfast*: the pretentious, arty folk with their gimcrack houses and "demented modish" paintings, who were determined "never to admire anything that was obviously beautiful, like a sunset or a pretty woman, but to find surprising loveliness in things which I thought hideous." Nor will he be reassured by Buchan's distaste for such writers as Proust, James, and Dostoievsky. Yet, alien as it may be, his mind had a range and seriousness that has to be respected. It was not only Scott, Tennyson, and Macaulay whom he was fond of (though his heartier characters were confined to quoting these three), but

also such varied writers—to select only a few of those most often cited in his pages—as Shakespeare, Hakluyt, Thomas Browne, Bunyan, Hazlitt, Walton, Thoreau, Whitman, Johnson, Chateaubriand, Calvin, and Augustine. Impatient with experiments in the arts as in politics, fearful of attempts to probe the unconscious in novels as in life, he was obviously limited in his æsthetic responses. Yet it can hardly be judged philistine to prefer Homer in the Greek to T. S. Eliot in English, "low-brow" to admire Tolstoy more than Dostoievsky, or "anti-intellectual" to write serious works of historical scholarship that are also refreshingly literate.

What is involved is a different cultural tradition, emerging in a different set of intellectual and literary manners. The English intellectual of Buchan's generation was loath to parade his intelligence; his Double First at the university had to be acquired without visible swotting or cramming. (Buchan's characters never admitted to memorising anything; they had "fly-paper memories" to which long passages of poetry or facts adhered effortlessly.) And his writing suggested not the anguish of creation but the casualness of civilised conversation. In this relaxed manner, Buchan was able to produce fifty-seven books in the interstices of his other more absorbing occupations—the law, interrupted by a short period of service with Milner in South Africa, then business, Parliament, and finally the Governor-Generalship of Canada.

Such productivity could only be attained if one wrote not merely *as* one spoke, but also *what* one spoke. This is the real clue to Buchan's (as to the Victorians') prodigious output. There are many to-day who are as rich in intellectual resources; there are few who feel so free to draw upon their capital. Buchan had confidence not only in his knowledge, but also in his opinions, attitudes, intuitions, and prejudices. What he wrote for the public was what he felt in private; he did not think to labour for a subtlety or profundity that did not come spontaneously, or to censor his spontaneous thoughts before committing them to paper. He had none of the scruples that are so inhibiting to-day. He was candid about race, nation, religion, and class, because it did not occur to him that anything he was capable of feeling or thinking could be reprehensible. His creative strength was the strength of his character.

What makes Buchan, and the ethos with which he is identified, so unpalatable to-day is not one or another cause for distaste: the idea that the good life is a matter of cold baths, rousing games, and indifferent sex; the apparent philistinism that put a high premium on success and a low premium on intelligence; an unseemly preoccupation with race and class; and a still more unseemly glorification of nation and empire. It is each of these and more: the sense of a temperament and mentality that is inimical to the prevailing "liberal imagination." The liberal celebrates the likenesses of men rather than their differences; individuals rather than race, class, or nation; the benevolent and malleable character of men rather than their recalcitrance. He chooses to understand rather than judge, and he is discreet where understanding fails him. He is as much repelled by intuition and prejudice as by the usages and prescriptions of tradition; he regards violence, like evil, as a negative quality, a temporary aberration, unreal both in its impulse and in its effect.

Buchan—Calvinist in religion, Tory in politics, and romantic in sensibility—has obviously nothing in common with all this. It is no accident that he was addicted to a genre, the romantic tale of adventure, which is itself alien to the liberal temper. For what kind of romance would it be that feared to characterise or categorise, to indulge the sense of evil, violence, and apocalypse? It is no accident, either, that the predominance of liberal values has meant the degeneration of a literary form so congenial to the Tory imagination and of which Buchan was so eminently a master.

M. L. RIDLEY
From "A Misrated Author?"
Second Thoughts
1965, pp. 3–44

He is often described as 'a mere writer of adventure stories'—this usually from would-be intellectuals, who would hardly recognize an adventure if they met one, and would move hurriedly in the opposite direction if they did. Anyway the statement is untrue. Much of Buchan's best work is not fiction at all, and even in fiction some of his best novels cannot, by any stretching of terms, be classed as thrillers. And again: 'He is so painfully obvious.' That is a comment characteristic and symptomatic of our time, when so many readers seem to prefer elaborate and often murky psychological analysis and a minimum of 'story' to any narrative of events. It is true that there is in Buchan very little avowed psychological analysis, and he makes clear his own position about this: 'The truth is, the pathological is too easy.' But there is plenty of acute psychological observation, and also at least one underlying theme which is not particularly 'obvious', though it is patently perceptible when one takes the trouble to perceive it.

But it is better to dismiss these, I think misguided, verdicts and examine what Buchan did in fact achieve in fiction and what his powers were. He is almost universally accepted as a master of the thriller, and as a kind of criterion, so that 'almost up to the Buchan standard' and the like are common-form critical phrases. But the odd thing is that his thrillers are by no means uniformly in the top class of that *genre*. As a 'simple' thriller *The Thirty-Nine Steps* is hard to beat. It moves with extreme velocity and retains its momentum throughout; it does not strain credibility too far, and has some admirable episodes and an effective climax; and the characters, though there is no subtlety in the drawing of them, are reasonably human. It was at once accepted as a classic of its kind, and goes on being so accepted, even in spite of the distorting maltreatment of film adaptation. . . .

Buchan's characters are a richly diversified company, drawn from many countries and from many walks of life, from peers to peasants, kings to roadmenders, princesses to cutpurses, Laputa to Shalah. I have heard Buchan called a snob, and that by people who would have cheerfully run a mile to shake hands with him (after he was raised to the peerage). Such sillinesses are usually best left to wither, without giving them the even momentary life of a challenge, but this particular one is the result not of deliberate falsification but of obtuse misinterpretation. What is true is that Buchan valued highly some virtues which a flaccid and disillusioned age does not value at all, and tries to preserve its self-respect by deriding; and he thought that he found those virtues particularly well displayed in a particular stratum of English society. But he took his virtues where he could find them, and he had far too wide an experience to suppose that any 'class' had a monopoly of quality, and far too wide a humanity not to enjoy drawing people from all classes. And he never condescends. He presents for special admiration, out of all his heroes, a barely literate Boer hunter; if he draws Prince Alexis, he draws with even warmer sympathy and understanding a tinkler laddie of no fixed abode, Fish Benjie, and a group of dead-end kids, the Gorbals Diehards from the Glasgow slums; he clearly feels deep affection, mixed indeed with some kindly amusement, but with even more admiration, for a retired grocer; alongside Sir Edward Leithen he put Lew Frizzel, and the sketch of Georgie Hamilton is as firm as the full-length portrait of General Hannay; and it may be observed that the general himself does not start at a higher social elevation than that of a mining engineer. . . .

And, finally, a word about Buchan's style. In his youth he was subjected to that discipline of the classical languages which, for a writer, nothing can replace, and at Glasgow he sat under Gilbert Murray, already one of the greatest of Greek teachers. 'To me his lectures were, in Wordsworth's phrase, like "kindlings of the morning". Men are by nature Greeks or Romans, Hellenists or Latinists. Murray was essentially a Greek; my own predilection has always been for Rome; but I owe it to him that I was able to understand something of the Greek spirit, and still more to come under the spell of the classic discipline in letters and life. . . . Faulty though my own practice has always been, I learned sound doctrine—the virtue of a clean bare style, of simplicity, of a hard substance and an austere pattern.' Without his 'predilection for Rome' he could hardly have written *Augustus*, but I think that he underrated his affinities with Greece. His son had no doubt about these: 'The most striking characteristic of his mind was its balance. He had developed to a high degree the virtue which the Greek called Sophrosyne. . . . Greek also was his conception of the proper nature and aims of the man of full stature. . . . He never abandoned a belief in the intrinsic value of individual character . . . [and this] ended in a love of life and a tenderness that was both Greek and Christian.' But whatever his affinities of temper may have been, his style, it seems to me, was pure Greek, and, at that, the Greek of Plato. He did not command, or wish to command, the rolling Ciceronian period, or the compressed trenchancies of Tacitus or Thucydides. He aimed at one thing only, precise clarity of thought expressed in the simplest clarity of language. He had also, innate—for it is hardly a thing which can with any certainty be acquired by practice—an almost faultless ear for rhythm. As a result, you will look long in Buchan for a sentence which is not limpidly clear, and even longer for an ugly sentence. The even ludicity of thought is a delight to the mind, and the sure rhythms are a continual pleasure to the ear.

. . . I have been concerned with trying to show that Buchan, simply as a novelist, is misunderstood and therefore seriously underrated. He has brought delight and often much-needed relaxation to millions of readers, and that is something abundantly worth doing. But he has something to offer deeper than refreshment for the weary traveller. The dusty wanderer cannot take his ease at his inn for more than a while, and then he must set out again on his journeying. And from book after book of Buchan's, as it seems to me, there shines out the spirit of the man, wisely and widely experienced, with a tempered optimism, loving youth and courage and honour, hating nothing but the faint-hearted and the foul, illuminating the road and defining the goal.

BASIL BUNTING

1900–

Basil Bunting was born in Scotswood, Northumberland, on March 1, 1900. Raised a Quaker, he resisted the draft in World War I and spent two years in prison as a result. After his release in 1919 he attended the London School of Economics. In 1923 he became assistant editor of the *Transatlantic Review*, where he worked alongside Ford Madox Ford. He spent much of the rest of the decade in Italy, where he became a protégé of Ezra Pound. Bunting's first book of poetry, privately printed in Milan in 1930, was so heavily influenced by Pound that the few critics who read it dismissed it as mere imitation.

Bunting did not publish again for twenty years. In the interim, he moved between Italy, England, the Canary Islands, and Iran, where he worked in the British Consulate and as a Middle East correspondent for the *Times*. He was a yacht captain for several years in the late 1930s; when World War II began he put aside his pacifism to fly in the Royal Air Force. His second collection of poems appeared in 1950 to almost no notice; he worked as financial sub-editor of the Newcastle *Chronicle* until the publication of his third book in 1965 brought him attention at last. Since then he has taught at the University of California at Santa Barbara, SUNY Binghamton, the University of British Columbia, Victoria, Durham, and Newcastle, from which he received an honorary doctorate in 1971. His long autobiographical poem, *Briggflats*, won a Levinson Prize in 1966.

Bunting married Marian Culver in 1930, and Sima Alladadian in 1948. He has two children by each. He lives in Greystead, Northumberland.

General

hast killed the urochs and the bison sd/Bunting
      doing six months after that war was over
as pacifist tempted with chicken but declined to approve
of war "Redimiculum Metellorum"
                    privately printed
to the shame of various critics
nevertheless the state can lend money
      and the fleet that went out to Salamis
      was built by state loan to the builders—EZRA
POUND, "Canto LXXIV," *The Cantos*, 1934, p. 431

A dislike of Bunting's poetry and Zukofsky's is possibly due to haste. Their verse is more thoughtful than toffee-lickers require. At intervals, months apart, I remember a passage, or I re-open my volume of excerpts and find something solid. It did not incinerate any Hudson river. Neither did Marianne Moore's when it first (20 years since) came to London. You have to read such verse slowly.—EZRA POUND, "Active Anthology," *Polite Essays*, 1937, p. 153

Secret I take it a commitment hushed to feed amicableness
    sealed between us *note* to feed us animate,
making us say one with those whose whole lore may adjure rite
    sacred,
    Corneli, the fact you may say repute me Harpocrates.—
CELIA ZUKOFSKY, LOUIS ZUKOFSKY, "Catullus 1025: quiquam to Basil Bunting," *Agenda*, Autumn 1966, p. 17

    . . . But they have named all the stars,
    trodden down the scrub of the desert, run the white
      moon to a schedule,
    Joshua's serf whose beauty drove men mad.
    They have melted the snows from Erebus, weighed
      the clouds,
    hunted down the white bear; hunted the whale the
      seal the kangaroo
    they have set private enquiry agents on to Archipiada:
    What is your name? Your maiden name?

    Go in there to be searched. I suspect it is not your
      true name.
    Distinguishing marks if any? (O anthropomet-
      rics!) . . .

This passage from Basil Bunting's *Villon*, written in 1925, renders a whole complex of traditional poetic antagonisms—to scientific positivism, to the interference of men in the life of nature, to the interference of technically aided administrations in the lives of individuals. The same poet, characteristically, has resisted the anti-poeticism that demands direct statement couched in the vocabulary and syntax of current prose usage. 'Poetry is seeking to make not meaning but beauty,' Basil Bunting has said; 'or if you insist on misusing words, its "meaning" is of another kind, and lies in the relation to one another of lines and patterns of sound, perhaps harmonious, perhaps contrasting and clashing, which the hearer feels rather than understands; lines of sounds drawn in the air which stir deeper emotions which have not even a name in prose. This needs no explaining to an audience which gets its poetry by ear.' Apart from the question of whether poetry should be read or heard—and the present revival of spoken poetry, on the whole, has favoured not Bunting's kind of poetry but the kind that conveys instant and obvious 'meaning' with little regard for 'beauty'—Bunting's statement defines the position of a poet who will not collaborate with the *Zeitgeist*, a position reminiscent of the modernism of 1912. His very use of the unfashionable word 'beauty' reminds us that the truths of modern poetry need not be the truths of newspapers, nor its concerns the concerns of politicians. Bunting's highly developed sense of place, and of particular ways of life rooted in particular localities, is another characteristic that sets his work apart from anything that could be described as a new 'international style' in poetry.—MICHAEL HAMBURGER, "Town and Country: Phenotypes and Archetypes," *The Truth of Poetry*, 1969, pp. 272–73

Bunting is a "quirkie bodie, capable o' making law no law at a'," in Galt's phrase. He is a catbird, and one must laugh with him—and at him—as he delights in doing himself, re/B. Bunting and his friends. Since I am nearly as much of a metrophobe as he is, we get along quite well. Basil these days looks a proper subject for the lens of Julia Margaret Cameron—in the mould of Alfred Lord Tennyson—but he hates the Kensington/Chiswick world she represented. Much of what he takes for canon he learned by the age of 22. For 60 years that knowledge has sustained him in his arrogant (and modest) Modernism. I think you get him very wrong, however, if you take him to be the statute of Ozymandias and all that. What he is is a very complicated, alienated poet, with opinions strictly out there on their own. A few of us listen very hard when he gives utterance. He both likes giving utterance and he hates it. He is self-dismissive and self-satisfied. There is more than a touch of the 'slovenly.' He often says precisely the opposite of what he stands for. One can only drink to that. What I value most is his hard, sharp music, and his insistence that poetry is made by privateers for "unabashed boys and girls."—JONATHAN WILLIAMS, "Pre–Amble" to "An Interview with Basil Bunting," *Conjunctions*, 1983, pp. 75–76

Works

Mr. Bunting's poetic care is measure. He is aware that quantity has naturally to do with the tones of words. His diction, as a result, tends to a classical selection, even when his themes are modern, as in his epigram to Narciss and in his sonnet beginning "An arles, an arles for my hiring." At the same time, reversing this relation, the past meets the present as in *Against Memory*:

> Ten or ten thousand, does it much signify, Helen,
>   how we
> date fantasmal events, London or Troy? Let Poly-
>   hymnia
> strong with cadence multiply song, voices enmeshed
>   by music
> respond bringing the savors of our sadness or delight
>   again.

The diction often seems to collect no more than the experience of classical poetry: "The distant gods . . . abstracts of our spirit," at the end of *While Shepherds Watched*, themselves "rabbits sucked by a ferret"; the preoccupied but outwardly integrated mythology of the *Chorus of Furies—Overheard—guarda, mi disse, le feroce Erine*:

> Let us come upon him first as if in a dream,
> Anonymous triple presence,
> Memory made substance and tally of heart's rot:
> Then in the waking Now be demonstrable, seem
> Sole aspect of being's essence,
> Coffin to the living touch, self's Iscariot.
> Then he will loathe the year's recurrent long caress
> Without hope of divorce,
> Envying idiocy's apathy or the stress
> Of definite remorse.

But Mr. Bunting would not be among the isolate instances of Englishmen concerned with poetry in this time, were his content only the product of a classical ear directing a polished manner. All his poems, and especially the *Villon*, are grounded in an experience, though the accompanying tones of the words are their own experience:

> Let his days be few and let
> His bishoprick pass to another,
> For he fed me on carrion and on a dry crust,
> Mouldy bread that his dogs had vomited.
> I lying on my back in the dark place, in the grave,
> Fettered to a post in the damp cellarage.
> Whereinall we differ not. But they have swept the
>   floor,

> There are no dancers, no somersaulters now,
> Only bricks and bleak black cement and bricks,
> Only the military tread and the snap of the locks.

His indictment of Bertillon in this poem is violence that an intelligent man confronted with historical fact has had to express, even it the name has joined the decorative scheme of his poem. The coda of the *Villon*—

> How can I sing with my love in my bosom?
> Unclean, immature and unseasonable salmon—

is the logical humility consequent on Mr. Bunting's bitterness. The rhetorical wrench of the last line is self-mitigated because the writer's metaphor has become the objective equivalent of his personal irony.

Mr. Bunting's adaptation of Lucretius' invocation to Venus even indicates a safer art and a more certain direction:

> Therefore, since you alone control the sum of things
> And nothing without you comes forth into the light
> And nothing beautiful or glorious can be
> Without you, Alma Venus! trim my poetry
> With your grace; and give peace to write and read
>   and think.

So much so that the French epigrams opening and closing his volumes and laying restraint on the extent of his expression (*Bornons ici cette carrière*) are unnecessary.—LOUIS ZUKOFSKY, "London or Troy," *Poetry*, June 1931, pp. 160–62

On the subject of *Poems*, Hugh Kenner once wrote: "Of these 54 pages some five may or should enter the corpus poeticum; a way of saying that Bunting's subjects and treatment have an interest outlasting the area in which they were conceived." (*Poetry*, September, 1951.) Certainly the best works and the best parts of them stand out a long way in *Loquitur* from those elegantly written pieces on tickling young ladies in the back of taxis. "The Well of Lycopolis", "Chomei at Toyama", "Vestiges", "Let them remember Samangan", "The Orotava Road", these are a few of the contexts where Bunting shows as a distinctly individual poet, where he makes good Kenner's claim that from Pound and Williams "he has learned techniques where others have borrowed voices". Pound's voice, however, certainly dogs him—even in "Samangan" usurers head the list of villainies and elsewhere Pound's presence overwhelms poet and reader:

> See! Their verses are laid
> as mosaic gold to gold
> gold to lapis lazuli
> white marble to porphyry
> stone shouldering stone, the dice
> polished alike, there is
> no cement seen and no gap
> between stones as the frieze strides
> to the impending apse.

Yet even here, where the poem begins in mere pastiche, in the four quoted lines which still carry on a Poundian distinction about stone-building from Canto 45, something different from Pound occurs with the gathering forces that lift through the concealed rhyme (seen/between) and in the rising tone and syntax of "the frieze [striding] to the impending apse". The new voice that has entered is one that we hear more clearly in other, more realised passages:

> Sea's over that island,
> weed over furrow and dungheap:
> but how I should recognise the place
> under the weeds and sand

who was never on it on land I don't know:
some trick of refraction,
a film of light in the water crumpled and spread
like a luminous frock on a woman walking
alone in her garden.

A lucid music empowers this—the unstressed final syllable of "island" taken up by "sand", and "sand" by the internal rhyme "land" spoken at full pace, the whole wound on a dramatic syntax where "I", the subject, is so beautifully divided from "who was never on land" by the fact of helplessness, the doubt of recognizing the place, which receives an answering musical pull in the sentence's close: "I don't know". In "The Orotava Road", a poem where, as Gael Turnbull was the first to point out ("An Arlespenny". *King Ida's Watch Chain*, Migrant Press), Bunting "makes use of a 'triplet' structure which, while anticipating W. C. Williams' use of a similar device, is distinctively his own", it is the surprise of the syntax which reinforces the music:

Four white heifers with sprawling hooves
trundle the waggon.
Its ill-roped crates heavy with fruit sway.
The chisel point of the goad, blue and white,
glitters ahead,
a flame to follow lance-high in a man's hand
who does not shave.

The delay of "who does not shave" brings us back to the man with renewed force—a journey of the mind's eye from goad tip to hand to driver—and the earlier delay of verb in

Its ill-roped crates heavy with fruit sway

shows a skill in handling spondaic clusters that marvellously accommodates classical metric to English, the held back verb "sway" tugging down the final spondee with something of the weight of that ill-roped and precarious burden of crates. Louis Zukofsky has noted, with this sort of effect in mind: "Mr. Bunting's poetic care is measure. He is aware that quantity has naturally to do with the tones of words." (*Poetry*, June 1931.) Tone and quantity certainly combine in the placing of "sway" and the resultant music in Bunting's best pieces earns Zukofsky's comment later in the same essay: "All his poems, and especially the 'Villon', are grounded in an experience, though the accompanying tones of the words are their own experience."— CHARLES TOMLINSON, "Experience Into Music," *Agenda*, Autumn 1966, pp. 11–13

One first picks up the track of Basil Bunting in 1931, in a letter from Pound to Harriet Monroe in which he also speaks of Auden as "*mutatis mutandis*, another James Elroy Flecker". Of course it is not Auden at all but Bunting himself, with his translations from Sa'di—

Night swallowed the sun as
the fish swallowed Jonas

—and his recondite reconstruction of the hedonist's Persia, who suggests to us now the author of *Hassan* and *The Golden Journey to Samarkand*. Bunting's long poem *The Spoils*, which appeared first in this magazine in 1951 and is now republished in England, offers precisely the discriminating welter of whining sensuality ("Condole me with abundance of secret pleasure") we like to associate with those Moslem epicureans so attractive to English poets since Fitzgerald:

By the dategroves of Babylon
there we sat down and sulked. . . .
Shade dimples under chenars,
resonant verse spilled
till the girls' mutter is lost

in whisper of stream and leaf,
a final nightingale
under a fading sky.

This is like the best of the *Cantos*, or anyway the prettiest: Turkish delight, and indigestible without something more fibrous along the way. In 1951 fiber evidently still meant the anti-Roosevelt line Pound had been following since the thirties (Bunting appears in the *Active Anthology*, 1933), and some of *The Spoils* is spoiled by the shrill "bastard Roosevelt" invective that waters down to paranoia: "counsellors of patience / lie in wait for blood, / every man with a net." Zukofsky quotes in his *Test of Poetry* eighteen perfect hexameters of Bunting's, an imitation of Lucretius which closes:

. . . Alma Venus! Trim my poetry
With your grace; and give peace to write and read
and think.

The peace was given, apparently, in the Middle East, where Bunting translated Firdusi and dropped out of sight. Early last year, of course, *Poetry* published his masterpiece, *Briggflatts*, in which Pound's music has been fused with the kind of understanding which surpasses peace, giving us the Northumbrian fantasia on themes of king-killing and masonry-as-meaning which enclose their own magisterial poetic:

Flexible, unrepetitive line
to sing, not paint; sing, sing,
laying the tune on the air. . . .

Briggflatts suggests an alternative convention of prosody, one afforded by "modernists" as centrifugal as Perse and David Jones and, taken with the best parts of *The Spoils* (over 400 lines), proves Pound to have been quite right, again, about the man to whom he wrote in 1936: "The poet's job is to *define* and yet again define till the detail of surface is in accord with the root in justice." Thirty years later, we can see what he meant.—RICHARD HOWARD, *Poetry*, June 1967, pp. 195–97

The structure of *Briggflatts* is symphonic, a development from the earlier long poems, such as "Villon" and "Aus dem Zweiten Reich," which have a simpler sonata form. The latter poems employ a basic pattern of Theme A (and development), Theme B, Recapitulation of Theme A. *Briggflatts* has a design more like that of a Sibelius symphony: fragments of themes are presented in the first four movements, gradually taking on more significance each time a fragment relating to the same block of thematic material is repeated, until in the fifth and final movement, the fragments are brought together in a resolution which combines all the basic subject matter of the poem, art and experience, love and memory, nature and the cosmos. . . .

Again the parallel with the musical form of the *Four Quartets* is conspicuous. It is no accident that two poets at the height of their powers should have chosen a musical solution to a thematic preoccupation of their whole lives. And what else but a form that approaches music could express the simultaneity of impressions in the memory that is one of the most important aspects of *Briggflatts*? Music undoubtedly possesses a quality that only the most subtly orchestrated of languages ever has, a quality that bears directly on the question of time. Language fixes one's ideas and impressions on the printed page; the reader can go back to a particular passage and give it a disproportionate effect in the whole. The flow of music is absolute—"you are the music / While the music lasts." Music can evoke in a way far more precise than the other arts, as it contains within itself the movements of states of consciousness and their superimposition. Music contains time and therefore vanquishes it.

In *Briggflatts*, with a greater mastery of individual voice than before, Bunting states his theme of time directly. The experiences of the poet-narrator are passed through all ages, all situations, culminating in the conclusion where form is theme. There is, however, a paradox in the fact that art, which is the most permanent of human creations, can only reflect the transience of existence. Bunting's poet can retrieve nothing from time but his own poems.—Anthony Suter, "Time and the Literary Past in the Poetry of Basil Bunting," *CoL*, Autumn 1971, pp. 525–26

HUGH KENNER
From "A Resurrected Poet"

Poetry, September 1951, pp. 361–65

Mr. Bunting's verse has been inaccessible since the *Active Anthology* (1933) went out of print; after eighteen years there should be a few hundred people to be interested in the present collection. What he has to offer that is not in the work of his elders doesn't depend on his having read different books, gone to a different school, and formed a preference for different women, adjectives, and cheeses. Neither Mr. Bunting's interest nor his readers' is focused on Mr. Bunting's insides. The reflection has preceded the poems, has preceded, as it were, the very mapping of the interests they articulate; the poem isn't a transcription of the poet's trying to think, nor a noise attending spiritual indigestion.

Let the reader not be put off by talk about thought; we are not in the presence of versified dogmatics:

Let them remember Samangan, the bridge and tower
and rutted cobbles and the coppersmith's hammer,
where we looked out from the walls to the marble
    mountains
ate and lay and were happy an hour and a night;
so that the heart never rests from love of the city
without lies or riches, whose old women
straight as girls at the well are beautiful,
its old men and its wineshops gay.

Let them remember Samangan against usurers,
cheats and cheapjacks, amongst boasters,
hideous children of cautious marriages,
those who drink in contempt of joy.

Let them remember Samangan, remember
they wept to remember the hour and go.

The sonority of this strikes the attention at once, but it isn't on sonority that Mr. Bunting habitually depends. The solidity of image, the absence of fuzz and duplication, the weighing of epithet, the continual interest of rhythms (none of them conspicuously borrowed), underlie single lines arresting and rich:

Whose steps wake your delight?

or

Here was glass-clear architecture
Gardens sacred to Tethys

and a range of tone that can extend in a single poem all the way from

Crack, rush, ye mountains, bury your rills!
Spread your green glass, ocean, over the meadows!
Scream, avalanche, boulders amok, strangle the
    dale!
O ships in the sea's power, O horses
on shifting roads, in the earth's power, without
    hoofhold!

This is the earthquake, this was
the great earthquake of Genryaku!

to

Summer? Cuckoo's *Follow, follow*—to
harvest Purgatory hill!
Fall? The nightgrasshopper will
shrill *Fickle life!*
Snow will thicken on the doorstep,
melt like a drift of sins.

And the thematic range of the collection extends with equal sureness from

We built no temples. Our cities' woven hair
mildewed and frayed. Records of Islam and Chin,
battles, swift riders, the ambush, tale of the slain,
    and the name Jengiz

to wry contemporary observation:

Capital is land upon which
work has been done (*vide* textbooks).
Capital is everything except the desert,
sea, untunnelled rock, upper air.
Breathed air
is Capital, though not rented:
70 million tons of solid matter
suspended in the atmosphere,
November, in London,
    not by an act of God.

It is probably the novelty of encountering verse not held together solely by a sense of the writer's personality that makes Bunting seem, at first, fragmentary. The reader brought up on the presently popular tradition of more or less dramatic introspection may need to be persuaded at some length that a thing is what it is, that anything honestly recorded has the incalculable value of honesty:

My jacket's wistaria flax,
my blanket hemp,
berries and young greens
my food.
(Let it be quite understood,
all this is merely personal.
I am not preaching the simple life
to those who enjoy being rich.)

This is from *Chomei at Toyama*, close reading of the whole of which may persuade us of the pleasure to be derived from writing that confines itself to discovering what are the essentials of the job in hand and setting them down.

Lofty city Kyoto
wealthy, without antiquities

precisely defines a quality; but six words are apt to be overlooked if one assumes a point to be unimportant unless dilated into witty rhetoric. Mr. Auden would have fashioned this distich into a whole chorus.

Bunting's extreme concentration is not unconnected with an air of contrivance. Not that his verse is the null product of a will to turn out so many lines on a theme; it is the contrivance of a man who knows what it is he means to contrive. Word never suggests word, mood is never prolonged because a groove held it. On the other hand, one has only seldom the sense that—as with Pound or Yeats—the right words are miraculously presenting themselves instant by instant. This is only to say that Mr. Bunting isn't (and doesn't claim to be) a major poet. He has done a few things right; his superiors (whom at his best he isn't inferior to) did more things well, and weren't betrayed into publishing their attempts on subjects a little beyond their skill. Bunting's virtue is that he always knows what he wants to do; he does it so deliberately that one occasionally notices the hand reaching for the next tool. The beginning of the *Villon* monologue—

> He whom we anatomized
> "Whose words we gathered as pleasant flowers
> And thought on his wit and how neatly he described
>   things"
> Speaks
> To us, hatching marrow,
> Broody all night over the bones of a deadman.

—is unnecessarily strained into patness: an attempt to crush the daisy-pickers who a page later are evaporated by the full heat of the poem. When the heat comes, however, the overlaboured irony of the opening not only suffers, it vanishes from the mind: one must quote enough to give the momentum—

> . . . Worn hides that scarcely clothe the soul,
> They are so rotten, old and thin,
> Or firm and soft and warm and full,
> Fellmonger Death gets every skin.
>
> All that is piteous, all that's fair,
> All that is fat and scant of breath,
> Elisha's baldness, Helen's hair,
> Is Death's collateral:
>
> Three score and ten years after sight
> Of this pay me your pulse and breath
> Value received. And who dare cite,
> As we forgive our debtors, Death?
>
> Abelard and Eloise,
> Henry the Fowler, Charlemagne,
> Genee, Lopokova, all these
> Die, die in pain.
>
> And General Grant and General Lee,
> Patti and Florence Nightingale,
> Like Tyro and Antiope
> Drift among ghosts in Hell,
>
> Know nothing, are nothing, save a fume
> Driving across a mind
> Preoccupied with this: Our doom
> Is, to be sifted by the wind,
>
> Heaped up, smoothed down like silly sands.
> We are less permanent than thought.
> The emperor with the Golden Hands
> Is still a word, a tint, a tone,
> Insubstantial—glorious,
> When we ourselves are dead and gone
> And the green grass growing over us.

After this the close of part 2 earns its admirable condensation:

> How many golden prints on the smudgy page?
> Homer? Adest. Dante? Adest.
> Adsunt omnes, Omnes et
> Villon.
> Villon?
> Blacked by the sun, washed by the rain,
> Hither and thither scurrying as the wind varies.

Mr. Bunting has learned from Pound, but gotten far beyond the early *Personae* at which most Poundlings stick. (His debt is rather to *Cathay* and *Propertius*). He has learned from W. C. Williams, and been sufficiently original to dissociate the assimilable techniques from the highly personal (and hence, to the imitator, far more tempting) astringencies. He has learned techniques where others have borrowed voices. His defects (occasional strain after a contrast; rhythm bogging while attention pauses on lexicographic concision) depend on virtues. He is alive to much more than the things he has read about, or the

commonplaces which assume a spurious uniqueness when they happen at length to *me*.

Of these 54 pages some 5 may or should enter the *corpus poeticum*; a way of saying that Bunting's subjects and treatment have an interest outlasting the area in which they were conceived.

KENNETH COX
From "The Aesthetic of Basil Bunting"
Agenda, Autumn 1966, pp. 20–28

The most obvious characteristic of Mr Basil Bunting's verse is its compression of language. This characteristic is so consistent and at times so extreme that, whatever the intention or the instinct at its origin, it is likely to strike the reader as a practice fortified by long use and possibly buttressed by some theory. Given a knowledge of Mr Bunting's famous pun *dichten = condensare* he may then suppose the objective to be a simple quantitative brevity, such as is recommended in those manuals which tell you to prefer short words to long and never to use two if one will do. But Mr Bunting's condensation covers a number of different techniques as well as processes which can hardly be described as technical at all. There are, it is true, times when what is written appears to be the result of a mere saving of unnecessary words, such as we aim at in composing a telegram, or to have a curt and offhand manner. Traces of these idiosyncracies persist throughout Mr Bunting's work but the method which gives his style its individual mark is not at all scrimping or casual. His aesthetic, his sense of the beautiful, does not depend on mechanical measurement, although the criterion of brevity may be used as others might use metre or consonance, to prompt revision and suggest improvements.

The foundation of the method is a close involution of the idea consisting in the use of phrases which are, as it were, knotted as tight as they can be yet are easily unloosed. It disdains any gradual leading up to the meaning or the fumbling which makes it necessary to qualify or supplement what has just been said. It is not concerned with progression, development or illustration: the meaning is given in full and at one go, in a quick and as far as possible inclusive shot. With this onceness there goes a paring away of inessential elements. In turning itself for the quickest presentation the idea drops the encumbrances of cliché and avoids the adventitious meanings which cling to it. The result, if successful, is clean, bare, limpid and perhaps a little awkward.

It may be desirable to add that the technique described does not require the meaning itself to be without nuance. There would be less merit in giving sharp expression to a crudity. It is the art of Mr. Bunting to give succinct and accurate expression to firm, delicate and uncontaminated observations. . . .

The concept of the turn (tropos, trope) lies at the basis of syntax. It is not merely a matter of deciding the order of words or, as in the political rhetoric of antiquity, the figure of speech which will best ingratiate the speaker with his audience. Presentation, in the obstetric sense of the term, is nevertheless its object. On which way up or which end first the writer presents his idea will depend the immediacy and the accuracy of its impact and the amount of delay in any delayed action he may have deliberately intended. The possibilities are numerous and the choice may be difficult. In the recent past the possibilities were reduced to the comparatively few stereotypes to which the writing of English had been restricted by the spread of schooling and the development of the media of communication: in the interest of making a thing known to a large number of people in a short time the number of tropes conventionally permitted to the written language was severely limited. A parallel social movement, partly democratic in impetus and partly due to the diffusion of English as a second language in other parts of the world, made the restriction seem convenient and even welcome. Writers who resisted or evaded these pressures owed the strength of their resistance to a deliberate disintegration of syntax practised on philosophical grounds or to the studies of living speech undertaken by the nineteenth-century philologists.

It is apparent all the same, from many instances in the history of literature, that the introduction of new tropes or the restoration of old ones is not a mere social or linguistic trick but the result of a reliving of ideas, sometimes agitated and prolonged, whose effect is to make the tropes already established look rhetorical and ridiculous. In presenting himself to the world through the medium of a language renewed in this way a writer compels himself to examine himself and cannot, it seems (the mechanism is obscure), perform the operation of stripping and reassembly without some moral discipline. There emerges in the end not only a spareness but also a purity of line.

Another method of attaining concentration of meaning, supplementing work on the fabric of the phrase, is the narrative or dramatic method, consisting in the clever selection and arrangement of what comes before. So prepared, a few words possibly unremarkable by themselves accumulate a charge which can shock. The principle will be familiar from Ibsen and the sagas.

If there is, as W. P. Ker thought he could discern at the origins of Old Norse and Old English verse, a basic difference between their movements and systems, then it is from what he called the Norse that Mr. Bunting's verse derives. Its continuous single-stroke movement promotes pointed observation and epigrammatic vehemence, in contrast to the longer line or couplet of the so-called English tradition which, by favouring the introduction of a second element, promotes balance, modification and antithesis. Unless singularly adapted to the matter, for instance in drama or argumentation, the second element is liable to duplicate or weaken whatever is in the first. So Pasternak found the power of expressing reality heightened by shortening the lines, not so much to develop any specific quality they contained as to escape the tyranny of a humdrum metre.

Whether or not this is a typically northern process, there is to be seen in the spareness and purity of Mr Bunting's line, especially manifest in his earlier work, the tempered and taciturn spirit of the border ballads. His compression of language can be regarded as a compression of emotion, as of speech through compressed lips. Such speech not only rejects fripperies, it keeps as close as it can to the feeling which generated it and to the object it describes.

The ground here, it will be recognized, has been trodden before. It is the tradition which appeared earlier in the famous words of the preface to the second edition of the *Lyrical Ballads*:

> The principal object, then, which I proposed to myself in these poems was to choose incidents and situations from common life, and to relate or describe them, throughout, as far as was possible, in a selection of language really used by men, and, at the same time, to throw over them a certain colouring of imagination, whereby ordinary things should be presented to the mind in an unusual way; and, further, and above all, to make these incidents and situations

interesting by tracing in them, truly though not ostentatiously, the primary laws of our nature. . . .

The mention of Wordsworth ought to cause only momentary surprise. For all its artistry the poetry of Mr Bunting stays, in the stark tradition he adorns, close to the state of inarticulateness. Such a state may arise from concentration, passion, madness, sleep or even stupidity: any of these can turn into a matrix of poetry, because free of sophistry. The resulting speech utters what has only just escaped being unspoken, almost as if speech were painful or inappropriate to the circumstances, and it bursts under strong pressure but strict control into the nearest expression capable of speedy termination. . . .

The re-emergence of this tradition may be of interest to those critics who stress Mr Bunting's acknowledged obligations to Ezra Pound and who ask to what extent and in what manner the example of the American master can be assimilated to a native heritage. A poetry which remains close to the state it describes gives rise to certain difficulties. How far can the close expression of reality be freed from the feeling of disgust? And what elements of colloquial speech is it possible to reproduce? It is also a disadvantage of the method that, with a rendering so close to the subject, firsthand knowledge of the object may be needed to appreciate the fidelity of the rendering. Who, who does not remember Churchill or see old newsreels, will get the picture of him *clowning with a cigar?*

One of the paradoxes of the situation is that a direct transcription of the vernacular easily looks false. Mr Bunting's Cockney imitation of Villon rings untrue. It is hard to say why: it seems that the feel of living speech comes through only when some of the subtlest elements of movement and intonation join in a meeting governed by rare and unpredictable conditions, similar to those which govern the evanescent existence of the elementary particles, and that these conditions commonly escape the meshes of the grammarian's net, fine as these are now. The prestige of Wordsworth's theory, the political movement of which it is part and our modern interest in radio and the tape-recorder may temporarily have obscured the truth that even the colloquial style is acquired by sedentary toil oblique stroke and by the imitation of great masters. The real, it seems, is not to be won by direct assault but is to be wooed with humility and display. It is demonstrable that the most authentic achievements of colloquial utterance usually crown a lifelong exercise in revision, imitation and translation. . . .

Few of Mr Bunting's rhythms depart from the limits ordinarily set by the internal movements of the human body—systole and diastole of the heart, expansion and contraction of the lungs—which set the norms for expression of the emotions. But there is also to be found in his verse a slower movement keeping time not with the movements or gait of the body but with the longer stronger motion of the sea. When drained of feeling or evoking a reality outside human life it is to this movement, as to a prenatal source, that his verse returns, for example in the coda to *Briggflatts*.

It may be doubted whether anyone can really (without losing his personality) step outside his own personal rhythms, whatever the nationality of the vocabulary he may temporarily employ. Mr Bunting's rhythms offer great variety within a small compass: the delights of perfect freedom of movement are difficult to combine with the satisfactions of remaining close to earth. His verbal concentration also precludes certain auditory effects. Although it may be lightened by playfulness, his verse is occasionally also clogged by the ornament the Arabs call *jinas*, correspondence of consonants without correspondence of meaning. (It differs from the *cynghanedd* of Welsh poetry in that it does not constitute an organic part of the structure of the verse but only knits it closer together.) In an example like

> Fear of being imputed
> naive impeded thought

the idea is not only in-turned but in-grown and a surgical operation is needed to release it.

After economy the next most notable characteristic of Mr Bunting's verse is risk. The omission of intervening or supporting structures exhibits both characteristics, while his choice of words tends towards the slightly unexpected. Part of this tendency is due to the continuous process of expelling poetic diction. The direction of his choice is towards the more familiar and the more sensuous word: ramparts no longer *hug* a town, they *cuddle* it. The constant undercutting of his expectations may excite in the reader a pleasure continually reactivated and mingled with a suppressed apprehension. When he sees that an exercise of skill and daring has been successfully performed his pleasure is complicated by relief that the danger has been avoided and by amusement that it could ever have been overestimated. . . .

Mr Bunting's verse is not only concerned with *the angle a slut's blouse / draws on her chest.* As in the example given above, it also honours those who themselves acknowledge and manage these perceptions. From the girl with *delicate ignorant face (preoccupied rather / by the set of her stockings)* it goes on to celebrate a Persian miniature painter, Italian fiddler, Cumbrian dog-trainer. This cultivation of the senses has two extraneous consequences of some importance. First, by progressively increasing the definition of the verbal record, the expression of observation drives the language to its primal resources, till it draws upon the qualities which bind words to things. Secondly, by monopolising the mind these observations act as a preservative against propaganda of all persuasions and so make possible the commemoration of innocence achieved in the first section of *Briggflatts.* . . .

The underlying themes of Mr Bunting's poetry are not easily brought to the surface because the volume of his preserved work is small and sudden perfections discourage thematic analysis. Certain deductions may be permitted. In its description of the external world much of his writing is concerned with appearances of desolation: the deserts of the Middle East, the borderlands of northern England, the Paris of Villon, the thirties, the sea. In these settings man comes close to facing the conditions beyond which life is not possible:

> Bound to beasts' udders, rags no dishonour,
> not by much intercourse ennobled,
> multitude of books, bought deference:
> meagre flesh tingling to a mouthful of water,
> apt to no servitude, commerce, or special dexterity.

If he survives he can say with the quiet arrogance of the bedouin: *What's to dismay us?* The impoverishment of the actual world stems the flow of the verses, reducing them to a pure trickle of which every drop is to be valued. Economy, the free use of few resources, is seen to be another aspect of the same concern, thematic as well as technical.

By another of the correspondences one comes to expect the idea of risk also appears thematically, most clearly in *The Spoils.* The dominant theme of this poem is that of opposition between the calculating and the reckless. The calculator (moneylender, administrator, policeman) imposes arbitrary rule and measure: the reckless (singer, soldier, seaman) gives without counting. The difference between them is determined by the presence of death. The calculator works to an end beyond the scope of an individual lifespan, but it is the risk of death that gives zest to life: without death life is not worth living. This bourgeois-romantic dichotomy is counterpointed by a secondary opposition running in the contrary direction. In spite of the care and precision of their operations the art of the calculating is rhetorical and false: *Roman exaggeration and the leaden mind of Egypt.* But the art of the gay in the shadow of death is cool and fine: it is by taking risks that we preserve proportion. The thesis is illustrated by reference to Persia and the second world war.

Briggflatts, somewhat unfairly, makes Mr Bunting's earlier poetry look like preparatory work. Its subject is repossession after long absence: *Heureux qui comme Ulysse.* . . . It returns to the north country with English both purified and enriched, the past and its studies absorbed. Here and there is a southern warmth, an eastern courtesy, the skill of a Latin poet in placing a long word, the audacious finality of Dante. . . . But in general the debts are present only as harmonics. Yet it is the long practice of the translator, the persistent testing of every word, which has probably made possible the unfailing discretion with which the life and appearance of the country is represented without trace of provincialism or lapse into the banal. In addition to romantic theory and symbolist technique it infuses into the native tradition the sensuality of oriental poetry and attains, not by imitation but by a revival of its primitive elements, the standard of the King James version of the Old Testament. . . .

Skills and accidents by which we make contact with poets distant and past, or by which we seem to establish a relation with the non-human world, convince us that in cultivating the art we are not just playing with words, toys of our own invention, but that we do indeed perform, in ways we cannot understand but know for sure, parts in a rite able to dignify and perpetuate our common life. It may also be allowed that in obeying its laws we do a little to appease the dead. The achievement of Mr Bunting is to have demonstrated yet again and by concrete example the classic conclusion of his early poem:

> The Emperor with the Golden Hands
>
> > is still a word, a tint, a tone,
> > insubstantial-glorious,
> > when we ourselves are dead and gone
> > and the green grass growing over us.

ANTHONY BURGESS

1917–

John Anthony Burgess Wilson was born in Manchester on February 25, 1917. He graduated from Manchester University in 1940, then spent World War II as musical director of an Army entertainment unit. After the war he taught at Birmingham University and at an Oxfordshire grammar school, worked for the Ministry of Education, played jazz piano, and wrote A *Vision of Battlements*, a novel that was not published until 1965. From 1954 to 1959 he served with the Colonial Service in Borneo and Malaya, where he wrote a semi-autobiographical trilogy, *The Long Day Wanes*.

Burgess's most prolific period began in 1959, when he was mistakenly diagnosed as having a brain tumor. Believing he had only months to live, he returned to England and wrote five novels. By the time he realized he would live, his literary career was firmly established. His next book, published in 1962, was *A Clockwork Orange*, a dystopian novel written in neo-Russian slang. It remains his best-known book, in part due to Stanley Kubrick's 1971 film version. Other Burgess novels of the 1960s include *Nothing Like the Sun* (1964), a historical fiction involving William Shakespeare, and *Enderby* (1968), a comical portrait of a harassed novelist. He also paid tribute to his hero James Joyce by writing *Re Joyce* (1965), a "key" to *Ulysses* and *Finnegans Wake*.

Burgess tackled several other media in the 1970s, including the theater (translations of *Cyrano de Bergerac* and *Oedipus Rex*) and television (the screenplays *Jesus of Nazareth* and *Moses the Lawgiver*). He taught at Princeton, Columbia, and City College, while continuing to write novels, criticism, non-fiction, musical compositions, and occasionally poetry. He has been married twice—in 1942 to Llewela Jones, who died in 1968, and in 1968 to philologist and translator Liliana Macellari. They reside in Monaco, Malta, and Italy.

Personal

Like most novelists, I like to regard my books as works of craftsmanship for sale, objects as well-made as I can make them. The deeper issues—aesthetic or social or metaphysical—are not my concern; they are strictly for the commentators. A carpenter makes a chair for both use and ornament; the professional novelist hopes that his offering will provide refreshment for the mind and at the same time raise the mind closer to the eternal values of truth and beauty (which, as Keats reminds us, can be regarded as the same thing—different views of reality). The problem of every professional craftsman is the reconciliation of these humble aims with the pressures of time. Only the amateur—carpenter or novelist—has all the time in the world; the professional sometimes has to hurry. If he is commissioned to write a book, that book must be delivered (just as a set of chairs must be delivered) by an agreed date. He must say: 'Tomorrow I go out of circulation for a while; I must start a new novel.' This, and his habit of gathering material in the hope that it may be useful for a novel, makes him seem cold-blooded to those who have a more romantic view of art—the Muse descending only when she decides to, the long wait—in an exophthalmic trance—for inspiration. Novels are created by men and women who put bottom to chair and pen to paper.

When I first began to write fiction it was, as with most novelists, a refined hobby that, as I got deeper into it, began to demand more time and application than was right for a hobby: it began to wish to be a full-time job. But there is probably no greater happiness in this world than that derived from writing, in a void, for pure pleasure—to see whether places and people, speech and action, can be fixed on paper and then, like a lesser divine creation, rise from that paper and live. When I wrote my first novel, A *Vision of Battlements*, I had no artistic aim other than to recall my wartime life in Gibraltar and stamp that life, in a suitably depersonalized form, on to paper. I was not even concerned about an audience. But when I wrote my first published books—the three which make up my *Malayan Trilogy* (called *The Long Day Wanes* in the United States)—I had a strong urge to communicate an image of a Far Eastern British protectorate in a phase of transition, and so I wrote for an audience (a primary one of Malayans, a secondary one of everybody else). I was encouraged by good reviews to wish to consider the writing of fiction as a secondary profession (my primary one was that of a Colonial Civil Servant), and so every book I wrote from then on was aimed at a cultivated readership and designed to further—through at least good craftsmanship—my reputation as a novelist. The subject-matter I chose was cognate with that of the three first published novels—the state of transition in British colonial territories; the impact of a self-indulgent England (which no longer cared about its dying Empire) on a sensibility much modified by living in the Far East. *Devil of a State* was about an imaginary caliphate in East Africa (a kind of fantasticated Zanzibar); *The Right to an Answer* (much influenced in its language by Nabokov, whom I had been reading for the first time) was a study of provincial England, as seen by a man on leave from the East, with special emphasis on the decay of traditional values in an affluent society.

Then I was invalided out of the Colonial Service and, back in England, found that literature had been forced upon me as a career: the days of the hobby and the semi-professional approach were over; I had to write in order to live. In a single year I wrote *The Doctor is Sick*, *The Worm and the Ring*, and *The Wanting Seed*, which were eventually published under the name of Anthony Burgess. I also wrote two other novels—*One Hand Clapping* and *Inside Mr. Enderby*—under the pseudonym Joseph Kell. The pseudonym was, I was told, necessary in order to hide evidence of over-production. Critics and publishers alike look sourly on the prolific writer, forgetting how large was the annual output of men like H. G. Wells, Henry James, Hugh Walpole and—to go farther back—Anthony Trollope, Sir Walter Scott, and Charles Dickens. For my part, I see only good in fecundity. I can never forgive E. M. Forster (who has set a puritanical standard of spare output) for writing only five novels and subsisting on the reputation they earned into old age. There are two good reasons for writing much, if one can. The first is the need to earn; the second is the fear of an untimely death, which will prevent the half-formed books in one's mind from being realized. We know not the day nor the hour. I may be killed in a train accident when taking this present book to my publisher in London. You can see whether or not this has happened by reading the blurb on the dust-jacket. If it is not mentioned, I am probably still alive. Anyway, we must all write what we can and, alas, as quickly as is consistent with good craftsmanship.

Critics say that there are certain persistent themes in my novels—the need to laugh in the face of a desperate future; questions of loyalty; the relationships between countries and between races. I am not qualified myself to discuss my work in terms of subject-matter; I have enough to do in trying to write well, which is not easy: the writer concentrates on his craft, the critic looks over his shoulder at his art, such as it is. All I can say is that the novel is a form to which I am committed, that I am interested in the progress of the novel, that it is the only important literary form we have left and that I am proud to be involved in its continuing life and development. I know that all my contemporaries would express a similar pride, while admitting to a certain desperation. Here is the daily treadmill; here is the job to be done. Are we doing it as well as we can? Should that sentence, which has already been rewritten ten times, be rewritten yet again? Is that character necessary? Is that scene really funny? Will people like the book when it is finished? More important, will they buy it?

As, I hope, this little handbook has shown, there are enough people in the world prepared to brave the novelist's depression and anxiety and self-doubt for the sake of the occasional elation and, more, for the sake of assisting in the evolutionary development of one of the noblest of the arts. The contemporary novel is not doing badly. Soon, when we least expect it, it will do not merely better but magnificently. Any one of us may, astonishingly, prove the vehicle of some great unexpected masterpiece which will burn up the world (meaning the people who read). That dim hope sustains us.—Anthony Burgess, *The Novel Now*, 1967, pp. 211–13

And a very happy New Year to you, too, Mr. Burgess!

The wish, however, is wasted on both sides, for this, to your night visitors, is a very old year. We—whispering, fingering, rustling, creaking, about your roach-ridden West Side flat—are that posterity to which you hopefully address yourself. Congratulations, Mr. Burgess: you have already hit your ball smack over the pavilion clock, not to mention the left-field wall on this American side of the Atlantic. If you awaken now with one of the duodenal or pyloric twinges of your poet Enderby (which are to us as gruesome a literature-lesson spicer as Johnson's scrofula, Swift's scatophobia, or Keats's gallop of death-warrant blood), do not fancy it is ghosts you hear, sibilant and crepitant about the bed. To be a ghost one has first to die.

But you are still very much alive, Mr. Burgess, in spite of the eager North American scholars who would regard you as dead and ready for decent interment in an elegant sarcophagus of scholarly exegesis. I'm sorry, Priscilla, that I cannot recommend examples of "early," "middle," or "late" Burgess, for I cannot honestly say he appears to be anywhere near the end of his revels. You see, for about a dozen years, he has had a disease uncommon among writers of serious fiction: it is called *fecundity*.

I would call your attention, children, to the fact that there

is in Mr. Burgess's appearance nothing to suggest a complacent sense of completed achievement. The photographs in recent articles that show a stocky little man are very misleading. If we could linger here until he rises in the morning, you would see he is about six feet tall and lean, without either the haunch or the paunch you might expect to see on a man who spends most of his time before that typewriter in the corner. No, Harold, Mr. Burgess does not write in the lavatory like Mr. Enderby, but maybe he should. Do you know what the word *impinge* means? Well, never mind, I'll tell you later.

You will notice, children, that his hands are rather large and powerful, more than strong enough to play a piano as well as an electric typewriter. Mr. Burgess, I might add, is very fond of typewriters, although, like a farmer, he dares not make a pet of one. But let us not talk of typewriters while we have the man himself slumbering before us. As you can see, his hair is half grey, but he still has it all and combs it forward Roman fashion across his high forehead. Regrettably, his most arresting features are presently concealed beneath heavy lids. His eyes, when he opens them, are sharp grey and extremely penetrating, although reddened somewhat by an almost perpetual stream of cigar smoke. That should give you some idea of how he *looks*, children, but can you guess how he *sounds*, when he wakes in the morning, lights his first cigar, and brews his first five-bag cup of tea? What's that, Priscilla? Like anyone else from England, you say? Like those announcers on NET who sound sort of vaguely superior? Yes and no, Priscilla. He does indeed sound very British, but one tends to be less aware of the Britishness, if you will, than the deep resonance of his voice. The sound of his voice rather enhances an overall effect of tremendous virile energy awaiting release. In fact, as one listens to him, one soon becomes less astonished that so many books have flowed out of him in such a short time.

You could not, of course, derive any sense of Mr. Burgess's dynamism from watching him at this moment. But if we could stay through the morning, you would surely see him at work, if not at that typewriter, then lecturing on some campus in Texas or Missouri, or conferring with theatre associates in Minneapolis or New York, or being interviewed by some professor with a tape recorder. About this word *impinge*, incidentally—what's that, Melanie? Yes, I realize tomorrow is your holiday. Of course, Mr. Burgess never takes a holiday; whether he is in Malta, Rome, Sussex, or New York City, he works seven days a week. No, Harold, he doesn't drink like Mr. Hemingway or Mr. Fitzgerald. Sometimes he does leave that machine humming to itself while he brews himself a strong cup of tea, but his rest breaks are few. Strong tea and cigar smoke are about all he will consume during a working day. Actually, he enjoys cooking and relishes fine wines, but any indulgence that might slow him down he leaves for after working hours.

Why does he do it? You mean, why this sense of urgency? Well, I suppose it's partly a vestige of his "terminal year." He was, you know, told that 1960 would probably be his last year on earth, and he spent that year producing as many books as he could before a supposed brain tumor did its work. But I tend to see in his commitment something more than a sense of life's brevity. What appears to be a more compelling motivation is simply creative desire itself—a determination to bring forth all the books within him. Regretting what he considers a late beginning as a writer, he means to leave you not only new fiction but as much drama, poetry, translation, and criticism as his remaining years will allow. . . .

Although he enjoys university teaching, he does not see himself as any sort of intellectual ("If I am one, I'm fighting against it all the time"). He does not want to become too much a part of the rarified, cerebral campus atmosphere in which the enwombed academic thrives. His attitude stems largely from his view of the nature of literature and indeed reality itself. To some extent, he agrees with the Shakespeare/Burgess composite hero in *Nothing Like the Sun* that literature is "an epiphenomenon of the action of the flesh":

> I don't think it's an intellectual thing. It's not made out of concepts; it's made out of percepts. People often think you're being trivial or superficial if you think it's important to describe a bottle of sauce or beer as neatly, as cleverly, as evocatively as you can. It's really more important to do that than to express an idea or concept. I believe the world of physical things is the only world that really exists, and the world of concepts is a world of trickery, for the most part. Concepts only come to life when they're expressed in things you can see, taste, feel, touch, and the like. One of the reasons I have a sneaking regard for the Catholic Church is that it turns everything into tangible percepts. There's no mystical communion with God as there is in Hinduism or Buddhism. Instead you get God in the form of a meal, which is right, which is good. When you die, they shove oil on your body. Oil is something your body has always given out, exuded. You're getting it back again. It's a Mediterranean idea, using this staple of life, this nourishing thing, oil. And I like the ring in marriage. One gets a shock in countries like Italy to find the old Fascism alive and people who talk about mystical concepts, about what Mussolini *really* meant, about *l'umanita, lo spirito umano*, and all that sort of thing. These are horrible metaphysical concepts which mean bugger all. You find this summarized best at the end of *Finnegans Wake*, where they're waiting for the coming, where you get this Berkeley-Bulkily-Buckley character who talks an idealistic mumble. Then you get St. Patrick with the shamrock. There it is, the God-given, the *Dieudonné*, the physical object. It's a thing in itself, just as the Cross is a thing in itself, but it's also a symbol of something bigger. These bloody far eastern religions with their lack of physicality, their incorporeal substances, they're sickening.

With regard to religion, Burgess still maintains a "renegade Catholic" stance that is oddly conservative in some respects. He despises liberal Catholicism, which seems to have become another religion in the process of gaining acceptance in the modern world. The ecumenical movement repels him, as do the liturgical changes and the use of the vernacular. He is disgusted by these innovations, as he says, "very much from the Catholic angle":

> But when I say that I am a Catholic now, I mean solely that I have a Catholic background, that my emotions, my responses are Catholic, and that my intellectual convictions, such as they are, are very meager compared with the fundamental emotional convictions. Certainly, when I write, I tend to write from a Catholic point of view—either from the point of view of a believing Catholic, or a renegade Catholic, which is what I think James Joyce's position. Reading *Ulysses*, you are aware of this conflict within a man who knows the Church thoroughly and yet has totally rejected it with a blasphemous kind of vigor.

To an extent, he subscribes to the Manichean heresy, although he agrees with the Church that it should be condemned as heresy. He shares the Manichean belief that there is a perpetual conflict between two forces that dominates the affairs of the universe, and whether the forces can be accurately labelled "good" and "evil" is by no means certain. They might as reasonably be designated by terms such as "right" and "left," or "x" and y," or even "hot" and "cold." All that is certain is that the opposed forces exist, are in conflict, and that earthly turmoils, such as the present conflicts between East and West, are relatively trivial affairs that merely "figure" the great cosmic clash. Like his character Hillier in *Tremor of Intent*, he believes that the man who is aware of this conflict and yet deliberately and cynically refuses to involve himself in it is a contemptible self-server. Although even America and Russia are beginning to realize that the Cold War has just been a game, and although the possibility of nuclear war between them is perhaps steadily diminishing, Burgess believes their rivalry reveals "an unconscious recognition that this is the nature of life—the two opposed forces, as exemplified in these big political blocs, the West and the East and their opposed ideologies. In this respect, I call myself a Manichee. I believe, if you like, that God and the Devil are possibilities, but it is not foreseeable, it is not inevitable that God should win over the Devil."

Although Burgess's world view is in many ways a pessimistic one, it has not prevented him from enjoying fully what the world has offered him. The spectacle of humanity in all its infinite variety of race and language is a constant source of wonder and pleasure to him, and the love he has known in human relationships is a great solace. Then there are the pleasures, although sometimes excruciating, of artistic creation, which for him include music as well as literature. He still composes music and has had the pleasure of hearing his own Concerto for Strings, some sonatas and quartets, and the incidental music for some plays and motion pictures performed. Most recently, his Symphony in C was performed at the University of Iowa. There is also for him the great sensual pleasure of listening with a trained ear to the works of others. The bitter disappointments, frustrations, and pain he has known cannot diminish the consolations of love and art, and indeed his view of life itself is wholly affirmative, even while his pessimistic view of the world allows the possibility that the "wrong god" may gain the upper hand in the great cosmic struggle. Like Christopher Howarth in *The Worm and the Ring*, he believes life must be blessed and praised in spite of every misery it may bring. The reader who shares to any extent this capacity to accept life on its own tragicomic terms will find his fiction an enriching experience.—Geoffrey Aggeler, *Anthony Burgess: The Artist as Novelist*, 1979, pp. 1–29

General

Heller, Barth, Purdy, and Vonnegut appear to believe with Beckett that "the supreme obligation of art is to its own impossibility," "that art is a 'fidelity to failure.'" Their novels, therefore, gradually self-destruct, leaving the reader alienated from the work, capable only of an ironic laugh of detachment from the human condition. "Laughing at our existence," says Hassan, "we exhaust its final possibilities." Each of these four authors writes novels of number.

For Anthony Burgess, on the other hand, as for Joyce, "The artist is a Promethean figure who ends by usurping the place of Zeus." Burgess writes in *Re Joyce*: "The fundamental purpose of any work of art is to impose order on the chaos of life as it comes to us; in imparting a vision of order the artist is doing what the religious teacher also does (this is one of the senses in which truth and beauty are the same thing)." It is not surprising that of twentieth-century fantasy writers Burgess most admires Nabokov and Joyce, because his use of fantasy is for their purposes rather than for the purposes of the Post-existential novelists of number. Burgess, like Joyce, is "a free-thinking fabulist." He needs his reader to be detached and observing, and so he needs fantasy rather than the techniques of realism, but he does not finally alienate his reader.

Burgess, like Joyce, wishes to manipulate "the commonplaces of language into a new medium that should shock the reader into a new awareness." His language has infinite reverberations. The important thing for Burgess is to keep the reader observing the pattern, yet involved, willing to fit the pieces of the jigsaw puzzle together, and then to believe in the picture. He does not take the reader towards nothingness, but towards an image of all-inclusiveness, where "everything is there at once." His purpose, like Joyce's, is the "atonement, at-one-ment, of contradictions." Burgess writes novels of nightmare.

Burgess, one of the most prolific of postwar British writers, is the author of sixteen novels published under his own name, of two published under the pseudonym Joseph Kell, and of a prodigious amount of criticism, among the best of which is his work on Joyce: *Re Joyce* and *A Shorter Finnegan's Wake*. Although almost all of Burgess's fiction illustrates the same basic philosophic stance, the kinds of fantasy he employs vary considerably. . . .

Burgess's novels deal with the same metaphysical questions as those of Heller, Barth, Purdy, and Vonnegut: the purpose of human existence, the nature of identity, the value and significance of language; but his answers—and he, unlike the previous novelists I have discussed, has answers—are not the Post-existential ones. As comments in various interviews and many of his novels indicate, Burgess is directly answering Sartre's and Camus' notion that there is no essential pattern in the universe and that the relationship between man and his universe is therefore irrational.

MF, perhaps, demonstrates most clearly that Burgess is answering the Post-existential view. The protagonist, Miles Faber, believes he can define himself through acts of will, create his own identity in the way Sartre suggests. He imagines he is completely free and seeks for the poems of a little-known writer in whose work he hopes to find "Words and colors totally free because totally meaningless." He learns, however, that "Nobody's free . . . choice is limited by inbuilt structures." Burgess reveals his interest in Existentialism also in his comments about his novels. For example, in an interview with Thomas Churchill, Burgess has stated that the central theme of *A Clockwork Orange* is "the idea of free will. This is not just half-baked existentialism, it's an old Catholic theme."

If Burgess's answer is the Catholic one—and he says himself that he "will not allow Catholicism to go over to the converts" nor "allow the Protestants to attack it," that what he writes "looks like Catholic writing"—it is certain only some Catholic doctrines interest him. Like Hillier, the hero of his novel *Tremor of Intent*, Burgess seems to have an Augustinian belief in the existence of evil and a sense of "what a bloody Manichean mess life is." Duality is the key to Burgess's view of reality; the essence of reality for him—and there are essences in Burgess's scheme as opposed to Sartre's—is its double nature. "Ultimate reality," says Hillier, "is a dualism or a game for two players." In religious terms this means that good and evil cannot exist without one another, "There is truly evil lying coiled in the good." But as Burgess realizes, "we don't believe in good and evil any more"; we need new terms. Each of the five Burgess novels illustrates this duality in new terms: *A Clockwork Orange* in psychological terms; *The Wanting Seed* in historical/sociological terms; *Tremor of Intent* in political

terms; *Enderby* in aesthetic terms; *MF* in terms of the relationship between society's structures and those of language.

The basic method of each Burgess novel is to present the reader with two visions, sometimes two antithetical world views, sometimes two apparently opposed aspects of one personality, and to invite him to make a choice. The choice often proves to be a false one; the two visions are a double vision, a dualism, inseparable parts of the one reality. The true choice lies elsewhere, between this duality and another negative value. The great evil in Burgess's view is to see life as unstructured and therefore capable of being completely controlled by man. The world is not neutral, not simply there. Burgess's use of the double vision is reminiscent of Vonnegut's, but there is an important difference between them. Vonnegut, a novelist of number, allows each vision to undercut the other, leaving the reader with nothing; Burgess, a novelist of nightmare, shows how the two visions are really one, leaving the reader with unity.— JEAN E. KENNARD, "Anthony Burgess: Double Vision," *Number and Nightmare*, 1975, pp. 131–33

Anthony Burgess . . . has written so many novels so fast that one is limited, for sheerly practical reasons, to mentioning only a couple of them. The Joyce-presence in Burgess is mostly linguistic, and perhaps beyond that musical; like Joyce, and like no other novelist in English, Burgess is fond of using language harmonically or impressionistically, and not just in nostalgic moods—he likes to strip words of their representational values and use them for their tonal values. This was apparent almost from the beginning. Without its special dialect, *A Clockwork Orange* would be not only a sparse but a muddled book, with its bare bones in evident disarray. There is a *1984* or *Brave New World* component in the book, a totalitarian society savagely conditioning its subjects into conformity; there is the urban gang-leader as outlaw-hero, a slummy Robin Hood; and there is Alex's particular hangup on classical music, which balances uncertainly in the middle of things—one moment a barbaric incitement to indiscriminate violence (in the rape of the two preadolescent *ptitsas*), one moment a nobler and more civilized vision, which is contaminated and degraded by being associated with violence. As a matter of fact, the whole conditioning-experiment which is the center of the novel is unconvincing, because it consists of giving Alex a representational overdose of what he obviously enjoys in everyday life, sadistic cruelties. (One is not convinced that—even with the help of drugs—the movies he's forced to see would revolt him; there's just as good a chance that they'd incite him.) In any case, having set up his alternatives—Alex *au naturel*, a bloodthirsty guttersnipe, versus Alex brainwashed, a whiny, sanctimonious guttersnipe—Burgess clearly was unable to resolve them, and so bundled his novel toward an inconclusive ending.

But the dialect of the novel performs several services for this rather crude fable. Being relatively opaque, it absorbs a lot of attention in its own right; it's a rich mixture of Russian conflated with English, Romany, rhyming slang, and Burgess-coinages, so that initially a lot of the meanings have to be guessed from the contexts. The reader is thus kept well occupied, not to say distracted; a good deal of his attention goes simply to the surface of the novel. Reading the book also involves a lot of back-and-forthing—that is, a word used in one context is given further meaning by its use in another context further on, which reflects back on its first usage. All this to-do on the linguistic surface of things blurs one's attention to the overall shape of the novel, and the scenes of gleeful sadism work to reinforce that desirable superficiality. It's a flat novel written in a thick, impasto style. The theme of music is integral to the novel, defined in this way; it makes for tonal unity on an immediate and impressionistic level, which is just another way of saying that the book is put together more like a movie than like a novel.

It is also a book, like those of Joyce, largely unconcerned with morality in any form. No doubt this was part of the reason for its popular success; it was an authentically cold book, at which a reader was entitled to shiver. Partly this was because of the society that Burgess envisioned, but partly also it derived from a personal artistic option within the book. One can almost feel the pathetic, beseeching figure of Poetic Justice imploring the novelist for admittance to his book and being roughly shouldered away. The writer whose book gives its title to Burgess's, whose house was vandalized and whose wife was raped by Alex and his droogs, is later allowed to play the samaritan to beaten Alex, and to suspect who it is that he's helping, but never to know it. The "brothers" to whom the story is recited are never identified, but we are bound to assume they are a new set of droogs of whom Alex, now a casehardened pro, has become or will become the leader. Droogery is thus unrebuked, even triumphant; if only by contrast with the alternatives, its appeal is allowed.

Music in this novel, which slants across all the categories, doesn't work in any logical way on the narration, nor is it an integral part of the plot, yet it's no less functional. In conjunction with the language, which is a major source of the book's vitality, it suggests a sphere of instinctual and uncorrupted response, such as neither *1984* nor *Brave New World* ventures to represent, and which contrasts with the asphalt jungle of the book itself. It's this intimation of the primeval and healthy barbaric, if only as a possibility within the corrupt, sick barbaric of the city slumster, that's distinctively Burgess and at the same time strongly Joycean.

Even more marked is the application of Joycean prose in a pure entertainment like *Tremor of Intent*. Burgess, like Joyce, is delighted by the linguistic patterns that form in the fading shadows of unconsciousness; and in this wholly implausible thriller, the most impressive and inventive passages are those where various characters (Hillier, Roper, Theodorescu, and a Russian KVD-agent) wander off for one reason or another into gaga-land, letting words, their sounds, and their associations take over for the common order of discourse, or imposing on them a whole new order of non-meanings:

> I was not surprised. In a way I was pleased [writes Roper]. My sense of betrayal was absolute. I fetched the barnaby out of the cheese-slice, fallowed the whereupon with ingrown versicles, then cranked with endless hornblows of white, gamboge, wortdrew, harimon, and prayrichard the most marvellous and unseen-as-yet fallupons that Old Motion ever hatched in all his greenock nights.

We couldn't, perhaps, take this wamble-speech in extended and uninterrupted doses, and Burgess doesn't give us a great deal of it. Even the *Clockwork Orange* dialect runs down perceptibly in the latter part of that novel, and the freakyspeak in *Tremor of Intent* is even more carefully spotted than that. Still, though it's only a dash of Joycean seasoning on books which are of a pretty common order, Burgess unmistakably uses that garnish, and not by any means to contemptible effect. Where Durrell escapes *from* Joycean structure in the course of the Alexandria novels, Burgess at the high point of his fictions escapes *into* Joycean language. The one author is no more interested in palimpsest-effects, narrative discontinuities, and classical analogues, than the other is in twilight states of consciousness; neither has much of a hand for parody, neither is a

self-vivisector. Both are entertainers, and in that capacity both are willing to settle for varieties of short-range effect that come close to claptrap—*coups de théâtre* with suave, ice-cold heavies and sultry, fire-lipped temptresses—all suffused with the aroma of musty theatrical trunks, from which they were just dragged. To point out that elements of Joyce served authors of this character is not to add very much to his permanent glory on the Homer-Dante-Flaubert scale, but it humanizes and facilitates him, suggesting the dimensions and directions of his work that were most readily domesticated. In neither case is there any question of pushing Joyce's work further than he himself carried it; on the contrary, Burgess and Durrell use only one aspect apiece of the Joycean enterprise, and handle it very gingerly in their own novels. Yet for the most part, that salt is what gives the rest of the dish its savor.—Robert Martin Adams, *AfterJoyce*, 1977, pp. 166–69

Works

THE LONG DAY WANES

Probably no writer today can distinguish better than Burgess the line between life and literature as it is set down in fiction. Yet in rethinking through *The Long Day Wanes* I find here precisely a thinning of effect. Crabbe, for much of the trilogy the author's reflector, is the immediate link to the riddle of Malaya, but in losing touch with the life about him he progressively becomes the outsider who frustrates our solving it. He is more and more the epitome of a literary creation rather than a person whom literature illuminates for us. I press this objection with the full knowledge that all literature is fabulation, and that what we think of as truth in a novel is as valid (or no more valid) than what we consider artifice. Still, art demands even more consistency than life, and the chief difficulty in the trilogy is in knowing when Burgess is practicing one or writing about the other. I suspect part of the difficulty is lodged in the historic tempo and framework of the novels and in our tendency to fall back on history to support judgments that literature should clarify without it. If our best hope of understanding Crabbe and Malaya comes from realizing that, like Crabbe, we really cannot understand things at all, then we are left with the uncomfortable realities of life winning out over the more comfortable ambiguities of literature. It is to history, not art, that we must look for any answers, a consideration that returns us to my opening paradox and places upon the reader the burden of penetrating where Burgess has so easily begun—inside.

The Long Day Wanes is therefore a personal statement, not prediction or prophecy, and in the end we should adhere to its spirit before its letter. Burgess wrote it as an insider for other insiders who may or may not have shared his views or feelings, but who could in any event fathom what he was talking about without undue analysis. He intended the trilogy as a comic ordering of a world primed on confusion and disorder and staggering toward unification. But revealing Malaya never meant explaining it—either to us or to his hero. The major irony of *The Long Day Wanes* is that what we may have admitted to comedy fifteen years ago is now open only to tragic implications and conclusions. It will take years more of history until the grim misunderstandings in and about the Far East prove stuff for the comic novelist; indeed, some muffled note of prophecy might yet sound through Burgess's triumph of comedy and pathos. Crabbe's personality, devastated by unconsolable ambiguities perhaps less private and personal than we care to believe, may be but a further step toward a finer and more complete devastation that is no longer ambiguous and for

which, unfortunately, there will be no consolation at all.—
ROBERT K. MORRIS, *The Consolations of Ambiguity*, 1971,
pp. 30–31

A CLOCKWORK ORANGE

In *A Clockwork Orange* Burgess goes on to explore the kind of
spiritual life that might, in fact, lead to damnation. This novel,
which is, I think, Burgess's most brilliant and blackest achievement, is set in a shabby metropolis at some unspecified time in
the future, where teenage gangs habitually terrorise the inhabitants. The story is told by one of them in the first person,
in a superb piece of mimetic writing. This narrator is morally
but not mentally stunted; he writes an alert witty narrative in a
special kind of slang that incorporates a large number of words
of Russian origin; one is never told the social or political events
that underlie this linguistic intrusion, but it is possible that
Burgess is trying to comment, in a mirror-image fashion, on
the current dominance of Americanisms in colloquial English
speech. The invention of this idiolect is an extraordinary
achievement; it is hard to read at first, but with a little persistence it can be mastered (the American Norton Library edition
contains a useful glossary); in fact, after a second reading of *A
Clockwork Orange* I found myself starting to think in it. One of
its functions is to keep at a certain distance the horrors that
Alex, the young narrator, so cheerfully describes: to say, 'we
gave this devotchka a tolchok on the litso and the krovvy came
out of her rot' is less startlingly direct than, 'we gave this girl a
blow on the face and the blood came out of her mouth'.

Alex is cheerful, even high-spirited in his life of crime:
older citizens, particularly of a square or bourgeois disposition,
are fit material for beating-up; books are to be destroyed, and
girls are to be assessed by the size of their breasts, and raped
where possible. In *A Clockwork Orange* none of this behaviour
is ascribed, as contemporary psychologists or sociologists would
have it, to a mindless protest against lack of love or cultural
deprivation or the alienating structures of capitalist society.
Alex makes it clear that he has chosen evil as a deliberate act of
spiritual freedom in a world of sub-human conformists. Despite everything—and this is, perhaps, the most disturbing
thing about Burgess's novel—Alex is engaging. His adventures
are often funny, or at least his way of describing them is: whereas Amis and Wilson keep comedy and horror on separate
planes in their fiction, Burgess, like Waugh, often fuses them.
In some respects Alex is not at all a stereotype delinquent. He
and his friends, having robbed and beaten an elderly couple in
a shop, make off with the takings and then buy innumerable
drinks and presents for a couple of old women in a pub, partly
to secure an alibi for themselves, but also out of pure generosity. Alex spurns pop songs and is a passionate listener to classical music, which inspires him to thoughts of violence and
rape, sometimes to the point of orgasm.

Alex does not, in short, reflect an exact sociological understanding of present-day youth and its problems. Burgess uses
him to illustrate his own quasi-theological conviction that men
do extreme evil because they choose to, and enjoy doing it,
rather than because they are reluctantly or unconsciously
forced to it by social conditioning. In presenting Alex, Burgess
has drawn on a familiar literary tradition. Marcuse has spoken
of the way in which bourgeois society

> remained an order which was overshadowed, broken,
> refuted by another dimension which was irreconcil-
> ably antagonistic to the order of business, indicting it
> and denying it. And in the literature, this other di-
> mension is represented *not* by the religious, spiritual,
> moral heroes (who often sustain the established

order) but rather by such disruptive characters as the
artist, the prostitute, the adultress, the great criminal
and outcast, the warrior, the rebel-poet, the devil,
the fool—those who don't earn a living, at least not
in an orderly and normal way. (*One-Dimensional
Man.*)

In the language of Baudelaire or Eliot this is the opposition
between the masses of the spiritually dead and null, and those
who, however evil they may be, are at least alive. Balzac's
Vautrin stands some way behind Alex, but his more immediate
literary antecedent is Pinkie in Graham Greene's *Brighton
Rock*, the articulate, lucid, cruel, young Catholic diabolist.
Alex is more alive, and less improbable than Pinkie; yet he
remains the embodiment of a literary idea, a late instance in
the milieu of the cosh and the bicycle-chain and the gang-
bang, of the romantic antinomian cultivation of evil.

Eventually Alex is caught by the police, and after being
roughed up by them and imprisoned, he is selected for a new
form of remedial treatment, since the prisons are now all
needed for political offenders, and common criminals are to be
rehabilitated and permanently 'cured'. Alex is given an intensive course of aversion-therapy; he is injected with a drug
and shown films of brutality and sexual assault, accompanied
by classical music. Eventually he is cured of his taste for all
three, since any hint of them causes uncontrollable nausea.
(The music is regarded by the authorities not as having any
aesthetic or spiritual dimension, but merely as something that
arouses unwelcome emotional excitement in Alex.) After the
course Alex is released, a good citizen, yet a person in whom
the capacity to choose has been wholly destroyed. In his
account of the therapy Alex undergoes, Burgess is describing
known techniques, and it is here that the novel acquires
philosophical profundity: in what sense is a man who has been
forced to be good better than a man who deliberately asserts his
humanity by choosing evil? For the behaviouristic pragmatism
that invents such procedures, the question is presumably
meaningless; but genuine humanists will recognise its urgency,
even if they cannot fully answer it. Towards the end of the
novel Alex gets caught up in a political plot against the government and is exploited by the opposition (very much as Ralph
Ellison's Invisible Man is used by the communists); in a final
unexpected twist of circumstances, the government reverses
Alex's treatment, and he ends the novel as a free individual
with all his criminal impulses—and his love of music—
restored. Many of Burgess's assumptions are, of course, vulnerable. The notion of 'spiritual death' is a powerful literary idea,
but it is existentially specious; it is merely a way of reinforcing
one's sense of the otherness of other people. Non-Augustinian
Christians as well as conventional progressives will want to
object to the extremity of Burgess's pessimism, as well as his
basically romantic conception of evil. Nevertheless, as an
embodied imaginative vision of life *A Clockwork Orange* is
hard both to forget and to refute, and in its emphasis on the
nature of human freedom in a totalitarian society the book has
philosophical as well as literary importance. As a novel of ideas
that projects a conservative and pessimistic view of human
nature, *A Clockwork Orange* seems to me to have a similar
quality and significance to William Golding's *Lord of the Flies*,
while being more humorous and less diagrammatic. One
wishes that it had achieved the same reputation.—BERNARD
BERGONZI, *The Situation of the Novel*, 1970, pp. 182–85

⟨*A Clockwork Orange*⟩ is constructed on a series of doubles:
there are two characters called Alex; two visits to the old men in
the library; two visits to the house of the author; two views of
Alex's friends, as criminals and as policemen. The clarity of the

pattern forces us to make comparisons. But Burgess's aim is our involvement. His use of the title of his own novel as the title of the author's book, which in a novel of number might have served to alienate us by means of the self-conscious art technique, is employed here to suggest that Burgess is F. Alexander, "another Alex," and therefore partakes equally of the violence. Throughout the novel Alex addresses his readers as "O my brothers," a phrase with obvious implications of complicity. Finally the teenage slang, Nadsat, that Burgess invented for the novel, serves to include us also. Initially strange, the words of the language are learned by the reader as he learns any language by being constantly exposed to them. He is, in fact, conditioned as Alex was; the effect of Nadsat on the reader functions as an ironic comment on the novel itself.—JEAN E. KENNARD, "Anthony Burgess: Double Vision," *Number and Nightmare*, 1975, p. 137

MF

MF is an incredibly difficult book; Burgess has more than fulfilled the prophecy he made to Jim Hicks in 1968: "The sort of things I write will be more and more involuted, more and more difficult, less and less saleable. This just has to be. You get fed up with existing technique. You have to do something more daring." Burgess has dared to put the reader in the position of solving a whole series of riddles, not just those which Miles has to solve, but the riddles of the book itself. The reader is obviously intended to be placed in a position parallel to that of Miles, just as in *A Clockwork Orange* Nadsat conditioned the reader much as Alex was conditioned. *MF* is full of scraps of foreign languages—Sanskrit, Welsh, Italian, Indonesian— of conundrums, some of which Burgess has invented and some of which belong in folklore, of palinlogues, of every possible kind of word game.

To understand what Burgess is attempting here it is helpful to refer to two comments in his book on Joyce, who, after all, practiced many of these games before he did. The first concerns the significance of riddles and talks of the relationship between the mysteries of the cosmos and those of language. To Burgess, as to Joyce, there is more than a metaphorical connection between them: "The difficulties of *Ulysses* and, very much more, of *Finnegans Wake* are not so many tricks and puzzles and deliberate obscurities to be hacked at like jungle lianas: they represent those elements which surround the immediate simplicities of human society; they stand for history, myth, and the cosmos. Thus we have not merely to accept them but to regard them as integral."

The second is a comment about himself and the relationship between languages:

> Waking literature (that is literature that bows to time and space) is the exploitation of a single language. Dream-literature, breaking down all boundaries, may be more concerned with the phenomenon of language in general. Living in the West, I have little occasion to use Malay, a tongue I know at least as well as I know French. In dreams, I am no longer in the West; with the collapse of space, compass-points have no meaning. Hence English and Malay frequently dance together, merging, becoming not two languages conjoined but an emblem of language in general.

In *MF* Burgess uses many languages as an indication of a fundamental structure basic to all languages. The fact that the reader does not need a translation is itself an illustration of Burgess's point.

The relationship between apparently dissimilar languages,

like the relationship between linguistic and social structures, is explained by Burgess in terms of the Lévi-Strauss theory that the mind of man has been operating in the same pattern since the beginning of time. This theory is obviously in opposition to the Sartrean denial of inherent structure in man or the universe and can very easily include the possibility of, though does not necessarily imply, what Burgess calls in *The Wanting Seed*, "a pattern-making demiurge." Merleau-Ponty points out in his article "From Mauss to Claude Lévi-Strauss": "Society itself is a structure of structures: how could there be absolutely no relationship between the linguistic system, the economic system, and the kinship system it employs?"

In the novel Burgess indicates the link between language and social forms by the similarity of the pronunciation of Keteki, name of the professor whose riddle Miles solves and who sends him on his journey, and Kitty Kee, nickname of Miles's sister whom he is forced to marry. Hence a parallelism is established between solving riddles and sleeping with one's sister. Throughout the novel Burgess draws the two concepts, "postures and language," together. Pardaleos explains: "We condemn incest because it's the negation of social communion. It's like writing a book in which every sentence is a tautology." Man's drive to reproduce himself is described as one of the "great structural machines throbbing away, those messages in code." As Burgess explains at the end of the novel: "Communication has been the whatness of the communication."— JEAN E. KENNARD, "Anthony Burgess: Double Vision," *Number and Nightmare*, 1975, pp. 146–48

NAPOLEON SYMPHONY

Mr. Burgess's very wide knowledge of and sensibility to literature (inside this kind of writer an autodidact don is always struggling to get out) makes him an admirable popularizer of works by—to risk the phrase again—"real authors," and he has adapted the Joycean stream of consciousness to a popular level for almost any use. *Napoleon Symphony* is in a good and modest sense a popular novel, using highbrow techniques in a not too demanding way, and throwing in plenty of eating (chicken marengo after the battle and Napoleon's favorite Chambertin), sex, and jokes, with all the agreeably ghoulish details of battlefields and frozen corpses. Seriousness of vision there is none, nor can there be any attempt at subtlety of insight. Facility— and Bloomian good nature—are all. Here, to illustrate the point, is Napoleon on the Queen of Prussia:

> "There was a moment, Talleyrand—" He mused, amused, bemused.

(One must interpolate at this point that one of Mr. Burgess's more self-indulgent practices is a kind of verbal doodling, less Joycean than lushly Euphuistic and Elizabethan, which sometimes cannot be restrained from breaking out into sections of verse, not seriously intended, one assumes, to underwrite the symphonic image, or to be admired in their own right, but to jolly along the pleasantly undemanding associations of Hardy's *Dynasts* or Tchaikovsky's *Overture*.)

> She was sitting in her carriage waiting, while the King was having a final word with young Alexander. Eyes full of tears, smiling bravely, so beautiful and so much *alone*—because that long-faced bastard she's married to is no good to man, beast, woman, Prussia, or anything else. There was a moment, I say, when I nearly jumped in there and gave her what she so obviously needed—passionate kisses on mouth and neck and bosom, a pair of strong arms around her. And then, of course, she would have gone on about dear suffering Prussia, and then I would have said,

Oh, have it all back, poor angel, what is a kingdom
compared to a woman's tears? The world well lost,
there's a play about that, I think. But I was strong,
Tallyrand, I did not yield.

This is boneless stuff, no skeleton of point beneath it. Is it
irony? he was not strong. Or pity? the great cannot yield to their
impulses and be human. Or a demonstration of the commonplace? history is a bundle of trivial and misshapen needs
and muffled impulses. All that really emerges is that Napoleon
is nicer than Talleyrand—the Blazes Boylan of the book—and
must be so, because it is his consciousness that author and
reader inhabit. Mr. Burgess's problem, which he cannot be
said to have solved, is that his more informed readers cannot
really need this kind of thing to imagine themselves into the
Napoleonic era, while all the sound knowledge—of corps commanders, horse batteries, Continental System—which he
strews so prodigally but inconspicuously around cannot do
much to edify his more popular readership.—JOHN BAYLEY,
"From the Ridiculous to the Ridiculous," *NYRB*, Sept. 19,
1974, p. 32

THE END OF THE WORLD NEWS

"Nothing odd will do long." One often thinks of Dr. Johnson's
famous remark when reading fiction, even going on to wonder
whether he was not entirely right in his judgment that *"Tristram Shandy* did not last."

My tastes in fiction are so largely "middlebrow" that I am
the worst possible judge of a multitalented innovator like Anthony Burgess. All his novels are hectically stylish, but *The
End of the World News* is not the best of them. It is presented
almost apologetically by John B. Wilson BA (Mr. Burgess's
"real name") as the first published posthumous work of an
unknown author, which he claims to have found in a carrier
bag from an Italian supermarket. In the preface we are reminded that President Carter was seen watching three television programmes at once, and *The End of the World News*
requires a similar hexoptical energy on the part of the reader. It
is really three quite different stories. One of them is a rather
vivid fictionalised life of Sigmund Freud, which, had it stood
on its own, would have made a very striking and sympathetic
historical novel. Another is an extraordinarily feeble script for a
Broadway musical based on Trotsky's visit to America. I quote
one of the lyrics to give some idea of its flavour. Olga, a New
York Trotskyite, sings:

> The new world hasn't been built yet,
> For its builders don't have much luck.
> The capitalistic flowers
> Have not begun to wilt yet,
> The proletarian hour's
> Not struck.

The third strand of the narrative is set in the future and is a
piece of science fiction. The planet earth is about to be crushed
by "the dreaded Lynx", an intruder from a distant galaxy. At
the end of this rag-bag, the whole narrative is discussed by a
seminar of American students, again set in the future. They
agree that the science fiction is completely "real" but they find
the "myths" of Freud and Trotsky quite unbelievable.

Lively as the book undoubtedly is, it was wasted on me. It
seemed impossible not to feel that Mr. Burgess had not served
up three half-finished books from his desk drawer, all wildly
disparate in character and stirred together carelessly. The idea
that the various strands of this narrative relate to one another is
little more than a literary confidence trick. Even if one blocks
one's ears to the siren common sense of Dr. Johnson, it is

difficult not to feel that Dickens's Mr Turveydrop knew a thing
or two about art: "Polish, polish, polish!"

The End of the World News is almost insolently un-
polished. Doubtless, had it been edited or reworked it could
have presented us with interesting comments on the nature of
illusion and reality. The seminar at the end is all too plausible.
We live in a world where whole schools of literary critics have
decided, and are teaching the gullible young to believe, that it
is impossible to determine the "verisimilitude" of a "text." And
Frank Kermode, one of the cleverest living critics, has expounded this view in his book *The Genesis of Secrecy*: there is
no way of telling, according to this view, whether a narrative is
"true" or not. Nor can we distinguish, to Professor Kermode's
satisfaction, between historians, novelists and evangelists. Henry James and St Mark were apparently up to the same sort of
game. The commonsense answer—"But St Mark believed
himself to be describing things which had actually taken
place"—would be howled down on all sides; no one more
anxious to bay and mock than New Testament scholars in holy
orders.—A. N. WILSON, "Faith and Uncertainty," *Enc*, Feb.
1983, p. 70

The End of the World News appears to be chaff. Mr. Burgess,
borrowing a term from his Riviera neighbor and literary spar-
ring partner, Graham Greene, calls it "an entertainment." He
doesn't seem to mean that it's lightweight—its 389 pages sit a
bit bulkily in the hand for that. He means to parody the forms
of writing that might survive the death of literature: the libretto,
the novel ripe for a television series and science fiction. In fact,
we get one of each here, spliced together by what Mr. Burgess,
masquerading as his own editor, calls sub-literary devices: A
character goes to the window in one story; a character is found
at the window in another; the whole mixture is offered as a
chronicle told to children in the far future. We don't have to
take the splicing seriously. Mr. Burgess simply alludes to the
problem of structure and then ignores it.

The three stories are a life of Freud ("novelised, or very
nearly televisualised," Mr. Burgess says), a musical about
Trotsky in New York in 1917 and a tale about a hefty planet
crashing into the earth and thus ending our world around the
year 2000. The stories "are all the same story: they are all about
the end of history as man has known it." This declaration is not
entirely to be trusted, since it appears in the cheerfully overblown blurb Mr. Burgess has written for himself—"the author . . . who is past all shame, is acting as his own puff-
er"—but it is not to be dismissed either. The stories are not all
the same, and they are not exactly about the end of history. But
they are all about dreams of ending, about old worlds that go
off with a bang, not a whimper, leaving us with less history
than we thought we had but maybe more than we can manage. . . .

The real answer to the theme question in the Burgess
novels may lie in the mess itself rather than in anything we can
do about it. That is the burden of the science-fiction story in
The End of the World News. Faced with imminent extinction,
the Commonwealth of Democratic Americas, as well as other
groupings in the world, constructs its space-age ark. The question arises, of course: Who is to go, who is to lift off into the
universe and leave the rest to the exploding end? Mr. Burgess's
strongly implied comment is that the question involves a double bind. Those who think they can answer it are not the fittest
to go; they are too rational or too gifted; they would preserve
only a purified breed, not the "dirty delightful world" we know,
not the "clumsiness and humanity and imperfection and

drunkenness" that Mr. Burgess has always celebrated as our only reliable truth.

On the other hand, those who can't answer might just be the people worth saving. Valentine Brodie, a science-fiction writer who missed the ark because he was out drinking, tries to get aboard before it takes off, and finds himself worrying. "He could smell and taste the end of the world like an apple. He said: 'Why the hell should we be saved?'" His companion, a fat, Falstaffian actor who once played Orson Welles on television, says, "Because that's not a question those scientific bastards would ever dream of asking. That's why." He's wrong about the scientists but right about himself. He ought to be saved because he is the kind of character—gluttonous, disorderly, lecherous, brave and kindly—whom no one is likely to find a reason for saving. In the end, though, he doesn't want to be saved, and he isn't.

The world won't end tonight, and Anthony Burgess doesn't think it will. His is not the scorching apocalypse of Lawrence or Yeats but a love song to what would be lost if the world went away: all its colors and tastes and smells and finally forgivable mistakes. It is an old song but a good one, made attractive not by its newness but by its steady virtue and the liveliness of Mr. Burgess's arrangement of it. "This is the end of the world," a character in the book says. "I presume anybody can join in." Sure. And we can also, in the words of Sam Goldwyn, include ourselves out.—MICHAEL WOOD, "A Love Song to What Would Be Lost," *NYTBR*, March 6, 1983, pp. 3, 25

STANLEY EDGAR HYMAN
"Anthony Burgess" (1962)
On Contemporary Literature
ed. Richard Kostelanetz
1964, pp. 300–305

Anthony Burgess is one of the newest and most talented of the younger British writers. Although he is forty-five, he has devoted himself to writing only in the last few years; with enormous productivity, he has published ten novels since 1956; before that he was a composer, and a civil servant in Malaya and Brunei. His first novel to be published in this country, *The Right to an Answer*, appeared in 1961. It was followed the next year by *Devil of a State*, and by *A Clockwork Orange* early in 1963. A fourth novel, *The Wanting Seed*, is due out later in 1963. Burgess seems to me the ablest satirist to appear since Evelyn Waugh, and the word "satire" is inadequate to his range.

The Right to an Answer is a terribly funny, terribly bitter smack at English life in a provincial city (apparently the author's birthplace, Manchester). The principal activity of the townspeople seems to be the weekend exchange of wives, and their dispirited slogan "Bit of fun" (prophetically heard by Mr. Raj, a visiting Ceylonese, as "bitter fun"). The book's ironic message is Love. It ends quoting Raj's unfinished manuscript on race relations: "Love seems inevitable, necessary, as normal and as easy a process as respiration, but unfortunately . . ." the manuscript breaks off. Raj's love has just led him to kill two people and blow his brains out. One thinks of *A Passage to India*, several decades more sour.

Devil of a State is less bitter, more like early Waugh. Its comic target is the uranium-rich East African state of Dunia (obviously based on the oil-rich Borneo state of Brunei). In

what there is of a plot, the miserable protagonist, Frank Lydgate, a civil servant, struggles with the rival claims of his wife and his native mistress, only to be snatched from both of them by his first wife, a formidable female spider of a woman. The humor derives mainly from incongruity: the staple food in Dunia is Chinese spaghetti; the headhunters upriver shrink a Belgian head with eyeglasses and put Brylcreem on its hair.

Neither book at all prepares one for the savagery of Burgess' next novel. *A Clockwork Orange* is a nightmarish fantasy of a future England where the hoodlums take over after dark. Its subject is the dubious redemption of one such hoodlum, Alex, told by himself. The society is a limp and listless socialism at some future time when men are on the moon: hardly anyone still reads, although streets are named Amis Avenue and Priestley Place; Jonny Zhivago, a "Russky" pop singer, is a juke-box hit, and the teenage language is three-quarters Russian; everybody "not a child nor with child nor ill" must work; criminals have to be rehabilitated because all the prison space will soon be needed for politicals; there is an opposition and elections, but they reëlect the Government.

A streak of grotesque surrealism runs all through Burgess' books. In *The Right to an Answer*, at one melodramatic point, a corpse grunts and turns over in its coffin. In *Devil of a State*, a political meeting is held in a movie theatre while polecats walk the girders near the roof, sneer down at the audience, and dislodge bits of dried excrement on their heads. By *A Clockwork Orange* this has become truly infernal. As the hoodlums drive to their "surprise visit," they run over a big snarling toothy thing that screams and squelches, and as they drive back they run over "odd squealing things" all the way.

Alex has no interest in women except as objects of violence and rape (the term for the sex act in his vocabulary is characteristically mechanical, "the old in-out in-out"). No part of the female body is mentioned except the size of the breasts (it would also interest a Freudian to know that the hoodlums' drink is doped milk). Alex's only "aesthetic" interest is his passion for symphonic music. He lies naked on his bed, surrounded by his stereo speakers, listening to Mozart or Bach while he daydreams of grinding his boot into the faces of men, or raping ripped screaming girls, and at the music's climax he has an orgasm.

A running lecture on free will, first from the prison chaplain, then from the writer, strongly suggests that the book's intention is Christian. Deprived of his capacity for moral choice by science, Burgess appears to be saying, Alex is only a "clockwork orange," something mechanical that appears organic. Free to will, even if he wills to sin, Alex is capable of salvation, like Pinky in *Brighton Rock* (*Devil of a State*, incidentally, is dedicated to Greene). But perhaps this is to confine Burgess' ironies and ambiguities within simple orthodoxy. Alex always *was* a clockwork orange, a machine for mechanical violence far below the level of choice, and his dreary socialist England is a giant clockwork orange.

Perhaps the most fascinating thing about the book is its language. Alex thinks and talks in the "nadsat" (teenage) vocabulary of the future. A doctor in the book explains it. "Odd bits of old rhyming slang," he says. "A bit of gypsy talk, too. But most of the roots are Slav. Propaganda. Subliminal penetration." Nadsat is not quite so hard to decipher as Cretan Linear B, and Alex translates some of it. I found that I could not read the book without compiling a glossary.

At first the vocabulary seems incomprehensible: "you could peet it with vellocet or synthemesc or drencrom or one or two other veshches." Then the reader, even if he knows no Russian, discovers that some of the meaning is clear from context: "to tolchock some old veck in an alley and viddy him swim in his blood." Other words are intelligible after a second context: when Alex kicks a fallen enemy on the "gulliver" it might be any part of the body, but when a glass of beer is served with a gulliver, "gulliver" is "head." (Life is easier, of course, for those who know the Russian word *golova*.)

Burgess has not used Russian words mechanically, but with great ingenuity, as the transformation into "gulliver," with its Swiftian associations, suggests. Others are brilliantly anglicized: *khorasho* (good or well) as "horrorshow"; *liudi* (people) as "lewdies"; *militsia* (militia or police) as "millicents"; *odinock* (lonesome) as "oddy knocky."

Burgess uses some Russian words in an American slang extension, such as *nadsat* itself, the termination of the Russian numbers eleven to nineteen, which he breaks off independently on the analogy of our "teen." Thus *kopat* (to dig with a shovel) is used as "dig" in the sense of enjoy or understand; *koshka* (cat) and *ptitsa* (bird) become the hip "cat" and "chick"; *neezhny* (lower) turns into "neezhnies" (underpants); *pooshka* (cannon) becomes the term for a pistol; *rozha* (grimace) turns into "rozz," one of the words for policeman, *samyi* (the most) becomes "sammy" (generous); *soomka* (bag) is the slang "ugly woman"; *vareet* (to cook up) is also used in the slang sense, for something preparing or transpiring.

The "gypsy talk," I would guess, includes Alex's phrase "O my brothers," and "crark" (to yowl?), "cutter" (money), "filly" (to fool with), and such. The rhyming slang includes "luscious glory" for "hair" (rhyming with "upper story"?) and "pretty polly" for "money" (rhyming with "lolly" of current slang). Others are inevitable associations, such as "cancer" for "cigarette" and "charlie" for "chaplain." Others are produced simply by schoolboy transformations: "appy polly loggy" (apology), "baddiwad" (bad), "eggiweg" (egg), "skolliwoll" (school), and so forth. Others are amputations: "guff" (guffaw), "pee and em" (pop and mom), "sarky" (sarcastic), "sinny" (cinema). Some appear to be portmanteau words: "chumble" (chattermumble), "mounch" (mouth-munch), "shive" (shiv-shave), "skriking" (striking-scratching).

There are slight inconsistencies, when Burgess (or Alex) forgets his word and invents another or uses our word, but on the whole he handles his Russianate vocabulary in a masterly fashion. It has a wonderful sound, particularly in abuse, when "grahzny bratchny" sounds infinitely better than "dirty bastard." Coming to literature by way of music, Burgess has a superb ear, and he shows an interest in the texture of language rare among current novelists. (He confessed in a recent television interview that he is obsessed by words.) As a most promising writer of the 60s, Burgess has followed novels that remind us of Forster and Waugh with an eloquent and shocking novel that is quite unique.

After *A Clockwork Orange*, Burgess wrote *The Wanting Seed*, which appeared in England in 1962 and will soon be published in the United States. It is a look centuries ahead to a future world almost as repulsive as Alex's. Perpetual Peace has been established, and the main effort of government is to hold down human reproduction. Contraceptive pills are universal, infanticide is condoned, homosexuality is officially encouraged, and giving birth more than once is a criminal act. We see this world as it affects the lives of Tristram Foxe, a schoolteacher, his wife Beatrice-Joanna, a natural *Urmutter*, and his brother Derek, Beatrice-Joanna's lover, who holds high office in the government by pretending to be homosexual. In this world of sterile rationalism, meat is unknown and teeth are atavistic, God has been replaced by "Mr. Livedog," a figure of fun ("God knows" becomes "Dognose"), and the brutal police-

men are homosexuals who wear black lipstick to match their ties.

As a result of all the organized blasphemy against life, in Burgess' fable, crops and food animals are mysteriously stricken all over the world, and as rations get more and more meagre, order breaks down. The new phase is heralded by Beatrice-Joanna, who gives birth in a kind of manger to twin sons, perhaps separately fathered by the two men in her life.

But the new world of fertility is no better than the world of sterility that it supplants. Soon England is swept by cannibalism (the epicene flesh of policemen is particularly esteemed), there are public sex orgies to make the crops grow, and Christian worship returns, using consecrated human flesh in place of wine and wafer ("eucharistic ingestion" is the new slogan). The check on population this time is a return to old-fashioned warfare with rifles, in which armies of men fight armies of women; war is visibly "a massive sexual act."

At the end, Tristram, who as a representative man of both new orders has been in prison and the army, is reunited with his wife and her children, but nothing has changed fundamentally. The cycle, now in its Augustinian phase with the emphasis on human depravity, will soon enough swing back to its Pelagian phase, with the emphasis on human perfectibility.

The Wanting Seed shows Burgess' familiar preoccupation with language. His vocabulary rivals that of Wallace Stevens: a woman is "bathycolpous" (deep-bosomed), a male secretary is "flavicomous" (blond), a Chinese magnate is "mactated" (sacrificially killed), moustaches are "corniculate" (horned). The book is full of Joycean jokes: in a long sequence of paired names for the public fertility rites, one pair is "Tommy Eliot with Kitty Elphick," which is, of course, Old Possum with one of his Practical Cats; war poetry is read to the army on Saturday mornings, on order of Captain Auden-Isherwood.

On her way to the State Provision Store to buy her ration of vegetable dehydrate, synthelac, compressed cereal sheets, and "nuts" or nutrition units, Beatrice-Joanna stops to take a breath of the sea, and Burgess' beautiful sentence is an incantation of sea creatures: "Sand-hoppers, mermaids' purses, sea gooseberries, cuttle bones, wrasse, blenny and bullhead, tern, gannet and herring gull."

Like any satirist, Burgess extrapolates an exaggerated future to get at present tendencies he abhors. These include almost everything around. He does not like mindless violence, but he does not like mechanical reconditioning either; he detests sterile peace and fertile war about equally. Beneath Anthony Burgess' wild comedy there is a prophetic (sometimes cranky and shrill) voice warning and denouncing us, but beneath that, on the deepest level, there is love: for mankind, and for mankind's loveliest invention, the art of language.

CHRISTOPHER RICKS
"The Epicene"
New Statesman, April 5, 1963, p. 496

Ten novels since 1956—that is the fact about Anthony Burgess. Some of his well-wishers think it looks irresponsible, but surely it is his fertility which makes one hopeful of a first-rate comic novel. He hasn't yet written it; no single one of his books focuses all the best in his writing. No doubt he has been embarrassed by the gratifying words of reviewers; to deserve them all, he would have to be a much better novelist than Dickens. His prodigality is in a sense undiscriminating, a fact which comes out glumly in his new British Council pamphlet,

The Novel Today. He does his best to protect himself against the suspicion that such pamphlets have the casually inflated hospitality of the party that Don Juan went to ('Also the 80 greatest living poets'), so he borrows a look of rigour: 'If the novel is not to be debased, we must practise an almost cruel stringency of judgement.' But far from being stringent, he even has to fall back upon 'may yet emerge as'. The pamphlet is merely jolly. The difference in liveliness between the pamphlet and the novels would define his kind of creative talent.

His reputation, like Waugh's and Greene's, seems to be of the sort that is bound to zoom and plunge. Since it is high now he is in his mid-forties (posh reviewer, interviewed on TV and radio, British Councillor), one must resist the envious urge to take a hand in turning fortune's wheel about. Anyway *Honey for the Bears* is one of his best books, and an oddly subversive one both politically and sexually. Paul Hussey is an antique dealer from Sussex, on a trip to Leningrad with his American wife Belinda. Business rather than pleasure, since they are smuggling in a lot of drilon dresses; they plan to make a thousand pounds, for the benefit of a friend who is a widow. Russia turns out to be disconcertingly like America (even in its RC-versy godliness), so that politically the book is about a Third Force that will combine and outdo them. Sexually it is about the same thing, since Paul and Belinda find out, or at last admit, that they are homosexual, though that hasn't stopped them from being heterosexual as well.

Does this seem old hat rather than subversion? I don't think so, and one might ask where the Tweedledum and Tweedledee feeling about Russia and America has yet found expression in a novel. Likewise, novels tend to be *either/or* about sex, dealing in the notion that so-and-so is *a* homosexual rather than homosexual, that he or she will prove to be *really* one or the other despite sad attempts at the wrong one. In fact the novelty of the book doesn't lie exactly there, but in its invincibly comic treatment of these two ideas of a Third Force. Instead of lordly moral claims to political sainthood, there is the idea that life won't be any more dangerous and is very likely to be more fun. And instead of the transcendental mysticism of Mr G. Wilson Knight's paean to bisexuality—'the seraphic intuition' of Byron, Lawrence and Christ—there is the idea that being able to enjoy both is to find more to enjoy and so to add to the public stock of harmless pleasure. That homosexuality is not wicked, not ethereally spiritual, not necessarily the source of anxiety or agony, not incompatible with other things, but a rather pleasant virtuosity—if this is not subversive, what would be? Paul and Belinda don't terribly mind when they find out about themselves. 'All things contain their opposite,' Paul keeps reflecting, but this is the first time that Mr Burgess has applied this to sexuality; in his first novel it was only political, the merry pre-war Marxist version of 'Green Grow the Rushes, Oh':

Two, two, the opposites
Interpenetrating though . . .

Mr Burgess has all the current awareness of how hard it is to pin anything on a novelist. When someone suggested that Patrick Standish in *Take a Girl Like You* is nasty like his creator, Kingsley Amis wrote a sharp note saying that Standish was a character in a book—as if the question of whether an author connived could be settled simply by his saying he didn't. (In fact Standish seems to me unswervingly criticized, but that needs to be demonstrated and not just pronounced.) So Mr Burgess might complain of misrepresentation, in which case it would be enough to claim that his novel is a humanely funny discussion of an unusual point of view. The jokes are not always good, but a pointed one leaps from the way in which the

Russians transliterate G and H; Paul Hussey becomes Pavel Gussey (no longer a shameful Hussey?), and more importantly homosexuality becomes gomosexuality—an excellent device for stripping it of spirituality, guilt, introversion.

The author's imagination, too, is released. One of the rare moments when Salinger's Buddy Glass is distinguishable from his brother Bluddy Gass comes when Buddy maintains that

> there is an enormous amount of the androgynous in any all-or-nothing prose writer, or even a would-be one. I think that if he titters at male writers who wear invisible skirts he does so at his eternal peril.

This is certainly a genuine part of what Mr Burgess is trying to say: in his pamphlet he claims that Angus Wilson's distinctive contribution to the novel has been 'taking seriously the homosexual sensibility'. Taking it comically might be his own praise, and this does not mean sneeringly. Throughout the novels he has apparently been trying to make up his mind about the epicene, and in the first one (*Time for a Tiger*) his prose took on a delighted and very uncensorious lilt as it observed androgynous Ibrahim: 'Undulating through the market, who so gay as Ibrahim?' No guilt for Ibrahim. The futurist fable, *The Wanting Seed*, begins with a world in which over-population has made homosexuality socially most desirable, so that the posters say 'It's Sapiens to be Homo' and 'Love Your Fellow-Men'. Such a situation is thought to be unfortunate because of the public vindictiveness about heterosexuality, but even here there is a notable absence of disgust. And when heterosexuality resumes its baby-bringing reign, we find that we just have King Stork.

All this has been about the ideas of the book, shocking in the same genial way as Fielding (both of them mildly suggesting that many kinds of sexual immorality don't in fact much matter). But the novel is inventive and gay as well. For me a clear advantage which it has over some of the earlier ones is that it abandons horror comedy, the mingling of black realistic violence and comic lightness. True, at one point a Russian policeman punches Paul, but then the policeman is at once genuinely contrite, and the novel as a whole has a straightforward and old-fashioned comic decorum. Many of the previous ones seem spoiled by their black comedy. Even if one accepts that in theory there is no reason why the two shouldn't mingle, it does seem that in practice it is a very great deal harder to do than one would guess from the sheer number of writers now engaged in doing it.

Waugh is presumably the most practised modern exemplar, but then his best moments are simply comic; the off-hand brutality seems to get less and less funny in re-reading. Among the golden opinions which Mr Burgess has won, a recurring one is the comparison with Waugh, and it even lured Miss Brooke-Rose into an iambic line: 'A Waugh without the underlying wounds'. But then if he hasn't the wounds, need he have the casually 'comic' violence and pain? The blurb of *The Doctor is Sick* pointed out that it is 'fundamentally more light-hearted than his previous ones'—that is, the story is just that of a man who is waiting for an operation on a brain tumour, who escapes from the hospital and the suffering it inflicts, who sees—or dreams he sees—his wife copulating, and so on. Of course there are straightforward comic things in that book; one of the best (allusive as so many of his best jokes are) comes when the hero stares in at a windowful of nudist magazines:

> There was the one Charlie had brought him: *Brute Beauty*. And there were others he had never seen before: *Valour*; *Act*; *Oh!* He rubbed his eyes, which were troubling him with an odd impairment of vision. Were those really *Air, Pride, Plume, Here*?

Anyone who has had enough of 'The Windhover' will think that Hopkins has had that coming to him for a long time. But that doesn't alter the fact that it would take stupendous powers to be able to yoke such heterogeneous material together, such pain and such humour. It is the same with *A Clockwork Orange*, an excellent book in so far as it protested against the idea that it is all right to 'cure' people of unfortunate tendencies by giving them emetic drugs and showing them films of their undesirable behaviour. (One thinks of the bulletins from the *Observer* which we're still getting about that 'cured' homosexual.) But far too much of *A Clockwork Orange* was desperate straddling, and what did its blurb mean by saying that 'the book can be read as a straight horror comedy'? Straight? We could do worse than return to the dull neo-classical idea that realistic horror and comedy are different genres. At any rate, *Honey for the Bears* shows how much more Mr Burgess can get said when he isn't also teetering in that rather meaningless and fashionable juggling act.

WILLIAM H. PRITCHARD
"The Novels of Anthony Burgess"

The Massachusetts Review, Summer 1966, pp. 525–39

Anthony Burgess published his first novel in 1956, his most recent one in the present year, a fact which becomes of interest only when it is added that in the intervening period he published fourteen additional novels.[1] No doubt the figure is already dated for there are no signs of slowing down; in a recent apologetic valedictory to reviewing theater for *The Spectator* he confessed ruefully to not having written a novel in six months or more. One raises an eyebrow at all this plenty, yet only one of the novels marks itself off as a casual, slight creation, nor does the astonishing rate of production signal slapdash composition. The five novels selected for consideration here represent a judgment of his best "early" and "later" work; no doubt any admirer will have his particular favorite to add to the list. Burgess is a comic writer, a term broad and common enough to cover supposed refinements of it such as satire, grotesque, or farce. None of the labels substantially promotes understanding of his work, nor does the knowledge that he, like all British comic novelists, is "the funniest . . . since Evelyn Waugh." If comparisons are desired, one would begin with the guess that the contemporary novelist Burgess most admires is Nabokov; beyond that one goes to Joyce, to Dickens, ultimately to Shakespeare as the literary examples most insistently behind his work. In *Nothing Like the Sun*, his novel about Shakespeare, the hero sees himself as a "word man," and his author is not likely to quarrel with the term as a description of himself. But then, like Nabokov or Joyce or Dickens or Shakespeare, he is more than just a word man: the brilliant exploration of a verbal surface will lead to the discovery of truths about life, of inward revelation. Or will it, does it in fact lead to such truths in the unfolding of Burgess' best work? The question is an interesting one to entertain, though only after we have first been moved and delighted by the books themselves and the continuing presence of their author.

I

Burgess is at his most direct and perhaps most simply appealing in his early novels about life in Malaya just before independence; published last year as a trilogy, *The Long Day Wanes*, the books are given continuity through the presence of Victor Crabbe, an embattled liberal school-master for whom

things get progressively worse. Crabbe is one of us: reasonable, guilt-ridden, alternately shabby and decent in his relations with others. In a word, colorless, though he looks colorless only when put next to the characters that surround him, grotesques such as Nabby Adams, an enormous police-official whose life is devoted to the insuring each day of his proximity to about two-dozen bottles of Tiger beer (*Time for a Tiger* is the first volume of the trilogy). Or, emerging from the words themselves, Crabbe's boss Talbot, married to a young and adulterous wife, but truly wedded to his stomach:

> 'My dear fellow, you ought to eat. That's the trouble with my wife. Thin as a rake, because she won't bother to order anything. She says she's not hungry. I'm always hungry. The climate has different effects on different people. I always have my lunch out. There's a little Chinese place where they give you a really tasty and filling soup, packed with chicken and abalone and vegetables, with plenty of toast and butter, and then I always have a couple of baked crabs.'
> 'Yes,' said Crabbe.
> 'With rice and chili sauce. And then a pancake or so, rather soggy, but I don't dislike them that way, with jam and a kind of whipped cream they serve in a tea-cup. Anne, what is there to eat?'

Crabbe's mild "Yes" is a typical Fred Allen-response to the antics performed by assorted characters throughout the trilogy. But we are asked to take Crabbe, unlike Fred Allen, seriously as a person. He is presented as a recognizably psychological figure, available for easy identification with on the part of any ordinary reader; his death terminates the trilogy and should evoke some feelings on our part. But the feelings do not appear. We accept Crabbe's fate, whatever it is, without much interest, because we are being so royally entertained elsewhere.

Robert Garis has demonstrated brilliantly how the art of entertainment, as it appears in Dickens' novels, is typically a "loud and distinct" one, apprehended firmly and easily by the reader.[2] In what Garis terms Dickens' "theatrical" art, the reader is happy to watch the artist-showman at his performance, and does not expect to receive complex insights into characters who have to be "taken seriously" as we take Anna Karenina or Dorothea Brooke seriously. The satisfied reader of Dickens delights in the showman's ability energetically to command a large and various number of acts by an inexhaustibly creative language. Burgess' comedy, particularly in his early novels, if not as loud and distinct (or expansive and assured) as Dickens', is as purely verbal in its workings; for example, all we need or want to know of the glutton Talbot is that he is gluttonous and that his poems are filled with highly nutritious images: we are satisfied to watch the pancakes and whipped-cream roll by. Or to delight with Nabby Adams in his acquiring, without payment, eight large unopened bottles of Tiger beer, and in his anticipation of "The hymeneal gouging-off of the bottle-top, the kiss of the brown bitter yeasty flow, the euphoria far beyond the release of detumescence." The novel-reader's desire to find out what happens next does not assert itself, for the narrator is in no hurry to press on toward exciting revelations. He contemplates instead, with the satisfaction of Nabby Adams viewing the bottles of Tiger, his own agile high-humored creations.

One of the most original and satisfying elements of Burgess' theatricality is a persistent literary allusiveness that teases us to make something out of it and then mocks our efforts. *The Long Day Wanes* invokes Tennyson's "Ulysses," but is Victor Crabbe an "idle king" who eventually drowns in the "deep [that] moans round with many voices"? Only a solemn explicator would be interested in displaying that connection, for the theatrical novelist is less interested in creating symbolic expressions of a complex truth about man than in making play with the words of writers who have expressed such truths. Although the trilogy is filled with allusions to "The Waste Land," their interest does not lie in suggesting that Victor Crabbe fears death by water (he does), but in the purely amusing way they are woven into the narrative and made to seem at once absurdly confected and perfectly natural: "This music crept by Syed Omar in Police Headquarters, sitting puzzled while others were going out to lunch." As Crabbe's wife reads "The Waste Land" to Nabby Adams and his Malayan sidekick, Nabby remarks

> 'He's got that wrong about the pack of cards, Mrs. Crabbe. There isn't no card called the Man With Three Staves. That card what he means is just an ordinary three, like as it may be the three of clubs.'

> And when they came to the dark thunder-speaking finale of the poem, Alladad Khan had nodded gravely.

> *'Datta. Dayadhvam. Damyata.*
> *Shantih. Shantih. Shantih.'*

> 'He says he understands that bit, Mrs. Crabbe. He says that's what the thunder says.'

This "contributes" nothing to the novel except as one more of the witty satisfactions which occur throughout the trilogy. The long day has indeed waned, and the play made with Eliot or Joyce shows us just how late in the game we are, how far from the epic worlds of our modern legendary authors. Far enough it seems so that we can be entertained by a contemporary's familiar use of them.

These isolated examples of entertainment have little to do with the presentation of the hero, Crabbe, who is brought eventually (like all Burgess' heroes) to some sort of reckoning. Typically, the reckoning involves a sexual humiliation; in this novel, Crabbe learns a shocking fact about his first love, then slips into the water while trying to board a launch. We view this event through the impassive gaze of a Malayan doctor who lets him drown, deciding that "Human lives were not his professional concern." There is no other significant comment on the scene. Although it is perfectly well to say that Crabbe is essentially a device for holding together loosely-related characters and episodes, he is also allowed an inner life we must take seriously—his psychological anxieties are given full expression. When it comes to ending the trilogy, the author doesn't seem to know how seriously he wants to take that life, so it is easier to show up the Malayan doctor's sophistry (if it is that) than to assign significance, however minor, to Crabbe's end. It may seem pedantic to accuse Burgess of trying to have it both ways, since *The Long Day Wanes* is a comedy of humours in which, with the exception of Crabbe's story, the narration is external and detached. But the problem is there, and it becomes more complicated when the theatrical novelist does his tricks through a first-person narrator.

This narrator appears as J. W. Denham in what is surely Burgess' most engaging novel, *The Right to an Answer* (1960). A civil servant in the Far East home on holiday in England for much of the book, Denham is over forty, has bad teeth and a cushy job, and can smell the TV-corruption of England in the late fifties. England is a mess because people have too much freedom, and Denham claims to have learned from Hobbes that you can't have both freedom and stability. By the end of the novel he does not pronounce on matters with the arrogant certainty of the opening pages, but it would be wrong to conclude, therefore, that Burgess has written a moral novel with a dramatic change of view. How much, really, can a narrator

learn who early in the book talks this way about Sunday dinner at his sister's:

> There was a smell of old dog in the hall, an earthy rebuke at least to the blurry misty pictures of dream-dogs on the walls. The honest black telephone shone coyly from behind flowery curtains—Beryl's home-made booth for long comfy talkie-talkies with women friends, if she had any. I noticed a poker-work poem of slack form and uplifting content: 'In a world of froth and bubble two things stand like stone: kindness in another's trouble, courage in your own.' Beryl's unimpaired high-school humour was indicated by a framed macaronic paradigm: 'Je me larf, tu te grin, il se giggle; nous nous crackons, vouv vous splittez, ils se bustent.' Beryl herself could be heard singing in the kitchen at the end of the hall—an emasculated version of 'Greensleeves'—and the fumes of heavy greens gushed out under the noise of the masher.

And on and on. Crackling with wordy Nabokovian irritation, the writing individuates Beryl so firmly that there is no temptation to see her as a representative of England's corruption. If this is satire, it is satire which, as Eliot would say, creates the object that it contemplates. Beryl's house is as unforgettably there as the love-nest Lolita's mother designs for Humbert. In neither case are we interested in using the descriptions to censure the ladies in some moral way; by the same token, any claims the narrator makes about his own moral progress will have to compete with his continuous and self-contained verbal brilliance.

At one point in the novel, Denham, playing the inept narrator, apologizes for the lack of action in his tale: " . . . you have had merely J. W. Denham on leave, eating, drinking, unjustifiably censorious, meeting people, especially Mr. Raj, recounting, at the tail of the eye, almost out of earshot, the adultery of small uninteresting people." Mr. Raj is an eager sociologist from Colombo who comes to Denham's home town to investigate the manners and to court an English woman. His most notable capabilities, however, are pugilistic and culinary: in Ted Arden's Shakespearean pub, Mr. Raj disposes of a vocal racist, and Ted muses as follows: "'Queer bugger that is. It Jack Brownlow, quick as a flash, right in the goolies. . . . I didn't let on when e did it so quick like. E did it real gentleman like.'" Eventually Mr. Raj moves in with Denham and his father, to cook Sunday afternoon curries that are too rich and deep for tears:

> We fell to. My father spooned in curry and panted. He frequently tried to stagger to the kitchen for fresh glasses of cold water, but Mr. Raj said, 'No, no. I will get. This is my privilege, Mr. Denhams both.' To my father all this was a new world; he ate with Renaissance child's eyes of wonder. 'I'd no idea,' he gasped. 'Never thought.' He was like a youth having his first sexual experience.

But all these pleasant events are shattered abruptly as Denham resumes his job in the East and leaves his father in the hands of Mr. Raj, who proceeds to kill him with the kindness of curry. This is one of a series of violent acts, including assault, rape, murder, and the suicide of Mr. Raj, which cause Denham to reexamine his earlier superiority to "the mess." Although after Mr. Raj's suicide Denham moralizes that these are "just silly vulgar people uncovering the high explosive that lies hidden underneath stability" he is allowed a meditation in the concluding chapter which places him in a different relation to these people. Denham disgustedly contemplates his body in the mirror, then moves to his equally unsatisfactory spirit:

It was the eyes I didn't like, the unloving mouth, and the holier-than-thou set of the nostrils. . . .The mess was there, the instability, but I wondered now if that sin against stability was really the big sin. What I did realize quite clearly was the little I'd helped, the blundering or not-wishing-to-be-involved plump moneyed man of leave inveighing against sins he wasn't in the position even to begin to commit. For surely that sneered-at suburban life was more stable than this shadow life of buying and selling in a country where no involvement was possible, the television evening, with the family round, better than the sordid dalliance that soothed me after work? . . . If poor bloody innocent little Winterbottom had died, and striving Mr. Raj . . . surely it was something that they invoked the word Love? Even the word was better than this emptiness, this standing on the periphery and sneering.

This seems to offer us a secure vantage-point from which to review the events with understanding. But are we convinced by it? What indeed would it mean to be "convinced" by it? Doesn't the analysis unjustly simplify Denham's earlier behavior, since that behavior has been presented to us through a style which delights? How can we accept "sneering" or "standing on the periphery" as adequate labels for the description of Beryl's house quoted earlier? Or, from the same chapter, is the following menu a sneer at the English Sunday meal?

> The meal was pretentious—a kind of beetroot soup with greasy *croûtons*; pork underdone with loud vulgar cabbage, potato croquettes, tinned peas in tiny jam-tart cases, watery gooseberry sauce; trifle made with a resinous wine, so jammy that all my teeth lit up at once—a ghastly discord on two organ manuals.

One quickly grows fond of those encased peas, that loud cabbage; the food, through these words, becomes not just awful but fascinatingly awful. Here, as in general, the imaginative vitality of Denham-Burgess' prose elbows aside the moralist who later repents of his hypercritical satiric self.

Denham's relationship to "the mess, the instability" represents a novelistic questioning of the satirist's relationship to life, to the materials of fiction. *The Right to an Answer* is unique in Burgess' work for the way it shows an aggressively comic and satiric intelligence taking us in through a casual first-person style of reporting. At the same time, or perhaps as a result of such aggressive dealing, the "I" repents of it, apologizes to us for putting himself outside the reek of the human. I am really no better than they are, probably not as good, he winningly admits. But if the apology is an engaging gesture of humility, it has things both ways only through a noticeable straining in the very prose of the book. When the narrator refers harshly, in the above passage, to "the sordid dalliance that soothed me after work," just how seriously can we take something which is referred to by a demonstrably witty intelligence as "sordid dalliance"? And does Burgess himself know how seriously he wants to take it? The attempt by a marvelous entertainer to discover a truth about life, to engage in moral reappraisal of himself, results in an uncomfortable sleight-of-hand effect that isn't quite quick enough to escape our notice. And the question remains: how much can the dark comedian afford to enlighten, with sincere reflection, the chaotic scene he has so wittily imagined?

II

This question, asked by the critic, is of course one the artist is under no obligation to answer. Burgess goes on to publish three novels (*Devil of a State*, *The Worm and the Ring*,

The Doctor is Sick) which in their individually interesting ways avoid the issue and which, for all their excellent goings-on, are not as solidly entertaining as *The Long Day Wanes*, or as humanly ambitious as *The Right to an Answer*. It is the three novels that appear in 1962–63 which present a truly experimental attempt to unite brilliance of entertainment with a seriousness toward human beings—more accurately, toward humanity. *A Clockwork Orange*, *The Wanting Seed*, and *Honey for the Bears* are (at least the first and last) Burgess' most popular books and they ask to be considered together. All of them concern the individual and the modern state; all of them are felt to have a connection with the quality of life in the 1960's, but they approach life obliquely by creating fantasies or fables which appeal to us in odd and disturbing ways. As always with Burgess' work, and now to a splendidly bizarre degree, the creativity is a matter of style, of words combined in strange new shapes. Through the admiration these shapes raise, rather than through communication of specifiable political, philosophical or religious ideas about man or the state, is to be found the distinction of these novels; for this reason it is of limited use to invoke names like Huxley or Orwell as other novelists of imagined futurist societies.

A Clockwork Orange, most patently experimental of the novels, is written in a language created by combining Russian words with teenage *argot* into a hip croon that sounds both ecstatic and vaguely obscene. The hero, Alex, a teen-age thug, takes his breakfast and morning paper this way:

> And there was a bolshy big article on Modern Youth (meaning me, so I gave the old bow, grinning like bezoomny) by some very clever bald chelloveck. I read this with care, my brothers, slurping away at the old chai, cup after tass after chasha, crunching my lomticks of black toast dipped in jammiwam and eggiweg. This learned veck said the usual veshches, about no parental discipline, as he called it, and the shortage of real horrorshow teachers who would lambast bloody beggary out of their innocent poops and make them go boohoohoo for mercy. All this was gloopy and made me smeck, but it was nice to go on knowing one was making the news all the time, O my brothers.

Although the American paperback edition provides a glossary, one doesn't need it to get along very well after the first few pages. In fact such translation is a mistake for it short-circuits the unmistakable rhythms of speech by which the sentences almost insensibly assume meaning. Moreover, though the book is filled with the most awful violence—what in our glossary or newspaper would be called murder, assault, rape, perversion—it comes to us through an idiom that, while it does not deny the connection between what happens in the second chapter and what the newspaper calls a "brutal rape," nevertheless makes what happens an object of aesthetic interest in a way no rape can or should be. Life—a dreadful life to be sure—is insistently and joyously deflected into the rhythms of a personal style within which one eats lomticks, not pieces, of toast.

The novel is short and sharply plotted: Alex is betrayed by his fellow "droogs," imprisoned for murder, then by a lobotomizing technique is cured of his urges to violence; whereas music, Beethoven in particular, had inspired him to heights of blood-lusts, he now just feels sick. Caught between the rival parties for state power he tries suicide, but lives to recover his original identity, as listening to the scherzo of the Beethoven Ninth he sees himself "carving the whole litso of the creeching world with my cut-throat britva." The book concludes on this happy note, for oddly enough it *is* a happy note; we share the hero's sense of high relief and possibility, quite a trick for the novelist to have brought off. And without questioning it we have acceded to the book's "message," as radical and intransigent as the style through which it is expressed:

> More, badness is of the self, the one, the you or me on our oddy knockies, and that self is made by old Bog or God and is his great pride and radosty. But the not-self cannot have the bad, meaning they of the government and the judges and the schools cannot allow the bad because they cannot allow the self. And is not our modern history, my brothers, the story of brave malenky selves fighting these big machines. I am serious with you, brothers, over this. But what I do I do because I like to do.

Doing what you do because you like to do it is what the Burgess hero—Crabbe, Denham, others—has done and has been punished for doing by his creator. But the hero of *A Clockwork Orange* is rewarded and endorsed in a way more recognizably human characters in a more "realistic" atmosphere could not possibly be. In the world of creative fantasy we can admire hero and event as they are shaped by language; our response is akin to the old-fashioned "admiration" proper to the heroic poem. By the same token the defense of self, no matter how twisted it may be, and the condemnation of the state, no matter how benevolent it pretends to be, is absolute. Such a simple and radical meaning is not morally complex, but it must be taken as a serious aspect of fantasy. Within its odd but carefully observed limits the book is entirely consistent, successful and even pleasing, Burgess' most eye and ear-catching performance.

Published a few months later, *The Wanting Seed* pleased critics a good deal less, the general feeling being that Burgess had overreached himself and produced a holge-podge book. It is true that nothing is alien to its virtuoso atmosphere: elemental poetry, broad jokes, science fiction and political philosophy consort together, couched throughout in a highly pedantic and jawbreaking vocabulary ("corniculate," "vexillae," "fritinancy," "parachronic"). But in this most Joycean of Burgess' novels, that virtuoso atmosphere is precisely what appeals. The novel takes the population explosion as fictional opportunity and imagines a society presided over by a Ministry of Infertility which encourages homosexuality ("It's Sapiens to be Homo" is their motto) and forbids any woman to bear more than one child. As in *A Clockwork Orange* the lawless individual is at odds with a "benevolent" state; the heroine, Beatrice-Joanna, married to Tristram Foxe, a history teacher, is having an affair with Tristram's brother, a government official. Beatrice-Joanna's rebellion consists in her refusal to accept the death of her son and her rejection of the doctor's sensible advice: "Think of this in national terms, in global terms. One mouth less to feed. One more half-kilo of phosphorus pentoxide to nourish the earth. In a sense, you know, Mrs. Foxe, you'll be getting your son back again." Emerging from the clinic, she walks down the great London street (once Brighton but now a part of Greater London) to the sea and perceives it with a special poetry granted her:

> If only, she felt crazily, poor Roger's body could have been thrown into these tigrine waters, swept out to be gnawed by fish, rather than changed coldly to chemicals and silently fed to the earth. She had a mad intuitive notion that the earth was dying, that the sea would soon be the final repository of life. 'Vast sea gifted with delirium, panther skin and mantle pierced with thousands of idols of the sun—' She had

read that somewhere, a translation from one of the auxiliary languages of Europe. The sea drunk with its own blue flesh, a hydra, biting its tail.

Then looking up at the Government Building she sees the figure of a bearded man: "A cynosure to ships, man of the sea, Pelagius. But Beatrice-Joanna could remember a time when he had been Augustine. And, so it was said, he had been at other times the King, the Prime Minister, a popular bearded guitarist, Eliot (a long-dead singer of infertility), the Minister of Pisciculture, captain of the Hertfordshire Men's Sacred Game eleven, and most often and satisfactorily—the great unknown, the magical Anonymous." A hodge-podge of style perhaps, but no more so than *Ulysses*: at one moment the scientific knowingness of a Buck Mulligan, then the moody broodings of Stephen Dedalus, followed by an inventive Bloomlike list. What holds the various styles together is a linguistic virtuoso who moves his characters up and down the map of England: to complain as one reviewer did that the hero and heroine were mechanical contrivances is not to the point, since more "character," more recognizably human dimension, would destroy the fable.

For proof of this, consider the block of chapters describing Tristram's attempt to join his wife in the North of England (he has just escaped from jail and she, pregnant, has fled to her brother-in-law, an old-fashioned Roman Catholic, to have what turns out to be twins). As the state moves from a Pelagian phase to an Augustinian one, a great famine impels man toward cannibalism, fertility rites, the genesis of drama, and from homo- to heterosexual love. Tristram observes these effects as he moves from Brighton to Wigan, but we have heard reports of them already, courtesy of Anthony Burgess the announcer:

> . . . In Stoke-on-Trent the carcass of a woman (later identified as Maria Bennett, spinster, aged twenty-eight) grinned up suddenly—several good clean cuttings off her—from under a bank of snow. In Gillingham, Kent, Greater London, a shady back-street eating-shop opened, grilling nightly, and members of both police forces seemed to patronize it. In certain unregenerate places on the Suffolk coast there were rumours of big crackling Christmas dinners. . . . The New Year commenced with stories of timid anthropophagy. . . . Then the metropolis flashed its own sudden canines: a man called Amis suffered savage amputation of an arm off Kingsway; S. R. Coke, journalist, was boiled in an old copper near Shepherd's Bush; Miss Joan Waine, a teacher, was fried in segments.

Some might consider this (especially the reference to imagined fates of Angries) a debilitating cleverness, fatal to Burgess' art; to me it seems admirably indigenous to his ruthlessly literary sensibility. But in any case, it must be agreed that an attempt to give a hero traveling through such a scene much "dimension" would result in an awkward and uncertain book. *The Wanting Seed* is neither: its inventiveness is large enough that we are content to follow the fortunes of heroine and hero without desiring some further "inward" reach of understanding. What is to be understood—taken in—is put before us in the theatrical manner spoken of earlier. Even the closing paragraphs of the book, coming as they do after the longest of journeys and bringing together the Tristram Foxes and their twins, united on the promenade at Brighton, even these paragraphs are less a moving tribute to a particular man or woman than they are a general and now mythicized embodiment of love, of possibility:

> She clung to him, the huge air, the life-giving sea,
> man's future history in the depths, the present tow-
> ered town, the bearded man at the pinnacle, all shut
> out from the warmth of his presence, the closeness of
> his embrace. He became sea, sun, tower. The twins
> gurgled. There were still no words.

And as if to formalize and make shimmery this closing atmo-
sphere, the narrator dons prophetic robes and plays a late
Shakespearean sage or Joycean lyricist, in language stolen from
Valéry:

> The wind rises . . . we must try to live. The im-
> mense air opens and closes my book. The wave,
> pulverized, dares to gush and spatter from the rocks.
> Fly away, dazzled, blinded pages. Break, waves.
> Break with joyful waters. . . .

This looks more vulnerable in quotation than it feels in the act
of finishing the novel, although one understands how such
writing might give rise to distrust or scepticism about its narrative poise. Burgess knows the extravagant overreaching that
attaches to grand incantations, and as a rule his fictions do not
make them. But *The Wanting Seed*, like *A Clockwork Orange*,
has it affinities with the heroic poem: "faring forward" is saluted by the Bard when he ends his tale with an imitative
gesture meant just as seriously as the cannibalistic jokes in-
spected earlier. In creative fantasy or fable, no suggestion that
its figures are merely human is in order: Alex prepares to resume his career as a hoodlum; Beatrice-Joanna and Tristram
prepare for—what? The fact is we are not interested in these
"characters," only the action in which they have figured. A
reader of *The Wanting Seed* must vouch to the extent that, like
it or not, it is very much a linguistic action.

By contrast, *Honey for the Bears* would seem to be a return
to the real world—the Soviet Union in 1963—where Paul
Hussey, an English antique dealer, and his American wife
Belinda are engaged in smuggling in and selling twenty-dozen
drilon dresses, the loot for which will be turned over to the
widow of a dead friend. A mysterious rash sends Belinda to the
hospital where she falls under the influence of a female Dr.
Lazurkina who analyzes Paul as a homosexual ("gomosexual"
without the "h" in Russian) and spirits Belinda off to the
Crimea for what promises to be a long talk. Paul makes his own
liaison with a bearded young Russian struggling to be hip and
properly disenchanted about the modern state: "'Russia or
America,' said Alexei Prutkov, 'what's the difference? It's all
the State. There's only one State. What we have to do is get
together in these little groups and start to live.'" But after an
unsuccessful attempt by Paul to seduce Alexei's mistress, and a
drunken party where Paul suggests the guests strip "stark bal-
lock naked," he is thrown out of Alexei's group with the
accusation "What you like, dig, is your own sex, and that's
what's so filthy and disgusting." Other humiliations and confusions follow (teeth knocked out, thrown into prison) until
Paul leaves Russia, this time smuggling out (as his wife) the son
of a Russian composer in disgrace named Opiskin, whose
works Paul's dead friend Robert had loved.

It makes little difference whether we call this "plot" (inadequately summarized here) brilliant or absurd, so long as the
detailing of it removes all suspicion that Burgess has abandoned
us to Real Life in the Soviet Union today. *Honey for the Bears*
is just as fantastic or fabulous as its two predecessors; characters
(possibly excepting the hero) are viewed externally as ever, and
their dimensions (and our sympathies) are thus severely limited. Stylistically the book moves at whirlwind pace with events
and thoughts rapidly telescoped through Paul Hussey's mind;

for example, on the first page we have this response to an
unknown aged master in a wheelchair:

> The face was trenched and riven, as by a killing life
> of metaphysical debauchery. That was it, decided
> Paul: a head that philosophy had unsexed, some final
> Shavian achievement. He had seen a head like it on
> television newsreels; an old proud eagle squatting in
> Whitehall among students, Banning the Bomb. But
> these oyster-coloured eyes surveyed with disdain the
> scruffy redbrick layabouts who nearly filled the Cul-
> tural Saloon, the nose twitched at them.

Paul's own "unsexing" is to come, when by the end of the book
he admits that he no longer knows what he is, sexually. And so
the novel invites us, as did the earlier *The Right to an Answer*,
to relate the satiric intelligence accorded Paul in the passage
above, to something he learns in Russia; more generally, to feel
a unifying of the style of entertainment with the content of
truth.

In the best single piece of writing about Burgess ("The
Epicene," *New Statesman*, April 15, 1963) Christopher Ricks
argues that this can be done, insofar as the book makes an
analogy between sexual and political behavior. Politically the
book presents America and Russia as equally monolithic and
insufficient states, and opts instead for what Ricks calls a
"Third Force." So, by analogy, homo and heterosexuality need
not be exclusive choices; without singing hymns to bisexuality
it can at least be entertained and admitted to be perhaps more
fun, more attractive to the individual who would be free. Ricks
points out correctly that this is a subversive message, but that it
is transmitted in an "inventive and gay" manner that takes the
fear out of it. And he goes on to claim that the book is more
humane and "says more" than Burgess' earlier minglings of
black violence with comic lightness. It would be pleasant to
take *Honey for the Bears* as evidence of this kind of novelistic
breakthrough, especially since at the moment it is the most
recent full-fledged novel Burgess has given us. But it is much
more problematic than Ricks suggests whether the "message"
about sex and about politics is convincingly worked into the
texture of the novel. There are difficulties in knowing just how
to take Paul's sexual humiliations with his wife and Alexei's
mistress—they are indeed fiascos, but do not recommend
themselves to us as, in book-jacket language, "outrageously
funny" or "wildly comic." They are no more comic than Paul's
difficulty in keeping his false teeth in place. On the other hand
the narrator makes no attempt to extend Paul sympathetic understanding. We are free, if we choose, to connect heterosexual
failure with Paul's memories of "poor, dead Robert," though
these memories are sentimental moonings we assume the narrator doesn't fully share. But even this is an assumption.
Burgess treats Paul any way the spirit moves him: now harshly,
now pathetically, now as a witty, perceptive satirical eye—all
depending on the exigencies of a moment. When we try to say
what these moments add up to the trouble begins. What they
claim to add up to is concentrated in two passages late in the
novel: in the first of these, Paul relates a dream to his cell-mates
about how there was a little man who lived between two greatly
opposing tsardoms. They bully the little man by giving him a
wife who accuses him of not being a real man, an adequate
protector. Like Belinda, the wife walks out. The second passage
makes the Paul-as-England identification explicit: "I'm going
back to an antique-shop, but somebody's got to conserve the
good of the past, before your Americanism and America's
Russianism make plastic of the world. . . . You'll learn about
freedom from us yet." Even as he says it he feels a "doubt," as

does surely the reader. For England (Rick's political "Third Force"?) is simply not *there* in the novel, any more than is Paul Hussey's inner life, which, we are told, has undergone some sort of change. Once more, the imagination of comic disorder proves stronger than the fable's attempt to make thoughtful sense out of it.

This is not cause for alarm, nor a gloomy note on which to conclude. When Ricks says, in the essay mentioned above, that Burgess has yet to write a really "first-rate comic novel" we may feel the standards are high indeed after reading through a group of novels distinguished by their abundant qualities of imaginative energy, creative invention, complicated wit, and verbal delight. Since *Honey for the Bears* Anthony Burgess has given us a number of books somewhat off-the-center of his literary vision: juvenalia, a fascinating novelistic sport about Shakespeare, books on language and on Joyce. In a recent *TLS* article titled "The Manicheans" he mused aloud on why the novel has not made more use of religious experience, and he specified further:

> I do not mean the tribulations of priests among the poor, or deanery gossip, or pre-ordination doubts; I mean rather the imaginative analysis of themes like sainthood, sin, the eschatological sanctions of behaviour, even that dangerous beatific vision.

One of the best ways to analyze sin is to become a comic novelist; there is every reason to suspect that the remaining themes will occupy Burgess in the novels to come. At any rate we can be grateful for the books we have. After Nabokov there is no other, but that is because, in part, Nabokov sees the world through imaginatively obsessed narrator-madmen who impose their strange shapes on reality. Burgess, despite the variety of narrators and situations in his fiction, speaks to us as one of us: a fallen man with the usual amount of ambition, irritation, guilt, decency and common sense. Given such ordinary qualities or modest sins, how can things go as wrong as they do for the heroes of these painful books? That they go not just wrong, but marvelously wrong, is the result of the one quality Burgess does not share with the rest of us or with his heroes—the art of the novelist.

Notes

1. Depending on how you count. His first three published novels, counted individually here, form a trilogy. Aside from titles mentioned in this essay there is a youthful attempt, recently published, called *A Vision of Battlements*, another early, slight fable, *The Eve of St. Venus*, and two novels published under the pseudonym Joseph Kell. Titled *One Hand Clapping* and *Inside Mr. Enderby*, the latter have been just republished under Burgess' name. A novel, *Tremor of Intent*, is scheduled for June.
2. Robert Garis, *The Dickens Theatre* (Oxford: Clarendon Press, 1965). Part I—"The Dickens Problem"—is filled with valuable observation about particular artistic styles and about literature in general.

GEORGE STEINER
"Scroll and Keys"

The New Yorker, April 13, 1981, pp. 156–62

These past decades, the authorized tone in English letters has been one of gray and acid sparseness. Novelists, playwrights, a tribe of minimalist versifiers have gone to the bank to borrow words. The interest rates have been punitive. So they have borrowed few, and, where possible, sharp-edged ones. English writers and reviewers have bridled at American copiousness, drawing inward like winter snails at the wasteful march-past of a millipede. Now, gradually, the mizzle may be lifting. The London theatre has exploded with a brilliantly prodigal, eight-hour version of Dickens' *Nicholas Nickleby*. As New Yorkers can witness, there is an almost ferocious extravagance of spirit, of histrionic means in Peter Shaffer's *Amadeus*. And there is Anthony Burgess.

Victorian confidence engendered kaleidoscopic individuals: bearded colossi who planted their umbrellas on alpine peaks, grew tumultuous orchids, learned languages as we slip into sweaters, composed tomes on a great variety of matters, thumped sonorous harmoniums in outsize conservatories, and advanced upon their ornate sepulchres with encyclopedias three-quarters read. Burgess is of this breed—almost a *monstre sacré*, were it not for his amused, self-observant humanity. He plays and composes music. He is a virtuoso linguist in respect both of the languages he knows and of his interest in the theory of language. He is one of the most incisive, just book reviewers busy in that precarious trade. He has published literary, art, and music criticism of distinction. He is a translator of awesome resource. (Currently, he and his no less gifted wife, Liana, are transposing *Finnegans Wake* into Italian.) Burgess has made filmmakers rich—witness *A Clockwork Orange*—and has been directly involved in script-writing and production. He has fed both quality and robust kitsch into the maw of television. There are not many name lectures in academe which he has not adorned by his erudition and zany authority; it was, at moments, from the piano, hammering out rags and chanting ditties in a finely charred voice, that he recently delivered the Eliot Memorial Lectures at the University of Kent. But A.B.—his fantasies often play on the permutations and linguistic associations that spring from these initial, dawn letters of our alphabet—would, I think, want to be considered first and foremost as a novelist, as an artificer of prose fiction. I say "artificer" because this is Joyce's word, his emblematic token, and Burgess is, with Beckett, Joyce's only legitimate heir.

The Burgess bibliography lists twenty-one novels. (There are rumors of esoterica under a pen name.) *The Long Day Wanes*, an autobiographical trilogy set in Malaya, launched the Burgess canon. It remains perhaps his most poignant, unguarded performance. *A Clockwork Orange* brought celebrity when it was made into a striking movie. But the fiction is subtler than Stanley Kubrick's package and points to that in Burgess's politics and alertness to science-fiction which connects his writings to those of Aldous Huxley and George Orwell. *Honey for the Bears* is both a political fable and an ingenious meditation on language. It is one of a cluster of works, fiction and nonfiction, in which Burgess seeks an imaginative grip on the ominous charms of the Russian tongue and of its native speakers. *Enderby*, *Nothing Like the Sun*, and *ABBA ABBA* form a sparkling trio. They are studies of the writer's odd condition, of the pathologies and carnivals of poetic inspiration. The first is a wry mirroring of Burgess himself; the second is just about the only convincing fictional recreation we have of the young Shakespeare; the third is a witty but also moving evocation of Keats in the season of his passing. *Napoleon Symphony*, a novel on Beethoven, combines Burgess's frank obsession with the titans of the past and his virtuoso knowledge of music, his rare cunning in finding a verbal counterpoint to musical effects (another decisive link with Joyce). *1985*, a "semi-fiction," begins where Orwell and *A Clockwork Orange* left off. *Moses* and *Man of Nazareth* are potboilers aimed at, occasioned by, more or less Neronian treatments on television and film. Yet even here there are touches of mandarin originality. All in all, a prodigious catalogue.

Take its several items, add to them ingredients from Burgess's nonfiction, from his monographs on Joyce and on the English language, from his portrait of Hemingway and other forays into Americana, top off with some of his acrobatics of translation, and you will have what Coleridge called, self-teasingly, an omnium-gatherum. Burgess's collectanea—another word beloved of listmakers and lexicographers—masks itself in the guise of a leviathan novel *Earthly Powers*. And there are spacious stretches of fiction in it. But it is Anthony Burgess's polymath persona, his cat's lives, the appetites of his intellect, the syncopations of thought and feeling so peculiarly his own which furnish the great creature with its life force and (partial) unison.

The opening sentence of the book is certain to enter into the teasing immortality of quizzes ("Identify the novel that starts . . . ") and of academic dissection: "It was the afternoon of my eighty-first birthday, and I was in bed with my catamite when Ali announced that the archbishop had come to see me." Merely at the surface, the sentence is a rococo masterpiece. Observe the ruse, the rallentando in the cadence. Note the arch dispersal of scabrous intimations: "afternoon," "cata-mite," the suggestive Ali. But it is also a sentence charged with pointers toward what will be the sources, the mimed and parodied presences, the sinews of plot and of tone in the enterprise as a whole.

Connoisseurs of Somerset Maugham's life and manner will almost "preconsciously"—and therein lies Burgess's control—pick up the underlying thread. They will know within moments that Burgess has undertaken the implausible task of composing the memoirs of an eighty-one-year-old panjandrum and world celebrity of letters who is a homosexual and, under the alias of Kenneth Marchal Toomey, none other than Willie Maugham. "Catamite" is a learned, exact term for a male lover of sullied motives, a male whore, but one about whom hovers a nuance of antique pederasty, of the idiom and mores known to curious readers of Suetonius and of Alexandrine scandalmongers. To aficionados of the more modern baroque, the entrance of the archbishop will give all sorts of subliminal signals: a hint of Ronald Firbank's and Aubrey Beardsley's louche ecclesiastical fantasies, an echo of Norman Douglas—like A.B. himself, a master of Mediterranean moods—and, above all, an annunciation à la Baron Corvo (F. Rolfe), the fin-de-siècle confidence man and occasionally magical dreamer whose *Hadrian the Seventh* remains, stubbornly, a kind of classic, and a vital source in Burgess's summa.

The "Maugham level" is adroitly sustained. "Willie" is himself often alluded to in the third person, and his tales of empire and sunset lust are subtly interwoven with Burgess's own Malaya. The style of the first-person narrative wickedly renders the aging carnivore's malice, sexual needs and panics, self-punishments, and bitchy hauteur. Here is a memorable study of an immensely successful middlebrow writer cursed with just that dram of unsparing lucidity which shows him, which makes him discern in the judgment of others, the final fiasco: the ephermerality of his most acclaimed works. Burgess's ability to slip into the old man's flaccid hide, to bring to fetid yet poignant expression the sexual lunges and humiliations of the old and of the invert, is uncanny. But writers have long been Burgess's meat, and they crowd this canvas: Joyce, Steinbeck, Huxley, J. B. Priestley, Arnold Bennett, either in propria persona or transparently referred to, together with dozens of lesser lights. Thus, if the actual narration is that of "Maugham" at the approach of death, one of the key episodes is an amalgam of W. H. Auden's rescue of Thomas Mann's daughter from Nazi Germany and of the weakness and vanity under Nazi pressure—a weakness and a vanity mercifully

observed—of P. G. Wodehouse. As is just now the fashion, actual political, literary, artistic, and underworld figures move in and out of the novel.

The other main strand in *Earthly Powers* is the saga of Don Carlo Campanati, half brother of Toomey—though "half brother" is not quite right, for it simplifies a consanguinity as arcane and doom-laden as that in Sophocles' *Oedipus*, a play A.B. has himself translated. Don Carlo is a larger-than-life invention in whom we recognize elements not only of Moses, Christ, Napoleon, and Beethoven as Burgess has portrayed them but, massively, of John XXIII. I have already cited *Hadrian the Seventh*; another precedent might be Zola's neglected but formidable novel *Rome*. But it is, of course, Anthony Burgess who has dreamed his own multiple energies and ironies, his politics of disenchanted utopia, and his fantasies of power into this priest, iron-nerved casino player (Burgess lives in Monaco), lover, theologian, master of mass media, dazzling linguist, and charismatic pontiff. The death of Gregory XVII—of a heart attack, suffered in Moscow during one of a series of triumphant world journeys—embodies not only the brusque, melodramatic end of Corvo's Hadrian but the motif of sudden eclipse at the height of perception, of creative strength, which haunts many of Burgess's books. Campanati—and the bells peal literally in his name—is among the most ambitiously conceived, intellectually exciting agents in recent fiction.

Dozens of subplots wind around these two main stems. I have mentioned Auden-Wodehouse and Nazi Germany. There is a detailed account of a recent, celebrated prosecution for blasphemy and obscenity in the London courts; there are well-documented imbroglios from the history of Diaghilev's Ballets Russes and of La Scala. Much of the latter part of the book is taken up by an often acute but hurriedly imagined presentation of the Manson case, of the mass suicide at Jonestown, and of a general slide of young America into mysticism and mindless violence. As with one of Beethoven's unwilling codas, so with *Earthly Powers* one has the impression not so much of a logical close as of a halt, reluctantly imposed, on a continuing pulse of energy.

This is a taxing novel. Not only because of the innumerable conundrums, acrostics, cross-echoes, veiled citations, and historical-literary references that make up its opulent texture. Not only because of a vocabulary in which terms such as "metathesis" and hints out of *Finnegans Wake* are common. Not only because a reader innocent of Christian soteriology, English metrics, and antique mythology will be deprived of numerous apprehensions and pleasures. *Earthly Powers* is taxing simply because it has set out to reclaim for the current art of the novel those domains of intellectual debate, of political modelling, of formal and anarchic religiosity, of adult confrontations with humbling sexuality and the wastage of death which have been, so very largely, yielded to high journalism, to discursive prose, and to the uneasy hybrid of "fact/fiction." Burgess honors his readers in purposing them to be almost as omnivorously aware and intelligent as he is.

At a first reading, one is not confident that the venture has "come off"—that the monster has, in Henry James's phrase, achieved "deep-breathing and organic form." And in the face of so much authority it is a reviewer's trivial pastime to note that only Pope Gregory is infallible. (Kafka's *The Castle* is given a false German gender; the last line in the haunting rag sung on page 442 contains an erratum; it is not primarily, I believe, failed plays for which the young Goebbels was known but a by no means untalented novel.) To be serious: there is here, and past cavil, a feat of imaginative breadth and of intelligence which lifts fiction high. The whole landscape is the brighter for it.

ROY CAMPBELL

1901–1957

Born in Durban, Natal, South Africa on October 2, 1901, Ignatius Roy Dunnachie Campbell left Durban High School at fifteen to join the Sixth South African Infantry. He was promptly arrested and returned to high school. He attended Oxford, failed his exams, and left for years of travel and adventure throughout Europe and Africa. During this time, in 1922, he met and married Mary Gorman; fished and poached in Wales; fought bulls, busted broncos, bred horses, and became a champion steer-thrower in Spain. Campbell also edited a satirical journal in South Africa, for which he was exiled. All the while, Campbell was writing his first volume, *The Flaming Terrapin*.

After settling in Spain with his wife and their daughter Teresa, Campbell converted to Catholicism and Fascism, fighting for Franco in the Spanish Civil War and reporting on it for the *London Tablet*. His political views made him a controversial figure—which delighted him—and his critical reputation has declined steadily since the mid-1930s. G. S. Fraser epitomized the moderate line on Campbell in the *New Statesman*: "Mr. Campbell is . . . a poet of striking and successful obvious effects. His tone is usually that of the harangue or even of the tirade . . . no hesitant, implicit ironies, no shy layers of meaning. He presents the poet not as the uneasy conscience of our sick society but as the fierce, rejected, tribal hero of a simpler day."

Campbell served in the British Army in Africa during World War II. A serious injury caused him to tone down his vigorous lifestyle, and he moved to London to join the BBC. In 1952 Campbell retired to Portugal, where he was killed in an automobile accident on April 22, 1957.

Personal

"They will never love where they ought to love," Burke writes in the fourth letter of the *Regicide Peace*, "who do not hate where they ought to hate." Mr. Roy Campbell, a faithful lover and a hot hater, a soldier, a sailor, a hunter, a bull-fighter, a horse-breeder, a critic, a translator, a champion of religion, a great brawny Carlyle-hero of a man, a South African and a Scot and a Latin rolled into one gigantic frame, a singer of sea-chanties, a master of pencil-sketching, a High Tory, a great drinker, a great talker, one of the fiercest and kindest beings alive—this adventurer is one of the few modern poets likely to be read a hundred years from now, or two hundred. It is his power of loving and hating which gives his verse its invariable strength and its frequent splendor.—RUSSELL KIRK, "The Last of the Scalds," SWR, 1956, p. 164

Fantastically brave and chivalrous, he had the simple heart and the faith of a child. His character was as extraordinary as his poetry, and he would have been more at home in the Tudor age than in this age of the barren grey creeds—of the dictators who could see mankind as "planet bacilli".

Born in Durban, fifty-four years ago, his whole character reflected the great stretches of grandeur, the exuberant color, of his native South Africa. In his autobiography (*Light on a Dark Horse*) he thanked Almighty God "for letting me loose in such a world, to plunder its miraculous literatures and languages, and wines; to savor its sights, forms, colors, perfumes, and sounds; to see so many superb cities, oceans, lakes, forests, rivers, sierras, pampas and plains, with their beasts, birds, trees, crops, and flowers—and above all, their men and women, who are by far the most interesting of all."

His adventures were as extraordinary as his character. Who but he would have had his motor charged (in an African forest) by a rhinoceros, who—which was unusual—won the battle and disappeared into the forest bearing the bonnet of the motor on its horn as a trophy.

He enjoyed battles. When last in Africa (at the time of the rhinoceros episode), he sent me a postcard depicting a sleeping lion, and bearing the words—"How is" (mentioning a weekly paper that had been giving me trouble) "behaving? I shall be in Europe again in a few weeks. Would you like me to come over?"

So he lived—in a whirlwind always—from the moment when he fought, as a child, with octopuses, and with sharks.—EDITH SITWELL, "Roy Campbell," *Poetry*, April 1958, pp. 42–43

General

Mr. Campbell's name turns up in lists, and his verse goes mechanically into the bigger anthologies, but the location and magnitude of what he does don't seem to get plotted. His verse, one gathers, is found stirring by rather inarticulate people. This isn't to say that it is written down to a public, or that Mr. Campbell is either unintelligent or dishonest. He writes to please himself, and he isn't a dull man. He has, however, a good deal more "biography" on his record than most poets, and, to complement it, rather less poetry in his verse than his talents would lead one to expect. This needn't be an inexorable equation; one doesn't write by abstaining from living. But the man of courtly and ritualistic action has been so much an anomaly in the lustrum 1920–50 that Mr. Campbell's muse has used up her energy being, so to speak, astounded at her own existence. She speaks most of the time in borrowed accents—rather absent-mindedly borrowed: Pope's, Rimbaud's, Baudelaire's. In a trance of astonishment she chants, astonished at the things that go on before her eyes, not caring especially whether the subject really gets caught up into the verse so long as we stay aware that she and Mr. Campbell are alive-oh.—HUGH KENNER, "A Narcissist of Action," *Poetry*, June 1953, p. 169

Wild creatures such as those of the South African veld, with their grace of movement and untamable spirit, have always served for Campbell as symbols of the life of freedom and independence which he would have for human beings, and his physical contests with them have been a source of spiritual exultation. This proud vision of beauty "volted with delight" is probably South Africa's most valuable gift to him. It is revealed in his scornful attitude towards the smugness and unadventurous mediocrity of modern city life, its meaningless pursuits and activities, its mechanical patterns and drab order of society, in both his prose—

> . . . The obscenity of the sham ideals of the crowd,
> the mental non-existence of the man in the street,
> the huge unwieldy paralysis of the gods, are flung
> before one in their grim reality. . . .
>
>   (*Voorslag* No. I)

—and his poetry:

> I sing the people; shall the Muse deny
> The weak, the blind, the humble and the lame
> Who have no purpose save to multiply,
> Who have no will save all to be the same:
> I sing the people as I watch, untamed,
> Its aimless pomps and generations roll—
> A monster whom the drunken gods have maimed
> And set upon a road that has no goal.
>
>   (A *Song for the People*)

It is also responsible for his glorification of the cattleman, the matador, and similar representatives of the desirable way of life, in *Taurine Provence* and *Broken Record* and so many of his poems. Campbell's ideal community would be a "gymnasium of athletic personalities", though presumably a community which would, at the same time, be susceptible to the appeal of the creative arts. . . .

Unlike many of his English contemporaries, Campbell gazes outward upon the world rather than inward upon himself, and the pettiness and materialism he perceives appal him. He seems to be preoccupied with the two contrasted modes of existence which, by means of an extensive range of symbols, he is never tired of presenting in his poetry—the life of the independent personality revelling in freedom, and that of the conventional, herd-minded, half-blind and already half-dead citizen. When others speak of freedom, he sees only a progressive humiliation of mankind. The typical figure on the one side is the horseman or herdsman; on the other "Charlot", Charlie Chaplin, shuffling in his thousands through city streets. And these have given rise to a whole series of representative figures with which the reader soon becomes familiar: equestrian—pedestrian; cattleman—shopkeeper; Sons of Cain—Sons of Abel; cowboys, toreros, vaqueros—Charlies, Tommies, Pommies, wowsers. The city itself is placed in opposition to "The Hill, the Pampa, and the Tide" by which humanity may perhaps be regenerated. Another term for those whose equestrian qualities may cleanse and revitalize society is "The White Commando". Christ, though sometimes represented as a great Albatross, is usually a great equestrian figure, the Prince of Herdsmen, the Herdsman King, or the red Torero.—Howard Sergeant, "Restive Steer: A Study of the Poetry of Roy Campbell," *ES*, 1957, pp. 105–8

Campbell was responsible for no technical innovations in verse; and it would be true to say that he left the English language where he found it. He achieved nothing new in his handling of it, his work made no apparent difference to the development of contemporary English poetry, or not the kind of difference that can be assessed by the test of the comparative analytic criticism now fashionable. Yet much the same complaint could be made of George Crabbe, who, in the age of Wordsworth, contributed nothing to the literary revolution of the time; for all that, Crabbe remains a poet we cannot ignore. And this is the case with Campbell, who is not to be fitted in as

a neat cog in the machine which future literary historians will inevitably construct and label 'The Development of English Literature in the Twentieth Century'. As Robert Graves has warned: 'Literature is a cumulative tradition: authentic poetry is a number of unrelated events, or poems.' That Campbell was an authentic poet there can be no doubt; that he was an 'unrelated event' will probably bother posterity less than his contemporaries. But, in another and more intangible sense, Campbell exercised an influence extraneous to the actual body of work he left behind him. As Vernon Watkins has pointed out, 'he maintained a singularly consistent role as inspired campaigner and champion of the under-dog', and, like Dr. Johnson, Campbell was in the habit of championing what he considered the real, rather than the obvious or currently fashionable under-dog. Further he affirmed, in his life and in his work, the validity of the poetic vocation, its serious character and its morality of delight, in an age when its existence is either denied or, by pedants and cultural organisations, polluted by various subtle and well-meant forms of standardization and commercialization. 'There are no substitutes for morality, honour, and loyalty, either in themselves (as we are so painfully learning) or as the substance of poetry.' In this sense Campbell was a Don Quixote whose courage and valour were dedicated to a vanished ethic, and whose values only seem comic or insane in the measure that the world is debased.— David Wright, *Roy Campbell*, 1961, pp. 42–43

Roy Campbell is another poet of a now unfashionable kind whose approach to the world is through his senses and emotions, and one should add emphatically his passionate will, rather than his intellect. He was notable among poets of his time for a strict traditionalism of form and of vocabulary, only mitigated (but more often in his satires than in his 'straight' poems) by expansiveness and a vigorous use of colloquial expressions, especially army slang. His rhetoric had more in common with early French and English romantic poets—with Victor Hugo and Byron—than with ⟨the⟩ complex and allusive diction of modern poetry. . . . His descriptive imagery, when he writes about zebras or wild horses on the Camargue, has a vividness of colour, a dash and directness that again might remind one of the Romantic period, of great painters of the exotic, like Delacroix. In his more strident and garish moments one remembers Keats's snarl at Byron,

>   . . . large self worshippers
>   And careless Hectorers in proud bad verse.

He was able to write in this romantic-pictorial-rhetorical tradition without affectation, because he did not really belong to the modern world of great grey cities, but rather to the traditional pastoral communities which still survive, if only precariously, relatively undisturbed on its edges. Born in South Africa, Campbell lived an adventurous life as cowboy, fisherman, farmer, hunter, soldier, in many parts of the world, before being killed about ten years ago in a motor accident in Portugal, where he had finally settled. He was apt to exaggerate his own pastoral simplicity; he had also been to Oxford and had shared a flat in London, at one time, with Aldous Huxley. He was a learned man, and an excellent translator of verse and prose from French, Spanish, Portuguese, and Provençal; but he had learned these languages by living and working among the people who spoke them rather than out of dictionaries.

. . . He liked the common man, especially the soldier, and when he was once asked in a questionnaire in what ways he differed, as a poet, from the ordinary man, he wrote: 'In nothing at all . . . in which, however, I differ very much from *the ordinary poet.*' He had a strongly combative temperament, which was at once his strength and his weakness. He has, as a poet, wonderful vigour, wonderful 'go', but everything he writes is very much in one tune, and his rapidly moving verses never slow down, as those of Yeats and Eliot and Graves do, to a halt from which we can take in his whole landscape. Campbell presents himself dramatically, as a figure in action, in conflict with others, but if the man on horseback (*Talking Bronco* was the title of a post-war volume of poems) has any doubts or worries, they are not communicated to the reader (except, sometimes, very indirectly, through a certain stridency in the assertive tone). A lack of inwardness and the concentration this brings breeds hardness. One of Campbell's most striking lines is 'I learned to inflict and suffer pain.'

In spite of his Christian beliefs, there are few passages in his poems which suggest that he had learned to inflict or suffer forgiveness.—G. S. Fraser, "The 1920s," *The Modern Writer and His World*, 1964, pp. 287–89

Works

Roy Campbell's *Selected Poems* appear in his fifty-third year and offer themselves as a sort of retrospective show that might accurately be billed as Three Decades of the Muscle Man. No poet writing in English has equaled Campbell's violence, though Robinson Jeffers must be entered in the competition. None has presented a mind—to me at least—more despicable, a mind compounded of storm-trooper arrogance, *Sieg Heil* piety, and a kind of Nietzschean rant sometimes mixed with a ponderously uncomical sense of satire.

The center of that mind—and of its poetic style—is all sledgehammers. It would be comforting to one's sense of liberalism to report that the result is all merely thud-thud. What must be reported instead is that the sledgehammers are sometimes magnificent as in the description of a dawn seen in the eyes of Campbell's magnificent Albatross:

> Then through the gloom wherein, like tiny spiders
> Webbed in their flimsy rays, the systems spawn,
> Up dim blue rocks of cloud, with scarlet fibres,
> Crawled the gigantic lichens of the dawn.

But if this adulation of brute splendor shines as a magnificence in the physical world, the same muscularity applied to human orders becomes a disaster. No poet in English has come nearer composing the entire litany for the storm trooper—the mystique of the superman, the paean to muscular arrogance, even the sentimental piety of the romantic thug. So, in the Dedication to Mary Campbell, the poet is described as born of his own disdain, emerging from the rabble to live by sterner laws and a god superbly stronger; he is plotted against and hated by the small ones, is murdered at last by their leaden blows, but dies trailing his scorn and knowing that in death the Valkyrie will descend to him.—John Ciardi, "Muscles and Manners," *Nation*, Dec. 10, 1955, p. 515

I am all for simple, sensuous and passionate utterance. I am sure Racine had a good idea when he read his stuff to his cook and rejected what she couldn't understand. I think *The Bible in Basic* reads just fine, although I still prefer the King James. But this is not the verse of William Barnes, or Toulet, or Robert Frost, or whoever you like who writes simply. It is doggerel. It is not conscious doggerel, of the type Goethe or Heine once wrote, and Mr. Auden sometimes uses so skillfully today. It is just plain doggerel. Not even like Robert W. Service (a much better poet with somewhat similar tastes in life if not in politics). What distinguishes it is its persistent, insistent ill-temper.

This has given Campbell a reputation as a satirist. To most vulgar people, Pope sounds like doggerel, and abuse sounds like satire. But this just means that there are a lot of people in the world like Roy Campbell—a lot of very coarse-grained people with tin ears. They just haven't worked it out in a political theory and they don't have a facility for rather clumsy rhyming, but there are lots and lots of people every bit as vulgar. Ill-temper is not satire. Ill-temper is not "savage indignation." As you can learn in any manual of the seven sins from a tract case, righteous wrath is not the sin of anger. Rocking-horse couplets that go bump at the end are not "skillful verse in the great traditions of English Poesy." You can't learn that in any manual. In the long run it requires sensibility to tell Campbell from Kipling.—Kenneth Rexroth, "Poets, Old and New" (1960), *Assays*, 1961, p. 226

The many love poems in *Flowering Reeds* and the poems deriving from natural scenes all show the effects of Campbell's careful blending of imagery and thought in a way that is not common in English poetry. It is only the metaphysical poets who use a similar technique and who develop their conceits with as much rigour, while Blake's symbolic imagery in poems like "The Sunflower," "The Sick Rose," and "London" has an even greater effect of simple yet universal suggestion than Campbell's symbols. His interest in conceits and symbols is not derived from the metaphysical poets alone, however. French poets such as Baudelaire, Rimbaud, Apollinaire, and Valéry are, by his own account, the central influence on his technique. This influence on *Flowering Reeds* is marked. . . .

In *Flowering Reeds* the number of short poems built around a central conceit illustrates Campbell's deep concern for technical restraint. Although all the short poems stand on their own as original works, the fact that the volume contains so many suggests how strenuously the poet was striving for control in many short pieces which are almost exercises in precision. His repeated turning to French sources and models shows too how far his interest was from current English trends or issues. The timeless quality of *Flowering Reeds* is remarkable for a poet in whose three previously published volumes are included *The Georgiad* and *The Wayzgoose*. Although he continued to experiment with symbols and images after 1933, he never recaptured the extended mood of lyric ease which is embodied in the volume he published that year.—Rowland Smith, "The Provençal Poems," *Lyric and Polemic: The Literary Personality of Roy Campbell*, 1972, pp. 103–17

GEOFFREY STONE
"Roy Campbell: Romantic Paradox"

The American Review, December 1936, pp. 164–76

At a time when half our poets speak so cryptically that they are not understood even by the critics who enumerate their obscurities, and when the other half seek to identify themselves with the voice of the subhuman creature to which industrialism has degraded the workman, Mr. Campbell declares:

> I will go stark: and let my meanings show
> Clear as a milk-white feather in a crow
> Or a black stallion on a field of snow,

and declares it on horseback, wearing a broad-brimmed hat. His posture is certainly the stock romantic one, but he is worthy of notice because he has invested it with vigor and even with dignity.

Now the romantic posture is intrinsically one of defiance toward society, though everyone join in it and grow weary in its stance. But Mr. Campbell is defiant of the latter-day romantics who surround him; he takes the position of the forebears to belittle the descendants. He began with the customary bourgeois-baiting and exaltation of the poet:

> Lashing his laughter like a knotted scourge,
> A poet of his own disdain is born
> And dares among the rabble to emerge. . . .
> (*Adamastor*, 1930.)

He has found, however, that the great public are not the only ones who cannot "learn to look on beauty unashamed"; the self-appointed intellectual élite are in no wise better, perhaps even worse, for they profane the shrine they profess to serve. Doubting them, he has examined sceptically their intellectual premises, and in the end rejected most current notions, to establish himself on a groundwork of ideas decidedly classical in view of the frank romanticism of his own poetry. The disparity between critical ideas and poetic practice is fairly common in an age whose prevailing sensibility often runs counter to the strictest logic. Messrs. Eliot and Wyndham Lewis have both been accused of this failing—unjustly, I think—and Mr. Campbell is an ardent follower of the second. In the case of Mr. Campbell, where the disjunction seems actually to exist, a personal explanation is perhaps to be sought; and this seems justified for the "I" of his poems is plainly to be identified with a young South African who lives in Provence and earns his living by fishing and bull-fighting. . . .

The collapse of the industrial-capitalist world is a frequent theme of Mr. Campbell's poetry, especially in *Mithraic Emblems*. Here again the romantic posture of defiance serves him well, and the cowboy seated upon his horse hears the voice of the rails speaking:

> From fog-red docks, the sink of rotting drains,
> Where, tipsy giants, reel the workless cranes:
> Where in dead liners, that the rust attacks,
> Sprung decks think back beyond the saw and axe,
> And masts put on the green of country lanes. . . .
>
> These tons of metal rusting in the rain
> (Iron on strike) are singing one refrain:
> Let steel hang idle, burning rust devour,
> Till Beauty smile upon the face of Power
> And Love unsheathe me from the rust again. . . .

In a number of other poems in the same book, Mr. Campbell repeats that steel will be delivered from rusty industrialism to flash again as the blue Excalibur of courage, gold will escape from the usurers to glow as the metal of beauty.

Mr. Campbell, it should be evident by now, is also a poet of honest hate. "A hater is always a lover too. Hate belongs to the same quality of appreciation as love. Nobody who does not hate can love." The last sentence remains equally true reversed, and in defense of what he loves Mr. Campbell has written some vigorous satire. His two longest satirical poems are *The Wayzgoose* and *The Georgiad*. The Wayzgoose "occurs annually in S.A. It appears to be a vast corroboree of journalists, and to judge from their own reports of it, it combines the functions of a bun-fight, an Eisteddfod, and an Olympic contest." To Mr. Campbell it is the occasion for a furious rout of the "counter-jumping" intellectuals of Capetown and Durban. *The Georgiad* revolves around a hero called Androgyno, who is reminiscent of Mrs. Woolf's Orlando, and of fifty other literary figures in England who exist off paper, if not with

much more reality. Androgyno's adventures result in satire of a strength and accuracy that only Wyndham Lewis (in another medium) equals today. Mr. Campbell employs the couplet of Dryden and Pope, and, as a careless though naturally very gifted craftsman, must suffer by the comparison, but he does convincingly show that satire is not in need of new forms to preserve its vigor; once more he suffuses the traditional forms with life by the very vitality of his own belief and shows that, while it is something consciously imposed from without, form is dead if it is not a reflection of the spirit. His satire, indeed, I would rank above his lyric pieces; but, given a poet of varied talent, it is perhaps inevitable in an age of numerous and conflicting standards that his satire should prove superior to other forms of verse, allowing as it does a greater didactic content by which to indicate its intellectual bias and straiten the interpretation to be set upon the poem's meaning. The intellectual nature of satire makes it depend less than the lyric upon words from which a common emotional response is expected. . . .

Mr. Campbell has a lot to account for on the debit side. His verse is plainly written in haste, and speed is a worthier attribute in the arena than in the muses' garden. For all his facility in language, he is apt to repeat too often a good phrase, as when in three different poems a train at night is found stitching the world with threads of fire. His scorn of the unworthy at times degenerates to mere bravado, bringing in its train statements that are not poetry but noisy rhetoric. Relying on a romantic intensity of feeling rather than a classical balance of form to sustain his poems, his verse too often tends to collapse under its own weight, or dissolve in the mind after the first impact of its rich imagery has passed. He has imposed his own rhythm on a fairly regular iambic line, but not always with that imagination which can convert a standard meter into something peculiar to a single poem. His emphatic rhyme is not without monotony, and to achieve a rhyme he will on occasion resort to stratagems that even Browning would not have condoned. As a result of all this, his verse is distressingly uneven, and will descend from a pure and perceptive lyric note to he-man swashbuckling. These things, of course, are consequent upon his romantic posture: though he inveighs against those who gaze into mirrors, his own verse bears too little testimony to interior discipline and partakes of the fitful nature of the moment's inspiration, with the inevitable attempt to justify the work simply because it is something personally and deeply felt. Yet in balancing the ledger, the ultimate figures must be on the credit side, I believe, and the reason, paradoxically enough, is romantic and personal. For the small residue of fine poetry that is to be found in Mr. Campbell's work comes, as it were, out of his native sanity, uncorrupted by our dominant industrialism and the morbid intellectual fashions it breeds. From his pose of romantic defiance has grown his defiance for all that originally supported that pose, and his vision of the poet as the lonely wayfarer seems to have led him back to the haunts of men.

Perhaps it is invidious to say that Mr. Campbell's promise remains yet to be fulfilled, but he himself has pointed to the direction his talent must take if its athletic exuberance is not to end in exhaustion. If "conscious power, privilege, and authority" are to be re-established in society, imposing their lawful dictates against the renegade by force when necessary, there must exist in the new society an élite which willingly submits to a similar discipline, rigorously applying it from within, and the poet who expresses the spirit of that aristocracy will by the example of his work show the wisdom and beauty of such restraint.

BERNARD BERGONZI
"Roy Campbell: Outsider on the Right" (1967)
The Turn of a Century
1973, pp. 198–202

In addition to Catholicism and French neo-classicism, another important influence on Campbell was his friend, Wyndham Lewis, painter, novelist and critic. Lewis was a subtler and more complex figure than Campbell, and attempts to describe him as a straightforward apologist for fascism go wide of the mark. Lewis was always seeking a hierarchical static society, in which art could flourish; and although he writes approvingly of fascism in *The Art of Being Ruled* (1926), he also shows himself very sympathetic to the Soviet approach; they both had the virtues of being ordered, elitist systems, in contrast to democratic untidiness. In 1930—three years before the Nazis came to power—Lewis published a book praising Hitler, which he subsequently repudiated, and although he never cared for what he saw as the comic-opera elements in Italian fascism, he adopted for a time in the mid-thirties a thoroughly pro-Axis position, seeing the European fascist powers as 'have not' nations struggling for a place in the sun against the joint hegemony of Soviet Russia and the Western democracies. This was a short-lived position on Lewis's part, as Geoffrey Wagner shows in his masterly study of Lewis. But it was at this point, corresponding to the outbreak of the Spanish Civil War, that the ideological alignment between Lewis and Campbell seemed to be most intimate.

The two men had been friends since the early twenties, and in 1930 they collaborated in a pamphlet, *Satire and Fiction*, which Lewis published when the *New Statesman* refused to print Campbell's enthusiastic review of Lewis's huge satirical novel, *The Apes of God*. There are several admiring references to Lewis in *The Georgiad* and *Broken Record*, and Lewis returned the compliment in his novel, *Snooty Baronet* (1932), where there is a portrait of Campbell as 'Rob McPhail', a South African who lives in Provence and works as a fisherman and bullfighter; he is described as 'one of the few authentic poets now writing in English', and Geoffrey Wagner has called McPhail 'perhaps the first thoroughly sympathetic character Lewis had created in his satire'. Lewis seems to have given a faithful account of Campbell's way of life in the south of France in the early thirties, although he is fairly derisory about Mithraism and tauromachy, which Campbell took very seriously. Campbell and Lewis had a common inclination to the politics of neo-classicism, as expounded by Lewis in such books as *The Art of Being Ruled*, *Time and Western Man* and *The Childermass*, and a deep contempt for egalitarianism and the flux and relativism of a debauched democratic society which overturned all hierarchical distinctions. Campbell praised *The Apes of God* for its stress on the 'masculine intellect' as opposed to 'the sentimental idealisation of "youth" for its own sake, of the feminine in the male, and the male in the feminine, the romanticism of the negrophilist . . . ' In the 'Author's Note' to *Flowering Rifle* he echoed this sentiment when he condemned the humanitarianism which 'sides *automatically* with the Dog against the Man, the Jew against the Christian, the black against the white, the servant against the master, the criminal against the judge'. Even though Lewis was not an exclusive intellectual influence on Campbell, he undoubtedly helped to give a particular articulation to Campbell's existing ideas and attitudes.

In 1936, soon after his escape from Toledo, Campbell compared Lewis in a letter to the defender of the Alcazar: 'Intellectually, you are Moscardò to the whole of Europe . . . ' In his reply Lewis wrote: 'I gloried in the title of *Moscardò*. You may rely on me to behave on all occasions in a manner no way inferior to that of the "Eagle of Castile".'[1] A few months later Lewis published *Count Your Dead: They are Alive!*, a vigorous apologia for Franco, which denounces the alleged pro-Soviet leanings of the Western democracies; it seemed that Lewis and Campbell were united in upholding a position which—outside Catholic circles—had few intellectual defenders in the English-speaking world. Nevertheless, their positions were to diverge before long. Lewis's later development makes it clear that his fundamental attitude to politics was very different from Campbell's, as the latter was ruefully to discover. Although Lewis was extremely interested in politics and wrote copiously on the subject, his basic criteria were aesthetic rather than social or ideological: he was primarily concerned with the kind of society in which great art could be produced, and he was prepared to abandon political and ideological positions according to his latest assumptions and insights. After his support for fascist nationalism in the thirties, he swung completely in the opposite direction during the Second World War and declared himself in favour of total internationalism and what he called 'cosmic man'. Lewis liked to present himself as an unchanging, monolithic figure, stemming the flux of a sickly, time-bound romanticism, but he was decidedly volatile and inconsistent where particular political questions were concerned. Thus, although he was bitterly anti-Soviet in the thirties, after the qualified admiration expressed in *The Art of Being Ruled*, we find him praising Stalin in his war-time letters, then becoming anti-Soviet again with the growth of the Cold War in the late forties.

Campbell, by contrast, was massively single-minded, and throughout the Second World War remained convinced that communism was the major enemy, and that Franco's crusade had been a wholly just and noble cause. (He claimed that after the Yalta agreement he threw away his British and American medals in protest against the betrayal of Eastern Europe to Russia; at a public occasion connected with the Festival of Britain in 1951 he wore only his Spanish Nationalist medals, saying that they were the only decorations he could wear without a sense of shame.) He must have been dismayed at his friend's blatant shifts of opinion, as when Lewis wrote to Mrs Campbell in 1944:

> I was glad to hear from Augustus that he has exchanged his requeté uniform for that of the Home Guard. The best Catholic opinion now—and I speak from very near the horse's mouth[2]—is that the requetés were on the wrong side in the land of the flowering rifle.[3]

Lewis, on his part, must always have had doubts about aspects of the poet's *persona*. Since a distaste for 'action' was at the core of Lewis's aesthetic philosophy, we can assume that Campbell's determined immersion in the role of man of action did not greatly appeal to him (one recalls Lewis's scathing remarks about Hemingway in *Men Without Art* (1934)). It is certain that he was not very sympathetic to Campbell's religious attitudes, whether Mithraic or Catholic: in 1942 he wrote to Augustus John: 'It is really capital news that he has got out of Spain, where he was liable, because of his over-fervent papist nature, to get involved in all kinds of abominable nonsense.'[4] In the epilogue to Lewis's book of short stories, *Rotting Hill* (1951), there is a portrait of Campbell *in propria persona* which combines sympathy with a certain detached observation, producing an effect close to pathos (the account corresponds exactly with the present writer's recollection of Campbell at about that time):

> Roy Campbell passed and he raised his large coffee-coloured hat. He walked as if the camp were paved with eggs, treading slowly, putting his feet down with measured care. 'Tis his war-wound imposes this gait on him of a legendary hidalgo. He was followed by a nondescript group, some say his audience. I noted a poetaster, a photographer, a rentier, and a B.B.C. actor. He is the best poet for six miles or more around. But he suffers from loneliness I believe. He is like a man who rushes out into the street when the lonely fit is on him and invites the first dozen people he meets to come up and have a drink. He led his band into 'The Catherine Wheel'.[5]

Campbell continued to admire Lewis, although he made no secret of his disappointment at Lewis's post-war advocacy of internationalism and 'cosmic man'; in *Light on a Dark Horse* he wrote of Lewis: 'I gradually came more and more under his influence till I started generating ideas of my own, and he went "cosmic".'[6] In a long review of a reissue of *Tarr*,[7] Campbell wrote of Lewis's books with unrestrained enthusiasm, saying that although Lewis had now lost faith in Western culture, he had once been its most vigorous defender, and that Lewis's current attitudes in no way affected the value of such works as *The Childermass* and *Time and Western Man*. Here, as on other occasions, Campbell was trying to fit Lewis into his own frame of reference, with its sharp polarities. In fact, as Wagner has shown, Lewis could never have accepted a purely Maurrassian view of Western culture; his lifelong admiration for oriental art, for instance, would complicate such an interpretation. At all events, Lewis appreciated Campbell's review; he wrote: 'To find you still at my side is a matter of the greatest satisfaction to me: and I hope we shall always remain comrades-in-arms against the forces of philistia.'[8]

Notes

1. W. K. Rose (ed.), *The Letters of Wyndham Lewis* (1963) p. 239.
2. At this time Lewis was teaching in a Canadian Catholic college.
3. *The Letters of Wyndham Lewis*, p. 374.
4. Ibid., p. 338.
5. *Rotting Hill* (1951) p. 302.
6. *Light on a Dark Horse*, p. 224.
7. *Time and Tide*, 7 July 1951.
8. *The Letters of Wyndham Lewis*, p. 543.

JOHN POVEY

"The Making of a Poet: *Adamastor*"

Roy Campbell

1977, pp. 88–90

Through the years in which he had been writing *Adamastor*, between 1924, when the first of these poems was written, and 1930, when the collection was put together, Campbell was developing a lyric gift that was unmatched in the contemporary English tongue. I do not think this is too excessive a statement. No one else had achieved this vivid, virile note, this authoritative power, coupled with the sensitivity to sensory experience. Everything appeared to suggest that this man was going to be a new force in English poetry, an invaluable antidote to the prettiness and etiolated intellectualism which had so filled the style of poetry at this particular period. On the one hand, T. S. Eliot had made his own revolution by

asserting that the nonpoetic could be the substance of poetry, that the damp souls of housemaids were as appropriate a subject for poetry as the women breast-high amid ripening corn, and that the scenes of slum evenings in the "Preludes" were as suggestive and impressive as the views of the Lake District had been to the earlier Romantics. Campbell came with his own revolution which, as it turned out, appeared to be an antagonistic one, but could well have been coupled with Eliot in introducing a change in English poetry. Campbell was asserting the possibility of sensual vehemence, of intensity for a poet, but not deriving this from the shallow and falsely poetic excess that had cluttered the remnants of Victorian verse. Campbell was trumpeting that it was possible to create a new and modern poetry which did not have the dry, prosaic, deliberately conversational flatness which was the calculated basis of Eliot or Pound's style.

The significant point is that at this time Campbell could have brought to English poetry a new vision. It is not for nothing that most revolutionary British poetry of the twentieth century is entirely the product of foreigners, often themselves living in exile. The major names are Yeats from Ireland, the Americans T. S. Eliot and Ezra Pound living in London and Italy. It is this non-Englishness which permits change because it allows their vision the detachment of internationalism. They were not trained in and therefore restricted by the excessive power of the great tradition of English poetic forms and styles. Such new, clear, intense voices from younger countries could make their vital revolution simply by speaking their own international voice, the voice of their own lands. They affected a revolution in English poetry almost unintentionally by being themselves rather than attempting to conquer any particular fortresses of English literary styles.

Here was a direction for Campbell to take. It was in one sense the road that Eliot had chosen. This is not to pretend that Campbell was even at this stage in his poetic career as potentially significant as Eliot. It is equally true that nothing that Campbell ever wrote could equal the power of "Gerontion" or the social impact of *The Waste Land*. Nevertheless, theirs was an identity; in Campbell too there was a new voice. If he could have been true to the intellectual ideal, the clarity of his African vision, then his success as a poet would have been assured, and through this success his influence and prowess would have been recognized and admitted. Unfortunately, many dominion poets from new lands come to the mother country, in the same way as people from parochial and minor areas of this nation go to the great metropolitan center, New York. Such travelers bring with them this same sense of the inferiority of their own environment, the sense that somehow they must adjust so that they can become part of the literary scene, or react in a grieved display of petulant bravado. In doing either, they deliberately and willingly forego the authentic freshness of vision which they should maintain and should cherish as the antidote against being swamped by the pressures of the conventionality of the literary fashion of the time. Campbell himself, in fact, did not allow himself to be swamped or changed directly by the disparagement which, to his anger and humiliation, he met with from the leading literary figures in the English Georgian movement, but his reaction drove him to write poetry of shrill satiric excess. It allowed him to dissipate his talents, quarreling and feuding with the minor literary figures which he should have had the good sense to ignore as being unworthy of his concern or interest. It also led him to take more and more virulent stands, both in his political and intellectual beliefs, and more specifically, in the poetry which he wrote, straining to gain the effects which would more than ever shock and dismay the poets whom he despised.

PAUL VINCENT CARROLL

1900–1968

Paul Vincent Carroll was born on July 10, 1900 in Blackrock, Ireland. His father was a school-teacher, and Carroll prepared for that profession at St. Patrick's Training College in Dublin from 1916 to 1920. It was the time of the Irish Rebellion and the Abbey Theatre, and Carroll became involved in both. In 1921 he left for Glasgow, hoping to teach without Church restraints, and did so for the next sixteen years. In 1923 he married Helena O'Reilly, with whom he had three children. He kept up contact with the Abbey, which produced his short play "The Watched Pot" in 1928. *Things That Are Caesar's* won the Abbey Theatre Award for 1931, and ran on Broadway the following year.

Carroll's greatest success came in 1936 with *Shadow and Substance*, a sharp satire on the Irish clergy. The off-Broadway production in 1938 won the New York Drama Critics Circle Award for Best Foreign Play, as did *The White Steed* the following year. After that, Carroll wrote a number of somber, symbolic plays that were equally disliked by critics and audiences. The exception was *The Strings, My Lord, Are False*, a 1942 drama of wartime Glasgow that became a hit in Dublin but not in New York. In 1943, Carroll founded the Glasgow Citizen's Theater, which occupied him for much of the decade.

Carroll had a burst of activity in the mid-1950s, commencing with his 1955 whimsical fantasy *The Wayward Saint*. In 1956 he dramatized the life of Jonathan Swift, his greatest influence, in the BBC teleplay *Farewell to Greatness*. His last play, *The Devil Came from Dublin*, produced in 1958, was another fantasy. Paul Vincent Carroll died on October 20, 1968.

General

The sombre fact that Eire's attitude to the recent world conflict was as of something remote and no direct concern of hers, has had a regrettable effect on her literature in general and her dramatic art in particular. It would hardly be an exaggeration to state that she has already entered on an alarming eclipse of letters that may well last for more than a generation, or at least until such time as she wisely decides to readjust herself to Britain, America and the new Europe that is emerging out of ruin and chaos. Her golden literary age has passed for the time being. It lasted from about the turn of the century until the disastrous death of W. B. Yeats in 1939.

During that splendid period, Eire led the world in dramatic achievement, challenged the artistic supremacy of the Moscow Art Theatre, won the unstinted admiration of her ancient enemy, and had a profound influence on the growth of the young American theatre. Behind these great victories was the artistic driving force of the Anglo-Irish tradition, in which the best of both stocks combined, without serious rancour, bigotry or petty blood feuds, to produce a dramatic literature that was intensely Irish, and yet profoundly international in its implications.

All that is now a glowing memory. Since the death of Yeats, the whole theatre movement has been in retreat, and the once famous Abbey Theatre has shrunk into a barn theatre of petty dimensions, haunted by the ghosts of the great figures whose portraits adorn its vestibule. Her artists and her brilliant actors are now either under the clay with Yeats or scattered over the globe, and like Lycidas they have not left their peer.

It was felt and hoped by all that the coming of Irish freedom would have meant a new and glowing lease of life for Irish dramatic art. There were numerous problems to be solved from within—all waiting for vivid dramatisation, and many external problems too that could be dramatically resolved in the glowing terms of the native art. There was in particular the problem of Eire's attitude to the Europe she had helped to civilise, now at bay before the German and Russian *diktats*. But to the dismay

of all, the reborn nation turned sulkily inwards, closed her frontiers to foreign thinking, looked askance at the remnant army of her artists, allowed her highly insular clergy, who persistently cold-shouldered everything in art that is not pietistic, to multiply their influence, and imposed on all writing a savage and senseless censorship.

The dramatic art was exempted by the official censors— probably with a cynical smile, for they knew they could successfully curb any iconoclastic playwright by the strong unofficial censorship of the clerics and their pious henchmen throughout the country. To illustrate how narrow and prejudiced this unofficial censorship can be, I may point out that one play of my own authorship which received on its production in the Art Theatre in Rome superlative praise in the semi-official organ of the Vatican, the *Osservatore Romano*, has been forbidden production in at least six little theatres in Eire by local clergymen who presumably have no objection at all to the subtle and glamorised pornography of American films. I point this out not as a personal grievance but as an indication of the crippling handicaps that confront any Irish playwright who dares to interpret what Yeats called "the wrong of unshapely things", or dramatically opposes the parochial ego of what A. E. prophesied would be "a smug peasant republic".

There can be no doubt whatever that the Irish leader, Mr. de Valera, had cast-iron arguments to justify his much-maligned policy of neutrality during the world war. The melancholy history of the nation would alone have made neutrality inevitable. But, as Bernard Shaw contended in his denunciation of Hitler, the greatest crime of a government is to fail to protect the artist from the swarms of petty-minded men around him. In this category, the Eire government fell far short of the Shavian axiom, for it delivered the Irish creative artists in literature and drama—or caused them to be so delivered—up to official and unofficial censorships, condoned the disastrous and retrogressive policy of the Abbey Theatre Directors by threatening to withdraw the miserable subsidy if a purely Gaelic policy were not rigorously enforced, looked upon native artistry more as a nuisance and a hindrance to the popular ego than as the only mature conception of nationhood, and connived at the deliberate destruction of the Anglo-Irish tradition in drama. In short, the day threatened that Yeats foresaw with "public life moving from violence to apathy, Parliament disgracing and debauching those who entered it, and men of letters living like outlaws in their own country".

This sorry state of decline and fall which still exists in Eire, and is in fact bound to worsen, has not given us any dramatic work of major importance, and this is not surprising. The new degenerate Abbey sternly rejected the work of the young iconoclasts and played safely with minor productions that steered clear of the clerical and national taboos. The Abbey audience, now bereft of its intellectual coteries, and composed mostly of courting couples, pious suburbanites and Gaelic language snobs, guffawed its way through kitchen comedies, watered-down revivals and domestic provincial dramas that skimmed discreetly over the evils and corrupt practices that had eaten into the moral, aesthetic and artistic potentialities of the nation.

But the more serious dramatist, whose premier function is to swim resolutely against the current of mass opinion, got a poor deal indeed, and some of them, those who did not escape abroad, turned to journalism, politics or the law. An honourable exception is George Shiels, who has over the years carved out a niche that is peculiarly his own in Irish drama. This charming writer of rich comedies is the Irish prototype of the Quinteros in Spain, or more accurately still, of the English Eden Philpotts. He is an expert in his dramatisation of the foibles and drolleries of rural characters, but although his comedies are reinforced with thinly veiled satire, he skilfully avoids major issues or controversial themes and is well content to gain limited objectives. His play, *The Rugged Path*, which deals with the Irish chronic weakness for smuggling and evasion of the law, drew crowds to the Abbey Theatre over many weeks during the war, and his new play, *The Caretakers*, currently running at the Abbey, which satirises the native amoral attitude to wills and land settlements, looks like adding fresh laurels to his comic genius. . . .

. . . ⟨G⟩enerally speaking, at the present time, two years after V Day, Eire cannot be congratulated on the state of her creative drama. All of it is cast in a minor mould and deals with minor themes. Frustration, pietistic snooping and sterility have temporarily marred its genius, and the unhappy playwright, flanked on all sides by taboos that he longs to smash, either conforms and writes within the narrow canons of his masters, or yields to the temptation to go abroad and carry his genius into lands where the censorious is trimmed to a healthy minimum and the writ of liberalism still runs freely in spite of privation and short commons.

To redeem the Irish drama and restore it to its former eminence, the native Irish playwright must again turn outwards to a critical examination of foreign dramatic thinking, with the essence of which he will impregnate his own native interpretations.

He must swim against the popular mass ego, despite the most strenuous opposition; he must, while bidding great and good luck to the new Gaelic drama, demand the restoration of the Anglo-Irish theatre, and he must free the once famous Abbey Theatre from the death grip of the political doctrinaire, the mere pietist, the oaf who takes his girl to eat chocolates in its stalls, and pernicious government patronage.

But tomorrow will not see these achievements. Nor the day after.—Paul Vincent Carroll, "The Irish Theatre (Post-War)" (1947), *International Theatre*, eds. John Andrews, Ossia Trilling, 1949, pp. 122–28

Carroll has portrayed a number of priests sympathetically, and his treatment of various types may be a key to his philosophy and to a theme recurrent throughout his work. That theme is the need for tolerance, for a feeling heart, and for understanding of individual needs. In *The White Steed* he contrasted two kinds of priests. In that play an old canon, who has lived close to the village and developed a live-and-let-live philosophy, is faced with his successor, the fanatical Puritan bent on turning the town inside out. The old canon finally triumphs and defeats the reformer in the name of humanity and tolerance. In *The Old Foolishness*, the local priest is an example of entrenched authority, intolerant and callously conventional. But the priest that tries to shelter the slum dwellers of Clydeside during the blitz, in *The Strings, My Lord, Are False*, is of heroic nature. His heart goes out to all kinds of people—a Protestant, a Jew, a radical, or a prostitute. In *The Wayward Saint*, the St. Francis-like canon is almost trapped by his own vanity, but he is warm-hearted and humane—if child-like. While his portrait is sympathetically satiric, by now one recognizes that Carroll is having a kindly chuckle at human and priestly frailty, and is again affirming our universal humanity.

The Wise Have Not Spoken presents a priest who raises another problem. The play is one of several that display, as stated, a strong feeling for the proletariat. Its meaning, at first, might seem ambiguous. A family is trapped on a poverty-stricken farm near the northern border. Faced with a hopeless future and eviction by the bank, they react in different ways to the situation. One member, a violent young Communist who has fought in Spain, is determined to defend the home with his gun. Contrasted to him is a boarder, a priest who has been "silenced" for attacking authority. Throughout the play the priest argues that man's future is not through change by force but through spiritual change. He tells the young revolutionary: "I see a greater republic than yours, Francis—it is the republic Christ envisaged." He is, however, a broken man. The Communist dies valiantly defending his home; the priest is killed as a rather pathetic bystander. As there is a good deal of vitality in the young man's characterization, one might at first wonder where his sympathies are supposed to lie, with revolutionary or priest.

But the speeches of the "silenced" priest concerning non-violence, on closer study, seem most earnestly meant, and there is further evidence of Carroll's views: *The Old Foolishness* also portrays a revolutionary who has lived by violence. He has fled the police, and his mistress, a golden-haired girl "with a wistful, shadowy personality," comes to his family's farm; there she ends up being adored by his brothers when she brings a moment of romance into their plodding lives. She eventually rejoins her lover and is married to him—but only after he has rather abruptly renounced his gun and developed a sense of humanity.

Proletarian though some of the plays are, they do not seem to me essentially to urge any definite social or political change; the change must be in man's feeling for his fellows, his inner values. Carroll once wrote of himself: "Since coming to maturity, I have had no political opinions. I like a system of government that leaves me alone to do what I want to do, so long as I conform to the ordinary natural laws. . . ." The "silenced" priest says to the revolutionary, "Are you not old or bitter enough to realize, Francis, that the government is the least important thing in the nation."

In remarking that the current Irish theater is dominated by the plays of Behan and his school, Carroll states that none of the work of this school has "beauty of language or the inspired emotionalism that makes a theatre *magnifique!*" Inspired emotionalism is more easily desired than attained, but this statement may suggest a quality that Carroll attempts to inject in his plays. It may take the form of angry sympathy for human suffering, or on the other hand open romanticism. In *The Old Foolishness* the local lads repeatedly hearken back to the exploits of Finn and other giants of pre-Christian Ireland in their dreams of fabulous individualism as an escape from the confines of modern life. The headnote to *The White Steed* and references in that play show Carroll's admiration for the deeds of Ossian, heroically riding through the land of little men. His stress, however, in regard to this romantic individualism, is upon a person's courage and refusal to kowtow.

In spite of his glorification of pagan folklore, Carroll says his faith is in the Christian ethic. While this gives further importance to the words of the "silenced" priest in *The Wise Have Not Spoken*, Carroll, judging by his plays, seems to think of the Christian ethic primarily in social and humanitarian terms. The sympathetic priests in his plays do not display any great interest in doctrine, and his work as a whole seems religious only in the broad sense of affirming humane values. Though he is obviously sincerely religious, Carroll seems to be more a man of strong feeling than one of doctrine or theory.

Satire of authority, and glorification of the free spirit are certainly not peculiar to Carroll's work in the Irish drama. Satire of the priest goes back at least to Synge's *The Tinker's Wedding*, and both elements appear through the later work of O'Casey. The difference as it appears to me, however, is that Synge's comedies contain little except satire—little compassion or sense of the individual. When Synge wrote serious drama, he was so concerned with writing formal tragedy that he reduced interest in his characters as individuals. In O'Casey's later work, the plea for the free spirit of the individual often seems either linked with a desire for proletarian solidarity or secondary to his bitter attack on his target. On the other hand, much of Carroll's work, while not showing any particular orthodox religious bent, displays a deep concern for the individual as an individual, and affirms the need for respect for many kinds of people. This affirmation, even with pre-Christian reference, does not seem incompatible with the Christian ethic and can easily be read in its terms.

It is this affirmation that lends warmth and dignity to Carroll's plays. Much criticism of the Irish drama has fallen in recent years into a stereotype, concerning itself too exclusively with the well-known. The same few plays continue to appear, and some of these have rather special appeal. As a result, interesting, if not always major work by other writers is being forgotten or not noted. It seems time possibly for a reappraisal, at least for another look.—Drew B. Pallette, "Paul Vincent Carroll—Since *The White Steed*," *MD*, Feb. 1965, pp. 378–81

Carroll has called himself "an enemy of photographic realism," but his enmity resembles his enmity toward the Church. He has never really cut the apron strings of Papa Ibsen, and he seems to realize that fact: he once wrote, "All my life I have had in me two irreconcilable crazes—my rigid insistence on the inviolability of the fourth wall, and on the other hand my almost overwhelming longing to cross the stage with the tabs in my hand, opening them as I go and say to the audience, 'Sit up now, folks, we're ready.'" Unfortunately, he never did allow himself such freedom; his deviations from realism have been only tentative excursions into fantasy, mysticism, and satire.

There had been hints of mysticism in *Shadow and Substance* and in *The White Steed*, and Carroll turned to fantasy in the alternately sad and funny one-act *Coggerers* (later retitled *The Conspirators*). This fine tragi-fantasy is set in the entrance hall of a Dublin library on Monday morning of Easter Week, 1916. In the hall are busts of Irish patriots—Mitchel, Lord Edward, Wolfe Tone, Emmet, and Parnell—and the busts speak as characters in the play, acting as a chorus for the big drama outside and for its microcosm inside, the death of the charwoman's son. Few plays in such a short space arouse such a moving and various body of emotions as this thoroughly successful little piece does.

Coggerers, despite Carroll's irritation with the theatre, was performed at the Abbey on November 22, 1937, as was his next long play, *Kindred*, which appeared on September 25, 1939. *Kindred* contained some elements of fantasy which were so unsuccessful that Carroll removed them on the second night. Still, the play failed in both Dublin and New York, where it was slated by some of Carroll's warmest admirers. It was his last play at the Abbey, and it has not been published.

The Old Foolishness, produced on May 7, 1943, at the Arts Theatre, London, is unlike those usually associated with Carroll, and might well be compared to O'Casey's late plays. Like them, it celebrates life, vigor, and beauty. Its realism is softened by a more romantic tone than can be found elsewhere in Carroll; even the comic speeches have an O'Caseyan lilting exaggeration. For instance:

Dan: . . . And did ye hear her tellin' Peter her mouth was for kissin'? Man, I dream of a fine lovely woman sayin' that to me! "Dan, me hero, take your face out of me scented hair, and crush me mouth." . . .

Tim: . . . You were born too far west, Dan.

Dan: So I was. Fastin', prayin' and bein' respectable, and the oul' foolishness buried in pagan ground. It must have been grand in the oul' days when ye lay back and said to your woman, "Dance, yous lovely divils, dance, or I'll chop your heads off."

By his Old Foolishness, Carroll meant that same vigorous pastoral past that O'Casey used as a touchstone of the good life. And against the Old Foolishness, Carroll pits some of the same adversaries—the narrow, life-quenching morality of the Church, the stony ideals of embittered patriotism, the dull safety of an arranged and loveless marriage.

The character who arouses the Old Foolishness in the men is Maeve McHugh, another of Carroll's women on a pedestal and his best girl's part since Brigid. In Brigid, he conveyed saintliness and simplicity; here he tries, pretty successfully, for romance. However, as in O'Casey's later versions of pastoral, the idyl is shattered by the modern world. The neighbors and the inevitable canon disapprove of the carryings-on, and the last scene is a dying fall that movingly makes Carroll's point—which is that the Old Foolishness must be caught on the wing, for it has no place in modern Ireland. The play's greatest fault is its length. If about ten pages could be judiciously cut, there would be little to criticize in this sadly humorous play. It is a pity Carroll did not explore this vein further.

Instead, the bombing of Glasgow deflected him into *The Strings, My Lord, Are False*, which was followed by a piece of grimly serious realism, *The Wise Have Not Spoken* of 1944. In the savagery of its theme, this play harks back to *Things That Are Caesar's*. Intending the play as a cutting criticism of Ireland, Carroll mentions the heavy hand of the Church, grasping politicians, emigration, and even the Rising and the Troubles. This time the good priest is a silenced priest, an outcast. The home of the MacElroys, the scene of the play, is an embryo Ireland from which much of the love and all of the beauty have fled. Though Carroll's points are fairly taken, some of the characters are so exaggerated, and the story is so intensely melodramatic, that the theme seems overstated. It is a black play whose theme might be summed up in Father Tiffney's speech:

> Laws, laws, laws. The modern Deity, the stop-gap of idiotic men. Christ made only one law—to love one another. It's not laws we want in this country, nor taboos, nor censorship—it's love, knowledge, dignity, an understanding of each other, a supernatural meeting-point as old as time, not a tower of Babel where fools, puritans, and scoundrels shout each other down. . . .Just look at this place—a warping, killing crookening rat-trap where the human mind and spirit are driven mad.

"—a warping, killing crookening rat-trap where the human mind and spirit are driven mad" is as savage an indictment as one might find outside of Swift, and this whole play seems impelled by a raw irascibility. The serious characters, Francis and Catherine MacElroy, both seem livid cries of pain. Francis, representing idealism reduced to violence, spends his time cleaning his gun and crying moodily for blood. Catherine has some strongly plausible moments toward the end, but mainly she is a thin symbol of sexual starvation and guilt. Though strong characters, both are exaggerations; the play is too bleak and black to be either good theatre or convincing statement. Still, it does give an insight into Carroll as a man neither completely housebroken by conventional morality nor ever completely emancipated from it.—ROBERT HOGAN, "Paul Vincent Carroll: The Rebel as Prodigal," *After the Irish Renaissance,* 1967, pp. 57–60

Works

You have to turn to the Irish for such a play as *The White Steed* or a proper production of it. Joxer in *Juno and the Paycock* had a name for it. It's a "darlin'" play, not in a saccharine or silly way, but "darlin'" in the sense of winning the heart by its eloquence, its radiant faith, its humanity, its rollicking humor, its wit and turmoil, and in the proud fiery manner of its breathing, in the oppressive air of this sorely troubled world, tales of legendary heroes who have never died.

As in the case of *Shadow and Substance,* Paul Vincent Carroll has written in the best Celtic tradition a play which is not only a drama in its own right but an allegory of Ireland. Once again his subject is a major problem of his country advanced in terms of a conflict waged within the Church itself. This time Mr. Carroll's pivotal character is not a proud aristocrat of the cloth, out of touch with his rough curates and his ignorant parishioners. He is Canon Matt Lavelle, a wise, lovable, peppery old codger who, paralyzed though he is, manages to triumph over the inhumanity, the rigid Calvinism, the committee of moral vigilantes, and the other snooping and coercive methods of such an essentially un-Christian force as Father Shaughnessy represents.

Out of this battle, fought in such a favorite setting of Mr. Carroll's as the living room of a Canon's Parochial House in County Louth, emerges a fable which, more than speaking dramatically for Ireland, has its unmistakable bearing upon the struggle men of good will are fighting everywhere at present against men of evil will.

What also emerges at the Cort in the person of Mr. Carroll's heroine is a rebellious maiden restoring the pride of the servile schoolteacher who falls in love with her. He has been brave only in his cups. Her bravery is nurtured on dreams of her country's ancient glories. As Niam did for Ossian in the days before the Christian Era, when Ireland was peopled with

mighty warriors and the land had not come to teem with a race of little black-haired men, Mr. Carroll's heroine makes room for her schoolteacher on the white steed she rides.

To synopsize Mr. Carroll's new play is to make a script, at once simple and effective, sound like the fuzziest of fuzzy allegories. It is to lose sight of the gaiety underlying its overtones; to ignore the pungency of its dialogue; to fail to indicate the compassion with which its meaning is pointed; and to overlook unfairly some of the characters Mr. Carroll has drawn with genuine skill.

Above all, it is to forget Mr. Carroll's wisdom as a dramatist. He is a propagandist, attacking egotism, persecution, and cruelty, who knows and avoids the dangers of "raving" and "raging." By his own confession, he is well aware of what he has described as man's "love of this battered imperfect thing called life." In the presence of a serious subject he does not forget the curative and persuasive powers of laughter. No wonder that in last Sunday's *Times* he could write with affection of the Aristophanes who is "still laughing," of Boccaccio and Rabelais still dancing, of Voltaire's "grand guffaw that still blows up the Seine and over the tops of Paris," and of Chaucer who "still goes roaring down to Canterbury." Mr. Carroll is himself a merry sage. His laughter, like his humanity, is a proof of his sagacity, even as *The White Steed* is a proof of how much he has grown in authority as a dramatist since he wrote so good a play as *Shadow and Substance.*

If he still has difficulty in establishing his young lovers, if he cannot quite make us believe in their affection for one another, or if once in a while his machinery creaks, if some of his village snoopers remain no more than broad types, Mr. Carroll, nonetheless, shows he is a man who can write from his heart and set ideas spinning in dramatic form. His dialogue is rich with all the music and wit of his race. Moreover, when it comes to his drawing of Canon Matt Lavelle and Father Shaughnessy he works with a master's skill.

The two performances of the evening which are unforgettable are George Coulouris' brilliant and unsparing playing of the detestable Father Shaughnessy, and Barry Fitzgerald's Canon Matt Lavelle. That very mortal saint, the Canon, may be a surefire part. Although from the certainty of his appeal he may seem the *Abie's Irish Rose* of stage clerics, Mr. Fitzgerald does not content himself with letting the part do his work for him. Dodging the obvious, he brings all his unction and his skill to giving a performance both lovable and memorable.—JOHN MASON BROWN, "Ireland and *The White Steed*" (1939), *Broadway in Review,* 1940, pp. 205–8

Apart from its skill in construction and the tremendous chances it offers to the actors—how I wish I could see that Canon through the eyes of Arthur Shields, and the Brigid of Phyllis Ryan—*Shadow and Substance* has for me the strange charm of half-familiar things. I know so well those healthy, jocular young priests. I know the very smell of the Canon's house with its rigid austerity, its reproductions of Spanish masters, the iron-blue mountains through the window, the smell of turf fires, and clean linoleum, and gravy on Sunday mornings. I know, too, his niece Thomasina, and the house she comes from. I know every virtuous peeping window in the little town with its hilly main street, and the problems of its inhabitants—for this is a play that is choc-a-bloc with problems. The very dishes that appear on the table in the Canon's house are enough to start off a whole new series of letters to the *Evening Mail* on the thorny subject of Irish cooking. The Canon's niece, Thomasina, is the perfect type for all time of the desperate and, to me, quite unfaceable problem of the country-girl who has become what we in the Gaelic League call Anglicised, what the West Briton would equally unfairly call Americanised, what her own neighbours would, I fancy, call simply foolish, and what in actual fact is unendurably cheapened, tedious, and embarrassing, the price we pay in the twentieth century for being able to buy diamond brooches at fourpence, and Outdoor Girl lipstick, food value guaranteed, from stores where all goods may be bought from the shelves.

Shadow and Substance, indeed, hits very hard at our worst faults, and what is alarming is that all these faults are not only recognisable to an honest Irishman, they are characteristic, and are to be met everywhere with startling frequency. The glaring defects of ignorance, sluttishness, bigotry, contrariness, are all here, together with that peculiarly typical and exasperating trick of deliberate, self-conscious, arch, unblushing, brazen, whimsy, sickening, prudish, presumptuous affectation of innocence, purity, childlike playfulness of heart, that astounding glorification of incompetence, and that ghastly "Sure I'm hopeless, but amn't I irresistible?" attitude with which every dweller in Ireland is familiar, and which to me is our one claim to utter and everlasting damnation. Not, mind you, that I think it necessarily a virtue in a writer to discover only the blemishes in his country-people. Indeed, the only fault I have to find with Mr. Carroll is the fact that, with the exception of a possibly over-idealised portrait of the little girl, there is not a soul in the play that presents what one might call the brighter side of the

Irish character. One feels there is no defect in us that is not obvious to Mr. Carroll, no scar or blot that we can hide from his far-seeing eyes. There are only two people in his world that he loves, and he has shut them up in a tragic house, in a circle of storm-ridden mountains where they live, the man dreaming of the clear-cut, grave, and courteous life he has left behind in Spain, the little girl dreaming of a flame, a star, a face, of something that fills her days and nights with ecstasy and drives her mad with loneliness. And all around are enemies—the other people, the ordinary ones. They are curiously like childhood's bogey-men, these people that never come on to the stage in *Shadow and Substance*. They are large and ungainly, and loud in their speech and heavy in their gait like the Philistines of Schumann's dream. No, Mr. Carroll doesn't like us *en masse*, so to speak. Who shall blame him indeed? All those years in Scotland, even, seem not to have revealed to him the irresistible quality of our charm, that lovely rainbow sheen as of Waterford lustre of shot silk in which we specialise, and which is known in all the leading establishments (head office Killarney, Co. Kerry) as the tear and the smile. Perhaps, however, one has to live in England to really know all about Irish charm. I have lived there a great deal, and I still have a firm belief in tear and smile. And better men than I have succumbed.— MICHAEL MACLIAMMOIR, "Problem Plays," *The Irish Theatre*, 1939, pp. 209–11

JOYCE CARY

1888–1957

Arthur Joyce Lunel Cary was born on December 7, 1888, in Londonderry, Ireland. At age nineteen he studied art in Edinburgh and Paris, where he issued a book of poems in 1908. He graduated from Trinity College, Oxford, in 1912, then fought in the Montenegrin Army in the Balkan War. He chronicled the experience in *Memoir of the Bobotes*, which was published posthumously.

Still longing for adventure, Cary joined the Nigerian political service in 1913. He became strongly opposed to colonialism in the process, publishing *The Case for African Freedom* in 1941. While serving with Nigerian troops in World War I he met Gertrude Ogilvie, whom he married in 1916. After the war they settled in Oxford and had four children. In 1932 he published the first of four books set in Africa, *Aissa Saved*. The last of these—*The African Witch* (1936) and *Mister Johnson* (1939)—attracted critical plaudits, as did the semi-autobiographical *A House of Children*, published in 1941. It won the James Tait Black Memorial Prize the following year.

Encouraged, Cary began the ambitious trilogy that made him famous: *Herself Surprised* in 1941, *To Be a Pilgrim* in 1942, and *The Horse's Mouth* in 1944. The latter became a best-seller, and was filmed in 1958. Each of the three major characters in the trilogy narrates one book, commenting on the other two characters from his or her own perspective. The first trilogy dealt with art; the second (*Prisoner of Grace*, 1952; *Except the Lord*, 1953; *Not Honour More*, 1955) dealt with politics. Cary completed only the first volume of a third trilogy with a religious theme, *The Captive and the Free*, in 1959. All three were designed to interlock in a grand nine-book structure.

Gertrude Cary died in 1949. That same year, Cary refused a CBE, explaining that the Crown should not be a judge of art. He did accept an honorary LL.D. from the University of Edinburgh in 1953. Three years later he delivered the Clark Lectures at Cambridge, which were collected, under the title *Art and Reality*, after his death on March 29, 1957.

General

Joyce Cary's most striking characters talk out loud, sometimes about themselves, but more often of life in general; and we learn from them as we learn about garrulous strangers met at a party, piecing together a rough impression of what they are

from the clues they let fall. Mr. Cary's method of character-drawing is not, however, consistent; of the important books, *Mister Johnson* is told quite objectively, without comment, in the third person; in *A Fearful Joy* the same basic method is used, but the impression given is that the narrator himself is a marked personality, never in the centre of the scene and within the action, but certainly standing just within the proscenium arch. In the trilogy, *Herself Surprised, To Be a Pilgrim* and *The Horse's Mouth*, first person narration *in character* is employed; these are Mr. Cary's histrionic books, giving the effect of three sustained *bravura* performances by an actor of superb confidence. In *Herself Surprised* it is Sara who speaks, the bonny, roseate, amoral cook who will inspire the painter Gulley Jimson, live with him and haunt his old age; in *To Be a Pilgrim* it is Mr. Wilcher, the disreputable, rather mad old gentleman who cannot be trusted in Hyde Park, but has a genuine love for Sara and would have married her, had not his relations intervened; in *The Horse's Mouth*, Mr. Cary's masterpiece to date, it is Gulley Jimson, the rowdy, randy painter, with the vision of a Blake, and the social conscience of a Charley Peace. They are set to talk; talk themselves into ecstasies and the sympathetic reader into a kind of fuddled and rapturous half-comprehension. Yet elsewhere the reader is allowed to see each in a different and more objective light. Sara's idea of Gulley is not quite Gulley's idea of himself; and Mr. Wilcher's self-explanation softens our original impression, given in *Herself Surprised*, that he is simply a dirty old person who would be better off in a home.

Now Mr. Cary's great gift is his visual sense; he is constantly enraptured by physical beauty, by the radiance of the natural world and the astonishing harmony of unrelated objects brought into relation by accident. It was either M. André Breton or Mr. Salvador Dali who remarked upon the fortuitous loveliness of a sewing machine and an umbrella upon a dissecting table. Mr. Cary's joy is in the unexpected pattern; for him, life is a delightful jigsaw liable to rearrange itself in an infinite number of ways, and to startle his eye with an infinite number of shapes and colours. Therefore, his best characters are those that see the most; which explains the success of Sara and Jimson, both creatures of extraordinary visual capacity, and the relative failure of Mr. Wilcher, whose interest lies in the peculiar and always unexpected working of his own wits.— PAMELA HANSFORD JOHNSON, "Three Novelists and the Drawing of Character," *ES*, 1950, pp. 89–90

It has been general critical comment that English fiction in the 1950s has shown a very high average level of technical intelligence, but that it has not produced masters: the novelist as great man, as oracle, sage, or prophet, as lonely dedicated artist, of the type of James, Conrad, Joyce, Lawrence, seems no longer to exist. The trick or device of the successful contemporary novelist is to seem a limited person, sensitively at sea and intelligently bewildered, like oneself. Some young critics, however, have seen a major figure in Joyce Cary, a retired colonial Civil Servant who published his first novel in 1930, after retiring from his job in Nigeria because of ill health. Cary was a man of unusual generosity and range of mind, a range which comes out in *Art and Reality*, a very fine set of meditations on the art of the novel, written on a slow and painful death-bed. He had thought seriously about politics, about religion, about art, about the truths of personal and social relationship. He wrote his most successful novels in trilogies, covering a series of events in turn from the points of view of three main characters concerned in them, and with each character impersonating not only a way of speaking and of seeing, but a philosophy of life. He wrote his original drafts at enormous length and then selected from them just enough material to cover, in sections, a life story. This method of dramatic impersonation (one model is the Defoe of *Robinson Crusoe* and *Moll Flanders*) had certain disadvantages as well as potentialities. A late novel, *Not Honour More*, purports to be written by a retired colonial administrator and soldier, Captain Jim Latter, when he is in jail awaiting execution for the murder of a Liberal politician who is a rascal and a lecher but also a man of genius (Cary was probably thinking of Lloyd George). Captain Latter personifies the bitterness of the ex-officer out of a job, with no real purpose in life, after the Great War. He is the type who would have become a supporter of Sir Oswald Mosley. He thinks and talks in conventional officers' mess phrases. He is rather proud of *not* trying to analyse his own loves, resentments, and angers. He has a streak of deviousness; he is not *only* a plain, blunt man, but also partly somebody acting, and a little over-acting, that part. He gives in the end an impression of staginess, as, to me, does the much more famous Gulley Jimson of *The Horse's Mouth*. I lived in Chelsea for more than ten years, and met lots of bohemian artists, but never one like Gulley going out on all four cylinders all the time. I never met one, either, who could quote Blake's prophetic books, *ad lib.*, and in fact it is my experience of painters that they have a rational distrust of being articulate and have a double attitude to literary men, surprised that the words come out so easily, but distrustful about seeing behind the words. If you wished to deride the book you would say that Gulley Jimson was a cinematic conception, if you wanted to praise it up you would say he was a poetic conception. I suppose that these impersonative novels of Cary's worry me because I start off reading what I think is going to be a realistic story and then discover that it is a moral fable. I think Cary may well be one of my blind spots, like D. H. Lawrence; but it is a different kind of blind spot; I feel the moral size of the man and yet the novel does not seem an adequate vehicle for it. The technique, after all, of the impersonative novel is a very primitive one, that of Defoe's *Moll Flanders*: it throws the task of adding irony, of making fine moral discriminations, on the reader; it runs the risks of monotony, undue repetitiveness, a lack of real suspense, a narrative structure of a string of similar episodes, all illustrating one not very complex character. One respects Cary, but one does not feel that he was a 'master' in the old sense.— G. S. FRASER, "The Novel in the 1950s," *The Modern Writer and His World*, 1953, pp. 166–67

Even if I do decide to go on with a book I may drop it at any moment in the first six months. And these novels themselves grow out of sketches and notes made at odd times which are not meant to turn into anything. They are made like a painter's, for my own interest, and most of them are never used—in fact, the majority are lost. But when I want to write a story or novel, I browse among the old notebooks and always find something of interest. I don't think I've ever begun a novel right off, from scratch. All my published books have been based on stories or notes that have been lying about in notebooks or jackets for a long time.

A Fearful Joy began from a story of a young girl who went to a dance and could not get any partners, a truly fearful position for any girl. She was, in fact, rather plain and prim, and a step-mother without taste had dressed her in a very unbecoming frock. Also her family had not had the sense to make sure that she went to her first dance with friends capable of seeing that she enjoyed it. They were busy with other things that seemed to them more urgent. No one in fact had been unkind to the girl, the point was simply how much young people can suffer, simply because no one of taste or intelligence happens to be about to give their sensible help and advice. Her failure at the dance was simply a piece of bad luck. . . .

I don't know why I abandoned this story but, years later, when I wanted to write a novel with a background of economic change and dealing especially with the role of the imaginative man in business and in invention, I remembered it. One of my characters in the novel was to be an ambitious young man, full of ideas for making a fortune and I said, 'Why shouldn't the young man at the dance be a man of enterprise and imagination looking for some capital to start his schemes? And this would suit me down to the ground because the girl in that story is a decent girl with decent standards but not much imagination and therefore not much grasp of the world in which she has been placed. She has never realised, for instance, that freedom itself, the free creative mind in action, means an everlasting revolution, everlasting change. She belongs, that is, to the kind of person who cannot accommodate herself to change, who begins to say in middle age that the world is going to the devil.' We all know the academician who says that art is finished because people don't like his pictures any more, or the critic who says the novel is finished because he doesn't like any novels written later than those he read about forty years ago. This nice, intelligent decent girl belonged to this type and would bring in just the right element of contrast to the lively imagination of the man. . . .

Another book of mine, or rather a whole trilogy, the last trilogy, dealing with the political scene in this same world of the imagination, began in a dialogue between two women, written in a notebook, I rather think somewhere in a train. There were two women, one called Aunt X and the other Niece Y. Niece Y has been proposed to by an ambitious young man in the village. She has refused him, she takes the whole thing as a joke and tells the Aunt about it. But the Aunt says, 'You are a very silly girl, that young man is going to have a future and you haven't got any future as you are. You think you are so pretty and clever but your looks aren't going to last and your cleverness is simply in amusing yourself and dodging responsibility. As you are going now you will make a complete waste of your life, but that young man would make something of you and give you a real career. What's more, he is very fond of you and will never let you down if he can help it.'

I had no recollection of this dialogue or when it was written; I say it was written in a train only because there were some notes next-door in the same notebook about cloud effects and field colours as seen from a train behind the jump of the telegraph wires, but it turned up while I was browsing among various notes and I said at once, 'Here is a good situation for my political novel. The ambitious young man will be my politician, the clever girl shall tell the story. What's more, since she does not love him and is pushed into marriage with him by Aunt X, she will have on her hands a real political job, in handling a husband so different from herself in ideas, in character, and in taste.'

Now this is important to my idea, because all human relationships have what I can call a political aspect, they have to be managed. Every lover, every parent, knows that, and if you listen to children in a nursery you will hear them entering into political relations with each other all day long. One says to the other, 'If you leave my horse alone, I won't knock down your fort.' Here you have an elementary social contract and we all know how much questions of justice and its opposite, special consideration, both crop up every day in handling children. I wanted in my political trilogy to have a completely political atmosphere, both in domestic and social relations; both in politics, strictly speaking (that is to say, the politics of my politician), and also the politics of marriage and the nursery. And the germ of them all was in that little piece of dialogue which stopped in the middle, which had no explanation or description to it, and which had not even developed into a short story.

Of course, a vast number of notes have never had any use and most of my stories and novels have never been finished.

Some of them have a beginning and end, but no middle; one, about artists, ran to about thirty thousand words and has most of the big scenes written or sketched. It could easily be finished in a few months. And it has a fascinating subject, the revolution of taste, of what is called fashion. It shows the old academician in a rage at what he calls the cult of ugliness, that is to say, of an art that he doesn't understand and couldn't understand if he tried. It shows the young artists studying abstraction under a modern master and quite convinced that every other kind of art is out of date. And it shows the indignation of their master the abstractionist at this new fashion just beginning to appear of pictures that are far from abstract, pictures like Francis Bacon's, pictures that tell a story. True, a new kind of story. But what a shock to all the schools for fifty years back—especially the abstractionists. And the Victorians themselves are coming back. Even Frith of 'Derby Day'. Yes, Frith. People will soon be collecting Frith and paying big prices for him. And artists who think themselves modern today will find themselves right out of date. For the trouble is that artists live much longer than artistic fashions. So that you often have about three generations of artists all furious with each other and despising each other's art, and only united in rage and hatred against the very latest school.

All artists live in this world of the revolution of taste—in fact, we all live in it and it affects us all. It is always producing new ideas in art, or industry or politics, and breaking somebody's heart; and very often ruining him and his family on top of that. And it's never going to stop. Even Russia is moving, Russian writers want to write something new, Russian women want the new fashions. . . .

Of course, that world, as I see it, is not merely a flux of senseless change. Underneath all the turmoil there are certain fixed and permanent things too. In daily life there is always affection, family love and responsibility, ambition, the things people really live for; and on the other hand you have always the same anxieties, loss, bitterness, and danger, the everlasting dilemmas of life. And so, in spite of changing fashion, the great art of the past in our galleries is still great: it expresses something that is eternal and not subject to fashion at all. Fashion is simply a new way of saying an old thing, of putting over something important that has been overlooked and forgotten.— JOYCE CARY, "Unfinished Novels" (1956), *Selected Essays*, 1976, pp. 111–15

> Although I did not know it, how could I, my mind was split . . . And until I had made a reconciliation I could not even write dialogue. I had no religion, no integrated ideas of the world. I believed vaguely in God and I believed vaguely in science, but I had never seen the need to reconcile the mechanism of the scientific idea and the free creative soul of the world.

To understand Cary's ideas and appreciate the argument of his novels . . . we need to reflect on the implications of this statement. For Cary seems to be saying that this opposition of Science to God and of Mechanism to Freedom constituted his most important source of spiritual and intellectual uncertainty. If, indeed, he was able to write fiction only after he had resolved this conflict—'made a reconciliation', as he put it—then Cary's specific conclusions in his individual novels and in his other writings would in some important way be related to that original dichotomy between Spirit and Matter, between Necessity and Freedom. It is not, therefore, simply a matter of recognising the place of the imagination or the recurrence of the ideas of freedom in Cary's work as his critics have sometimes tended to do, but of giving these ideas their full philosophical status and of accepting that a total world-view is derivable from them. It is certainly one implication of Cary's own statement that he believed the reconciliation he sought would resolve the philosophical and aesthetic problems which he would encounter in writing fiction.

Fortunately, it is not difficult to place Cary's task in relation to the ideas of earlier philosophers, especially Kant. Indeed the problem which Cary was trying to resolve for himself was the same that Kant encountered when he wanted to reconcile the *necessity* of classical philosophy with the idea of the *freedom of the self* enjoined by the practical reason. As Copleston has put it, Kant's philosophy was an 'original attempt to solve the problem of reconciling the two realms of necessity and freedom, not by reducing the one to the other, but by finding their meeting-point in the moral consciousness of man'. This reconciliation is, in fact, derived from the empirical philosophy of Hume as revolutionised by the transcendental criticism of Kant. In so far as man's existence is subject to time-conditions, Kant argued, his actions form part of the mechanical system of Nature and are determined by antecedent causes. That is *necessity* or mechanism. Rebelling, however, against empiricist mechanism, Kant argued that 'the very same subject, being on the other hand conscious of himself as a thing-in-itself, considers his existence also in so far as determinable only through laws which he gives himself through reason'. Kant's solution came in the form of a paradox:

> It does not involve a contradiction to assert on the one hand that the will, in the phenomenal realm (of visible action), necessarily obeys the laws of nature, and to this extent is not free; and on the other hand, that, as belonging to a thing-in-itself, it is not subject to such laws and accordingly is free.

Cary phrases his in a similar vein:

> The creative soul needs the machine, as the living world needs fixed character, or it could not exist at all. It would be merely an idea. But by a paradox we have to accept, part of this fixed character is the free mind, the creative imagination, in everlasting conflict with facts, including its own machinery, its own tools.

In Kant, then, Cary found his own answer to those 'scientific' philosophies—of Darwin, Nietzsche, Spengler, Freud and Marx—which were, in a sense, parallel to the Newtonian 'mechanism' of Kant's time. Man needed a 'spirit' to counteract the supremacy of matter; a transcendental 'God' to challenge the material God of the scientists. Moreover, God may be dead, in the sense, according to Nietzsche, that Science has triumphed and made Providence unnecessary. But a universe without a unifying principle parallel to the moral will of man, or to God, would be a meaningless and absurd one. In Kant, Cary found a philosophy in which the 'truths' of human freedom and the existence of God, though not scientifically demonstrable, are introduced as 'implications' of the moral nature of man. When Cary was asked by the *Paris Review* interviewers whether he was a 'determinist', he answered pointedly:

> Everyone but a lunatic has reason for what he does. Yes, in this sense I am a determinist. But I believe, with Kant, that the mind is self-determined. . . . Of course, anyone can deny the freedom of the mind. He can argue that our ideas are conditioned. But anyone who argues so must not stop there. He must deny all freedom and say that the world is simply an elaborate kind of clock. He must be a behaviourist.

There is no alternative, in logic, between behaviourism, mechanism, and the personal God who is the soul of beauty, love and truth.

In a way, Cary's novels are his own way of giving expression to this philosophical position within the framework of art. Cary was himself very reluctant to embrace the title of 'philosophical novelist'. 'I have been called a metaphysical novelist, and if that means that I have a fairly comprehensive idea of the world I'm writing about, I suppose that's true'. And also: 'I do not care for philosophers in books. They are always bores'. But these statements do not amount to a rejection of philosophy. As Cary himself put it, his novels aim at a kind of truth which 'is not to be grasped, any more than any other kind of reality, by the brain alone, in contemplation, but only by a combination [of] thought and feeling'. Whereas the philosopher's job is to 'make sense of life to the mind', it is the novelist's to make sense of it 'to the senses'. Yet, in *Art and Reality*, in reflecting on 'the mind-body gap which all idealist philosophers and mechanists are eager to get rid of', Cary argues that 'even to our experience', this gap is not 'fixed' but 'varies from individual to individual and continually shifts'. And again: 'The individual mind appears to itself cut off from the general real except in so far as it can intuit that real'. In these statements, Cary is clearly offering a significant alternative proposition to both the idealists and the mechanists. If these propositions also inform the fiction, they will not appear explicitly in an occasional situation or dialogue, or directly as independent disputations, but will condition the interpretation of situation, character and even structure.—MICHAEL J. C. ECHERUO, "Ideas," *Joyce Cary and the Dimensions of Order*, 1979, pp. 3–5

Works

THE FIRST TRILOGY

The basis of Anglo-Irish writing is intoxication, from Somerville-Ross to Shaw and from Shaw to Joyce onwards. It is also experimental. The experiment consists in exploding a strong personality among traditional material. The business of experiment, these writers seem to say, is to adapt. So when Sara (in the *First Trilogy*), the garrulous West Country cook, tells her tale with her ready words and her twisted mingling of prudery, honesty and sly lechery, she is really an adaptation of *Moll Flanders*:

> Miss Rodwick was a good soul. She would bring me daffodils and tulips, and if they were the short ones or the little ones, as Miss Slaughter said, why should I poison a gift with looking beyond it, especially in the country where, God knows, a bad thought about a neighbour is as good as grease in your soup. Miss Rodwick gave many a start of pleasure and asking nothing in return. . . .

Sara is Nature herself, unscrupulous, untidy; and yet she is more than Nature, for she has faith. It is in all the dominant Cary characters. If she is inclined to overdo herself, in a literary phrase—for she has a touch of Irish literariness—she has a sort of soul which confidently, if deleteriously moves on in its earthly pilgrimage. The moving-on is everything. We are to see her through the eyes of her other lovers, in *The Horse's Mouth* and *To Be a Pilgrim*, and when one of them accidentally kills her by pushing her down the cellar steps, she is (as always) capable of one more revelation. She has (she realises in a moment of naive wonder, excitement, even of satisfaction) been murdered! She has had one more earnest of the mystery of love and life.

The Horse's Mouth is the most popular of Mr. Cary's adaptations. It is adapted from Smollett, crossed with Surtees and Somerville-Ross; it has none of Smollett's ambiguous attitude to physical disgust and is applied to the unlikely subject of an artist's life and ideas. The trilogy seeks to cover the complete spiritual life of the period. The farce and fantasy of this book could hardly be thicker, but it suffers (as the whole trilogy does) from an excess of loquacious imagination. Mr. Cary's wonderful appetite and invention cannot stop themselves. And we are never quite convinced that Gulley Jimson, the raging old Bohemian crackpot, maddened by old age and in and out of every kind of roguery, is strong enough to sustain the theories of Blake which are splurged on the riotous pages. The saving thing in the book is Mr. Cary's continuous eye for picaresque circumstance and local character. Coker, the grim barmaid, always wronged by Nature, is a wonderful counterpart to Sara, now turned into a genial, boozing, humbugging and thieving old tart, lost in the raucous mythology of her memories and affections.

But Jimson—and this would be Mr. Cary's fundamental point—has faith. His starved broken body, his cracked mind, his immoral will, are ready to "go on" on their own. Guilt? Conscience? The devil? Sin? Between revelation and cunning, between holding his tongue and winking his eye and occasionally using his fists, this Protestant is sure he can get away with it and palm off a soiled soul.

This crucial question of faith is gravely and explicitly treated in *To Be a Pilgrim*, which suffers from an excess of commentary over incident, but which is an ambitious and important novel. Its object is to see the personal lives of a family over two generations, pre-1914 and post-1914, through the eyes of a man with strong political and religious intuitions. He is now an old, dying lawyer, an evangelical Protestant who believes "there is no rest for the soul except in the love of God and His Beauty and His justice, that man is condemned to be a pilgrim in an unexplored wilderness." A worried and solid old sinner who has been Sara's lover in his old age—she has been his housekeeper—he views in loneliness the rise of a hostile generation and fights tenaciously for self-interest and the old values. This novel is raised above the picaresque level of the other two by the complexity and seriousness of its moral conflicts, and it has the intricacy of reflected points of view. Mr. Cary is a master of movement back and forth in the novel. Through the unsteady mind of the angered old man he is able to put the past, the middling past and the present dramatically side by side; and the main business of the plot, which is to show the old man defending his property from the young whom he loves but disapproves of, enables him to keep the book firmly in the present. Old Wilcher's fight is sympathetically treated, for in his obdurate contempt for the free-loving and divorcing young, he has experience and time on his side. Mr. Wilcher's experience may be misleading, his beliefs may be reckless, irate, or irrelevant, but the character they come from has been toughened by introspection. He is a formidable and battered relic of property and faith; and it is all the better that he is an old lecher with romantic delusions, who has worried girls in the park.

An old man, of this moral interest, has not, I think, appeared in the English novel before, and certainly not in the novel of character. But Mr. Cary's achievement is to have done something to restore character to its lost place in the English novel. Here again, he has adapted. Character begins, for the novelist, where surprise begins, and Mr. Cary's surprises take the breath away. Mr. Wilcher's sister Lucy appears to be the conventional tomboy of the country house; suddenly she is converted to a vulgar hallelujahing sect, called the Benjamites, marries the womanising leader of it, plunges into religious masochism and makes a fierce spiritual life out of dreadful material. Edward, the brilliant political brother, rises the more he is ruined by debt and women, and fails as a Cabinet Minister in the Thirties because he is suddenly seduced by culture. The homely quarrelling Anglo-Indian couple begin as a pair of the conventional dullards of army life and end as comics. Amy's death, when she refuses the consolations of religion, is a wonderful scene ("I am going now, Tom. Yes, I think that's all—except oh yes—my summer dress at the cleaners"). The young alcoholics of the Twenties are, again, a surprise. And then, in the next generation, there is the trite niece, with her advanced ideas and her incompetence, who goes through her own obstinate transformation. Surprise is the road into human nature or the road round it; its aim, in Mr. Cary's rehabilitation of character, is to make character round. His commentary itself is never journalistic; it comes from a man who thinks on his own.— V. S. Pritchett, "Books in General," *NSN*, Oct. 24, 1951, pp. 464–65

THE AFRICAN NOVELS

Aissa Saved is dominated by Aissa, and I intend to consider her in due course, but there appears in that work no one man who can represent what always needs to be represented in a Cary novel—the creator, the artist, the revolutionary: the free man, making a free world for himself. But there are fragments of this man in the missioner Carr, who more than half stupidly but also kindly will impose a picture-book Christianity upon the Africans; in the District Officer Bradgate who plunges himself into the enterprise of building a bridge; and, above all, in the young African boy Ali who is en route by way of education to freedom. In fact, Ali was the germ of *Aissa Saved*. In the Carfax preface Cary records having known such a boy. He walked a hundred and thirty miles without sleeping, to help Cary make a map. This journey, which nearly killed the boy, was striking as "the effect of education on this rather shy and not very clever boy. . . . I was anxious to contrast Ali's standards and ideas with those above him. This, of course, involved questions of local ethics, local religion, the whole conflict of those ideas in a primitive community; and also the impact of new ideas from outside." But, in the course of writing the book, "Aissa gradually became the heroine because she was more central to a deeper interest, that of religion." Actually, I think Cary did not know how to handle Ali, who does not appear at all until nearly half-way through the book, and whose rôle is very small.

Ali, who is sixteen, is the son of the local Waziri—that is, the prime minister—and he has been to the government school. He explains to his fellow-countrymen who are anxious to make a sacrifice to the goddess of mountains and fertility, and who wish to put Aissa to death because they think she is a witch, that "witches had no power over rain which fell from the clouds when they were made cold, and besides all knew very well that it was a wrong thing to condemn anybody without a proper trial before judges." Ali indeed has his moments, but they are few. The most effective occurs at the riot, when he is reduced from a man of high moral dignity to a frightened boy. Ali will impartially save the life of a pagan as he has formerly saved the life of the Christian Aissa, because it is a matter of right; when he is struck down, he is so frightened that he crawls away saying, 'Don't tell them—don't tell them.' But Ali, sandwiched among some seventy characters in a very short novel, is given little opportunity to become more than a sketch for a portrait.—ANDREW WRIGHT, "The World as Character," *Joyce Cary*, 1958, pp. 77–79

In his work as magistrate, Cary felt all the attraction that the drunk and disorderly have for the sober and responsible. In the man who ran foul of the law Cary first began in Africa to recognise the maker, the free soul creating its own world with all the pain and delight of artistic effort. And he was to make this the main theme of all his novels.

It is clearest of all in *Mister Johnson*. Johnson thrusts aside legalities in the fulfilment of his dreams; Rudbeck, compelled to try Johnson while sharing his vision of the great trade road to Kano, in the end also defies the law in order to preserve Johnson's dream world and so, paradoxically, his freedom. Behind Johnson's dealings with Rudbeck lie several actual relationships of Cary's Borgu days. The clerk, Mr Graves, who was appointed to the Divisional Office a few months before Cary left, had none of Johnson's ebullience, but Cary was led to identify himself closely with him by the fact that they were the only two men of Western education in a vast tract of bush. Even when Mr Graves makes a mess of the accounts and calls down on himself some fearsome Irish imprecations, these are characteristically prefaced with 'I've found out Graves's chief fault. Like me—as you said once—he thinks he knows everything.' Much more was contributed to the Johnson-Rudbeck relationship by Cary's delight in Tasuki, the road foreman, who also appears under his own name in the novel.

A more complex relationship which helped to shape *Mister Johnson* was Cary's friendship with his political agent, Musa. He was an educated Moslem, somewhat cynical and effete by nature, whose handsome features were sketched in many letters. He and Cary worked in a close partnership until, in August 1919, Musa was accused of corruption. The affair which led to Cary having to try his closest associate was a Caryish blend of the ludicrous and the calamitous: it concerned the entitlement to a state umbrella, 'a dashed old brolly', which a minor chief was alleged to have obtained by bribing Musa. Musa got off for lack of evidence; but it seems that Cary was left with a lasting guilt about this intrusion into his political agent's sphere of enterprise, and 20 years later he dedicated *Mister Johnson* to Musa with the quotation 'Remembered goodness is a benediction'.

No word could be more evocative than this last of a time in Joyce Cary's career when, amid many vexations and frustrations, he wrote down in his diary that 'life is a birthday present'. In this, his African experience is in sharp contrast to Conrad's. Both novelists made a journey to the interior, but Cary found no horror. Rather, he discovered with delight his own creative freedom and the anything-but-peaceful coexistence of other Blakean freedoms in people like Tasuki, Musa and Lafia. Another ten years of reading and thinking were needed to define the discovery, and then Joyce Cary was ready to write what he himself termed the Comedy of Freedom.—M. M. MAHOOD, "Joyce Cary in Africa, 1913–1920," NSN, Oct. 1, 1960, p. 478

The African Witch is Cary's largest, most comprehensive African novel. He catches up, in a wide-ranging panorama, diverse specimens of both native and British life, in an effort to give the inconclusiveness of *An American Visitor* a less personal basis. "My book," he says in his preface to the novel, "was meant to show certain men and their problems in the tragic background of a continent still little advanced from the Stone Age, and therefore exposed like no other, to the impact of modern turmoil. An overcrowded raft manned by children who had never

seen the sea would have a better chance in a typhoon." It is very much a novel about an intractable continent, whose multiform problems are quite beyond the poor powers of its British managers and of its British-educated leaders like the young Rimi prince, Louis Aladai. Cary's panoramic ease of movement and range serve his purposes remarkably well. And the ambiguity of the swarming continent, the inaccessibility of saving truths, the scarceness of effectual sympathy inherent in Cary's subject make that subject an ideal one for his indeterminate vision. At the close, Africa sinks back unavoidably into its savage juju practices, every noble European aspiration having quite flickered out.

There is a considerable range of British inadequacy. The Resident, Burwash, is a bumbling, imperceptive official, terrified of taking a false administrative step or employing an unfortunate phrase in reports to his superiors. Much of the finest energy and passion of the Britishers goes into their games, polo and bagatelle, sometimes played, symbolically enough, when things to which they are oblivious are about to descend upon them. The stupid arrogance and racial bigotry of such younger Englishmen as Prince and Honeywood are repulsive, and, at the very least, tactically impossible for colonials. A streak of vicious racial hatred turns up, surprisingly, in one of the more sympathetically treated Britishers, Captain Rackham, though it has a sexual basis which is perhaps responsible for its intensity. In love with Judy Coote, a former don who is Louis Aladai's old friend from Oxford days, but finding himself more and more drawn to Honeywood's athletic and beautiful sister, Dryas, Rackham is in something of a personal turmoil. When he learns that the Anglophile Louis has been isolated in the bush overnight with Dryas and that they have been seen dancing, he attacks the young Rimi prince with his fists, thereby making necessary his own resignation from the colonial service. Judy Coote, for all of her learning, wisdom, and good will, is as little able to manage her relationship with Rackham as she is to realize her prescriptions for Aladai and the Rimi. Most regrettable of all is Dryas Honeywood's disastrously well-bred conscience. Her physical aversion to the Negro Aladai, because she is ashamed of it, compels her to be unnaturally kind to him. This strange debt to her dislike of Aladai misleads him where he is blindest—in his adoration of British goodness and graciousness—and precipitates his encounter with Rackham.

The Africans are certainly no better. Elizabeth, Louis Aladai's sister, for whom the book is named, is an imposing juju priestess who prevails against all her enemies and shows some signs of rather mystifying supernatural powers. But she is a figure of darkness and murderous ignorance. Aladai himself is a gifted young idealist eager to bring the blessings of European learning and art to his enslaved people; but he is a divided and ineffectual figure, torn this way and that by hybrid loyalties to England and Rimi. After Rackham beats him, all his intellectual and emotional refinement dissolves, and he sinks into the most brutal savagery under the influence of Coker, a native rabble-rousing preacher obsessed with blood and human sacrifice. Eventually, Aladai is willing to believe only in British betrayal. The other Africans are largely dominated by Elizabeth's juju, which, though a formidable force, destroys more easily than it either heals or creates.

Cary's effort to portray the chaos of African administration, the discrepancy between vast problems and infinitesimal human capacities, is notably successful. Africa is too much for everyone in the novel to grasp or control. In a world where confusion constantly proliferates and people, no matter how dedicated, or gifted, or assertive, constantly fail to master more than a few rudimentary subjective ideas, Cary is on his home grounds. Commitment would be out of place for him, the point of the novel being that commitments do not work in Rimi. There is not even any reason to believe that any figure in the novel knows very much about what has happened or about its implications.—ROBERT BLOOM, "The Uses of Irresolution," *The Intermediate World*, 1962, pp. 52–54

An American Visitor develops the theme of love and sacrifice explored in *Aissa Saved*. Marie's act of faith, when examined closely, is the obverse of Aissa's. Aissa sacrifices her child and herself for love of Jesus; Marie, unknowingly and involuntarily, sacrifices Bewsher to the concept that God is love. In an earlier version of the crucial scene Marie does not hide the pistol but takes out the magazine and gives the gun to Bewsher unloaded; she does it because, as she says to Bewsher, "You won't change now after all the years when you've never used violence. Don't you see that you're safer when you go as a friend when God's spirit is with you." Though these words are not used in the published version, they are implicit in the situation. Marie's sacrifice is as futile as Aissa's, but it arises from the same impulse of faith. Both Marie and Aissa are victims of events beyond their control.

What prevents Marie and Bewsher from being tragic figures at the end is that they are seen from the point of view of Cottee. For a moment Cottee is moved by the compassionate figure of Marie at Bewsher's grave and is transported by the scene "into another state of being, where men and women were born to heroic destinies, and life was the magnificent stage of their glories and their suffering." But "this fit of poetical fervour" dissolved "like a transformation scene," and Cottee thinks, "This ugly little woman a tragic queen, Monkey Bewsher a hero, it was absurd." Cary did not want to romanticize Marie and Bewsher, and Cottee's analysis serves the same function as Marlow's analysis of Lord Jim in Conrad's novel.

It would be a mistake, however, to view Cottee as Cary's spokesman. Cottee is no Conradian narrator analyzing the romantic temperament from the security of a rational code of conduct. As the representative of the new civilization, he is as vulnerable as Bewsher, who attempts to oppose the revolution, and Gore, who hopes to make peace between the two factions but who must eventually give in to change. Cottee rides the tide of change and thus wins over Bewsher. He triumphs (and profits) because the revolution triumphs: "how could any man hope to fight against it when it came with the whole drive of the world behind it . . . ?" His cynicism is revealed in his pity for men like Bewsher and Gore: "man only had one life and if he wanted to enjoy it he had better suit his taste to his times and not try to change the times to suit his taste." Although he foresees a new civilization evolving out of the ruins of the old with new values and new standards that "might take forms more austere and rigid than anything known to them," Cottee cannot see the point to the Russian story of the old lady who tried to save her beautiful cabinets and china and thus assured their being destroyed by the revolutionary soldiers. To him she is holding to outmoded values; the cabinets and the china are replaceable. He cannot understand that these particular objects are unique, are irreplaceable, no matter how many new things are made and created. He cannot understand the irony of the woman's attempt to save her beautiful things by appealing to the soldiers' nonexistent finer instincts—"What did she expect?" is his comment.

Cary has achieved a balance of forces among the various points of view in the clash of ideas. His is a Huxleyan detachment (the early Huxley, that is) rather than a Conradian commitment. It enables him to realize both the absurdity and the idealism of Marie's faith, the anachronism and the romantic

heroism of Bewsher's devotion to the Birri's cause, the ineffectuality and the humaneness of Gore's middle-of-the-road policy, and the vulgarity and the truth of Cottee's revolution. It is this ability to see all sides that enables Cary to explore the complex war of ideas and cultures with sympathetic detachment.

It is Cary's ability to portray contradictory ideas and views objectively and convincingly that Robert Bloom calls Cary's "indeterminateness," an "intellectual irresolution" that deprives his novels of a moral center. I believe it is more understanding of Cary's multiple view of reality to suggest that this empathic ability to submerge his own view of reality is related to Keats' idea of the negative capability: "A poet is the most unpoetical of anything in existence, because he has no Identity—he is continually in for and filling some other body." Thus, Cary portrays sympathetically the views of both the primitive Aissa and the emancipated Marie Hasluck, the evangelistic Carrs and the rationalistic Bradgate, the romantic Bewsher and the materialistic Cottee. And in *The African Witch* he presents convincingly all sides of the racial and religious conflict. Cary's "neutrality" in the war of ideas is not intellectual irresolution but is the objective detachment necessary in the novel of ideas with its contrapuntal technique of contrasting ideas and attitudes in dramatic conflict with each other.—CHARLES G. HOFFMAN, "There's a War On," *Joyce Cary*, 1964, pp. 23–25

Mister Johnson has a sustained lyrical quality which arises from a quite remarkable unity of conception. Like several of Henry Green's novels it has something of the quality of a fairy tale; the world presented, though unmistakably related to the real world, has a self-consistency, a completeness, which beguiles the reader into an almost uncritical acceptance of its reality. When E. M. Forster writes about India we are all the time aware of an outside observer battling with problems which he may not—he is quite aware—fully understand: Joyce Cary's novel works in precisely the opposite way. Certainty is established. This *is* Nigeria, at any rate for the purposes of the book. The opening of *Mister Johnson* has the flavour of an objectivity which is almost that of the anthropologist. There are no ifs and buts about this writing.

The theme of *Mister Johnson* is the effect of the imposition of an alien code of morals and manners upon a native culture. Mister Johnson—the 'mister' is a title of social respectability—is a young African who becomes a Government clerk in an outpost in the Nigerian bush. He is a character of unbounded vitality, optimism and fecklessness. He is a 'big man', a civilised man, removed from and despising the pagan savages yet far more deeply one of them than he is one of the elect. He is an absurd figure with his patent shoes and total incomprehension of the civilisation he respects, deeply pathetic in his complete vulnerability, enormously sympathetic and amusing in his superb vitality and courage.

I do not see how within its appointed limits *Mister Johnson* could be better done. Humour and compassion are blended, not in the sentimental fashion of the following of an amusing scene by a pathetic one, but through the conveying at the same time of the pathos and the humour of the same situation, so that one laughs and cries at once. . . .

The strength of *Mister Johnson* springs, I think, not only from Joyce Cary's firm and compassionate grasp of the nature of Johnson's tragedy but also from his remarkable insight into the function of myth among primitive peoples. Johnson is not merely a passive figure in this novel, the pathetic victim of imperialism and its by-products; he has a vitality of his own, potentialities of his own, expressed partly in his unfailing resourcefulness in playing the counters he does not understand but chiefly in his deep understanding of his own people and one-ness with them. The tragedy of Johnson the little clerk is pathetic enough; that of Johnson the poet-hero is far more profound.

This aspect of *Mister Johnson* recalls another remarkable work of art of this century, J. M. Synge's *The Playboy of the Western World*. The theme of *The Playboy* is that of the un-heroic victim who has heroism thrust upon him through the needs of the people for a myth to enrich their barren lives. Christy Mahon, who murdered his dad, becomes a living myth and thereby changes the lives of the people. And when the climax comes and he is exposed by the appearance of the father whom he is supposed to have murdered, the myth has done its work and changed him from a coward to a hero. The people lose their playboy but Christy finds himself.

Joyce Cary's use of the theme is, of course, different, but the emergence of Johnson as poet and myth-maker, organising and heightening the labour of the road-workers, shows an insight akin to Synge's. The relation between art and work in primitive society and the nature of tribal magic are brilliantly illuminated and in the terms not of the sociological text book but of a lyrical art.

There is, I think, an underlying weakness in *Mister Johnson*, a weakness most fully emerging in the final pages of the book when Johnson is shot by his hero the District Officer, Rudbeck. The limitations of Rudbeck and of the colonial administrators in general have been clearly expressed in the book. The final episode carries, in one sense, an appalling irony for it is clear that Rudbeck himself is totally unaware of the implications of what he has done. In the last sentence of the novel he is kidding himself into a day-dream version of the nightmare. Yet there is about these final pages an incomplete dissociation of the writer from Rudbeck's own sentimental attitudes. Rudbeck shoots Johnson as he would shoot a suffering dog to whom he feels a special responsibility and although the horror of this act is conveyed it is somewhat blunted by the underlying paternalism of Joyce Cary's own attitude. It is at this point that the lyrical approach wavers for we are forced now to evaluate the whole situation in terms more complex than the novel has hitherto demanded. Some rather fundamental questions begin to creep in. Is this an entirely just appreciation of the African situation? Does it not leave out something essential, that rising tide of African national consciousness and effectiveness which today one knows to be a vital element in the cultural and political issues of West Africa? Is not the whole novel conceived within a paternalist attitude—the attitude of the liberal imperialist—inadequate to the fullest and profoundest treatment of the subject? And is not the security, the confidence, the fairy-tale quality of the treatment based perhaps on a *false* confidence, an over-simplification?

I do not think these questionings affect the fundamental value and success of Joyce Cary's novel. It is a lyrical statement of a theme, not a sociological investigation, and its artistic vitality is in the end answer and justification enough.—ARNOLD KETTLE, "Joyce Cary: *Mister Johnson*," *Introduction to the English Novel*, Vol. 2, 1969, pp. 160–65

THE SECOND TRILOGY

Modern British comedy, whether that of Evelyn Waugh in the novel or of Alec Guinness in the films, tends to be satiric and sadistic. It is filled with violence and death, murder and corpses; its humor comes from the mixture of finesse, manners, niceness and hatred. It is nostalgic, also, and while it pokes fun at the Edwardian fathers it expresses a passionate envy of their

stable dignity. Mr. Cary's comedy, in books like *The Horse's Mouth* and *Herself Surprised*, is not of this fashionable kind but is more tranquil and indulgent; it is far less social and class-conscious and it is devoid of snobbery. Liberal, humanistic, it accepts the contemporary, it defends the possibilities of the man of the present, denies that it is so very bad to be what we are or that we are born to be condemned with the times. It asserts that there are powerful and original natures to be found still, that genius exists, that striving is not necessarily monomania, happiness not extinct, hope not unjustified. "The marvel is that millions deny all hope and boast themselves wise," Mr. Cary's Nimmo earnestly says in *Except the Lord*.

There is no comedy at all in this latest novel of his, I am sorry to report. Of course, there is no reason why a novelist should be required to write always in his best vein. On the contrary, he should be encouraged to diversify his talents and deny himself no attitude or point of view, serious or comic. But this book, the story of the childhood and early manhood of the son of an evangelical West Country stableman, is not one of his best. Neither wide nor deep enough, it does not invite the reader's imagination to displace its full weight. No notable character emerges; the episodes are too brief. The book takes the form of the personal record of a national leader, and its style is more appropriate to a memoir than to a novel. I feel that Mr. Cary has accepted the convention too completely for the sake of its color; he ought not to have been so faithful to it. "I feared her government over me," Nimmo writes of his sister Georgina. The word "government" is an authentic one, and it is all very well to be authentic, but it does not do to sacrifice fullness for it, and our longing to know more of Georgina and her brothers is not satisfied by it. We learn of the father's arrest in a miner's riot and of his broken leg but through the narrow apertures of the memoir we cannot see, and consequently experience a considerable disappointment.—SAUL BELLOW, "A Personal Record," *NR*, Feb. 22, 1954, pp. 20–21

The moral ambiguity of Nina Nimmo is part of the complexity of the political trilogy that includes *Prisoner of Grace* (1952), *Except the Lord* (1953), and *Not Honour More* (1955). She is at once one of the most anomalous and yet credible characters Cary created. No one, least of all she, could explain the "logic" of her conduct. Sara Monday is female affection and adaptability; Nina is both and more. She is the irreducibly human who loves as she hates, and has a sense of involvement in comically grotesque actions from which she neither wills to be nor can be free.

Nina writes "her book" because of revelations to be made in the press about Chester, her former husband. This device seems unpromising. But once the story begins, staccato-like, illogical, cutting off actions not really delineated much less explained, the reader becomes a prisoner of Nina's need to protect Jim, her irascible, stupid, honor-ridden lover, and to protect Chester, crafty, driven, sincere, and with a touch of genius. She justifies her *ménage à trois.* . . .

Some critics have found Nina a self-indulgent liar, and it is true that as a liar she has few peers. But she is something more than this. She knows life beneath the proprieties, and she knows that politics, of which she is a symbol, never, or rarely, black or white, is filled with delusion, cant, false rhetoric, compromise, pride, sincerity, and profound commitment to ideals.

This political trilogy may, in the long run, come to appear Cary's major achievement, more moving and more convincing than the earlier trilogy. If this proves to be the case, the character Nina will be one of the keys to its success. She pursues her version of justice in a madly unjust world, the possible in a world of impossibilities, and even attempts to mediate between irreconcilable views, such as those of Chester and those of Jim Latter. . . .

Walter Allen says, and undoubtedly he is right, that Cary represents the English Protestant Nonconformist tradition. In an interview Cary once said he believed in a personal God who actively involves Himself in human affairs. If He did not exist, there was no accounting for the universe or man's dual needs for beauty and justification. Cary was assured of God's presence. The title *To Be a Pilgrim* is from Bunyan:

> Who would true valour see
> Let him come hither;
> One here will constant be,
> Come wind, come weather.
> There's no discouragement
> Shall make him once relent
> His first avowed intent
> To be a pilgrim.

The Nonconformist tradition explains Wilcher and Jimson and Nimmo—and it explains Cary's preoccupation with William Blake. Allen says: "The Protestant or Nonconformist tradition, though its manifestations change from generation to generation, has been one of the most potent and formative in English life, in politics no less than in religion."

The individual, responsible only to God, suspicious of priest, ritual, and orthodoxy, goes his lonely way. To the non-believer he appears more than a little mad, an egotist, and often a hypocrite. He passes beyond the Slough of Despond, he climbs hills to catch sight of God's dawn, and refuses to sell his soul to Mammon.

In another century, Cary might have been a preacher. Moral tags seem to be just beneath the surface of his views— "Judge not, that ye be not judged," or "The ways of God are exceeding strange"—but he restrains himself from uttering them in the older way. Yet the half-suppressed fury, the icon-oclasm, the search for one's *own* God; are there, in Gulley Jimson's drive to create, come hell or high water, in Wilcher's scruples at the same time he is facing up to his own dishonesty and pettifogging ways, and in the ambiguous moralizing and self-seeking of Nimmo.

In his last novel, Cary turned to Nonconformity again, very explicitly, as though making one final effort to understand his own subject.

> When in his soliloquies at the front of the stage, his eyes, roving over the audience, seemed to meet mine, they sent forth an indescribable thrill—it seemed that something flashed from the very center of evil into my deepest soul.

In that combination—a man marked by poverty, deep religious belief, and profound family affections—we have one clue to Nimmo, the dedicated politician. In his awareness of the mesmeric effect of work we have another. And lastly, there is his admission that he felt an "indescribable thrill" at being confronted by evil.

Nimmo is not a simple character. As a young union man he is shocked by duplicity, yet he can accept his own dishonesty, and even the political usefulness of violence. He can be very proper, and he can be obscene. He can be courageous and he can fake a heart attack for a temporary advantage. He is indifferent to Nina, and woefully dependent upon her. He can cajole, blackmail, lie, and see his own role as dedicated statesman in an aureole of religious light. Cary seems to be saying that Nimmo is *all* of these things, and no single characteristic or action cancels out the others. Nina, out of a higher social class, does not understand him because she does not *feel* his

childhood. And Jim Latter, for whom everything is black or white, can see him only as a devious scoundrel, a flannel-mouthed liar, and a political opportunist.

In his narrative *Not Honour More*, we get a further look at Nimmo, from the point of view of a soldier who happens also to be more than a little mad. . . .

Latter's narrative, in laconic, soldierlike prose, is dictated to Policewoman Martin as he awaits execution. The style is effective because, one, the reader has already had two earlier versions of the events, and, two, Latter is so obviously lacking in either complexity of mind or plain mother wit.

The three volumes represent Cary's view of the political world, its dependence on human relationships, the driving force of sex, and of religion. Latter is a persistent type, a believer in simple answers, and so is Nimmo, a "wrangler," as Cary called him. Nina too is a persistent type, picking her way, making choices in a world full of dilemmas and joyous possibilities. In the three novels, Cary once again presents the rush, the anguish, and the splendor of human life.—WILLIAM VAN O'CONNOR, *Joyce Cary*, 1966, pp. 36–41

The fierce moral indignation which *Prisoner of Grace* arouses in so many readers is due largely to its structure. Starting with the ruthless machiavellism of Chester, the novel moves to a second stage where Cary dwells on events showing the enormous difficulties of political life, the endless struggle to balance personal ambition against the public good and, moreover, the ingratitude of voters to even a successful government; in the third and final movement, the main characters reach the nadir of corruption in their private lives as Chester is driven by crude appetites which he seeks to satisfy without regard to persons, place or time. The structure thus predisposes our minds to condemn Chester and just when we are beginning to re-examine our first impressions, Cary shows us a new and far more revolting kind of depravity in the man's private life. The effect is to reduce if not destroy the impact of his exemplary services and his patriotic fervour in the middle section of the novel.

The curious thing is that Cary obviously wants us to sympathize with his hero. If we read the trilogy in its chronological order, we can understand Chester's unrelenting drive for political success; but that order also leaves us wondering how with his strict upbringing he can behave the way he does without a pang of conscience. Even Nina's explanation that politics and religion and sexuality are inextricably mixed in the mind of Chester seems pitiably inadequate. Perhaps Cary unconsciously diminished sympathy for his hero in a bid to achieve structural unity in the trilogy. For unlike the strange move from *To Be a Pilgrim* to *The Horse's Mouth* in the First Trilogy, the transitions from one novel to the other in the Second Trilogy are carefully and convincingly prepared. Thus the moral and psychological violence of the closing pages of *Prisoner of Grace* fully prepares us for the physical violence of *Not Honour More*, just as the closing words of Nina in her narrative actually foreshadow the manner of her death at the end of the trilogy.— S. H. KAHV, "Domestic and Political Conflicts," *A World of Everlasting Conflict*, 1974, pp. 272–73

ROBERT BLOOM
From "*Not Honour More*"
The Indeterminate World
1962, pp. 170–80

The essential characteristic of realism in medieval and modern western literature, Erich Auerbach tells us, has been the serious, problematic, or tragic treatment of random everyday life—an undertaking which goes counter to the classical rule of differentiated levels of style.[1] The novel has, of course, been an outstanding vehicle of such a realism, and Cary, for all his comic proclivities, belongs solidly to this tradition. In *Not Honour More*, however, and in the second trilogy generally, he undertakes the consideration and portrayal of a great public figure and public issue, in addition to private, everyday existence. He does not, it is true, achieve in Chester Nimmo anything like the nobility and magnificence of the public figure in Greek tragedy; this disparity arises, in some measure at least, out of the changes which public life has undergone over the centuries and is very much a part of the meaning of the trilogy. Modern democratic public life, that is, offers, on the whole, shoddier possibilities; but it serves, still, to enlarge the scope of *Not Honour More* and to confer on it a magnitude that we do not ordinarily associate with the novel of personal, or even social, life.

The significance of *Not Honour More* is very much conditioned by an interplay between public and private considerations. Cary has designed the novel in alternating sections which focus on the private problem of adultery and on the public problem of the General Strike of 1926. Andrew Wright notes that "in the course of the book the two focuses become one."[2] This is an astute and helpful remark; yet we cannot comprehend the whole burden of the novel unless we realize that it is, in a sense, equally true that in the course of the book the two focuses remain two. Out of a constant pull between public and private obligations emerges the terrible, murderous frustration of the novel's narrator, Jim Latter, the meaning of the novel, and what we must take to be its contribution to the trilogy.

The pattern of alternated focus is fairly clear-cut. Cary has Jim begin his narrative, which is dictated in prison while Jim awaits trial for murder, with a private episode. On May 1, 1926, Jim unexpectedly returns home to Palm Cottage from hunting. As we know from *Prisoner of Grace*, Chester Nimmo has been visiting the Latters for about two years, writing his memoirs—of which *Except the Lord* is a first installment—waiting for an opportunity to re-enter public life, and forcing himself sexually on a reluctant but cooperative Nina. As he enters the Cottage Jim catches Chester "interfering" with Nina and shoots, wounding Chester slightly. Jim escapes with Nina's help, makes a statement to the press, then discovers that Chester has publicly denied that any attempt has been made on his life. On the following day Jim confronts Chester again, but allows himself to be talked out of immediate revenge by the wily politician. Before he can satisfy himself about the true nature of Chester's relations with Nina and work out his personal revenge, Jim becomes involved in political developments in the restless Tarbiton area, and the novel enters a public phase. . . .

During this period, Jim's major concern as head of the specials is to preserve order by regulating picketing and preventing mob violence. With the General Strike under way, his greatest obstacle is the Communists and their local leader, Pincomb, who are eager to exploit all the possibilities of agitation and revolution which the Strike affords. Jim begins to suspect, after Nina has been seen at Pincomb's headquarters, that a bargain has been struck between Chester and Pincomb. The suspicion is eventually confirmed. Jim learns later that in return for Communist support, Chester has agreed to allow the Communists to picket, and thus destroy, Potter's, a very old independent shipbuilding firm which is on the brink of financial ruin, but whose employees do not wish to strike. On May 10, Pincomb, after inciting a Communist crowd in front of

Potter's and encouraging a menacing revolutionary situation, is injured and arrested by Maufe, one of Jim's specials. The Communists immediately charge Maufe with an unprovoked criminal assault, though there is evidence that Pincomb and his two bodyguards have resisted arrest. The Emergency Committee, however, suspends Maufe for his action. Jim, who considers Maufe a heroic benefactor of the community and the nation, resigns his position in protest. So ends the first public phase.

After resigning Jim returns late at night to Palm Cottage expecting to find Nina, with whom he has become reconciled, alone. Instead, he finds her with Chester in her bedroom. After hearing Chester's torrential rambling defense, Jim, now resigned to Nina's infidelity and indifferent to Chester, agrees, out of pity, to drive with them to the Town Hall, where Chester claims that the political errand which brought him to the Cottage can be corroborated. Just before they enter the Hall, Nina, to whom Jim has not spoken at all, attempts suicide by leaping under a moving vehicle. As Jim waits, with Chester, for news of her condition, he consoles himself with Nina's ultimate honesty: she refused to enter the Town Hall, he thinks, because she was through with lies and tricks. Full of forgiveness, he invites Nina to accompany him to Africa, after her recovery, where they can escape the corruption and complication of English public life. She agrees. Before they leave, while Nina is convalescing, they seek refuge from publicity in the loneliest spot that Jim knows.

> We wanted peace for a week. We were sick of the rackets and the ramps.
> Sick of the gimme game, the grab boys, the bunkum and the spoof. But we found pretty quick that in England you can't get out of it. Perhaps not in Europe. It's soaked into everything. It's crept into the last cracks.[3]

A photographer sneaks up on them as they lie in the sun and "Nina's thin white face with her great eyes, looking as terrified as a child who's seen a ghost, went all round the world." So the desperate attempt to withdraw into private life fails.

The closing section of the novel occurs, consequently, in a public context. Although the Strike is over, Maufe has been brought to trial for his assault on Pincomb, who is now permanently disabled by a blow to his head. Nina is summoned to testify, for it develops that she has played a crucial role in the affair. The key witness for the defense, a man named Bell, asserts that Pincomb struck Maufe first, resisted arrest, and injured his head by falling and striking it against a curb. Bell maintains that he passed this information on to Chester and that Chester must have received it because he sent Nina to see Bell and confirm the testimony. Since Chester is supporting the charges against Maufe, this is highly embarrassing evidence. However, Nina's testimony at the trial saves the old politician. She recalls hardly anything of her conversation with Bell; and when Chester's letter instructing her about the Bell interview is read in court, it turns out to be not the least incriminating, though Bell's original report to Chester is missing. Jim is suspicious, but he does not press her; since her suicide attempt she seems to have put all chicanery behind her.

Shortly before the trial ends and just a few days before their departure for Africa, Nina and Jim are sorting their belongings at Palm Cottage. Jim notices that two collections of letters—Chester's and Nina's to each other—have been lying about, and that Nina seems unable to make up her mind about disposing of them. Jim takes the line that they are none of his business, though he suspects that they contain the whole truth about the Maufe affair. Nina, to her credit, does not destroy or hide them, though she has a number of opportunities to do so. This restraint comes to an end when Jim receives a phone call informing him that Maufe has been convicted and given a three-year sentence. Just as Nimmo's car pulls up—he has come to collect his letters—Jim asks Nina for permission to examine the correspondence, knowing that this is his last chance to uncover the truth about the Pincomb-Nimmo-Maufe affair. She consents, asking him only to remember that it was all before "the accident"—her word for the attempted suicide. The correspondence reveals that Bell's report was actually received but that Chester has hinted that it be suppressed; that Chester refused Bell police protection, though Bell was threatened by the Communists; and that Chester was quite eager to have Maufe convicted in order to gather for himself the support of the Labor Party while he was trying to form a new government in London.

Filled with a kind of public rage at the way in which Maufe has been victimized, Jim turns on the newly arrived Chester with a razor and chases him into a lavatory. Chester manages to lock himself safely in, but he dies soon after from a heart attack. When Nina, not knowing this, pleads with Jim for Chester's life, Jim indicates that he is going to execute her as well. She says that he must not mind the letters since they were written before her "accident," in effect, before her conversion to honorable dealing and truth. But Jim interrupts to explain, in the manner of an inarticulate Othello, that there is nothing personal in his proceeding:

> "My darling," I said, "it isn't what you said about me—it's about the fearful thing you and Nimmo have done. Perhaps you think it wasn't very much to betray Maufe and to join in with the liars and cowards and tricksters against an honourable man, against the honour of England. But that only makes it worse—it only proves what I say, that the rottenness has gone too far" (p. 221).

And a moment later he reflects, "[Nina] couldn't understand she was up against something bigger than either of us or anyone's happiness. The truth. And nothing could change it."

Despite the banality and bombast of Jim's utterance here, it is clear that he conceives of himself as a disinterested instrument of justice, cleansing, in one supreme necessary gesture, some part of the public life of England. Not adultery, not sexual jealousy, he tells us, but political corruption and subversion of the truth impel him. Although Jim's disinterestedness, like Othello's, takes some of its vehemence from personal considerations, on the whole, his willingness to forgive Nina before the Maufe conviction must persuade us that his motives are largely those that he all but inarticulately expresses. It is the public Nina, the conspirator with Chester for Communist support and for the sacrifice of the courageous Maufe, whom Jim kills, not the unfaithful wife. Her attempt, from the time of her "accident," to withdraw from the machinations of political life, to flee publicity and England altogether, is a touching indication of her decision to purge herself of trickery and maneuver; so too is her refusal to destroy the incriminating letters. Jim is aware of this effort and prizes it. But Nina enters upon it too late in life and is not prepared, even after resolving to live honorably and privately, to deny her assistance to Chester. We know that her suppression of evidence at the trial in order to save Chester occurs after she has resolved to make a new life with Jim. She cannot repudiate her public role even in the full sweep of her private retreat.

This alternating focus—from the private matter of adultery to the General Strike, then to Nina's attempt at suicide and extrication from public life, and finally to the Maufe trial and its consequences—gives the novel its structural outlines and creates the pull which, as we shall see, acts decisively on its major figures and on our view of them. We would do wrong, though, to suppose that Cary is making anything like a mechanical or absolute separation between public and private interests. Throughout the novel charges of private interest in public decisions, as well as the reverse, occur. The intermingling acts to reinforce the main conflict by making it ubiquitous. It also provides the conflict with specific occasions on which to manifest itself in Nina, Chester, and Jim.

Nina's situation in this novel culminates her development in *Prisoner of Grace*, where she first becomes a victim of the divisiveness which works her moral destruction. Cary makes it fairly clear that her allegiance to Chester is essentially a public allegiance to a great leader. She becomes so completely a prisoner to his political efficacy that at the close of *Not Honour More*, when she knows that Jim is at the point of killing her, she has courage and devotion enough to beg Jim to remove the dead Chester from the lavatory because it is horrible that so great a man, revered by millions of people all through the world, should be left in such a place. Yet we gather that she does not love Chester; her sexual services to him are merely a vouchsafing of inspiration to the public man. Her love, her personal feeling and allegiance, are presumably all for Jim. She asserts this in *Prisoner of Grace* and Jim accepts it in his own narrative. The private attachment, however, is consistently overcome. She protects Chester through all the adulterous sequences in *Not Honour More*, runs shoddy, fawning errands for him during the Strike, seeking to reconcile the alienated Jim and keep him from discovering too much about the Pincomb-Nimmo bargain, and, in the end, perjures herself in order to convict Maufe. In sum, the public consideration—that is, Chester's career, his mission to save a tottering England—is powerful enough to impose a public morality on most of her private life. Expediency, trickery, deceit, the justification of means by ends infect all her dealings with Jim. Her two efforts to recover the decency and truthfulness appropriate to a love relationship—her suicide attempt and her reluctance to destroy the letters—are merely the last remains of that fatal divisiveness in her nature which she can never completely elude, even when it threatens Chester's career. Cary conceived her in division. At the close, he has Jim kill the public aspect of her and ask forgiveness of the private.

The public-private pull affects Chester as well. It is from him, after all, that Nina learns to forgive herself almost any transgression in the name of some larger, higher dedication. We have seen this dedication take the form, in *Prisoner of Grace*, of an obeisance to God, with Chester making political decisions as the appointed instrument of his Creator. In *Not Honour More*, however, he pitches his justifications in a lower key, for they are largely directed at Jim, who is likely to be more revolted than persuaded by religious claims. Instead of invoking God, Chester invokes the public cause, the public danger, as his sanction. His importance to the nation during the General Strike crisis must excuse, he implies, any merely personal consideration. Thus, when Jim, pistol in hand, confronts him after catching him with Nina the first time, the question of adultery drops quickly out of Chester's sight. "Don't talk about your honour," Chester says to Jim,

> what is it worth? The country is tottering on the edge of revolution and you seize this moment to gratify a private spite. At last you see your chance to ruin the man who has never done you anything but kindness—a man over seventy, in any case condemned to die. But you can't wait to dance on my

grave and vilify my memory, like all the other jackals who have preyed upon me in life—you are resolved to drag me in the dirt during my last months. And this at the cost of your country. My dear Jim, at least allow yourself to believe that I am not speaking a vain thing. You saw the Press this morning—if not, the papers lie there on the bed. I have some influence still. Say if you like that I have done nothing to deserve this position, but you can't deny or ignore it. Since this last week the whole picture has changed, at this moment my intervention could be decisive. Forgive me if I say that you don't realize the situation (pp. 66–67).

And again, when Jim returns to Palm Cottage after resigning as head of the specials and finds Chester with Nina, Chester wanders, during the course of his excuse, into the public domain. He has just returned from London, he says, where the Prime Minister would have nothing to do with his proposal to form a new government to deal with the Strike emergency. Forgetting completely the immediate issue—his presence in Nina's bedroom—he gives what amounts to a public speech:

> For this is war. War for the soul of England—the very heart of liberal Europe. And we are ready. Lloyd George will serve. I will serve. In any capacity. We do not demand guarantees. This is not a time for haggling. And always remember this, if we threw our weight with the workers we could tell the Tories to get out, we could toss them into the Thames. And make such a revolution the world has never seen—it would transform history—and who would dare to say we were not justified. We have been flouted and ignored—the men who brought this country through the agony of the war—the most tremendous, the most bloody in the history of man. Our experience is despised by the miserable pettifoggers and timeservers who are paltering with a crisis equally beyond their imagination and their powers (p. 166).

Characteristically, Cary makes it quite impossible to tell whether Chester is genuinely distressed by, and preoccupied with, his recent public failure in London—which, to add to the difficulty, has its own personal aspect as well—or whether Chester is merely trying to distract Jim's attention from the issue of adultery. In *Not Honour More* Cary allows us our closest look at the mature Chester; but the wily old politician remains, despite this, a mystifying figure. Chester's dialogue, at its lengthiest and most eloquent, is quoted verbatim by Jim, whose own narrative style verges on a kind of headlong military illiteracy. The improbability of such accurate recall and duplication may be something of a threat to the novel's verisimilitude, but the danger is well worth the gain. Chester's genius for intrigue, persuasion, and manipulation is fully rendered. We come to understand the greatness, even if it is nothing more than inspired audacity, which Nina responds to and which enslaves her. And Cary conveys, too, the way in which Chester, as a public figure, can at once trample the personal lives of others, vindicate himself to himself, if not to Jim, yet all the while be desperately dependent upon the private ministrations of a woman like Nina, who is willing, at terrible cost, to replenish and restore him. There is something of Zeus's need of the mortal Leda in Chester's proceedings, and something, too, of Zeus's inhumanity.

Cary has the public-private theme reach its climax in the novel's first-person narrator, Jim Latter. It is not for nothing, as Mark Spilka has pointed out, that Cary's very name for his protagonist makes him an unmistakable spiritual descendant of Conrad's Lord Jim. A gentleman soldier, Cary's Jim has

ordered his life around such conceptions as duty, truth, love, justice, and honor; and he insists, sometimes frenetically, upon their reality and their survival even in a corrupt and ugly age. If this makes him appear, at times, antiquated and ludicrous, the fault, we are often inclined to feel, is not entirely his own. While Chester and Nina have allowed the looser morality of public life to govern their personal relationships, Jim steadily insists on the reverse. He wishes public life, even the national life, to base itself on the same code which governs a gentleman's conduct. The whole novel takes its title from what Jim calls "Colonel Lovelace's great poem." At fourteen he had explained its meaning to ten-year-old Nina, who, at that time, he says, "didn't laugh at an idea because it was true or fine" (p. 126). Whatever the new wisdom that Nina has imbibed, for Jim "I could not love thee, dear, so much, Loved I not honour more" is still the climax of "the most beautiful and true of all poems." As an essentially private person with a history, in *Prisoner of Grace*, of ineffectual and frustrating dealings with the British government, Jim is bound to be outraged by Chester, and by Nina too, at least to the extent that she puts on Chester's knowledge with his power. Since the book is narrated by Jim, we view most of its events with his sense of outraged honor, and we share, if only tentatively, in his violent denunciations of a corrupt world. Our commitment to Jim and his code may be a little uncertain and uneasy, but the narrative mode tends to insist on it, at least for the duration of the novel. The trilogy is perhaps another matter.

Notes

1. *Mimesis*, trans. Willard Trask (New York: Doubleday Anchor, 1957), pp. 37–40 and *passim*.
2. *Joyce Cary*, p. 151.
3. *Not Honour More* (London: Michael Joseph, 1955), p. 189. Subsequent references will be made to this edition, with page numbers cited parenthetically.

GOLDEN L. LARSEN
From "The Contemporaneity of Joyce Cary"
The Dark Descent
1965, pp. 3–18

Among the generation of writers preceding Joyce Cary and using the technique of "multiple reflection of consciousness", remarked Erich Auerbach in *Mimesis*, there is a pervasive mood that leaves "the reader with an impression of hopelessness. . . ."[1] Although Auerbach thought he saw a phoenix rising out of the ashes in the "wealth of reality and depth of life in every moment to which we surrender ourselves without prejudice" as given in Virginia Woolf's *To The Lighthouse*, his total evaluation of these writers, particularly of James Joyce, reflects a despair almost as deep as that of the novels he describes.[2] But the crucial question here is whether Joyce Cary's work represents a possibly inferior continuation of the same gloomy theme of his predecessors or provides a new perspective and a new hope (if not a solution).

This question provides the basis for the discussion in this section. What is being sought is a working hypothesis about Cary's own sources of insight so that the actual labour of analysing his novels might be approached consistently from the same angle—the angle, it is hoped, from which Cary himself worked. This is not to fall into the fallacy of interpreting only according to the supposed intentions of the author, for it must be evident that on occasion he wrote better than he knew.

Rather, it would appear that only when the critic begins from a philosophical base at least as broad as the writer's can he hope to uncover the richer hidden significances. If other interpreters of Cary's works have failed in this respect, one suspects that it is partly because they have too often fallen back upon the obvious analogies between Cary and earlier novelists in the English tradition or have used indiscriminately the vocabulary of romanticism (imagination, freedom, individualism, and so on) without looking underneath to see whether the words have a special applicability to the novels of Cary or, perhaps, any applicability at all.

Perspective seems essential for formulation of this working hypothesis and may be attained by comparing briefly his treatment of the African scene with that of Joseph Conrad. Conrad appears to be a particularly good choice for a number of reasons. First of all, he came from the generation of writers referred to by Auerbach and dealt with essentially the same problems that confronted them (and Cary as well), but his experimentation was less radical. For this reason he is obviously more readily comparable with Cary, who, although an innovator of sorts, never deviated far from the traditional novel form. Second, there is the obvious advantage of both writers having treated what might be called the "African problem". Finally, Andrew Wright has made the comparison almost necessary by asserting in one place that in "The Heart of Darkness" is posed "most centrally the question which Cary asks"[3] and in another that Cary's "interest in an exotic setting is of the same order as Conrad's; it is metaphysical: Cary does not in fact acknowledge Conrad as one of his masters."[4] These remarks, while casually tossed out and never really developed, have the damaging consequence of misleading association, as if Cary were in fact simply a shadow of the master. This discussion, on the other hand, will emphasize the differences between the two writers and will, in fact, attempt to prove that these differences reflect diverging philosophical orientations, differences in their respective conceptions of the limits of knowledge—their conceptions of the real. The suggestion made here then is that the novels of Joyce Cary differ in their conception from those of Joseph Conrad and that this difference is a mark of his contemporaneity, and, perhaps, of his peculiar significance.

The epistemological problem posed by Conrad can best be got at through the pronouncements of his own master, Henry James. For it was James, in his introduction to the New York edition of *The American*, who attempted to define the boundaries of realism and consequently the areas of the novelist's responsibility and in at least one instance applied those standards to a novel by Conrad:

> The real represents to my perception the things we cannot possibly *not* know, sooner or later, in one way or another; it being but one of the incidents of their quantity and number, that particular instances have not yet come our way. The romantic stands, on the other hand, for the things that, with all the facilities in the world, all the wealth and all the courage and all the wit and all the adventure, we never *can* directly know; the things that can reach us only through the beautiful circuit and subterfuge of our thought and our desire.[5]

The challenge to the novelist's genius is greatest, according to James, "when he commits himself in both directions; not quite at the same time or to the same effect, of course, but by need of performing his whole possible revolution, by the law of some rich passion in him for extremes."[6] But even the romancer will achieve the "greatest intensity . . . when the sacrifice of community, of the 'related' sides of situations, has not been too

rash."[7] James's own "passion for extremes" remained subtly contained and obliquely arrived at within the manifold and related sides of the community. Scorning shallow and sterile sensationalism of the sort of Robert Louis Stevenson, he insisted that the greatest threat to the moral life can be found in the "common and covert" dangers "that 'look like nothing' and that can be but inwardly and occultly dealt with, which involve the sharpest hazards to life and honour and the highest instant decision and intrepidities of action."[8] His own admitted failure in *The American* to keep the "commodious car of the imagination" fastened firmly to the balloon of experience was never repeated, and in *The Ambassadors* he attained a sort of balanced perfection in making the point-of-view technique exfoliate the meaning of the tensions involved. But it is not unreasonable to think that when James spoke of that ideal genius whose need it is to perform "his whole revolution" he knew the risks of that passion to the artist's production. The obscurities, the involutions of style, the strain to discover hidden meanings in his last works can only be justified by most readers by their awareness of James's own deliberateness. His knowledge that the novelist must keep one foot on the ground only invited him to find out how high he might kick the other in the air without losing balance. James's own way of living dangerously is best expressed by himself in his observation that "the panting pursuit of danger is the pursuit of life itself, in which danger awaits us possibly at every step and faces us at every turn. . . ."[9]

. . . James's perceptive and disquieting judgement of *Chance* found strong support, except in a more sweepingly generalized way, in a classic example of critical impatience—E. M. Forster's comment in *Abinger Harvest*:

> What is so elusive about him is that he is always promising to make some general philosophic statement about the universe, and then refraining with a gruff disclaimer. . . . No creed, in fact. Only opinions, and the right to throw them overboard when facts make them look absurd. Opinions held under the semblance of eternity, girt with the sea, crowned with the stars, and therefore easily mistaken for a creed.[10]

And even F. R. Leavis, in spite of his general high regard for Conrad, found serious lapses into the vague and indefinite.[11] In the interest of fairness to Conrad, however, it should be pointed out that these judgements by no means represent the opinions of all critics of him. Robert Penn Warren, for example, in an excellent essay argued convincingly for Conrad's philosophical astuteness in *Nostromo*.[12]

At any rate, complete unanimity of agreement among his critics about a particular work is not necessary to the point being made here, for it is clear that in some novels at least—particularly those narrated by Marlowe—Conrad worked deliberately through manipulation of narrative devices, such as the narrator-within-narrator one in *Lord Jim*, language, and ambiguous symbolism to attain a sort of indefiniteness or remoteness from empirical reality. And it is precisely in the use of these technical devices that Cary's artistic orientation, and consequently his thought, can be seen to differ from Conrad's. Cary began with the omniscient point of view in *Aissa Saved* and employed the same approach in the succeeding three novels, in which he was clearly more concerned with communicating his "idea" than in solving technical problems. In *Mister Johnson* he retained the omniscient point of view but made an important attempt to have technique support idea by using the present tense. In the other two "growing-up" books he employed both present and past tense in combination with the omniscient point of view and then in the trilogy shifted to a first-person narrator technique. Although not a radical innovator, Cary was constantly experimenting with various narrative techniques in an attempt to make the meaning unmistakably clear to the *ideal reader*—that is, the reader who is fully equipped intellectually and emotionally. For him there are no mysteries.

As for style, the prose of *Aissa Saved* is direct, simple—almost austere—in direct contrast to the emotionally charged subject matter, a fact that suggests his awareness even that early of the value in effect and meaning of such a counter-balanced tensional relationship. Although in the three novels that followed the action is cluttered with characters, complications, and philosophizing, the style remains fluent and clear, and beginning with *Mister Johnson* it is beautifully adapted to the demands of the particular novel.

In their use of symbols the two writers differ significantly too. The sea in *Lord Jim*, for example, can be assigned a multiplicity of values from the most obvious to the most conjectural and esoteric, and when Jim journeys to Patusan the jungle is likened to the sea and takes on the same ambiguous significance. By careful analysis some acceptable equations can be made for them, and yet there still remains a residuum of undefinable value. One of Cary's favourite symbols also is water. A river appears in each of the four African novels; the sea dominates *A House of Children*; tides and river appear in *The Horse's Mouth*. But he assiduously guarded against any kind of vague suggestiveness by closely identifying symbol with immediate action and character predicament. It can be stated as a general rule that while Conrad's symbols are expansive and suggestive, Cary's are delimiting and definitive.

While extensive comparison of their respective works seems unwarranted, at least some confirmation of the validity of these generalizations is possible by considering the following passages, the first from Conrad's "The Heart of Darkness" and the second from Cary's *Aissa Saved*:

> Dark human shapes could be made out in the distance, flitting indistinctly against the gloomy border of the forest, and near the river two bronze figures, leaning on tall spears, stood in the sunlight under fantastic head-dresses of spotted skins, warlike and still in statuesque repose. And from right to left along the lighted shore moved a wild and gorgeous apparition of a woman. . . . She was savage and superb, wild-eyed and magnificent; there was something ominous and stately in her deliberate progress. And in the hush that had fallen suddenly upon the whole sorrowful land, the immense wilderness, the colossal body of the fecund and mysterious life seemed to look at her, pensive, as though it had been looking at the image of its own tenebrous and passionate soul.[13]

> Women while walking clapped their hands and sketched the movements of the ritual dance, jerking their hips, bending their knees, many of the younger men and women, too eager and excited to wait for the drums, were dancing fiercely, leaping, squatting; the sweat ran down their backs, they were already in a trance, their eyes fixed, their muscles jigging like parts of a machine. They threw off their loin cloths and did not even hear the yells of encouragement from the crowd, who themselves carried away by the sight of them began also to leap, whirl, utter shrill cries which sounded like a defiance and an appeal. Not only the debtors, beggars, prostitutes, lepers, diseased wretches, ruptured children, syphilitic girls, idiots and outcasts, but those who seemed strong and

well and to have no cares, leapt and grimaced with fierce, greedy cries and wild gestures which seemed to throw off heavy burdens of fear and anxiety; which said: "I don't care for anybody, I don't care for anything. I'll do what I like this time."

> Only the old men and women with bodies twisted by work and disease, their grey faces hollow like rain-eaten stones, continued to look on, or pretending to join in, shuffled with bored, patient looks like those who perform a duty without much hope of profit.[14]

For Conrad the jungle and the woman exist only as a mystery, as something at once alluring and threatening, inexplicable. His woman moves deliberately, slowly, magnificently while the jungle appears to assume human attributes, looking upon her as though she were an "image of its own tenebrous and passionate soul." The lines between the human and the natural are blurred, the movement of the prose is slowed down, and the language is sufficiently emotionally charged and generalized to suggest a stillness of live subject transformed into eternal symbol. The impact of *The Heart of Darkness* depends upon this kind of symbolic projection, upon the unspeakable mystery, the great abyss.

Joyce Cary's point of view, on the other hand, comes closer to that of the cultural anthropologist (but without the scientific abstractness), especially in the earliest novels, when he saw primitive society as exactly that: a society with its own customs, ceremonies, and, as a result, its own tensions, its nobility and its corruption. His women lose their identity, not by being transformed into ambiguous symbols, but, instead, by becoming part of a ritual, a communal erotic orgy born out of fear and anxiety. The frenzied, leaping dancers, with their "shrill cries which sounded like a defiance and an appeal," are expressive of another and different attitude toward fecundity: the vital life impulse seeking expression out of the depths of its own ignorance. The collapse of personality back into the anonymity of tribe is at once a threat to individuality and from the point of view of the natives a protection against the inexplicable forces of nature. Ambiguity lies in the uncertainty of the motives of the dancers while the language moves with the speed of the dancers' feet.

Closely related to his propensity for symbolic reduction is Conrad's view of history. In spite of his manipulation of time sequence in *Lord Jim*, for example, he placed the weight of meaning upon that scene in Patusan when Jim and Brown come together face to face—the moment of revelation of the hero's identity to himself. This concentration or compression of meaning is not only effective but, as Dorothy Van Ghent pointed out, also derives from "a closed and static system, incapable of origination though intensely dramatic in its revelations."[15] Miss Van Ghent also showed in her essay on the novel a close similarity between the concept of flawed character in Greek drama and the "flaw" in Jim's character and between their respective dramatic renditions of meaning. According to her:

> The word "epiphany" implies manifestation of divinity, and this meaning of the term can serve us also in analysing Conrad's method and his vision, if we think of the "dark powers" of the psyche as having the mysterious absoluteness that we associate with the daemonic, and if we think mythologically of man's destiny both as being carried within him, and, *in effect*—since his acts externalize his destiny—as confronting him from without.[16]

It is clear that the direction of movement of a character so conceived will be away from the secret self but in a large curve that ultimately directs the character back upon himself. This circular movement exactly describes the shape of Jim's soul-journey as he moves from hesitancy of confrontation in childhood to an open breach in the *Patna* incident and a return to the green world of Patusan—the second chance.

Although any explanation of the reasons for Conrad's view of history, with its exaggerated emphasis upon the single moment of revelation, will in a sense falsify his position as an artist, such an explanation would most certainly have to consider his relationship to the naturalistic movement. Paul Tillich called the modern naturalistic view non-historical and compared it with the Greek non-historical or circular conception:

> Modern European naturalism since the Renaissance is different from Greek naturalism in so far as it has overcome, under Christian influence, that dualistic and tragic element in Greek thinking which drives the human soul beyond the world and history to seek for salvation from the tragic circle, in the immovable "One". Modern naturalism is monistic and describes the world as a unity and totality, either in mathematical terms, as Spinoza and Leibniz do, or in organic terms, as Bruno and Shaftesbury do, or in dynamic terms, as Nietzsche and Bergson do, or in sociological terms, as Spengler does. For all these people the future signifies the evolution of all possibilities as implied in the present stage of the world. There may be infinite varieties, there may be self-destruction or circular motion or infinite repetition; but in no case is the directed line of history decisive. Billions of years of physical time frustrate any possible meaning for the utterly small sum of historical years. In the mathematical type, time has been made a dimension of space. He who knows the mathematical world formula in principle knows all the future. In the organic and dynamic types of modern naturalism, time is considered a deteriorizing force. In the organic and historical process, life becomes more complex, more self-conscious, more intellectualized. It loses its vital power and is driven toward self-destruction. In Spengler's prophecy of the decline of the West the great cultures are posited like trees beside each other. They arise, grow, decay, and die like trees, each for itself. There is no universal history, crossing the life-and-death curve of each culture, overcoming the spatial "Beside" by a temporal "Toward". On this basis even the tragic outlook of Greece tries to return. In nationalism the gods of space revolt against the Lord of time. Nation, soil, blood, and race defy the idea of a world-historical development and a world-historical aim. This recent development shows that a non-historical interpretation of history, even if arising in Christian countries, must return to paganism in the long run, for Christianity is essentially historical, while paganism is essentially non-historical.[17]

Without necessarily agreeing with Tillich's Christian existential bias, one can see his explanation provides a valuable hint as to Conrad's own dilemma. Like Hardy, Conrad saw the inevitable direction of naturalism but, unlike Hardy, who chose to make the implied pessimism the dominant mood of his novels, he attempted to lift man out of the "tragic circle", not through escape into the transcendental "One", but through his "dream"—his social ideals. Actually the problem was not solved for him by this simple method, however, for Conrad's attitude towards civilization itself was clearly ambivalent. His revulsion against the brutality of Kurtz's experience is balanced against the brutality of imperialism, and the morbidity of Kurtz's self-destruction is balanced against the impotency of the unviolated Intended. In his dramatization of Lord Jim's unresolvable dilemma Conrad epitomized the broader drama of the apparently unresolvable conflict between traditional humanistic values and nineteenth-century evolutionary theory and naturalism. Like his characters, Conrad appears to be trapped in a circular pattern of finding, ironically enough, in his own civilized personality an affirmation of his ever-present animal nature, although it is submerged in the unconscious of the individual and the assumptions of society. . . .

The argument might be stated even more forcefully by saying that Conrad's attempt to solve the problem posed by naturalism resulted in a retreat rather than a resolution—a retreat into the self, an annihilation of the conscious and social part of man in order to partake of the unconscious, and an obliteration of time in order to partake of the eternal. In this respect, then, he is typical of many of the great novelists of the twentieth century who, in their pessimism, assumed an "internal eternal" reality, a "Satanic" stance diametrically opposed to the transcendent eternality of Christian or philosophic idealism. It is Protestantism deprived of its God. The words of Auerbach quoted earlier are especially descriptive of the novels of Joseph Conrad: "There is often something confusing, something hazy about them, something hostile to the reality which they represent. We not infrequently find a turning away from the practical will to live."[18]

The distinctive fact about Joyce Cary is that he resolved the dilemma that confronted his master, as he referred to Conrad, by turning away from an obsessive concern with the "threat" of nature and the unconscious and toward a recognition of man as *creator* and doer. And here again one is tempted to compare his outlook with that of some twentieth-century anthropologists. Consider, for example, Cary's treatment of time as it is related to cultural development in the following passages from *Mister Johnson*, a novel in which for the first time he realized the full meaning of his insight:

> Jirige is a new town, planted three years before to serve the ferry, but it has already created for itself a little desert surrounding it on all sides. Every tree has been cut or burnt down. The soil has been cropped and then left to blow about in dust. Close to the mat walls of the three compounds, large rubbish heaps throw a powerful stench of fish refuse down wind. These rubbish heaps are also village latrines. The paths to the village wander through and over them. No one has planted a shade tree, much less a fruit tree, but the sticks supporting the mat walls have insisted upon taking root, so that in the village itself, thanks only to Nature, there are patches of green leaf and blue shade.
>
> At eight o'clock in the morning this village is just waking up. Women are beating corn and fetching water; a dirty child with a large sore on its chin is sitting on the largest rubbish heap and holding a goat. Two men are dawdling toward the shore, holding themselves with crooked languor as if just out of hospital. Infinite boredom and disgusted resignation are expressed in their languid, crippled progress. (p. 25)
>
> Fada is the ordinary native town of the Western Sudan. It has no beauty, convenience or health. It is the dwelling place at one stage from the rabbit warren or the badger burrow; and not so cleanly kept as the latter. It is a pioneer settlement five or six hundred years old, built on its own rubbish heaps, without charm even of antiquity, even of smell. But neither

has it the freshness of the new. All its mud walls are eaten as if by smallpox; half of the mats in any compound are always rotten. Poverty and ignorance, the absolute government of jealous savages, conservative, as only the savage can be, have kept it at the first frontier of civilization. Its people would not know the change if time jumped back fifty thousand years. They live like mice or rats in a palace floor; all the magnificence and variety of the arts, the ideas, the learning and the battles of civilization go on over their heads and they do not even imagine them. (p. 99)

The examples of the two villages, strikingly similar even though one is five or six hundred years older than the other, illustrate Cary's conviction that civilization is the product of the creative powers of man, that social and moral values of the highest sort exist only in a society with a sense of pastness and antiquity. In other words, to have a civilization is to grasp an essential dimension of reality—the dimension of time. The pagan, Cary said in *The African Witch*, knows only one world. "One lived among men, trees, and beasts. One reckoned with them, handled them, fought them, loved them; and, when one died, one was born again a man, a tree, or a beast, to begin again with loving, fighting, and striving for the glory and the honour of creatures" (p. 178). He is, as Cary expressed it, "alive to the last jump of his pulse" and consequently has immense creative potential but is thwarted by his own limited perspective. The world of the pagan is largely a spatial world— what Cassirer called "space of action" as opposed to abstract space of geometry[19]—and his art forms of dance and song, improvised renditions of immediately felt emotions, are limited in depth and without lasting quality. . . .

Joyce Cary's interest in Africa and primitive forms of life was close to that of modern anthropologists in so far as he saw it objectively in its society-forming aspects and attempted to link these patterns with the forms of contemporary civilized society. It is interesting to note, for example, the number of points of agreement between his observations about primitive culture and those of Ernst Cassirer.[20] A more important link between him and Cassirer is their mutual agreement with the Kantian dictum of the powers of the imagination of the mind as an active creative and shaping force rather than as a *tabula rasa* on which sense data are inscribed. He most certainly would have subscribed to Cassirer's belief that "man's outstanding characteristic, his distinguishing mark, is not his metaphysical or physical nature—but his work. It is this work, it is this system of human activities, which defines and determines the circle of 'humanity'. Language, myth, religion, art, science, history are the constituents, the various sectors of this circle."[21]

To return then to the comparison between Joyce Cary and Joseph Conrad. One can easily see that the closed system of the latter is superseded (although not necessarily displaced) by the open system of the former; the circular movement of *Lord Jim* is replaced by the linear movement of *Mister Johnson*. Therefore, as he criticized Conrad for getting his fusion of form and content effected in the air in *Chance*, Henry James might very well have criticized Cary for (to adapt an excellent statement Cassirer used to describe the realm in which language operates) moving "in the middle kingdom between the 'indefinite' and the 'infinite'," or, in other words, for not effecting the complete revolution between the realistic and the romantic realms of being. This criticism would be especially valid in the first novels, where the story always threatens to lapse into mere anthropological and sociological theorizing. But it becomes less valid in those novels where Cary realized more clearly the dramatic potential of his idea.

Notes

1. Erich Auerbach, *Mimesis: The Representation of Reality in Western Literature*, trans. Willard Trask (Garden City, New York, 1957), p. 487.
2. *Ibid.*, p. 488.
3. Andrew Wright, *Joyce Cary: A Preface to His Novels* (London, 1958), p. 31.
4. *Ibid.*, p. 58.
5. Henry James, Preface to *The American* (New York, 1922), pp. xv–xvi.
6. *Ibid.*, xv.
7. *Ibid.*, xvii.
8. *Ibid.*
9. *Ibid.*, xvi.
10. E. M. Forster, *Abinger Harvest* (London, 1936), pp. 134–135.
11. See F. R. Leavis, *The Great Tradition* (London, 1948), p. 180.
12. Robert Penn Warren, "'The Great Mirage': Conrad and *Nostromo*", *Selected Essays* (New York, 1958), pp. 31–58.
13. Joseph Conrad, "*Youth*" and Two Other Stories (London, 1923), pp. 135–136.
14. Joyce Cary, *Aissa Saved* (London, 1952), p. 54. Citations from Cary in this text are to the Carfax edition (Michael Joseph) with the exception of the last three published novels, which are not included in that edition. Those novels not included are *Except the Lord* (Michael Joseph), *Not Honour More* (Michael Joseph), and *The Captive and the Free* (Michael Joseph).
15. Dorothy Van Ghent, *The English Novel: Form and Function* (New York, 1961), p. 234.
16. *Ibid.*
17. Paul Tillich, *The Protestant Era* (Abridged Edition), trans. James Luther Adams (London, 1957), pp. 22–23.
18. Auerbach, p. 487.
19. Ernst Cassirer, *An Essay on Man* (New Haven, 1944), p. 45.
20. See, for example, Cassirer's chapter "The Human World of Space and Time" in *An Essay on Man*, pp. 42–55. Also compare the analysis of the pagan world by Cary presented above with this comment by Cassirer: "To mythical and religious feeling nature becomes one great society, the society of life. Man is not endowed with outstanding rank in this society. He is a part of it but he is in no respects higher than any other member. Life possesses the same religious dignity in its humblest and in its highest forms. Men and animals, animals and plants are all on the same level. And we find the same principle—that of the solidarity and unbroken unity of life—if we pass from space to time. It holds not only in the order of simultaneity but also in the order of succession. The generations of men form a unique and uninterrupted chain. The former stages of life are preserved by reincarnation. The soul of the grandparent appears in a newborn child in a rejuvenated state. Present, past, and future blend into each other without any sharp line of demarcation; the limits between the generations of man become uncertain."—*Essay*, p. 83.
21. Charles W. Hendel, Introduction to Ernst Cassirer's *The Philosophy of Symbolic Forms*, I, trans. Ralph Manheim (New Haven, 1953), p. 68. There is a danger in pressing the analogy too far, however. Cary would hardly have concurred with Cassirer's ultimate emphasis upon science and reason. For an analysis of this aspect of Cassirer's philosophy see William K. Wimsatt and Cleanth Brooks, *Literary Criticism: A Short History* (New York, 1957), p. 703.

GILES MITCHELL
From "*Herself Surprised*:
The Design of a Permanent Character"
The Art Theme in Joyce Cary's Trilogy
1971, pp. 23–34

In Sara Monday, Cary reveals what he calls a ". . . human constant . . . a part of reality objective to us, that is, a permanent character of the world as we know it . . . ".[1] Cary is not writing of Sara here but of the nature of "elemental characters" in whose existence we must believe else[2] ". . . the world would probably vanish into nothing".[3] Sara is in this sense Nature. In a more specific sense she is basic, pre-moral or perhaps supra-moral female nature. It will be one of the purposes of this study to show precisely, if possible, the human constant in Sara. The discovery of the elemental constant in Sara gives Thomas Wilcher a new vision of society and Gulley Jimson a new vision of God. Sara is taken into the minds of both men as a reshaping force. To these two men she is not only flesh, wife, mistress—raw material, but also pattern. To Wilcher she is for many years a companion and mistress; later she becomes for him the ancient design wrought by all pilgrim spirits from Chaucer's Wife to Bunyan's Christian. To Jimson she is for years mistress, wife, and the female of females, original woman. Later she becomes a symbol of universal being and the subject of his most ambitious painting.

The critic's first task in working with *Herself Surprised* will be to determine how Sara appears to the critic rather than to Wilcher and Jimson. To say so is to imply, of course, the belief that this novel does not depend on either of the other two novels for its aesthetic integrity. A valid, although naturally limited view of what Sara is as material and pattern can be deduced from a reading of her novel alone. The question "What is the meaning of Sara Monday?" may therefore be profitably considered at this point.

Sara herself is not interested in the problem of identity, the problem which engages so many protagonists in the modern novel. Although she has an intuitive knowledge of self that allows her to achieve a high degree of personality integrity, she is not interested in self-analysis of the sort that so afflicts Mrs. Dalloway, for example. Sara is, really, not interested in motive at all. She says at the end of the story that she knows herself better than ever before, but she does not. Her own story suggests that she does not, and the subsequent books in the trilogy confirm the fact that she does not. If she were deeply interested in knowing herself, she would probably, given her lack of education and her puritan background, see herself as irrevocably fallen from innocence. However, near the end of her story, while living with Wilcher at Cravens Gardens, she remarks on her feeling of maiden innocence: ". . . I would be gay all evening, as if I'd been a young girl coming from a party or from the Communion; not yet knowing my own self or the traps of the world . . .".[4]

Writing the story reveals little of herself to Sara. Apparently she is not aware of her real motives for writing it. She is glad enough of the opportunity to sell her book to the papers, for the money will defray Tommy's school bills; and the arrangement of material in the first few chapters suggests vaguely that she is writing with serial publication in mind. Chapter one, for example, ends with the suggestion that her husband may leave her because of her uncontrollable whimsicality. Chapter two ends with the hint that she is going to try to justify a life of practical expediency necessary to the happiness of unpretty women. The third chapter ends with the implication that the reader may look forward to an account of the fall of a respectable woman, but after chapter six the technique of ending each chapter with a promise of exciting things to come is abandoned, and from that point on, most of the chapters are arranged after a rather casual, primarily chronological fashion, each enclosing an episode which is, in the main, pleasant to Sara's memory. In spite of her obvious failure to present an analytical account of her criminal motives and acts and by her cheerful unawareness of discrepancies in her tale, Sara does, however, characterize herself as a person whose identity is supremely worth investigation by the proper reader. It is true that Sara is cognizant of the fact that she is sometimes involved in a moral dilemma, but such knowledge is not painful to her: "If I did wrong with Mr. Hickson so often, I can't believe I did but right" (p. 38). What Hickson has given

her, among other things, is a negative example in himself of the results of too much analysis: He thinks about his life so much that he can get no joy out of it (p. 40). Sara attempts neither to understand nor to exonerate herself in logical terms. When Monday accuses her of having affairs with Hickson, the garden boy, Jimson and perhaps others, Sara does not deny his charges, partially because they are very likely true and partially because she realizes that it is emotionally and intellectually simpler to let Monday blame himself than for her to try to present a complex of explanations. Therefore she merely tells him that she cannot trust herself. "I don't know what I am", she truthfully adds (p. 73).

There are three important ways in which Sara does know herself. She knows in a simple, fundamental way when and why she is lost, when and why she is found and when and why she is happy. She recognizes, accepts and rejoices in her instinctive need for a man to care for. It ought to be noted that Sara never mentions her maiden name; she is interested in herself only as a wife. After driving Jimson away, following the funeral of Monday, by her emphatic refusal to marry him, she begins to feel uneasy. She begins to worry about whether he is working and about how he is otherwise managing (p. 103). She begins to feel a pressure in her chest. A few days after deviously letting him know where she is to be found, she sees him and knows what the pressure was about (p. 105). The result is that she "marries" him and achieves a sense of belonging and being; she feels "like a woman" (p. 107) instead of "like a truck, which goes where it is pushed and knows not why" (p. 107). When because of a punch in the nose she leaves Jimson and goes to Queensport, she feels that she has "no business to be there alone" (p. 135). When she returns to Jimson to the one room that she shares with him at Miss Slaughter's, she feels once more that she is in her "own home" (p. 142). She feels this way partially because she has taken over the duties of housekeeper and cook, and when she can clean a house, she creates it and thus it becomes hers. Therefore she says, "I found myself singing over my pots, delighted every day" (p. 142). Sara believes that her "true place" in the world is the kitchen (p. 182). Although Sara may at times be a bit devious when her joy in living is threatened, she is at bottom honest both in living her life and telling her story. It is doubtful that the newspaper people who buy her story are going to be greatly pleased with it. There are no lurid details of any kind in it. Sara is not promiscuous in the usual sense, and she does not dwell on the physical pleasures of the few bedroom scenes mentioned. There is really very little, other than an occasional pious platitude, to make the book appealing to the public. Fortunately, Sara is being paid in advance.

Not only does Sara not see herself as having been promiscuous, but she does not sentimentalize her experience. She does not have to do so; she knows for certain that she has had a great deal of happiness, for she is an experienced practitioner of the art of loving life. She does not delude herself into mistaking any of the forms of pseudo-love, as Fromm calls it,[5] for the real thing. The realism of Sara's view of herself is shown in many ways, one of the most significant of which is this avoidance of the "abstractification of love in terms of time".[6] Sara is a remarkably full illustration of Fromm's theory of the kind of person who knows how to love. The four chief elements in the makeup of such a person are the following: self-knowledge, discipline, concentration, patience. That Sara establishes, through a creative love, a highly successful relationship with the world there can be little doubt. Her kind of self-knowledge prevents destructive illusions; her knowledge is an "intuition, the essence of any art",[7] an intuition which is a blend of her simple theory and her practice of a disciplined life. Although Sara regards herself as having been at times self-indulgent, and though she sees her love of ease as having been the cause of her downfall, the real truth is that she is a disciplined person and thus is a "productive"[8] person. She always enjoys "a thing done right" (p. 137) whether in dressing, cleaning, cooking, or love-making. Even when angry with Jimson, if she sees that she is going to yield to his amorous advances in spite of herself, she will decide to make the event as pleasurable as possible: "So I had to do as he wished, and since to do so without kindness and kisses is a mean dirty thing, I let myself be friendly" (p. 141). Her love of seeing a thing well done is so great that while she is in the midst of her first great cleaning of Tolbrook, she refuses to consider going back to Jimson even though he urges her to return. Sara is not compulsive, not a perfectionist. Her labor at Tolbrook is based on an organic relationship with the house-hold objects. Compulsiveness, being based on fear, is mechanistic, but "the creative person unites himself with his material".[9] Sara is *Weib*, mother, lover, producer; she is not "the indolent, luxurious classical mistress". Sara realizes that she knows how to love. While sitting in the newly-cleaned kitchen at Tolbrook, she remembers "what Jimson said about my true home being the kitchen, and that I was a born servant in my soul, and my heart gave a turnover and I felt the true joy of my life" (p. 182).

Sara invites comparison with Molly Bloom in such a way as to give a certain specificity, or rather a certain emphasis, to Sara's identity. The literary kinship of the two women revealed in *Ulysses* and in *Herself Surprised* in itself alone confirms Jimson's final view of Sara as a symbol of fecundity, among other things. Both women justify their sexual adventures by insisting that they are merely creatures of nature, for which not they but God is answerable. Sara so insists at least fifteen times and by implication numerous other times. Molly is explicit on this score at least three times and by implication throughout her entire monologue. Sara's justification in one passage is couched in language much like that in one of Molly's: "Providence must answer for our shapes . . ." (p. 26). ". . . I suppose that's what a woman is supposed to be there for or he wouldn't have made us the way he did . . .".[10] The word "nature" is frequently used by Sara and Molly in their generous reflections on fleshly desire. Both women greatly admire their own bodies. Sara at age forty-six, in her bath, looks admiringly down at her body and bewails her loss of youth and love. Molly while making chamber music, looks longingly down at her body and yearns for a true lover. Both comment occasionally on their best features, their breasts and thighs, which are large and fertile. The women particularly admire their breasts. "They excite myself sometimes",[11] Molly says. Each sees likenesses between her body and those in classical statuary. Both have husbands who are slightly depraved. Bloom's mild fetishism is parallel to Wilcher's occasional exhibitionism. Neither woman cares greatly for other women, but are completely absorbed in their men. Neither gets along well with daughters. Each is so grief-stricken at the loss of an only male child that she can bear to allude to the loss only once. Both want to find sons. Sara will find a son in any male child who will allow her to do so; she has three such in the course of her life. Molly wants a son in Stephen Daedelus, but having perhaps less delicacy than Sara, she wants him as a lover also. Although Sara is not as complex in terms of overt symbolism as Molly is, both are symbols of the eternal female, of life force. Each retains her essential innocence by giving herself to life. Joyce is surely referring to Molly's special kind of innocence when he calls her Madonna Bloom.[12] Sara's book is a work in praise of earthly life and love. Molly's monologue "is a vision of abundance".[13] She is "earth . . . life force . . .".[14] She is "sane full amoral fertilisable untrustworthy engaging shrewd prudent indifferent *Weib. Ich bin das Fleisch das stets be-jaht*".[15] Another aspect of fecundity shared by these women is that both are richly lactescent during the nursing season. Sara nurses her babies for a full nine months and could nurse them

longer if she wished; yet her breasts remain full and beautiful. Jimson sees them symbolically and draws what is apparently the traditional vein of fertility across them in one of the bath pictures.[16] Molly's breasts are so full that Bloom himself must give her relief orally, and he wishes to milk them into his tea. Tindall sees a sacramental significance in certain of Bloom's libations, and although he does not mention this one (not allowed by Molly in any case), it seems probable that Bloom's desire for such a drink may suggest not only an aspect of the man's spiritual isolation but also an aspect of the woman's failure to realize herself spiritually.

It would indeed be willful for the critic to insist that Cary consciously wishes his readers to compare Sara and Molly. There are no overt allusions to *Ulysses* in *Herself Surprised*. If there is such an allusion in the trilogy, it occurs at the end of *To Be a Pilgrim*, where it seems likely that Cary wishes one to contrast Molly with Ann Wilcher.

The antiquity of Sara's essential being as a constant by which the true female may always be known is suggested in the observation by Andrew Wright that Sara has a Biblical counter-part in Sarah, the wife of Abraham. Wright here comments on an aspect of Sara's capacity for surprise not mentioned by other critics. When Abraham's Sarah, at the age of ninety-one, hears that she is to bear a son, she "laughed within herself, saying, after I am waxed old shall I have pleasure?"[17] Both these women are wanderers. Both allow themselves to be used by their husbands. The Biblical Sarah's services to the Pharaoh are, to say the least, of a dubious nature; yet Abraham profits materially by them. Monday flourishes as a result of Sara's relationship with Hickson, and Jimson "rents" Sara to Wilcher. Both women apparently submit themselves deeply to their men in a way never found by most other women, and although Sara keeps her own integrity, she, like the women in Lawrence's novels, is never able to achieve perfect equilibrium in her love relationships. Like Lawrence's women, she lives in a mutable, tragic world. The literary figures with whom Sara may be profitably compared are all wife types. Even Molly can say yes to Bloom for all her life, even though she is at present engaged in an affair with Blazes Boylan. Cary strongly repudiates any suggestion that his Sara is at all like Moll Flanders—"that old bawd".[18] Moll Flanders is one of the most immoral and one of the least likeable women in literature, whereas Sara is "the most engaging woman in contemporary fiction".[19]

It is inevitable that the most engaging woman of pre-modern literature be called to mind by a study of *Herself Surprised*. Chaucer's Wife of Bath, like Sara, is a highly creative woman ever on the alert for an opportunity to be happy. Like Alison, Sara has been, for most of her life, a firm believer that the generative force of life has its basis in the flesh. Alison believes that the chain of Eros ascends from the "Venus Chambre" to God, and although Sara does not try to erect a philosophical rationale for her love of the flesh, it is to be noted that her religious affections are most strong when she is carrying on a satisfactory sexual affair. Sara and Alison are both "al Venerien", and therefore have a proper regard for their sexual attractiveness and at the same time have been properly admired by others for this quality. Ironically, the man each loved the best "was of his love daungerous". Having loved passionately, both women have a painful awareness that "age, alas hath / al wol envenyme". But yet not all: They both, at the end of their stories, still hope to find a workable love.

In a sense, Sara's story is an announcement to the world through the press that she knows how to be a good wife, that she is a skillful cook and housekeeper, that she is a warm lover and in general a circumspect human being. Alison's tale is a statement of her longing for the security of ideal love. What she will find is the love of God. Sara, however, is to be redeemed through love in this world only. Like the Wife, she has five husbands whose lives with her make a story of the reconciliation of human nature to an ideal mode of conduct. Sara, unlike the Wife of Bath, is nevertheless not on her way to the City of God but to a life of brutal poverty which will end in a violent death at the hands of Jimson. Sara does not live in the carefully structured, Christian world of the Wife of Bath. Sara does finally find herself a young husband—a neurotic widower with whom she is not happy. She ends her life with an old husband, a brutal creature with whom she has nothing in common except a fear of a pauper's grave. Alison seems in her prologue to be able to argue her way into heaven by the sheer vitality of her rhetoric and by her brilliant distortions of the Pauline pronouncements on marriage, just as she has dominated her husbands by the force of her character and by her wiles. The point is that she lives in a world where she can be finally and completely saved. The world of the comic experience in Chaucer's tales is framed by the larger worlds of the knight and the parson, and as the Wife draws near to Canterbury, she is to participate in a saving act of penance to which the parson directs her. The prison chaplain merely tells Sara that she is getting what she deserves and no more. Sara's world is one of fearful insecurity and chance, a world in which at the crucial moments in her life she finds herself somehow surprised; for she cannot tell, really, whether she is saved or damned. Therefore she keeps her serenity and loves her life.

Although she is a wanderer who during her adult life has but one abode that one would normally call home, Sara's psychic energies are not vitiated through helpless diffusion. Wherever she is at any given time (except for the brief interlude with Rozzie) she knows enough about what she is to know what she wants. Her consistent and frequent use of domestic imagery shows her great love for and preoccupation with homey things. The fact that Sara in her metaphors so readily sees colors, forms, smells in domestic terms suggests her ability to make the world her home, that home is a creative image in the heart, an image which cannot be destroyed but only modified. Since she has no sense of history and since she, unlike Wilcher, has little of material value to be destroyed, she sees change itself as an organically creative thing. "Things change", she says, "like mold in a bread bin" (p. 39). To maintain such a view is Sara's way of surviving destruction. Sara sees herself as having been acted upon, especially by her men, but the truth is that she makes a profound and in part aggressive commitment to what Cary sees as the basic psychic conditions of the female role. These conditions are not primarily but only partially those which require passiveness. Sara's love is as active as her imaginative power is vital. The significance of this vitality, for the ultimate purposes of this art trilogy, is revealed in her artistry as lover, and in her power of metaphor, which makes circumstances conform to an imaginative ideal. . . .

It is the design which this process follows that shows Sara to be artistic pattern. It has been noted above that Sara's intuitive powers are so disciplined, so concentrated in terms of her purpose to function fully as a female that the essence of her being blends with the raw material of her experience to produce a shaped life. Before this shape can be fully seen, the process in which essence and material become blended at a given point in Sara's life must be studied. The place which best illustrates the unifying power in Sara occurs not long after she becomes cook at Tolbrook. She is sitting in her kitchen at the end of a long day, feeling the joy of her work, reveling in the beauty of her surroundings. Because the passage is crucial to an understanding of Sara as a kind of artist-figure, it needs to be quoted in its entirety.

> So here I am, I thought, mistress of my own world in my own kitchen, and I looked at the shining steel of the range and the china on the dresser glittering like jewels, and the dish covers, hanging in their row from the big venison one on the left to the little chop one on the right, as beautiful as a row of calendar moons, and the kitchen table scrubbed as white as beef fat and the copper on the dark wall throwing out a glow to warm the heart, and the blue delf bowls like pots of precious balm.

> And then beyond where the larder door stood ajar you could see bottles of oil and relish and anchovies and pickles and underneath the lid of the big flour bin as white as its own lovely flour; I call it a treat for queens to sink your hands in new wheaten flour. And next the larder, the dark scullery door with a wink within the brass taps to say: "Your servants, madam," and a slow drip from the one or other to tell me: "We are ready this minute and never will fail," and next the scullery, the kitchen pantry. I could not see its glass-fronted cupboards as fine as the British Museum, or its china and glass in thick heaps like the treasures of Aladdin. I could not see them, but I felt them like kingdoms in my charge. And, indeed, *I felt bits of myself running out from the grand kitchen into pantry and scullery and larder and beyond into the passage and the stillroom and even to the wood cellar and the boot hole as if I was really a king or queen whose flesh is brought up to be the father of all his countries, and not to forget the little byelands even when they are on the dark side of the sun. You would say that I was putting out in buds like a shallot* [Italics mine] with my big kitchen heart in the middle and my little hearts all around in the empire of those good faithful offices, all fitted up as they were . . . . Well, I thought, if you tied a knot of all the roads and railways and pipes and wires in the world it would come to a kitchen in the middle of it. And so close and neat, there wouldn't be room in it for a single piece of useless nonsense or vain furniture. For the great beauty of my jewels was that every one of them was needed . . . my shining armor was to keep dinners warm and my regiments were to cut up chickens and ducks . . . . (pp. 182–184).

Sara achieves the organic unity described in this passage in two ways principally, one of which is the force of her being; the other is her use of figurative language. It ought to be noted that at this point Sara is alone, forsaken by Jimson and, in effect, by her daughters. She is living in an ancient decaying manor from which the family have long since vanished. Yet Sara at this time feels herself to be at the very center of life; at the center of the kingdom of life, she rules as queen. At the center of a great house, she is servant. At the center of the natural world, she is a shallot surrounded by burgeoning flowers which make seasoning for the food which becomes in another metaphor the regiments commanded by Sara in her war on chaos. The kitchen, which grows metaphorically out of Sara's flesh, a flesh designed, "brought up", to give life to the world, becomes the center of all active life. The world flows out of Sara's flesh to shape itself IN METAPHORIC FORM into a pattern which is "close and neat". The process is an upsurge of the power of rebirth. The design is the formal design of art.

Sara is both form and matter. She has been absorbing the matter all her life; it has been growing in her for years. This matter has been absorbed specifically in her flesh by the force of the sort of experience which she describes as having with Jimson when they go to the Ancombe fair: "My flesh was so full of the dust and the warmth and the beer and the shaking" (p. 129). The flesh which for many years has taken into itself such generative matter as earth, heat, and Jimson's love will later reproduce this matter in artistic form. The reproductive process described in the kitchen scene is the climax of Sara's life as well as of her book.

Notes

1. Joyce Cary, *Art and Reality: Ways of the Creative Process* (New York, Doubleday and Company, Inc., 1958), p. 19.
2. *Ibid.*, p. 20.
3. *Ibid.*
4. Joyce Cary, *Herself Surprised* (New York, Harper and Brothers, 1941), p. 200. Subsequent quotations from this novel will be followed by page number.
5. Erich Fromm, *The Art of Loving* (London, George Allen and Unwin, 1957), p. 99.
6. *Ibid.*, p. 101.
7. *Ibid.*, p. 4.
8. *Ibid.*, p. 125.
9. *Ibid.*, p. 17.
10. James Joyce, *Ulysses* (New York, The Modern Library, 1946), p. 762.
11. *Ibid.*
12. Jacques Mercanton, "The Hours of James Joyce, Part II", *The Kenyon Review*, XXV (Winter, 1963), 100.
13. W. Y. Tindall, *A Reader's Guide to James Joyce* (New York, Noonday Press, 1959), p. 234.
14. *Ibid.*
15. *Ibid.* Tindall is here quoting from Joyce's Letters. Compare Cary's statement that Sara's ". . . morals were the elementary morals of a primitive woman, of nature herself, which do not change; and she was supremely indifferent to politics, religion, economics". Quoted by Lord David Cecil. "The Novelist at Work: A Conversation Between Joyce Cary and Lord David Cecil". *Adam International Review*, XVIII (Nov.–Dec., 1950), 15. Note further the statement by Jimson that "when you knew Sara, you knew womankind, and no one who doesn't know womankind knows anything about the nature of Nature". Joyce Cary, *The Horse's Mouth* (New York, Harper and Brothers, 1944), p. 264.
16. It is possible that Cary is here remembering Browning's Bishop, who has a lump of *lapis lazuli* "Blue as a vein o'er the Madonna's breast". Cary shrinks from suggesting—except in the most subtle possible way in *The Horse's Mouth*—a comparison between Sara and the Holy Virgin.
17. Quoted by Andrew Wright in an essay appended to *Herself Surprised*, p. 112.
18. *Ibid.*, p. 284.
19. Carlyle King, "Joyce Cary and the Creative Imagination", *Tamarack Review*, No. 10 (Winter, 1959), p. 49.

G. K. CHESTERTON

1874–1936

Gilbert Keith Chesterton was born in London on May 29, 1874. He attended St. Paul's, where he wrote and edited a magazine called *The Debater*, the Slade School of Art, and the University of London. In 1896 he took the first of several publishing jobs, and began writing the torrent of reviews, articles, essays, and books that would continue throughout his life. His more than 100 volumes included poetry (notably *The Ballad of the White Horse*, 1911, and *Lepanto*, 1915), essay collections (such as *All Things Considered*, 1908), philosophy (*What's Wrong with the World?*, 1910, which set forth his theory of "Distributism"), criticism (of Stevenson, Browning, Blake, and Dickens, to name a few), history (*A Short History of England*, 1917), fiction (ranging from the luminous nightmare *The Man Who Was Thursday*, 1908, to the celebrated "Father Brown" detective stories), and autobiography.

He also wrote several successful plays (at the urging of Shaw), reams of journalism, and weekly columns for the London *Daily News* and the *Illustrated London News*. The latter continued with scarcely a break for twenty-five years. Chesterton, his younger brother Cecil, and Belloc founded the journal *Eye Witness* in 1911; Chesterton edited it as the *New Witness* from 1916 to 1923, and as *G. K.'s Weekly* from 1925 to 1936.

In 1922 Chesterton converted to Catholicism after which point the religious content in his work became more explicit. Among his later books are biographies of St. Francis (1923) and St. Thomas Aquinas (1933). In 1934 he was named Knight Commander With Star of the Order of St. Gregory, and was a Fellow of the Royal Society of Literature.

Chesterton married Frances Blogg in 1901. They lived in Beaconsfield, where he died on June 14, 1936.

Personal

All men one may say, or very nearly all men, have one leading moral defect. Few have one leading Christian virtue. That of Gilbert Chesterton was unmistakably the virtue of Christian charity: a virtue especially rare in writing men, and rarest of all in such of them as have a pursuing appetite for controversy—that is, for bolting out the truth.

He loved his fellow-men. Through this affection, which was all embracing, he understood the common man; and that virtue, which was so conspicuous in all his private life and broad river of daily speech, was both a strength and a weakness to his fame.

It was a strength because it gave him access to every mind; men will always listen to a friend; and so much was he a friend of all those for whom he wrote that all were prepared to listen, however much they were puzzled. I shall always remember how once in America a man said to me, a man who I believe had never seen Chesterton in the flesh: "When I read of his death I felt the shock one feels upon the loss of a daily and beloved acquaintance."

The drawback, however, of this virtue of charity as regards

its action upon his fame was that it prevented the presence in what he wrote of that acerbity or "bite" which gives an edge or rather a spearhead to every effort at persuasion. It preserved him from enmities. He had no enemies; and in a society such as ours in Modern England, a society which above all demands comfort and ease, this gave him a universality of appeal but furnished no occasion for attack. You do not rise from the reading of one of Chesterton's appreciations with that feeling of being armed which you obtain from the great satirists and particularly from the masters of irony.

He wounded none, but thus also he failed to provide weapons wherewith one may wound and kill folly. Now without wounding and killing, there is no battle; and thus, in this life, no victory; but also no peril to the soul through hatred.

Of the personal advantage to himself of so great and all-pervading a charity, too much cannot be said; but I believe it to be a drag upon his chances of endurance upon paper—for what that may be worth—and it is worth nothing compared with eternal things. Christendom would seem to be now entering an ultimate phase in the struggle between good and evil, which is, for us, the battle between the Catholic Church and its opponents. In that struggle, those will stand out in the future most vividly who most provoked hostility. To his lasting advantage in the essential things of the spirit, of his own individual soul, he did not provoke it.

He was aided in the preservation of such serenity by the gradualness of the approach he made to the right side of the battle. His name and writings were already familiar before his conversion, to a general public, which had no idea of the Faith. They were thus familiar and accepted long before he threw down the last challenge by fully accepting the Creed, the Unity and the temporal disabilities of Catholic allegiance. He had before his reception acquired, as it were, a privileged position which permitted him to be still listened to after he had crossed that frontier of the Faith beyond which lies all that his fellow-countrymen oppose.

Herein he was blessed and may be justly envied by those who are condemned by their Faith to exclusion and exile. In the appreciation of a man rather than of a writer virtue is immeasurably more important than literary talent and appeal. For these last make up nothing for the salvation of the soul and for an ultimate association with those who should be our unfailing companions in Beatitude: the Great Company. Of that Company he now is; so that it is a lesser and even indifferent thing to determine how much he shall also be of the company, the earthly and temporal company, of the local and temporarily famous.

What place he may take according to that lesser standard I cannot tell, because many years must pass before a man's position in the literature of his country can be called securely established.

We are too near to decide on this. But because we are so near and because those (such as I who write this) who were his companions, knew him through his very self and not through his external activity, we are in communion with him. So be it. He is in Heaven.—HILAIRE BELLOC, *On the Place of Gilbert Chesterton in English Letters*, 1940, pp. 79–84

More interesting than either the sceptical Belloc's submission to authority or the introspective Baring's unexplained conversion from atheism is the growth of religious conviction in Chesterton. By this is not meant his entry into the Roman Catholic church, which did not take place until he was forty-eight years of age and had been for most of his adult life a prominent and orthodox Anglican. The Roman Catholic community of England hailed his entry with such jubilation—

priests wrote triumphantly to each other in such extravagant terms as 'a man-child is born to Jesus Christ'—that they might have been celebrating the conversion of an African witch-doctor rather than the entry of an established Anglo-Catholic apologist.

Of much more interest is the way in which, as a young man, Chesterton developed from an agnostic, deeply disturbed by the artistic and moral decadence of the English society in which he grew up, into a belief in Christ's divinity and acceptance of orthodox Christianity. It is a complicated, tangled growth, which was certainly nurtured by his wife Frances, a frail, frequently ailing woman, as ardent in religion as, it seems probable, sexually frigid, to whom he was chivalrously and uniquely devoted; the first person he had met, he said, who actually practised religion.

But the growth was not rooted there. It was rooted in a sensitive adolescence in which he was appalled at some sin of his own—enormous or imagined so—of which throughout his life he gave a few dark hints; it probably contained a strand of latent homosexuality, and some looming evil which seems to have been a kind of diabolism. In the closing years of adolescence it drove him almost to the point of mental breakdown. Years later, shortly before he was received into the Roman Catholic church, he wrote in a letter to Father Ronald Knox, the Oxford intellectual who had taken part in his instruction: 'I am in a state now when I feel a monstrous charlatan, as if I wore a mask and were stuffed with cushions, whenever I see anything about the public G.K.C.; it hurts me; for though the views I express are real, the image is horribly unreal compared with the real person who needs help just now. I have as much vanity as anybody about any of these superficial successes while they are going on; but I never feel for a moment that they affect the reality of whether I am utterly rotten or not; so that any public comments on my religious position seem like a wind on the other side of the world; as if they were about somebody else—as indeed they are. I am not troubled about a great fat man who appears on platforms and in caricatures; even when he enjoys controversies on what I believe to be the right side. I am concerned about what has become of a little boy whose father showed him a toy theatre, and a schoolboy whom nobody ever heard of, with his brooding on doubts and dirt and daydreams, of crude conscientiousness so inconsistent as to be near hypocrisy; and all the morbid life of the lonely mind of a living person with whom I have lived. It is that story, that so often came near to ending badly, that I want to end well.'— DUDLEY BARKER, *G. K. Chesterton: A Biography*, 1973, pp. 16–17

How Chesterton became the kind of writer he was makes, biographically speaking, a curious story. As we learn from Maisie Ward, he did not reach puberty until he was eighteen or nineteen—evidently he suffered from some mild glandular disorder, as one might have guessed from his later fatness. The fact was clearly important. For to come to puberty so belatedly, when in most other respects you are in the midst of adult life, must be a very strange, and perhaps shattering, experience; and so it proved with Chesterton. He became a victim of phantasmagoric sexual obsessions, which convinced him of the close and immediate presence of the devil. And, more to the point, it gave to the intellectual movements of the day, in which he had already taken a cheerful debating-society interest, a sulphurous flavour of diabolism for him. His reaction was to combat them with the weapons of his childhood—with a toy-theatre medievalism, pasteboard swords and debating-society high jinks. It was a reaction of genius, restoring his moral balance and leaving his intellect untrammelled and free. None the less it left him with some extremely odd, and rather comic, misconceptions. It prevented him from having much real notion of what Ibsenism, or Zolaism, or Symbolism or Schopenhauerian pessimism were about. It even left him feeling that there was something sinister, and metaphysically subversive, in Impressionist painting—at least, he thought that his own 'black night of the soul' might partly be laid at its door.— P. N. FURBANK, "Chesterton the Edwardian," *G. K. Chesterton: A Centenary Appraisal*, ed. John Sullivan, 1974, pp. 16–17

General

Does it never occur to Mr. Chesterton that frequently a dignity, a justness, a clarity might be obtained by the elimination of some, at first sight, brilliant remark? He has a 'debonair' way of throwing into articles and essays such irrelevant items as cows, maiden aunts, lamp-posts, and stars, until we are left gasping and 'winded' in the race after his meaning. 'Ergo,' we sit down half-way there—wherever 'there' may be—laugh with what breath is left in us, and watch Mr. Chesterton plunging splendidly along until he is a mere speck in the distance. From *Twelve Types*, for example, we take in hazard the following sentence: 'When Will. Morris says that "love is enough," it is obvious that he asserts in those words that all science, politics, ambition, money, houses, carriages, concerts, gloves, walking-sticks, door-knockers, railway-stations, cathedrals, and all other things one may choose to tabulate, are unnecessary.' It is exhilarating and great fun but it is not literature. There may be a subtle relationship between the ashes in the reader's pipe and the Assyrian Empire; it is interesting to think so; but it is most uninteresting to labour a proof thereof.

Quite legitimately Mr. Chesterton might retort that his style has made him, and is part of himself. True, doubtless; but the line of demarcation between style and affectation, the real and the spurious, is faint. Could he not do with a little less . . . gunpowder, shall we say? A heavy charge spreads the shots, and at present he is so busy loading and discharging his ammunition that he grows careless with regard to the important question of aim. Fewer shots, well trained and directed, would be more effective, although we are far from suggesting that he never hits the mark. On the contrary, there are sentences and whole paragraphs of his which grip, as we have already noted. 'Heaven, so infinite is its care, may shake with anger from bound to bound at the sight of a caged bird.' That appeals; it is passionate and challenging—one of the splendid indiscretions which compensate for a deal of loose firing. The charming digression—and his digressions are often charming—on railway-signals and language in *G. F. Watts*; the chapter vi. in *Robert Browning*, with its insight and fascinating comparison of the probable manner in which Meredith and Browning would treat a given subject; his description of the old 'bric-à-brac' shop in *The Ball and the Cross*, and many other detached portions of his writings, move us to willing admiration. Occasionally we find a phrase incomparably fine, such as 'Morning lifted itself laboriously over London,' or 'The long tide of sunset-light'; or, as in his last *Daily News* article, discussing the desolation of a Lancashire moorland, we get an inspiring thought—'It is not the ugliness that I criticize. I don't mind being ugly, but I have a strong objection to being sad.' When we read *Defendants* or *Twelve Types*, we ask for more; but when, for the sake of a weekly article, we discover arguments upon the relation of Byzantine architecture to penny loaves, fishes, bicycles, or whatever whimsy enters the writer's mind we cry off—distortion has limits.—W. L. RENWICK, "The Chesterton Manner," *AcL*, Feb. 18, 1911, pp. 206–8

Mr. Chesterton, as an anti-Modernist, compromises himself perhaps more vitally than as an anti-Socialist. His notion that he is an anti-Socialist is founded on the erroneous superstition that he was once a Socialist. An early fancy for Socialism no more makes a man a Socialist than an early fancy for the architecture of St. Sophia's makes him a Moslem. In the spirit of the schoolmaster who offered Coleridge a little essay on Method to cure his discursiveness, I recommend my own tracts to Mr. Chesterton to cure his delusion that social salvation is attainable by a combination of personal righteousness with private property in the form of a picturesque allotment. When Mr. Chesterton combines a knowledge of the law of rent with his regard for the law of God, he will become a Socialist for the first time; and his Socialism will stick.

But anti-Modernism is another matter. The law of rent and the law of value are, unfortunately, still in the technical sphere: they are not in the air: they are known only to those who have cared enough about the intellectual soundness of their politics to make a special study of economics. Diners-out do not talk of Gresham's law, or Ricardo's law, or Jevons's law, any more to-day than they did when they dined with Shakespear at the Mermaid, with Johnson at the Literary Club, or with Dickens at Tavistock House. But they do talk about Evolution and Natural Selection (often, alas! confusing them damnably) and about Eugenics, about Darwin and Mendel, Bergson and Butler, Hertz and Marconi, aeroplanes and trinitrotoluene. Now it is not conceivable that Mr. Chesterton is as ignorant of these matters as Shakespear, Johnson and Dickens. He cannot believe that Marconi is a bookmaker with whom certain politicians had shady dealings; that Galton was a prurient blackguard who invented the word eugenics as a mask for disgusting improprieties; that Evolution is a silly and blasphemous attempt to discredit the Garden of Eden; that motor-cars are nuisances, aeroplanes toys to which Chinese kites are far superior, and war still an affair of battle-axes mightily wielded by armour-plated athletic giants. Yet Mr. Chesterton has written a good many sentences which seem to mean either these things or nothing. I will even go so far as to say that it will serve him right if future professors, specialising in the literature of the Capitalistic Era, explain to their students that they must not rely on traditional dates, as it is clear from internal evidence that though Wells and Bennett and Chesterton are dated as contemporaries, Chesterton must have died before the middle of the nineteenth century, and may perhaps be placed as early as the fifteenth or sixteenth as a master of the School of Rabelais. Wells and Bennett, on the other hand, could not possibly have come earlier than the post-Ibsen period. "As against this," we may conceive the future professor lecturing, "it is alleged that one of Chesterton's best books is a monograph on Shaw, who is dated as a contemporary of Wells. But the best authorities are agreed that this extraordinarily enlightened author was one of the pioneers of the twenty-fifth century, and that the allusions to him in the books of the nineteenth and twentieth centuries are later interpolations, the pseudo-Chesterton book being probably by Shaw himself, a hypothesis which fully accounts for its heartfelt eulogy. It has been objected that the writer does not seem to have read Shaw's works; but this is clearly an intentional mystification, very characteristic of the freakish founder of the Shavians."— GEORGE BERNARD SHAW, "The Case against Chesterton," *NS*, May 13, 1916, pp. 133–36

Chesterton's bibliography consists of one hundred volumes, the "quiet resolute practice of the liberty of a free mind," as Mrs. Ward admirably expresses it. Out of this enormous output time will choose. Time often chooses oddly, or so it seems to us, though it is more reasonable to suppose that it is we ourselves who are erratic in our judgements. We are already proving our eccentricity in the case of Chesterton: a generation that appreciates Joyce finds for some reason Chesterton's equally fanatical play on words exhausting. Perhaps it is that he is still suspected of levity, and the generation now reaching middle-age has been a peculiarly serious one. Mrs. Ward should at least alter that opinion: she dwells at great length on Chesterton's political opinions. He cared passionately for individual liberty and for local patriotism, but the party which he largely inspired has an art-and-crafty air about it today. He was too good a man for politics: he never, one feels, penetrated far enough into the murky intricacies of political thought. To be a politician a man needs to be a psychologist, and Chesterton was no psychologist, as his novels prove. He saw things in absolute terms of good and evil, and his immense charity prevented him admitting the amount of ordinary shabby deception in human life. At their worst our politicians were fallen angels.

For the same reason that he failed as a political writer he succeeded as a religious one, for religion is simple, dogma is simple. Much of the difficulty of theology arises from the efforts of men who are not primarily writers to distinguish a quite simple idea with the utmost accuracy. He re-stated the original thought with the freshness, simplicity and excitement of discovery. In fact, it was discovery: he unearthed the defined from beneath the definitions, and the reader wondered why the definitions had ever been thought necessary. *Orthodoxy*, *The Thing* and *The Everlasting Man* are among the great books of the age.—GRAHAM GREENE, "G. K. Chesterton," *Spec*, April 21, 1944, p. 364

Ten or twenty years ago, the form of nationalism most closely corresponding to Communism today was political Catholicism. Its most outstanding exponent—though he was perhaps an extreme case rather than a typical one—was G. K. Chesterton. Chesterton was a writer of considerable talent who chose to suppress both his sensibilities and his intellectual honesty in the cause of Roman Catholic propaganda. During the last twenty years or so of his life, his entire output was in reality an endless repetition of the same thing, under its laboured cleverness as simple and boring as "Great is Diana of the Ephesians". Every book that he wrote, every paragraph, every sentence, every incident in every story, every scrap of dialogue, had to demonstrate beyond possibility of mistake the superiority of the Catholic over the Protestant or the pagan. But Chesterton was not content to think of this superiority as merely intellectual or spiritual: it had to be translated into terms of national prestige and military power, which entailed an ignorant idealisation of the Latin countries, especially France. Chesterton had not lived long in France, and his picture of it—as a land of Catholic peasants incessantly singing the *Marseillaise* over glasses of red wine—had about as much relation to reality as *Chu Chin Chow* has to everyday life in Baghdad. And with this went not only an enormous over-estimation of French military power (both before and after 1914–18 he maintained that France, by itself, was stronger than Germany), but a silly and vulgar glorification of the actual process of war. Chesterton's battle poems, such as "Lepanto" or "The Ballad of Saint Barbara", make "The Charge of the Light Brigade" read like a pacifist tract: they are perhaps the most tawdry bits of bombast to be found in our language. The interesting thing is that had the romantic rubbish which he habitually wrote about France and the French army been written by somebody else about Britain and the British army, he would have been the first to jeer. In home politics he was a Little Englander, a true hater of jingo-

ism and imperialism, and according to his lights a true friend of democracy. Yet when he looked outwards into the international field, he could forsake his principles without even noticing that he was doing so. Thus, his almost mystical belief in the virtues of democracy did not prevent him from admiring Mussolini. Mussolini had destroyed the representative government and the freedom of the press for which Chesterton had struggled so hard at home, but Mussolini was an Italian and had made Italy strong, and that settled the matter. Nor did Chesterton ever find a word to say against imperialism and the conquest of coloured races when they were practised by Italians or Frenchmen. His hold on reality, his literary taste, and even to some extent his moral sense, were dislocated as soon as his nationalistic loyalties were involved.—GEORGE ORWELL, "Notes on Nationalism" (1945), *Collected Essays, Journalism and Letters*, eds. Sonia Orwell, Ian Angus, 1968, pp. 365–66

Real acquaintance with the bulk of Chesterton's writing uncovers a figure no more congenial to progressive thinkers of our day than he was to those of his own. (Until I re-read "The Secret Garden", I had not realized that thinkers could be called progressive, and gently derided on that score, sixty years ago.) Not that he fits into any stereotype of the reactionary: he was too much his own man for that, inveighing against imperialism and the power of the rich as stoutly as any liberal, if not quite from that standpoint. But, to give a few examples, he was against rationalism, the spread of science, sociology (partly for its scientific pretensions), introspection, what might be called unmorality, and George Moore. He was for the normal man, doctrine, vulgar conviviality, the past, England and Sherlock Holmes. And much more besides: in particular, his patriotism was qualified by a deep respect for other nationalities, such that no other English writer I know has written about Americans or Frenchmen with so much perceptive generosity.

Chesterton's stance on most matters could be summed up very roughly as follows. What is simple, generally agreed, old and obvious is not only more likely to be true than what is complex, original, new and subtle, but much more interesting as well: a prescription calculated to alienate almost any type of progressive thinker. His work is full of celebrations of the commonplace, from the descriptive passages in his fiction that show us we have never properly looked at a suburban street before, to critical insights like the one enabling him to see that the distinctive genius of Shakespeare lay in his being sublimely ordinary. No clever paradox, this, but triumphantly argued out, and incidentally carrying the uncomfortable rider that what we think of as the artistic temperament is a hallmark of the second-rate.

As a critic, Chesterton is always provocative, perhaps too regularly so. Perhaps he did too much use the work of other writers as raw material for the exposition of his own ideas. But at his best, on Browning or Dickens, he passes with honours the first test of any critic, that of being able to praise convincingly, to extend the grounds on which some author or work can be enjoyed. He writes with an energy and humour that remain fresh even when his subject has become faded by time. So, too, in his polemical essays, where the dust overlying one or another long-defunct controversy will suddenly be blown away by a joke, a gust of insight—often of the chillier sort—or the force of a prediction: religion and reason (to take a case), conventionally thought of as foes, are to Chesterton really cousins and allies, allies seen as withering and dying side by side in a welter of assorted superstitions—a truism in 1972, but surely a remarkable forecast in 1908. In an age of prophets, he stands up adequately when measured against Shaw and Wells;

indeed, if a prophet's prophecies are supposed to bear some relation to the event, rather better than adequately.

Even to (I should guess) the majority of his admirers, Chesterton's verse has become reduced to a handful of anthology pieces, at the head of which stands "Lepanto"—as an exhilarating battle poem a major sin of his against the progressive light, though it does avoid the aggravating offence of being also patriotic: no Englishmen were present when the forces of the Papal League under Don John of Austria defeated the Turks and their allies by sea in 1571. However: it is in his fiction that I find Chesterton's genius best and most characteristically displayed. (Here I am far from sure I have the majority with me.) The novels and stories, especially the stories, dramatize virtually the whole range of the themes and interests met with in his other work. Further, the polemical tone and forensic style of much of that other work reappear—modified, to be sure—in the fiction, alongside the elements of narrative, in which he was only periodically interested, and of description, at which he was a master.—KINGSLEY AMIS, "Introduction" to *Selected Stories of G. K. Chesterton*, 1972, pp. 12–14

But among critics whose interest in Chesterton is extra-literary, those who perhaps have done the most serious damage to his artistic reputation are a group which might be called the professional Catholics. For them, Chesterton is an institution to be defended rather than an author to be discussed. A characteristic which defines their attitude is an aggressive defensiveness towards him as a writer who needs their protection combined with an astonishing ignorance and uncertainty about the writing they are trying to protect. Bernard Bergonzi, who betrays something of the same attitude himself in his somewhat exaggerated attempt to avoid it, seems to have them in mind when he describes the way many of his co-religionists refuse even to discuss a question such as the anti-Semitic element in Chesterton's writing. He might have added that the refusal to evaluate Chesterton as a writer often goes with a refusal to tolerate any criticism of him as a literary artist. At the first hint of criticism there is as it were an immediate closing of ranks, which is followed, as often as not, first by a perfunctory tribute to his personal qualities, and then by an evident eagerness to change the subject. This attitude may be explained in terms of the altogether understandable gratitude which an embattled minority feels towards a writer whom they regard as their champion. But whatever its explanation as a cultural phenomenon, there is no doubt that those who share this view have helped to create an impression of Chesterton which they are the first to resent. Their preference for what appears to be his most controversial work and their refusal to discuss it in any detail has had the effect of fostering an antagonism for him which is equally unbalanced and uncritical. It is significant, for example, that Orwell, who shows signs of knowing a surprising amount about his work, should nonetheless regard him as the leader of a group which in its discipline and like-mindedness corresponds almost exactly to the Communist Party.—IAN BOYD, "Philosophy in Fiction," *G. K. Chesterton: A Centenary Appraisal*, ed. John Sullivan, 1974, p. 42

Works

POETRY

Of all the modern poets there is only one whose verse is always full of the voice of battle, and that is Mr. Chesterton. In the *Dynasts*, though we watch Trafalgar and Leipsic and Waterloo, it is from a height too far removed to hear the sound of the charges and the cannon, and Hardy has seen to it that the song or shout of victory shall be thin and paltry enough in our ears.

But Mr. Chesterton's verse, even when it is not concerned with historic battles—Ethandune, Lepanto, the Marne—has generally the sound of a battle within it. There are drawn swords from the first page to the last, material, intellectual, and spiritual; the swords of Arthur and Roland, of Ben Tillett and Paul Deroulède, of the Mother of God and Michael the Archangel. Everything is spoken of in terms of war, either actual or potential. For even when there is no enemy the state of being described is a state where man is strung to a high pitch of expectation and his delight is already militant. The babe unborn in one poem looks forward to 'leave to weep and fight', and his old men die either in conflict or in the joy or fear of conflict. Man must be either a hero or a coward.

If it were not that the vocabulary of this poet is in itself so largely taken from battle and the things of battle, it would be sufficient to say that his verse always seems to be dealing with a crisis. But all poetry, in its nature, tends to deal with crises, either for their accentuation or resolution; and this more universal word scarcely fits so well the part which man himself takes, according to Mr. Chesterton's poetry, in the resolution of the critical moment. Here, if anywhere in English verse, he is a fighting animal, and here he is scarcely anything else. Whether that dream in which he has seen himself and his affairs as important be true or false, the knowledge of a mystic or the rationalizing of a madman, it is certainly as important that he appears here. Mr. Chesterton and Mr. Housman hold up between them all the philosophies; man conquers or he endures.

To speak of Milton in this connexion would seem absurd—for Mr. Chesterton's theology is as Catholic (in the Roman sense of the word) as Milton's was Puritan, his politics as democratic as Milton's were aristocratic, and his sense of enjoyment as universal as Milton's was ascetic; and yet there is perhaps no English poetry which in the matter of combat Mr. Chesterton's verse so much resembles. Both these poets deal with the combat in its cosmic, mundane, and localized forms, and as Milton conducted (ostensibly, at any rate) campaigns against Satan, the Philistines, the Bishops, and the King of England, so Mr. Chesterton has attacked the Dragon, the Danes, the Turks, the Prohibitionists, and Lord Birkenhead. Both of them have fought for definite and enunciable principles. Both of them, though rarely, have suggested in the middle of their warlike and triumphant verse the state which is beyond warfare, and which opens upon the soul when, and whether, the last battle has been won or lost. It might almost be added that neither of them has felt, or at any rate has allowed himself to express, what his opponent really wanted; but the charge could hardly be sustained. For Milton has been accused for generations of understanding only too well what Satan wanted; and it is certain that some of Mr. Chesterton's opponents know less clearly even than he for what intellectual end they are striving.

All the magnificent imagery of forlorn hopes and last charges and final stands and broken swords which Mr. Chesterton has strewn about his poems does not conceal the fact that he is, on the whole, on the side of the big battalions. Nor would he desire to conceal it; on the contrary, he asserts it—it is his claim and his song throughout. He is on the side of God and the people. But, in a sense, both of his great allies are voiceless and unarmed. It is he who is their song and weapon; and his weapon is his song. It is always the few whom he attacks, but it is the few in possession, the pseudo-scientists, the politicians, the usurers, King Dives. In this large simplification it is probable enough that he seems to do a good deal of injustice. It is probable that the people will not always be grateful for what he offers them, and that (for example) a good deal of spurious democracy and comfortably-vicarious combativeness may strengthen themselves on these noble poems. But that is not his business. And as against that, the lucidity of some of the topical poems can be appreciated by minds which are far enough from the causes for which he stands. It is not necessary to have an opinion on the Welsh Disestablishment Bill to appreciate the folly of the remark that it 'had shocked the conscience of every Christian community in Europe', which gave rise to the famous *Antichrist, or the Reunion of Christendon: An Ode*. Nor need one be in obedience to Rome to appreciate the worth of that negligible periodical which claimed that the Church of Rome was troubled by the opposition of Sir Arthur Conan Doyle and Mr. Dennis Bradley—

> If she must lean on lesser props
> Of earthly fame or ancient art,
> Make shift with Raphael and Racine
> Put up with Dante and Descartes,
> Not wholly can she blind her grief,
> But touch the wound and murmur sadly,
> 'These lesser things are theirs to love
> Who lose the love of Mr. Bradley'.

And there are other things of the same kind. These things, poems and provocations alike, have their place in the gaiety of the created universe.

These poems, however, are not Mr. Chesterton's most important, however dearly they may be loved. Nor, merely because of their shattering rightness, is there felt in them that combination of the forlorn hope and the big battalions which gives quite peculiar force to some of the others. It derives, at least in part, from the tradition and creed of Christendom to which Mr. Chesterton's entire genius and loyalty has been devoted: the creed of God crucified. But it is strengthened by the fact that some such paradox is discoverable in the world everywhere. The Incarnation and the Passion recur everywhere in this poetry. But there recurs also the poetic sense of the danger in which single and helpless things stand—and this is the correlation of the one, as the general struggle, and especially that struggle in which defeat is practically certain, is the correlation of the other. For one of the facts that makes the combination of which we have spoken possible is simply that the big battalions are made up of an infinite number of forlorn hopes. Few things have occurred to bigger battalions of men than, for instance, romantic love. But the sense of it is universal because it is individual. And to each experience Mr. Chesterton implicitly attributes such apocalyptic values, and casts about it a rain of such gigantic terms, that it takes on the appearance of an ultimate romantic war.

> Little I reck of empty prides,
> Of creeds more cold than clay;
> To nobler ends and longer rides
> My lady rides to-day.
> To swing our swords and take our sides
> In that all-ending fray
> When stars fall down and darkness hides,
> When God shall turn to bay.

There has never been a poet who took sides more vigorously than Mr. Chesterton. 'God turning to bay' is the continual theme of this verse—it occurred in the *Napoleon of Notting Hill*, published years before—but it is a proof of its integrity that the phrase does not, as so easily it might, become a mere stupid reiteration. Some have held it to be blasphemy—as in Walt Whitman's lines:

> Silent and amazed even when a little boy,
> I remember I heard the preacher every Sunday put
> God in his statements,
> As contending against some being or influence—

but to Mr. Chesterton it has been the centre of poetic life, and it is for the sake of that tradition that he has spent so much energy on insisting that nothing worth having is to be gained by a false unity,

> When man is the Turk and the Atheist,
> Essene, Erastian Whig,
> And the Thug and the Druse and the Catholic
> And the crew of the Captain's gig.

(But it is, of course, possible to believe that the seven types named—and others—are, precisely, the crew of the Captain's gig.)

But all these poems of war and battle, all this sympathy with the weak and suffering, all this defiance of the rich and learned, all this wit and humour and theology and traditionalism—does it after all make poetry? In the sense that it is all part of the Muse's preoccupation, all part of the things that she can and must do, it is as much poetry as Pope's attack on Addison or Shelley's couplet on Castlereagh; and it will be unfortunate if poetry is ever so limited as to omit such admirable labours. Nevertheless, they are rather her indulgences than her life. They are not of the nature of her great achievements; they are collateral, not direct, inheritors of her kingdom.—CHARLES WILLIAMS, "Gilbert Keith Chesterton," *Poetry at Present*, 1930, pp. 97–102

Like most poets he is praised to-day by his admirers for the wrong reasons. Charity would suggest leaving the uncritical Chestertonian to his illusions, but prudence insists that the bubble must be pricked, because of the curiously exclusive nature of misguided praise. If a man is praised for the wrong reasons he will almost certainly not be praised for the right reasons. This is attested in the present instance by the abject refusal of Chestertonians to see that interest in their idol as a significant figure must centre not on his cleverness or heartiness but on his perceptivity.

Consider, for example, the opening of one of the best of Chesterton's poems, *Gloria in Profundis*:

> There has fallen on earth for a token
> A god too great for the sky.
> He has burst out of all things and broken
> The bounds of eternity:
> Into time and the terminal land
> He has strayed like a thief or a lover,
> For the wine of the world brims over,
> Its splendour is spilt on the sand.

The paradoxes here are perhaps more directly and explicitly rooted in the Incarnation than any considered in the last chapter, and a little thought will justify any of them. Our concern here is with the mode of their poetic realization, and the judgment must be that the realization is not poetic at all, but intellectual. The alliteration (via Swinburne) and the hearty rhythmic thump (via Kipling) exert a hypnotic influence in their own right and direct attention *away from* the intellectual content. There is no development of imagery: one must pause, shutting one's ears to the sound, to think out the aptness of the thief, the lover, and the wine-cup as analogues for Christ; and each image exists in isolation, without connections before and after. The latter is also true of each stanza; the four stanzas of the poem may be arranged, without serious confusion, in any one of twenty-four possible orders. In sum, the reader is confronted with a cluster of epigrams while a brass band drums at his ears.

The reader who will compare this poem, or any Chesterton poem he likes, with, say, the fourth part of T. S. Eliot's "East Coker" (in *Four Quartets*) will have no difficulty perceiving the radical difference. . . .

This radical difference in the mode of working of the two poets cannot be brushed aside by calling the demonstrable differences merely finicky or ascribing Eliot's superiority to more laborious craftsmanship. Indeed the latter argument tells exactly the other way. Chesterton is simply uninterested in the job a serious poet undertakes. The merit that can be claimed for his verse, once the careful reader has shut his ears to the sound-effects and deciphered the relevance of the array of images, is simply the merit owing to any triumphal celebration. Read in this way, as celebrations of cosmic fact, his poems take on their full meaning; but it is a philosophical, not a poetical meaning, and a noisy rather than a perceptive celebration.

That he should write in this way is the inevitable consequence of the way he perceived. The conflicts reflected in the language are not in his mind but out in front of him, in the things; he admires them, he does not feel involved in them. His analogical vision was both total and in an odd way painless. It unfits him for poetry; it equips him admirably and beyond question for philosophy and exposition.—HUGH KENNER, *Paradox in Chesterton*, 1947, pp. 104–7

FICTION

> Because He does not take away
> The terror from the tree . . .
> (Chesterton: *A Second Childhood*)

Edgar Allan Poe wrote stories of pure fantastic horror or pure *bizarrerie*; he invented the detective story. That is no less certain than the fact that he did not combine the two genres. He did not inflict on C. Auguste Dupin the task of solving the ancient crime of the Man of the Crowd or of explaining the image that terrified the masked Prince Prospero in the chamber of black and scarlet. On the other hand, Chesterton lavished such *tours de force* with passion and joy. Each story in the Father Brown Saga presents a mystery, proposes explanations of a demoniacal or magical sort, and then replaces them at the end with solutions of this world. Skill is not the only virtue of those brief bits of fiction; I believe I can perceive in them an abbreviation of Chesterton's life, a symbol or reflection of Chesterton. The repetition of his formula through the years and through the books *(The Man Who Knew Too Much, The Poet and the Lunatics, The Paradoxes of Mr. Pond)* seems to confirm that this is an essential form, not a rhetorical artifice. These notes are an attempt to interpret that form.

But first we must reconsider some facts that are perhaps too well known. Chesterton was a Catholic, he believed in the Middle Ages of the Pre-Raphaelites ("Of London, small and white, and clean"). Like Whitman, Chesterton thought that the mere fact of existing is so prodigious that no misfortune should exempt us from a kind of cosmic gratitude. That may be a just belief, but it arouses only limited interest; to suppose that it is all Chesterton offers is to forget that a creed is the underlying factor in a series of mental and emotional processes and that a man is the whole series. In Argentina, Catholics exalt Chesterton, freethinkers reject him. Like every writer who professes a creed, Chesterton is judged by it, is condemned or acclaimed because of it. His case is not unlike that of Kipling, who is always judged with reference to the English Empire.

Poe and Baudelaire proposed the creation of a world of terror, as did Blake's tormented Urizen; it is natural for their work to teem with the forms of horror. In my opinion, Chesterton would not have tolerated the imputation of being a contriver of nightmares, a *monstrorum artifex* (Pliny, XXVIII,2), but he tends inevitably to revert to atrocious observations. He asks if perchance a man has three eyes, or a bird three wings; in opposition to the pantheists, he speaks of a man who dies and discovers in paradise that the spirits of the angelic choirs have, every one of them, the same face he has; he speaks of a jail of mirrors; of a labyrinth without a center; of a man devoured by metal automatons; of a tree that devours birds and then grows feathers instead of leaves; he imagines *(The Man Who Was Thursday,* VI) "that if a man went westward to the end of the world he would find something—say a tree—that was more or less than a tree, a tree possessed by a spirit; and that if he went east to the end of the world he would find something else that was not wholly itself— a tower, perhaps, of which the very shape was wicked." He defines the near by the far, and even by the atrocious; if he speaks of eyes, he uses the words of Ezekiel (I:22) "the terrible crystal"; if of the night, he perfects an ancient horror (Apocalypse 4:6) and calls it a "monster made of eyes." Equally illustrative is the tale *How I Found the Superman.* Chesterton speaks to the Superman's parents; when he asks them what the child, who never leaves a dark room, looks like, they remind him that the Superman creates his own law and must be measured by it. On that plane he is more handsome than Apollo; but viewed from the lower plane of the average man, of course— Then they admit that it is not easy to shake hands with him, because of the difference in structure. Indeed, they are not able to state with precision whether he has hair or feathers. After a current of air kills him, several men carry away a coffin that is not of human shape. Chesterton relates this teratological fantasy as a joke.

These examples, which could easily be multiplied, prove that Chesterton restrained himself from being Edgar Allan Poe or Franz Kafka, but something in the makeup of his personality leaned toward the nightmarish, something secret, and blind, and central. Not in vain did he dedicate his first works to the justification of two great gothic craftsmen, Browning and Dickens; not in vain did he repeat that the best book to come out of Germany was *Grimm's Fairy Tales.* He reviled Ibsen and defended Rostand (perhaps indefensibly), but the Trolls and the creator of *Peer Gynt* were the stuff his dreams were made of. That discord, that precarious subjection of a demoniacal will, defines Chesterton's nature. For me, the emblems of that struggle are the adventures of Father Brown, each of which undertakes to explain an inexplicable event by reason alone. That is why I said, in the first paragraph of this essay, that those stories were the key to Chesterton, the symbols and reflections of Chesterton. That is all, except that the "reason" to which Chesterton subjected his imaginings was not precisely reason but the Catholic faith or rather a collection of Hebrew imaginings that had been subjected to Plato and Aristotle.

I remember two opposing parables. The first one is from the first volume of Kafka's works. It is the story of the man who asks to be admitted to the law. The guardian of the first door says that there are many other doors within, and that every room is under the watchful eye of a guardian, each of whom is stronger than the one before. The man sits down to wait. Days and years go by, and the man dies. In his agony he asks, "Is it possible that during the years I have been waiting, no one has wanted to enter but me?" The guardian answers, "No one has wanted to enter this door because it was destined for you alone. Now I shall close it." (In the ninth chapter of *The Trial* Kafka comments on this parable, making it even more complicated.) The other parable is in Bunyan's *Pilgrim's Progress.* People gaze enviously at a castle guarded by many warriors; a guardian at the door holds a book in which he will write the name of the one who is worthy of entering. An intrepid man approaches the guardian and says, "Write my name, sir." Then he takes out his sword and lunges at the warriors; there is an exchange of bloody blows; he forces his way through the tumult and enters the castle.

Chesterton devoted his life to the writing of the second parable, but something within him always tended to write the first.—JORGE LUIS BORGES, "On Chesterton," *Other Inquisitions*, 1964, pp. 82–85

It may seem odd to class a man who has difficulty in rolling his umbrella and does not know the right end of his return ticket among the Supermen of detection, but Father Brown belongs among them through the knowledge given to him by God. Logicians of the detective story complained with some bitterness that Chesterton outraged all the rules they had drawn up, that he did not tell you whether all the windows were fastened or whether a shot in the gunroom could be heard in the butler's pantry. But the very merit of Chesterton is his ability to ignore such things, to leave out everything extraneous to the single theme he wants to develop, and yet to provide a clue that is blindingly obvious once we have accepted the premises of the story and the character of Father Brown. A dog whines because a stick sinks in the sea, the red light from a closed door looks like "a splash of blood that grew vivid as it cried for vengeance," the priest of a new religion does not look round when he hears a crash and a scream, and these are geniune clues by which we may solve mysteries. And when we have accepted Father Brown, then we are bound to accept also his right to draw religious and social morals from the cases he investigates.— JULIAN SYMONS, *Mortal Consequences*, 1972, pp. 79–80

Whether they are very good or only workmanlike, the Father Brown stories owe their attraction to things outside pure puzzle. They insinuate themselves in the mind by being seen, most often, as journeys. People move from street to street, from valley to hill, from cold weather to snow and, if we except 'Israel Gow', the journeys are set in a low key out of loving respect for the commonplace. The London scene is always beautifully done, intimately, sharply, with eloquence or sentiment. The lights in a small shop in Camden Town will shine from a distance, like the butt end of a cigar. Chesterton's journeys are always small—the everyday ones. Another advantage is that his narrative is a series of criticisms. One thoughtful quarter of an hour is demolished by what happens in the one that follows it. Chesterton's eye for the normal and commonplace was, of course, quite abnormal. He sees that one of the characteristics of the commonplace is that it is a surface, therefore a disguise. It is so normal to pass a coat stand that one cannot be blamed for not noticing a body is hanging on it. Father Brown has a sharp clerical brain, a feeling for the turn of the screw and an unastounded sense of the human drama. Who more likely to commit a crime of jealous passion than the postman who is compelled by his job to deliver his rival's letters? In the Father Brown stories Chesterton made paradox work for him. Elsewhere it became a nuisance, but here it had the theatrical value of the trap-door.—V. S. PRITCHETT, "Pugnacious Paradoxes," *NS*, Jan. 19, 1973, p. 95

Chesterton himself did not attach great importance to the Father Brown stories. Ordered in batches by magazine editors and publishers, they were written hurriedly for the primary purpose of helping to finance his Distributist paper, *G. K.'s Weekly*. And though they have proved to be the most popular of Chesterton's writings, critical attention to them has been casual. This is partly because they are detective stories; and the detective story is commonly dismissed, without argument, as a very low form of art. That it is also a very difficult and demanding form, in which many clever writers have failed, is not regarded as relevant. Nor is there much respect for the innovators in this genre, or much comment on their remarkable

rarity. If there were, Chesterton's reputation would stand very high; for his detective stories, while they may not be the best ever written, are without doubt the most ingenious. But to show ingenuity and originality in the detective story is for the superior critic merely to have a knack for a particular sort of commercial fiction. It is not the sort of thing he takes seriously. And Chesterton himself, it seems, would have agreed with him. . . .

Again and again in these stories Chesterton shows how much the common dislike of Catholicism is (or was) due to dislike of 'religious externals'. But the deeper religious meaning of these stories is to do with something more important than cultural considerations. The abundance of quacks, mystagogues, sorcerers in them is not only due to the desire to point a contrast with Father Brown. It is to illustrate, in terms proper to the genre in which Chesterton is writing, his belief that what Christianity has shown is that the age-old effort of man to grasp the Divine is bankrupt. Man cannot come to God. Christianity says that God came to man. This was what Chesterton was saying over and over again, in different tones and with varying degrees of humour or earnestness. Orwell claimed that writers like Chesterton seem to have only one subject: that they are Catholics. One might as well retort that Orwell's only subject seems to be that he was not one. Either the Catholic faith is relevant to the whole of life, or it is relevant to none of it. That, at any rate, was Chesterton's position.

In the end, then, the priest's 'steady humble gaze' owes its power to more than observation. When he realized that the doctor did the murder, he 'looked him gravely and steadily in the face'; and the doctor went away and wrote his confession. He is an atheist, and he begins in his confession: '*Vicisti, Galilaee!*' But he goes on at once 'In other words, damn your eyes, which are very remarkable and penetrating ones.'

The religious meaning is central in the best of these stories. But some of them contain a good deal of effective social satire also. I have already mentioned 'The Invisible Man', that ingenious fable of the people who 'don't count'. Wells, we know, had another idea of the 'invisible man'; and Ralph Ellison has another. Seeing the invisible in Chesterton's story means what Ellison means: discovering human brotherhood. Some of the incidental themes in this story are interesting, especially considering its date. We note that the victim Isidore Smythe is a characteristically modern man, who not only has a fast car, but more remarkably, a complete staff of robots to wait on him. Another parable, with a keen edge of social satire, is another well-known story, 'The Queer Feet'. The point of this story, as a detective story, is that a gentleman's coat looks the same as a waiter's; but the stratagem of Flambeau, the owner of the 'queer feet' which now saunter like a gentleman and now scurry like a waiter, is possible only because of the great gulf fixed between gentlemen and waiters. It is the 'outsiders', first of all Death (the dead waiter at the beginning of the story), then the crook Flambeau, and finally the shabby Father Brown, who point the satire on the Twelve True Fishermen. Chesterton, like Kipling, vividly describes the ritualism of English upper-class life; but he sees it more ironically than Kipling. The members of the select club The Twelve True Fishermen parody the twelve apostles, who were fishermen, and fishers of men like Father Brown, who can bring the reformed criminal back from the ends of the earth with 'a twitch upon the thread'. Light and amusing as the story is, it is an exposure not only of social class, but of plutocracy employing the traditions of social class, to eliminate brotherhood. Yet all the Fishermen are very likeable, and the story ends with an amusing touch. After their silver has been recovered, thanks to Father Brown, their first thought is to invent a new addition to their ritual by way of commemorating its recovery. The members will in future wear green coats, to distinguish them from waiters.

But the most memorable of the stories are not witty parables like these, but imaginative fairy tales. What some readers remember most in the Father Brown stories is Chesterton's powers of description. His liking for a twilight setting—dawn or dusk—has been noted; and so has the constant sense we have that the action is taking place in a toy theatre, where the weird and wonderful backcloth dominates everything, and the tiny puppets that gesticulate in fight or dance in front of it seem faceless and featureless. And these backcloths have a décor which links Chesterton to Swinburne and the Decadents. His moral and religious outlook could not be more different from theirs; but his imagination has been formed on their work. Lurid, or fanciful, or grotesque decoration dominates stories like 'The Wrong Shape' or 'The Dagger with Wings'. Of course this decoration is there in part to distract us. A classical detective story exists to fool the reader; and Chesterton likes to avert our attention from the 'simple centre' to the 'rococo excrescences'. These are Chesterton's own expressions, which come from an incidental brief discussion of *Hamlet* in 'The Queer Feet'. Every successful crime, he says, like every successful work of art, has at its centre something simple. It is Chesterton's task as conjurer to arrange this scene, with bizarre figures in a bizarre setting, so that we shall miss the explanation of the mystery, which always turns on some straightforward, mundane motive. (In more than half the stories the motivation for the crime is nothing more metaphysical or *outré* than greed.)—W. W. ROBSON, "Father Brown and Others," *G. K. Chesterton: A Centenary Appraisal*, ed. John Sullivan, 1974, pp. 58–69

Chesterton's first book of fiction, *The Napoleon of Notting Hill* (1904), is in outline, and on the face of it, a romance about the future. The date indicated is 1984, but this coincidence, though doubtless odd, is unilluminating. Those twin concerns, to diagnose the contemporary world and through doing so to sound a warning about what it may turn into, characterize Orwell's novel and much orthodox science fiction besides; they find no more than a very incidental place in the Chesterton work. This indeed opens with an attack on prophecy and shows us, first, a society 'almost exactly like what it is now', then, later, a creation of pure and free fancy. (We could capture the book for science fiction only by taking what C. S. Lewis called 'the German view' that any and every romance about the future must fall within that category.)

The product of Chesterton's fancy is a London in which, by a kind of reversion to a medievalism that never existed, the various boroughs, while owing ultimate allegiance to the Crown, become independent city-states. Each has its Provost with his attendant group of heralds, its flag, its citizensoldiery—armed with no more than sword and halberd—in their distinctive uniforms, its manufactured traditions and mottoes, its ambition and honour. Notting Hill, having ignominiously defeated an aggressive coalition of Bayswater and the Kensington boroughs, acquires a twenty-years' hegemony over all London, only to perish by a combined final onslaught, a set battle in Kensington Gardens.

This sounds like a straightforward, if idiosyncratic, chronicle of adventure and action. In fact, it is both more and less than that, a verdict that may prove not quite so hideously dull as it sounds if I amplify it by suggesting that in this first novel are to be found all its author's important concerns as a writer of fiction, concerns at times cumulative and mutually

helpful to marvellous effect, now and then disastrously at odds, but concerns that always recur in his tales and give them their unique flavour and place in the canon.

The preludial attack on prophecy mentioned above consists of some sensible and provocative remarks couched in, often buried under, a style that wavers from the jocular to the facetious. Two concerns are at work here, or, to put it perhaps more appropriately, two men: Chesterton the Polemicist and Chesterton the Buffoon.

The Polemicist, thickly or thinly disguised, turns up virtually everywhere in Chesterton's fiction, and it must be said of him at once that he is rarely less than entertaining and often lends argument an elegance and an epigrammatic sting worthy of the best of the author's avowed polemical writing. Here, the argument is about nationalism and politics generally, it is conducted from more than one point of view, and most of it has nothing to do with the rest of the story; indeed, after the principal debate one of its chief participants, Juan del Fuego, a Nicaraguan grandee about as authentic as his name, is reported to have dropped dead. Right at the end of the book, the Polemicist puts in a secondary appearance to advance the not very inflammatory point that the humorist and the idealist, or the clown and the fanatic, are the two essential parts of the whole, sane man.

The clownish half of this synthesis corresponds to the figure I have called the Buffoon, to some tastes a mildly dismaying companion. He is actually incarnated in the character of Auberon Quin, an owlish minor civil servant who finds himself elected King—by what must have been a very arbitrary process. Until then he has been able to do little more than mystify and bore his friends with a string of elaborately pointless anecdotes; now he can mystify and bore all the people of London by decreeing that they build walls round their municipalities and parade in grotesque costumes sounding tocsins. At last—rather late, in fact, there appears a man who takes the whole charade seriously.

This is Adam Wayne, the youthful Provost of Notting Hill, tall, blue-eyed and red-haired. Red hair in Chesterton's men is a badge of unworldliness and chivalry (in his women it belongs to the sedate and serious-minded). Here we have the fanatical half of the synthesis, and at this point, too, a third Chesterton takes a hand in the shaping of the story. Aware of the deficiencies of the title, I dub the newcomer Chesterton the Melodramatist, meaning no disparagement, intending only to allude to that fusion of the grand and the histrionic, the magnificent and the magniloquent, which we find in the poems of Housman or the music of Tchaikovsky, and which we can respond to, even be deeply moved by, without necessarily ranging it alongside the work of Tennyson or Beethoven. . . .

In *The Napoleon of Notting Hill*, the status of Chesterton the narrator is sufficiently indicated by denying that role an initial capital. There is a story holding at any rate its second half together, there are some fine moments of military action and expectation, but the main job of the narrative is to bridge the gaps between the returns of the various other roles. The closing scene, at the end of which Wayne and Quin set off like—perhaps a bit too much like—Don Quixote and Sancho Panza to roam the world, is right, is a triumph, but it is the triumph of the Melodramatist with some useful support from the Polemicist. No self-respecting, or mere, storyteller would have permitted himself a finale so blatantly implausible; implausible not just by ordinary commonsense standards, but even by the bizarre ones of what has gone before. (A look at the text compels the unanswerable question: Where had everyone else disappeared to?)—KINGSLEY AMIS, "Four Fluent Fellows," *G. K. Chesterton: A Centenary Appraisal*, ed. John Sullivan, 1974, pp. 28–33

The year 1925 produces an essay with a long list of 'DONT'S' for the detective writer. The main points that emerge are first, that the reader desires to be deceived; and second, that the character must do the murder, in other words there should be no extenuating circumstances such as the use of professionals, gangs, spies and so on. The intent is to avoid any fudging of the moral issue that murder is a sin. The idea is repeated almost 10 years later in an essay of 1934. He states that detective stories need criminals and crime, and must not 'ignore the existence of sin'. Because the plot is really moral the stories are concerned with conscience and acts of will. There must never be 'that arbitrary gesture of self ablution and self-absolution with which some characters in modern stories conclude the confession of their lives'. The emphasis is on the criminal's act of choice and the need to expose it. A year later he says that the murderer should commit his crime for reasons 'immediately, though erroneously, satisfactory to his soul and his inner life'. The act of will is at the root of the distinction between insanity and criminality. He condemns as heresy 'the perpetual itch to describe all crime as lunacy'. The criminal may have lost his innocence but he still has free will. The insane has lost 'more than innocence he has lost essence'; he has lost the acknowledgement of an external authority. Crime is always a matter of choice, therefore the criminal's soul may always be saved.

While the criticism shows plainly how Chesterton viewed the subject matter and technique of the detective story, it does not touch specifically on the methods of the detective except as he is linked with the mystic. To examine his ideas on method we must go to the detective stories themselves. The first collection of detective stories that Chesterton publishes is *The Club of Queer Trades*. The stories, while all centred on an event, are really concerned with how the mind of the detective, Basil Grant, works. The main plan of the short stories is similar to the Sherlock Holmes story. We have a Watson in the narrator. The action takes place out of a comfortable bachelor apartment in central London, and is nearly always initiated by a sudden arrival on the step of a mystery that needs to be solved. However, the whole intent is to reverse the Sherlock Holmes method of thought. The book is not a parody but a demonstration of a different kind of thinking. The rational is not satirised but merely shown to be ineffective. The author speaks of the 'fantasies of detective deduction' that are worthless in the face of a moral problem.—LYNETTE HUNTER, "Inner Landscapes: 1900–1935," *G. K. Chesterton: Explorations in Allegory*, 1979, pp. 138–39

ESSAYS AND BELLES LETTRES

I admit that I have always found Mr. Chesterton's style exasperating to the last point of endurance, though I am aware that there must be many people who like it. In a chapter in this book, on "The Style of Stevenson," Mr. Chesterton remarks: "I am one of those humble characters for whom the main matter of style is concerned with making a statement." To which one might reply that the matter is concerned with the statement, but that the style is concerned with making it clearly, simply, and in good taste. In his matter Mr. Chesterton is apt to make too many statements; in his style he is concerned rather to agitate than to clarify, to impress rather than to persuade. And readers like myself find his manner rather offensive to their vanity. For he seems always to assume that what his reader has previously believed is exactly the opposite of what Mr. Chesterton knows to be true. Readers who like an easy formula may find this attitude delightful; for they have only to stand on their

heads to find themselves in agreement with Mr. Chesterton. But we are not all so completely immersed in ignorance, prejudice, and heresy as Mr. Chesterton assumes. To assume that one's readers are in total spiritual and intellectual darkness is easy, and dispenses the author from any great intellectual effort himself: as Mr. Wells thinks that we are all quite ignorant of Evolution, and Mr. Belloc is convinced of our total ignorance of European history, so Mr. Chesterton believes that we have never heard of Catholicism except possibly through Kingsley's *Westward Ho!* It would not so much matter if it did not mean that able writers, who might produce work of enduring value, become ephemeral. If they wrote primarily for *themselves*, they would be at the same time writing for the best people everywhere, people known and people obscure, without distinction of class or set.

If Mr. Chesterton does not seem to make the most of Stevenson's "cheerfulness," it is, I suspect, in my own case, due largely to the fact that I find Mr. Chesterton's own cheerfulness so depressing. He appears less like a saint radiating spiritual vision than like a busman slapping himself on a frosty day. He makes a great deal of Stevenson's restoration of the child's point of view. After Mr. Wyndham Lewis's recent fulminations against the child-actors, this policy requires rather more bolstering up than Mr. Chesterton has given it. He says, for instance, that in our "characteristic contemporary literature there is an almost complete absence of joy. And I think it would be true to say, in a general fashion, that it is not childish enough to be cheerful." Mr. Chesterton's fashion is *too* general. The modern world is, in another general fashion, childish, and, like childhood, is rather anarchistic. There is something very childish about Chicago, and I dare say Chicago is also joyful. I should be very glad to be joyful, but I should not care for any joy to be obtained at the price of surrendering my life's experience. Of course, Mr. Chesterton is wrong in supposing that one can speak about such matters "in a general fashion." There is one authoritative sense, to be respected, in which we are admonished to be like little children. Mr. Chesterton seems to think that we must execute these instructions by a romp. Hence his regular outbursts of heavy-weight Peter-Pantheism.—T. S. ELIOT, "There Must Be People Who Like It," *NA*, Dec. 31, 1927, p. 516

In many respects *Autobiography* is the finest book G. K. C. ever wrote. All the old graces of style are here, heightened and deepened by intimate revelations of his spiritual adventures. It is gay with the gaiety of his lightest essays, and wise with the wisdom which, as he claimed, comes only with "second childhood." Again he is seen in his favourite role of Defendant of ancient or derided virtues. Once more the case for Orthodoxy is presented in its most subtle and sophisticated guise. What's Wrong with the World, according to Chesterton's final testament, appears to be much the same as when he engaged in battle royal against the Evils of Eugenics, the Superstitions of Divorce, and the menace of the Servile State. If Mr. Belloc had not already used the title, "The Path to Rome" might fitly have summed up the general trend of this book which, in various aspects is also another Short History of England—at any rate, of the men and movements most closely connected with the author's career. To his co-religionists *Autobiography* may well seem a personal document of the highest value. To others, who loved the man and gloried in his writings, but for whom the Roman road has no attractions, the question may often intrude: did Chesterton take the Wrong Turning? That is not a question that need be debated here, though references may have to be made to the influence of his theological beliefs on his work as an artist.

For it is as an artist—and not as a democrat, a reformer or a Catholic—that G. K. C. achieved his most lasting claim to fame. One recalls memories of that glad, confident morning when Chesterton first burst into the arena of Liberal journalism and set Fleet Street alight with a display of verbal fireworks which both coloured and illuminated the literary scene. Squibs, crackers and rockets there were in abundance, but it was soon to be proved that the new young author was also a master of the "set piece." In such high-spirited fantasies as *Napoleon of Notting Hill* and *The Flying Inn*, and in the critical monographs on Dickens, Browning and Shaw, which followed, we discovered that we had, now rapidly coming to the forefront of letters, a man with a fresh pair of eyes and an original point of view. And the young among us devoured his articles with the avidity with which small boys devour hot jam tarts.

At that period (the beginning of the century) the Liberal creed was suffering badly from the dourness of its prophets and the sourness of its scribes. For a long time the devils of Imperialism and eroticism had been having all the best tunes, alike in poetry and prose. When Chesterton entered the lists, with *The Wild Knight* and *The Defendant*, followed by a continuous stream of literary broadsides in the papers, he was hailed as "the cleverest devil of them all"—who was most definitely on the side of the angels. Reading Chesterton in those days was like reading a more exuberant Emerson. Both uttered spiritual truths in sparkling epigrams, and both possessed that mystical insight which pierces through the outward shows of things to the heart of reality.

The parallel cannot be pursued any further, because in Chesterton's outlook on life there was rarely any of the transcendental gravity and sedateness which characterized the Sage of Concord. An omnivorous sense of humour pervades every page signed by G. K. C.; while a good deal of his verse also is distinguished by its note of rollicking fun. Indeed, with the possible exception of Bernard Shaw, there is no figure in our literature who has been productive of so many serious ideas clothed in such mirthful form as that of Gilbert Keith Chesterton. One may be hostile to his Catholic propaganda, smile at his fervour for the Middle Ages, discount his social and political gospel, and shy at many of his literary judgments. And still one would have to accord him a very prominent place in the gallery of English comic writers (in the Thackerayan sense); and acknowledge his title as a prince of essayists. That title was seldom better deserved than in the various articles he wrote for THE FORTNIGHTLY. He was at the top of his form in such contributions as "English Literature and the Latin Tradition" (August, 1935), and in his penetrating appreciation of Walter de la Mare, which appeared in July, 1932. The old crusading spirit—embellished by many of the familiar flourishes—is also still very much alive in "The Virtues of Revolution," an essay published in the May number of the same year.—HUBERT WARING, "G. K. C.: Prince of Essayists," *FR*, Nov. 1937, pp. 589–90

Our day has seen the emergence of two kinds of literary critic, the documentor and the cryptologist. The former with meticulous accuracy collects and publishes every unearthable fact about an author's life, from his love-letters to his dinner invitations and laundry bills, on the assumption that any fact, however trivial, about the man may throw light upon his writings. The latter approaches his work as if it were an anonymous and immensely difficult text, written in a private language which the ordinary reader cannot hope to understand until it is deciphered for him by experts. Both such critics will no doubt dismiss Chesterton's literary criticism as out-of-date, inaccurate

and superficial, but if one were to ask any living novelist or poet which kind of critic he would personally prefer to write about his work, I have no doubt as to the answer. Every writer knows that certain events in his life, most of them in childhood, have been of decisive importance in forming his personal imaginative world, the kinds of things he likes to think about, the qualities in human beings he particularly admires or detests. He also knows that many things which are of great importance to him as a man, are irrelevant to his imagination. In the case of a love-poem, for example, no light is thrown upon either its content or its style by discovering the identity of the poet's beloved.

This Chesterton understands. He thought, for example, that certain aspects of Dickens's novels are better understood if we remember that, as a child, Dickens was expected to put on public performances to amuse his father, so he informs us of this fact. On the other hand, he thought that we shall not understand the novels any better if we learn all the details about the failure of Dickens's marriage, so he omits them. In both cases, surely, he is right.

Again, while some writers are more 'difficult' than others and cannot therefore hope to reach a very wide audience, no writer thinks he needs decoding in order to be understood. On the other hand, nearly every writer who has achieved some reputation complains of being misunderstood both by the critics and the public, because they come to his work with preconceived notions of what they are going to find in it. His admirers praise him and his detractors blame him for what, to him, seem imaginary reasons. The kind of critic an author hopes for is someone who will dispel these pre-conceived notions so that his readers may come to his writings with fresh eyes.

At this task of clearing the air, Chesterton was unusually efficient. It is popularly believed that a man who is in earnest about something speaks earnestly and that a man who keeps making jokes is not in earnest. The belief is not ill-founded since, more often than not, this is true. But there are exceptions and, as Chesterton pointed out, Bernard Shaw was one. The public misunderstood Shaw and thought him just a clown when, in fact, he was above all things a deadly serious preacher. In the case of Browning, Chesterton shows that many of his admirers had misunderstood him by reading into his obscurer passages intellectual profundities when in fact the poet was simply indulging his love of the grotesque. Again, he shows us that Stevenson's defect as a narrator was not, as it had become conventional to say, an over-ornate style but an over-ascetic one, a refusal to tell the reader anything about a character that was not absolutely essential. As a rule, it is journalism and literary gossip that is responsible for such misunderstandings; occasionally, though, it can be the author himself. Kipling would certainly have described himself as a patriotic Englishman who admired above all else the military virtues. In an extremely funny essay, Chesterton convincingly demonstrates that Kipling was really a cosmopolitan with no local roots, and he quotes in proof Kipling's own words. . . .

Chesterton's literary criticism abounds in such observations which, once they have been made, seem so obviously true that one cannot understand why one had not seen them for oneself. It now seems obvious to us all that Shaw, the socialist, was in no sense a democrat but was a great republican; that there are two kinds of democrat, the man who, like Scott, sees the dignity of all men, and the man who, like Dickens, sees that all men are equally interesting and varied; that Milton was really an aesthete whose greatness 'does not depend upon moral earnestness or upon anything connected with morality, but upon style alone, a style rather unusually separated from its substance'; that the Elizabethan Age, however brilliant, was not 'spacious', but in literature an age of conceits, in politics an age of conspiracies. But Chesterton was the first critic to see these things. As a literary critic, therefore, I rank him very high.—W. H. AUDEN, "Foreword" to *G. K. Chesterton: A Selection from His Non-fictional Prose*, 1970, pp. 13–15

DRAMA

Mr. Chesterton's play ⟨*Magic*⟩ has run straight into me at a point at which I am most irritable. If there is a thing I detest, it is the temper of mind, now excruciatingly common, which associates table-rapping, being banged, pushed, and pinched in the dark, and the gasping, maundering trances of mediums with religion. By all means "research" if you like, but if the reality of your faith or the strength of your religious emotions depends upon the degree to which such phenomena impress you, your soul is in a bad state. Mercifully, the best-sifted evidence collected hitherto does not go far to proving the "psychic phenomena" are the work of the spirits of the dead. Were it otherwise, the answer to the question, "O Death, where is thy victory?" would certainly be "Up 'Julia's' sleeve." A new prosaic terror would have been added to this microbial planet if the after-life were what the tinkling of guitars in shut cupboards, the bumping of tables, and the tumultuous blatherskite of automatic speech and writing suggest. Mr. Chesterton is most anxious we should attribute these phenomena to demons, and regards traffic with them as defiling and damnably dangerous. This attitude pleases me as little. He would like to revive the belief in possession, witchcraft, incubi and succubae, and perhaps in afrites and banshees, though, I gather, he is not set upon stimulating the belief in fairies who can sit in acorn cups, or in nixes and trolls. The reason he wants to stimulate these beliefs is that he conceives them to be bound up with a belief in a religious view of the universe. No poltergeists, no parsons, is practically the argument with which the necromantic conjurer silences the clergyman who admits that, if he were given a naturalistic explanation of the red light turning blue, he would prefer it to any other. Now, of course, it is true that anyone who believes that there are magicians about who with the help of devils can make (a temptation the conjurer resisted) a champagne bottle jump out of a cellar into the hand of a thirsty man in the street, will have no difficulty in believing in the "supernatural"; but that he will be nearer being religious I doubt, or that the world in which such occurrences took place is really more likely to be a divine creation. Mr. Chesterton is impressed with the disasters which come from doubting too much; he therefore advocates swallowing practically anything ("poor De Rougemont," the Duke would have added). After all, the people who can believe anything are most on the spot in practical matters, he argues. "Are you not easy in your mind in allowing this youth's sister who believes anything to nurse him?" the conjurer asks the doctor. The doctor admits she is a most sensible girl. But Patricia keeps her beliefs in fairies, demons, and magic in a separate compartment, like the people who talk about spiritualism in drawing-rooms. If she believed in magic in the wholehearted way a Fijian believes, would the doctor have been so easy in his mind about her being a good nurse? Would Mr. Chesterton himself be quite at peace in leaving together in the same house a patient recovering from typhoid, a really enthusiastic Christian Scientist (they make a considerable effort to believe enormous things), and a cold plum pudding?

It is the mystic, not the believer in magic, the easy swallower of spectres and Glamis mysteries, who is often remarkable for his grip upon facts; and the main point I wish to make about Mr. Chesterton's idea in this play is that magic runs as

counter to mysticism as anything well can; while as soon as we have ceased to be satisfied with explaining thunder as the rumbling of Jove's chariot wheels (Mr. Chesterton's own example of a plausible hypothesis), and have abandoned that kind of attitude towards things, the only path to a religious conception of the world lies through mysticism.

I have discussed the ideas in this play, not the play itself; for Mr. Chesterton himself cares much more for them than for it. He described his play as amateurish. The first act was admirably good. I only wish other people's acts were as amateurish.—DESMOND McCARTHY, "Black and White Magic," *NS*, Nov. 15, 1913, pp. 180–81

H. G. WELLS
From "About Chesterton and Belloc"
The New Age, January 11, 1908, pp. 209–10

In many ways we three are closely akin; we diverge not by necessity but accident, because we speak in different dialects and have divergent metaphysics. All that I can I shall persuade to my way of thinking about thought and to the use of words in my loose, expressive manner, but Belloc and Chesterton and I are too grown and set to change our languages now and learn new ones; we are on different roads, and so we must needs shout to one another across intervening abysses. These two say Socialism is a thing they do not want for men, and I say Socialism is above all what I want for men. We shall go on saying that now to the end of our days. But what we do all three want is something very alike. Our different roads are parallel. I aim at a growing collective life, a perpetually enhanced inheritance for our race, through the fullest, freest development of the individual life. What they aim at ultimately I do not understand, but it is manifest that its immediate form is the fullest and freest development of the individual life. We all three hate equally and sympathetically the spectacle of human beings blown up with windy wealth and irresponsible power as cruelly and absurdly as boys blow up frogs; we all three detest the complex causes that dwarf and cripple lives from the moment of birth and starve and debase great masses of mankind. We want as universally as possible the jolly life, men and women warm-blooded and well-aired, acting freely and joyously, gathering life as children gather corn-cockles in corn. We all three want people to have property of a real and personal sort, to have the son, as Chesterton put it, bringing up the port his father laid down, and pride in the pears one has grown in one's own garden. And I agree with Chesterton that giving—giving oneself out of love and fellowship—is the salt of life.

But there I diverge from him, less in spirit I think than in the manner of his expression. There is a base because impersonal way of giving. "Standing drink," which he praises as noble, is just the thing I cannot stand, the ultimate mockery and vulgarisation of that fine act of bringing out the cherished thing saved for the heaven-sent guest. It is a mere commercial transaction, essentially of the evil of our time. Think of it! Two temporarily homeless beings agree to drink together, and they turn in and face the public supply of drink (a little vitiated by private commercial necessities) in the public-house. (It is horrible that life should be so wholesale and heartless.) And Jones, with a sudden effusion of manner, thrusts twopence or ninepence (got God knows how) into the economic mysteries and personal delicacy of Brown. I'd as soon a man slipped sixpence down my neck. If Jones has used love and sympathy to detect a certain real thirst and need in Brown and knowledge and power in its assuaging by some specially appropriate fluid, then we have an altogether different matter; but the common business of "standing treat" and giving presents and entertainments is as proud and unspiritual as cock-crowing, as foolish and inhuman as that sorry compendium of mercantile vices, the game of poker, and I am amazed to find Chesterton commend it.

But that is a criticism by the way. Chesterton and Belloc agree with the Socialist that the present world doesn't give at all what they want. They agree that it fails to do so through a wild derangement of our property relations. They are in agreement with the common contemporary man (whose creed is stated, I think, not unfairly, but with the omission of certain important articles by Chesterton), that the derangements of our property relations are to be remedied by concerted action and in part by altered laws. The land and all sorts, of great common interests must be, if not owned, then at least controlled, managed, checked, redistributed by the State. Our real difference is only about a little more or a little less owning. I do not see how Belloc and Chesterton can stand for anything but a strong State as against those wild monsters of property, the strong, big private owners. The State must be complex and powerful enough to prevent them. State or plutocrat, there is really no other practical alternative before the world at the present time. Either we have got to let the big financial adventurers, the aggregating capitalist and his Press, in a loose, informal combination, rule the earth, either we have got to stand aside from preventive legislation and leave things to work out on their present lines, or we have to construct a collective organisation sufficiently strong for the protection of the liberties of the some-day-to-be-jolly common man. So far we go in common. If Belloc and Chesterton are not Socialists, they are at any rate not anti-Socialists. If they say they want an organised Christian State (which involves practically seven-tenths of the Socialist desire), then, in the face of our big common enemies, of adventurous capital, of alien Imperialism, base ambition, base intelligence, and common prejudice and ignorance, I do not mean to quarrel with them politically, so long as they force no quarrel on me. Their organised Christian State is nearer the organised State I want than our present plutocracy. Our ideals will fight some day, and it will be, I know, a first-rate fight, but to fight now is to let the enemy in. When we have got all we want in common, then and only then can we afford to differ. I have never believed that a Socialist Party could hope to form a Government in this country in my life-time; I believe it less now than ever I did. I don't know if any of my Fabian colleagues entertain so remarkable a hope. But if they do not, then unless their political aim is pure cantankerousness, they must contemplate a working political combination between the Socialist members in Parliament and just that non-capitalist section of the Liberal Party for which Chesterton and Belloc speak. Perpetual opposition is a dishonourable aim in politics; and a man who mingles in political development with no intention of taking on responsible tasks unless he gets all his particular formulæ accepted is a pervert, a victim of Irish bad example, and unfit for decent democratic institutions. . . .

I digress again, I see, but my drift I hope is clear. Differ as we may, Belloc and Chesterton are with all Socialists in being on the same side of the great political and social cleavage that opens at the present time. We and they are with the interests of the mass of common men as against that growing organisation of great owners who have common interests directly antagonistic to those of the community and State. We Socialists are only secondarily politicians. Our primary business is not to impose upon, but to ram right into the substance of that object of Chesterton's solicitude, the circle of ideas of the common man, the idea of the State as his own, as a thing he serves and is served by. We want to add to his sense of property rather than

offend it. If I had my way I would do that at the street corners and on the trams, I would take down that alien-looking and often detested inscription "L.C.C.," and put up, "This Tram, this Street, belongs to the People of London." Would Chesterton or Belloc quarrel with that? Suppose that Chesterton is right, and that there are incurable things in the mind of the common man flatly hostile to our ideals; so much of our ideals will fail. But we are doing our best by our lights, and all we can. What are Chesterton and Belloc doing? If our ideal is partly right and partly wrong, are they trying to build up a better ideal? Will they state a Utopia and how they propose it shall be managed? If they lend their weight only to such fine old propositions as that a man wants freedom, that he has a right to do as he likes with his own, and so on, they won't help the common man much. All that fine talk, without some further exposition, goes to sustain Mr. Rockefeller's simple human love of property, and the woman and child sweating manufacturer in his fight for the inspector-free home industry. I bought on a bookstall the other day a pamphlet full of mis-representation and bad argument against Socialism by an Australian Jew, published by the Single-Tax people apparently in a disinterested attempt to free the land from the landowner by the simple expedient of abusing anyone else who wanted to do as much but did not hold Henry George to be God and Lord; and I know Socialists who will protest with tears in their eyes against association with any human being who sings any song but the "Red Flag" and doubts whether Marx had much experience of affairs. Well, there is no reason why Chesterton and Belloc should at their level do the same sort of thing. When we talk on a ceiling or at a dinner-party with any touch of the celestial in its composition, Chesterton and I, Belloc and I, are antagonists with an undying feud, but in the fight against human selfishness and narrowness and for a finer, juster law, we are brothers—at the remotest, half-brothers.

Chesterton isn't a Socialist—agreed! But now, as between us and the Master of Elibank or Sir Hugh Bell or any other Free Trade Liberal capitalist or landlord, which side is he on? You cannot have more than one fight going on in the political arena at the same time, because only one party or group of parties can win.

And going back for a moment to that point about a Utopia, I want one from Chesterton. Purely unhelpful criticism isn't enough from a man of his size. It isn't fair for him to go about sitting on other people's Utopias. I appeal to his sense of fair play. I have done my best to reconcile the conception of a free and generous style of personal living with a social organisation that will save the world from the harsh predominance of dull, persistent, energetic, unscrupulous grabbers tempered only by the vulgar extravagance of their wives and sons. It isn't an adequate reply to say that nobody stood treat there, and that the simple, generous people like to beat their own wives and children on occasion in a loving and intimate manner, and they won't endure the spirit of Sidney Webb.

GEORGE BERNARD SHAW
"The Chesterbelloc: A Lampoon" (1908)
Pen Portraits and Reviews
1931, pp. 75–86

Our friend Wells is mistaken. His desire to embrace Chesterton as a vessel of the Goodwill which is making for Socialism is a hopeless one for other reasons than the obvious impossibility of his arms reaching round that colossal figure which dominates Battersea Park. Wells is an Englishman, and cannot understand these foreigners. The pages of Who's Who explain the whole misunderstanding. Turn to Wells, Herbert Geo., and you learn at once that he is every inch an Englishman, a man of Kent, not in the least because he was born in Bromley (a negro might be born in Bromley) but because he does not consider himself the son of his mother, but of his father only; and all his pride of birth is that his father was a famous cricketer. It is nothing to Wells that he is one of the foremost authors of his time: he takes at once the stronger English ground that he is by blood a Kentish cricketer.

Turn we now to Chesterton, Gilbert Keith. He is the son of his mother, and his mother's name is Marie Louise Grosjean. Who his father was will never matter to anyone who has once seen G. K. Chesterton, or at least seen as much of him as the limited range of human vision can take in at once. If ever a Grosjean lived and wrote his name on the sky by towering before it, that man is G. K. C. France did not break the mould in which she formed Rabelais. It got to Campden Hill in the year 1874; and it never turned out a more complete Frenchman than it did then.

Let us look up Belloc. The place of his birth is suppressed, probably because it was in some very English place; for Belloc is desperately determined not to be an Englishman, and actually went through a period of military service in the French artillery to repudiate these islands, and establish his right to call himself a Frenchman. There is no nonsense of that kind about Chesterton. No artillery service for him, thank you: he is French enough without that: besides, there is not cover enough for him on a French battlefield: the worst marksman in the Prussian artillery could hit him at six miles with absolute certainty. Belloc's sister is a lady distinguished in letters: she is also in Who's Who, which thus betrays the fact that one of their ancestors was Dr. Priestley. Also that Belloc is the son of a French barrister and of Bessie Rayner Parkes. You cannot say that Belloc is wholly French except by personal choice; but still he is not English. Beside his friend Grosjean he seems Irish. I suspect him of being Irish. Anyhow, not English, and therefore for ever incomprehensible to Wells.

Before shutting up Who's Who turn for a moment to Shaw, George Bernard. He, you will observe, is the child of his own works. Not being a Frenchman like Chesterton, for whom the cult of *ma mère* is *de rigueur*, and not being able to boast of his father's fame as a cricketer, like Wells, he has modestly suppressed his parents—unconsciously; for he never noticed this piece of self-sufficiency before—and states simply that he was born in Dublin. Therefore, also eternally incomprehensible to Wells, but, on the other hand, proof against the wiles of Chesterton and Belloc, I cannot see through Chesterton: there is too much of him for anybody to see through; but he cannot impose on me as he imposes on Wells. Neither can Belloc.

Wells has written in this journal about Chesterton and Belloc without stopping to consider what Chesterton and Belloc is. This sounds like bad grammar; but I know what I am about. Chesterton and Belloc is a conspiracy, and a most dangerous one at that. Not a viciously intended one: quite the contrary. It is a game of make-believe of the sort which all imaginative grown-up children love to play; and, as in all such games, the first point in it is that they shall pretend to be somebody else. Chesterton is to be a roaring jovial Englishman, not taking his pleasures sadly, but piling Falstaff on Magog, and Boythorn on John Bull. Belloc's fancy is much stranger. He is to be a Frenchman, but not a Walkley Frenchman, not any of the varieties of the stage Frenchman, but a

French peasant, greedy, narrow, individualistic, ready to fight like a rat in a corner for his scrap of land, and, above all, intensely and superstitiously Roman Catholic. And the two together are to impose on the simple bourgeoisie of England as the Main Forces of European Civilization.

Now at first sight it would seem that it does not lie with me to rebuke this sort of make-believe. The celebrated G. B. S. is about as real as a pantomime ostrich. But it is less alluring than the Chesterton-Belloc chimera, because as they have four legs to move the thing with, whereas I have only two, they can produce the quadrupedal illusion, which is the popular feature of your pantomime beast. Besides, I have played my game with a conscience. I have never pretended that G. B. S. was real: I have over and over again taken him to pieces before the audience to shew the trick of him. And even those who in spite of that cannot escape from the illusion, regard G. B. S. as a freak. The whole point of the creature is that he is unique, fantastic, unrepresentative, inimitable, impossible, undesirable on any large scale, utterly unlike anybody that ever existed before, hopelessly unnatural, and void of real passion. Clearly such a monster could do no harm, even were his example evil (which it never is).

But the Chesterbelloc is put forward in quite a different way: the Yellow Press way. The Chesterbelloc denounces the Yellow Press, but only because it dislikes yellow and prefers flaming red. The characteristic vice of the Yellow Journalist is that he never says he wants a thing (usually bigger dividends) or that his employer wants it. He always says that the Empire needs it, or that Englishmen are determined to have it, and that those who object to it are public enemies, Jews, Germans, rebels, traitors, Pro-Boers, and what not. Further, he draws an imaginative picture of a person whose honour and national character consist in getting what the Yellow Journalist is after, and says to the poor foolish reader: "That is yourself, my brave fellow countryman." Now this is precisely what the Chesterbelloc does in its bigger, more imaginative, less sordid way. Chesterton never says, "I, a hybrid Superman, and Grand Transmogrificator of Ideas, desire this, believe that, deny the other." He always says that the English people desires it; that the dumb democracy which has never yet spoken (save through the mouth of the Chesterbelloc) believes it; or that the principles of Liberalism and of the French Revolution repudiate it. Read his poem in the *Neolith* on the dumb democracy of England: it would be a great poem if it were not such fearful nonsense. Belloc is still more audacious. According to him, the Chesterbelloc is European democracy, is the Catholic Church, is the Life Force, is the very voice of the clay of which Adam was made, and which the Catholic peasant labours. To set yourself against the Chesterbelloc is not merely to be unpatriotic, like setting yourself against the Daily Mail or Express: it is to set yourself against all the forces, active and latent (especially latent) of humanity. Wells and I, contemplating the Chesterbelloc, recognize at once a very amusing pantomime elephant, the front legs being that very exceptional and unEnglish individual Hilaire Belloc, and the hind legs that extravagant freak of French nature, G. K. Chesterton. To which they both reply "Not at all: what you see is the Zeitgeist." To which we reply bluntly but conclusively, "Gammon!"

But a pantomime animal with two men in it is a mistake when the two are not very carefully paired. It has never been so successful as the Blondin Donkey, which is worked by one Brother Griffith only, not by the two. Chesterton and Belloc are so unlike that they get frightfully into one another's way. Their vocation as philosophers requires the most complete detachment: their business as the legs of the Chesterbelloc demands the most complete synchronism. They are unlike in everything except the specific literary genius and delight in play-acting that is common to them, and that threw them into one another's arms. Belloc, like most anti-Socialists, is intensely gregarious. He cannot bear isolation or final ethical responsibility: he clings to the Roman Catholic Church: he clung to his French nationality because one nation was not enough for him: he went into the French Army because it gave him a regiment, a company, even a gun to cling to: he was not happy until he got into Parliament; and now his one dread is that he will not get into heaven. He likes to keep his property in his own hand, and his soul in a safe bank. Chesterton has nothing of this in him at all: neither society nor authority nor property nor status are necessary to his happiness: he has never belonged to anything but that anarchic refuge of the art-struck, the Slade School. Belloc, like all men who feel the need of authority, is a bit of a rowdy. He has passed through the Oxford rowdyism of Balliol and the military rowdyism of the gunner; and he now has the super-rowdyism of the literary genius who has lived adventurously in the world and not in the Savile Club. A proletariat of Bellocs would fight: possibly on the wrong side, like the peasants of La Vendée; but the Government they set up would have to respect them, though it would also have to govern them by martial law. Now Chesterton might be trusted anywhere without a policeman. He might knock at a door and run away—perhaps even lie down across the threshold to trip up the emergent house-holder; but his crimes would be hyperbolic crimes of imagination and humour, not of malice. He is friendly, easy-going, unaffected, gentle, magnanimous, and genuinely democratic. He can make sacrifices easily: Belloc cannot. The consequence is that in order to coordinate the movements of the Chesterbelloc, Chesterton has to make all the intellectual sacrifices that are demanded by Belloc in his dread of going to hell or of having to face, like Peer Gynt, the horrible possibility of becoming extinct. For Belloc's sake Chesterton says he believes literally in the Bible story of the Resurrection. For Belloc's sake he says he is not a Socialist. On a recent occasion I tried to drive him to swallow the Miracle of St. Januarius for Belloc's sake; but at that he struck. He pleaded his belief in the Resurrection story. He pointed out very justly that I believe in lots of things just as miraculous as the Miracle of St. Januarius; but when I remorselessly pressed the fact that he did not believe that the blood of St. Januarius reliquefies miraculously every year, the Credo stuck in his throat like Amen in Macbeth's. He had got down at last to his irreducible minimum of dogmatic incredulity, and could not, even with the mouth of the bottomless pit yawning before Belloc, utter the saving lie. But it is an old saying that when one turns to Rome one does not begin with the miracle of St. Januarius. That comes afterwards. For my part I think that a man who is not a sufficiently good Catholic to be proof against the follies and romancings of Roman Churches, Greek Churches, English Churches, and all such local prayer-wheel-installations, is no Catholic at all. I think a man who is not Christian enough to feel that conjuror's miracles are, on the part of a god, just what cheating at cards is on the part of a man, and that the whole value of the Incarnation nowadays to men of Chesterton's calibre depends on whether, when the Word became Flesh, it played the game instead of cheating, is not a Christian at all. To me no man believes in the Resurrection until he can say: "I am the Resurrection and the Life," and rejoice in and act on that very simple and obvious fact. Without that, belief in the gospel story is like belief in the story of Jack the Giantkiller, which, by the way, has the advantage of not being three different and incompatible stories. I should say, too, that a man who is not Individualist

and Liberal enough to be a staunch Protestant, is not an Individualist nor a Liberal at all. That is, in the Chestertonian sense of the words. There is a sense in which you can be a Catholic and burn Jews and Atheists. There is a sense in which you can be a Christian and flog your fellow-creatures or imprison them for twenty years. There is a sense in which you can be a Protestant and have a confessor. But not on the Chestertonian plane. Chestertonesse *oblige*.

Chesterton and Belloc are not the same sort of Christian, not the same sort of Pagan, not the same sort of Liberal, not the same sort of anything intellectual. And that is why the Chesterbelloc is an unnatural beast which must be torn asunder to release the two men who are trying to keep step inside its basket-work. Wells's challenge to Chesterton is finally irresistible: he must plonk down his Utopia against ours. And it must be an intellectually honest and intellectually possible one, and not a great game played by a herd of Chesterbellocs. Nor must it be an orgy of uproarious drunkards—a perpetual carouse of Shakespears and Ben Jonsons at The Mermaid. This may seem rather an uncivil condition to lay down; but it is necessary, for reasons which I will now proceed to state.

It is the greatest mistake in the world to suppose that people disapprove of Socialism because they are not convinced by its economic or political arguments. The anti-Socialists all have a secret dread that Socialism will interfere with their darling vices. The lazy man fears that it will make him work. The industrious man fears that it will impose compulsory football or cricket on him. The libertine fears that it will make women less purchaseable; the drunkard, that it will close the public-houses; the miser, that it will abolish money; the sensation lover, that there will be no more crimes, no more executions, no more famines, perhaps even no more fires. Beneath all the clamour against Socialism as likely to lower the standard of conduct lies the dread that it will really screw it up.

Now, Chesterton and Belloc have their failings like other men. They share one failing—almost the only specific that they have in common except their literary talent. That failing is, I grieve to say, addiction to the pleasures of the table. Vegetarianism and teetotalism are abhorrent to them, as they are to most Frenchmen. The only thing in Wells's earnest and weighty appeal to Chesterton that moved him was an incidental disparagement of the custom of standing drinks and of the theory that the battle of Waterloo was won at the public-house counter.

Now it will be admitted, I think, by all candid Socialists, that the Socialist ideal, as usually presented in Socialist Utopias, is deficient in turkey and sausages. Morris insists on wine and tobacco in "News from Nowhere"; but nobody in that story has what a vestryman would call a good blowout. Morris rather insists on slenderness of figure, perhaps for the sake of Burne-Jones (who was *his* Belloc). As to Wells, his Utopia is dismally starved. There is not even a round of buttered toast in it. The impression produced is that everybody is dieted, and that not a soul in the place can hope for a short life and a merry one. What this must mean to Chesterton no words of mine can express. Belloc would rather die than face it.

I once met a lady who had a beautiful ideal. Even as Tintoretto chalked up on the wall of his studio "The color of Titian, and the design of Michael Angelo," this lady wrote on the fly-leaf of her private diary, "The intellect of Chesterton, and the figure of Bernard Shaw." I think her bias was rather towards Chesterton, because she concluded, rather superficially, that it is easier to change a man's body than his mind so instead of sending to me a file of the Daily News and a complete set of Chesterton's books to Chestertonize me, she sent to Chesterton—anonymously, and with elaborate precautions against identification—a little book entitled, if I recollect aright, Checkley's Exercises. Checkley's idea was that if you went through his exercises, your maximum circumference would occur round your chest, and taper down from that to your toes in a Grecian slenderness of flank. I glanced through Checkley and saw that the enterprise was hopeless. His exercises were to be performed without apparatus; and they mostly consisted in getting into attitudes which only a hydraulic press could get Chesterton into, and which no power on earth or in heaven could ever get him out of again. But I, the vegetarian, can do them on my head.

And now I will tear the veil from Chesterton's inmost secret. Chesterton knows about me. I am the living demonstration of the fact that Chesterton's work can be done on a teetotal and vegetarian diet. To Chesterton Socialism means his being dragged before a committee of public health and put on rations from which flesh and alcohol are strictly eliminated. It means compulsory Checkley until his waist will pass easily through a hoop for which his chest has served as a mandril. He sees that all his pleas and entreaties will be shattered on Me. When he says, "Look at Charles James Fox: he was the English exponent of the principles of the French Revolution; and he ate and drank more than I do—quite disgracefully, in fact," they will say, "Yes; but look at Bernard Shaw." When he pleads that a man cannot be brilliant, cannot be paradoxical, cannot shed imagination and humour prodigally over the pages of democratic papers on ginger beer and macaroni, he will get the same inexorable reply "Look at Bernard Shaw: he does not drink even tea or coffee: his austerity shames the very saints themselves; and yet who more brilliant? who more paradoxical? who more delightful as a journalist? And has not he himself assured us that the enormous superiority shewn by him in doing everything that you do and writing epoch-making plays to boot, is due solely to the superiority of his diet. So cease your feeble evasions; and proceed to go through Checkley's first exercise at once."

Whoever has studied Chesterton's articles attentively for a few years past will have noticed that though they profess to deal with religion, politics, and literature, they all really come at last to a plea for excess and outrageousness, especially in eating and drinking, and a heartfelt protest against Shavianism, tempered by a terrified admiration of it. Therefore I will now save Chesterton's soul by a confession.

True excess does not make a man fat: it wastes him. Falstaff was not an overworked man: he was an underworked one. If ever there was a man wasted by excess, I am that man. The Chesterbelloc, ministered to by waiters and drinking wretched narcotics out of bottles, does not know what a real stimulant is. What does it know of *my* temptations, *my* backslidings, *my* orgies? How can it, timidly munching beefsteaks and apple tart, conceive the spirit-struggles of a young man who knew that Bach is good for his soul, and yet turned to Beethoven, and from him fell to Berlioz and Liszt from mere love of excitement, luxury, savagery, and drunkenness? Has Chesterton ever spent his last half-crown on an opera by Meyerbeer or Verdi, and sat down at a crazy pianet to roar it and thrash it through with an execution of a dray-horse and a scanty octave and a half of mongrel baritone voice? Has he ever lodged underneath a debauchee who was diabolically possessed with the finale of the Seventh Symphony or the Walkürenritt whilst decent citizens were quietly drinking themselves to sleep with whiskey—and diluted whiskey at that?

Far from being an abstinent man, I am the worst drunkard of a rather exceptionally drunken family; for they were content

with alcohol, whereas I want something so much stronger that I would as soon drink paraffin oil as brandy. Cowards drink alcohol to quiet their craving for real stimulants: I avoid it to keep my palate keen for them. And I am a pitiable example of something much worse than the drink craze: to wit, the work craze. Do not forget Herbert Spencer's autobiography, with its cry of warning against work. I get miserably unhappy if my work is cut off. I get hideous headaches after each month's bout: I make resolutions to break myself of it, never to work after lunch, to do only two hours a day; but in vain: every day brings its opportunity and its temptation: the craving masters me every time; and I dread a holiday as I dread nothing else on earth. Let Chesterton take heart, then: it is he who is the ascetic and I the voluptuary. Socialism is far more likely to force me to eat meat and drink alcohol than to force him to take overdoses of Wagner and Strauss and write plays in his spare time. Let him, I say, throw off this craven obsession with my fancied austerity, and instead of declaring that he is not a Socialist when he clearly does not yet know what he is, accept Wells's challenge, and make up his mind as to how he really wants the world to be arranged under the existing conditions of human nature and physical geography.

Wells, like Sidney Webb and myself, is a bit of that totally imaginary Old Victorian England which Chesterton invented in his essay on G. F. Watts. He is intellectually honest. He does not pretend to be the English people, or Democracy, or the indigenous peasant European, or "the folk," or Catholicism, or the Press, or the French Revolution, or any of the other quick changes of the Chesterbelloc. His song is

My name's *not* John Wellington Wells;
And I *don't* deal in magic and spells.

He keeps the facts as to WELLS, Herbert Geo. and his difficulties and limitations, and the worse limitations of his much less clever neighbours, honestly and resolutely before you. With wit enough, imagination enough, and humour enough to play with the questions raised by the condition of England quite as amusingly as the Chesterbelloc, he works at it instead, and does what he can to hew out and hammer together some planks of a platform on which a common unliterary man may stand. I also, with a stupendous endowment for folly, have put my cards on the table—even some that are unfit for publication. Webb is far too full of solid administrative proposals to have any time or patience for literary games: when he gets taken that way he puts his witticisms into my printers' proofs, and leaves me to bear the discredit of them and to be told that I should be more serious, like Webb. But, on the whole, we have all three dealt faithfully with the common man.

And now, what has the Chesterbelloc (or either of its two pairs of legs) to say in its defence? But it is from the hind legs that I particularly want to hear; because South Salford will very soon cure Hilaire Forelegs of his fancy for the ideals of the Catholic peasant proprietor. He is up against his problems in Parliament: it is in Battersea Park that a great force is in danger of being wasted.

O. W. FIRKINS
From "A Burlesque of Macaulay"
The Forum, November 1912, pp. 597–607

Twenty years ago one would have said that the style of Macaulay, except as a qualifying force, had disappeared from English literature—that it belonged with the sackbut and the virginals, with the baldric and the coat-of-mail, among the curiosities of history. But the fact of death is not always established, in literature at least, by the fact of inquest, and one of the alertest of our younger writers has taken the relic from its cabinet, reset and refurbished it, and found its merits preferable to the praise of originality. The old marks of Macaulay, the short, forcible sentence with the velocity and the impact of a missile, the clash of a word upon its repeated self like jingling castanets, the old readiness, if not quite the old richness and remoteness of allusion, the controversial zest, the glow of conflict, the impatience of half-truths and half-certainties, the insistence that all assertions shall be sweeping and all demonstrations final, the old and more than the old fertility of comparison and the relish for the homely simile that rivets and clamps the idea, the fearless use of balance, the terse, casual sarcasm which, like the scythe on the chariot, does execution as an incident of transit—all these traits, for the most part unabated and altogether unabashed, reappear to-day in the style of Mr. Gilbert K. Chesterton.

But the later writer has not been content with a duplication of his prototype; he has gone further and evolved a serious style which might have passed without question as a burlesque of Macaulay. He has added a daredevil and boisterous tone (confined, it is true, to things intellectual), a curious and motley word-play, from the pun up, of which now the felicity, now the triviality, is electrifying, a more than Macaulayesque pertinacity in hounding a thought to its death and baiting it after its surrender, and a delight in paradox which assimilates his pages to those circus billboards in which acrobats figure in every form of topsy-turviness and contortion. In spite of some higher and less strident traits, such as the searching epithet that rather distils than describes an object, and a fancy whimsical even to elfishness, the total effect remains, in one word, shrill: it is exaggeration passing into caricature; it is Browne super-added to Dickens.

There are vehicles in which the whir and whiz of the mechanism destroy for the time being the sense of surroundings and the interest in destination. The perception of message, of substance, almost of mind itself, in Mr. Chesterton's work is swept away at the outset by the deadening and deafening effect of his omnipresent and overbearing style. Later on, we perceive in his make-up an analyst and a logician. His pursuit of generalizations is unflagging; he is never happy with a fact until he has matched it with a principle. He is not only willing to introduce philosophy into the brief newspaper sketches of which he has republished several volumes (*Tremendous Trifles, All Things Considered, Alarms and Discursions*); he is unwilling to leave it out. He has an eye for objects and the gift of picture, but a case of pure description or pure record in these sketches is hardly discoverable. His mind moves like a shuttle from picture to theory and from theory to picture, providing an illustration for every thesis and an hypothesis for every fact; but it cannot abide long and easily in either the abstract or the concrete; it does not pass naturally like a poet's from picture to picture, nor like a mathematician's or metaphysician's from theory to theory. Like Emerson, like the great maxim-writers, he stands for the philosopher as distinct, in point of fact divided, from the systematizer. He can scarcely write a treatise; his *Orthodoxy* is a chain of papers; his critiques are successions of insights. He divagates even in newspaper sketches; he always rambles when he is short of time.

The logician is hardly less conspicuous. The swiftness, the deftness, the crispness, are, in this field also, extraordinary; the author runs up and down the logical rigging of the syllogism, the analogy, or the dilemma with the agility of a sailor or a cat. The reader is committed to revolutionary or discomfiting conclusions before he has had time to catch his bearings or to get his breath; everything is proved, proved off-hand, proved completely, proved redundantly; errors go down before his spear at a touch, but knowing he is Chesterton. Yet nothing, in the long run, is more suspicious than the appearance of universal cogency. The claim, like that of infallibility, is discredited by its very compass. Every man who grasps the mixed and doubtful nature of about half the truths in the moral world knows that an aspect of conclusiveness cannot be at the same time universal (or even widespread) and genuine. An opening is made for extreme reactions, for suspicions of trickery and superficiality, which, in some cases and notably in Mr. Chesterton's, are only partly justified.

An actual test of the logic proves that if Mr. Chesterton belongs to the class of generals who claim victories even when they are beaten, he belongs also to the class who win victories. His reasoning at its best is annihilative; it makes an end both of the topic and the antagonist. His refutations, in particular, are sometimes of incredible cogency and address. He can expose the contradictions in the multifarious arguments of the diverse assailants of Christianity with unequalled brilliancy and effect; he can puncture the Nietzschean "superman" ambiguity with a dexterity that is exhilarating, he can riddle the "up-to-date" or "modernist" fallacy in a score of careless but irrefutable sentences. On the other hand, no man is more prone to defend the idlest errors on the flimsiest grounds; he makes mistakes from which five minutes' thought should have saved a stupid man. Never was a mind at once so acute and so unwary, as no mind so original ever succumbed so often to the obvious. The latter fact may be explained by a style which gives a glaze of originality even to a platitude, and the former, possibly, by the faith that his unwariness will lead him into no trap from which his acuteness will prove insufficient to release him. We should exaggerate little in affirming that the chances are about even that a dictum of Mr. Chesterton's will turn out to be a truism magnificently restated, a brilliant but fallacious novelty, or an insight of real originality and power. . . .

Criticism, for Mr. Chesterton, is a mere study of the human spirit as disclosed in literature, whether as conveyed in its contents or exemplified in its methods; it is a section of philosophy. We may summarize his own philosophy in half a dozen propositions.

First: he upholds a Christianity, orthodox and ritualistic but otherwise undefined, on grounds drawn chiefly from man's psychical needs and barely touching the historical argument. This means collision with the experts and the evolutionists who try his Christianity in a double sense. Second: his defence of a great popular tradition blends naturally with the glorification of the common man, evinced not only in the democratic ideal of government, but in a firm trust in the righteousness, authority, and sanctity of the universal instincts of which the common man is the depositary. The existence of paradox in Mr. Chesterton is therefore itself paradoxical, since it contradicts the universal beliefs whose authority he concedes. Third: as "progress" so-called is drawing men away from Christianity, or at least orthodoxy, he naturally insists that advance need not be amelioration, and that the location of an idea in time has no effect upon its value; on the abstract question he is here quite irrefutable. Fourth: he is a liberal in politics, but an individualist by temperament; he upholds a robust nationality, undiluted with cosmopolitanism and purged of the imperialistic virus. Fifth: he dilates on the wonder latent in the normal and the common, and reveres the ignorance, even the folly, on which these wonders fall with their primal force. Sixth: he preaches a militant and hardy optimism expressing itself in loyalty to what he calls in a beautiful phrase "the flag of the world."

Three observations may be made on this philosophy. First of all, it is a somewhat curious blending of the instinctive and the conventional. There is enough of elemental, primordial humanity in this creed to impart a real piquancy to the discovery that its holder reveres tradition, upholds convention, and has even a kind word for artifice. The explanation, however, is simple: the first or primary attitude of men toward convention is poetic and reverent, the second slavish, the third rebellious or disdainful; the third of these attitudes is a protest against the second; Mr. Chesterton has adhered to the first.

We are struck, in the second place, by the absence of novelty and audacity in these propositions: a platform of this kind could be submitted without perturbation to a New England village tea-party or to the British House of Lords. Many of Mr. Chesterton's statements, many of his secondary opinions, are novel and sensational, but the paradox that impregnates his constitution reappears in the fact that his cardinal tenets are unoriginal and unexciting. The novelty lies in the circumstance that he has brought the radical temper to the support of the conservative idea; he neither skulks nor truckles nor propitiates; in assurance, in dexterity, in gayety, in the very levity and wantonness of courage, he outruns his coolest antagonists. He has shown that a sally of the garrison may have more impetus than an assault of the besiegers.

The final comment on these articles of faith is that they gain approval even where they fail to win assent; their manly, tonic, and invigorating quality impresses even the unconvinced. A man who preaches an impassioned and romantic Christianity, and who adds to that the Jeffersonian doctrine of democracy, the Wordsworthian and Tolstoyan doctrine of the majesty of the untutored man, the Carlylean doctrine of wonder, the Emersonian doctrine of the spirituality latent in all objects, the Dickensian faith in the worth and wisdom of the feeble-minded, the Browningesque standard of optimism, affects us as a man with whom, whatever his vagaries and harlequinries, it would be wholesome and inspiriting to live. . . .

Mr. Chesterton's attitude toward religion is the most original and interesting thing in his constitution. A person ignorant of the term might gather from the Chestertonian allusions that religion was some fine old English sport like falconry or archery which a thankless nation had suffered to lapse into unmerited neglect. He even brackets the church with the tavern and beer with the Bible in his half-whimsical lists of the excellent and desirable things in life. He finds himself both religious and jocular—disposed even to combine religion with jocularity. The normal man would accept such incongruities as personal and casual, and would no more try to reconcile them than to harmonize his love of Plato with his love of oysters: Mr. Chesterton insists that the combination is primordial and cosmic. Laughter is the sign of that perfect adjustment of the individual spirit to the nature of things of which religion is the source. He goes so far as to make his maddest burlesque (the novels, *The Man Who Was Thursday*, *The Ball and the Cross*, *The Napoleon of Notting Hill*) the vehicle for his most solemn meditations, and even suggests humor as the unrevealed mystery in the spirit of Jesus Christ.

The opening for ridicule is obvious—too obvious indeed to be worth accepting—but in the fact itself combined with the simplicity of its avowal there is, for the thoughtful mind, something that is touching and reassuring. The grotesque touch is the touch that certifies for the very reason that it is for the hypocrite and the dilettante the touch that invalidates, and this

half-grimace has the power to conduct us into the presence of an unassailable sincerity. Moreover, the impossibility of such an avowal from the sober respectabilities in literature, from Johnson or Burke, from Scott or Macaulay, from Tennyson or Arnold, reveals to us in a flash that Mr. Chesterton belongs to the race, though not to the class, of the great pregnant, primal, wilful temperaments, the Richters, the Heines, the Sternes, the Lambs, the Burnses, the Carlyles. In this trait or union of traits, a temperament, otherwise not exceptional, lays hold at the same moment of the seriousness that gives depth and the grotesqueness that bestows individuality. After this we are pleased rather than surprised to find this brisk and bounding personality capable of awe, capable even of passages which only just fall short of lofty religious exaltation. . . .

It is obviously too early to discuss the question of Mr. Chesterton's absolute value, his value for posterity. It is idle to forestall a verdict in the absence of half the evidence and of all the jurors. Two suggestions, however, are in place.

The style of an author, even when convicted of misrepresentation, does not cease to represent him; it still largely determines his effect upon mankind. Mr. Chesterton has been unfortunate in this point. Whether his style was a piece of mischief (a by no means impossible hypothesis), or the means which his love of excitement took to indemnify itself for the moderation of his doctrines, or an attempt to transfer to paper the seismic properties which he divined and extolled in the universe, it is certain that it presents a serious and sincere man in the likeness of a trickster and a mechanician. The deeper and richer notes in his diapason come to us dulled and confused through the charivari of epigrams and antithesis by which he reconvinces himself and his reader five or six times on a page that Mr. Chesterton is the cleverest of men. The danger is that the reader will content himself with this concession.

Granting that the style is unfair to the real seriousness of the man, it is proper to ask whether a still higher seriousness would not have prevented the adoption of that style. Granting that he mixes religion and mirth without hurt to his religion and with vast profit to his individuality, the question remains as to the nature of the inhibition which has made such a combination impossible to three-fourths of the evangelists and prophets. Is Mr. Chesterton the possessor of a deeper feeling and a finer insight like that which enabled Shakespeare in *King Lear* to blend tragedy and comedy in a fashion impracticable to his weaker rivals? There is nothing in the nature of things to interdict the possibility, but there is also nothing in the nature of Mr. Chesterton to make its application plausible in the present case. Rather, his fine, fresh, boyish, untrammelled temper would suggest that the difference is explicable through his exclusion from an order of experience which subdues and saddens in the measure of the depth and enrichment it confers. It is this exclusion which may constitute for this robust and pungent intellect the drawback to greatness and the bar to immortality.

MAURICE EVANS
From "Style and Argument"
G. K. Chesterton
1939, pp. 147–54

Chesterton's use of concrete illustration by analogy introduces the question of his methods of argument. We are not concerned here with his general methods of stating a case. It is sufficient to mention that, like Aldous Huxley, he generally begins with a study of human needs and then erects a religious or social system to fit them. Our main concern is rather with the illegitimate use to which Chesterton frequently puts his admirable command of word and image, so that proof appears where, in fact, none exists. Analogy is obviously a very dangerous weapon in this respect, for what begins as illustration may, after sufficient development, be accepted as proof. For example, a simile may be introduced and elaborated for some time. It is then suddenly related back to the argument in a completely new fashion and one feels that the argument is inevitably clinched. An illustration will establish this point more clearly. In *Orthodoxy* Chesterton is discussing mysticism and reason. Mysticism is the acceptance of what we cannot understand, and the main source of our happiness, while reason implies an attempt to understand everything. It produces clarity and consistency, but limits the rich diversity of life and ultimately leads to madness. He then illustrates the contrast by analogies of the sun and moon. "Like the sun at noonday mysticism explains everything else by the blaze of its own victorious invisibility." It is too bright for us to see and yet warms and cherishes the whole of our life. Reason, on the other hand, is as clear and cold as the moon: "But the circle of the moon is as clear and unmistakable . . . as the circle of Euclid on a blackboard." After thus establishing the simile through the links of warmth and brightness, cold and clarity, he suddenly relates the simile back to the main argument by the entirely unexpected connection of reason, madness and the moon: "For the moon is utterly reasonable; and the moon is the mother of lunatics and has given to them all her name." A satisfactory sense of finality is produced and it is difficult to feel that the argument is not proved. We may quote a rather more flippant example from the same book. Chesterton is establishing a connection between democracy and tradition which, he says, is "the democracy of the dead . . . an extension of the franchise". "The ancient Greeks voted by stones", he continues, "and these shall vote by tombstones; it is all quite regular and official for", to clinch the argument unexpectedly, "tombstones, like ballot-papers, are marked with a cross."

A slight extension of this method of suggestion is Chesterton's use of a metaphor as a literal fact on which an argument may be based. For example, he observes that the American mentality is child-like and loves "to watch the wheels go round" (*Generally Speaking*). Then taking the metaphor literally, he argues from it: "watching the wheels go round" implies that they will return back to the same place, or if they move on, they will move in a rut. Therefore, Americans are conservative. This may be the case, but there is no logical connection in the argument. The childlike interest in working things does not in fact imply a conservative outlook, and the conclusion is deduced from the metaphor, not the fact for which it stands. Similarly, Chesterton answers the argument that democracy will not work by saying that it does not work, it plays (*What's Wrong with the World*), where the metaphor is again taken in a literal sense.

It is interesting to analyse Chesterton's exploitation of imagery to suggest a conclusion by almost imperceptible allusions. When dealing with some neutral subject, he uses significant imagery in order to arouse an emotional anticipation of what is to follow, and to prejudice our thoughts in a particular direction. To quote *Orthodoxy* once more, and the conflict of reason with mysticism, Chesterton has shown how reason leads to madness, but has made no mention of religion as yet. Nevertheless, biblical language is introduced to prepare the way: "Curing a madman is not arguing with a philosopher; it is casting out a devil." From such preparation the subsequent argument for religion becomes more convincing. We can see the same thing happening in *The Ball and the Cross*, when

dawn is described in language carrying religious associations. "Both the men, according to their several creeds, felt the full thunder of the psalm of life . . . and every bird that rose with that sunrise caught a light like a star upon it, like the dove of the Holy Spirit." It is essentially a Christian dawn and the atheist Turnbull seems unnatural and out of place.

By such word-play as this, Chesterton tampers with the facts and illegitimately prejudices the argument. His logic is often equally faulty, only escaping criticism by the bewildering speed of attack. He begins with some statement from which he argues so rapidly, leaving the original statement so quickly behind, that he has established a new position before we have time to question the old. Such quick generalization is extremely intimidating. For example, Chesterton is defending the supernatural by arguing that the evidence in its favour should be considered as impartially as evidence for anything else. "You reject the peasant's story about the ghost either because the man is a peasant or because the story is a ghost story. That is, you either deny the main principle of democracy or you affirm the main principle of materialism, the abstract impossibility of a miracle." This is so much dust thrown in one's eyes. By dragging in the patriotic associations of democracy, he screens the fact that we may reject the ghost story for a host of other reasons which would still exist if the man were not a peasant. For example, there might be insufficient evidence, or it might come from a strongly prejudiced source. But the sweeping nature of the assumptions incline one to ignore the fallacy.

By way of variation, Chesterton attacks by pushing the opposite argument to its logical conclusion and so proving a *reductio ad absurdum*. For example, he attacks those who disbelieve in the miracles of St Francis by saying that we deny the miracles now and shall deny St Francis next, relegating him to mythology. Or again, in denying evolution, he argues that by humanism we were not allowed to sit on a man: by vegetarianism we cannot sit on an animal: next we shall not be allowed to sit on a chair. Obviously the logical conclusion has no bearing on the facts of the case.

There is, also, much proof by bad or doubtful history to which Chesterton does not quite commit himself. He says in support of the Catholic Church that "he would not be surprised" if the Renaissance should come to be regarded as a barbarian interlude in history; or "he would not be at all astonished" to discover that all great scientific movements were originated by the Church. Similarly, he makes vast political generalizations which could never be proved either way, as, for example, when he declares that Catholic countries are always happier than Protestant ones.

It might seem from such an arraignment that Chesterton's arguments are never to be trusted. Yet, on the whole, he is a clear and acute thinker, extremely quick to discover bad arguments in his opponents. He concludes *A Miscellany of Men* with a very just and very angry attack on popular looseness of thought, giving a list of catch phrases in general use which mean nothing at all. A statement such as "give one patriotism that is free of all boundaries", for example, is a contradiction in terms; while "Progress" is only a means to an end "going somewhere", not an end in itself. Elsewhere, he very aptly analyses the confusion of ethical and financial values in the phrase "making good"; or points out the stupidity of bringing the Church up-to-date by telling youth about the present and future, "not about what happened two thousand years ago" (*All is Grist*). That is, to retain the Church after destroying the only reason for its existence.

Chesterton's contempt for such common newspaper catchwords is unbounded, and most refreshing. He is an especial adept at discovering the unquestioned assumptions of the modern world, and pointing out their relative illogicality. He is particularly aggressive towards what he calls the modern "scientific mysticism" and the materialistic assumption on which it is based. "The world of to-day", he declares in *The Thing*, "does not know that all the novels and newspapers that it reads or writes are in fact full of certain assumptions that are just as dogmatic as dogmas . . . they are not felt as being preached, and therefore they are not called propaganda." He gives as an amusing instance a story in which the hero, on seeing a ghost, makes the sign of the cross. This is at once denounced as Catholic propaganda; but if the hero merely remarks "This is the twentieth century", no one takes any notice. Yet in that statement is contained the dogma of materi-

alism and the assumption that ghosts are impossible. For that reason he calls Shaw with all his rationalism "a heathen mystic", upholding values quite as unprovable as those of Christianity.

Chesterton was one of those writers to whom self-expression is easy and who find a keen and masterly pleasure in the handling of words. Apart from other aspects, his writings are triumphs of literary virtuosity, and he has none of that paralysing timidity which would rather be sterile than run the danger of being sentimental. He glories in the sudden violent assault, the grand climax or the purple patch: and if he does at times exaggerate, it is through that exuberance of energy which produced Elizabethan fustian.

AGATHA CHRISTIE

1881–1976

Agatha Mary Clarissa Miller was born on September 15, 1890, in Torquay, Devon. She was an isolated, lonely child, raised largely by her mother. At sixteen she studied voice and piano in Paris; at twenty-four she married Archibald Christie, who soon rose to the rank of Colonel in the Royal Air Corps. They had one child. Agatha worked as a Red Cross nurse in World War I, then after the war accepted a dare from her sister to write a mystery novel. The result was *The Mysterious Affair at Styles*, published in 1920, which introduced the fussy Belgian detective Hercule Poirot. A subsequent Poirot novel, *The Murder of Roger Ackroyd* (1926), broke a cardinal rule of mystery writing—Christie became famous after the controversy, and after "disappearing" for ten days the same year (Kathleen Tynan's novel *Agatha* offers a fictional chronicle of those ten days). She divorced her husband in 1928, and in 1930 married archeologist Max Mallowan. Their expeditions to the Middle East inspired some of her most famous novels, including *Death on the Nile* and *Murder in Mesopotamia*, and the non-fiction account *Come, Tell Me How You Live* in 1946.

By the time of the Second World War, Agatha Christie had become an institution. Not only Poirot but Miss Jane Marple, Parker Pyne, and several other detectives solved her intricate puzzles, presented not only in print but on stage and screen as well. *Witness for the Prosecution* and *And Then There Were None* appeared in all three media. *The Mousetrap* was a stage original that has run continuously since 1952, becoming the longest-running play in history. Christie also wrote poems, collected in 1973; romances, under the pseudonym "Mary Westmacott", and an autobiography, published posthumously in 1977. She caricatured herself as "Mrs. Ariadne Oliver" in 1972's *Elephants Can Remember*. Christie received the Grand Master Award of the Mystery Writers of America in 1954, an LL.D. from the University of Exeter in 1961, a CBE in 1956, and a DBE in 1971.

Agatha Christie died in Wallingford on January 12, 1976. She had killed off Hercule Poirot the previous year in *Curtain*.

General

I have been told by the experts, however, that this endless carrying on of the Doyle tradition does not represent all or the best that has been done with the detective story during the decades of its proliferation. There has been also the puzzle mystery, and this, I was assured, had been brought to a high pitch of ingenuity in the stories of Agatha Christie. So I have read also the new Agatha Christie, *Death Comes as the End*, and I confess that I have been had by Mrs. Christie. I did not guess who the murderer was, I was incited to keep on and find out, and when I did finally find out, I was surprised. Yet I did not care for Agatha Christie and I hope never to read another of her books. I ought, perhaps, to discount the fact that *Death Comes as the End* is supposed to take place in Egypt two thousand years before Christ, so that the book has a flavor of Lloyd C. Douglas not, I understand, quite typical of the au-

thor. ("No more Khay in this world to sail on the Nile and catch fish and laugh up into the sun whilst she, stretched out in the boat with little Teti on her lap, laughed back at him"); but her writing is of a mawkishness and banality which seem to me literally impossible to read. You cannot *read* such a book, you run through it to see the problem worked out; and you cannot become interested in the characters, because they never can be allowed an existence of their own even in a flat two dimensions but have always to be contrived so that they can seem either reliable or sinister, depending on which quarter, at the moment, is to be baited for the reader's suspicion. This I had found also a source of annoyance in the case of Mr. Stout, who, however, has created, after a fashion, Nero Wolfe and Archie Goodwin and has made some attempt at characterization of the people that figure in the crimes; but Mrs. Christie, in proportion as she is more expert and concentrates more narrowly on the puzzle, has to eliminate human interest completely, or, rather, fill in the picture with what seems to me a distasteful parody of it. In this new novel, she has to provide herself with puppets who will be good for three stages of suspense: you must first wonder who is going to be murdered, you must then wonder who is committing the murders, and you must finally be unable to foresee which of two men the heroine will marry. It is all like a sleight-of-hand trick, in which the magician diverts your attention from the awkward or irrelevant movements that conceal the manipulation of the cards, and it may mildly entertain and astonish you, as such a sleight-of-hand performance may. But in a performance like *Death Comes as the End*, the patter is a constant bore and the properties lack the elegance of playing cards.—EDMUND WILSON, "Why Do People Read Detective Stories?" (1944), *Classics and Commercials*, 1950, pp. 234–35

Agatha Christie maintained, after her very earliest books, an air of slightly sardonic detachment from the events of which she wrote. One feels it to be an attitude characteristic of an astute professional author. The sellers' market in crime fiction which lasted throughout the 1920s and 1930s permitted the publication of many books that not only lacked literary merit but, by being gauchely imitative, brought into ridicule a number of contrivances that had been used with discretion and therefore effectively by more capable writers. By 1926 when *The Murder of Roger Ackroyd* consolidated Mrs Christie's reputation, already it was inadvisable to postulate crimes committed by hypnotists, men armed with South American blowpipes, purveyors of untraceable poisons, and butlers. Murders of, or by, identical twins and long lost brothers were also questionable propositions. The last chapter gathering of suspects calculated to encompass the dramatic self-betrayal of the guilty party was not yet discredited, but a few sophisticated readers were beginning to wince at each recurrence of the device.

A less shrewd practitioner than Mrs Christie would have been tempted to bar all those elements of crime fiction that had become absurdities in the eyes of intelligent people. But she seems to have been well aware that intelligence and readership-potential are quite unrelated. So she hedged her bets. While preserving the essential artificialities, unlikelihoods and clichés of the bestselling whodunnit, she evolved a style of narration that hinted, just delicately enough not to offend British sensitivity to 'sarcasm', at self-parody.—COLIN WATSON, "The Little World of Mayhem Parva," *Snobbery with Violence*, 1971, pp. 173–74

As a prose stylist Christie is hardly distinguished. From the beginning she wrote in a neutral, simple fashion using short sentences and brief paragraphs which do not tax the reader. Occasionally, however, she uses her lack of a prose style to spring traps on the readers: this is the case with the intrusion of figurative description in *And Then There Were None*, as well as the irritatingly simple-minded style adopted for *Easy to Kill*. If Christie has any particular claim to literary originality, though, it is because of her use of point of view. The important lesson which she learned early and well was that detective stories work chiefly because of the way in which they are told. Using Hastings as the narrator in *The Mysterious Affair at Styles* shows that from the beginning she liked Conan Doyle's method of hiding the obvious from the reader by using an obtruse narrator. She also realized, in the early twenties, that this technique was old hat and she started to poke about for alternate styles of narration which would obscure the facts which needed to be withheld until the conclusion. In *The Man in the Brown Suit* she mixed straight narration with extracts from two diaries, covering the facts by switching the point of view. This mixture

of points of view, although it is not always so obvious, appears in most of the non-Hastings novels—and in *The ABC Murders* which Hastings narrates—written subsequently. The point of view of a typical Christie novel of the period usually shifts among 1) straight third person narration describing people and events from the outside, 2) third person narration over the shoulder of a particular character following him or her around, 3) selectively omniscient narration which probes some of the characters' minds, and 4) dramatic presentation of dialogue with little more than speech tags supplied. By switching from one point of view to another, Christie manipulates her readers in several ways. First, she gives the readers the false confidence that they can sympathize with and trust the judgments of the character whom the narrative follows. Almost equally important is the impression which the readers receive from the omniscient passages: they falsely believe that they receive insight into all of the characters' thoughts, while this never happens. By tossing together these different points of view, Christie can keep her important facts back and fool her readers almost every time.— LEROY PANEK, "Agatha Christie," *Watteau's Shepherds*, 1979, pp. 62–63

Agatha Christie has taken a common term of criticism applied to women novelists in the Victorian era—narrowness of experience—and shown how the deficiency can be turned to good account. Miss Marple's own experience of life is neither wide nor deep, but she has a very productive familiarity with other people's. She has spent a lifetime observing the untoward in St Mary Mead. Her method of detecting works by extension—applying the principles that got to the bottom of a small contretemps like the disappearance of a quantity of shrimps from the fishmonger's—and analogy: '"I always find one thing very like another in this world," said Miss Marple.' This is presented as an endearing mannerism:

'And perhaps he reminded you of someone?' prompted Sir Henry, mischief in his eye.
    Miss Marple smiled and shook her head at him. 'You are very naughty, Sir Henry. As a matter of fact he *did*. Fred Taylor, at the fish shop. Always slipped in an extra I in the shillings column . . .'
        (A *Murder is Announced*, 1950)

Miss Marple attributes her successes to specialized knowledge, by which she means knowledge of the characters involved; she has just sufficient gumption to repudiate the term 'feminine intuition' which is bandied about on several occasions. It is not intuition but accuracy of thought which leads her, time and again, to a pertinent conclusion. Otherwise she behaves with impeccable femininity, according to the popular and pejorative definition of the term: she simpers, flutters, flatters, dithers, and is subject to apparently meaningless digressions in conversation. Invariably she exasperates the bluffer and more stolid type of policeman: 'For about ten seconds Inspector Neale stared at Miss Marple with the utmost bewilderment. His first idea was that the old lady had gone off her head. "Blackbirds?" he repeated.' But the old lady's confusion is on the surface only, to amuse the reader who knows what is coming. Miss Marple's thoughts are always in order and the significance of her remarks will soon strike the Inspector with appropriate force: 'Craddock caught his breath. She'd got it! She was sharp, after all.'

In fact Jane Marple is both sharp and fluffy, intelligent and muddle-headed, timid and resolute, inquisitive and fastidious, self-effacing and persistent, unworldly and cynical. Her character is composed of contradictory elements for maximum effect. If she had a counterpart in real life it was the author's Victorian grandmother who was continually surprised by human gullibility. But the requirements of detective fiction supervened before a note of realism could be transcribed. It is well-known that Agatha Christie was not so much a novelist as the inventor of a novelty, a peculiarly intricate and entertaining type of puzzle. All the complexity and originality she could muster went into the construction of the story; her characters, apart from a handful of principals, are rarely more than cyphers. The principals—Poirot, Jane Marple, Mrs Oliver, Tommy and Tuppence Beresford—have a greater number of personal characteristics and mannerisms and this causes them to stand out although they lack substance. They have, however, exactly the right degree of presence to fulfil the function enjoined to them.—PATRICIA CRAIG and MARY CADOGAN, "Grandmotherly Disguise," *The Lady Investigates*, 1981, pp. 165–67

Works

There was yet another Christie whom nobody knew, or so few as to amount to almost nobody. This was Mary Westmacott. Even today, and even in book circles, there are more who do not know than who do know her true identity.

The Westmacotts bear as little relation to women-type novels as to Winnie-the-Pooh. One cannot but wonder if any of those who proffered opinions had ever read her work. Had they, they would know that in its own way, each of these books, whose heroes lead lives of quiet desperation and whose villains are villainous only in that they do not understand, presents a fragment of the human comedy. Each tells a tale of the procession of days which add up to the years, and which resolve not in a crashing dissonance but in a whimper. And life goes on, but down a different lane and to a different bird call.

These are works in which Christie is trying to fathom herself and those who were a part of her world. The stories are the revelations of a woman of perception, a woman who is searching human emotions to preserve and heighten moments which must be remembered. She is writing of men and women whose dreams bleed when pricked, who are not beset by the gods or the fates, but who are made bereft by human frailties and a wanton expenditure of the loving heart.

Not by any catch-phrases can Westmacott be put into a Christie category. The books are not concerned with 'breathless romance, intrigue and suspense . . . tangled lives and star-crossed passions . . . dangerous secrets', as has been written of them. Westmacott was a distinctly different person from the mystery writer, Agatha Christie.

The six books are actually all a part of the same book. In the whole they are the fictionalized autobiography of Dame Agatha. Properly the autobiography begins with the second, *Unfinished Portrait* (1934). Christie could not have given many interviews before that time, at least not about her childhood and youth, or the Mary Westmacott identity would have been revealed immediately. In *Unfinished Portrait*, Larraby, a portrait painter, frames the story, thus making the pretence that it is a story, not a personal revelation. Yet there can be no doubt that Celia, the unknown woman he presumably met and spoke with, is Christie, so much younger than others of her family that she is in effect an only child, the beloved of her mother.—DOROTHY B. HUGHES, "The Christie Nobody Knew," *Agatha Christie: First Lady of Crime*, ed. H. R. F. Keating, 1977, pp. 123–25

Agatha Christie, by herself, wrote twelve full-scale plays (one published, not performed) and three in a single act. She collaborated in another full-length play; four more, from her novels or short stories, were adapted by other hands. It was fitting, I think, that her final one-acter, *The Patient* (1962), depended on its curtain-line. Whatever else was wrong, no-

body sustained a problem as she did, or solved it so quickly without a tedious explanatory huddle. This was her Midas gift to the theatre. 'Upon my soul,' exclaimed Dickens's Barnacle Junior, 'you mustn't come into the place saying you want to know, you know.' Agatha Christie's fans did want to know. In the later plays they may have found it a lagging wait. Never mind: having been in at the death they insisted on a post-mortem verdict. . . .

Dame Agatha's strength in the theatre was her power of plotting. She could do most things with a body, but it became increasingly hard to animate the gap between death and revelation. Usually people and dialogue were functional, though at times, as in the whole of *Witness for the Prosecution*, in much of *The Mousetrap*, in the second acts of *The Hollow* and *Ten Little Niggers*, in the incidental comedy of *Spider's Web*, and in *The Unexpected Guest*, the stage could flash swiftly to life. Very few detachable lines keep a play in memory; humour often stiffened to mannerism. Someone says in *Verdict*: 'I've never been to an inquest in this country. Are they always like this?' A doctor replies: 'Oh, they vary, you know; they vary.' So did the Christie plays.

That admitted, Agatha Christie had more narrative impulse than anyone of her day. Frequently her end would justify the means. She was a technician when, among critics, the word had mildewed. Our pleasure in her major puzzles was the pleasure of a testing anagram, of an exact mortise-and-tenon, of filling the space at 27 down and closing an awkward corner. In fine, the pleasure of solution, the answer to a precisely stated challenge. In the matter of life and death within her world of artifice, she could be past-mistress of the artificial: no leopardess, no organ at midnight, not even a vault. She failed when her heart was not with the problem (*Towards Zero, Go Back for Murder, Verdict*). When she had persuaded herself she could soon persuade others: in the period's most rubbed jargon, there might not be many 'insights', but the machine did 'work'.—J. C. TREWIN, "A Midas Gift to the Theatre," *Agatha Christie: First Lady of Crime*, ed. H. R. F. Keating, 1977, pp. 133–54

The thriller depends very heavily upon suspense, but it also depends on surprise. The collision with the unexpected occurs in almost every thriller—the ordinary traveller is an enemy agent, the First Sea Lord is not the First Sea Lord but an international plotter in disguise, the kindly gentleman helping the hero is really the Master Crook, the hero traps foreign villains but a trap door bangs open and he is dropped into the Thames. They were, after all, called shockers. Christie's consistent purpose in her thrillers as well as her detective novels was to shock the readers with the denouement. "The least likely suspect" formula with which Christie has been tagged is really "the most surprising solution" formula. She continuously worked out solutions which would surprise, and, because they infuriated many people who hollered about "playing fair," shock. When one of the detectives commits the murder, when the narrator is the murderer, when the "victim" is the one, when everyone in the plot has bashed, stabbed, or shot the corpse, the reader must be surprised and in most cases shocked—in a more emphatic way than one is shocked in the thriller. In thrillers we expect it, for the whole fictional world is hostile to the hero struggling toward his goal. Detective stories supposedly have more normal values, where crimes occur because of explainable, domesticated motives. When the detective story's narrator whom we have trusted turns out to be a blackguard, or a subsidiary detective turns out to be a murderer, and all of our best guesses are wrong, we are shocked (but not too deeply, for this is, after all, fiction) and surprised, because we never expected it to happen. Thus the surprise ending for Christie functions not as the solution to a puzzle which we might have, or could have solved, but as a diversion—and diversion was the overriding purpose of Christie's straight detective tales as well as her thrillers.

Plenty of readers have overlooked the lifeless prose, the meagre atmosphere, and the cardboard characters because Christie entertains them by surprising them at the end with something which they did not expect. Christie's work in the thirties centered on variations of plot formulae which she adjusted so that she could continue to pull off what seemed to be new surprises. Her plot patterns, however, are really fairly simple, and she invented them early and merely worked out variations over and over throughout the period. Her favorite plot is that in which a detective is the guilty party. The idea goes back to *The Secret Adversary*, and it is the reason that so many of her books have subsidiary detectives in them who either help Poirot or go off detecting with another character. Simply, they intend to mislead the chief detective and the readers by gaining their confidence and feeding them malarkey. Thus, detective figures are the culprits not only in *The Secret Adversary* and *The Man in the Brown Suit*, but also in *Peril at End House*, *The Boomerang Clue*, *Murder in Three Acts*, *The ABC Murders*, *Murder in the Air*, *A Holiday for Murder*, *And Then There Were None*, and *Easy to Kill*. In each case someone who apparently helps to investigate the crime is actually the criminal. A variant of this criminal-as-detective plot appears in the novels in which the narrator commits the crime—it is a variant since we expect the narrator of the story to be interested in solving the crime and to be on the right side. Christie introduced this gambit in *The Man in the Brown Suit*, which followed *The Secret Adversary*, the first criminal-as-detective plot. We can almost see her looking for a variant. She carried this device to its fullest fruition in *The Murder of Roger Ackroyd*, where, instead of having the criminal narrate only parts, he narrates the whole novel. Finally, she reversed the process in *The ABC Murders*, in which the narrative of Cust seems to be that of the criminal, but turns out to be Christie's ruse to cover the straight criminal-as-detective plot. I have already provided lists of the works in which Christie employs her other stock plot devices: murder in disguise and murder with an accomplice. These are really about all of the patterns which she used in the twenties and thirties. Throughout the period she works with these basic formulae, using them in variations: sometimes combining two basic devices, sometimes, as in *Murder on the Calais Coach* and *And Then There Were None*, extending the idea to its furthest limit. The total effect of the plotting, however, is to provide sanitary thrillers in the guise of regular detective stories in order to divert her audience.

One final point about surprise, upon which all of Christie's books depend for their effect. Ought we to have tried to figure it out? Can or should one read her books the same way that we would read the early Ellery Queen novels? I think not. First of all, in the comments which Christie puts into the mouths of her detective novelists, Mr. Clancy and Mrs. Oliver, she discredits this approach. During the formative years of the twenties Christie seems, in fact, to shrug off the puzzle story which presents the readers with clues which they are to find and attempt to interpret. Few of Christie's novels, if any, when examined with any sort of objectivity, can be considered as puzzles which the readers are supposed to solve. They do not yield the solution to the enigmatic circumstances until the final chapters when Christie chooses to present it herself. Otherwise they would lose all of their force.

Consider the case of *And Then There Were None*. In this novel ten people die while they are trapped on an isolated island to which they have been lured by person or persons unknown. At the end of the book readers hear the musings of police officials who cannot solve the murders. The police continue at sea until a note in a bottle washes ashore and outlines the truth about the events on the island (which exemplifies the readers' position—or the position which Christie would like her readers to be in). If this is a puzzle story, where are the clues which should lead the readers to a logical interpretation of the facts and events which have been presented? There is no material evidence, there are no meaningful alibis, and the crimes have no internal similarities (poisoning, sandbagging, pistol shot, hanging, drowning, and stabbing all appear). The physician who pronounced the deaths could have been in cahoots with any one of the victims. All of the characters are in the same circumstance: each is accused of having committed a murder in the past by a mysterious recording. The psychological evidence is useless; the narration penetrates the consciousness of some people (including the murderer) but this does nothing to reveal the truth. Any of the victims could have feigned death and done the murders. Most of the characters have vocations which might lead them to this sort of mass judgment and execution, but this is moot, since each of us judges countless people daily, and this hardly makes us murderers. Upon what clues ought we to base our solution if we try to figure it out before the book provides it? There is, given retrospect, one clue—Christie describes one death (the fake one) in figurative language while she depicts the others in physical detail. Ought we to see that? I would like to say of course not, but I will waffle and say I think not. We don't see the miniscule, isolated clue for any number of reasons, but chiefly because the novel is three quarters thriller. If this were a *bona fide* puzzle detective novel, there would be ten deaths to be thought through and solved; instead, here, there are ten episodes in a thriller plot which pushes the readers on to the end even if they would otherwise incline to look for and analyze the events and facts in the story. With only one hundred and seventy-one pages in the book, divided into extremely short chapters, we know that we can finish the book tonight if we go on, and that she'll give us the answer at the end without making us think, and the chapters fly by so quickly, why bother? Not many people really do try to puzzle out the answer. It is the psychology. It is the thriller psychology and not that of the puzzle story: all of the facts are not in our possession.—LeRoy Panek, "Agatha Christie," *Watteau's Shepherds*, 1979, pp. 50–54

H. DOUGLAS THOMSON
From "The Orthodox Detective Story"
Masters of Mystery
1931, pp. 193–205

*T*he Murder of Roger Ackroyd* is dedicated "To Punkie, who likes an orthodox detective story, murder, inquest, and suspicion falling on every one in turn." Punkie must have derived no little entertainment from Mrs. Agatha Christie's novels, for she is in many respects a paragon of orthodoxy. She believes in a clean, slick murder and plenty of swift, exciting, low-brow action. Her detective, Poirot, belongs to the old school of super-detectives who keep things pretty much to themselves, and spar incessantly with the arrogant tribe of police inspectors. In Captain Hastings she has held the mirror up to Dr. Watson. The dedication shows that she is an advocate of the most unlikely person theme. As a final example of her orthodoxy, she is the perfect matrimonial agency in pairing off the right couples.

But granted that Mrs. Christie writes "down" rather than

"up," that she keeps her crow a crow—in Mr. St. John Ervine's phraseology—and does not seek to make it a flamingo, that she does not cast about her for spurious effects, it is not difficult to discern a delicious vein of satire in her stories. Even before she essayed the burlesque of *Partners in Crime*, she had a hankering to poke fun at the various schools of detective fiction. She is certainly well read in the Classics, as the adventures of Tommy and Tuppence show. It is almost as if she had set herself to learn all she could about the methods and technique of "How to Write a Detective Story for Profit"—and had then proceeded to pull legs.

Mrs. Christie is not a criminologist. She is not even a first-rate detective. Compared with Mr. Crofts she is in this respect a babe-in-arms. For the grouping of data, for the building up of a case from "purposeful" *minutiæ*, for the effects of belladonna on rabbits she has no time. And evidently she has felt unequal to the strain of assiduous bluffing. Her description of the data is, therefore, of the sketchiest. In lieu thereof she gives us a plethora of motives. Most of her *dramatis personæ* have quite a few motives concealed on them—motives white and black, motives satisfactory and unsatisfactory, so they be only motives. Mrs. Christie's skill lies in playing off motive against motive, and thus character against character; for her characters are often merely pegs on which to hang these motives.

Neither does Mrs. Christie usually bother her head with character study. The recognised types are quite sufficient to be going on with; big-game hunters of the Ethel M. Dell variety; hard-boiled Americans after Mr. Edgar Wallace; fencers and blackmailers of the Oppenheim School; private secretaries and so forth. . . .

In *The Mysterious Affair at Styles* Mrs. Christie evolved a scheme which she evidently felt would bear repetition. The murder was postponed for a few chapters to allow the reader to play the eavesdropper to conversations inevitably heated and inevitably interrupted. The murder out, she will probably toss a coin to decide on whom first to turn the searchlight of suspicion. It's really in a way immaterial, as they've all got to go through it. The plot gathers speed from the discovery of at least two significant incidents big with motives for the murder. This means that suspicion will rest in turn on all those implicated in these events. During this time Poirot flits about like a Tchehov character, casting the pearls of his innuendo before the pig-headedness of Hastings. The inquest will quicken Poirot's steps, for it means the veering of suspicion from the first star suspect to the second (the second being equally guiltless). All this time you will be feeling a shade uncomfortable. Two love affairs will be going on in full swing; not of the type, however, to arouse Evoe's nausea, for at least two of the lovers will be under a cloud. By a process of elimination, the field will be reduced to one or two "favourites." Then comes Poirot's hour. Not all the king's horses will prevent him from holding a salon. Certainly it is impressive, with all the characters as his audience, to begin his exegesis with a *Messieurs, mesdames*. Impressive, too, is the grand climax when he points his finger to the villain, and the chair is overturned in the confusion.

The *Mysterious Affair at Styles* is a very good example of our old friend the "double bluff"; but it is different from the ordinary species in that the very person responsible for directing suspicion at the start on the real criminal is actually an accomplice of the latter. Thus we have the amusing situation of the villain wishing to be arrested as soon as possible. He relied on securing an acquittal while the evidence was fragmentary and while he had, through the male impersonation of his accomplice, an unobjectionable alibi. Poirot was equally anxious in the circumstances to delay his arrest. . . .

The Murder of Roger Ackroyd is Mrs. Christie's masterpiece. Indeed it is one of the best half-dozen detective stories ever written. The stage version, *Alibi*, had a very successful run, and Mr. Charles Laughton, as Poirot, was responsible for a brilliant piece of character acting. *The Murder of Roger Ackroyd* is the perfect example of "the most unlikely person" *motif*. Logically, the most unlikely person to be the villain in the detective story is the detective. But this distortion causes a flaw in the construction. There has to be a second investigator to detect the detective. Mrs. Christie, however, hit on a character as "unlikely" to be the murderer as the detective himself. She chose the Dr. Watson: Dr. Sheppard this time, not our old friend Captain Hastings.

The extraordinary cleverness of this idea grows on one. It cannot have been a flash in the pan, but must have been born only after much labour. And never did an idea need such careful fostering. There are at least three points which demonstrate Mrs. Christie's cunning.

(1) When the narrator is not the detective, he is expected to flounder. We do not expect the candid, nothing-to-hide Wills Crofts manner. This is largely because Sir Arthur Conan Doyle has taught us not to give Dr. Watson the credit of understanding Sherlock's methods. Mrs. Christie took advantage of our education. Here Dr. Sheppard's dullness was assumed because he *had* something to conceal.

"I tried my best," said Dr. Sheppard, in the middle of the story, "to read his (Poirot's) mind. As I know now, I failed in this latter task. Though Poirot showed me all his discoveries—as, for instance, the gold wedding ring—he held back the vital and yet logical impressions that he formed. As I came to know later, this secrecy was characteristic of him. . . . I played Watson to his Sherlock. . . . But after Monday our ways diverged." The parting of the ways mentioned in the last sentence refers, of course, to Poirot's process of inference and is not a confession on Mrs. Christie's part of illicit secrecy.

(2) Mrs. Christie deceived us in a second particular by profiting from our association of ideas. Doctors, thanks to the nobility of their calling, thanks also to the sentimentalism of Sir Luke Fildes, have as a class an enviable reputation—country doctors in particular. The popular idea of a doctor is of a Dr. Watson—of a large but infinitely gentle soul with a bushy moustache. And when the narrator in the detective story is a doctor and has a wife called Caroline, one's previous impressions hold sway.

(3) Thirdly, it never enters our minds to suspect the narrator. We regard his existence possibly as an artistic necessity. It is, of course, a weakness in the plot that the villain should chronicle his villainy; and Mrs. Christie, if hotly challenged, might find herself, *mirabile dictu*, at a loss for a satisfactory motive. It is amusing to find that she felt it necessary to mention that Dr. Sheppard kept his notes well "written up." To commit a murder first and then write a detective story about it is certainly one way of finding a plot.

DAVID I. GROSSVOGEL
From "Death Deferred"
Art in Crime Writing, ed. Bernard Benstock
1983, pp. 4–14

I have analysed elsewhere (*Mystery and Its Fictions*, 1979) the (relatively) innocent world of which, and within which, Agatha Christie first wrote. In that innocent world, the detective-story writer did not propose so much a solvable problem as a disposable one. Agatha Christie's first readers read her in order to purchase at the cost of a minor and passing disturbance the comfort of knowing that the disturbance was *contained*, and that at the end of the story the world they imagined would be continued in its innocence and familiarity.

The nature and consequences of that disturbance are crucial, for ultimately they are the key to Agatha Christie's huge popularity and her yet-enduring readership. A sense of Dame Agatha's climate in her early works will be obtained instantly through contrast with the hard-boiled variety mentioned in later chapters. In the latter, a relatively sordid private eye does battle with openly sordid forces loosed by the urban chaos. That private eye—Sam Spade, Philip Marlowe or Mike Hammer—encounter what is intended to be 'real' corruption, whether in a politician, a sexuality (most frequently a woman's against which is successfully matched the demonstrative virility of the detective), a corpse. This 'reality' entails a specificity; the detective performs acts that particularise him even though they have nothing to do with the functional gestures required of him by the case he is on: he drinks, he makes love, he lets all and sundry know that he is 'tough'. He walks the back alleys of a city whose surfaces are fully analysed. As Zola discovered a century before, such 'slice-of-life' realism not only entails specificity, it also assumes a burden of 'truth' which, more often than not, it feels able to demonstrate only by exposing its seamier parts.

Agatha Christie was far more stylised. For her, the game was merely a puzzle (or a series of interlocking puzzles) told in the form of a story. The story required people, of course, but their creation was left largely to the imagination of the reader.

Writing in the years immediately after the end of the first world war, Agatha Christie was instinctively striving for a delicate balance, but one that was still possible at that time. It consisted in an intrusion upon the reader's ideal world, but an intrusion not so intense as to cast doubt on its eventual dissipation. She achieved this balance by identifying accurately her middle-class audience and its hankering for an Edwardian gentility.[1] Dame Agatha offered these readers recognisable posters of a world which they had experienced only through posters: they were offered a journey to a land that they knew well, but only in the world of their social fantasising and bygone dreams of empire. Poster and book served the selfsame purpose: they preserved the awareness of a world that must have existed for someone; it was a far better world than the known world and doubly comforting because of a suspicion that if it had indeed existed once, its days were now numbered. . . .

Murder within this English pastoral was not so much an evil act as one whose consequences would be unfortunate for a prescribed moment. Whereas a Mike Hammer or a Sam Spade might right their little piece of the corrupt, urban jigsaw puzzle while the complex itself remained corrupt and awaited the private eye's attention to the next area of his concern, murder upon the mead was more in the nature of a washable and cathartic stain. For a while, these good people would become each and every one suspect (Agatha Christie, who built her reputation early on a disregard for established rules, showed as little unwarranted sentimentality here: however much tradition might have endeared a particular type to the reader, none was above suspicion). Within this dream of rural England, murder was trivial enough; the corpse upon which Philip Marlowe stumbled might not have had quite the stench of Laius', but in St Mary Mead or Styles St Mary the murder itself was antiseptic—already a part of the cleansing process (there were always half a dozen compelling reasons to kill the victim—and

as many evident suspects). It was the wake of the murder that made things momentarily disagreeable: the country inn would lose its ruddy bonhomie; the vicarage might be pressed uncomfortably close to moral quandaries; and, worst of all, aliens would walk the pristine land. For just as the reader was able to people fully a world to which he aspired, the reader would temporarily jeopardise through his own malaise the harmony of the world he had conjured from his fiction. And here again, Dame Agatha remained supremely aloof, giving the reader only such few and accurate stimuli as were needed. . . .

It was within a world distracted only momentarily by this kind of curable malaise that was born the detective destined to become one of the most famous of the genre: Poirot was able to dissipate the uneasiness, but he was also created and shaped by it to a great extent.

Like his prototypes, Dupin and Holmes, this sort of detective demonstates a perfect intelligence within a multitude of flaws. The structural reason for this contrast results from a fundamental identity between the fictional detective and his circumstances: that detective is the reader's assurance that his expectation of an end to a number of small annoyances will be met—the detective's acuity is therefore absolute; but the reader's concession in that contract requires that a semblance of doubt be maintained for as long as it takes to tell the tale—all else in the detective is therefore flawed.

However, the strangeness of Dupin and Holmes confirmed their intelligence even as it removed them from the common world of mortals; Dupin and Holmes dwelt in remote worlds, isolated by books, drugs, laboratory or musical instruments—all awesome objects that extended the awesomeness of their brains. Poirot's flaws, on the other hand, represented a compendium of what marred the idyllic landscape once it became the temporary site of the sombre event that brought Poirot into it. When Agatha Christie first described Poirot, he was in fact a part of the negative consequences that followed the transgression of the bucolic dream.

To start with, Poirot was a foreigner, another alien note within the pastoral harmony. The evidence of his foreignness was multiple, but because of the specific area of Poirot's first trespass, it was peculiarly unEnglish. Starting with his ridiculously short stature, most of his obvious traits were intended to amuse, but also to annoy, his English reader:

> Poirot was an extraordinary-looking little man. He was hardly more than five feet, four inches, but carried himself with great dignity. His head was exactly the shape of an egg, and he always perched it a little on one side. His moustache was very stiff and military. The neatness of his attire was almost incredible. I believe a speck of dust would have caused him more pain than a bullet wound. Yet this quaint dandyfied little man who, I was sorry to see, now limped badly, had been in his time one of the most celebrated members of the Belgian police.

Hastings' initial awareness and dismissal of the physical Poirot spoke for his reader, and Hastings' voice was subsequently echoed by countless others—villains, chambermaids, gardeners, romantic leads: just about everyone was to be taller than Poirot, treating him until the final moment of revelation and awe with either amused contempt or patronising tolerance.

Lack of stature made Poirot's aping of British virtues something halfway between a joke and an affront: dignity sounded like an unseemly overstatement in one so short, while the military moustache became a ridiculous attribute. As for Poirot's sartorial fastidiousness, something that would have been praiseworthy in an Englishman of more normal size, could at best be quaintly dandifying in an undersized foreigner.

But Poirot added to even these shortcomings. Having been denied the grace of British birth, he compounded his misfortune by refusing to hide it, indulging an unBritish propensity for exuberance and exaggeration. He was from the first a boaster, one given to stressing the subject pronoun through the apposition of his own name, and using his hands with abandon for even greater emphasis. And to bring the picture to its full dejection, this master of the little grey cells never learned to speak English correctly. To the end, Poirot's sentences were marred by Gallicisms, even though they became more probable over a lifetime than the porcine 'Ah! Triple pig!' or 'you remain there like—how do you say it?—ah, yes, the stuck pig' that flavoured his original speech.

Poirot's very intelligence, before even his unseemly boasting about it, was yet another exaggeration, and one which he displayed with equal lack of tact in his all too apparent egghead. Aloof as ever, but knowing full well from which vantage point *she* observed her creation, Dame Agatha named him after the least favoured of vegetables (*poireau*: the leek, which also means 'wart' in French) and then stressed the dismissiveness by pairing it with a singularly grandiloquent Christian name, Hercule—itself turned into still another overassertion by the diminutive size of its bearer. . . .

Why then her continuing popularity? A part of the answer was intuited by the directors (Sidney Lumet, Don Guillermin, Guy Hamilton) who have recently turned into films *Murder on the Orient Express*, *Death on the Nile*, *The Mirror Crack'd*, peopling them with old-time actors now seldom seen on the screen—Lauren Bacall, Richard Widmark, Bette Davis, David Niven, Angela Lansbury, or, in a new, Queen-Motherish avatar, the enduring Elizabeth Taylor. These actors represent the cinema of a shinier moment, over a third of a century ago, before they were swept aside by the new forms of the present cinema. Seeing them once again on the screen, we re-enter that world briefly. This is especially felicitous casting for Agatha Christie, since we now regress through her books to something more real than the times she described: the period pieces that those descriptions themselves have become now attract us. There may have been a time when Agatha Christie mediated for her reader unattainable worlds: now her archaic books have become those worlds. We acknowledge our present discontent in retrospections that make us smile at what once constituted the measure of our passing cares, the sense of how comfortable we felt in a world of referable absolutes (after all, Dame Agatha herself tells us in her autobiography that she came to the detective story out of a comforting sense that Evil could be hunted down and that Good would triumph—an avowal that explains not a little her sombre mood within, and tenuous gap on, the world that followed the second world war).

In that world, our present one, a residual pull of psychological gravity draws us to the evidence that we once had faith in the possibility of control, of knowledge and of the power of reason against the irrational. We are still drawn to the old writings of Agatha Christie.

Notes

1. See the anonymous 'Commentary' in *The Times Literary Supplement*, 18 Sept. 1970.

Arthur C. Clarke

1917–

Arthur C. Clarke was born on December 16, 1917, in Minehead, Somerset. In 1936 he moved to London to work as a civil servant. During World War II he served as a radar instructor with the R.A.F. After the war he studied at Kings College, London, graduating with first-class honors in physics and mathematics in 1948. From 1949 through 1950 he worked as associate editor of *Science Abstracts* magazine; since 1951 he has written full-time.

Clarke's first published story, "Rescue Party," appeared in John W. Campbell's *Astounding* in 1946. In 1948 he published his first novel, *Against the Fall of Night*, in *Startling Stories*; this work was subsequently revised for publication in book form as *The City and the Stars* in 1956. Although Clarke continued to write and publish novels and short stories throughout the 1950s, probably his best known works from that period are "The Sentinel" (1951) and *Childhood's End* (1953), the latter being considered by many to be a groundbreaking novel about contact with aliens and human transcendence.

By the 1960s Clarke had begun to focus more heavily on non-fiction. In 1962 he received UNESCO's Kalinga Prize for writing on scientific topics; in the same year, he was honored by the Franklin Institute for having been the first to propose the concept of the communication satellite in a technical paper published in 1945. Meanwhile, having moved to Sri Lanka in 1956 in order to pursue his interest in underwater research, much of his writing—fiction and non-fiction—came to focus on this other frontier of human exploration.

Nonetheless, Clarke is best-known for his science fiction. In 1968, he and Stanley Kubrick developed *2001: A Space Odyssey* from the short story "The Sentinel," with Clarke writing the novel of that name at the same time as Kubrick wrote the screenplay and directed the film. In 1972 Clarke won the Science Fiction Writers of America's Nebula Award for "A Meeting with Medusa" (1971), and two years later won another Nebula along with the Hugo Award from the World Science Fiction Convention for *Rendezvous with Rama* (1973). In 1982 he published *2010: Odyssey Two*, a sequel to *2001*.

Arthur C. Clarke has been married and divorced once, and has no children.

General

Arthur Clarke is another dreamer to make good into the starry empyrean beyond the sf field. His escape velocity has been fueled by reserves of technical knowledge, and his career resembles in many ways the schoolboy dream of success. It has been said, unfairly, that Bradbury's science fiction is for those who do not like sf; but no such monstrous charge can be levelled at Clarke's writing. More than any other sf author, Clarke has been faithful to a boyhood vision of science as saviour of mankind, and of mankind as a race of potential gods destined for the stars. If Stapledon has successors, Clarke is the foremost. Egotistical in many ways, he has throughout his career remained humblingly true to that early faith, and to science fiction as the literature of the gods.

His literary abilities are traditional, and his prose workaday. But he rises to a certain strength when he manages to unite the thinking and dreaming poles of his nature (to amalgamate the Wellsian and the Burroughsian, as it were). This he achieves in several masterly short stories—especially in "The Nine Billion Names of God," justifiably famous—and in two novels, *The City and the Stars* (1956) and *Childhood's End* (1953). In the latter especially, a rather banal philosophical idea (that mankind may evolve into a greater being, an Overmind) is expressed in simple but aspiring language that vaguely recalls the Psalms, even down to the liberal use of colons; when this is combined with a dramatised sense of loss, Clarke's predominant emotion, the result has undeniable effect.

This passage is from the end of *Childhood's End*, when Karellen, a member of a menial alien race, has seen man vanish from Earth, and prepares to return to his own distant planet:

> For all their achievements, thought Karellen, for all their mastery of the physical universe, his people were no better than a tribe that had passed its whole existence upon some flat and dusty plain. Far off were the mountains, where power and beauty dwelt, where the thunder sported above the glaciers and the air was clear and keen. There the sun still walked, transfiguring the peaks with glory, when all the land below was wrapped in darkness. And they could only watch and wonder: they could never scale those heights.
>
> Yet, Karellen knew, they would hold fast until the end: they would await without despair whatever destiny was theirs. They would serve the Overmind because they had no choice, but even in that service they would not lose their souls.
>
> The great control screen flared for a moment with sombre, ruby light: without conscious effort, Karellen read the message of its changing patterns. The ship was leaving the frontiers of the Solar System: the energies that powered the Stardrive were ebbing fast, but they nad done their work.

Arthur Clarke's success story lies in the main beyond the scope of a mere literary critic. His early work on earth satellites and his informed commentaries on the Apollo space launchings during the sixties and early seventies have made him almost as much a part of the space race as Cape Kennedy itself. He is also celebrated as co-author of the Stanley Kubrick film *2001*, one of the great cult successes of its day.—BRIAN W. ALDISS, *Billion Year Spree*, 1973, pp. 259–61

. . . One of the major images which emerges about Arthur C. Clarke is that of "hard science fiction" writer. When all is said and done, Clarke's authentic commitment seems to be to the universe and, like Asimov, to the underlying sets of laws of behavior by which the mystery inherent in it will probably be explained.

How is it, then, that he is associated with mysticism, mythology, theological speculation, and "cosmic loneliness"? Hard science fiction, if nothing else, usually needs to come to closure, in its qualities of validity and consistency, with specific explanations and scientific justifications. Yet much of Clarke's fiction pushes the mind outward and ever open. If this is accomplished by an explication of assumed or searched-for universal laws, it is understandable and consistent with science-based extrapolation.

But this is substantially different from the overall impression actually left upon most readers of Clarke's science fiction—that there is a search underway for universal ideas which transcend time, space, and cultures. If these ideas exist, the way to discover them may not be through the explication of universal laws but rather through the discovery of root metaphors and symbols. The universe may not appear, therefore, as simply a set of problems to be solved rationally but rather as a still mysterious place, to be creatively—and respectfully—explored and appreciated. In this sense, one of Clarke's familiar, if not quintessential, themes—that humanity's loneliness in the universe will be remedied by contact with other-world living beings—can be reinterpreted to mean that living things are really not separated by space but by consciousness.

This perspective implies that the human being is not *homo sapiens*—the rational being—but that the human being is *homo ludens*—the playing thing. Although *homo ludens* seems to imply a more creative, open role for the human being in the face of a universe which is imperfectly understood, Clarke's fiction, or at least much of it, seems to suggest that the universe may be playing with humanity. It is in this connection that contradictions arise between Clarke's optimism and pessimism concerning human destiny.

Clarke's optimism is not that of a scientific expert convinced of the effectiveness of his tools, confident of the knowledge upon which he stands, and certain of the existence of universal laws which, if only discovered, can further explain remaining mysteries. Instead, his optimism is that of a mystic, convinced of the inevitability of the transcendent and sure of the positive direction in which it moves. And his pessimism is not that of the scientist who has lost faith in the usefulness and efficacy of his tools; rather, it is the pessimism of one who appreciates the awesomeness of the universe and is able to anticipate the "tricks" and surprises which it may have in store for humanity. Moreover, it is not the pessimism of "I have seen the future—and it doesn't work!"; rather, it is the pessimism of "I have seen the future—and it is all too familiar, but I am not sure that humanity can stand the potential surprises!"—JOSEPH D. OLANDER, MARTIN HARRY GREENBERG, "Introduction" to *Arthur C. Clarke*, eds. Joseph D. Olander, Martin Harry Greenberg, 1977, pp. 7–8

Works

Shaw saw man as at the top of the evolutionary chain with no one above him. Having dared ⟨in *Back to Methuselah*⟩ the anti-secular feat of smuggling God back into the universe in the guise of a life force, Shaw could not take the more dangerous step of readmitting Michael, Raphael, and Beelzebub also. Science seemed to say that beings more knowing, more powerful than man could not exist. So Shaw gave man and his descendants 30,000 years of hard intellectual, creative effort to get free of the bondage to matter. What Shaw said man could do over these next 30,000 years, Clarke (in *Childhood's End*) simply assumed had already been done somewhere in the universe in the billions of years during which the evolutionary process has already been at work. With that simple shift, the problems of Shaw's rather bumbling life force fall away. What more natural than to assume that if matter has reached the selfconscious stage here on our comparatively young planet, it did so eons ago on one of the older worlds? And if the intellect's next possible evolutionary stage is as a disembodied community of organically unified minds, what more reasonable to conclude than that, in the long history of the universe, this evolutionary stage also has already successfully been reached? Not as the result of the desires of some forward-dreaming spirit, but as the inevitable, eventual result of the combination of the laws of physics and the laws of chance. So, what Shaw dreamed of happening eventually through the efforts of both man and some mystical entity, Clarke could declare had already happened through ordinary evolutionary means. Thus we can again surmise that the heavens may be filled with beings above as well as below man in the hierarchy of the universe. Superior intellects of satanic stature may exercise a lordship over man in his present state. Beyond those Overlords controlling them, however, may be the Overmind, the collective bodiless intellect of Shaw's Ancients, that has "long ago," Clarke says, "left the tyranny of matter behind." This Overmind may be superior to the intellectual Overlords by virtue of its ability to achieve a psychic community of being, and it may have a kinship with mankind by virtue of our common psychical natures. Surely it is possible that a deity of this sort—not all-powerful, not all-knowing, not equal to the universe but a product of it—seeking greater power, greater knowledge, a greater dominion—"trying to grow, to extend its powers and its awareness of the universe"—could take a collective interest in man, shield him from evil, and manipulate his evolutionary progress in such a way as to insure the elevation of the human race into the unity of its own mystical body. This, of course, is what occurs in *Childhood's End*, and, apart from the fact that the whole thing is fantastic, we have no compelling reason to fault it on the grounds that it runs contrary to the best conception we have of our universe. Here, in *Childhood's End*, when the human race, guarded by limited angels who are shut out from union with the Overmind, passes through the dissolution of this earth to enter a transformed state, we can satisfy our feeling that we humans count, that we are distinctive creatures on the evolutionary chain, of greater importance than monkeys, fish, and the amoeba, a transitional link between a world of dust and a world of mind.

If we need to know that we have a home in the universe, that somebody big up there is looking out for us, *Childhood's End* allows us to believe it without sacrificing our scientific stance. However much luck it may have taken for the first intellectual-psychical species to become the nucleus for the mental whirlpool of the Overmind—that "vortex," "spinning like the funnel of a cyclone"—our little human species can feel that we have more than blind chance on our side. We have the wisdom the Overmind has gained through its own original elevation and the skill it has developed in guiding, with increasing success, the elevation of other kindred species. However mankind may first have become differentiated from its anthropoid ancestors—and we can go to *2001* for one answer to that question—we can be confident that the next stage of our development is being carefully monitored and that we will have whatever help we need in order to mutate successfully.

There is no mistake about our needing the help. There is no guarantee in Clarke's evolutionary system any more than in Shaw's, that every mutation will survive. The universe as natural process is just as indifferent to the results it gets in Clarke's world as in the world of Huxley or Wells. As Clindar of Clarke's "Moon-Watcher" recalls, "The universe was as indifferent to intelligence as it was to life; left to themselves . . . dawning minds had less than one chance in a hundred of survival. Most of them achieved no more than a tragic consciousness of their doom, before they were swept into oblivion." And Karellen assures mankind that had the human race been left to make the transition from flesh to mind by itself, it never could have found its way safely over the abyss. "Across that abyss, there is only one bridge. Few races, unaided, have ever found it. Some have turned back while there was still time, avoiding both the danger and the achievement. Their worlds have become Eylsian islands of effortless content, playing no further part in the story of the universe. That would never have been your fate—or your fortune. Your race was too vital for that. It would have plunged into ruin and taken others with it, for you would never have found the bridge."

It is evident, therefore, that a theory of a universal evolutionary process that has been going on as long as can be imagined is an absolutely liberating theory. In *Childhood's End* it allows Clarke to lock God the creator out of the universe while letting god the creature in. It lets Clarke reintroduce the ancient view of humanity as the object of a heavenly concern. He can yoke together both the callousness of natural selection and the comfort of a special dispensation. When the last man on earth witnesses the passing away of the earth and the elevation of man's descendants to godhead, the emotion he feels, we are told, "wasn't joy or sorrow; it was a sense of fulfillment, achievement. . . . Good-by, Karellen, Rashaverak—I am sorry for you. Though I cannot understand it, I've seen what my race became. Everything we ever achieved has gone up there into the stars." It is not surprising that Jan's description of Earth's last moments seems familiar to us: "'The light! From *beneath* me—inside the Earth—shining upward, through the rocks, the ground, everything—growing brighter, brighter, blinding—' In a soundless concussion of light, Earth's core gave up its hoarded energies. . . . There was nothing left of Earth: *They* had leeched away the last atoms of its substance." St. Peter anticipated these last moments this way in his Second Epistle: "the heavens will pass away with a loud noise, and the elements will be dissolved with fire, and the earth and the works upon it will be burned up . . . the heavens will be kindled and dissolved, and the elements will melt with fire!" Religion, science, and the imagination make a heady cocktail.

In *Childhood's End* descendants of the human race achieve the apotheosis that Shaw's Ancients desired. The manner by which the elevation to divinity is achieved, it is clear, is totally alien to the philosophy Shaw espoused. Though Shaw called himself a religious man, and in his view he was, his position vis-à-vis the evolutionary process was that of the humanist who sees man as the maker of his own good. Shaw's humanity *is* the measure of all things thus far; it is its own deity and is responsible as deity for the world it creates. Man is the sole means of his salvation. He needs only to call upon his own creativity to solve all the problems existence throws across his path. The humanity of *Childhood's End* is no such self-sufficient entity. Clarke's conception is not humanistic but theocratic; his universe is hierarchical. Clarke's people cannot get to heaven on their own. They must be rescued from their inadequacies. It is grace given from above and not meritorious works from below that gain them everlasting life.

Another essential difference between Shaw's conception

and Clarke's is also clear. Shaw's people have to strain with Nietzschean effort to reach a higher level of existence. Shaw demands that man use his intellect, his imagination, his will, to fight his way forward. The burden Clarke places on humanity is light. His men do not need to struggle to amend their faults. The superrace, treating men as inferiors, simply compel men to become civilized, communal creatures. Men do not turn themselves into new beings; they are remade docile and decent by the gifts from the superrace. In *Childhood's End* the meek and the mild, the common as well as the elite are equally lifted up. Salvation is universal, not selective. If Clarke's man exercises his intellectual curiosity and investigates the atom, space, or the paranormal, such scientific research will get him in trouble. He encounters warnings to Keep Out. He is to leave all that alone. It is not seek and you shall find, nor gird up your loins and struggle, but sit still, neither spin nor toil, and all shall be provided by those who know what it is that you need. . . .

It might seem that with a work like *Childhood's End* the effort to render Darwinian theory in a form that would be comfortable to man would at last have succeeded. There was here no need to play at espousing evolutionary theory as Bulwer-Lytton had done, nor to blur the final lessons of the theory as Wells had futilely attempted. Clarke had only to enlarge Darwinian theory, not reject it, in order to allow mind to exist apart from body, and the psychic to coexist with the material. Nevertheless while Clarke's friendly world thus proves to be possible—relying on an evolutionary process and a conception of nature that makes all kinds of things possible—in a world of so many possibilities it is also possible that the friendly creation of Clarke is only the fabrication of a writer of fiction. There's the rub. Where all things are possible, what is impossible—including the possibility that the Wellsian view—man is finished—is the true one? *Childhood's End* could appear in 1953 and show that a mellowed science and a corrected religious view can come together; but in 1958 and in 1980 people will be searching the skies for flying saucers and other signs that big brother really does care. The crisis of the spirit that Jung noted in 1958 persists. Literary visions that show that the world does have a place for man do not have the power to exclude all other visions. Thus Arthur Clarke may write a *Childhood's End* that warms the innermost feelings of willing believers, but Clarke doesn't have to believe what he writes. Indeed he can explicitly insist, as he does on the copyright page of *Childhood's End*, "The opinions expressed in this book are not those of the author." Why should they be, unless Mr. Clarke really knows what the world is like and, like Mr. Shaw, thinks he ought to tell us.

When we have come this far, we have passed the point where literary visions can hope to show us what the world and the evolutionary process are certainly like. To help us now we need literary visions that show us how we can be human in a world where we cannot know what the world is certainly like. On this quaking ground we may find our firmest stand. Nor do we much need an art that merely demonstrates that the world is finally unknowable. We need one that convinces us that we can know that and still walk unhesitatingly forward.—EUGENE TANZY, "Contrasting Views of Man and the Evolutionary Process: *Back to Methuselah* and *Childhood's End*," *Arthur C. Clarke*, eds. Joseph D. Olander, Martin Harry Greenberg, 1977, pp. 187–92

That the universe is also likely to prove too immense for any species with any machines is to Clarke's point (in *2001: A Space Odyssey*). He wants to use the insufficiency of the ma-

chine partnership to argue that there is room for another step in the development of a being capable of dealing with the cosmos. He wants to use the fact that other steps have been taken, that the race has survived and has partnered with the machine, to argue that there may be an evolutionary design in the universe. Not a plan imposed from above, as in Kubrick's film, as in that line-up of planets and monoliths with which the race has to get square, but a growing "tapestry," the product of a "weaver" who has himself evolved, a design that gives us all a chance of not having lived in vain, of having contributed.

Clarke's second monolith is not a teaching machine; it is, as is Kubrick's, a giant black slab. This time Clarke wants the aspect of suggestion, the idea that the physical may mean something beyond itself. He calls attention to the block's "geometrical perfection," its ratio of "1 to 4 to 9—the squares of the first three integers," and says that it is "naive" to imagine that the series ends "in only three dimensions."

He wants the actions of the book to be similarly suggestive. He wants the manufactured sea of white which makes one of Saturn's moons look like an eye to turn out to be something of an eye, the observation post from which our evolution has been monitored. He wants Bowman's awakening from hibernation, his coming back safely from "the furthest borders of sleep," "the nearest borders of death," to be a forecast of his awakening from death at the close of the novel, his rebirth as a "Star-Child." He wants us to see why Bowman tires of the "romantic composers," of Sibelius, Tchaikovsky, Berlioz, and even Beethoven, as he sails on alone after the deaths of Poole and Hal. Bowman finds peace "finally," "as so many others [have] done, in the abstract architecture of Bach, occasionally ornamented with Mozart," because such music most clearly suggests that there may be a design in the universe.

Clarke's third monolith, the one Bowman finds on the moon of Saturn, turns "inside out" when he tries to land on it in a space pod. It acts "exactly like one of those optical illusions" where what was the top is suddenly the bottom, the tower suddenly a tunnel.

He wants a similar experience to happen to the reader. He wants us to see that the argument points both ways, that as the end of the novel confirms that the path of evolution is from flesh and blood through the machine to spirit, so the humans who have always speculated that it was so have been right. At the close of the book we learn that the extraterrestrials who left the monoliths were at "the limits of flesh and blood" when they first visited Earth. Later they "transferred" their brains "into shining new homes of metal and plastic," and have since "learned to store knowledge in the structure of space itself," to become "free at last from the tyranny of matter." Now they "rove at will among the stars and sink like a mist through the very Interstices of space."

Knowing that such is the pattern, we can look back at those biologists who argued that no "really advanced beings" would continue to "possess organic bodies" and see that they were right. They were right to say that such beings "would replace their natural bodies" with "constructions of metal and plastic," and they were also right to take a cue "from the beliefs of many religions" and suggest that the "robot body, like the flesh and blood one, would be no more than a stepping-stone to something which, long ago, men had called 'spirit.'" As does *Childhood's End*, Clarke's *2001* turns the fact of evolution inside out in order to confirm a version of some of the race's oldest beliefs.

Kubrick's film also confirms old beliefs, to be sure, but the beliefs are not the same. There is no reason to suppose the fetus at the end of the film has discovered anything but his own superior nature, whereas Clarke's Star-Child discovers that he is at one with the beings who have watched over humanity's evolution. He has more individuality than the children at the conclusion of *Childhood's End*, but he is also part of an Over-mind.

Clarke's *2001* is much concerned with loneliness. In fact, the voyage of Bowman and Poole could be considered something of an exercise in it. Poole feels so distant from his family that he cannot appreciate their birthday greetings. When the *Discovery* swings around behind Jupiter, the two astronauts feel so cut off from Earth that their "loneliness" is suddenly "over-whelming." And after the deaths of Poole and Hal, Bowman's loneliness is, of course, extreme. It is not, however, as extreme as in the film. Clarke's Bowman re-establishes contact with Earth, something Kubrick's does not, and so he still feels part of his race right up to the point when he enters the Star Gate. Moreover, in the novel, the voyage is something of a prepara-tion for the sense of union at the end. We find out that the extraterrestrials first came to Earth (as to many other systems) because "when they looked out across the deeps of space, they felt awe, and wonder, and loneliness." We are told that the Star-Child will "always be a part of the entity" which has made him. We see the Star-Child rescued from his panic at realizing the depths of time as well as space by remembering that he will "never be alone." We understand why he destroys the orbiting bombs when he returns to Earth, for, given his wider sense of kinship, the one thing we may be sure of about the Star-Child is that he will be less patient with parochialism than we are.

But the final difference between Clarke's *2001* and Kub-rick's is that Clarke's hopes that, whatever the future may hold, the race will not have lived in vain. He does not know what a Star-Child would do, but he hopes that the evolution thus suggested, the evolution beyond the bomb, will happen. He hopes that the descendants of Moon-Watcher and his cousins will not pass as meaninglessly as the dinosaurs seem to have done. We may not have any more understanding of the Star-Child than Moon-Watcher would have of us, but our having had to have been in order for the Star-Child to be is terribly important to the novel. The design is that evolution goes from flesh to machine to spirit, and each of the steps is both neces-sary and legitimized by the result. The machine step, which is the surprising one, is justified by exactly what Kubrick fears in such a change: Clarke's Bowman becomes as emotionless as a robot as he journeys on alone. As Kubrick's Bowman gets further and further from the family of humans, he confronts the universe on a more and more individual basis. He is the young man growing up, discovering that the universe and him-self are more and better than he had been taught. Clarke's Bowman, on the other hand, is able to hurry through the machine stage of evolution because the distance from other humans brings him closer to a universal perspective. He gives up listening to recordings of plays because the problems they deal with seem "so remote," "so easily resolved with a little common sense." As I pointed out before, he finally can only listen to the patterns of Bach. He becomes, without having had to identify completely with a machine, as free of human emo-tions as a creature of the universe ought to be.

Clarke feels obligated to remove some of the sting from Poole's death by pointing out that his body is sailing ahead of the *Discovery*, that he will be "the first of all men to reach Saturn." The "worst job" Bowman has after he kills Hal is getting rid of the bodies of the crewmen Hal killed. Their deaths seem so pointless, so preventable. They too, we are told somewhat desperately, will "all reach Saturn" before Bowman.

The consolation for the death of the individual, we know

from Clarke's other fiction, especially *Childhood's End* and *The City and the Stars*, is the continued growth of the race. Moon-Watcher's being taught to use tools is a major breakthrough, but even more important is the fact that the teaching monolith has "twisted" "the very atoms of his brain" "into new patterns"—patterns "his genes" will pass on "to future genera-tions." The next great breakthrough is learning "to speak." With that, the former man-apes win "their first great victory over Time." Now "the knowledge of one generation" can "be handed on to the next." Moon-Watcher has "no real remem-brance of the past" before the monolith works on him; after-ward the race learns "to grope towards a future" using knowledge acquired in the past. The book itself posits a future that is an extension of the past's one great fact—the fact of evolution.

Clarke's real wish is that the past continue to be contained in the future, as *Childhood's End*'s Overmind absorbs all of our planet and its buried dead. The extraterrestrials, who are the model of what our race may become, not only pass on from generation to generation the memory of the experiments that have started on planets like Earth, but also remember, even though they have become "lords of the galaxy" and "beyond the reach of time," their own origins "in the warm slime of a vanished sea." They have not forgotten, though they have be-come "godlike," those who went before, even back to the first forms of life out of which their race arose.

The Bowman of the novel re-establishes, as I have said, contact with Earth after he disconnects Hal. He broadcasts back everything that happens to him right up to the point when he enters the Star Gate. Clarke does not want even that much of human experience to be lost. He wants somehow to com-pensate for the "thirty ghosts" that stand behind "every man now alive" (for that is the "ratio," he explains in the novel's Foreword, "by which the dead outnumber the living"). He is even careful to use the popular idea that one's life flashes before one's eyes at the moment of death to insist that "nothing" of Bowman's life is "being lost; all that he had ever been, at every moment of his life, was being transferred to safer keeping. Even as one David Bowman ceased to exist, another became im-mortal."

2001 the novel, in other words, is not about the revolt of the machines, but about the two things Clarke seems to think we mortals would most like to know in a universe in which we can only hope that the odds are in favor of the race's survival: that we are not alone and that we have not lived in vain.— JOHN HOLLOW, *Against the Night, the Stars*, 1983, pp. 143–48

Arthur C. Clarke was never going to write another book after *The Foundations of Paradise*, but he has. Like the film to which it is a sequel, *2010: Odyssey Two* is a sprawling, frag-mented tale. But it lacks verve.

And verve is what it has to have. The central proposition is still that there are godlike powers in the Universe which have manipulated us for their own purposes. If there is someone out there who has been looking for a way to be an atheist and deist at the same time, this is an exciting premise. Otherwise, it is a stultifying one, and always has been.

The whole premise behind romantic fiction is its attempt to show that the universe is susceptible to human intervention, and I defy anyone to show me any notable stretch of Clarke prose—anything longer than a sentence or two—that is not intensely romantic. So what you have to do is show people becoming as gods or overcoming the gods. And it's true that

Bowman comes back from the abode of the gods and is as a demigod. But he had yet to *earn* any of that; it's all gifts, no one asked him whether he wanted them—the implication is that he would just as soon not—and he is still firmly under the thumb of the masters.

Furthermore, it turns out that despite all this backing-and-forthing, the ultimately triumphant race from the Solar System might be the one from the oceans of Europa; despite the multi-millenia invested in human evolution and Terrestrial ecology, the secret masters for some reason now start up an ecology on Europa which will have to produce a civilization lacking fire. The idea, it seems to me, is to call all of human striving a mere exercise, lacking specific validity and worth. From the point of view of whatever secret masters there be, this may be perfectly rational. From the viewpoint of a human reader, however, while this thought may be majestic it is not one to take to the heart.

This is the essential story in *2010*; everything else is window-dressing, and meaningless as well.

There is a possible intellectual conspiracy between Dimitri Moisevich and Heywood Floyd to maintain intellectual purpose in human space exploration. Don't bother getting interested in it; all subsequent events would have occurred as shown whether the Russian and the American had ever met in the antenna complex over the Arecibo radio telescope bowl or not. Clarke is sending us a picture for our gallery of true-life science wonders; he is not advancing the plot.

There is Floyd's second marriage. It comes apart offstage, for no discernible reason, since his *very* tentative romance with the Soviet cosmonaut is a phfft at first instance. It accomplishes *nothing* dramatic; it simply occurs. It's a page from an expedition's daybook. Floyd is of course terribly upset because now he will lose the love and companionship of his son. While Floyd is on Earth and the marriage is not only ongoing but almost 100% satisfactory, Clarke takes no opportunity to show us any special bond between the boy and the ousted bureaucrat, or any special strain on the marriage. When the marriage

breaks up, Floyd is out at the orbit of Jupiter, as part of the international expedition to repair Hal the schizoid computer, recover the abandoned spaceship left when the masters seized Bowman, and check out the monolith still hanging around out there. In no way does the divorce affect his performance or attitude, or anyone else's performance or attitude.

There is the Chinese expedition to Europa. This is an utterly self-contained episode. Although Clarke writes in a few bridges to the main storyline, every word of that material could be cut, no other word would need to be cut, and the reader would never know anything had been omitted.

What this is, in other words, is an open idea on which the author has hung counterfeit, non-functioning appurtenances of the closed-idea story.

I have no doubt that many readers will proclaim this a terrific book, citing its "large" concepts as counterpointed by its "poignant" freight of "human incident." I say no; I say it's counterfeit. I say it's an old open idea: Suppose there *are* omnipotent things lurking in the closet! I say that the characters in this book are homunculi rather than humans, moving on tried-and-true tracks borrowed from a dozen other books supposedly concerned with character and human situation. And I think that as demonstrated here, these simulacra are less likeable and less worthy than frankly two-dimensional representations would have been.

The best parts of the book—the only poetic, moving parts—are the pictures from science. Beginning with the post-card from the telescope, Clarke brings us a succession of sweeping, breathtaking vistas describing the wonders of the universe. He is in some ways more a film-maker than Stanley Kubrick or even than someone who can tell a coherent story in film. As for the rest of it—the supposed story, the supposed human interaction, the supposed relevance to what you and I are as distinguished from what we fear, or worship, or both, all I can say of this book is that it seems unlikely Clarke was burning to do it. Money talks in a monotone.—ALGIS BUDRYS, "Books," *F&SF*, March 1983, pp. 37–39

AUSTIN CLARKE

1896–1974

Austin Clarke was born on May 9, 1896 in Dublin, the city where he was to live for most of his life. His family, most of whom were ardent nationalists, taught him a fierce love of Ireland and its traditions. Clarke attended Belvedere College, then University College, where he earned a B.A. in 1917. His first book of poetry, *The Vengeance of Fionn*, was published the same year to considerable praise. Like most of his work, it was based in Irish history and mythology. Clarke lectured at University College for four years, receiving an M.A., then turned to journalism. From 1923 to 1937, he lived in London, where he reviewed books for the *Observer*, the *Times Literary Supplement*, and several magazines.

Clarke returned to Dublin in 1937, and produced the ambitious *Night and Morning* the following year. An attempt at a long autobiographical poem ended in frustration, and Clarke put aside poetry. In its place, he plunged into theatrical work, founding a troupe which broadcast his verse plays as the Dublin Verse Speaking Society and presented them on stage as the Lyric Theatre Company. During this time he wrote several novels and critical essays; he also acted as president of Irish P.E.N. for six years and the Irish Academy of Letters for two years. He received an honorary doctorate from Trinity College.

In 1955 Clarke began his most fertile and celebrated period with the publication of *Ancient Lights*, his first poetry in almost two decades. From then on the poems flowed, characteristically dense, satirical, with intricate rhymes. "I load myself with chains and try to get out of them" was Clarke's own description. Austin Clarke died on March 20, 1974. He was married and had three sons.

G. K. CHESTERTON

AGATHA CHRISTIE

ARTHUR C. CLARKE

AUSTIN CLARKE

JOSEPH CONRAD

IVY-COMPTON-BURNETT

BARON CORVO (FREDERICK ROLFE)

PADRAIC COLUM

General

One of the problems confronting the contemporary writer is to determine what part of his present experience and that of society is of lasting importance. History has speeded up; change is an overnight experience: what is of significance? Clarke's talent is not so delicate that he need worry about saving his words for the major theme of the time. He writes about what is important to him and the result is often the recording of apparently casual history as it flashes by, unnoticed or ignored by other poets. If in the future a reader wants to know how an Irish poet viewed, for example, labor troubles, ecumenism, sex, education, pollution of stream, landscape, mind, he will not need to read collateral literature. With Clarke, in a sense, the footnotes are the poems themselves.—Richard Weber, "Austin Clarke: The Arch Poet of Dublin," *MR*, Spring 1970, p. 297

In his early poetry, Clarke is attempting to find his own voice, congenial form and subject matter. At first he consciously attaches himself to Irish tradition by using legendary subject matter and by trying his hand at narrative poetry. Never really feeling at ease with narrative, he turns to the shorter lyric and temporarily abandons the legendary Celtic material for more contemporary subject matter. In striving to find himself, in his search for a valid and independent voice, he is thrown up against two issues: one structural, one thematic.

The thematic problem is one of finding the mean between the historical and the contemporary—between the local and the universal. Yeats had inaugurated the occasional poem; he had lifted it to full dignity by giving maximum intensity to the occasion it celebrated. Clarke did not want to follow in Yeats's footsteps, yet he saw the limitations of the thematic possibilities of the Celtic-Romanesque mode and the pitfalls awaiting him in the too narrow confines of the local: its slackening into the provincial, the obscure. Although Clarke's early poetry before 1936 betrays an awareness of this problem he does not find any solutions. As he recently said, he soon realized that Joyce did not avoid obscurities—his readers faced up to the difficulties of his work without lessening their total respect for it—and therefore, he rationalized, there was no reason why his own readers could not and would not do the same. And so, as we shall see, Clarke was to focus solely on Ireland, dealing with its problems in a Swiftean mode: bitter satire softened only by the underlying love of the country so critically examined.

The structural problem saw the beginnings of its resolution in these early years. One of Clarke's closest friends and literary advisors, Æ, watched him battling with questions of rhyme and prosody and encouraged him to go back to the assonantal measures of the Gaelic. With Æ's support Clark began in the late 'twenties and 'thirties what was to become a life-time project: the creation of a valid Anglo-Irish prosody with its roots in Gaelic but its sound suited to and designed ultimately for twentieth century English.—Susan Halpern, *Austin Clarke, His Life and Works*, 1974, p. 60

Works

POETRY

In the poems in *Pilgrimage*, Austin Clarke, through some strange process, has been able to identify himself with the Gaelic poets of the seventeenth and early eighteenth centuries, times which in Ireland were an extension of the medieval period. He writes in the temper of these dispossessed men, as if he were actually trudging the roads they trudged, crossing the waters they crossed, and, like them, separating themselves from the people they sing to by dealing with the most tragic figures in their tradition. The landscape is blurred with rain; the light is the light before or after a storm:

> Grey holdings of rain
> Had grown less with the fields,
> As we came to that blessed place
> Where hail and honey meet,
> O Clonmacnoise was crossed
> With light; those cloistered scholars
> Whose knowledge of the gospel
> Is cast in metal of pure voices,
> Were all rejoicing daily,
> And cunning hands with cold and jewels
> Brought chalices to flame.

He uses assonance in the place of full rhyme, and by using assonance so deliberately and with such ability he makes an innovation in verse-structure. "Assonance," he has written, "takes the clapper from the bell of rhyme." He assures us that these vowel-correspondences—and there is no doubt but that he is right in his contention—permit lovely words neglected for the reason that there are no rhymes for them to take the tonic place in the line. If he wanted to back up this innovation, he could make quotations from an Irish critic of thirty or thirty-five years ago: William Larminie declared that "the unnecessary burthen of rhyme" should be shed from poetry in English; his formula for the new departure was "quantity sweetened by assonance, and assonance strengthened by quantity." Austin Clarke makes no attempt to write quantitative verse. But he has made himself an adept in the use of assonantal sounds. And by following this sound he is able to create a new pattern in verse. Such poems as *The Planter's Daughter* and *Aisling* have music as lovely as it is unfamiliar—like the notes of the bog-lark or the curlew. This distant, haunting music has come from the union of English and Irish poetry.

The effects which he achieves are not an external accomplishment, although he was probably given a direction by the critic I have quoted, William Larminie. These muted verses belong to the world of half-lights, remembered visions, and lost forms of lapsed civilizations, to that "Romanesque" Ireland whose architecture and sculpture are beginning to be appreciated, where the Woman of Beare pleases the captains of armies and the lawyers who break lands, where Queen Gormlai makes her "learned and pitiful ditties," and where monks on an island of a western lake throw themselves on beds of nettles to get rid of some tempting vision, or where, in the seventeenth and eighteenth centuries, a poet on a desolate mountain-side meets her who is the spirit of poetry and the spirit of the land. There is a poem which shows all his curious accomplishment and his power of creating in the Gaelic mode: it is the *Aisling* which brings his *Pilgrimage* to a close. Austin Clarke as he re-creates this form, as curious and as special as one of the rarer forms of Provençal poetry, evokes, too, the world of the last Gaelic poets.—Padraic Colum, "Introduction" to *The Collected Poems of Austin Clarke*, 1936, pp. 15–17

One of the most interesting aspects of his modern side is that Clarke's most recent book, a single narrative poem called *Mnemosyne Lay in Dust* (1966), approaches the spirit of confessional poetry as closely as any work that has yet appeared in the British Isles. Though written in the third person, this book has an autobiographical ring to it. It has to do with the hysterical breakdown and amnesia, hospitalization, and recovery of one 'Maurice Devane,' Clarke's relatively youthful protagonist. Formally, it represents a culmination of Clarke's entire development. After his early period of romantic work, he has for years cultivated an astringently compressed style employing certain rhyming and alliterative devices that appear eccentric in

English but that are precisely that 'influence of Irish versification' to which Montague refers. The remarkable turn, achieved in old age, that *Mnemosyne Lay in Dust* represents is clearly the result of a fusion of resolutions, artistic and psychological.

Clarke may have been influenced by the confessional movement, as well as by the painful but eventually triumphant private experience he describes in the poem, but this late reflowering of his art seems firmly rooted in his own earlier practice. He can be uncomfortably plain in his simple, unsqueamish factual presentation, as in Section VI of the sequence, which deals with a fit of depression that led to Maurice's being put for a while in a padded cell. . . .

Revelations concerning his own self, which he is struggling to re-create, mingle in this poem with the sights and smells of Dublin, inside and outside the hospital, and with a vivid sense of both the literal nature and the strangeness of the other human beings whom Maurice observes from his vantage point. The poem is the full-bodied realization of a world, yet it never loses its subjectivity. The visions that come to Maurice in his traumatized state and the lyrical interpretations of his experience, sometimes (as in Section III) fearful and depressed, sometimes (as in VIII) tragically and prophetically buoyant as Yeats was in, say, 'Lapis Lazuli,' exalt the poem into self-transcendence.—M. L. ROSENTHAL, "Contemporary Irish Poetry," *The New Poets*, 1967, pp. 268–70

Austin Clarke's main themes are four: the Irish past, fragile, remote; the chill of religious restraints; outrageous things in the papers; the precariousness of his own reason. Since (as Yeats assured us) "manifold illusion" hoops civilization's staves around an emptiness, such themes will threaten an insecure community, and Clarke's failure to be more heard of is explicable. When you've picked your way into his packed, difficult verse you find something you don't want to be told.

The verse is packed and evasive because it must achieve its air of control without recourse to the declamatory tones of certainty. What it is certain of is all nuance: that Ireland's religion thwarts, but not, for instance, that Ireland "would be better without its religion." (Reflect that Ireland is unimaginable without its religion.) . . .

Our tongue's most consummate declaimer, Yeats could make someone as scrupulous as Clarke feel tongue-tied. Clarke once heard AE say, "The old man is talking to himself." He recalls the scene in AE's study:

> I saw behind him
> Gold-leafed, with their dark blue or olive bindings,
> The *Collected Poems* of William Butler Yeats,
> Macmillan'd in a row.
>   I wondered were they
> A Purgatory the poet had ghosted from hatred,
> Incessant, inner circles, of repetition
> Systematised by metaphysics, late
> Excuse for fantasies, that never let him
> Be still when he became a man of letters,
> Discovered in old age the physical.
> "His lyrics are Saturnian rings illumined
> By colder fire."
>   "What of our common ill?"
> Do they explain it?"
>   "If rhetoric can last,
> Then all that lonely, premeditated art must."

It is AE speaking of Saturnian rings and rhetoric, Austin Clarke asking about his constant theme, "our common ill." Dublinborn, raised a Catholic, slowly, quietly embittered to the point of a mid-life mental breakdown, he did not think his case was in any way special.

In an odd way he is Yeats's furtive shadow. His first work, published in 1917 at twenty-one, inaugurates, like *The Wanderings of Oisin*, a project of retelling the old stories: of Fionn, of Concobar, of Cuchulinn, of Maeve. That was why Beckett and Kavanagh dismissed him as antiquarian. The narratives halt, but there are rich splendid passages. He kept this up for a dozen years. Then, like the Yeats of *Responsibilities*, he moved to contemporary epigrams. Then *Night and Morning* (1938) commences a regime of bitter self-examination ("Martha Blake" is part of that). Then Yeats dies, and for seventeen years, save for theatre projects that entailed writing plays of his own and staging Yeats's Austin Clarke is silent.— HUGH KENNER, *A Colder Eye*, 1983, pp. 246–48

DRAMA

The most immediately obvious way in which Clarke has enlarged the scope of verse drama—as Yeats understood the term—is by introducing humour into it. Any humour in Yeats' plays is confined strictly to prose; verse is for more serious things. Clarke, on the other hand, is not afraid to call *Black Fast* "A Poetic Farce," and the same sub-title might be given to *The Son of Learning*. *The Kiss* is too subtle for such a gross word as "farce" to be applied to it, but it is deliciously amusing. The more serious plays, too, have their humorous side in a sense, for Clarke's formula is to follow every climax with an anti-climax.

Then too, Clarke has found new subject-matter. Yeats' plays are pagan even when they deal with Christian times: Clarke prefers to emphasize the Christian elements in such of his fables as are borrowed from history, while at the same time giving them a twist of his own. Besides, his plays of the religious life deal with a subject-matter which Yeats could never, as a Protestant, either know or understand. Yeats' Catholic Church consists almost entirely of saints; Clarke knows that, laity apart entirely, the Church is made up less of saints than of everyday, run-of-the-mill clergy, monks and nuns in their various degrees. And, whereas the saint can afford to be an individualist, the rank-and-file of the Church Militant have to stick pretty close to army regulations. Discipline, the rule of the order, is particularly stressed in his two plays about nuns, *The Flame* and *Sister Eucharia*.—VIVIAN H. S. MERCIER, "The Verse Plays of Austin Clarke," *DM*, April–June 1944, pp. 39–40

FICTION

In the middle of his career, before his return to Ireland in 1937, Clarke first turned to prose narrative. *The Bright Temptation* was published in 1932; another work, *The Singing Men at Cashel*, in 1936; both were full-length volumes. He has noted that he deliberately called them romances because he was aware that they were not truly novels; they merged fantasy with a narrative akin to that used for historical novels. His shift to prose, he said, had two purposes: to revive interest in the Celtic Middle Ages, a period practically unknown in Ireland, and to make a little money—since opportunities for reviewing at that time were proving meagre. He did not make as much money as he had hoped, and no more prose romances were forthcoming until sixteen years later when *The Sun Dances at Easter*, his third and last prose romance, was published.

There seems to have been a very clear third reason for writing prose that Clarke, so used to wedding the propagandistic to his work, had been hesitant to mention. Beyond romantic reconstruction of the medieval monastic society lies a deliberate comment on present-day Ireland which crops up time after time, persistently maintaining an obbligato throughout all three works. This third purpose, especially, has not gone unnoticed by earlier critics: 'Obviously the poet is examining, from his own peculiar stance, the moral and religious structure of Ireland, using history as his stalking-horse: the "drama of racial conscience" is restlessly in progress.' More than being charming historical romances about medieval Ireland, these works are protests of a satirical nature against the complacency of the Irish of Clarke's own day.—SUSAN HALPERN, *Austin Clarke, His Life and Works*, 1974, p. 176

If there is a major flaw in Clarke's prose "romances," it is that too often art surrenders to polemics. There are many passages of graceful, beautiful prose and many others of remarkable comic vigor. But, at the same time, there are far too many instances in which the prose becomes annoyingly shrill and dogmatic. Too often the characters' speeches degenerate into harangues.

. . . ⟨I⟩n his prose "romances" he too frequently engages in a kind of literary ventriloquism, forcing angry sermons through the lips of characters who in the context of his narrative are wholly unsuited to the task of preaching. Not only that, but in each of these prose works Clarke's relentless condemnation of what he regards as the moral perversity of the Irish Catholic Church gradually wears upon the reader and, unless he shares the author's intense aversion to Irish Catholicism, eventually bores him. One may be amused at first to have it suggested that Irish hermits taught "wild creatures, big and small, to behave themselves" sexually or that in Irish monasteries male and female animals were carefully segregated during mating season lest they be the cause of impure thoughts among the inmates. But when the same observations are repeated again and again with little variation, the novelty loses its effect. In the end, perhaps, one is more convinced that the author has little affection for Christianity, especially as it is practiced in Ireland, than that the given "romance" is successful as a work of art.—RICHARD J. LOFTUS, "Austin Clarke: Ireland of the Black Church," *Nationalism in Modern Anglo-Irish Poetry*, 1964, pp. 267–68

CRITICISM

One reason why Clarke may have almost disregarded his work as a critic is the position in which he saw himself in relation to the tradition of criticism in Ireland. He acquired his seminal ideas about Irish literature at the beginning of the century while a university student from his teacher, the poet Thomas MacDonagh; since then, Clarke worked to clarify the definition of Irish literature. Throughout Clarke's career the validity as well as the dignity of Irish national poetry was one of his greatest concerns. His analysis of the growth of Irish poetry is a product of the Irish tradition as well as of his own theory of literature.

Poetry in Modern Ireland begins with a credo of Irish literary independence. Clarke contends that, essentially, there has been no poetic revival during the early years of this century but that Irish literature has had a continuous tradition.

> Owing to present confusion and neglect, the particular conditions of our poetry are often misunderstood—indeed the fact that critics speak of an Irish literary revival shows in itself a certain measure of inaccuracy. We do not speak of an English, French, or American literary revival and, in the strict sense of the word, therefore, it is inaccurate to speak of an Irish literary revival. The movement which expanded so quickly, so imaginatively, at the beginning of the present century was the result of a gradual development. We can trace that development back to the eighteenth century when the English language spread more widely throughout Ireland and the native language and its literature were in decline.

Although Clarke believes this is a moot question, nevertheless it has remained a complex and often debated issue.

Clarke's theory is the following: when all Europe was turning to realism, poets in Ireland turned to Irish mythology; theirs perhaps was a delayed reaction to romanticism but it was, in any case, individual and independent. Irish verse, which had become highly political, was reformed and the ground for the Celtic Twilight laid: 'This mingling of landscape and lore, this topographical excitement, as we might call it, was the expression of a new emotional experience.' When this experience became coupled with a mood of mystery, the Celtic Twilight was born. Clarke credits the rapid spread of the Celtic Twilight to Æ (George Russell), but although he reveres Æ, Clarke contends that the vogue of the Celtic Twilight at the turn of the century temporarily concealed the real direction of Irish poetry which was being fostered by the translations of Douglas Hyde and George Sigerson, enthusiasts who were trying to honour, to save and to rejuvenate the Irish language.

The revival of the Irish language and the growth of nationalism ushered in what Clarke called a 'folk phase' which included in its ranks most of the greats of the first quarter of the century: Pearse, MacDonagh, Stephens, and Higgins. Although the *national* quality of this poetry was not glaringly obvious, Clarke sees nationalism as one of its most important attributes; 'these poets, while avoiding obvious comment, reflected indirectly the impoverished state of our country during centuries of alien rule.'—SUSAN HALPERN, *Austin Clarke, His Life and Works*, 1974, pp. 136–37

MAURICE HARMON
From "The Later Poetry of Austin Clarke"
The Celtic Cross
eds. Ray B. Browne,
William John Roscelli, and Richard Loftus
1964, pp. 39–55

Austin Clarke grew up during the exciting years of pre-revolutionary Ireland. He witnessed the Easter Rising of 1916, the Anglo-Irish War, and felt the attraction of that romantic and idealistic period. Like other writers of his generation—Sean O'Faolain, Frank O'Connor, and Liam O'Flaherty—he was deeply affected by the violence, the bitterness, and the disillusion brought about by the Civil War; and he has not lived happily in the kind of Ireland that emerged from the days of youthful vision. Like theirs, his work reflects the change from romance to realism, from idealism and hope to something occasionally bordering on despair. It is a rebellion against what Frank O'Connor has called the "subjective, idealistic, romantic literature"[1] of the Irish Literary Revival.

He began in the manner of a Celtic Revival poet. His early work—*The Vengeance of Fionn* (1917), *The Fires of Baal* (1921), *The Sword of the West* (1921), and *The Cattledrive of Connaught and Other Poems* (1925)—are epic narratives showing the influence of Yeats, Samuel Ferguson, and William Larminie. They are romantic and idealistic in tone, with a lyrical, impressionistic beauty, and reveal a delicate metrical skill. Like Yeats, Clarke went back to Irish myth and saga, to the Cuchulain and Ossianic cycles. But gradually he worked out an important, personal handling of the old material. Where Yeats had formulated a dichotomy between the pagan, aristocratic past and the democratic present, Clarke presented a contrast between the Christian, medieval past and the dogmatic, Catholic present. Yeats had largely ignored the religious issues and after 1916 tended to concentrate on the Anglo-Irish middle nation of the eighteenth century in preference to the rising, unattractive middle class of his own time. With Clarke the religious question is central, for personal and national reasons, and it is closely associated with the native middle class whose rise to power is the greatest social event of Irish history. . . .

In his novels and plays, in particular, Clarke uses the medieval scene as a framework of reference for satirical comment on his own time. He opposes the medieval, monastic Church of masculine intellect to the centralizing, dogmatic Church of modern Ireland and seeks out a form of Christianity in which men of his complex nature and far-reaching intellect can exist within the Church. He has natural affinities with the greater intellectual liberty that was possible for the individual before the Council of Trent (1546–63). "Pilgrimage" is indicative of his attitude, although it does not express the full range of his relationship to the medieval scene. Clearly it provides him with a form of escape from the problems of his own life. But where the theme of flight in the early poems was vague and indefinite as to motivation and destination, here it is related to sexual temptation. The method is indirect but the material is personal. Thus, in "Celibacy" he uses the person of the ascetic monk persistently harassed by temptation in the form of a woman. It is a traditional story associated with many of the Irish hermits, and Clarke's treatment retains some of the humor with which the situation is now often treated in conversation. As a result the poem works in a complex manner. It dramatizes the temptation with sympathy and through the direct account of the hermit, but is also comments ironically on his story and becomes satirical of the whole situation. Clarke can view the subject as a personal one but also as one previously experienced, not unique but typical. The conjunction of past and present, impersonal and personal, absurd and exaggerated, gives the poem at least three levels of interpretation. His view of the past is derived from such a scholarly familiarity that he moves with great ease and freedom in the remote period. He has sympathy for the ascetic rigors of the Celtic Church in its earlier forms and finds in them reflections of puritanical Catholicism in his own time. And when the earlier church grew rich he finds in its various manifestations of complacent power convenient analogies for the Irish Church of his time and its treatment of the individual. Insofar as its excesses are unattractive, he can be satirical about them and use them as absurdly magnifying mirror-images for his own age. And when the individual, particularly the poet, is rejected by the early Church or State, he can present him in terms of the poet's position in modern society and comment upon his treament at the hands of authority. . . .

Many of these poems are concerned with the conflict between the desire for freedom of action and self-expression and the regulations of the Church. The most personal, dominated by religious images and the contrasting images of natural freedoms, are the result of a genuine spiritual need. Clarke is inescapably attracted to the idea of sin, guilt, and damnation; he cannot ignore conscience and feels the need for repentance. The stern morality and the simple faith of the Irish Church fail to satisfy his needs. But his work is not limited to a self-centered interest. It is human and passionate in its concern for the

dignity of man. His identification with the spoiled priest who embraced the Renaissance is not casual or accidental. It lies at the heart of his work. He is concerned with the outcast, the misfit, the mistreated, and with the individual who does not conform or blend with his environment. As well as his own religious and sexual problems there is his awareness that the drama of the individual soul is very often the drama of the racial conscience. He knows that the difficulties he experiences represent more than personal condition. Others are likely to feel the same influences and be disturbed by the same tendencies. Since the courageous and painful poetry of *Night and Morning*, his sense of public responsibility has become more pronounced. The ancient Irish bards were concerned with public utterance, with eulogy, satire, and elegy, and in the final three books of *Later Poems*—*Ancient Lights* (1955), *Too Great A Vine* (1957), and *The Horse-Eaters* (1960)—Clarke has written much satirical comment on public issues and events. He has moved away from the middle ages as a setting and concentrates on his own time. . . .

The quiet humor and gentle irony of the recent autobiographical poems attest Clarke's courage through the years. Burdened with great difficulties in his personal life and harassed by frustrations in the life of the country, he has continued to produce poetry, prose, and drama of distinction. His work as a whole is a skillful, varied, and complex response to his own time, and while the later poetry is only a part of that achievement, it can serve as evidence of his imaginative range and technical ability.

Notes

1. Frank O'Connor, "The Future of Irish Literature," *Horizon*, V, (January 1942), p. 58.

RICHARD J. LOFTUS
"Austin Clarke: Ireland of the Black Church"
Nationalism in Modern Anglo-Irish Poetry
1964, pp. 260–76

Of all the "new school" of Irish writers who gained a measure of recognition in the nineteen-twenties, only Austin Clarke may be said to have made an important contribution to modern Irish verse—a contribution deliberately ignored by most Irish intellectuals and virtually unknown outside of Ireland. For one thing, he succeeded, where so many others had failed, in making effective use of elements of Gaelic prosody in English-language verse. Colum and Higgins alike tried to combine assonance with the regular end-rhyme conventions of English verse; and in so doing they invariably softened and romanticized the tone of their verse. Clarke, too, in his earlier poetry is guilty of much the same sin of excess; in "Music Healers," for instance, a revised version of a poem that first appeared in *The Sword of the West*, he has Emer address her husband, the hero of the *Táin*: "'Cuchullin, it is I/ Without lie, though I cry'af05" (*Poems*, p. 69). In *The Cattledrive in Connaught*, the last of his narrative poems, however, Clarke ignores end-rhyme entirely and relies on assonance for his sound pattern. In his more mature poetry he has come to regard end-rhyme as simply one device in the overall sound pattern, to be used or not according to need.[1]

Nor are Clarke's achievements limited to matters of prosody. He soon left behind the flaccid romanticism of his youthful verse and by 1929, with the publication of *Pilgrimage*, he was producing a harsher, much more potent kind of poetry.

Clarke's poem "The Young Woman of Beare"—the Old Woman of Beare, a well-known figure in folk stories, was reputed to have had seven periods of youth before age came upon her—may well have served as a prototype for Yeats' Crazy Jane poems. The peasant woman upon whom Clarke based his characterization resembles in some ways the old woman of Gort who, Yeats tells us, served as a model for Crazy Jane. . . .

One does not find in Clarke's work, prose or poetry, any sustained intellectual justification of his art such as Yeats provides in *A Vision*. One could not accuse him of accepting the ideal of "bog wisdom," yet certainly the faith that motivates him is a simple one. He is for good, by which he means freedom of the individual, particularly in matters of sex but also in matters of intellect; and he is against evil, which takes in all the restrictive elements of Irish society but especially the Catholic Church. Clarke's reference to "the black church" in the title of his autobiography is significant. Literally the phrase refers to a Protestant church on Mountjoy Street in Dublin near Clarke's childhood home. But there is another, more important meaning as well. As a child Clarke had absorbed the street-lore about the grim, forbidding structure—"that anyone who ran round the church three times after dark would meet the Devil himself on the third round." Then, one Sunday two little Protestant girls, who were visiting his family, took him in hand and led him into the dreadful structure. "I was filled with astonishment," he comments, "for the interior of the church was as bright as its exterior was dark. I had known only the dimness of old city [Catholic] churches, the rich gleam of stained-glass windows in the transept with all their saints and instruments of torture. . . . But through the lancets of the Black Church came a plain and temperate daylight which showed all clearly."[2] "Black Church," as Clarke knows well, is a common street term used by Dubliners when referring to Protestant churches; and, as the anecdote of the church on Mountjoy Street and numerous other episodes in *Twice round the Black Church* suggest, the term says much more of those who use it than of the Protestant places of worship to which it is applied. For Clarke, the Irish Catholic Church is "the Black Church," the church that destroys the light of intellectual and emotional freedom and that condemns the Irish people to the darkness of ignorance and puritanism.

Clarke is not a poet of great vision. No doubt the time was past when Irish poets might give themselves to the task of defining what the new Ireland might become. The British garrison had long since departed; the new Ireland was an established fact, a reality. For the poet determined to dedicate his art to his native country—and Clarke has been just as determined to do this as were Yeats and Pearse and Colum—there remained little choice but to look at the reality and to comment upon it. This is precisely what Clarke has done in his more recent verse, *Ancient Lights* (1955), *Too Great a Vine* (1958), *The Horse Eaters* (1960), and *Flight to Africa and Other Poems* (1963). The result is a sustained, bitter satire against the Irish Catholic Church and the ruling middle-class establishment. James Stephens had dabbled in satiric verse; and Yeats, in his poems about Parnell and Casement and in those inspired by the Abbey Theatre controversy in the first decade of the century and the Lane affair in the second decade, showed that he, too,

could write in anger. But Stephens' satires are tempered by his humor, those of Yeats by his sense of aristocratic dignity and by the rhetorical discipline of his art. Clarke's later poetry knows no such restraint. Gone are the backdrop of medieval Ireland, the neopagan ideals, the occasional burst of comic humor. What remains is a savage rage that Ireland has not known since Swift in the seventeenth century and the Gaelic bards of an earlier age, Angus na n-aor Ó Dálaigh (Angus "of the Satires" O'Daly) and Tadhg Dall Ó Huiginn (Blind Teigue O'Higgin), both of whom were supposedly murdered by enraged victims of their satires.[3] . . .

Clarke maintains that his comments on Irish life are accurate and just; and he can produce newspaper clippings to substantiate many of the incidents about which he writes.[4] No doubt the incidents of the poems are based on facts. Thousands of Irishmen do travel to Lourdes each year. Irish Catholics do molest Protestant evangelists, though they do not always escape justice as easily as Clarke would have it. The Irish government did cancel legislation to provide free obstetric care—and fired the Minister of Health, Dr. Noel Browne, who proposed it—after the Irish Catholic hierarchy denounced it as socialistic. But in Clarke's verse the incidents are invariably subjected to ironic distortion and exaggeration. Nor could one say that the composite picture of Ireland which emerges from his poetry is a valid one. He is motivated by an unrestrained personal hostility. His point of view is savagely one-sided. Were he a historian, one could hardly credit him.

But, of course, Clarke is not a historian but a poet. The accuracy or inaccuracy of his social criticism is largely irrelevant to an objective judgment of his artistic achievement. His art is not of the first order: its range is much too narrow, its tone at times too shrill. Nevertheless, these late satires are impressive; and what makes them so is the passionate rage that informs them. Ireland and Irish verse had become, as James Stephens predicted, "bitter and angry and defensive." Clarke is the most bitter, most angry, most defensive of the Irish poets; and his work, more than that of any other Irish writer, proclaims the estrangement of the Irish artist from his society. His poetry is not profound, but it is extraordinarily intense. He sees only one "evil"—a monstrous religious establishment that devours the country's wealth and condemns its people to intellectual ignorance and sexual frustration. He is obsessed with this violent vision of a black church and a bitter nation.

Notes

1. Robert Farren, *The Course of Irish Verse*, pp. 155–58, analyzes Clarke's expert use of assonance.
2. *Twice round the Black Church*, pp. 23–24.
3. Vivian Mercier, *The Irish Comic Tradition* (Oxford, 1962), pp. 134–35, writes that Ó Dálaigh was reportedly killed by a servant of one of his victims, Ó Huiginn by six men of the O'Haras whom he had satirized for raiding his house. Lady Gregory, *Poets and Dreamers* (London, 1903), p. 3, says that Ó Dálaigh was killed when the servant of an Irish chief stuck a knife in his throat and that Ó Huiginn had his tongue cut out. Austin Clarke, *Too Great a Vine: Poems and Satires* (Templeogue, County Dublin, 1957), p. 27.
4. Clarke showed me a number of these clippings when I visited him in Dublin.

PADRAIC COLUM

1881–1972

Padraic Colum was born on December 8, 1881 in Longford, Ireland, where his grandmother told him the stories and legends that began his lifelong romance with folklore and the spoken word. Although Colum did not attend college, he later received honorary doctorates from Columbia University and Trinity College. At seventeen, he went to Dublin and worked as a clerk at the Irish Railway Clearing House. He became involved with the embryonic National Theatre Society, and there met the leading figures of the Celtic Revival: Yeats, Synge, Lady Gregory, and A.E. (George William Russell). Colum later became a close friend of James Joyce as well.

In 1903, banking heir Thomas Hughes Kelly gave Colum a five-year scholarship for writing. He wrote several plays, which became the first successful presentations of Yeats' Irish National Theatre, co-founded and edited the *Irish Review*, and began to publish his poetry. Colum married the critic Mary Maguire in 1912, and the next year began to retell folk tales for children. This brought him his greatest fame. "The story-teller must have respect for the child's mind and the child's conception of the world, knowing it for a complete mind and a complete conception," Colum told his biographer Zack Bowen.

In 1914 Colum embarked on an eight-year journey through the United States, where he collected folk tales and gave frequent readings of his work. He returned to Ireland in 1922, but soon left for Hawaii, where he adapted Hawaiian legends at the invitation of the Hawaiian legislature. Colum moved to New York City in 1933. In 1939 he and his wife began teaching comparative literature at Columbia University. Colum remained there for the rest of his life, teaching and publishing his tales, essays, and poems, which he often read aloud. Mary Colum died in 1957; Colum died on January 12, 1972.

Personal

Padraic Colum's new novel, *The Flying Swans*, came out last week, and in a burst of friendly enthusiam there was an attempt to set him up as a sort of benign elder statesman, contemplating a monument. *The Flying Swans*, it was said, would be published just fifty years after the date of his first book. It would represent his fortieth work, or perhaps his fiftieth, and would be the major effort of a lifetime—which, incidentally, had consumed a full decade of that lifetime.

"It took well over ten years to write, if you date back to when I put down the first notes. But while I was writing it, I also did quite a lot of other things—a treasury of Irish folklore, the life of an Irish statesman, two plays, a book of verse.

"As a matter of fact, anything that prolongs the time allowance for writing a novel is all to the good. The longer you have, the better you get to know the characters. Maybe one trouble with the novels today is that the authors don't live with them nearly long enough.

"This applies to writing plays, as well, but not to verse. You just toss verse off. It belongs to only a moment in your life, and isn't like the people of a novel, whose daily life you share."

Back a couple of uneasy generations, Mr. Colum was one of the Irish writers who were revolutionaries or patriots, depending on where you sat. As to what the "young fellows" had then, while they dreamed of nationalism, the future and the Abbey, and as they meanwhile wandered Dublin. . . .

"There was the tremendous benefit of living in a small city. You could walk the streets and would meet everybody. Suppose you were writing a poem and got stuck. You took a walk and ran into Yeats or whoever. You stopped. You said, 'Here's a poem. What's wrong with it?' Like as not, he could read it once and tell you.

"Another thing I had in my time—the drawing room, the salon. That no longer exists, but it was a wonderful place for conversation. When I was growing up, there were the salons that Shaw and Wilde both knew."

Forty or fifty books—the true count is rendered even more hopeless by the addition of what Mr. Colum describes as "innumerable" books for children—and fifty-four years of writing. Could he estimate the total number of words?

"No number goes so high. I trained myself to write steadily, by writing newspaper editorials. Now I'm just in the habit. I get up, write until lunch. After that there are chores around here, and later I write again. At night I take a walk in Central Park. They say it's dangerous, but I've never found it so.

"One thing I've never outgrown, writing plays. I'm a sort of Sunday playwright, and do them for pleasure as well as with hope. One may go on, off-Broadway, this fall. But the theatre's a pretty uncertain sort of thing, so I just plug along. At the moment, my wife and I are doing a book on Joyce. Not a formal biography, but as we knew him day-to-day, in Dublin and in Paris afterward."

Pleasure reading? Detective stories, to a certain extent, and—listen to this—"The English ones are best." The Irish trouble clearly is over.—LEWIS NICHOLS, "Talk with Padraic Colum," *NYTBR*, June 23, 1957, p. 15

Mr. Colum, who is small and well-made and has a beautiful voice and gray hair that flies up and away in all directions, and who wears a porkpie hat as if it were a crown of the Kings of Tara, got off to such an early start that he'd made a secure place for himself in Irish literary history by his early twenties. He and Synge were among the discoveries of the Abbey Theatre, and his play *The Land* was the third the Abbey ever put on and the first to be a success. "In those days, sixty years ago," he told us the other afternoon, over a cup of tea and a plate of cinnamon toast, "it was the fashion to be writing stories and plays in the country speech. Yeats, Lady Gregory, Synge, and all were doing it, but the truth of the matter is that I was the only one of the lot that knew what the real country speech sounded like. I wouldn't want to say a word against Synge's language, which is exquisite, very fine, but has no more to do with how people actually spoke than Oscar Wilde's dialogue in his comedies has to do with how people spoke in London drawing rooms in the eighteen-nineties. You might say I had the advantage of the disadvantages that Yeats and others didn't have—I was born in a workhouse and knew common speech from my birth. I always say I was born in a workhouse to make a romantic story; the fact is, my father was the master of a workhouse, which isn't *quite* so good, not being quite so bad." . . .

"⟨James Joyce⟩ was two or three months younger than I," Mr. Colum said. "We became good friends not in our student days but after. He used to give fine parties in Paris, when he had the money—the best was good enough for James Joyce! Whenever Nora's back was turned, there'd be another bottle of his favorite white wine. Joyce was convinced that the proper sacramental wine was white—I don't know why. He had a theory for everything, and would willingly have set Rome straight on sacramental wine, had Rome but asked. We Dubliners are like the Florentines who were so fiercely proud of their mention in the *Inferno*. To be a contemporary of Joyce and not be mentioned in *Ulysses* is a disgrace. I come off easy in it—in the National Library scene somebody says of me, 'He has that queer thing called genius.' Joyce later made a sneering remark about me in a satire on poets, but it often slips my mind—I remember the praise and forget the sneer!"—UNSIGNED, NY, June 19, 1962, p. 25

General

Concerning Colum the writer one does not ask, Is he Irish? The query rather is, What is not Irish in him? He is of Catholic country family, with a mind like—what shall I say?—like one of those firkins of butter they find in bogs. None know what year long since they were laid in cool, wet places, and not remembered; only that it *was* long since and that still to-day they are here, are still as fresh as this morning's churning, and carry from an age that used be, in a land still here, the sweetness of grass once chewed to the milk that made them. Such is Colum's mind: an ancient mind full of newness. . . .

I have heard of poets in England who could see very little in Colum, and who wondered politely at our constant praise of him. They may be right; he may have little for them; but I never heard an Irishman decry him. We yield to his work as to something in the Irish grain—our climate's kind of light, the prevailing direction of our winds, our own sorts of stone and soil. His feeling for high moods in politics might strike an outsider as at issue with the quiet of his mind, but for us it is additional proof that he is Irish; for, quiet mind or brawling mind, the Irishman follows the public action with interest. . . .

Colum's verse, like Campbell's, is a house full of people, with fields and roads around it which are filled with people as well. He does not so often make his own thoughts into poems, preferring to project inside them the women and men he knows and moves among. This is a way of saying that he cultivates the dramatic lyric, which has been for many hundreds of years an indigenous form in Ireland. He is a finer dramatist than Campbell, and fitted of right into the company of the early Abbey Theatre; and the bent for drama shows in his poems; they are not only dramatic lyrics, but often have a dramatic framework, being written in sets, where each reacts on the others.

Many a poet is compelled by his own nature to brood on that of his fellow-man; but not every such poet broods affectionately. Colum's style is warm, human, friendly; and the friendliness shows in many of his subjects and comments. He

wrote with love of Casement, Griffith, Kuno Meyer and other notable people; but, besides these, of the unnoted country folk of his youth.— ROBERT FARREN, *The Course of Irish Verse in English*, 1947, pp. 98–104

Padraic Colum has been acknowledged as a master of the Irish faerie: the quaint and leprechaunish peasants have been celebrated by him in prose and verse. This is simply not true. His tales for children include fairy stories, but Colum is the vigorous, hard-headed spokesman of the true peasant, the recorder of the historic fate of Ireland; and even in the books for the young he has never talked down but has sought to hand down both the historic and mythic past. As poet and playwright and essayist—and now as novelist—he speaks the true spirit of his nation and has the versatility of a scholar-poet. Most important, he has written poems that would astonish those who know only the set anthology pieces—"The Plougher," "A Drover," and "An Old Woman of the Roads." Devin-Adair is the publisher of *The Collected Poems of Padraic Colum*: it is a proud book, and it ranks its begetter among the authentic poets of Ireland.— WILLIAM TURNER LEVY, "Padraic Colum, Poet," *LR*, Summer 1958, p. 493

To dismiss Colum's style as merely straightforward, accurate, or simple, as many critics have done, is to do the craftsmanship of the poetry a considerable disservice. The way Colum says things is very often beautiful and his poetic scenes and the characters as delightful as they are unassuming and familiar. His language is unpretentious and his verse forms are predominantly lyrical and rhyming with heavily accentuated iambs and tripping anapests, the sort of poems that on first reading tend to inspire song rather than thought. . . . ⟨T⟩here is no obscurantism for its own sake, no complicated syntax to unravel, few ingenious conceits to dazzle the mind, and a scarcity of literary allusions to provide grist for the scholarly mill. I suspect the forthrightness of the poet's style has been the principal cause of the dearth of literary criticism about his poetry, since the fashionable critics are now more explicative than descriptive. . . .

Colum thinks of himself as one of the few authentic national poets of Ireland because his upbringing is rural and Catholic, as opposed to the Protestant ascendency backgrounds of poets like Yeats, AE and Lady Gregory, whose links with the peasant people are at best studied and vicarious. Much of Colum's poetry retains its roots in the Catholic peasantry of the Irish Republic, dealing occasionally with the joys and aspirations of the people but far more with their sorrows, hopelessness and disintegration. Always, however, his people are uncomplicated and readily understandable and his language sparse and accurate.

Colum cannot be considered typical of any particular modern tradition. Hailed as a poet of the Irish Renaissance, his poems lacked the nationalistic didacticism which plagued other Irish poets, whose vision of things was colored by recollections of an unblemished past and the certainty of a utopian future. During the years following World War I, a period of realism, surrealism, Dadaism and naturalism, each with its own limitations on subject matter and emphasis on a particular variety of experiment, his poems bordered on the sentimental, and were more often about the beautiful, the remote and the wondrous than the ugly, the despairing and the hopeless. The present age is returning to the inner truths of symbolism and Plato's world of forms, while Colum, unlike his contemporaries, is perfectly at home in the world as it "appears," that is, presents itself to his senses. The tendency in modern poetry is to seek the truth behind what we see, to get a meaning of the world by interpreting the objects and events around us as symbols or indicators of the truth which lies behind and above. For Colum, however, the truth of things resides in the accurate perception of them. Things are as they appear, and misunderstanding or failing to grasp their essence can only be due to faulty perception. His poetry is designed to enhance perception by clear delineation and description.—ZACK BOWEN, *Padraic Colum*, 1970, pp. 25–27

Works

POETRY

With a true instinct Padraic Colum found a title which not only fitted the particular collection of poems to which it was given, but was also a proclamation of the author himself. The fresh tang of "wild earth" comes into literature again with these songs of a peasant lad who still carries in his memory the simple, strong odour of the soil on which he was reared. He does not look at nature with the somewhat sophisticated eyes of the city-bred poet, who at best must bring to the contemplation of natural beauty a mentality coloured by the literary and philosophical theories of his *milieu*. We have already had occasion to notice how beautifully the charm and the secrets of nature may be revealed to one who seeks them, equipped with the necessary gift of vision and sympathy. We may rejoice at times, when highly cultivated art and intuitive simplicity combine to give us poetry which satisfies our sense of natural and artificial perfection. We cheerfully grant the necessary licence to the poetic artificer, so long as he shows himself conscious of the peculiar, innate quality of his material. The poet is measured by the skill and congruity of his selection and elaboration. Padraic Colum made but the slightest claim upon our artistic tolerance. With a minimum of artistic liberty he produced the maximum effect, giving us the stark poetry of life as it is felt by those living close to the soil:

> Sunset and silence; a man; around him earth savage,
>   earth broken:
> Beside him two horses, a plough!

Such is the landscape in which his figures move. The poems are concerned only with these elementals, the plough, the land, the beasts of the field, and the human creatures who live for and by them. Colum excels in depicting the intimate relation of these primordial factors of civilisation, and he knows how to sum up existence, as it seems to men struggling daily in contact with primitive forces. The peasant speaks in such lines as:

> O! the smell of the beasts,
> The wet wind in the morn,
> And the proud and hard earth
> Never broken for corn.

If he allows himself to comment upon these pictures, he does so in terms as simple as they are profound:

> Slowly the darkness falls, the broken lands blend with
>   the savage;
> The brute-tamer stands by the brutes, a head's
>   breadth only above them.
> A head's breadth? Ay, but therein is hell's depth, and
>   the height up to heaven,
> And the thrones of the gods and their halls, their
>   chariots, purples and splendours.

There is a rugged strength in such poems of ploughers and sowers and herdsmen, admirably reflected in the hexameters just quoted. They are never marred by the obtrusion of merely literary effects. In all *Wild Earth* there is not an allusion which betrays the background of a literature other than that which one expects in the Irish countryside. The much-admired *Poor*

Scholar of the Forties supplies the only legitimate atmosphere of learning, with its pathetic reference to an essentially Irish tragedy. The author had doubtless personal memories to assist him in evoking that pitiable figure. There is a suggestion of autobiography in the verse:

> And I must walk this road that winds
> 'Twixt bog and bog, while east there lies
> A city with its men and books,
>   With treasures open to the wise,
> Heart-words from equals, comrade-looks;
> Down here they have but tale and song,
> They talked Repeal the whole night long.

Another aspect of this absence of literary allusion is the freedom of Colum's poetry from any suggestion of imitation. It is possible for a more keen than friendly critic to ascribe a model to a large number of poems written in Dublin within the past decade. There is, of course, a trace of over-emphasis in such a proceeding, which makes no allowance for the unconscious influences of our literary atmosphere, tending inevitably to lend an air of homogeneity to the work of the younger poets. Many have, it is true, deliberately echoed their elders, especially in their first books, but this evidence of a weakness common to all beginners must not be insisted upon too harshly. So far as Padraic Colum is concerned, he appears to have escaped completely even the suspicion of being a borrower. *Wild Earth* presents no analogies with anything written by his immediate predecessors. The young poet had neither Yeats's passion for the music of verse, nor the mystic vision of A. E. Unlike his contemporaries he does not oscillate between the two, being as far removed from the one as the other. The impression conveyed by his work approximates rather to that Douglas Hyde's *Songs of Connacht*. Not that Colum's Catholicism ever becomes articulate, as in Hyde's *Religious Songs*, or that he displays any of the dialectic energy of the *Love Songs*. His thought is as devoid of specific religious colour as his language is devoid of that Gaelic exuberance which Synge caught from the same sources as Hyde. What then, it may be asked, is left of the suggested resemblance between *Wild Earth* and Hyde's translations? Very little, it must be confessed, that is tangible. There is, however, an undoubted kinship of spirit between the poet of the Midlands and the poets of the West in *The Songs of Connacht*. Probably it is their common origin which unites them. They all sing the same song of peasant life, the emotions they render, the scenes they describe, belong to an identical rural civilisation. Writing of the peasantry from the inside, while unspoiled by urban sophistications, Colum responded to the deeper race tradition which still survived from the days when the Connacht poets were similarly inspired. He has brought once more the peasant mind into Anglo-Irish poetry, which is thus renewed at the stream from which our national traditions have sprung, for it is the country people who still preserve the Gaelic element in Irish life, the beliefs, the legends and the usages which give us a national identity. So long as he continues to cherish those impressions of early life, so long as he retains his original imprint, Padraic Colum will contribute an essential part to the growth of the literature created by the Revival. Fortunately he has not lost that eagerness of mind peculiar to the imaginatively young. He still can view things with a certain fresh, all-consuming curiosity which lends a specially naïve charm to his work. He is at his best when he is simple.—ERNEST BOYD, *Ireland's Literary Renaissance*, 1922, pp. 262–65

Commend me to Mr Colum among the Irish poets! He has the eye for externals, which do not with him lose their outline in a crepuscular reverie, blending a ghoulish dream-world with the archetypal actualities of nature, until we know not whether we be looking at moods or mountains! His is the mind, not of the mythologist, but of the folk-lorist; and if we were disposed to look for an explanation of this we might find it, I think, in his Catholic piety. His faith I am far from sharing; but I can recognize that it has kept his mind open to the actualities of life and nature in Ireland, an objectivity which has not been characteristic of Ireland's Protestant poets, with Mr Yeats at their head: for it is the Protestants who have filled Irish literature with an ambiguous twilight, peopled with phantom divinities and shadowy beings, which every Catholic knows perfectly well were driven once for all from the green fields of Erin before the uplifted crozier of St Patrick. Irish Catholicism has in fact always looked askance at the wonder world of Celtic mythology. In the early days of the Irish Literary Movement the evocation of the Gael's pre-Christian past had almost amounted to a threat to the organized religion of the country; the situation was saved, however, by the firm religiosity of the Catholic population, much as in Russia the anti-capitalistic Revolution was stayed by the self-interested conservatism of the peasant.—JOHN EGLINTON, "New Poems by Padraic Colum," *Dial*, Feb. 1928, p. 124

Padraic Colum champions the cause of peasant Ireland. The nationalism which informs his verse bears little resemblance to the nationalism given expresssion by Yeats, A. E., or the Rising poets. He is concerned neither with creating a national mythology from which his countrymen may draw spiritual strength nor with justifying Ireland's sacred cause of rebellion against the Gall. Ultimately, Colum's nationalism derives from the stuff of everyday existence, from the simple people and the homely properties of the Irish country scene. . . .

As early as 1913, in his introduction to the anthology, *Broadsheet Ballads*, Colum commented on the nature of the popular tradition of folk songs and ballads: "There is an idea that popular poetry is an impersonal thing, an emanation from the multitude, but I think this is an illusion. The multitude may change or may interpolate, may coarsen or may improve, but the song has been made by an individual." It is as just such a poet of the people that Colum regards himself. In his attempt to create a popular Irish epic, *The Story of Lowry Maen*, he assumes the role of a storyteller of old Ireland, stopping on his way to the fair to recite his tale in the house of an aristocrat. Similarly, in most of his poems he puts upon himself the robes of the popular bard; his songs and ballads are concerned with the problems of the country folk and, in an important sense, they also are addressed to an audience composed of country folk. Colum intended that his poems should be recited aloud and even sung—as indeed they are—by the people of the Irish countryside.

Colum's poetry, like much of his early drama, represents an attempt to achieve "expression of the national character" as he perceived it in the people of the countryside (*Poems*, p. v). His verse is crowded with what Strong terms the "common furniture" of life, or, more specifically, the common furniture of Irish peasant life—the quaint (one cannot avoid the word) characters, the homely proprieties of hearth and pasture. But his art embodies more than realistic detail, for Colum, more than any modern Irish poet writing in English, with the possible exception of Joseph Campbell, captures in his verse the underlying spiritual naïveté of the peasantry. In this respect, his portrayal of the Irish peasant is more accurate, more true to life, than either Yeats' portrayal or that of Padraic Pearse. Yeats employed folk materials to give substance to his occult vision and Pearse used them to support his own peculiar belief in mystical nationalism. Colum, on the other hand, is innocent of any extrinsic design; the attitudes and beliefs of the peasantry are presented in his verse for their own sake and are recorded in the form in which he found them among the people. Mary Sturgeon perceived this quality in the early work of both Colum and Campbell: "they are innocent of ulterior purpose and free from the least chill of philosophical questioning into origin or ends."

The nationalism which is given expression in Colum's verse provides a kind of antithesis for the nationalism in Yeats' verse. Yeats in his poems and plays argues the case for an aristocratic society in which men are ruled by the law of natural passion; and Yeats justifies his plea by appeal to traditional cultural and literary values that have found acceptance in western civilization from the age of Plato and Aristotle and by appeal to the esoteric symbolism of occult mysticism. Colum, on the other hand, defends the social ideal of the Irish peasantry—and by implication the social ideal of the Irish middle class—and glorifies the humble life of a people whose moral code centers on the suppression of natural passion. He rejects both traditional aristocratic values and the validity of mysticism—whether, as with Yeats, founded on occult tradition or, as in the case of Plunkett, on orthodox Christian tradition; to substantiate his eulogy of the peasantry Colum invokes the physical realities of everyday life. Yeats "discovered" Colum in 1904 and certainly Yeats' early, sentimental verse on peasant life—for example, "The Ballad of Moll Magee"—influenced the younger poet in the formulation of his artistic objectives. But Yeats and Colum soon came to the parting of the ways. Yeats fought for the survival of the Abbey Theatre; Colum dissociated himself from the Abbey and turned to Arthur Griffith and the zealous patriots who were to beleaguer the theater movement in the name of nationalism. In certain respects, the national ideal which finds expression in Colum's poetry fits too well Yeats' definition of "whiggery": a leveling mentality "That never looked out of the eye of a saint / Or out of a drunkard's eye." The image of passionless moderation is not inappropriate, for Colum seems to advocate the kind of moral values which Pearse condemned as incompatible with Christ's teachings—"Thou shalt not be extreme in anything—in wrongdoing lest thou be put in gaol, in rightdoing lest thou be deemed a saint"—and which the contemporary Irish novelist, Honor Tracy, ridicules by quoting this supposed fragment of an Irish sermon: "What we have to do, my dear brethren, is stay on the straight and narrow path between right and wrong."—RICHARD J. LOFTUS, "Padraic Colum: The Peasant Nation," *Nationalism in Modern Anglo-Irish Poetry*, 1964, pp. 165–97

DRAMA

Padraic Colum was the first of the peasant dramatists, in the strict sense of the word; he was, that is to say, the first to dramatise the realities of rural life in Ireland. Where Synge's fantastic intuition divined human prototypes, Colum's realistic insight revealed local peasant types, whose general significance is subordinate to the immediate purpose of the dramatist. Together they define the limits within which our folk-drama has developed, for none of the later playwrights has added anything to the tradition initiated by Padraic Colum and J. M. Synge. With rare exceptions, which will be noticed, their successors have failed to give personality to their work, contenting themselves with certain general formulae, whose elaboration leaves them as far from the restraint of Colum as from the flamboyancy of Synge. For, it is interesting to note, the former dramatist is the direct antithesis of the latter, nor has he been at all influenced by him, in spite of the disparity of their respective successes. Synge's fame and work made resistance difficult for all but the most original of his young contemporaries. But

Colum has remained, at the cost of popular recognition, faithful to the spirit of *Broken Soil*, whose almost simultaneous appearance with Synge's first play precluded any possibility of imitation. . . .

It would be misleading to leave the dramatic work of Padraic Colum without making clear his innocence of any avowedly didactic purpose. A brief analysis of his plays involves the use of phrases which are perhaps more convenient than accurate. *The Land* and *Thomas Muskerry* envisage certain phases of Irish life which constitute the "problems" of our sociologists, but the latter need not suspect him of any intention to anticipate their conclusions. The effort of the dramatist is not to propound or solve social questions, but is directed, as he says, "towards the creation of situations." "For character conceived as a psychological synthesis he has only a secondary concern." In thus defining the attitude of the playwright, Colum clearly demonstrates the character of his own work. The three plays that have been mentioned are primarily attempts to situate the Irish peasant in such circumstances as to bring out the essential drama of rural life. Coming from the Midlands, and viewing the world from the standpoint of the peasantry, he saw at once the naturally dramatic situations in which they revealed themselves most characteristically. These restrained and faithful pictures, from which every exaggerated or adventitious element is eliminated, have a quality which recalls Ibsen in their almost purely intellectual action. Colum even avoids the melodramatic *dénouements* which the author of *Hedda Gabler* did not disdain.

In this last respect, but in that only, the later peasant playwrights approach more closely to Ibsen. The majority, indeed, show so marked an affection for violent effects and purely external drama, that the local setting of their work seems fortuitous. The drama of Padraic Colum, on the other hand, is peculiarly Irish, and has its very basis in peasant conditions. One cannot imagine Conn Hourican, Murtagh Cosgar or Thomas Muskerry transplanted to another soil, their roots are too deep. Unlike so many of their successors on the stage of the National Theatre they could not develop just as well in London, Liverpool or New York. The greater part of our pseudo "peasant" drama is merely melodrama with an Irish accent. The situations are not inherent in, or peculiar to, our national life, but are adapted. They might serve equally as well to illustrate the tragedy of an English slum or the dramatic possibilities of popular politics in the United States. Even where the national and literary quality of the work done by his successors is beyond dispute, the achievement of Padraic Colum only gains by comparison. Without any predecessors of importance, he shares with Synge the right to be considered the most original of our folk-dramatists. W. B. Yeats has said that Synge wrote of the peasant "as he is to all the ages; of the folk-imagination as it has been shaped by centuries of life among fields or on fishing grounds." If it be admitted that, in this manner, Synge transcended the limits popularly ascribed to the peasant play, then, indeed, Padraic Colum is the first of our peasant playwrights. By confining himself to the realistic interpretation of everyday country life he gives us the complement of Synge's transmutations. Together their work completes, as it initiated, the dramatic realisation of peasant Ireland.—ERNEST BOYD, *Ireland's Literary Renaissance*, 1922, pp. 335–43

FICTION

I would not recommend this contemplative book ⟨The Flying Swans⟩ to the kind of reader who expects a novel to give him a roller-coaster ride, on which, once pinned down by the safety bar, he is swept breathless up dizzy heights and hurtled screaming down dizzier depths, until the vehicle deposits him, retching and staggering, on firm ground once more. This is rather the kind of book that one lays aside from time to time in order to daydream over one's own youth. Yet Ulick O'Rehill, the future sculptor, finally chooses reality and responsibility in preference to the daydreaming fecklessness of his father and thus rejects the man who has rejected his mother, his younger brother and himself.

In the long run, when this novel's characters and incidents have faded from the reader's mind, one abiding influence will remain with him—its style. Perhaps it would be more correct to call it a language rather than a style, that collective language of the first generation of the Irish literary revival. The most recent generation of Irish writers seem to have lost it completely. To them Gaelic is Gaelic, English is Oxford or Hollywood, and Irish English is a bastard dialect never spoken off the stage of the Abbey Theatre. As a result, their novels and plays are unreadable, their poems readable but not speakable.

But here, with scarce-diminished vigor, that sinewy style rides once more, giving—in narrative as well as dialogue—the old sense of a language reborn, of an English grafted on Gaelic, almost every phrase of which has been formed, not by pen or typewriter, but on the living lips of men. "Oisín in the wake of the Fianna" says the Gaelic proverb for survivors of a great generation. But Padraic Colum is an Oisín not yet fallen from his horse, an Oisín who still miraculously retains his youth and strength.—VIVIAN MERCIER, "Sinewy Style of the Irish Literary Revival," *Com*, July 19, 1957, pp. 404–5

Almost all of Colum's fiction grows out of its Irish milieu, and similarly most of his nonfiction is an elaboration on the country, its people and its customs. There have been excursions to Hawaii, France and America but the bulk of his work concerns his home. Because of this preoccupation he has become for many Americans the window on the Irish scene, the chronicler of its folklore and customs, a sort of literary tourist bureau. Though this role had its inception in his early poetry and plays, he has striven to maintain it through his novels, biographies and essays.

Just as his subject matter is predominantly Irish, his style can also be generally described as familiar and colloquial. His most characteristic stylistic trait is his abundant use of the present tense narration in fiction as well as nonfiction. This together with a first person narrator places him in the role of a storyteller sitting by a turf fire spinning out tales of things familiar to him and wondrous to his audience. This posture that Colum tries to maintain in his work is one he is well suited to. The particular criteria of excellence in evaluating Colum's work are not the normal currency of contemporary literary critics, because few other serious writers attempt what he is doing, and our appreciation of it has fallen into disrepair through disuse. . . .

As the patterns of Colum's prose become apparent we are able to see certain tendencies running throughout the material discussed in this chapter: First, his penchant for defining, describing, analyzing, and illuminating his country. Through the speech which he captures with such accuracy, through his vivid descriptions and through his lifelike characterization, the Ireland of the late nineteenth and twentieth centuries comes alive in his novels, biographies and essays. Relaxed familiarity coupled with humor and first person present tense narration make his style both distinctive and easy to read. This ease of comprehension tends, as in the case of his poetry, to belie the intricacy of structure and design in his novels and to underscore the portrait of the unassuming author in his essays.—ZACK BOWEN, *Padraic Colum*, 1970, pp. 90–121

IVY COMPTON-BURNETT

1884–1969

Ivy Compton-Burnett was born in Middlesex on June 5, 1884. From 1902 to 1907 she attended the University of London's Royal Holloway College. Her first novel, *Dolores* (1911), was quite unlike her subsequent books, and she came to dismiss it as juvenilia. Soon after its publication came a series of events that "smashed up my life," as she would later put it. First her father died; then both her brothers; and finally two sisters in a suicide pact. Compton-Burnett herself grew quite sick. Unable to write, she spent years of convalescence weaving tapestry chair seats.

Her turning point came in 1921 when she met and moved in with Margaret Jourdain, a leading expert and writer on English furniture. Jourdain encouraged and inspired Compton-Burnett, who produced the novel *Pastors and Masters* in 1925. This book set the pattern for those to come: it was an oblique, witty tale of family tension in an English country house, told with much dialogue and little description. Her next, *Brothers and Sisters* (1929), started a wave of critical and commercial success that crested with 1947's *Manservant and Maidservant*, her own favorite. *Mother and Son* won the James Tait Black Memorial Prize in 1957.

Compton-Burnett lived alone after Jourdain's death in 1951, traveling only to add to her prized collection of Alpine flowers. She received an honorary doctorate from the University of Leeds in 1960. In 1951 she received a CBE; in 1967, she was made a Dame Commander. She died in London on August 27, 1969.

Personal

The first time I saw Ivy Compton-Burnett was at a party given to watch the Oxford and Cambridge Boat-race from Chiswick Mall. The setting was appropriate, because this fixture always peculiarly evokes in the mind a sense of the late nineteenth century, and the 'varsity men' of that era, rather than the undergraduates and sporting events of today. In early or later life these are the people, with their womenfolk—one uses that word advisedly—who make up the population of the Compton-Burnett novels, most of which suggest in period the years not long before the turn of the century.

Miss Compton-Burnett herself was wearing a black tricorne for the Boat-race. She looked formidably severe. I think she was severe. She saw life in the relentless terms of Greek tragedy, its cruelties, ironies, hypocrisies—above all its passions—played out against a background of triviality and ennui. Later we met on two or three occasions, but I never knew her well, and always felt the sort of constraint experienced as a child talking to an older person, whom one suspected could never understand the complexities of one's own childish problems. This was absurd in a way, because we shared a lot of literary likes and dislikes (she wrote to me of Emily Brontë: 'Posterity has paid its debt to her too generously, and with too little understanding'), and we might be said to have 'got on' together very well.

I think the explanation of my sense of unease was no more and no less than what has been said; Ivy Compton-Burnett embodied in herself a quite unmodified pre-1914 personality, so that one was, in truth, meeting what one *had* encountered as a child. The particular interest and uniqueness of this is in relation to the immense individual revolutions and transformations that must, in fact, have taken place within herself, all without in the smallest degree affecting the way in which she faced the world. No writer was ever so completely of her books, and her books of her.—ANTHONY POWELL, "Ivy Compton-Burnett," *Spec*, Sept. 6, 1969, p. 304

In her life, Dame Ivy liked pleasantness in those about her. 'Nothing goes deeper than manners', she wrote in her last book, 'They are involved with the whole of life. It is they that

give rise to it and come to depend on it. We should all remember it!' Good manner were expected—and exacted—and good looks were appreciated in her guests.

> 'It doesn't follow that people have personality because they are plain.'
> 'Or that they haven't because they are good-looking.'
> *(Brothers and Sisters)*

She was gracious in welcoming new-comers brought to visit her by established friends. They were expected to contribute to general conversation and not to address each other instead of their hostess. After her two hip operations, she had to forego the luncheons *à quatre* and the Saturday Tea parties because her 'Helps' found them too much: life followed art tragically in her domestic affairs at the end. But many visitors will remember Tea—the operative meal in so many of the novels—at the dining-room table in later years when she liked them to make a hearty meal. Gifts of chocolates and flowers (if not chrysanthemums) were appreciated, and she saw to it that flowers were put in water at once or small plants dug into the bed of soil that ran along the top of her stone balcony.

Dame Ivy's intense interest in trivialities sometimes surprised—even shocked—her visitors; friends appreciated it for one of the paradoxes of her personality as a woman and a writer.

Dame Ivy had no author's vanity in the usual sense. If it was very difficult to get her to talk about her methods of work or to discuss literary influences she had a proper pride in the recognition she received in later years and was always ready to discuss the matter of sales.

She did not suffer fools or bores gladly, but was tirelessly indulgent to children and ready with generous sympathy to friends in trouble. *Ventosa* may have seemed an apt description of a feature immobilized in some photograph, but in real life any first impression of up-tightness was quickly dispelled by Dame Ivy's look of lively interest, a 'twinkle in the eye' and an easy, if not an expansive, smile at the absurdity of things. Only when a young reporter sent to interview her enquired her age did the *ventosa* snap close like a sea-anemone about his impertinence.—R. GLYNN GRYLLS, *I. Compton-Burnett*, 1971, pp. 26–27

One might think from her books that Ivy was a good conversationalist. She could not be called that. She was more a good listener. She was hospitable, she loved her tea parties with her friends all talking round her, but she herself was 'a sealed fountain'—the phrase is Edward Gosse's—interested, courteous, putting in her word, the still centre. Sometimes we were five or six round her table at tea, and one or two led the talk and kept it going at a fairly cracking pace, with the rest of us flinging in a word now and then, and Ivy often doing no more than that, though she always followed every word with close attention. She loved vivacious talk. She once told me how she loved to hear Rose Macaulay and Ernest Thesiger together, when Rose 'seemed to bubble over with high spirits'. . . .

The two women, Ivy and Margaret Jourdain, were as close in spirit, as mutually sympathetic, and as devoted, each to the other, as two friends could be. To a third person they were unlike in every way. Ivy was small and spare, and had a rather tight, neat appearance. She always wore long, black dresses with a white edging at the neck, and these black clothes seemed not to change, summer or winter. In very cold weather she wore little velvet jackets—there was a pink velvet one I liked especially. Such things as cardigans or sweaters were not in her world.

Margaret was heavier in build, and her clothes, which were very good and in a style of her own period—I am not quite certain which—had a draped look. I remember seeing her once in the Library of the Victoria and Albert Museum. She rustled and flowed between the bookshelves, a harmony of soft pinks and greys and E flat, so that heads were turned.

In manner, too, they were quite different. Ivy had a strict, almost schoolmistressy manner, but Margaret was languorous-seeming, with a charming graciousness. Ivy's voice was weak, Margaret's had a good, full tone; she spoke with a cultured drawl that was very attractive.

Both had their hair folded away in a band. Ivy's was always tucked in neatly, but Margaret's hair, which was fairer, was less disciplined and had a look of having been pushed under the band here and there in a haphazard fashion. I always disliked Ivy's head-band. One had no idea as to her brow—whether it was wide or high or low, because the band stayed firmly just above her eyebrows.

Margaret had a kindness of manner that Ivy seemed to lack. She was certainly not without kindness, but her wall of reserve was formidable, her dignity impregnable—interviewers always spoke of 'her iron dignity'. Her mask of strictness had a subduing rather than an encouraging effect. She could be awesome, many felt awe in her presence and said so. I felt a certain coldness in those early years; she had beautiful manners but she could correct one sharply and Margaret, who had an altogether warmer manner, would rush in quickly with some soothing remark. Perhaps Ivy thought I should have the wits to counter a rebuke, but I never had any wits, alas, in Ivy's presence. When I first knew her I had to struggle against an overmastering shyness. I felt at ease with Margaret always, hardly ever with Ivy.

Between the typing of *Manservant and Maidservant* and the typing of her next novel *Two Worlds and their Ways*, I was working fairly regularly for Margaret and I was often at the flat for tea. In those days tea at Braemar Mansions was something of an ordeal and different in every way from the tea-parties I so much enjoyed later. I remember very well my first tea there, and my extreme nervousness.

The flat was a large one, and one followed the maid down a fairly long passage to the door of the sitting-room. One was announced and always most graciously received.

This room which I came to know so well, was 'large and light and chill, and furnished with few and stately things . . . good to look at, less good to live in'. I quote from *Manservant and Maidservant*. One wall was taken up with two large French windows, floor to ceiling high and opening on to the balcony. This balcony was Ivy's joy, it extended along two walls of the flat and one could walk on to it from the bedrooms or kitchen as well as from the sitting-room. The balcony railing held a trough and this was Ivy's garden, and always gay with flowers from spring to autumn. On this first visit there were petunias in bloom. I thought they were flowers that needed less water than most flowers, and said so. Ivy corrected me. They had to be watered twice a day. Later I became more involved with Ivy's garden, but on this first day I was more interested in the room and its furniture.

There was a beautiful eighteenth-century bookcase on the left of the door. I saw in it a set of Jane Austen, and a set of Shakespeare, books by Fielding and Sterne, the *Dialogues* of Plato, Plato's *Republic* and a volume of Sophocles. I always regret that I never talked to Ivy about Plato. As a student I had to read the *Dialogues* and the *Republic* and I still have copies of my favourites—the *Phaedo* and the *Symposium*. I had to read them in Jowett's translation. Ivy, of course, had studied them in the original. I was a reader, she was a scholar and I think I had an inferiority complex. Ivy loved Jane Austen—she put *Pride and Prejudice* first, but I preferred *Emma*. I liked Henry James, Ivy had read one or two of his books and had no great liking for him. He was not one of her authors.

One expected more books, but really there were very few. Later, however, as Ivy became better-known, especially among contemporary novelists, there were always the newly-published books of friends lying about. Ivy would pick up the book and say: 'So-and-So has sent me his latest novel. Have you read it?' There were always some on a table in the hall, and on the table in the sitting-room.

The fireplace was opposite the door and there was a small, and very beautiful little bureau, of the Davenport kind, on the right of the fireplace. This was Ivy's desk, and I imagined her sitting there writing her novels until she told me she always wrote her books 'sitting in one or other of the two armchairs', and never sitting at the desk. These armchairs were on each side of the fireplace, and the sofa between them formed a set, and the three pieces were covered with the same material which for many years, certainly during the last years of her life, was black. Beautiful period chairs, two or three of them Hepplewhite, stood against the wall, and there were Hepplewhite chairs in the dining-room. The curtains at the huge windows were of rose-coloured silk; they were very old, worn and even torn in places. Later, these were changed. A table stood between the two windows, and this was laid for tea.

We sat and talked before the maid brought in the tea-pot. I admired the fireplace which I could see, from the urn and the scrolls, was Adam. Margaret said they had it in the flat at Linden Gardens and had decided to bring it with them.

'We wished we had left it,' Ivy said. 'They had to knock the wall down, almost, there, to bring it here, and then almost knock the wall down to install it here and remove the other one. It was an expensive business.'

It was a collector's room, a room one could talk about. The two small, elegant fire screens on their tall stands which stood against the wall facing the window, an armed Hepplewhite chair between them, were later to appear in more than one photograph of Ivy. There was only one picture in the room, a rare Japanese mirror painting in an exquisite blue. Margaret was later to write on these paintings.

When the maid put the tea-pot and hot water on the table

Ivy pulled a chair out for me, and I looked at it for a moment with interest. By now Margaret had seen me looking at this and that and was pleasantly ready to answer my questions. So I said: 'I saw a chair just like this in the V. and A. Museum the other day.' It was a very beautiful chair. Margaret nodded, and told me it was a copy, but an old copy. The chair I had seen was Elizabethan, so I sat down cautiously.

The tea table had an unusual appearance. There were two loaves of bread, one brown, one white, a dish of butter, a bowl with lettuce in it, a dish with a cucumber on it and there was a homemade cream cheese. In front of Margaret's plate was a small plate with two or three oatmeal biscuits—these were for her. I wished I had them in front of me. But Ivy had other plans for me.

'I hope you like bread and butter,' she said, as she cut the loaf. 'There is no cake. Will you have brown or white?'

Ivy put a slice of brown on my plate. Then she cut a good inch of cucumber and put that on my plate, took up a handful of lettuce, shook a quantity of water over the Persian rug, and put that on my plate.

'Take some cream cheese,' she commanded. 'There, in front of you.'

All resistance gone, I did as I was told. I was kept very busy with my lettuce and cucumber and cream cheese and bread and butter, and was rather slow. Ivy, on the other hand, managed it all with brisk efficiency and obvious relish, shredding her cucumber finely, breaking up her lettuce, spreading cheese over her slice of bread, helping us to tea, keeping the conversation going and popping more cucumber or lettuce on one's plate if one didn't watch out.

Margaret took no part in these antics. She watched us with her lazy smile, crumbling her oatmeal biscuit while we ate our cucumber.

'Have some more cucumber?' Ivy said.

'No thank-you very much . . . it was delicious.'

'Ivy eats cucumbers as soon as they appear in the shops,' Margaret said.

'They have a very short season, really,' Ivy said.

I asked if she had always liked them, and Ivy said yes, always.

'And meringues,' Margaret said. 'The nice sticky kind.'

'Oh, you can't get them now,' Ivy said.

Tea at Braemar Mansions was a long drawn-out meal. It changed with the years, more drawn-out, I think never under two hours—and much less of a meal—the usual tea food, cake, toast (Ivy loved toast), but one was allowed a biscuit if one liked. I can't say just when Ivy gave up the lettuce and cheese and cucumber teas, but suddenly, to my huge relief, they were of the past. And the scene for tea shifted from the sitting-room to the dining-room.

When I look back to that time, when Ivy sliced up her cucumbers and enjoyed her lettuce and cream cheese, while Margaret looked on with her delightful, lazy smile, I am sure it was a time when Ivy was happiest.—CECILY GREIG, *Ivy Compton-Burnett: A Memoir*, 1972, pp. 27–35

General

Miss Compton-Burnett has freed herself from all irrelevances in order to write the pure novel. And like Miss Austen she has a dislike for merely descriptive writing, which she uses with even greater economy. The village which is to be the scene of action is undescribed and, except for Moreton Edge in *Brothers and Sisters*, is not even named. Characters are often tersely but completely described, in terms which do not remain in the

memory, and it is necessary to turn back if we wish to remind ourselves of their appearance. . . .

Dialogue, to which in *Emma* Jane Austen had begun to give a far more important place, is the staple of this writer's work. It is a dialogue of a power and brilliance unmatched in English prose fiction. In her early and immature book, *Dolores*, the machine creaked audibly at times, but already functioned with precision. The style of that book is crude, bare and rather alarming. It is not like real English: it is like the language of translation. It reminds one of English translations of Russian novels and of Greek tragedy, and one may conjecture that both of them had formed an important part of her reading. Such a style is uneuphonious and harsh, but conscientiously renders a meaning— and that is what, like a translator, Miss Compton-Burnett already did, with a remarkable exactitude.

This ungainly, but precise language was later evolved into a dialogue, more dramatic than narrative, which, whether in longer speeches, or in the nearest equivalent in English to Greek tragic stichomythia, is an unrealistic but extraordinarily intense vehicle for the characters' thoughts and emotions, and enables their creator to differentiate them sharply, and, whenever she wishes, to condemn them out of their own mouths. Its nearness to or remoteness from ordinary spoken language will vary from place to place. There is no single formula that will cover it, and the author has indicated that no kind of 'figure in the carpet' is to be sought: 'it is simply the result of an effort to give the impression I want to give'.

'The key', says one critic, 'is the realization that her characters speak precisely as they are thinking.' This key will not unlock more than a part of her work: part of the utterances of her good characters, and the utterances of exceptionally simple or straightforward characters.

For she excels particularly at the revelation of insincerity on all its levels: from that of characters who tell flat lies, to that of characters who have deceived themselves into believing what they say. In between are characters such as Dominic Spong, who are more than half-aware and are wholly tolerant of their own smarminess and their own insincere ways of talking: 'if I may approach so great a man upon a comparatively flimsy subject.'

Her idiom sometimes approximates to what one might actually say if one were in the character's skin and situation, but also to what one might think and conceal; to what one might think of saying and bite back; to what one might afterwards wish one had said; to what one would like other people to think; and to what one would like to think oneself. It is unlikely that these alternatives are exclusive.—ROBERT LIDDELL, "The Novels of I. Compton-Burnett," *A Treatise on the Novel*, 1947, pp. 148–50

Miss Compton-Burnett is, in fact, about as fastidious and detached as a writer can become and continue to set pen to paper—her dialogue, lively and witty as it is, gives the effect of having been delicately unwound, like a live nerve, from the lips of her troubled speakers, and I am assuming that it isn't rapped out on a typewriter—and it is probably no accident that the inhabitants of the big, cold houses and wet countryside of her novels are invariably more suspicious of praise than of blame.

. . . ⟨Of⟩ all living writers Miss Compton-Burnett makes, I should think, the least concession to contemporary taste. She is neither obscure nor naturalistic. Her characters do not talk as real people talk, in starts and grunts and groans; they bubble up like never-failing springs. There are no streams of consciousness, only streams of conversation. Quietly, but ever so firmly, Miss Compton-Burnett hints that Joyce and Proust and Hemingway are all very well in their place but that there are hundreds of other ways to write a novel, and that the method of Jane Austen is, with certain remarkable modifications, good enough for her.—BRENDAN GILL, "Ivy Compton-Burnett and the Gift of Gab," NY, June 19, 1948, pp. 84–86

Miss Ivy Compton-Burnett is the most original novelist now writing in English. Her novels are all alike but they are unlike anyone else's in method or matter; yet she remains traditional and without the taint of experimental conceit. One can take her simply as a comfort, an exponent of the comedy of manners, very much in the fashion of Jane Austen, working upon a small corner of late Victorian family life. She can be regarded as an artificial and hard-headed writer like Congreve or Firbank. If we begin by laughing at the wit and devastations of her stylised dialogue, we are likely to end by saying that it is not stylised at all, but is the real speech fitted to the recognisable mind of a few isolated upper-class families of the period. At a certain point of decadence, groups of people acquire the skill and habit of speaking their own epitaphs ("Living? We leave that to our tongues"), cremating their own experience and keeping it in elegant, funerary urns. Miss Compton-Burnett's people chatter like the dead in their graves. Her novels are elegies written in the churchyard or mausoleum of family life.

. . . ⟨I⟩t is not as silly as it might sound to compare her with the revolutionary in Mr. Hemingway. Both novelists rely on speech rather than narrative; both depend on characters which are anonymous and little described; both remove a good deal of scenery and interpretation from their stories; but whereas Mr. Hemingway sought the lowest common denominator in the dumb ox whose moral and emotional development is well below the technical knowingness of his own acts, Miss Compton-Burnett has created a number of instructed and even agreeable vipers whose moral self-consciousness is equal to every crime or folly they may have fallen into. For creatures who at some time in their lives have committed incest, adultery, murder, suicide, who have tyrannised without mercy, who have indulged to the limit "the forgeries of jealousy" and the inexhaustible suction of possessive love, they are preposterous in self-knowledge and deadly in ironical sting:

> Experience has done something for us but it has destroyed our natural feeling and now we have to fabricate it—the dying are judges of the real thing.

They please because they share our universal human stupidity and are muddled and insincere in the acts of their lives; they startle us, because of the effrontery with which they ignore their crimes and the stoicism with which they catalogue the consequences in epigrams which—they well know—have been distilled out of pain, tears, even blood. Such a ruthlessness is Elizabethan; it is made tolerable by a sociable if iron mirth, in which monster and victim recognise that there is a difference between our terrible demands and the fancy dresses we necessarily put on them. . . .

Some readers of Miss Compton-Burnett have found her novels flat and monotonous and think it difficult to distinguish one character from another. There is a continuous demand on the attention of the reader who becomes exhausted by the drill of epigram and paradox. The difficulty with the characters is largely due to the fact that her novels are very much alike. There is the vague country house, the family asylum, generally ruled over by an elderly tyrant, male or female; there are the victims, there is a brilliant chorus of servants and there is cross-talk from precocious children; all speak on the same high sentments level—a good joke in itself—and there is the inevitable, appalling revelation of what, for the sake of appearances, has been left to fester beneath for years. Yet, as Mr. Liddell shows, within this repeated pattern, the variations of character are really rich for the patient reader. There is more than one kind of tyrant for this moralist who, if she is horrified by the lust for power, is equally shocked by the insincerities of those who have been forced in some way, albeit unjustly, to compound with it or evade it. It is no commendation of the meek that they inherit the earth.—V. S. PRITCHETT, "Miss Compton-Burnett," NSN, March 5, 1955, p. 328

It is more than thirty years since Miss Compton-Burnett published her first novel and revealed to the world her brilliant and peculiar talent. If my memory serves the revelation was gradual. No prominent critic trumpeted his 'discovery' of her. There was no dizzy succession of reprints. Her renown spread in intimate, fastidious circles as each reader sought to communicate and share his delight. I who lived (and live) rather far from fastidious circles was not drawn into the almost secret society of her admirers until the publication of *Brothers and Sisters* in 1929. Since then I have remained steadfastly devoted, but because of the impact of first love *Brothers and Sisters* has for me a unique eminence and I tend to regard it as quintessential of her art. Not that there has been any great change in her matter or manner. She has established her own enclosed garden in which in due season her flowers unfold, each perfectly true to type and almost identical. I have never got on with Professor Tolkien's 'Hobbits.' Those who do, I presume, enjoy something of the same experience as the readers of Miss Compton-Burnett, the entry into a timeless Wonderland directed by its own interior logic, not distorting, because not reflecting, the material world.

Miss Compton-Burnett's readers have now, I think, greatly multiplied. I wonder whom they comprise. Her fellow-writers certainly, for her technical skill is masterly. In the Thirties a number of English novelists, reacting perhaps against the vogue for Proust, sought to tell their stories as much as possible in dialogue. Mr. Henry Green is one of the most notable of these but he quite often allows himself the luxury of rich and poetic descriptive passages. Miss Compton-Burnett austerely restricts herself to the minimum of bare stage directions. She is the least sensuous of writers. There is no flavour of food or wine, no scene-painting of landscape or architecture, no costume, no visual image even of the characters; ages are stated; height, bulk, strength or infirmity gently suggested; sometimes a moustache or a beard is mentioned, but there is never anything approaching a portrait.—EVELYN WAUGH, "Op. XV," *Spec*, Aug. 16, 1957, p. 223

In a sense it can be said that Miss Compton-Burnett is more successful in handling Greek themes in a modern social context than T. S. Eliot in *The Family Reunion* (which is more similar to Miss Compton-Burnett's novels than has ever been observed), for she does not mix her levels of probability and keeps within the stylistic convention she sets herself. On the other hand, Eliot allows himself the assistance of choruses and of breaks into lyrical utterance which comment on and give extra depth of meaning to the action.

Miss Compton-Burnett's art, making use of no such devices, and at the same time denying herself the novelist's privilege of commenting in his own person on the significance of the action, is craftsmanlike but limited in scope. We admire the skill; we are astonished at the wit; we wonder at the imagination that can contrive such themes in such settings; but (dare it be admitted?) with the sixteenth novel in the same style and with the same rigid limitation of scope we get a little weary. At least I for one find myself at times wishing that somebody would thow a stone into this perfect glass-house and let in some air.—DAVID DAICHES "Amid Edwardians, a Greek Curse," *NYTBR*, Jan. 31, 1960, p. 5

She is interested in the pains of dependence and the lust for power, and on the deadly hurts which, never renouncing the most frigid conventions of politeness, the members of a large ingrown family can inflict on each other. The younger members of the family depend upon and resent their elders. Either the father or the mother is usually a tyrant, and the parent who is not a tyrant is usually a weakling or a fool. The characters exist to torment, to dominate, or to undermine each other; the obvious real-life solution of escaping from each other is ruled out, because nobody would dream of working for a living. The tension often leads to some central episode of crime or wickedness: the poisoning of a mother by her son, the exposure of an invalid to the night air so that she dies, or at the very least the breaking of a heart and the crushing of a will. But obvious consequences are, at least for a time, suspended; the son announces at table he has poisoned his mother, the remark is civilly ignored as evidence of hysteria; though perhaps everyone secretly believes him. The simplest way of describing Miss Compton-Burnett's tales is as Victorian thrillers, such as might have been invented by Miss Braddon, presented with a comic artifice that might have appealed to George Meredith. Comparisons that have been made with a much greater novelist, Jane Austen, seem to me quite off the mark. Jane Austen's world is one in which the soul can breathe, and, in its miniature range, it gives one a Shakespearean sense of life's gravity, order, and fullness. Miss Compton-Burnett's world is not sane and rich in that sense; it is a narrow, enclosed, obsessed world and though its flavour is very distinctive, a little of it is enough at a time. One cannot read two Compton-Burnett novels in succession, for her world is one of the imagination, a powerful but narrow allegory of hell in which one breathes a little more freely when she turns from the world of the totally lost, the adult members of the family, to the conversation of the servants and the children.—G. S. FRASER, "Looking Back and Forward in the 1940s," *The Modern Writer and His World*, 1965, pp. 151–52

The Compton-Burnett novels deal with a form of life that has largely, if not entirely disappeared, though I suspect that even to this day pockets of something very similar could be found; perhaps not so much in the country, where the novels tend to be located, as in residential suburbs and seaside towns. As with all good writers, a fair amount of nonsense has been written about her subject matter, so that one hesitates to generalise for fear of adding to it, especially in these days when so many people are obsessed with the subject of 'class'.

However, let me risk suggesting that, between a still lively aristocracy merging effortlessly into an enormously proliferated middle-class, both keenly aware of what is going on round them, large gloomy moderately rich families in largish, though not immense, houses in the country, going as a matter of course to Oxford or Cambridge, interested in acquiring property or money, yet lacking almost all contact with an outer world, living in a state of almost hysterically inward-looking intensity, have become pretty rare. If we add to that the Compton-Burnett conditions that such families take little or no interest in sport, and none of the sons enter the army or navy, the field is again narrowed within the terms of reference.

This is the usual Compton-Burnett setup, and certainly it had once a being. My reason for thinking it not wholly extinct is partly on account of the vitality of the novels themselves—if people were ever like this, there must be people always like this;

partly because one will suddenly be confronted—in a railway carriage, for example—with a great burst of overheard Compton-Burnett dialogue. However, whether or not they remain in any appreciable number, such persons form the core of the novels as they are, a social category accepted without question by the author. The men have a classical education, the women a good knowledge of standard poets. It is a 'cultivated' society, but not, one would say, an 'intellectual' one in anything like the contemporary sense. Professional writers play only a small part, artists none at all, though the children draw and paint.

The matter of 'class' is touched on here chiefly because it is almost always made such a feature by Compton-Burnett reviewers. In fact, she is not a novelist greatly concerned with class differences and nuances, as was, for example, Proust, or even Dickens. All novels must be written from a given point of view. The Compton-Burnett novels concentrate minimally on an aspect that is usually allowed undue prominence in their criticism. They are primarily concerned with human passions, and the ruthless manner in which these are usually satisfied. For an investigation of that sort, an accepted routine of manners must always be a great convenience to any novelist.—ANTHONY POWELL, "Ivy Compton-Burnett," *Spec*, Sept. 6, 1969, p. 304

The dominant theme in Dame Ivy's novels is vanity: the demand for attention, whether admiration or pity, and this is served by the exercise of power, for power is only important when it is acknowledged and self-esteem thereby satisfied. Power may stem from authority or fame; sometimes from sex, that is, as the result of a personal attraction which holds another in thrall, as with the young second wives that widowers tend, unsuitably, to marry to bolster their vanity, like Duncan Edgeworth in *A House and its Head* and Miles Mowbray in *A Father and his Fate*.

The sexual act itself is treated as unimportant, except for what leads up to it and what follows from it. There may be momentous consequences from a moment's indiscretion (Dame Ivy's births often seem to result from instant and immaculate conception), as in *A Heritage and its History* where Simon has to lose his right to the property which he loves and would serve well, because of an heir who is really his own child, and the cousins who are in love and cannot marry because they find they share a father. Rhoda, the grandmother, comments: 'It has been so much to follow from so little.' . . .

But Dame Ivy recognizes the tragedy attendant on power: the tyrant forfeits the affection of those about him by accepting the responsibility his power brings and its corruption of him. Those who opt out may show a certain charm at first but this wears thin when they refuse the opportunity to play their part in the world, like the younger brothers, Hugo in *The Mighty and Their Fall*, and Dudley in *A Family and a Fortune*.

The exercise of power is shown at its most direct in the bullying of families by their rulers (fathers and mothers), who submit them to excessive demands of affection and submission, and inflict unnecessary economies on the household. . . .

Most important in its relation to power is money. Dame Ivy is fascinated by the influence exerted by the sudden acquisition of money: the way it corrupts the recipient and those about him. 'Riches are a test of character and I am exposed,' says Dudley in *A Family and a Fortune*, the novel based most fully on the subject. . . .

Dame Ivy had complete understanding of the vanity of the artist. In *A God and His Gifts*, Hereward Egerton, the bestselling novelist, does not want his son, Merton, to follow in his footsteps for fear he might overtake him, and on his side Merton despises his father's success and wants to devote himself to 'serious' work. In *Daughters and Sons*, this theme is more deeply explored with the father, John Ponsonby's, obsessive jealousy of his daughter, France's, success.

She tinctures with pity her understanding of the scholar whose passionate desire to bring a book to birth leads him to steal one from the bedside of his dying friend, as in *Pastors and Masters* where Nicholas Herrick succumbs to the temptation.—R. GLYNN GRYLLS, *I. Compton-Burnett*, 1971, pp. 7–15

Works

With each novel, Miss Compton-Burnett adds to her gallery. Figures she has already, in another novel, created, she is content—and content with deliberation—to rename and to put, in *Parents and Children*, to a this time purely formalized use. For the Cranmer family (with the exception of Faith, who is new), for the three mysterious Marlowes and for the three eldest of the nine Sullivans, Miss Compton-Burnett seems to rely, and rightly, on our progressive acquaintanceship with one kind of person—what one might call the illustrative rather than the functional character. In *Parents and Children*, these play subsidiary parts. In *Parents and Children* the high light falls on, and genius is evident in, the younger Sullivan children and their immediate world. Especially James and Nevill. I know no children like James and Nevill; there may be no children like James and Nevill—in fact, the point of this author's genius is that it puts out creatures to which it might defy life to approximate. James and Nevill, of a beauty divorced from sentiment, *are*, in *Parents and Children*—one cannot question them; they are more living than life. There are also Honor, Gavin, the tearful, complex, articulate Isabel, and Venice—this last more lightly, though as surely, touched in. To say that this book depicts the repercussion of grown-up crisis on children would be incorrect. The children's intensive, moment-to-moment living is for each a solitary crisis, that each maintains: grown-up sense of crisis, grown-up drama do no more than splinter upon these diamond rocks. It is the strength of Lady Sullivan, the strength of Miss Mitford, the strength of Hatton that they recognize the children's inviolability.

In this novel, as in the others, relationships remain static. The dialogue, in less than half of a phrase, in the click of a camera-shutter, shifts from place to place. The careless reader, for instance, must look back twice to discover at which point the departing Fulbert's carriage drives off. Scenes, on the other hand, are played out without mercy, to an attentuation felt by each of the characters. Most notably, the scene of Fulbert's departure. 'Well, it cannot go on much longer, boys,' Fulbert says to his elder sons, as they all stand in the hall. 'If there were any reason why it should stop,' says Graham, 'surely it would have operated by now.' Luce says: 'The train will become due.' The train is the only artificial interference, by Time.

Is this a book for now? Decidedly, yes. And for the 'now' not only of already avowed readers of Miss Compton-Burnett. *Parents and Children*, coming at this juncture, is a book with which new readers might well begin. Miss Compton-Burnett, as ever, makes a few concessions; she has not, like some of our writers, been scared or moralized into attempts to converge on the 'real' in life. But possibly, life has converged on her. Elizabethan implacability, tonic plainness of speaking, are not so strange to us as they were. This is a time for *hard* writers—and here is one.—ELIZABETH BOWEN, "Ivy Compton-Burnett: I" (1941), *Collected Impressions*, 1950, pp. 84–85

As a title, *Elders and Betters* is ironical: everyone in this novel is the same age, and nobody is admirable. In a Victorian novel, the characters fail to impose upon the reader; here, they fail to impose upon each other. The revolution, foreseeable, long overdue, has arrived—without disturbing a single impalpable cup on the impalpable drawing-room mantelpiece. It has been succeeded by this timeless anarchy, in which meals are served and eaten, visits paid, engagements to marry contracted and broken off. Everything that was due to happen in the world the Victorians posited, and condoned, has happened—but, apparently, there is still more to come: such worlds are not easily finished with, and Miss Compton-Burnett may not see the finish herself. For one thing, that disrespect for all other people underlying Victorian manners (as Victorians showed them) has not yet come to the end of its free say, and fear has not yet revenged itself to the full. The passive characters, almost all young men, marvel at the others, but not much or for long; they return to marvelling at themselves. Only the callous or those who recuperate quickly can survive, but in *Elders and Betters* everyone does survive—except Aunt Jessica, who commits suicide after the scene with Anna. In this we are true to the masters; in the Victorian novel people successfully die of their own death-wishes (as Aunt Sukey dies in *Elders and Betters*), but nobody ever dies of an indignity.

Miss Compton-Burnett shows, in *Elders and Betters*, that she can carry weight without losing height. She has been becoming, with each novel, less abstract, more nearly possible to enclose in the human fold. *Elders and Betters* is, compared, for instance, with *Brothers and Sisters*, *terre à terre*; but with that I greet a solid gain in effect. The more she masters what I have called her logic, the more material she can use. Her technique for melodrama has been by degrees perfected, and is now quite superb: I know nothing to equal Chapter X of this book—the duel in Aunt Sukey's death-chamber, after Aunt Sukey's death. Only second to this is the lunch-party, at which two families voice their disgust at old Mr. Calderon's engagement to Florence, the governess's young niece. There is an advance, too (again, a logical one), in the articulateness of employed persons: nothing protects the Donnes against Cook and Ethel, with whom even Anna is placatory. The importance of money has not budged, but dependence is now felt by the monied side—also, there is, with regard to employed persons, either a weakening or a belated dawn of grace. In one of the earlier novels, it seemed consistent that a child of the house should laugh every time the governess eats; in *Elders and Betters*, a child suffers because he has left a governess out in the dusk and rain. And religion, the worship in the rock garden, for the first time enters the scene.

The post-Victorian novel, in Miss Compton-Burnett's hands, keeps its course parallel with our modern experience, on which it offers from time to time, a not irrelevant comment in its own language. To the authority of the old, relentless tradition, it has added an authority of its own.—ELIZABETH BOWEN, "Ivy Compton-Burnett: II" (1944), *Collected Impressions*, 1950, pp. 89–91

Miss Compton-Burnett is immensely unfair to most other contemporary British novelists. Using the same traditional material that so many of them use (hearts of oak and heads to match) she turns out a notably superior work of art for export. Her apparently effortless skill shows them up. They seem to be breathing too hard by comparison. The unfairness of it all is apparent in this sparkling novel ⟨*Bullivant and the Lambs*⟩ about a seedy little coterie of county gentry living in the numbing, secure twilight of Queen Victoria's reign.

It is her talent as a novelist to make the almost inanimate more than articulate. In less adroit hands her story of the Lamb family and Bullivant, their knowing, Stanley-Baldwinish butler, might be as spectacularly dull as the bleak outline of their lives. Nothing much ever happens to them; nothing much ever will. Their main and characteristic concern is with droughts and the state of the fire on the hearth—a European preoccupation that must go back in a straight line, without alleviation, to quite primitive times.

Occasionally, someone gets the constructive idea that the father, Horace Lamb, who is for long stretches nothing but a dreary morass of rectitude, should be violently abolished. Occasionally, his sardonically dependent (if not dependable) cousin Mortimer considers running away with Charlotte, Horace's not-quite-long-enough-suffering wife. Occasionally, there seems a chance that the wonderfully drawn and tragically perceptive children may have a shot at the true capture, instead of only the desperate pursuit of happiness.

In the end, though, they generally get nowhere. And they get there at a measurelessly sedate pace, a pace set by the slow beat of hearts unfulfilled. The main trouble seems to be that no one has finally the courage of appropriately felonious convictions.

Yet Miss Compton-Burnett gives their existence point and depth and luster. She does that by concentrating on the drama that lies in commonplace, everyday things. Her story is told in flowing dialogue uncluttered with descriptive passages or sage reflections. It is superb dialogue, far better than the kind that human beings really talk. The prose of naturalism never gave poetry to the comedy of manners.

Her style has been compared to Evelyn Waugh and Richard Hughes, which is a friendly, if not particularly helpful, thing to say, and to Angela Thirkell, which is closer as a judgment, though perhaps unnecessarily severe. Well, Trollope and Peacock and Meredith may send ghosts to help her write about the cook and the scullery maid and the pantry boy, about the principal characters and about the male and female spinsters under the tutor's roof. It would seem apparent that Miss Compton-Burnett had heard of the incomparable Jane Austen if only from the commendable way she avoids ladling in historical background. But her style is her own. Please let her keep it that way.—CHARLES POORE, "The Lambs and Their Smug Shepherd," *NYTBR*, June 20, 1948, p. 5

Miss Compton-Burnett expresses the wish that this early book ⟨*Dolores*⟩ should not be considered among her novels, as she regards it as *juvenilia* and outside the stream of her important work.

It would, however, be a pity if this novel were not eventually reprinted with a prefatory essay; for the relation which it bears to her later works is in about the same proportion as the relation of *Les Plaisirs et Les Jours* to *A la Recherche du Temps Perdu*. It is apart from the mainstream of her work in two important respects. Firstly, whereas the later novels have a preponderance of dialogue and singularly little commentary and narrative, *Dolores* has a preponderance of commentary and narrative and singularly little dialogue. What dialogue there is, however, strikes sharply on the ear and with all the familiar surprise; it is quite individual, standing out as if it were printed in phosphorus from a text that bears the marks of derivation from other works of fiction.

This leads us to the second point: that *Dolores* has several derivative sources—from *Middlemarch* (there is an echo of the Dorothea–Casaubon story), from *Scenes from Clerical Life*, and, more oddly, from *The Professor, Villette*, and even from *Jane Eyre*. At this time Miss Compton-Burnett *was* striving

after visual effects; and when she attained them, they had something in common with Charlotte Brontë's emphatic chiaroscuro. With *Pastors and Masters* she deliberately reduced visual effect almost to nothing; but lately has begun to develop it once more.

The most interesting point of comparison between *Dolores* and the succeeding novels is the reversal of theme. *Dolores* concerns a plain, intellectual young woman who immolates her whole life upon the altars of other people—often, in a manner doing more credit to her staying-power than to her good sense. But the thesis is this: that to sacrifice oneself for the good of others is beautiful and ennobling. Fourteen years later, the thesis had altered—and this new thesis, either dominant or subsidiary in every novel Miss Compton-Burnett has written since, is as follows: that to sacrifice oneself for the good of others is splendid for others but horrible for oneself.

Though *Dolores*, like a good many first novels, is stamped with the influence of other books, to the student of Miss Compton-Burnett it is entirely fascinating, for her voice is in it, her wit glimmers sparse but bright where wit is least to be expected, and her force, her chill and her curious authority are clamped like hydraulic pressure upon the whole of it.—PAMELA HANSFORD JOHNSON, *I. Compton-Burnett*, 1951, pp. 24–25

In her early novel *Dolores* (published in 1911), the father, Cleveland Hutton, is hardly seen as a tyrant. His selfish claims on his daughter, Dolores, are always liable to break up the academic career she has made for herself, and he is not uncritically viewed. But the daughter's sacrifice is, in this immature book, seen as noble—almost in the spirit in which Tennyson saw that of Jephthah's daughter or of Iphigenia. With her mature mind the author sees such sacrifices as horrible, and this youthful work (interesting for the seeds of further development which can be discerned in it) must be regarded as outside the canon of her work.—ROBERT LIDDELL, *The Novels of I. Compton-Burnett*, 1955, p. 24

⟨*Brothers and Sisters*⟩ is the infernal language of enclosed people who are talking each other to death, people inhabiting some dry hole of life which their good ancestors have hollowed out for them and furnished securely, all in high purpose. It is a language of a worn-out stock turned upon itself and upon its members within its narrow, hallowed trench: blood kin. Its career is relentless and unrelieved, turning up fresh losses and shocks and damning news as it chops on and on, and cutting under old layers of secrets and deceptions.

Miss Compton-Burnett's is a rhetoric created by prisoners of conversation where vocal self-explanation is the only action of the bound and the captive: the only freedom lies in a verbal attitude toward disaster, and the choice vocabulary is limited to concepts of irony, tragic wit, self-pity, condescension. Her rarefied, elliptical, telescoped and bitten-off style is mannered beyond Gertrude Stein's anywhere or Virginia Woolf's in "The Waves" but recalls gentler overtones from the very different worlds of these two women.

How to describe this strange style and its grasp upon the reader? What is compressed as tightly as gunpowder to make a bullet must, because it is forced into a tight mixture of irreducible minimum, expand to its natural dimension and potency in some other place. This seems rather the natural and rightful demand of essences and concentrates. Where the inevitable diffusion and return to natural volume of her style occurs is in the mind of the reader where Miss Compton-Burnett fires her explosive compounds. This accounts for a reader's lagging behind her sentences or being snagged onto them for long lulled periods and for a feeling of suffocating closeness; but it is the very source of her striking power and explains the detonation of her savage wisdom into largeness and eventual fullness.

The author is observing her characters from a position deeply buried in the structure of their situation and so the writing appears directionless until one can find out what point of view is being taken. This obscures the reader's focus for a while for he has no help of time, of description, of narrative. But when a shape comes clear out of this stubbed thicket of conversation, it is constructed of perversely antic devices of Websterian melodrama in grand style—a key, a locked cabinet holding a terrible letter than divulges the doom of a household, the burning of a will, a photograph album revealing life-long secrets that taint forever. Her style and the breathless formal convention her novels take reproduce the very situation her characters are involved in: stratagem and high-toned cunning within family prison-life.

This novel is a picture of the devious, devilish and intricate results of the intermingling of brother and sister, illustrated by several sets of them living in an English village and especially in Moreton Edge, a manor house on the rim of the village inhabited by the Staces for generations. All these brothers and sisters are involved or on the point of getting involved with each other, treating their fathers, where there are any, like unfortunate pranks of nature and their mothers as something to win out over, which they do not.

When it turns out that mother and father Stace are themselves half-brother-and-sister, and this through the discovery of a dusty letter left long ago by Grandfather Stace, progenitor of all the woe that has followed, heretofore vaguely intoned ominous forecast materializes. Irony doubles back on itself and, twice strengthened, delivers that psychic blow which often turned Greek and Elizabethan tragedians' characters into madmen, but not Miss Compton-Burnett's. Commenting on their dreadful situation as brilliantly as ever, they harness their Sophoclean destiny with the bridle of cruel wit and trot on, conversing, into their future hells.

There seems little doubt that this extraordinary author binds one of the tightest knots in literary history; but the labored loosening of it is rewarding and its secrets at the core staggering.—WILLIAM GOYEN "Small Talk on the Way to Damnation," *NYTBR*, Nov. 18, 1956, pp. 5, 36

Miss Compton-Burnett, I hardly dare to say, is a little off form in ⟨*A Heritage and Its History*⟩. I do not dote on her novels but it is possible to see her extraordinary distinction without doing so. She shares with very different writers—Salinger and Wodehouse, for instance—the knack of infecting one with a dialect; just before going to sleep one can, after reading one of her books, entertain oneself with endless conversations, automatically witty. Her books are what they are. But I owe it to myself to add that this is not infallibly what they ought to be. And debts of this nature are never left unpaid. In the last novel, *A Father and His Fate* (a better book than this, I think), one character explains why he has been whispering (uselessly, for in this world everything is overheard): "What is there about any of it fit to be uttered aloud?" This is true of all Miss Compton-Burnett's fiction. In her artificial hell nothing goes without saying provided it can be said in the infernal dialect. All speak it, servants and children included, because they breathe it in with the poisonous air. Every remark, false, sentimental, cruel or apparently generous even, breeds a malicious consequence by a sort of hellish logic. . . .

The skill with which Miss Compton-Burnett handles her outrageous plot is wonderful; she is entirely mistress of her conventions. There is one paragraph of expository prose in the book. On the whole, though, this one has less bite, its hell is less amusing, than some of the earlier ones. At times the dialect seems to move closer than we like to Wodehouse, the conversation free-wheels. People compare her with Jane Austen, one can see why; but in the end this is as absurd as comparing Hobbes with Hooker. Yet she is not grossly flattered by the collocation of names. She is literally inimitable; she has cheated all the lawgivers of modern fiction; and it is quite impossible to imagine a future time in which a few people will not read her.—FRANK KERMODE, "Fiction Chronicle," *PR*, Summer 1960, pp. 553–54

Pastors and Masters is a study in various kinds and varying degrees of parasitism, with people living off other people; it is a study of exploiters and exploited, of tyrants and victims, in many guises. Yet there is a *necessity* (the word is the author's) in all this; the exploited need their exploiters and are bound to them in many ways. One is reminded of the *Origin of Species* and the chain of interdependence of species upon species for survival. In fact, one of the principal movements or patterns in Miss Compton-Burnett's novels involves a symbiotic relationship in spite of the victim's efforts to escape the emotional overlordship imposed upon him into an emotional fulfillment of his own. . . .

Miss Compton-Burnett has set before us a world which we cannot take lightly or simply. We are shocked by the fact that even so petty a crime as plagiarism escapes without the conventional poetic retribution, and outraged by the indestructible hold the exploiters have on their victims. At the same time we are made to view the criminality and the exploitation with a sense of admiration: our normal sense of values seems to be suspended. In this novel the suspension is embodied in the idea of the genius vs. the ordinary person. The ordinary people, in the long view of the book, are the good people, those who do things for themselves, even those who are creative. The genius is the man like Nicholas, who has the gift of getting the best out of others, as Emily herself suggests at the time the plot is getting under way, in reference to Nicholas' use of Mr. Merry as schoolmaster (she is ignorant at this point of how much Herrick hopes to get out of someone else's writing!). The genius is capable of sustaining deception when he practices it, in the face of reason and goodness. The contest between Nicholas and Bumpus, which begins as one of creativeness, ends as one of fraudulency. The man who has *some* creativeness in him—Bumpus at least had written one novel—and some decency by conventional moral standards to confess his temptation, comes off second best. The reader's sympathies, controlled finally by Emily's reaction to the ultimate revelation, or concealment, remain finely poised between horror and admiration, between a sense of outrage and a sense of the ridiculous.

Having throughout the novel hoped and waited for Emily's declaration of independence, the reader ultimately realizes the more valid aesthetic satisfaction of having seen the frightening strength of moral weakness, the unshakable power against which understanding is the only defense available to the morally strong. Our reaction to Miss Compton-Burnett's picture of the fixed necessities governing human relationships reminds us, in a way, of our response to the inevitability of tragedy. The writer's artistic integrity enhances our appreciation of sanity and moral strength even in showing that it is the morally weak who inherit the earth. For Emily's insight and moral integrity are still preferable to Herrick's kind of genius (as well as to conventional Christian do-gooding, as we shall see later). Her triumph in maintaining dignity while protecting her brother in his weakness renders Herrick's genius somewhat foolish and pathic.—Stanley B. Greenfield, "*Pastors and Masters: The Spoils of Genius,*" *Crit,* Winter 1960, pp. 68–71

Novels by Miss Compton-Burnett can no more be read for their narrative impetus or their development of character than those problems in which Harry is taller than Dick, who is shorter than Bill. Miss Compton-Burnett gives her characters more distinguished names but scarcely more distinguishing marks. You are not invited into their consciousness: you are set the problem of working out their relationships—including, as a rule, their blood relationships.

The dialogue—that is, virtually, the whole novel—is full of lesser conundrums of its own. It's not always easy to identify the speaker: Miss Compton-Burnett plays fair but close to the chest; she will give you the information only if it's absolutely impossible to deduce it from other sources. Whatever the clues you employ, they won't be individual tones of voice. Everyone in her novels speaks in the same idiom, and the idiom itself is instinct with conundrums. Miss Compton-Burnett's speakers seem to be applying a course of remedial exercises to the relaxed muscles of English syntax. They invent, as it were, private equivalents to a preceding direct object and test the reader's alertness to the agreement of the adjective. 'I shall not see the life as ordinary,' says the hero of her new novel. 'None is so to me.' 'How do you see your own life?' asks his interlocutrix. 'It is even less so to you?' Give a *full* account, one seems to be being bidden between the lines, of the significance of the second 'so'.

To my senses, Miss Compton-Burnett is not exactly an artist. She is something less valuable but rarer—the inventor of a wholly new species of puzzle. It is probably the first invention of the kind since the crossword, which it far outdoes in imaginative depth. Indeed, it is only a touch less profoundly suggestive than chess or formal logic. An extra attraction is that, though her novels are not themselves works of art, the rules of the puzzle are allusions to literary forms and conventions. Reading them is like playing some Monopoly for Intellectuals, in which you can buy, as well as houses and hotels, plaques to set up on them recording that a great writer once lived there.

The social nexus in which Miss Compton-Burnett assembles her speakers is such a memorial—to Jane Austen. The centre, the permanent set, in the new novel is a baronet's home in the country; the milieu consists of those grouped round the magic 'Sir'. At the start, the baronet's son Hereward is refused by a tenant, marries instead the daughter of the neighbouring house and brings her to live in the baronet's. Hereward is a popular novelist, which occasions a discussion in which the baronet and his butler gently disparage novels—a tacit allusion to the novels passage in *Northanger Abbey*. But the resemblance to Jane Austen is never more than allusion-deep. The composure of Jane Austen's prose is adaptable to expressing every nuance of social and individual idiom, whereas the sedateness of Miss Compton-Burnett's is wooden-featured. Where Jane Austen is concerned above all with her heroines' consciousness, Miss Compton-Burnett shuns—indeed positively and in panic flees from—the idea of entering anyone's consciousness. Only one paragraph in *A God and his Gifts* makes any attempt (and it is a sketchy one) to give the reader direct access to what someone feels.

In flight from the novelist's freedom to wander into minds, Miss Compton-Burnett is logically driven to embrace the restrictions of a dramatist. Her allusion now is to classical drama, whose conventions she abides by to the extent of having major events happen off-stage—though in her new book some curiously intimate ones, including a proposal, happen in pub-

lic. Her text is as bare as Racine's of furniture or handkerchiefs, and you might say her speakers resemble his in all speaking alike; the trouble is that hers don't speak poetry. Their language is in fact a let-down. They exchange big, imprecise banalities, seeing paths plain before them, keeping a light touch, letting things loom large. Still, they toss these clumsinesses about with some grace, achieving the form if not the content of wit. It's like reading a Wilde comedy in algebra, the aphorisms reduced to 'All a's are really b's. Only y's ever think them z's.' Occasionally a speaker strikes off at least a common-sense-ism. When the baronet dies, his widow is offered the consolation of yet another banality. 'You will live in the past. That will always be your own': and she has the wits, if not quite wit, to reply 'I have lived in it. But then it was the present. And that was much better.'

The setting is not so much subject to the conventions as plain conventional—'book-lined'. Period is not indicated—you can't make much of the absence of cars and telephones when so few material objects are present anyway; the butler, however, has a presence which seems unmistakeably Edwardian. (He is named, by the wittiest stroke in the book, Galleon.) The devices of the plot-making seem borrowed from the Edwardian theatre. Where except in a mustachio'd melodrama would a man betray, as Hereward does, that he is the real as well as the adoptive father of a child by letting himself be overheard exclaiming above the child's head 'blood of my blood, and so deeply deprived from me'?

Indeed, Miss Compton-Burnett creates a positively farcical pile-up of skeletons tumbling from the Edwardian cupboard. Piecemeal it is disclosed to his family (an allusion to the strip-technique of the *Oedipus Rex*) that Hereward is a man of unconfinable sexual appetite and charms. He, not the baronet (who is financially dependent on his son's royalties), is the head of the family, the boss stag in the herd who takes all the females as his right. This, since the herd is rather restricted and close-knit to begin with, involves him in the near-incest of taking his wife's sister and his sons' wives; when these have children by him, apparent cousins are really half-siblings (liable, of course, in the restricted milieu, to fall in love with one another) and the close-knit family has become inextricably inter-ravelled.

As a matter of fact, Hereward's unions always *are* fertile. I take it Miss Compton-Burnett is tacitly referring to the doctrine of pagan theology that gods never mate fruitlessly; for by the end Hereward's family have explicitly recognised him as the god of the title, identifying the paradox of their continuing respect for him with the paradox of the Greeks' basing their own restrictive sexual morality on a lecherous and incestuous pantheon. Presumably the particular god concerned is Zeus: the incest in Zeus's own ancestry is represented by the fact that Hereward's parents are distant cousins; Hereward is a Zeus with no need to usurp his father, having reduced him to financial impotence, but when, on the baronet's death, the butler greets the son as 'Sir Hereward' we understand that Zeus has come into his inheritance.

Inside this classical box, Miss Compton-Burnett's Chinese puzzle implicitly places another. The situation is an outline of Freud's theory of the primal horde. Indeed, I suspect Hereward's name of being compounded of 'herd' and 'horde'. The situation is, however, pointedly worked *out*, and not worked, in psychoanalytical jargon, *through*: and that the reader is not called on to involve his emotions is, I suppose, why the book remains an admirable and diverting puzzle rather than a work of art.

Miss Compton-Burnett's technique is all directed to avoiding the need for technique, just as her dialogue is to avoiding the need for a consciousness. It is, in fact, the technique of a *faux naïf* painter—one who, unable to render either adults or children, depicts both as charmingly wooden dolls. Miss Compton-Burnett's children and servants charm and astonish the reader by speaking as gravely and syntactically as her educated adults: the real sleight of hand is that her educated adults are not flesh and blood, either. Time Miss Compton-Burnett treats exactly as the neo-primitive painter treats perspective. Not only does she make no indications of period to start with: generations elapse at the turning of a page, and still Miss Compton-Burnett gives not the least sign or sense of change either in period or in personalities. Her eighteen novels make a pretty, quirky terrace inhabited by grave dolls, each villa an ingenious little puzzle box, depicted, without perspective and with a most meticulous absence of technique, by the cunningly *naif* hand of a Grandma—no, Moses has the wrong connotations: Grandma Oedipus.—BRIGID BROPHY, "I. Compton-Burnett" (1963), *Don't Never Forget*, 1966, pp. 167–70

EDWARD SACKVILLE-WEST
From "Ladies Whose Bright Pens . . ."
Inclinations
1949, pp. 86–89

Miss Compton-Burnett's progress in her art has been more considerable than might appear, in view of the curious and no doubt deliberate uniformity of her novels. For, like a sculptor obsessed by the human figure, she recommences the same task in each successive book, and relies for variety on the endless combinations of spoken language. Her characters are comparatively few and reappear constantly under different names; but each incarnation reveals some new facet of experience. Her first book, *Dolores* (published in 1911), is indeed not very characteristic and is chiefly interesting for the few glimpses of her later style which it contains. A lachrymose, amateurish book, it occasionally startles one with things like this:

> "How do you do, Mrs. Cassell?" said Mrs. Blackwood. "We were all beginning to wonder if anything had prevented your coming."
>
> "How do you know we were, mother? We have none of us said so," said Elsa.

This foreshadows the portentous domestic tyrants of *Brothers and Sisters*, *A House and Its Head* and *Daughters and Sons*, as well as the disillusioned, completely intelligent, but dutiful children who suffer under them.

With *Pastors and Masters* (1925) the mature style is already formed in all essential features: it only remained for the artist to exploit the potentialities of so remarkable an invention. Her own view of the matter is set out, in modest but very illuminating fashion, in a dialogue with Miss M. Jourdain published in *Orion*. But to the present writer the effect of her art recalls the aims of the Cubist movement in painting, at its inception. Like a Picasso of 1913, a Compton-Burnett novel is not concerned with decoration or with observation of the merely contingent, nor is it exhibiting the author's personality or in exploiting a romantic dream. It is constructive, ascetic, low in tone, classical. In enquires into the meanings—the syntactical force—of the things we all say, as the Cubist enquired into the significance of shapes and planes divorced from the incidence of light and the accidents of natural or utilitarian construction. These novels contain very few descriptive passages, and none where description is indulged in for its own sake, or for Im-

pressionistic ends; and in this connection it is significant that Miss Compton-Burnett seems to scorn the aid of images. This does not, I think, strike us at the time of reading; it is not until we take up some other book that we realise to what extent nearly all novelists rely on metaphor and simile to enliven their scene. . . .

But it is her zeal for measuring the *temperature* of emotion—the graph described from moment to moment by the action of the plot on the alert sensibilities of her characters—which is responsible both for the continuously witty surface of her writing and the deeper truth of her picture. Like Henry James, Miss Compton-Burnett is much concerned to preserve an amusing surface, as well as a polite one; and this remains true of the tragic passages in her books. Indeed, in those which deal with the most frightful happenings (*Brothers and Sisters*, *Men and Wives*, *More Women than Men*, *A House and Its Head*) the comic relief is more pronounced and more evenly distributed than in the later novels, of which the plots are considerably less lurid. But it is her anxious attention to Truth which, more than anything else, gives to her books their quality of timeless relevance. Her wit has many sides, but it excludes absolutely the wise-crack, the smart epigram, the modish or private sally. "People don't feel as much as you want them to." This assumption is fundamental to all these novels: it is the arrow on the thermometer which marks 98.4°. And the movement of the book is the to-and-fro rhythm of a tug-of-war between those who do not wish to feel too much and those who are determined to make them feel more than they can bear—until the rope breaks.

I do not want to give the impression that I consider these novels faultless. In common with other important artists Miss Compton-Burnett has a number of failings which are perhaps inherent in her very personal idiom. They are easily described:

(1) She tends to fill her canvas too rapidly, and this mistake is aggravated by the perfunctory way in which she describes her characters, so that we are in constant danger of forgetting or confusing them. It must, however, be pointed out that in her later novels this fault is less apparent.

(2) She cannot manage masculine men. Her males are either overtly effete (e.g. Alfred Marcon in *Daughters and Sons*), or possessed by a feline power-mania (e.g. Duncan Edgeworth in *A House and Its Head*).

(3) Her plots are not easily remembered in detail, or distinguished one from another. This is not a serious charge, for her emphasis lies elsewhere; but it argues a certain rigidity of imagination and probably has some connection with

(4) Her subsidiary characters are often (but by no means always) too 'flat'. Even regarded as a chorus, they are too dim in outline and tend, moreover, to be always of the same type.

(5) Her chief characters do not develop in the course of the book, they only loom larger or dwindle, according as the author lengthens or shortens her opera-glass.

(6) When action supervenes, she skates over it as quickly as possible, in the manner of Jane Austen. At such moments a kind of deadly calm descends on the page; which is in a way effective, but tends to spoil what in music is called the balance of parts.

These faults, although they add up to something, do not seriously affect the brilliance and gravity of these amazing books, or the intense satisfaction that arises from submitting oneself to Miss Compton-Burnett's regime. If her novels are tiring to read, that is because the non-stop rallies, the wonderful patness, the immense logical sequences, make it difficult to decide where to put the book down, when it becomes necessary to attend to something else. Once launched on the stream one must attend completely to every word, until the end is reached. But although these difficulties render her work no light undertaking for the reader, the reward is proportionate—not only in the illumination of so much in life that other, and perhaps more scopious, novelists agree to ignore, but in irresistible laughter. For these books are, one and all, monumentally funny.

PAMELA HANSFORD JOHNSON
From *I. Compton-Burnett*
1951, pp. 7–42.

Home Truths

The peculiar charm of Miss Compton-Burnett's novels, the charm that has won her not merely admirers but addicts, lies in her speaking of home-truths. She achieves this by a certain fixed method. One character propounds some ordinary, homely hypocrisy, the kind of phrase from which mankind for centuries has had his comfort and his peace of mind. Immediately another character shows it up for the fraud it is, and does it in so plain and so frightful a fashion that one feels the sky is far more likely to fall upon the truth-teller than upon the hypocrite. In these books there is always someone to lie and someone to tell the truth; the power of light and the power of darkness speaking antiphonally, with a dispassionate mutual understanding. . . .

Do young people, like Daniel and Graham, adolescents like Isabel, children like Marcus, really speak in this measured and extraordinary fashion? Of course they do not. Miss Compton-Burnett's almost incessant dialogue has very little relation indeed to human speech; it is the speech of the secret understanding in all its rightness and all its crudity. Occasionally the Parents (or masters) speak in the convention of ordinary converse: the Children (or servants) speak only with their minds. What seems to be the recorded speech of the lips is really only the recording of that swift comprehension which can hardly find utterance in conscious thought. This is why Miss Compton-Burnett's writing appears so strange to the reader who comes upon it without warning, a gentle tea-cosy madness, a coil of vipers in a sewing-basket.

Yet readers who come to know her fascination will discern one startling fact; that this piercingly wise, discreet, mannered Victoriana conceals abysses of the human personality. There are monsters in her books, men and women a hundred times worse than the Murdstones, because they are indestructible—and incombustible also; they do not carry their own fire and brimstone about on their persons.

It is important to realize that the novels of Miss Compton-Burnett are *terrible*; though she uses the comic technique she is not a writer of comedies, and the reader who approaches her with Jane Austen in mind is either going to get a violent shock or to enjoy her in a happy state of total incomprehension. Her method is always a mask for her theme; indeed, if some of her themes were set out in a normal, unstylized manner, some of her books would find their way into the locked cages of sensitive librarians. Behind the veil of witty patter, question and response, the human horror stands up straight. If we do not always notice quite what a horror it is, this is because she allows her characters to beard her lions—even her worst monsters are always baited, always challenged. But in the end they devour the small and valiant prey, and no keeper ever comes in the last chapter to lock them up or shoot them down. In these books there is never a Fortinbras, never a Richmond, never a Mal-

colm. Evil is achieved, and the results of it are assimilated into the life from day-to-day, and the victims of it stand in the third and fourth generation.

The Question of Justice

The important fact is that she has an entirely revolutionary conception of *dénouement*. Othello slays himself, Dmitri Karamazov goes to Siberia, Mr. Rochester is blinded, and Mr. Dombey reforms. Anna Donne enjoys Jessica's money and marries Jessica's son. This is the most severe shock launched at any reader by any novelist since the novel first took shape; and at a first reading the effect is scarcely perceptible. Truth, in this case, is not only stranger than fiction but is less acceptable. In the Bible, which is full of simple truths, the wicked flourish like the green bay tree; in life the wicked not infrequently die in great material comfort amid a host of admiring and affectionate friends and relations.

It must be noted that, writing in a century which has seen the compassionate and objective exploration of personality in depth, and which has emphasized (not infrequently with rather mechanical results) the consolatory and guilt-allaying discoveries of Freud and his successors, Miss Compton-Burnett believes in pure wickedness. Indeed, she seems to believe in it more than in anything else. She has three kinds of characters, good, bad, and weak: sometimes they are good and weak, sometimes bad and weak, but the weaklings are no more presented as complex beings than the monsters are presented as such, so we cannot regard them on their own as a class objectively studied.

Emotion and Intellect

A few of her characters exist in their own right: Anna Donne, Aunt Matty, Dudley and Aubrey Gaveston, Horace Lamb and Harriet Haslam we remember as individuals. The others exist only through the content of the remarks they make and have no human outline. This weakness is due partly to her lack of visual presentation, and partly to a lack of interest in anything but the verbal sword-play, except upon those rare occasions when pity or contempt have deepened into more violent emotions. Sometimes, in a flash, we see a person move: we do not see the face, but we do see the characteristic behaviour of the body:

> Blanche entered with outstreched arms and stumbled slightly over nothing apparent, as she hurried forward.

The truth is that the *pace* of Miss Compton-Burnett's novels is singularly rapid; there are enrichments for which at this speed, she literally has no time. The action in her books is, for the most part, reported, as in the convention of Greek drama; but there is a prodigious amount of it. Something has to be sacrificed; and that something is too often the quality that makes a character visible to the mind's eye, or turns a roomful of fencing shadows into a genre-piece mobilized by light.

If these novels were merely exercises for the intellect their worth would be infinitely less; but the more closely they are studied, the more humane (in a peculiar sense) they must appear. They examine, in fact, the major emotions of the heart and the major experiences of life, but examine them in the restricted terms of drawing-room intercourse. Miss Compton-Burnett's understanding of tyranny, rage, frustrated pride, obsessive greed, and the whole scope of *normal human wickedness* is incomparably greater than Jane Austen's: her emotional range is, in fact, incomparably more vast. What she lacks, and what Jane Austen has, is the element of pure delight and joy in the small pleasures of the daily round, and the element of real satisfaction in the common, day-by-day manifestations of human affection and generosity. Miss Compton-Burnett has wit. She has a sense of the ridiculous. She has high spirits. She has no joy.

One of the elements that give so odd a flavour to her work is that she is humane without being kindly. She is neither kindly nor unkindly; even in A *Family and a Fortune*, where a degree of warmth does break in, she is usually content to point to a condition of victimization without appearing to feel too strongly about it. Interference, one feels, is not her *métier*, even interference by the instinctive uprush of compassionate indignation. She does not appear to believe that there is much to be done about the human condition. The battle is to the strong; the weak go to the wall. She is sorry for the weak, but has no great hope of any amelioration of their driven and chivvied lot. She watches and she records; sometimes in pity, more often in contempt, but never with much participatory feeling.

A Summing-Up

Writing of a dying age (it dies hard), she stands apart from the mainstream of English fiction. She is not an easy writer nor a consoling one. Her work is an arras of embroidered concealments beneath which the cat's sharp claws flash out and are withdrawn, behind which the bitter quarrels of the soul are conducted 'tiffishly', as if cruelty and revenge and desire, the very heart itself, were all trivial compared with the great going clock of society, ticking on implacably for ever behind the clotted veilings. She is not to be mildly liked or disliked. She is a writer to be left alone, or else to be made into an addiction. Her addicts do not, one imagines, come together in groups to admire her work. It would be possible, of course, to spend an evening remembering what Horace said and how Marcus answered, how Honor and Gavin dealt with their new governess, who made the remark that being useful was not nice, except for other people: but the home-truths by which Miss Compton-Burnett's addicts are made and retained are not proper topics for public discussion. They are embarrassing; they would dry up the founts of ordinary, consoling, hypocritical human intercourse and make people pick their words so dry that friendships would wither away and no desire endure save to find the clock-hand at that hour which makes the good-nights possible.

ANGUS WILSON
"Ivy Compton-Burnett"

The London Magazine, July 1955, pp. 64–70.

Miss Compton-Burnett's isolation from contemporary novelists is surely a most exact measure of the failure of the modern English novel. This failure is now a very worn-out critical theme. It threatens to become the most tedious of King Charles's heads and it should undoubtedly be avoided by any critic who does not wish to become as boring as Mr Dick. It inevitably arises, however, in any estimation of Miss Compton-Burnett's work.

The debate on the English novel's decline now runs like clockwork. We are cut off from our traditional roots, says the critic, the soil from which our greatness sprang has been weakened by artificial experiments. Without experiment, comes the reply, there can be no new growth, the soil will be clogged and choked with weeds. Surely, says the inevitable third and sensible critic, we may make use of all that experiment has taught us, may indeed experiment ourselves, without

losing contact with our good old English tradition, the true husbandry needs old and new alike. The simile, though undistinguished, is, I think, justly used, for the debate on the decline of the novel has the same familiarity, the same echo of stale wireless discussions as the debate on the use of artificial manures. Yet, if the sensible third voice is right and I think we must concede it to be so, Miss Compton-Burnett seems alone in following its call. Her novels are deeply entrenched in the great tradition of the English novel, or rather, in the great traditions, for this much vaunted single tradition is an invention of obtuse and undiscriminating traditionalists. Miss Compton-Burnett is also a great experimentalist: she has rigorously adapted form and language to accord with her aims, which is surely the only serious experiment to be considered. And yet she stands so alone in a wilderness of dreary imitated dead experiment and dismal imitated dead tradition. The unique vigour, the formidable strength of her books does not come only from her ethic, her healthy acceptance of life, but is a direct expression of her creative vitality. Her living art, which should be an oak in a contempory forest, stands out in its isolation, almost theatrically monolithic, like Stonehenge on Salisbury Plain.

To praise so highly is not indeed to say that the greatness of her achievement can be easily estimated, nor even that it can be absolutely asserted. She inherits and uses so many of the themes and manners of the nineteenth-century golden age of the novel. She has explored and made her own the aesthetic ethic, the touchstone of goodness in taste, decorum and sincerity which was once for all stated by Jane Austen and then miraculously expanded by James and not inconsiderably ornamented by Virginia Woolf and Forster. She can make humours into personalities compelling our childish horror, demanding our sympathy by their own childish pathos. Here she moves easily in the world not only of Sir Walter Eliot and Lady Catherine de Burgh, but of Mr Pecksniff and Mr Dorrit, of the Duc de Guermantes and the Baron de Charlus. She explores the stuff of personality, its fictions and its onion peelings of reality: and like the great nineteenth-century novelists, she exploits hypocrisy and false sincerity in humanity in order to discuss truth. These connections with the great novelists have, I think, been remarked upon by other critics. What, so far as I know, has not been noted is her likeness to a more improbable nineteenth-century writer—Oscar Wilde. There is, nevertheless, something strangely akin in their combination of the language and wit of high comedy with the plots of melodrama. She does not, of course, lapse so easily into the language of melodrama as Wilde, but there are purple passages in her work which are by no means intended ironically. Finally, it seems to me, that in the total statement of her novels, in what is insufficiently but conveniently described as her 'acceptance', she develops straight from the great agnostic artists of the last century. I use the word 'artists' here to denote the spiritual battle fought out in a Christian society. It seems customary to call her ethic pagan, and Mr Liddell, her latest critic and great admirer, tries to define her novels in the terms of Greek tragedy. The attempt seems to me too grandiose and too remote, by asserting the wrong 'too much' about her work he ends by making too little of it. To use the word 'pagan' about any modern person is at best a vague term of differentiation, allowable perhaps to Christians confused by varieties of unbelief: to use it as a term of praise is unhistorical and misleading. It does not help in understanding Housman or Hardy, it helps even less in understanding Miss Compton-Burnett. The Christian surrounding of her world is more decayed, more perfunctory than that of George Eliot, and her answer is at once less consciously and culturally agnostic than George Eliot's, and also less unconsciously Christian than the burden of Evangelical duty that George Eliot carried. Nevertheless the Christian ruins are the backcloth of her family dramas—Establishment, orders of society, feeble ends of Christian ethics. When she portrays belief she does so with the same understanding and dignified rejection as George Eliot. For all her craggy isolation, for all the icy winds that seem at times to howl through her dialogue, there is a warmth, a sense of comedy at its highest level remaining at the end of many of her novels that makes her acceptant view of life seem strangely like the human realism of Tolstoy's best novels.

I have purposely allowed myself to bandy great names so freely, for it is only so, I think, that we can begin to see the difficulties of estimating Miss Compton-Burnett's place as a novelist. Her intention is very high, her handling of the dialogue medium she has chosen is masterly, her range is only in a rather superficial sense narrow, yet there are few, I think, who could happily feel that her total work, or indeed any of her individual novels, is great in the sense that we apply this word to Jane Austen, Dickens, George Eliot, Tolstoy or Proust. In some degree this is simply the difficulty of applying to a contemporary author judgement which is made up of qualities observed in novelists of the past. This difficulty, however, should not be very serious with Miss Compton-Burnett, whose work as we have seen bears such a close relationship to those very novelists. In some degree we may be unwilling to apply the word 'great' to a novelist whose works are unlikely ever to be popular as were those of Dickens or George Eliot. That there is some element of this in our difficulty seems likely when we compare her to Henry James—the comparison seems at once more allowable than any of the others we have made. Nevertheless I doubt if we will feel satisfied to place them on the same level. Yet if we do admit this distrust of an author with a limited appeal to be more than a sentimentalism, we shall have to explain what element is lacking in an unpopular author that contributes to 'greatness'. We cannot make the naïve charge of limited range of observation or of social scene, for we should have to reject our corner-stone, Jane Austen. Some critics, I suppose, would claim that Miss Compton-Burnett has lived cut off from her time; not only in the narrow sense that she does not write of contemporary life or that her world is a dead social unit—the late Victorian family—but on a deeper spiritual level. She has not been touched, they would suggest, by the fresh vision of original sin that has come to us in the last forty years. It is surely exactly this modernity of vision, however, which separates her agnosticism from that of George Eliot, as it does Mr T. S. Eliot's Christianity from Victorian Christianity. Finally, there are those who would refuse her greatness simply because she was working in the medium of the novel. The novel is a dead art, they would assert, we cannot therefore expect any more great novelists. Most of such critics, however, would admit that the novel is only dead if we are speaking of its traditional form, its future lies in new developments which will free the imagination. It can hardly be on this ground then that Miss Compton-Burnett can be denied greatness, for no one has rejected the old forms or evolved a new one more satisfactorily.

The truth, I believe, does not lie in any of these usual generalizations about content or form. Miss Compton-Burnett is unique not only in her difference from contemporary novelists and her superiority to them, but unique among novelists generally. And it is the peculiar quality of her remarkable talent that she immediately invites comparison with the great and yet cannot attain that status. From *Pastors and Masters* onwards— I see no reason to discuss *Dolores* since she does not do so

herself—she consciously asserts her concern with the highest themes of the novel and demonstrates her special approach to them. It is a consciousness of importance, a direct statement of intention that allows for a thousand nuances, a host of subtleties, but allows of no serious development. Development comes not from conscious overtones, but from unconscious themes and conflicts and symbols. With *Pastors and Masters*, with Henry Bentley and the Merrys, she emerged full grown before a world that had no practice in recognizing such a phenomenon. That her reputation has grown as more and more discerning critics have discovered her adult powers is not surprising, nor that those who have recognized her should proselytize her work and judge their friends by their reception of it. An adult writer of high seriousness is not so common a phenomenon that we can make her less than a touchstone of taste. There have, of course, been changes in her work; she has developed her children, she has developed her servants, in her latest novel, *Mother and Son*, she develops a cat, she allows herself an occasional comment now amid the flow of brilliant dialogue and the odd truncated personal descriptions, her style, though still curiously jerky in places, moves more easily. But these are not developments of the inner core of her writing; she need never have introduced what Mr Liddell calls her choruses of children and servants, she need never have smoothed out the awkwardnesses of her sentences, and she could still have ranked with the greatest. As it is, from the very first, we have had enough and more than enough to satisfy us, novels being as they are today. Nevertheless we have not had that inner development, that gradual unconscious change that we find between *Nicholas Nickleby* and *Our Mutual Friend*, or between *Scenes of Clerical Life* and *Middlemarch*, which we rightly associate with great novelists. Like other changes, these are not necessarily to be called progress; *The Ambassadors* is not necessarily better than *Portrait of a Lady* nor *Mansfield Park* than *Pride and Prejudice*. If it is for progress that we ask, it may well be said that *More Men than Women* is better than *Pastors and Masters*, and *A Family and a Fortune* or *A House and Its Head* better still. Indeed, in point of omission of distracting elements and of formal arrangement, her latest novel *Mother and Son* excels all the others. Fundamentally, however, her novels remain the same: she presents us with a whole view of life and conveys that whole view in a subtle and convincing way, but she does not tell us more of it or show it to us from another side, or make us feel or think about it more deeply than she did from the very start. It is thus, I think, that her work misses greatness, but misses it probably so narrowly that we are constantly urged to set her novels beside the masterpieces of the past.

This sameness of statement, complete yet never new, is surely the reason why many critics of discernment fail to appreciate her work. There are many readers, of course, who lack either wit or intellectual discipline to make contact with her novels. There are, however, people of wit and intelligence who find the dish monotonous, or others again like Miss Hansford Johnson who appreciate her work but can yet, as Mr Liddell is at pains to point out, lose their way in the labyrinth of her plots. This, I believe, is because of this underlying sameness, for there is certainly no other monotony. Each book contains characters so different, so completely lifelike that any attempt, like Mr Liddell's, to categorize them into tyrants or victims tells us nothing of any importance about them. Matty Seaton, cruel, brutal, that occasional real life person who is larger than life, clever and understanding, refuses to be categorized as a tyrant, and she certainly has nothing to do with the other tyrants, Harriet Haslam or Sophia Stace or Miranda

Hume or Duncan Edgeworth or Sir Jesse Sullivan. It is useless for the critic to try his usual trick of categorizing the events or the characters, for life is not susceptible to moral category, has no finality of event except death and that, as Miss Compton-Burnett never ceases to tell us, is only final to those who die and even then in quite different ways. There are, of course, goats and sheep, and in accordance with the great tradition of Miss Austen they are betrayed by nuances alone, but these nuances are not such constant tests in Miss Compton-Burnett's world as in Jane Austen's, not even so constant as they are in Forster's or Virginia Woolf's. There are the great 'humorous' figures like Sophia or Josephine or Matty or Rosebery Hume, figures with the outlines of Dickens's world, but though we know them to be somewhere on the wrong side of the fence, we must never build our fences too exactly. In Rosebery, the son of her new novel, *Mother and Son*, a certain sort of moralizing, humourless, playful, heightened speech speaks against him or at the most calls for our pity, yet in Justine Gaveston we can see that the same tone speaks for 'goodness', and in Luce Sullivan for something in between. It is this ambiguity of personal values, I think, that makes the nature of her plots so essential to her novels. Much objection has been made to what is called their 'melodrama'—incest, illegitimacy, occasional murder. They are, of course, familiar mechanisms of novel narrative and if Miss Compton-Burnett used them purely formally as mechanical devices I do not think it would be objectionable. She has, however, in her radio discussion with Miss Jourdain, stated that she believes them to be real ingredients of a great deal of family life— sometimes as skeletons revealed, sometimes as skeletons for ever hidden. This view I entirely accept. It has been my experience that most middle class families have some 'secret' of this kind in their midst. On grounds of realism also, then, they do not seem to me objectionable. If, however, we examine the nature of this 'melodrama' more closely we will find surely that it is an integral element in the whole ambiguity which is at the centre of her view of human values. The revelation of incest and of illegitimacy must mean that the members of a family have to see themselves anew as different people in exactly the most important sense that exists in the family unit—they are no longer sons and daughters, or they are not only sons and daughters of their parents but brothers and sisters as well. And if, as so often happens, they later find that the revelation was untrue, they must once again revert to their former view of their personalities, but the former view can never be what it was before because they have learned in between to see the whole of their world from a different angle. It is, of course, the common theme of Shakespearean comedy. Its final effect is to question at its roots the whole conception of 'personality', to consider it only as relative. And this, of course, is the essential of Miss Compton-Burnett's attitude. What, in fact, are we to make of personality or event at all, when illegitimacy so often proves us to be other than we thought, or when false report has made us digest a cataclysm that never occurred? Perhaps, we are led to conclude that relationship, the fundamental family relationship which rules her books, does not matter at all, when Christian and Sophia are sister and brother as well as husband and wife, or seem to be; or when Edmund Lovat seems to have married his daughter and has not; but who could say that it did not matter to Rosebery that Miranda was his mother even if Julius was not his father. Sometimes relationship is vital and sometimes it is not, is the answer. And so it is with everything else, with death, with malice, with arrogance, with charity, with patronage, with plain speaking, with lying, they may be good or they may not, they may be final or they may be transient. Nothing can be judged except in

its context, and then only with reservation. In *Mother and Son*, for example, Miranda praises her son in these words, 'He would not do little wrong things behind my back; he would not do them any more than the great ones; and that is a rare thing'. Yet in the same book, Hester Wolsey does great wrong and her friend Emma Greatheart says, 'I will think the one thing, that she has known the depths, and that I have seen her knowing them. It is a good thing experience is ennobling. I believe she is becoming a little ennobled.' If we cannot judge of the good and the bad, we cannot also judge of the important and the unimportant. We can know, perhaps, that Dulcia Bode and Faith Crammer are as unimportant as they are comic, but this is exceptional levity on the author's part. Who can say whether Rosebery who looms so large is more important, even as a literary character, than his supposed father Julius, or Matty Seaton than her sister Blanche? We might as well try to judge between Vronsky and Anna, Karenin or Levin. The manner in which Miss Compton-Burnett so wonderfully suggests real life is, in fact, so similar to that of Tolstoy—Levin's sudden perception of religious truth which seems momentarily so decisive and yet is the next moment gone, the falsity of the apparently basic moments in Anna's life with Vronsky—change and false change, climaxes that are transient, chance remarks that are final, trivialities that take up more attention and energy than death or disaster. It is not that Miss Compton-Burnett is less plumb at the centre of life than her great predecessor, but only that Tolstoy gives us aspects of this centre from a hundred different revolving mirrors that almost bewilder us by their changing reflections, while she has only one mirror, clear and full, but unchanging. It is, nevertheless, a mirror to be deeply grateful for.

KINGSLEY AMIS
From "One World and Its Way"

The Twentieth Century, August 1955, pp. 171–75

This author's entire strategy is comprised in first setting out a few scenes of talk, which may be of any length and come in any order; and then, a good long time after the initial situation has been established, somebody listens at a door or finds a letter, a switch is thrown and a new situation takes immediate charge, though without causing or revealing any significant change in the characters involved. . . . There is something almost lazy about this procedure; it exempts the author from having to construct any chain of incident such as is likely in fact to determine change and progress in human lives, substituting a mere arbitrary framework within the divisions of which no development is called for. One danger of such a method is that large stretches of any given book are liable to escape being clipped together by these devices and will hence be called upon to justify themselves. Miss Compton-Burnett is too gifted not to be able to pull this off time and time again—one immediately remembers such things as the marvellously invigorating battles between the governess Mildred Hallam and her two young charges in *Darkness and Day*. But even she could not make the Miss Buchanan scenes in *Manservant and Maidservant*, for instance, anything more than a pendant, a simple addition, to what goes on in the rest of the book: a skilful and amusing addition, again, but so disproportionately large that one began to be troubled lest Miss Buchanan would drop a letter or a photograph revealing her to be somebody's mother. An inferior book like *Two Worlds and Their Ways* can turn into padding, into addition, before it is much more than half over, though the virtuosity of the dialogue, as always, remains undiminished to the end, while even a masterpiece like *The Present and the Past* is too long by some twenty pages. One might sum up these points by saying that the real objection to the author's method is not that her books are held together by melodramatic, or improbable, or reduplicated events, but that they are not so held together.

My second main line of argument can also take *Mother and Son* as its starting-point. When Julius tells Miranda his secret, she says:

> . . . Our time is over; we have only the past that we have seen. What am I to say to you, Julius, in my last hour, on the brink of the grave? That I forgive you, my husband. What else can I say? What other word can pass lips so soon to be closed? And I say them fully. But I thank God that I have not dealt with you, as you have dealt with me.

Having said this, she dies, and Rosebery at once says:

> Father, she is dead! She is gone from me, my mother! Why have you done it? Why did you think of yourself? Why could you not keep your secret? What did it matter, your personal burden, the weight on your own mind? Why did you put it on her in her weakness and age? It was for you to spare her, not to think of easing yourself. You have done an ill thing.

It is not enough, agreed, to say about this that real people never talk (or talked) like that at a moment like that, although to say so is to imply a charge not easily answered, and certainly not answered by pleading, with Mr Liddell, that real people in the Compton-Burnett period expressed themselves better than we do, and that these are clever people too. If one asks what sort of people do talk like that, one might mention, again with Mr Liddell, people in verse drama, and he has produced an astonishing effect by interlarding Euripides (in English, of course) with Compton-Burnett stage-directions. But this is irrelevant, because Miss Compton-Burnett—and I hope to obtain agreement here—is not writing verse drama, where the conventions are utterly different. (The temptation to regard these novels as Attic tragedies must be resisted at all points: why suggest that the servants in some of the books provide a choric commentary? We don't want a chorus.) The other kind of people who talk as Miranda and Rosebery do are people in other novels, some of them not-too-good novels—there is a perilous resemblance to the kind of way some of Mr Charles Morgan's characters go on. And that is fatal. There may be times for people in a book to talk like people in a book, but at moments of emotional crisis it is best avoided. It is often avoided in Miss Compton-Burnett's better novels, and this is an important way in which they establish themselves as better.

There is really not as much in common as all that between this general type of Compton-Burnett dialogue, such as usually occurs in duologue and in what Mr Liddell calls 'the great tragic speeches', and the other, more familiar type where a larger number of characters sit round a table and indulge in communal dialectics. Reviewers have noticed an unrealistic level of aphorism in these exchanges, most conspicuous where children or servants participate, but again to point this out is not quite adequate on its own. What is striking is less what the characters say than the remarkable number of kinds of thing they do not say. To imagine what would have to happen before a Compton-Burnett character could say 'You bore me' or 'What a pretty dress' or 'Give me a kiss' or 'Oh my God' is an

instructive experience. The majority of these conversations are marathon tennis-matches in which the ball always lands in court. Any given return may be a smash, a screw-shot or a plain lob to the base-line—very occasionally it may come off the wood—but no ball ever rebounds from a player's head instead of his racquet, or gets angrily kicked into the net, or is chucked over the wire into the cabbage-patch. Quite a lot of the time the players are virtually interchangeable, maintaining as they do a close verbal and syntactical continuity in their collocutions, and holding their favourite idioms in common: two examples are the extended 'that' substitution ('Nurse is at a loss. She often finds herself that') and the *cliché-critique* introduced by some such formula as 'Why do people always talk as if *x* were a good (or bad) thing?' And in most of the novels one could count on the fingers of one hand, or even on its thumb, the number of times anyone refuses to play.

I think I can probably fudge up a couple of comments on this policy of rigorous limitation and exclusion in dialogue. The first one is just that it takes an almost overweening audacity to discard at the outset the most powerful card in the hand of the novelist interested in character-drawing, that of differentiation by mode of speech. It is true that some characters are thus differentiated—Dulcia Bode (*A House and Its Head*) and Cassius Clare (*The Present and the Past*) are good instances— but on the whole the lack of variety is enervating, much more so than any lack of realism. A butler and cook who are no more than over-articulate can perhaps be accepted, but a butler and cook who reproduce the conversational techniques of their master and mistress are merely ventriloquial. Here, too, I think, lies an important source of the repetitiveness of character discussed earlier: how is one to differentiate two tyrants, or two governesses, or two children, or two footmen, who talk the same? And this applies within books as well as between them. To keep separate in the mind the schoolgirls of *Two Worlds and Their Ways* requires a concentration—during reading— incommensurate with the reward offered, and in several other novels the issue is thickened and impeded by similar 'doubling-up' of characters. My second comment is just that the danger in stylizing the procedure of dialogue in this way, and in thus tending inevitably to reduce the status of the individual character, is that of finally turning the whole thing, not indeed into a solemn game, but into a frivolous game. Loss of seriousness is for some reason the dragon that lurks in the path of the writer who opts for other modes than a selection of the language really used by men. To read almost any piece of Compton-Burnett 'communal dialectics' is to experience a pleasure as intense as most available literary pleasures, and yet page after page, sometimes scene after scene (the servants' conversations in *Darkness and Day* provide the most extreme example), is marked by the triviality inseparable from fantasy.

There are two things which decisively rescue a great part of Miss Compton-Burnett's work from this danger. One is her comic sense; the other a dyad composed of her hatred and her pity. To any of her readers, not only her devotees, her comedy will hardly need illustrating, though her liking for subject-matter generally considered tragic may obscure the importance and extent of the wonderfully amusing passages in even the more harrowing books, such as *Manservant and Maidservant*. Her hatred and her pity, her hatred for cruel irresponsible spite and sentimental righteous folly, her pity for their victims, for the downtrodden servant, the hounded companion and above all the child goaded to tears in the name of love and duty— these things too need no emphasis. The relevant point here is that these two passions are realistic passions. They work not through, but alongside and apart from, an arbitrary method of construction and a technique of dialogue which is too often de-individualizing and at times undisciplined. Miss Compton-Burnett is a writer of the wildest internal contradictions and not the least of these is her ability to turn out novels—two or more of which are masterpieces—that conceal under great homogeneity of tone a conglomeration of all but incongruous elements.

The above may seem a sufficiently left-handed tribute to a writer I enjoy and admire. I do not think it really is. Our most original living novelist will not best be served by having an affectionate bloom rubbed over such flaws as, by reason of its vitality, her work inevitably bears. It is only after those flaws have been probed that they can be understood and finally dismissed.

ANTHONY WEST
From "Ivy Compton-Burnett" (1955)
Principles and Persuasions
1957, pp. 225–32

The big moment of *Mother and Son*, by Ivy Compton-Burnett, a British writer whose reputation is growing at a reckless pace, comes when an elderly gentleman named Julius Hume kills his wife, Miranda, by confessing to her that the supposed nephews and niece she has been bringing up in her home are not his brother's children at all but the fruits of an extramural enterprise of his own. He chooses to make this disclosure in the presence of Rosebery Hume, whom he presumes to be his legitimate son. The crisis of the scene runs as follows:

> "What am I to say to you, Julius, in my last hour, on the brink of the grave? That I forgive you, my husband. What else can I say? What other word can pass lips so soon to be closed? And I say them fully. But I thank God that I have not dealt with you, as you have with me."
>
> Miranda's voice ended on its hissing note. Her hands shook, and she pressed them on the arms of her chair. Her breath came shallow and rapid, and as her son approached, she suddenly threw up her arms, turned eyes on him with no sight in them, gave a long, deep sigh and was silent.
>
> "Father, she is dead! She is gone from me, my mother! Why have you done it? Why did you think of yourself? Why could you not keep your secret? What did it matter, your personal burden, the weight on your own mind? Why did you put it on her in her weakness and age? It was for you to spare her, not to think of easing yourself. You have done an ill thing."

The gentlemen exchange stilted recriminations over the cooling body for a couple of minutes, and then a surprising revelation is offered; a Miss Hester Wolsey, the old lady's recently engaged companion, has been in the room through the whole thing. "Yes," she says, "I have been here all the time. I had not the chance to go." If it seems unlikely that Mr. Hume would not notice this comparative stranger before making his confession, it seems positively unnatural that she should remain immobile and inactive to the point of invisibility during her charge's seizure. The bare minimum of human feeling would require that she step forward to take the old woman's pulse to find out if she had merely fainted, had had a stroke, or was really *in extremis*. But we are not dealing with realities of human feeling; we are dealing with a heightened reality, or

some such thing, so the companion pops up like a rabbit out of a hat when Miss Compton-Burnett needs her. . . .

It is the argument of the many admirers of Miss Compton-Burnett that she is not dealing with the mechanistic realism that would lead any normal household to exhale this persistent eavesdroper with extreme rapidity; she deals with a larger wisdom that can be attained only by discarding humdrum superficialities. Thus, in place of plausible action leading to plausible developments of character, one gets a dialectical pillow fight in which people batter each other from one position to another with maxims of the La Rochefoucauld variety; that is to say, profound untruths stated with an air of authority.

. . . What one is face to face with is not the devastating insight into human relationships that should spring from events of the order of the death scene and the discovery of paternity which are the core of this book but the mildest conventions of an almost repulsively parochial society dressed up to look like courageous explorations. That is perhaps the secret of the current British vogue for Miss Compton-Burnett's work; it has an air of being utterly ruthless, but it leaves everything disturbing and challenging severely alone. The vogue for this sort of thing was established by the nostalgic resurrection of Henry James as a great reputation. James's visions of country-house England, and his pictures of English and French life, meant very little when they were new because they were manifestly at variance with the experiences of his contemporaries. They began to acquire validity of a kind after the First World War, when the horrors of the new order lent a pleasant glow to the Edwardian period. The dingy 'twenties, with their steady erosions of private life by threatening political and economic events, were succeeded by the decades of misery when mass movements and mass events, such as the depression, took complete charge of private life, and the Jamesian heyday became a golden age to be looked back on with intense longing, the longing with which Talleyrand and other men of his generation looked back on the last years of the *ancien régime*. The Master's novels gave a picture of life before the Flood, when people could concentrate on their own affairs in the warm sunlight of a stable and happy world that existed only as a background. It is worth noting that James's rise in esteem corresponds almost exactly with the fall in esteem of the Edwardian writers whose work gives, in setting and background, an authentic picture of their far from ideal times and also with the development of a theory that setting and background are unimportant accessories of the drama of relationships.

Miss Compton-Burnett has in her novels evolved a stylistic trick that exploits this conception to the logical end. The background is almost entirely eliminated, as scenery was in certain avant-garde theatrical productions of thirty years ago, and what little exists emerges only by implication from the dialogue. The language—one never spoken by any human race before or since the Flood—announces that one is faced with a period piece, and a ticket at the corner of the bare stage announces that the year is 1897. Its detail is up to the reader, and he can construct it in accordance with his own fantasies and so exempt himself from the harsh realities of his own times—if there had been no horrid wars, if his parents had not had to give up their comfortable old Georgian house (now the local telephone exchange), if servants were still easy to get, if incomes had kept their value and taxes had stayed at a reasonable level, he, too, might be living in one of the teeming three generation family warrens that Miss Compton-Burnett describes again and again. Her novels are, however, realistic in the sense that they are not for those who go climbing socially in their fantasies; unlike those of Henry James, which cater to readers who prefer to transport themselves up the social ladder in their daydreams, they picture the ideal world of those who will admit to being middle-class. But basically this kind of fiction functions exactly on the level of the lighter kind of historical novel, taking the reader out of his own epoch and transporting him to whatever he sees as his particular golden age—the "stap-me, Sir Harry" eighteenth century, or the Good King Charles merrie seventeenth, of the franker purveyors of dream stuff. The dreams, though, are milder, being concerned not with swashbuckling or womanizing but with such refinements as having plenty of maids in aprons on hand to do the dirty work. Their flavor is exquisitely conveyed by the opening sentence of James's *Portrait of a Lady*: "Under certain circumstances there are few hours in life more agreeable than the hour dedicated to the ceremony known as afternoon tea." The remark sets the tone of artistic seriousness in which the question of whether or not Lord Warburton or Caspar Goodwood will succeed in arousing the passions of sexually timid Isabel Archer is explored for four hundred and thirty pages. It is rather a comedown from Lord Warburton, with his hundred thousand a year, his seat in Parliament, his half-dozen houses, and his fifty thousand acres, to poor Julius Hume and his bourgeois ambiance, but they at least inhabit the same spiritual realm. One may recall the delicacy and restraint with which Mr. Hume's wife, the mother of *Mother and Son*, died: she "gave a long, deep sigh and was silent." Death is after all a little thing that stops one character talking and gives a new turn to the talk of the others; such are the values of afternoon-tea letters.

BERNARD McCABE

From "Ivy Compton-Burnett, an English Eccentric"

Critique, Winter/Spring 1960, pp. 60–63

I am prepared to defend a high estimate of Miss Compton-Burnett's sense of comedy, and of her sense of drama—such scenes as the clash between Anna and Jessica in the death-chamber in *Elders and Betters*, or between Duncan and his cuckolding nephew, Grant, in *A House and Its Head*, are genuinely exciting. Or again, the accounts of the "ordinary pathos of childhood"—the persecuted little boys in *Manservant and Maidservant*, the lonely ten-year-olds in *Parents and Children*—are genuinely moving, as, in a different way, is the death of Blanche in *A Family and a Fortune*. And this list could be extended. But in themselves such scenes are not enough; the question recurs: even if we admit that there is enough in Miss Compton-Burnett to justify the effort that her idiosyncrasies demand of the reader, is there anything more? It is time to ask a broad critical question. Large claims have been made for her work, in England, and particularly in France, where she has at least one notable "objectivist" disciple in Nathalie Sarraute. Is there then, beyond the idiosyncrasy, a moral awareness of life of the distinctively comprehensive quality that we expect from a great novelist?

First it must be emphasized, against her detractors, that her books *are* concerned with real life. Where she might appear to be most vulnerable she is in fact the least so. Despite the persistent artifice of her presentation of it, her closed world is not so remote and artificial as it may at first seem. The only extended public statement that Miss Compton-Burnett has been known to make—it was in the course of a published "conversation" with a woman friend—includes the remark, "I do not feel that I have any real or organic knowledge of life later than 1910. I should not write of later times with enough grasp

or confidence. . . ." But her grasp of her chosen world is real and organic enough. To those who would object that families, particularly Victorian families, simply do not behave in the way that Compton-Burnett families do, Mr. Liddell very appositely quotes the case-histories of a few Victorian families whose stories have become public knowledge: those of the Ruskins and the Tennysons and the Brontës and the Barretts, for example, and he might have mentioned Edmund Gosse's account of life with father.

The insight goes beyond immediate domesticity. The moral decay that Miss Compton-Burnett probes has a social and economic background—although it is remarkable how often reviewers will say that she imagines a world remote from the realities of work and money. It is true that the heads of families rarely do go out to work, and seem not much concerned with the source of the wealth that allows them to maintain their large establishments; but the economic dependence of their victims is heavily stressed, as are the neurotic results of the static idleness that afflicts almost everybody. The cultivated appearance of indifference to money is yet another of the falsehoods that Miss Compton-Burnett's revelations ironically destroy. All the hidden wills and anxious heirs, not to mention the overworked servants and underfed governesses, are part of a pre-1914, bourgeois world on the edge of dissolution, economic as well as moral. In the early *Brothers and Sisters*, the scandal-driven family actually leaves its country mansion and moves to London to seek obscurity. In the later novels there is nothing so explicit: the family somehow survives, but the mention of the workhouse in *A House and Its Heritage* is not only a joke; we have the feeling that the next generations will have to abandon their mansions. (As, incidentally, they have abandoned their faith: clergymen in these novels are either hypocrites or fools, and the understanding characters share Miss Compton-Burnett's uncompromising scepticism.)

What is Miss Compton-Burnett saying about her world? The resemblances that her novels bear in atmosphere, plot and various technical narrative methods to theatrical performances, and more specifically to Greek tragedy, have been pointed out by several critics, and Miss Compton-Burnett (I suspect with a suspicion of a tongue in her cheek) occasionally allows characters in the novels to underline the parallel. Such resemblances can only, in the end, be of incidental academic interest. What is more important, as these critics note, is a fundamental difference in attitude from that of the Greek tragedians—never is there a suggestion of moral retribution for the crimes and guilts that are revealed. After the most shocking discoveries, life is somehow resumed. The books never end in any cathartic denouement; there is a slow fade-out, with everybody talking. For the truth that Miss Compton-Burnett discovers about people is finally no more than ironic. Understanding is the instrument with which she controls or withstands evil—"being with the same people from the beginning makes for so much understanding"—and in the end it is on the quality of her understanding that Miss Compton-Burnett must be judged.

The obvious criticism seems, as usual, to be the best. Her world is too cerebral, and this quality excludes too much of what complete moral awareness demands. Not that feeling is absent—almost all her characters become objects of pity, for example; yet here, significantly, the persistent element of ironic detachment makes genuine *compassion* out of place. Passion plays no real part, for although Miss Compton-Burnett cannot be said to shirk the fact of physical sexuality, she is somehow too matter-of-fact about it. Reticence is, no doubt, a neglected virtue today, yet one has the impression that the acts of love or passion necessary to furnish the innumerable bastards in her stories must have been as perfunctory and mechanical as the other recurring gestures that her characters make in order to advance the plot—opening hidden drawers, dropping incriminating letters. Once again, the fact that the restriction is deliberate does not make it any the less disturbing.

Members of the Compton-Burnett cult do not hesitate to place her beside Jane Austen, a dangerous comparison to risk. One suspects that they are the kind of critics who admire Miss Austen primarily for the elegance of her wit rather than for her wisdom—and the distance that separates the two writers might usefully be summed up as the distance between wisdom and *knowingness*. Miss Compton-Burnett relies too exclusively on a limited kind of understanding, a clever, rapid, ironic, pinpointing knowingness, characteristic of her "understanding" personages. It would be perhaps naïve to look for a moment of comprehending repose in these novels, for despite her serious intentions, and the depths of imaginative understanding that have developed through the years—compare Simon Challoner in her last book with the Reverend Henry Bentley in her first—her perceptions seem too often closer to those of Restoration comedy than to those of Greek tragedy. If we look for positive statement beyond the ironic defensive wit, one assertion appears again and again, an aggressive statement of individual independence that the most persecuted and the most guilt-ridden characters equally fall back on in moments of great stress: their right to exist as they are, without in the end any obligation to anyone but themselves. This is the last, unanswerable line of defense, and when it is reached, and this happens frequently, we have those sudden shocks, those violent repudiations of any basic authority that constitute the final irony of the family, or, presumably, of the human social situation as Miss Compton-Burnett sees it. These momentary anarchic assertions are complementary to a deterministic resignation—"Things can only be done by us according to our natures and our understandings. It is useless to expect more"—and it is the reiteration of these two attitudes, and her evident attachment to them that more than anything else suggests an essential immaturity and consequent limitation in Miss Compton-Burnett's approach to moral situations. Her art thrives on a paradox—the family is often a bitter joke, and its members must realize and accept the fact that appearance is not reality—but it is a paradox with which we are, after all, familiar, and it is not such an eccentric view of life as her novels somehow contrive to make it appear. For these formidably clever and highly amusing books do not in the end escape this epithet—"eccentric" is the right word—although we should use it with all respect for its implications and note, perhaps, the special pieties attached to the word in Miss Compton-Burnett's native land.

D. W. JEFFERSON
From "A Note on Ivy Compton-Burnett"

A Review of English Literature, April 1960, pp. 19–24

Implicit in Miss Compton-Burnett's choice of methods is an ironical sense of the history of the novel. Her art has all the air of a studied adjustment to a period of decline, resisting decline but only by the use of extreme measures. At her best she is a good example of T. S. Eliot's conception of the 'individual talent' in relation to tradition, the tradition which can only be attained with great labour; for her extreme measures consist in the development of an entirely new set of possibilities in the forms of the literary and social past, so that certain

elements in the latter are stretched beyond all expectation and enjoy a surprising modernity of function.

She belongs mainly to the literary line of Jane Austen, but her varied technique includes many ingredients from elsewhere. Some of her passages of narrative are in a solemn quasi-biblical style. It is interesting, in the episode of Dudley's flight in *A Family and a Fortune* (Ch. 8), to see the effect of such phrases as 'taking her only course and trusting to his aid,' modified by the sharp observation in the words that follow, describing poor Miss Griffin's walk: 'Her short, quick, unequal steps, the steps of someone used to being on her feet, but not to walking out of doors, made no attempt to keep time or pace . . .' The stately but off-centre idiom of her servants' hall dialogue ('Tabby, that is rushing in where angels would hesitate') is reminiscent of the garbled English of the socially inferior characters of some of the older novelists. There is a slightly Dickensian flavour in the fictitious tales of family calamity with which the nursemaid Mullet beguiles her small charges in *Parents and Children*, and also in the pathetic wish of Miriam, the plump housemaid in *Manservant and Maidservant*: 'I should like to have a real illness. It seems it might pull me down and make me different.' The formalised word-play which pervades her work has a general affinity with that of Jane Austen's predecessors, the wits of the eighteenth century, though she follows none of them in detail. She inherits their regard for a clear-cut vocabulary and neatness of implication. Her use of a 'set speech' idiom for portentous disclosures takes us back to early conventions of fiction. And the list could be developed further. . . .

Miss Compton-Burnett's novels abound in characters with infirmities beguiling to the modern mind. Her conservative idiom enables her to give a light and pleasing sophistication to her portrayal of them. The following conversation between two women is from *Pastors and Masters* (Ch. 3):

'. . . He couldn't propose to me.'
'Why not?'
'Why, I should think he couldn't. I haven't thought about it. I should think it is one of the things he doesn't do. We all have them.'
'But you could manage yourself, dear. People can,' said Theresa.
'Yes, of course they can. I've noticed that. And he could accept me, I am sure. I know he would spare me embarrassment. Dear William!'
'But he wants to marry you, doesn't he?'
'As much as he can want to marry anyone. Anyone who is a woman. And that is not very much.'
'Oh, dear! These dons and people!' said Theresa.
'Yes, it is something of that way. I knew you knew all the time. I might tell you it is that way with me, too . . .'

All Miss Compton-Burnett's novels contain intelligent characters with habits of thought that may be called 'modern'. Through their penetration and vigilance, manifested in innumerable significant passages of dialogue, she has herself been one of the notable teachers and moulders of attitudes—the attitudes are partly a matter of 'style'—of her age. By placing these characters in a world based on the country-house life of the late nineteenth century, at the same breakfast table with representatives of Victorianism, sometimes at its most untamed, she achieves a formalised, exaggerated and very entertaining version of a familiar clash between the generations. In so far as she is on the side of modern sceptical honesty against entrenched complacency, dishonesty and tyranny, she can be included among novelists congenial to readers of 'progressive' outlook. But the social implications of her art are somewhat complex. For example, the fact that so many of her characters not only do no work but also refrain from having a 'full life' might seem to reflect something inadequate in their class; but it is relevant that these people are often very nice and usually gifted with intelligent self-awareness. The characters who crave for a full life and devour experience, like Mrs. Doubleday, tend to be devourers of other people too. Her art is so ironical throughout that any attempt to extract a straight moral concerning 'class' or 'decadence' from it would be unwise.

Miss Compton-Burnett is far from being the first novelist to succeed by evading the encroachments of certain kinds of realism: those of the human sciences, and of journalism and mass media generally, together with the less specialised kinds which developed in the nineteenth century; but perhaps no writer has made this gesture quite so pointedly. The peculiar limitations of her art—its spareness, its dryness—may be regarded partly as assets if we see them as an ironical reflection on the age which drives the artist to such disciplines to avoid banality; while its wanton ingenuity, its almost insolent virtuosity, demonstrate the liveliness of its resistance to such an age. The importance of her gesture for us will depend in a large measure on how far we think the novel *is* in decline, and on how far we associate the decline with the decay of social and cultural forms, including language, and with the growing exposure of the human subject matter to approaches alien to the imagination.

FREDERICK R. KARL
From "The Intimate World of Ivy Compton-Burnett"
The Contemporary English Novel
1962, pp. 204–12

In nearly every one of the novels, there is movement toward a revelation that will, inevitably, make the characters aware of what they are and what the situation is. The revelation takes the form of a recognition scene (many critics have thus compared Miss Compton-Burnett's novels with Greek tragedy), but the recognition itself does not appear to change the characters. In Greek tragedy, the recognition was the climax of the rising action, entailing a meeting between the protagonist's past and future—for what he has been will now determine what he will be. After the recognition scene, the character passes into a decline that is in some ways the equivalent of Christian contrition, except that there is ultimately no salvation. His exile is from his self; he must pay for the rest of his life for something he was unable to control.

This, obviously, is not the pattern in Ivy Compton-Burnett's novels. True, she shares with the Greek tragedian his awareness of the importance of the recognition scene, but she has reworked the materials of the tragic vision so that further comparison is valueless. Frequently, the revelation amuses the reader more than it changes the character. Instead of facing the revelation, the character merely tries to hush up the news and live with it. The incestuous pair in *Brothers and Sisters* are treated comically, as they are in *Darkness and Day*. First, we are led to believe that Edmund and Bridget Lovat are father and daughter, but later we find they are half brother and sister—and thus their marriage should not seem outrageous. If only Oedipus and Jocasta had been siblings! Meanwhile, their incest has become a source of common gossip among the chil-

dren and servants. No one, however, is particularly upset, for incest serves as well as anything else to gossip about.

Furthermore, in Miss Compton-Burnett's world there is no repentance, no Christian charity which will reward the good person, no Christian revenge which will punish the bad. There are no amenities whatsoever. If one has been incestuous, it is discreet to keep the news to oneself and continue living. If the news does get out, then one hopes that the other fellow has done something even worse so that incest will not disturb him. If one has had illegitimate children in the past, then he usually finds that his husband or wife has committed a similar folly, and the two indiscretions cancel each other. If one loves his brother's wife or fiancée, he finds that another woman can be provided for the brother, perhaps a maid or governess. . . .

The lack of repentance and salvation makes possible the comic play of the novels. If the amenities are meaningless, the law of the jungle must prevail. And all this against the background of a Christian society! The surface of behavior is impeccable, but beneath lie arrogance, vanity, jealousy, and excessive pride—all the characteristics of normal people. Miss Compton-Burnett's characters are always themselves. And just as no force from within can change them (only circumstances change, they remain the same), so no force from the outside can alter them. They are fixed by their characters and doomed, to some extent, by their heritage. They resist progress with the fierceness of people who recognize that change means death, although not to change is also a kind of death. Their death throes, however, are often comic.

The chief weight of this amoral world falls on the children. They are the beneficiaries of the muddle that adults make of their lives; but rather than learn from their sad experiences, these children perpetuate similar lives in their own children. The cycle of infamy is endless. For someone to have learned from his experience would be for him to deny what he is. His individuality consists of denying that his children's claim on life might be superior to his own; the struggle between the two, consequently, becomes one of life and death, with the children hanging on through desperation.

Lest the reader feel sorry for these children, Miss Compton-Burnett has made them monsters who speak and understand in an adult way. Unlike the Victorian children who had to be seen but not heard, Miss Compton-Burnett's children are constantly uttering witticisms to dissipate their parents' evil. In a society in which even the family becomes an institution supporting injustice, the children must conspire with each other to float above the backwash of their parents' past. Like Dickens' long-suffering youngsters, they too must endure the absurdity of their elders, but they have weapons and armor that Dickens could not have conceived. By hiding beneath couches or in doorways, they become aware of everything; and, with the servants, provide a chorus-like comment upon their parents. Their revenge comes from understanding exactly what is happening to them, and at a suitable time they torture the adults by withholding affection and love. Precisely as their elders use love to gain what they want, so the children themselves form alignments and use love, withdrawn or extended, as an offensive weapon in their struggle for survival.

In a tragic or semi-tragic novel, the child must become the victim of adult duplicity; in the comic novel, however, the adult becomes the child's victim. And yet the weapons of each side in Miss Compton-Burnett's novels are so fierce and the moves so predatory that comedy gains a new dimension. This is comedy based on torture, cruelty, and selfishness, in which no one can afford to relent because to survive he must continue being what he is. Graham Greene's dialogue between man and God, with the ensuing conflicts, becomes in Ivy Compton-Burnett's hands the everyday conflicts between the generations, between parents and children, between grandparents and their children, between aunts and nephews and nieces. . . .

Miss Compton-Burnett's method of narration is perfectly coordinated with the subject matter. By bringing two or three families together as the whole of society, she makes their interplay the sum of all essential forces in the world, until nothing else seems to matter. Her conversational method creates, as it were, an external stream of consciousness, in which the characters overtly voice what the traditional novelist usually explains about them. Consequently, in a literal way, we see what they are—there is nothing to hide, for the very nature of their communication forces complete disclosure of their thoughts. Only infrequently do the characters enter into a conspiracy to withhold information. More often, the characters reveal everything they know, and their disclosures suggest the limits of their cruelty.

This aspect of the method is effective, for its very freakishness becomes a way of complementing the eccentricity of Miss Compton-Burnett's characters. The stream of consciousness has been transformed into a spray of epigrams. The conversational method that Henry Green was seeking in his last two novels, *Nothing* and *Doting*, has been a staple of Miss Compton-Burnett's work for thirty years. Most novelists assume that their characters will hide certain things about themselves, since they are ashamed of their iniquity. For Ivy Compton-Burnett, however, iniquity is not a marginal characteristic of a chosen few but the substance of the whole world. To feel shame indicates a commitment to a morality of good and evil, but to be unaware of shame is to show allegiance to an amoral world in which a generous action is repaid not by kindness but by retribution, in which a sympathetic word is offered—for a gain, in which the old must survive by fighting their children for their rights.

The method suggests, then, that if a character has a thought of any kind, he will shape it into words. And even more, into an epigram. The conversational idiom, however, does result in emotionally flaccid people, although this consequence does not disturb the author. Her characters are not emotional beings under any circumstances; they react with reason, and reason is their only god. For the reader, nevertheless, there is a curious sameness of character and narrative, perhaps because we tend to remember literary creations by their emotions. In these novels, however, no survivor grieves for the deceased, no one is horrified to see what his children have turned into, no one questions that a mother has the right to destroy her son(s), no one is particularly upset to discover incest or infidelity. The emotions are so well controlled that the most startling revelation will not elicit surprise. Life itself seems frozen.

The conversational idiom of the characters helps establish their complacency. Their epigrams are rapier thrusts cleaned of all sweat and all effort—the thrust is cool and straight to the mark, as though they had spent their lives polishing their marksmanship for precisely this situation. Even the children are untouched by the grossest of deceptions. In *Daughters and Sons*, for example, the daughter of John Ponsonby, a popular novelist, accepts unquestioningly that her father's writing career is finished, and that he must be protected from this knowledge. Accordingly, she turns her own novel over to a publisher, receives a large sum of money, and then pretends that the money has been sent her father by an admirer. Mr. Ponsonby inadvertently thinks the money comes from the family governess and marries her, setting off a whole series of misunderstandings. Yet, Frances, the novelist-daughter, calmly accepts that her father is written-out and that she must sacrifice herself for him. An ancient ritual is carried out in modern dress.

This very lack of emotion or surprise creates a good part of the horror—a kind of intellectual sport—which an Ivy Compton-Burnett novel generates. The glitter of the conversation helps form a tight wall around the characters, as the novelist herself has built precisely such a wall around her society. The epigrams convey an exclusive quality, as though these are special people who cannot react or speak in any other way. In *Two Worlds and Their Ways*, these sallies occur on every page. For example:

> "Is your family musical, Mr. Spode?" said Juliet, with no suggestion of a change of subject.
> "My mother is one of those people, who do not know one note from another. That means that they do not concern themselves with notes. I do not know about my father. He died when I was born."
> "What?" said more than one voice.
> "It appears to have been the case. There is a primitive people, whose men take to their beds, when their wives have children. It seems that my father followed that course, and never rose again."
> "So your mother is a widow?" said Mr. Bigwell.
> "That is one of the consequences."
> "We must remember that Mrs. Cassidy is present."
> "I did remember it. I was trying to cause her some amusement."
> "Thank you so much," said Juliet. "You have quite taken my thoughts off our disgrace." (p. 179)

This is a special language, one that is sheathed and unsheathed like a sword or dagger, a language that, so to speak, lies in wait for its victim, scores a light hit, and then moves away preparatory to another strike. Consequently, because the children in these novels can survive only by answering back, their conversational abilities are phenomenal. They speak like adults, indeed like special adults—like Henry James and La Fontaine. Their use of language stylizes them, gives them the brittleness and nervousness one expects of children whose parents "use" them. They rebel without illusions, conspire without shame, and survive without love. And while they fail to gain our sympathy, they do win our amazement.

Despite the virtues of the conversational method—its literalness, its sharp definition of issues, its penetration into the thoughts of the characters—despite these, its deficiencies are apparent. Miss Compton-Burnett's characters all seem cut from the same mold; the children all have the same awareness of evil, and the parents and grandparents all demonstrate the same predatory expedience. When a mother in one novel says, "My good, dear children," or something similar, she is preparing to sacrifice them at the first need, and the mother in the next novel is little different. A widower makes a "wife" of his eldest daughter, and a widow makes a "husband" of her eldest son. To gain a life, one must crush a life. A flat sameness is evident both in character development and plot, and it precludes Miss Compton-Burnett's being a creator of memorable characters.

Another factor, and one that drives to the heart of the creative process itself, is the lack of motivation in her characters. Here the novelist allows the surface to be definitive: either the character explains himself or he does not. There is no "background filler" to provide the explanatory material which the character himself is unaware of. Part of the unreality of the conception is that the character maintains almost total awareness of himself: what he is, how he got that way, what direction he is to take. There are no uncertainties. The author assumes that the background of the elders was the same as that of the children, and that the cycle perpetuates itself.

An almost total reliance on dialogue further weakens characterization by making people float, as it were, on the rhythms of their speech. Miss Compton-Burnett's characters seem to have no substance except what their words give them. They are little more than mouthpieces, wits, talking heads, disembodied streams of words. And yet strikingly, despite the brilliant flow of words, there are no characters who are expert in their work. Her writers are second-rate, her professionals marginal and uninvolved in their work, her "intellectuals" uninterested in pursuing ideas. Every ideal is in decline.

There is of course little doubt that Miss Compton-Burnett is indebted to the fiction of Henry James, perhaps more so than to that of Jane Austen. Like James, she is interested in late-Victorian attitudes, and, again like him, she is concerned with revealing the hypocrisy that the age has disguised as hearty materialism. Both have placed limitations on the range of the novel so that they could probe in depth, and both have emphasized characters whose lives are built on sand or based on misconceived relationships that are no longer viable.

Miss Compton-Burnett's restrictions on the range of her novels seem an epitome of the contemporary English novel, which has forsaken adventurous forms and broad content for the small, intensive work. Often like the Greek tragedian in her attempt to convey the doom that waits for the successful man, she is unlike him in her inability to project individual ills upon the social framework. The "sickness" of her characters is theirs alone, a condition of their lives, and there is no other life. Perhaps this is her main point. Despite her fierce brightness, the inner world of her typical characters is as moribund as that of a Beckett bum; for both, love, hope, faith, and desire are meaningless values in a world that only language can define.

MARY McCARTHY

From "The Inventions of I. Compton-Burnett" (1966)
The Writing on the Wall and Other Literary Essays
1970, pp. 112–44

Detection seems to be natural to the English novel; this is true even in Jane Austen, where a Wickham or a Frank Churchill is "found out." The traditional English novel, from Fielding on, deals in lost-and-found identities, concealment and discovery. Unlike the Continental novel (or the American), it is a kind of commodity with a warranty of unfailing reader-interest contained in the plot, which works like a factory mechanism—the mills of the gods. One of the mischievous originalities of Compton-Burnett is to have pursued this insular tendency to the extreme, making it her trademark. She produces Compton-Burnetts, as someone might produce ball bearings. (Dickens produced Dickenses, but Flaubert did not produce Flauberts.) Hence the uniformity of labeling in her titles and the open-stock patterns of her incidents and dialogue. The author, like all reliable old firms, is stressing the *sameness* of the formula: senior service. Her books have a magic in-gredient—forgettability, which makes them just as good the second time. She has no imitators. The formula is a trade secret. When she consents to give interviews about her work,

Compton-Burnett is cryptic, like an oracle or a hermit inventor. . . .

There is something in her work that seems to encourage false generalizations about it. She has designed her books as curios, and the fate of a curio is to be ranged on a shelf. Though easy to read, she is a hard writer to grasp. Her books slip away from you, and the inclination, therefore, is to "place" them conveniently. Most criticism of her is replete with lists—of "good" characters and bad ones, flat characters and round ones, "likeable" persons and tyrants; her critics are prone to count, divide, and classify, not always accurately, to measure the ratio of dialogue to description on a page. This counting, these laborious measurements, as of an unknown object—a giant footprint or a flying saucer—denote critical bafflement. Doubtless by her own wish, she remains a phenomenon, an occurrence in the history of letters. It would appear to be hubris to try to guess her riddle.

Her work is strewn with big, amateurish-looking clues, like planted evidence to mislead professional pryers in search of meanings, wider applications, influences. She has a fondness for naming her people after the English Poets (no resemblance intended; that is the point), and one of her old women is named Regan—by mistake; her father had thought that Regan was one of Shakespeare's heroines. The English Novelists too, like a private joke, keep nudging each other in these texts, while the anxious reader asks himself what is the point of allusions to Smollett, Maria Edgeworth, Jane Austen, Miss Mitford, Mrs. Gaskell, George Eliot, Dickens. Is he missing something important? Where is the connection with the story? Many clues lead to Shakespeare (King Lear and his daughters, for instance, in A *Father and His Fate*), and the reader is early put on the scent of Oedipus, the Jane Austen trail having grown cold. The "incest theme," already prominent in *Brothers and Sisters*, reappeared in *Darkness and Day*, as though to confirm suspicion. Did the quirky author, hidden like one of her characters in the folds of her narrative, hope to overhear critics fondly talking about Greek tragedy in Victorian dress and the "stichomythia" of her dialogue?

The incest theme is surely a red herring. The coupling between blood relations (or between people who imagine they are blood relations) is never anything but a twist of the plot. The author is capable of the fullest realism in her treatment of the passions, including the sexual ones, but when she shows incest, it is not a passion but an accident. She is strong on presenting temptation, but we never see a character being *tempted* to commit incest, as we do in the case of murder. Anyone who thinks that incest is the "subject" of Compton-Burnett has failed to see her real interests and the real idiosyncrasy of her mind.

Her books are not like other books; they are, as she might say, books apart. They do not "relate" to their material in the ordinary literary way, but crab-wise. The subject of any given Compton-Burnett is simply a cluster of associations and word-plays, while the plot is usually made up of arithmetical puzzles and brain-twisters. . . .

Compton-Burnett's people, including the sympathetic ones, are more often than not sententious, prone to balanced utterance, quotations from Shakespeare and the Bible, which are questioned by the lighter and more rebellious spirits. Bullivant is a polished orator, and great promise is shown by the three-year-old Toby in *The Present and the Past*, when he conducts the mole's funeral service, copying what he has heard in church. To "talk like a book" in Compton-Burnett is not (contrary to what is said by some critics) a proof of inauthenticity. It is a gift.

Quotations and adages are the chief worldly provisions of Compton-Burnett's people and particularly valued by the lower orders, who have fewer of the other kind. It is this that gives her work a grim sadness, as well as monotony: the sense of a ship-wrecked Band of Hope marooned on a desert island (England or the planet) with Bartlett's *Familiar Quotations*. Her people are survivors, battered floating bottles or time-capsules containing the remnants of human wisdom in aphoristic doses. "It is in the books," says a character in *A God and His Gifts*. "All human life is in them." As though this were not a credit to literature but a melancholy criticism of life.

The power of speech possessed by Compton-Burnett's servants is an eerie thing. Their voices, coming from near at hand, strike the ear with an effect of surprise, like talking animals in a fairy tale—the frog prince in the spring, or the horse's head hanging on the wall, or the speaking fish caught by the poor fisherman. Like those talking animals, the voices waiting at table have the faculty of omniscience, being given to warning and instruction. And the hands and bodies attached to them swiftly execute tasks, as in the fairy tales, beyond the power of ordinary mortals, *i.e.*, the leisured classes. These froggy, fishy attendants wear a menial livery, being bound by an enchantment, and when they remove it, on their day off, they are changed back into human beings.

Something of the kind is true of Compton-Burnett's children. Their treble contributions make you jump, like a sound coming from an improbable quarter. Audibility equals visibility in Compton-Burnett. Children who are not heard are not seen, just as a servant, waiting at table, usually remains invisible until his voice is raised. One by one, the characters at table materialize in a ghostly way, like lights turning on. Until they gave tongue, you did not know they were there; their place on the stage was dark. It is the *unexpectedness* of the voices that creates an effect bordering on the supernatural and reminds the reader of a sentient world all around him, listening, in the shadows. Children and servants are astral bodies. . . .

It is said (sometimes as a compliment) that Compton-Burnett has no interest in social problems. The world she has made, because there are no factories or slums in it, is mistaken for Jane Austen's "little bit of ivory." But the poor in Compton-Burnett are, precisely, made conspicuous by their absence—to be inferred by the reader, if he is paying the slightest attention, from the horrible scarves, shirts, and petticoats charitably knitted and sewn for them by the idle classes. The toiling, spinning masses are invisible and unheard, like the silent chorus of schoolboys whose marmalade is being watered. Remarks are made *about* them, and the worst are the "feeling" ones: "We should remember the less fortunate people when we are in want of nothing ourselves." Compton-Burnett has as much belief in philanthropy as Karl Marx himself. Whatever her voting habits, in her writing she is a strict economic realist with no partiality for the well-to-do. Her writing is extraordinary in its lack of social snobbery. Here she is far ahead of Jane Austen and of most of her own contemporaries. She does not even have an interest in social climbers, a sure sign of secret snobbery in an artist. That is probably why her books, despite the swarms of servants in them, have not found a larger public. They evoke "a vanished world" of privilege too unsparingly. Nor can a liberal reader flatter himself that the disappearance of a servant class has lent these novels a "documentary" interest; conditions have changed, but the condition has not.

What flashes out of her work is a spirited, unpardoning sense of injustice, which becomes even sharper in her later books. In her own eccentric way, Compton-Burnett is a radical thinker, one of the rare modern heretics. It is the eccentricity

that has diverted attention from the fact that these small uniform volumes are subversive packets. If their contents had to be reduced still further, boiled down to a single word capable of yielding a diversity of meanings, the word might be "necessity." From strict to dire. From "constraint or compulsion having its basis in the natural constitution of things" to "the condition of being in difficulties or straits, esp. through lack of means; want; poverty." Not omitting its uses in phrases and proverbs or "a bond or tie *between* persons, *Obs. rare*." It is a deep word, like her works.

CICELY GREIG
From *Ivy Compton-Burnett: A Memoir*
1972, pp. 21–23

Her perennial, and one as troublesome to her (and now to me, the only quirk I inherit from her) as speedwell or buttercup in a garden was the word *that*. The word occurred in her sentences and was crossed out on almost every page. I can only give examples from her last novel, unfinished at the time of her death, but much of it gone over in her careful way. This novel was written during the last years of her life, and she had not finished it, nor her revision of it when she died, two months after her eighty-fifth birthday. But the discipline is there on every page she revised.

⟨Following⟩ are three sentences all written originally with the word *that* in them.

'It is nothing that you would understand.'
'You know what I have asked for, and you know that I will have it.'
'We must see that you don't have too much of it.'

All three *thats* are crossed out.

But sometimes, having crossed out her *that*, she re-wrote it. Here is a passage where both *thats* were crossed out, but in a later revision she restored the first.

'Mater has found us a greater trial in her life than we knew.
'It does not mean that we have found her any less of one.'
'I suppose we should remember that she had to bring us up.'

She disliked our outworn words and phrases. She might use them in conversation, and she wrote them in her manuscripts. But she crossed them out in revision. The *of course* in the following sentence has a line through it, and so has the first *that*.

'It does suggest that there is something about you that we missed in our family life. Though of course that may hardly be the sphere for it.'

Vague words are crossed out. In this sentence *somehow* is crossed out.

'Hermia had a look of being somehow unusual.'

In place of *somehow* Ivy wrote *personally*, a stronger word, and more typical of Ivy. She had a precise and exact mind. She was familiar with our modern talk, our idioms, our way of working words to death—words like *basically*, for instance. She read the novels of her contemporaries, English and American, and we often discussed them. Sometimes a word like *impact* occurs in her writing, another well-worn word of our time. The word comes in her last book and she has crossed it out and used the word *impression* in its place. Her revision of the following sentences shows how she can use words as we lesser mortals use them, but in revision she crosses them out.

'To someone who was *actually* a stranger . . .'

'The large school in town *that* is not doing *too* well.'

The words in italics were rejected.

Her sentences have a distinctive lilt to them. When a word occurs out of tune, as it were, it is crossed out.

'My grandmother was never to lift *up* her head again.'

'We know *very* little as yet,' said Sir Robert.

'There seems *to be* no room for doubt.'

'And *it is* not only powers *that* are in question,' said Eliza.

The words in italics are all crossed out.

She corrected me when I, unconsciously, corrected her. I typed *judgment* because that is how I write it.

'I like the *e*,' Ivy said, in her quiet way.

I always thought she used commas rather freely. I left some of them out, thinking they could not all have been meant. With a pencilled manuscript, and one with many rubbings-out and corrections, one gave oneself the benefit of the doubt. But Ivy rescued them all. I left commas out in *Manservant and Maidservant* (before I knew better) and heard no more until her next manuscript was in my hands. There was one of her little notes:

'Do not leave out any commas. They are all necessary.'

Joseph Conrad

1857–1924

Joseph Conrad was born Teodor Konrad Korzeniowski on December 3, 1857 in Berdiczew, Poland. He came from a family of landowning aristocrats. As a man of letters, his father had translated Shakespeare into Polish from both French and English. Conrad's early years, however, were filled with unrest. His father was a member of the National Committee, an underground organization which supported Polish independence from Russia. In 1862 Conrad's father was arrested by Russian police and the family was forced into exile in Vologda, Russia. On the journey the young Conrad nearly died.

Shortly after their arrival in Vologda, Conrad's mother died. Although these years were rigorous and marked by intense solitude, Conrad took refuge in books. Due to his father's illness and melancholy over his wife's death, the two were eventually allowed to return to Poland. However, Conrad's father also died shortly after their arrival, leaving him to be raised by an uncle.

In 1874 Conrad left Poland and went to sea under the French flag. Many of his adventures provided fodder for his later writings. He sailed to the West Indies, ran guns in Central America, and was almost mortally wounded in a duel. When he recovered he went to England that same year, knowing little or nothing of the language. From that point on he sailed exclusively on British ships to various places in the East, such as Bangkok.

1886 was a key year for Conrad. He became naturalized as a British subject and achieved the position of Master Mariner. He also wrote his first story, "The Black Mate," for a competition in the magazine *Tit-Bits*.

In 1888 Conrad received his first command. After visiting his uncle in the Ukraine, he set sail as the Commander of a river steamer in the Belgian Congo. The journey had a profound impact on Conrad and later served as the basis of *Heart of Darkness*. He returned from the Congo exhausted and ill, retiring from the sea in 1894.

It was at this time that he began to write. In his solitary lodgings in London he completed two novels, *Alamayer's Folly* and *The Outcast of the Islands*. Both brought him the admiration of many of the literary giants of his time: Henry James, H. G. Wells, Stephen Crane, and Ford Madox Ford.

In 1896 he married Jessie George, then twenty-three. They had two sons, Borys and John. The family lived in a succession of rented homes while Conrad wrote. The novels which appeared between the years of 1897 and 1919 are generally considered his greatest: *Lord Jim*, *Nostromo*, and *Under Western Eyes*, among others.

Although he received much critical acclaim, financial rewards for his work were not forthcoming in his lifetime, and he often wrote under physical and psychological strain. He died on August 3, 1924.

Personal

What is so elusive about him is that he is always promising to make some general philosophic statement about the universe, and then refraining with a gruff disclaimer. Dealing, even in the slightest of these essays ⟨*Notes on Life and Letters*⟩, with vast and eternal issues, he won't say whether such issues lead or don't lead to a goal. "For which may I put you down, Mr. Conrad, for the One or the None?" At such a question Mr. Conrad roughens into a shrewd sailorman promptly. He implies that the One and the None are highly interesting, but that it is more important to distinguish a bulwark from a bollard. . . .

He never gives himself away. Our impertinence is rebuked; sentence after sentence discharges its smoke screen into our abashed eyes, yet the problem isn't settled really. Is there not also a central obscurity, something noble, heroic, beautiful, inspiring half a dozen great books; but obscure, obscure? While reading the half-dozen books one doesn't or shouldn't ask such a question, but it occurs, not improperly, when the author professes to be personal, and to take us into that confidence of his. These essays do suggest that he is misty in the middle as well as at the edges, that the secret casket of his genius contains a vapour rather than a jewel; and that we need not try to write him down philosophically, because there is, in this particular direction, nothing to write. No creed, in fact. Only opinions, and the right to throw them overboard when facts make them look absurd. Opinions held under the semblance of eternity, girt with the sea, crowned with the stars, and therefore easily mistaken for a creed. . . .

He does not respect all humanity. Indeed, were he less self-conscious, he would probably be a misanthrope. He has to pull himself up with a reminder that misanthropy wouldn't be quite fair—on himself. Observe . . . why he objected to being charged with cynicism. Cynicism may be undeserved by the poor victims, but that didn't occur to him. He objected because "it is like a charge of being blind in one eye, a moral disablement, a sort of disgraceful calamity," because he was touched in his pride. It becomes a point of honour not to be misanthropic, so that even when he hits out there is a fierce restraint that wounds more deeply than the blows. He will not despise men, yet cannot respect them, and consequently our careers seem to him important and unimportant at the same time, and our fates, like those of the characters of Alphonse Daudet, "poignant, intensely interesting, and not of the slightest consequence."

Now, together with these loyalties and prejudices and personal scruples, he holds another ideal, a universal, the love of Truth. But Truth is a flower in whose neighbourhood others must wither, and Mr. Conrad has no intention that the blossoms he has culled with such pains and in so many lands should suffer and be thrown aside. So there are constant discrepancies between his nearer and his further vision, and here would seem to be the cause of his central obscurity. If he lived only in his experiences, never lifting his eyes to what lies beyond them: or if, having seen what lies beyond, he would subordinate his experiences to it—then in either case he would be easier to read. But he is in neither case. He is too much of a seer to restrain his spirit; he is too much Joseph Conrad, too jealous of personal honour, to give any but the fullest value to deeds and dangers he has known.—E. M. FORSTER, "Joseph Conrad: A Note" (1920), *Abinger Harvest*, 1936, pp. 137–40

What is there you can write about him now that he is dead?

The critics will dive into their vocabularies and come up with articles on the death of Conrad. They are diving now, like prairie dogs.

It will not be hard for the editorial writers; Death of John L. Sullivan, Death of Roosevelt, Death of Major Whittlesey, Death of President Coolidge's Son, Death of Honored Citizen, Passing of Pioneer, Death of President Wilson, Great Novelist Passes, it is all the same.

Admirers of Joseph Conrad, whose sudden death is an occasion for general regret, usually think of him as an artist of the first rank, as a remarkable story teller and as a stylist. But Mr. Conrad was also a deep thinker and serene philosopher. In his novels, as in his essays etc.

It will run like that. All over the country.

And what is there that you can say about him now that he is dead?

It is fashionable among my friends to disparage him. It is

even necessary. Living in a world of literary politics where one wrong opinion often proves fatal, one writes carefully. I remember how I was made to feel how easily one might be dropped from the party, and the short period of Coventry that followed my remarking when speaking of George Antheil that I preferred my Stravinsky straight. I have been more careful since.

It is agreed by most of the people I know that Conrad is a bad writer, just as it is agreed that T. S. Eliot is a good writer. If I knew that by grinding Mr. Eliot into a fine dry powder and sprinkling that powder over Mr. Conrad's grave Mr. Conrad would shortly appear, looking very annoyed at the forced return, and commence writing I would leave for London early tomorrow morning with a sausage grinder.

One should not be funny over the death of a great man, but you cannot couple T. S. Eliot and Joseph Conrad in a sentence seriously any more than you could see, say, André Germain and Manuel Garcia (Maera) walking down the street together and not laugh.

The second book of Conrad's that I read was *Lord Jim*. I was unable to finish it. It is, therefore, all I have left of him. For I cannot re-read them. That may be what my friends mean by saying he is a bad writer. But from nothing else that I have ever read have I gotten what every book of Conrad has given me.

Knowing I could not re-read them I saved up four that I would not read until I needed them badly, when the disgust with writing, writers and everything written of and to write would be too much. Two months in Toronto used up the four books. One after another I borrowed them from a girl who had all of his books on a shelf, bound in blue leather, and had never read any of them. Let us be exact. She had read *The Arrow of Gold* and *Victory*.

In Sudbury, Ontario, I bought three back numbers of the Pictorial Review and read *The Rover*, sitting up in bed in the Nickle Range Hotel. When morning came I had used up all my Conrad like a drunkard, I had hoped it would last me the trip, and felt like a young man who has blown his patrimony. But, I thought, he will write more stories. He has lots of time.

When I read the reviews they all agreed *The Rover* was a bad story.

And now he is dead and I wish to God they would have taken some great, acknowledged technician of a literary figure and left him to write his bad stories.—ERNEST HEMINGWAY, "Conrad, Optimist and Moralist" (1924), *By-Line Ernest Hemingway*, 1967, pp. 132–33

"I wonder if it's the end," I was reading in a letter dated May 30, the last that I received from him; cordial as usual, and like the others penetrated by that sort of bitter liveliness, that slightly unwilling charm, which gave a sea-tang to his friendly impulses; but marked already with a mysterious solemnity, with the presentiment of death.

That letter touched me to the quick like a farewell. I felt myself in arrears with him. I had gone a long time without seeing him again, without writing him. Had I ever been able to tell him—what I wrote him immediately—all the affection, admiration, veneration, which despite so much absence, so much silence, I had never ceased to feel for him? He was the only one of my elders that I loved and knew. . . .

Claudel was the one who made me aware of Conrad. I am still grateful to him. After a lunch together, as some other companion was speaking enthusiastically about Kipling, Claudel with a slightly disdainful smile threw out the name of Conrad. Not a one of us had yet heard of him.

"What should we read of his?" some one asked.

"Everything," said Claudel. And he cited *The Nigger of the Narcissus, Youth, Typhoon, Lord Jim. . . ."* None of these books had been translated as yet. I immediately took note of their titles and at my first contact with them was completely won over.

Shortly after, on a trip to England, I had the opportunity of meeting the author in person. Valery Larbaud (if my recollection is correct) went with me. Miss Tobin, a charming young English woman whom Larbaud knew, was to introduce us. Conrad was living then in Kent at Capel House, a small country place near Ashford; it was there that he received us. I lingered several days in the vicinity; returned to Capel House the next year, and we were soon the warmest and best of friends.

Conrad did not like to talk about his life; a sort of modesty, a lack of regard for himself restrained him and kept him silent on his past. His memories of the sea seemed to him now only the raw material for his art, and, because the requirements of his art, as they became involved, constrained him to transpose, to depersonalize and distance from himself by fiction everything he had experienced personally, he was singularly awkward, both in his books and in his conversation, as a raconteur; only in fiction did he feel at his ease.

The sea to him was like an old abandoned mistress whom only an engraving, the picture of a superb sailing vessel in the hall of Capel House, recalled nostalgically to memory.

"Don't look at that," he said as he drew me into the parlor while I was studying that symbol of his first love. "Let's talk books."

Conrad had married, "settled down"; lived with his wife and children, but by and for books. How well he knew our authors. He admired Flaubert and Maupassant and enjoyed talking about them. He especially liked our critics and Lemaître most of all. He didn't care much for Barrès; it's not hard to imagine what this perfect example of man uprooted thought of theories of *déracinement.* As he pronounced opinions only on what he knew, his judgments were very firm; but as they accorded with mine, our conversations went smoothly. On one point only we could not agree: the name even of Dostoievsky made him shudder. I think some journalists, by awkward comparisons, had intensified his exasperation, as a good Pole, against the great Russian; with whom nonetheless he had some subtle points of resemblance, but whom he detested cordially and whom one could not mention without calling up anew his vehement indignation. I should have liked to know what it was he disliked in Dostoievsky's books, but could get from him only vague imprecations. . . .

Nothing was more cordial, purer, or more virile, than his laughter, than his appearance, than his voice. But like the sea in its moments of calm you felt him capable of violent passion, of tempests. Great as was his curiosity for the dark places in man's soul, he detested any exhibition of the underhanded, the equivocal, or the vile. And I think what I liked best in him was a sort of inherent nobility, rugged, disdainful, and a little despairing, the same quality that he gave Lord Jim and that makes that book one of the most beautiful that I know, one of the saddest too, and at the same time one of the most uplifting.

Somebody else will have to speak of the instruction to be drawn from his works, especially since it is the fashion now to search out the lessons in everything. I think the works of Conrad are as profitable as it is possible for art to be today, when on the one hand the study of man tends to turn novelists away from life, and on the other hand the love of life tends to discredit letters. Nobody had lived more savagely than Conrad; nobody had then submitted life to so patient, sensitive, and knowing a transmutation into art.—André Gide, "Joseph Conrad" (1924), *The Art of Joseph Conrad*, ed. R. W. Stallman, 1960, pp. 3–5

Suddenly, without giving us time to arrange our thoughts or prepare our phrases, our guest has left us; and his withdrawal without farewell or ceremony is in keeping with his mysterious arrival, long years ago, to take up his lodging in this country. For there was always an air of mystery about him. It was partly his Polish birth, partly his memorable appearance, partly his preference for living in the depths of the country, out of earshot of gossips, beyond reach of hostesses, so that for news of him one had to depend upon the evidence of simple visitors with a habit of ringing doorbells who reported of their unknown host that he had the most perfect manners, the brightest eyes, and spoke English with a strong foreign accent.

Still, though it is the habit of death to quicken and focus our memories, there clings to the genius of Conrad something essentially, and not accidentally, difficult of approach. His reputation of later years was, with one obvious exception, undoubtedly the highest in England; yet he was not popular. He was read with passionate delight by some; others he left cold and lustreless. Among his readers were people of the most opposite ages and sympathies. Schoolboys of fourteen, driving their way through Marryat, Scott, Henty, and Dickens, swallowed him down with the rest; while the seasoned and the fastidious, who in process of time have eaten their way to the heart of literature and there turn over and over a few precious crumbs, set Conrad scrupulously upon their banqueting table. One source of difficulty and disagreement is, of course, to be found, where men have at all times found it, in his beauty. One opens his pages and feels as Helen must have felt when she looked in her glass and realised that, do what she would, she could never in any circumstances pass for a plain woman. So Conrad had been gifted, so he had schooled himself, and such was his obligation to a strange language wooed characteristically for its Latin qualities rather than its Saxon that it seemed impossible for him to make an ugly or insignificant movement of the pen. His mistress, his style, is a little somnolent sometimes in repose. But let somebody speak to her, and then how magnificently she bears down upon us, with what colour, triumph, and majesty! Yet is it arguable that Conrad would have gained both in credit and in popularity if he had written what he had to write without this incessant care for appearances. They block and impede and distract, his critics say, pointing to those famous passages which it is becoming the habit to lift from their context and exhibit among other cut flowers of English prose. He was self-conscious and stiff and ornate, they complain, and the sound of his own voice was dearer to him than the voice of humanity in its anguish. The criticism is familiar, and as difficult to refute as the remarks of deaf people when *Figaro* is played. They see the orchestra; far off they hear a dismal scrape of sound; their own remarks are interrupted, and, very naturally, they conclude that the ends of life would be better served if instead of scraping Mozart those fifty fiddlers broke stones upon the road. That beauty teaches, that beauty is a disciplinarian, how are we to convince them, since her teaching is inseparable from the sound of her voice and to that they are deaf?—Virginia Woolf, "Joseph Conrad" (1924), *The Common Reader*, 1925, pp. 309–11

I made the acquaintance of Joseph Conrad in September 1913, through our common friend Lady Ottoline Morrell. I had been for many years an admirer of his books, but should not have ventured to seek acquaintance without an introduction. I traveled down to his house near Ashford in Kent in a state of somewhat anxious expectation. My first impression was one of surprise. He spoke English with a very strong foreign accent, and nothing in his demeanor in any way suggested the sea. He was an aristocratic Polish gentleman to his finger tips. His feeling for the sea, and for England, was one of romantic love—love from a certain distance, sufficient to leave the romance untarnished. His love for the sea began at a very early age. When he told his parents that he wished for a career as a sailor, they urged him to go into the Austrian navy, but he wanted adventure and tropical seas and strange rivers surrounded by dark forests; and the Austrian navy offered him no scope for these desires. His family were horrified at his seeking a career in the English merchant marine, but his determination was inflexible.

He was, as anyone may see from his books, a very rigid moralist and politically far from sympathetic with revolutionaries. He and I were in most of our opinions by no means in agreement, but in something very fundamental we were extraordinarily at one.

My relation to Joseph Conrad was unlike any other that I have ever had. I saw him seldom, and not over a long period of years. In the outworks of our lives, we were almost strangers, but we shared a certain outlook on human life and human destiny, which, from the very first, made a bond of extreme strength. I may perhaps be pardoned for quoting a sentence from a letter that he wrote to me very soon after we had become acquainted. I should feel that modesty forbids the quotation except for the fact that it expresses so exactly what I felt about him. What he expressed and I equally felt was, in his words, "A deep admiring affection which, if you were never to see me again and forgot my existence tomorrow, would be unalterably yours *usque ad finem.*"— BERTRAND RUSSELL, "Joseph Conrad," *Portraits From Memory and Other Essays*, 1956, pp. 86–7

. . . Contradictions abounded in him. "Enigmatic," "mysterious," "elusive" were terms liberally applied to a man no term adequately fitted; his complex novels, human commentaries to be read on several levels, were as hard to classify. "A truly great novel is a tale to the simple, a parable to the wise, and a direct revelation of reality . . . to the man who has made it part of his being," wrote John Middleton Murry in 1924. In that sentence was summarized, Carlos Baker has suggested, "the triple power which Conrad brought to the art of the novel." With the meaning in his work depending on what each reader grasped, his novels received manifold interpretations. What views he held, what make of man he was, also ran the gamut of opinion. . . .

Mankind was Conrad's theme, all aspects of it, weaknesses and strengths. To cope with that large theme he had the equipment of a mind so extensive in its range that it drew from Rothenstein, his friend for twenty years, the comment "Conrad understood everything." One after another, those who knew him sought to describe his intellectual power. Bertrand Russell told of the exhilarating impact of his talk with Conrad at their first meeting in 1913: "We seemed to sink through layer after layer of what was artificial, till gradually both reached the central fire. It was an experience unlike any other that I have known . . . I came away bewildered, and hardly able to find my way among ordinary affairs." More than forty years later he would write of Conrad: "His intense and passionate nobility shines in my memory like a star seen from the bottom of a well. I wish I could make his light shine for others as it shone for me." To Galsworthy the "storehouse of his subconscious self was probably as interesting and comprehensive a museum as

any in the world." A voracious reader and trilingual, the extent of his knowledge was a source of awe to Stephen Crane, made him the "brilliant conversationalist" so "formidable in argument" Cunninghame Graham knew. To Curle, a frequent companion in his later years, he had "for great subjects a great outlook," a "philosophical detachment from the cries of the moment." With friends he would talk for hours on a subject, "winding into its ramifications and letting it bear him on gradually into reminiscence and by-paths that were enthralling."

A superior intellect was one factor in the comprehensiveness of Conrad's work, the versatility which has given him a special standing of his own. The uniqueness inducing the New York *World* to say of him that "he was like no predecessor and he leaves no followers behind him" was to some extent due to a combination of circumstances unknown to any other writer of modern times. A man with an extraordinary mind and acute sensitivity, he was exposed to a series of dramatic experiences lasting two decades of a global wandering more extensive in time and space than the myth-producing voyages of Ulysses. His wide outlook is more attuned to the present space-dissolved age than it was to the insular period he knew. In today's shrunken world, where East and West are within a traveler's sunrise-to-sunset reach, it has become accepted truth that, regardless of what areas of the earth they inhabit, men share common traits and motives. This, plus the fact that life is more frankly discussed than in his Victorian day, has given Conrad's novels more meaning than they had for readers in his lifetime.— JERRY ALLEN, "The Men," *The Sea Years of Joseph Conrad*, 1965, pp. 305–10

General

. . . Conrad's marvellous gift of language was, in the end, dramatic. When he talked his sense of phonetics was dormant, but the moment it came to any kind of performance the excitement would quicken the brain centres that governed his articulation. It was, indeed, the same with his French. When conversing desultorily with the writer, he had much of the accent and the negligence of an aristocratic, meridional lounger of the seventies. . . . But when at Lamb House, Rye, he addressed compliments to Mr. Henry James, you could imagine, if you closed your eyes, that it was the senior actor of the Théâtre Français, addressing an eulogium to the bust of Molière. . . .

It would be disingenuous to avoid the subject of language. This is the only matter on which the writer ever differed fundamentally from Conrad. It was one upon which the writer felt so deeply that, for several years, he avoided his friend's society. The pain of approaching the question is thus very great.

Conrad's dislike for the English language, then, was, during all the years of our association, extreme, his contempt for his medium unrivalled. Again and again during the writing of, say, *Nostromo* he expressed passionate regret that it was then too late to hope to make a living by writing in French, and as late as 1916 he expressed to the writer an almost equally passionate envy of the writer who was in a position to write in French, propaganda for the government of the French Republic. . . . And Conrad's contempt for English as a prose language was not, as in the writer's case, mitigated by love for English as the language for verse-poetry. For, to the writer, English is as much superior to French in the one particular as French to English in the other. . . .

Conrad's indictment of the English language was this, that no English word is a word; that all English words are instruments for exciting blurred emotions. "Oaken" in French means "made of oak wood"—nothing more. "Oaken" in English connotes innumerable moral attributes: it will connote stolidity, resolution, honesty, blond features, relative unbreakableness, absolute unbendableness—also, made of oak. . . . The consequence is that no English word has clean edges: a reader is always, for a fraction of a second, uncertain as to which meaning of the word the writer intends. Thus, all English prose is blurred. Conrad desired to write prose of extreme limpidity. . . .

We may let it go at that. In later years Conrad achieved a certain fluency and a great limpidity of language. He then regretted that for him all the romance of writing was gone—the result being *The Rover*, which strikes the writer as being a very serene and beautiful work. . . . In between the two he made tributes to the glory of the English language, by implication contemning the tongue that Flaubert used. This struck the writer, at that time in a state of exhausted depression, as unforgivable—as the very betrayal of Dain by Tom Lingard. . . . Perhaps it was. If it were Conrad faced the fact in that book. There are predicaments that beset great Adventurers, in dark hours, in the shallows: the overtired nerve will fail. . . .We may well let it go at that. . . .

> For it would be delightful to catch the echo of the desperate and funny quarrels that enlivened these old days. The pity of it is that there comes a time when *all* the fun of one's life must be looked for in the past. . . .

Those were Conrad's last words on all the matters of our collaborations here treated of. They were, too, almost his last words. . . . For those who can catch them here, then, are the echoes. . . .— FORD MADOX FORD, "Conrad on the Theory of Fiction," *Joseph Conrad: A Personal Remembrance*, 1924, pp. 171–77

Sir,—Will you please allow me to correct a few of the most fantastic statements regarding my husband made in Ford Madox Hueffer's book, which was reviewed in your columns a few weeks ago?

If Mr. Hueffer intends a personal remembrance as a tribute to the dead friend with whom he claims to have had such close acquaintance, why endeavour on every page to show the vast difference between himself and his friend, and always to the detriment of that friend: his inferiority in intellect, character and ability? To those who knew Joseph Conrad personally these statements would have their real value, and to those who had also the privilege of even a slight acquaintance with Mr. Hueffer these few lines would be quite unnecessary. . . .

During the years that Mr. Hueffer was most intimate with Joseph Conrad—between 1898–1909—Ford Madox Hueffer never spent more than three consecutive weeks under our roof, and when we returned the visit we always, with few exceptions, had rooms in a cottage close at hand. After 1909 the meetings between the two were very rare and not once of my husband's seeking. The author of *A Personal Remembrance* claims to have been Joseph Conrad's literary adviser, also his literary godfather! That claim is, like nearly everything else in that detestable book, quite untrue. I have heard my husband say more than once that he found Mr. Hueffer a mental stimulus, but that was in the early days—days before even Ford Madox Hueffer himself became aware of the great dignity he claims—that of being the greatest English stylist.—JESSIE CONRAD, Letter to the Editor, *TLS*, Dec. 4, 1924, p. 826

Despite the great interest shown recently in Joseph Conrad's fiction, there has appeared comparatively little comment relating the ideas on literary technique expressed by Ford Madox

Ford in his several chapters on Conrad to the latter's own remarks in his letters, essays, and notes to his first Collected Edition. These remarks, when brought together and evaluated, go far to provide a basis for Conrad's literary intentions and suggest criteria by which to judge his early artistic successes as well as his later generally less successful work. They demonstrate almost conclusively that when Conrad forsook the theories he worked out with Ford and those expressed in his early letters and essays, especially in the now famous Preface to *The Nigger of the "Narcissus,"* his work became thin and uninteresting, losing the range and texture of his best fiction. They demonstrate further that when he wrote his Author's Notes, from which several critics have been tempted to derive his aesthetic, he was already shucking off many of the early ideas in favor of the very practices he had once repudiated. Conrad's notes were almost frivolous for a major novelist intent on the seriousness of his craft, and they were obviously conceived more to establish rapport with his newly-won popular audience than as a guide to his artistic intentions. If we want insight into the major Conrad, we must return to the critical comments thrown out when he was an apprentice writer still excited by the ideas he and Ford had agreed upon, a time almost twenty years before the debility set in which marked his last years of creative work and which carried over into the notes written during the same period. . . .

Ezra Pound said that what Flaubert had done to change French prose, Conrad and Ford did to transform English prose, and he, Pound, was trying to do in order to reshape English poetry. Conrad's use of *phanopoeia*—the piling up of imagistic details which replaced, in part at least, a direct narrative—was, said Pound, the way of the Imagists. The breakup of the conventional novel's narrative into small scenes makes the scene function as an image in poetry, in a way like the images in Pound's own early poetry. . . .

Ford and Conrad, in their numerous sessions together, worked out their idea of the "planned novel," in which each step in the novel points toward a predetermined effect and leaves nothing to chance. Every word and every action, they said, must carry the story forward—what they called a novelistic *progression d'effet*—wherein the intensity increases as the story develops. This attempt to convey increasing urgency and intensity in the story would involve, said the authors, an assiduous study of all factors relevant to the pace of the novel. One idea, however, always predominated: to unsettle the conventional narrative sequences which had hitherto prevailed in the novel, and by so doing to create new interest in what the two authors feared was now a faded genre. This method meant slow and calculating work, paying unflagging attention to the effect of each scene and character, and maintaining always strict control. Conrad with his enthusiasm for the French novel and possessing the French penchant for experimentation and analysis was especially fitted for this role.

What was achieved with narrative structure and character development, the collaborators realized, could also be effectively accomplished with speech. Conrad and Ford, perhaps influenced by Flaubert's experiments with interrupted speech, decided that to avoid boredom long speeches must be broken down, interspersed with narrative, and bolstered by little "jumps" in the pace of the novel. These "jumps" would provide, they said, a "consistent succession of tiny, unobservable surprises" which would alleviate the monotony of incessant speech. . . .

Accordingly, Conrad conceived of the novel as history, psychology, sociology, fiction, and poetry cast into one structure and informed by the power of the imagination. Of course, this emphasis on inclusiveness meant that the novel had to become the receptacle of a large vision of human experience. Ford wrote that he and Conrad had agreed "that the novel is absolutely the only vehicle for the thought of our day. With the novel you can do anything; you can inquire into every department of life, you can explore every department of the world of thought." In making his characters themselves narrate the story, and thus, so to speak, create the novel, Conrad was moving toward a representation of history in the making. *Chance* and *Nostromo,* with their various points of view which carry the narrative backward and forward, are a sort of literary history in which the "facts" of the story are fictitious while their arrangement aims at historical and social truth. . . .

Central to Conrad's conceptualization of his material was the emphasis he and Ford placed on the sense of the incongruous, which, they said, should be based on the use of contrasts and comparisons. The incongruous situation could, through overlapping and repetition, dramatize combining or contrasting characters and themes, and at the same time keep the author at an objective distance from his material. *Lord Jim,* for example, is full of characters whose personalities are symbols of segments of Jim himself. Likewise, in *Nostromo* and *Victory,* we find characters and situations that hold the novel in balance through their interaction with previous characters or situations. Further, Heyst and Jones (*Victory*) complement each other like Jim and Brown (*Lord Jim*) and in some ways like Decoud and Nostromo. In *The Secret Agent,* the idiot boy Stevie, who draws circles of perfection when disturbed, is an ironic contrast with the "normal" anarchists who want to destroy while he wants to create.

This is how Conrad attained objectivity, imaginatively and not discursively, precisely without being journalistic, clearly without being obvious. When Conrad wrote to Hugh Clifford that no single word or method is adequate—that the "imagination of the reader should be left free to arouse his feeling"—he was of course suggesting that really big themes come through the novelist's awareness of all the potentialities of his subject matter. . . .

For Conrad, if art and beauty were to unite as moral factions, then there would have to be virility as well as verbal skill, sincerity as well as devotion, responsibility as well as sensitivity, and integrity as well as involvement. Conrad was harsh to those he thought pseudo-artists, those who went through the motions without the substance, the fire, the restraint and the detachment that could transform everyday facts into an artistic vision and the particular into the universal. If the imagination were to bear fruit, it must be an imagination rooted in responsibility, a conception of the world in moral terms that is presented indirectly through a non-didactic surface that derives every nuance and possibility from the arrangement of the material.—Frederic R. Karl, "Joseph Conrad's Literary Theory," *Crit,* Fall 1960, pp. 317–35

Works

THE NIGGER OF THE "NARCISSUS"

The entire book occupies well under two hundred pages. And within this brief span Conrad has presented his subject in every manner known to narrative art, from every conceivable angle of vision, from every conceivable point of view, physical and psychological. His subject is the *Narcissus* and everything about that boat during a six months' voyage. And he seems to have started out with the intention of "putting across" that subject by the mere magic of the written word. The Oriental

style is very much in evidence throughout, whether in description, psychology, or meditation.

> On men reprieved by its disdainful mercy, the immortal sea confers in its justice the full privilege of desired unrest. Through the perfect wisdom of its grace they are not permitted to meditate at ease upon the complicated and acrid savour of existence. They must without pause justify their life to the eternal pity that commands toil to be hard and unceasing, from sunrise to sunset, from sunset to sunrise; till the weary succession of nights and days tainted by the obstinate clamor of sages, demanding bliss and an empty heaven, is redeemed at last by the vast silence of pain and labour, by the dumb fear and the dumb courage of men obscure, forgetful, and enduring.

But Conrad's instinct outran his theory. He began his story in the omniscient manner of the traditional author, and for a long space it is all told in the third person. There is no suggestion at all that the person writing was anywhere on that boat as witness or participator in the action. Then suddenly . . . there is a shift from the third to the first person. It is a question of the attitude of the crew to James Wait, and suddenly the crew are no longer "they" and "them" but "we" and "us." It would appear that the writer is one of the crew and sharing their experiences and emotions. The first person is maintained pretty steadily through ten pages, and then we return to the third. And throughout the rest of the book there is a constant alternation between the objective third person and the first person which implies participation by the writer. Very often there is a shift from the third person to the first on one page and back again on the next.

Generally speaking, we may say that the most vividly realized passages are those in which the writer identifies himself with the crew (or possibly with the officers) by the use of the first person. It is clear that, however blindly Conrad may have started out in the objective manner, his instinct led him inevitably to the technique of identification. But there is no indication until the very end of the story of who this writer is who makes himself so anonymous a member of the group described as "we," nor even very certainly whether he is an officer or one of the crew. It is only in the last three pages that he becomes individualized as "I," sharply distinguished from the common sailors, whom he so much admires and regards in comradely fashion, but with the unmistakable air of a superior.

Thus in *The Nigger of the Narcissus* we see Conrad actually in process of learning, of accidentally stumbling upon a trick which was to serve him so very well in the greatest of his later stories. To experiences which he had personally lived through he was trying to apply the traditional impersonal manner of fiction, and only as it were in spite of himself fell into the personal manner of one who was there. In later stories we shall see him applying the personal manner of one who was there to what were largely fictitious inventions.—Joseph Warren Beach, "Impressionism: Conrad," *The Twentieth Century Novel,* 1932, pp. 351–52

. . . *The Nigger of the "Narcissus"* is an allegory of temptation and endurance, a microcosm of the moral world of relationships and responsibilities. And since, as in all myth, principles as well as patterns of action are reiterated across space and time, the social motif of *The Nigger of the "Narcissus"* is referable to the individual psyche, and the novel, under this aspect, is an adventure of the soul.

It is the third aspect, the mythic, never openly acknowledged by Conrad himself, which gives to the novel its vibratory temper and its perennial interest. Conrad's fraternal loyalty to the nautical facts of the case is finally subordinate to his transcendental theme, fortified throughout the novel by its equivalence in symbolic action. Geography and meteorology combine with crises of human conduct and with analogues of the metaphysical cycle to produce a rich complex of correspondences. . . .

Leaving one continent for another, the *Narcissus* sails *out* of darkness *into* darkness, since Conrad's moral geography was opposite in value to Herman Melville's, for example. The sea, "the unstable element," was, to Conrad, the amniotic ocean of life, itself: like life uncertain, incalculable but enchanting and worthier of men's challenge than the land. In all Conrad's novels, the land is the home of the enemy. The jungle, the forest, the city: these are his symbols of treachery. The sea, however disastrous or inclement it may become, is as neutral and as irrefutable as the life-cycle; it is the given, if "destructive element," and in the face of it man's duty is, like Singleton's in this novel, to "steer with care." . . .

The *Narcissus*, a creature of light, was born in darkness, "in black eddies of smoke, under a grey sky, on the banks of the Clyde. The clamorous and sombre stream gives birth to things of beauty that float away into the sunshine of the world to be loved by men." When she leaves Bombay with her yards hoisted she becomes "a high and lonely pyramid, gliding all shining and white, through the sunlit mist. The tug turned short round and went away towards the land [resembling] an enormous and aquatic black beetle, surprised by the light, overwhelmed by the sunshine, trying to escape with ineffectual effort into the distant gloom of the land . . ." Upon arrival in the Thames at the end of the voyage, the *Narcissus* re-enters the cloud: "the shadows of soulless walls fell upon her, the dust of all the continents leaped upon her deck, and a swarm of strange men, clambering up her sides, took possession of her in the name of the sordid earth. She had ceased to live." . . .

By not accepting the moral dichotomy of land and sea as a highly charged metaphor, the reader of *The Nigger of the "Narcissus"* might well accuse Conrad of sentimental sophistry; accepting it, he will be in a position to appreciate how effectively it is co-featured with the other symbolic properties—particularly with the permeating use of color contrasts. White and black, pink or blue and black, light and shade, sun and cloud, gold and darkness—within the total form, these oppositions are vitally operative, usually accompanied by relative variations of weather. So much is this tonality the index to Conrad's alignment of moods and forces that its most pertinent appearances are well worth isolating before taking up considerations less purely visual. . . .

In *The Nigger of the "Narcissus,"* what Conrad's imagery substantiates above all is the apocalyptic nature of the novel's outline. The four Empedoclean elements, the polar variants of night and day, hell and heaven, West and East, encompass the cosmological pyramid which is the subject. In "the living movement of the whole," Conrad's symbolism subscribes to no single order of religious values; it synthesizes universally recurring emblems in man's expression of his destiny and places them at the service of the novel's contingent subject, the moral effects of illusion. . . .

Metaphysically, Wait serves a purpose comparable to that of El Negro in Melville's "Benito Cereno": he is the *spirit* of blackness, archetype of the unknown forces from the depths. With this important difference, however: he is not sensationally demonic but, rather, insidious and emanating. His role is a rehearsal, in Conrad's literature, of that "barbarous and superb

woman" in "Heart of Darkness" who, as the steamboat leaves with the damned and moribund remains of Kurtz, stretches "tragically her bare arms after [them] over the sombre and glittering river." Wait, by a form of adjuration less explicit, more accessible to the gullibility of simple men, all but deprives the crew of their will to live. Consentient with the natural perils that haunt its progress, he accompanies the *Narcissus* across the waters of strife, casting his spell on the probity of the crew's endeavors.

A symbol of postponement, his name is cardinal token: Wait. Conrad plays upon it when the Nigger belatedly joins the ship, shouting "Wait" to the astonished officer who takes the word as an insolent injunction rather than as a name. Wait's burial at sea re-emphasizes the tenacity of his inertia, for when the plank is first raised to slide his body overboard, he holds fast until one of the sailors, after screaming "Jimmy, be a man! . . . Go, Jimmy . . . ," gives the corpse needed impetus with a light push. But *Wait* has also, by virtue of the Nigger's retarding and oppressive action, the force of the other spelling, *weight*. (Immediately following his plummet from the deck, "The ship rolled as if relieved of an unfair burden.") From his bed-ridden vantage point, supine and seemingly helpless, he drags on the initial resistance of the men like an anchor, beguiles their sympathy, gradually vitiates their resolution by the pathos of his induced condition. (Naturalistically, his eventual death may be construed as psychogenic.) His appeal is to the slacker in each man's heart, awakening the desire to rebel, abandonment of duty and luxury of irresponsible rest. . . .

The iconography of *The Nigger of the "Narcissus"* was not accomplished without a dangerous compromise between the naturalistic, biographical material and its symbolic transmutation. Fearful of overstressing the subaqueous world of the underconsciousness, the symbol-producing level of the psyche which, in fact, was the most dependable source of his inspiration, Conrad overloaded his mundane treatment of the crew. As separate units of consciousness they are beautifully deployed for angels of relationship, but no one can deny that their professional virtues are overwritten, almost to the detriment of the narrative's aesthetic integrity. It is clear, in this direction, that Conrad had difficulty in serving myth and memory with equal justice. His narrator-perspective is awkwardly handled. The novel gets under way in the third person; in the middle of the second chapter it switches abruptly to the viewpoint of first person plural and remains there until the coda section, when it becomes first person singular. Presumably an unspecified member of the deck crew has carried the narration; in this case the contents of the thoughts of Mr. Creighton and of the cook, and many of the conversations, between Allistoun and his officer or between Donkin and Wait, for example, are impossibly come by. And, with this handicap, the gilded sermonizings on the crew's high endeavor are doubly hard to accept. If Conrad was solicitous for the phenomenal level of his narrative, he might at least have supplied a recorder to whose endowments his own opulent prose would have been more apt. However, this novel was an early trial in the marriage of subject with its coordinating agencies; Conrad's craft was not yet wholly adequate to sustain an unfailing integrity of means. . . .

The Nigger of the "Narcissus" is a fable with many layers of interconnection. "A work that aspires, however humbly, to the condition of art, should carry its justification in every line." So begins the preface to this work and in so far as the novel, itself, seeks to establish "the power of occult forces which," Conrad concedes elsewhere, "rule the fascinating aspects of the visible world," it does carry its justification. Without the other

dimensions, it would be merely a tale of ships and men burdened by an iridescent futility of expression. As it is, the
metaphors which significantly cluster at every magnetic point
in the narrative illuminate the infernal core of its theme as, on
the equator, the *Narcissus* floats in the aurora of the lightning,
"like a charred ship enclosed in a globe of fire."—VERNON
YOUNG, "Trial by Water: Joseph Conrad's *The Nigger of the
'Narcissus'*" (1952), *The Art of Joseph Conrad*, ed. R. W. Stallman, 1960, pp. 109–20

The Nigger of the "Narcissus" (sixty years after the event) is
peculiarly beset with dangers for the critic. For Conrad has
become fashionable rather suddenly, and comment on this
story has passed almost without pause from naïve recapitulation
to highly sophisticated analysis of "cabalistic intent." The older
innocence is suggested by Arthur Symons' complaint that the
story had no idea behind it, or by a journeyman reviewer's
remark that James Wait had no place in this record of life at
sea. An example of recent sophistication is Vernon Young's
important essay "Trial by Water," in the Spring 1952 issue of
Accent. A single sentence will suggest its bias: "Fearful of overstressing the subaqueous world of the underconsciousness, the
symbol-producing level of the psyche which, in fact, was the
most dependable source of his inspiration, Conrad overloaded
his mundane treatment of the crew." The comment is provocative; it leads us to wonder whether the crew isn't, for this
fiction, too numerous. Yet we must rejoin that the crew is very
important, and that many of the book's greatest pages have little
to do with this subaqueous world. There remains the vulgar
charge, yet real menace, that the critic may oversimplify
a novel by oversubtilizing and overintellectualizing it—not
merely by intruding beyond the author's conscious intention
(which he is fully privileged to do) but by suggesting patterns of
unconscious combination which do not and cannot operate for
the reasonably alert common reader. Much of any serious story
works on the fringes of the reader's consciousness: a darkness to
be illuminated by the critic's insight. But that insight remains
irrelevant which can never become aesthetic enjoyment, or
which takes a story too far out of its own area of discourse. I say
this with the uneasy conviction that criticism should expose
itself to as many as possible of a novel's suasions, and that it is
only too easy (above all with a Conrad or a Faulkner) to stress
the abstract and symbolic at the expense of everything else.
One might begin by saying that *The Nigger of the "Narcissus"*
recasts the story of Jonah and anticipates "The Secret Sharer"'s
drama of identification. This is a truth but a partial truth. And
how many partial truths would be needed to render or even
evoke such a mobile as this one? Touch one wire, merely
breathe on the lovely thing and it wavers to a new form! In the
pursuit of structured meaning—of obvious purpose and overtone of conviction and "cabalistic intent" and unconscious
content; of stark symbol and subtle cluster of metaphor—one is
tempted to ignore the obvious essentials of technique and style.
One may even never get around to mentioning what are, irrespective of structure or concealed meaning, the best-written
pages in the book. They are these: the arrival of James Wait on
board, the onset of the storm, the overturning of the ship, the
righting of the ship, old Singleton at the wheel, the quelling of
the mutiny, the death of Wait and his burial, the docking of
the ship, the dispersal of the crew.

It seems proper for once to begin with the end: with that
large personal impression which an embarrassed criticism often
omits altogether. *The Nigger of the "Narcissus"* is the most
generalized of Conrad's novels in its cutting of a cross section,
though one of the least comprehensive. It is a version of our

dark human pilgrimage, a vision of disaster illumined by grace.
The microcosmic ship is defined early in the second chapter
with an almost Victorian obviousness: "On her lived truth and
audacious lies; and, like the earth, she was unconscious, fair to
see—and condemned by men to an ignoble fate. The august
loneliness of her path lent dignity to the sordid inspiration of
her pilgrimage. She drove foaming to the south as if guided by
the courage of a high endeavour." Or we can narrow the vision
to a single sentence near the end: "The dark knot of seamen
drifted in sunshine." The interplay of light and dark images
throughout conveys the sense of a destiny both good and evil,
heroic and foolish, blundered out under a soulless sky. If I were
further to reduce the novel to a single key-word, as some critics
like to do, I should choose the word *grace*. In thematic terms
not the sea but life at sea is pure and life on earth sordid. Yet
the pessimism of *The Nigger of the "Narcissus"* is (unlike that of
The Secret Agent) a modified pessimism, and the gift of grace
can circumvent thematic terms. Thus England herself is once
imaged as a great ship. The convention of the novel is that the
gift of grace may fall anywhere, or anywhere except on the
Donkins. The story really ends with the men clinging for a last
moment to their solidarity and standing near the Mint, that
most representative object of the sordid earth. . . .

So the novel's vision is one of man's dignity but also of his
"irremediable littleness"—a conclusion reached, to be sure, by
most great works in the Christian tradition. In *Heart of Darkness*, *Lord Jim*, and "The Secret Sharer" we have the initiatory
or expiatory descents within the self of individual and almost
lost souls; in *Nostromo* we shall see the vast proliferation of
good and evil in history and political institution. But *The Nigger of the "Narcissus"* presents the classic human contradiction
(and the archetypal descent into self) in collective terms, reduced to the simplicities of shipboard life. The storm tests and
brings out the solidarity, courage, and endurance of men
banded together in a desperate cause. And the Negro James
Wait tests and brings out their egoism, solitude, laziness, anarchy, fear. The structural obligation of the story is to see to it
that the two tests do not, for the reader, cancel out.

Presented so schematically, Conrad's vision may seem
truly Christian. But this is indeed a soulless sky. In the restless
life of symbols sunlight is converted, at one point, to that
inhuman Nature which Man must oppose. The Norwegian
sailor who chatters at the sun has lost his saving separateness
from Nature, and when the sun sets his voice goes out
"together with the light." The "completed wisdom" of old
Singleton (one of the first Conrad extroverts to achieve some of
his own skepticism) sees "an immensity tormented and blind,
moaning and furious. . . ." And in one of the novel's central
intellectual statements (the first paragraph of the fourth chapter) the indifferent sea is metaphorically equated with God, and
the gift of grace is defined as labor, which prevents man from
meditating "at ease upon the complicated and acrid savour of
existence." The dignity of man lies in his vast silence and
endurance: a dignity tainted by those who clamor for the reward of another life. The message is rather like Faulkner's, and
these good seamen are like "good Negroes." But here too, as in
other novels of Conrad, man's works and institutions must
prepare him to profit from even such grace as this. From our
human weakness and from the eternal indifference of things we
may yet be saved . . . by authority, tradition, obedience. Thus
the only true grace is purely human and even traditional.
There are certain men (specifically Donkin) who remain untouched. But such men exist outside: outside our moral universe which is both dark and light but not inextricably both.
And James Wait, as sailor and person rather than symbol? I am

not sure. He seems to suffer from that "emptiness" which would be Kurtz's ruin: "only a cold black skin loosely stuffed with soft cotton wool . . . a doll that had lost half its sawdust."

This, speaking neither in terms of gross obvious intentions and themes nor of unconscious symbolic content but of generalized human meaning and ethical bias, is what *The Nigger of the "Narcissus"* says. This is its reading of life.—ALBERT GUERARD, JR., "On *The Nigger of the 'Narcissus'*" (1958), *Conrad*, ed. Marion Mudrick, 1966, pp. 18–21

LORD JIM

The general lines of the story are given in miniature in the first chapter. Jim, having developed a romantic view of himself as one who will meet crises with calmness and determination, is not shaken in this faith by his failure to reach the cutter of his training ship when it puts out to effect a rescue. In the main crisis of the first part of the novel the failure is repeated under circumstances where he offends most unequivocally against "the obscure body of men held together by a community of inglorious toil and by fidelity to a certain standard of conduct." His crime is described in terms which are reminiscent of some passages of *Heart of Darkness*—in terms of what, in that story, is called "sordid farce." . . .

Jim's offence is one upon which the Court of Enquiry can have no mercy. But he insists on what, to many of the spectators, seems like trying to brazen it out. Brierly's question: "Why eat all that dirt?" sums up the feeling of most of them. His hope, however, is that he can rehabilitate himself; as in his first failure in the training ship, he is still sure that at bottom he is ready for any emergency, that he has only been betrayed by circumstances. He will not accept his weakness and stay in a place where men knew his story, and so he is driven farther and farther eastwards in the search for a refuge where he can start with a clean sheet and establish himself as a trustworthy man.

Finally, in the jungle settlement of Patusan, he rises to be "Lord Jim," one whose authority and honour are never questioned and on whom all the natives are dependent. It seems that he has successfully isolated himself from his past, in a place where

> The stream of civilization, as if divided on a headland a hundred miles north of Patusan, branches east and south-west, leaving its plains and valleys, its old trees and its old mankind, neglected and isolated.

But, despite the fact that he has achieved "the conquest of love, honour, men's confidence," his past comes in search of him. Gentleman Brown and his crew of cut-throats penetrate the "wall of forests" which shuts Jim in his isolation. Physically the people of Patusan are more than a match for Brown, but mentally Jim is helpless before this man who combines with his ferocity "a vehement scorn for mankind at large and for his victims in particular" and who "would rob a man as if only to demonstrate his poor opinion of the creature." Everything that Brown says recalls Jim's past weakness, undermines his certainty that he has put behind him a cowardice that was only momentary. . . .

In enlarging the simple story of the pilgrim ship episode, however, Conrad makes a more significant addition than the second half of the story; he introduces Marlow, who, although he does not appear as storyteller until the fifth chapter, is the person to whom we naturally look for commentary and judgment. Judgment we find in plenty—but, far from clarifying the

moral issues, Marlow's reflections only succeed in making them more confused. . . .

The reason for this uncertainty is clear; it is because Marlow, Conrad's mouthpiece, is himself bewildered. As in *Heart of Darkness*, which Conrad wrote while recasting the novel, Marlow plays a greater part than might at first be thought. We may reasonably wonder whether the feelings which brought *Heart of Darkness* to birth may not be the chief cause why *Lord Jim* developed from a simple short story into a complex novel, for there are many resemblances between the relationship of Marlow and Kurtz and that of Marlow and Jim. . . .

Here, as in the short story, the experience of Marlow goes far beyond that of the man whom he cannot disown. Kurtz is only a "hollow man"; Jim himself is, by comparison with Marlow, naïve, a romantic thinking in the terms of a boy's adventure story.

But the muddlement goes farther than this. I have so far begged the question by saying "Marlow, Conrad's mouthpiece." In fact the confusion seems to extend to Conrad's conception of the story, and this reveals itself in some of the rhetoric given to Marlow. A good deal of this is imprecise and some is little more than a vague and rather pretentious playing with abstractions. It is in these terms that he speaks of the approaching catastrophe:

> *Magna est veritas et* . . . Yes, when it gets a chance. There is a law, no doubt—and likewise a law regulates your luck in the throwing of dice. It is not Justice, the servant of men, but accident, hazard, Fortune—the ally of patient Time—that holds an even and scrupulous balance. . . . Well, let's leave it to chance, whose ally is Time, that cannot be hurried, and whose enemy is Death, that will not wait.

There are many such passages, and they give the impression rather of a man who is ruminating to obscure the issue than of one thinking to clarify it. But they are not "placed"—Conrad, that is, does not so present them that we see them as deliberate, part of the portrayal of a man who is bewildered. They come rather from his own uncertainty as to the effect at which he is aiming. There is, very clearly, a conflict in his own mind; he raises the issue of the sufficiency of the "few simple notions you must cling to if you want to live decently," but he does not, throughout the book, face it consistently.

Lord Jim is, at bottom, concerned with the same preoccupations as *Heart of Darkness* and other works of this period, but Conrad has chosen to treat them in such a way that he inevitably feels more directly concerned. As he says in the concluding words of the "Author's Note": "He was 'one of us.'" The uncertainty which remains even at the end of the book as to what judgment we should pass on Jim and the passages of imprecise rhetoric are, I believe, an indication that his feelings are too deeply and too personally involved for him to stand above the bewilderment in which he places Marlow. The fixed standards of the simple sailor are those which, above all others, Conrad finds it difficult to treat with detachment. He was too aware of the depths of treachery and cowardice of which men are capable not to cherish whatever seems to provide a defense against them, and at times we have the impression that, just as much as Marlow, he is himself fighting to retain a faith in the efficacy and total goodness of the "few simple notions." . . .

In this pessimism and scepticism he resembles very closely that side of Dostoevsky which is seen in the questioning of Ivan Karamazov and the radical doubt of Kirillov and Raskolnikov. What we do not find in Conrad is the positive side of Dostoevsky's thought which is manifested, for instance, in the further development of *Crime and Punishment*, where Raskolnikov finds that his logically justified decision to kill the old woman is an unnatural violation of those parts of his personality which his logical thought has not taken into account. Conrad's view of human nature is, in fact, fundamentally more pessimistic, more "nihilistic" than that of Dostoevsky. He has in his best novels and stories a conception of evil which is not vague and mystifying and which is not a matter of good people and bad people. It is precise and it is conceived profoundly in terms of the maiming power of Charles Gould's silver mine, the "hollowness" of Mr. Kurtz and the self-deception and fear of Mr. Verloc. But he has no conception of a goodness just as profound (and sometimes just as hidden), rooted in a complex human nature, and though he could echo with approval Nostromo's "God for men—religions for women," the God is not apparent in his work; he takes no comfort from supernatural hopes of improvement or redemption.

That this was a painful state of mind for him is clear. Though he is pessimistic, he is never cynical; we cannot but take seriously the fate of Mrs. Gould or Captain Whalley or Winnie Verloc. As he said, speaking of Mr. Kurtz: "I have not treated him with the easy nonchalance of an amateur. Believe me, no man paid more for his lines than I have."

We do believe him and we can understand why, seeing no positive values to counter the force of his negative criticism, he took refuge in the unreal and unquestioned goodness of Lena and old Peyrol. For, in essence, this is Conrad's situation: he is intensely and continuously aware of the existence of a world of moral and spiritual values, yet every quality, every virtue, every position in which he might hope to rest in security, is at once undermined; the "impenetrable darkness" covers the world. He is in the position—and it is not an uncommon one for writers of the last fifty years—of feeling the reality of a moral and spiritual order sufficiently for it to condemn normal feelings and normal idealisms, but of having no beliefs that can give him hope that the forces of evil will be overcome.

His protagonists, therefore, face their problems and suffer their torments against a static background which condemns them; their struggles are futile and their fate predetermined.—DOUGLAS HEWITT, "*Lord Jim*: Conrad and the 'Few Simple Notions'," *Conrad: A Reassessment*, 1952, pp. 55–62

When *Lord Jim* is approached from the perspective of its narrative structure and its design of recurrent images it reveals itself to be not less but more problematic, more inscrutable, like Jim himself. I have elsewhere argued that temporal form, interpersonal relations, and relations of fiction and reality are three structuring principles fundamental to fiction. *Lord Jim* is an admirable example of the tendency of these in their interaction to weave a fabric of words which is incapable of being interpreted unambiguously, as a fixed pattern of meaning, even though the various possibilities of meaning are rigorously delimited by the text.

To begin with the structure of interpersonal relations: Victorian novels were often apparently stabilized by the presence of an omniscient narrator, spokesman for the collective wisdom of the community, though, as my Victorian examples here demonstrate, such a narrator never turns out to be unequivocally the basis of the storytelling when a given Victorian novel is interpreted in detail. Such a narrator, if he were ever to exist, would represent a trustworthy point of view and also a safe vantage point from which to watch the hearts and minds of the characters in their relations to one another. Conrad, as many critics have noted, does not employ a "reliable" narrator. In *Lord Jim* no point of view is entirely trustworthy. The novel is a complex design of interrelated minds, no one of which can

be taken as a secure point of reference from which the others may be judged.

The first part of the story is told by an "omniscient" narrator who seems like the narrator of a novel by Trollope or by George Eliot. This first narrator of *Lord Jim* has the same superhuman powers of insight, including direct access to the hero's mind, that is possessed by those earlier Victorian narrators. He relinquishes that access early in the story, as though it could not provide a satisfactory avenue to the truth behind Jim's life. He then returns in chapter 36, after Marlow's narrative to his almost silent auditors is over. He returns to introduce the man who receives the letter which is Marlow's "last word" about Jim. The bulk of the novel is made up of Marlow's telling of Jim's story to the group of listeners in the darkness who are the reader's surrogates. Those listeners stand between the reader and Marlow's telling. "He existed for me," says Marlow, "and after all it is only through me that he exists for you. I've led him out by the hand; I have paraded him before you" (ch. 21).

Many sections of the story are told to Marlow by Jim. In these the reader can see Jim attempting to interpret his experience by putting it into words. This self-interpretation is interpreted once more by Marlow, then by implication interpreted again by Marlow's listeners. The latter appear occasionally as intervening minds, as when one of them says: "You are so subtle, Marlow" (ch. 8). This overlapping of interpretative minds within minds is put in question in its turn, at least implicitly, by the "omniscient" narrator. He surrounds all and perhaps understands all, though he does not give the reader the sort of interpretative help provided by the narrator of *Middlemarch* or of *The Last Chronicle of Barset*. Even so, this narrator may have been brought back briefly near the end of the novel to suggest that the reader might be wise to put in question Marlow's interpretation of Jim, even though the narrator cannot or will not provide the reader with any solid alternative ground on which to stand. . . .

Lord Jim is made up of episodes similar in design. In each a man confronts a crisis testing his courage, the strength of his faith in the sovereign power enthroned in a fixed standard of conduct. In each case someone, the man himself or someone else, interprets that test, or rather he interprets the words which the man's reaction to the test has already generated. There is even a parody of this pattern early in the novel, as if to call attention to it as a structuring principle or as a universal way in which men are related to one another. Just as Marlow seeks out the chief engineer of the *Patna* in the hospital "in the eccentric hope of hearing something explanatory of the famous affair from his point of view," so the doctor who is tending the engineer after his brandy debauch says he "never remember[s] being so interested in a case of the jim-jams before." "The head, ah! the head, of course, gone, but the curious part is that there is some sort of method in his raving. I am trying to find out. Most unusual—that thread of logic in such a delirium" (ch. 5). The reader of *Lord Jim*, like the doctor, must seek the thread of logic within a bewildering complexity of words. With these words Conrad attempts to express a truth beyond direct expression in words, "for words also belong to the sheltering conception of light and order which is our refuge" (ch. 33), our refuge from the truth hidden in the darkness. In the sequence of discrete episodes which makes up the novel, no episode serves as the point of origin, the arch-example of the *mythos* of the novel, but each is, by reason of its analogy to other episodes, a repetition of them, each example being as enigmatic as all the others.

A similar complexity characterizes the temporal structure

of the novel. Jim says of his memory of watching the other officers struggle to get the *Patna*'s boat in the water: "I ought to have a merry life of it, by God! for I shall see that funny sight a good many times yet before I die" (ch. 9). Of an earlier moment before the officers desert the ship he says: "It was as though I had heard it all, seen it all, gone through it all twenty times already" (ch. 8). Each enactment of a given episode echoes backward and forward indefinitely, creating a pattern of eddying repetition. If there are narrators within narrators there are also times within times—time-shifts, breaks in time, anticipations, retrogressions, retellings, and reminders that a given part of the story has often been told before. Marlow, for example, like the Ancient Mariner, has related Jim's story "many times, in distant parts of the world" (ch. 4). The novel is made up of recurrences in which each part of the story has already happened repeatedly when the reader first encounters it, either in someone's mind, or in someone's telling, or in the way it repeats other similar events in the same person's life or in the lives of others. The temporal structure of the novel is open. *Lord Jim* is a chain of repetitions, each event referring back to others which it both explains and is explained by, while at the same time it prefigures those which will occur in the future. Each exists as part of an infinite regression and progression within which the narrative moves back and forth discontinuously across time seeking unsuccessfully some motionless point in its flow. . . .

I claim, then, that from whatever angle it is approached *Lord Jim* reveals itself to be a work which raises questions rather than answering them. The fact that it contains its own interpretations does not make it easier to understand. The overabundance of possible explanations only inveigles the reader to share in the self-sustaining motion of a process of interpretation which cannot reach an unequivocal conclusion. This weaving movement of advance and retreat constitutes and sustains the meaning of the text, that evasive center which is everywhere and nowhere in the play of its language.—J. HILLIS MILLER, "*Lord Jim*: Repetition as Subversion of Organic Form," *Fiction and Repetition*, 1982, pp. 31–39

HEART OF DARKNESS

Heart of Darkness, to present its theme bluntly, is an impression, taken from life, of the conquest by the European whites of a certain portion of Africa, an impression in particular of the civilising methods of a certain great European Trading Company face to face with the 'nigger.' We say this much because the English reader likes to know where he is going before he takes art seriously, and we add that he will find the human life, black and white, in *Heart of Darkness* an uncommonly and uncannily serious affair. If the ordinary reader, however, insists on taking the subject of a tale very seriously, the artist takes his method of presentation more seriously still, and rightly so. For the art of *Heart of Darkness*—as in every psychological masterpiece—lies in the relation of the things of the spirit to the things of the flesh, of the invisible life to the visible, of the sub-conscious life within us, our obscure motives and instincts, to our conscious actions, feelings and outlook. Just as landscape art implies the artist catching the exact relation of a tree to the earth from which it springs, and of the earth to the sky, so the art of *Heart of Darkness* implies the catching of infinite shades of the white man's uneasy, disconcerted, and fantastic relations with the exploited barbarism of Africa; it implies the acutest analysis of the deterioration of the white man's *morale*, when he is let loose from European restraint, and planted down in the tropics as an 'emissary of light' armed to the teeth,

to make trade profits out of the 'subject races.' The weirdness, the brilliance, the psychological truth of this masterly analysis of two Continents in conflict, of the abysmal gulf between the white man's system and the black man's comprehension of its results, is conveyed in a rapidly rushing narrative which calls for close attention on the reader's part. But the attention once surrendered, the pages of the narrative are as enthralling as the pages of Dostoevsky's *Crime and Punishment*. The stillness of the sombre African forests, the glare of sunshine, the feeling of dawn, of noon, of night on the tropical rivers, the isolation of the unnerved, degenerating whites staring all day and every day at the Heart of Darkness which is alike meaningless and threatening to their own creed and conceptions of life, the helpless bewilderment of the unhappy savages in the grasp of their flabby and rapacious conquerors—all this is a page torn from the life of the Dark Continent—a page which has been hitherto carefully blurred and kept away from European eyes. There is no 'intention' in the story, no *parti pris*, no prejudice one way or the other; it is simply a piece of art, fascinating and remorseless, and the artist is but intent on presenting his sensations in that sequence and arrangement whereby the meaning or the meaninglessness of the white man in uncivilised Africa can be felt in its really significant aspects. If the story is too strong meat for the ordinary reader, let him turn to 'Youth,' wherein the song of every man's youth is indeed sung.—EDWARD GARNETT, "Mr. Conrad's New Book," *AcL*, Dec. 6, 1902, pp. 606–7

Thanks to Mr. Kurtz, Conrad's magnificently proportioned Marlow never need pay the full price himself for so costly a victory and a vision. And this is the debt to Kurtz that he acknowledges and that he meets, however modestly, in that cautious ethical realm which Marlow clasps for his safety. For, having lived through Kurtz's extremity, Marlow can retain his own more yielding—and more compromising—resistance to extremity, more fearful than ever of its consequences but now fully aware of the vistas it opens onto for him who dares embrace it. And Marlow can move beyond his own "vision of grayness." Kurtz has, at great expense, made the tragic vision available to his less venturesome but still sensitive fellows: in his relation to Marlow, he is an allegory of the role that the visionary and the literature in which he figures are to play for those of us who are interested but not ourselves committed totally. And where the tragic visionary is concerned, of course totality is all.

Heart of Darkness is effective as an ideal archetype of the literature of the tragic vision, giving us an exemplary version of the relations between representatives of the ethical and of the tragic realms. The categories it so clearly schematizes frame most of Conrad's work and reach beyond to many others'. . . .

As I have here posed the ethical-tragic relation, it would seem that it is in the ethical resistance to the tragic that moral strength resides. But it is just the paradoxical nature of this strength that constitutes the central problem of *Heart of Darkness*. The key to the novel turns on Conrad's complex attitude toward the twin classical qualities that Marlow terms "innate strength" and "restraint." Two points seem immediately clear: as surely as Marlow does have them, Kurtz does not; and these qualities are severely tried—and especially needed—in Africa, that is, in the primitive reaches of pre-civilization or in the Dionysian darkness of pre-consciousness. We must examine the sources of Marlow's inner strength and of Kurtz's lack of it. The problem is perhaps most neatly posed in the passage in which Marlow, sailing down the river, is attracted and tempted by the frenzied dancing and howling of the natives on the banks. Will he join them? (This, after all, is to be the essence of Kurtz's sin.) Marlow admits that he feels a stirring deep within him, feels a call to his primitive humanity in the spectacle. He cannot ignore the call, but rather rejects it in full realization of its significance and its attraction. . . .

The source of Marlow's restraint, then, is finally just a healthy practicality, a preoccupation with the most worldly of things because these are explainable, are tangible causes for tangible effects. This notion of diehard practicality persists through the story since it is what is lacking in Africa and what Africa most challenges. The many incidents which befall Marlow on his trip to the scene of action are all fearful indications of the same omen: the cause-and-effect pragmatics of civilization has been replaced by a nightmarish futility. The shelling of the coast by the man-of-war, the landing of soldiers, the "objectless blasting," the bustling activity, all seem pointless and ineffectual. It is like "some sordid farce acted in front of a sinister blackcloth," with "a touch of insanity in the proceeding, a sense of lugubrious drollery." The surf and the Negroes rowing boats are comforts. They have a meaning: "For a time I would feel I belonged still to a world of straightforward facts." Significantly, when the natives later attack Marlow's boat, they are dispersed by nothing so fitting as gunfire but rather by something as seemingly unrelated as the sound of the steam whistle. The world of European efficiency cannot absorb the jungle's unreality into itself. Modern equipment gives us especially eloquent testimony. The farthest accomplishments of the reasonable and utilitarian world, this equipment, sent literally to *realize* Africa, lies all around, rusted, decayed, broken, as we are continually reminded. . . .

We should see by now that Marlow's conception of strength takes a strangely paradoxical nature: it consists in the relentless retention of artificial props. To hold onto one's crutches brings the restraint that makes him strong; to try courageously to walk without them results in the lack of restraint that we are so often told weakens Kurtz. The problem is hardly a simple one. There is, for example, the problem of "the fool" whom Marlow has just defined for us. If the mere retention of the props of modern society constitutes strength, then the paragons of strength in the tale are such nonentities as the company manager or that "miracle," the chief accountant (he of the "high starched collar, white cuffs . . . snowy trousers . . . varnished boots . . . green-lined parasol . . . penholder behind his ear" who was annoyed at the sick because their groans impaired the efficiency of his computations). Clearly these are the fools Marlow spoke of who are too insensitive to be aware that there is any problem, any temptation in their situation. And of course these men cannot be expected to understand Kurtz at all. Thus they reject him completely but uncritically, and reject him in the practical rather than in the moral realm, since for them he can be evil only insofar as he represents a threat to their interests, their "aesthetic" pursuits. As beings who do not partake of the ethical, they can hardly be said to possess moral strength; for this strength can hardly exist where there is ignorance of moral alternatives. Marlow, on the contrary, is completely aware of the alternatives, their respective claims and consequences. His rejection of Kurtz, made in the moral realm, is yet critical of itself, so that it reveals both admiration and sympathy together with its repulsion. Marlow chooses the crutches, knowing them to be crutches, and thus knowing also that his choice must shut him off from areas of vision which are Kurtz's. He has chosen morally, but the moral criterion remains worldly and pragmatic: it just wouldn't do to act otherwise and would constitute a breach of civilized faith. By so choosing, he has insured himself against the tragic—but

insured himself against the glory of its vision as well as the horror of its devastation. . . .

When Marlow was speaking of the inborn strength that led him to resist the dancing natives and traced its source to the devotion to practical necessity, he insisted—man of the world that he is—that "Principles won't do. Acquisitions, clothes, pretty rags—rags that would fly off at the first good shake." And so it was with Kurtz. But his story would allow Marlow to go further: the slavish devotion to principle is finally an identification with it, allowing one to make oneself into the god, the embodiment of what he has worshiped. The rest, of course, is demonism and destruction, the overassertion of self finally without even the pseudo humility of the idealistic claim to have lost oneself in service. So Kurtz, relentless as he is in his pursuit of absolute integrity of motives, becomes a pure representative of the force of imperialism that in its arrogance victimizes itself: he becomes what he is at last as a symbol of that impure mask of disinterested virtue which disguises the ugliness of man playing god before man. However lofty the initial undertaking, in the extreme it must lead to the bowing down and the sacrificing by those supposedly being served.—Murray Krieger, "Joseph Conrad: Action, Inaction, and Extremity," *The Tragic Vision*, 1960, pp. 155–62

In 1890 Joseph Conrad, having voyaged down the coast of Africa, disembarked at Boma and continued on in a smaller boat to Matadi. From there he went overland to Kinshasa, then by steamer to Stanley Falls, in order to collect a company agent named Klein. The materials of this journey, carefully recorded in his diary, were later published as "Heart of Darkness." In 1925, thirty-five years later, Carl Jung set out for Mombassa and journeyed by boat, caravan, steamer, narrow-gauge railroad, and wood-fired paddle-wheel to visit Masai, Bugishu, and other African villages. His experiences were recorded in a diary and later recounted in *Dreams, Memories, and Reflections*. These journeys into literal and symbolic interiors of Africa and of self provide uncanny parallels. Both diarists deplored the exploitation of the Africans by the imperialist West; both felt the danger, not in savagery itself, but in the potential for savagery in civilized man when boundaries of rational society are lacking. Both were almost swept out of their conscious existences: Marlow longed to go ashore for a howl and a dance, and Jung did go, dancing and swinging his rhinoceros whip wildly. Both men wrote of the positive aspects of the unconscious, which could lead to psychic growth with the integration of the primitive, instinctive self; both wrote of the negative aspects of the unconscious, which could lead to the destruction of the psyche. Conrad the artist and Jung the psychologist found strikingly similar symbols to describe their discoveries from their voyages. Jung's journey to Africa, his most impulsive and subjective journey, confirmed his theories and settled his doubts about the "validity and universality . . . of the 'collective unconscious,'" whereas Conrad uncovered truths about the unconscious that were not to be articulated in psychological terminology until years later with the publication of Jung's *Archetypes and the Collective Unconscious*. . . .

Jung states that the primitive sees reality as whatever is experienced, including delusions, fantasies, dreams, "for in the primitive world things do not have the same sharp boundaries they do in our 'rational society.'" Men have archetypal memories, however, of a forgotten prehistoric past, which a naive attempt to relive would constitute a "relapse into barbarism." The attraction of Africa tempts modern man to revert to forgotten and primitive impulses, all the more powerful and difficult to resist because unconscious. The tensions produced by this urge cause him "either to succumb utterly and become a pale, effete version of the primitive or to reject and hate the dark man who has served to evoke it." The intense rejection results in prejudice and hatred. For Jung, man's "first duty was to his own culture, place and moment in time."

What protects the man who is neither foolish nor exalted from atavistic behavior are, for Conrad, such things as valuable work (through attending to duty, Marlow found surface "truth enough" to save him), the fellowship of the craft, and faithfulness to one's code ("the strongest bond laid upon the self-will of men"). Even the cannibals on the steamer have their taboos that prevent them, even though starving, from eating the persons aboard. But for a man like Kurtz, who had no restraint, the wilderness claimed him, "found him out." It had caressed him, "gotten into his veins, consumed his flesh, and sealed his soul to its own by the inconceivable ceremonies of some devilish initiation." He was lost. Split from his civilized personality, isolated from the claims of his past, he became an insatiable shadow "of splendid appearances, of frightful realities"—a diabolic egomaniac. Jung puts it this way: when outer restraints fail, "the light of consciousness is extinguished, and the dark sea of the unconscious breaks in." In his medical practice Jung occasionally treated a patient with such ego superiority (a Kurtz?) that Jung refused to stir up the unconscious because to do so would have shattered the patient's personality. . . .

For Conrad as for Jung, these inhabitants ⟨archetypes⟩ of the unconscious mind can be both positive and negative, can lead to psychic growth or to psychic destruction. After the Congo voyage, Conrad's view of primitive peoples changed from seeing them as merely cunning, avaricious, immoral, and expendable to viewing them with respect, some fear, and even awe. Marlow finds in them "truth stripped of its cloak of time," truth which neither his civilization, acquisitions, nor principles are sufficient to deal with, and he tries to integrate this truth by articulating it: "I have a voice, too, and for good or evil mine is the speech that cannot be silenced." Marlow says that the most one can hope for from life is "some knowledge of yourself," and he has to come to terms with aspects of himself he had not known existed. Marlow, having looked over the edge of the abyss, having stepped over the "threshold of the invisible," was "permitted to draw back [his] hesitating foot." He determines to go back to the "world where events move, men change, light flickers, and life flows in a clear stream. . . . I wasn't going to dive into it; I would have enough to do to keep my head above the surface." He will, however, order the experience into art, which for Conrad is "rescue work carried out in darkness against cross gusts of wind . . . out of native obscurity into a light where the struggling forms may be seen, seized upon, endowed with . . . permanence in this world of relative values." In so doing, the artist of words constructs a conception of existence to creep under, "for words also belong to the sheltering conception of light and order which is our refuge." Jung says that "if the translation of the unconscious into a communicable language proves successful, it has a redeeming effect. The driving forces locked up in the unconscious are canalized into consciousness and form a new source of power." . . .

Both Conrad and Jung are quite aware of the negative aspects of the confrontation with the unconscious. Conrad's picture of the deterioration of Kurtz could serve as a case study for Jung's theories. The "unspeakable rites" in which Kurtz has participated must have taken vengeance on him when he, as though a veil had been rent, cried out twice, "The horror! The horror!" Marlow feels that the wilderness had "whispered to him things about himself which he did not know," and in

kicking himself "loose of the earth," he had fallen to the bottom of an abyss. "Being alone in the wilderness, it [his soul] had looked within itself and . . . had gone mad." When Marlow goes to Kurtz's "intended" to tell her of his death, he has a vision of Kurtz in which he sees him as a "shadow darker than the shadow of the night." . . .

But in the end Kurtz does achieve a moral victory, at least as Marlow sees it, by summing up his life and recognizing the horror of it. When Marlow lies to the intended, it is because to tell her the truth "would have been too dark—too dark altogether."—GLORIA L. YOUNG, "Quest and Discovery: Joseph Conrad's and Carl Jung's African Journey," *MFS*, Winter 1982–83, pp. 583–88

NOSTROMO

Let us turn, at long last, to *Nostromo*, the novel. In this book Conrad endeavored to create a great, massive, multiphase symbol that would render his total vision of the world, his sense of individual destiny, his sense of man's place in nature, his sense of history and society.

First, *Nostromo* is a complex of personal stories, intimately interfused, a chromatic scale of attitudes, a study in the definition and necessity of "illusion" as Conrad freighted that word. Each character lives by his necessary idealization, up the scale from the "natural" man Nostromo, whose only idealization is that primitive one of his vanity, to Emilia Gould, who, more than any other, has purged the self and entered the human community.

The personal stories are related not only in the contact of person and person in plot and as carriers of variations of the theme of illusion, but also in reference to the social and historical theme. That is, each character is also a carrier of an attitude toward, a point of view about, society; and each is an actor in a crucial historical moment. This historical moment is presumably intended to embody the main issues of Conrad's time: capitalism, imperialism, revolution, social justice. Many of the personal illusions bear quite directly on these topics: Viola's libertarianism, with its dignity and leonine self-sufficiency and, even, contempt for the mob; Charles Gould's obsession in his mission; Avellanos' liberalism and Antonia's patriotic piety; Holroyd's concern with a "pure form of Christianity" which serves as a mask and justification for his imperialistic thirst for power; even the posturing and strutting "Caesarism" of Pedrito Montero, whose imagination had been inflamed by reading third-rate historical novels.

All readers of Conrad know the classic picture of imperialism at its brutal worst in "Heart of Darkness," the degradation and insanity of the process, and remember the passage spoken by Marlow:

> The conquest of the earth, which mostly means the taking it away from those who have a different complexion or slightly flatter noses than ourselves, is not a pretty thing when you look into it too much. What redeems it is the idea only.

In "Heart of Darkness" we see the process absolutely devoid of "idea," with lust, sadism, and greed rampant. In *Nostromo* we see the imperialistic process in another perspective, as the bringer of order and law to a lawless land, of prosperity to a land of grinding poverty. At least, that is the perspective in which Charles Gould sees himself and his mine:

> What is wanted here is law, good faith, order, security. Anyone can declaim about these things, but I pin my faith to material interests. Only let the material interests once get a firm footing, and they are bound

to impose the conditions on which alone they can continue to exist. That's how your money-making is justified here in the face of lawlessness and disorder. It is justified because the security which it demands must be shared with an oppressed people.

This passage and Gould's conception of his own role may be taken as the central fact of the social and historical theme of *Nostromo*. But how does Conrad intend us to regard this passage? Albert Guerard, Jr., in his careful and brilliant study of Conrad, says that the mine "corrupts Sulaco, bringing civil war rather than progress." That strikes me as far too simple. There has been a civil war but the forces of "progress"—i.e., the San Tomé mine and the capitalistic order—have won. And we must admit that the society at the end of the book is preferable to that at the beginning.

. . . We may remember that Conrad most anxiously meditated the epigraphs of his various books, and that the epigraph of *Nostromo* is the line from Shakespeare: "So foul a sky clears not without a storm." It is innocent to think that this refers merely to the "storm" which is the action of the novel, the revolution that has established the order of material interests in Sulaco. If the sky has cleared at the end of that episode, even now in the new peace we see, as Dr. Monygham sees, the blacker and more terrible thunderheads piling up on the far horizon.

"Heart of Darkness" and *Nostromo* are, in one sense, an analysis and unmasking of capitalism as it manifested itself in the imperialistic adventure. Necessarily this involves the topic of revolution. The end of *Nostromo* leaves the sky again foul, and in the years immediately after finishing that novel Conrad turns to two studies of revolution, *The Secret Agent*, begun in 1905 and published in 1907, and *Under Western Eyes*, begun in 1908 and published in 1911. These books are in their way an analysis and unmasking of revolution to correspond to the already accomplished analysis and unmasking of capitalism and imperialism. In the world of revolution we find the same complex of egotism, vanity, violence, and even noble illusion. . . .

Nothing, however, is easy or certain. Man is precariously balanced in his humanity between the black inward abyss of himself and the black outward abyss of nature. What Conrad meant by and felt about man's perilous balance must already be clear, if I can make it clear at all. But now I shall speak of *Nostromo* as an image of this.

The setting of the story, the isolation of Sulaco, is in itself significant. The serrated wall of the Cordillera, hieratic and snow-capped, behind the Campo, the Azuera and the Golfo Placido define a little world that comes to us as complete—as a microcosm, we may say, of the greater world and its history. Man is lost in this overwhelming scene. The story of the two gringos, spectral and alive, on the peninsula of Azuera is, of course, a fable of greed and of the terrifying logic of material interests unredeemed. But it is also a fable, here at the threshold of *Nostromo*, of man lost in the blankness of nature. At the center of the book, to resume the same theme, we find the story of Decoud, who loses his identity into the "world of cloud and water, of natural forces and forms of nature." When he commits suicide, he falls into the "immense indifference of things." Then at the very end of the novel, in the last paragraph, Dr. Monygham, in the police-galley, hears the wild, faithful cry uttered by Linda, the name of Nostromo: "Never! Gian' Battista!"

It was another of Nostromo's successes, the greatest, the most enviable, the most sinister of all. In that true cry of love and grief that seemed to ring aloud

from Punta Mala to Azuera and away to the bright line of the horizon, overhung by a big white cloud shining like a mass of solid silver, the genius of the magnificent capataz de cargadores dominated the dark gulf containing his conquests of treasure and love.

This, too, is a fable: the passionate cry in the night that is a kind of triumph in the face of the immense indifference of things.—ROBERT PENN WARREN, "The Great Mirage: Conrad and *Nostromo*", *Selected Essays*, 1941, pp. 43–56

The guilt and redemption which dominate the book are worked out specifically in terms of Christian myth and theology. To overlook this is to miss one of the most central sources of unity in the novel.

The silver of the San Tomé mine from which the curse upon the land emanates is a vastly powerful but ambiguous force. It has the potential to make Costaguana a kind of paradise, but on the other hand it is a strong temptation that drives men to cruelty and barbarism. There is no neutral point in the struggle between the two tendencies inherent in the mine. Like Eden, Costaguana must be a successful paradise or its inhabitants must be under a curse. It has not been a paradise since the first Europeans set foot there in search of treasure.

In the beginning of *Nostromo* the curse of the mine rests only upon the Gould family in the form of an unworked concession. But when Charles Gould and his wife Emilia decide to make the mine operative, they, like Adam and Eve, extend the curse to all of Costaguana. The dual nature of the mine's potential and the parallels with Eden are made quite specific in the physical description of the mine. It is a lush mountain garden with a pure waterfall later "dammed up above" to make sluices for working the mine. Don Pepe, the overseer, calls it "the very paradise of snakes." The allusion to Eden becomes unmistakable when Don Carlos Gould says to his wife, "It is no longer a paradise of snakes. We have brought mankind into it, and we cannot turn our backs on them to go and begin a new life elsewhere. . . ." But it is she who feels the responsibility for extending the curse beyond herself and more than Don Carlos seeks to ease the suffering it has brought. When she and her husband began their plans to make the mine operative, they thought they were making the cause of "an absurd moral disaster" into a "serious and moral success," but the problem remains with them only on a much larger scale.

When the curse of the silver manifests itself in the form of the greed that leads to the Monterist revolution, Mrs. Gould's compassionate instincts come into conflict with her husband's attitudes. As Decoud explains in his letter to his sister, "Don Carlos's mission is to preserve unstained the fair name of his mine. . . ." His idea of a "moral success" is law and order above all else. "Haunted" by the "fixed" idea "of justice," he will do anything to keep the mine out of the hands of the corrupt Monterists. He is prepared, if necessary, to blow up the mine, out of the territory of the republic, an action that will bring political reprisal and misery to Sulaco. So strong is his passion for justice that even his wife is not exempt from it. He is even willing to "bring heaven down piteously upon a loved head." Mrs. Gould's mission is "to save him from the effects of that cold and overmastering passion." This is only possible through the agency of Nostromo. Unless he is successful in keeping the most recent shipment of silver out of the hands of the Monterist revolutionaries and securing aid against them, her compassion cannot win out over her husband's rigid demands for justice.

Nostromo thus becomes the agent of mercy protecting

vulnerable humanity caught between the opposed forces of corruption and stern justice. To save the mine and abort the revolution, Nostromo must take the curse of the silver, "The curse of death" as he calls it, upon himself. Like Christ who undoes the curse brought upon the world by Adam and Eve, he performs an act of vicarious atonement. . . .

By his later actions Nostromo assumes the guilt for both a failure to confess and a lack of faith. In his case they are combined in an act of secrecy which determines that he shall die like a thief. He has only to have enough faith in the reliability of other men to tell them what has happened to Decoud and the silver and he will avoid all the suspicion and guilt with which he is later surrounded, but he chooses instead to keep silent. . . .

In one sense Nostromo's sin of secrecy is Adam's sin of possessing forbidden knowledge. Though the knowledge of the silver is not in itself damning, Nostromo makes it so by turning it into a guilty secret in defiance of love and duty. In the scene in the custom-house when Nostromo makes his decision to keep his secret, he is presented as a guiltless Adam who becomes more and more Satanic as he becomes more committed to secrecy.

As he begins to experience the vanity which sets his mind against his fellow men, he is described in terms suggesting both Adam and Satan: "Nostromo tasted the dust and ashes of the fruit of life into which he had bitten deeply in his hunger for praise." The fruit he eats suggests the forbidden fruit of Adam, but the taste is that of the dust and ashes which Satan is condemned to eat for his part in corrupting man. After he has met Monygham who further wounds his vanity by assuming the silver lost, his feelings are described in terms suggestive of Satan's fall. "The sense of betrayal and ruin floated upon his sombre indifference as upon a sluggish sea of pitch." The mind of the previously innocent and incorruptible Nostromo has now become a kind of hell. In the necessity to come to grips with Monygham's plan to tell Sotillo that the silver is on the Great Isabel, he gives way to "hissing vehemence." And finally, as he commits the first act of deceit to keep the silver a secret by offering the counterplan to tell that the silver has been lost in the sea, the process is complete: Monygham calls him a "Devil of a man!"

While Nostromo is depicted as Adam succumbing to temptation and assuming the characteristics of Satan, another undercurrent of suggestion keeps us aware that in assuming this sin he is atoning vicariously for all of Costaguana. His unexpected return to shore when "everything seemed lost in Sulaco" is looked on as a miracle of rebirth bringing deliverance. Giorgio Viola experiences it as "a return to life." Monygham calls it a "marvelous" reappearance. To him "Nostromo's return was providential. He did not think of him humanely, as of a fellow-creature just escaped from the jaws of death. The capataz for him was the only possible messenger to Cayta, the very man." He says again later that Nostromo is "the only man." Nostromo, himself, alludes to his accomplishment in saving the silver, saying, "if that silver turned up this moment. . . . That . . . would be a greater miracle than any saint could perform." And he speaks of his arrival with Barrios as a "return in triumph."

The act of faith necessary to make salvation complete comes from Dr. Monygham. He accepts Mrs. Gould's assertion that Nostromo told her nothing as absolute pardon for Nostromo. As soon as she speaks, the light of the "temperamental enmity to Nostromo" goes out of his eyes. Paradoxically, however, he does not give up his belief that Nostromo has somehow saved the silver that was lost. He alone believes

that Nostromo has performed the "miracle greater than any saint could perform" and yet affirms his innocence. His act of faith not only completes Nostromo's absolution but provides the belief in the act of sacrifice that makes it effective. . . .

The presence of a theological structure unifying *Nostromo* not only helps us to order the threads of the plot, it also suggests a relationship between Conrad and the reader somewhat different from the one we are accustomed to thinking about. Encouraged by the dramatic presence of his famous narrators, Conrad's readers have for the most part been content to see themselves as listeners to a story. Their job has been the familiar one of judging character, weighing motives, responding to description, and following the action. To be sure most of them have felt the need to participate actively in the telling to evaluate testimony and correct the biases of the various points of view. But even in this complex process readers have involved themselves primarily in a transaction with the personae of the stories. Conrad's presence, except in the degree that he is equated with his narrators, is not felt. But as soon as the words we read begin to have suggestions about a larger structure of which the characters of the novels are themselves unaware a new element is present. . . .

This aspect of Conrad confirms his position as one of the first of the moderns, the forerunner of Joyce and Eliot rather than the technically superior contemporary of Hardy. In manipulating a parallel between the present action and the religious structures and in involving the reader as a mind that must actively perceive patterns beyond the overt action, Conrad made innovations in the British novel as great as those Yeats made in poetry. All this is not to say of course that those elements of setting, plot, character, and narration for which Conrad has been so frequently praised do not remain a major part of his attraction. It is only to say that along with them, often providing the unity for his complex actions, there is often another structure to which we should respond. To see this structure and its implications in *Nostromo* is to approach a little closer to the heart of Conrad.—DOUGLAS MCMILLAN, "*Nostromo*: The Theology of Revolution," *The Classic British Novel*, eds. Howard M. Harper, Jr. and Charles Edge, 1972, pp. 168–81

THE SECRET AGENT

It is good for us English to have Mr. Conrad in our midst visualising for us aspects of life we are constitutionally unable to perceive, for by his astonishing mastery of our tongue he makes clear to his English audience those secrets of Slav thought and feeling which seem so strange and inaccessible in their native language. They are not inaccessible, those secrets, not in the least; through the gates of literary translations we can all enter into the alien spirit of those distant peoples; but so poor is the imagination of most of us that we linger outside, puzzled and repelled by their strange atmosphere and environment, even when mirrored clearly by art. Mr. Conrad, however, is to us as a willing hostage we have taken from the Slav lands, in exchange for whom no ransom could outweigh the value of his insight and his artistic revelation of the world at our gates, by us so imperfectly apprehended. By *The Secret Agent* he has added to the score of our indebtedness, and he has brought clearly into our ken the subterranean world of that foreign London which, since the death of Count Fosco (Count Fosco, the villain of Wilkie Collins's *The Woman in White* ⟨186⟩, was a secret agent for a foreign government), has served in fiction only the crude purpose of our sensational writers. . . .

In tracing the outline of this appallingly futile tragedy the

reviewer may remark that Mr. Conrad's possession of a philosophy, impartial in its scrutiny of the forces of human nature, is
the secret of his power—we had almost added, of his superiority to contemporary English novelists. The laws that govern
human nature are often as disconcerting to our self-esteem as
they are chastening to our spiritual egoism. And our English
novelists, unlike the Slav, are apt to work too assiduously on
the side of the angels, and hold, avowedly or in secret, an
ethical brief. But the advantage of keeping the earthly horizon
on a low plane is that there is more space around and beyond,
in the picture, for the background of those eternal elements
which both govern and dwarf man's petty endeavour. Mr.
Conrad's achievement in his novels and tales of seamen's life in
the Eastern seas, was, in fact, a poet's achievement; he showed
us the struggle of man's passionate and wilful endeavour, cast
against the background of nature's infinity and passionless purpose. And in *The Secret Agent* Mr. Conrad's ironical insight
into the natural facts of life, into those permanent animal
instincts which underlie our spiritual necessities and aspirations, serves him admirably in place of the mysterious backgrounds of tropical seas and skies to which he has accustomed
us. He goes down into the dim recesses of human motive, but
though his background is only the murky gloom of old London's foggy streets and squares, the effect is none the less arresting. His character sketches of Michaelis, the ticket-of-leave
apostle of anarchism, of Karl Yundt, the famous terrorist, the
moribund veteran of dynamite wars, 'who has been a great
actor in his time, on platforms, in secret assemblies, in private
interviews,' but who has never, strange to say, put his theories
into practice; of Comrade Ossipon, who lives by exploiting the
servant-girls whom his handsome face has seduced; and of the
Professor, the dingy little man whose ferocious hatred of social
injustice inspires him with a moral force that makes both his
posturing comrades and the police shudder, acutely conscious,
as they are, that he has both the will and the means to shatter a
streetful of people to bits—these character sketches supply us
with a working analysis of anarchism that is profoundly true,
though the philosophical anarchism of certain creative minds
is, of course, out of the range of the author's survey. And not
less well done is the scrutiny of the official *morale* and personal
incentives that govern the conduct of those guardians of social
order, Chief Inspector Heat and the Assistant-Commissioner of
Police. The two men, who have different ends in view, typify
the daily conflict between Justice as a means and Justice as an
end, which two are indeed rarely in harmony.

But Mr. Conrad's superiority over nearly all contemporary
English novelists is shown in his discriminating impartiality
which, facing imperturbably all the conflicting impulses of
human nature, refuses to be biassed in favour of one species of
man rather than another. Chief Inspector Heat, the thief-taker
and the guardian of social order, is no better a man than the
inflexible avenger of social injustice, the Professor. The Deputy Commissioner of Police, though a fearless and fine individual, moves our admiration no more than does the childlike idealist, Michaelis, who has been kept in prison for fifteen
years for a disinterested act of courage. Whether the spy, Mr.
Verloc, is more contemptible than the suave and rosy-gilled
favourite of London drawing-rooms, M. Vladimir, is as difficult a point to decide as whether the latter is less despicable
than the robust seducer of women, the cowardly Comrade
Ossipon. And, by a refined stroke of irony, the innocent victim
of anarchist propaganda and bureaucratic counter-mining is
the unfortunate and weak-witted lad, Stevie, whose morbid
dread of pain is exploited by the bewildered *agent provocateur*,
Mr. Verloc, in his effort to serve the designs of his Embassy,

and preserve both his situation and his own skin. Finally, as an
illustration of our author's serene impartiality, we may mention that the real heroine of the story is concealed in the trivial
figure of Mr. Verloc's mother-in-law, whose effacement of self
for the sake of her son, Stevie, is the cause contributory to his
own and her daughter's ruin. For Mr. Verloc, growing desperate, sends the half-witted lad with an infernal machine to blow
up Greenwich Observatory, and, Stevie perishing, Mr. Verloc
is attacked by his wife in a fit of frenzy and killed.

While the psychological analysis of the characters' motives is as full of acumen as is the author's philosophical
penetration into life, it is right to add that Mr. Verloc and his
wife are less convincing in their actions than in their meditations. There is a hidden weakness in the springs of impulse of
both these figures, and at certain moments they become
automata. But such defects are few. Mr. Conrad's art of suggesting the essence of an atmosphere and of a character in two
or three pages has never been more strikingly illustrated than in
The Secret Agent. It has the profound and ruthless sincerity of
the great Slav writers mingled with the haunting charm that
reminds us so often of his compatriot Chopin.—EDWARD
GARNETT, *Nation*, Sept. 25, 1907

Responses to Conrad's *Secret Agent* have ranged from total
capitulation to coolish approval; and it is not at all yet clear
what position in the future hierarchy of his works it is destined
to occupy. A reconsideration needs no apology.

First, we can accept the virtue of the writing throughout
and of the different scenes considered in themselves as scenes.
Any blemishes here are incidental. We may tire of hearing
Comrade Ossipon called "robust" and we may find a speech or
two of the Assistant Commissioner to the Home Secretary (in
spite of the latter's appeal for brevity) clotted and obscure. And
of course there are mistakes in the English. But all these are
small matters; and the only serious mistake of detail is in the
psychology of Ossipon. Granted his previous presentation, is it
likely that he would have been haunted permanently by the
thought of Mrs. Verloc's death and permanently put off his
amorous adventures? I can find nothing in his previous states of
mind to justify such fidelity to an impression. I suspect that
Conrad here unconsciously sacrificed psychological probability
to certain demands of plot, to which I shall refer later. But in its
context of the last chapter this blemish does not count for
much; it affects our pleasure in reading very little, for it coexists
with so much else to think about.

Next, I can only concur in most of the praise that writers
have bestowed on Conrad's ironic method, on his success in
keeping his dreadful story within the bounds of comedy. His
prevailing ironic method is to make very large the distance
between the way things appear to the persons in the story and
the way they are made to appear to the reader. The theme of
Verloc's hat provides typical instances. Verloc's hat and heavy
overcoat, constantly worn indoors, are powerful agents in
building up Verloc's character; they are symbols of his physical
and mental frowstiness. Then, rather more than halfway
through the book, Conrad gives us the reasons for Verloc's
habit of retaining his clothing: "It was not devotion to an outdoor life, but the frequentation of foreign cafés which was
responsible for that habit, investing with a character of un-
ceremonious impermanency Mr. Verloc's steady fidelity to his
own fireside." And of course Verloc has no notion of this
discrepancy between appearance and reality. The culminating
chapter containing the murder ends thus:

> Then all became still. Mrs. Verloc on reaching the
> door had stopped. A round hat disclosed in the mid-

dle of the floor by the moving of the table rocked
slightly on its crown in the wind of her flight.

These words are perfect in deflating the murder—that is, as it
concerns the victim. The grotesque rocking of the inverted
bowler resembles and mocks Verloc's precarious state of mind
in the last weeks, just as its dethronement from the eminence
of his head duplicates and minimises his own downfall. The
hat figures for the last time when Ossipon, now convinced that
he is the victim of a plot to murder him, returns with Winnie
Verloc to the house in Brett Street. He is standing in the shop
looking through the glass of the door into the parlour, where
Verloc lies, apparently asleep; Ossipon is still under the illusion
that he had been blown to pieces in Greenwich Park:

> But the true sense of the scene he was beholding
> came to Ossipon through the contemplation of the
> hat. It seemed an extraordinary thing, an ominous
> object, a sign. Black and rim upward, it lay on the
> floor before the couch as if prepared to receive the
> contributions of pence from people who would come
> presently to behold Mr. Verloc in the fullness of his
> domestic ease reposing on a sofa.

There is, of course, more than one kind of irony here. For
instance, there is the contrast between the appearance of
domestic ease and the reality of its opposite. But the main irony
consists in the fantastic distance between what Conrad instructs
the reader to think of, the likeness of the hat to a beggar's
inviting coins, and Ossipon's vision of it as a symbol of chaos
come again. And by achieving that distance Conrad makes the
reader very happy indeed. . . .

But *The Secret Agent* is pervaded by another kind of irony,
and one which, like the first kind, helps towards making the
book a unity. It is the irony of great plans having trivial results
and of the weightiest results being effected by trivial means. It is
the kind of irony that encourages men to keep their eyes open
and not to expect too much logic and tidiness from life; and
Shakespeare gave it its classic embodiment in *Much Ado About
Nothing*. There Claudio and Hero are the chief figures in the
main plot, although they are less fitted to be so than Benedick
and Beatrice. Through a freak of fate their story nearly ends in
disaster, but not quite. They arouse unnecessary passions in
other people, and all the pains that these folk take to clear up
the trouble are futile because the fantastic incompetence of
Dogberry and his fellows anticipates the carefully directed
efforts of their betters: "What your wisdoms could not discover,
these shallow fools have brought to light." Beatrice, the potentially tragic figure, and with a brilliant intellect, not only wastes
her efforts in setting Benedick against Claudio, but has her love
awakened by a trick that a much less brilliant person might
have evaded; and the trick itself may have been superfluous
since Benedick and Beatrice are in fact deeply attracted to each
other. Conrad writes in the mode of *Much Ado*; since this
seems to be a new contention, I had better go into the details.

The first hint of expectations being falsified occurs in the
opening scene at the (German or Austrian?) Embassy. There,
Privy Councillor Wurmt questions the vigilance of the English
police, but the vigilance turns out to be embarrassingly greater
than he had ever expected. Later, in the same scene, Vladimir
announces that England must be brought into line with the
Continent in the way she deals with revolutionaries: in the end
his action only helps to perpetuate the difference of methods.
Chief Inspector Heat hopes to use the explosion of the bomb to
justify the imprisonment of Michaelis, whom he dislikes seeing
at large; but this dislike awakens the suspicions of his superior
and leads to a rebuff. The domestic set-up of the Verlocs is a
humble and small scale affair, yet it makes itself felt in embassies and offices of state; while in turn the feelings thus aroused
there are destined to lead nowhere. The mother of Mrs. Verloc, thinking that her presence in the Brett Street house may
ultimately annoy Mr. Verloc and finally lead to his turning
against her mentally deficient son, heroically contrives to retire
to an almshouse. Her act is rich in unforeseen consequences. It
leads first to Mr. Verloc's taking more notice of Stevie and
finally to his using him to deposit the bomb that blows Stevie
up, and second to Winnie's sewing the address of the house
under Stevie's coat collar, an act which identifies him as the
blown-up man. Mrs. Verloc did another thing to help Stevie.
She joined with her daughter in impressing on him the
measureless "goodness" of Mr. Verloc. Thus impressed they
thought he would be more docile in Mr. Verloc's presence and
hence more acceptable. It was through Stevie's blindly loyal
belief in this "goodness" that he let himself be persuaded to
carry the bomb and so meet his death. The Assistant Commissioner of Police hoped that the Greenwich explosion might
become a *cause célèbre* and show up the iniquities of foreign
embassies; and immediately, with Verloc's death, it lapsed into
impenetrable obscurity. Most obvious of all, Verloc's efforts to
pacify Winnie over Stevie's death serve instead to enrage her
into committing murder. And lastly there is Ossipon, whose
exposure to the same process is the *coda* of the novel. Ossipon,
as well as affecting to be a revolutionary, was the *gigolo* of a
steady succession of mature women not without means. He
expected Winnie Verloc, widow of a man obviously possessed
of means, to take her place in the succession. Finding her a
murderess and haunted by the horror of her end, he is put off
women altogether and takes to drink instead. I have questioned
the motivation of this part of the novel, but in ironic idea it is
strictly in accord with the rest. Thus, the theme of ends mis-
carrying goes right through and can hardly not have been
intended by its author to be a means towards unity of impression.—E. M. W. TILLYARD, "The Secret Agent Reconsidered," *EC*, July 1961, pp. 309–18

UNDER WESTERN EYES

A new work by Mr. Conrad is a literary event of the first
importance. It is now three years since *A Set of Six*—that
volume of stories which marked so distinct a change in his
technique—was published, and one must not therefore be surprised to find that *Under Western Eyes* carries us still further on
the fresh path. One need expect no longer, save in occasional
sentences, the exuberant and monotonous vocabulary, that
sea-like and sonorous ebb and flow. No; for that exotic style he
has exchanged one very distinguished, it is true, very expressive, very artistic, but altogether less striking. It is the
atmosphere which we miss (that impalpable thing which has
no necessary relation to place), the atmosphere from which
emerged people of an invincible reality, the atmosphere which
gave us Jim, Mrs. Gould, and Winnie Verloc. It was in his
tropical books especially that it became so enthralling. The
strange glow which hung over the tropics hung over his figures
as well; the languor of Southern nights which stole into his
words stole into the hearts of his people. Everything seemed
surrounded by a mysterious and patient force, amidst which
life, dimly conscious of it all, went on increasingly with an
ironical intensity of joy and suffering. An immense power
appeared to brood over the vanities and struggles of men, an
impassive and relentless purpose to await them at every step.
The fleetingness of individual life, the disenchantment of desire, the passing away of hope, were contrasted with the stillness of the forest, the might of the ocean, the teeming prodigality of the earth. Such is the kind of atmosphere of novels like

Lord Jim and *Nostromo*, of stories like 'Heart of Darkness,' 'Youth,' 'An Outpost of Progress,' and 'The End of the Tether.' It was a romantic realism, colouring life with an extraordinary vividness. And such is not the atmosphere of *Under Western Eyes*. It is not simply that it is a novel of Europe instead of the tropics, for the typical Conrad atmosphere can be seen in European tales such as 'The Return,' 'To-morrow,' and *The Secret Agent*—it is something much more. *Under Western Eyes* is the work of a great writer for whom psychology is swallowing romance, of a great artist for whom form is becoming more and more impersonal, of a great creator whose creations are beginning to lack energy. The sentences are perfectly modulated, the whole style is exact and finished, but there is that something lacking which used not to be lacking. There are probably in this book a greater mastery of the detail of language, a nearer approach to complete avoidance of exaggeration, than in any of his books, but there is less of original genius. It is curiously as if he had been trying to model himself on Henry James, and in the effort had lost part of his own personality.

But *Under Western Eyes*, though not one of Mr. Conrad's typical achievements, is a remarkable book. . . .

Perhaps the finest part of the book is devoted to the midnight betrayal of Haldin, reposing trustfully in Razumov's bed. And the only result of it all is that Razumov is convinced that he is himself suspected by the Government. In a powerful scene between him and Councillor Mikulin, who has charge of the inquiry, a scene strangely reminiscent of those between Raskolnikov and the terrible Porphyrius in *Crime and Punishment*, he endeavours to probe their intention concerning him. Caught thus in the web of suspicion, he consents to go as a Government spy to Geneva, where there is a notorious colony of Russian conspirators. Here, as fate would have it, he meets with Haldin's mother and sister, who consider him a hero, as he is believed to have been Haldin's associate and helper. On all hands, indeed, he is greeted warmly, though as somewhat of an enigma. For he cannot hide the bitterness of his animosity nor the gnawing of the remorse which has been fully roused by contact with Miss Haldin. She is presented as a beautiful and strong nature whose trust in Razumov is unbounded. Slowly, under the awakening of his conscience, this life of lies grows impossible to him. It is not till all chances of his ever being discovered have disappeared, till he has felt that he is falling in love with Miss Haldin and that his love will be returned, that he resolves to confess. The end of the book is tragedy, not of an exalted but of a pitiful description. The novel is, as Mr. Conrad truly says, 'the sustained psychology of a mood,' and, as such, all other figures are subsidiary to the main one, and, in spite of their force, appear somehow insubstantial.—Richard Curle, *MG*, Oct. 11, 1911, p. 5

In an author's note on *Under Western Eyes*, written in 1920, Conrad himself is interestingly reticent about the purpose of this narrative device. It has, he admits, been heavily criticised since the book first appeared, but he will make no attempt at this late point to justify its existence: it is enough to say that the language-teacher proved 'useful' for his artistic purposes. The uses he then specifies, however, seem less than adequate justification for the technique: they simply concern one or two issues of plot-credibility—the need to produce 'the effect of actuality', to create a credible eye-witness, and so on—which seem curiously disproportionate to the insistence with which the device is employed in the novel. There is an awkward problem about the language-teacher's role in *Under Western Eyes* and a clue to it may be found in another of the book's disturbing emphases: its claim to a dispassionately neutral handling of its own subject-matter. . . .

We can note, to begin with, that neutrality in the narrator's sense of avoiding evaluative judgements can, of course, be as much a mode of commitment as explicit partiality: by withholding judgement at a crucial point, it can silently endorse a questionable attitude. Aside from that relatively subtle form of deception, however, there are more obvious ways in which the novel's claim to strict neutrality seems less than justified. In the first place there is the treatment of the anarchists themselves: Sophia Antonovna, Peter Ivanovitch, Madame de S——, Necator and the rest. 'Nobody', says Conrad, 'is exhibited as a monster here—neither the simple-minded Tekla nor the wrong-headed Sophia Antonovna. Peter Ivanovitch and Madame de S—— are fair game. They are the apes of a sinister jungle and are treated as their grimaces deserve. As to (Necator), he is the perfect flower of the terroristic wilderness. What troubled me most in dealing with him was not his monstrosity but his banality.' The whole statement is significantly ambiguous: 'monstrosity' is disowned in the first sentence only to re-appear as 'apes' in the second and be implicitly confessed in the last. In fact, the novel's actual descriptions of the revolutionaries undeniably confirm the hollowness of this disclaiming of caricature. Madame de S—— has 'the rigour of a corpse galvanised into harsh speech and glittering stare by the force of murderous hate'; Ivanovitch is a megalomanic fraud; Necator is portrayed as a gross, sinisterly squeaking obscenity. The only really admired revolutionaries are Miss Haldin and Sophia Antonovna, but the first is attractive for her character rather than her beliefs, and the magnetism of the second is significantly qualified. . . .

In none of these cases can there be any question of 'neutrality': what we have instead is the indulgence of a half-repelled, half-fascinated loathing of social revolution which, as the mechanically over-emphatic language used to describe Madame de S—— reveals, has a tone of uncontrolled fantasy and fear. The truth is that the novel is shot through with two, almost contradictory, political attitudes. On the one hand there is a form of genuinely sceptical detachment generated by a sense of inevitable stalemate, of the equal absurdities of both anarchy and autocracy. 'In this world of men', Razumov reflects, 'nothing can be changed—neither happiness nor misery. They can only be displaced at a cost of corrupted consciences and broken lives—a futile game for arrogant philosophers and sanguinary triflers.' When this viewpoint is dominant, the sympathies withheld from both conservatives and radicals are directed toward Razumov, as the helpless tool of them both. But although it is in fact true that Razumov is exploited by both sides of the political struggle, as a double-agent used by both Councillor Mikulin and the anarchists, it is also noticeable that a good deal less attention is directed towards his role as an unwilling agent of autocracy. What we see, in the main, is his destruction at the hands of the radicals; and in this sense, the novel's official thesis of 'neutrality', disparaging both parties alike, is in practice dominated by a second attitude: its anti-revolutionary bias. . . .

The treatment of Razumov himself is one of the most striking examples of the novel's ambiguities of feeling. 'Razumov', says Conrad, 'is treated sympathetically. Why should he not be? He is an ordinary young man, with a healthy capacity for work and sane ambitions. He has an average conscience. If he is slightly abnormal it is only in his sensitiveness to his position.' As a judgement on Razumov before his encounter with Haldin, this seems accurate enough: we are told that he is an amiable and generous man with 'an instinctive hold on normal, practical, everyday life'. But it is difficult to see how a man of this kind—'ordinary', 'average', and only 'slightly' abnormal—could have grown so rapidly into the cruel, arrogant, malicious egoist whom the novel actually presents. There is a tension between what the novel shows us of Razumov and what it says of him: and the latter portrayal is a good deal more admirable than the former. The truth is that the novel, in pointing out reasons for genuine sympathy with its protagonist—his loneliness, his previously attractive character, his reasonable ambitions and their tragic collapse—lulls us at the same time into a tolerant attitude towards his less engaging traits: his violence, selfish cynicism and autocratic sneering. The formal motive for this leniency is, once again, the need for neutrality. . . .

What is in fact at work, in the relationship between the narrator and Razumov, is a kind of double-detachment. Both men are politically disengaged, but to the extent that both take their stand, if anywhere, on 'practical, everyday life', they share a common, anti-revolutionary front. In this sense there is a good deal of Razumov in the narrator himself (as there is, quite evidently, in Conrad); but in order to avoid commitment to the cynicism and negation which underpin Razumov's detachment, the narrator must in turn detach himself from this position, stressing the Russian's inscrutability. By doing so, he can protect the 'sanity' of his own decent English empiricism from the risks of a corrosive scepticism; but having established that defensive margin between himself and scepticism, he can then, through the character of Razumov, indulge it to the full, in a way which severely criticises his own 'decent' conventionality. The novel, by the use of its narrator-device, can therefore satirise the limits of British empiricism by the portrayal of passionate experience beyond its scope, without permitting that empirical position to be undermined; it can indulge, through Razumov, a wholly un-English nihilism without allowing that stance to be fully affirmed. . . .

Conrad, of course, was continuously preoccupied with a conflict between the structures of English rationality and kinds of experience which those structures failed to encompass. What is interesting about *Under Western Eyes* is the unique ambivalence of this conflict, directly registered in the structure of the novel. It is, at base, an ambivalence which suggests a profound uncertainty in attitude: an uncertainty which is projected into, and half-concealed by, the 'scrupulous impartiality' which the novel strives to sustain. That impartiality is meant to suggest a neutral balance between conservative and anarchist, yet it is more than once disturbed by an uncontrolled impulse to caricature the latter; it is meant to indicate the limits of English pragmatism, yet it does this only in a way which leaves that pragmatism essentially confirmed. *Under Western Eyes*, like many of Conrad's works, contrasts the structures of civilised thought with alien experience; but whereas in other of his novels there is a genuine dialectic between the two, so that alien experience is allowed radically to question civilised structures which in turn gain fresh validation from the encounter, no such dialectic is really present here. It appears to be there, but disappears on analysis. In this novel, the foreign reality of Russia is not ultimately allowed to undermine the Western attitudes of the narrator; it reveals the limits of those attitudes, but, precisely because it is a *foreign* reality, recedes then into a distant, inscrutable realm which presents no active challenge to conventional English wisdom. The English narrator and the Russian revolutionaries live in different worlds, and that, really, is all there is to say; there is no question of either world gaining a point of critical purchase upon the other. The posture of neutrality—the bemused recognition that Orientals are different—is at one point a target for satire; but at another point it helps to keep the revolutionary world safely at arm's length. That deliberate distancing is evident, as we have seen, in the caricature of the anarchists, which is a symptom of the refusal

to allow English experience to be effectively questioned. Since it is Razumov, and not the narrator, who provides us with these parodic descriptions of revolutionaries, the narrator's 'neutrality' is preserved; but since much of his narrative dramatises the thoughts of a virulently anti-revolutionary Russian, it is not preserved at the expense of castigating radicalism.—TERRY EAGLETON, "Joseph Conrad and '*Under Western Eyes*'", *Exiles and Emigrés*, 1970, pp. 21–31

CHANCE

Mr. Joseph Conrad's *Chance* is none the less a signal instance of provision the most earnest and the most copious for its leaving ever so much to be said about the particular provision effected. It is none the less an extraordinary exhibition of method by the fact that the method is, we venture to say, without a precedent in any like work. It places Mr. Conrad absolutely alone as a votary of the way to do a thing that shall make it undergo most doing. The way to do it that shall make it undergo least is the line on which we are mostly now used to see prizes carried off; so that the author of *Chance* gathers up on this showing all sorts of comparative distinction. He gathers up at least two sorts—that of bravery in absolutely reversing the process most accredited, and that, quite separate, we make out, of performing the manœuvre under salvos of recognition. It is not in these days often given to a refinement of design to be recognised, but Mr. Conrad has made his achieve that miracle—save in so far indeed as the miracle has been one thing and the success another. The miracle is of the rarest, confounding all calculation and suggesting more reflections than we can begin to make place for here; but the sources of surprise surrounding it might be, were this possible, even greater and yet leave the fact itself in all independence, the fact that the whole undertaking was committed by its very first step either to be 'art' exclusively or to be nothing. This is the prodigious rarity, since surely we have known for many a day no other such case of the whole clutch of eggs, and these withal of the freshest, in that one basket; to which it may be added that if we say for many a day this is not through our readiness positively to associate the sight with any very definite moment of the past. What concerns us is that the general effect of '*Chance*' is arrived at by a pursuance of means to the end in view contrasted with which every other current form of the chase can only affect us as cheap and futile; the carriage of the burden or amount of service required on these lines exceeding surely all other such displayed degrees of energy put together. Nothing could well interest us more than to see the exemplary value of attention, attention given by the author and asked of the reader, attested in a case in which it has had almost unspeakable difficulties to struggle with—since so we are moved to qualify the particular difficulty Mr. Conrad has 'elected' to face; the claim for method in itself, method in this very sense of attention applied, would be somehow less lighted if the difficulties struck us as less consciously, or call it even less wantonly, invoked. What they consist of we should have to diverge here a little to say, and should even then probably but lose ourselves in the dim question of why so special, eccentric and desperate a course, so deliberate a plunge into threatened frustration, should alone have seemed open. It has been the course, so far as three words may here serve, of his so multiplying his creators or, as we are now fond of saying, producers, as to make them almost more numerous and quite emphatically more material than the creatures and the production itself in whom and which we by the general law of fiction expect such agents to lose themselves. . . .

What shall we most call Mr. Conrad's method accordingly but his attempt to clarify *quand même*—ridden as he has been, we perceive at the end of fifty pages of *Chance*, by such a danger of steeping his matter in perfect eventual obscuration as we recall no other artist's consenting to with an equal grace. This grace, which presently comes over us as the sign of the whole business, is Mr. Conrad's gallantry itself, and the shortest account of the rest of the connection for our present purpose is that his gallantry is thus his success. It literally strikes us that his volume sets in motion more than anything else a drama in which his own system and his combined eccentricities of recital represent the protagonist in face of powers leagued against it, and of which the dénouement gives us the system fighting in triumph, though with its back desperately to the wall, and laying the powers piled up at its feet. This frankly has been *our* spectacle, our suspense and our thrill; with the one flaw on the roundness of it all the fact that the predicament was not imposed rather than invoked, was not the effect of a challenge from without, but that of a mystic impulse from within.

. . . *Chance* is an example of objectivity, most precious of aims, not only menaced but definitely compromised; whereby we are in presence of something really of the strangest, a general and diffused lapse of authenticity which an inordinate number of common readers—since it always takes this and these to account encouragingly for 'editions'—have not only condoned but have emphatically commended. . . . They can have done this through the bribe of some authenticity other in kind, no doubt, and seeming to them equally great if not greater, which gives back by the left hand what the right has, with however dissimulated a grace, the attempt is made disproportionately to impose it. There is no danger for the play of the cart before the horse, no disaster involved in it; that form being *all* horse and the interest itself mounted and astride, and not, as that of the novel, dependent in the first instance on wheels.

The order in which the drama simply says things gives it all its form, while the story told and the picture painted, as the novel at the pass we have brought it to embraces them, reports of an infinite diversity of matters, gathers together and gives out again a hundred sorts, and finds its order and its structure, its unity and its beauty, in the alternation of parts and the adjustment of differences. It is no less apparent that the novel may be fundamentally *organised*—such things as *The Egoist* and *The Awkward Age* are there to prove it; but in this case it adheres unconfusedly to that logic and has nothing to say to any other. Were it not for a second exception, one at this season rather pertinent, *Chance* then, to return to it a moment, would be as happy an example as we might just now put our hand on of the automatic working of a scheme unfavourable to that treatment of the colloquy by endless dangling strings which makes the current 'story' in general so figure to us a porcupine of extravagant yet abnormally relaxed bristles.—HENRY JAMES, "The New Novel," *Notes on Novelists*, 1914, pp. 271–80

The meeting probably took place in James's London apartment at 34 De Vere Gardens, Kensington—it is there that Conrad later remembered that he had chanced upon the Pepys epigraph for his next book, *The Nigger of the "Narcissus"*. But Conrad was then living in Essex, and occasion for the two to meet very often was lacking. Eighteen months later, however, James and Conrad were brought closer together. In the summer of 1898 James became the lessee, and later the owner, of Lamb House, in Rye; and in October, the Conrads moved to the Pent, a Kentish farmhouse some fifteen miles to the east, and fairly close to Sandgate, where H. G. Wells was living. The Fords soon moved nearby, and there followed a period of

quite close literary frequentation, of which many picturesque episodes have been recorded: Wells tells of Conrad "driving a little black pony carriage as though it was a droshky and encouraging a puzzled little Kentish pony with loud cries and endearments in Polish"; Mrs. Conrad recalls Henry James taking the Conrad's small son on his knee, and forgetting "his existence, now and then giving him an absent-minded squeeze", while baby Borys, with an "instinctive sense of Henry James's personality . . . sat perfectly resigned and still for more than half an hour"; and one also hears of James, nearly sixty, accompanied by Edmund Gosse, bicycling some ten miles across the marshes to have tea with H. G. Wells.

Few of the friendships then formed were destined to survive; and there is no Rye school of novelists to rival the Lake School of poets. Conrad's feelings toward H. G. Wells cooled soon after he had dedicated *The Secret Agent* (1907) to him, though the rupture was not as violent as that of Wells and James, nor even as the earlier quarrels of Wells and Ford. James, never very fond of Ford, broke with him completely at the time of his conspicuously messy divorce (1910); Conrad's relationship with Ford became a good deal less intimate after the years of collaboration; and although there was no breach, Conrad saw very little of James after 1906. . . .

By 1915 it had become apparent to many critics that Conrad was James's chief rival for the title of the greatest contemporary novelist; and then in *Chance* Conrad made his closest approach to a Jamesian novel. John Cowper Powys, for example, comments that "No work of Conrad's has so close an affinity with the art of Henry James . . . the disturbing vibration, the intense malice of provoked curiosity . . ." And—as we shall see—*Chance* has many other Jamesian elements; including the irony that Conrad's most Jamesian novel should have achieved a popular and financial success such as had for thirty years now eluded James, and at the same time provoked James to strike the last sad note in his dealings with Conrad.

We do not know whether Conrad finally had lunch with James, though the two men probably did meet again. But later that year James proposed to the *Times Literary Supplement* an article which was to contain his only published critique of Conrad. It appeared under the title "The New Generation" (19 March and 2 April 1914), and was reprinted in *Notes on Novelists* under the equally misleading title of "The New Novel".

The article—which is not James at his best, and which also provoked James's breach with Wells—divides the novelists into the very young, and the not-so-young. Among these latter James lists Maurice Hewlett, John Galsworthy, H. G. Wells, Arnold Bennett, and Conrad. All but the last of them are presented as following what James calls the "fatal error" of Tolstoy, "the great illustrative master-hand . . . of disconnexion of method from matter"—they all think only of their matter not of their art. Conrad, on the other hand, is presented as the prime—and unique—example of the other extreme. . . .

James's main objection to the narrative method of *Chance* is that it compromises the reader's sense of the reality of the events by drawing attention to the narrators rather than to the narrative. . . .

This view of *Chance* seems to me not to take account of Conrad's aims, and since James singles out the novel's ending for special attention, I would like to suggest that the method of narration here is in fact a response to the "challenge from without", to the imperatives of the story itself.

Very briefly, *Chance* is told through three major informants. The primary narrator, whose words constitute the novel, is an unnamed "I" who reports his conversations with

Marlow. Though technically a secondary narrator, it is Marlow who is chiefly responsible for assembling the stories of the fictional protagonists: the Fynes, Flora, her father, De Barral, and her lover, Captain Anthony; Marlow's interminable colloquies also interpret the psychological and moral dimensions of the story, in what James felicitously terms "a prolonged hovering flight of the subjective over the outstretched ground of the case exposed". Then there is the third narrator, Powell, who meets the first two narrators at the beginning by chance, and who was second mate of Anthony's ship when the events of the last half of the novel occurred. . . .

Much may be said against *Chance* and its narrative method: some obtrusive artificiality, a tendency to sentimentalize, and moments of fatiguing garrulousness; but the charge that its mode of recital is gratuitously imposed seems itself to be gratuitous.

James and Conrad must have looked at the treatment of *Chance* in the "New Generation" essay from very different points of view. James would certainly have felt that he was innocent of envy or malice, and he could point to passages where Conrad was implicitly accorded a higher literary status than any other author treated: Conrad alone is called a "genius"; and *Chance* is described as the work of "a beautiful and generous mind" with "a noble sociability of vision". But, as Conrad must have seen, what James gives with one hand he takes away with the other, and in much more detail. Imperceptive about the reasons for the method of *Chance*, James, no doubt impelled by the rhetorical requirements of his polar opposition between Conrad's concentration on method, and the infatuation with mere matter of the other contemporary novelists, does not mention earlier works in which Conrad might have figured as offering happier examples of harmony between form and content.—IAN WATT, "Conrad, James and *Chance*," *Imagined Worlds*, ed. Maynard Mack and Ian Gregor, 1968, pp. 301–17

VICTORY

When, indeed, such a novel as *Victory* unfolds itself in sound and vision before the imagination, with its rhythms and cadences, music and silences, its unrestricted freedom in time and space, its wisdom and balance and simpleness out of complexity, we begin to realise to what an immeasurable extent life on the world is coloured and quickened by the imagination, how easy it is to recognise, how difficult and unusual to discover.

Every reality is something compounded, the outcome of a collusion between the seer and the thing seen. And the simplest work of art—of fiction—is a thing infinitely more abstruse. So that to say that *Victory* is 'true to life' amounts not only almost to ignoring Mr. Conrad altogether, but is an exaggerated compliment to one's everyday consciousness as his reader. For just as form and content in a work of art (or of nature humanly seen) are inseparable, so the originality of a novelist consists not in how he has copied the life we know, but in the life that he has himself created—the life of which, without his witness, we should be ignorant. It is his all of life that is indivisibly his. If Axel Heyst and Lena, if the German hotel-keeper Schomberg ('in a state of rapid moral decomposition'), and that ineffable 'gentleman' and 'brigand' Mr. Jones were handed over to some other practitioner, they would not be merely re-dressed up; they would in themselves cease to exist. And to make a précis of *Victory*, to say that it is the story of the conflict between heart and mind in a man doomed by destiny to the trammels of philosophic doubt and a passionless integrity

in the presence of a selfless love and innocence and of an evil as violent and as confined in spiritual space, so to speak, as an atom of radium, is nothing better than to write a name and a date upon a tombstone. We realise sooner or later that Mr. Conrad alone could create *for us* the naïve, fearless, submissive, all-sacrificing Lena, the rancid German, Schomberg, the ivory, silvery philosopher of Despair, Heyst senior, 'silenced destroyer of systems, of hopes, of beliefs,' and that devil of two instincts, lust and violence, Ricardo, just as he alone could float before our eyes Samburan amid its archipelago in the remote waters of an unfamiliar world:

> The islands are very quiet. One sees them lying about, clothed in their dark garments of leaves, in a great hush of silver and azure, where the sea without murmurs meets the sky in a ring of magic stillness. A sort of smiling somnolence broods over them; the very voices of their people are soft and subdued, as if afraid to break some protecting spell.

It is an originality that is manifest even in a phrase, as when the peculiar timbre of Lena's voice is described as possessing 'a modulation of audacity and sadness'; or even in just three words for ever individualising Mr. Jones's 'dark sunken stare.'

This is only to insist on a commonplace. It may humble us to realise that Mr. Conrad's Lena could not of herself 'in real life' reveal to us her spiritual loveliness, that we should have discovered most easily in Heyst what is for ever troubling us in his appearance in his story—those bronze horizontal moustaches, that large white brow, that suave manner and volubility—and probably have missed his tragic, dauntless bearing, his despair, in face of the 'Great Joke'—Life. But in the acceptance of a gift humility does no harm. We may be positively shocked at a plane of consciousness whereon evil is at the same time so hideously substantial and violent and yet so spectral; troubled in face of a beauty so densely mantled with the moods and emotions of sadness, isolation, solemn ecstasy and despair; and remain unsolaced by a presentation of virtue which reaps no reward but that of death. 'Let Heaven look after what has been purified.' But what is this but the recognition of genius? What, indeed, is genius but a power of receptiveness so individual that its revelation in the form of art is the revelation of a new universe?

Mr. Conrad's universe is haunted. The humility of *his* acceptance takes strange disguises of irony and scorn, indignation and laughter. But these are only the clothing of his truth. 'Real bad people get over me somehow,' says Lena. 'I have said to the Earth that bore me: "I am I, and you are a shadow."' 'And by Jove, it is so,' says Heyst. Shadow it may be, but 'It will bite you if you give it a chance.' 'Formerly,' explains the unnamed narrator, 'in solitude and silence, Heyst had been used to think clearly and sometimes even profoundly, seeing life outside the flattering optical delusion of everlasting hope, of conventional self-deceptions, of an ever-expected happiness.' And it is this same victim of blessedest disillusionment who with his last breath cries, 'Ah, Davidson, woe to the man whose heart has not learned while young to hope, to love—and to put its trust in life.'

It is an emptier stage even than that of *Hamlet* on which Mr. Conrad's curtain descends. And yet his story leaves us in the presence of what we long for most just now in the tormented conflict between the chequered good and evil of nations and individuals—for the reassurance of the spirit of love and of life—Victory.—WALTER DE LA MARE, WG, Oct. 2, 1915

Revisiting *Victory* today, one cannot help being struck by its "existentialist" qualities—by how much it shares the intellectual preoccupations and postures notable in continental literature during recent decades. Here, for instance, is an elaborated image of human isolation: the isolation not only of man from man, but even more of man from his metaphysical environment—Axel Heyst, the rootless drifter, who has settled alone upon a singularly remote little island, near an abandoned coal mine, there to meditate in silence his late father's reflections upon "the universal nothingness" and "the unknown force of negation." Here, too, is the familiar counterattack upon metaphysical isolation, the unsteady impulse toward human fellowship—those compassionate gestures toward Morrison and the girl called Lena which belie Heyst's habitual detachment and are the source of his misfortunes and maybe of his redemption. Here is the articulated obsession with the feeling of existence and of nonexistence, as clues both to character and action. "If you were to stop thinking of me, I shouldn't be in the world at all," Lena says to Heyst; and, "I am he who is—" announces plain Mr. Jones, in a breath-taking moment which, in context, has an overpowering propriety. Here are modes of nihilism yielding to modes of self-annihilation, in the oddly similar catastrophes of both hero and villain. Here, in short, is a tale of violence that oscillates richly between the fundamental mysteries of being and nothing. Conrad, we are inclined to say, is the still insufficiently acknowledged grandfather of the most recent literary generation.

To say so is not necessarily to praise Conrad; and it is more likely, indeed, to impose upon him a false identity. *Victory* is not—and it cannot be discussed as—a novel of ideas, for example, in the manner of Malraux's *The Walnut Trees of the Altenburg*. Nor is it a calculated work of metaphysical revolt, like Camus' *The Plague*. Conrad did of course display attitudes, and he had a stiff little set of convictions. But E. M. Forster has rightly, if unsympathetically, made the point that Conrad had no "creed"—no coherent order of intellectual principles—and no more than other novelists writing on English soil did Conrad possess that occasional French and German talent for making the war of thought itself exciting. He wanted to exploit the power of words, as he said, in order "to make you hear, to make you feel—before all to make you *see*"; and the end of each of his best novels was simply its own composition. He did not believe with Malraux that art is "a rectification of the universe, a way of escaping from the human condition"; and he would scarcely have understood Camus' parallel and derivative contention that "the novel is born simultaneously with the spirit of rebellion and expresses, on the aesthetic plane, the same ambition." *Victory* dramatizes basic aspects of truth and being; but as regards the human condition, its main aim is only to observe it in the way of art—with that idle but no less intense and sustained attention for which Conrad accurately thought he had a natural ability, and with which he recalled observing the living model for *Victory*'s heroine.

The novel's final word—"Nothing!"—is, accordingly, less a cry of appalled metaphysical recognition than the quiet acknowledgment that the adventure is over and the art that described it has peacefully exhausted itself. It is in the mood less of Camus' *Caligula* than of Shakespeare's *Hamlet*: "The rest is silence." The drama is done, and everybody who had a significant part in it is dead. Lena is dead, accidentally shot by Mr. Jones. Heyst has died by fire; Jones has died by water; and both deliberately, as it seems. Ricardo has been killed by Jones's second try at him; and Pedro has been dispatched by Wang, the houseboy. "There are more dead in this affair," Davidson remarks to the Excellency, "than have been killed in

many of the battles of the last Achin war." The bungalow and the other two houses are burned to ashes; the boat has drifted out to sea; a corpse lies rotting on the scorched earth. To close the account, only the word "nothing" needs to be uttered.

And yet. If there is no metaphysical vision or purpose at work in the novel, there can nevertheless be felt running through it something like a metaphysical tide. Or better, perhaps, one senses the active presence, the dangerous undertow, of a metaphysical current giving the story its energy and its direction. In the same way, if the tale is not plainly intended as an allegory, one feels in it nevertheless something like an allegorical swelling, as though everything were about to become bigger than itself. That very impression affects the nerves of the persons in the book. "I have a peculiar feeling about this," says Mr. Jones. "It's a different thing. It's a sort of test." In the long list of Conrad's writings, *Victory* also comes to us as a different thing and a sort of test. It is Conrad's test of the nature of fiction: in general, of the ability of drama to move toward allegory while retaining intact its dramatic form and essence; and in particular, of the ability of fiction to move toward drama while retaining its identity as fictional narrative. It is a test of the way truth and reality can become the subject matter of a novel which hangs on to its novelistic nature. And the result, in my judgment, is indicated by the last word Conrad actually did write in this book, as he tells us: the single word of the title.

Victory (1915) is itself the last of those works both Conrad and his critics have agreed to call major; and it ranked with *Nostromo* (1904) as Conrad's personal favorite. Conrad's appraisal of his writings was, I think, both sound and suggestive. He always had a special fondness for *The Nigger of the Narcissus* (1897), recognizing it for what it was, his first genuine artistic accomplishment; and his satisfaction with *The Secret Agent* (1907) was grounded correctly in his belief that he had succeeded, in that novel, in treating "a melodramatic subject ironically," as he wrote in the copy he gave his friend Richard Curle. But he disagreed with readers and critics who thought that *Lord Jim* (1900) was his best book; he felt the tale did not justify the great length of the novel, and suspected that he should have stuck to his original idea, which was to restrict the narrative to the pilgrim ship episode. The most he could say for *Under Western Eyes* (1910) was "rather good." We should probably speak more warmly, but the pain of composition clings to the pages of *Under Western Eyes*; and the congealing of the action (for example, in Part III) is for long stretches greater than all the interpolated reflections on the art of fiction can overcome. About *Chance* (1913), in a manner not uncommon with authors, he began to talk deprecatingly the moment it became so huge a success. But he remained steadfast in his conviction that his two supreme efforts were the vast tale of the South American seaboard and the tight little story of Axel Heyst.

Surely he was right. *Nostromo* was, as Conrad knew, his largest canvas and his "most anxiously meditated work." It is also one of the greatest novels in English, with a greatness so complex and extensive that only belatedly and partially has it become appreciated. *Victory* is a triumph of a different kind, of a nearly opposite kind. Here Conrad has presented almost all the themes that interested him, but he has refracted those themes through the closely observed conduct of a tiny group of people in a tiny and absolutely isolated setting. *Nostromo* and *Victory* thus stand in a relation similar to the relation between *King Lear* and *Othello* (or perhaps like that between *The Possessed* and *Crime and Punishment*). Both *Nostromo* and *King Lear* comprehend more of the world and of human experience than the mind can comfortably contemplate; both are made up of a variety of parallel plots and involve several different groups of persons; in each we discover what Francis Fergusson calls "action by analogy," and the action so richly exposed in its multiplicity of modes reveals something not only about the individuals concerned but about the hidden drift of history, the secret and tragic movement of the universe. Both works engage the artist's most disturbing power—the prophetic power—which is of course not the ability to read the particular and immediate future, but the ability to read the future implicit in every grave and serious time, the future man is perennially prone to. In *Victory*, on the other hand, as in *Othello*, the action emerges directly from the peculiar temperaments of a few eccentric individuals. What happens, both artistically and psychologically, happens as a result of the impact of one unique personality upon another. This is not to deny any largeness to *Victory*; it is only to identify the source of the special largeness it does reveal. It is to say that the novel shows an allegorical swelling rather than an allegory, and that the creative force is less a pre-existent design the characters are re-enacting (for example, the myth of Eden, of the man and the woman in the garden and the invasion by the serpent) than the jarring effect of the human encounters.—R. W. B. LEWIS, "The Current of Conrad's *Victory*" (1959), *Trials of The Word*, 1965, pp. 149–53

THE SHADOW LINE

In Mr. Conrad's art the very antithesis of subjective and objective becomes unthinkable. His method here, as always, is psychological. He makes us see his changing pictures as they change in the minds of his characters. *The Shadow-Line* is more bare and simple than his earlier stories in the same vein. The old efficiency of phrase is found (with occasional lapses, such as: 'a perpetual consciousness of unpleasant physical sensations in his internal economy,' and 'consigning' so-and-so 'to eternal perdition'). But there is not all the old magic. There is something abrupt, casual, in the treatment. It is as if we were being told: 'This is the fact, whether it moves you or not'—and in consequence we are not moved. There are books, and books by writers much inferior to Mr. Conrad, which one reads with a thrill of excitement. Out of *The Shadow-Line* I, at any rate, can get no excitement whatever. But it is interesting throughout, beautiful in places; there is much of it that no one but Mr. Conrad could have written.

> With her anchor at the bow and clothed in canvas to her very trucks, my command seemed to stand as motionless as a model ship set on the gleams and shadows of polished marble. It was impossible to distinguish land from water in the enigmatical tranquillity of the immense forces of the world. A sudden impatience possessed me.
>
> 'Won't she answer the helm at all?' I said irritably to the man whose strong brown hands grasping the spokes of the wheel stood out lighted in the darkness; like a symbol of mankind's claim to the direction of its own fate.

That is the beginning of the voyage: the irony of the last sentence is typical of Mr. Conrad's art.—GERALD GOULD, NSN, March 31, 1917, p. 618

Conrad's last masterpiece, *The Shadow-Line*, is one of his most typical works. The story—about how the young narrator suddenly throws up a satisfactory job as first-mate of a steamer trading in Eastern seas, only to find himself unexpectedly thrust into his first command, which turns out to be one of unique difficulty—is characteristic. Characteristic because its

subject is a sea voyage; a voyage, moreover, that is, as Conrad wrote, "exact autobiography," an example, like *Heart of Darkness* and *The Nigger of the "Narcissus,"* though even more literally so, of "my personal experience . . . seen in perspective with the eye of the mind"; while the nature of the personal experience, moral initiation, is one of Conrad's dominant literary themes.

. . . Conrad disliked titles that were "too literal—too explicit"; but a shadow-line has just the right degree of suggestive mutability and indeterminacy of application to stand as a nautical metaphor for a transit through one of what Johnson called "the climatericks of the mind." A shadow-line is not a definite boundary that one crosses consciously, whether in space, like a line of longitude, or in time: Conrad isn't dealing with the rather obvious temporal indicators of adulthood—political or legal, like the 21st birthday; religious, like the first communion; or biological, like sexual maturity. The shadow-line is inward and social; approaching it one is only aware of some vague atmospheric change, and one may not know its cause; yet although it is mysterious and elusive, projected almost at random through the chance collisions of the individual with his endlessly varying environment, it has a compelling universality. The narrator, fleeing, as he puts it, from "the menace of emptiness," is really fleeing from the shades of the prison house that lie ahead; and he tries to alter his course because pursuing the present one—his career as first mate—obviously involves renouncing many other aspirations; it means acknowledging an end to the youthful dream that one will, one day, be able to achieve everything; it means, alas, beginning to be like everybody else. . . .

At first, we observe, the narrator pays as little attention to Giles's gloomy prognostications as to the later warnings of the friendly doctor at Bangkok; unreasonably but understandably he clings to the belief that once out of harbour all will be well because the sea is "pure, safe and friendly." Such security, however, is more than anyone should count on; the crew's health actually gets worse as the lack of wind makes it impossible to pass the island of Koh-Ring; and the nadir is reached at the end of the fourth chapter when the narrator discovers that the remaining five quinine bottles actually contain a worthless white powder. He informs the crew of the catastrophe, fully expecting to be overwhelmed by their anger and reproach: actually, the "temper of their souls or the sympathy of their imagination" surprises him; and it is their stoic resignation, their refusal to see things personally, which does most to turn him away from his egocentric sense that all is merely a plot aimed against him personally—a plot by which he has been "decoyed into this awful, this death-haunted command."

Before then there had already been some signs of human interdependence, and of the narrator's growing awareness of it. In contrast to the moral intransigence he had showed towards the steward at the Officers' Home, he had listened to his sick first mate Burns's plea "You and I are sailors," and allowed him, sick as he was, to come back from hospital on to the ship, even though Burns, like Hamilton, had been his rival for the command, and was now so broken in body and mind that his mere presence on board ship was a serious hindrance. But when the crisis comes, Mr. Burns isn't wholly a dead loss: he steadies the narrator by telling him that it's "very foolish, sir" to feel guilty about the quinine; and he unwittingly seconds Giles's earlier advice about keeping to the east side of the Gulf of Siam.

It is, however, to the clear-sighted persistence of Ransome that the protagonist is most indebted. In the fifth chapter, after two weeks of being virtually becalmed, Ransome points out "a broad shadow on the horizon extinguishing the lower stars completely," and the narrator realises that there are not enough fit men to prepare the boat for the coming squall. Overwhelmed by the depth of his "contempt for that obscure weakness of my soul [under the] stress of adversity," he goes below in a state of paralysed remorse and confesses in his diary: "What appals me most of all is that I shrink from going on deck to face it . . . I always suspected I might be no good. . . . " Gradually, however, he becomes aware that Ransome is lingering "in the cabin as he had something to do there, but hesitated about doing it." Hesitates long enough to make the narrator ask "You think I ought to be on deck," to which Ransome replies "without any particular emphasis or accent: 'I do, sir.'"

It is the final nudge into the realisation that command means self-command. They go on deck, and the narrator finds in "the impenetrable blackness" a sense of "the closing in of a menace from all sides."

It is in this crisis that we are closest to the Jungian analogy suggested by Guerard. The darkness of the night and the narrator's despair certainly receive sufficient emphasis to suggest a symbolic intent; and even to lend some support to the interpretation of *The Shadow-Line* as essentially concerned, like "The Secret Sharer," with an "archetypal . . . night journey" which eventually causes the protagonist to subdue those aspects of his personality "which interfere with seamanship."

"The dark night of the soul" seems to be getting even more of a nuisance than the "Dark Lady of the Sonnets" used to be. The objection is not that it doesn't exist—metaphors exist once they are made—but rather that the seductive concreteness of the phrase deludes its hierophants into thinking that they have gained more than they have when the analogy has enabled them to reduce the literary work to less than it is: in the present case, to find *The Shadow-Line* inferior to "The Secret Sharer" primarily because, being much longer, its resists reduction to a single symbolic paradigm even more vigorously.

Actually, Conrad's emphasis in *The Shadow-Line* is not specifically on the forces which interfere with seamanship, but on something much more general—on "an ordeal . . . which had been maturing and tempering my character." It is true that the narrator often feels that he is a failure as captain: but this, and his consequent sense of guilt, is, as far as we can judge, a subjective—and typical—reaction to the difficulties of a first command; from the time that the doctor in Bangkok compliments him on his "very judicious arrangements," we have no reason to doubt that the narrator is right in saying that "the seaman's instinct alone survived whole in my moral dissolution."

The darkness and immobility of the night do not, of course, in themselves require symbolic explanation. The increment of suspense and pictorial vividness would be justified for its own sake; it is in keeping with Conrad's frequent use of darkness for his narrative climax; and it may well have been dark when the actual events occurred which served as basis for the story. But if one looks for larger meanings, for symbolic representations of universal elements in man's relations to his fellows and to the natural world, there are several which are clearly relevant to the main implications of the narrative. The calm before the storm, and the intensified darkness that precedes dawn, are well enough established commonplaces of human experience; and here they derive a particular significance from the fact that the calm is the climax of the long period of calm since leaving port, and that the darkness is the climax of the longer inner darkness which began when the leading edge of the shadow-line began to trouble the narrator's youthful horizon.

The calm, of course, has its psychological parallel in the narrator's prolonged inward lethargy, a parallel to which Conrad draws attention in the epigraph; in Baudelaire's sonnet "La Musique" the poet's quest for "ma pâle étoile" is most deeply menaced, not by tempests but by the "calme plat" which is the "great mirror of his despair." More widely, the alternating rhythm of calm and storm is the equivalent in the natural order of a human perspective to which Conrad was uniquely attentive—the duality of rest and work; of the solicitations of inertia and the impulsions to action. In the beginning the narrator's deepest yearnings, in his inarticulate revulsion from the "mortal coil," were for repose; later, on his way to the harbour office, he found "something touching about a ship . . . folding her white wings for a rest," and then heard that Captain Ellis had attributed his delay in coming to "funking . . . too much work."

Once at sea, the solicitations of the most extreme form of inertia, death, increasingly pervade the consciousness of the narrator. In the brilliant passage where he goes down to tell Burns about the quinine, for instance, he at first mistakes his glimpse of Burns trimming his beard with a pair of scissors as an attempt at suicide; while shortly afterwards Burns's ageworn look causes him to reflect: "Enviable man! So near extinction." Later, when Ransome comes to report on the darkening sky, the narrator thinks that the message must be that "Someone's dead"; and when he finally goes up to prepare for the squall he welcomes the utter calm and darkness of the night as an image of death. . . .

It was this particular implication of the shadow-line which led Conrad's wife to object to his title on the grounds that it suggested the Psalmist's "valley of the shadow of death." But death is only one of the terrors which occupy the narrator's mind as he waits in the "blackness which had swallowed up our world" for the heavens to declare themselves; most obviously he experiences an unforgettable reminder of man's precarious exposure to the unpredictable power of the natural order as a whole; and the importance of this exposure to the idea of the shadow-line was suggested in a letter which Conrad wrote to his relative and intimate friend Marguerite Poradowska: "One always thinks oneself important at twenty. The fact is, however, that one becomes useful only on realising the utter insignificance of the individual in the scheme of the universe."

On the other hand, confronting his own "utter insignificance" in the natural order heightens the narrator's awareness of his need for the support of his fellows. This is brought home, for instance, in the scene when, after the mainsail has been hauled up close and the mainyard squared, Ransome comes to report, and then, suddenly "stepped back two paces and vanished from my sight" out of the light of the binnacle lamps. . . .

Here the vivid realization of complete human isolation in "the darkness before creation," evokes the historical dimension of the theme of human solidarity; the narrator, having been deprived, first through the loneliness of command, and then through darkness, of the support of his fellows, is brought face to face with the long tradition of civilisation since the creation, and his own utter dependence on it.—IAN WATT, "Story and Idea in Conrad's *The Shadow-Line*," *CQ*, Summer 1960, pp. 121–29

MARLOW

Marlow was one of those born observers who are happiest in retirement. Marlow liked nothing better than to sit on deck, in some obscure creek of the Thames, smoking and recollecting; smoking and speculating; sending after his smoke beautiful rings of words until all the summer's night became a little clouded with tobacco smoke. Marlow, too, had a profound respect for the men with whom he had sailed; but he saw the humour of them. He nosed out and described in masterly fashion those livid creatures who prey successfully upon the clumsy veterans. He had a flair for human deformity; his humour was sardonic. Nor did Marlow live entirely wreathed in the smoke of his own cigars. He had a habit of opening his eyes suddenly and looking—at a rubbish heap, at a port, at a shop counter—and then complete in its burning ring of light that thing is flashed bright upon the mysterious background. Introspective and analytical, Marlow was aware of this peculiarity. He said the power came to him suddenly. He might, for instance, overhear a French officer murmur "Mon Dieu, how the time passes!" . . .

Picture after picture he painted thus upon that dark background; ships first and foremost, ships at anchor, ships flying before the storm, ships in harbour; he painted sunsets and dawns; he painted the night; he painted the sea in every aspect; he painted the gaudy brilliancy of Eastern ports, and men and women, their houses and their attitudes. He was an accurate and unflinching observer, schooled to that "absolute loyalty towards his feelings and sensations", which, Conrad wrote, "an author should keep hold of in his most exalted moments of creation". And very quietly and compassionately Marlow sometimes lets fall a few words of epitaph which remind us, with all that beauty and brilliancy before our eyes, of the darkness of the background.

Thus a rough-and-ready distinction would make us say that it is Marlow who comments, Conrad who creates. It would lead us, aware that we are on dangerous ground, to account for that change which, Conrad tells us, took place when he had finished the last story in the *Typhoon* volume—"a subtle change in the nature of the inspiration"—by some alteration in the relationship of the two old friends. " . . . it seemed somehow that there was nothing more in the world to write about." It was Conrad, let us suppose, Conrad the creator, who said that, looking back with sorrowful satisfaction upon the stories he had told; feeling as he well might that he could never better the storm in *The Nigger of the "Narcissus"*, or render more faithful tribute to the qualities of British seamen than he had done already in *Youth* and *Lord Jim*. It was then that Marlow, the commentator, reminded him how, in the course of nature, one must grow old, sit smoking on deck, and give up seafaring. But, he reminded him, those strenuous years had deposited their memories; and he even went so far perhaps as to hint that, though the last word might have been said about Captain Whalley and his relation to the universe, there remained on shore a number of men and women whose relationships, though of a more personal kind, might be worth looking into. If we further suppose that there was a volume of Henry James on board and that Marlow gave his friend the book to take to bed with him, we may seek support in the fact that it was in 1905 that Conrad wrote a very fine essay upon that master.

For some years, then, it was Marlow who was the dominant partner. *Nostromo, Chance, The Arrow of Gold* represent that stage of the alliance which some will continue to find the richest of all. The human heart is more intricate than the forest, they will say; it has its storms; it has its creatures of the night; and if as novelist you wish to test man in all his relationships, the proper antagonist is man; his ordeal is in society, not solitude. For them there will always be a peculiar fascination in the books where the light of those brilliant eyes falls not only upon the waste of waters but upon the heart in its perplexity. But it must be admitted that, if Marlow thus advised Conrad to shift his angle of vision, the advice was bold. For the

vision of a novelist is both complex and specialised; complex, because behind his characters and apart from them must stand something stable to which he relates them; specialised because since he is a single person with one sensibility the aspects of life in which he can believe with conviction are strictly limited. So delicate a balance is easily disturbed. After the middle period Conrad never again was able to bring his figures into perfect relation with their background. He never believed in his later and more highly sophisticated characters as he had believed in his early seamen. When he had to indicate their relation to that other unseen world of novelists, the world of values and convictions, he was far less sure what those values were. Then, over and over again, a single phrase, "He steered with care", coming at the end of a storm, carried in it a whole morality. But in this more crowded and complicated world such terse phrases became less and less appropriate. Complex men and women of many interests and relations would not submit to so summary a judgement; or, if they did, much that was important in them escaped the verdict. And yet it was very necessary to Conrad's genius, with its luxuriant and romantic power, to have some law by which its creations could be tried. Essentially—such remained his creed—this world of civilised and self-conscious people is based upon "a few very simple ideas"; but where, in the world of thoughts and personal relations, are we to find them? There are no masts in drawing-rooms; the typhoon does not test the worth of politicians and business men. Seeking and not finding such supports, the world of Conrad's later period has about it an involuntary obscurity, an inconclusiveness, almost a disillusionment which baffles and fatigues. We lay hold in the dusk only of the old nobilities and sonorities: fidelity, compassion, honour, service—beautiful always, but now a little wearily reiterated, as if times had changed. Perhaps it was Marlow who was at fault. His habit of mind was a trifle sedentary. He had sat upon deck too long; splendid in soliloquy, he was less apt in the give and take of conversation; and those "moments of vision" flashing and fading, do not serve as well as steady lamplight to illumine the ripple of life and its long, gradual years. Above all, perhaps, he did not take into account how, if Conrad was to create, it was essential first that he should believe.—VIRGINIA WOOLF, "Joseph Conrad" (1924), *The Common Reader*, 1925, pp. 313–18

Read as a unit, Conrad's Marlovian fictions—*Youth, Heart of Darkness, Lord Jim*, and *Chance*—differ markedly from what they are in isolation. In the four works taken together, Conrad's primary narrator, Marlow, himself becomes the moving center of an episodic, larger fiction in which characters and incidents spin off and revolve about him, as in one of the inner circles *Lord Jim* seems to emit characters like Brierly and the German captain, Brown and the French lieutenant—all aspects of the whirling, prismatic protagonist of one experiential focus. Conrad's seemingly depersonalized narrator emerges over the course of several works first as character and then as protagonist. In the beginning of *Heart of Darkness*, Marlow says, "'I don't want to bother you much with what happened to me personally,'" which provokes the narrator to comment that Marlow showed "in this remark the weakness of many tellers of tales who seem so often unaware of what their audience would best like to hear." Yet Marlow immediately indicates that his purpose in recounting his Congo experience is to have his listeners "understand the effect of it on me." Marlow's tales are self-revelatory above all.

Conrad constructs the Marlovian tales on two main series of relationships and two dynamic sequences. First, Marlow interacts both with the protagonists of his narratives and with the narrators who frame him; second, temporal revelations portray not only the young Marlow, Kurtz, Jim, and Flora, but also Marlow's own picaresque journeying from one narrative stage to the next. The stories within the stories express an independent reality and validity like that which Chaucer creates in *The Canterbury Tales*—and as great a symbiotic interdependence with the framing context. The narrated tales are beguiling in their own terms, for each dramatizes an extraordinary sequence of adventures and misadventures in which an energetic questor reaches, with varying degrees of success, toward identity and control. The four narrated sequences lose in chronological ordering but gain in significance by being filtered through what James calls the "interpreting consciousness"—Marlow's plus at least one other. Yet the four also exist—and perhaps most fundamentally, certainly most organically—as temporal stages in the development of Marlow himself. For through Marlow, Conrad achieves at once the intimacy and distance he sought in the shifting perspectives of *The Nigger of the "Narcissus."* It is our task, then, to consider how this oddly constructed tetralogy—growing much longer and more cumbersome each step of the way—negotiates the personal, moral, and aesthetic evolution of its central spokesman.

Youth and *Heart of Darkness* are both narrated by an anonymous former seaman, one of the five characters (along with the director of companies, the lawyer, the accountant, and Marlow) who recall and verbalize a similar past. "Between us there was, as I have already said somewhere [in *Youth*], the bond of the sea. Besides holding our hearts together through long periods of separation, it had the effect of making us tolerant of each other's yarns—and even convictions." But *Youth*, the earliest of the four, is straightforward and its dualism assumes a traditional order; like Pip in *Great Expectations*, an older and more reflective Marlow both narrates and comments upon the active, uncontemplative innocence of his own younger self. Yet the structure of *Youth* is far simpler than that Dickens employs, for the younger and older Marlows are virtually identical. No lesson has been learned, no initiatory trauma separates the two; it is only that one is older, more experienced, and consequently sadder. For all its vitality and vibrance, its humor and bravura, its briefly but fully realized characters, *Youth* is slight because in it Marlow experiences no crisis beyond the physical; consequently, he has no moral lesson to teach or learn. . . .

Lord Jim, the greatest of the four Marlovian tales, is unique in including an extra narrative layer, a multifarious commentator who begins with ostensible objectivity to portray the title character—"He was an inch, *perhaps* two, under six feet, powerfully built, and he advanced straight at you with a slight stoop of the shoulders, head forward, and a fixed from-under stare which made you think of a charging bull"—parlays that "perhaps" into a full-scale attack on the validity of just such narration—"They wanted facts. Facts! They demanded facts from him, as if facts could explain anything!"—and then merges into an auditor-narrator analogous to the one in *Youth*, *Heart of Darkness*, and *Chance*: "And later on, many times, in distant parts of the world, Marlow showed himself willing to remember Jim, to remember him at length, in detail and audibly. Perhaps it would be after dinner, on a verandah draped in motionless foliage." The main difference between the multifarious and personal voices lies in the breadth of "many times" and the vagueness of that last "perhaps"; but from this point until the return to multifarious narration at the end of Chapter 35, the narrative perspective of *Lord Jim* is identical in form

and effect to that of the other three tales: a companion of Marlow's narrates Marlow's narrative.

. . . The narrator's mocking attitude speaks through the hollow rhetoric of "valorous deeds," "the success of his imaginary achievements," "gorgeous virility, the charm of vagueness," "heroic tread," as well as the climactic self-deception of "There was nothing he could not face," and the devastating betrayal of trust implicit (and retrospectively explicit) in "keeping *perfunctorily* his eyes ahead." As elsewhere, the narrator here verges on turning into the sarcastic presiding genius of *The Secret Agent*. The intense derision directed at Jim—increasingly obvious with each rereading—requires counterbalancing if Jim is to be afforded any sort of sympathetic response. Thus, Conrad conceals from his reader what everyone else knows—that the *Patna* failed to sink—and abandons the frame narrator by offering Marlow as intercessor between Jim and us.

One further important distinction between the narrators of *The Secret Agent* and *Lord Jim* is that the latter never really engages in dry, ironically detached, and near-solipsistic narration and manipulation. Rather, when Marlow passionately declares to Jewel that Jim is not good enough (because no one is good enough), it seems clear that he speaks also for the novel's uncertain multifarious narrator who, in the novel's first line, announces Jim's height as *perhaps* five feet ten inches and then rails out against facts just before the anonymous listener and Marlow take over the narration. Such a narrator is far removed from that of *The Secret Agent*, who accepts as valid the irony of facts and the triviality of all human endeavor. . . .

In both *Youth* and *Chance* Marlow wryly but enviously shakes his head over the bravura successes of youth, but such nostalgia, while valid once, becomes brittle and artificial after the confrontation with youth's flagrant excesses of ideas and imagination, and its consequent heart-rending doom, in *Heart of Darkness* and *Lord Jim*. James Baldwin has noted that "people who shut their eyes to reality simply invite their own destruction, and anyone who insists on remaining in a state of innocence long after that innocence is dead turns himself into a monster." An analogous perversity reduces Marlow in *Chance* to anachronism, a banal commentator on the subject he admittedly knows least—women. For *Chance*'s title is misleading: the novel's small philosophical energy expends itself primarily on the subject of women rather than accidents of fortune. Like *Youth* and unlike *Heart of Darkness* and *Lord Jim*, *Chance* lacks a moral core and Marlow a moral stance. The problems of its plot are situational; they bear no relationship to the crisis of nightmare and conscience Marlow, along with Kurtz and Jim, experiences in *Heart of Darkness* and *Lord Jim*. Though used in various ways, "chance" primarily means coincidence rather than providence, happenstance rather than moral and symbolic aptness. Thus Powell tells us that he got his first chance by chance—a casual display of verbal irony indicative of the novel's lack of profundity and wit. The story is the vehicle not for symbolic, philosophical, or moral exploration, but for what Marlow calls "the commonest sort of curiosity," for he finds what he narrates only mildly interesting, and his lack of temperamental involvement utterly denies any tension at the novel's core. . . .

Marlow's attitudes toward *Chance*'s central concerns—the sea and women—are also disturbing, for his complacent categorization of each confronts endless contradictions while remaining unchanged. As with *Typhoon*'s Captain MacWhirr, the sea in *Chance* is defined as free from all moral challenge, "free from the earth's petty suggestions," offering professional satisfaction plus adventure with its simple, direct claims. Thus, life on the *Ferndale* (as on the *Narcissus*, the *Patna*, and the

Sephora—in fact, most of Conrad's ships) must be seen as aberrant, its unrestfulness atypical of the sea but very like that associated with the land. In *Chance*, this aberrance is compounded by the marriage of Flora and Anthony, for another of Marlow's ex cathedra pronouncements blithely generalizes about marriage and then marriage at sea. "'With what we know of Roderick Anthony and Flora de Barral I could not deduct an ordinary marital quarrel beautifully matured in less than a year—could I? If you ask me what is an ordinary marital quarrel I will tell you, that it is a difference about nothing. . . . There are on earth no actors too humble and obscure not to have a gallery, that gallery which envenoms the play by stealthy jeers, counsels of anger, amused comments or words of perifidious compassion. However, the Anthonys were free from all demoralizing influences. At sea, you know, there is no gallery. You hear no tormenting echoes of your own littleness there.'" Once again, Marlow remains unperturbed by the failure of his definition and picture to square with each other. . . .

One central question remains concerning the Marlovian narratives. Is Marlow himself aware of and controlling the attitude implicit in his perspective—and thus as cynical as *The Secret Agent*'s narrator from first to last? Or is he as unconscious of many of his words' implications as is the professor of languages who narrates *Under Western Eyes*? By and large, *Chance* does not raise such questions because in it Marlow's sarcasm and sympathy are both distinct and superficial. But *Heart of Darkness* and *Lord Jim*, which are, in Booth's word, "seamless," remain two of Conrad's inscrutable fictions because they both raise such questions and seem to deny all the possible answers. Yet whether or not Marlow is fully a party to the plot, Conrad is surely at great pains to frustrate the part of us craving certitude. In one sense, Conrad (an ironist in all his major fiction) is simply having fun at our expense and Marlow's; yet he is also recognizing that our deepest experiences never sort themselves out neatly: they berate and confound us with their multiple moral claims; they perversely demand contradictory responses of us—and in the process truth and validity must sort themselves out as best they can. Our most difficult and important task may well be to dismiss the ambivalent "possibly" Marlow offers *Lord Jim*'s "privileged man" as wholly inadequate, and yet to perceive that it lies at the heart of truth—if, that is, one may even speak of truth as having a heart. Marlow's journey, though it finally loses the momentum that is its raison d'être, derives its validity by becoming what it seeks—the way into the self-confronting realm of modern art and life, where the artist, burdened by tradition like all of us, nonetheless asserts his claim to "making it new," to striking out for unknown territories of the human psyche like the bold, free, but criminal Leggett of *The Secret Sharer*. Marlow agrees with Jim that his clean slate is a magnificent chance and then adds, "But chances are what men make them, and how was I to know?" The only answer to such a question must be the quest implicit in the question.—ALLAN WARREN FRIEDMAN, "Conrad's Picaresque Narrator: Marlow's Journey from *Youth* to *Chance*," *Multivalence*, 1978, pp. 112–40

F. R. LEAVIS
From "Joseph Conrad"
The Great Tradition
1948, pp. 173–90

An announcement once appeared in a quarterly, against the name of the present writer, of an article to be entitled *Conrad, the Soul and the Universe*. The exasperation registered

in this formula explains, perhaps, why the article was never written. For that Conrad has done classical work is as certain as that his classical status will not rest evenly upon his whole *œuvre*, and the necessary discriminations and delimitations, not being altogether simple, clearly oughtn't to be attempted in any but a securely critical frame of mind. He has, of course, long been generally held to be among the English masters; the exasperation records a sense that the greatness attributed to him tended to be identified with an imputed profundity, and that this 'profundity' was not what it was taken to be, but quite other, and the reverse of a strength. The final abandonment of the article may have been partly determined by Mr. E. M. Forster's note on Conrad that appeared in *Abinger Harvest*:

> 'What is so elusive about him is that he is always promising to make some general philosophic statement about the universe, and then refraining with a gruff disclaimer. . . . Is there not also a central obscurity, something noble, heroic, beautiful, inspiring half-a-dozen great books, but obscure, obscure? . . . These essays do suggest that he is misty in the middle as well as at the edges, that the secret casket of his genius contains a vapour rather than a jewel; and that we needn't try to write him down philosophically, because there is, in this direction, nothing to write. No creed, in fact. Only opinions, and the right to throw them overboard when facts make them look absurd. Opinions held under the semblance of eternity, girt with the sea, crowned with stars, and therefore easily mistaken for a creed.'

—This might well have gratified the exasperation, and made its expression seem unnecessary.

Mr. Forster, however, doesn't attempt discriminations or precisions (his note is a reprinted review of *Notes on Life and Letters*). And he doesn't suggest those manifestations of the characteristic he describes in which we have something simply and obviously deplorable—something that presents itself, not as an elusively noble *timbre*, prompting us to analysis and consequent limiting judgments, but as, bluntly, a disconcerting weakness or vice. Consider, for instance, how *Heart of Darkness* is marred.

Heart of Darkness is, by common consent, one of Conrad's best things—an appropriate source for the epigraph of *The Hollow Men*: 'Mistah Kurtz, he dead'. That utterance, recalling the particularity of its immediate context, represents the strength of *Heart of Darkness*:

> 'He cried in a whisper at some image, at some vision—he cried out twice, a cry that was no more than a breath—
> "'The horror! The horror!'"
> 'I blew the candle out and left the cabin. The pilgrims were dining in the mess-room, and I took my place opposite the manager, who lifted his eyes to give me a questioning glance, which I successfully ignored. He leaned back, serene, with that peculiar smile of his sealing the unexpressed depth of his meanness. A continuous shower of small flies streamed upon the lamp, upon the cloth, upon our hands and faces. Suddenly the manager's boy put his insolent face in the doorway, and said in a tone of scathing contempt—
> "'Mistah Kurtz—he dead.'"
> 'All the pilgrims rushed out to see. I remained, and went on with my dinner. I believe I was considered brutally callous. However, I did not eat much. There was a lamp in there—light, don't you know—and outside it was so beastly, beastly dark.'

This passage, it will be recognized, owes its force to a whole wide context of particularities that gives the elements here—the pilgrims, the manager, the manager's boy, the situation—their specific values. Borrowing a phrase from Mr. Eliot's critical writings, one might say that *Heart of Darkness* achieves its overpowering evocation of atmosphere by means of 'objective correlatives'. The details and circumstances of the voyage to and up the Congo are present to us as if we were making the journey ourselves and (chosen for record as they are by a controlling imaginative purpose) they carry specificities of emotion and suggestion with them. There is the gunboat dropping shells into Africa:

> 'There wasn't even a shed there, and she was shelling the bush. It appears the French had one of their wars going on thereabouts. Her ensign dropped limp like a rag; the muzzles of the long six-inch guns stuck out all over the low hull; the greasy, slimy swell swung her up lazily and let her down, swaying her thin masts. In the empty immensity of earth, sky and water, there she was, incomprehensible, firing into a continent. Pop, would go one of the six-inch guns; a small flame would dart and vanish, a tiny projectile would give a feeble screech—and nothing happened. Nothing could happen. . . .'

There is the arrival at the Company's station:

> 'I came upon a boiler wallowing in the grass, then found a path leading up the hill. It turned aside for the boulders, and also for an undersized railway-truck lying there on its back with its wheels in the air. One was off. The thing looked as dead as the carcass of some animal. I came upon more pieces of decaying machinery, a stack of rusty nails. To the left a clump of trees made a shady spot, where dark things seemed to stir feebly. I blinked, the path was steep. A horn tooted to the right, and I saw black people run. A heavy, dull detonation shook the ground, a puff of smoke came out of the cliff, and that was all. No change appeared on the face of the rock. They were building a railway. The cliff was not in the way of anything; but this objectless blasting was all the work going on. . . .'

There is the grove of death:

> 'At last I got under the trees. My purpose was to stroll into the shade for a moment; but no sooner within it than it seemed to me that I had stepped into the gloomy circle of some Inferno. The rapids were near, and an uninterrupted, uniform, headlong, rushing noise filled the mournful stillness of the grove, where not a breath stirred, not a leaf moved, with a mysterious sound—as though the tearing pace of the launched earth had suddenly become audible. . . .'

By means of this art of vivid essential record, in terms of things seen and incidents experienced by a main agent in the narrative, and particular contacts and exchanges with other human agents, the overwhelming sinister and fantastic 'atmosphere' is engendered. Ordinary greed, stupidity and moral squalor are made to look like behaviour in a lunatic asylum against the vast and oppressive mystery of the surroundings, rendered potently in terms of sensation. This mean lunacy, which we are made to feel as at the same time normal and insane, is brought out by contrast with the fantastically secure innocence of the young harlequin-costumed Russian ('son of an arch-priest . . . Government of Tambov'), the introduction to whom is by the way of that copy of Tower's (or Towson's) *Inquiry into Some Points of Seamanship*, symbol of tradition,

sanity and the moral idea, found lying, an incongruous mystery, in the dark heart of Africa.

Of course, as the above quotations illustrate, the author's comment cannot be said to be wholly implicit. Nevertheless, it is not separable from the thing rendered, but seems to emerge from the vibration of this as part of the tone. At least, this is Conrad's art at its best. There are, however, places in *Heart of Darkness* where we become aware of comment as an interposition, and worse, as an intrusion, at times an exasperating one. Hadn't he, we find ourselves asking, overworked 'inscrutable', 'inconceivable', 'unspeakable' and that kind of word already?— yet still they recur. Is anything added to the oppressive mysteriousness of the Congo by such sentences as:

> 'It was the stillness of an implacable force brooding over an inscrutable intention'?

The same vocabulary, the same adjectival insistence upon inexpressible and incomprehensible mystery, is applied to the evocation of human profundities and spiritual horrors; to magnifying a thrilled sense of the unspeakable potentialities of the human soul. The actual effect is not to magnify but rather to muffle. The essential vibration emanates from the interaction of the particular incidents, actions and perceptions that are evoked with such charged concreteness. . . .

By such means as it illustrates we are given a charged sense of the monstrous hothouse efflorescences fostered in Kurtz by solitude and the wilderness. It is a matter of such things as the heads on posts—a direct significant glimpse, the innocent Russian's explanations, the incidents of the progress up the river and the moral and physical incongruities registered; in short, of the charge generated in a variety of highly specific evocations. The stalking of the moribund Kurtz, a skeleton crawling through the long grass on all fours as he makes his bolt towards the fires and the tom-toms, is a triumphant climax in the suggestion of strange and horrible perversions. But Conrad isn't satisfied with these means; he feels that there is, or ought to be, some horror, some significance he has yet to bring out. So we have an adjectival and worse than supererogatory insistence on 'unspeakable rites', 'unspeakable secrets', 'monstrous passions', 'inconceivable mystery', and so on. If it were only, as it largely is in *Heart of Darkness*, a matter of an occasional phrase it would still be regrettable as tending to cheapen the tone. But the actual cheapening is little short of disastrous. Here, for instance, we have Marlow at the crisis of the episode just referred to:

> 'I tried to break the spell—the heavy, mute spell of the wilderness—that seemed to draw him to its pitiless breast by the awakening of forgotten and brutal instincts, by the memory of gratified and monstrous passions. This alone, I was convinced, had driven him out to the edge of the forest, towards the gleam of the fires, the throb of drums, the drone of weird incantations; this alone had beguiled his unlawful soul beyond the bounds of permitted aspirations. And, don't you see, the terror of the position was not in being knocked on the head—though I had a very lively sense of that danger too—but in this, that I had to deal with a being to whom I could not appeal in the name of anything high or low . . . I've been telling you what we said—repeating the phrases we pronounced—but what's the good? They were common everyday words—the familiar vague sounds exchanged on every waking day of life. But what of that? They had behind them, to my mind, the terrific suggestiveness of words heard in dreams, of phrases spoken in nightmares. Soul! If anybody had ever

struggled with a soul, I am the man. And I wasn't
arguing with a lunatic either. . . . But his soul was
mad. . . .

—That the 'admirer of Mr. Kurtz,' the companion of the narrator here, should be the fantastically sane and innocent young
Russian is part of the force of the passage.

This final account of Kurtz is associated with a sardonic
tone, an insistent irony that leads us on to another bad patch,
the closing interview in Brussels with Kurtz's 'Intended':

> 'The room seemed to have grown darker, as if all the
> sad light of the cloudy evening had taken refuge on
> her forehead. This fair hair, this pale visage, this
> pure brow, seemed surrounded by an ashy halo from
> which the dark eyes looked out at me. Their glance
> was guileless, profound, confident, and trustful. She
> carried her sorrowful head as though she were proud
> of that sorrow, as though she would say, I—I alone
> know how to mourn for him as he deserves.'

It is not part of Conrad's irony that there should be anything
ironical in this presentment of the woman. The irony lies in
the association of her innocent nobility, her purity of idealizing
faith, with the unspeakable corruption of Kurtz; and it is developed (if that is the word) with a thrilled insistence that recalls
the melodramatic intensities of Edgar Allan Poe. . . .

Conrad's 'inscrutable', it is clear, associates with Woman
as it does with the wilderness, and the thrilling mystery of the
Intended's innocence is of the same order as the thrilling mystery of Kurtz's corruption: the profundities are complementary.
It would appear that the cosmopolitan Pole, student of the
French masters, who became a British master-mariner, was in
some respects a simple soul. If anyone should be moved to
question the propriety of this way of putting it, perhaps the
following will be found something of a justification:

> 'Woman and the sea revealed themselves to me
> together, as it were: two mistresses of life's values.
> The illimitable greatness of the one, the unfathom-
> able seduction of the other, working their im-
> memorial spells from generation to generation fell
> upon my heart at last: a common fortune, an un-
> forgettable memory of the sea's formless might and of
> the sovereign charm in that woman's form wherein
> there seemed to beat the pulse of divinity rather than
> blood.'

This comes from a bad novel, one of Conrad's worst
things, *The Arrow of Gold*. It is a sophisticated piece of work,
with a sophistication that elaborates and aggravates the deplorable kind of naïvety illustrated in the quotation. Not that the
author's talent doesn't appear, but the central theme—and
the pervasive atmosphere—is the 'unfathomable seduction' of
the 'enigmatic' Rita; a glamorous mystery, the evocation of
which (though more prolonged and elaborated) is of the same
order as the evocation of sinister significance, the 'inconceivable' mystery of Kurtz, at the close of *Heart of Darkness*. If any
reader of that tale had felt that the irony permitted a doubt
regarding Conrad's attitude towards the Intended, the presentment of Rita should settle it.

'Woman' figures in *The Rescue*, the book that in publication preceded *The Arrow of Gold* (both came out just after the
1914 war, though *The Rescue* belongs essentially to Conrad's
early period). The glamour here is a simpler affair—less sophisticated and more innocent. But if *The Rescue* lacks the
positive badness of *The Arrow of Gold*, it is, on a grand scale,
boring in its innocence. The seduction of Woman as represented by Mrs. Travers is less insistently and melodramatically
'unfathomable' than in the later book, but cannot sustain the
interest Conrad demands for it; so to say that it is, in the formal

design, adequate to balancing Heroic Action as represented by
Lingard—King Tom, idealized seaman-adventurer—is not to
say anything very favourable about the whole. *The Rescue*, in
short, is an Academy piece— 'sombre, colourful, undeniably a
classic' the reviewers may have said, and its Grand Style staging
of the conflict between Love and Honour (a kingdom at stake)
against a sumptuously rendered *décor* of tropical sea, sunset,
and jungle is, in its slow and conscientious magnificence,
calculated to engender more deference than thrill, and so can't
even be recommended as good boy's reading—though it offers
little to adults. The book, in fact, is not altogether a surprising
kind of thing to have come from a sailor of pertinacious literary
talent and French literary education. The reason for bringing it
in just here is to enforce the point that Conrad, for all his
sophistication, exhibits a certain simplicity of outlook and attitude. About his attitude towards women there is perceptible, all
the way through his literary career, something of the gallant
simple sailor.

The sailor in him, of course, is rightly held to be a main
part of his strength. It is not for nothing that *Heart of Darkness*,
a predominantly successful tale, is told by the captain of the
steamboat—told from that specific and concretely realized
point of view: appraisal of the success of the tale is bound up
with this consideration. But the stress up till now has fallen
upon Conrad's weaknesses. It is time to ask where the strength
may be found in its purest form. There will, I think, be general
approval of the choice of *Typhoon* as a good example. But I am
not sure that there is as general a recognition of just where the
strength of *Typhoon* lies. The point may be made by saying that
it lies not so much in the famous description of the elemental
frenzy as in the presentment of Captain MacWhirr, the chief
mate Jukes and the chief engineer Solomon Rout at the opening of the tale. Of course, it is a commonplace that Conrad's
distinctive genius comprises a gift for rendering the British
seaman. But is it a commonplace that the gift is the specific gift
of a novelist, and (though the subtler artist doesn't run to caricature and the fantastic) relates Conrad to Dickens? . . .

It is to be noted further that these backgrounds in their
contrast with the main theme of the tale afford a far more
satisfactory irony (it is, in fact, supremely effective) than that,
in *Heart of Darkness*, of the scenes at Brussels. At the same
time it is to be noted that there is in *Typhoon* no sardonic
Marlow, commenting on an action that he is made to project;
whereas, though *Heart of Darkness* is given from the point of
view of the captain of the steamboat, that captain *is* Marlow—
Marlow, for whom Conrad has more than one kind of use, and
who is both more and less than a character and always something other than just a master-mariner. For comment in *Typhoon* we have the letters home of Solomon Rout, the chief
engineer, and the letter of Jukes to his chum. In short, nothing
in the story is forced or injected; the significance is not adjectival, but resides in the presented particulars—the actors, the
incidents and the total action: we are given the ship, her cargo
and her crew of ordinary British seamen, and the impact on
them of the storm. . . .

In *The Shadow Line*, also in common recognition one of
Conrad's masterpieces (it is, I think, superior to *Heart of Darkness* and even to *Typhoon*), we have the same art. It has been
acclaimed as a kind of prose *Ancient Mariner*, and it is certainly a supremely sinister and beautiful evocation of enchantment
in tropic seas. But the art of the evocation is of the kind that has
been described; it is not a matter of engendering 'atmosphere'
adjectivally, by explicitly 'significant' vaguenesses, insistent
unutterablenesses, or the thrilled tone of an expository commentator, but of presenting concretely a succession of particulars from the point of view of the master of the ship, who,

though notably sensitive, is not a Marlow, but just a ship's master; an actor among the other actors, though burdened with responsibilities towards the crew, owners and ship. The distinctive art of a novelist, and the art upon which the success of the prose *Ancient Mariner* essentially depends, is apparent in the rendering of personality, its reactions and vibrations; the pervasive presence of the crew, delicately particularized, will turn out on analysis to account for the major part of the atmosphere. . . .

> 'I approached him with extended hand. His eyes, not looking at me, had a strained expression. He was like a man listening for a warning call.
>
> '"Won't you shake hands, Ransome?" I said gently. He exclaimed, flushed up dusky red, gave my hand a hard wrench—and next moment, left alone in the cabin, I listened to him going up the companion stairs cautiously, step by step, in mortal fear of starting into sudden anger our common enemy it was his hard fate to carry consciously within his faithful breast.'

These things are worth many times those descriptions of sunsets, exotic seas and the last plunge of flaming wrecks which offer themselves to the compilers of prose anthologies.

This is at any rate to confirm the accepted notion of Conrad to this extent: that his genius was a unique and happy union of seaman and writer. If he hadn't actually been himself a British seaman by vocation he couldn't have done the Merchant Service from the inside. The cosmopolitan of French culture and French literary initiation is there in the capacity for detachment that makes the intimate knowledge uniquely conscious and articulate. We are aware of the artist by vocation, the intellectual who doubles the seaman, only when we stop to take stock of the perfection of the rendering and the subtle finish of the art.

But this fine balance, this identity, isn't always sustained. In Marlow, who (as remarked above) has a variety of uses, the detachment is separated off. As a main participant in events though, by his specific rôle as such, a detached one, he gives his technical function a dramatic status in the action, and the author a freedom of presence that, as we have seen, constitutes a temptation. Elsewhere Marlow is frankly a method of projection or presentation—one that we learn to associate with Conrad's characteristic vices and weaknesses. In *Youth*, for instance, one of the best-known of the tales, though not one of the best, he goes with the cheap insistence on the glamour, and with that tone which, here and in other places, makes one recall the formula of the early reviewer and reflect that the prose laureate of the British seaman does sometimes degenerate into a 'Kipling of the South Seas'. (And this is the point at which to note that Conrad can write shockingly bad magazine stuff—see the solemnly dedicated collection called *Within the Tides*.)

In *Lord Jim* Marlow is the means of presenting Jim with the appropriate externality, seen always through the question, the doubt, that is the central theme of the book. Means and effect are unobjectionable; it is a different matter from the use of Marlow elsewhere to pass off a vaguely excited incomprehension as tremendous significance. But *Lord Jim* doesn't deserve the position of pre-eminence among Conrad's works often assigned it: it is hardly one of the most considerable. There is, in fact, much to be said in support of those reviewers who (Conrad tells us) 'maintained that the work starting as a short story had got beyond the writer's control', so that what we have is neither a very considerable novel, in spite of its 420 pages, nor one of Conrad's best short stories. The presentment

of *Lord Jim* in the first part of the book, the account of the inquiry and of the desertion of the *Patna*, the talk with the French lieutenant—these are good Conrad. But the romance that follows, though plausibly offered as a continued exhibition of Jim's case, has no inevitability as that; nor does it develop or enrich the central interest, which consequently, eked out to provide the substance of a novel, comes to seem decidedly thin.

The eking out is done mainly from the world of *Almayer's Folly*, *An Outcast of the Islands*, and *Tales of Unrest*, those excessively adjectival studies in the Malayan exotic of Conrad's earliest vein. Those things, it had better be said here, though they are innocuous, and no doubt deserved for their originality of setting some respectful notice when they came out, will not be urged by judicious admirers of Conrad among his claims to classical rank. In their stylistic eloquence, which suggests a descent from Chateaubriand, their wearying exoticism, and their 'picturesque' human interest, they aren't easy to re-read.

No, *Lord Jim* is neither the best of Conrad's novels, nor among the best of his short stories. If, on the other hand, his most considerable work had had due recognition, it would be known as one of the great novels of the language. For *Nostromo* is most certainly that. And it complicates the account of Conrad's genius in that it doesn't answer to the formula arrived at above. He is not here the laureate of the Merchant Service, the British seaman happily doubled with the artist—an artist whose 'outsideness' with regard to the Merchant Service is to be constated only in the essential degree of detachment involved in an adequately recording art.

THOMAS MOSER
From "The Exhaustion of Creative Energy"
Joseph Conrad
1957, pp. 179–212

The literary history of Conrad's very last years seems, on the surface, to be one of orderly continuation of old habits of mind and, at the same time, a development of new interests. Conrad's last two "Author's Notes," to *The Arrow of Gold* and *The Rescue*, certainly convey a sense of culmination and fulfillment. All his life he has waited for the right moment to render into art one of his most memorable personal experiences, his love affair with "Rita," and now the moment has come to give the public *The Arrow of Gold*. For twenty years *The Rescue* has awaited the appropriate time for its completion; that time is 1919. His French biographer, G. Jean-Aubry, tells us that Conrad had "dreamt over ever since 1907" a "Napoleonic romance" and that he was fulfilling this dream in the twenties with *The Rover* and the unfinished *Suspense*. M. Jean-Aubry concludes that Conrad's "imagination was still vitally active."[1] It is of course fitting that Conrad should die while at work on a novel, but Richard Curle finds it "tragic" that he did not finish *Suspense*, since even as a fragment it "will take its place among the recognized masterpieces of this remarkable man."[2] Even thirty years after Conrad's death, Mr. Paul L. Wiley shares this generous view of Conrad's final efforts. He finds that the "main thematic structure of Conrad's work [is] completed" in his last phase; moreover, although one does detect a change in tone, that change "is best accounted for by changing inspiration and not by declining energy."[3]

This chapter proposes, regretfully, to show that the productions of Conrad's last years are virtually without a redeeming feature. They reveal that Conrad has exhausted his creative energy. He has no longer anything to write about and must rework old materials, cling to someone's memoirs, or, in the case of *The Rover*, spin nearly three hundred pages out of almost nothing. Even more seriously, the last novels show that Conrad has finally lost control of the basic tools of his craft. He can no longer focus on his subject: the novels contain many beginnings but virtually no endings. The characters lack substance, and Conrad can only assert their emotions and ideas—he cannot dramatize them. The prose of the last works is very faulty. When Conrad tries his hardest to make a scene important, the prose drifts into thin, vague pretentiousness. Although Conrad writes awkwardly at times in all of his novels (least so perhaps in *Lord Jim* and the shorter sea pieces), the prose of the last novels stumbles on every page. Sometimes he cannot even execute a sentence. Besides the specific faults in technique, the last novels give a general feeling of weariness. All the characters, young and old, seem very tired, eager to sit or lie down. Moreover, the difficulty with which their creator manipulates them indicates clearly the source of their fatigue.

To demonstrate the weakness of the last period, we shall discuss the novels separately, dealing only with *The Arrow of Gold* (1919), *The Rover* (1923), and *Suspense* (1925). We shall omit *The Rescue* since its history is so complicated. . . . Yet all our comments on the other novels will apply with equal force to the dictated later half of *The Rescue* (Part IV, Chapter V, to the end). These will be brief because such dissection is essentially unpleasant and because any reader making a resolute effort to forget who wrote these books will immediately perceive that they are failures. . . .

In reading *The Arrow of Gold* we perhaps react first to its radical lack of form. It has virtually no center of interest, no basic conflict to be resolved, no climax toward which to move. Rather it has a series of possible narrative strands, each of which Conrad picks up, examines, speculates on, and drops. The novel begins with a long conversation among the young seaman, George, and two adventurers, Blunt and Mills, involved in the Carlist revolt in Spain. The latter do most of the talking, each telling what he knows about the mysterious Carlist patriot, Rita de Lastaola. Their ostensible purpose is to arouse George's interest to such an extent that he will join their conspiracy and smuggle guns to the revolutionists in Spain. Now this could be an effective means of engaging the reader's interest, except that Conrad seems not to have his purpose very firmly in mind. Most of the time the two older men are unaware of George's presence. Any possibilities inherent in a situation whereby George may be trapped into a dangerous assignment are lost in the ensuing scene, which describes the three men lunching with Rita. The dangerous work is not alluded to, except that the narrator (George) remarks after the lunch that "in those four hours since midday a complete change had come over me. For good or evil I left that house committed to an enterprise that could not be talked about. . . ."

At this point in the novel we seem to have arrived at its real center of interest, the love affair between George and Rita. Yet in truth little interest rises from it, since one senses few obstacles to be overcome. George does not slowly awaken to awareness of his feelings for Rita. . . .

Conrad tries to create interest by giving George a rival, Blunt, with his accomplice, that "wonderful old woman," his mother. In what reads like a parody of Henry James, Conrad laboriously describes the battle of wits between the scheming mother and George, who appears to be a threat to her son's chances of winning Rita and, especially, Rita's fortune. Once again, Conrad does nothing with the situation. Rita rejects

Blunt's proposal, without Blunt and George coming into any kind of conflict. Son and mother drop out of the novel on page 213. One hundred and thirty-three pages later, we are told in a few sentences that Blunt shot George in a duel. We must attribute this artless conclusion to what Mr. Guerard calls the "heavy hand of actuality."[4] Conrad's own Marseilles experience ended in his being wounded in a duel. Therefore the novel must end the same way, no matter how improbably. . . .

The Arrow of Gold constantly overwhelms the reader with its pretentiousness. On almost every page, we see Conrad trying to convince us that what happens in his story is more important, more meaningful, than we might suppose. This pretentiousness appears most frequently in those passages proposing the infinity and eternity of the love between George and Rita. . . .

The pretentiousness of *The Arrow of Gold* appears in less obvious ways; through, for example, George's comments on some of the other characters. He frequently points out rather absurd occasions: Mills's eyes grow wider "than I had ever seen them before" (he has known Mills only a short time and this is their first real conversation together); Rita speaks "in a louder tone than I had ever heard her use before" (he has known her about one half hour, has heard her speak no more than a dozen sentences). George also conveys a sense of self-importance through his frequent assertions of powerful emotions. Within three pages, while George is listening to Blunt and Mills, he is "extremely embarrassed," "positively annoyed," "horribly vexed," and "suddenly extremely delighted." In his first meeting with Rita, George experiences "astonishment" at seeing her; two pages later he is equally "astonished" to see a newspaper man with white hair; at Blunt's departure he feels "extreme surprise." On learning that there are new roomers in the house he lives in, George experiences "intense surprise" and is "astonished," all within one sentence. The reader, incidentally, discovers ultimately that these new roomers have no bearing at all upon the plot. . . .

The source of Conrad's bafflement in *The Arrow of Gold* is not far to seek. The sheer mechanical faultiness of the prose and the general exhaustion and despair of the characters betray fatigue too great for creativity. Inept prose ranges from simple clumsiness to downright gibberish. Sometimes the awkwardness results from a tangled arrangement of clauses: "she whom the quayside called Madame Léonore closed her outstretched hand before my face and opened it at once to show its emptiness *in illustration of her expressed opinion*." (The italics here and throughout this chapter are mine.) Much more frequently, however, the clumsiness seems directly the result of the older Conrad's difficulty in fusing two related ideas. In fact, one of the most characteristic constructions in the later prose is a complex sentence containing an "as to" clause:

> *As to* him whom we may regard as Mills' victim it is obvious that he has never harboured a single reproachful thought.
>
> I was feeling quite inanimate *as to* body and frightfully stimulated *as to* mind all the time.
>
> He advanced towards me, correct, supple, hollow-eyed, and smiling; and *as to* his costume ready to go out except for the old shooting jacket which he must have affectioned particularly, for he never lost any time in getting into it at every opportunity.
>
> But *as to* the sound of the four magic letters of her name I was not very likely to hear it fall sweetly on my ear.

Conrad has some of the same difficulty with other connectives: "A waiter approached for orders and it was then, *in relation to* my order for coffee, that the absolutely first thing I learned of Captain Blunt was the fact that he was a sufferer from insomnia." At least once Conrad makes no attempt to provide a connection but simply puts two ideas side by side. This is a description of the carnival celebrants: "They were people of the poorer sort (white calico with red spots, costumes)." On another occasion his confusion appears in an ambiguous handling of pronouns:

> But all the same the revelation turned many things into dust; and, amongst others, the sense of the careless freedom of my life. If that life ever had any purpose or any aim outside itself I would have said that *it* threw a shadow across *its* path. But *it* hadn't. There had been no path.

Some of the sentences in *The Arrow of Gold* simply break in half:

> I only learned that for at least five mixed reasons, none of which impressed me profoundly, Doña Rita had started at a moment's notice from Paris with nothing but a dressing-bag, and permitting Rose to go and visit her aged parents . . .

> I shall never forget that grey dress with ample skirts and long corsage yet with infinite style, the ancient as if ghostly beauty of outlines, the black lace, the silver hair, the harmonious, restrained movements of those white, soft hands like the hands of a queen—or an abbess; and in the general fresh effect of her person the brilliant eyes like two stars with the calm reposeful way they had of moving on and off one, as if nothing in the world had the right to veil itself before their once sovereign beauty.

Sometimes the prose of *The Arrow of Gold* seems downright slovenly. We notice the redundancy of this sentence: "I felt suddenly the . . . whole woman go inanimate all over!" Slovenliness carries over into inattention to details. On page 286 we find "an eight-branched candelabra standing on a little table" (presumably borrowed from the climax of *Victory*); thirty pages later George overturns "the little table, bearing the six-branched candlestick." Clearly, at the time that Conrad needed him most, he had no one to furnish the kind of editorial assistance that Garnett had provided in the nineties.

Most novels contain a few slips in prose, but the pervasive faultiness of *The Arrow of Gold* indicates that we are reading not the Conrad we know but a very different and very tired writer. His fatigue appears not only in his style but in the weary actions of all his characters. Time and again we see them seated head in hand. During the long opening scene with Blunt and Mills, George lies on the divan and Blunt sits with his elbow on a table. In the next scene, the luncheon at Rita's, the whole party sits glumly at the table, Rita leaning on her elbow, her head on her hand. A later scene between Rita and Blunt takes place with Blunt leaning against the mantelpiece "on his elbow with his head in his hand." George talks to Rita "with my elbows on my knees and my head in my hands." The vigorous Madame Léonore can be seen "leaning with mature grace on her elbow," and Mrs. Blunt talks to George "leaning her elbow on the table and supporting her head on her old, impeccably shaped, white forearm." George discovers Rita in his bedroom "enveloped in the skins of wild beasts," with her "precious head repos[ing] in the palm of her hand." . . .

Imperfect as *The Arrow of Gold* is, it remains, nevertheless, the best executed of the last three novels. We need merely note briefly how generously *The Rover* and *Suspense* partake of

the poor qualities of *The Arrow of Gold*. Both lack narrative focus and convincing characters. Both suffer from frequent passages of pretentious and essentially meaningless rhetoric and from extremely faulty prose. Finally, both reveal a gallery of exhausted and demoralized characters.

Like *The Arrow of Gold*, *The Rover* focuses briefly on several possible centers of interest but settles on none. In the first pages of the novel, Conrad draws our attention frequently to Peyrol's clumsiness and we shortly discover the cause: a money-belt full of gold. We then learn how Peyrol had got such loot, and we see him carefully hide it at the bottom of his sea chest at his new home, Escampobar Farm. The later Conrad then characteristically abandons the gold for 246 pages. (At the end of the book the Réals find the money in a well and turn in over to the French government.) In the early pages interest focuses, too, on Peyrol's strong feeling of communion with this portion of the south of France where he had been born but which he had left nearly fifty years before. Again the idea, which has real possibilities, remains undeveloped. Between Chapters Three and Four eight years pass and a nocturnal prowler becomes the new interest. We soon discover that he is a spy from an English corvette lying offshore, and that he has been captured by Peyrol. The Englishman proves to be an old acquaintance of Peyrol's piratical days, whom Peyrol recognizes. This encounter arouses in Peyrol deep feelings of nostalgia for his old life as one of the "Brothers of the Coast." Yet he does not reveal his identity to the Englishman; he allows him to escape and never thinks of him again.

In addition to these three undeveloped fictional ideas, there are two more obvious subjects in *The Rover*: the rivalry between Peyrol and Réal over Arlette, and Réal's mission to trick the English navy by putting into their possession false French documents. The love story, like the George and Rita affair, does not inspire belief. Conrad, in fact, hardly attempts to dramatize the relationship between Arlette and Peyrol; he simply asserts at frequent intervals that violent and incomprehensible passions are engulfing one or all of the trio. Perhaps because of our recollections of the fine sea stories of the early period, we may respond more favorably to the account of Peyrol fulfilling Réal's mission by sailing his tartane, with the documents aboard, in such a way as to be caught by the English corvette. This story of three strangely assorted men in a small boat on a dangerous mission of political intrigue is, however, rather an old one. Twenty years before *The Rover*, Conrad told the story in *Nostromo*, about Nostromo, Decoud, and Hirsch. At about the same time, he described its autobiographical source in *The Mirror of the Sea*, where he tells of Dominic Cervoni, his traitorous, evil cousin, and himself aboard the *Tremolino* on an unsuccessful mission on behalf of the Carlists. In *The Arrow of Gold*, he mentions the story again and also, incidentally, "a money-belt full of gold." The version in *The Rover* probably depends heavily for its effectiveness upon the nostalgia of faithful Conradians. The account conveys little sense of action and conspicuously lacks the details of seamanship which so enrich the sea stories through "The Secret Sharer."

The Rover must stand or fall upon the credibility of its central character, old Peyrol. Conrad tries very hard to make him into a dignified and admirable figure. In fact, he uses some of the techniques that he had first employed with Singleton a quarter of a century before. He calls our attention frequently to Peyrol's "Roman" profile, and attempts to make him into something of a mythic figure with a face "like a carving of stone." His profile preserves the "immobility of a head struck on a medal." Yet Peyrol is *not* Singleton. Even though Singleton comes to understand that he is old and will die, the thought of retiring never enters his mind. It is unthinkable that a true Conradian seaman would spend eight years idling in a farm-yard. Peyrol may have a Roman profile, he may look longingly at the sea, he may sneer at landsmen, yet the question remains: why did he give up? Why must he wait eight years before he suddenly feels the "longing for a great sea victory for [his] people?" The voyage on the tartane is, after all, a rather easy way out of a tedious and perplexing existence. The seamen of *The Nigger of the* "*Narcissus*," "*Youth*," and *Typhoon* do not perform their heroic actions in a brief voyage on a lovely after-noon. And only such dubious heroes as Willems and Jim find their solution to life's problems in a quick and painless death by gunshot.

The prose of *The Rover* partakes of all the faults we have noticed in *The Arrow of Gold*. Since there are fewer and shorter love scenes, there are (happily) fewer and shorter passages of rhetoric about love. Yet we can easily find enough to know that Conrad has not really made any recovery:

> She dazzled him. Vitality streamed out of her eyes, her lips, her whole person, enveloped her like a halo and . . . yes, truly, the faintest possible flush had appeared on her cheeks, played on them faintly rosy like the light of a distant flame on the snow.

If the instances of love rhetoric diminish, the mechanical faultiness becomes, if anything, more conspicuous in *The Rover* than in *The Arrow of Gold*. . . .

Finally we find in *The Rover*, as in *The Arrow of Gold*, a pervading sense of weariness which infects all of the characters. It has perhaps a certain appropriateness in *The Rover* since the central figure and one of the important minor characters, Catherine, are both old. Nevertheless, their weariness results not only from age but also from despair. As in *The Arrow of Gold*, the most characteristic pose of the characters is seated, head in hand. At various points in the book we find Peyrol, Catherine, and Arlette in that position. More often, Peyrol and Réal sit facing each other with their arms folded on their chests. Young Réal habitually sits on a bench "with hardly a movement, for hours." When Peyrol and Réal are not sitting, they can be found leaning against a mast or a wall. The thirty-eight-year-old Scevola appears to be perpetually tired: "the pa-triot dragged his dirty clogs low-spiritedly in the fresh light of the young morning." He spends much of his time "lying open-eyed on his tumbled pallet in raging sulks about something." Sooner or later virtually every character despairs. The young lieutenant feels sick of life, "the desperation of a man under torture." Peyrol reaches "that depth of despondency" in which there is "nothing more before him but a black gulf into which his consciousness sank like a stone." Scevola resembles a "sick child," while Catherine, who tells Peyrol she is "tired of life," staggers under "the weight of her accumulated years." In short, *The Rover* hardly conveys the sense of serenity which its admir-ers have attributed to it.

Suspense, Conrad's unfinished last novel, represents that venture into historical fiction which he had contemplated since 1907. It is curious that Conrad had for so long aspired to write a historical novel, for his talent does not seem to point in that direction. The early Conrad deals with setting, costumes, man-ners, and public events not so much for their own sake as for their capacity to reveal what happens inside his characters. Even *The Nigger of the* "*Narcissus*," which explicitly memori-alizes a passing phase of life dramatizes the *spirit* of that life more than its outward manifestations.

The early Conrad, nevertheless, does use history for his psychological purposes. We think, for example, of *Lord Jim*.

John D. Gordan shows clearly that the Patusan portions of that book owe much to Conrad's reading in histories of Rajah Brooke of Sarawak. But Conrad there completely assimilated his sources. Mr. Gordan, in the light of his own painstaking study of all the books about Brooke available to Conrad, says that "it is impossible to tell exactly which he knew. He may have known them all equally well."[5]

Finding the source of *Suspense* has proved no such prob-lem. Less than a year after its publication, Miss Mildred Atkin-son, in a letter to the *Times Literary Supplement*,[6] showed that the source of *Suspense* is the *Memoirs of the Countess de Boigne*. Conrad does not, however, use the *Memoirs* as he does the history of Rajah Brooke, simply for hints about characters and events. Rather, the *Memoirs* furnish character relation-ships and even actual wording. Miss Miriam H. Woods quotes six passages from *Suspense*, some of paragraph length, one of almost a page, which follow the *Memoirs* virtually word for word.[7] The *Memoirs*, in fact, supply practically all that is new in *Suspense*. We have already seen that *Suspense* tends to move in the same weary circle as the later love stories, complete with hero, heroine, and voyeur-villain. Some of the scenes appear to be faint echoes of Conrad's previous work: the salon scene, for example, seems to arise from a forty-five-year-old memory of the Carlist intrigue, filtered twice, through *Nostromo* and *The Arrow of Gold*. As history, *Suspense* gives us little sense of the past, and, except for the *Memoirs* material, it contains none but the most obvious historical details. In other words, Conrad, at the end of his career, was using history, not as an adventure into a new kind of writing, but as a crutch for exhausted creativity.

In his introduction to *Suspense*, Richard Curle indicates that Conrad himself, though he had written nearly 300 pages, did not really know where the center of interest would lie. He discussed *Suspense* with Curle the day before he died and told him: "I see five or six different lines of treatment."[8] Certainly, a reading of *Suspense* does not reveal any signs of a true subject emerging. Rather, as in *The Arrow of Gold* and *The Rover*, we find only a series of hints of emerging subjects, but no real development. Among the possible narrative "lines" we find these: the Count de Montevesso, Doctor Martel, and Cante-lucci appear to be involved in a conspiracy to release Napoleon from Elba; Doctor Martel seems also to be in the service of the French Bourbons; the Count, out of jealousy over his wife, is plotting against Cosmo; the Count has a strangely paternal attitude toward his "niece," Clelia, which will need fuller ex-planation; and, finally, Cosmo is involved with Attilio in an adventure the nature of which is a complete mystery.

By far the most intriguing of *Suspense*'s many subjects is the hint that Cosmo and his beloved Adèle are, unbeknownst to them, children of the same father. This would be the only time in Conrad's career in which he consciously dealt with incest, a subject which we have already seen lurking beneath the surface of a great many of his love stories. At any rate, Conrad has clearly prepared in *Suspense* for the revelation that Cosmo and Adèle are half-brother and -sister. Early in the novel we learn that Cosmo's father, Sir Charles Latham, had, as a young man touring Europe, gained "great social recogni-tion in Paris and Versailles" but had "suddenly" left France for Italy. He spends "some months" in Florence, then "suddenly" determines to go home. . . .

Cosmo's characterization proves to be even less satis-factory than that of Peyrol or of George. He is the last in the new category of boy-heroes. Like the others, Cosmo appears to be moving from simple naïveté to complex maturity, but he in fact already evinces a kind of sophistication. Cosmo's most characteristic scene, a secret, "serious" conversation with Adèle, recalls scenes between George and Rita in the first half of *The Arrow of Gold*. While these scenes abound in sophisticated conversation with sexual overtones, they do not suggest maturity. Yet some critics of Conrad admire the later boy-heroes: Mr. Wiley finds that Conrad "establishes a basis of reference to the norm of conduct" through them.[9] We may agree that they are normal enough, but we would insist that it is important for their creator to recognize their immaturity. The early Conrad realizes that vulnerable heroes like Jim and Decoud are false; the later Conrad does not seem to understand that Powell, the young captain, George, Carter, and Cosmo remain throughout their stories rather talkative adolescents.

If Cosmo appears adolescent, he has, like George and Peyrol, little more physical and mental vigor than an ailing old man. Cosmo's every movement seems a tremendous effort. The novel abounds in staircases which Cosmo must toil "up and up." Like George, he has difficulty tying his neckcloth. He falls "heavily" into chairs and cannot endure the sound of a drum coming through his window. Up and about, he slips off into open-eyed sleep, but in bed, he sleeps fitfully. He has difficulty writing his sister a letter, and discovers, when he finally settles down to the task, that "it required all his courage to keep on, piling up words." He trembles with "doubts and apprehensions" when he wakes up in the morning and needs "keen, pure air" to rouse his "vitality." A feeling of immense depression constantly distracts him from the life about him, so that he loses the track of conversations with his beloved Adèle and with the fascinating Doctor Martel. . . .

Conrad's ill health unquestionably aged him early and it had perceptible effects upon his use of language. R. B. Cunninghame Graham, who had known Conrad since the earliest years of his writing career, noticed that although his flow of vigorous and idiomatic English never failed, and his vocabulary only grew richer as the years passed by, his accent (once slight) "became more marked, and certain turns of phrase appeared, that . . . were not English."[10] Ill health had still another effect upon Conrad's language; gout crippled his hand and wrist until he had to dictate his last novels. Doubtless that dictation added considerable strain to Conrad's creativity. When he was dictating *The Arrow of Gold*, his invalid wife could hear every word upstairs because the process so unnerved him that he shouted at his typist sitting only a few feet away.[11] He became wrought up over his difficulties with *Suspense* to the point of trying to write with a pen and dictate at the same time. . . .

If we are not conscious of the marked decline in the quality of his art after 1912, we may tend to mix indiscriminately in our minds early and late ideas and characters simply because of superficial resemblances. Explicit statements about self-recognition and initiation in *The Shadow Line* and *The Arrow of Gold*, about skepticism and romanticism in *Victory* and *Chance*, may lead us to believe that these novels embody the same profound perceptions as the great early works. Apparent resemblances between Anthony and Jim, Heyst and Decoud, Peyrol and Singleton, between the two young captains in *The Shadow Line* and "The Secret Sharer," may cause us to respond in much the same way to all of them. If this happens, it means that through insensitive reading we have deprived ourselves of the enjoyment and understanding which Jim, Decoud, and the other fine early characters can afford us. In the same way, imprecise attention to technique may lead us, as it has led a number of others, to think *Chance* the most complex of Conrad's novels, rather than the most cumbersome, and to

read the opening pages of *The Arrow of Gold* as ingenious plotting rather than confused narration.

It is indeed difficult to conquer the impulse to find greatness in all the works of a man we sense to be great. Yet this impulse is pernicious. It has brought forth complicated mythical and allegorical interpretations of novels that probably ought not even to have been published. Such lack of discrimination is perhaps less reprehensible, however, than the approach that insists that literary greatness lies only in explicitly, unequivocally affirmative works. This approach has led to gross overrating of inferior Conrad and to dismissal of some of his best works as "minor." To fail to perceive the vast differences in his quality or to hunt for that quality in the wrong places means that one listens not to Conrad's voice but to one's own. And to be deaf to the true Conrad is to be deprived of one of the finest voices in our literature: pessimistic, skeptical, ironic—but also courageous, sympathetic, profoundly human.

Notes

1. *Life and Letters*, II, 166.
2. Introduction by Richard Curle to *Suspense* (New York, 1926), pp. vi–vii.
3. Wiley, pp. 132–133.
4. Guerard, p. 24. (Although Conrad insisted throughout his life on the myth of the duel, it is now generally accepted that his wound was self-inflicted. Author's note.)
5. Gordan, p. 65.
6. Mildred Atkinson, *Times Literary Supplement*, no. 1,258 (Feb. 25, 1926), p. 142.
7. Miriam H. Woods, "A Source of Conrad's *Suspense*," *Modern Language Notes* 50:390–394 (1935).
8. Introduction by Curle to *Suspense*, p. vi.
9. Wiley, p. 198.
10. Preface by R. B. Cunninghame Graham to *Tales of Hearsay* (New York, 1926), p. ix.
11. R. L. Mégroz, *Joseph Conrad's Mind and Method* (London, 1931), p. 90.

FREDERICK CREWS
From "Conrad's Uneasiness—And Ours"
Out of My System
1975, pp. 42–62

Predictions about the future ranking of authors should be made with the greatest tentativeness or not at all. In retrospect it is easy to see that literary value in any given age has been glimpsed through a haze of ideology (it wasn't long ago that *By Love Possessed* was thought by many to be the Great American Novel). The academy, that home of disinterested taste, cannot be appealed to as a referee; there a swelling GNP of discreet praise for every "major author" is bound to be heard, and one author may be favored over another simply because he lends himself to a more labored approach. Joseph Conrad is a case in point: he was trilingual, he was influenced and influential, he did some obscure things that need to be "researched," he studded his works with symbols, and he exuded a moral portentousness that both invites and resists analysis. Most "Conradians" would find it hard to separate these professional conveniences from the question of Conrad's ultimate merit. Those of us who are involved in the quaint modern industry of explaining literature are assailed sometimes by a doubt as to whether we even know what we like. To say what some future generation would like is quite beyond our power;

the closest we can come is to try to define for ourselves the shape and limits of an author's imaginative world.

For Conrad, however, this is evidently a difficult undertaking. Everyone recognizes—in passing—that his fiction is pervaded with uneasiness, but something about Conrad urges his critics to hurry on to the "moral issues" which are taken so very seriously. One can read a great deal of commentary before coming across any sustained discussion of the wishes and fears that lie behind his art, energizing it and yet warping it into something quite distinct from dramatized philosophy or nautical tale-spinning. We are told over and over that Conrad preferred responsibility and discipline to self-indulgence, but what must have been painfully defensive for Conrad somehow comes out sounding merely thematic. The final Conradian gesture, whether of courage or duty or tragic pessimism or human solidarity, gets more of the attention while the mental turmoil that precipitated it gets lip service. What is engaging about Conrad for me and I daresay for others is the part of his imagination that is prior to this withdrawal into gesture—the part that Marvin Mudrick refers to darkly, without explanation, as Conrad's "suppressed . . . nightmares."[1] But it is one thing to sense this fact and another to bring it into critical focus. On the whole the "close analysis" of our time has been devoted not to understanding anxiety but to mollifying it.

A prime instance is F. R. Leavis' widely quoted chapter on Conrad in *The Great Tradition*. Leavis is made uneasy by Conrad's "adjectival insistence upon inexpressible and incomprehensible mystery,"[2] but it wouldn't occur to him to inquire *why* Conrad writes this way. He is too busy showing that despite his imperfections Conrad is a great novelist, since he produced "work addressed to the adult mind." What the adult mind seems to approve is a combination of tangible realism (a "vivid essential record, in terms of things seen and incidents experienced by a main agent in the narrative, and particular contacts and exchanges with other human agents . . . ") and bracing moralism ("he does believe intensely, as a matter of concrete experience, in the kind of human achievement represented by the Merchant Service—tradition, discipline and moral ideal . . . "). Leavis wants to convince himself that behind the expansive adjectives sit good English nouns, "firm and vivid concreteness" and characters "each having a specific representative moral significance." This clinging to the palpable and the banal is in a curious sense a plausible response to Conrad, who wanted to see his fiction as Leavis sees it and would have been ungrateful for such cooperation.[3] Whereas most critics merely underrate the atmosphere of guilt and depression that encircles Conrad's world, Leavis is positively determined to ignore it. His favorite novel, *Nostromo*, has "a certain robust vigour of melodrama . . . completely controlled to the pattern of moral significance." "There is plainly no room in *Nostromo* for the kind of illustrated psychology that many critics think they have a right to demand of a novelist. . . ." In short, there is plainly no room in Leavis for Conrad.

The American academic reply to Conrad's problematic quality is more businesslike and complacent than Leavis': explication replaces value judgment. Take, for example, the three casebooks in which scholars quarrel politely over what "Heart of Darkness" truly means. The specific job is to decide whether Conrad wanted us to be just like his narrator Marlow or to look down on him as morally inadequate. Since Conrad was in fact much too involved with Marlow to conceive of either of these cautionary ideas, the issue is agreeably difficult to settle; recourse must be had to patterns of imagery and allu-

sion, in which, it is supposed, the author's lessons have been imbedded. Thus for one critic the allusions to the *Aeneid* constitute the hidden key; for another it is the allusions to the *Inferno*; for another it is the allusions to Buddhism, which show us some remarkably flattering things about Marlow which are not even hinted in the literal plot.[4] Depending on whether they find Marlow a satirized "persona" or a saint, the critics discern that "Heart of Darkness" is really a grail quest or a protoexistentialist essay or an attack on Christian hypocrisy or a critique of imperialism. In fundamental respects these interpretations are alike. All are concerned with some equivalent of salvation—a subject whose appeal these days seems restricted almost exclusively to people on the academic ladder. All take for granted the greatness and the single-minded didacticism of Conrad's novella. None tries to think of Conrad as a troubled man who worked amid the prejudices of his age and the exigencies of his own nervous mind. The critics have paid him their highest compliment: he has been graduated from an author to an Assignment.

It should be noted, however, that the most refreshing exceptions to this trend are provided by Americans who share their colleagues' feeling that Conrad's mysteries can be decoded. The pivotal issue is whether Conrad himself grasped the deeper consistencies of his art. In *Joseph Conrad: Achievement and Decline*, Thomas Moser concluded with a certain embarrassed surprise that Conrad's celebrated "later affirmation" makes excellent sense as a pseudoaffirmation, a whistling in the dark. By exposing a disparity between statement and emotional tone, Moser threw into question the whole genteel enterprise of understanding Conrad through his "views." Not surprisingly, Moser's book has been something of a black sheep among Conrad studies, but now it has been confirmed and expanded in many directions by Bernard C. Meyer's *Joseph Conrad: A Psychoanalytic Biography*. It is a telling reflection on literary study today that this book, which aspires merely to say what Conrad personally was like, should provide insights into his fiction that go beyond anything offered by his professional critics. Being a psychoanalyst, Dr. Meyer takes for granted a continuity between the author's psychic life generally and the symbolic world of his fiction; this simple assumption, without which no incisive criticism is possible, has not been drummed out of him by graduate training in "English."

In making Conrad fully and plausibly human for the first time, Dr. Meyer's book will give a jolt to many critics whose readings, though they purport to be independent of biographical trivialities, in fact rely heavily on a sentimental view of the stoical mariner Conrad. It ought to be harder from now on to take this line. The Conrad who recommended stoicism was in his private life a hypochondriac and at times a suicidal defeatist; the Romantic lover of the sea was bored to fury whenever he had to pass much time on it; the lover of truth had a way of lying about his past; the defender of chivalry made babyish demands on his wife and resented the existence of his children. Conrad's idolators will have to ponder such incidents as his tossing his infant's clothes out a train window, or his retiring to his room for three weeks when the family maid died and writing melancholy letters from "Your boy" to his wife downstairs. It seems cruel to mention these long-available details of petty behavior, which could probably be matched from any great writer's life, but the cruelty is toward a false image and not toward Conrad, whose dignity consisted precisely in his struggle to overcome his emotional incapacities.

Paradoxically, I suspect that a certain iconoclasm toward the beauty of artists' lives may be conducive to an honest respect for their art. However eager we may be to look up to a novelist for moral guidance, this wish is clearly not what involves and holds us in his fiction. If fiction teaches a lesson it is only as a by-product of something more crucial, a shared experience; not ideas but fantasies entice us into someone else's imaginative world. It is no coincidence that Moser and Meyer, with their interest in aspects of Conrad's work that contradict his deliberate moral intentions, can make better sense of verbal nuances and oddities of plotting than other critics have done. No moral or formal commentary can account for the fact that Conrad's best work, in Mudrick's words, produces an effect of "obstruction and deadlock, an opposition of matched and mutually paralyzed energies." Conrad's most significant level of discourse is the unconscious level, where inadmissible wishes are entertained, blocked, and allowed a choked and guarded expression.

The atmosphere of Conrad's fiction is only partly one of physical challenge; there is always an opposite pull toward easeful death. The source of this urge is obviously his own depressive tendency, which he fought, disguised, and tried to negate in his art as in his life. And yet he is a consistently autobiographical writer; the effort to shout down his deepest impulses entails an incessant recasting of his psychic history. As Dr. Meyer points out, "almost without exception Conrad's heroes are motherless wanderers, postponing through momentary bursts of action their long-awaited return to a mother, whose untimely death has sown the seeds of longing and remorse, and whose voice, whispered from beyond the grave, utters her insistent claim upon her son's return."[5] The fathers of these heroes, like Conrad's own father, tend to have outlived the mothers for a while and then died or departed, leaving the sons to brood over their intimidating high-mindedness and disastrous fanaticism. This concern with the posthumous grip of the parents amounts to an oblique assigning of blame for the inhibition which characterizes Conrad's protagonists and is never adequately explained on "realistic" grounds. Conrad tells us in effect that his characters cannot involve themselves emotionally because they suffer from fixation; they are too busy fending off resentments and longings toward the departed elders to permit themselves anything more than the most furtive encounters with their contemporaries.

It is startling to see how all the peculiarities of the Conradian world fall into place in this perspective. Like Hemingway, Conrad wavered between a maudlin *Weltschmerz* and a defensive assertiveness about the importance of manly style; the two attitudes are psychologically consistent in that one is an antidote to the other. The value of action for such a writer is measured by the inertia that must be overcome to achieve it. Manhood is always in doubt, and its reconfirmation can only be made believable in an exclusively masculine ambience hedged with rules and physical difficulties. Hence the otherwise inexplicable feeling in Conrad that nautical duty and discipline and trial constitute a welcome respite from something more fearsome. In a word, that something is sexuality. Conrad can permit himself to imagine a love relationship only if it is a matching of racial opposites—that is, if it contains an alibi to the accusation of being latently incestuous. When the lovers are of similar background they lock themselves in what Dr. Meyer calls a morass of inhibition, "all the while engaging in a ruminative chatter that at times approaches sheer double-talk." But Conrad's precautions do not stop there. His heroes, for all their exotic adventures, amount to virtual eunuchs, while his heroines tend to be awesome, androgynous, self-sufficient

monoliths who can be fought over but not fertilized. His heroes' mortality rate rises sharply as they approach these Brobdingnagian ladies, who evidently pose a menace more forbidding than any hazard of the male world. Death is at once a symbol of castration and the surest escape from it, a flight from incest and a return to it— and, of course, by killing off his heroes Conrad spares himself the awkwardness of trying to depict love scenes when his mind is possessed by fantasies of this sort.

The critics have been hard pressed to say why Conrad succeeds despite his evasions, which they prefer to minimize. But the question has been wrongly put: Conrad's evasions themselves serve a function within his economy of "mutually paralyzed energies," and criticism should be able to say what the function is. Conrad's uniqueness does not consist in the virtues for which he is most often praised—vivid detail, evocative scenery, suspense, moral concern, a sense of the heroic— but in the fact that he carries these traits along in a nose dive toward self-destruction. He is simultaneously terrified at existence and a connoisseur of its heightened moments, at once a nihilist and a raconteur. This tension is sustained by the "adjectival" rhetoric which looks so foolishly obfuscating when it is extracted for analysis. Even the memorable sentences, the ones that strike us as profoundly true, serve to mediate among Conrad's contrary impulses. Take, for instance, his haunting remark in *Nostromo* that "in our activity alone do we find the sustaining illusion of an independent existence as against the whole scheme of things of which we form a helpless part." That is classic Conrad, not only because it contains a flash of tragic insight but also because it blurs responsibility: to think of oneself as helpless within a metaphysical void is to assign an external cause for one's prevailing depression. I suggest that this quasi-confessional mode is Conrad's forte and that we are more affected by it than we may care to admit. Conrad indulges our fears of isolation, neglect, and victimization by malign higher powers—the fears of an anxious infant—without locating their source. There is something luxurious about the Conradian *Angst*; it comforts us because it is shared, indeed it is built into the order of things, and we combat it with the fellowship of our orphanage. Underlying everything is the seductive, unmentionable thought that it is not so bad after one's fitful strivings to sink back into the maternal nothingness.[6]

This is not to deny what everyone feels, that Conrad is a stoic writer, but rather to identify his chief antagonist as the despairing side of his own mind. The external sources of gloom, "the solitude of the sea" and "the inscrutable eyes of the Most High" (I am quoting the Author's Note to *Almayer's Folly*), are not so much combated as they are sought out as metaphors of preexisting inhibition—and very precise metaphors at that, since psychologically they amount to allusions to the parent figures with whom Conrad is unceasingly involved. The real agon in Conrad is the struggle against inhibition. It is no small point in his favor that he always tried to resist the impulse— indulged, for example, by Henry James—to pretend that his taste for sexless irresolution was a superior achievement of some sort. Every Jamesian plot puts a thick moral varnish on the necessities of the Jamesian temperament, but Conrad did what he could to oppose the passivity which usually has the final say in his works. Common human experience was sacred for Conrad, as it distinctly wasn't for James, because he grasped at it for rescue from the real destructive element, his instinct for failure.

When this aspect of Conrad's fiction is perceived, he is apt to appear a psychological ironist, a student of the way the misfortunes of nervous, lonely dreamers are determined, not by the cruel fates as they imagine, but by their own masochism. There is evidence for such readings; what is doubtful is that Conrad expected them. His engagement in his plots would seem to have more to do with self-exculpation than with dispassionate analysis. The semblance of irony is thrown up by his need to review his misgivings about himself, but when the misgivings become too insistent they must be replaced by muddle. Conrad typically diverts our interest from the hero's gloomy mind to his lush surroundings, which are stocked with misplaced energies; we expect confessions and instead we get tropical storms. The very fact that the plots are so crammed with adventure is comprehensible in this light. The hero is kept too busy staving off real "savages" and villains to spare time for self-inquiry, and in most cases we are finally meant to think of him as a victim of hard luck. Thus Conrad avails himself of projection—into the landscape, into "the whole scheme of things of which we form a helpless part"—in order to blunt an insight which would amount to self-analysis. Conrad the celebrated realist brings to mind Genet's sardonic definition of verisimilitude: "the disavowal of unavowable reasons."

For the comfort of disavowal Conrad pays a price in stereotyped characterization, melodramatic incidents, and the overworking of exotic props. (The three traits are really one, the negation of what is complicated, personal, and paralyzing by what is simple, alien, and active.) Not surprisingly, the works that have stood up best—nearly all of which were written in the so-called "Hueffer decade" of 1899–1909, when Conrad felt himself to have an ally against despair—are those which come nearest to self-confrontation. In *Lord Jim*, for example, though it is never stated in so many words that Jim is to be held responsible both for his aberration on the "Patna" and for his passively accepted "punishment" in Patusan, Conrad at least allows us to infer the logic connecting the two parts of the story. By dividing his own mentality into Jim and Marlow, furthermore, he is able to muster a degree of detachment from Jim's tendency to blame external forces for his doom. In contrast, the author of such late novels as *Chance*, *Victory*, and *Suspense* sides with Jim; in Albert Guerard's words, "evil and failure in this new cleansed moral universe are presumed to come from outside rather than from within."[7] Significantly, the most conspicuous change occurs in Conrad's treatment of women. Though he never at any period recognized that misogyny is more an affair of male psychology than of female sin, in his later phase he felt compelled both to idolize womankind and to denigrate it with slanderous generalities, both to try his hand at idyllic love scenes and to wilt them with the abhorrent language studied by Moser. It is evident, as Dr. Meyer has shown in detail, that Conrad's later fiction is ridden by the same mechanisms of denial and projection that come to dominate his psychic life after his total breakdown in 1910—during which, according to Mrs. Conrad, he let loose a "stream of disjointed accusations concerning my moral and spiritual character."[8]

As an example of the way these deep constraints can mar an otherwise promising novel, consider *Victory*. Among critics who take Conrad's "later affirmation" at face value it is regarded as a near masterpiece.[9] Yet the whole novel is built upon an anomaly which Conrad seems unable to control: as the hero gets (verbally) more committed to involvement in the world, his remarkable passivity is not overcome but intensified. In effect Axel Heyst does nothing to defend himself and his

mistress Lena from the four villains whose chief business seems to be to persecute him. The atmosphere of muffled depression which has accumulated over many chapters is discharged through a series of weirdly static *tableaux* in which Heyst has no efficient part. This immobility is contagious; the main villain, Jones, turns out to be almost as much a bystander as Heyst, and what they witness is confusing in the extreme. Whatever passion Conrad had intended to explore is shunted off onto the lecher Ricardo and Lena, who is promoted rapidly from a meek and threatened chorus girl to a typical Conradian Amazon, statuesque and immensely powerful. She mesmerizes Heyst, Jones is terrified at the thought of her, and the would-be seducer Ricardo addresses her in a way that makes one reach for Krafft-Ebing. "What you want is a man," he tells her, "a master that will let you put the heel of your shoe on his neck." Instead of indicating that there might be something a bit odd about such a relationship, Conrad proceeds to a climactic scene that is perverse in every sense. Lena succeeds in acquiring Ricardo's knife, not to protect herself but to secrete it between her legs so that "the dreaded thing was out of sight at last," while Ricardo shows the nature of his sexuality by crawling across the room and timidly begging Lena to stick out her foot: "Ricardo, clasping her ankle, pressed his lips time after time to the instep, muttering gasping words that were like sobs, making little noises that resembled the sounds of grief and distress." When things have reached such a compromised point it is understandable that Conrad should halt them with a gunshot that seems to have been fired by Heyst but in fact has been fired by Jones, and that seems to have merely wounded Ricardo but in fact kills Lena. No wonder, too, that after this charade the familiar objects of Heyst's room should appear to him "shadowy, unsubstantial, the dumb accomplices of an amazing dream-plot ending in an illusory effect of awakening. . . ."[10]

Viewed as fantasy, all the literal peculiarities of *Victory* belong together: the rescue of the mother-Magdalen (that is Lena's name) from a paternal seducer (Schomberg); the flight of the incestuous pair to an island retreat where further aggressors arrive to renew the father's claim; the mother's transformation, under this threat, from ward to protectress, while the hero-son becomes more infantile; the pseudosolution of denying female "castration" (Lena's acquisition of the knife, plus the eroticization of her foot); and a self-immolation that is meant to cancel all filial presumption. Implausible as these strategies may sound to "literary" ears, they are common in Conrad's art—in his life, too, for that matter. But their immediate importance for *Victory* is that they explain its bizarre episodes and Conrad's failure to see how they must strike the reader. He cannot detach himself adequately from Jones's anti-feminine ravings and Ricardo's fetishism because, quite simply, they are his own; all he can do is to foist them off onto exaggeratedly "other" antagonists of his exaggeratedly Christlike hero. To perceive what Conrad must have been wrestling with in the act of writing is to see why he repeatedly assures us, with subtle cavils, of Heyst's respect for his father's memory, and why Heyst behaves as if he were not so sure of his unimpeachable right to Lena, and why Lena herself is uncomfortably convincing in her pretense of wanting to abandon Heyst. The novel's aesthetic incompleteness is a consequence of its censored self-debate: the details that stand out as blemishes are coherent only as replies to charges that Conrad has suppressed in the interest of his dubious tranquillity.

It may be possible now to appreciate the link between

Conrad's artistic freedom and his capacity to manage psychological insight. Given his makeup, he had to deal regularly with obsessional themes, and he could never distance himself from them in the manner, say, of Thomas Mann. But he could, at his best, harmonize them with a plot which was manifestly "about" a psychic bondage of some sort, even if it had to end in equivocations. The trouble with *Victory* is that Conrad wants no part whatsoever of the forces that are tyrannizing over his plot; the result of his divided purpose is a sulky and confusing reticence. In all his finest novels and tales he is moving toward, not away from, a recognition that character is destiny. In these works the charged language, the undercurrent of double entendre which was bound to be present anyway, works with the momentum of the plot, and we are carried through an experience that feels single and whole.

Here, however, Conrad's cultural remoteness from us becomes pertinent. Conrad was on the whole a good Victorian, which is to say that he was earnestly overwrought about maintaining order and decency in his mind, and was apt to mistake the effects of repression for the structure of the universe. Even in his own time he was not a "modern." He lived long enough to call Lawrence's writings "Filth. Nothing but obscenities"; and he used his resonant prose to shore up semblances of the piety which all the great modern writers began by smashing. There was no real choice involved in his continuing to work his customary vein, telling fireside tales of adventure after Joyce and Lawrence and Yeats and Eliot had turned their backs on the philistine public of their day. Conrad and the *hypocrite lecteur* needed each other's company; in order to have access to his creativity he had to believe he was engaged in validating common mankind's good opinion of itself.

His critics, by and large, have shared this opinion, and some have gone so far as to suggest that it is precisely his conventionality that guarantees his stature: Conrad still tells a story, he speaks to Everyman, he still believes in virtue, etc. It is questionable whether this popular reasoning, which ignores everything latent and cherishes the hollowest conscious avowals, really protects Conrad's standing; it seems rather to turn him into the complacent bore he sometimes aspired to be. To put supreme value on obstacles which he set against the deepest current of his art is to forfeit any hope of explaining his power. It would be better to take account of his Victorianism from the beginning, which means above all to recognize that the Conradian experience, while intense and cathartic, is built around taboos that have lost much of their sacredness. Given the Victorian rules of the game, Conrad's grandiose but barely sustained duplicity with himself can be understood as the enabling condition of his narrative energy.

In order to pose this issue concretely, let me return in some detail to "Heart of Darkness," which is surely Conrad at his best. This is not to say that its intellectual content is especially profound or even clear; on the contrary, the one definite point that emerges from the cacaphony of explication is that the appeal of this story cannot rest on its ideas. I suppose it was by working in an irresolute state that Conrad managed to keep the source of his inspiration so extraordinarily open. What matters, in any case, is that nearly everyone can respond to the symbolic experience at the base of his plot and feel the consonance between overt and latent emphasis. As a deliberately "psychological" tale, a pilgrimage toward some debasing revelation about human character, "Heart of Darkness" is not immobilized by totally contradictory intentions in the manner of *Victory*. Marlow tells us explicitly that Kurtz is "the nightmare of my choice,"[11] and no subtle inferences are needed to establish his ambivalence toward Kurtz. We see, for example, that he yearns to hear Kurtz's voice but cannot stand to hear of the natives' obeisances to him; we see him hanging on Kurtz's dying words but refusing to approach the corpse or witness its disposal; and we see that he is willing to lie on Kurtz's behalf even though he regards him as a degenerate. It is Marlow himself who finally concludes, "I had no clear perception of what it was I really wanted," and who surmises that he has had an "unconscious loyalty" to Kurtz. Thus, though we are not meant to decipher exactly what is meant by "the horror," "the fascination of the abomination," and so on—indeed, though Conrad expects us to share Marlow's and his own feeling of being assailed by "something altogether monstrous, intolerable to thought and odious to the soul"—we know at least that Marlow's adventure amounts to an uncanny self-unfolding.

No one, to my knowledge, has bothered to define the psychological content of this adventure,[12] but it is hardly obscure. Just consider: a sunken, ascetic narrator who fervently believes that women should be kept quarantined "in that beautiful world of their own, lest ours gets worse," tells us that he felt irrationally compelled to visit a dark and mysterious continent, a "confoundedly big" and "dumb thing," "and I had heard Mr. Kurtz was in there." Since childhood he had yearned to visit this area, and now at great risk and in the face of Kurtz's hostility he arrived via a river described as "an immense snake uncoiled, with its head in the sea, its body at rest curving afar over a vast country, and its tail lost in the depths of the land." After passing jungle of "vengeful aspect" whose rank and matted vegetation appeared ready to "sweep every little man of us out of his little existence," he eventually found the much-respected Kurtz in a state of depravity, accompanied by a savage mistress in a wilderness "that seemed to draw him to its pitiless breast by the awakening of forgotten and brutal instincts, by the memory of gratified and monstrous passions." Now withered and helpless, and rescued by the narrator from "certain midnight dances ending with unspeakable rites," Kurtz acknowledged "the horror" of his experience and died, after which the narrator found himself strangely interested in protecting the dead man's reputation—especially in the eyes of a marmoreal, mourning lady who overrated him.

If such a plot were recounted to a psychoanalyst as a dream—and that is just what Marlow calls it—the interpretation would be beyond doubt. The exposed sinner at the heart of darkness would be an image of the father, accused of sexual "rites" with the mother. The dreamer is preoccupied with the primal scene, which he symbolically interrupts. The journey into the maternal body is both voyeuristic and incestuous, and the rescue of the father is more defiant and supplantive than tender and restitutive. The closing episode with the "phantom" woman in a sarcophagal setting would be the dreamer-son's squaring of accounts with his dead mother. He "knows" that parental sexuality is entirely the father's fault, and he has preserved the maternal image untarnished by imagining that the father's partner was not she but a savage woman, a personification of the distant country's "colossal body of the fecund and mysterious life." But given the anxiety generated by his fantasy of usurpation, he prefers to suppress the father's misdeeds. Such a tactic reduces the threat of punishment while reestablishing the "pure" mother-son dyad. Only one complaint against the sainted mother is allowed to reach expression: the son tells her with devious truthfulness that the dying sinner's last word ("horror!") was "your name."

I do not want to review the abundant evidence that this "dream" is indeed the shaping force in "Heart of Darkness";

this fact will prove if anything too apparent to an unprejudiced reader who goes over the story with attention to its language and the stages of its plot. Derivatives of the primal scene await the hero everywhere: the African bush swarms with "naked breasts, arms, legs, glaring eyes," "a black and incomprehensible frenzy," "a great human passion let loose," "the inconceivable ceremonies of some devilish initiation," and so forth. In such surroundings the threat of castration from the two classic sources, the father's wrath and the mother's body, is relentless:

> I avoided a vast artificial hole somebody had been digging on the slope, the purpose of which I found it impossible to divine. It wasn't a quarry or a sandpit, anyhow. It was just a hole. . . .Then I nearly fell into a very narrow ravine, almost no more than a scar in the hillside. I discovered that a lot of imported drainage-pipes for the settlement had been tumbled in there. There wasn't one that was not broken. It was a wanton smash-up. At last I got under the trees. My purpose was to stroll into the shade for a moment; but no sooner within than it seemed to me I had stepped into gloomy circle of some Inferno. . . .

To look at such a passage with comprehension of its plentiful symbolic detail is to have removed oneself from Marlow's literal difficulties; the text threatens to become no longer a story but a clinical document.

Conrad specialists have yet to face this eventuality, but their reaction can be predicted. Nothing is more repugnant to most literary scholars than the thought that their favorite author was prey to obscene wishes and worries. When simple incredulity does not dispel the evidence, they attempt a more sophisticated accommodation: "Freudian insights" are welcomed into the roomy mansion of criticism to coexist peacefully with insights of every other sort. Each "meaning" is taken as further testimony to the author's conscious art; if it becomes necessary to recognize that, say, castration anxiety is a feature of the text, then the author can be credited with a prescient exposé of his hero, who is now seen to lack masculinity *and* divine grace. Thus the last and least sincere stand against mental strife is a specious hyper-Freudianism which takes for granted a pre-Freudian writer's conscious manipulation of psychoanalytic categories as if they had been common knowledge all along. By means of such sophistry an aloof, tastefully dehumanized notion of creativity can be upheld while token deference is being paid to the irrational.

Perhaps, then, it is worthwhile to belabor the obvious point that "Heart of Darkness" is in the most agitated sense an autobiographical work. Far from criticizing Marlow, Conrad was using him to recapitulate and try to master the Congo experience he himself had sought out and undergone in 1890—an experience that led not to philosophical conclusions but to a physical and nervous collapse. Conrad's Congo interlude presents exactly the interpretive problem for his biographers that "Heart of Darkness" does for his critics; in both cases he went out of his way to make a real journey coincide with an unconscious investigation of his morbidity. It could be shown that "Heart of Darkness" is packed with family allusions so private that no concept of "conscious art" could make use of them. In various ways Kurtz amounts to a vindictive reconstruction of Conrad's father,[13] and the story alludes not only to the Congo voyage but also the childhood period of exile in Russia after Conrad's mother, like Kurtz's Intended, had retired to a "sepulchral city" with "an ashy halo," leaving Conrad to cope with a father who inspired what Zdzislaw

Najder calls "admiration and contemptuous pity."[14] Then Conrad like Marlow must have "resented bitterly the absurd danger of our situation, as if to be at the mercy of that atrocious phantom had been a dishonouring necessity."[15] Whether or not this cryptic aspect of the story is recognized, it should be clear to everyone that Conrad as well as Marlow is rattled by the idea of Kurtz, who is melodramatically overdrawn and yet scarcely permitted to appear.

In a broader sense we can see that Conrad's involvement in the unconscious allegory of "Heart of Darkness" explains its combination of hallucinatory vividness and garbled ideas. The whole account of European imperialism in the Congo is brilliantly convincing, not because of any developed ideology on Conrad's part, but because in his struggle with Oedipal "savagery" he feels within himself the pathology of men who want both to improve the brutes and to exterminate them. Because he thinks incessantly of usurping the father's power and privilege, he grasps the zeal to lord it within a cutthroat bureaucracy and to "tear treasure out of the bowels of the land." No one is better at investing real observations of folly and sadism with the fever of a mind that has already imagined the worst criminality and severest punishment. What he cannot do, however, is relinquish this charmed mood or think clearly about its basis. Since everything that is necessary to Marlow's sanity is necessary to Conrad's, he cannot crawl out of Marlow's mind even for a moment. Hence the difficulty he has in conceiving of the Congolese except as objects of persecution or diabolical headhunters; he too shares the need for bogeymen whose howls and dances will be, not signs of a culture, but simply abominations. He cannot even have Marlow say without hedging that Christianizing the Congo is a mistake, for he still aspires to put down the heathen in himself. In short, Conrad finds no point of repose from which to assess the ordeal he puts us through. All he can muster as a substitute are dabs of moral philosophy—treasured like scripture by his critics—to plaster over his confusion about the causes of his melancholy.

To a certain degree, then, "Heart of Darkness" *is* a clinical document, a record of persisting misery. This is not to deny its power as art but on the contrary to suggest where its power must lie. Despite some details which owe their significance to memories that have not been made available in the text, the anxiety of the whole story comes across unmistakably. We do not yet have an aesthetics of anxiety—indeed, the New-Critical enterprise can be construed as a skirting of the problem, a defensive anchoring of emotion in "objective correlatives" and self-referring tensions—but in reading a deeply ordered work of anxiety we seem willing to concede the suitability of its "adjectival" and "vaporous" language to hidden referents. If we feel "Heart of Darkness" to be somehow coherent despite its patent vagueness and its air of near hysteria, this is because a return of the repressed is not lost on us. We know it is right for Marlow, with his prurient interest in his elders' misdeeds, to be drawn into a journey that leads to knowledge of certain midnight dances ending with unspeakable rites, and on the same level of awareness we know he must make amends for having entertained such a revelation.

I doubt whether any biographical knowledge about "Heart of Darkness" or any critical account of its logic will make its disguised content too available for dramatic illusion to be sustained. Such information only helps to explain why the story seizes us anew with every reading. To say this, however, is not to say that Conrad's sensibility is our own. Nihilism, which in Conrad is surreptitious and nicely padded with scenic effects, has become aggressively explicit in the serious literature of our day, and anyone who prefers Conrad's mode is likely to be conscious of doing so nostalgically. The most awesome and permanent Conradian secrets, the unseen magnets which bind every detail in the field of his plots, are now matter for offhand jokes: "I was on my way to my mother," says Beckett's Molloy, "whose charity kept me dying."[16] A contemporary writer could be forgiven for envying Conrad's relative ignorance, which enabled him to be earnest about fending off vice and to write stories that merge self-realization with believable and intrinsically lively adventures. Nothing is more symptomatic of the present predicament than that Molloy, the man who is wholly at peace with his bodily self, should have nowhere to go but around in a circle on his autoerotic bicycle. Lesser writers than Beckett, having forfeited much of the power of latent reference, are rapidly exhausting the power to shock. Aesthetic complexity would seem to be one of the casualties of desublimation.

If this is so, then we have Conrad's neurosis and the style of his culture to thank, not of course for his genius, but for the special quality of his appeal. In the manuscript of "Heart of Darkness," immediately after Marlow's plea that women be kept apart in their beautiful world, Conrad had added a typically lurid but singularly revealing outburst: "That's a monster-truth with many maws to whom we've got to throw every year—or every day—no matter—no sacrifice is too great—a ransom of pretty, shining lies. . . ." That he decided to suppress the remark instead of merely editing out some of its agitation may indicate nothing more than a shrewd assessment of his readership, but that he wrote it in the first place is a mark of his true inner situation. Lying to (and about) women, the quintessential article in the Victorian modus vivendi, was so important to Conrad for his own reasons that he found himself actually putting the requirement into so many words; his curse and opportunity was his need to deal at close range with the gaping monster of his fantasies. Whoever begrudges him his distracting maneuvers has not sufficiently understood the precariousness of the civilized equilibrium he sought to maintain. In retrospect Conrad's lurking skepticism about the strength of conscious decency looks so warranted by public events that we may feel tempted to credit him with a clairvoyant modernity, a vision of general collapse, but precisely because he writhed under the nightmare of history he could not be its interpreter. He did not formulate contradictions, he lived intensely with them and transcribed them into the terms of art. To demand of him something more static and placid, as the bulk of our criticism has implicitly done, is only to manifest in a subtle way what our civilization is now proving with brutal plainness: an incapacity even to imagine what it is like to be human and oppressed.

Notes

1. Marvin Mudrick, ed., *Conrad: A Collection of Critical Essays* (Englewood Cliffs, N.J., 1966), Introduction, p. 10.
2. F. R. Leavis, *The Great Tradition: A Study of the English Novel* (1948; rpt. Garden City, N.Y., 1954), p. 216.
3. But for Conrad the matter wasn't so easy. "Even writing to a friend—to a person one has heard, touched, drunk with, quarrelled with—does not give me a sense of reality. All is illusion—the words written, the mind at which they are aimed, the truth they are intended to express, the hands that will hold the paper, the eyes that will glance at the lines. Every image floats vaguely in a sea of doubt—and the doubt itself is lost in an unexplored universe of incertitudes" (*Letters from Conrad, 1895–1924*, ed. Edward Garnett [London, 1928; rpt. Indianapolis and New York, 1962], p. 155). This is Leavis' "gallant simple sailor" whose genius was "a unique and happy union of seaman and writer" (Leavis, pp. 223, 229).

4. "Although qualified to enter nirvana, like the true Bodhisattva, Marlow remains in the world to work for the salvation of all people. In his stage of enlightenment he teaches what his descent into the imperfections of the human soul has taught him—egoless compassion. Cancelling out all personal desire and fear, he has made available to humanity the gift of complete renunciation. To every suffering, striving creature, trapped in the karmic processes (enslavement to matter), he offers the inexhaustible wisdom of selflessness" (William Bysshe Stein, "The Lotus Posture and *Heart of Darkness*," Norton Critical Edition of *Heart of Darkness*, ed. Robert Kimbrough [New York, 1963], p. 199).
5. Bernard C. Meyer, *Joseph Conrad: A Psychoanalytic Biography* (Princeton, N.J., 1967), p. 69.
6. For a fuller psychoanalytic discussion of this side of Conrad, see Norman N. Holland, "Style as Character: *The Secret Agent*," *Modern Fiction Studies*, 12 (Summer 1966), 221–231.
7. Albert Guerard, *Conrad the Novelist* (Cambridge, Mass., 1958), p. 257.
8. Jessie Conrad, *Conrad and His Circle* (New York, 1935), p. 27.
9. Leavis, for instance, feels cheered by a novel containing so many "upright, sensitive and humane individuals . . . —'we sailors,' the feeling is . . . " And he reminds us that Heyst, whatever his problems may have been, does make a "tragic pronouncement in favour of trust in life" (Leavis, p. 252)—shortly before committing suicide, but no matter.
10. Joseph Conrad, *Victory* (1915; rpt. New York, n.d.), pp. 372, 375, 377.
11. *Heart of Darkness* (note 4 above), pp. 65–66. Hereafter cited parenthetically as *HD*.
12. See, however, Richard F. Sterba's perceptive "Remarks on Joseph Conrad's *Heart of Darkness*," *Journal of the American Psychoanalytic Association*, 13 (July 1965), 570–583.
13. Both Kurtz and Korzeniowski—the names are alike—are intellectuals and versifiers; neither can be properly said to have a profession; both have dabbled in journalism and written pamphlets; both have messianic political ambitions and a mixture of refinement and demagoguery; both are accused of disrupting the orderly domination of a victimized territory; both die far from home, maintaining almost until the end a grandiloquent intention to return and prevail; both are remembered as prematurely withered and helpless, yet oppressive; both are famous for their arresting voices and their ability to persuade; both seem addicted to self-pity; both refuse an offer of rescue; both leave literary remains; both profess a high-minded Christianity but have experimented with dissipation. The family of Kurtz's "Intended" objects to her engagement to him; so did Evelina Bobrowska's family object to her engagement to Apollo Korzeniowski. These parallels, all of which can be inferred by checking "Heart of Darkness" against Jocelyn Baines's biography of Conrad, receive further credence from Bernard Meyer's conclusion that "there was something of his father in every story [Conrad] had written" (Meyer, p. 285).
14. Zdzislaw Najder, *Conrad's Polish Background* (London, 1964), p. 11.
15. Of these allusions to childhood dependency one deserves special interest, not only because it has been a crux but because it epitomizes the privacy and anguished sincerity of the story's autobiographical reference. Marlow finds Kurtz attended by a remarkably boyish Russian, a "harlequin" with a peeling nose, who sits at Kurtz's feet and tries to think the best of him, as the well-bred, inwardly forgiving Conrad must have done with his father in Russia. This figure of submission had formerly been rebellious against his father, an arch-priest; he "had run away from school, had gone to sea in a Russian ship; ran away again; served some time in English ships; was now reconciled with the arch-priest. He made a point of that" (*HD*, p. 54). Beyond question this is Conrad's own story, with the difference that Conrad finds reconciliation less feasible. But the image of the obedient harlequin has a still more precise origin in Conrad's memories. In the letter I have quoted as an epigraph he lamented his post-Congo depression and compared himself wistfully to the "Polichinelle"—or Pulcinello—of his childhood. This gentlemanly toy, he explained, had put up with all manner of tender abuse from its master. Despite such indigni-

ties as a broken nose and missing eye (the symbolism is obvious), and the licking off of its paint, the harlequin had "received my confidences with a sympathetic air. . . ." When Conrad, near the end of his tale of filial usurpation, tried to introduce an image of the reformed son, his latent cynicism hit upon this figure. To obey was to be a clown, a "polite little Pole" whose nose and eye were forfeit to the paternal avenger. See J. A. Gee and P. J. Sturm, eds., *Letters of Joseph Conrad to Marguerite Poradowska, 1890–1920* (New Haven, 1940), pp. 37–39.

16. Samuel Beckett, *Three Novels* (New York, 1965), p. 22.

JOHN BATCHELOR
From "Conrad"
The Edwardian Novelists
1982, pp. 28–55

In Conrad the young hero is there to be admired but also to be educated. The hero is himself both an ideal image of man, a *kouros*, and an immature seeker, the hero of a *Bildungsroman* or novel of initiation and development.[1] In Conrad these young heroes—Willems, young Marlow in *Youth*, Jim in *Lord Jim*, Powell in *Chance*—must relate themselves to mature men in the course of the difficult process of establishing their own manhood. It has been suggested that this pattern in Conrad's work reflects his own relationships with two older men, his father and his uncle.[2]

Bound up with the question 'What is a man?' is the question 'What is the significance of his life?' Conrad's imagination is that of an atheist using Christian concepts, as is perhaps inevitable for someone brought up in early childhood as a Catholic. The great works of his central period, *Heart of Darkness*, *Lord Jim*, *Nostromo* and *Under Western Eyes*, ask these questions *together*. 'What is man? What is the significance of his life?' circle the male figures of these narratives. The answers are oracular, and consist of the questions rephrased: 'Need man's life have a meaning? Need man have an identity?'

So much has been written on Conrad, he is now so much an academic heavy industry, that with him more than with most major figures it is important to recover the freshness of the amateur reader: to stand back from the works and ask oneself 'Why do I read Conrad? What do I find in him?'

My own answer to that would be that I find in him the *loneliness* of human beings caught and communicated with a vividness unsurpassed in any other writer. . . .

II. The Nigger of the Narcissus *and 'Youth'*

A man tries his strength against the sea. This primitive formula, which has attracted the poetic imagination from Homer to Hemingway, is the strong base on which *The Nigger*, 'Youth', 'Typhoon', 'Falk' and much of *Lord Jim* and *Chance* are constructed, and stands in the background of the more complicated contest taking place in *Heart of Darkness*. In *The Nigger* (1897) 'Old' Singleton, the oldest seaman on board, 'through half a century had measured his strength against the favours and the rages of the sea'. The respective strengths of Singleton and Captain Allistoun are challenged by the sea and the unsettled state of the crew. The sea is as 'mischievous and discomposing as a madman with an axe.' Singleton sees it as his lifelong partner and comments on Allistoun's combativeness: 'The old man's in a temper with the weather, but it's no good bein' angry with the winds of heaven.' But Singleton's strength is over-taxed by the gale. As the oldest of the 'children' in the forecastle he becomes abruptly conscious that he himself will die:

'Old! It seemed to him he was broken at last. And like a

man bound treacherously while he sleeps, he woke up fettered by the long chain of disregarded years. . . .He looked upon the immortal sea . . . and he saw an immensity tormented and blind, moaning and furious, that claimed all the days of his tenacious life, and, when life was over, would claim the worn-out body of its slave.'

For the crew the trial of strength is a struggle with their own weaknesses. James Wait, the cowardly and morally sick 'Nigger' seaman appeals to 'the latent egoism of tenderness to suffering,' and unfits the crew for their work: 'through him we were becoming highly humanised, tender, complex, excessively decadent.' Donkin appeals to egoism of another kind, envy of the officers and a desire to upset the ship's working order: 'inspired by Donkin's hopeful doctrines they dreamed enthusiastically of the time when every lonely ship would travel over a serene sea, manned by a wealthy and well-fed crew of satisfied skippers. . . .'

The story reflects the current belief that the urban working class was morally and physically degenerating. The men of Singleton's generation, 'who could understand his silence' were 'those men who knew how to exist beyond the pale of life and within sight of eternity. They had been strong, as those are strong who know neither doubts nor hopes.' That generation of primitive heroes has been replaced by the present crew of the *Narcissus*, 'highly humanised', 'excessively decadent'. Stevie in *The Secret Agent* is identified by Ossipon as a degenerate partly because he has thin prominent ears: Donkin in this story has the same physical feature: 'His big ears stood out, transparent and veined, resembling the thin wings of a bat.'

The Nigger closes by asking a question: 'Haven't we, together and upon the immortal sea, wrung out a meaning from our lives?' The experience of the sea defies and finally expels degeneracy—Donkin is given a bad discharge—and enforces the traditional moral sanction of the primitive fable, man against the sea. After lifting this simple contrast into a full light Conrad ends his story by inverting its antithetical shape and simultaneously enlarging its meaning. . . .

The Nigger can be seen as a story organised round four major figures: Wait and Donkin, the destructive elements, and Singleton and Allistoun, the sustaining figures who hold the ship through the memorable and lovingly written gale in chapter 3.

In this pivotal chapter the four central figures interact and reveal each other. Allistoun 'seemed with his eyes to hold the ship up in a superhuman concentration of effort,' while Singleton at the wheel steers for thirty hours, 'forgotten by all, and with an attentive face. In front of his erect figure only the two arms moved crosswise with a swift and sudden readiness, to check or urge again the rapid stir of circling spokes. He steered with care.' When the *Narcissus* is blown on her beam ends Donkin, who has hitherto established a kind of power for himself among the sailors, is revealed as cowardly and useless, screaming 'curses' and 'filthy words' at the skipper for his refusal to cut the masts and abruptly silenced by the hostile reaction he provokes: 'One of his rescuers struck him a back-handed blow over the mouth.'

Jimmy, sick in his cabin, has to be rescued from drowning and displays a hysterical cowardice which succeeds in demoralising the men where Donkin has failed: 'He screamed piercingly, without drawing breath, like a tortured woman; he banged with hands and feet. The agony of his fear wrung our hearts so terribly that we longed to abandon him, to get out of that place deep as a well and swaying like a tree, to get out of his hearing, back on the poop where we could wait passively for death in incomparable repose.'

Between the strength of Allistoun and Singleton and the cowardice of Donkin and Jimmy Wait a fifth figure, the young Charley, is thrown into prominence in a moment of extraordinary tenderness: 'Between two bearded shellbacks Charley, fastened with somebody's long muffler to a deck ringbolt, wept quietly, with rare tears wrung out by bewilderment, cold, hunger, and general misery. One of his neighbours punched him in the ribs asking roughly: "What's the matter with your cheek? In fine weather there's no holding you, youngster." Turning about with prudence he worked himself out of his coat and threw it over the boy. The other man closed up, muttering: ""Twill make a bloomin' man of you, sonny." They flung their arms over and pressed against him. Charley drew his feet up and his eyelids dropped.'

This has an obvious and direct relevance to the theme of initiation into male maturity. As the chapter closes the maturing process in Charley has begun. The sea has forced him to relinquish his cheeky, privileged persona for one humbler and more timid: 'Charley, subdued by the sudden disclosure of the insignificance of his youth, darted fearful glances.'

Despite its many strengths, its magnificent storm passages, its strong five-part structure, its carefully studied interplay between the major figures and the confidently 'known' quality of the masculine world that it presents, *The Nigger* is finally less perfect a form than 'Youth' (1902). The floating narrator in *The Nigger* has access to all the minds but is anchored in none until he surprisingly speaks in the first-person at the end of the story. In 'Youth' Conrad establishes the narrative device which contributes incalculably to the success of two of his major performances, *Heart of Darkness* and *Lord Jim*.

'Youth' begins, as *Heart of Darkness* begins, with a group of four mature men listening to a fifth man, Marlow, telling a story. Marlow is still in the merchant navy, the others were sailors as young men and have now gone into safe land jobs: law, industry, accountancy. Both stories begin with a frame, an anonymous outer narrator who establishes the relaxed, affectionate male solidarity of the after-dinner audience and introduces Marlow. The outer narrator of 'Youth' doesn't know Marlow well; this is perhaps the first occasion on which they have met. We are to imagine *Heart of Darkness* as being narrated at a later date, since here the outer narrator (clearly the same person) is well acquainted with Marlow although not, it seems, a close friend. In *Lord Jim* the after-dinner situation is taken for granted—it is sketched in perfunctorily at the end of chapter 4, as though the reader is expected to supply it from his memory of the earlier stories. The outer narrator here has the important function of establishing an omniscient and detached view of Jim in the first four chapters, before Marlow's special pleading takes over in chapter 5.

The identity of Marlow has been much discussed in criticisms of Conrad. He may well be based on Cunninghame Graham, whose own prose has the unrevised, colloquial quality that Conrad revises in Marlow. Or he may be conceived loosely as any man of action who recalls his experiences, like Captain Fred Burnaby, author of *A Ride to Khiva*, which went through many editions in the Victorian periods and is read by young Marlow in 'Youth' and greatly preferred to Carlyle's *Sartor Resartus*.

Whatever the source for Marlow, he was a timely gift to Conrad's art: a pragmatist and man of action, unsubtle but reflective, affectionate as well as self-seeking. A contrast to, without being an antithesis of, the intensely sensitive, ambitious, over-scrupulous and self-pitying, not to say neurotic, personality of his creator.

The primitive myth, in which a man tries his strength against the sea, is at its simplest in 'Youth.' The middle-aged Marlow recalls his younger self, at the age of twenty, making his first voyage to the East. The whole enterprise is beset with comic misadventure. The ship, the *Judea*, is an old wreck which tries to put to sea three times with its cargo of coal for Bangkok and eventually has to be dry-docked, recaulked and completely refurbished. The voyage then begins; ominously, the rats choose this moment to leave the ship. The sailors laugh at the rats' stupidity; they stayed with the ship while it was a leaking ruin, they are leaving it now that it is reconditioned and safe. But the rats are proved right: the danger now is not the ship but the cargo. The cargo of coal has been re-loaded too often in bad weather during the work on the *Judea*, it has been broken up and become damp and produces gas which ignites on the voyage. After long delays caused by the obstinacy of the old skipper, Captain Beard, whose first command this is, the crew abandon the burning ship and the young Marlow sails into an Eastern port at the tiller of *his* 'first command': a lifeboat manned by two exhausted sailors and sailing under an improvised rig consisting of an oar, a tarpaulin and a boat-hook.

The weeping Charley in *The Nigger* is told at the height of the storm that the experience will 'make a bloomin' man of you, sonny.' His successor, the twenty-year-old Marlow, sails his life-boat to an unknown Eastern port: 'I did not know how good a man I was till then.'

The firm narrative frame provided by the Marlow device is strengthened by the carefully established contrast between the middle-aged man, an ironist with few illusions left, and the idealistic younger self. From one point of view 'Youth' can be seen as ironic: the foolish ardour of the young Marlow is balanced against the foolish obstinacy of old Captain Beard, overprotective towards his wife, endangering his crew by refusing to allow them to leave the burning *Judea* until the ship is fully ablaze.

Once the reader is engaged with the excitement of the story's central contest, though, the irony seems unimportant. In 'Youth' the sea is like chaos at the beginning of creation, 'white like a sheet of foam, like a caldron of boiling milk.' The energy of the sea forces Marlow to measure his own young strength against it while the ship becomes a gallant old female whom the young sailor defends. . . .

III. Heart of Darkness: *action and lying*

'Youth' was an exposed work, carrying its significance on its surface. The middle-aged man recaptures the moment of maturing and self-discovery in his own younger self. In later works the interest in this moment of self-discovery—in Lord Jim and Razumov—will be extended and bound up with the unanswerable epistemological questions which themselves give a generative force to Conrad's art. In 'Youth' the process of initiation is finite, the personality is fully knowable. The young man who 'did not know how good a man I was till then' has reached the East and won his long-drawn battle with the sea; at the same time he has undergone a quasi-sexual consummation with the East. An 'aromatic' puff of wind reaches him from the land, 'impalpable and enslaving, like a charm, like a whispered promise of mysterious delight.'

'Youth' leaves one quite clear as to what the story has been 'about'. *Heart of Darkness* permits no such confidence. The reader himself is forced into the epistemological wilderness in this wrestle with the text; the normal premises, the normal contractual relationship between writer and reader have been discarded. The reader is not permitted to know which of the two figures, Marlow and Kurtz, is the 'subject' of the story, nor to know how reliable Marlow is as narrator. He is a simple Englishman of action with enough sensibility and experience to communicate his story at the level of primitive narrative but with at the same time a limitation of outlook and sophistication which enables the novelist constantly to hint that the story's significance lies beyond and behind the narrative surface. In the three major Marlow narratives, *Heart of Darkness*, *Lord Jim* and *Chance*, all the most sophisticated uses to which the device of the limited narrator can be put are explored. In this Conrad is working within a well-established English tradition, if one thinks of Ellen Dean and Lockwood in *Wuthering Heights*, Esther Summerson in *Bleak House*, the soldiers who narrate Kipling's barrack-room stories, the children who provide the frames for the stories in Kipling's *Pack of Pook's Hill* and *Rewards and Fairies*. . . .

Heart of Darkness can be read as a modernist fiction, perhaps the first consistently self-referential fiction in English.[3] Its surface can be taken as a system of signs and secrets, mysteries leading to other mysteries none of which are explained. The journey of exploration itself is a literary metaphor, an analogy illustrating the way the mind moves through a text responding to its images and signs.

In reading *Heart of Darkness* one encounters opposing principles which may be termed 'action' and 'the lie'. Action is irreducible. In the world of the epistemological crisis a man's words, intentions, concepts of himself are all vulnerable while his actions are irrefutable as well as irreversible. . . .

Marlow finds relief, or therapy, in action against the stagnation and malice that he finds among the Belgian traders. He must restore his sunk steam-boat. (The manager of the trading station has probably scuttled it to impede Marlow's career, since he jealously imagines that Marlow, like Kurtz, has been selected for rapid promotion by the Head Office back in Brussels, the whited sepulchre). . . .

The quest for Kurtz brings in the other opposing principle, 'the lie'. 'I would not have gone so far as to fight for Kurtz, but I went for him near enough to a lie. You know I hate, detest, and can't bear a lie, not because I am straighter than the rest of us, but simply because it appals me. There is a taint of death, a flavour of mortality in lies—which is exactly what I hate and detest in the world—what I want to forget. It makes me miserable and sick, like biting something rotten would do.'

Marlow's progress through the story is a movement towards knowledge of Kurtz and of the nature of the heart of darkness, a movement which is blocked at almost every turn by lies, shams, impostures. The colonialists have imposed on the continent a fraudulent linguistic frame, a verbal umbrella like Orwell's Newspeak under the protection of which they can exercise any degree of tyranny. Chained together in workgangs, the Africans are 'called criminals'; when shelled by the French man-of-war ('it appears that French had one of their wars going on thereabouts'), they are 'enemies'; when they are dying in the 'grove of death' they are former 'workers' (the text adds: 'They were not enemies, they were not criminals, they were nothing earthly now'). When Marlow finally reaches Kurtz's inner station to find Kurtz's house surrounded by severed heads on posts, Kurtz's naive young Russian disciple explains that these are the heads of 'rebels'. Marlow's mind revolts: 'Rebels! What would be the next definition I was to hear? There had been enemies, criminals, workers—and these were rebels.'

The celebrated imagery of 'hollow men' in the story is directly related to this pattern of fraudulent language. The word 'Kurtz' is itself a lie: 'Means short in German—don't it?

Well, the name was as true as everything else in his life—and death. He looked at least seven feet long.' The ambitious brick-maker with a forked beard—who sees himself as competing with Marlow for the favour of the company and rapid promotion—is a 'papier-mâché Mephistopheles'; 'if I tried I could poke my forefinger through him, and would find nothing inside but a little loose dirt.' Marlow decides to play up to the illusion in the mind of this 'young fool' and feels himself become a fiction, a 'pretence.'

Kurtz is 'hollow at the core,' and the hollowness within him and the other hollow men is identified with the 'wilderness', which is itself an increasingly potent word in the story: it is the vacuum left behind a word when the word is part of a lie, the vacancy inside Kurtz which 'invades' Kurtz and 'speaks' to him.

The mass of commentary on *Heart of Darkness* reveals two major emphases. One tradition sees it as a major piece of anti-imperialist fiction.[4] Another sees it as a story about private sensibility which reflects especially the new interest of the 1890s in psychology and reflects also the Darwinian intellectual background of the period.[5]

A recent critic in this tradition, C. B. Cox, confidently reads *Heart of Darkness* as a 'journey into the wilderness of sex'.[6] An earlier notable sexual and psychological approach to this story is in the important 'psychoanalytic biography' by Bernard Meyer.[7]

Heart of Darkness plainly does reflect late Victorian anxieties over matters of major topical interest: the status and function of the Empire in a period when its mid-Victorian Christian justification was on the ebb, and the subversive and unassimilable pressures of the demands for sexual freedom and a humanist morality. In some ways Conrad is more representative of the 1890s and the Edwardian period than any native-born writer could be; a sensitive outsider responsibly and minutely observing the major concerns of the age. Eloise Hay quotes Flaubert's doctrine, 'The artist should have neither religion, country, nor even any social conviction', and comments that Conrad 'had neutralised himself in all three of these points by the time his writing life began'.[8] The surface of his life shows the case for this view: he had left Poland, he had married into the English lower middle-class, he was no longer a practising Catholic. But part of the pressure of evolutionary and psychological thinking in the 1890s is towards the position that one cannot, and should not, sever one's roots. These intellectual currents thus have a conservative as well as a radical effect by forcing the individual to acknowledge his place in the natural order and come to terms with his own biological history. . . .

From a broad view of Conrad's work one may judge that he sees subversion (Donkin and Wait, the anarchists in *The Secret Agent*) as a major threat to the 'feeling of fellowship', the 'conviction of solidarity'. But *coercive* authority—the Russian regime in *Under Western Eyes*, the British penal system in *Chance*—is equally fatal to human solidarity. The right ordering of human societies depends upon a form of authority which is simultaneously absolute and dependent on consent.

An ideally run merchant ship may approximate to such a society, but in its perfect form this social ordering would presumably be found in Christianity ideally expressed. . . .

In *Heart of Darkness* it is possible to see Conrad writing as a non-Christian who still innately is sharing specifically Christian responses to the paradox of authority and then seeking to clarify them in secular terms. Kurtz makes himself into a god and establishes his own liturgy:

'His—let us say—nerves went wrong, and caused him to

preside at certain midnight dances ending with unspeakable rites, which— as far as I reluctantly gathered from what I heard at various times—were offered up to him—do you understand?—to Mr Kurtz himself.'

Marlow himself is forced to acknowledge Kurtz as a deity:

'I had, even like the niggers, to invoke him—himself—his own exalted and incredible degradation. There was nothing either above or below him, and I knew it. He had kicked himself loose of the earth. Confound the man! He had kicked the very earth in pieces.'

I am not suggesting, as some have, that Conrad is in a sense condoning and covertly approving Kurtz's self-deification.[9] Kurtz's epiphany is presented in language of recoil: 'unspeakable rites', 'incredible degradation'. The wilderness possesses Kurtz in what could be a diabolical parody of an account of God invading the life of a saint: 'The wilderness . . . had taken him, loved him, embraced him, got into his veins, consumed his flesh and sealed his soul to its own by the inconceivable ceremonies of some devilish initiation.' If one substituted 'God' for 'the wilderness' and removed the word 'devilish' the passage could almost have been lifted from, say, the agonies of St Margaret Mary preceding her vision of the Sacred Heart. But of course the word 'devilish' cannot be removed. Conrad is determined—at all costs, as it were—that the act of veneration shall be perceived as a monstrous evil. He is like a former alcoholic writing about the perils of drink.

It seems to me, then, that in this story Conrad is writing with the temperament of a theist and the convictions of an atheist, and that this traps him in a contradiction which runs like a bottomless fissure through *Heart of Darkness* and helps to account for the difficulty and evasiveness of the surface of the text. The visible expressions of the religious impulse are there to be hated and rejected. At the same time the story begins and ends with the questions forced by Conrad's title: what lies at the heart of man's intellectual darkness? What is the significance of the totality of his being? These are ultimate questions about the nature of life: religious questions, in short. That Conrad should ask such questions is consistent with the view that he is a man of *repressed* religious impulses. This is distinct from the suggestion made by the 'savage god' adherents[10] that he is a man of *secret* religious impulses. The latter suggests a respectable citizen who is a secret drinker, but the right analogy for Conrad is a former alcoholic who has become a strict teetotaller.

One would guess that the writing of this story came as an exhilarating release, the unblocking and unlocking of a hidden region of the creative self. The title and theme address themselves to the problem of whether it is possible to arrive at and communicate a total world-view. The question then has sub-sections: is the world-view attainable from the advanced evolutionary vantage point of Western man? Or from that of primitive man engaged in the struggle for survival? Or, possibly, from that of man in the act of worship? It is as though the former alcoholic were to test himself by asking himself, cautiously, whether he wants a drink, and the answer comes in the form of a passionate and cathartic rejection.

Marlow's maleness, his generous virility, fills the vacuum left by the hollowness and negation surrounding him in *Heart of Darkness*. The deadness and hollowness of the traders is contrasted with the vitality of the Africans: 'They shouted, sang; their bodies streamed with perspiration; they had faces like grotesque masks—these chaps; but they had bone, muscle, a wild vitality, an intense energy of movement, that was as natural and true as the surf along their coast.'

The fascinating whiteness that Conrad as a child had seen at the centre of Africa 'in 1868, when nine years old or there-

abouts' [*A Personal Record* (1912)] has given way to a 'darkness' which is alive while Brussels is a white sepulchre. Black is energy, white is death; the equation is not mechanical or rigid, but it is sufficiently clearly marked to give its own additional richness to the text. The doors of the trading company offices leading into the darkness are opened by a white-haired secretary.

The elegant white-suited, clean-collared clerk, 'amazing', sits in the middle trading-station on the Congo keeping his ledgers accurately while a groaning man dies at his feet. The ivory itself, the goal of this cruel and incompetent imperialism, takes its place in the black-white symbolism which is rounded off by the grouping of peripheral female figures in the story: in Brussels, the whited sepulchre, two women, one old and fat, one younger and thin, knit black wool 'guarding the door of Darkness.' The black girl, 'savage and superb, wild-eyed and magnificent' sums up the vitality of the savages in her sexual passion and loyalty to Kurtz. She gives way in turn to her rival the 'Intended', the white girl in a black setting, dressed in mourning but characterised by her 'forehead, smooth and white' which 'remained illuminated by the unextinguishable light of belief and love.' This pattern of imagery has been much discussed and is familiar. The point arising out of it which is of interest to me is that Conrad is a *macho* novelist in this story as in much of his other work. The women are unimportant. They are part of the frame; but the story does not pretend to be interested in heterosexual relationships as such: 'They—the women I mean—are out of it—should be out of it. We must help them to stay in that beautiful world of their own, lest ours gets worse.'

As Marlow here implies, the important relationships are between men.

Kurtz's blacks 'adored' him, the naive young Russian is possessed by him: 'The man filled his life, occupied his thoughts, swayed his emotions.' But Marlow comes closer to him than these idolators: 'I knew him as well as it is possible for one man to know another.'

Kurtz at least has purposiveness. He has come to the colony a romantic idealist, 'humanising, improving, instructing,' preparing his grandiloquent and philanthropic report for the International Society for the Suppression of Savage Customs: 'By the exercise of our will we can exert a power for good practically unbounded.' The surprise post-scriptum, 'Exterminate all the brutes!' indicates purposiveness of another kind. The Kurtz that Marlow meets has become hollowed out by wickedness, but he is still more of a 'man' than the 'pilgrims' with their 'staves' and the flabby manager with his petted overfed black 'boy' from the coast who is allowed to cheek the agents without reproof.

The manager is devoid of normal human drives, the pilgrim's 'staves' are like impotent reified phalluses, emblems of the purposelessness of their lives; 'strolling aimlessly about . . . with their absurd long staves in their hands.' The French gun-boat shelling the bush is attended by another symbol of sexual impotence: 'Her ensign drooped[11] limp like a rag; the muzzles of the long six-inch guns stuck out all over the low hull; the greasy, slimy swell swung her up lazily and let her down.' The six-inch guns have shrunk through the successive drafts of the story; in the Ms. they are 'ten-inch' and in *Blackwoods Magazine* 'eight-inch'. One of Conrad's editors has suggested, rather convincingly, that the sexual symbolism here is overt and refers to a specific European male's anxiety about the superior sexual potency of black men.[12]

Marlow is romancing when he describes Kurtz's cry, 'The horror. The horror!' as a moral victory. Marlow is a generous, virile temperament who will create moral positives where they don't exist. He prefers outright wickedness to 'hollowness'. Violence and greed are 'strong, lustly, red-eyed devils, that swayed and drove men—men, I tell you'. Among the Belgian traders he encounters 'a flabby, pretending, weak-eyed devil of a rapacious and pitiless folly.' In the sharpest contrast with this shabbiness and pretention is the nobility of the starving cannibal crew of the steamer. Marlow wonders why they do not fall on the white men and eat them: 'They were big powerful men, with not much capacity to weigh the consequences, with courage, with strength. . . . And I saw that something restraining, one of those human secrets that baffle probability, had come into play there.' The key to the human secret is in Marlow himself. Marlow is innately modest and is unable to see himself. It doesn't need much ingenuity for the reader to see that Marlow himself is, in reality, all that the naive Russian imagines Kurtz to be: a philanthropic, hard-working, morally upright being—in short, that rare phenomenon in the *serious* (as against popular) literature of that period, the good imperialist. It is Marlow's leadership that restrains the cannibals, Marlow's superiority that inspires envy and rage in the manager of the central station and the Mephistophelean brick-maker, Marlow's bearing and obvious honesty that inspire confidence in the 'Intended'.

The lie marks a change, perhaps the beginnings of 'corruption' but equally to be regarded as a gain in flexibility. Marlow is a pre-lapsarian Lord Jim, a 'limited' narrator in the sense in which a good man seeking to describe a wholly evil universe is limited—he can't believe the full iniquity of what he sees.

Marlow speculates that self-knowledge 'came to [Kurtz] at last,' with his dying cry, 'The horror! The horror!' It seems equally likely, though, that this is the last and most provoking of the story's evasions. The reader's understanding of this final cry is heavily coloured by Marlow's commentary: 'It was an affirmation, a moral victory paid for by innumerable defeats, by abominable terrors, by abominable satisfactions. But it was a victory! That is why I have remained loyal to Kurtz to the last.'

Why? How can Marlow know that this is 'a victory'? Marlow is too generous a man to be able to tell the story of Kurtz with full understanding. His own virility balances the hollowness of Kurtz, the lack of sexual drive in the manager, the externalised phallic symbols of the pilgrims' staves and the heads on stakes.

He has already warned the reader that his experience of meeting Kurtz will prove incommunicable: 'I've been telling you what we said—repeating the phrases we pronounced—but what's the good?' Here we have unconscious proof, so to speak, of that failure. 'Affirmation', 'moral victory', 'abominable terror', 'abominable satisfaction', these are all evasions, words and phrases indicating nothing except the fact that there is a mystery still concealed. The action/lying antithesis is brought into focus with Kurtz's cry. The words 'The horror! The horror!' tell the reader nothing, their function is not to communicate but to provoke and stimulate further questions, to drive the reader and Marlow yet further on their collaborative quest for the story's 'whole meaning' or 'kernel.'

'The horror' is the last of Kurtz's lies; a form of words that compels respect, has an air of oracular communication, and reveals nothing. The 'whole meaning' for Marlow is to be found in Marlow's own actions: his life has been decisively changed by the loyalty that Kurtz has generated in him. He finds the Intended and tells her his own deliberate lie, performs the action that has the flavour of death for him, thereby revealing the extent to which Kurtz's imprinting has affected him.

IV. Lord Jim: *creative love*

. . .Conrad was developing a philosophy of the reality of action at the time of writing *Lord Jim*; witnesses the passage of *Heart of Darkness* and the letter to Blackwood of 1902 that I have referred to above: his work is based on 'action observed, felt and interpreted with an absolute truth to my sensations', and for Marlow, in *Heart of Darkness*, action enables a man to know himself: 'Your own reality—for yourself, not for others.'

Within Conrad's epistemological wilderness the actions of the self and the appearances of the physical world are the only evidences. There may well be constants, parameters, which are more stable than the welter of subjective experience would suggest. But the narrating mind has only the subjective experience to go on. There is a further inherent paradox, of which Conrad was increasingly aware as he developed the use of Marlow as narrator, in that the narrating mind is itself a constant, a parameter, the subjective factor that continually modifies the observed instabilities of the experienced world. Where everything else has become elusive and contingent the printed word remains a fixed fact, a self-evident constant, a parameter of the simplest kind.

In *Heart of Darkness* Marlow was a 'Buddha' and the way he tells the story suggests that he has arrived at this Buddha-like state as a result of the experience described in the story, the maturing 'immersion' of the exploratory journey and the disturbing encounter with Kurtz. This Buddha becomes a priest, confessor and father-figure to Jim in *Lord Jim*. Marlow's own identity as a man is of critical importance: Jim's story is one of a tragicomic near-miss transformed into surprising romantic success by the maieutic influence of a lucky friendship. The cycle of aspiration to an unattainable self-image is broken by Marlow's love for him which enables him not so much to come to terms with himself—the image of the 'veiled familiar at his side' suggests that he can do this only at the moment of death—as to win achievement with the energy generated by neurotic conflict.

Since Marlow speaks in the first person the reader's sense of his identity has to be intuited from his style. When speaking of 'style' one is discussing two related matters: the restricted sense of the word refers to the organisation of sentences, the large sense to the temperament of the man presenting the tale as sensed in the manner of the telling.

The temperaments of the mature male figures surrounding Jim give the reader alternative modes of approaching this truth while simultaneously hinting that a clear formulation of such a truth may not in the end be possible. Brierly, Doramin, Chester, the German skipper, the French Lieutenant, Jim's father, Brown, Stein as well as Marlow himself are all more mature men than Jim whose styles form a pattern, inviting the reader to make analogies which may well be false. The first law of the epistemological wilderness is that the self is isolated and can know nothing beyond its own frontiers. But this novel is full of male characters who seem to assert the opposite: that the self is a comprehensible, socially determined entity, that Jim's difficulty is a matter of vanity, refusal to face facts, oversensitivity to criticism.

Marlow likes rogues, 'bad company'; he reminds the after-dinner group to whom he tells his story that they are 'respectable thieves of commerce', and of Jim's association with the officers of the *Patna* he remarks tolerantly that 'there are times when a man must act as though life were equally sweet in any company.' Marlow also likes Jim's company, and Jim likes Marlow's. Jim is deified in Patusan, 'Tuan' Jim, and this moral sanction enables him to impose an order which in turn reinforces the deification. In a more sophisticated way Jim 'worships' Marlow: Marlow is the point of reference in his mind which validates his own being, the man whose good opinion he must retain even after they have separated for the last time. And in still broader terms Marlow venerates Jim as emblematic man, reminding him of his youth's belief in the ideal of human solidarity now much flawed and battered by 'bad company': 'He came from the right place; he was one of us. He stood there for all the parentage of his kind.'

With the exception of Jim's father and Gentleman Brown the white males in the novel have much in common with each other. They are men of action, adventurers in a world heavily weighted in their favour by the late-Victorian expansion of Europe's commercial and political power. Divided though Conrad may seem about the morality of imperialism, in one sense this whole book is an expression of it: without the conditions created by imperialism the setting for *Lord Jim* and the code of virtue by which Jim measures himself—the unspoken code which is never formulated—would vanish, and the underlying assumption of *Lord Jim* is to that extent identical with the code of Kipling's subalterns and schoolboys who are being trained to survive and conduct themselves well as imperial administrators. He looks like one of Kipling's 'clean-run' subalterns and he has gone wrong initially by deserting his *country*, not his ship: by taking exployment with a 'native-owned' in preference to a British line.

Yet it would plainly be wrong to suggest that the high Victorian ideal of empire is in some sense, even unconsciously, the final moral referent of *Lord Jim*. It may well be the hidden ultimate referent of the intensely self-regarding Brierly; it is possible that after witnessing Jim's humiliation Brierly sees Jim's failure to live up to the imperial ideal reflected in himself, and finds the experience intolerable. But if this is true of Brierly it is no more applicable to Jim's own inner struggle than are the French Lieutenant's rigid code of honour or the tame domestic English Christianity of Jim's father. In any case, since life is process and a 'destructive element', no code can be final. In this case the visible expression of the authority of empire is as ugly as Gentleman Brown's quasi-imperial rapacity: the court of which Brierly is a member is a cold and ungenerous mechanism, with a chief magistrate who looks like a dying invalid. The chill of the courtroom and the pallor of this magistrate are contrasted with the joyous indifference of life outside, the brilliant sunshine, the smells and clamour of an eastern port.

If there is an ultimate moral referent for Jim we need not look for it in the values and order laid down for the British Empire. Yet it is obvious—indeed, it is a truism without which the novel could not exist—that Jim perceives himself as a moral being.

One way to express Jim's experience is to see it in religious terms as a private revelation, binding but incommunicable. Marlow's anxiety in his presence goes to support this: 'He was not speaking to me, he was only speaking before me, in a dispute with an invisible personality, an antagonistic and inseparable partner of his existence—another possessor of his soul. . . . He appealed to all sides at once—to the side turned perpetually to the light of day, and to that side of us which, like the other hemisphere of the moon, exists stealthily in perpetual darkness, with only a fearful ashy light falling at times on the edge.'

Marlow senses that Jim has access to a moral and psychological truth, something that both enables him to see a 'moral order' beside which all manmade codes look like interim and clumsy mechanisms, and also brings into play the whole of his (and Marlow's) being, the daylight self and the 'other hemisphere'. One might object that Conrad's language is rhapsodically inexplicit at this point, but it seems to me that the diction is exactly right for Marlow's temperament as it responds to Jim: the 'style' in both senses is appropriate. The discomfort and mixed feelings, the embarrassed use of 'Inconceivable' are consistent with what one intuits of Marlow. His pain here is the pain of a rational man exposed to a friend who has had a religious experience.

The right order of things exists only in Jim's head, locked up with his private revelation. His good work in Patusan is an approximation to that order, and certainly owes much to the way both empires and ships should be governed in the real world— Doramin and Dain Waris as first and second mates, Jim as the heroic young skipper—but it transcends both these models. Jim is Christ-like, forgiving Brown, refraining from the use of power, unapproachable. Marlow tells his story as hagiographers recorded the lives of the saints, because its central figure was distinguished by remarkable action and has access to an inner truth. The book itself, the product of the pragmatic narrator's attempt to organise the records of a man now dead, is like a gospel or even a church, a meeting place between sacred and secular, between men caught in the web of circumstance and the isolated self which has received an intense, transfiguring illumination.

If Jim is finally unknowable, can the view of the novel as a *Bildungsroman* hold? Certain aspects of him, his movement from unsuccessful to successful arenas of action and his growth from boy to man are confidently grasped by Marlow's consciousness. As he discusses him with Stein he calls Jim 'the youngest human being now in existence' and speaks of the 'insolence' of his youth: 'Youth *is* insolent; it is its right—its necessity; it has got to assert itself, and all assertion in this world of doubts is a defiance, an insolence.' As he takes leave of Jim in chapter 23 Marlow becomes aware that Jim has been becoming adult through his reversals, that his youthfulness is receding. They are intimate 'as though his risk set off against my years had made us more equal in age and in feeling. . . . He exerted himself to soothe me as though he had been the more mature of the two.'

On the *Patna* and in the subsequent jobs that Marlow has made shift to find for him—with Denver in the rice mill, in Bangkok with Yucker, as water-clerk in various far-Eastern ports—Jim is the victim, the bound man whose actions are determined.

In Patusan he is at last a free man asserting his own will. The difference is immediately registered. The boy who lacked the will to join the cutter from the training-ship or to stick to his duty on the *Patna* becomes the man who discovers the instinctive will to rescue himself from the murderous old Rajah Allang by leaping over a palisade. He then runs like a machine until he finds himself buried in mud in a creek, and with his eyeballs, 'bursting' and chest straining he demonstrates a primitive will to survive, 'culminating in one mighty supreme effort in the darkness to crack the earth asunder, to throw it off his limbs—and he felt himself creeping feebly up the bank.' He reenacts in his own person the evolutionary struggle and is reborn from the slime a mature and self-determining man.

To explore further the use of freedom in the novel is to come up against a paradox. Freedom brings responsibility which in turn brings a new kind of bondage: 'The land, the people, the friendship, the love, were like the jealous guardians of his body. Every day added a link to the fetters of that strange freedom.' . . .

The normal attributes of human success have proved

short-lived. Stein strikes a match: '"Friend, wife, child", he said, slowly, gazing at the small flame—"phoo!" The match was blown out.'

In Stein's stoical view of the world it is right to detach oneself from human beings and collect butterflies. The butterfly is a perfectly adapted product of evolution: '"Look at the accuracy, the harmony. And so fragile! And so strong! And so exact! This is Nature—the balance of colossal forces. Every star is so—and every blade of grass stands *so*—and the mighty Kosmos in perfect equilibrium produces—this. This wonder; this masterpiece of Nature—the great artist."' Stein's chapter, the twentieth chapter of the novel, is the pivot of the structure, the axis on which are hung the two parts of the hinged diptych in which the two aspects of Jim, his youth and maturity, are presented. The image of the butterfly could be taken as making a point about the structure of the novel, with the identity of Jim held at its centre. The analogy can only be tentative, though, Stein's butterfly leading as it does to his carefully qualified account of man himself. Whereas the butterfly is perfectly adapted, man is 'amazing', an aberration in the creator's plan, 'making a great noise about himself, talking about the stars, disturbing the blades of grass.' His celebrated image of the 'destructive element' catches up the themes of survival and rebirth in the story of Jim: '"A man that is born falls into a dream like a man who falls into the sea. If he tries to climb out into the air as inexperienced people endeavour to do, he drowns— *nicht wahr?* . . . No! I tell you! The way is to the destructive element submit yourself, and with the exertions of your hands and feet in the water make the deep, deep sea keep you up."'

In this complicated metaphor the surface of the sea replaces the meeting-point of the 'colossal forces' as the point of balance, and man at this point of balance (replacing the butterfly) is held in his place by his own small action—his will—working with the destructive element to sustain himself by treading water.

Equally the destructive element is an image of the narrative itself, simultaneously dissolving and renewing the identity of Jim, the central figure. Marlow's problem is the problem of seeing Jim clearly. Stein helps to define the parameters of the problem. Man has a soaring and diving spirit, 'he wants to be a saint, and he wants to be a devil' and he is 'romantic, romantic' which is both good and bad. Marlow's problem is not exactly clarified by Stein's thinking, but the terms of the problem are extended. Listening to Stein, Marlow reflects that 'at that moment it was difficult to believe in Jim's existence', meaning his social existence—parson's son, sailor, disgraced exile—but that 'his imperishable reality came to me with . . . an irresistible force!' as though 'we had approached nearer to absolute Truth, while, like Beauty itself, floats elusive, obscure, half-submerged.' Jim's 'reality' has been the subject of Marlow's quest from the beginning: 'He was not—if I may so say so—clear to me.' This paragraph about Truth and Beauty is the most elusively phrased, and the least characteristic, of Marlow's inquiries into Jim's nature. Marlow is not helped, the phrases remain emblems of intangible standards borrowed from

Stein's reminder that man is Romantic: absolute Truth, Beauty itself are watchwords of literary romanticism. . . .

As disaster finally overtakes him Jim sits down to write to Marlow: 'It was then, I believe, he tried to write—to somebody— and gave it up. Loneliness was closing in on him' (Marlow considers briefly the possibility that Jim is writing to Stein, another instance of Marlow's modesty). Marlow and Jim have set up for themselves overlapping mythologies in which each is the central figure in the world-view of the other. If Jim is Marlow's foster-son, Marlow is for Jim the experienced judge of right action, a guarantor of the possibility of goodness in a fallen world, the man to whom he turns in his extremity. He seems to see his relationship with Marlow as mystical; the good conduct of his own life will permit him to 'keep in touch with' a man whom he will never see again. But loneliness closes in; the novel leaves Jim at the moment of his death isolated, out of Marlow's reach. It finally communicates the bleakest and most central of Conrad's insights, the ultimate loneliness of human beings.

Freedom and bondage, pragmatism and romanticism, isolation and solidarity, order and worship; ostensibly *Lord Jim*'s diptych form holds in balance the contrasting elements of these linked antitheses. In the experience of reading, though, the last emphasis always falls on romanticism, isolation, self-worship and freedom *in* bondage. The balance of idealism and action is not a real balance; it is the idealism in which we are interested, and the subjective presentation of idealism and the problems which it has created that yields Conrad's most vivid and strenuous writing.

Notes

1. See J. H. Buckley, *Season of Youth: The Bildungsroman from Dickens to Golding* (1974).
2. See R. R. Hodges, *The Dual Heritage of Joseph Conrad* (1967).
3. See the rather different but very interesting discussion of the novel's self-referential features in Jeremy Hawthorn, *Joseph Conrad: Language and Fictional Self-Consciousness* (1979).
4. See Raymond Williams, *The English Novel from Dickens to Lawrence* (1974), Irving Howe, *Politics and the Novel* (1957), Eloise Knapp Hay, *The Political Novels of Joseph Conrad* (1963), Jeffrey Meyers, *Fiction and the Colonial Experience* (1973).
5. See Tom Gibbons, *Rooms in the Darwin Hotel*, and above, p. 3.
6. C. B. Cox, *Joseph Conrad: The Modern Imagination* (1974), p. 46.
7. Bernard Meyer, *Joseph Conrad: A Psychoanalytic Biography* (1967).
8. E. K. Hay, *The Political Novels of Joseph Conrad* (1963), p. 1.
9. See K. K. Ruthven, 'The Savage God: Conrad and Lawrence', *Critical Quarterly* 10, 1 and 2 (Spring and Summer 1968), pp. 39–54.
10. See Ruthven, op. cit.
11. 'dropped', 1946, 'drooped' Ms. and modern editions.
12. Robert Kimbrough, private communication: editor of the Norton Critical Edition of *Heart of Darkness* (1971). This point is perhaps weakened by the fact that the measurements refer, of course, to the *width*, not the length, of the barrels, and Conrad may well have made these changes simply because six-inch guns were the appropriate armoury for a small gun-boat. (I am indebted to John Bayley for this *caveat*.)

BARON CORVO
Frederick Rolfe
1860–1913

Frederick William Serafino Austin Lewis Mary Rolfe, known as Baron Corvo, was born in London on July 22, 1860. He left school and his strict Protestant family at age fourteen. Rolfe taught and tutored until 1886, when he converted to Catholicism. He studied for the priesthood from 1887 to 1888 at St. Mary's College, Oscott, and from 1889 to 1890 at Scots College in Rome. He was expelled from each institution for non-payment of debts and "lack of vocation."

Rolfe moved to the Italian *palazzo* of the Duchess Sforza-Cesarini, whom he later claimed had recognized him as her long-lost grandson and given him the title of Baron Corvo. For the rest of his life, Corvo would dress eccentrically, favoring vaguely Middle Eastern garb; work little, preferring to live off the largess of wealthy patrons (and often living in poverty as a result); and write prolifically, most notably for the celebrated *Yellow Book*. His first published work was a long poem about a boy martyr, *Tarcissus*, which appeared when he was twenty.

A Royal Literary Fund grant in 1902 enabled him to write his most popular novel, *Hadrian the Seventh*, an autobiographical fantasy which takes the Corvo figure from the priesthood to the Papacy. Corvo's work after the turn of the century included poetry, a history of the Borgias, a translation of Omar Khayyám, and many paintings and photographs. From 1908 to 1913 Corvo lived in Venice, sometimes on a gondola (in London in the 1890's he had lived on a sandhill). He wrote several books with explicitly homosexual themes that were published after his death on October 26, 1913.

Personal

Ten years of desultory suffering followed upon Rolfe's adoption of literature as a profession. His work was widely applauded, but brought him little money; for not only circumstances, but his own nature, fought against him. The rejection of his clerical ambitions, and his consciousness of being a man apart, had combined to produce a chronic sense of persecution and injustice which made him bitterly suspicious of all men, and resentfully ungrateful to those who befriended him. Henry Harland, Trevor Haddon, Sholto Douglas and a dozen others who put themselves out to assist the struggling author found themselves, after a time, treated as enemies instead of friends, for, like those credulous believers who see an omen in every chance event, Rolfe saw the hand of an enemy in every misfortune, and where he saw an enemy, he struck. He wasted time and temper in unnecessary quarrels, and began to be shunned as a malevolent ingrate.

Yet during that decade of his London career he wrote some remarkable books, only now beginning to find their mead of praise and appreciation: *Chronicles of the House of Borgia*, an historical study shot with tart epigrams and curious knowledge; *Don Tarquinio*, an account of twenty-four hours in the life of a young nobleman in the company of the Borgia, A.D. 1495; *In His Own Image*, described as 'the most amazing, fantastical, whimsical, bizarre, erratic and harebrained of books'; a translation of Omar into 'diaphotick verse'; and, above all, *Hadrian the Seventh*. Elsewhere I have paid full tribute to Rolfe's masterpiece, one of the most remarkable books in the English language. Those who have not read it are fortunate, in that their first reading is still to come. It is autobiography dramatized, and portrays 'Fr. Rolfe's' early life as he wished it to be remembered, and his future years as he would have liked them to be. *Hadrian* was too excellent to be disregarded; it was, indeed, widely praised, but brought no money to its harassed

writer, who retired to Oxford to act as secretary to the one friend with whom he never quarrelled, Dr Hardy, the late principal of Jesus College, Oxford.

It was at this point in Rolfe's life (1905, 1906) that he began the friendships with Mgr. Robert Hugh Benson and Mr C. H. C. Pirie-Gordon, which led to his last work, the present book. Collaborations in literary projects were started with both the new-found friends, but, like all Rolfe's friendships, these were not made to last; and the break came when 'Fr. Rolfe,' after being taken by another friend to Italy for a month's holiday, fell so much in love with Venice and Venetian life that he flatly refused to return to England. Instead, he settled down in a Venetian hotel, ignored his mounting bill, and appealed for help to his friends at home. Help was offered on condition that he returned to England, a condition with which he flatly refused to comply. His letters became more frequent and more abusive, till at last they were destroyed unopened by Benson. Even his relations with his solicitors, whom he had persuaded into making him an allowance pending the decision of a lawsuit and the expected success of one of his books, came to an end in a shower of comically bitter correspondence, and Rolfe was left penniless in Venice.

After a time he was turned out of his hotel; later he managed to secure fresh credit; later still he was turned out again. He became a byword among the English residents, both for his ingratitude, his poverty, and a suspicion of his perversion.—A. J. A. SYMONS, "Introduction" to *The Desire and Pursuit of the Whole*, 1934, pp. vi–vii

I am sure he had some cause for paranoia: he was shabbily treated by R. H. Benson, and by some others. But there is a converse to the dictum with which I began this note, and it is this: 'Remember that people who feel persecuted have usually done something to be persecuted for'. Perhaps not much: but something. And perhaps a great deal. I think no one can read

Victor Hall's account of the rise and fall of the friendship between Mrs van Someren, her husband and Rolfe, without feeling that hers is the word to accept.

The paranoid personality very often has the power to give a significant, penetrating quality to literary expression. This can be very clear and brilliant, as in the case of Rolfe, clear and heavy, as in the case of Martin Luther, or insistent and turgid, as in the case of Hitler: but the quality is much the same. It is surprisingly easy when reading Rolfe to accept him on his own valuation: to accept even the screams of revenge, of abuse, of denunciation. One feels there must be something in it.

And, of course, there is: there is black tragedy in it, his personal tragedy, none the less to him because it was so largely self-wrought. *The Desire and Pursuit of the Whole, Hadrian the Seventh, Nicholas Crabbe*, they are very tragical mirth, hot ice, and wondrous strange snow. In the world of his own creation, he is very much the hero: so much so, that all the rest are the merest supporting players. No one can stand up to him. The terrible little man towers a mile high out of the desert of his own life.

I am not sentimental enough to think that had Rolfe and I known each other, we should have rubbed along nicely; to think that I might have been the one person to understand him; mine the hand to remain unbitten. His English friends in Venice seem to me to have been marvels of patience; I should not have done half so well as they. Yet, with a year between my birth and his death, I feel safe in admitting his attraction for me. Like most paranoiacs, he achieves a real touch of splendour.—Pamela Hansford Johnson, "The Fascination of the Paranoid Personality," *New Quests for Corvo*, eds. Cecil Woolf and Brocard Sewell, 1961, p. 9

General

What is it about Corvo that compels us to become his enthusiasts? Not that we number so many in our ranks! Although there is an increasing readership for *Hadrian*, we ought not to exaggerate the actual number of people who have read any, let alone all, of the works of Corvo. Despite the fact that *The Quest* has gone through many editions, and in its Penguin form, has reached hundreds of thousands of readers, this wonderful book *about* Corvo has not brought very many readers *to* Corvo or to the narrow shelf of his books. In all likelihood, the number of actual Corvinists (those who have a strong and devoted interest in Corvo) is still extremely limited, perhaps to less than two hundred readers and collectors.

Here, perhaps, is an indication of part of the answer to our question. Corvo's life must always occupy the centre of the stage. Despite the exquisite refinement of his style, his unusual perception of colours and shapes and movements, the fullness of his research, the utter individuality of his characters, and the stark revelation of intense emotions which characterize his best writing, none of his works could ever have achieved for him the place that he aspired to reach, and that he *has* reached through the fascination of his life-story. Perhaps only *Hadrian* (and that only in part—the chapters dealing with Sant and Mrs Crowe are far less effective and meaningful than the enduring portrait of Rolfe-Rose) has some seeds of imperishable appeal. And even (or especially) *Hadrian* has an attenuated significance if the book is read without close knowledge of the life-story which forms its background.

Rolfe-Corvo will never achieve major status in any history of literature. His books are, at the best, for the delectation of those who like the unusual taste, who share some of the author's tendency towards the bizarre and the peculiar. If they

had been written by another sort of person, a natural sort of man, a family man, with a normal household composed of wife and children, and with all the accoutrements and encumbrances of middle-class respectability, I doubt that there would be very much interest in them or in their author. But that would be impossible, because only Corvo could have needed to write the books as they were written: the wish-fulfilment of an unbearably frustrated man.

It is the fantastic and unbelievable life of the man himself that binds Corvinists to him. The books are important largely because they reveal the man, the twisted soul, the tormented spirit, the emotional cripple. Rolfe-Corvo might have been, rather than a writer, an artist, or a chemist, a poet, or a photographer, and still he would fascinate us (presuming that he had persisted in his blessed habit of letter-writing!) Or he might have been a physician, or a student of Egyptian hieroglyphics, or an authority on North American Indian mythology. The net result would still have been Rolfe-Corvo: the man against the world, against convention, not in any picayune way, but writ large against the sky. Only Corvo of all the misguided originals ever known could have conceived himself as Supreme Pontiff!

I have difficulty in finding a label for our small fraternity of Corvo-enthusiasts (so did those who organized the Corvine Society). We are not devotees, or disciples, or followers. Far from it! Who could or would aspire to emulate the personality and character of this homosexual-ingrate-wretch! Yet there *is* an emotional tie to him, I am certain, stronger by far than the somewhat generalized respect and admiration we have for a Wordsworth or a Browning. Can any single word describe what we feel towards Corvo? What happens, I suspect, is that his life-story touches a complicated chord in our inner being, and reaches into the (largely unconscious) pool of our own fears, wishes, loyalties, aggressions, and apprehensions.

Corvo is, perhaps, attractive to some of us because we wish that we were free to become Corvo-like. Every shred of logic and reason and common-sense and conscience we possess holds us back, so we continue to act out our conventional, respectable rôles. But we have discovered a perverse (and, I think, unconscious) pleasure in identifying ourselves with this man who refused to submit to any sort of compromise, who insisted that the world and its people and institutions had to revolve around him, who tossed away every chance of material success and comfort because he persisted in being himself. We all, many times, particularly to-day when international unrest impinges upon every thoughtful person's mind, want to escape from the real world and its real problems, to run away and to live in a world of our own making; we dare not, and we know that it is not even possible, because our real problems are within us. But Corvo was different—it was his problems (the result of his peculiar psychological make-up) which helped him escape from the world and live his own utterly selfish life, while damning everything that stood in his path. Still, in a way, we who curb our anger and smother our hostility, we who refrain from taking advantage of others, we who show consideration for our neighbours, must secretly envy Corvo's ability to treat others as dust.

But I must not press this aspect of Corvo's appeal too far. Perhaps we are more aware of another facet: the attraction of Rolfe-Corvo to our pity and compassion for the under-dog, the disenfranchised, the disinherited, the friendless. Corvo's need for help was so self-evident that it drew many people towards him, people who were to rue the day they ever touched the life of this man, half-genius, half-demon, who was prepared to squeeze his benefactors dry to the last guinea, and was willing to give in return only the wit of his conversation, the privilege of assisting a needy writer, and the opportunity to submit to his own dominating personality. Very possibly there are Corvinists to-day who would be willing to be dehydrated by this man (we are surely being impoverished by the prices asked and obtained for his manuscripts and autograph letters); but he is dead . . . so we pay the homage of the present to the man from the past in the only way we know. Even more, in a certain sense, I think we expiate society's guilt towards this man for whom no secure place could be found in his entire life-time. Neither the Church, nor the world of scholarship, nor the market-places of literature would accept his gifts of talent, passion, and creativity. Somewhere there should have been a way and a haven for him to live and work—yet I cannot imagine what it might be, unless in some library perhaps, with a vast store of mediaeval manuscripts and relics, and with a chief not too importunate for speed in cataloguing and filing. So we make up to Corvo, atone to him, in a sense, for all the care which he was denied in life.—RABBI BERTRAM W. KORN, "The Anatomy of Corvinism," *New Quests for Corvo*, eds. Cecil Woolf and Brocard Sewell, 1961, pp. 65–68

Works

Rolfe's first literary effort, *Stories Toto Told Me* (1898), was a retelling of the Lives of the Saints by a fascinating Sicilian boy. Its bizarre style and quaint originality was praised by the discerning, and more *Toto* stories appeared in 1901 under the title *In His Own Image*. The same year saw the publication of the extraordinary *Chronicles of the House of Borgia*. The book revealed both Rolfe's pedantry and his poetic imagination, his great sympathy for the classical learning of the Italian Renaissance and the boldness of his ingenious historical surmises. It was an essay in a new way of writing history; the style is brilliantly epigrammatic, the vocabulary orchidacious, full of fancy coinages and strikingly vivid images, the spellings individual, the system of punctuation highly original.

Brilliant and original as these writings were, from the monetary point of view they were complete failures. By 1903 Rolfe had reached the zenith of despair. He lived day and night with the horror of being turned out into the street. Then an event occurred (the death of the Pope) which not only fired the smouldering faggots of his imagination into incandescent flame, but in doing so gave to English literature a unique novel—*Hadrian the Seventh* (1904). Since his conversion Rolfe had remained true to his own supreme desire to become a priest, and he suspected a conspiracy of stupidity, error and ill-will frustrating him. Now the papacy was vacant what had been denied him in life could be realized a hundredfold in imagination. Scorned by authority for the humble office of priest, he would show how admirably fitted he would be, as Pope Hadrian VII, to occupy the throne of Christ's vicegerent on earth.

This remarkable novel, simpler in style than anything he had written so far, is a piece of literary exhibitionism representing the fulfilment of a secret wish organized in dramatic form. All Rolfe could never be was projected into the idealized self-portrait of George Arthur Rose, raised to the papacy after living for many years as an excommunicant. The book fulfilled a dual purpose. It enabled Rolfe in imagination to take an exquisite revenge on all his ecclesiastical enemies, who are mercilessly satirized, and to glorify himself in the person of Hadrian—enlightened, tolerant, urbane, still possessed of a feline wit, and with a strange power of detecting cunning and hypocrisy in the minions of the Church. Rolfe's special knowledge of Church procedure was shown in the chapter describing a

Roman Conclave. The new Pope's philosophy is that of the personal responsibility of the individual. He proclaims the dogma of Equality as scientifically, historically and obviously false and impracticable, a diabolic delusion for the ruin of the soul. He astonishes the world by an Epistle to all Christians, and shows his unworldliness by selling the Vatican treasure for a vast sum, which he gives to the poor. Hadrian's career of spiritual glory is abruptly terminated by the machinations of a repulsive socialist agitator, who, failing in an attempt at blackmail, shoots the Pope as he is returning to the Vatican. His epitaph is one that Rolfe would have chosen for himself: "Pray for the repose of His soul. He was so tired."—S. DIANA NEILL, "Aesthetes and Social Realists," *A Short History of the English Novel*, 1951, pp. 251–52

What a genius for folly Rolfe had! It makes his literary gifts look commonplace, though he gave to his novels all the store of curious learning, all the gorgeous but off-hand style, all the headlong and self-betraying fancy that hard and careful work could stimulate. To everyone who tried to befriend him as he capered and agonized across the *fin de siècle*, he opened the treasuries of his hatred: you would shelter him, or pay his bills, and there would be scenes, with Rolfe pitiless in his shabbiness and hunger; there would be letters, endless, complicated letters, letters full of heartfelt obscenity, letters full of cold analysis that might almost make you believe you had acted from the foulest motives, letters to your family, neighbors, superiors; then there would be what Rolfe called his "severe postcards"; there would be novels, with your name slightly altered.

The Desire and Pursuit of the Whole is such a novel, a love story. It was Rolfe's last book, carefully written while he was starving in Venice; after he died in 1913, the four manuscripts of it, all done out in the fine calligraphy he was so proud of, were locked away in England—simply unpublishable under the libel laws—until his biographer, A. J. A. Symons, found them. This is its first publication in America. Even now one character has had to be edited.

The title is Plato's definition of love, taken from his allegory of the incompleteness of the single soul; the incomplete pursuer is Rolfe himself, under the name of Nicholas Crabbe. Crabbe, his fortune in the hands of disloyal lawyers and a crooked, implacable priest in England, robbed and ostracized by the English colony in Venice, patiently writing letters to the plotters, living on a few pennies' worth of breadstuffs a day and sleeping at night in a moored gondola, is in love. He loves Venice, and he loves a young gondolier, a strange beautiful creature called Zildo. Zildo is technically a 17-year-old girl, but is as flat and muscled as a boy, and has been raised as a boy. Crabbe has saved him-her from an earthquake; and the poor orphan becomes at first his bodyservant and at last—still in boy's habit—his Completing Half.

Thus this is three simultaneous books: the reverie of a homosexual, the revenge of a paranoiac, and the impressions of an Englishman in Venice. Apparently there is no question that Rolfe was a homosexual paranoiac and a brilliant writer. There is something wrong, though, with Rolfe's paranoia. It is true that he conferred on himself the title of Baron Corvo of Corvicastro; that he abbreviated his name "Fr. Rolfe" in hopes of being taken for a priest (he had tried twice to be ordained); that he claimed poor Kaiser Wilhelm for his godfather; that he wore a ring with a sharp metal spur on it with which he was going to tear the faces of the "bravos" the Catholic hierarchy was sending to kidnap him, so they could be recognized by their scars and caught. Those were theatricals, not madness; and they suggest that the paranoia itself was largely theatrical, a device for shocking. The distortion in the book is too regular; the effect of a madman's vision is too perfect; there is no breaking of the voice, no real cry for help.

Rolfe, with his quaint style tricked up from lexicons, was not a *very* brilliant writer, but this is a fascinating book, showing us a man diligently becoming what we all hate and fear, and thus showing us ourselves.—DONALD BARR, "A Definition of Love," *NYTBR*, July 19, 1953, p. 4

In all the literature of curiosa few twentieth-century books are as permanently entrenched as Frederick Baron Corvo's *Hadrian The Seventh*, which made its third appearance in this country last month. (Written in 1904, it was first published here in 1925.) Although formally *Hadrian the Seventh* is a novel, in actuality it is a rather thickly disguised autobiography, based on the author's astounding capacity for wishful thinking.

The hero—and no character has ever been more accurately labeled—is one George Arthur Rose, an Englishman who once studied for the priesthood, only to be expelled from the seminary and then—twenty years later—belatedly called to Holy·Orders and elected to the Papacy. It requires a singularly impish sense of humor to imagine an Englishman as Pope, but Baron Corvo is up to it. He himself is the unsuccessful half of George Arthur Rose—the divinity student who is sent home. But in *Hadrian the Seventh* he becomes Pope, and in this sense the book is pure fantasy. George Arthur Rose is Walter Mitty born fifty years too soon.

Not to reform the church (to which he was attached only in the most neurotic sense), as he pretended to do, but to release his paranoia—that was Corvo's purpose, and one to which he succeeded in the manner of a man excising an ingrown toenail. Yet for all its interest as a reflection of a sick mind, Baron Corvo's novel has its own scheme of values. It does, in a somber but no less sensational way, what "The Cardinal" did in throwing open the back doors of the Church, admitting us to the politics of the Vatican, as he imagined them. Its style is variously mock-heroic and sardonic ("the sour oppressive septic odour of architectural and waxen human antiquity," he could write of the Sistine Chapel), its characters twisted into shape by Corvo's overbearing ego until they stand out like those gargoyles which are found on both German pipes and French cathedrals. There is too much spitefulness in *Hadrian the Seventh* to make it an *ex cathedra* study of the Papacy. As a pipe dream, however, it is quite admissible and it will survive as one of the most preposterous stories ever written.—DAVID DEMPSEY, "Repeat Performances," *NYTBR*, Dec. 8, 1953, p. 31

Frederick Rolfe's "spoiled priest" and self-appointed Baron Corvo, was a literary con man who had better luck at victimizing patrons than at negotiating with publishers. The latter are the targets of this satirical novel, which now appears in print for the first time although its author died as long ago as 1913. Publication of the book had to wait until the models for its principal characters had passed beyond the possibility of lawsuits.

In the present novel there is none of the brilliant fantasy that distinguishes Corvo's best book, *Hadrian the Seventh*, and the tone of *Nicholas Crabbe* is often annoyingly nasty. But in spite of the usual quota of archaisms and Corvo-minted words, the narrative is for the most part lively, and the story contains some highly readable sardonic episodes. Among other things, it provides new information about Corvo's own life, subject of one of the most piquant literary biographies of our time, A. J. A. Symons' *The Quest for Corvo*.

The autobiographical Crabbe appears elsewhere in Corvo, notably in his Venetian romance, *The Desire and Pursuit of the Whole* (first published 1934). *Nicholas Crabbe*, an earlier work probably written in 1905, is set in London at the turn of the century. In this chronicle of persecutions, whatever sympathy is aroused for Crabbe he repeatedly loses through his eagerness to bristle at the rebuffs which are the lot of all except the most readily successful authors. It is hard to feel sorry for this odd crustacean of the Grub Street tideflats who has a habit of nipping the hand that feeds. Not that the publishers and editors in the story are willing to feed Crabbe much in the way of royalties. When they accept his work, for very low fees, they mutilate it or tormentingly delay its publication. Now Corvo has his posthumous revenge on the whole pack of them.

Students of the period will recognize more than one literary pundit in this lampoon. But Corvo-Crabbe will be remembered longest by the general reader. Despite his mockery of others and his self-pity, he manages to project very strikingly the *fin de siècle* atmosphere; and the strutting little *littérateur* in his quest after the Divine Friend, has the magnetism of the pathetically comic.—HARRY T. MOORE, "Strutting Litterateur," *NYT*, Feb. 15, 1959, p. 18

During a brief period of creative energy Rolfe wrote some half-dozen novels, but several of them were so abnormal or so libellous that publishers were afraid to accept them. The second that got into print was *Don Tarquinio*, an historical romance recording one day in the life of a Roman patrician at the end of the fifteenth century. Rolfe had previously published a massive history of the Borgias, based upon laborious research; and some of the same material lends authenticity to the novel, which is presented as a transcript of the hero's memoirs, written in his older years. Described on the title page as "A Kataleptic Phantasmatic Romance," it depicts a versatile young political outlaw, a great athlete and a great lover, who hobnobs with Lucrezia Borgia, rescues her brother Cesare from captivity, and wins the patronage of their father, Pope Alexander VI. Rolfe's gift for sensuous description of physical beauty, particularly color and texture, was never shown to better advantage than in such passages as his picture of Indian boatmen whose flesh "resembled the color of a field of ripe wheat when some delicate zephyr sways the stems in the sun, not more than half revealing poppies; but their eyes were like pools of ink, fathomless, upon glittering mother-o'-pearl," or of page boys who "in liveries resembling vermilion skins from toe to throat to wrist, bearing armorials on their tabards, displayed at the prow the double-cross, golden, and the high Estense gonfalon."

The only other novel by Rolfe published in his lifetime came out seven years later, when he was dying in Venice in miserable penury. Entitled *The Weird of the Wanderer*, and attributed to the joint authorship of "Prospero and Caliban" (Rolfe's contemptuous way of indicating that the idea had been suggested by one of his transient friends), it was an effort at necromantic fantasy in the manner of Machen or Blackwood. An Englishman named Nicholas Crabbe tries to establish communication with the dead through ancient Egyptian spells, and instead finds himself carried back into an earlier incarnation when he was Ulysses.

Rolfe gained virtually no recognition during his lifetime, and after his death he was promptly forgotten. Twenty years later, however, interest in his work began to stir, and eventually four of his manuscripts were put into print. One of them, *Hubert's Arthur*, was again attributed to "Prospero and Caliban," though in its final form it was obviously all written by

Rolfe. He attempts to revise history by imagining what would have happened if Prince Arthur, Duke of Brittany, had not been murdered by his uncle King John in 1203. The narrator, Hubert de Burgh, tells how he spirited the young prince away from the wicked king, after which Arthur killed another claimant to the throne in single combat, became monarch of England, and recovered Jerusalem from the infidels. According to A. J. A. Symons, who prepared the book for publication, the style was "meant to be an enriched variant upon that of the *Itinerarium Regis Ricardi* and of William of Tyre, with an admixture of Maurice Hewlett." When occasionally a modern colloquialism intrudes, there is always a footnote giving the supposed original Latin phrase. Rolfe's prejudices were so strong that his portraits of historical characters are fully as virulent as those of his personal enemies in his other books.

Of the other recovered manuscripts the earliest in date of composition, though the last to be published, was *Don Renato*, perhaps written even before *Hadrian the Seventh*. Like *Don Tarquinio*, it claims to be a translation of a manuscript journal, written early in the sixteenth century in a macaronic jargon of Italian, Latin, and Greek. This pretense justifies Rolfe in parading his most egregiously precious vocabulary, entailing the provision of a glossary to define such words as "galbanate," "lacertose," and "hestern," as well as pedantic footnotes and a long introduction discussing the sources and inspiration of the book and the author's theory of historical fiction. The narrator of the story is a superstitious, pedantic, sybaritic priest, "a verbose, genial busybody," as the author calls him; and his "diurnal" gives an amazingly plausible impression of life in the heyday of the Italian renaissance.

The other two posthumous books are further installments of the fictionized autobiography that started with the early chapters of *Hadrian*. The hero's name has changed from George Arthur Rose to Nicholas Crabbe, but his personality is unaltered. Devoutly believing in astrology, Rolfe made a virtue of having been born under the sign of Cancer, claiming that the crab signified his tough shell, his inner softness, and his oblique manoeuvres. *Nicholas Crabbe, or The One and the Many* deals with the impecunious years in London while he was trying to establish himself as a professional author, and contains scurrilous caricatures of the editors and publishers whom he regarded as his persecutors. Rolfe kept a file of all his letters, and some of them are incorporated almost verbatim in the novel. The principal events concern a beautiful youth expelled from Oxford, whom the "grimly imperscrutable" but inwardly sensitive and affectionate Crabbe finds starving as a telegraph messenger and takes to his lodgings to be nursed through a temporary siege of blindness. Upon recovery the young man deserts his protector in favor of a rich officer in the Guards, leaving Crabbe penniless and in debt, "festering in his shell . . . all alone with The Alone."—LIONEL STEVENSON, "Elegant Wits, Cynical Satirists," *The History of the English Novel*, Vol. II, 1967, pp. 165–67

Rolfe was a student of literature, history, religious doctrine and language. He was also an astute observer of current affairs. Minor glimpses of this are caught in letters and articles, but *Hadrian* provided for him the scope for prophecy in the affairs of the world. The political unrest of major powers, terminating in a world war and revolution, is predicted. But the threads of upheaval do not end here. In a sense, Rolfe can be compared with Hitler. The doctor who diagnosed the disease which killed A. J. A. Symons in 1941 wrote to him about *Hadrian* during his last months: 'Hitler's Neuordnung bears an astonishingly close likeness to the ethnological settlement of Europe which Rolfe fathers on the Kaiser.' This parallel is not unfounded. Rolfe, as Hadrian and as himself, deplored Socialism. At the time he first became aware of it, Leo XIII had already embarked on his campaigns against the new 'religion'. Yet he lived to see Socialism and Communism spread across Europe. So heavy was its gain at the expense of Catholicism that, some years later, Hitler found himself in a position to defy the church, after he had, with the pope's aid, secured power.

Each character in the novel is a real person or some one Rolfe knew about in some way. Trevor Haddon appears as Alfred Elms, 'an English Catholic painter' arriving in Rome to set the pope's image on to canvas. 'Hadrian knew him for a vulgar and officious liar: detested him. . . . Also, He loathed the cad's Hercomeresque-cum-Camera-esque technique and his quite earthy imagination: from that palette, the spiritual, the intellectual, the noble, could not come.' Rolfe himself needed no camera to perpetuate the images of others. He needed nothing save his memory and the glowingly colourful words at his command.

Hadrian's first act in the story is to give the Blessing to the people of Rome, anticipating Pius XI by eighteen years. He consorts with world powers, prays in Greek, designs his own crucifix and lives on a few shillings a day. His thoughts are put down with his 'beloved Waterman.' When at last he is shot, one of his first thoughts is of Flavio, his little yellow cat. Reminiscent of the Nowt's assassination at Sewers End by the Saint (John Holden), Hadrian speaks to Sir John Devine (Holden again): 'Dear John, take this cross—and Flavio.' By the end of the book, Rose-Rolfe's *saison en enfer* has been unfolded with sparkling brilliance. The bright sunlight 'on warm grey stones, on the ripe Roman skins, on vermilion and lavender, and blue and ermine, and green and gold, on apostolic whiteness and the rose of blood' then becomes subdued in the hues of death. 'The bloodstain streamed down the Pope's white robes with the red stole of universal jurisdiction. The slender hand with the two huge rings ascended. The shy brown eyes fluttered; and were wide, and very glad.'

With all its blemishes, *Hadrian the Seventh* presents a truly living and breathing personality. With an embarrassing stutter at times, suddenly shrill-voiced or emotionally spouting as a man possessed, Rolfe never ceases to have something to say. The unevenness in the story is the natural unevenness of any one person's day-to-day life. Written at a time when Rolfe was employing make-up to appear younger than his forty-two years, Rose strikes out at his reflection: 'Strip, man, strip stark.' And in *Hadrian* Rolfe lays bare his naked soul. . . . Rolfe possesses the writer's greatest gift: timelessness in expression. This is true of all of his major books, save one. In *Nicholas Crabbe* he speaks as a new author, wanting 'to do a thing which would justify his reincarnation as a crustacean'. The only book of his which has not fully escaped the date of its composition is *The Weird of the Wanderer*, whose subject is reincarnation.

A departmental mind was one curiosity of his personality. Perhaps the best example of this involves his *Chronicles of the House of Borgia*. Its publication in 1901 entirely dissatisfied him and caused his friendship with the publisher, Grant Richards, to cease. Yet four years later, in July 1905, he wrote to Richards, asking 'if I can be of any assistance to you'. He asked that the past be forgotten and added, 'if my help in any other way would be useful, I should have liked you not to be embarrassed by any false delicacy about asking, for it'. In December he made a few possible publishing suggestions to Richards. He was sincerely trying to help and said: 'Please note that I am not concerned with this. I am merely . . . "voicing a felt want," in a hint which perhaps may be useful to you.' At the same time that these letters were written to Richards, Rolfe was meeting young Harry Luke at Oxford. Seeing a copy of his Borgia book on Luke's shelves, Rolfe inscribed in it: 'An insult to the public intelligence.'—DONALD WEEKS, "Introduction" to *Corvo*, 1971, pp. xi–xxix

The name of Frederick Rolfe is not commonly associated with poetry. Yet among the recollections of Rolfe by his contemporaries are a number of allusions to his considerable facility in writing verse, and in an obituary notice he is characterised as 'a poet whose lighter verse was seldom refused by the magazines'. But apart from one sonnet, reprinted in 1961, no specimen of his poetry is readily accessible and Rolfe students have hitherto passed it by with no more than casual attention.

. . . In the verses written in early youth, the immaturities can be explained by literary inexperience. They justify themselves as do the maiden efforts of any seriously considered writer. The later verse is harder to justify, particularly in view of Rolfe's mastery of prose; he probably believed that metre and rhyme lend to poetry a certain impact which prose is obliged to seek in other and less obvious ways. . . .

Certainly he is limited in range. The forms he chooses are brief. Like Swinburne, Austin Dobson and Dowson, he generally employs such difficult verse forms as the rondeau, the ballade and the sestina, developed by the French in the Middle Ages and popularized by Charles d'Orléans and François Villon. His longest poem is less than four pages. The pattern of rhymes of such old forms and the length and number of their lines are rigidly fixed by tradition, and demand the highest discipline. There is no denying the technical skill of some of the poems or their force or colour, though the phrasing here and there is rather awkward and stilted. Of the other defects of these verses it is unnecessary to speak, for they are obvious.

Looking at the poems broadly, we find numerous anticipations of what Rolfe was to say in later years. The poems have the same theological and historical themes that underlie and unify much of his maturer work. Substantially all of Rolfe's poems fall under the head of what could loosely be called religious poetry, one aspect of which is his consistent worship of beauty, both concrete and abstract. His favourite topic in the youthful verses is the boy saints of the early church. His appreciation of and delight in the vitality and appeal of boyhood are obviously deeply felt and often poetically expressed. His writing and painting reveal a constant fascination with the same subject. It is not surprising that he should have made boyhood a dominant theme in his verse, which shows a general preoccupation with innocence and 'purity'.

In truth the young Rolfe was not a poet. The real Rolfe is in his prose: in his novels and short stories and in his letters. Few of the poems can claim to be more than verse, but few are devoid of interest; they show him to be sensitive, perceptive, spiritual, earnest, and there is in several of them a sense of adventure and search, a youthful striving to explore a new area of literary expression. To judge them technically is of little purpose. They command our attention as an archaeological record, and it is the insight they provide of the evolution of a writer's mind that gives the collection its permanent value. For printing them, the authority of the author himself might be claimed; in one of his letters Rolfe said 'I always write for publication'.—CECIL WOOLF, "Introduction" to *Baron Corvo: Collected Poems*, 1974, pp. 11–13

GRAHAM GREENE
"Frederick Rolfe: Edwardian Inferno" (1934)
Collected Essays
1981, pp. 130–33

The obscurity and what we curiously believe to be the crudity and violence of the distant past make a suitable background to the Soul. Temptation, one feels, is seldom today so heroically resisted or so devastatingly succumbed to as in the days of Dante or of Milton; Satan, as well as sanctity, demands an apron stage. It is, therefore, with a shock of startled incredulity that we become aware on occasion even today of eternal issues, of the struggle between good and evil, between vice that really demands to be called satanic and virtue of a kind which can only be called heavenly.

How much less are we prepared for it in the Edwardian age, in the age of bicycles and German bands and gold chamber ware, of Norfolk jackets and deerstalker caps. How distressingly bizarre seems the whole angelic conflict which centered around Frederick Rolfe, self-styled Baron Corvo, the spoilt priest, who was expelled from the Scots College at Rome, the waster who lived on a multitude of generous friends, the writer of genius, author of *Hadrian the Seventh* and *Don Tarquinio* and *Chronicles of the House of Borgia*. When Rolfe's fictional self prayed in his Hampstead lodging:

> God, if ever You loved me, hear me, hear me. *De Profundis ad Te, ad Te clamavi.* Don't I want to be good and clean and happy? What desire have I cherished since my boyhood save to serve in the number of Your mystics? What but that have I asked of You Who made me? Not a chance do You give me—ever—ever—

it is disquieting to remember how in the outside world Mr Wells was writing *Love on Wheels*, the Empire builders after tiffin at the club were reading 'The Song of the Banjo', and up the crowded stairway of Grosvenor House Henry James was bearing his massive brow; disquieting too to believe that Miss Marie Corelli was only palely limping after truth when she brought the devil to London. For if ever there was a case of demonic possession it was Rolfe's: the hopeless piety, the screams of malevolence, the sense of despair which to a man of his faith was the sin against the Holy Ghost. 'All men are too vile for words to tell.'

The greatest saints have been men with more than a normal capacity for evil, and the most vicious men have sometimes narrowly evaded sanctity. Frederick Rolfe in his novel *Hadrian the Seventh* expressed a sincere, if sinister, devotion to the Church that had very wisely rejected him; all the good of which he was capable went into that book, as all the evil went into the strange series of letters which Mr Symons has described for the first time ⟨*The Quest for Corvo*⟩, written at the end of his life, when he was starving in Venice, to a rich acquaintance.

> He had become a habitual corrupter of youth, a seducer of innocence, and he asked his wealthy accomplice for money, first that he might use it as a temptation, to buy bait for the boys whom he misled, and secondly, so that he might efficiently act as pander when his friend revisited Venice. Neither scruple nor remorse was expressed or implied in these long accounts of his sexual exploits or enjoyments, which were so definite in their descriptions that he was

forced, in sending them by post, so to fold them that only blank paper showed through the thin foreign envelopes.

These were the astonishing bounds of Corvo: the starving pander on the Lido and the man of whom Mr Vincent O'Sullivan wrote to his biographer: 'He was born for the Church: that was his main interest.' Between these bounds, between the Paradise and the Inferno, lay the weary purgatorial years through which Mr Symons has been the first to track him with any closeness. Mr Symons's method, unchronological, following the story as he discovered it from witness to witness, lends Rolfe's vacillating footprints a painful drama. Continually, with the stamp of an obstinate courage, they turn back towards Paradise: from the rim of the Inferno they turn and go back: but on the threshold of Paradise they turn again because of the devilish pride which would not accept even Heaven, except on his own terms; this way and that, like the steps of a man pacing a room in agony of mind. It is odd to realize that all the time common-or-garden life is going on within hailing distance, publishers are making harsh bargains, readers are reporting adversely on his work, friends are forming hopeless plans of literary collaboration. Mr Grant Richards and Monsignor Benson and Mr Pirie-Gordon and the partners of Chatto and Windus beckon and speak like figures on the other side of a distorting glass pane. They have quite a different reality, much thinner reality, they are not concerned with eternal damnation.

And their memories of Rolfe are puzzled, a little amused, a little exasperated, as if they cannot understand the eccentricity of a man who chooses to go about sheathed in flame in the heyday of the Entente Cordiale, of Sir Ernest Cassel, and Lily Langtry.

Mr O'Sullivan wrote of Rolfe to Mr Symons as a man 'who had only the vaguest sense of realities', but the phrase seems a little inaccurate. His realities were less material than spiritual. It would be easy to emphasize his shady financial transactions, his pose as the Kaiser's god-son, his complete inability to earn a living. It is terrible to think what a figure of cruel fun a less imaginative writer than Mr Symons might have made of Rolfe, turned out of an Aberdeen boarding house in his pyjamas, painting pictures with the help of magic-lantern slides, forced to find employment as a gondolier, begging from strangers, addressing to the Pope a long indictment of living Catholics. But against this material reality Mr Symons with admirable justice sets another: the reality of *Hadrian the Seventh*, a novel of genius, which stands in relation to the other novels of its day, much as *The Hound of Heaven* stands in relation to the verse. Rolfe's vice was spiritual more than it was carnal: it might be said that he was a pander and a swindler, because he cared for nothing but his faith. He would be a priest or nothing, so nothing it had to be and he was not ashamed to live on his friends; if he could not have Heaven, he would have Hell, and the last footprints seem to point unmistakably towards the Inferno.

NOEL COWARD

1899–1973

Noel Coward was born on December 16, 1899 in Teddington, Middlesex. He acted professionally as early as 1911 and wrote his first play, *The Rat Trap*, at the age of twenty. In 1920 he appeared in the first production of his play *I'll Leave it to You*. But not until *The Vortex*, which appeared in 1924, did Coward receive popular acclaim. He authored and appeared in the play, which was staged in Hampstead. By the standards of its day the play, which concerned an alcoholic, probably verged on indecency. It was an overnight sensation, however, and moved quickly to London where Coward established himself as both a playwright and actor.

Perhaps his most famous play, *Cavalcade*, opened in 1931. The play was closely rivalled by *Blithe Spirit* which ran for nearly 2,000 performances. Coward was as eclectic as he was prolific. Aside from writing no less than fifty plays, he also penned some twenty-five films, numerous songs and poems, a ballet, two autobiographies, a novel, and several volumes of short stories. He held a post in the Enemy Propaganda Office in Paris during World War II, and in 1943 appeared in London as a highly-successful cabaret entertainer. He continued to write and act steadily virtually up until the time of his death on March 26, 1973.

Personal

He always had the gift of being able to plunge into a conversation or to start one when silence fell at a luncheon or dinner table. Most of us avoid the subject when introduced to, say, someone who has had a leg amputated; but not Noel, who would immediately say, 'Tell me, *how* did you come to lose your leg?' and he was right, the other person was invariably quite happy to tell him. At this same Garden Party he noticed that Queen Mary, when he was presented to her, hesitated slightly for something to say and as usual he plunged. Anything. 'How beautiful the gardens look, Ma'am. I've never seen anything so lovely,' and they were off—to the Queen's relief, he felt. From then on there was never any shyness between them. Years later, when Princess Elizabeth and Prince Philip gave their first dinner-party at Clarence House and he found himself next to Queen Mary at table, he broached, of all things, the subject of the Abdication and asked the question he had been longing to ask: 'Is it true, Ma'am, that you said, "Here's a pretty kettle of fish"?' She said, 'Yes, I think I did,' and from then on, he said, they had a lovely time. They must have had, because Queen Mary also asked him to sit next to her during the film shown after dinner, and later Queen Elizabeth the Queen Mother told him she had telephoned the next day to say how much she had enjoyed Mr Coward's company, and what a bright and clever young man he was. This pleased him greatly, being fifty-two at the time.—COLE LESLEY, "Tonight at Eight-Thirty", *Remembered Laughter*, 1976, p. 175

General

The versatility of the man makes me gasp. It is, perhaps, or certainly, a perilous versatility. To compose and sing and play; to write and act and produce; these are strangely diversified if cognate gifts. To use them all at will without showing the amateur in any is to be in one mind and body a Ministry of All the Talents. Before long Noel Coward will have to pick one gift and make the utmost of that. Otherwise he must fritter genius away in multiplying talent. Meanwhile the absurd richness of endowment is a cause for envious admiration.

I am excited by the adventurous youth in what he does and how he does it. It seems to be drawn from an unfathomable well of young daring, and it is likely that the Noel Coward of sixty five will be as debonair and reckless as the Coward of to-day.

He has brought new life to the British theatre and new arrangements to the English language.

He is young and strong and brilliant, armoured in self-confidence, but independent and thinking for himself.

With it all he is learning to be merciful.—*SR*, Jan. 28, 1933, p. 92

Almost from the beginning Noel Coward, chief patentee of the dramatic possibilities of his times, hated what he was dealing in. Not all the time, of course; he is occasionally subject to a natural clannish admiration for the insouciant glitter of jazz-age high jinks. He can be almost dazzled by the smarter aspects of post-war "sophistication" as if he had borrowed the romanticizing spectacles of Michael Arlen. It is the presence of this element of admiration which bewilders the spectator when *Design for Living* is labelled satire. However its characters malign themselves, they are the standard Coward types of *Private Lives*, rather more sentimentalized, and their creator is very fond of them. Yet this comradely enjoyment of his contemporaries' flippancies often carries over into a frenetic horror of the galvanic, tinselled recklessness of the world that succeeded the war. It was his vibration between these two points of view and his competence in expressing both which made him versatile in spirit as well as in technique.—J. C. FURNAS, "The Art of Noel Coward," *FR*, Dec. 1933, p. 710

Works

DRAMA

The Vortex was the first play in which Mr. Coward showed signs of more feeling and thought than are to be found in a charade. His earlier plays left on the minds of those who saw them an impression of hasty improvisation. They seemed to have been written in a great hurry by a fluent and unusually quick-witted young man whose knowledge of life was considerably less than his ability to laugh at it. One could suppose them to have been thrown together on a wet afternoon to amuse the younger members of a country house-party. But *The Vortex* was a play of a different sort from those early pieces, and the public was quick to see the difference. It had not given much support to the early flippancies, but it gave a great deal of support to *The Vortex*, and it may, therefore, claim with justice that its reputation for shallowness was less justified, even in those days, than it was supposed to be. The public seriously

supported Mr. Coward's work the moment it saw some signs of seriousness in him. The play has almost every fault. It is shapeless, in spite of Mr. Coward's extraordinary sense of the theatre, and its characters are ill-drawn and insufficiently set out. We do not *know* them as we know the people in *Hamlet*. They rush before us and rush away again, and we are left in some bewilderment about them. While they are before our eyes, they cause excitement, but after their departure, we wonder why so much fuss was made about them. Our indifference is the result of our ignorance of the characters. We know as little of them at the end of the play as we knew at the beginning. Coleridge said of Edmund Kean that "to see him play is like reading Shakespeare by flashes of lightning," but to read any author, and especially such an author as Shakespeare, by flashes of lightning is to get a very queer view of him. Our feeling after seeing and particularly after reading, *The Vortex*, is that we have seen the people only in flashes of limelight. We might identify them in a court of law, but we would not, if we were conscientious, take our oath on it. To read the play,—and here it had better be confessed that Mr. Coward does not make good reading,—is to feel less assured about the characters than when they have been seen on the stage.—ST. JOHN ERVINE, "The Plays of Mr. Noel Coward," *QQ*, Spring 1935, pp. 8–10

In contrast to the many comedies which Coward wrote, there are about eight serious plays, one of which received considerable critical, as well as public, acclaim. *The Vortex* (1923) is Coward's first success of any importance and shows him as a playwright developing rapidly into a mature dramatist after only three years. *I'll Leave it to You* was written in 1920. The sordid events of *The Vortex* seem to be convincing, and one feels that this is the Mayfair set without the light-hearted treatment. Florence Lancaster, a faded beauty, who wished to remain lovely and desired, enjoys the adulation and attention of younger lovers and ignores her son, Nicky, who becomes addicted to drugs as a defense against his mother's immorality. Nicky's fiancee is whisked away by the masculine charms of his mother's latest lover, resulting in a long last-act dialogue in which " . . . debauche son upbraids debauchee mother, ending up with his head in her lap," thus giving some hope that this society of matron and son may yet find themselves. If this seems to be more of the 1960's than of the 1920's, so be it. An indication of the success of this play may be found in these words of Coward: " . . . I sat nightly at the end of the play receiving people and giving them drinks and cigarettes, and listening to their praise. So much praise." *The Vortex* was highly successful as one critic put it. "It reflected society life so accurately that the theatre was shy of being such a perfect mirror."—CLARENCE RALPH MORSE, "Mad Dogs and Englishmen," *ESRS*, Spring 1973, pp. 34–35

MUSICAL THEATRE

Romance might be dead in his world, but it was by no means dead in Noel Coward. It remained as a corroding residue and presently began to eat its way to the surface, appearing first in the mere prettiness of shows like *This Year of Grace*, workmanlike musical comedy stuff for a leading lady with a sweet face and a mild soprano. Then, in *Bitter Sweet*, it cropped up as a curious nostalgia after the days when love was love. Here he confronts the younger generation with an operetta romance of the approved type. Being completely panoplied in cocktails, jazz and dancing, they miss the point completely; the ageing heroine's song of love is immediately converted into jazz rhythms and the younger generation exit in the throes of the Charleston. The audience, however, is not allowed to miss the point. A dozen times the distressing contrast between Strauss's spacious days and the degenerate times of Irving Berlin flounces across the footlights into the audience's laps: "You none of you know anything or want anything beyond noise and speed," says Lady Shayne to her young guests, "Your dreams of romance are nightmares, your conceptions of life grotesque." If you dissect away the lavender and old lace from *Bitter Sweet*, you find a young romantic seeking any port in a storm, so bewildered that he is able even to believe that the year 1900 was a thing of candy-box beauty. Before *Bitter Sweet* he might have been mistaken for a moralist; after *Bitter Sweet* it is plain that his outraged feelings were the sequel to his congenital romanticism and he shows unmistakable signs of being a sentimentalist, in spite of his own assertion that his plays display "a distrust of sentimentality amounting to hatred."—J. C. FURNAS, "The Art of Noel Coward," *FR*, Dec. 1933, p. 13

Coward is the grand master of verbal triviality. He has never been one to turn the cliché inside out; his art consists rather in piling cliché on cliché until the total banal effect makes its comic impact. 'The Use of Topography in the Metasomatic Wit of Noël Coward' would make a first-class American university English thesis *e.g.*, 'Very flat—Norfolk'; 'You can see as far as Marlow on a clear day, so they tell me'; 'She went to Brighton with the worst intentions but never got further than Haywards Heath', etc. I sometimes think he will live longest in literature as a grubbing-ground for the scholiasts of AD 2558 and be published in the form of gobbets, learnedly annotated like a Loeb edition. Lines such as 'I think Rajahs bumble up a house-party so terribly' will be mauled over as fiercely as a fragment of Menander.

Yet at his best, and on his own entirely theatrical terms, Coward is a supreme entertainer. *Hay Fever* and *Private Lives*, *Hands Across the Sea* and *Present Laughter*—these contain his moments of purest comedy; its quintessence is to be found on the Las Vegas long-player and many of the other tunes he has written over the past thirty years: *Poor Uncle Harry* (missionaries), *I Wonder What Happened to Him* (the Raj), *Don't Put Your Daughter on the Stage, Mrs Worthington* and that splendid number which, very pompously, he appears to have withdrawn at the time of the 1945 Election—*Imagine the Duchess's Feelings, When Her Youngest Son Went Red!* My own favourite—because it subsumes in some 30 lines a whole branch of English fiction and even life itself—is the one about how, in the bar of the Piccolo Marina, Life Came to Mrs Wentworth-Brewster and how she was never the same woman again.—JOHN RAYMOND, "Play Orchestra, Play," *NSN*, Oct. 25, 1958, p. 553

The fall of Winston Churchill in 1945 was a timid joke compared with the fall taken in that year by Mr Coward, when the Labour Party romped home. There is no other historical figure, not even Harold Macmillan, who has taken such a battering from history since that time. *Present Laughter*, which was published in 1943, now seems like a despairing cry as darkness fell. Democracy was upon us all, but it lay heaviest on Mr Coward. All the same, being a man of considerable courage, he looked around for weapons. With the same care that he chooses the wrong targets, he selected the wrong weapons. His technique as a writer and musician, a technique he rightly loves and cherishes, became coarsened and unwieldy. He did something which has proved disastrous to him as an artist of the theatre: he raised his voice. The mob was at the gates and he made the mistake of trying to address it. He has continued to

shout at it for seventeen years, and is doing so at this moment at the Savoy Theatre in *Sail Away*. . . .

The action of the show takes place on board a ship on a European pleasure cruise. The last thing Mr Coward would wish to be reminded of, it seems, at the moment is a square. Yet he has chosen the inside of a ship for the action of his musical, and nothing can be squarer than that. The designer, Mr Sainthill, has gone all out for right angles. The dance director, Mr Layton, has obliged with straight lines. The desperate faces of the actors face us square-on in this inexorable geometry. The result is that we get the lot on the nose.

The characters. There seem to be thousands of them, although I notice they all go on one page of the programme. Miss Elaine Stritch plays the lead, a woman called Mimi Paragon, a cruise hostess. She does so with wit, pathos and a lost look.

The music. It is big band stuff, with the subtlety of a steam-roller in the Hammersmith Palais-de-danse. The lyrics. A little of the old acid here and there, but the gift for writing love songs (oh, those sweet 1930s, with Hitler and 'Where Are the Songs We've Sung?') nowhere apparent.

The final impression? A lot of common young men in common clothes. Sir, this is butcher boy stuff, and you know it.

Made unhappy by the whole affair, I picked up *Present Laughter*, a play Mr Coward wrote in those gay days when the world was merely on the brink of war. It was like reading an old love letter.

Look at this: Act II, scene one. Garry talking to his valet, Fred.

> *Fred*: Well, I'm off now. Got everything you want?
> *Garry*: You're very dressy. Where are you going?
> *Fred*: Tagani's.
> *Garry*: Where's that?
> *Fred* (laconically): Tottenham Court Road.
> *Garry*: Is it a dance hall or night club or what?
> *Fred*: Bit of all sorts, really. Doris works there.
> *Garry*: What does she do?
> *Fred*: Sings a couple of numbers and does a dance with a
>   skipping rope.
> *Garry*: Very enjoyable.

Dear Fred. So uncomplicated. So free. And, most important of all, so safely alive on Mr Coward's stage. Now, however, Fred is in the audience. And there he is dangerous, mixed up and in bondage. History has put him there and very much confused Mr Coward. Gone is Garry's affectionate conversation, and in its place is a baffled voice shouting, 'Fred, get back here on the stage at once, where I can understand you!' But Fred stays put—the thousand Freds did the night I was there—smoking his cigar and saying to his Doris, 'S'all a bit outadate, int it?'

A dramatist selects his material, his method and his audience, in that order. Mr Coward's mistake is that he is doing this, but backward. It cannot but lead to the gravest errors of taste. And these Mr Coward commits in abundance. He is against the playwright as social realist, but nothing could be more unreal than Mr Coward's view of present-day society as exemplified in a work such as *Sail Away*.

To stay sane under such an assault as this musical makes it is as well to remember that *Hay Fever* and *Private Lives* are the two best comedies written in English since *The Importance of Being Earnest*. Also that *Bitter Sweet* and *Conversation Piece* rank with the best Johann Strauss operettas. Keeping this in mind, and remembering that Mr Coward is a very young man, let us look to the future.—JOHN WHITING, "Coward Cruising," *Lon*, Aug. 1962, pp. 64–66

The subject matter of the musical plays is traditional: the vicissitudes of true love. Some end sadly—in *Bitter-Sweet*, Carl Linden is killed in a duel; in *Operette*, Roxanne nobly renounces her aristocratic lover so that his army career will not be ruined by marriage with an actress. These endings are no innovation; Victor Herbert's *Sweethearts*, with its pathetic ending, dates from 1913. On the whole, however, true love triumphs over the obstacles set in its way—a statement that is just as true of *Bitter-Sweet* and *Operette*; for Sarah Linden's life is still a graceful memorial to her love for Carl, and Roxanne's renunciation is a mark of truly unselfish love. Such is the world of the musical play and there is little mark of Coward's world-weary sophistication. Indeed, only "Family Album" makes something of a break with tradition. Gathered in the parental home after the funeral of their father, the Featherways reminisce about their childhood. Thanks to an ample supply of madeira and to the relief felt at the passing of the family tyrant, they finally reveal their hatred of their father, all to the ironic accompaniment of simple, sentimental music box melodies. But "Family Album" is more an anecdote than a play, and the music is incidental.

What is true of the subject matter is also true of the writing in general. Except for some reticence about expressing deep emotional feeling, a reticence even more pronounced in and typical of Coward's non-musical plays, the dialogue contains little that is distinctive.—MILTON LEVIN, "Words and Music," *Noel Coward*, 1968, pp. 33–34

And the songs. The very best of Noel Coward's lyrics seem to me the best in the language since Gilbert. Lorenz Hart and Cole Porter are his only competitors. But Hart was a sort of refugee from the Algonquin Club, Dorothy Parker in drag; Cole Porter's lyrics are usually too well enmeshed with the score, too smooth or too clever, ultimately without an individual stamp, like a society orchestra leader. The best of Coward's efforts have the canniness of the gambler who stops while he's ahead. Also a striking singularity and venturesomeness. Imagine creating "I've Been to a Marvelous Party" or "Down With the Whole Damn Lot!" or "Mad Dogs and Englishmen" during the days when Harry Richman sang "I cried for you, now it's your turn to cry me. . . ."—ROBERT MAZZOCCO, "Whipped Cream," *NYRB*, March 14, 1968, p. 29

Blithe Spirit is, perhaps, the climax to Coward's writing career, for in addition to the thoughtfulness given to the role of Madame Arcati, he attempts a perilous dramatic venture in creating the ghostly Elvira. Putting a ghost upon the stage and tightly incorporating its actions into the plot of a drama which deals with earthly inhabitants and their foibles is difficult. The problem arises from the fact that the playwright must make the audience believe in this ghostly device, regardless of its incredulous nature. Coward, through the use of the medium, Madame Arcati, gives a naturalness to the return of a spirit from the other world. He combines Elvira's existence with those of the living by making her actions, mannerisms, and speech the same as the other characters. Elvira, although a ghost, is a lovely, malicious phantom of no conscience and much charm. Coward, here, proves his skill in writing actable parts by creating a role which is more difficult than most to develop.—CLARENCE RALPH MORSE, "Mad Dogs and Englishmen," *ESRS*, Spring 1974, p. 27

SHORT STORIES

There is much to admire. He was master of the shifting point of view, and managed the difficult balance between comedy and tragedy. No one has written better of theatrical professionals in our time. He could update a myth and make it pertinent today: "Pretty Polly," one of my favorites, can be read as a recasting of the Cinderella story, with the young Indian Amazahudin as an improbable fairy godmother. Finally, the stories are often hilarious—as when a boorish major explains, "A man who has a light hand with a horse has a light hand with anything." To which the Cowardian narrator gently replies, "Except pastry."

The stories fall into two categories: those based on autobiographical experience ("What Mad Pursuit?" and "Mr. and Mrs. Edgehill," in which Coward makes a cameo appearance as a world-weary English lady of society); and those which more or less are imaginary ("Aunt Tittie" and "The Kindness of Mrs. Radcliffe"). There also are satires ("A Richer Dust" and "Star Quality"). Whatever the impetus or mode, his stories display literary excellence and, not surprisingly, a sense of drama.

Their themes are boredom, loneliness, loyalty, resignation, aging, fame, fate and inhumanity—all of which somehow coalesce in his ship-of-fools novelette, "Bon Voyage," which concludes this collection. Yet despite their weighty subjects, these stories are entertainments by a great entertainer. Readers who enjoy them should next turn, or return, to *Pomp and Circumstance* (1960), Coward's extended fictional romp in the South Seas, which is as funny as the best of Evelyn Waugh.

But had Coward written nothing other than these twenty light, wry stories, he would have made a bid for fame. The text of the present edition gathers, in order of publication, the stories from *To Step Aside*, *Star Quality*, *Pretty Polly Barlow and Other Stories* (1965), and *Bon Voyage* (1962), all out of print in this country. This is the first complete collection of Coward's stories, and cause for celebration. It is also further proof that he was, as Bennett Cerf proclaimed, "The man who could do everything."—ROBERT PHILLIPS, "Preface" to *The Collected Stories of Noel Coward*, 1983, pp. viii–ix

---

HOMER E. WOODBRIDGE
From "Noel Coward"

The South Atlantic Quarterly, July 1938, pp. 239–50

Noel Coward's sequence of one-act plays, *Tonight at 8:30*, has again proved that he is a masterly entertainer, and raises the question whether actually or potentially he is anything more. Though he is now thirty-seven and has written some nineteen full-length plays, besides revues and shorter pieces, he is still the *enfant terrible* of the theater. He has gained a sort of naughty eminence as the author of farcical comedies of sex which have more or less scandalized the conservatives, but his greatest popular successes have been in widely different fields. One was a family tragedy, one a sentimental romance with musical setting, one a partly historical pageant. The nine short plays included in *Tonight at 8:30* are a timely reminder that his instrument is by no means a one-string fiddle; his work has shown great versatility as well as exceptional technical skill. The one-act pieces range from tragedy in *The Astonished Heart* through realistic drama of various types in *Still Life*, *Fumed Oak*, and *Hands Across the Sea*, to farcical comedy in *Ways and Means*, and costume comedy with musical accompaniment in *Family Album*. Only one of them, *We Were Dancing*, is a deliberate exploitation of sex. All of them, with the possible exception of *Shadow Play*, are examples of expert dramatic story-telling. In the sheer mechanics of dramaturgy, in the skill which can put a story before an audience with the greatest economy of means and the maximum of dramatic effect, Mr. Coward has few living superiors. And in accuracy of observation, in the power for instance to transplant to the stage an English railway refreshment room with its attendants and patrons, he sometimes approaches perfection. That refreshment room in *Still Life* recalls the early morning innyard scene in *Henry IV, Part I*, by its authentic tang of reality. Here at least, in the talent which enables him to reproduce an everyday scene with the atmosphere and feeling of the place, Mr. Coward is more than a mere entertainer. . . .

In these plays Mr. Coward pays one of the penalties of his versatility. He can write fluent doggerel, and can compose "catchy" tunes; and he is unable to resist the temptation to exercise these powers. (He exercises them in two of the one-act pieces of *Tonight at 8:30*.) It would be foolish to find fault with him for exploiting these talents, if he had not proved that he is capable of much better things.

Mr. Coward's third line of escape from the mood of painful disillusion that dominates his serious plays is through farcical comedy, especially the type that is chiefly concerned with sex. To this group of his plays belong *Fallen Angels*, *Hay Fever*, *Home Chat*, *Private Lives*, and *Design for Living*. As a group these plays are superior to the melodramas and sentimental romances, because there is no sham about them, and no false sentiment. An exception should perhaps be made of *Home Chat*, in which the heroine's indignation at the very natural suspicions of her husband and friends is carried to an unnatural extreme, and can scarcely be accepted as sincere. The play failed disastrously on the stage, because the action turns upon her sincerity, and the audience declined to believe in it. Mr. Coward attempted to combine realistic comedy in the first part with farcical development later, and the audience was doubtless puzzled and annoyed. But the other plays are sheer entertainment of a rather special and original sort. There is little characterization in them, and not much plot; the interest depends on the skilful treatment of a situation and its implications, and upon lively swift flowing dialogue. All except *Hay Fever* play upon the theme of sex adventure. They owe something to French farce, and it is worth noting that two of them, *Hay Fever* and *Private Lives*, have appeared in French versions. We have had nothing quite like them in earlier English drama. Twenty-five years ago Mr. Shaw attempted a farcical comedy of sex, and wrote a preface showing wherein all previous efforts in this direction had failed. According to him, "conventional farcical comedies are always finally tedious because the heart of them, the inevitable conjugal infidelity, is always evaded." His play, *Overruled*, though short, is also tedious; it begins somewhat in the manner of a Coward piece, but Mr. Shaw gets interested in a discussion of the ethics of infidelity, and forgets his own recipe. Incidentally, his characters are as colorless as Mr. Coward's; it is impossible to remember them individually. Mr. Coward perhaps recalled Shaw's advice; at any rate, he follows it better than Shaw does, and his farcical comedies do not, as a rule, "shirk their subject."

They have been compared to the comedies of the Restoration period, but the differences are at least as conspicuous as the resemblances. The resemblance, indeed, scarcely goes beyond the fact that the people in Restoration comedy, like Mr. Coward's, are amoral and are chiefly occupied with sexual intrigue, which is treated pretty frankly. But the plots of the Restoration plays are usually involved and complex, with three or four distinct intrigues; they stress character much more heavily than Mr. Coward does, and usually include several eccentric types. Most of them contain an important element of satire, and they are generally much coarser in style. Anyone who has seen *The Country Wife* can verify these points; or anyone who has read *The Relapse*, or *Love for Love*, or *Love's Last Shift*. Lamb's famous defense of the old comedy on the ground that its world was an unreal one, remote from actual life and morals, is much more applicable to Mr. Coward's comedies than to Wycherly's or Congreve's. In every respect but in the style of dialogue, the Restoration playwrights are far more realistic than our contemporary. They give us more of the color and variety of life than he does—eccentricities, complications of human relationship, even moral scruple. His comedies represent the extreme of abstraction from reality; we are in a world where people have absolutely nothing to occupy them except the game of sex. Mr. Coward has truly said that these farcical comedies require expert acting, because the tempo must be exactly adapted to the spirit of every audience. But there is another reason, of which he is perhaps not so definitely aware: the plays require trained and excellent actors, because in themselves they are empty. The actors must supply most of the suggestions of character, must put life and color into the barely outlined sketches. . . .

The real question about Mr. Coward is whether some one of his numerous minor talents will finally seduce and betray him. A few years ago he seemed in some danger of becoming a mere writer of sentimental operettas and revues. At present his facility in handling farcical dialogue seems more likely to lead him astray. As Gilda in *Design for Living* says of Leo's play, "He flips along with easy swift dialogue, but doesn't go deep enough." His weakness has always been in the creation of character; but in *The Vortex*, *This Was a Man*, and *Cavalcade* he proved that he has powers of characterization which he has never fully developed. He ought not to be content with writing the most amusing sex farces of our time; his best talent is for realistic and satiric drama. *Tonight at 8:30* gives some hope, at least, that his mind is turning to his real job.

DONALD DAVIE

1922–

Donald Alfred Davie was born in Barnsley, Yorkshire, on July 17, 1922. His education at St. Catherine's College, Cambridge, was interrupted by six years in the Royal Navy during World War II. He learned Russian while stationed in the North Sea, and developed an interest in Eastern European literature that led him eventually to translate the poetry of Boris Pasternak. In 1946 Davie returned to Cambridge, earning a B.A., an M.A., and in 1951, a Ph.D. He has remained in academia, teaching English and American literature at Cambridge, Trinity College, the University of Essex, the University of Southern California, the University of California at Santa Barbara, Stanford, and since 1978, Vanderbilt. He received a Guggenheim Fellowship in 1973.

As poet and critic, Davie's chief concern is summarized in the title of his 1952 book: *Purity of Diction in English Verse*. Writes Davie, "If the poet who coins new metaphors *enlarges* the language, the poet who enlivens dead metaphors can be said to *purify* the language." In the 1950s, he was associated with the group of poets known as "The Movement," and his poetry was published in the pivotal *New Lines* anthology. In addition to writing poetry, Davie has edited numerous anthologies and collections.

He lives in Nashville with his wife, Doreen, whom he married in 1945. They have three children.

Personal

I was brought up to think that libertarian principles were so ingrained in the English tradition that in England, if nowhere else, totalitarianism would be quickly unmasked and vigorously resisted. I was taught to take pride in having been born to that strain in the English tradition, the strain of the English Dissenters, in which such promptness and boldness could most be counted on, indeed to excess. But in the last dozen years, since I myself awoke to how state socialism is totalitarian, I have listened in vain for any cheep of protest from the English tradition I am heir to, the tradition of Oliver Cromwell and John Bunyan. And I have accordingly clung the more fondly to the images of individuality that were created, far outside England, by the masterful artificers of Renaissance Italy. Just so, but heroically, did Osip Mandelstam, hounded by Stalin in the 1930s, cling to the witnesses of Dante and Ariosto, obscurely comforting himself by the assurance that the waters of his own Black Sea flowed into and out of the Mediterranean, washing the shores of Italy and Greece. From my North Sea the waterways were altogether more devious and longer. And accordingly I had to overcome several sorts of guarded suspiciousness in myself, and constrictions of sensibility, before the Mediterranean light could bathe and brace and heal. More than twenty-five years ago I put this in a poem which has for epigraph what I remember my mother saying when I was too cocky as a child: 'Mr. Sharp from Sheffield, straight out of the knife-box!'

Americans are innocents abroad;
But Sharp from Sheffield is the cagey kind
And—out of the knife-box, bleeding—can't afford
To bring to Florence such an open mind.

Poor Mr Sharp! And happy transatlantic
Travellers, so ingenuous! But some
Are so alert they can finesse the trick,
So strong they know when to be overcome.

Now must he always fall between these stools?
Blind, being keen; dumb, so as not to shrill;
Grounded and ground in logic-chopping schools;
So apt in so inapposite a skill?

Beleaguered and unsleeping sentinel,
He learned the trick of it, before the end;

Saw a shape move, and could not see it well
Yet did not challenge, but himself cried, 'Friend!'

I write these verses out again because the turning-point that they register seems now, down the perspective of years, even more momentous than I knew it to be when I wrote them.—DONALD DAVIE, "Italophils," *These the Companions*, 1982, pp. 126–27

General

It is true that I am not a poet by nature, only by inclination; for my mind moves most easily and happily among abstractions, it relates ideas far more readily than it relates experiences. I have little appetite, only profound admiration, for sensuous fullness and immediacy; I have not the poet's need of concreteness. I have resisted this admission for so long, chiefly because a natural poet was above all what I wanted to be, but partly because I mistook my English empiricism for the poet's concreteness, and so thought my mind was unphilosophical whereas it is philosophical but in a peculiarly English way.

Most of the poems I have written are not natural poems, in one sense not truly poems, simply because the thought in them could have been expressed—at whatever cost in terseness and point—in a non-poetic way. This does not mean however that they are worthless, or that they are shams; for as much can be said of much of the poetry of the past that by common consent is worth reading and remembering. Nevertheless I have taken a decision to write no more poems of this kind, only poems which are, if not *naturally*, at all events *truly* poems throughout.

For a true poem can be written by a mind not naturally poetic—though by the inhuman labour of thwarting at every point the natural grain and bent. This working against the grain does not damage the mind, nor is it foolish; on the contrary, only by doing this does each true poem as it is written become an authentic widening of experience—a truth won from life against all odds, because a truth in and about a mode of experience to which the mind is normally closed.

My 'Obiter Dicta' is a poem which wins through to sensuous immediacy, to poetic concreteness, by asking what sort of abstractions appeal to me, and answering that question in the only possible way, by a concrete fantasy. Instead of discriminating attractive ideas from other less attractive (which is the sort of operation to which my mind lends itself most readily), I ask in that poem by what criterion I find some ideas more attractive than others. I answer that I like ideas which are *stony*. This represents (I hope) a true poem won out of precisely that which is most inimical to it, free play among abstractions.

'A Gathered Church' actually follows out the process of thus winning to the concrete through the abstract—the church I was brought up in represents itself to me in the first place as a pattern of doctrines and doctrinal cruxes; only after giving these their head, in a free play and snip-snap of ideas and distinctions, can I win through to an apprehension of Dissent as embodied and made concrete in the personality of my grandfather.

'Under St Paul's' by contrast conceals the true movement of my mind, presenting as a deduction from concrete experience what was in fact the source of the poem (the idea of Candour), to which the concrete experience of the cathedral as a building was subsequently attached, not without difficulty. Yet perhaps this is to be less than fair to myself. As in 'The Fountain' and 'Killala', the idea and the sensuous experience struck me independently, and only in the process of writing did I recognize a harmony between them, and a rightness about splicing them together in the poem. All the same by and large it is certainly true that the idea comes into my mind more readily than the sensuous experience which not only can stand, but must stand, as its symbol.—Donald Davie, Note to "With the Grain," *Collected Poems 1950–1970*, 1972, pp. 301-2.

The place of Donald Davie in the British poetic scene is an interesting one. His poetry, particularly the earlier work, strikes one at first as coldly intellectual and distant. His criticism responds to new currents, both British and international, without seeming to be deeply and significantly informed by them; though it is always intelligent and relevant, it tends to let go of issues before they are fully and sympathetically encompassed. Nevertheless, one grows to see that the 'defects' of detachment have enabled him to cultivate a valuable openness at the same time. . . . This has happened, it seems to me, because the work is at once clear and witty, involved in the deeper issues of the age and of contemporary consciousness, and devoid of false attitudinizing. It has depths as well as surfaces, and survives contemplation. It provides one instance of the fact that British sensibility is beginning once more to take hold of the relevant considerations for a living poetry.—M. L. Rosenthal, "Contemporary British Poetry," *The New Poets*, 1967, pp. 209–10

. . . ⟨F⟩or Davie the ideal poet is a "judicious and fair-minded" citizen who doesn't make irrational, irresponsible and subversive claims to personal or political revelation like Blake or D. H. Lawrence. But what he is overlooking, though he must know it, is that if poetry provokes us to action—political or otherwise—it does so only in a very indirect way. It is not a question of electing Lawrence to office, it is a question of how far his honest revelation of the primitive in himself (and of his possibly fascistic rejoicing in it) may alter our understanding of ourselves and the world.

. . . ⟨W⟩hen you start writing poetry, if you are a real poet, you are going to end up in regions at which you didn't guess, you will follow your senses through into strange and irresponsible embodiments. And there is no doubt in my mind that Davie, whatever his social theories, is such a poet.— Thom Gunn, *NYTBR*, Jan. 3, 1973, pp. 5, 26

Works

Mr. Davie makes it clear ⟨in *Articulate Energy*⟩ that he is attempting a fundamental account of the poetic strategies that have prevailed since Pope's Great Anarch dropped the curtain and engulfed us in the romantic night-world: "The point I want to make is this: in the 17th and 18th centuries poets acted on the assumption that syntax in poetry should often, if not always, carry a weight of poetic meaning; in the 19th and 20th centuries poets have acted on the opposite assumption, that when syntactic forms are retained in poetry those forms can carry no weight. I have sought only to make those assumptions explicit, so that we may know just what we are doing, and what we are turning our backs upon, when we agree with the symbolists that in poetry syntax turns into music. Is Pope's handling of poetic syntax really so irrelevant to the writing of poetry today? And are we really so sure of ourselves that we can afford to break so completely with the tradition he represents?"

Since twentieth-century poetry has all along conducted its affairs on the principle that we can afford to sacrifice much of the nineteenth, Mr. Davie's lumping of these poets and those in one regretful but firm dissent seems open to suspicion. So does his principal strategy, a joining together of Susanne Langer, T. E. Hulme, and Ernest Fenollosa, whose interests don't overlap, to make a sort of tripartite *advocatus diaboli* whose principles, with a little adroit give and take, will blanket twentieth-century literature, and, with a little dampening, smother it. . . .

Mr. Davie's unpromising procedure nevertheless opens enough incidental doors to convince us that he has something of fundamental usefulness to say. He is absolutely right in focusing our attention on the eighteenth century if we want to see the beginnings of a landslide; that was also, we recall, where Pope cautioned us to look. It may also be deduced that the standard accounts of post-symbolist poetry are in a state of confusion, since a poetry answering in essence to those accounts would deserve all Mr. Davie's suspicions.—Hugh Kenner, "In the Wake of the Anarch" (1956), *Gnomon*, 1958, pp. 181–83

Donald Davie's first book was a cool, rather tough work of literary criticism, *Purity of Diction in English Verse*, published in 1952. This was ostensibly an academic study of the procedures of various minor eighteenth century poets, together with reflections on later poetry; it contained some admirable literary history, and was full of worthwhile hints for the student of Augustan verse. But *Purity of Diction*, despite its bland scholarly guise, had a barely concealed polemical purpose. It represented Davie's reaction against the dominant assumptions of twentieth century poetics: that the essence of poetry lay in metaphor, and particularly in the bold or violent collocation of images, and that syntax must inevitably be distorted or broken in the interests of poetic immediacy. The minor Augustans whom Davie admired had used metaphor sparingly, and 'arresting' images hardly at all; they preserved in their diction a tone that was carefully balanced between cultivated speech and literary usage (and which Davie saw as closely related to desirable moral qualities of poise and balance); and they employed a compressed, energetic syntax which, though based on the syntax of prose, was capable of a wide range of poetic effects: Davie's interest in syntax was to be expanded in his next critical work, *Articulate Energy* (1957). Occasionally the contemporary relevance of his scholarly investigations was made overt; in *Purity of Diction* he remarked, 'there is no denying that modern poetry is obscure and that it would be less so if the poets adhered to the syntax of prose'.—BERNARD BERGONZI, "The Poetry of Donald Davie," *CQ*, Winter 1962, p. 293

I first encountered Donald Davie through the challenging and inventive criticism found in the pages of his *Purity of Diction in English Verse* and *Articulate Energy*. Davie's imaginative selection and juxtapositions of poems were woven into continuous arguments that never disposed of those poems by wrapping them up in interpretative tinfoil ("well, now that's done and I'm glad it's over!") but helped them instead to open out and open up to the reader. The books were exhilarating stimulants to one's own critical practice; they provided a standard of loving care directed at the art of poetry which the critic never presumed was less than indispensable. In his newly-published book of criticism (*Thomas Hardy and English Poetry*, Oxford University Press) the belief is still that the poet "is what society cannot dispense with", and Davie practices on Hardy, and some modern and contemporary poets who are indebted to him, the kind of scrupulous, unfailingly lively attention we now expect from him as our right. It was probably because of my high regard for this criticism that, becoming aware of Davie as also a poet who had then published two volumes (*Brides of Reason*, 1955; *A Winter Talent*, 1957), I took the "also" literally and considered the poetry a pastime out of which had come some delightful, slight efforts, very much subordinate to his larger labors as a critic. The publication of Davie's collected poems has made me reconsider my priorities to the extent of realizing that a body of work of this magnitude can't be taken as "also" to anything else, no matter how good the something else may be.—WILLIAM H. PRITCHARD, "Donald Davie's Poetry," *Poetry*, Aug. 1973, p. 289

The Shires was leapt on rather gleefully by most English reviewers when it appeared: how silly he was to think he could get away with this, try for a modern *Poly-olbion*, one poem for each shire. If good poems are necessarily responses to human situations, in justice one would have to admit that the air in *The Shires* is something pretty thin, the "situations" gasping to be put in quotation marks. How can one care very much about the following musing which takes up the last two of the four stanzas of "Leicestershire":

> Perhaps the Leicester Poetry
> Society is still calling
> Its week-end schools together;
> It's my fault if I've fallen
> Out of touch with its sponsors.
>
> At Loughborough, I remember,
> A man too little regarded
> (Dead since), V. C. Clinton—
> Baddeley afforded
> Several views of Yeats.

No doubt, but the chap was never alive for us, and nothing in the poetry makes him so in our eyes despite the musing poet. Some of the shires fail, as it were, to jog Davie into rich enough reverie or rhetoric. Yet, and even though it's right in general to suspect appeals to the volume "as a whole" (thus redeeming individual poems from failure), this one is special enough, with its forty shire-poems in alphabetical order, Bedfordshire to Yorkshire, to disarm a too scrupulous worry over whether an individual poem really succeeds or not. They *do* help each other out.—WILLIAM H. PRITCHARD, "The British Looking-Glass," *Parn*, Spring/Summer 1976, p. 232

THEODORE WEISS
From "Between Two Worlds or On the Move"
Parnassus: Poetry in Review, Fall/Winter 1974, pp. 113–17.

Anyone acquainted with Donald Davie's work will not be surprised at my calling it one of the more considerable ventures in literature in our time. He has from the start, with *Purity of Diction in English Verse* (1952), attempted to counteract what he regards as the most pernicious tendencies in modern poetry. And though with twenty years elapsed, symbolism, the brand of Romanticism he objected to, hardly dominates today, many qualities he reprehended still prevail in American poetry—the intuitive, the improvisatory, the fragmentary as against reason, syntax, order. Challenging modern poetry's failure to exploit traditional verse's resources, Davie has stressed the grievous losses of expression and content poetry sustains when it abandons the poetic past. On the other hand, one of Davie's striking traits is his openness of mind, his sympathy, despite his basic reservations, for poets like Charles Olson and Edward Dorn. "To *move*, to *keep moving*" (Davie's italics), an "imaginative response," has been his comportment, if not his strategy, in his work as in his life. Yet whatever detours he may undertake, the conservative standpoint persists throughout his work. Because of that standpoint and what he understands by it, his work generally reflects the quality he most appreciates and wishes restored: a generous civility. Whatever demurs I may have for Davie's position, I admire his struggle toward honesty, his intelligence, his defense of the quieter, less impressive, since less assertive, virtues. The struggle he is involved in is nothing other than that of poetry and life itself, not only in a wounded, diminished England, but in the world at large. . . .

Several decades ago, being an excellent critic would have provided Davie with the certification poets were expected to have: knowing about poetry proved the poet's trustworthiness as a poet. Today, except in the universities, and often not in them, the reverse obtains. With the fierce insistence on instinct, the magical, "the dark and mysterious," if a man is that learned, especially in past English poetry, how can he be free to create new work? Of course learning, and of the most obtrusive kind, hardly impeded Pound and Olson. But theirs, existing chiefly programmatically, always came at one with enormous certainty and powerful exclamation. In short, as the reaction set in against New Criticism and its devotion to English poetry, the Pound and Olson variety of learning appealed precisely for its cantankerousness, its often shrill authoritarian tone. Davie, however, though as unorthodox in his championings as Pound and Olson, has usually been modest, making points for poetry as seemingly remote and irrelevant as that of the late 18th century in England.

But if Davie's defense of the unpopular "center" has, like much modern English poetry, seemed too mild, especially for an age as tempestuous as ours (one further reason for his urging modesty), we might do well to heed the English view that American poets are frequently forced, melodramatic, sensational. Davie is definitely not a world-shaker. He knows the world is being shaken more than enough. He does not want to change his reader or life itself. Rather, he wishes to preserve the precarious, precious stuff and the equally precarious democratic society that he feels alone makes life of any decent sort possible. So if he has written enthusiastically on Pound, Olson, Dorn, he has also recognized the hazards and costs of such work. I am reminded of a statement by Picasso that Françoise Gilot quotes in her *Life with Picasso*.

> . . . as soon as art had lost all link with tradition, and the kind of liberation that came in with Impressionism permitted every painter to do what he wanted to do, painting was finished. When they decided it was the painter's sensations and emotions that mattered, and every man could recreate painting as he understood it from any basis whatever, then there was no more painting; there were only individuals.

Davie would, I think, agree with this observation; and coming as it does from one of the greatest experimenters painting has known, it might give us pause. But I would go farther. Modern poetry, dismissing established conventions and the tradition behind them, has established a new orthodoxy; out of the eccentricities and the powerful, idiosyncratic style of a Pound, a Williams, an Olson, younger poets have tried to make a style of their own. Or a very limited style indeed.

As Davie points out in his first book, the Romantics already rarely recognized more than one kind of poetry. But Davie does appreciate the "web of responsibilities" enmeshing the poet mindful of the importance of poetic diction. For such a poet—and here's the rub for us—even as he is sure of his audience, must share its basic assumptions. "Strength of statement" is primary to him; his poetry must possess the virtues of good prose (shades of Pound and Eliot). Pure diction in its "economy in metaphor," achieving "judgment and taste . . . preserves the tone of the center, a sort of urbanity." Unfortunately a poet seeking these qualities may win his reader's respect but never his love. For it is not the appeal of a powerful individual at work. Borrowing Eliot's definition of Dante's diction as "the perfection of a common language," Davie says we find this perfection not in the great English poets, who apparently ignore or exceed it, but in the good ones. So he cites Gower and Greville and Denham, Parnell and Goldsmith, Johnson and Cowper. One wonders how many present American poets would be persuaded by such examples or by the good sense that a poet look not for greatness but goodness. . . .

Belatedly Davie acknowledges historical changes as well as the effect of changes in men's philosophy and conduct on language. He also rightly insists on the reverse. This is the tantalizing question: which affects which first. Nevertheless, abandoning syntax in poetry, as Davie sees it, amounts to throwing away "a tradition central to human thought and conduct. . . ." "Throw away" sounds immensely deliberate, if not cavalier. But so he says of Pound. And he abruptly links Pound's abandoning of syntax with his fascism.

> By hunting his own sort of 'definiteness' (truth only in the particular), he is led to put his trust not in human institutions but in individuals. Similarly he pins his faith on individual words, grunts, broken phrases, half-uttered exclamations. . . . Hence his own esteem of the definite lands him at last in yawning vagueness, the 'intuitive' welcome to Mussolini. . . .

Or "one could almost say, on this showing, that to dislocate syntax into poetry is to threaten the role of law in the civilized community." This statement is tantamount to the old charge of the "treason of the clerks." And indeed soon after Davie instances Valéry's admission that he attends more to the composition of a work than to the work itself as a "*trahison des clercs* on the grand scale." Despite his respect for history Davie has paid little attention to modern historical circumstances or to

the prevailing poetry that Pound and his associates violently and justifiably reacted against. Davie does not apparently believe that language in poetry, as it ages, hardens, and seals itself off more and more from contemporary experience and a changing world, becomes useless if not dangerous. Rather, principally concerned with coherence, he inclines to the language and its laws as an innate, lasting thing. A page later he seems to relent: Eliot may have "done all that was practicable and renovated only so much as is appropriate to the present day." But persisting in his desire for a pure diction, Davie maintains that such diction was damaged by the appearance of the "improvisor," "a heroic figure of the Romantic movement throughout Europe." Through him poetry went from the notion of the maker and the poem as a made object to the poet as "legislator, seer, scapegoat and reporter." Men moved from poetry as "artificial" to an enshrining of the "natural." And the equating of the natural with the spontaneous, the amorphous, the artless, and the personal "is still a potent force in the writing and reading of poetry." Still indeed. This statement is more apt today than ever.

BERNARD BERGONZI
From "Davie, Larkin, and the State of England"
Contemporary Literature, Summer 1977, pp. 345–60

I shall say at once that Larkin seems to me a "better" poet than Davie; that is to say, I find more poems to move and console me in Larkin's three slender volumes than in Davie's much more extensive body of work. This is partly a matter of inherent skill; though possessing none of Davie's intelligent experimentalism, Larkin is a more naturally assured craftsman. He is a narrower but deeper poet. . . . Yet if Davie is a lesser poet than Larkin, he is also, to invoke an impure but beguiling category, in some respects a more interesting one.

The interest arises less from the character of Davie's poems, taken separately, than from the total impression one gets from all his writing of a powerful literary personality struggling with obsessions and endeavoring, with unexpected success, to balance or combine attitudes usually thought of as contradictory. Thus, Davie is emphatically a moralist, imbued with the rigorous spirit of the Cambridge English school of the forties and fifties. His first critical book, *Purity of Diction in English Verse* (1952), found admirable moral qualities in the lexical restraint and controlled syntax of eighteenth-century poetry and was offered as a lesson in the neoclassical virtues to Davie's contemporaries. In his own poetry Davie embodied this lesson in the sharp, cool, ironic observations of *Brides of Reason*. Yet he is also an aesthete, who believes with Henry James that "it is art that *makes* life, makes interest, makes importance." He was unable to remain satisfied for long with exclusively moral and social criteria for poetry; its significance, in the end, was ontological:

> The metaphysicality
> Of poetry, how I need it!
> And yet it was for years
> What I refused to credit.
> ("Or, Solitude," *CP*, p. 202)

Davie's ideal in these matters is that pure realm where art and morality become indistinguishable. Few of us, however, can inhabit it for long.

In one allegiance Davie is, unashamedly, a provincial

Englishman, strongly attached to his Yorkshire roots and the nonconformist religious tradition in which he was brought up, even if he is no longer a believer. This allegiance is personally exemplified in his affectionate memory of his father, to whom he has devoted several poems. In poetic terms it shows itself in Davie's admiration not just for minor eighteenth-century poets in general, but for hymn-writers such as Isaac Watts and Charles Wesley, in particular. Against this aspect of Davie—English, provincial, traditionalist—one must set quite different allegiances, which are cosmopolitan, global, and modernist. It is this, above all, which soon marked Davie off from the unambitious poetics of the Movement. He admires and imitates Pound and Pasternak, and is drawn to the heroic style, in life and art, of the early masters of modernism. However much his imagination is rooted in Pennine landscape, it constantly turns to the large unpeopled spaces of America and Russia. Davie spent some time in Russia during the Second World War, learned Russian, and later came to read and translate Pasternak's lyric poetry. Its influence is noticeable in *Events and Wisdoms* of 1964, which I think is Davie's best single collection of poems. Martin Dodsworth, an acute English critic who reads Russian, has praised the quality of Davie's translations of the *Dr. Zhivago* poems and has described the effect of Pasternak in helping Davie to find a looser, though still formal, mode of verse after his tight poetry of the fifties.[1] Pasternak's short lines, regular but not stiff stanzaic forms, and frequent exclamations are a noticeable feature of *Events and Wisdoms*.

Pound's influence on Davie is more pervasive. Indeed, Davie's interest in Pound, deeply admiring but never wholly approving, would be worth a study in itself. It has so far resulted in several articles and two books—*Ezra Pound: Poet as Sculptor* in 1964 and *Pound* in the Fontana Modern Masters series in 1975. As early as 1952 Davie was taking issue with Pound about the improper fragmentation of syntax in the *Cantos*, and in 1975 he was still worrying about the problem, though now concluding that it would be equally honorable to reject or accept Pound's procedures. In 1955 Davie wrote, "I honour the poets, English, Irish and American who revolutionized English poetry thirty years ago; and indeed it seems to me that one of those poets, Ezra Pound, has influenced me more deeply and more constantly than any other poet of the present century."[2] Davie reveres Pound for taking the art of poetry with true seriousness, as opposed to English amateurism. He finds, too, in Pound's imagist poetics a regard for the integrity of nature, seen and respected as something nonhuman, and accepted in its quiddity. He finds forerunners of this attitude in Ruskin and Hopkins and Hardy, and prefers it to the symbolist procedures of Eliot, in which the world of things is swallowed up in the all-embracing consciousness of the poet. . . .

From the early sixties Davie became increasingly concerned with America as a poetic subject. Like his Russia, Davie's North America was something of a landscape of the mind: empty, vast, silent, uncluttered with humanity—the pristine vision of the first explorers rather than the contemporary USA. He envied the American poets their freedom of imagination, reversing the traditional American envy of Europe for its cultural achievements and possibilities. At the same time, Davie, in his second, Californian exile, cannot forget England,

as we see in his sequence *The Shires* (1974). In some recent poems Davie's concern with England is less ideal or metaphysical, and more overtly political. Davie's politics, though, are quite other than the left-liberal, social democratic variety professed until recently by most English intellectuals. His distaste for contemporary England has a heroic-modernist basis and is directed at many things: the drab complacency of postimperial Britain; an industrialized and polluted landscape; social egalitarianism; civic philistinism; and the fatuities of the "Swinging London" cult of the sixties. In "Epistle. To Enrique Caracciolo Trejo," Davie brings together his cultural and personal discontents at the end of four unhappy years at the new University of Essex and hints at his own further expatriation:

> Still in infested gardens
> The year goes round,
> A smiling landscape greets returning Spring.
> To see what can be said for it, on what
> Secure if shallow ground
> Of feeling England stands
> Unshaken for
> Her measure to be taken
> Has taken four bad years
> Of my life here.   (*CP*, p. 213)

In some poems Davie's attitudes harden into a cold right-wing disdain; as, for instance, "New Year Wishes for the English":

> May the humanitarian
> Blackmail be paid no longer;
> Instead may you work a little.
> May you have, against the incessant
> Rain of the new, the all-new,
> Indifference as an umbrella.
>   (*CP*, p. 210)

In "England," a not very successful long poem written on the occasion of his departure to California, we find similar thoughts, combined with fragments of autobiography, and historical and geographical references inspired by the transpolar flight. Once he had embraced a new expatriate condition, though, Davie was able to write about his country in a more affectionate and relaxed way, in *The Shires*. . . .

Davie likes and cultivates the "open-ended" poem that does not return neatly and predictably to its starting point but moves onward and outwards like an arrow-shower or a river flowing into the sea. I shall conclude this essay in a similar way, suggesting a new and perhaps farfetched comparison, drawn not from poetry, but from war and public affairs, and not from England or America, but from France. During the Second World War Charles De Gaulle and Henri Philippe Pétain mutually repudiated and condemned each other as traitors to their country. In the more generous perspective of history, however, it has been said that each was serving France in his own way: one as the sword, one as the shield. Energy: endurance.

Notes

1. Martin Dodsworth, "Poetry in the Grass," *The Review*, No. 14 (Dec. 1964), pp. 23–30.
2. *Poets of the 1950's: An Anthology of New English Verse*, ed. D. J. Enright (Tokyo: Kenkyusha, 1955), p. 47.

C. DAY LEWIS

1904–1972

Cecil Day Lewis was born on April 27, 1904, in Ballintupper, Ireland. His father was a curate in the Church of Ireland and his mother was a collateral descendant of Oliver Goldsmith. She died shortly after the Reverend Day Lewis moved his family to Nottinghamshire and became a vicar in the Church of England.

In 1923 Day Lewis enrolled in Wadham College, Oxford. It was there that he became associated with what was loosely called the "Auden Group," consisting of W. H. Auden, Stephen Spender, and Louis MacNeice. Day Lewis co-edited *Oxford Poetry* with Auden in 1927.

After leaving Oxford he taught at a number of schools in England and Scotland. In 1928 he married Mary King and the couple had two children. He produced three major volumes of poetry in rapid succession between the years of 1929 and 1935: *Transitional Poem, From Feathers to Iron,* and *The Magnetic Mountain*. During that period he also wrote a volume of criticism, *A Hope for Poetry*, and published the first of many highly regarded detective stories under the name of Nicholas Blake.

In 1951 Day Lewis was appointed Professor of Poetry at Oxford. That same year he divorced his first wife and married Jill Balcon. He continued to produce both poetry and prose and also translated Virgil's *Aeneid*. In 1968 he succeeded John Mansfield as Poet Laureate of England until his death on May 26, 1972.

General

All genuine poetry is in a sense the formation of private spheres out of a public chaos: and therefore we would remind those who annually criticize us for lack of homogeneity, first, that on the whole it is environment which conditions values, not values which form environment; second, that we must hold partly responsible for our mental *sauve-qui-peut*, that acedia and unabashed glorification of the subjective so prominent in the world since the Reformation. . . .

The psychological conflict between self as subject and self as object, which is patent in the self-consciousness and emotional stultification resultant from the attempt to synchronise within the individual mind the synthesis and the analysis of experience. Such appears to be the prime development of this century, our experiment in the 'emergent evolution of mind.' Emotion is no longer necessarily to be analysed by 'recollection in tranquillity': it is to be prehended emotionally and intellectually at once. And this is of most importance to the poet; for it is his mind that must bear the brunt of the conflict and may be the first to realize the new harmony which would imply the success of this synchronization.—W. H. AUDEN, C. DAY LEWIS, "Preface" to *Oxford Poetry*, 1927, pp. v–vi

The literary myth goes that in the Thirties in England a group of undergraduates—called the Oxford group and consisting of W. H. Auden, Cecil Day Lewis and myself, and then later joined by Louis MacNeice—started a so-called movement in verse. The facts are that we never met as a group, never referred to ourselves as a movement; curiously, the original three didn't meet each other collectively until September 1949, in Venice. . . .

We had, nevertheless, much in common. We were all contemporaries; we were all at Oxford; we were all young. Auden's room at Oxford was more or less familiar to each of us.

We admired *The Waste Land*, which set up a barrier between our generation and much modern poetry that preceded it and—perhaps without our being fully aware of this—set our generation the problem of getting out of the wastes. Among Auden's views at this time were hatred of politics, condemnation of all literary movements and the idea that poetry should be impersonally clinical. There is no doubt that these thoughts influenced his friends. . . .

Day Lewis wrote some rather embarrassing "red" poems—to the delight of those who like to hold his past against him. MacNeice wrote the poetry of a civilized, scholarly man who loves Greece and hedonistic values, but who feels touched by the necessity of choosing between public right and public wrong. As for me—I wrote a poetry of pity for the unemployed and the victims generally. It did not please the politicians. . . .

The lesson of the Thirties is that above all what the young writer needs today is on the one hand his own individuality and on the other—to strengthen this—some sense of having colleagues. Where we were particularly fortunate was in being young at a moment when it was possible to take up an attitude toward a human cause without losing our individuality.—STEPHEN SPENDER, "It Began at Oxford," *NYTBR*, March 3, 1955, pp. 4–5

He has always been a poet with a fine sense of structure, a various command of rhythms, but with a thinnish feeling for texture and with a tendency to stretch the surface of a poem too thinly, also, over a predetermined framework. The fairies who presided at his birth made him both ingenious and copious, gave him a craftsman's conscience also, but an uninvited and malicious fairy added: "You will be able to catch *almost* exactly the note of any poet you admire!" Through his poems of the 1930s, one hears again and again the voices of Yeats and of Auden. As with a very skillful verse translator, one feels: "Yes:

but after all it is better in the original!" With the outbreak of the Second World War, Day Lewis commenced a slow mutation of his poetic character from radical rational Utopian to conservative sentimental Arcadian. He turned his admirably conscientious craftsmanship to versions of Virgil and Valéry which are, ironically, among his most truly original works. He wrote a long poem, *An Italian Journey*, in which, using Clough and Browning and Hardy, he turned the bad fairy's gift into a blessing: producing not diluted imitation, but admiring parody or critical *pastiche*. Two ways of thinking of him would be as the hermit-crab, needing some tougher dead creature's shell to tuck its tail into; or as the poet as role-player. Hardy and Browning preside over this present volume. He can reproduce Hardy's halting exactitude:

> It was as though her room, her world
> Had blurred with fog, and she
> Was feeling her way from chair to clock,
> From vase to mahogany table, less
> By sight than by memory.

In a poem on the Glasgow genteel murderess, Madeleine Smith, who died in 1928 in the United States seventy-one years after a "Not Proven" verdict (she had poisoned her lover with arsenic in cocoa) had left her legally free but socially and morally ostracised, he catches the sharpness of the English of the Lowland Scot as expertly as Browning might have done:

> Sir, I am dying. Let the douce
> young medico Syrup his verdict, I
> am not deceived.

It is a pretty problem for the critic: if the two poems I have quoted *were* by Hardy or Browning, one would place either of them in the high middle reaches though not at the top of the Hardy or Browning canon. But they aren't, they are by Mr. Day Lewis, and somehow the backward-looking, benign, wistfully agnostic, country-loving Tory of the 1960s doesn't ring *quite* true, any more than the up-boys-and-at-'em assistant pack-leader to Auden rang *quite* true in the 1930s either. The bad fairy is still around.—G. S. FRASER, "Three British Poets," *NYRB*, June 25, 1964, p. 14

Works

POETRY

The first part of *Transitional Poem* is a series of discussions of general philosophical problems conducted from a constantly shifting point of view and through ever changing fables. There is no conclusion, no resolution of the separate statements. The second part is concerned with the problem of right action; the poet is seeking to find out where he ought to offer loyalty, what ethical system should command his allegiance:

> It is becoming now to declare my allegiance,
> To dig some reservoir for my springtime's pain,
> Bewilderment and pride, before their insurgence
> Is all sopped up in this dry regimen.

The preface to this section is a significant quotation from Whitman:

> Do I contradict myself?
> Very well then, I contradict myself;
> I am large, I contain multitudes.

The discussions in this second part are as unfocused as those in the first. The poet proceeds from speculation to speculation. The tentative quality of the thought is even more apparent here:

> In heaven, I suppose, lie down together
> Agonised Pilate and the boa-constrictor
> That swallows anything: but we must seize

One horn or the other of our antitheses.

> When I consider each independent star
> Wearing its world of darkness like a fur
> And rubbing shoulders with infinity,
> I am content experience should be
> More discontinuous than the points pricked
> Out by the mazy course of a derelict,
> Iceberg, or Flying Dutchman, and the heart
> Stationary and passive as a chart. . . .
> But an eccentric hour may come, when systems
> Not stars divide the dark; and then life's pistons
> Pounding into their secret cylinder
> Begin to tickle the most anchorite ear
> With hints of mechanisms that include
> The man. And once that rhythm arrests the blood,
> Who would be satisfied his mind is no
> Continent but an archipelago?. . .

The questions are left unanswered, the moral problems suggested are not solved, but the section ends with an acceptance of experience, of life, as the best position to take up while deciding:

> Charabancs shout along the lane
> And summer gales bay in the wood
> No less superbly because I can't explain
> What I have understood.
> Let logic analyse the hive,
> Wisdom's content to have the honey:
> So I'll bite the crust of things and thrive
> While hedgerows still are sunny.

This confident acceptance of the natural world is something far removed from anything we find in Eliot and is an indication of the direction which the younger poets are to take. Their criticisms, at least in their early poetry, are based on an underlying optimism.

The third part of *Transitional Poem* is concerned with the more general psychological problem of keeping the personality integrated and unified during the process of search and opens with a quotation from Herman Melville: "But even so, amid the tornadoed Atlantic of my being, do I myself still centrally disport in mute calm." This is the ideal rather than the actual situation. Again there is the same rapid movement from point to point, only this time the search is for a common denominator, as it were. There is the rejection of all factors that represent only a part of the personality:

> Farewell again to this adolescent moon;
> I say it is a bottle
> For papless poets to feed their fancy on.

And there is the search for the integrating unit:

> Where is the true, the central stone
> That clay and vapour zone,
> That earthquakes budge nor vinegar bites away,
> That rivets man against Doomsday?

The final section of the poem is, in the poet's own words, "an attempt to relate the poetic impulse with the experience as a whole." It is perhaps the most difficult section of the poem to see as a whole; the ambiguity of the symbols, the tentative nature of the fables, suggest more than they explain; it seems clear that the poet is not yet in a position to make any summing up. It is, in fact, a "transitional poem," in which all meaning is bound to be in some degree ambiguous and all symbols ambivalent. Throughout the whole poem the writing is somewhat loose, even at times sloppy. Day Lewis is too often content to surrender his language completely to the casual wanderings of his mind so that his poetry lacks the cogency that comes from discipline.—David Daiches, "Poetry in the 1930's," *Poetry and the Modern World*, 1940, pp. 196–99

Almost half the poems (in *Short is the Time*) directly reflect a decade of war or the more tangible aspects of The Times. The poet tries hard to avoid brass and neon glare, flourishing baton, head too deeply bowed, and tear too facile, and to keep the finger pointed not at special villains but at a civilization which must be its own scapegoat; yet these poems are not his best controlled. At times "Humankind stands forth" from "The Cause," as Lewis puts it in "Word Over All," his poetica; the theme of "The Assertion," for instance, is that our agonized world is the proper context for asserting that "men are love," that "love's no laughing matter" but may be evidenced in violence and may offer both "kindness" and "bloody correction." But often the issue is slight, or first-rate imagery is not properly used to sustain tone and structure. "Landscapes"—the parks of "cash Conquistadors" and "Towns . . . choked with desperate men"—becomes a too mechanical diptych; "Bombers" ends in a lesson; "The Nabara," a Spanish-war sea-story, focuses the recurring problem of what is "in the words," so to speak, and what we breathe into them of the air of our times. The motivation is provided by "freedom," a powerful cachet during World War II; yet it needs no cynic to guess that history may date the term and thus empty the poem of its heart.

The problem of motivation and structure is underlined by certain poems in which Lewis is at his best—those which generalize aspects of modern life ("Newsreel," "Sex Crime") or deal directly with large, permanent human concerns ("Overtures to Death," "Departure in the Dark," "Ode to Fear," "Fame," etc.). The final issue is whether he is satisfied with the methods and effects of immaturity or will impose the discipline of maturity, and this appears simultaneously in what he says and in the way he says it. Two poems, for instance (No. 7 of "O Dreams, O Destinations," "The Rebuke"), mourn "The flame that once we knew," the heat that "threw up mountains," later replaced by a half-hearted appetite for half-loaves. "Who cares a damn for the truth that's grown / Exhausted naggling for its own?" he asks. This nostalgic ache equates growing up with desiccation and retreat.

Again, "In the Heart of Contemplation" and "Questions," both of which utilize their preparatory imagery very skillfully, give calls from thought to action: "Nothing is innocent now but to act for life's sake" and "[When will you] pierce reflection's heart, and come alive?" are the final lines. . . .

When Lewis can stay away from the rhetorical flourish, keep to the proper materials of which he has no lack, submit to the discipline of his form, and let the hot metal of enthusiasm be poured into firm molds instead of splashing all over the shop, he can write first-rate poetry. "Newsreel" and "Departure in the Dark" both keep the eye on the object and unravel the commonplace to bare essential experience. "The Image," an application of the Perseus-Medusa story, uses myth as a mode of formal organization. "Angel" is best in his witty style, an offhand but tightly integrated personification of Death, who is not a hanging judge but a "spoilt girl in ermine": we fear "That bitch's casual favors." "Ode to Fear" is a maturely articulated statement of the terrifying powerlessness felt in the face of a threatening, distorted world which signifies "endemic guilt," "our guilt at the root."

There we have Lewis the profound observer, a large cut above the denouncer and the exclaimer. This insight contributes to most of his best poems; it burns with Learish intensity in "Sex Crime." "On point," he says, "to . . . the red, collusive stain." The sting of our dark spot which will not out, drives the poet to utterance after utterance on disaster and

death.—R. B. Heilman, "Some Milestones in a Poet's Growth," *NYTBR*, Aug. 5, 1945, pp. 5–25

In *From Feathers to Iron*, Day Lewis explores the mythical levels of the private for analogies with the public; the emergence into the public and communal, in fact, is the goal of the personal. In *The Magnetic Mountain*, on the other hand, we witness what Spender called the usurpation of the personal by the public—the willful coercion of the personal by the rational demands of the public. The public experience demands a social revolution, to which the personal, instinctual desire for rejuvenation must conform. The point of view is altered, therefore, by the shift from lived experience to ideological (or at least social) conviction.

Strangely enough, and perhaps unfortunately for the poem, *The Magnetic Mountain* does not dramatize that journey to and beyond the frontier, which it seems to promise. Revealingly, the poem's stress is on the sublime structure of the mountain rather than on the inner compulsion of the quester. There is no longer time to indulge the private sphere, no longer any significance in his personal anxiety or in the harrowing fear attendant upon uprootedness. The poem begins with its commitments fully made; its strategy is to defend and amplify those commitments: the ideal of the mountain which exists not in history but in men's desire for order and peace.

In this sense, the magnetic mountain is the symbol of the human spirit: it is an ideal beyond time and space, the gravitational center of man's need for community from which history has alienated him. Its origin lies in Romantic aspiration, but it offers to Day Lewis a way out of the isolate ego, and, in this sense, it is the symbol of man's deep-seated personal desire for self-transcendence. The magnetic mountain is nothing less than the primordial human community, a pastoral future. That the ideological hope supersedes and ultimately silences the intuitive, instinctual drama of the private mind should not prevent us from recognizing Day Lewis' desire, once again, to keep the two levels in exact balance. The poem's failure to achieve this balance is a good index of the age and of the demands it made upon the individual poet.

In this regard, the poem's guiding spirits are significant. Of the four epigraphs to the four parts, only the first, from Day Lewis' friend Rex Warner, is explicitly political; and even it celebrates the "Heart's heyday" in the "movement of masses." The others, from Blake, Lawrence, and Hopkins, place the emphasis on spiritual as opposed to social radicalism, or they suggest that the one precedes the other. Lawrence, in fact, was the guiding spirit to Day Lewis' early "romantic humanism." In *A Hope for Poetry* Day Lewis confessed, as we have noted, the strange intermixture of Lawrence and Marx in his attempts to marry the intuitive and the rational, the private and the public. Yet he had to admit (as Christopher Caudwell later argued) the irreconcilable conflict of the Lawrencean and the Marxist views—the former "driven ill and mad, a failure unable to recreate a satisfactory social group for the nucleus of his own individuality"; the latter offering the "most whole-hearted attempt ever made to raise the individual to his highest powers by a conditioning of his environment," yet succumbing to all the evils of an impersonal and depersonalizing system.—Joseph N. Riddel, "The Poetics of Action," *C. Day Lewis*, 1971, pp. 69–70

PROSE

Reading this serious, witty and extraordinarily perceptive little book (*The Poetic Image*) is an experience rarely, in these days, available, for we live in an age when the secular dogmas of poetry are often fanatically held to and when the free play of mind over the whole realm of poetry is too often inhibited by preconceptions as to what poetry must be and do in order to be acceptable to the modern canon. Mr. Lewis is not content to let sleeping dogmas lie, and he limits his preconceptions to a single pair.

The first is that, next to a whole-souled act of worship, the poetic act is at its best the most profoundly satisfying of all the means which man has discovered for the vindication of his species.

That most good poets, and all great ones, have known this open secret, which is what keeps them at poetry, does not mean that they have often been explicit about it. Nor have they customarily stressed the dark corollary: that there are few experiences more frustrating to the poet than his realization of the discrepancy which exists between the visionary genesis and the verbal exodus of a given poem. The first assumption underlies the whole book. The second assumption, which is that the image stands at the deep center of the poetic act, is what the book sets itself to document.

What is the poetic image? Mr. Lewis is not dogmatic, or indeed supremely systematic, in giving his answers, since he knows that the image, like poetry itself, is always larger in meaning and more extensive in its ramifications than any generalization which can be made about it. Primarily, perhaps, imagery is a quality implicit in language: every word, said Emerson, was originally a poem—by which he meant an available image. But when the image is, so to speak, born out of the language-matrix, it performs functionally in several important ways: to communicate, to reveal, to inform, to actualize and to intensify.

The image is quick-summarizing means of communication between the poet and the reader; but it is also the fleet, unbidden messenger flashing between vision and incarnation. It acts functionally to link the artificial or mind-made "world of poetry" (what Yeats partly meant by the gold-enameled bird in "Sailing to Byzantium") to the world of the actual. It reveals hitherto unobserved patterns in the actual while simultaneously assisting in the development of patterns in the world of artifice. Or, to put the matter differently, it serves the poet as a means of drawing back from the actual in order more strongly to come to grips with it.

So bald and incomplete a set of summary definitions does scant justice to the felicity and fecundity of Mr. Lewis' presentation, nor is it possible, short of an extended essay, to do more than suggest in barest outline the thronging virtues of this little book. Of these the greatest, perhaps, is the variety of vantage points, both past and present, from which Mr. Lewis surveys his problem. One finds here a field of fresh ideas to rove in.—CARLOS BAKER, "A Poet Considers His Technique," *NYTBR*, Dec. 28, 1947, p. 8

The Buried Day is a subtly written, precise account of the growth of imagination. All things conspired to make an artist: the tempestuous, lonely father, the long, sensuous summers in the garden of Monart rectory; the beauty of landscape and the inhumanity of boy to boy at Sherborne, the public school of which another memorable account has been given by John Cowper Powys. Auden drove iron into Day Lewis's art, but he did not alter its essentially private, nearly pastoral quality.

It is this quality that gives Day Lewis his special place in the famous triad of "Marxist" poets—Auden-Day Lewis-Spender. Though he was a member of the Communist Party and jeopardized his teaching career in order to express his radical sentiments, he continued to live in the country, a jealous guardian of private feeling. His politically inspired verse

has in it an odd tolerance and coolness of vision, as if the cycle of the seasons and the sensuous reality of landscape had always been to the poet more vital than the claims of political crisis.—GEORGE STEINER, "Mirrors on the Wall," *Rep*, Oct. 27, 1960, p. 63

From most of the news stories about the appointment of Cecil Day Lewis as Poet Laureate of Great Britain, you would gather that he is one of those lyric dons who dash off an occasional detective story in their lighter moments. In fact the poet is, as "Nicholas Blake," a hard-working professional in crime, who has written a novel almost annually since 1935, and is also one of England's two or three leading reviewers of crime fiction. Blake's stature among mystery novelists is at least as high as that of Day Lewis among poets; he has excelled both in the straight detective puzzle and in the broader study of crime and character, as well as in happy blends of the two methods. And it seems particularly fitting that he should celebrate his laurels by publishing his best novel in a dozen years, *The Private Wound*.

The narrator, an Anglo-Irish novelist visiting County Clare in the disturbed year of 1939, says that his story "began as an idyll, continued into low comedy, and ended in tragedy." It is an intensely penetrating study of sexual passion (and, incidentally, a model of how to write sexy without writing dirty). It is also a powerful story of murder and its aftermath, strengthened by a subplot of Irish politics, and constantly illuminated by the author's lightning flashes of insight into the peculiar relation between the Irish and the English (he himself is both) and the even more incredible relation between man and woman, which few male novelists have understood so well.—ANTHONY BOUCHER, "Criminals at Large," *NYTBR*, April 7, 1968, p. 20

D. E. S. MAXWELL
From: "C. Day Lewis: Between Two Worlds"
Poets of the Thirties
1969, pp. 100–127

Belief, whether a fully developed metaphysic or a complex of unformulated attitudes, is one of the links securing a poem to the experiences of ordinary human life. A similar relationship obtains between the work of literature as aesthetic creation and the concrete reality around it—the source of Virginia Woolf's innumerable atoms of sensation which fall into the shape of Monday or Tuesday. The poet apprehends this reality more exactly than most men and has the unique ability to verbalise his perceptions. But he is dealing with a world jointly inhabited by him and his audience; it is this world, however transfigured, that his audience will expect to recognise: and more particularly the language, the habits, the unvoiced codes of feeling and behaviour of its own time and place. The idiom of literature responds to these properties: and the thirties poets insisted that it should, recording the realities of the time in a diction explicitly of the times. But not merely recording. The poet was also to judge. His statements would indicate a means of controlling to proper ends the world of experience which supplied his subjects. Correct, that is, a precisely contemporary, diction was an agent in the process of perception and judgment. There is nothing really new in any of this. Any innovating poet fashions a style relevant to new circumstances so far unapprehended by the imagination. The questions are whether the thirties poets were not embarking on a task already accomplished by Eliot, Pound and the later Yeats; and whether in fact they took innovation any further.

Certainly they claimed a radically distinctive manner. Its contemporary quality appears in specific details of linguistic connotation, perhaps not always too easily recognised now. The years between now and the thirties cover much more sweeping economic, political and social reorientations than the lapse of time might suggest. 'Arterial roads' is of course still a perfectly comprehensible phrase, and was long before the thirties. But it no longer has either the currency it had in the thirties or the same associations: with the first real era of popular motoring and the summer weekend exodus from cities by car; with highways being adapted to a fast and crowded flow of traffic, with reckless driving, multiple accidents, a habit of aimless release—at its most nightmarish the situation depicted in the last few paragraphs of Patrick Hamilton's *Mr Stimpson and Mr Gorse*. In Auden's 'Consider this and in our time', these associations translate the reader from the social particulars to their brusquely abstracted psychic underlay; from 'Escaping humming down arterial roads' to 'the prey to fugues' and 'the explosion of mania'. How superbly, in those lines, Auden has managed the shift to an intenser witness of his scene.

It is by just this use of particulars that poetry isolates the inwardness of a period; by this means, paradoxically, it achieves its necessary escape from a vision too narrowly vested in the assumptions of its times. . . . As Johnson remarked in another connection, 'a man might write such stuff for ever, if he would *abandon* his mind to it'. Anthologies from Tottel to *Best Poems of 1920*, periodicals from eighteenth-century miscellanies to the 'little magazines' entomb, with its betters, verse that has not got beyond mere modishness. The difference between that and the apotheosis of a mode is the difference between Donne and Cleveland; between the conclusions of Pope's *Dunciad* (especially in its 1728 context) and of Otway's 'To Mr Creech';[1] between Eliot's 'taxi throbbing waiting' and Rupert Brooke's 'keen/Unpassioned beauty of a great machine'. Properly, the surface particulars are there, but as the basis of universalising images, fusing into one the poet's ideas and feelings, objective reality and his way of seeing it. The precipitate is myth, the total synthesis which dramatises the poet's vision of human life. Myth, in this sense, is clearly of the poet's own making; his rendering is its essence.

But certain situations, certain patterns of experience, certain conjunctions of circumstance and character—archetypal myths—seem to have an integrity and energy of their own, almost irrespective of the precise nature of their embodiment in a literary work. As George Steiner has said, 'Even a prose version in modern speech of *Antigone* or *Macbeth* holds the imagination spellbound.'[2] The dialect of a period and of the personal sensibility can stir one of these archetypes to life within a poem. It happens in Frost's 'Stopping by Woods' (the dark wood and the social haven); in Emily Dickinson's 'There is a morn by men unseen' (the return from exile on earth to the afterlife); and elaborately in *The Waste Land*. The poem thus opens out on a lengthened perspective of human experience; not just on acquired knowledge of mythical lore; on the mythical structures of the unconscious too.

The poets of the thirties may give the impression that they have constituted these resources into a composite myth, undifferentiated from poet to poet. They had much in common: their political thinking, their personal backgrounds, the society of their era. Their poetry contains a whole body of shared images and attitudes which makes sense on their being regarded as a 'school'—Auden, Spender and Day Lewis partic-

ularly—even if not one formally set up in the Continental manner. As both Spender and Day Lewis have pointed out, although each of the three poets knew the other two, the three never met until 1947, and so could not have legislated themselves into a kind of poetic commando. Their affinities are none the less undeniable. But the composite myth, as closer inspection reveals, has a protean constitution. Entered by way of different poets, it falls into the several alignments which their individual sensibilities determine. As I have briefly indicated, Day Lewis gives it a distinctively heroic cast. His 'Props of an English scene', as he calls them in *The Magnetic Mountain*, were partly the odds and ends of the standard décor; in his best poems they bring to life a scene disturbingly shadowed by the emblematic drama latent in its surface particulars.

Day Lewis's poems assemble a contemporary landscape with figures. Across it, in common with many of the thirties poets, he is given to saluting his personal friends. Auden and others turn up (unnamed but identifiable) in *Transitional Poem*, in the last poem of *From Feathers to Iron*, R. E. Warner and Auden here and there in *The Magnetic Mountain*. 'Wystan and Rex my friend', 'Wystan, lone flier', 'Wystan, Rex, all of you who have not fled' stand for the reformist band of apostates from their class, the clear-eyed elect 'Bringing light to the dark-livers'. Critics have found this practice offensive. It is certainly rather naive, more self-conscious than its eighteenth-century precedents, in Swift, say: it rarely has the aplomb with which Yeats carried it off; perhaps because behind the author's friends the poems imply a bigger audience, the revolutionary masses. But though one might pretend, one had no assurance that the masses were really listening, while neither Yeats nor the eighteenth century had any such uncertainty of address. Auden, in re-working his poems, has eliminated the name-dropping, or replaced the Stephens and Christophers by cryptic pseudonyms like 'Maverick' and 'Pretzel'. But it was a harmless enough mannerism and in a small way perhaps added to the impression of a mysterious confederacy of initiates.

Day Lewis also recruits once-familiar names from the social history of the times, hired *bourgeois* apologists—'Professor Jeans spills the beans/Dean Inge tells you a thing'—or radical martyrs—'What Wainwright wrote with his blood or Rosa in Prison'. The anti-masque of villains also has the depersonalised cast of Morality types, mentioned in the previous section, who exhibit the stigmata of social privilege or neurotic distempers: politicians, press barons, clerics, middle-class suburbanites. . . .

This extensive use of actual events and people recalls the potted biographies and 'Newsreels' of John Dos Passos: the poet, in fact, was seeking to imitate the appearances of society in something the way of the novelist. So we find the generic thirties scene—or the aspect which seemed to dominate it—fixed in brief vignettes from city and countryside, capturing a mood from a scene in the manner we associate with the cinema, by abrupt caesuras of image as the viewpoint tracks over a landscape. . . .

This kind of 'location shot' gives body to what is really a generalised scene. If the poet had particular roads, a particular city centre in mind, it is more for their typical than their individual qualities. In the topography of the parody poems 'Come live with me' and 'Hush thee my baby' of *A Time to Dance*, the physical objects are pure types. The docks, the canals, the factory hooters are not meant to have any 'local habitation', made physically present by sensuous detail. Instead of by anatomising landscape, these poems disclose the pattern of a way of life by annotating the flat locutions, linguistically domesticated in the twenties and thirties, of Labour Exchanges, Means Tests and Depressed Areas. This new cant stood for shabby realities incongruously lodged in the setting recalled from the parodies' originals. . . .

One may object that poetry is not sociology. But it can say more about the nature of a society than elaborate tables of statistics and questionnaires. In the various ways described, *From Feathers to Iron, The Magnetic Mountain, A Time to Dance, Noah and the Waters* and *Overtures to Death* create a poetic chronicle of their society. Is it consistent with the mythological interpretations it is called upon to support?

The subject of *From Feathers to Iron* is the anxieties and hopes of the prospective father and mother. The heightened sense of 'birth and death in our bones', of promise and threat, gives the experience its critical significance. Poem 27 opens wth an oppressive scene of impending storm. . . . Images of mountaineering and warfare in the next section elaborate the suggestions of menace. The final part discloses the actual occasion, the birth itself, with the nervously intervening *'But if '* in Poem 27 finally allowed to complete its sense and the last lines accepting the possibility of death . . . .

The Magnetic Mountain is recognisably the same world as *From Feathers to Iron*. Its political orientation is more overt and without the central private mataphor. The first of its four parts consists of five poems of which three celebrate the elation of flight, departure. The spirit thus emancipated glimpses the new lands commanded by the magnetic mountain. Its rich deposits transfigure the known universe; Arcadia here is a myth formulated in the concepts of pure and applied physics. . . .

As re-constituted in *Collected Poems, A Time to Dance* consists of these and other separate poems leading up to the title poem; 'A Time to Dance' is partly a narrative of the Parer–M'Intosh flight from England to Australia, partly an elegy on the death of L. P. Hedges, a fellow-schoolmaster. In the original volume it introduced a sequence setting depression England ('despair gathered together at street corners') against the airmen's spirited adventures and the 'radiant energy' of the dead friend, 'our dynamo, our warmth'. A chorus of the unemployed comments sardonically on 'flash talk of the spirit outshining death'; 'Two Songs' and 'A Carol' (given these titles in *Collected Poems*, where they precede the narrative) illuminate their plight. The poet then likens the 'radiance struck/From a deep mourning hour' of his personal loss to the strength accumulated in the martyrdoms of industrial life; and points the analogy which the pilots' technical skills and doggedness hold for the struggle of the workers. They are a metaphor of Engels's dictum, quoted in the poem, 'Freedom is the knowledge of necessity'. The remaining poems, in pseudo-jazz idiom, urge the poet's audience to love, unity, and the revolutionary spirit. The last thirty lines revert to the more formal manner, and *Collected Poems* retains these as an 'Epilogue'.)

The poems preserved are no doubt those that stand best on their own. Verses like 'Yes, why do we all, seeing a Red, feel small?[3] and 'Revolution, revolution/Is the one correct solution' flourished in a climate which we can re-construct but hardly re-inhabit naturally. In the original arrangement, however, the sequence as a whole had an uninhibited aggressiveness which it is a pity to lose. But it was inseparable from its occasion and that has gone. The sequence lived off it rather than perpetuated its life; and it has not quite the dexterity that might have produced entertaining mockeries of the popular song. The narrative and the elegy are fine poems in their own right, celebrating the heroic spirit better than the directly propagandist glosses added to them.

Noah and the Waters is open to similar criticisms. The author's foreword described it as 'something in the tradition of the medieval morality plays', dramatising in modern terms 'the choice that must be made by Noah between clinging to his old life and trusting to the Flood'. After the opening choruses three Burgesses plead with Noah to avert the Flood, then with the Waters of the Flood to undo the havoc they are causing. *The Voices in the Flood* ('Waters of the world, unite!') reject all entreaties: appeals for moderation, offers to compromise ('No doubt there was much that needed, that cried out for, destruction'), accusations of being foreigners, threats ('My poison-gas outfit will make them froth'). Noah sides with the Flood and they 'go out in a running fight,' with the Burgesses. . . . The trouble, as Julian Bell observed, is that the action fails to dramatise the choice so delicately balanced here and elsewhere in the lyric passages. It turns a critical engagement of the emotions into roustabout farce; language surrenders its functions to horseplay. More might be salvaged from *Noah and the Waters*, but it displays that weakening of concentration which Day Lewis has attributed to the demands of his political chores.

The first ten poems of *Overtures to Death*, the last collection Day Lewis published in the thirties, exude an oppressive, despondent atmosphere. In 'Maple and Sumach', 'Regency Houses' and 'Two Landscapes' an autumn setting has the season's jaded melancholy, transferred to (or transferred from) and symbolising a debilitated human vigour. The landscapes and the Regency houses are the elegant but faded properties of a condemned society, evocative of loss, decay, not the triumph of their being supplanted. . . .

Overtures to Death reveals some of the outlines of Day Lewis's later poetry. 'Passage from Childhood' delicately unfolds the solitary evasions of a sensibility damaged in childhood. It anticipates the interest of 'Cornet Solo', 'O Dreams, O Destinations', 'Juvenilia' and other poems of youthful recollections issuing into later life with a significance not grasped in the original experience. There is a marked turning away here to a much more 'subjective' area of consciousness. A number of the poems which conclude *Overtures to Death* suggest the same switch of attention. 'Behold the Swan' describes an October lake scene, its serenity abruptly shattered by the sudden outthrust of energy as a swan takes off in noisy flight. At the end the poem says of the beating wings and stretching neck, 'They are a prophecy'. But like 'Maple and Sumach', 'February 1936' and 'Regency Houses' the poem is primarily descriptive, with the 'moral' appearing very briefly as a tailpiece. One can construe it politically only because of what one knows from the poetry generally. The poet has responded to a quality in the scene which awakens a fundamentally personal emotion. Any ulterior social attitude it might be used to signify pulsates much more weakly than the immediate personal feeling. In this collection, too, the style has shed or modified most of the features that previously marked it: the elliptical syntax, the reminiscences of Anglo-Saxon models, the syncopated rhythms. And with these the frequent echoes of Hopkins, Wilfred Owen, Eliot have faded also. . . .

His later poetry retains a strongly public element. He writes with assurance about 'public affairs'—as in his war poems; and the communal world of extrinsic objects and events is firmly present, as in the scenery of *An Italian Visit*. The colloquialism is toned down, but its idioms and intonations still invigorate the cadenced, lyrical periods and set in relief the more elevated style. We hear this counterpoint in 'Two Travellers' and the sequence 'Florence: Works of Art' in *An Italian Visit* adopts the vernacular offhandedness fashioned in the thirties. One in particular of its poems, 'Perseus Rescuing Andromeda: Piero di Cosimo' reenters the world of updated myth and fairy tale which had harboured the ogres of the thirties. Its prefatory initials. W.H.A., are intended as a clue to the reader that like the other Florence poems it is deliberate Auden pastiche. The later poetry also maintains the heroic stance of the political poems. The seasons, the individual's experience of life appear still in images of movement and crisis. And again, the modern setting assumes the exemplary patterns of myth— 'The Image', 'The Revenant'—now without the specific political application.

Despite the evident differences between the two, the poetry Day Lewis wrote during and after the war is recognisably the descendant of the poetry he was writing in the thirities. The earlier verse does not fully represent his achievement—in translation, for example. But it is a distinguished body of poetry. It gives real emotional substance to the bickerings induced by marxist dialectic and the crude simplifications of the party line. The literary debate, though solemn, was not uniformly edifying nor even very sensible. Day Lewis's poetry, however, gives the abstractions—art as propaganda, the *bourgeois* predicament, documentary realism—a flesh and blood presence. They exist in the events, personalities and appearances of the time: in the shabby towns of an industrial wasteland denied the machines of the new technology; in the sad landscapes of a countryside neglected or despoiled; in the heartless antics of the complacent or ill-disposed; and in the patterns of ideas and emotions which these formed in a troubled conscience not quite sure what was to be done but recording its dilemmas in terms of heroic conflict. The attitudes expressed are attractive; the passage of time has not obliterated their relevance. The poems uncover old myths in their images of the present; and refresh traditional forms—ballad, parable, narrative—with new techniques and contemporary language. It is not a 'communist' poetry; but it is a poetry which could hardly have existed without the communist entrance into the England of the thirties.

Notes

1. J. C. Ghosh (ed.): *The Works of Thomas Otway* II, pp. 439–40, ll. 57–77.
2. *The Death of Tragedy*, p. 47.
3. The version in *A Time to Dance*, which ends, 'He is what your sons could be, the road these times should take', perhaps shades the odds a little compared with the original ending. The poem appeared in *Left Review* for November 1934, when it was called 'The Communist', and ended, 'He is what your sons will be, the road these times must take.'

WALTER DE LA MARE

1873–1956

Walter John de la Mare was born in Charlton, Kent, on April 25, 1873. His father died when de la Mare was four, and he was brought up by his mother. The family eventually moved to London and de la Mare became a chorister at St. Paul's Cathedral, where he was also educated. In 1890 he became a clerk at the Anglo-American (Standard) Oil Company, where he stayed for nearly twenty years. During his spare time, however, he began to write stories and poems, publishing them in *The Cornhill, Pall Mall Gazette*, and other periodicals. He was, however, so diffident as to the quality of his work that he initially used the pseudonym "Walter Ramal." His *Songs of Childhood* was published in 1902, and his first novel, *Henry Brocken*, appeared in 1904.

In 1899 he married Constance Elfrida Igpen, by whom he had two sons and two daughters. In 1908 the Asquith government granted de la Mare a Civil List pension, and he was able to leave the Standard Oil Company and become a full-time writer. In 1943 his wife died, he became a Companion of Honour in 1948, and in 1953 he received the Order of Merit. From his home in Twickenham he produced an astonishingly variegated body of work, including poetry, novels, tales, essays and reviews, one play (*Crossings: A Fairy Play*, 1921), and an odd collection of prose and poetry (*Desert Islands and Robinson Crusoe*, 1930). He received honorary degrees from Oxford, Cambridge, St. Andrews, Bristol, and the University of London.

Personal

After I was demobilised, at the end of the first world war, I went up to Cambridge, and it was there I first saw Walter de la Mare, who came to lecture to us. His manner, at once grave and shy, was what one might have expected. But the look of him was astonishing. Who could have anticipated the sight of that massive head and that strong and almost saturnine profile? It was the face of a benevolent Roman Emperor, fit to be graved on some enduring coin. There was no hint of misty churchyards and lingering twilight in those powerful Latin features. His deep voice fell pleasantly and persuasively on my ears, but my eyes still stared in surprise.

A year or two afterwards, when I used to go out to Anerley with Edward Davison, I met the poet in a very different setting—at home, with a crowd of youngsters playing charades. (I fancied myself at charades, as author, actor or producer.) I came to know his fascinating trick of asking odd questions, which gave our imaginations a lift. All of us youngsters delighted in him, not only because of his work but also because he was one of those rare persons who never make the young awkwardly conscious of their youth and lack of experience. You seemed to start—though of course you really did nothing of the kind—on level terms with him. When he asked you one of his odd questions, he really waited for your answer. Unlike most men of genius, he did not impose his brilliant personality upon you, flattening you out to give himself more height and grandeur, but deftly lifted you apparently to his own stature of thought, feeling and experience. (What a wonderful schoolmaster he would have made!) We were an aggressive gang,

WALTER DE LA MARE

C. DAY LEWIS

NOEL COWARD

MARGARET DRABBLE

LAWRENCE DURRELL

ARTHUR CONAN DOYLE

LORD DUNSANY

ready to tear down reputations, but we all loved Walter de la Mare.

He made no conscious attempt, however, to be the lovable literary figure, just as he has never made any attempt to build up a great reputation as a representative writer, as one of the giants. He seems to me never to have had in him that hard core of ambition which was certainly there, for example, in Yeats, whose every cry in the Celtic twilight, whose every turn and twist in his mythology and symbolism, was devised to add to his literary stature. (This is not to deny the splendid genius of Yeats, of course, but merely to point to a certain Irish hardness that is entirely missing in de la Mare.)—J. B. PRIESTLEY, "What Lovely Things," *Tribute to Walter de la Mare on His Seventy-Fifth Birthday,* ed. W. R. Bett, 1948, pp. 15–16

W. J.—for so I soon came to call him—built much of his conversation around questions. 'Do you agree . . . ?', he would begin; or, after relating some strange fact or series of events, he would end with the challenge—'How do you account for that?' His questions were of various kinds. They were never Socratic questions, designed to lead the answerer on, and finally expose his ignorance. Some were rhetorical, and to these he did not expect an answer: indeed many of his questions were, as he admitted, unanswerable. Others were prompted by a desire to obtain information or to get the listener's opinion: others, again, were designed to encourage someone in the company to talk. The topics of his conversation were joined together by what psychologists call free association: one thing suggested another by some mental process which often was not logical at all. For example, talk about plagiarism reminded him of a poem he had written called 'The Owl'; this led him to talk about the owl's hooting, and this to a comparison between boys' and women's voices. Thus his conversation was as wayward as the flight of a butterfly. But perhaps a flying-fish is a more appropriate simile, for it flashed out into the light, and fell back into silence; and one could not tell in what direction it would next appear. But in addition to this pursuit of fancy he would reminisce about his childhood, and about people, particularly writers, whom he had known in later life.

His talk was highly idiosyncratic: perhaps it can best be described as a soliloquy for two; and in this form it could not survive in a larger company. Hence, though he much enjoyed entertaining a larger party, his conversation on such occasions was less memorable. He was prepared to be entertained as well as to entertain; and guests would start topics which had to receive some attention, so that the peculiar continuity of his own thought could never fully develop, though he was adept at bringing any conversation round to one of his favourite themes. This, I think, must be the reason why I have few records of the tea-parties at which several other guests beside myself were present. Indeed as time went on he seemed to prefer to see me alone. There was an exception, however, to his rule of 'two's conversation': he did not count members of my family as enlarging the party enough to necessitate any change in his conversational style. Perhaps they were already well-trained listeners. W. J. enjoyed the company of young people, and they became devoted to him; and when any of them came with me the talk went on as usual, and they from time to time became the target for questions.

Though I describe W. J.'s talk as a soliloquy for two it must not be thought that he was a monopolistic talker: the emphasis is as much upon the 'two' as upon the 'soliloquy', and, as I came to know his mind, I learned what in my own sphere would interest him, and how to cast a fly over the flying-fish, and bring them to the surface.

I have spoken of his favourite themes. Poets and poetry,

words and the writing of fiction naturally figured largely in his conversation: the other subjects upon which he enjoyed talking were those of his own poems and stories—time, memory, childhood, dreams, apparitions, horror, death and the unknown future, the unseen, and the mystery of life. . . .

Tea was the ideal occasion for these talks with W. J.: indeed he had invented the term 'tea-talk' for them. They retained something of the atmosphere of 'going out to tea' in childhood—a more exciting social event, perhaps, than any luncheon or dinner party of later life, and I am sure he was conscious of this. Then, a tea-talk is by its nature limited in time: after dinner you can talk all through the night, if you like; but not after tea. A tea-talk has something of the restrictions of an art-form, and the transience of mortality. The party will come to an end: the conjurer will pack away his magical properties; and you will be 'called for'—by Time if not a punctual grown-up. And it is as a conjurer that I think of W. J.—a Prospero who knew that

> We are such stuff
> As dreams are made on

but none the less real for that.—RUSSELL BRAIN, "The Little Nowhere," *Tea with Walter de la Mare,* 1957, pp. 16–19

> de la Mare? I knew him well,
> that old poet of visionary loveliness,
> remember how he looked at me, probingly,
> from dark, kind eyes, taking my hand,
> the words he spoke of mystery and wonder
> as if Somebody beyond was listening.
> He was a gentle man, no stiffness or rancour,
> passionate about children, the world's injustices,
> his warm spirit searching for reality,
> catching its gleam in flower and bird,
> shine on snow, sea shores and water meadows,
> and all the small phenomena of common day.

> Haunted by presences in the dark shades,
> evil decked up in clothes of innocence,
> did not deceive himself, recoil from their menace.
> Hungry for truth asked unanswerable questions,
> intrigued more with 'Why?' than with 'How?';
> once said his poems were visitors
> making some of them stay for ever.

> I see him now moving about the Twickenham house
> leaning on walking stick, breath short, smiling still,
> a Listener longing for the eternal hour,
> his own Traveller, Eden his home.

> Yes, I remember him well, and hear him now
> calling me to walk in fields of asphodel,
> beckoning me to sundown and dewfall in the lost
> Hesperides.
> I shall answer his 'Come Hither'.

—LEONARD CLARK, "Listening and Travelling," *Tribute to Walter de la Mare,* by Edmund Blunden and Leonard Clark, 1974, p. 5

General

What, after all, is the great globe itself but undiscovered or perhaps re-discovered country to every newcomer? What is life but a cryptogrammatical chart as yet uncompleted in the delineation of which Destiny or Providence helps us to guide the faltering pen? Who even can deny us the privy hope, if not conviction, that we walk and slumber, not, as it might appear, on a giddy ball chiefly consisting of metal in what is called Space—an exceedingly difficult pill for any self-respecting fancy to swallow; but on an endless sea-ridden plain whose furthermost bourne is called Death? Our jaded, sated greed for fact is largely a fallacy, A green meadow may be El Dorado and all the Indies to a simple, ardent and unexacting heart. The Well at the World's End *may* be found in one's backyard. Better be busy with the bucket while its waters are sweet. Thou art— what thou dost gaze upon. Thou dost gaze upon what thou art. To a tortured imagination the homely Thames may wander black as Acheron; to a happier, not Naaman's Jordan itself is a more miraculous stream. And if, possibly, one sometimes wearies of the old familiar places, of Greenwich time and terrestrial latitudes, how easy to take pencil and brush and idly map out the place where one *would* be. No need to be specific; no call to give it even a name. It would be quite unnecessary even to write a book about it. It would fetch not forty-four farthings in open auction. It would be only a poor thing, but it would be one's very own.—WALTER DE LA MARE, "Maps Actual and Imaginary" (1920), *Pleasures and Speculations*, 1940, p. 347

He is one of those writers who have a few obvious characteristics known to everybody, characteristics that are complacently indicated by the reviewer whenever such writers publish a book; but if we wish to press forward and examine him more closely, he becomes curiously elusive, almost playing Ariel to our Caliban. There is no difficulty if we are simply prepared to enjoy and not to analyse, for we can always recognise his hand; the work is all of a piece, and no one who has once known it can fail to appreciate that curious perfume and that most melodious twang. Superficially, his work may appear somewhat fragmentary and casual, the spasmodic creation of a gifted dilettante—a few bundles of short lyrics, some short tales, and a fantasy or two, so many lovely and quaint odds and ends; but nothing could be further from the truth, for actually his work is one of the most individual productions this century has given us, every scrap of it being stamped with its author's personality and taking its place in the de la Mare canon. If Mr. de la Mare were to wander into half a dozen literary forms that so far have not known him, if he were to bid farewell to poetry and fiction and do nothing but essays, criticism, and even history, the new work would promptly link up with the old and take on a quality different from that of any other essays, criticism, or history, so marked is his individuality. Nevertheless, he remains to criticism an elusive figure, whose outline and gestures are not easily fixed in the memory—a shadowy Pied Piper.

One fairly common misconception must be brushed aside before we can begin to examine Mr. de la Mare, and that is the notion that he is primarily a creator of pretty fancies for the children. Because he has occasionally produced a volume for children, many persons regard him merely as the latest and most delicate of nursery poets, an artist for the Christmas Tree. Nor is this notion, except in its crudest form, confined to the uncritical, for even at this late hour there is a tendency on the part of many critics to treat Mr. de la Mare as if he were not an artist with a unique vision, a man of strange delights and sorrows, but a rather gentlemanly conjurer they had engaged for their children's party. There is, of course, an element of truth in this view, but at the moment it is hardly worth while disengaging it, though, as we shall presently see, this element of truth happens to be of supreme importance. Regarded as a general view this popular misconception is so preposterous that if we go to the other extreme, if we argue that Mr. de la Mare is a writer that no child should be suffered to approach, we shall not be further from the truth. We could point out that his work is really unbalanced, decadent, unhealthy, poisonous fruit for any child's eating. Consider his subjects. *The Return* is the story of a man who is partly possessed by an evil restless ghost, who comes back from a meditation among the tombstones in the local churchyard, wearing the face of a long-dead adventurer—a nightmare. The poetry is filled with madness and despair, wonders, and witchcraft, lit with a sinister moonlight; some crazed Elizabethan fool sitting in a charnel-house might have lilted some of these songs. The *Memoirs of a Midget* is the history of a freak who moves elvishly in the shadow of some monstrous spirit of evil; it is a long dream that never turns to the waking world, but only changes, when it does change, to nightmare. The tales in *The Riddle* are worse; they are the chronicles of crazed or evil spirits, Miss Duveen, Seaton's Aunt, and the rest; their world is one of abnormalities, strange cruelties and terrors, monstrous trees and birds and dead men on the prowl; their very sunlight is corrupt, maggot-breeding. And is this, we might ask, the writer of pretty fancies for the children; as well might we introduce Webster, Poe, and Baudelaire into the nursery and schoolroom. Such an account of Mr. de la Mare as an unwholesome decadent is manifestly absurd, but on the whole it is probably less absurd than the more popular opinion of him as a pretty-pretty children's poet. Yet we can use his work for children as a kind of jumping-off place in our pursuit of him.—J. B. PRIESTLEY, "Mr. de la Mare's Imagination," *LM*, May 1924, pp. 33–34

Every reader of Mr. de la Mare's prose or poetry is acquainted with numberless instances in which an unearthly radiance is imparted to familiar things. The slow, searching motion of silver moonbeams in the silence of the night; the strange loveliness of earth when masked by a fall of snow; the beauty that may linger about a mossy, indecipherable gravestone, hidden away among swaying grasses, beneath its coverture of overarching yews—these are things which, once Mr. de la Mare has shown them to us, the grateful heart is never likely to forget.

It is the privilege of the imagination, however, not only to transfigure familiar things but also to range at will over worlds that are remote and strange. Here, too, Mr. de la Mare is perfectly at home. With superlative ease he visualises the fight of a snake with some bird of prey in the heart of the tropics, or watches the meeting of a languorous Eastern potentate with a loathsome leper in the depths of a lonely forest. It is nothing to him to imagine what princesses in Tartary or Arabia may be doing, or a company of dwarfs or apes on some lone island of the South Pacific. Having a true relish for the travels of Sir John Mandeville, Mr. de la Mare loves to toy with the rubies and amethysts of Mandalay, Guadalajara and Solikamsk, and to summon before him, with a gesture of delight, "the puma, pelican, Patagonian papalja, and pretty Poll."

It must not be supposed, however, that all is lovely and of good report in the imaginative realm to which he penetrates with so much courage. The other world, as Mr. de la Mare conceives it, is tenanted by the obscene, the sinister, and the grotesque no less than by the beautiful and kindly. If you press too far into that region you never know when some "monstrous porcine cacodemon" may come hoofing towards you out of unknown deeps. Much of this writing reminds us of the tales of Edgar Allan Poe, or the grisly shapes that look out on us from the drawings of S. H. Sime.

Mr. de la Mare has made a profound study of the sense of guilt and the fear that attends on guilt. It is a dreadful thing to be caught unexpectedly with stolen apples in your pocket, or to be suddenly confronted, in the silent recesses of a supposedly empty house which you have invaded, by a woman who holds a loaded revolver to your eyes. Our author is evidently well acquainted with "the terror that walketh by night." He has also an uncanny power of mingling the human and the fantastic and showing what it must be like to feel oneself a ghost and a man at the same time. He has shudderingly traversed and mapped out for us some of the most bleak and inhospitable tracts of the human mind. His pages provide us with minute psychological studies of a youth whose soul within him is jellied with paralysing fear at the thought of pulling a crimson-pleated bell-handle that dangles above his head; a man who has become firmly convinced that he is possessed, body and soul, by the ghost of a French Huguenot who commited suicide a century before; and a trembling old verger who struggles desperately with spectral terrors in the aisles of a lost cathedral shrouded in sea-borne mists on an abandoned coast.

Sometimes this feeling of disillusionment and despair takes appalling forms. What if the whole universe be a monstrous death-trap, a hideous masquerade, and the age-long upward strivings of humanity doomed to end at last in ghastly frustration and defeat? Frenzied apprehensions of this kind beset the minds of many of Mr. de la Mare's characters, and we are frequently taken right up to the brink of that yawning precipice of the mind beyond which madness lies. Yet in some cases full health is recovered by the homeliest means. One of the finest of his stories tells of a woman who is obsessed by horrible nightmare visions of souls being shovelled away grossly to make up a festering muck-heap somewhere in the void, but who is ultimately restored to complete sanity and peace of mind by nothing more than the neighbouring farmyard companionship of a pile of ripe manure covered with sweet flowers.

What all these things may signify for the ultimate interpretation of the universe Mr. de la Mare does not attempt to say, and he suggests that we are wiser not to ask. The world is simple and beautiful enough to be enjoyed to the utmost, if only we will resist the temptation to explain it overmuch.

> Leave this vain questioning. Is not sweet the rose?
> Sings not the wild bird ere to rest he goes?

After all we contrive to say about it, life remains an enigma. It "emanates from no discernible whence and vanishes out into no detectable whither." It may be, as one writer suggests, that Mr. de la Mare is trying to describe things for which human language is as yet inadequate, since they can only be apprehended in a glass darkly. Certainly he gives us the impression that he wishes us to believe in this real existence of a supernatural world which is more than the projected image of our own minds. "What are we all but the ghosts of something?" There must in this universe be abiding realities which so far are "only distantly dreamed of by the time-driven, thought-corroded congregations of man." We can only at present grope our way fumblingly among these mysteries, feeling ourselves to be trespassers and intruders, exposed to the scrutiny of unseen eyes, and having our movements watched by concealed "listeners," of whose existence we are mostly unaware.

In any case, we must go on groping, and, if we are hardy and courageous in our search, who knows what discoveries may yet be granted to us? "Illuminated by the imagination," says Mr. de la Mare, "our life—whatever its defeats and despairs—is a never-ending, unforeseen strangeness and adventure and mystery. This is the fountain of our faith and of our hope."—R. H. Coats, "The World of Walter de la Mare," *FR*, Oct. 1927, pp. 489–91

Every great writer, like every great teacher, makes certain assumptions about life. Joseph Conrad, for example, earnestly opposed (in the ordinary sense) didacticism in fiction; yet, says Conrad, "every subject in the region of intellect and emotion must have a morality of its own if it is treated at all sincerely;

and even the most artful writer will give himself (and his morality) away in about every third sentence." If the reader cannot understand the assumptions made, or cannot grant them even as the frame of reference of a work of art, then—there is no help for it—the writer's world is closed to him. De la Mare, too, has his assumptions, and, gentlest of men though he is, there are "hard sayings" among them.

"Realism," for example, "in the accepted sense," is only, as he sees it, "a kind of scientific reporting." "What is called realism is usually a record of life at a low pitch and ebb viewed in the sunless light of day . . ." Nature itself "resembles a veil over some further reality of which the imagination in its visionary moments seems to achieve a more direct evidence." There are the senses, of course. But the senses "can tell us only what they are capable of being sensible *of*." And this is quite inadequate, for "what we see and hear is only the smallest fraction of what is." Even when you have found a material explanation for a given set of phenomena, "it doesn't follow . . . that they didn't mean something else too."

Some of these quotations are from de la Mare's stories; some of them are from Mr. de la Mare speaking *in propria persona*. None of them, I think, misrepresent him; for, as I have already suggested, his is a notably varied yet remarkably single voice. And it should not be difficult, I think, to guess along what lines a writer who makes such assumptions would be likely to proceed.

If he is a serious writer, he must, necessarily, first of all seek to pierce "the veil," to "achieve a more direct evidence" of the things that matter than the senses can give. And, be it carefully noted at the outset, there is no element of "escapism" in this. "How," asked the wise London *Times* reviewer of *The Connoisseur*, "How can you be said to be fleeing the real, or the actual, when you are merely opening your eyes to what the simplest fragment of it, in your view, involves?" De la Mare has never fled through the veil to the comforting delights of a Never-Never Land; there are dreadful terrors in Tishnar—greater terrors indeed than any he could have encountered had he been content to remain earth-bound. But the essential point is that had Walter de la Mare stopped where, say, Mr. Maugham stops, that would have been, for him, the real "escapism"; for on that basis he must have left out not merely *a* segment of human experience but what seems to him *the* most important segment of all.

Now, obviously, the man who would pierce the veil must approach it at some point where it promises to be pierceable. Where do these points of entry lie? They are somewhat differently located, no doubt, for different writers. But there can be no question of where they lie for de la Mare. He finds his points of entry through dreams; through childhood ("Children . . . live in a world peculiarly their own." "They are not bound in by their groping senses. Facts to them are the liveliest of chameleons. Between their dream and their reality looms no impassable abyss"); through adventures, "psychic" or what-you-will, on the frontiers of consciousness; and, as has already been indicated, through the use of the artistic imagination ("An imaginative experience is not only as real but far realer than an unimaginative one"; for it is "in our individual imagination" that "the essential truth for each one of us lies").

And with this we have come, I think, very close to the themes and motives of the de la Mare fantasy; close enough, at any rate, to be clear in our own minds that none have been idly or arbitrarily chosen. To take a specific example, de la Mare has not written about children rather than about businessmen because he "likes" children better. He may, to be sure, "like" children better than businessmen. But his "liking" or not "liking" is a quite irrelevant consideration. He has been driven to the use of certain symbols, certain materials, because only through them can he express an apprehension of life which, in the last analysis, he did not choose, but which was chosen for him.—EDWARD WAGENKNECHT, "Introduction" to *Collected Tales of Walter de la Mare*, 1950, pp. x–xii

Works

POETRY

Except in the personal sense—and the charm of his gracious personality would surely surround him with friends, whether he wanted them or not—Walter de la Mare is, like Hardy, a lonely figure in modern English poetry—no other poet of our time has a place more notably apart from his contemporaries. You might almost read an allegory of this aloofness into his "Myself":

> There is a garden grey
> With mists of autumntide;
> Under the giant boughs,
> Stretched green on every side,
>
> Along the lonely paths,
> A little child like me,
> With face, with hands like mine,
> Plays ever silently. . . .
>
> And I am there alone:
> Forlornly, silently,
> Plays in the evening garden
> Myself with me.

only that one knows he is happy enough and not forlorn in his aloneness. You may trace, perhaps, here and there in his verse elusive influences of Coleridge, Herrick, Poe, the songs of Shakespeare, or, now and then, in a certain brave and good use of colloquial language, of T. E. Brown, but such influences are so slight and so naturalised into his own distinctive manner that it is impossible to link him up with the past and say he is descended from any predecessor, as Tennyson was from Keats. More than with any earlier poetry, his verse has affinities with the prose of Charles Lamb—of the Lamb who wrote the tender, wistful "Dream-Children" and the elvishly grotesque, serious-humorous "New Year's Eve"—who was sensitively wise about witches and night-fears, and could tell daintily or playfully of the little people, fairy or mortal. But the association is intangible; he is more unlike Lamb than he is like him. And when you compare him with poets of his day there is none that resembles him; he is alone in his garden. He has had imitators, but they have failed to imitate him, and left him to his solitude. . . .

He began late, as poets go, for he was nearly thirty when his first book came out, and about forty before he began to be given his due place among the poets of his generation. He was so slow in arriving because he came without noise, intrinsically unconventional but not fussily shattering the superficial conventions of others, making no sensational approach, not attempting to shock or to startle. I don't think his verse ever had the instant appeal of a topical interest, except such of it as grew out of the war, and nothing could be more unlike the orthodox war poetry than that strange, poignant lyric of his, "The Fool Rings his Bells"—

> Come, Death, I'd have a word with thee;
> And thou, poor Innocency;
> And Love—a lad with broken wing;
> And Pity, too:
> The Fool shall sing to you,
> As Fools will sing. . . .

Its quaintness, sincerity, tenderness and grim fancy are spontaneously in keeping with the lovely or whimsical dreamings, the wizardries and hovering music of his happier songs. He may not have lived in seclusion, unfretted by the hard facts of existence, but the world has never been too much with him, so he can still hear the horns of elfland blowing over an earth that remains for him

> a magical garden with rivers and bowers,

haunted by fays and gnomes, dryads and fawns and the witchery and enchantment that have been in dusky woods, in misty fields, in twilight and midnight places since the beginning of time. Howbeit, even the ghostly atmosphere of "The Listeners" is pierced with a cry that is not of the dead, for in his farthest flights of fantasy he is not out of touch with nature and human nature, and it is a glowing love of these at the heart of his darkling visions and gossamer imaginings that gives them life and will keep them alive.—ARTHUR ST. JOHN ADCOCK, "Walter de la Mare," *Gods of Modern Grub Street*, 1913, pp. 73–80

It is almost impossible not to compare Mr. de la Mare with Mr. Yeats. Of both poetries it is a temptation to use the word 'magical', for these two poets, more than any others living, are adept in the incantation through words of these indefinable emotions and unassociated passions. 'No—but opopanax and cinnamon;' what a satisfying line that is, yet its intellectual content is of the smallest! and Mr. de la Mare can do similar things. Both of them begin with faery—though with different realms of that world; both of them have moved into a world of profound humanity. But there the resemblance ceases. For it might be held that, though the reader derives an equally intense satisfaction from the later work of both poets, he receives from Mr. Yeats the communication of a rich and unappeased longing, while from Mr. de la Mare he receives a rich and appeased content. In Mr. Yeats's work there exists—a word may be borrowed from his own criticism—the 'antitype' of his desires, and from the half-loved, half-loathed encounter arise his moving lines. But Mr. de la Mare's work has neither type nor antitype; there is in it no vibrant conflict, and what conflict there is, is in it almost awfully subdued to a farther peace. There emerges from his verse the imagination at least of a state beyond Time.

A number of these poems, nevertheless, are about things that imply conflict—fear and parting and madness, and even more evil possibilities. A number of them again are about death. But it is not death understood, as it is normally understood by most of us, as a state devoid of experience and empty of realization. Whatever our intellectual beliefs may be, the word death generally suggests a 'naughting' of all that we know. We may expect to know other things and even dimly hope to know lovelier; but such expectation and hope are slender emotions. In Mr. de la Mare's poems there is a state of removed ecstasy; it is as though death had become, not a gate to experience, but itself a rich experience, a summing-up and transcending of all present beauty and richness. It is removed in two senses; first, it is—as it must be in poetry—not something to be looked forward to in time and with the natural mind, but to be felt here and with the 'holy imagination' which Blake perceived to be the Saviour of men; it is therefore something more removed than a promise, being a state which exists already within us, but into which we have not entered. And secondly, it is a state which is beyond, and beyond in the sense of including, those other experiences of fear and mistake and terror. These, which are separate poems, are elements of the whole; transforming these into beauty, Mr. de la Mare has persuaded us of an inclusive ecstasy.

In this most passionate verse there is one thing perhaps

lacking, and yet it seems ungracious to speak of it. If it is spoken of at all, it must be not in complaint or regret but merely as a warning to some readers. Not even Mr. de la Mare can give us everything, and the thing he has not condescended to give us is philosophy. This statement implies no pride on his part, but it does imply that this beauty will not of itself shape itself in metaphysical thought, or anyhow not in rationalized metaphysical thought. The emotion is too intense, it seems, to do so, yet some such modification might be a relief. It is, normally, when the intensity of emotion no longer exists that we turn to thought, or perhaps the turning is itself a natural lowering of the emotion. Normally, but not necessarily; certain great and passionate minds have had intellect as well as feeling enlarged and influenced. But that hardly happens here—though such a phrase should be modified with all the 'perhapses' possible. For it is, by whatever road he has reached it, from *beyond* thought that this communication comes, and thought in itself could never find the way to know it.—CHARLES WILLIAMS, "Walter de la Mare," *Poetry at Present*, 1930, pp. 84–86

De la Mare uses delicately and sometimes magically the ordinary vocabulary of the romantic poets ("lorn as curlew's in the hush/Of dewfall"); but he has a feeling for terse, homely, concrete phrasing that is not ordinary, and a surprising Hardyish willingness to use awkward and ineffective abstractions because he spontaneously thinks of a subject in those terms. He uses the most flagrantly Poetic diction, half for old-fashioned manners and half for love: he seems to share the Collegiate Dictionary's frightening belief that a poem is "a composition in verse, characterized by imagination and poetic diction." Similarly he thinks the gaudiest trappings of Elizabethan tragedy intrinsically valuable, and his fervidly romantic and dramatic speeches in blank verse are close to those of Kipling's mock-Elizabethan play-scenes. (His poems are *about* part of the pre-1914 world, not our own—though there is something prescient in their gloom.) When he writes in the grand manner it is with a certain innocence, as children act out an execution; he is genuinely unassuming, a mouse in a corner, and never thinks to tell you, as better but vainer poets do: "Now I am going to be humble."

It is easy to complain that de la Mare writes about unreality; but how *can* anybody write about unreality? From his children and ghosts one learns little about children and nothing about ghosts, but one learns a great deal of the reality of which both his ghosts and his children are projections, of the wishes and lacks and love that have produced their "unreality." (We read religious poems not to learn about God but to learn about men.) At the very least de la Mare is a perspective of reality, a way of sight, that satisfies the limitations he and his readers share, and that exposes to his readers the limitations that are peculiar to de la Mare—or to themselves. He has made himself a fool for the sake of Faerie, for the sake of everything that is irrational, impractical, and at the same time essential; and because he has persisted in his folly his best poems—limited and extravagant as they are—are full of the personal distinction, the involuntary individuality that are marks of a real poet. But his poetry represents our world only as the flickering shade-pattern of leaves upon an arm can represent the arm; the hard hot flesh in the sunlight has nothing to stand for it but vacancy.—RANDALL JARRELL, "A Verse Chronicle," *Poetry and the Age*, 1953, pp. 153–54

FICTION

The Return . . . is, of course, a fantasy, but it differs from the later work not so much in its theme as in its treatment, which brings it nearer to the ordinary realistic fiction of the time than

the later stories are. The style is not so mannered, not so subtly cadenced and bright with imagery, as the style of the other two volumes, and it does not lure us on to forget this world of offices and the witness-box as the later one does, but really has the contrary aim of making the one fantastic stroke credible. Mr. de la Mare has not boldly entered his own world, and the result, for all the art he has plainly lavished on the story, is unfortunate; the story itself is one, or at least is of the kind, that we are more accustomed to seeing treated comically, in the manner, say, of Mr. Anstey, than treated tragically as it is here, and though this would not have mattered in the least had the author lured us away into his own world, it matters a great deal when he is making terms with this one. For example, seeing that the translated Lawford and his wife are compelled to deceive every one about them in the most elaborate fashion, we wonder why it did not occur to them that Lawford, who was his own master and not without means, could easily settle the matter by quietly slipping away from the district for a time. This procedure would not have pleased Mr. de la Mare, it is clear, but it was the obvious thing to do. And the author, by his method of treatment, aiming at some kind of verisimilitude, invites such questions, which would be mere prosaic quibbling, nothing more than evidence of the questioner's lack of imagination, if they were raised in connection with one of the later stories. Then again, Mrs. Lawford, a commonplace, conventionally-minded wife, is the kind of character the ordinary realistic novelist sketches in between a few puffs of his (or her) cigarette; but just where such inferior chroniclers are happily in their depth, Mr. de la Mare is well out of his, and Mrs. Lawford is appalling, a crude monster from a first novel by a third-rate writer. Her friend and their conversations are on the same level of crudity. In short, the conventional element, which would not be present at all in the later stories since the whole pack of characters, with their houses and furniture, would be subtly translated, is so badly done that it almost wrecks the fantasy, which is presented with some characteristic strokes of genius. Here, then, the normal, with its commonplace tangle of adult relations and interests, has baffled our author's imagination.—J. B. PRIESTLEY, "Mr. de la Mare's Imagination," *LM*, May 1924, pp. 38–39

That obsession with death that fills Mr de la Mare's poetry with the whisper of ghosts, that expresses itself over and over again in the short story in the form of *revenants*, has never led him to accept—or even to speculate on—the Christian answer. Christianity when it is figured in these stories is like a dead religion of which we see only the enormous stone memorials. Churches do occur—in 'All Hallows', 'The Trumpet', 'Strangers and Pilgrims', but they are empty haunted buildings. . . .

What an odd world to those of us with traditional Christian beliefs, is this world of Mr de la Mare's: the world where the terrible Seaton's Aunt absorbs the living as a spider does and remains alive herself in the company of the dead. 'I don't look to flesh and blood for my company. When you've got to be my age, Mr Smithers (which God forbid), you'll find life a very different affair from what you seem to think it is now. You won't seek company then, I'll be bound. It's thrust on you'; the world of the recluse Mr Bloom, that spiritualist who had pressed on too far ignoring the advice that the poet would have given him.

> Bethink thee: every enticing league thou wend
> Beyond the mark where life its bound hath set
> Will lead thee at length where human pathways end
> And the dark enemy spreads his maddening net.

How wrong, however, it would be to give the impression that

Mr de la Mare is just another, however accomplished, writer of ghost stories, yet what is it that divides this world of Mr Kempe and Mr Bloom and Seaton's Aunt, the dubious fellow-passenger with Lavinia in the train, the stranger in Crewe waiting room from the world of the late M. R. James's creation—told by the antiquary? M. R. James with admirable skill invented ghosts to make the flesh creep; astutely he used the image which would best convey horror; he was concerned with truth only in the sense that his stories must ring true—while they were being read. But Mr de la Mare is concerned, like his own Mr Bloom, to find out: his stories are true in the sense that the author believes—and conveys his belief—that this is the real world, but only in so far as he has yet discovered it. They are tentative. His use of prose reminds us frequently of a blind man trying to describe an object from the touch only—'this thing is circular, or nearly circular, oddly dinted, too hard to be a ball: it might be, yes it might be, a human skull.' At any moment we expect a complete discovery, but the discovery is delayed. We, as well as the author, are this side of Lethe. When I was a child I used to be horrified by Carroll's poem *The Hunting of the Snark*. The danger that the snark might prove to be a boojum haunted me from the first page, and sometimes reading Mr de la Mare's stories, I fear that the author in his strange fumbling at the invisible curtain may suddenly come on the inescapable boojum truth, and just as quickly vanish away.

For how they continually seek their snark, his characters—in railway trains, in deserted churches, even in the bars of village inns. Listen to them speaking, and see how all the time they ignore what is at least a fact—that an answer to their questions *has* been proposed: how intent they are to find an alternative, personal explanation: how they hover and debate and touch and withdraw, while the boojum waits. . . .

In all these stories, it seems to this admirer that we have a prose unequalled in its richness since the death of James, or dare one, at this date, say Robert Louis Stevenson. Stevenson comes particularly to mind because he played with so wide a vocabulary—the colloquial and the literary phrase, incorporating even the dialect word and naturalising it. So Mr de la Mare will play consciously with clichés (hemmed like James's between inverted commas), turning them underside as it were to the reader, and showing what other meanings lie there hidden: he will suddenly enrich a colloquial conversation with a literary phrase out of the common tongue, or enrich on the contrary a conscious literary description with a turn of country phrase—'destiny was spudding at his tap root'.

With these resources at his command no one can bring the natural visible world more sharply to the eye: from the railway carriage window we watch the landscape unfold, the sparkle of frost and rain, the glare of summer sunlight, the lights in evening windows; we are wooed and lulled sometimes to the verge of sleep by the beauty of the prose, until suddenly without warning a sentence breaks in mid-breath and we look up and see the terrified eyes of our fellow-passenger, appealing, hungry, scared, as he watches what we cannot see—'the sediment of an unspeakable obsession', and a certain glibness would seem to surround our easy conscious Christian answers to all that wild speculation, if we could ever trust ourselves to urge that cold comfort upon this stranger travelling 'our way'.—GRAHAM GREENE, "The Short Stories," *Tribute to Walter de la Mare on His Seventy-Fifth Birthday*, ed. W. R. Bett, 1948, pp. 73–77

The critics of poetry tell us that de la Mare had remarkable technical virtuosity. Here, in verse and prose, he has his strong resemblance to Poe. He knew that there is no point in a macabre story unless it is made more macabre, and that the final macabre moment is the one that relates it to common and not exceptional experience. The last sentence of *Seaton's Aunt* is an example of a technical and a feeling capacity that gets the last drop out of a situation. The essence of Seaton is that he was a nonentity who never had more than the half-hearted interest of the narrator. He was slowly killed by his old Aunt, the vampire, because he had not the will or the guts to live. He died. He was buried. That is mere horrifying anecdote. What follows is, alas, life:

> There was precious little use in pottering about in the muddy dark merely to discover where he was buried. And yet I felt a little uneasy. My rather horrible thought was that, so far as I was concerned—one of his extremely few friends—he had never been much better than "buried" in my mind.

We are living graveyards of the unwanted. It required an extra refinement of the whole conception of this story to make the macabre tragic.

Yes, the art was in de la Mare's stories, but what was their degree? There is an obvious difficulty for us here. The events of the last 50 years have made a mess of literary criticism. De la Mare was enclosed in a manner which history has driven out. He wrote in a Period room. He was the Artist, the Romantic, the Puritan oblivious in the room. We find a prose that has come down through Meredith and Stevenson, Edwardian, decorative, studied, a velvet jewelled by what will occasionally strike us as the art-jewellery of *mots justes*, whereas we have grown up among prose like clear, common, regular rain. We cannot begin a story with the phrase: "Away into secrecy frisked a pampered mouse". It is too rich for us, like lobster, though in fact de la Mare knew how to write the plain, bare factual prose that can set the poetic image off. In saying this we are merely saying that we did not start writing in the Nineties ourselves. A more serious difficulty is that in the last twenty or thirty years studies in the macabre, in guilt, fear and horror, have been taken into regions even less secure. De la Mare belongs to the tradition which makes us feel more complacently safe, as children feel, the more we are terrified. There is pleasure in the torture. There is reassurance even in the guilt. No one has left the back door open. Whereas in the stories of Kafka and his disciples, cruelty, self-torture, guilt, the horrors, are comfortless; they take us into a universal wretchedness and lead us whimpering on out of literature to modern religious sensibility and its self-pitying, bleeding God. That is an extra turn of the screw which de la Mare's generation did not have to give. Of course, guilt and fear are guilt and fear and hell is hell, whatever the disguises, but they do not now seem to us as *enclosed* as they are in de la Mare's art. . . .

The stories of de la Mare are not archaisms. They are romances in the sense that he has seen through the first-class waiting room at Crewe, or the kitchen cupboards and the knife-powder in the villa or the scene in the London tea-shop. They are contemporary romances in which, whether the scene is vulgar or beautiful, it has its own brute force. He has responded, in the elaborate and elusive way of certain artists, to the imbroglio of what he knew about his time. He has, in Matthew Arnold's sense, "criticised" the Edwardian agglomeration, every yard of shot satin. His obvious refuge as a poet and a writer of stories, was in loneliness, in shutting himself away, for good or evil. There is always (he conveys, now with delight, now with horror) another room within. This was a temperament less suited to stories which involved "normal" life, for there he moved into the prosaic, unhaunted world of the ups and downs of life, the soluble psychological problem.

There his power of evocation was dulled by common sense and forgiveness. But the stories I have named are masterpieces of innocence or wickedness which are beyond any question of forgiving and forgetting. Their evils and delights are as absolute as magic, as dense as rituals.—V. S. PRITCHETT, "Walter de la Mare," NSN, June 30, 1956, pp. 767–68

WORKS FOR CHILDREN

When the first illustrated edition of *Peacock Pie* appeared in December 1916 with Heath Robinson's amusing and delightful drawings, the *Times Literary Supplement* hailed the poems as '. . . the purest poetry for children ever made; Blake and Stevenson not forgotten'. Later on, in 1932, in his essay, *Lewis Carroll*, Walter de la Mare was to say,

> Yet writers who had the nursery in view, and even long after William Blake had sung of innocence, remain for the most part convinced that what is good for the young *must* be unpleasant. Their rhymes like their prose were "nearly always in a moral, minor or miserable key". They prescribed not simples, syrups and cordials, but brimstone . . . A reaction, it is clear, was bound to follow, and that reaction has perhaps reached its extreme in a good deal of the nursery literature of our own day, which is as silly, if not worse, as theirs was dismal.

Walter de la Mare—and the work of W. B. Yeats has been borne in mind—is the greatest writer of English lyrical poetry (particularly for children) of the first half of this century. It is tendentious and futile to label this poetry as being merely 'minor' or 'Georgian' or 'romantic'. And it is patronising and insulting to say of this poetry that it is little more than 'accomplished'. Yet this is what some critics, who have lost their sense of wonder, have said of it because it does not measure up to what *they* say poetry ought to be. . . .

His work is always found on the shelves of children's libraries, and librarians continue to recommend successive generations of children to read it. His poetry and his stories for children are firmly established in the schools of this country, of the Commonwealth, and of America. Eleanor Farjeon wrote of her visits with Walter de la Mare to

> . . . Girls' Schools and Children's Libraries, he to read his poems and I to sing my nursery rhymes, for I was always shy of reading aloud in public, or indeed of appearing on any platform for any reason. Oddly enough, I felt he liked support almost as much as I needed it, and even asked me to split his occasions with him. Children adored his presence among them, but I sometimes wondered if his small rapt listeners heard him beyond the third row, for he read his poems to them in the same reflective voice with which, in the intimacy of his room, poetry fell with ease into the talk. He would tell them, "This one is called 'The Little Green Orchard' . . . and here's another one . . . and another . . . and here's another . . ." Once, when I had written describing a prize-giving I had braced myself to attend alone, he wished he had been there "disguised as a little creature with blue ribbons in her hair and a muslin frock"; and in turn described one of his own recent prize-givings at a girls' school—"and it was awful to feel the smile from the heart steadily stiffening into the plaster of Paris of habit—and *yet* to be coming from the same place, I believe".

. . . Walter de la Mare wrote steadily for sixty years, seeking to perfect his craftsmanship and to develop that rare talent to the full; he succeeded in doing so in a score or so of poems

and in a dozen or so of tales. These wear the bloom of immortality. How many writers ever do as much, for all the books they write? His imagination was unique, particularly in his own day, though of the same cast as Coleridge's and Poe's; he was blessed with foreknowledge and an uncanny understanding of children and their world; he knew by heart as well as by intellect what are the salient characteristics of childhood. Neither was he led astray by the more paradisal aspects of childhood, by the 'trailing clouds of glory'. He saw it, as D. H. Lawrence did, and Wordsworth did not, as a whole thing, divine, elemental, wayward, unfathomable.

. . . He wrote *The Three Mulla-Mulgars*, one of the finest long stories for children ever written—a book of poetic truth and beauty, tender, fresh, and shimmering with the light of its faraway snows. There are also a fairy play, *Crossings* (written for a boys' school), some fifty short stories (including twenty or so for children), re-writings of traditional and Bible tales for children, any number of critical essays ranging over a wide field and displaying unusual insight and knowledge, anthologies of poems for children in schools, four massive and masterly anthologies for grown ups: *Desert Islands, Early One Morning in the Spring, Behold, This Dreamer, Love*, and one, *Come Hither*, of poetry only, 'for the young of all ages': these are concerned with the world of poetry, exploration, childhood, dreams and love. They would have made a reputation in themselves. And it is unlikely that they will not be read and used as sources of reference for years to come.

His extraordinary imagination is further illustrated by *A Child's Day* and *Flora*. In *A Child's Day* he wrote rhymes to illustrate a set of fine photographs of a child, portraying her at work and play from dawn to dusk. And in *Flora* he composed poems to accompany the aquarelle drawings of Pamela Bianco, a child herself, barely in her 'teens.—LEONARD CLARK, "Walter de la Mare," *Three Bodley Head Monographs*, ed. Kathleen Lines, 1960, pp. 115–20

De la Mare wrote many poems with an audience of children specifically in mind, and, in his collected works, these have been published in a volume by themselves. This has a practical convenience, but it must never be forgotten that, while there are some good poems which are only for adults, because they presuppose adult experience in their readers, there are no good poems which are only for children. Human beings are blessed with the power to remember; consequently, to grow old means for us not to discard but to accumulate; in every old man, there still lives a child, an adolescent, a young man and a middle-aged one. It is commonly believed that children are, by nature, more imaginative than adults, but this is questionable. It is probably the case only in cultures like our own which put a higher social and economic value upon practical and abstract thinking than upon wonder and images; in a culture which put a high value on imagination and a low one on logic, children might well appear to be more rational than adults, for a child is not, by nature, more *anything*. In all cultures, however, there is one constant difference between children and adults, namely, that, for the former, learning their native tongue is itself one of the most important experiences in their lives, while, for the latter, language has become an instrument for interpreting and communicating experience; to recapture the sense of language as experience, an adult has to visit a foreign country.

What the child, and the child-in-the-adult, most enjoys in poetry, therefore, is the manipulation of language for its own sake, the sound and rhythm of words. There is a deplorable tendency in the United States, which I hope and pray has not spread to the United Kingdom, to think that books for children should use a very limited vocabulary, and that verses for them should be written in the simplest and most obvious meters. This is utter nonsense. The surest sign that a child has a feeling for language is that he talks like an affected adult and always uses a polysyllabic word when a monosyllabic one would do.

As a revelation of the wonders of the English Language, de la Mare's poems for children are unrivaled. (The only ones which do not seem to me quite to come off are those in which he tries to be humorous. A gift like Hilaire Belloc's for the comic-satiric is not his; he lacks, perhaps, both the worldliness and the cruelty which the genre calls for.) They include what, for the adult, are among his greatest "pure" lyrics, e.g., *Old Shellover* and *The Song of the Mad Prince*, and their rhythms are as subtle as they are varied. Like all good poems, of course, they do more than train the ear. They also teach sensory attention and courage. Unlike a lot of second-rate verse for children, de la Mare's descriptions of birds, beasts, and natural phenomena are always sharp and accurate, and he never prettifies experience or attempts to conceal from the young that terror and nightmare are as essential characteristics of human existence as love and sweet dreams. There is another respect in which, as all writers of good books for them know, children differ from grown-ups; they have a far greater tolerance for didactic instruction, whether in facts or morals. As Chesterton observed:

> The child does not know that men are not only bad from good motives, but also often good from bad motives. Therefore the child has a hearty, unspoiled, and unsatiable appetite for mere morality, for the mere difference between a good little girl and a bad little girl.

Without ever being tiresome, de la Mare is not afraid to instruct the young. What could be more practically useful than his mnemonic rhyme *Stars*, or more educative, morally as well as musically, than *Hi!*?

> Hi! handsome hunting man
> Fire your little gun.
> Bang! Now the animal
> Is dead and dumb and done.
> Nevermore to peep again, creep again, leap again,
> Eat or sleep or drink again. Oh, what fun!

—W. H. Auden, "Walter de la Mare" (1963), *Forewords and Afterwords*, 1973, pp. 388–90

JOHN FREEMAN
From "Walter de la Mare"
English Portraits and Essays
1924, pp. 96–114

IV

There are two worlds with which the imaginative mind may be concerned: one is the world which it creates by itself and of itself, the world which has no other reality than an immaterial reality; and the other is the common moral and material sphere with which all men are necessarily confronted. Most artists are concerned with one only of these worlds. Blake beheld and apprehended the imaginative and immaterial alone, Browning the moral and material alone. In his earlier poetry Mr. de la Mare was preoccupied—haunted, even—by the imaginative world, which he saw often as a bright, sometimes as a dark sphere, chequered with sunlight and moonlight falling between shadows, and peopled with those fantastic figures—in human shape or winged—which spring suddenly

from the fulness of the mind. But in *Motley* he dwells no longer utterly in that brilliant and flushing world; he is compelled by a new urgency to absent himself from felicity and breathe the air of commoner reality. He begins to meet the questions that we all meet, the difficulties, the desolation, the despair; he tries to apprehend the world in which we all move—what it is, who are they that throng it, and the eternal whence and whither of their passage. Part of the peculiar intimacy which *Motley* allows to the reader comes from the fact that the poet is so sharply and so bitterly aware of the exile from the imaginative world. It is an intermitted exile, and so these departures and returns, despairs and renewals, yield him and us the solace of an exquisitely human tenderness. The painfulness is not yet prolonged, the edge of bliss resumed is not yet dulled, and in this alternation between the two spheres lies the open secret of the beauty of *Motley*. So he passes from:

> When music sounds, all that I was I am
> Ere to this haunt of brooding dust I came;
> While from Time's woods break into distant song
> The swift-winged hours, as I hasten along—

to the sorrowfulness of:

> Some win peace who spend
> The skill of words to sweeten despair
> Of finding consolation where
> Life has but one dark end;
> Who, in rapt solitude, tell o'er
> A tale as lovely as forlore,
> Into the midnight air.

Speech so plain as this makes interpretation vain, and not less vain when you read, in a poem itself called "The Exile":

> Betrayed and fugitive, I still must roam
> A world where sin, and beauty, whisper of Home.

It is far from being a matter for disappointment or remonstrance that Mr. de la Mare has won this painful freedom of passing between two worlds.

V

Although I have spoken of part of Mr. de la Mare's mind being uttered in prose, it is not possible to survey his work in isolated fragments, and therefore a reference to the prose falls conveniently here. *Henry Brocken*, indeed, is a prose exercise of his poetic instinct, unwisely diverted into this medium, rather than an exercise of powers which could find utterance in prose alone. It is an essay upon the eternal theme of the wanderer, a journey backwards through the imaginative kingdom of other writers—Poe, Charlotte Brontë, Cervantes, and so on; and thus is akin to the "Characters from Shakespeare's Plays" which were found in his second volume of poems. Admirably written, with a fervid ingenuity and a fondness like that of a child for remembered stories, *Henry Brocken* reveals its author only in that fondness. *The Three Mulla-Mulgars* followed for the delight of many children, but with a reminder that the literary preferences of the child are beyond prediction. Happy are they whose perfect childishness finds an equal wondering joy in *The Pilgrim's Progress* and *The Three Mulla-Mulgars!* I cannot pretend to show why other children do not find satisfaction in either, and nevertheless slake their capricious appetites with *Peacock Pie*, a tale of Tchehov, Mr. Hudson's *Purple Land*, and Mangan's *Dark Rosaleen*. Maybe it is the slight allegorical hint, the touch of the emblem, that repels the graceless children who do not care for Mr. de la Mare's story of the three monkeys; maybe it is an inexplicit but acute sense of the gulf between the fantastic and the imaginative.

When the third novel, *The Return*, was published, there was found little of the merely fantastic and nothing that might have gone into verse. *The Return* was an essay in quite another manner, and suggested that the author had strayed into a field over which the spirit of Henry James had passed. There was no lack of welcome for this novel but, for all its welcome, it slid very quietly into the minds of readers, and perhaps needed more than a single reading before its singular beauty and strength could be realised. It is the story of a man who, recovering from an illness, strays one afternoon into a graveyard and sits by the unconsecrated grave of one Sabathier; drowsing there, and awakening into a sense of strangeness, he grows conscious of something akin to demoniacal possession, which touches not simply his mind but changes also his face into the abhorred likeness of the buried outcast. Consummate is the skill with which this incredible possibility is made convincing to the victim, his sceptical wife, his friends, and—most difficult of all—to the reader. The single, profound impression of interfusing spiritual and physical is not maintained equally throughout the book, but this metaphysic dominates the whole without rendering the story less than imaginative. The difficult abyss between imagination and invention might be surveyed in the first and second parts of *The Return*; certainly, in the first, imagination is absolute. Spiritual horror peers through, and spiritual beauty expels the horror, and the story of that wrestling with principalities and powers and the rulers of the darkness of this world pierces and dismays the reader. It is the more wonderful since this tragic battle is set within a commonplace suburban home, with a detestable wife and a too briefly seen, adorable child for witnesses.

. . . That the evil metempsychosis is defeated is the least significant fact in the story; the significance lies in the struggle, the lonely courage, the beauty springing up in the bleakness of a narrow and material neighbourhood. To speak in an image of *The Return* is to say that in the cold, owlish darkness of the mind a light shines, making that darkness suddenly crystal with beamy reflections—every wet spray beaded with tiny mirrors yet with no clear light anywhere. Oddly enough, where the story is apparently autobiographical, it diminishes the impression of the rest; but perhaps it is not odd that voluble characters should be a distraction, even if one of them speaks with the roving and restless curiosity which so exactly suggests the author's talk. But even when these incessant verticulations are most bewildering, deep and simple things are said—"The more one thinks about life the worse it becomes," and that of poor Sabathier, "What peace did he find who couldn't, perhaps, like you, face the last good-bye?" . . .

VI

In looking at Mr. de la Mare's most recent work in verse and prose, I cannot evade an impression that the change which was lightly apparent in *Motley* has been strongly developed in the brief intervening years. In *The Veil* he is seen often painfully far from his imaginative sphere, reverting to it in desire but bitterly alienated; treading the harsher ways of the common sphere, unable to accept it, unable to escape from it, seeing it as a moral enormity and that other as a spiritual sweetness, but no longer passing as it were at will from this to that. The simplicities and the ingenuities of joy have alike waned; doubts rise and do not sink again, but are met by affirmations, or softened by consolatory whispers. The heart of furious fancies has been startled by a vision that is no cloudy fancy—the callous, rude-carven image of time, with change and sorrow in tributary posture at his feet. Enchantment is forgone or forgotten, and interpretation begins.

The publication of *The Memoirs of a Midget* had already prompted such misgivings as these, when *The Veil* following

showed that the new attitude was not a casual one, or a dramatic assumption, but an inward change or growth. Had the author wanted to prove the unkindness of fate or circumstance towards the tenderest of sensitive things, the natural cruelty of human hearts, the sadder cruelty of egoism, his choice of theme and his treatment of character would have made the new novel an exhaustive proof. But he did not want to prove anything, certainly not anything desperate, bitter, relaxing; and hence it seems that the melancholy frustations of *The Memoirs of a Midget*, and the mere insistent painfulness, are but an involuntary utterance of the unhappiness with which Mr. de la Mare, stung by a sense of the irreconcilable, has contemplated life in its ruins—life of which all the beauty and energy have dwindled into the simple "making the best of a bad job." A midgetary Jude the Obscure might hardly breathe an air of crueller sorrow than the poor nymph of our author's imagination; the parable of life is moralised to a purpose as sombre as that of Mr. Hardy himself, whose spiritual influence, indeed, is the only one to which the younger writer has made obeisance.

A careful reader will look for a development in style when the change of spirit is so conspicuous; and here also the prose and verse bear witness. The prose of *The Memoirs of a Midget* is highly concentrated, and takes small heed to the weakness of mortality; it is so tense, so packed, so vividly and restlessly pictorial, that you rise from a prolonged reading with eyes smarting as though you had peered too closely at a pattern which a midget only might study with ease. In this minute agility the mind sees no point of rest, and while the prose thus matches the extravagant consciousness, the very ecstasy of self-consciousness, of the star-crossed Midget, it fatigues or bewilders the grosser reader. And in considering the "style" of the book in more than a restricted technical sense, the humblest admirer may be disconcerted by the incessant moralisation of the Midget's world, a moralisation to which not herself alone but most of the characters—that is, most of the women—contribute. Might not the disease of thought have been soothed a little? Might not the moral impression have been silently presented in circumstance and character, instead of in explicit challenge and pleading? To utter such doubts is to say again that the first part of this novel triumphs in its silence, and the second fails because of its too obstinate questioning. . . .

The chief technical influence seen in Mr. de la Mare's verse before *The Veil* was that of Coleridge, whose wave-like music and translucent brightness are echoed and reflected even in certain of the latest poems, such as "Sunk Lyonesse";

And the ocean water stirs
In salt-worn casemate and porch.
Plies the blunt-snouted fish
With fire in his skull for torch.
And the ringing wires resound;
And the unearthly lovely weep,
In lament of the music they make
In the sullen courts of sleep.

But the influence of Coleridge is chief no longer, and now (if any be chief where none is very strong) it is Mr. Bridges who affects his verse most plainly, with that manner of strange rhythm and odd phrasing which the Poet Laureate has used to test the affection of those that love his earlier work. With the conception, let us say in short, the style has become intellectualised; both are less instinctive, more deliberate; there is less to charm, more to stimulate, though it be only curiosity or perplexity that is stimulated. "Sweet and amusing," in Gilbert White's phrase, are the earlier verses, but the later are dark in spirit and harsher in style. It may be that they are transitional and that the next volume will extend the movement at which it is possible to look too doubtfully now, forgetting that the present has grown out of the past and will itself soon be a station of the past; for criticism limps and stumbles at best, and can seldom anticipate the motion of an original mind. Sometimes it may luckily forecast the flight of the creative instinct, sometimes predict the course of the rational mind; but an impossible felicity is wanted to discover the future of such an alternation or fusion of the two as Mr. de la Mare's latest work suggests.

Nor is it possible to attempt conclusions upon his present position in English poetry. His task as a lyrical writer is far different from that of Mr. Hardy and Mr. Doughty. The largeness of conception upon which the vast events of *The Dynasts* are so easily borne, and which informs scarcely less amply the shorter poems of Mr. Hardy, is no more within Mr. de la Mare's range than is the elemental, mythopoeic movement of *The Dawn in Britain*. But it is his work, before that of any other contemporary, that springs to the memory if it be asked what lyrical, what purely subjective poems may best endure the neighbourhood of these epical nobilities. And there is satisfaction in noting how general has been its acceptance, how warm its welcome. Recognition has not needed the waspish provocation of attack; criticism has been but praise, never a whisper of dissent has broken the concord; and we may point to his poetry for current evidence that the best that is given to readers is the most honoured of all giving.

RODOLPHE LOUIS MÉGROZ
From "Walter de la Mare"
Five Novelist Poets of To-day
1933, pp. 28–57

The reader of the story of *Come Hither* will recall how a much more complicated and detailed allegory of human life is completely concealed under the simple and evocative appearance of the story, even the names being cryptograms, Thrae being Earth; the Ten Laps, the Planets; Sure Vine the Universe; Mr. Nahum, Human, and so on, while the room in the round tower, in which the boy makes so many discoveries, as Miss Taroone explains, is the human mind or the head. These devices are a clever *jeux d'esprit* of the poet, and not in themselves significant; but they emphasise his double mindedness when he shares the child's vision and comprehends it in a more elaborate philosophy. It is from such a standpoint as this that a reader will best appreciate the scheme and content of *Henry Brocken, His Travels and Adventures in the Rich, Strange, Scarcely Imaginable Regions of Romance*. The too simple impression created by the sub-title is speedily corrected when the reader discovers that the very regions of "romance" explored by Henry Brocken, include the world of Jane Eyre as well as of the Sleeping Beauty, of the *Pilgrim's Progress* as well as *A Midsummer Night's Dream*. And how they are explored! Francis Thompson reviewed this book in 1904, and found in it a "true sense of dream, an alluring play of fantasy," "poetic richness and grace," phrases not undeserved and all pointing to that other aspect of de la Mare, as a poet of dream. What is true of the music and atmosphere of many of his child poems and the fantasy of *The Three Mulla-Mulgars*, applies to *Henry Brocken*. By recreating the childish vision he also recreates something of the imagery and atmosphere of the dream world. There are many instances but none more memorable than that where the hero reaches the land of the Houyhnhnms. There

are few translations of dream imagery in English literature so vivid as this. De la Mare however becomes his own rival in passages of his first novel, *The Return*, stories in *The Riddle* volume, and still later in *The Connoisseur* volume. In the last there is a story called "The Wharf" which describes a woman's nightmare. It is the kind of dream which is remembered as something unpleasant and rather silly, and if repeated to anybody at breakfast is a five minutes wonder.

The reason is that if enough of the experience can be recalled, it cannot be expressed but only badly reported. But in reading "The Wharf," you see the woman before and after the dream, and the dream itself becomes your own. You enter the woman's mind while the author's gently insinuating sentences uncover the darkness. The writer's craft is shown not by simply describing the nightmare—that alone could be a visionary poem—but in selecting a sufficient sequence of events to set the strangeness firmly in our daily life. . . .

The elaborate tales in *The Connoisseur* and *On the Edge* are sometimes the common murder story written by an artist (e.g. "Missing," "Mr. Kempe," "Crewe" and even "A Recluse"—the sinister recluse or solitary is a favourite theme of the author); the story of domestic life or of apparently ordinary people, but charged with wonder ("The Nap," "The Wharf," "Disillusioned," "At First Sight," "Willows," "An Ideal Craftsman," which, but for its unusual idea, might have gone with the murder stories, "The Picnic"); the purely ghostly and atmospheric, which of course includes several of those already mentioned, and also "The Green Room," and that masterly evocation of mediaeval superstition, "All Hallows." In his maturity de la Mare moves more easily from ironic observation to fantasy, or even to mysticism, sometimes with an appalling sense of both evil and of naked goodness or purity of heart that is like a dangerous flame in this familiar world of mixed motives.

His vision occasionally, his method often recalls Henry James, though de la Mare has James's insight with more poetic imagination, being capable of a deeper passion of awareness. At least it can be said that his extremely skilful narrative craft, whether devoted to sinister or to beautiful mysteries of the human heart, remind a reader of *The Craft of Fiction* of Mr. Percy Lubbock's fine description of how James, by repeated touches gradually loosens and then suddenly detaches whole the full meaning of a situation. It is a method that few modern authors have the patience or the intelligence to practise.

De la Mare's music and the potency of his carefully chosen words are of course peculiarly his own and do not resemble James's. But even in a simply ghostly tale like "Out of the Deep," possibly because he is telling the story backwards in the retrospective manner, one is continually reminded of James by superficial resemblances. . . .

In a longer study of ghostly fiction an interesting line of investigation might be followed to show the relation between the dream described in the narrative, such as the dream apparition of Catherine in *Wuthering Heights* or some of the dreams described by the Midget in her *Memoirs*, and these waking hallucinations rising "out of the deep." Clearly they are psychologically similar; but when the perception or hallucination is told as something dreamed by a fictional character the reader is further removed from the ghostly atmosphere and feels more secure. The haunting Sabathier in *The Return* is surely somewhere between the ghost which fills the stage and the ghost in the related dream. He leads a separate existence concurrent with that of Arthur Lawford and the people who live around Lawford, but the course of his separate career runs closer and closer into Lawford's own, until his haunting presence and partial possession of the living man is as disturbing and fearful as the apparition of the most unpleasantly inevitable of ghosts. Undoubtedly *The Return* richly deserved the "Polignac Prize," but it is much more like a *tour de force* than anything else de la Mare has written. The vague suggestion left to the reader at the end that the startling change in Lawford's appearance *may* have been due to imagination is rather unsatisfying after the persuasive explanations and speculations of his friend Herbert have drawn us deeper and deeper into sharing Lawford's conviction of being possessed, body and mind, by another man—a man whose tombstone declared that he had died in 1739. . . .

In the later ghostly stories however, de la Mare relies more upon a suggestion of some reality, beautiful or horrible, external to the mind of the narrator. "Mr. Kemp" and the murderer in "Missing," who blurts out his story to the narrator (*The Connoisseur*), and Mr. Bloom, in "A Recluse" and that other uncaught murderer in "Crewe" (*On the Edge*), are represented not as ghosts or as possibly imagined by the narrator but as concrete characters embodying their author's sense of evil which is as profound as James's or Conrad's. Perhaps this sense of evil in so powerful an imagination is the necessary relief to the sense of beauty and the capacity for mystical knowledge, which seems to have developed greatly in de la Mare's mature work. It is displayed most obviously in the philosophic—one might almost say religious—fantasy which is the title piece of *The Connoisseur* volume. This is not everybody's meat. In its inconclusive and unshaped state—it is a series of strange stories linked by the reappearance of an aged saint—a subtle and sublimated version of the undying Wandering Jew perhaps—the fantasy is full of beauty and wisdom, and the style shows de la Mare's evocative and ornate manner at its extreme. The charge of being "woolly" which has been levelled at de la Mare's style originates from the dislike of this packing of sentences with suggestive words, with nuances of description and suggestion until the sentences seem almost to come to a standstill.

First it should be remembered that the style in much of his work is comparatively simple, and people who try to dismiss such a creative writer by any sweeping generalisation have obviously not read much of him. When his style is loaded with descriptive phrases and hints of subtle sensations, though a hasty reader may find it difficult, any term like "woolly" completely misdescribes it, because the heavy sentences are full of matter. Words are rarely wasted or used without effect, and the effect is often unforgettable. The modern cant of simplicity has no power to derogate from the original and rare creative power of de la Mare's richest prose, though one cannot expect that such work as *The Connoisseur* should ever be popular. The packing of prose with the suggestions that it is the function of poetry to convey probably belongs to the delicate psychological probing of a distinctively modern type of fiction of which Henry James may be regarded as the pioneer. . . .

As I have tried to indicate, de la Mare's complicated and subtle stories are merely the final result of continuous development, and the evolution of the mystical strain of wisdom has come with the externalising of his perceptions so that they tend to reach further into the minds of people different from himself. Complete artistic success, to which nobody living has come so near as de la Mare, in this modern subtlety of interpretation may well require a gradual growth from such a poetic craft as de la Mare's, with its patient and passionate quest of lost horizons within the mind. In his mature fiction the artist has merely become more objective in comtemplation.

DYLAN THOMAS
"Walter de la Mare as a Prose Writer" (1946)
Quite Early One Morning
1954, pp. 149–55

"What I say is, keep on this side of the tomb as long as you can. Don't meddle with that hole. Why? Because while some fine day you will have to go down into it, you can never be quite sure while you are here what mayn't come back out of it.

"There'll be no partings there—I have heard them trolling that out in their chapels like misselthrushes in the spring. They seem to forget there may be some mighty unpleasant *meetings*. And what about the further shore? It's my belief there's some kind of a ferry plying on that river. And coming back depends on what you want to come back *for.*"

So an old, smallish man, muffled in a very respectable greatcoat at least two sizes too large for him, mutters in a dark corner of the firelit station waiting-room in Walter de la Mare's uneasy story, "Crewe."

How many of the nasty ghosts, from the other side of the razor's edge, from the wrong room, from the chockablock grave, from the trespassing hereafter, from the sly holes, crawl over and into the seedy waiting-rooms, the creeping railway carriages, the gas-lamped late Victorian teashops the colour of stewed tea, where down-at-soul strangers contrive their tales and, drop by drop, leak out the shadows of their grey or black, forlorn, and vaguely infernal secrets. The ghosts of Mr. de la Mare, though they reek and scamper, and, in old houses at the proper bad hours, are heard sometimes at their infectious business, are not for you to see. But there is no assurance that they do not see you.

And remember, in Mr. de la Mare, the scarecrow that suddenly appears in a cornfield behind a house where lately a man has hanged himself. "'Does the air round the scarecrow strike you as funny at all?' I asked him. 'Out of the way funny—quivering, in a manner of speaking?' 'That's the heat,' he said, but his lip trembled." And the shocking, hallucinatory mask of face and head lying on Mr. Bloom's pillow. And the polluted, invisible presences that seep through the charnel-house of Seaton's bloated and grave-emptying Aunt. Here in this house, and in all the other drenched, death-storied houses, down whose corridors and staircases the past hisses, and in whose great mirrors you see behind you a corridor of hinted faces, and in whose lofty beds you share your sheets and nightmare with an intangible, shifted fellow or the sibilant echo of a sound you wish had never been made, most things that happen are ordinary, or very nearly ordinary, and vile. These are houses suspended in time; and timelessness erupts in them.

Mr. de la Mare's *first* world of childhood is as "phantasmal" and "solitary" as Hans Andersen's, but rarely so cruel—or so alive. We grow to know that a huge mythological distance separates that world where Kay and Gerda breathe for ever and that in which the child-alone of de la Mare's tall tales goes about his dreams, loves, and surprises. The country whose habitations, whose great sleepy meadows of March mornings, blue and tumultuous and bleak, faraway cold towers and pinnacles, whether of clouds or hills, valleys and spelled woods, grey-green dells, mistletoed and mustard-seeded avenues, that the children of his earliest stories people, infest, and to high music, moon, glide, and meander through, this is a country of books. Hans Andersen's characters move in a magic that was not, beforehand, composed, pictured, or written down, but is created, there and then, by their lovely motion, and for themselves alone to inhabit. But in, for example, *Henry Brocken*, the first of de la Mare's long tales, the world through which the beguiled boy wanders on his mild Rosinanta is made of the trees and climates, moors, mornings and evenings, groves, hills, suns, stars, and gardens, of written, remembered words, of Bunyan's allegory and Swift's satire, of the poetry of Wordsworth, Herrick, Shakespeare, Poe, and Keats. Here enamoured Henry Brocken, in the library country, roving deep in the coils of the necromantic ball, meets Lucy Gray, Jane Eyre, Julia, Electra, Dianame, Anthea, Nick Bottom, the Sleeping Beauty, Gulliver, La Belle Dame Sans Merci, Annabel Lee. But, overdecorated, remote, rooted in "reverie," that favourite woollen-headed word, the adventure is all shades. Henry Brocken is a bookish and starry-eyed mood on a borrowed horse. The fabled earth is cloud. Clouds are reflections and echoes of sea waves that rhyme with other words. Rarely just pretty or arch, the way of the story is too often sadly sweet and single-noted.

But as Mr. de la Mare went on writing, his children went on growing. They did not grow into youths, but into children. They lost that lorn and dewy wonder, and when they moved, though always on odd errands, they did not rustle like the pages of an old book turned in a lamplit brown study by a wan, near-tenuous, but inky hand. "Homesick," "forlorn," "lost," and "silent"—these words were used less often, though the nostalgia for the "mournful gaiety" of the past, the loneliness, the silence, and the delirium still were there.

It was through Mr. de la Mare's perception of the very natural oddity and immediacy of childhood that a story like "The Almond Tree" emerged, most movingly, out of the tapestried and *unnatural* "farness" of *Henry Brocken*.

Nicholas in "The Almond Tree" is, in Mr. Forrest Reid's words, "the first of a line of strange, wayward, intelligent, dangerously sensitive, infinitely alive small boys." In later stories, his name changes, he is older or younger, sadder or gayer, more darkly cunning or more coldly innocent, now embroiled and tangled in briary thickets of love, now critical and aloof, faintly smiling, in fear and evil occurrences; but always his eyes are the same. It is through these eyes we see the astonishing systems, the unpredictable order, of life on the edge of its answer or quivering on a poisonous threshold.

Only on slight occasions do Mr. de la Mare's children come into contact with each other. We see them, nearly always, in their relation to abnormal men and women. And of his children, it is only the small boys who become real. The little girls live in a distant, and more fragile past.

A "*more* fragile" past; for he is loyal, always, to old Ways and Days, old houses, regions; customs, scents, and colours. His children loiter, wonder, and perceive; his men and women suffer, love, and are haunted; his weathers happen; his dead-behind-the-wainscot blow and scamper, in a time and place that was before he was born. The life of his countryside is that which his mother remembered hearing *her* mother tell of, and of which she told him when he was a child. His imagined memories of childhood are all of a timeless past before his own.

Mr. de la Mare's stories first appeared about 1900. One of the first reviewers to recognise his awakening genius was Francis Thompson. Through all those intermediary years he has written long and short stories, for children, about children, for grown men and dead men, for the unborn, for a livelihood, for nothing, for the best reward, through innocence and with wide

and deep skill, for pleasure, for fun, from suffering, and for himself.

His influences? Sir Thomas Browne, de Quincey, Ecclesiastes, Henry James, Emily Brontë, Stevenson, Poe, Traherne. And, in later life, Julian Green perhaps? His style? It is his stories. At the very beginning, he was fond, I think, of a rather flowery verbosity; he used a lot of clichés, but they were always the right ones. There was the suggestion of something, even in a young man, old-maidenish about his attitude to the love of men for women. Country terror was a little cosy, so that you felt not that something nasty had happened in the woodshed but that there were quite hellish goings on among the wool-baskets in the parlour. The period and place about which he writes? Somewhere in rural England, say anywhere after 1830 and just before the afterlife. In his more mature dramatic stories about grown-up human relationships, he often used a convoluted monologue manner that occasionally suggested the ghost of a landbound Conrad talking from behind a pot of ferns. A fault of the prose style, always avoided in the verse, was a gravy-like thickening of texture. And his elaborate language, fuller than ever of artifice and allusion when it was seemingly simple, did not suit, to my mind, the more or less straightforward, or the grotesque, fairy story. His *real* fairies are as endearing as Dracula. And his subject, always, is the imminence of spiritual danger.

JOHN ATKINS
From *Walter de la Mare: An Exploration*
1947, pp. 7–17

The ground plan of Walter de la Mare's mind is simple. It is in the elevation that complexity raises the chief problems for mind and eye. The ground plan is long and narrow. Due East is a tomb—with the head towards Egypt. Due West is a vast hall—with its axis towards Virginia. No-one, not even the servants, ever frequent the tunnel connecting the two extremes. When there is communication the messenger hurries through, looking neither to left nor right. Occasionally he glances over his shoulder to catch a last glimpse of the place he has left. Soon, he knows, he will be back, but on the way there is nothing but the ordinary, the dead-alive and the usual paraphernalia of a rational existence.

The tenant spends most of his time in the tomb. It is a cramped existence, but why go outside when there is so much to be observed within? Has he not got himself, his own mystery and its insistent questioning? But sometimes even this will pall, and he craves for space. But it is not simply a space in which he may stretch his legs; it must be a space in which he can stretch his mind. No vulgar *Lebensraum* of the body, but a natural temple for the spirit. So he goes as quickly as he may to the other extreme. It is a peculiar place, this hall. Although it must have walls and windows unto the world beyond (for who ever heard of a ground plan without boundaries?) it appears to be limitless. The human eye, range as it will, can see no frontier. But it is a very stimulating waste.

Naturally, the tomb and the waste are mutually compensatory. They are the two poles of de la Mare's psychological duality. And this duality is the core of, and provides the clue to, all his work. His obsession with the tomb and with life on the other side is apparent to even the most casual reader. His best novel, *The Return*, begins in a churchyard and is haunted by the churchyard throughout, as Shakespeare's *Julius Caesar* is haunted by the spirit of Caesar. The tendency came to a head when he devoted a whole book, *Ding Dong Bell*, to thoughts and emotions resulting from visits to cemeteries.

Put as baldly as this it might appear that de la Mare is an unnaturally morbid and unbalanced person. Nothing, of course, could be less true. His delightful books on Childhood, Dreams and Desert Islands refute any such accusation. Despite his admiration for the writings of Poe, he is no Poe himself. Yet the two share many interests. But these interests are not peculiar to them; they are widespread and at certain times in history have been almost universal. At other times some men have retained another epoch's curiosity, while their fellow men have gone a-whoring after money or philosophical concepts or aesthetic aims. These men, the de la Mares and Poes, have always put what they believed first things first; and these things have been Life and Death.

De la Mare's tomb points towards Egypt because the Ancient Egyptians preceded him in his absorption in the phenomenon of death. Their social lives were ruled by the never-forgotten fact that life was not eternal (in this world, at least) and that when life is important, so is death. They constantly reminded themselves of this by various rituals, even going to the extent of having a mummy carried around the table before they dined. Children's toys included midget mummies. Death will always get you, so don't pretend he isn't there. De la Mare is Egyptian in this respect, for he also can never forget it, although the conventions of our time force him to be less candid and more subtle. But any enclosed space reminds him of a tomb. Anything with walls is a grave-symbol. His walls are never on the defensive against the mind's expanding, roving spirit. Rather are they being battered from the outside by the unknown menace. It is quite natural that the sick girl in her dream fantasy (in "What Dreams May Come") likens the butler who is guiding her through the strange house to Cheops in his pyramid. This is no place for Ariel.

Ariel belongs to the waste. Part of *Henry Brocken* (though by no means all) is pervaded by a sense of space. It is the spirit's relief, its occasional necessary holiday, but like a sombre Fate the tomb is always beckoning. No other civilisation has ever been so conscious of death as the Egyptian. Since then it has been left to individuals to wrestle with this only certainty of life. For anyone who considers it at all seriously it must become an important conditioning factor in one's outlook and behaviour. Poe allowed it to overwhelm him until he became America's most distinguished neurotic. De la Mare, thanks to his strong inner resistance, remains distinguished but not a neurotic.

But the case of these two men is doubly interesting, because they provide evidence that certain individuals have the power to stand up successfully against the climate of the civilisation in which they live. De la Mare, living in an age of science and rationalism so far as his own social circle is concerned, retained a belief in emotional perception and the inner eye. He has been attacked, usually by people with nothing of his vision and understanding, but he has made no attempt to alter his course. Always behind him has been his dæmon. Similarly with Poe. In the period of America's greatest expansion, living in the sparsely populated State of Virginia, the contemporary of Fenimore Cooper, he yet preferred to centre his tales around coffins, prisons, enwalled cats and entombed hearts, both the latter being symbols of freedom. He also had his dæmon. . . .

What then, is the relation between these two writers? On the outermost layer it is obviously one of teacher and taught, admired and admirer. But behind this is a subtle shift of ground. De la Mare is not content merely to copy Poe's method. What he has done is to analyse Poe's work into its constituents of subject and atmosphere. But instead of retracing ground and adapting atmosphere and sensation to his own time, he has made them the subjects of his work. Thus most of his stories are really concerned, not with human beings in a particular psychic state, but with the psychic state itself. Naturally, he has to employ human beings, otherwise his stories would be essays and would not reach the public he wishes to reach—those readers who keep clear of psychological treatises. The atmosphere is the hero and, as is to be expected, the human characters are often no more than cyphers, unreal and not very human. Poe's first consideration was the individual, though always the individual under stress. De la Mare has used Poe as a stepping stone in his advance into the unknown land which lies somewhere between life, death, sleep, dream, wake and revery. That is all we know of its topography.

And now we come to that apsect of these two writers which is most obvious, and which has already been referred to. Few others have managed so efficiently the horror theme. It is this, more than anything else, that brings the two together. But it is only the subject that is common, for in its treatment and presentation they are in constant divergence. Poe's horror is visual and extremely objective; de la Mare's can only be sensed by some hidden instrument of the mind and is intensely subjective. This does not mean that he writes impersonally of horror, or tries to analyse states of mind of the horrible or horrified; he is never so explicit as this, never presents horror as does a film magnate, but allows a sensation of alarm and apprehension to creep across the reader's mind. Poe's situations are horrible to the least and most sophisticated minds; his devices, the living in the tomb, the pit and the pendulum, are frightening even to the most insensitive. But de la Mare, with his mastery of nuance and suggestion, palms his menace off on to the reader like an expert salesman. His harmless Victorian furniture and harmlessly eccentric old ladies (Seaton's aunt, for example) are objects and people we know and meet almost daily without the smallest shudder, yet he transforms them into dark threats and menacing witches.

What he has done, in effect, is to establish the existence of a subterranean link between horror and beauty. This Poe never did. In his world of maniacs we would be foolish to expect anything but the unnatural. But de la Mare presents us with his prim old ladies, sensitive little girls, old-fashioned drawing rooms and (a constantly recurring setting) railway carriages. The writer of detective stories and thrillers has used all these, but how differently! The old lady is so obviously the reassuring agent of an international spy ring, the little girl's mind is so obviously deranged; the drawing room is a murder trap, and the most important fitting in the railway carriage is the communication cord. Everything has its focus, and the labels are there for all to see. But there is nothing like this in the stories of de la Mare. Gradually one becomes conscious of an eeriness which it is impossible to attribute to any one trick, but which must derive somehow from an expert use of words. And that is about all that can be said.

EDWARD WAGENKNECHT
From "Walter de la Mare, Book Reviewer"

Boston University Studies in English, 1955–56, pp. 213–36

As to Mr. de la Mare's general approach to critical writing, it should be stated emphatically that he has nothing of the dilettante spirit that one often expects to encounter in the critical essays of creative writers. Works which require scholarly examination receive it, and judged even by professional standards, these reviews stand up well. Nevertheless the insights of the creative artist are much in evidence. As everyone who knows de la Mare's work is aware, intuition and imagination are more important to him than logic, and an imaginative experience quite as "real" as anything we may undergo in the flesh. This point of view is quite as clear in his critical writings as in his poems. . . .

De la Mare did most of his critical work in a day of somewhat leisurely reviewing, when reviewers were given space to turn about in, and were not expected to write so that he who runs may read. He does not confine himself to stating his conclusions; he traces the process by which he arrived at them. He gives details. He always tells his reader a good deal about the content of the book, though he never confines himself to content; when he seems to be doing this, he is really presenting his own judgment by implication (through his tone, choice of quotations, etc.), as he often prefers to do when the judgment is unfavorable. On the other hand, he never loses himself in details, for he also gives us the general truth which the details illustrate, and this is often a truth whose significance applies to much more than the volume under consideration. Naturally he is free from all the vulgar faults of the professional reviewer: he is never cruel; he is never "smart"; I cannot recall so much as one cutting witticism at the author's expense; he keeps his mind upon the object, not upon himself. With equal success he has resisted the corruption of kindliness: he praises warmly where praise is deserved, condemns without rancor when condemnation is called for, and discriminates between strength and weakness wherever discrimination is the order of the day. He is never more inclined to blame because the author is unknown and undistinguished, nor is he ever less exacting because the author is a writer of established reputation or even a personal friend.

. . . As reviewer, de la Mare encountered good and bad poets of both varieties; he was always content to take them on their own terms and judge them by reference to the standards they had set for themselves. Thus he dismisses Charles Stratford Catty as a mere traditionalist, allows considerable merit to Horace Holley's *Post-Impressionist Poems*, though he is clearly not in sympathy with its radical form and never quite sure what "post-impressionist means," and gives E. Scott Huelin's, "free verse" experiments a neatly balanced notice.

De la Mare's dislike of obscurity in poetry is particularly interesting in view of the fact that his critics have sometimes made this charge against him. He complains of obscurity specifically in connection with Meredith, Judith Lytton, T. Sturge Moore, Evelyn Underhill, J. Middleton Murry, and even Robert Frost. The fullest discussion is in connection with Murry. Admitting that "The charge of obscurity against a poet is a boomerang that may return not to the critic's feet, but at his head," de la Mare distinguishes between obscurity "in manner or in matter." A poem "may express its theme inadequately, or in a needlessly involved fashion; or the theme it expresses may be so remote from or alien to our minds that we cannot imaginatively share it." The first kind of obscurity he finds in "some of the later poems of Meredith and of Browning." Its effect is to limit the reader to "an inexact or faulty translation. In the latter case (as possibly in certain mystical poetry) it is merely our own powers of understanding that are at fault." So far as Murry himself is concerned, de la Mare admits that "he is not attempting the easy," and that "what is vital to him is profound and moving," yet he thinks that

he seldom succeeds in meeting us mind to mind, in making us see, in sufficing ear, imagination and heart. The cast of his mind is intellectual, an intellectuality subtle and sensitive, but his poetic medium is usually too stubborn for it. He cannot, that is, as if spontaneously, make something beautiful, free, self-contained, transparent. Intellect and emotion are constrained into his verse; they are not set free by it. What gold there is, is for the most part still in the ore.

. . . De la Mare's most elaborate consideration of the novel as a form was made in connection with his review of Percy Lubbock's book, *The Art of Fiction*. He seems to feel here that Lubbock overstressed the importance of analysis in reading fiction. Unlike buildings, vases, and statues, novels do not yield a sense of form at a glance. The reader cannot be completely aware even of the subject of the book until the last page has been turned. "It is the last gesture, the unforeseen crisis, the quiet descent of the climax that counts." Mr. de la Mare does not object to the analysis as such. Indeed he suggests that a good novel may well be read twice—"once purely for what it does to us of its, and of our own, sweet will," and again "for sheer joy in the means whereby it did it." He adds that "the former is the poetic attitude toward the universe; the latter the scientific." The analytical process is "an inversion, so to speak, of the process which created the book. . . . The reader's mind is like the Valley of Jehoshaphat: he breathes, and the dry bones live." For

> A novel is not a mere copy of life. It is a representation, a simulacrum of life arranged, condensed, amplified, balanced, annotated, and, in a sense, explained. Since, then, it is not a mere reflection but a picture, we may accept it as such, and enjoy its very artifices, which, if it is to be successful, must be so exquisitely concealed.

Fascinating as this experience is, however, de la Mare would not be de la Mare if, even here, he did not subordinate science to poetry. First of all, "a work of art should . . . take the mind captive—enchant the imagination." It is only when the reader is willing to put "his spirit in pawn" while he is reading a book that he can emerge from the experience changed. Read a great novel thus—say *Wuthering Heights*, *Madame Bovary*, *Jude the Obscure*, or *Lord Jim*—and the world will never look the same again. . . .

It is not surprising that ghost stories should have bulked rather large among the fiction de la Mare reviewed, but until we remind ourselves that this is a field in which, being a master, he might have been expected to be hard to satisfy, we may be surprised that he should find so many of them unsatisfactory. Algernon Blackwood's *Julius Le Vallon*, for example, is a book in which there is too much not discovered but merely made up: "A story of lively promise reaches a zenith rather too closely resembling a spiritualistic *séance*." W. F. Harvey's "The Beast with Five Fingers" is rejected because it deals largely in physical horror: "It may stir the scalp, it will not haunt the memory." For a third example, take Anne Douglas Sedgwick's very Jamesian novelette, *The Third Window*, "a cocoon of the finest silk spun out of that inward self which is the bliss of the novelist." Though de la Mare appreciates the skill with which it has been wrought, he finally rejects it. He knows that "all men and women . . . are spirits," but he still has difficulty with a story in which the ghost seems more substantial than the living lovers, "and yet so singularly uninteresting that he is in the worst sense unreal." If this was intended, he thinks it "a dubious extreme of refinement."

Such theory as he has formulated about the ghost story, de la Mare has given us most notably in his review of two collections of stories by Sir Thomas Graham Jackson and M. R. James and in his long introduction to his son Colin's anthology, *They Walk Again* (Faber and Faber, 1931). He begins the review by stressing heavily the importance of setting in the ghost story. "The scene must be in ordinary life and 'have an air of reality.'" This rules out the Dunsany type of story and such tales as those connected during recent years with H. P. Lovecraft and his followers, where, characteristically, the reader is carried off to an imagined world which has little or no connection with this one. For de la Mare it is the incursion of another world *into* this one which supplies the thrill.

> The reader's imagination . . . must be furtively quickened by a series of almost imperceptible hints, decoys, innuendoes, into a peculiar sensitiveness. The strings must be turned before they will echo the Banshee. Our journey over the borderland and into that stagnant, electric, sinister atmosphere must be as quiet and gradual as the coming on of night. As quiet and gradual must our ultimate exit be into the common air. To explain away a ghost is as clumsy a piece of philanthropy as to place an icy sitz-bath at the bedside of a somnambulist.

This does not mean, however, that the characters are not important. They "should be tinged with the queer, the erratic, or somehow rarefied—by beauty perhaps, or occupation or habits or history; and they must have the right names. . . ." He tends to agree with M. R. James (and to disagree with Sir Thomas Graham Jackson) that a ghost must be malevolent. "Nowhere else taste so sweet the juices of revenge, or shines innocence so blandly when the cloud releases the moon." James's own ghost stories de la Mare praised, though he does enter one caveat: "Gross tastes may prefer a fruitier vintage, thick blood require a more potent rennet; Dr. James is a connoisseur."

In his introduction to *They Walk Again*, Mr. de la Mare is largely concerned with comparing the ghost story and the detective story. Both, he thinks, may well appeal to the same reader. "For my part, if by a stroke of good fortune the evening postman brought me two books, each of them a masterpiece of either kind, I should read the ghost story first, but perhaps a little more rapidly than usual, in order to get busy with the crime." Both types of story involve a hunt or a mystery, but in the detective story the interest ends with the solution. "Little more than the rational powers are involved, the faculty that pieces a puzzle together. Not usually much imagination, still more rarely any profound stirring of the waters or fine aesthetic sensibility." With the ghost story all this is quite different. "Facts as mere facts" are "not the quarry" here. "We must be made to believe in it. At its best it gives us imaginative truth. As with all fine fiction its illusion is its sovereign charm." My article has been read to little purpose if this preference of de la Mare's is not, his termperament and his convictions being what they are, at this point inevitable to every reader. I am not aware that he has ever quoted these words of Lafcadio Hearn's, but I feel sure that he would agree with them: "There is something ghostly in all great art, whether of music, sculpture, or architecture. It touches something within us that relates to infinity." To that note all Walter de la Mare's work, whether critical or creative, beautifully vibrates.

WILLIAM JAY SMITH
From "Master of Silences"

Poetry, November 1957, pp. 112–16

Walter de la Mare remained during his later years a towering, but dim, figure. England, which paid him tribute, did so often for the wrong reasons; America, which with references to his delicate "magic" had relegated him to the purgatory of schoolroom anthologies, had forgotten almost that he existed. For many he was a poet writing out of a past, and with a poetic diction, which had little, if anything, to say to the modern world. For all the truly complex nature of his work, he seemed to present no problems. And because he seldom raised his voice in his poems, and indeed spoke at times in a whisper, his qualities had to be listened for; few people had the patience. In de la Mare's lines on Vaughan, he might have been writing for himself:

> So true and sweet his music rings,
> So radiant is his mind with light
> The very intent and meaning of what he sings
> May stay half-hidden from sight.
>
> His flowers, waters, children, birds
> Lovely as their own archetypes are shown;
> Nothing is here uncommon, things or words,
> Yet every one's his own.

Nothing is uncommon in the special universe of Walter de la Mare, but his intent and meaning may not be immediately grasped.

Certainly the setting of many of his poems is not unfamiliar—the rambling Victorian house where in a cob-webbed chair a little girl, the picture of health and innocence, has just fallen asleep. Moonlight streams in through the window; a face appears and disappears; a horseman gallops away, swallowed up in mist. The characters who move in and out of the rooms and in and out of the poems are ghosts; only the child is alive, but she, too, is close to death in sleep. Outside in the garden worms and snails creep from under mossy stones; far off, the sea breaks on the gray sand.

It may be that it is too familiar; everything about it is a bit too English, the haunted atmosphere too cozy; one would rather that the ghosts did not all stay to tea. But to object at this point is to lose sight of de la Mare's special qualities. The house—and how often the word itself occurs in his work—is for him the very habitation of the mind. Old, decaying, abandoned, it is like the mind haunted by memory, it is the voice of an eternal silence, choosing its speech in our almost involuntary utterances:

> Very old are we men;
> Our dreams are tales
> Told in dim Eden
> By Eve's nightingales. . . .

Walter de la Mare lived more and more in his dreams, he said, as he grew older; and the area which he explores is that between sleep and waking, past and present, life and death. The darkness within the house is balanced against the dark without: when the face at the window has vanished, all that remains is the gray night which shines on in its "chaos of vacancy". . . .

Walter de la Mare gazed within, as the title of that superb collection of lyrics, *Inward Companion*, published in his seventy-sixth year, indicates:

> Why, inward companion, are you so dark with anguish?
> A trickle of rancid water that oozes and veers,

Picking its sluggish course through slag and refuse,
Down at length to the all-oblivious ocean—
What else were apt comparison for your tears?

And while his gaze became ever more probing and his understanding of the complexity of the psyche ever keener, he concerned himself with a dream-enriched, dream-haunted world, not with a world of explicit nightmare. Everything he wrote has in it somewhere, as Horace Gregory points out, the chill of ice, but, I think, of ice that is ready to melt away before a warmth which is conveyed at times only in the tone of voice. Rarer than anything in life, one poem states, are good nature and good sense; and he possessed too much of both to be able to gaze directly—for very long, at least—at blood-curdling horror. His style—the record of the workings of that inner eye, which he said sees clearly but never fixedly—is "lucent, dewy, rain-sweet" (his adjectives for the prose of Isaak Walton); and as a writer for children he is closer certainly to Madame d'Aulnoy than to the Brothers Grimm. His children's stories have the delicacy, wit, and luminous mystery of certain French or Japanese, as opposed to German, fairy tales.

Nor is he completely at home in the field of nonsense; he lacks the zany spirit of Edward Lear. In his stories, for all their fantasy and implied unearthly terror, he never truly abandons the real world; nor in his children's poems does he ever allow good sense to become nonsense. In his *Stuff and Nonsense* he tried; and although many of its stanzas are rollicking and ingenious, the words do not somehow tumble from his tongue; it is the least successful of his children's books. Always, however, he moves majestically in the intermediate area between nonsense and sense:

Who said, "All Time's delight
    Hath she for narrow bed;
Life's troubled bubble broken"?
    That's what I said.

The words seem to rise from time itself as from the depths of those prehistoric vats which he describes in one of his stories. The *b*'s in the second last line, together with the short *u* sounds, suggest a mumbling attempt to say what cannot be said, to ask more than life can answer; they evoke also, with the question itself, the sound of the bubbling water carrying off the dead Ophelia. The voice of the speaker, the Mad Prince, becomes at once the voice of the child asking the impossible and of the adult reaching farther back than one can reach, the voice of a universal unconscious.

Far-off experience de la Mare brings into focus; his best children's poems shimmer with the unreasoning clarity of early morning:

Why does that bluebottle buzz?
Why does the sun so silent shine?—

We hear not only the bluebottle, but, more miraculously, the very sound of sunlight itself. *Peacock Pie*, which is, in its own way, as perfect as *Inward Companion*, is similarly concerned with the ultimate questions of existence. In it problems are simply stated, as they would be by a child, but they are life's problems none the less:

Do diddle di do,
    Poor Jim Jay
Got stuck fast
    In Yesterday

Because de la Mare can look back so clearly at life's first moments, he can hear in language those rhythms basic to all times and epochs. No poet of the century has used such a variety of stanzas and meters or has made more subtle use of off-beat folk rhythm and of the nursery lilt to which at passionate moments every lover, even the savage Swift, returns.

The ripples move slowly outward on the pool as we read over the poems of Walter de la Mare and the world begins to glow as if it had only just emerged from dream, shining forth with all its miniature perfections. And if we listen carefully, we can hear his voice, resonant and forever-questioning, speaking to us from the edge of that mysterious darkness, of which he wrote so well, and into which he now has gone.

DORIS ROSS McCROSSON
From "A Final Estimate"
Walter de la Mare
1966, pp. 141–45

Walter de la Mare's novels suggest that the imagination is unable, in this existence at least, to comprehend the mystery of life; to apprehend, to be aware of its beauty and strangeness, is all the imagination can hope to do. Yet, no matter how briefly, it is in the imagination that we truly live.

The novels show that de la Mare was not a follower of any particular philosophy, but that in his easy eclecticism he came closest to the Idealists, either borrowing from or paralleling the speculations or methods of Plato, Schelling, Coleridge, Blake, Lewis Carroll, and George MacDonald, among others. The one attribute de la Mare held in common with all of them was a fundamental belief in the imagination. A point of difference with some of them was that he did not attempt to construct a system. Nor did he possess, apparently, the religious faith that led George MacDonald, for one, to believe that he had found at least a partial explanation of the inscrutable mystery.

These two qualities—they cannot be called failures—may be among the reasons for de la Mare's having abandoned the novel form and for his concentrating instead on the short story, the poem, and the anthology. On the one hand, a novel must be structured to present a sustained and developing vision: "spots of time" cannot be developed into a coherent novel. The short story and the poem are forms in which a brief vision can be more effectively presented. That is to say, his vision after *Memoirs of a Midget* was not one that could be sustained in a longer medium: perhaps that is why *At First Sight*, his last attempt in the novel, is essentially a short story. . . .

The realization that man in life is isolated, that "the inmost self of each one of us is a livelong recluse,"[1] is the conclusion de la Mare reached in his novels and suggested in his poems and short stories. It would have been a melancholy one had he not also retained his belief that man can live in the imagination. Henry Brocken does so until the time he begins to question, to attempt to comprehend; and the three Mulla-Mulgars have limitless faith in the moonstone, or the imagination, which ultimately leads them to the very doors of the true reality.

The Return represents a turning away from children's stories to adult themes. It and the last two novels can be considered together; for in them the sense of isolation becomes most apparent; and, although the search for reality is pursued in them, they are a more sophisticated investigation of time, dreams, love, and death. As a true representative of this century, in *The Return* de la Mare discovers that time is relative; what is measured by the clock is not necessarily of any consequence. There is in this realization the hint of Blake's idea that it is possible to know "eternity in an hour." Of course, many others before de la Mare had experimented with time, notably Lewis Carroll and George MacDonald, and H. G. Wells on a less metaphysical level. Charles Williams, his contemporary, was to write in *Shadows of Ecstasy* that "Every second is an infinity, once you can enter it."[2] One recalls, of course, the experiments with time in the novels of Dorothy Richardson, Virginia Woolf, and James Joyce.

De la Mare's second discovery in *The Return* is that love is one path by which man can realize that ideal: through the power of love, man truly lives. This is not sexual love, but rather a mutual perception of reality through the power of the imagination. It is, perhaps, in E. M. Forster's terms, the ability to "connect." *At First Sight* is almost a reiteration of this theme; but, instead of abolishing the artificial barrier of time as *The Return* does, the lovers in the latter novel are solidly anchored in time. Both these novels conclude with the parting of the lovers. The reason for the separation in *The Return* is obvious: the lovers were living on three separate planes of consciousness (or of time)—Grisel's, Arthur's, and a third level when they are together. But they cannot remain on this last level because the other two levels had not merged with the one. Grisel's was more dream than life; Arthur's level was more in life than in dream. These terms can be converted into death (life) and dream (death), if one wishes. Lawford cannot remain on Grisel's level because, as George MacDonald suggests in *Lilith*, one must be spiritually ready to do so. If the term "spiritual" is understood without the usual religious connotations, the reason for Lawford's unreadiness is apparent: he cannot remain with Grisel because his Self is as yet an unknown quantity.

This spiritual unreadiness can be clarified by reference to *Memoirs of a Midget*, de la Mare's statement concerning the reality of the imagination as it applies to knowledge of the Self. The midget has a highly developed sense of identity, but she is incomplete for she lacks what Lawford had found—love. The self is not sufficient unto the Self, the midget learns. She gropes for communication with another imagination through which she can find the Ideal, but the one face of beauty, Fanny, which recalls it to her, she perforce cannot touch. This is not for the reason that Fanny is another woman; they cannot communicate because Fanny lacks imagination and self-

knowledge. On the other hand, the midget cannot "connect" with Mr. Anon, her physically repellent lover. She must live to learn, as de la Mare implies she may have, that real beauty is in the spirit, not in the corporeal shell.

Although this explanation may serve to elucidate the reason for Lawford's and Grisel's separation in *The Return*, it does little to explain the separation in *At First Sight* of Cecil and his beloved without some widening of its scope. Cecil's eye-shade and the hints of Miss Simcox's unsavory past must be taken into account. Cecil had never seen anyone, physically or imaginatively, until he looked into the face of his beloved. Then, shortly thereafter, she drowns herself in the river, which can be regarded as a symbol of eternity, or of the imagination, or of the unconscious; for all three terms are related and mean ultimately the same thing to de la Mare. These two events suggest that Cecil was unprepared to live in the imagination for he had never tried to do so before, and that Miss Simcox is also unprepared for she too had lived unimaginatively in the past: she must purge herself of the wounds inflicted by existence. In other words, she is like the suicide, Sabathier; and Cecil is like the midget in that he discovers beauty is not enough. Conrad, in *Lord Jim* wrote in straightforward language what de la Mare implies: "A man that is born falls into a dream like a man who falls into the sea. If he tries to climb out into the air as inexperienced people endeavor to do, he drowns. . . . The way is to the destructive element submit yourself, and with the exertions of your hands and feet in the water make the deep, deep sea keep you up."

One concludes that de la Mare believed that, although reality is apprehended in the imagination, the quality or duration of the experience depends upon the ability of the imagination to discover both the Self and other selves. Man must live imaginatively, then, but he must "venture into the world without, and the world within." Only with the imagination can man push back the frontiers of the unknown: this was de la Mare's hope and his faith.

Notes

1. *Desert Islands and Robinson Crusoe* (London, 1930), p. 27.
2. Charles Williams, *Shadows of Ecstasy* (London, 1931), p. 202.

Nigel Dennis
1912—

Nigel Forbes Dennis was born on January 16, 1912, in Surrey, England. His family moved frequently; Dennis was educated at Plumtree School in Southern Rhodesia and Odenwaldschule in Germany. After graduating, he went to London, where he worked as a freelance writer, door-to-door salesman, and crossword puzzle constructor. In 1934 he began a fifteen-year stay in the United States, during which time he reviewed books from *The New Republic* from 1937 to 1938, and for *Time* through the 1940s. Dennis also translated the works of Austrian psychologist Alfred Adler, who became a profound influence on Dennis and his writing.

Dennis continued to write for *Time* and other journals after returning to England in 1949, but he resolved to concentrate on fiction. His first serious book (Dennis disowns the first few), *Girls and Boys Come Out to Play*, established Dennis as a promising and inventive novelist. For many critics, that promise was fulfilled by his second novel, *Cards of Identity*, a biting, outrageous satire which Dennis adapted for the stage in 1956. *Cards* takes literally Adler's notion that "every personality is a self-constructed fiction," attacking psychiatry and religion in the process.

Dennis' next play, *The Making of Moo*, was a blast at organized religion, an expression of Dennis' committed atheism. His third play, *August for the People*, was a Shavian savaging of the very idea of democracy, and correspondingly quite unpopular.

Dennis' 1965 biography of Jonathan Swift won him the Royal Society of Literature's Heinemann Award for that year. Since then he has produced a number of book reviews for the London *Sunday Telegraph*, a book of poetry, and, in 1972, *An Essay on Malta*. Dennis currently lives in Malta with his wife, Beatrice. He has two daughters by a previous marriage.

General

The eighteenth-century skeptics long ago discovered that their best weapon against the citadels of folly and superstition was a coolly outrageous literalness: and in the presence of even greater affronts to common sense and daily experience Dennis has developed a modern version of their tactics. Of course the truth and the tones—and the jokes—of reason are rather unfashionable today, but they are obviously the weapons most likely to enlighten a generation which, in Trilling's phrase, worships "the apocalyptic subject and the charismatic style" precisely because they are so intimately adapted to an age when "Higher Criticism" of the last century has been succeeded by the Higher (and hired) Bull of this. For reasons which Dennis explains: "once the reality begins to fade, the symbol is needed to recapture it. If all barristers had brains, there would be no need for wigs." As we have less and less common ground in religion, or in tradition in general, or even in our conception of the nature of the individual, we find a growing appeal in various apocalyptic views of the psychological, religious, and social reality, views which somehow short-circuit the evidently unsatisfactory pictures of ourselves and the world which observation discloses: and this in turn offers a glorious opportunity to various professional soothsayers who—assisted by a strategic obscurity of discourse—offer to relieve the individual of the burden of understanding and of improving his real situation.

To do anything about this, the first need, and the one which incidentally does much to account for Dennis' style, is to learn from "the unpopular men and women known as 'linguistic analysts'" that "we need not fear if we resolve to speak clearly." Dennis' criticism of the Freudian movement, for example, shows how half the confusion arose from using words and symbols based on the current mechanistic images of reality; while most of the rest of the trouble came from the age-old tendency for the individual to seek a self-flattering image of himself as one set apart by his exclusive and privileged access to the Real Truth. The psychoanalysts are the lineal successors of earlier priesthoods: oracles, not of theological Grace, but of the omens of the Unconscious.

Here Dennis' argument seems to me largely true and certainly salutary. We've had enough of pseudo-Freudian gamesmanship; if the Unconscious is what it says, how come everybody knows all about it? And anyway, shouldn't we be grateful it is *unconscious*, if half the stuff one hears about it is true?

In his analysis of theological one-up-manship Dennis' chief target is the fashionable neo-Augustinianism of our time, which he links convincingly with the equally apocalyptic view of man's position on earth in other modern doctrines such as Communism and Existentialism. "Both Mr. Eliot and M. Sartre" he comments, "might expect to find their strongest supporters among housewives, who have dreamed for centuries that evil is preferable to mediocrity. . . . Is not the doctrine of Original Sin struggling to survive . . . by cooking itself up—by becoming Artificial Sin?"

And what—positively—does it all add up to? That we should not be ashamed of common sense. That we should try to be more serious about ourselves and our world. That we should apply both to the confessional and the psychiatrist's couch the

anathema which Pelagius pronounced on the irrational abdication of personal and social responsibility implied in Augustine's "Give what Thou enjoinest, and enjoin what Thou wilt." Dennis, in short, is making a timely plea for "a small shrine dedicated to the worship of Pelagius." By all means; and another to St. Dennis.—IAN WATT, " 'Very Funny . . . Unbelievably Tough,' " *NR*, Aug. 29, 1960, pp. 18–19

Cards of Identity (1955) contains the imaginative projection so sorely lacking in most novels of the forties and fifties and is one of the few recent works of fiction to suggest a broad range of satire. Dennis's first novel in 1949, *A Sea Change* (or *Boys and Girls Come Out to Play*), offered little basis for the present work. That book was concerned with political life in the Polish Corridor on the eve of the second world war as it affected Max, a political writer, and Jimmy Morgan, a callow young boy seeking his identity. Dennis ironically draws the contrast between the heroic Max of the newspaper world and the puny Max as seen by Jimmy. Only in this way—in the shifting Maxes—does Dennis suggest the theme of the later novel, concerned as it is with changing identities.

With *Cards of Identity*, however, Dennis obtained a sharp focus for his ironic view of the world, although to probe identity as such is of course not original. Nevertheless, Dennis has returned to the theme of the great novelists of the earlier part of the century, Kafka, Joyce, Conrad, Lawrence, and Mann, in whom the search for one's identity is the cosmic quest for what one is. The form the search takes is a metaphysical confrontation of man with the universe, and the novel that successfully catches this encounter moves into an imaginative re-creation of man's potentialities. . . .

Dennis's novel is a comic tour de force, and unlike the work of the Angries, with whom inexplicably he has been misidentified, it is not narrow. Striking out fiercely in several directions, Dennis's attack is clearly upon all aspects of life. He joins with the major satirists of the past, Voltaire among them, as a fearless castigator of social and political nonsense. As satire or comedy, *Cards of Identity* is trenchant, but unfortunately its ideas are projected not so much from people as from other ideas. Satire has of course always been concerned more with ideas than with character, and on this very ground Dennis leaves something to be desired. The satirist has to avoid the temptation to caricature. This pitfall Dennis fails to escape, and the novel, for all its breadth and incisiveness, becomes an intellectual sport, a literary eccentricity.

This drawback—a large one, indeed—is doubly unfortunate, for Dennis reveals the verbal and mental gifts as well as the ability to perceive levels of hypocrisy which are the essence of great comic novelists. We find some of these qualities in early Waugh and others in Anthony Powell, especially in the *Music of Time* series, but neither Waugh nor Powell has been fully able to generate important situations. Of the three, Dennis seems at the moment the best equipped. In *A Sea Change*, he demonstrates the ability to write about people, although the novel fails to succeed for lack of sharp focus. In *Cards of Identity*, he has the focus, as clear as anything in the novel of the last two decades, but lacks the humanizing quality which would give concrete significance to the material. To combine the two qualities, the ability to probe individual human beings and yet to keep all society in focus, is to write the large novel, comic or otherwise, so sorely lacking since the death of Joyce, Lawrence, and Conrad. Of contemporary novelists still working seriously, few seem better qualified than Dennis to catch satirically the major currents of contemporary life; in brief, to become a comic conscience. As we see from the past, the effective satirist is able to turn nonsense into metaphysical concepts and hypocrisy into philosophical speculation. How much more mature this is than the protests of the Angries or the puerile antics of their "heroes" in rebellion against forces they are too arrogant or limited to understand!—FREDERICK R. KARL, "The Novels of Powell, Wilson, and Dennis," *The Contemporary English Novel,* 1962, pp. 249–53

Works

BOYS AND GIRLS COME OUT TO PLAY (A SEA CHANGE)

Boys and Girls won the Anglo-American Novel Contest in 1949—but the Americanism is not obtrusive (nor would it matter if it was). The car, naturally enough, is an 'auto', has a 'hood' and not a 'bonnet', gears are 'shifted'. Only phrases like 'He went to sleep for a half-hour' remind us that Mr. Dennis worked for the *New Republic* up till 1949. We are spared the more Teutonic aspects of the American language—'gotten'— and the love of extending words to their utmost limits— 'transportation' for 'transport'. The real trouble, as I see it, is that here we have two books in one. A conventional modern novel where two at least *semi*-sympathetic characters 'find themselves'—and a satire on various theories and their applications. Willi Morgenstern, for example, is a monomaniac who would do credit to Peacock, with his lecture on Hitler and The Potato (*Answeisung der Nationalische-economie Deutschlands vom Standpunkt seiner Kartoffelzonen*). As a character, he would be at home in *Cards*. Here he seems out of place. One can sympathize with Jimmy Morgan, and even with Divver—and for this very reason one feels that they too are refugees—from a naturalistic novel that hundreds of people might have (and have) written.—GAVIN EWART, "Nigel Dennis—Identity Man," *Lon,* Nov. 1963, p. 38

Of Jimmy Morgan, the central figure in *Boys and Girls Come Out to Play,* a young man who suffers occasional epileptic seizures but who has thrown away the drug that, by doping him, is supposed to prevent the attacks, Dennis says: "For, the last two weeks had introduced him into a new world of the most disillusioning kind. Where he had once heedlessly dozed far into the morning, he now awoke, like any normal grown-up man, with a violent palpitation of the heart and a sharp sense of horror at the prospect of another day." If this is the way the "normal grown-up man" returns to living reality, then it is little wonder that he seeks a savior and an externally imposed self-transformation.—JAMES OLNEY, "*Cards of Identity* and the Satiric Mode," *SN,* 1971, p. 381

CARDS OF IDENTITY

In formulating the problem upon which *Cards of Identity* is based, Mr. Dennis may have got suggestions from many foreign sources, Kafka, Pirandello, my *bête noir* Dostoievsky, even the "existentialists," but his treatment is purely English, in the tradition of writers like Ben Jonson, Peacock, and Wyndham Lewis. His book is very funny and unbelievably tough, a jolly farce which, nevertheless, makes all those naturalistic novels in which men beat each other up, women die of syphi-

lis, and no lavatory would dream of flushing seem the work of vegetarian social workers. Mr. Dennis has come to the same conclusion as the sociologist David Riesman, namely, that 20th century society is "other directed" and he does not approve.—W. H. AUDEN, "Am I That I Am," *Enc,* April 1955, p. 68

Cards of Identity came in 1955, after a long gap; but it was worth waiting for. Here there is no silly nonsense about 'characters in the round'. There are no 'lovable people' or 'recognizable human beings'. Nobody could 'sympathize' with any of the protagonists. Only Lolly Paradise (the clueless nephew), the hysterical Dr. Towzer, and the unidentifiable Mrs. Chirk (or Finch) are even halfway pleasant—and for them one feels only vaguely sorry. By one brilliant stroke the author has freed himself from the greatest problem confronting a novelist: how to people a fantasy with 'real' characters, whose hopes and fears we can understand and feel, who are, in fact, as much like real human beings as possible. By simply choosing to regard all human behaviour and all human characteristics as parts of a façade—and interchangeable ones at that—according to the 'Great Theory' of Identity, Mr. Dennis has opted out of that dim half-world where fictional characters struggle to become flesh and blood. He thus makes a strength out of what, for an ordinary novelist, would be a weakness. He is not like Mr. Huxley, whose early novels at least would justify a charge of Cruelty to Characters; there is little or no emotion, certainly no hatred. Instead there is interest in the characters as *types*, with the implication that all real human beings, in real life, also try as hard as they can to type-cast themselves. Like advertising men, they strive to build up a 'brand image', and very consciously 'each man in his time plays many parts'.

Cards shows great vitality and great control, from the very start. Nor does the 'first subject' take long to appear. Like an oboe solo announcing an important theme, Miss Paradise in her opening row with her brother Henry declares: 'Everything about you seems to belong to another person. It's like being with a stranger.' The writing, dialogue and all, is on the Powell-Connolly level. The hallucinated, larger-than-life observation is Wyndham Lewis-with-a-difference. 'He opened a drawer and took out an old-fashioned pair of binoculars. . . . Grasping an extensive wheel between the lenses he wound away until the apparatus thrust forward like twin cannon.' Comic generalization is another forte: '. . . the moment of reading out the will is one of the few occasions when capital drops its striped trousers and reveals itself as none other than naked cash'.—GAVIN EWART, "Nigel Dennis—Identity Man," *Lon,* Nov. 1963, p. 39

Nigel Dennis's *Cards of Identity* is an ambitious satire, partly allegorical, which is weakened in the end by the purely negative values underlying it. The Identity Club has its yearly conference at a large country mansion and, using modern techniques of psychological persuasion, the members of the Identity Club persuade the owners of the mansion and the local doctor to accept the roles of old family servants. Papers are delivered, anecdotes about identity-changing or the assumption of fantasy identities are told, and the performance of a mock-Elizabethan play leads eventually to the murder of the Club President and his suppression by a younger and more ruthless rival. The satire is ambivalent; it is partly satire on modern means of mass persuasion, and on the uneasiness which many people feel today unless they can adapt themselves to a stereotyped role. But the cruel and frivolous members of the Identity Club seem to be regarded by Mr Dennis with a certain Nietzschean complicity, and the ruthlessness of the whole scheme is in the end distasteful. Mr Dennis lacks that basic sympathy with the human weaknesses which make up human nature—which Mr Golding and Mrs Spark possess. Nigel Dennis's first novel, written many years earlier, *Boys and Girls Come Out to Play*, about a young man's desperate escape from a family of progressive philanthropists, though imperfect in itself, may throw some light on the attitudes behind *Cards of Identity*. That remains a disagreeable and rather over-elaborated but powerful and sourly amusing book. Its nearest earlier equivalent is perhaps Wyndham Lewis's powerful but again bitter and top-heavy satire, *The Apes of God*.—G. S. FRASER, *The Modern Writer and His World*, 1964, pp. 172–73

That there is a crisis in the English sense of cultural identity is obvious, and what I have called the neurotic stance of much recent literature is one way of responding to it. But two novels, one of the fifties and one of the sixties, seem to me outstanding, both as works of fiction and as attempts to face directly the question of identity. The first of these is Nigel Dennis's *Cards of Identity*, published in 1955 and surely one of the most brilliant novels of its decade. . . . In its most universal sense *Cards of Identity* is a very funny and penetrating fable about the problem of identity, a problem that is, of course, familiar in many of the most distinguished works of the Modern Movement: one may refer, for instance, to Kafka or Pirandello. In sociological terms this topic ravages a large part of the Western world, particularly America, and is capable of endless commentary and explanation. In American fiction the paradoxes of identity are constantly invoked, and provide central themes for the novels of Barth and Pynchon. *Cards of Identity* appeared some years before their work, and is one of the few English treatments of this topic, which, because of the protective influence of the English ideology that traditionally made sure that everyone knew his place, has been less acute in this country than in others. (Yet there is a classic earlier treatment of it in *Alice in Wonderland*, which is interestingly echoed here and there in *Cards of Identity*.) Nigel Dennis's novel is set in an English country house, where a body called the Identity Club is holding its annual meeting. In some ways it reflects the conditions of the late forties and early fifties, a period of ration-books and identity cards and continuing post-war privations. The case-history delivered by Father Golden Orfe about an ex-communist turned monk, writing his memoirs in a monastery, all of whose intimates have had a similar communist past is, though entertaining, very much a product of the era of Whittaker Chambers and *The God That Failed*. On the other hand the story of the Co-Wardens of the Badgeries, and the sad farcical events that took place while they were ceremonially leading a symbolic stuffed badger across London in the funeral procession of the Lord Royal, is still a valid satire on the more absurd manifestations of English public traditionalism. . . . In its comic, inventive and somewhat heartless fashion, *Cards of Identity* probes at contemporary dilemmas: its satirical examination of the way in which the traditional symbols of English identity are losing their validity is an important part of its meaning.—BERNARD BERGONZI, "The Ideology of Being English," *The Situation of the Novel*, 1970, pp. 71–74

A HOUSE IN ORDER

A House in Order is the latest expression of Nigel Dennis's disenchantment with the world, a sharp hiss of contempt for what he all too clearly sees as the absurdity of mankind and the hollow mockery of its most hallowed institutions and values. It need hardly be said that his assault is both penetrating and vitriolic, calculated to chafe the latent prejudices of even the most tolerant reader at some point or another. Indeed, almost

alone among modern English satirists, Mr Dennis exhibits in his work the sort of Swiftian malevolence that begs little of disarming humour and is only concerned to ridicule and wound the object of his attack. He neither tempers his spite with drollery nor emulates those celebrated television pranksters whose self-conscious charm is, no matter how wicked their posturing, designed to placate and win the affection of even the prissiest audience. Where they merely caper like so many delinquent children striving to gain the attention of a slightly shocked but inwardly amused parent, Mr Dennis is out to draw blood, slashing the pretensions of the *avant-garde* as ruthlessly as he dissects the stupidity of the po-faced bigots of our society. Nothing, thanks be to Moo, is sacred to him. In consequence, it may be that, like Kafka, he is more respected than read, a situation which, I fancy, this book, although considerably less involved and elusive than *Cards of Identity*, will do little to rectify. A subtle and demanding parable of the essential hypocrisy of human standards, it provides little of the slick entertainment value we have come to expect from satire and will, I suspect, leave most readers uneasily aware that they have been numbered among the fallen rather than among the angels. This is, to say the least, a bit harsh for a generation reared on satirists who have done nothing more than flatter our progressiveness at the expense of Aunt Sally's prejudices.— FRANK MCGUINNESS, *Lon*, Nov. 1966, p. 103

Nigel Dennis is one of the most accomplished and idiosyncratic of living English novelists, and in his most recent novel, *A House in Order*, he continues to dwell on the question of identity in a way that is at once more personal and less culturally specific than in *Cards of Identity*, though it is an equally distinguished work. The subject could not be more restricted: during a war between two unnamed powers a prisoner is kept confined in a greenhouse near a building which houses a minor army administrative unit. He cannot be moved, as he is an object of contention between two branches of the military establishment, though neither side is interested in his personal welfare. In civilian life this man's hobby was gardening, and with immense patience he starts cultivating the small plants he finds in the greenhouse and the garden outside where he is allowed to take exercise. In time the prisoner becomes attached to his place of confinement, despite the physical privations he undergoes, and he uses the plants to keep not only his house but his mind in order, and to preserve his sense of self. The story has, of course, many symbolic or allegorical implications about the Human Condition in general, but Dennis advances them without destroying the credibility of his narrative. The humour which distinguished *Cards of Identity* is, though necessarily subdued, certainly present in *A House in Order*. The book is noticeable for the way in which it depicts the prisoner's plight without any sense of nightmare. He preserves his sanity, and at the end of the novel he is restored to his own country and a greenhouse of his own, although he looks back nostalgically to the days of his incarceration as to some vanished ideal order. Dennis may have manifested a certain English loss of nerve, or kind-hearted regard for his character: I can imagine a French or American novelist keeping the man a prisoner for good.—BERNARD BERGONZI, "The Ideology of Being English," *The Situation of the Novel*, 1970, pp. 74–75

EXOTICS

Nigel Dennis devotes almost half of *Exotics* to his clean uncluttered version of the Gilgamesh Epic. It walks an even, sensible line between the archaic and the prosaic, eschews any recreation of mythic grandeur by lyrical density and wisely allows the exclusion of doubts and guilts to establish a pristine, amoral semi-divinity. The effect is, curiously, of a flight from the rationalism and evangelicalism which the public school confers on classical antiquity, and a search for a parallel myth, less spartan, more stoic, and, incorruptibly, aware of the injustice of things.—RAYMOND DURGNAT, "Men of Two Worlds," *PoR*, Winter 1970–71, p. 366

NIGEL DENNIS
From "Preface" to *Two Plays and a Preface*
1958, pp. 7–12

I

The worshipping by Laplanders of large stones with eccentric shapes has so died out that, today, no Epstein could excite a Lapp's devotion. The cause of this falling-away is education: God is worshipped as a solid only by backward people; once educated, the mind reaches out only for what cannot be grasped, recognizes only what cannot be seen: sophistry adores a vacuum.

Vacuous worship brings solid advantages. The first, without any doubt, is that it makes worship far more difficult—which, in turn, means that ordinary people have no idea of what it is about and must ask better men to tell them. The second is that in being able to understand something so difficult, higher minds see that their minds *are* higher and attain to extreme self-confidence. The Invisible is always their goal because it offers unlimited opportunities for intellectual expansion. Only, for example, a Being who cannot outwardly be touched can haunt the sage with the notion that he may be touched inwardly by It. Only the Invisible has the requisite elasticity, and can be twisted and twined by the mind so flexibly that it can give a binding, if not neat, appearance to the most cumbersome of confessions. Only an Invisible can make daring sorties into plain visibility: by so doing two or three times every few thousand years, it can intensify, by means of simple contrast, its characteristic condition of being out of sight. The temptation to put flesh on the Invisible more often, to make live-bait of it, is a strong one; but any succumbing to it is not only a regression to savage solidity but provocative of scepticism. For the principle advantage of the Invisible is that so long as it cannot be seen, its presence cannot be denied. Any student of philosophy can show that a stone, however oddly shaped, is merely a sensory illusion; but no sceptic, however skilled, can poke his shooting-stick through the rails and give a reflective prod to nothing. Hume remarks the fact that the major heresies of the Christian religion were attempts to make it 'less contrary to plain sense'; this is *why* they were heresies; they made arguable, and thus uncertain, what was literally beyond doubt. A religion may make rational forays and expeditions on a tremendous scale, but it must always be able to withdraw to an interior castle on a desert island, and pull the ladder up.

It is here that satire enters the picture. By some marvellous Providence, some immensely-shrewd bit of Invisible planning, arrangements have been made for the satirical spirit to share the interior castle of the theologians. Theological man and satirical man have lived in adjoining cells ever since civilization began: the ravens have not brought to the theologian a single loaf or fish of which the satirist has not eaten half. The points they have in common are almost too obvious to mention. Each puts on a grand march-past of intellectual floats, led by Miss Idea with her whirling stick and springy pink knees, but each always knows, at heart, that he is pursuing his brutish way with no more than an animal faith in the rightness of his ferocity. Neither has any interest in everyday justice, fairness,

decency, accuracy: each is out simply to make his theme as glorious as possible. This means that dramatic exaggeration—often presented with a perfectly straight face but wearing funny clothes—is the particular speciality of both satirist and theologian: indeed, there is no more perfect description of the satirical justification than Tertullian's well-known ejaculation: 'It is certain, *because* it is impossible.'...

II

During the 'twenties and 'thirties, the satirist went through a worrying time: it seemed to him that religion was disappearing and leaving him an orphan. If this had happened, he would have had nothing to slander but social behaviour, which has always been the chopping-block of pure comedy, not satire, because it belongs to the world of eminently Visible things and any Ideas it has are too low to bother with. Today, the satirist is ashamed to think that he was ever nervous: the religious date-palm is not only going strong but has thrown out countless new branches, all foaming in spring with blooming religionettes.

Religion itself cannot be held responsible for this return: it has not undergone any attractive changes. The world, however, has undergone so many unattractive ones, and become also so unpredictable and complicated, that the lure of the ever-malleable Invisible has again become tempting to all minds that have passed beyond the Stone Age verities of Lapps. Yet, disappointment in the visible world is never enough by itself to bring about a religious revival; there must also be a strong conviction among those who return to the faith that they themselves are responsible for having made things go wrong: this is not always untrue. Those who are in this position today are the Radicals of yesterday who believed, for the first time in human history, not only in the earthly brotherhood of man but in the doctrine that each person is intimately responsible for the sufferings of all other persons. The catchword, which originally referred to the universal fate of death, and not to the nature of life, was the famous dictum: 'No man is an island, compleat unto himself.' This, forced and tugged out of its original context by Holy Rollers of the Donne-Stalin axis, came to mean that each time a distant stranger was tortured, garrotted or shot in the neck, persons in Wimbledon and Yonkers must feel responsible for the act. There was a certain commonsense in this nonsensical doctrine, in that there was a real propriety in believing that a brotherhood of man could not be described as such unless the brothers were prepared to stand by one another. But, on being tested, the doctrine turned out to be largely a hideous means of frustration and self-persecution. The powerful brothers in the fancied brotherhood continued briskly to torture, garrott and shoot, leaving the nicer, impotent brothers to bear the responsibility and feel the guilt. This they did with a will, and are still doing. Moreover, many of them decided that the earthly brotherhood idea had been a personal blunder from the start, resting on a too-materialistic base, and thus added the guilt of having made a basic mistake to the misery they felt about its consequences. The more extreme characters among these sinners—those who had dirtied their hands badly by furthering the brotherhood in ugly ways—are the ones who are now scrubbing away at their hands in public, confessing relentlessly and finding in religion a means of obtaining more intense self-condemnation at the Highest Level. Many of the less extreme characters have not turned to religion: they have merely been reduced to struggling on as best they can with the remnants of their old beliefs, and doing so in silence. This apparent half-heartedness is much to be respected: it is perfectly honourable to be puzzled. But precisely because silent puzzlement is undramatic, the literary stage is left empty, to be abused by the more agonized, noisier wowsers and barkers—a Salvation Army that never wearies of translating simple, human error and disappointment into massive, indecent transgressions against the body of Christ.

JAMES OLNEY
From *"Cards of Identity* and the Satiric Mode"
Studies in the Novel, 1971, pp. 385–87

No matter what his ostensible subject—auctions, or doctors and nurses, or the national health system, or sex, or religion, or national tradition, or police, or psychiatrists, or Communism, or Shakespeare, or whatever—Dennis, exemplifying in his presentation that unity-in-diversity that is peculiar to satire, is always hammering away at the one inclusive theme of identity. He never relaxes the intensity of his scorn and ridicule, never ceases poking a finger in his victim's one eye, and—this especially—never lets himself be caught hinting at a real and possible positive; for one of the satirist's cardinal rules is: "Always keep it negative."

Not only does the satirist shy away from the danger of offering positives, but in fact he seldom speaks directly in his own voice about anything. Dennis characteristically makes objective presentations entirely from outside character and action (*Cards of Identity*) or, as in *A House in Order*, creates a persona that is not, in any essential way, to be identified with himself. "To play this game properly," Dennis advises in his book on Swift, "the true author must never interrupt the pretended one; that "I" that is Jonathan Swift must never make a sudden personal appearance in territory that has been given over to one of his pseudonyms" (p. 32). Perhaps a better example than *A House in Order* of this persona device is offered by an article, "Of Unhappiness and War," that Dennis published as co-editor of *Encounter.* An exercise in Swiftian irony of the "Modest Proposal" variety, the article is based on the premise that American liberals are happy only when miserably unhappy, specifically when they are revolted by governmental policy (thus they were in their days of glory under Coolidge and Hoover); their greatest happiness-cum-revulsion/unhappiness is with the war in Viet Nam, and Johnson (this was published in February 1968), a great leader of the liberals, has sacrificed billions of dollars and thousands of lives in a commendable effort to keep his liberals happy, i.e., unhappy. The question that the writer ponders in conclusion is whether Johnson will be willing to make the liberals *really* unhappy/happy by turning over Southeast Asia to the Communists in an entirely ignominious and degrading capitulation. Dennis appears throughout this essay not as himself but as a good-hearted and helpful observer, inclined to the liberal side in his political sentiments, who modestly seeks to serve the best interests of everyone involved, and especially of the liberals; and, as will be obvious, he manages to have it both ways, eating his cake and keeping it too, by hazarding nothing positive.

One might suppose that in *Cards of Identity,* if the central question really is "Who am I?" Dennis might want to pursue

from within the efforts of the individual to establish and realize his identity. This is what Joyce does in the impressionistic record of *A Portrait of the Artist* or in the interior monologue of *Ulysses,* where there is little else but the subjective; this is what Virginia Woolf does also and a hundred other novelists intent on sketching an answer to the question of identity. Dennis's treatment, however, is unfailingly exterior. Indeed, another thing, as I have already implied, that distinguishes the satirist's art from the novelist's is the small regard shown by the former for characterization, which is perhaps achieved in any fullness only through the inner view. One reason that *Cards of Identity* so completely eschews the inside is that it is not really concerned with answering the question "Who am I?"; rather it pursues those who do offer to answer this question at large and those who require an answer from someone else: the book is dedicated not to the internal but the external, to the objective rather than the subjective. No living person, taken from his own point of view, is entirely—or perhaps at all—despicable, and this is good reason for the satirist to refuse to identify with any interior point of view and, going a step further, to avoid creating full and living characters. "Dogmatically," Wyndham Lewis says, speaking as a satirist, "I am for the Great Without, for the method of *external* approach. . . ."[1] Never, in *Cards of Identity,* does Dennis try to evoke the Within; never do we penetrate a character's mind and his thoughts so as to make them our thoughts; never do we have a sense of any character's individuality or his essential being (which is anyhow in question: is there such a thing?) It would be to destroy his very intention if Dennis went within a character, or within characters generally, to analyze their inmost, private motives and personalities. "Tout comprendre," according to the French proverb, "c'est tout pardonner." When we begin to understand the characters, we begin to excuse and to forgive them, and that is not at all to Dennis's purpose, for he has no desire to pardon anybody. Seeing them from without, the reader lacks totally in sympathy for the rogues and ninnies of *Cards of Identity.* As the characters are not made a part of his empathic field, the reader can laugh and ridicule (along with the author, who is *in* his book only in its consistent tone of mockery and ridicule, irony and sarcasm) and can condemn the sin without worrying about the sinner. The satirist, unlike the "true, compleat" novelist, is not interested in his characters for their humanness. He is not drawn to create character because he loves to create life, to feel a character come alive under his hand. He is almost always more interested in ideas than in people, and his characters are to be *used* rather than simply to be. Putting the distinction in gross terms, one might call the great novelist a creative genius, the great satirist a critical genius.

Notes

1. Quoted by Robert C. Elliott, *The Power of Satire* (Princeton Univ. Press, 1960), p. 225.

DENIS DEVLIN

1908–1959

Denis Devlin was born on April 15, 1908, in Greenock, Scotland; his parents returned to Ireland when he was ten. He attended Belvedere College, All Hallows College, Munich University, the Sorbonne, and University College, where he taught from 1932 to 1935. There he also produced his first volume of poetry with classmate Brian Coffey. In 1935 he joined the Irish foreign service, which employed him for the rest of his life. Devlin was stationed in Washington and London through the 1940s, then became Ambassador to Italy in 1950. He published few poems after his acclaimed second volume appeared in 1937; most of his work was published posthumously. Many of his translations and autobiographical writings remain unpublished.

Inez Boulton called Devlin the "inheritor of the Irish poetic tradition . . . [he] brings to his work its feeling for rhythm and cadence, Celtic mother wit, and rich religious background." Devlin's poetry developed over the years from a sprawling proliferation of wild images to tightly-constructed classical verse. He was modest and reserved, a devout Catholic whose religion often figured in his art. Devlin was married in 1946, and had one son. He died in Dublin on August 21, 1959.

Personal

We read in a letter from one of his boyhood friends, the last friend, in fact, who was summoned to the death bed, that, as a boy, Denis was notably courteous and had "an unfailing good humour of a conscious quizzical kind," and that he had "a way of standing still when listening, with his arms hanging by his sides," and that there was a college cartoon of him "represented as a penguin with a cherrywood pipe stuck in his mouth." Suddenly that boy in the stance of courteous immobility and the man are one and the same, and the years flee aside and leave that image. For we know that late one night in 1935, when he had just been appointed Cadet in the Department of External Affairs, he stood a long time on the canal bridge on Baggot Street in Dublin and debated with a friend whether he should abandon the formal study of literature—for literature, he said, represented the "higher life." And Brian Coffey, with whom Denis had joined in publishing that first book of poems, reports that though poetry was never an "idol" for Denis, he once had heard him cry out: "God, please let me write a poem!" It is not hard to imagine with what characteristic admixture of humor and humility he uttered that youthful cry.

We have such youthful images, gathered from here and there, and they seem to give a new dimension, after death, to the man who was a generous friend, gay and ready to break into a poem or to sing a ballad; who had, as an old friend puts it, "the strong moralist's desire for justice" and a profound sense of "his religious relationship to Our Lord"; who was the seasoned diplomat; and who also continued, with rare devotion and joy, his pursuit of the "higher life" of literature.—ALLEN TATE and ROBERT PENN WARREN, "A Preface" to *Selected Poems*, 1963, p. 12

General

⟨Devlin's⟩ poems are steeped in many traditions—myths, rituals, histories, religions, oracles, wars, martyrdoms, sensualities. They are romantic and highly discursive, tapestries of many colors, many moods, unified not so much by the abstraction of intellectual argument as by the all-encompassing ego which believes itself to be the unifying principle. Here indeed, is the flesh and blood of poetry. . . . Denis Devlin wanders far afield, filling the gaps with a largesse of tangible imagery—magniloquent heavens, firefly instinct dreamed out into law,

Orpheus, voiceless beasts, Byronic intuitions, "The loosened universe flowing," cliffs of ice, antlered forests, self-deluded larks, webbed tensions of memory, visible and invisible architectures.—MARGUERITE YOUNG, *NYTBR*, July 21, 1946, p. 12

Mr. Devlin, inheritor of the Irish poetic tradition, brings to his work its feeling for rhythm and cadence, Celtic mother wit and rich religious background. But he adds modern youth's re-examination of the past and awareness of the significant part that science now plays in man's universal orientation. Using greater economy of language than most of his Celtic forebears, he attains a strength of structure sometimes lacking in even the greatest of them. The bone structure of a philosophy is here more clearly defined than in other Irish poets, beneath that metaphorical process which is the flesh of all poetry.

Lough Derg, the poem from which the book takes its title, is the story of an Irish abbey, ancient and famous as a place of religious pilgrimage. The reference to Dante in it is not merely metaphorical but historical: tradition has it that Dante once stayed in retreat there. "Est Prodest," one of the loveliest poems in the book, is full of the deeply religious background and demonstrates the view of modern occultists that praise is more efficacious than prayer. The poem "Annapolis" shows Devlin's keen observation of the American scene. In "Diplomat" and "Memo from a Millionaire," the poet becomes the social critic with a light touch. "The Victory of Samothrace" and "Venus of the Salty Shell" are effective poems on subjects that because of their triteness are difficult to handle, but which in this case are handled exceedingly well.

Among the best poems are "Picture in a Window," "Eve in My Legend" and "Wishes for Her."—INEZ BOULTON, "Celtic Nova," *Poetry*, Dec. 1946, p. 169

Like most Irishmen of his generation, Devlin had closer ties with France than with England, and his education in modern poetry was mostly French. The influence of Valéry is pervasive; and there is little of Yeats. His originality is not spectacular; it is subtle and subdued, consisting in a slight modification of the language and conventions of his immediate elders. He wrote a few bad poems, many good poems, and perhaps three great poems. These are "The Passion of Christ," "From Government Buildings," and, above all, "Lough Derg," a poem that may rank with Stevens' "Sunday Morning," Eliot's "Gerontion," and Crane's "The Broken Tower." In all these poems, the poets are exploring the difficult region where doubt and faith have been conducting an inconclusive dialectic since the middle of the last century.—ALLEN TATE and ROBERT PENN WARREN, "A Preface" to *Selected Poems*, 1963, p. 13

Devlin was by profession a diplomat in the Irish foreign service, and his poems remind us of the posts he occupied: Washington, Rome, Ankara. Even more they remind us of the education of a young Irishman in the years after Independence, split so acutely between the home nation and France. Some poems with extended, sonorous lines remind us of Perse, and remind us also that Devlin was one of Perse's best translators; other poems, compact and difficult, remind us of Valéry. The native strains combine the wit of the Anglo-Irishman (Swift) with the lyricism of the Gael (Yeats), and display the anguished religious susceptibility of both. In spite of these reminders of other poets, however, we do not lose sight of Devlin. He is a distinct intelligence. Is he more than that? It's difficult to say. Possibly he vacillated too much among the styles he admired. Possibly he was incapable of the final risk of poetry, an assertion of the ultimate creative ego. Beyond intelligence, the outline of sensibility remains shifty; the *poet* is obscure.

Tate and Warren believe that Devlin wrote "many good poems and perhaps three great ones", namely *The Passion of Christ*, *Lough Derg*, and *From Government Buildings*. Certainly these are the big poems—two religious, one ethico-political—and certainly they contain many fine passages; but for me—here I take the plunge—they lack the strength of vision, rhythm, and feeling (the tripedal base of poetic faith) which would be required to sustain them as whole poems. I am interested particularly in the rhythm. We are told that Devlin was a lover of balladry and used to sing Irish songs, and this is evident in his slighter poems. Did he, for his more powerfully felt poems, intentionally break up the cadences of native idiom under some influence of fashion? Such a presumption would be unworthy; more likely he sought instead a style which would be personal, intrinsic, and inwardly supported. But in entering that Minoan cave—the rhetoric of a self—he may have dropped somewhere the golden thread which would have maintained his connection with the once-heard voice; he may have ended in a dissension of silent voices.—HAYDEN CARRUTH, "Silent Voices," *Poetry*, Dec. 1963, pp. 191–92

Works

"Lough Derg" takes its title from that part of Donegal where annually Irish pilgrims gather to pray. The poem is composed of nineteen six-line stanzas, rhymed *ababcc*, a modification of rhyme royal, or perhaps an adaptation of the stanza, *aabccb*, of "*Le cimetière marin*." In other ways the poem suggests a derivation from, but in no sense an imitation of, Valéry. Like "*Le cimetière marin*," it poses a universal religious conflict which, in Valéry, Mr. Yvor Winters has described as a sense of the "flaw in creation"; in "Lough Derg" the conflict moves within a definitely Christian orbit: a civilized Irishman of the Catholic faith meditates on the difference between the scepticism of faith and the simple, fanatical faith of the Irish peasant—with whom he partly identifies himself—praying at Lough Derg. It is a sufficiently commonplace subject, yet one that still seems to give rise to great poetry, and has become almost a contemporary genre,.—ALLEN TATE and ROBERT PENN WARREN, "A Preface" to *Selected Poems*, 1963, pp. 13–14

In 'Lough Derg,' the poet's contemplation of his own sophisticated religiosity in the light of the naïve devotion of most of his countrymen involves considerations similar to those of Clarke's 'Repentance' but is far more complex. As Devlin handles the problem, it becomes a subject with every sort of intellectual repercussion. The poem expresses the workings of a fine mind seeking an acceptable balance among its own motives. Devlin, though hardly as dynamic as Hart Crane, approaches him in his continuing effort at self-identification.—M. L. ROSENTHAL, "Contemporary Irish Poetry," *The New Poets*, 1967, p. 273

Denis Devlin's first volume of *Poems* (in collaboration with Brian Coffey) appeared in Dublin in 1932. Since then, residence abroad, the vicissitudes of publication and his undoubted quality as a poet have combined to earn him a reputation which stands much higher elsewhere than in his own country. . . .

Up to the present Devlin's reputation has rested mainly on two volumes of poems—*Intercessions* (London, 1937) and *Lough Derg and Other Poems* (New York, 1946). But it has been much enhanced by his splendid translations of the important French poet, St. John Perse. These translations appeared in America under the titles, *Rains* (1945), *Snows* (1945), and *Exile and Other Poems* (1949). . . .

The Heavenly Foreigner is unquestionably Devlin's most considerable poetic achievement to date. It is a complex poem, making what may seem unusual demands upon the reader. But they are the legitimate demands of a poet, and the reader who concedes them will find himself well rewarded. On a careful reading, superficial obscurities vanish ⟨and⟩ new imaginative horizons open in "the casual unwilled depths of the poem," complexities of thought and feeling fuse into a glowing lyricism. Indeed, certain sections of this long poem, taken out of context, have the smooth charm of anthology-pieces:

> Come back! come back! your absence cause for tears.
> Come back! no cause for fear.
> Youth's faithfulness with which I failed you most
> Is changed now to a gentler way of seeing
> So well I can be faithful to a ghost.
> Mostly there's one that loves and one lets love:
> But our two appetites devoured their food;
> Yet join me in this company I keep:
> Not life but below it or above
> Where bodiless blind eyes seem to weep.

On one level *The Heavenly Foreigner* communicates as a love-poem, rich in poignant and tender moods. But sexual love is the incidental and minor theme, as it was in the Catharist songs of the Troubadours. The deeper preoccupation is with the problems of Time and human destiny, the anguished alliance of flesh and spirit. What God had joined Descartes has put asunder, and the wound still festers.

> The world glows with mortal divinity;
> The red turns gray,
> The ash creeps up on the flame,
> O heavenly foreigner! your price is high.

This is the heart of the matter. Devlin's poetry is the product of a cultured and flexible mind, and in handling these fundamental themes he shows a rare power of stating abstract ideas and philosophical concepts in terms of poetry. Bergson can tell us: "Duration is the continuous progress of the past which gnaws into the future and which swells as it advances. The piling up of the past upon the past goes on without relation. . . . In its entirety, probably, it follows us at every instant. . . . Doubtless, we think with only a small part of our past, but it is with our entire past . . . that we desire, will and act."

The poetic statement is equally valid:

In the memory, years interweave; they do not follow
  one another
Like jealous ambassadors in the Mayor's procession.
All years flow from a hundred streets
Intemperately towards the mansion
Last year no less than this
For her mercurial year threads through them all
  since;

And only the poetic imagination strives to arrest the flux,
to crystallise past, present and future in

. . . an instant preconising eternity
Borne between our open eyes
With no perceptible bank of land between
Nor oblique eyesight deciding other objects were
  there.

The word "oblique" occurs more than once in the poem
and it suggests an important element in Devlin's approach to
his material. This is his faculty of observing from the corner of
the mind's eye, which has the effect of adding another dimension to his vision:

. . . the fiery circle cataracting outerworld
Showed in cold, peaceful stars to our little world
In his circular band of frisky, divine air
In which we build basilicas
And sicken at the sight of two-headed calves.

It is this faculty, too, which makes much of his imagery at once
surprising and satisfying, as in the line

Rodents in the corn like the black gas in the heart of
  the sun

or in this passage where the permanent dilemma is recognised
and accepted:

                                              Yet
If in such heaven my difference should compose,
And in such temporal harmony of health and harm
Flood of perfection flood back over me, there,
There in that bubble I'd exaggerate
A wet meniscus of discontent
And all my activity lie
Chaffing between diameter and arc.

In the varying moods of the poem Devlin displays great technical virtuosity—in his skilful use of internal assonance and half-
rhymes, Biblical cadences, traditional modes and passages of
straight prose. His handling of cliché is particularly effective,
and I doubt whether any contemporary poet can load the banal, colloquial phrase with such overtones of pathos and irony.

I feel that certain passages are marred by technical weaknesses and unresolved difficulties of syntax, but these are minor
flaws in a work which proves Denis Devlin to be a real force in
the development of modern poetry. The extent of his achievement in *The Heavenly Foreigner* depends finally on whether
this long poem makes, on its own esthetic terms, an intellectual and emotional synthesis.—NIALL SHERIDAN, "Introduction" to *The Heavenly Foreigner*, 1967, pp. 68–71

FRANK L. KERSNOWSKI
From "The Fabulous Reality of Denis Devlin"

Sewanee Review, Winter 1973, pp. 113–22

Denis Devlin . . . is one of the most impressive poets to
come out of modern Ireland. What may have kept Devlin
from wider approval is what irritated Austin Clarke about his

poetry: his similarity to intellectual poets of the Continent.
Devlin has translated St. John Perse, and his own progression
has been from a surrealistic portrayal of disgust to a mythic
celebration of love. In his presentation of a psychological reality, metaphor becomes reality. He searched for ontological
relationships which could raise him above the enforced fears
and the miserable squabbles of opportunists.

Seemingly every Irish writer must struggle with the demands of a church-trained conscience. Devlin's early poems
are illustrative:

Stinkarum, stankarum, buck,
The old Scholastics say
That the body is filth and muck
and will be dust one day.
Riddle-me, riddle-me, rin
Why do skeletons grin?
There is no rest on the journey,
And death is the wages of sin.

These two light and ironic ballad stanzas, with others, give the
expected conclusion to the discussion which is the body of the
poem: the tempted joy of love and the conditioned rejection of
it. His unwilling acceptance of a view of the body as vile tells of
the conclusion of the dialogue. If one metaphor, theme,
occurs most frequently in Devlin's first two volumes it is, in
various form, death-decay. . . .

Devlin's ambivalence about the feminine power clearly
exists, for woman is the Church and also a desirable physical
being. But more basic is his view that the feminine is an all-
powerful deity which the male must reject or be destroyed by.
The sources of this view, though ideology may be a better term,
are two obvious ones: the Church which he has shown as
turning man away from the world (equivalent to the feminine)
and the example of Eliot. Eliot's mingling of realistic details in
an unexpected manner is the basic technique of surrealists.
This is found in Devlin's poems frequently. . . .

The poems in Devlin's next volume, *Lough Derg,* retain
the mythic structure and allusions, but do so ecstatically. Except for occasional sardonic comments upon the ways of the
wealthy, diplomats, and others intricately involved in the workings of socio-economic man, Devlin's remaining poems
present the ecstasy of man. He is no longer consumed with
loathing for the workings of the Church. Without praising its
puritanical bias, he can wonder at that which differs in structure and goal from his own life. In the title poem of the
volume, he recounts the yearly pilgrimage to the lake and the
top of Croagh Patrick, the sacred mountain. Though he differs
from the people around him by the fact of his awareness, he
does in his own terms achieve their joy and humility before the
divine: "All is simple in their world,/The incomprehended rendered fabulous." While the people around him kneel to their
God, the poet's mind celebrates a union of soul and body that
allows the animal appetite to feed the spirit as exemplified by
druids and Christ of the Renaissance painters. Though he retains his censure of belief that destroys the physical:

                              O earthly paradise!
Hell is to know our natural empire used
Wrong, by mind's moulting, brute divinities.

The poetry becomes a religiously eclectic celebration of loved
life. The resemblance to Eliot's *Four Quartets* does not seem
accidental; and as one can for Eliot, one can question the
orthodoxy of Devlin's Christianity.

The importance of Jansenism, with its denial of free will
and assertion of man's corruption, may well make a discussion
of Irish Catholicism difficult to speak of in such a term as

orthodox. For the repression of the animal in the human becomes so extreme that man must become an apostate or be
destroyed. Devlin's inability to accept the Church's dicta is
apparent in "Jansenist Journey" and is flatly stated in "West
Pier": "Aboriginal anger and Christian terror/Wound happiness." Devlin's understanding of religion, again, resembles
Eliot's historical reconstruction, though to a completely different conclusion. Neither the anguish of the aware nor the brute
belief of those who blindly follow belongs to Devlin. Instead,
he has constructed a belief combining the pagan goddess with
the Christian worship of the separate soul. . . .

The heady ecstasy of many poems in *Lough Derg*—
"Welcome My World", for example—becomes quieter in the
last poems. In these poems Devlin reveals his conquest of
Jansenist morbidity through his acceptance of life, love, and
death as each being valuable for its own sake. He is not the
young man for whom life is seen as the reflection of death.
Instead, Devlin writes from his understanding of joy, his expectation of death. Judging from the many poems he wrote
about the complex and miraculous nature of woman, he came
to his enlightenment through a woman perceived and accepted
as divine mortality. . . .

Life and destruction still exist separately for Devlin, but
they no longer contend with each other. Instead, they are
contraries which mingle with interdependence. The ascetic
and the sexual do not struggle to destroy one another, and life
becomes sacred. To achieve this understanding, however,
Devlin sacrificed much that the Judaeo-Christian tradition had
led him to believe, much about the dominance of the male,
much about the nature of the divine. . . .

The central figure in the traditional society was the
woman. This importance has existed for Devlin since his early
poems in which he portrayed her with Eliotesque repugnance
as the carrion-consuming vulture. In "The Heavenly Foreigner" the woman is no longer the source of corruption, but of
ecstatic understanding. Again, for Devlin, she is an ontological, rather than literal, figure.

How she stood, hypothetical-eyed and metaphor-
        breasted
Weaving my vision out of my sight
Out of my sight, out of my very sight,
Out of her sight
Till the sight it sees with is blind with light
Other than hers, other than mine
Till it unravels
And there's only a light smoke in my hands . . .

Yet Devlin continuously asserts the presence of the mortal,
literal, woman in conjunction with the mythical force.

I know there is one thing, which is you, it is the
        unique
Which also in part is she,
You, not seen by her,
You, not to be reduced by my eyes' famine of her.

Mythic belief, then, has not destroyed his love of the unique
and literal, but has destroyed his fear of them. Becoming aware
that all great beauty and love partake in a fundamental and
divine ritual of existence, he no longer viewed the mortal as
diseased because it grew in its imperfection into the fixed state
of death. . . .

Understandably, Devlin did not become one of the people
he wrote of in "Lough Derg" for whom "all is simple and
symbol in their world,/The incomprehended rendered
fabulous." He was a civilized European who came to see the
history of Ireland and the soul of man without the guilt-
inspired fear and reticence so prevalent in his early poems. Yet
he did achieve a complex and, I believe, more fabulous world
than those who did not share his struggle. Though Devlin's
inquiry and his desire for joy took him to beliefs that would be
strange to many of his countrymen, he discovered the living
divine within himself and those he loved. He does not seem to
have abandoned Christianity. Like Charles Williams, whose
magical writings about love resemble Devlin's, he sought in
various cultures a belief founded on the permanence of the
divine in the temporary body of humanity.

KEITH DOUGLAS

1920–1944

Keith Castellain Douglas was born on January 24, 1920, at Tunbridge Wells, Kent. At the age of six
he was sent to his first boarding school, Edgeborough at Guilford. Shortly thereafter his father
abandoned the family, leaving the young Douglas to be raised single-handedly by his mother, often
under difficult circumstances. Douglas entered Christ's Hospital on nomination at age eleven and,
by the age of sixteen, published one of his poems in *New Verse*.

In 1938 Douglas won a scholarship to study English literature at Merton College, Oxford.
While at Oxford he joined the Officer Training Corps, which made him available for military
service. Douglas was called up in 1941 and stationed in the Middle East. His experiences as the
Commander of a Crusader Tank there were later recorded in a war journal *Alamein to Zem-Zem*.

Later that same year Douglas had several poems published in *Eight Oxford Poets*. He kept in
close contact with friends in England, sending them poems which appeared in *Poetry London*. In
1943 he returned to England and rather hurriedly prepared what was to be his first—and last—
collection, *Bête Noire*. Douglas himself proclaimed: "I can't afford to wait because of military
engagements which may be the end of me." On June 9, 1944, he was killed in Normandy while
gathering information behind enemy lines.

Personal

Douglas would have approved of the brief, terse obituary note written by his friend Bernard Spencer for the little magazine, *Personal Landscape*, which we edited in Cairo: and to which Douglas had contributed a number of fine poems. It was as simple and bare as a war communiqué. Douglas, who above all loathed rhetoric and affectation, would have been grateful. Almost the only personal detail about his work was the phrase 'He considered himself as being in the tradition of Wilfred Owen'. We knew that we had lost a poet of this high calibre but it is doubtful whether his companions-in-arms were aware of the fact; for them he was a brave and experienced officer of the line, a severe loss to a crack unit. This too he would have found completely appropriate and just. He was as devoted to his temporary profession as he was to his private gift and enjoyed both as fully as he was able in the short time allotted to him. There was neither self-delusion nor self-pity in his attitude. Life itself was so rich, so infinitely variegated, so full of sap, that he did not permit himself to think beyond the moment. How wise he was! He took things as they were, extracting every ounce of experience from them, and at the same time converting them into prose and poetry. Everything was enjoyable, even fear, horror and physical discomfort. Here and there in the poems he clearly previsioned his approaching death, but gaily and without reluctance. The only thing was time—would there be enough of it to enable him to capitalize on so rich a gift? Perhaps the very excellence of his work owes something to this sense of urgency; certainly it lends his prose an incomparable vividness and impact. Smooth, unhesitating and pointed, it conveys all his own enthusiasm and generosity: and it is the mirror of his conversation. . . .

It is not possible to know what Douglas would be writing today were he still alive; I suspect that the gradual maturing of this exceptional poetic gift might have given him by now an extra dimension, perhaps more metaphysical and less brilliantly impressionistic. But conjecture is fruitless. His work stands there in the niche he has carved for himself, perfect and self-subsisting. It is of the rarest quality and executed with an astonishing technical maturity. It is not the work of a virtuoso but the early work of a real master. We have every right to regret that his time ran out so quickly.—LAWRENCE DURRELL, "Introduction" to *Alamein to Zem-Zem*, eds. J. Waller, G. S. Fraser, J. C. Hall, 1966, pp. 11–13

General

Incidentally you say I fail as a poet, when you mean I fail as a lyricist. Only someone who is out of touch, by which I mean first hand touch, with what has happened outside England—and from a cultural point of view I wish it had affected English life more—could make that criticism. I am surprised you should still expect me to produce musical verse. A lyric form and a lyric approach will do even less good than a journalese approach to the subjects we have to discuss now. I don't know if you have come across the word Bullshit—it is an army word and signifies humbug and unnecessary detail. It symbolizes what I think must be got rid of—the mass of irrelevancies, of 'attitudes', 'approaches', propaganda, ivory towers, etc., that stands between us and our problems and what we have to do about them.

To write on the themes which have been concerning me lately in lyrical and abstract forms, would be immense bullshitting. In my early poems I wrote lyrically, as an innocent, because I was an innocent: I have (not surprisingly) fallen from that particular grace since then. I had begun to change during my second year at Oxford. T. S. Eliot wrote to me when I first joined the army, that I appeared to have finished with one form of writing and to be progressing towards another, which he did not think I had mastered. I knew this to be true, without his saying it. Well, I am still changing: I don't disagree with you if you say I am awkward and not used to the new paces yet. But my object (and I don't give a damn about my duty as a poet) is to write true things, significant things in words each of which works for its place in a line. My rhythms, which you find enervated, are carefully chosen to enable the poems to be *read* as significant speech: I see no reason to be either musical or sonorous about things at present. When I do, I shall be so again, and glad to. I suppose I reflect the cynicism and the careful absence of expectation (it is not quite the same as apathy) with which I view the world. As many others to whom I have spoken, not only civilians and British soldiers, but Germans and Italians, are in the same state of mind, it is a true reflection. I never tried to write about war (that is battles and things, not London can Take it), with the exception of a satiric picture of some soldiers frozen to death, until I had experienced it. Now I will write of it, and perhaps one day cynic and lyric will meet and make me a balanced style. Certainly you will never see the long metrical similes and galleries of images again.

Your talk of regrouping sounds to me—if you will excuse me for exhibiting a one-track mind—like the military excuse of a defeated general. There is never much need to regroup. Let your impulses drive you forward; never lose contact with life or you will lose the impulses as well. Meanwhile if you must regroup, do it by re-reading your old stuff.

Of course, you will never take my advice nor I yours. But in these tirades a few ideas do scrape through the defences on either side. Perhaps all this may make it easier for you to understand why I am writing the way I am and why I shall never go back to the old forms. You may even begin to see some virtue in it. To be sentimental or emotional now is dangerous to oneself and to others. To trust anyone or to admit any hope of a better world is criminally foolish, as foolish as it is to stop working for it. It sounds silly to say work without hope, but it can be done; it's only a form of insurance; it doesn't mean work hopelessly.—KEITH DOUGLAS, Letter to J. C. Hall (1943), *Complete Poems*, ed. Desmond Graham, 1978, pp. 123–24

Works

When his Collected Poems were first published in 1951, by Editions Poetry London Ltd, with notes and introduction, edited by John Waller and G. S. Fraser, he appeared primarily interesting, to most of his readers, as a 'war-poet', and as such seems to have been largely forgotten. Now, twelve years later and eighteen years after his death, it is becoming clear that he offers more than just a few poems about war, and that every poem he wrote, whether about war or not, has some special value. His poetry in general seems to be of some special value. It is still very much alive, and even providing life. And the longer it lives, the fresher it looks.

. . . 'Encounter with a God' is dated 1936. It is quite limited in scope, and comes properly into the category of Juvenilia, but it accomplishes its job, not an easy one, as brilliantly and surely as anything Douglas ever did. And the qualities that create and distinguish his most important later work are already there.

It is not enough to say that the language is utterly simple, the musical inflection of it peculiarly honest and charming, the technique flawless. The language is also extremely forceful; or rather, it reposes at a point it could only have reached, this very moment, by a feat of great strength. And the inflexion of the voice has a bluntness that might be challenging if it were not so frank, and so clearly the advance of an unusually aware mind. As for the technique, insofar as it can be considered separately, there is nothing dead or asleep in it, nothing tactless, and such subtlety of movement, such economy of means, such composition of cadences, would do credit to any living poet. And behind that, ordering its directions, the essentially practical cast of his energy, his impatient, razor energy.

In his nine years of accomplished writing, Douglas developed rapidly. Leaving his virtuoso juvenilia, his poetry passed through two roughly distinguishable phases, and began to clarify into a third. The literary influences on this progress seem to have been few. To begin with, perhaps he takes Auden's language over pretty whole, but he empties it of its intellectual concerns, turns it into the practical experience of life, and lets a few minor colours of the late 1930 poetry schools creep in. But his temperament is so utterly modern he seems to have no difficulty with the terrible, suffocating, maternal octopus of ancient English poetic tradition.

The first phase of his growth shows itself in the poem titled 'Forgotten the Red Leaves'. He has lost nothing since 'Encounter with a God', but gained a new range of imagination, a new ease of transition from image to image. Yet in this particular poem the fairyland images are being remembered by one still partly under their spell, indulging the dream, and this mode of immaturity is the mark of this first phase, which lasts until he leaves Oxford in 1940.

Before he leaves, a poem titled 'The Deceased' heralds the next stage. Here, the picturesque or merely decorative side of his imagery disappears; his descriptive powers sharpen to realism. The impression is of a sudden mobilizing of the poet's will, a clearing of his vision, as if from sitting considering possibilities and impossibilities he had stood up to act. Pictures of things no longer interest him much: he wants their substance, their nature, and their consequences in life. At once, and quite suddenly, his mind is whole, as if united by action, and he produces poetry that is both original and adult. Already, in this poem 'The Deceased', we can see what is most important of all about Douglas. He has not simply added poems to poetry, or evolved a sophistication. He is a renovator of language. It is not that he uses words in jolting combinations, or with titanic extravagance, or curious precision. His triumph lies in the way he renews the simplicity of ordinary talk, and he does this by infusing every word with a burning exploratory freshness of mind—partly impatience, partly exhilaration at speaking the forbidden thing, partly sheer casual ease of penetration. The music that goes along with this, the unresting variety of intonation and movement within his patterns, is the natural path of such confident, candid thinking.

There is nothing studied about this new language. Its air of improvisation is a vital part of its purity. It has the trenchancy of an inspired jotting, yet leaves no doubt about the completeness and subtlety of his impressions, or the thoroughness of his artistic conscience. The poem titled 'Egypt', for instance, could be a diary note, yet how could it be improved as a poem?

The war brought his gift to maturity, or to a first maturity. In a sense, war was his ideal subject: the burning away of all human pretensions in the ray cast by death. This was the vision, the unifying generalization that shed the meaning and urgency into all his observations and particulars: not truth is beauty only, but truth kills everybody. The truth of a man is the doomed man in him or his dead body. Poem after poem circles this idea, as if his mind were tethered. At the bottom of

it, perhaps, is his private muse, not a romantic symbol of danger and temptation, but the plain foreknowledge of his own rapidly-approaching end—a foreknowledge of which he becomes fully conscious in two of his finest poems. This sets his writing apart from that of Hemingway, with which it shares certain features. Hemingway tried to imagine the death that Douglas had foresuffered. Douglas had no time, and perhaps no disposition, to cultivate the fruity deciduous tree of How To Live. He showed in his poetry no concern for man in society. The murderous skeleton in the body of a girl, the dead men being eaten by dogs on the moonlit desert, the dead man behind the mirror, these items of circumstantial evidence are steadily out-arguing all his high spirits and hopefulness.

Technically, each of the poems of this second phase rests on some single objective core, a scene or event or thing. But one or two of them, and one in particular, start something different: the poems are 'On a Return from Egypt' and 'Simplify Me When I'm Dead'. Their inner form is characterized not by a single object of attraction, but a constellation of statements. In the second of these poems, more liberated than the first, Douglas consummates his promise. Here he has invented a style that seems able to deal poetically with whatever it comes up against. It is not an exalted verbal activity to be attained for short periods, through abstinence, or a submerged dream treasure to be fished up when the everyday brain is half-drugged. It is a language for the whole mind, at its most wakeful, and in all situations. A utility general-purpose style, as, for instance, Shakespeare's was, that combines a colloquial prose readiness with poetic breadth, a ritual intensity and music of an exceedingly high order with clear direct feeling, and yet in the end is nothing but casual speech. This is an achievement for which we can be grateful.—TED HUGHES, "Introduction" to *Selected Poems*, ed. Ted Hughes, 1964, pp. 11–14

Introducing Douglas's *Selected Poems* in 1964, Mr. Ted Hughes gave the opinion that 'he offers more than just a few poems about war, and that every poem he wrote, whether about war or not, has some special value. His poetry in general seems to be of some special value. It is still very much alive, and even providing life. And the longer it lives, the fresher it looks'. It is good to find a poet of a later generation writing thus of Keith twenty years after his death. For myself, I will shelter behind the ample solidity of Samuel Johnson when in his short life of the poet William Collins he brought back what he had written on Collins in earlier years. The critical notice that follows is dated winter 1944, and the reader will easily adjust it in minor points to the present time; like Dr. Johnson in the case of Collins, I think it is clearer than what I might write now, notwithstanding all the fuller 'materials'.

'As the poems of Keith Douglas are as yet uncollected (though there is a volume in preparation), it is not easy to express a full opinion on them; but one especial characteristic is clear—they were the work of a painter-poet, and highly pictorial. His thoughts and fancies were curious, his emotions were not everybody's, and he strove to present these in sharp designs of image and allusion. His observation of the arts, no matter what the period or the place, was extremely keen, and provided him when he wrote verse with these figures and their strong colours. As yet, his topics were principally personal, yet his mind's eye saw in them the recurrence of experience of wider range and longer date than his own. We must grieve that it happened with him as with some young writers of the generation before, writers whom he honoured; it was war which brought him towards the maturity of his poetry. Some of his latest pieces are, I think, his best; the complexity which overlaid much that he meant has gone, and he is governed by the great argument of the time—that becomes the rhythm and the feeling of his lyrics. But still the singular touch of his pictorial sense signs the poems.

'He hated decoration without anything behind it, but his verse is decorative, and, thinking of it, I think of figureheads and lamias, or of the masks which he devised so eagerly; yet it was his real aim in pleasing the imagination thus to impress truths of human affairs which he came at in his independent way. He did not wish to startle with novelty, but to fashion his work as best suited his kind of thinking, whether that was un-anticipated or after all of an ancient kind. The very look of his manuscripts is interesting as a help to understanding his poetic mood; they are written freely and gracefully, as though he saw his abstractions as definitely as physical objects. And this he maintained throughout his varied circumstances on active service'.—EDMUND BLUNDEN, "Introduction" to *Collected Poems*, eds. J. Waller, G. S. Fraser, J. C. Hall, 1966, pp. 19–20

In July 1943, while resting with his regiment after active service in the Western Desert, Keith Douglas wrote from Tripolitania to M. J. Tambimuttu, accepting a proposal that a volume of his poems should be published by Editions Poetry London. Back in England that December to train for the invasion of Europe, Douglas set about preparing the collection, for which he received a contract in February 1944. In March he gave it the title *Bête Noire*, and by April he had handed to Tambimuttu—along with the typescript of his war narrative *Alamein to Zem Zem*, and the illustrations he had done for both books—the hundred poems he wished to include in the volume. He had worked with great urgency because he was laying the ground for what he believed would be, not a first collection by a poet of twenty-four, but his life work.

From the first, Douglas had insisted that he should himself choose the poems for the collection, that they should be dated and arranged in sections, and that he should write a preface to explain the phases his work had passed through. The fact that in a few weeks at the beginning of 1944, working under difficult conditions, he was able to determine the scale of the collection, its arrangement, the dating of most poems, and the final text of many, has had an important effect on subsequent editions of his work. Only his 'Note on Drawing for the Jacket of *Bête Noire*' survives as a preface, but the phases of his work are clear.

At school, in December 1936 Douglas copied his poems into an exercise book under the headings 'Earlier Efforts', 'Transitional Stage', 'Translations', and 'Later Style'. The distinctions were firm. By sixteen he had already moved from the literary and Arcadian to the more intimate and modern. By the time he left school he had established the tones and approaches which were to remain in his work: a wry, alert acceptance ('On Leaving School'); a formal release of sentiment ('Villanelle of Gorizia'); a trenchancy of statement ('.303'); a wit drawn from shrewdness ('Encounter with a God'); a buoyant metaphorical speech ('Pleasures'); and over all a questioning detachment which looked steadily through each experience.

At Oxford the schoolboy's pleasure at each new challenge of form gave way first to a more sustained attempt to establish a single style. In his poems of 1938 and 1939 Douglas developed an ornate, descriptively metaphorical manner. Through his conventional images, however, appear the concerns of the time: the shadow of war, and of an insecurity which made happiness and an attachment to tradition necessary bulwarks against fear. The lyric voice, most often carried through his distinctively rhymed six-line stanzas, is increasingly threatened in the later group of Oxford poems, those of 1940, by the adventurousness of cynical wit and by the reductiveness of idiom. The conflict was to remain, but after the first few poems Douglas wrote in the Army, the ground on which it was fought was transformed.

From Sandhurst through to Palestine Douglas was insistently testing a new mode of impersonality—the metaphysical. Poems of perception, tracing a train of thought from curiosity through to speculation, focussed clearly on the coexistence of youth and mortality, the living and the dead, growth and decay, the physical and the abstract. Douglas's hard-earned ability to end poems with lyric poise had given way to conclusions which were intensifications of conflict, ways of opening the speculation to its emotional consequences. Direct lyric experience was now confined to the use of the 'Song' as form.

In Egypt in 1942, Douglas again allowed his poems immediate contact with his surroundings. 'Egyptian Sentry, Corniche, Alexandria' hovers between the descriptive and the speculative: 'Egypt' and 'Christodoulos' sharply confront the world as it is, with renewed toughening of diction and manner. It was only after the experience of the desert fighting, however, that Douglas discovered the nature of the art he now desired, writing to J. C. Hall in letters of 1943 of his commitment to 'reportage' and 'extrospective writing', a suppression of direct feeling to allow the intensities to focus. In the poems written at El Ballah he scrutinized notions of heroism and the meaning of the battlefield's dead. The dead were inhabitants of two worlds, the desert battlefield and the world outside; they compelled attention and gave nothing; they were supremely immune and supremely defeated; above all they were possessors of a secret they could not pass on. Then, in the poems written mainly in Tunisia, he tested the detachment with which he had encountered the dead. Writing in a tone pitched between cool observation and lyricism, he inquired into the place of feeling in war: of compassion for the civilians of 'Enfidaville'; of dismissive affection for the heroes of 'Sportsmen'; of helpless insensitivity in 'Vergissmeinnicht'; and of the murderer's cold power in 'How to Kill'. Each poem was a report on experience, but with Douglas in a dual role, as victim/killer, satirist/eulogist, observer/centre of feeling. Lucidly and with a control which was more disquieting than a show of emotion, he had enabled his poetry to live on the nerve of experience.

In England in 1944 Douglas tried to explore the consequences of such discoveries in 'Bête Noire' (which was to have been the title poem of his collection), but achieved only fragments and an account of his failure. His last completed poem, sent to Tambimuttu just before he was enmeshed in the top-security preparations for the invasion of Europe, was a return to lyricism, but a lyricism created so as to speak directly, to allow feeling its own voice. 'On a Return from Egypt' was not the announcement of a new phase but a culmination of the processes which had shaped Douglas's whole work.—DESMOND GRAHAM, "Preface" to *Complete Poems*, 1978, pp. viii–ix

ARTHUR CONAN DOYLE

1859–1930

Arthur Conan Doyle was born on May 22, 1859, in Edinburgh. He was educated at Stonyhurst Academy and the University of Edinburgh, where he studied medicine. In 1880 he visited the Arctic on a whaling expedition, and then toured West Africa. In 1885 he became an M.D., and also married Louise Hawkins; they had two children. Doyle began a medical practice, but abandoned it in 1891 for full-time writing: his Sherlock Holmes saga had begun in 1887 with *A Study in Scarlet* in *Beeton's Christmas Annual*, and attained immediate popularity. Many subsequent tales were published in *The Strand*. In 1894 Doyle made an extensive lecture tour of the United States, and visited Egypt in 1895. He was a war correspondent in the Boer War, and was knighted in 1902.

Louise Doyle died in 1906, and Doyle married Jean Leckie the next year; they had three children. Early in World War I Doyle was sent by the government to Italy on a mission, and throughout the war he wrote a history of the conflict, ultimately published in six volumes.

The horrors of the war turned Doyle from an agnostic into a spiritualist, and he began to vigorously preach the cause throughout England, continental Europe, Australia and New Zealand, the United States, Canada, and South Africa. He joined the Society for Psychical Research, established the Psychic Bookshop in London, and held séances in the homes of various illustrious people. He died on July 7, 1930.

Aside from the Sherlock Holmes tales, Doyle wrote several historical novels (which he regarded as his most serious work), tales of horror and proto-science fiction, scholarly articles on medicine, and much on spiritualism.

Personal

I'm having lunch with Conan Doyle today. He has written a spiritualistic novel which starts in the July *Strand*.

Conan Doyle, a few words on the subject of. Don't you find as you age in the wood, as we are both doing, that the tragedy of life is that your early heroes lose their glamour? As a lad in the twenties you worship old whoever-it-is, the successful author, and by the time you're forty you find yourself blushing hotly at the thought that you could ever have admired the bilge he writes.

Now, with Doyle I don't have this feeling. I still revere his work as much as ever. I used to think it swell, and I still think it swell. Do you remember when we used to stand outside the bookstall at Dulwich station on the first of the month, waiting for Stanhope to open it so that we could get the new *Strand* with the latest instalment of *Rodney Stone* . . . and the agony of finding that something had happened to postpone the fight between Champion Harrison and Crab Wilson for another month? I would do it today if *Rodney Stone* was running now.

And apart from his work, I admire Doyle so much as a man. I should call him definitely a great man, and I don't imagine I'm the only one who thinks so. I love that solid, precise way he has of talking, like Sherlock Holmes. He was telling me once that when he was in America, he saw an advertisement in a paper: "Conan Doyle's School of Writing. Let the Conan Doyle School of Writing teach you how to sell"—or something to that effect. In other words, some blighter was using his name to swindle the public. Well, what most people in his place would have said would have been "Hullo! This looks fishy". The way he put it when telling me the story was: "I said to myself, 'Ha! There is villainy afoot'."—P. G. WODEHOUSE, Letter to William Townend (April 28, 1925), *Performing Flea*, 1953, p. 31

The last and, for him, perhaps the most important cause Conan Doyle ever took up was that of Spiritualism. Although he had lost his Catholic faith, he had never failed to believe in God. Indeed, not only was atheism unthinkable to him, so was

religion as a static system, a communication between man and God in which the last important word had already been said. In *The Stark Munro Letters*, that autobiographical novel published in 1895, there is already apparent his lifelong concern with the problem of religion; correspondence published eight years earlier in the magazine *Light* suggests that even at that time he was among the many who then took a deep and serious interest in the activities and possible powers of mediums. In a letter, written in 1910, he said of Spiritualism, 'I . . . cannot easily dismiss it, in spite of the presence of frauds.'

Whatever experiences prompted it, there is no question that he went through a full conversion to Spiritualism in the course of the First World War. In a letter written in May 1915 he said, 'You know what I think of death. It is a most glorious improvement upon life, a shedding of all that is troublous and painful and a gaining of grand new powers. . . .' By 1917 he was lecturing audiences on what he called 'the new revelation'. As the war came to an end, he was working on two books on the subject, *The New Revelation* and *The Vital Message*. From then on he spent a great deal of his time and energy in lecturing throughout Britain, Australia, the United States, Canada and Europe. Perhaps the deaths in the war of his brother, Innes, once the small page at the door of his surgery, and of his son, Kingsley, gave his beliefs a decisive and personal impetus.

He recognised a failure which in this century has become increasingly apparent—that of the traditional churches to answer the spiritual needs of the more and more highly educated, more and more materialist (in both the popular and the philosophical sense) people of the Western, developed nations. He wanted to develop a new religion, compatible with the notion of human progress upon which he, in common with most of the middle classes born during Victoria's reign, predicated all his ideas about man's condition. For what was different in his case was that he included religion in that notion of progress, instead of opposing the two as the scientific materialists did. This naturally involved an altered notion of religion—in his belief, it should be a religion based upon the certainty of an individual future in another world. This in turn meant that the ancient sanctions of heaven and hell were to be done away with; such a conclusion might, even after all those years, have come as a relief to one who had been brought up under the stern discipline of Jesuits. This led him to formulate a new morality, based on the realisation 'not as a belief or a faith, but as a fact which is as tangible as the streets of London, that we are moving on soon to another life, that we will be very happy there, and that the only possible way in which that happiness can be marred or deferred is by folly and selfishness in these few fleeting years'.

It was this message that he preached up and down the world during most of the Twenties. In 1928 he travelled through South Africa, Rhodesia and Kenya, in the following year through Holland and the Scandinavian countries. He came home from Sweden on a stretcher, having had a mild heart attack. Soon after he spoke again, at an Armistice commemoration. As a result, he had a second, more severe attack. Perhaps, like all big men who have once been very strong and fit, who have always exercised and carried themselves well, he could not believe that he was really ailing. On the other hand, it may be that, secure in his beliefs, he remained unconcerned. Early in July 1930 he had another heart attack and died, upright in his armchair, at half past eight the following morning.—PETER BRENT, "Conan Doyle," *The Edwardians*, 1972, pp. 91–92

General

If anyone were to affirm that Arthur Conan Doyle was a thoroughly representative man of his epoch, I do not see how the statement could be seriously called in question. He published his first story in the year of the Victorian Jubilee, and enjoyed the renown and social popularity which during the Nineties fell in abundant measure to the writer of successful tales. Of Scottish birth and Irish extraction, he was a complete patriot of the John Bull type. He wrote the only vindication of the Boer War that found a public throughout the world. He was wholly at one with the crowd in times of excitement or stress. The last Christmas of the Great War he devoted to the preaching of the sacred duty of hatred. He had a fine emotional sense of justice, which impelled him to work as passionately on behalf of such victims of the criminal law as Edalji and Oscar Slater as for the ending of the Congo atrocities. In the latter half of his life he reversed both his political and religious beliefs. True to his character, he turned in wartime with evangelistic ardour to the propagation of Spiritualism. And he was the creator of the only character in English fiction since Robinson Crusoe which has become a universal possession of the English-speaking peoples.

Conan Doyle, naturally, was more than a little tired of his detective long before he condemned him to his first death in the Alpine crevasse, and, as everyone could have guessed, he had no wish to be remembered as the creator of Sherlock Holmes. He wished to be known and honoured as an apostle of Spiritualism, the bringer of a new hope to the modern multitude—"a bright view of death," as the Bishop of London once put it in another connection. If remembrance was to be his as a writer, Conan Doyle hoped that it might be on account of such historical romances as *Micah Clarke* and *The White Company*. But his destiny is more ironical than most. It would be absurd to imagine that his fame can rest upon anything but Sherlock Holmes.

We need not be surprised at his own attitude and hope. They are precisely what we should have expected. But it has seemed to me that nearly all the comments upon this matter by the obituarists have missed the mark. We have been told that Doyle created the best-known character in English fiction of the past hundred years, or that Sherlock Holmes and Dr. Watson had passed as types into popular speech, "a compliment paid to few authors since Dickens." As a matter of fact the thing can be stated far more strongly than that. Sherlock Holmes is not one of a number of fictitious characters known more or less to all the readers of books. He stands by himself. Everybody knows him. You would find it almost impossible to believe it if any person you came across—the bus-driver, the charwoman, or the errand-boy—did not instantly understand an allusion to Sherlock Holmes. Dickens alone, it is true, among the novelists, has come within measurable distance of Conan Doyle's achievement, but he has not equalled it. He gets nearest with Oliver Twist, who is very nearly a common possession of our people. Pickwick, Micawber, Sam Weller himself, are not in the same world of familiarity. Gulliver belongs properly to fairyland. Don Quixote, of course, is universal, but not to everybody is he a concrete personality or type. Shakespeare has only one character of the universality we are here thinking of—Shylock. Sherlock Holmes is known to our world, someone has said this week, as Napoleon and Charlie Chaplin are known; and Chaplin will be forgotten, while the kingdom of Holmes is clearly imperishable.

Conan Doyle, for all his clumsiness of style, was a capital story-teller. One need not suppose that a time will come when *Rodney Stone* and other books of his will not be read. But I hold, with Mr. Desmond MacCarthy, that for his own generation Conan Doyle has been liked and valued first of all as a writer of "good bosh." Mr. MacCarthy's distinction is as serviceable in its way as any other pair of literary opposites—for instance, as Realist and Romantic, or De Quincey's famous antithesis between the literature of knowledge and the literature of power. The ephemeral stuff we must have: even a pontifical Ruskin, writing for his choicest schoolgirls, conceded so much. Very well, then, says Mr. MacCarthy, let us keep clear the frontier between good bosh and the other kinds. Sherlock Holmes is very good bosh; and perhaps we may hope to have the completed proof of this view when the rival biographies of Dr. Watson are available.

Of Conan Doyle, "the St. Paul of Spiritualism," there would seem to be very little to be said from the outside. During the dozen years or so that he was writing, speaking, and travelling on behalf of his creed—or, as he called it, his knowledge—I did not come upon a single statement from him that one could think of as an utterance of the writer who had made the weighing of factual evidence a pastime for the multitude. When he exchanged his detective's quarters in Baker Street for the psychic bookshop in Westminster, Conan Doyle became another creature. We had to take him then as a believer to whom any medium, no matter how mercilessly shown up, was a revealer of truth, and "ectoplasm" as actual as tarmac. Two years ago he wrote to Henry Arthur Jones in order to assure him that "the bodily warmth and homely comfort" for which the playwright was longing as he drew near the end was exactly what he and his associates were offering. He added:

> I have a hundred descriptions if I have one from those who have gone before, and they all talk of their homes, their libraries, their pursuits—the joy of using every human faculty to the utmost in an extended field of action. You will write there as here, and I will (*sic*) probably continue to bore my friends with my views.

And so on, just as we should anticipate from one who had talked across the gulf with Cecil Rhodes and Lenin. His friends assure us that they are confident of hearing from this energetic and lovable man, as soon as he has rested from the fatigue of his crossing. They will hear. Nothing in the immediate future could be much more certain than that. Indeed, it would be a task of the simplest for the Sunday papers to set up the first message in advance.—S. K. RATCLIFFE, "Arthur Conan Doyle," *NS*, July 12, 1930, p. 442

Conan Doyle's attitude toward his gigantic child—an attitude in which toleration, resentment, bitterness, and resignation alternated—illustrates one of the tragedies of his long and successful life. Tragedy in the Jamesian sense, that is—the author's lifelong struggle to kill off a character who was making him much money, in order to devote himself to what he took to be more important work. For in the beginning the doctor planned no such career for the detective as Holmes has had. *A Study in Scarlet*, published in 1887, was a potboiler, and the second Holmes adventure, *The Sign of Four*, was of the same boiling. Similarly, a little later, *The Adventures of Sherlock Holmes*, and its sequel, *The Memoirs of Sherlock Holmes*, served their purpose, as far as Doyle was concerned, when they paid his bills. And they were really all he had to say about Sherlock Holmes. He was frankly tired of the fellow as early as 1894. Old inhabitants will remember with what appalling finality he killed the detective off in the last story of the *Memoirs*.

Yet five volumes were to follow. Public horror and indignation harassed him until, in 1902, he yielded to supplication and gave the world *The Hound of the Baskervilles*. Another surrender, in 1905, brought us *The Return of Sherlock Holmes* and the glad tidings (for the *Hound* had been a memory, not a new adventure) that the detective was not dead at all. He never *had* been dead! There are still living in the world many citizens who remember the ecstasy of that moment. Holmes had retired, however, to his bee farm in Sussex, and Conan Doyle again had reached an end to such ephemeral matters as these melodramatic chronicles of crime and detection. But *The Valley of Fear* appeared in 1917, and *His Last Bow* (it wasn't) just two years later. In *The Case-Book of Sherlock Holmes* there was an indubitable end, however; and three years later Conan Doyle was dead.

It is an odd story and perhaps it is a fable for writing men and women. One senses its resemblance to von Chamisso's fable of *Peter Schlemyl* or *The Shadowless Man*. Peter Schlemyl's shadow, in the old allegory, became independent of its master, waxed wealthy, and eventually hired him as a silent, obsequious attendant. The shadow had discovered that its own lack of a shadow caused inconvenient comments. It is certain that Conan Doyle feared some such loss of personal identity; at very least he felt that other and better work than his Holmes tales was suffering an unjust obscurity. Many times he confessed that he had come "almost to hate poor Sherlock"; but, as suggested, his most drastic effort to rid himself of the detective—by causing him to disappear over the Reichenbach Fall—was not regarded by the public as justifiable homicide. The uproar was prodigious. "You beast!" "You brute!" his readers cried at him; and Holmes reappeared. There was money in him, of course; and better money than ever, we may be certain, after the resurrection. But there is no doubt that several times over the long years of the detective's career his creator would cheerfully have shown him the door.

It was Conan Doyle's idea that he was an historical novelist; and so he was—one of the best the world has known. By such tales as *The White Company*, *Micah Clarke*, *The Refugees*, *Uncle Bernac*, and *Rodney Stone*, he takes rank with the greatest writers in that field. *The White Company* already is a classic, and probably it is immortal. Loving Holmes, one yet understands his creator's emotion. But would *The White Com-*

pany and *Micah Clarke* rank higher in the world's esteem if Sherlock Holmes had never lived in Baker Street? It seems only silly to believe so. They will last—along with Sherlock—and, if anything, will be helped by the detective, whose fame will constantly draw new readers to everything that carries the signature of Arthur Conan Doyle. It is a little surprising perhaps that Doyle, himself, was not able to realize this. Certainly the tales of Sherlock Holmes are not the author's greatest performances. They are not great at all—only Sherlock Holmes is *great*. But, after reading the nine volumes that comprise the Holmes saga, there will always be readers who will turn to those other titles on the long list, where they will make the acquaintance of some very attractive gentlemen of fortune.

But to the end Sir Arthur resented his most popular creation. "I do not wish to be ungrateful to Holmes, who has been a good friend in many ways," he wrote in his autobiography; and thereafter he went on to criticize the detective rather sharply. "My most notorious character," he called him, with wry humor. Sir Arthur's own favorite among his stories was *Sir Nigel*, which again reveals how notably a writer may be mistaken about his own work; for the novel, although good, is not a patch on *The White Company*, a masterpiece.—VINCENT STARRETT, "From Poe to Poirot," *Books Alive*, 1940, pp. 199–202

In his emotional reactions, Doyle was a super-typical Victorian, a bluff Imperialist extrovert who congratulated himself on having "the strongest influence over young men, especially young athletic sporting men, of any one in England (bar Kipling)," and therefore felt it a duty to volunteer for the South African War. Twenty years later, he condemned the "liquid putrescence" of the Russian Revolution and said that Post-Impressionism and Futurism were part of "a wave of artistic and intellectual insanity" sweeping across Europe. Yet Doyle was also a man of generous impulses, even when they ran counter to his own beliefs. He drew up the petition for Roger Casement's reprieve, and did not flinch when he was shown the *Black Diaries*, remarking with his characteristic common sense that "as no possible sexual offence could be as bad as suborning soldiers from their duty, I was not diverted from my purpose" by the apparent revelation of Casement's homosexuality. It seems at first sight astonishing that this Victorian philistine should have created an egocentric drug-taking hero so alien from his own beliefs. The answer to this puzzle has already been suggested. The passion for absolutes of belief and behavior, the desire to wipe the slate clean of error and impurity through some saving supernatural grace, shows constantly in Victorian life below the surface of stolid adherence to established order. The influence of Nietzsche and Wagner was widespread, and affected even those who thought, like Doyle, that Nietzsche's philosophy was "openly founded in lunacy," affected indeed those who had never heard of Nietzsche. Part of Holmes's attraction was that, far more than any of his later rivals, he was so evidently a Nietzschean superior man. It was comforting to have such a man on one's side.—JULIAN SYMONS, "The Case of Sherlock Holmes," *Mortal Consequences*, 1972, pp. 64–65

Conan Doyle's potentiality for achieving medical renown is better documented in his scientific medical writings. This is especially evident in publications relating to infectious diseases. He strongly supported prophylactic measures for smallpox by compulsory vaccination, in spite of considerable public opposition, and for typhoid by inoculation, in spite of the recalcitrant military hierarchy. Conversely, he was the first to caution against the overwhelming and world-wide acceptance of tuberculin as a cure for tuberculosis in 1890. Conan Doyle based his conclusion on a carefully reasoned consideration of its clinical effects and of pathological changes in lung tissue.

Remarkable was Conan Doyle's grasp of the significance of the newly emerging science of medical bacteriology. As a general practitioner, in 1883, he wrote that bacteria were undoubtedly the cause of many human diseases—this, at a time when only a few were so demonstrated. He also predicted the eradication of bacterial diseases several generations in the future—as has occurred recently for smallpox.

Medical training and experience continued to influence Conan Doyle's activities after he changed his profession to that of full-time writer. Many of his causes were related to needs for physical and psychological well being. He supported daylight saving time because sunlight would contribute to health. His campaign against the spread of venereal disease by prostitution was based more on the need to prevent disease than on moral issues. He supported vivisection, if done humanely, because of its major contributions to the amelioration of human disease and suffering. Even in his all-pervading dedication to spiritualism he applied medical concepts, such as the study of the pulse during a trance.

Nor can his literary output be separated from his medical orientation, which permeated many of his works. The blustering, egocentric professors Challenger, Ainslee Grey and von Baumgarten were drawn from his medical teacher, Rutherford, and his medical confrere, Budd. Many commentaries pertain to the derivation of the name of his master sleuth, Holmes. It has been suggested that the source was Oliver Wendell Holmes, physician, writer and anatomist, although Conan Doyle himself has stated that "I don't know how I got that name." Nonetheless, the attributes of Sherlock Holmes are based on two physicians—Joseph Bell, the surgeon, and Conan Doyle, the general practitioner.

Much prominence has been given to the medical aspects of the Holmesian *Canon*, mostly adulatory and nonevaluative. A critical analysis reveals, however, variability in the caliber of medical knowledge. Conan Doyle's appreciation of poisons was no better than can be expected from a generalist of his time. His orientation to alcohol and cocaine addiction was beyond the limits of both the cultural environment and the medical concepts of his time. The emphasis on infectious diseases in his scientific writings is reflected in the inclusion of numerous such afflictions in the *Canon*.—ALVIN E. RODIN, JACK D. KEY, *Medical Casebook of Doctor Arthur Conan Doyle*, 1984, pp. 303–4

Works

THE SHERLOCK HOLMES TALES

In looking over the work of Dr. Doyle during the past three or four years, one realises with the keenest sort of regret the unfortunate mistake he made in putting an end to Sherlock Holmes. The originality, the dramatic attractiveness of this character, were so striking that it is only now in looking back through the tales of *The Adventures* and *The Memoirs*, that we appreciate how utterly inferior they were in construction and dialogue. Since he wrote *The Study in Scarlet* Dr. Doyle has been learning much about craftsmanship. Sherlock Holmes in the author's hands to-day might not be any more striking and vivid a creation, but he would assuredly stand out from a better setting. We should probably have considerably less of his friend and alleged historian, the very tiresome bore, Watson. The latter was always quite incorrigible in his expressions of polite astonishment. When after Holmes, for the three hundredth time, had deduced alimony, a bad digestion and a West End

scandal from an inspection of a visiting-card or an old hat band, Watson broke into his conventional volley of superlatives, the whole matter became just a little wearisome. For a time after Dr. Doyle's first success and popularity there were strong indications of a general fizzling out of his originality. Upon one occasion he practically rewrote, with new characters and a few minor changes, a story which he had told a few years before. In the case to which we refer the second story was called "The Illness of Signor Lambert"; the first was included in the volume which bore the title *Round the Red Lamp*. There were many such indications of waning strength. But of late he [Doyle] seems to be coming up again; one might sum it up by saying that he is getting his second wind. Much of his very recent work is marked with all his early fire and spontaneity, and yet there are many of these later tales which we lay down with disappointment simply because we feel how much better they would have been woven about the strange gifts, the personality, the omnipotence and omniscience of Sherlock Holmes. A notable story of this kind was "The Story of the Lost Special," which appeared in the columns of an English magazine about two years ago, but which, to the best of the recollection of the present writer, has not yet been brought out in book form. It was simply the story of a train—locomotive, tender and two passenger-coaches—which, running in broad daylight through one of the most thickly populated districts of England, disappears without leaving the slightest clue of importance as to its fate. One could not readily conceive more startling and daring a plot, yet when the mystery is ultimately cleared away the whole thing seems possible enough, and had the explanation been brought about, as it should and might easily have been, by Sherlock Holmes and the science of deduction, the story would have taken rank with the very best that have come from Dr. Doyle's ingenious pen.—ARTHUR BARTLETT MAURICE, "The Romance of the Ring," *BkmL*, May 1900, pp. 224–25

Evidently, I am growing old. Sherlock Holmes is dead, and to young readers it may be that he is not even a dear memory. But I was at an impressionable age when he burst upon the world; and so he became a part of my life, and will never, I suppose, be utterly dislodged. I cannot pass through Baker Street, even now, without thinking of him. Long ago I had decided exactly which were the two windows of the sitting-room where Watson spent his wondering hours; and, only the other day, I had a rather heated dispute with a coæval who had also long since "placed" that sitting-room—"placed" it, if you please, on the side of the street opposite to that where it really was (need I say that I mean the right-hand side as one goes towards Regent's Park?). My sentiment for Sherlock Holmes was never one of reverence unalloyed. Indeed, one of the secrets of his hold on me was that he so often amused me. I would have bartered a dozen of his subtlest deductions for that great moment when he said (presumably on the eve of his creator's departure for a lecturing tour in America) "It is always a joy to me to meet an American, for I am one of those who believe that the folly of a monarch and the blundering of a minister in far gone years will not prevent our children from being some day citizens of the same world-wide country under a flag which shall be a quartering of the Union Jack with the Stars and Stripes." I learned that speech by heart, years ago; and, to this day, I generally try it on any American to whom I am introduced—sometimes with most surprising results. Sir Arthur (then mere Mr.) Conan Doyle's own attitude towards life, and his own extraordinary versions of the familiar things around us—what would Sherlock have been without these assets?—MAX BEERBOHM, "At the St. James's Theatre" (1905), *Around Theatres*, 1930, p. 481

I fear that Mr. Sherlock Holmes may become like one of those popular tenors who, having outlived their time, are still tempted to make repeated farewell bows to their indulgent audiences. This must cease and he must go the way of all flesh, material or imaginary. One likes to think that there is some fantastic limbo for the children of imagination, some strange, impossible place where the beaux of Fielding may still make love to the belles of Richardson, where Scott's heroes still may strut, Dickens's delightful Cockneys still raise a laugh, and Thackeray's worldlings continue to carry on their reprehensible careers. Perhaps in some humble corner of such a Valhalla, Sherlock and his Watson may for a time find a place, while some more astute sleuth with some even less astute comrade may fill the stage which they have vacated.

His career has been a long one—though it is possible to exaggerate it. Decrepit gentlemen who approach me and declare that his adventures formed the reading of their boyhood do not meet the response from me which they seem to expect. One is not anxious to have one's personal dates handled so unkindly. As a matter of cold fact, Holmes made his *début* in *A Study in Scarlet* and in *The Sign of Four*, two small booklets which appeared between 1887 and 1889. It was in 1891 that "A Scandal in Bohemia," the first of the long series of short stories, appeared in *The Strand Magazine*. The public seemed appreciative and desirous of more, so that from that date, thirty-six years ago, they have been produced in a broken series which now contains no fewer than fifty-six stories, including "The Adventure of Shoscombe Old Place," to appear in next month's *Strand Magazine*. These have been re-published in *The Adventures*, *The Memoirs*, *The Return*, and *His Last Bow*, and there remain twelve published during the last few years which Sir John Murray is about to produce under the title of *The Case-Book of Sherlock Holmes*. He began his adventures in the very heart of the later Victorian Era, carried it through the all-too-short reign of Edward, and has managed to hold his own little niche even in these feverish days. Thus it would be true to say that those who first read of him as young men have lived to see their own grown-up children following the same adventures in the same magazine. It is a striking example of the patience and loyalty of the British public.

I had fully determined at the conclusion of *The Memoirs* to bring Holmes to an end, as I felt that my literary energies should not be directed too much into one channel. That pale, clear-cut face and loose-limbed figure were taking up an undue share of my imagination. I did the deed, but, fortunately, no coroner had pronounced upon the remains, and so, after a long interval, it was not difficult for me to respond to the flattering demand and to explain my rash act away. I have never regretted it, for I have not in actual practice found that these lighter sketches have prevented me from exploring and finding my limitations in such varied branches of literature as history, poetry, historical novels, psychic research, and the drama. Had Holmes never existed I could not have done more, though he may perhaps have stood a little in the way of the recognition of my more serious literary work.

There has been some debate as to whether the Adventures of Holmes, or the narrative powers of Watson, declined with the passage of the years. When the same string is still harped upon, however cunningly one may vary the melody, there is still the danger of monotony. The mind of the reader is less fresh and responsive, which may unjustly prejudice him against the writer. To compare great things to small, Scott in his autobiographical notes has remarked that each of Voltaire's later pamphlets was declared to be a declension from the last one, and yet when the collected works were assembled they were found to be among the most brilliant. Scott also was

depreciated by critics for some of his most solid work. Therefore, with such illustrious examples before one, let me preserve the hope that he who in days to come may read my series backwards will not find that his impressions are very different from those of his neighbour who reads them forwards.—Sir Arthur Conan Doyle, "Mr. Sherlock Holmes to His Readers," *Strand*, March 1927, pp. 281–84

. . . Every writer owes something to Holmes. And every critic of The Novel who has a theory about the reality of characters in fiction, would do well to consider Holmes. There is no rich humanity, no deep and cunning psychology and knowledge of the human heart about him; he is obviously a formula. He has not the reality of any great character of Dickens or Thackeray or George Eliot or Meredith or Hardy; or Jane Austen or the Bröntes or Virginia Woolf or James Joyce: yet, as I suggested, he is just as real to us as Falstaff or the Wellers. He is not even a very good detective. But I am not sure that Sir Arthur Conan Doyle is not one of the great dramatic writers of his age. And France, in the person of Arsène Lupin (about whom I hope to write at length) has rendered homage to him. What greater compliment could France pay to England, than the scene in which the great antagonists, Holmes and Lupin, are lying side by side on deckchairs on the Calais-Dover paquebot, and the London Commissioner of Police, walks up and down the deck unsuspecting?—T. S. Eliot, "Books of the Quarter," *Critn*, April 1929, p. 556

The Sherlock Holmes stories, almost as much as the Alice books or as Edward Lear's nonsense, were the casual products of a life the main purpose of which was something else, but creations that in some sense got detached from their author and flew away and had a life of their own. Conan Doyle, it seems, worked conscientiously to document his historical romances, which he considered his serious work, but he regarded Holmes and Watson as the paper dolls of rather ridiculous and undignified potboilers, and he paid so little attention to what he wrote about them that the stories are full of inconsistencies, which Doyle never bothered to correct. He forgot Watson's Christian name and later on gave him a new one; he shifted the location of his wound; he began by making an ignorance of literature an essential trait of Holmes's personality and then had him talk about Petrarch and Meredith; and he even, on one occasion, changed the season abruptly from July to September. (It is an odd evidence of Holmes's vitality that some of his admirers should have gone to the trouble of attempting to account for these discrepancies, as if Watson and Holmes had been real men, and that they should actually have published their conjectures in a volume called *Profile by Gaslight*.) Doyle had become so impatient with his hero by the end of the second series in the *Strand Magazine* that he got rid of him by killing him off, totally without preparation, in a manner that was little short of frivolous. But Sherlock Holmes was like a genie let out of a bottle; there was no way of getting him back and, once at large, he was always available to minister to his master's wants. Doyle eventually brought Holmes back to life and wrote five more volumes about him. For perhaps the only time in his life, he had hit upon a genuine spell.

Whence had he mustered this spell and what elements had been mixed to make it? Well, there was Poe, of course, and there was also unquestionably R. L. Stevenson's *New Arabian Nights*. "The Adventure of the Hansom Cab" and "The Adventure of the Superfluous Mansion" must have suggested both the Sherlock Holmes titles and the formula of taking people to unexpected places and having them witness mysterious happenings. But Doyle, though much less "literary" than Stevenson, somehow got solider results, which depended on quite different qualities from Stevenson's suave Oriental tone and the limpid iridescence of his fantasy. For one thing, Stevenson was weak on character, whereas Doyle had produced two real personalities. And, for another, Conan Doyle had created his own vein of fantasy, which was vivider, if rather less fine, than Stevenson's. You see the force of his imagination exemplified in a curious way in some of those stories in which the dénouement is inadequate or disappointing. A young woman goes to work in a country house where she will be extravagantly overpaid if she will consent to have her hair cut short, to wear a dress of electric blue, to sit in certain places at certain times and to allow herself to be made to laugh uproariously at a succession of funny stories told by the master of the house; a professional interpreter of Greek finds himself suddenly shanghaied in a cab and taken to a stuffy London house with velvet furniture, a high white marble mantelpiece and a suit of Japanese armor, where a man who wears glasses and has a giggling laugh compels him to put questions in Greek to a pale and emaciated captive, whose face is all crisscrossed with sticking plaster. Neither of these stories—"The Copper Beeches" or "The Greek Interpreter"—quite lives up to its opening evocation. The way of accounting for the sticking plaster seems, indeed, entirely unsatisfactory, and since Watson tells us that this "singular case" is "still involved in some mystery," we are almost inclined to suspect that the affair concealed something else which the detective had failed to penetrate; but the images have exercised their power—a power that is partly due to their contrast with, their startling emergence from, the dull surface of Victorian London.—EDMUND WILSON, "'Mr. Holmes, They Were the Footprints of a Gigantic Hound!'" (1945), *Classics and Commercials*, 1950, pp. 267–69

In my opinion, Holmes is one of the truly great comic characters in our literature; but it is doubtful if Doyle himself would have agreed with this statement or even if he would have taken it as a compliment. Admittedly, Holmes was not conceived in comedy, like Falstaff and Micawber; he can only be considered comic in retrospect, if at all—like Captain Ahab. His comic quality seems to me to be this: he is the classic caricature of the Amateur Detective, in whose person the whole art of detection is made ridiculous. I don't believe that Doyle consciously intended this ridicule—and yet it is what makes Holmes lovable and immortal.

It is hard to love the Amateur Detective, either in fiction or in real life. That a man should hound his fellow-men for pay is quite bad enough; and we, his paymasters, must all share in his guilt. But that an unpaid dilettante should do the same thing for his own amusement is infinitely worse. No amount of fine phrases about civic responsibility can alter that simple human truth. The more the Amateur Detective tries to justify his hobby, the more contemptible he becomes.

But Holmes is different. He isn't contemptible and he needs no justification. He has the sanction of his own peculiar kind of madness. Like Captain Ahab, he is possessed by the insanity of the chase. Holmes's Moby Dick is Dr Moriarty, the arch-criminal; and Doyle's instinct was sound when he made Moriarty turn to bay and kill Holmes, just as the White Whale killed Ahab. I find Holmes's subsequent resurrection both embarrassing and unnecessary—for Doyle could easily have pre-dated his later stories about Holmes, just as he did pre-date *The Valley of Fear* in order that Moriarty could reappear in it. . . .

In his Sherlock Holmes stories, Doyle became one of the great exponents of the romance of London at the turn of the century—city of Night, pea-soup fogs, gaslight, hansom-cabs and opera-hats. Robert Louis Stevenson was before him in this field, with his *New Arabian Nights*. G. K. Chesterton was his successor. Hollywood took over the London they had created, slightly modernized it and put it again and again upon the screen. When, at last, it became outmoded (since, nowadays, most films about London are actually made there) a leading English newspaper lamented the fact, saying: 'We have lost a city that we had learned to know almost as well as our own.'—CHRISTOPHER ISHERWOOD, "*The Speckled Band* by Arthur Conan Doyle," *Exhumations*, 1966, pp. 88–90

If a man is proclaimed as superior to others, his superiority must be demonstrated. It is a weakness in many of Holmes's disciples that their genius is announced but not proved. Here Doyle is supreme. We learn gradually the astonishing extent of Holmes's knowledge, his monographs on a hundred and forty different varieties of pipe, cigar, and cigarette tobaccos, on the ear, on the Polyphonic Motets of Lassus, his analysis of a hundred and sixty ciphers, his ability to recognize the type of any newspaper at a glance. It is true that we are told about these studies rather than reading them, but the claim made in *A Study in Scarlet* that "by a man's finger-nails, by his coat-sleeve, by his boots, by his trouser-knees, by the callosities of his forefinger and thumb, by his expression, by his shirt-cuffs—by each of these things a man's calling is plainly revealed," is justified again and again. A single instance may be allowed to serve for the dozens in the stories. Given a battered old felt hat of which Watson can make nothing, Holmes is able to deduce that the owner is highly intellectual, was fairly well-to-do but is now poor, and has been going downhill probably under the influence of drink. "This may account for the obvious fact that his wife has ceased to love him." Holmes not only makes these deductions, but explains them in plausible detail. Would it be possible sometimes to reach different conclusions? No doubt, but the pleasure one gets from this opening up of a fine machine so that every cog in it can be seen revolving is hardly to be overestimated. Other writers try to mystify with one conclusion drawn from a fact unnoticed by the reader, where Doyle gives us a dozen, and almost always the deductions are those we might have made ourselves. This is perfectly exemplified in what is perhaps the most famous single short passage of Holmesian dialogue:

> "Is there any other point to which you would wish to draw my attention?"
> "To the curious incident of the dog in the night-time."
> "The dog did nothing in the night-time."
> "That was the curious incident."

A baffling fragment? The explanation is perfect. The dog did not bark, although somebody had entered the stables where he was on watch, and had taken out a horse. The significance of the incident is that the intruder must have been somebody well known to the dog. The passage shows, incidentally, a sensibility to phrasing which is not often noticed as one of Doyle's characteristics. Change the words "in the night-time" to what might superficially seem the more natural "during the night," and the sentences run much less happily.—JULIAN SYMONS, "The Case of Sherlock Holmes," *Mortal Consequences*, 1972, pp. 66–68

Of course the Holmes stories are detective stories, but they might be more accurately, if more cumbersomely, described as adventure stories involving a crime, or an apparent crime, and concentrating attention on a detective, his friend and chronicler, and the relations between the two. As such, they are not without flaws. There is implausibility: ten generations of Musgraves—a fast-breeding lot to have produced that number in little more than two hundred years—must have been successive victims of almost catatonic incuriosity not to have seen the sort of thing their ritual pointed to. And a good many modern readers will find a creakiness in the convention that makes the narrator of a flashback use the same fully dramatizing style as the author himself does in his own narrative. This is just about acceptable from Holmes, ever a dealer in histrionics, but it comes oddly from, say, Hall Pycroft, the amiable but commonplace stockbroker's clerk.

No matter—the device is of real service for the achievement of two virtues Doyle was very interested in: compression and its adjunct, pace. The same interest led him to be sparing of flat description. One of the attractions the stories have increasingly acquired over the years is their portrayal of late-Victorian London, the Home Counties, moorland country; yet it is remarkable how fleeting are the hints by which these are conveyed to the reader. Set-pieces like the famous picture of the Reichenbach Falls in 'The Final Problem' are fine but rare. It is partly the desire for economy which produces those memorable character-sketches, of old Trevor in 'The "Gloria Scott"', for instance, of the sinister Hudson in the same tale, of Reginald Musgrave. Doyle was too conscientious a craftsman to try to get away with stereotypes, but he denied himself the space in which, after the modern fashion, characters might have been made to reveal themselves by small degrees. (A reading of the Sherlock Holmes stories shows up, among other things, the demerits of that modern fashion.)—KINGSLEY AMIS, "Introduction" to *The Memoirs of Sherlock Holmes,* 1974, pp. 8–9

OTHER TALES

The Lost World alone, and the series of stories that followed it, would have been enough to assure Conan Doyle's literary reputation. They are stories based on scientific imagination, and spring from the same source of inspiration as the detective-stories, which also exploit the wonders of science. . . . But science fiction and the detective-story develop in opposite directions. In the latter there is a problem to be solved, and the circumstances of the plot produce the train of reasoning. In the former, on the contrary, the plot or narrative develops out of a train of reasoning or a hypothesis; the interest lies in illuminating the rational process or justifying the hypothesis. The atmosphere of science fiction had appeared in Conan Doyle's work before the Professor Challenger cycle. It impregnates certain stories, some of them tinged with occultism: for instance "Lot No. 249," written in 1894. One might also instance "Playing with Fire" (1900), "The Leather Funnel" (1903) and "The Silver Mirror" (1908). It would however be going too far to see these stories as forerunners of *The Lost World.* Not until 1912 does Conan Doyle emerge as one of Jules Verne's most talented disciples. There is something of the detective story in *The Lost World,* but it is also linked to the historical novels: Conan Doyle's evocation of prehistoric times clearly shows the fascination that the past had for him.

We make the acquaintance of the eccentric, dictatorial Professor Challenger right at the beginning of the book. He has returned from a journey to Amazonia, and claims to have come within range of a 'lost world' where certain species of prehistoric animals still exist. Confronted by the amused incredulity of his colleagues, Challenger organises an expedition consisting of Professor Summerlee (his most fiery opponent), Lord John Roxton the explorer, and a young journalist called Malone, who is the narrator of the adventure. After a rather long voyage and a several days march into the South American interior, the four men arrive in sight of the 'lost world'. It is a high table-land, completely cut off from the rest of the world by a precipice and a deep moat-like valley. The explorers cut down an enormous tree, and make an improvised bridge; but they have hardly reached the plateau when, as a result of the malevolence of one of the porters, the tree-trunk falls to the ground, leaving them imprisoned on the plateau like Robinson Crusoe on his island. They are 'in truth as far from any human aid as if they were in the moon'. The story does in fact roughly resemble the Robinson Crusoe myth, and there are two details of *The Lost World* which bring out its relationship with Defoe's novel. Challenger's plateau is not devoid of human life, any more than Crusoe's island is. Defoe's adventure with cannibals is matched by Conan Doyle's with the ape-men (representatives of the famous 'missing link'). In both cases the novelist profits from the occasion to introduce an episode of strategic importance. In both cases the explorers become allies and protectors of 'noble savages', who treat them as idols as a result. In *The Lost World* Challenger and his companions come to the rescue of a tribe of very primitive Indians, and with their help engage the ape-men in pitched battle. Their numerical inferiority is more than made up for by their superiority in arms and strategy, and the ape-men are ousted from the lost world. Conan Doyle is here symbolising the beginning of human life on the earth; but, like Defoe, he has also tried to demonstrate the absolute superiority of the white man. . . .

Conan Doyle wrote two more stories about Challenger, and in 1925 he figured in an apologia for spiritualism in novel form. In *The Land of Mist* the explorer finds himself in an unaccustomed situation. Usually the pioneer or defender of revolutionary theories, he now has to play the part of the incredulous rationalist. His unexpected capitulation in its own way represents Conan Doyle's spiritual development.

Apart from this novel, we meet Professor Challenger again in three stories with scientific themes: "The Disintegration Machine," "When the World Screamed," and "The Poison Belt." The first is based on the theme of the apprentice sorcerer, and also modelled on popular farce (the robber robbed, the biter bit, etc.); it shows how a diabolical invention turns against the inventor. The second is more unusual; it describes an experiment devised by Challenger to discover whether the terrestrial globe is, as he maintains, by nature animal, and endowed with sensibility. "The Poison Belt" was written towards the end of 1912. . . .

While the heroes of his historical novels expressed certain emotional or sensitive aspects of Conan Doyle's personality, Challenger—like Sherlock Holmes—is a manifestation of his intellectual side. But whereas Sherlock Holmes rationalises and explains the world in ever more logical terms, Challenger explores the domain of the marvellous, without attempting to understand it. The hero of *The Maracot Deep* can be considered as one of Challenger's reincarnations. The characters of this story are grouped like those in *The Lost World,* and have similar roles given them; the sub-title of the book is 'The Lost World under the Sea.' All we have to do is substitute Maracot for Challenger, Scanlan for Roxton, and Headley for Malone. As for Summerlee, he has no counterpart in this story, one of the last Conan Doyle wrote. Its theme is submarine exploration. Maracot has had a diving-bell constructed, and he and his two friends take their places inside it. As the result of a broken cable, the three explorers descend into an abyss nearly 10,000 yards deep. Resigned to imminent death, they are however delivered from their prison by men who have ascended from a city built on the floor of the ocean. They are descendants of the people of Atlantis, who had succeeded in escaping from the catastrophe several thousand years earlier. They had built a shelter, and their civilisation had survived and adapted itself to new conditions. The story of the three earth-dwellers' adventures ends with a description of the way of life and civilisation of Atlantis, reminiscent of modern utopias. Huxley's famous *Brave New World* was only written four years after *The Maracot Deep*, and there are several remarkable similarities between the two books.—PIERRE NORDON, "Professor Challenger," *Conan Doyle*, tr. Frances Partridge, 1966, pp. 328–35

In 1912 Doyle produced another hero in the person of Professor Challenger. If Sherlock Holmes was the hero of a young writer, Challenger was that of a middle-aged one, and as soon as the reader encounters him he realizes that Doyle has produced a winner, a fully-rounded character, consistent and believable and far removed from the bellicose and cardboard Gerard or the pageant figures of *Sir Nigel*. If there is something of Doyle in Sherlock Holmes, there is even more in Challenger, though he owed his genesis to recollections of the physiologist William Rutherford, who had taught at Edinburgh during Doyle's time there as a medical student.

Like Doyle, Challenger is a big strapping man, contemptuous of weaklings. Challenger is also a bully who takes great pleasure in throwing journalists out of his house, and to hell with the aftermath. He is the key man in a well-contrasted quartet: the peppery sardonic Summerlee, the white hunter Lord John Roxton with quaint Woosterish vocabulary, Challenger himself, and the narrator, a neatly characterized journalist, brave, naïve and eager to hero-worship in the same way as Watson.

The background of *The Lost World* is scientific, zoological, geographical. For once, Doyle did not have to delve into history to get his facts right, and make certain that the data were injected into the stories to prove that he had done his homework. The scientific material had been thoroughly assimilated long before, perhaps as early as his student days, and he presents it in a convincing manner, not trying to impress the reader. He was naturally interested, and it shows, whereas in certain of the Holmes stories Doyle has to pretend that Holmes is well up in, for example, music and other matters with which he himself is not intimate, and thus overplays his hand. The scene in which Challenger is putting the journalist Malone to the test, throwing nonsense questions at him, is masterly. Although the questions are nonsensical, they are not so much so as to be foolish: 'I suppose you are aware that the cranial index is a constant factor . . . and that the germ plasm is different from the parthenogenetic egg . . . and that telegony is still *sub judice*?' The average reader would pass these by, at one with the unfortunate Malone, and would be shocked when Challenger roars that Malone is an imposter, 'a vile, crawling journalist, who has no more science than he has decency in his composition!' . . .

There is more straightforward description in *The Lost World* than is usual in Doyle in his lighter vein, a dangerous process in magazine serials where the reader is tempted to skip over long sections with no dialogue. But Doyle manages it because he makes the description interesting, interesting because he was fascinated by the great rain forests of the Amazon as they existed in his imagination. He could stretch his reader, because his audience would have no means of knowing whether Doyle was accurate, and by drawing ever so lightly on its capacity for suspended judgement he could fill in the various prehistoric animals on the unexplored plateau.

The Brazil that Doyle pictured was a fantasy land that had ceased to exist more than half a century earlier, and he had probably got his information from his boyhood reading (*The Naturalist on the River Amazons* by H. W. Bates had been published in 1863, and was widely known, reissued in the Everyman Library in the 1900s). The Amazon of 1912 was not the awesome neglected wilderness of Bates, and Manaos was a metropolis of 40,000 people, with a magnificent opera house, hotels that rivalled Paris in splendour, and was fully lit by electric. Yet Doyle saw it as a picturesque village; so much we can gather from his brief reference to it, and the comment by the narrator that 'here we were rescued from the limited attractions of the local inn', as though it was some Sussex village with five hundred inhabitants.

Prehistoric animals living on top of a plateau in company with ape-men and Indians was a pretty fancy, but although Doyle explicitly tries to deal with the improbability of it, especially the question of supplying enough food for the vast creatures, he is not altogether convincing. He speculated that the prehistoric creatures survived by eating each other. It takes six days for the party to circle the base of the plateau, so the area of the lost world is not very great. When the four travellers arrive on top of the plateau, the beasts are very busy breaking down huge trees; and they have been presumably breaking down trees throughout the hundreds of thousands of years they have been stuck up there. Their section of tropical forest would not have lasted very long at that rate. . . .

The glaring faults of his weird stories, what he himself termed 'real Creepers', appear to a lesser extent in his Sherlock Holmes tales. Many of them are due to a lack of imagination; instead of imagination he had fancy. And what in another man would be a sterling quality weighed against him as a writer of weird and supernatural stories—his personal bravery. There is no instance of Doyle being scared of anything. The oldest and strongest emotion of mankind is fear, and the oldest and strongest fear is fear of the unknown. The unknown, whether it was the Egyptian mummy or a spirit form materializing in a corner of the room, had for him a prurient fascination. What has been called by H. P. Lovecraft 'the thrill of the chimney-corner whisper or the lonely wood' was outside his experience, but not outside his knowledge. He tried to diagnose what a typical horror-story reader was like, and often failed.—RONALD PEARSALL, *Conan Doyle: A Biographical Solution*, 1977, pp. 129–38

NOVELS

The Refugees . . . is one of his most remarkable productions. Like *Micah Clarke*, in which he champions the Puritans in England, in *The Refugees* he champions the Huguenots, who were the Puritans of France. One of the most vivid representations of the court of Louis XIV is to be found in Part I of *The Refugees*. The fall of Madame de Montespan is powerfully depicted, and the rise of her rival, Madame de Maintenon, who became the wife of Louis XIV, and through whose influence the final expulsion of the Huguenots from France took place, is graphically told. Indeed, the interest of the reader is so centred in the court at Versailles that the complete transition in the second part of the book to the forts and woods of Canada, whilst it forms the acme of contrast, is rather a disillusionment. But the real meaning of the book is to show that the violent measures adopted by the Catholic Church to penalise all who questioned the authority of the Church was to drive hundreds of thousands of the best citizens of France from beyond her borders. In this book, as in *Micah Clarke*, two of his earliest productions, Conan Doyle is revealed as the champion of the weak against the strong. The men and women who followed the Duke of Monmouth in the abortive rising in the West of

England, and who became in after-years the victims of Judge Jeffreys, were the counterpart in thought and action of the Huguenots who sought refuge in England and other countries.

The White Company was accepted by James Payne as the serial story for *The Cornhill Magazine*. He read during a whole year the books relating to the period of Edward III—a period in English history which he regarded as the real beginning of the English nation. This was the period above all others that he loved to depict. The archer, with his dare-devil love of adventure, and Sir Nigel Loring, who was always hankering after "a small feat of arms," with Hordle John and others, give ample scope for his descriptive powers. The story opens at Beaulieu Abbey in the New Forest, and is speedily transferred to France, where in the fourteenth and fifteenth centuries the ardent spirits alike of England and Scotland sought fame and fortune. It was at this period the Hundred Years' War began, and the heroic du Guesclin appears in the narrative. Du Guesclin anticipated to some extent the extraordinary martial feats accomplished later by Joan of Arc. This tale has always been a favourite and is now in its fiftieth edition.

Micah Clarke and *The White Company* always retained a foremost place in Sir Arthur's affections. They were the first-fruits of his early literary activity and laid the foundations of his fame. How diligent a worker he proved himself to be is borne out by the fact that at his death he left to posterity upwards of fifty books, many of them being large volumes.—JOHN LAMOND, *Arthur Conan Doyle: A Memoir*, 1931, pp. 41–43

To read *The Stark Munro Letters* is to learn much about Sir Arthur Conan Doyle; to know his life is to understand *The Stark Munro Letters*. For this book is essentially an autobiographical account of Doyle, fresh from medical school, and his attempts to establish a medical practice. The characters and places in the story are thinly disguised substitutes for the real, and most of the accounts are recollections of actual events.

The novel is a remarkable mixture of provocation, profundity, and entertainment, and as such it elicits a variety of reactions from its readers. It is *selectively* autobiographical and tells us what Doyle has chosen to recall about his medical life, his doubts, and his struggles in those formative years. . . .

The Stark Munro Letters recounts, often in close detail, the events in Dr. Doyle's life as he endeavoured to establish himself in practice. Although the book was written about ten years after the actual experiences which it describes, its careful attention to detail reflects Doyle's accurate memory and his habit of keeping diaries and notebooks, for in his writing he relied heavily on personal experiences. He believed that good writing could be realistic, that realism could be as entertaining as pure fantasy. This was a trend in literature that was to become more prevalent—romantic realism—and Conan Doyle was to be one of its most famous exponents.

In 1891, while convalescing from a severe attack of influenza, in the quiet moments of contemplation that this provided, he jotted down some of his thoughts (and doubts) about religion. There was an intellectual and emotional conflict raging within him on this subject—between what he had been told by his family and the Church on one hand and what he had learned in his scientific education on the other. Truly it was bothersome and most disturbing. Could it ever be satisfactorily resolved? These innermost thoughts about religion and science he put into a notebook, and, two years later, he decided to combine them with some of the events in his own life. On recollection, his attempts to start a medical practice had been filled with interesting occurrences. Of course, his entire life was characterized by unusual and remarkable experiences—the medical part was no exception. There was that outrageous, half-charlatan, half-quack former classmate he had worked with at Plymouth; there were the events that had led to his moving to Southsea in Portsmouth and setting up his own practice; and then there was his wife Louise and their marriage. Yes, all these could be combined and interwoven. It should make an entertaining and thought-provoking book. It would also question some of the old, well-established religious dogma; they certainly needed some critical scrutiny.

A few of the incidents in this novel are fictional, particularly the account of Lord Saltire and his lunatic son in Letter IV (which actually happened to a friend), but in essence *The Stark Munro Letters* is autobiographical. James Cullingworth, the main character but scarcely the hero, is in reality George Budd, Jr., a medical-school acquaintance. John Stark Munro is Arthur Conan Doyle. The young Paul is actually Doyle's younger brother Innes. The resident patient, Fred La Force in the book, is a tragic young man named Jack Hawkins, and the patient's sister Winnie La Force, whom Stark Munro marries, is Louise ("Touie") Hawkins, Doyle's first wife. Munro's mother, with her passion for truthfulness and honesty, her penchant for cleanliness, her disapproval of the "bankrupt swindler" Cullingworth, and finally her wholehearted approval of John's wife, is of course Doyle's own mother, Mary Foley Doyle—"The Mam" as he called her throughout her life—and the affection and high regard he had for her are stressed repeatedly throughout the letters. Herbert Swanborough, a former classmate now living in Lowell, Massachusetts, to whom the letters are written, has no real-life counterpart. . . .

There is another theme which stands out clearly in *The Stark Munro Letters*—the restless probings and searchings of an intelligent, well-educated young man in a period of scientific awakening and the conflict of what to believe intellectually or to accept theologically. Darwin, for example, claimed that man resulted from evolution, not by the Almighty's creation. The teachings of Spencer, Mill, and Huxley also influenced him greatly. Doyle finally decided that the theory of evolution could be merged with the Bible to establish a coherent and acceptable philosophy. He was bothered by the self-assurance of both scientific scepticism and religious dogma; his entire life showed this mental conflict between science and the supernatural. How could he reconcile the intense religious beliefs of his relatives with the natural wonders that he had experienced on his Arctic voyage, with his readings and conversations, and with his education at Edinburgh University? To him, Nature was the true revelation of the Deity. He sought a romantic idealism that would be acceptable in any church, by any group. But even more important to any searching mind, particularly a bright, sensitive yound mind, there is, in these struggles to establish what can be accepted and what must be rejected, the need for someone who can listen and share in these emotional and intellectual machinations. Stark Munro protests the absence of support from his father:

> . . . [T]here is little intellectual sympathy between us. He appears to think that these opinions of mine upon religion and politics which come from my inmost soul have been assumed either out of indifference or bravado. So I have ceased to talk on vital subjects with him.

Letters to an imaginary person, in this instance Herbert Swanborough, provide an ideal escape. If the letters were answered, the story would be different: there would be two sides. If the letters were written to someone else, such as his mother, to whom Doyle had written since first leaving home at age nine to go to school at Hodder and Stonyhurst, there would be the bias of an emotional attachment. No—let the recipient be distant and imaginary, someone whose life flows in a placid, quiet stream; now the letters and their contents can be unhampered, without restraint. His comments about religion even assume a type of exorcism. As he writes to Bertie in Letter V:

> I was so delighted, my dear chap, to have your assurance that nothing that I have said or could say upon the subject of religion could offend you. . . . I have no one to whom I can talk upon such matters. . . . Those whom I love best are those who have least sympathy with my struggles.

And so Bertie becomes an *alter ego,* a sounding board for these innermost conflicts, still water into which Munro can spill the "broken torrent" of his convictions. Munro thinks Bertie's life and religious orthodoxy must be comfortable, simultaneously expressing his doubts about eternal punishment and the absolutism of one and only one religious faith. Yet he is convinced that there is a Supreme Being—how else could there be so many wonders of Nature, so much variation, and so many problems? Must there not be a single guiding force to unite them? In Letter III, he explains how he solves part of this dilemma: " . . . [G]ood old Carlyle came to the rescue; and partly from him, and partly from my own broodings I made a little hut of my own, which has kept me snug ever since, and has even served to shelter a friend or two besides." And for the future as influenced by Charles Darwin: "Is it not glorious to think that evolution is still living and acting—that if we have an anthropoid ape as an ancestor, we may have archangels for our posterity?"—C. Frederick Kittle, "Afterword" to *The Stark Munro Letters,* 1982, pp. 195–209

G. K. CHESTERTON
"Sherlock Holmes" (1901/1907)
A Handful of Authors
1953, pp. 168–74
I

The return of Sherlock Holmes to the *Strand Magazine,* some years after his death, put a finishing touch to the almost heroic popularity of a figure whose reality was like the universally admitted reality of some old hero of medieval fable. Just as Arthur and Barbarossa were to return again, men felt that this preposterous detective must return again. He had emerged out of the unreality of literature into the glowing reality of legend, and in proof of this he has inherited the most widespread and pathetic of the characteristics of legendary heroes; that characteristic which makes men incredulous of their death. A slight and fantastic figure in a fugitive and ironical type of romance, he may seem too insignificant a subject for such a description. Nevertheless the fact remains that Mr. Conan Doyle's hero is probably the only literary creation since the creations of Dickens which has really passed into the life and language of the people, and become a being like John Bull or Father Christmas. It is remarkable to notice that although we possess many writers whose popularity is attested by enormous sales and general discussion, there is hardly one of them except Conan Doyle in this instance whose characters are familiar to everyone as types and symbols, as Pecksniff was the type of hypocrisy or Bumble of officialism. Rudyard Kipling, for example, is undoubtedly a popular writer. But if we were to go up to any man in the street and say that a particular problem would have puzzled Strickland he would receive it with a very different expression of countenance to that which he would wear if we said that it would puzzle Sherlock Holmes. Mr. Kipling's stories give inexhaustible intellectual delight, but the personality which we remember is the personality of the story, not the personality of the character. We remember the action, but forget the actors. In no other current creation except Sherlock Holmes does the character succeed, so to speak, in breaking out of the book as a chicken breaks out of the egg. The characters of Dickens had this capacity. The *Pickwick Papers* only prepared Sam Weller for us; after the book was written, Sam Weller is greater than the book. We can apply his philosophy for ourselves; we can continue his adventures in our dreams.

The fact that Sherlock Holmes alone has succeeded in familiarising himself at once with the cultured and the uncultured and turned his name into almost as descriptive a word as Dr. Guillotin or Captain Boycott, involves certain conclusions, which are for the most part worthy and reassuring. The phenomenon corrects finally, for example, much of the foolish and foppish talk about the public preferring books because they are bad. The stories of Sherlock Holmes are very good stories; they are perfectly graceful and conscientious works of art. The thread of irony which runs through all the solemn impossibilities of the narrative gives it the position of a really brilliant addition to the great literature of nonsense. The notion of the greatness of an intellect, proved by its occupation with small things instead of with great, is an original departure; it constitutes a kind of wild poetry of the commonplace. The intellectual clues and cruces upon which the development of each story turns are perhaps incredible as fact, but they are thoroughly solid and important as logic; they are such problems as a great lawyer might extract from two bottles of champagne; they are full of the very revelry of reason. The figure of Conan Doyle's detective is, in its own wild and trifling way, good literature.

Now, there are in London more than nine hundred and ninety-nine detective stories and fictitious detectives, nearly all of which are bad literature, or rather not literature at all. If, as the saying goes, the public likes books because they are bad, it would not be the fact that the one fictitious detective who is familiar to the whole public is the one fictitious detective who is a work of art. The fact of the matter is that ordinary men prefer certain kinds of work, good or bad, to certain other kinds of work, good or bad, which they have a perfect and obvious right to do. They prefer romance, farce, and everything that concerns the material diplomacy of life, to psychological delicacies or the more secret humours of existence. But, preferring a certain thing, they prefer it good if they can get it. The man in the street may prefer ale to crème de menthe, but it is nonsense to say that he prefers bad ale to good ale. He does not read George Meredith because he does not want that kind of book, however good it is, and he would not want it however bad it was. Surely we all know that there are hundreds of pigmy Merediths eternally engaged upon their unsightly embroideries and their bungling dissections. Bad literature is not confined to romance. The whole army of men in the street is scarcely so large as the army of young gentlemen who make it their business to despise the man in the street. Yet the sonnets of these young symbolists and the novels of these young psychologists are not sold like hot cakes upon bookstalls or read aloud in uproarious inn-parlours. The man who writes such literature as *The Egoist* has no right to expect to be as popular as Conan Doyle any more than a man who made incomparable astronomical telescopes would expect them to sell like umbrellas.

But it would be odd to deduce from this that the ordinary man has a weird and occult tenderness for a bad umbrella.

II

All English people have read the stories about Sherlock Holmes. Work like this is so good of its kind that it is difficult to endure patiently the talk of people who are occupied only in pointing out that it is not work of some other kind. The specific quality of a story of this sort is strictly what may be called wit; it is obliged to have some definite invention, construction and point, like a joke in the comic papers. Such work is inexpressibly superior to most mediocre serious work. There has to be something in it; it cannot be an entire imposture. A man can pretend to be wise; a man cannot pretend to be witty. His jokes may be much worse in your opinion than they are in his opinion; but after all they must be jokes; they cannot be entirely shapeless mysteries, like many modern works of philosophy.

Many men can make an epic who could not make an epigram. What is true of the comic anecdote is true also of that extended anecdote, the sensational story with a point to it. All real philosophy is apocalyptic, and if a man can give us revelations of heaven it is certainly better than giving us horrible revelations of high life. But I would rather have the man who devotes a short story to saying that he can solve the problem of a murder in Margate than the man who devotes a whole book to saying that he cannot solve the problem of things in general.

Sir Arthur Conan Doyle certainly weakened his excellent series of stories by being occasionally serious; especially he weakened it by introducing a sort of sneer at Edgar Allan Poe's Dupin, with whom he sustained no comparison. Sherlock Holmes's bright notions were like bright Cockney flowers grown in very shallow soil in a suburban garden; Dupin's were flowers growing on a vast, dark tree of thought. Hence Dupin, when he quits the subject of crime, talks in the tongue of permanent culture of the relations of imagination to analysis or of the relations of the supernatural to law. But the greatest error of the Sherlock Holmes conception remains to be remarked: I mean the error which represented the detective as indifferent to philosophy and poetry, and which seemed to imply that philosophy and poetry would not be good for a detective. Here he is at once eclipsed by the bolder and more brilliant brain of Poe, who carefully states that Dupin not only admired and trusted poetry, but was himself a poet. Sherlock Holmes would have been a better detective if he had been a philosopher, if he had been a poet, nay, if he had been a lover. It is remarkable to notice (I assume that you are as intimate with Dr. Watson's narratives as you should be)—it is remarkable to notice that the very same story in which the biographer describes Holmes's inaccessibility to love and such emotions, and how necessary it was to the clear balance of his logic, is the very same story in which Holmes is beaten by a woman because he does not know whether a certain man is her fiancé or her lawyer. If he had been in love he might have known well enough.

The only real danger is that Conan Doyle, by spreading the notion that practical logic must be unpoetical, may have encouraged the notion, too common already, that imagination must be absent-minded. It is a false and dangerous doctrine that the poet must be absent-minded. The purely imaginative man could never be absent-minded. He would perceive the significance of things near to him as clearly as he perceived the significance of things far off. In the highest imaginative sense man has no right whatever to forget his tea-cup because he is thinking about Plato. If he does not understand his tea-cup which he has seen, how shall he understand Plato whom he has not seen? The best and last word of mysticism is an almost agonising sense of the preciousness of everything, the preciousness of the whole universe, which is like an exquisite and fragile vase, and among other things the preciousness of other people's tea-cups. The last and best word of mysticism is not lavishness, but rather a sublime and sacred economy.

The perfect mystic would be always socially alert. The perfect mystic would be always correctly dressed. To such heights of transcendentalism some of us may find it difficult to soar; and such honest and unselfconscious failure, though it is certainly a weakness, is not an unpardonable or inhuman one. Some of the best men in the world—Dr. Johnson, for instance—have been specially remarkable for being conventional in theory and unconventional in practice. But if once a man is unconventional in theory, then the situation is atrocious. It almost certainly means either that a man has no morals or that he has no brains. The type of man does exist who says clearly and deliberately that he does not want to observe the little laws that surround him, that he is proud of being absent-minded, that he is proud of his disdain of detail. Whenever this occurs it certainly arises in another and most literal sense from absence—of Mind.

The real moral of the popularity of the adventures of Sherlock Holmes lies in the existence of a great artistic neglect. There are a large number of perfectly legitimate forms of art which are almost entirely neglected by good artists—the detective story, the farce, the book of boyish adventure, the melodrama, the music-hall song. The real curse of these things is not that they are too much regarded, but that they are not regarded enough; that they are despised even by those who write them. Conan Doyle triumphed and triumphed deservedly, because he took his art seriously, because he lavished a hundred little touches of real knowledge and genuine picturesqueness on the police novelette. He substituted for the customary keen eyes and turned-up collar of the conventional detective a number of traits, external and pictorial, indeed, but honestly appropriate to the logical genius, traits such as an immeasurable love of music and an egotism which was abstract and, therefore, almost unselfish. Above all, he surrounded his detective with a genuine atmosphere of the poetry of London. He called up before the imagination a new and visionary city in which every cellar and alley hid as many weapons as the rocks and heather-bushes of Roderick Dhu. By this artistic seriousness he raised one at least of the popular forms of art to the level which it ought to occupy.

He wrote the best work in a popular form, and he found that because it was the best it was also the most popular. Men needed stories, and had been content to take bad ones; and they were right, for a story in itself is a marvellous and excellent thing, and a bad story is better than no story, just as half a loaf is better than no bread. But when a detective story was written by a man who refused to despise his art, who carried all their dreams to fulfilment, they preferred him to the bungling and irresponsible authors who had catered for them before. It is no discredit to them that psychologies and philosophies had not stated their need for the rush of a climax and the fascination of a riddle. It would be as reasonable to blame men for not accepting cats as watch-dogs, or using pocket-knives as fire-irons. Men must have detective stories; they must have farces and melodramas and comic songs. For anyone who is honest enough to take trouble and invoke inspiration over these other forms, the road lies open to rich and many-coloured fields of undiscovered art.

PIERRE NORDON
From "The Character of Sherlock Holmes"
Conan Doyle, tr. Frances Partridge
1966, pp. 215–20

If he had not been linked with the collective consciousness and the sensibility of his readers, if he had not been in harmony with the ideological climate of the day, Sherlock Holmes would never have become an integral part of civilisation, as he is today. In so far as that climate impregnated Conan Doyle's ego, Sherlock represents that ego. And how could we identify ourselves with the hero if he did not emerge from the stories with sufficient consistency and a convincing enough individuality? Before making an inventory of the psychological contents of his character, we must first approach it from the periphery: contents is the appropriate word, because Sherlock Holmes was at first a mere outline, a type, a shape, an abstraction, before ever he developed a more complex interior and really began to exist. It seems as though Conan Doyle had always had two quite distinct images of Holmes in mind. Technically speaking, he is the 'detective'—that is part of the mechanism of the plot. Before being placed in 'a situation' he has to 'function'; but no aesthetic value necessarily attaches to this functional aspect. Hamlet would not have been Hamlet if he were simply an avenger. It is probably because they have been unable to go further than Conan Doyle in giving their characters inner life, that subsequent detective-writers have so rarely succeeded in creating an original or convincing detective who is not a copy of Holmes. But Sherlock Holmes has another aspect, at first sight somewhat disconcerting and at odds with his essential function, but clearly important to his creator for it is already apparent in 'Sherrinford Holmes', the first sketch for Sherlock: 'a sleepy-eyed young man—philosopher—collector of rare violins. An Amati. . .'[1]

This psychological dualism is not found in Poe's Dupin; it harks back to a *fin de siècle* dandyism, first connected with a detective by Stevenson in *The Dynamiter*, a work written shortly before the appearance of Conan Doyle's hero:

> 'Do you then propose, dear boy, that we should turn detective?' enquired Challoner.
> 'Do you propose it? No, Sir,' cried Somerset. 'It is reason, destiny, the plain face of the world, that commands and imposes it. Here, all our merits tell; our manners, habits of the world, powers of conversation, vast stores of unconnected knowledge, all that we are and have builds up a character of a complete detective. It is, in short, the only profession for a gentleman.'

With perspicacious humour, Stevenson here clearly suggests a relationship between the detective as a social type and a middle-class ideology concerned with dignity, security and liberalism.

But in all the portraits of Holmes in the Adventures, this dualism is manifest—these two basic systems are always in opposition. Quite early on in the stories, we come across frequent comparisons of the detective to a fox-hound: 'I was irresistibly reminded of a pure-blooded, well-trained fox-hound as it dashes backwards and forwards through the covert, whining in its eagerness, until it comes across the lost scent.'[2]

Why a fox-hound? Because it calls up an image of exactly that controlled alertness which should be second nature to a detective in Holmes's own view, and also the most traditional of English sports—for we must not forget that Holmes is a gentleman. The metaphor emphasises the functional side of his character, and, by its allusion to hunting, that he belongs to the upper class. The fox-hound image seems so to have obsessed the narrator, that if he, or rather Watson, is to be believed, Holmes becomes almost literally metamorphosed, when he is in his own element, or his own field of action:

> Sherlock Holmes was transformed when he was hot upon such a scent as this. Men who had only known the quiet thinker and logician of Baker Street would have failed to recognize him. His face flushed and darkened. His brows were drawn into two hard, black lines, while his eyes shone out from beneath them with a steely glitter. His face was bent downwards, his shoulders bowed, his lips compressed, and the veins stood out like whip-cord in his long, sinewy neck. His nostrils seemed to dilate with a purely animal lust for the chase, and his mind was so absolutely concentrated upon the matter before him, that a question or remark fell unheeded upon his ears, or at the most only provoked a quick, impatient snarl in reply.[3]

Here we see a man transformed with all speed into a fox-hound before our very eyes, until he seems almost to have lost the power of speech and be reduced to expressing himself by sounds. But the fox-hound motif recurs insistently: 'Holmes hunted about among the grass and leaves like a retriever after a wounded bird.'[4] 'See the fox-hound with hanging ears and drooping tail as it lolls about the kennels and compare it with the same hound as, with gleaming eyes and straining muscles, it runs upon a breast-high scent!—such was the change in Holmes since the morning.'[5] 'In an instant he was tense and alert, his eyes shining, his face set, his limbs quivering with eager activity. He was out on the lawn, in through the window, round the room, and up into the bedroom, for all the world, like a dashing fox-hound drawing a cover. . . . Then he rushed down the stair, out through the open window, threw himself upon his face on the lawn, sprang up and ran into the room once more, all with the energy of the hunter who is at the very heels of his quarry.'[6]

In contrast to this imaginary and almost stereotyped vision of Holmes in action, or as a countryman, we have Holmes the Londoner. Here is a personality as entirely different as is Doctor Jekyll from Mr. Hyde—an absent-minded, taciturn, disturbing morphia-addict who is also a rather Bohemian, fastidious, sceptical music-lover. It is not so much a contrast between two aspects of the same person as one between two ways of life and modes of consciousness, the first sensitive and impressionable, the second intellectual. And this very coexistence of two antithetical sides to Sherlock Holmes's character is essential to his status as a hero:

> My friend was an enthusiastic musician, being himself not only a very capable performer, but a composer of no ordinary merit. All the afternoon he sat in the stalls wrapped in the most perfect happiness, gently waving his long thin fingers in time to the music, while his gently smiling face and his languid, dreamy eyes were as unlike those of Holmes the sleuth-hound, Holmes the relentless, keen-witted, ready-handed criminal agent, as it was possible to conceive. In his singular character the dual nature alternately asserted itself, and his extreme exactness and astuteness represented, as I have often thought, the reaction against the poetic and contemplative mood which occasionally predominated in him.[7]

The picture of Holmes in his room in Baker Street, lying propped among a heap of cushions, with clouds of tobacco smoke rising through the dimness, evokes the characteristic pose of the 'decadents'. Cushions, tobacco—Holmes needs a special sort of environment and special stimulants in order to think; and he is a creative as well as an analytic thinker, as we shall have occasion to show. His addiction to morphine and cocaine (disapproved of by Watson) and to tobacco (which he tolerated) are the only links connecting him with the romantic idea of the artist, the decadent poet. It is easy for Watson, as a doctor, to trace the effects of narcotics in his friend's gaze—a gaze which clearly expresses Holmes's two modes of mental functioning, the extrovert and sensory, and the purely speculative. When he is under the influence of narcotics, Watson finds him even more mysterious than usual. As soon as he sees that dreamy look in Holmes's eyes, suspicions are aroused that were first hinted at in *A Study in Scarlet*:

> For days on end he would lie upon the sofa in the sitting-room, hardly uttering a word or moving a muscle from morning to night. On these occasions I have noticed such a dreamy, vacant expression in his eyes, that I might have suspected him of being addicted to the use of some narcotic, had not the temperance and cleanliness of his whole life forbidden such a notion.[8]

Holmes's gaze, so faithfully rendered by Sidney Paget, soon becomes one of his most striking characteristics, indispensable to our image of his personality: 'Holmes sat in his big arm-chair, with the weary, heavy-lidded expression which veiled his keen and eager nature.'[9]

As for the objects with which he surrounds himself in his Baker Street rooms, they tell us as much about him as clues do about a criminal, emphasising his interest in science and crime, and suggesting the intimate and endearing side of Watson's hero in terms that are sometimes not far from caricature:

> The rough-and-tumble work in Afghanistan, coming on top of a natural Bohemianism of disposition, has made me rather more lax than befits a medical man. But with me there is a limit, and when I find a man who keeps his cigars in the coal-scuttle, his tobacco in the toe-end of a Persian slipper, and his unanswered correspondence transfixed by a jack-knife into the very centre of his wooden mantelpiece, then I begin to give myself virtuous airs.[10]

Of all the objects associated with Holmes, the most familiar is of course his pipe. Is that because he prefers it to a cigar? No: it seems to mean more to him than a mere means of absorbing tobacco. It is, above all, the companion of his long, studious nights. The difficulties of some investigation on which Holmes has begged Watson to accompany him, have overcome the doctor's powers of resistance and he has fallen asleep in his chair:

> So he sat as I dropped off to sleep, and so he sat when a sudden ejaculation caused me to wake up, and I found the summer sun shining into the apartment. The pipe was still between his lips, the smoke still curled upwards, and the room was full of a dense tobacco haze, but nothing remained of the heap of shag which I had seen upon the previous night.[11]

The pipe is a necessary adjunct to his spells of thought, measuring their duration by the time taken to smoke a pipeful of tobacco.

> 'What are you going to do then?' I asked.
> 'To smoke,' he answered. 'It is quite a three-pipe problem, and I beg that you won't speak to me for fifty minutes.'[12]

Thus Holmes's simple outline developed a certain number of clear and unforgettable features, impressing our minds as vigorously as the drawings of *Punch* which flowed from Dicky Doyle's pen. Holmes is right when he says, 'art in the blood is liable to take the strangest forms'.[13]

However, neither of these two aspects of this outline are so much heroic, in the true sense of the word, as picturesque and remarkable. Holmes's vocation as a fictional character, willed and designed by his creator, destines him to follow a certain career and play a certain part, even though the stages and episodes in it are only potential. He must therefore possess a certain number of attributes, and his figure must be set against an aesthetic or ethical background which brings out its essentially heroic quality, independent of the heroism of the adventures themselves.

One of these is his herculean strength, whether of muscle or endurance. We see Holmes being engaged as a stable-boy in order to get information about Irene Adler, and verifying a hypothesis with a harpoon. We see him twisting a poker in his powerful hands, and intimidating enormous men; and in *The Sign of Four* a professional boxer greet him as a colleague and regrets that he never became a pugilist. He is probably not addicted to any one sport (how could he possibly find time?) nor to any form of physical training; yet the drain upon his energies involved in the investigations in *The Hound of the Baskervilles* and 'The Final Problem' is never too much for his strength. The opening of 'The Reigate Squires' gives Watson the chance to talk of his friend's 'iron constitution', which 'however had broken down under the strain of an investigation which had extended over two months, during which period he had never worked less than fifteen hours a day, and had more than once, as he assured me, kept to his task for five days at a stretch'.[14]

Holmes's physical energy is backed up by his quite exceptional acuteness of the senses. His sensitive ear, which partly explains his love of music, enables him always to be the first to detect the approach of some criminal for whom he and Watson are lying in wait. In "A Scandal in Bohemia" he recognises the disguised voice of Irene Adler wishing him a rapid and ironical good-night, even though it is only slightly familiar to him. But his piercing sight is his most precious possession. From tobacco-ash to mud-stains, there is nothing he cannot identify, read and decipher with speed.

Notes

1. Draft for *A Study in Scarlet* (C.D.B.A.).
2. *A Study in Scarlet*, HOL. I, p. 29.
3. *The Boscombe Valley Mystery*, HOL. II, p. 92.
4. *The Dancing Men*, HOL. II, p. 628.
5. *The Bruce-Partington Plans*, HOL. II, p. 980.
6. *The Devil's Foot*, HOL. II, p. 45.
7. *The Red-Headed League*, HOL. II, p. 45.
8. HOL. I, p. 10.
9. *The Engineer's Thumb*, HOL. II, p. 205.
10. *The Musgrave Ritual*, HOL. II, p. 396.
11. *The Man with the Twisted Lip*, HOL. II, p. 142.
12. *The Red-Headed League*, HOL. II, p. 43.
13. *The Greek Interpreter*, HOL. II, p. 478.
14. *The Reigate Squires*, HOL. II, p. 417.

BONNIE MENES
From "Sherlock Holmes and Sociology"

The American Scholar, Winter 1980/81, pp. 101–3

Sherlock Holmes is the defender of social norms; he enters a case not when a law, but when a norm, has been broken. In story after story this is so. Two people who love each other are kept from marriage. This is not illegal; it isn't even immoral. Wages should be commensurate with work; an exorbitant wage is cause for investigation. There should be no secrets between a husband and wife, yet one spouse in a marriage is acting mysteriously. Two people are scheduled to marry, but one fails to show up at the altar. No public crime has been committed, no private transgression even, but an unspoken social rule has been broken. A man, defender of home and family, is missing and thus unable to defend his home and family. Social fabric is torn. Holmes, in each instance, is called in.

Sherlock Holmes is no mere defender of the law. Like many another modern detective in literature, Holmes often finds himself an unwitting accomplice in a man's death, or the advocate of deliberate deception or disruption of one kind or another. The London in which Conan Doyle sets Holmes down is a complex place, so complex that Holmes himself, for his own good reasons, must sometimes actually break the law. But he rarely enters a case only because a law has been broken, a crime committed. More often he enters before any crime has taken place, before the murder, before the blackmail. Or perhaps there is no clear crime at all; it is only that someone or something is missing. Miss Violet Hunter, in "The Adventure of the Copper Beeches," engages Holmes for advice on a position she has been offered as a governess: the salary is surprisingly high and her future employers demand that she wear blue and cut her hair. Jabez Wilson, in "The Red-Headed League," would like to know why his well-paying position has been eliminated.

Strange business, unhappy coincidences, suspicious circumstances—these are what propel Sherlock Holmes into action. What is illegal is not necessarily, for him, what is of interest. "We have in this case one singular incident coming close to the heels of another singular incident," Holmes explains in "The Adventure of the Norwood Builder," "[and] the police are making the mistake of concentrating their attention upon the second, because it happens to be the one which is actually criminal. But it is evident to me that the logical way to approach the case is to begin by trying to throw some light upon the first incident—the curious will, so suddenly made, and to so unexpected an heir."

More important, once on a case Holmes does not invariably enforce the law. Sometimes he turns lawbreakers over to the authorities, but sometimes not. What is more, Holmes is quick to reprimand his own clients, to berate them when he does not approve of their behavior, even to refuse a client's gratefully outstretched hand. Holmes is often referred to as "a specialist in crime"; yet his is a special kind of specialty—it is in logic, not law. He is not a policeman and as far as possible from prosecutorial. Justice is always served, but the Baker Street logician never brings men to justice. In "The Boscombe Valley Mystery" Holmes chooses not to enter the courts:

> "Well, it is not for me to judge you," said Holmes, as the old man signed the statement which had been drawn out. "I pray that we may never be exposed to such a temptation."
>
> "I pray not, sir. And what do you intend to do?"
>
> "In view of your health, nothing. You are yourself aware that you will soon have to answer for your deed at a higher court than the assizes. I will keep your confession, and, if McCarthy is condemned, I shall be forced to use it. If not, it shall never be seen by mortal eye; and your secret, whether you are dead or alive, shall be safe with us."

Sherlock Holmes does not represent positive law, because he does not always agree with the law and because he himself frequently goes beyond the law. Holmes hangs out no shingle but dwells in shadow and, often, deceit. He keeps secrets, which is one of the reasons his clients seek him out. The police would laugh, they tell him; the police would not understand. As the headmaster puts it in "The Adventure of the Three Students": "When once the law is evoked, it cannot be stayed again, and this is just one of those cases where, for the credit of the college, it is most essential to avoid scandal." In fact, it is only thanks to Watson and the press—scandalous jumblers of the important division between public and private—that Sherlock Holmes is known as widely as he is, or so Conan Doyle leads us to understand.

If Holmes is not public defender, neither is he a private eye, a sleuth checking up on cheating wives. Morality is private and, as such, Holmes deems it none of his business. He takes a scientific view of his cases. He leaves it for others to unravel the morality behind their courses of action. He does not fight evil; he investigates problems. The universe is too much a puzzle to him to impose his own moral views on it. As he remarks in "The Adventure of the Cardboard Box":

> "What is the meaning of it, Watson?" said Holmes, solemnly, as he laid down the paper. "What object is served by this circle of misery and violence and fear? It must tend to some end, or else our universe is ruled by chance, which is unthinkable. But what end? There is the great standing perennial problem to which human reason is as far from an answer as ever."

Neither goodness nor justice but social order is Sherlock Holmes's desire. The idea of law, of life bounded by order and regularity, lies beneath all positive law, moral sanctions, social norms. Positive law and rules of morality are kinds of norms, and Holmes does uphold them on occasion. But for the most part his actions are in the social realm. You will not find the rules that guide him in the statutes or prayer books; the kind of order he upholds is unwritten. While it is neither legally nor morally right to murder, Holmes does not, in "The Adventure of Charles Augustus Milverton," mourn a murdered man:

> "Well, I am afraid I can't help you, Lestrade," said Holmes. "The fact is that I knew this fellow Milverton, that I considered him one of the most dangerous men in London, and that I think there are certain crimes which the law cannot touch, and which, therefore, to some extent, justify private revenge. No, it's no use arguing. I have made up my mind. My sympathies are with the criminals rather than with the victims. . . ."

At the end of each case in a Sherlock Holmes story, disorder is redressed, not necessarily in legal or moral terms, but socially a balance of sorts has been restored. Thus Watson concludes, at the close of "The Adventure of the Dancing Men": "Of Mrs. Hilton Cubitt I only know that I have heard she recovered entirely, and that she still remains a widow, devoting her whole life to the care of the poor and to the administration of her husband's estate."

In some of Holmes's unsolved cases, a social balance is not restored, seemingly because he—or, more precisely, Conan Doyle—does not consider the broken norm a valid one at the outset. In "A Scandal in Bohemia" Holmes is outwitted by an actress who has the means to blackmail the king of Bohemia. Scandal is of course a social phenomenon, and one might have expected all parties to join together to uphold the prestige and reputation of royalty. But Holmes has little respect for royalty, and his lack of respect is reflected in the fact that the case goes unsolved. "The Yellow Face" has to do with a woman conspiring to keep her mulatto child, offspring of her former marriage to an American black. Holmes implicitly approves of her keeping the child and thus does not succeed in solving the case, and hence in restoring the normative order. Inevitably Holmes shows a blind spot in cases that entail norms which he feels should be changed or are in fact changing. As the defender of social norms, he fails or loses interest when the norms he is asked to defend are in his view indefensible.

The social realm, distinct from law and distinct from mor-

als, has a powerful attraction for Sherlock Holmes. Everywhere he upholds the family relationship, and in many instances he upholds property relations. He is busied with thoughts of class and social structure, isolation, and the significance of the urban landscape (to use a bit of contemporary jargon). He is not himself a sociologist, but as a defender of social norms of a kind that does not exist outside fiction, his work is of the utmost interest to sociologists.

MARGARET DRABBLE

1939–

Margaret Drabble was born in Sheffield, Yorkshire, in 1939. Her sister is the well known novelist A. S. Byatt. She began writing novels early, after a brilliant undergraduate career at Newnham College, Cambridge. After leaving university she married an actor, Clive Swift, whom she met there. Drabble had done some acting and intended to make a career of it, but the birth of her first child caused her to leave the stage and turn to writing novels instead.

Drabble has stated that her books "are mainly concerned with privilege, justice, and salvation," and that she likes to relate "a good traditional tale." She writes in the central tradition of the English novel, closest perhaps to its 19th-century exponents, Thomas Hardy (on whom she has edited a study) and George Eliot, whom some critics consider her principal model. Although her narrative techniques are traditional, the world she narrates is a very modern one. Her early novels (A *Summer Bird-Cage, The Waterfall*) were interior and subjective, centered around their female protagonists. In *The Ice Age* (1977), she projects a panoramic examination of British society in crisis during the mid-1970s. In this book, as one critic has written, "she incorporates the ever-increasing junk pile of public disasters into a thematic background that never appears journalistic."

Drabble has remained extraordinarily prolific while raising three children. She has written a biography of Arnold Bennett, a writer for whom she feels a particular sympathy, and has won numerous prizes for her novels. She divorced her husband in 1975 and currently lives in London. In 1980 Drabble was awarded the CBE.

Personal

The solipsistic thing, nobody exists but me, I find offensive. I can't afford to think that reality doesn't exist. I've got to go to the shops, and I've got to get the supper. I think that once you've had a baby, it's terribly hard to pretend that reality doesn't exist. Somehow life becomes so basic, and you know other people are there. Having children gives you an access to an enormous common store of otherness about other people. This is how I learned that other people really existed. I used to be very solipsistic at university. I used to be appallingly selfish. I still am in some ways; I just can't get away with it as I used to. And I used to be terribly interested in my own brain and what it was perceiving and whether there was any outside reality. I used to read Hume and Berkeley and wonder about all that, and I could get myself into a state where I believed that the outside world wasn't there. And when I had children, I realized it was just very permanently there forever.

. . . And there are certain acts in the house that give me the feeling of authenticity as though I'm a real person, things like every morning opening the blinds. I always enjoy it, and putting the milk bottles out. I'm not a very tidy housewife, and I don't enjoy dusting because it just goes on and on, and the house is always a mess because everyone is always tramping

through it, but there are certain things I enjoy. I remember Angus Wilson once saying that he knew when he was in a bad psychological state when he didn't enjoy shaving in the morning. He said there's something so repetitive and ritualistic and good about shaving, and I feel that way about getting the house warmed up and going downstairs in the morning and making it all start happening. I'm very good in the morning. I get up feeling good. Some people don't; they hate getting up in the morning; they prefer the evening. But I like the feeling of everything coming to life. So I suppose it is creative, in a way. Certainly Virginia Woolf says this in A *Room of One's Own*, that the way one has one's house is an act of creativity, and it's so obvious that there are some houses that one feels at home in and some that one may like the look of but wouldn't want to live in. It's interesting that there are different levels of lifestyle that one can go into and be happy in, and with friends it's interesting whose house you can be in. I hate staying with people overnight. I like to be in my own place, and also one has to be so polite staying in other people's houses. But there are one or two friends that I don't mind staying with at all because there's something similar. They're feckless about the same things and fussy about the same things and have the same priorities, I suppose. It's interesting trying to work out which prejudices came from where.—MARGARET DRABBLE, Interview with Dee Preussner, *MFS*, Winter 1979–80, pp. 575–76

General

Englishmen do not love intellectual girls. They like bright girls, they respect intelligent girls, but their wariness of a girl with a trained and articulate mind borders on a fear which extinguishes all other emotions. Sarah, Emma and Rosamund are all intellectuals—that is to say that their response to any situation is generally simultaneous to their analysis of it. If they fall in love or out of bed their instinct is at once to examine, codify, write footnotes and marginal comments. It is the candour and accuracy with which Miss Drabble makes them do all this which makes them so interesting and real. The vivid creation of a new heroine is not sufficient reason to account for the passionate feelings so many people entertain about Margaret Drabble's novels. There are a number of other characteristics shared by all her books and I'd like to enumerate a few of them.

First, there is the raciness of the writing. The instant translation of experience into response and then into analysis is carried out with an astonishing self-confidence. Her critics might call this aggressiveness, which, whilst it will brook no obstacle, often disregards subtleties and contradictions which would give other more fastidious or imaginative novelists a good deal of pause. Things as they are, and as they seem subjectively, is what she writes about. This again antagonises her critics: how can anyone be so self-assertive when writing about anxiety?

Then there is the sense of occasion, the set pieces which include some of her most memorably simple and vivid pieces of narrative writing. Each of the novels contains at least two of these dramatic explosions. Best of all, perhaps, is the row in bed at the beginning of *The Garrick Year* which ends with the husband David punching through the William Morris wallpaper, through the plaster and laths—into a void. Reading it first it seemed merely a brilliant account of a quarrel. Re-reading it, two things stand out: first the economy—the whole scene takes three paragraphs when memory suggested it was half a chapter. (In rather the same way in retrospect the descriptions of nature in Thomas Hardy's novels seem to last for pages, but are in reality brief and few.) And secondly there is the true tact of the artist in suggesting larger issues, which may be taken up or not by the reader as he pleases. The wall may represent marriage, entrenched, decorated, and serviceable, but subject to collapse at a single determined or violent gesture.—JULIAN JEBB, *Lon*, May 1967, pp. 85–86

Miss Drabble in some ways bears comparison with Iris Murdoch and Muriel Spark; she is as intellectually serious as they, though not as witty, and warmer than either. But, in sharp contrast to these two plotmakers, she does not *encompass* her material; rather, she seems half lost within it—mystified by her characters, ruminative where she should be expository, expository where she should be dramatic, shamelessly dependent upon coincidence, lackadaisical about locating her theme, and capable, for long stretches, of blocking in episodes devoid of dynamic relevance to what one takes to be the action. The plot of *The Realms of Gold* appears to be this: a pair of perfectly suited middle-aged lovers break, and are slow to reunite because a postcard is held up by a mail strike in Europe. As the postcard (declaring, "I miss you. I love you") languishes at the bottom of a letterbox, the book happens; that is, a number of familial and professional gatherings are described, while the heroine's heart is distinctly elsewhere, and the reader's attention threatens to wander also. The unseen mailman who finally moves the missive is the novel's active agonist; the other characters conduct a three-hundred-page holding action. When at last the lovers do reunite, they are relieved and, sim-

ply, pleased; their circumstances, through no doing of their own, are enough improved for them to marry, and they do. "Invent a more suitable ending if you can," the author writes, in a last plea for the reader's collaboration, or indulgence.—JOHN UPDIKE, "Drabbling in the Mud," *NY*, Jan. 12, 1976, p. 88

Of all the contemporary English women novelists, Margaret Drabble is the most ardent traditionalist. Her sense of connection to female tradition, "the sexual doom of womanhood, its sad inheritance," comes first of all from her own past. Drabble described her childhood at the annual meeting of the Brontë Society in 1974: "I was brought up in Sheffield, on the edge of countryside very similar to the country round Haworth. My family was of the same size and constitution as the Brontë family; my siblings and I were interested in writing, and in our childhood composed magazines and stories together." Both Drabble and her sister A. S. Byatt have used material from the Brontë novels and legend as controlling myths in their own writing; Drabble has also written extensively about nineteenth-century women novelists, and about Virginia Woolf and Katherine Mansfield. Her full-length biography of Woolf's Edwardian literary adversary, Arnold Bennett, underlines her personal commitment to nineteenth-century social realism. "I don't want to write an experimental novel to be read by people in fifty years, who will say, oh, well, yes, she foresaw what was coming," she said in 1967. "I'm just not interested. I'd rather be at the end of a dying tradition, which I admire, than at the beginning of a tradition which I deplore." The women in Drabble's novels are unselfconsciously named for the great Victorian heroines, as if the supply of women's names were, after all, very small: Rosamund, Clara, Emma, Lucy, and Jane. It is as natural for a character in a Drabble novel to gossip about nineteenth-century heroines as to discuss her own childhood; in fact, more so. Heroines rather reticent about their own sexuality will decide that "Emma got what she deserved in marrying Mr. Knightley. What can it have been like, in bed with Mr. Knightley?"

For Drabble's heroines, at least up to Rose Vassiliou in *The Needle's Eye* (1972), there is a kind of peace in the acknowledgment of, and submission to, female limitation. In *The Millstone*, Rosamund Stacey, a Ph.D. candidate living in a posh apartment that her parents have loaned to her, becomes pregnant in a single encounter with a man she admires but has no claims upon. Rosamund is pretty, self-disciplined, and courageous; but, in bearing a child, she is brought to admit that she has lost control of her own destiny. She is humbled, first by her body, which forces a reluctant admission of femaleness upon her, then by the startling strength of her love for the child. In the maternity clinic, Rosamund feels her oneness with the shabby, exhausted women who wait with her to see the doctors: "I was one of them, I was like that too, I was trapped in a human limit for the first time in my life, and I was going to have to learn to live inside it."

Children are the compensation for feminine surrender. Drabble is the novelist of maternity, as Charlotte Brontë was the novelist of the schoolroom. The interaction between mother and child, the love that comes unbidden like the operations of grace, is for Drabble the most instructive and surprising human relationship. For a Drabble heroine, a room of one's own is usually a place to have a baby, but it is at the same time a testing-ground for resilience and charity and wisdom. Thus Drabble finds a female resolution to the feminine conflict between biological and artistic creativity. Pregnancy is a way of knowing, a process of education that not only helps Rosamund work "with great concentration and clarity" on her thesis, but also makes real to her the abstractions of the human condition: "I had always felt for others in theory and pitied the blows of fate and circumstance under which they suffered; but now, myself, no longer free, myself suffering, I may say that I felt it in my heart." Men, particularly successful men, are magnetically attracted to the company of these knowing women; in *The Waterfall* James is literally seduced by watching Jane convalesce from childbirth in a warm room at the top of an empty house.

Yet childbirth is not a victory; it is an acceptance of the compensations of giving in and giving up, of the "necessary pleasure of feeling from time to time the warm sense of defeat." Drabble's heroines are well aware of the boundaries of their world, and wryly, distantly amused by their own futile efforts to escape. At the conclusion of *The Garrick Year*, Emma tells no one that she has seen a snake clutching at the belly of a sheep on a family picnic in Herefordshire: "One just has to keep on and to pretend, for the sake of the children, not to notice. Otherwise, one might just as well stay at home."

As the novelist, of course, Drabble always notices and proclaims the presence of the snake her heroines gamely pretend not to see. By the end of *The Needle's Eye* (1972), however, the gap between novelist and heroine has almost closed; graceful resignation to feminine destiny, to the curse of Eve, has come to seem much more masochistic and despairing. Rose decides to live with a husband she despises, once more "for the children's sake"; but this time she feels that she has made a suicidal decision prompted only by duty, and that the "price she had to pay was the price of her own living death, her own conscious dying, her own lapsing . . . from grace."

Drabble herself has speculated about the extent to which Rose's martyrdom is connected to her personal need to force the ideology of marriage on a fiction straining to go beyond it. "I haven't written a novel since Clive and I separated," she told Nancy Hardin in 1972, "and I'm very interested to see what comes out next. I wrote the whole of *The Needle's Eye* when we were still together. And I might not have made it end like it did if we had separated first. I might have allowed her her freedom." A good deal of Drabble's strength and ability to grow comes out in the simplicity of this admission. Like her sister Antonia Byatt (now working on a four-volume novel), Drabble has been increasingly ambitious, serious, and open-minded; her work is the record of a feminine consciousness expanding and maturing. In some respects she has been clinging to a tradition she has outgrown. *The Needle's Eye* is evidently the end of a prolonged phase in Drabble's writing; perhaps she will now allow herself more freedom, more protest.—ELAINE SHO-WALTER, "Beyond the Female Aesthetic," *A Literature of Their Own*, 1977, pp. 304–7

From her early novels about the lives of young women leaving University, marrying, bearing children, coping with frigidity and nappies, to her current preoccupation with personal release from the prisons of family and society, Drabble has constructed, if not an autobiography, something in the way of a chronicle of a specific female generation. A fictionalized, English *Passages*. If Anthony's turn to God at the end of *The Ice Age* evokes the *nouveaux philosophes* and a rising personalist and antipolitical religious sensibility, the subject matter of her earlier novels constituted an open invitation to female identification, reinforced by an eye for interiors, clothing, and trends, that linked them with women's magazines such as *Nova* or the upgraded afternoon television soap-operas that have flourished in the United States since the women graduates of

the early nineteen-sixties found themselves at home with small children. As the embryonic women's movement, particularly in its more liberal, consciousness-raising manifestations, testified, many of the middle-class women of that generation shared a deep concern with the discovery of a self and the elaboration of a language in which to express it. Drabble's career as a novelist belongs to that phenomenon as surely as do those of Anne Roiphe, Lois Gould, and a host of others. Sarah, of *A Summer Bird-Cage*, has just come down from University and is making up her mind about getting married while holding a job and observing the marriages of her sister and friends; Emma, of *The Garrick Year*, is already married and coping with two children, her husband, and her first affair; Rosamund, of *The Millstone* (*Thank You All Very Much*, in the American edition), is completing a dissertation and bearing an illegitimate child; Clara, of *Jerusalem the Golden*, is finishing a degree, trying to shake off her past (mother and town), and having her first affair; Jane, of *The Waterfall*, is coping with young motherhood and a distintegrated marriage, enjoying her first adultery and orgasm; Rose, of *The Needle's Eye*, is fighting with her husband over the custody of their children and eventually will reconcile with him, for them; and Frances, of *The Realms of Gold*, having made it out of the domestic morass, is trying to consolidate true love.

The novels constitute dimensions of a female life, by no means fully identical to Drabble's own. More and more, they also constitute a running commentary, not so much on contemporary life, as on the trendy, shared representations of that life. Like a cheery and talented magpie, Drabble collects the latest themes: families and anthropology in *The Realms of Gold*; families, property speculation, and inflation in *The Ice Age*; and—predictably enough—health in the novel now in process. The quasi-photographic aspect of Drabble's technique, with its rigorous refusal of interpretation and causation, helps to account for the ambiguous and mirroring quality of her pictures of female and social being. Like Jane in *The Waterfall*, she registers the lack of an encompassing meaning. But, in accepting the erosion of absolute standards by which to judge or to condemn behavior, in this instance adultery, she rashly espouses a phenomenological personalism. The events of the novel themselves seem to pass judgment on the transgression: Jane and James embarking on an illicit, lie-based vacation, with their two children along, with Jane passing as her cousin Lucy, James' wife, have a terrible accident which leaves James unconscious and severely wounded. Judgment? Not at all. The accident was an accident. Presumably, a pure accident can be an act of God, but, if such, it was unmediated by the normal texture of meaning and prohibition.

Thus Frances, reflecting in *The Realms of Gold* on the simultaneous discovery of her Aunt Con's gruesome death and her nephew Stephen's disappearance, decides for coincidence, not connection. Drabble frequently insists on accident as a factor in plot. The point is the repudiation of cause and seems decisively related to her attitude to Freud. Let others read in judgment, should they so choose. Drabble rests her case on coincidence of act (adultery) and event (accident). That coincidence does not, however, stand naked. On one side, Drabble weaves the texture in which judgment would have been: the sensibility of morality, the yearning for meaning remain where once law held sway. In *The Ice Age*, she reverts frequently to the possibility that accident may mask choice—self-destructive choice. But she leaves the issue open: a possibility among others. And against accident she postulates salvation, as in Jane's first orgasm, powerfully and movingly described in a scant two pages worthy of any literature of salvation, and succeeded by her gradual healing and learning to live as a woman. Or Anthony's discovery of God while in prison.

Thus love, true sexual love, or maternal love, fills the place of salvation. Drabble, in her endorsement of love as personal salvation, avoids a crude hedonism. The ambiguity of *The Waterfall*'s ending amply confirms this residual reticence, as does Drabble's consistent emphasis on love as meaning and connection—not mere gratification. But the exclusive, accidental, personal, and even selfish quality of individual fulfillment underscores the limitation of Drabble's vision. Limitation not because happiness is wrong, as in some outmoded puritan discourse, but because, by accepting the social context in which it can only be so fleetingly personal, Drabble consistently portrays it as occurring at others' expense: much as freedom from rather than for, her heroines' happiness comes against rather than with. To be sure, traditionally, salvation has had highly personal connotations—the relationship of the individual soul to God. And the bourgeois novel, that great tradition Drabble reveres, similarly focussed upon the individual destiny. But traditional modes of salvation, like so many bourgeois novels, assumed that the destiny of the individual had a higher purpose with respect to the community at large. The marriage of a Jane Austen heroine contributes to a vision of proper social order, independent of whether or not one shares the politics or ideology upon which the vision rests. In Drabble's work, order—be it human or divine—proves elusive and problematical. Yet, paradoxically, Drabble heroines remain very much in and of society—ready to enjoy its privileges and advantages, provided they do not come at too high a personal price. Their alienation, can such a term be applied, consists in repudiating bourgeois-puritan constraints upon individual fulfillment while continuing to accept the social substance of the world, the corruptions and injustices of which are registered as meaningless fetters on personal happiness. Anthony's salvation in *The Ice Age* conforms to this pattern in its total personalism—he escapes from the mesmerizing entrapment of the market only through a vision he doubts ever being able to share. This conflation of the specific interconnections of capitalist society and of human interconnectedness reveals the depth of Drabble's largely unconscious nihilism—the mirror image of her heroines' narcissism.—ELIZABETH FOX-GENOVESE, "The Ambiguities of Female Identity: A Reading of the Novels of Margaret Drabble," *PR*, 1979, pp. 235–38

Fate is a word and a concept which pervades Margaret Drabble's fiction. In *The Millstone* it took on vaguely Freudian, or at least deterministic, overtones, as Rosamund sought to explain and excuse her frigidity in terms of her early childhood experiences. In *Jerusalem the Golden*, it is the burden of heredity which Clara would wrongly like to shrug off. In *The Waterfall*, it becomes more complex and closer to the thematic core of the novel, but at least on one level it is gender. For Jane Gray, as for Freud, "anatomy is destiny".

Jane's ideas about fate should be distinguished from Drabble's, who reflected in her interview with Nancy Hardin that she's "kind of Greek with a Greek view of the gods". When Jane thinks of Oedipus and fate, however, she is recalling not Sophocles but Seneca who, as Moses Hadas points out, "is concerned not to justify the ways of gods to men or of men to gods, but to display the capacity for emotional intensity exhibited by characters endowed with extraordinary passions". When Jane ventures to think about the ways of gods to men, she quickly becomes personal:

> What right had any deity to submit mortality to such obsessive, arbitrary powers? The meaningless vio-

lence of the world—the Lisbon earthquake, the *Titanic*, Aberfan—has given thought to better minds than mine, but at least these disasters are external, and can be ascribed to a hostile, ill-ordered universe: not so the violence of our own bodies, as unwilled, as foreordained, as the sliding of mountains, the uprooting of trees, the tidal waves of the sea.

The "fate" that Jane acknowledges has its seat in her "guts" and she claims to be powerless to resist it. "I do not accuse myself of weakness of will. There had been nothing else to do. There had never been a question of choice. There had been nothing in me capable of choosing. I had done what I had to do, I had done what my nature was. . . ." What my *feminine* nature was, she should have said. For as Drabble's language makes clear, Jane is governed by her female sexuality.—ELLEN CRONAN ROSE, *The Novels of Margaret Drabble*, 1980, pp. 52–53

The label "middle-aged" may equally well be applied to Drabble's own vision, for in many of her works she focuses on the compromises and disappointments of adulthood, especially resignation to the fact that one's youthful dreams will never be realized. Although in her later novels she presents certain middle-aged characters who have learned to be content with "life's modest satisfactions" (*Needle's Eye*), the protagonists of her earlier works and some of the younger characters in her later works are acutely distressed by the deflation of these dreams.

The experience of coming to terms with the bleak realities of adult life is the focus of Drabble's first novel, *A Summer Bird-Cage*. The action, which takes place during the year after the protagonist graduates from Oxford, consists of a series of experiences that open her eyes to the discrepancy between her undergraduate dreams and the real world. While at the university Sarah had envisioned a life of moral and aesthetic beauty, friendship, love, and equality, but the life she encounters as a working girl living in a London bedsitter is a far cry from this. Her friendships, in college so lofty and generous, now easily become threatened by petty bickering, for she and her friends find it hard to remain above meanness and irritability when they have to worry about money and scraping along. She is also dismayed by the education she receives about marriage. At Oxford she carried on a sublime, idealistic love affair and is still involved in it long-distance while her boyfriend is spending the year on a fellowship at Harvard. However, her ideals regarding marriage are dealt a severe blow by her exposure to the inadequate marriages of various friends and relatives, many of which deteriorate because of lack of money, a sudden pregnancy, or misunderstanding about roles. But, most important, she discovers that life after college is inevitably a downhill course for women of her generation. Although the novel's action takes place in the early 1960s, women think in terms of either a career or marriage, not both. Yet Sarah, intensely alive both intellectually and emotionally, wants both: "I should like to bear leaves and flowers and fruit, I should like the whole world." She explains to someone who asks her why she has not embarked on an academic career, "You can't be a sexy don." She therefore postpones making a commitment to either marriage or a career for as long as possible, for she knows that as soon as she chooses one she will have to relinquish her dreams of the other.

In other novels Drabble offers portraits of young women who have in fact made the choice of marriage and suffer bitterly from the ensuing constriction of their horizons. Emma Evans, a young wife and mother, forced to give up the prospect of an interesting career in London and move to the provinces because of her husband's job, grimly reflects, "I could hardly believe that marriage was going to deprive me of this too. It had already deprived me of so many things which I had childishly overvalued: my independence, my income, my twenty-two inch waist, my sleep, most of my friends . . . and many more indefinite attributes like hope and expectation" (*Garrick Year*).

Janet Bird and Jane Gray have also been sorely let down by marriage and its accompanying restrictions. They have consequently grown indifferent toward life. Emma sums up this feeling of lost possibilities when she muses, "what had happened to me, that I, who had seemed cut out for some extremity or other, should be here now bending over a washing machine to pick out a button or two and some bits of soggy wet cotton? What chances were there now for the once-famous Emma, whose name had been in certain small exclusive circles the cause for so much discussion and prediction?"

Drabble's theme of the disappointment of youthful dreams is particularly poignant when she applies it to working-class characters. In her short story "The Gifts of War" (1970), the protagonist's adult life, which consists of penury, hard work, and a violent marriage, is a grim contrast to the future she had envisioned as an adolescent. With bitter irony the woman recalls the hopes she and her girlhood friends once harbored:

> [she was] penniless then as now, but still hopeful, still endowed with the touching faith that if by some miracle she could buy a pair of nylons or a particular blue lace blouse or a new brand of lipstick, then deliverance would be granted to her in the form of money, marriage, romance, the visiting prince who would glimpse her in the crowd, glorified by that seductive blouse, and carry her off to a better world. She could remember so well how hopeful they had been: even Betty Jones, fat, monstrous, ludicrous Betty Jones had cherished such rosy illusions. . . . Time had taught Betty Jones: she shuffled now in shoes cracked and splitting beneath her weight. Time had taught them all. The visiting prince, whom need and desire had once truly transfigured in her eyes, now lay there at home in bed, stubbly, disgusting, ill, malingering, unkind: she remembered the girl who had seen such other things in him with a contemptuous yet pitying wonder.

Eileen Sharkey, Rose Vassiliou's nineteen-year-old neighbor in *The Needle's Eye*, is another working-class girl with similar notions about escaping her squalid, tedious existence. She dreams of being a "Spanish duchess, or a wicked woman, or a make-up girl at the B.B.C." Mistakenly assuming, as does the protagonist of "The Gifts of War," that love and marriage will effect the glorious life she desires, she hurls herself into an affair and gets pregnant. But the man won't marry her and she is left facing her dreary life, stuck in it forever, she realizes, now that she is saddled with a baby. Rose, gazing at Eileen's glum, depressed countenance, sadly observes, "There she sat, nineteen, finished, excluded forever from what she might want to be." Rose further reflects on what a terrible moment it is when "one abandons possibility. Gone was Eileen the wicked lady, driving around in taxis, wearing fur coats, drinking cocktails: gone was Eileen the make-up girl with false eyelashes and a pink overall: gone was Eileen the garage man's girl, taking trips up the motorway in a fast car."

Drabble, then, repeatedly emphasizes the powerlessness of human beings against the inimical conditions of life. While this concern appears in all of her fiction, it does not become the central focus of a work until *The Ice Age*. Drabble here makes use of the medieval wheel-of-fortune concept, presenting a wide range of characters who have recently plummetted

from fortunate to unfortunate situations. Anthony Keating has suffered a sudden, premature heart attack and lost a great deal of money in the recent property slump. Alison Murray's teenage daughter has been imprisoned and sentenced to hard labor for her part in a fatal accident in a Balkan communist country. Kitty and Max Friedmann were celebrating their Ruby wedding anniversary in a Mayfair restaurant when an IRA bomb exploded, killing Max and maiming Kitty. Len Wincobank, a fallen real-estate tycoon, has been banished to prison for having bribed a town councillor in an effort to redeem a property investment. The particular woes of the individual characters are set against the background of the public woes of contemporary Britain: the collapsing economy, workers' strikes, the Irish troubles, and Britain's shrinking international prestige and power.—Mary Hurley Moran, "Drabble's Dark Universe," *Margaret Drabble*, 1983, pp. 23–26

Works

NOVELS

In a number of respects *The Millstone* presents a twentieth-century version of a moral fable. It is contemporary in its reliance on existential themes and on the burdens of choice falling on the individual, yet it resembles the earlier moral fable in that it can serve as an object lesson for young women of the present time—a lesson in freedom as possibility. As a result of Rosamund's commitment to her pregnancy and subsequently to Octavia, she achieves a true synthesis both within herself and with the outside world. Rosamund's growth of character is accomplished by her own experiencing of inner depth. With her particular millstone, with the accompanying lonely and emotional handling of her burden, Rosamund is forced to stop and to become aware of herself. On her way into space and time Rosamund Stacey changes the workings of her inner world and, in relation to the outside world, changes herself. As a result of her millstone, she regains the lost dimension of depth in her own life. She learns to love. Given who she is and the basic honesty of her confrontations with the world, she paradoxically opens for herself the possibilities of freedom. As Camus' Sisyphus finds joy within the confinements of his existence, so does Rosamund when she accepts the "no choice" of her predicament:

> As so often in life, it was impossible to choose, even theoretically, between advantage and disadvantage, between profit and loss: I was up quite unmistakably against No Choice. So the best one could do was to put a good face on it, and to avoid adding to the large and largely discussed number of sad warnings that abounded in the part of the world that I knew. I managed very well, and the general verdict was, Extraordinary Rosamund, she really seems happy.

With Rosamund's confrontation of the "no choice" situation she launches her personal movement from naivete to knowledge and more, for Rosamund in telling her story reaches out to others in order that they might profit from what she has learned. The point of view of *The Millstone* is that of a feminine "I" narrator who views and describes herself in a scene of complexity and who as a consequence comes to understand and to define her own values in more concrete terms. Indeed, *The Millstone* can be viewed as an updated version of what might appear to be a humorously loving version of didactic literature for the education and edification of today's young women, as well as the portrayal of one young woman's growth of self-understanding.—Nancy S. Hardin, "Drabble's *The Millstone*: A Fable for Our Times," *Crt*, Autumn 1973, pp. 25–26

The direction in which Rosamund's "moral fable" finally moves, I think, is of questioning the Christian/Rousseauian/Marxian ethic underlying the modern welfare state. Man is not master of his fate and the notion of universal brotherhood is a lie. "Whoso shall offend one of these little ones which believe in me," the passage in Matthew reads from which the title of the novel is taken, "it were better that a millstone were hanged about his neck, and that he were drowned in the depths of the sea." And who is it that offends him? The hosts of babes crying in the wards make their accusatory reply. And whom do they believe in? Octavia's radiantly smiling face as she greets her mother, who had "deserted" her for a day, provides an equally certain answer. The state as God cannot escape responsibility and hence hanging with a millstone of guilt. For a child the true God is the parent, and only through the parent's love can the millstone be avoided. For the millstone is part of man's satanic machine; the mother, part of divine Nature's.

As if to make certain that this point shall not be lost on the reader, the novel concludes on Christmas Eve, with another "accidental" meeting of George and Rosamund. Rosamund, the suggestion seems to be, is Mary, a "virgin" who has given birth to a child; George is Joseph, a father who is nevertheless not a father. The message of this modern Christmas, however, is not one of universal love and brotherhood. Sitting across from George, Rosamund feels sorely tempted to break out into screams once more, this time of "I love you." But she restrains herself. The spark of love requires enormous voltage and the space it can leap is very small; it extends to Octavia but not to George. The Christmas message here is "love thyself," or love extensions of thyself, for that is all you can ever love. Even George, it appears, could once have entered into this narrow circle of possible love because he so very much resembles Rosamund. At the time of their brief physical encounter Rosamund had already sensed this, wondering if her reticence were not matched by his. Now the identification is explicit. "I neither envied nor pitied his indifference," she reflects, as they both gaze upon the sleeping child, "for he was myself, the self that but for accident, but for fate, but for chance, but for womanhood, I would still have been." The love for George has been displaced by love for Octavia, because finally Octavia, even more than he, is herself.—PETER E. FIRCHOW, "Rosamund's Complaint: Margaret Drabble's *The Millstone*," *Old Lines, New Forces*, ed. Robert K. Morris, 1976, pp. 107–108

The heroine of *The Realms of Gold* is an archaeologist, who has travelled in such realms, but her real realm of gold is her middle age. Frances at forty—rather younger, but not too much, than our other middle aged heroines—is 'as lively as anything, digging her garden, painting walls, writing articles, riding' because she has laid firm hands on the freedoms of the twentieth century, demanding her own divorce, using her disliked ex-husband's second wife as a competent carer for her children when she wants to go abroad, and choosing her own true love. Her creator gives Frances a little help by decreeing that her lover's wife shall turn lesbian, a novel device, as convenient and improbable as the death of Mr Casaubon. (There is no doubt about it, Mr Casaubon would have lingered well into his nineties with proper care—Mr Lydgate's, not George Eliot's.)

This novel spares nothing—Frances' scarred body, by childbirth and exertion, her coarse hair, her bad teeth; her lover would not mind them, he was not so much better himself. But perhaps love so true could have seen her through before—with her own husband, or her lover with his wife—if the loss of beauty is to be easily borne. This was a book in a hurry, no getting away from it.

It has points in it of great value. If women are, and indeed they are really going to be forty, with twenty or thirty good years to go before they can consider getting old, then they have until forty, if they care to take the time, to make all the arrangements for their lives which they used to have to complete in their early twenties; they have extra good years to get love, children, work gathered under their roof.

Then it was a book dealing with a theme extremely rare today, perhaps because it is so hard to handle, of happy love; where the presence of the beloved is a paramount good, where there is time and to spare.

However, reading about Frances Wingate bounding about so confidently and affectionately I wondered just what Margaret Drabble was up to. It is a defiantly, blatantly optimistic novel from a professed pessimist. My mind kept returning to Charlotte Brontë's plea to fathers, where she promises that if they will relieve, by letting them work outside the home, the torture of women's boredom their daughters will be their 'tenderest props in age'—that men will gain much and lose nothing by the change. Is *The Realms of Gold* up to the same thing? Is it saying that if the world will help women to work, love them through their less glamorous years, help them in youth not to be housebound and alone with children, let them in fact have a nice time—oh, then the world will see how loving women will be to men, how gay they will remain, how much money they will earn, how they will never grumble or cling? Charlotte Brontë was writing about a state she didn't herself believe could ever really come about. She was pretty much of a pessimist. And she was wrong; it came in the end.—ANTHEA ZEMAN, "New Roads to Madness," *Presumptuous Girls*, 1977, pp. 149–50

The Garrick Year records the process by which female identity often is destroyed. The sphere in which Emma is visible shrinks as the novel progresses. Instead of being engaged in television broadcasting—and therefore being everywhere visible—she spends her energies in a clandestine love affair, being everywhere hidden. Unable to consummate the affair, choosing motherhood over sexuality, Emma, at the end, is trapped in absolute privacy, neither seeing herself clearly nor allowing herself to be seen by others:

> But as I passed, walking slowly, supported by David, I looked more closely and I saw curled up and clutching at the sheep's belly a real snake. I did not say anything to David: I did not want to admit that I had seen it, but I did see it. I can see it still. It is the only wild snake that I have ever seen. In my book on Herefordshire it says that that part of the country is notorious for its snakes. But "Oh well, so what," is all that one can say, the Garden of Eden was crawling with them, too, and David and I managed to lie amongst them for one whole pleasant afternoon. One just has to keep on and to pretend, for the sake of the children, not to notice. Otherwise one might just as well stay at home.

At the end of this rather weak novel, Drabble indicts her heroine for the self-indulgence in her confusion: the image and therefore Emma's pat dismissal of it are disturbing. What Emma sees suggests a perverse and consuming motherhood, precisely what she herself has suffered throughout the novel. Her failure to think seriously about the implications of that image reflects her failure to take seriously the implications of her own life: she has already announced that she is going to repeat the sacrifice of her own interests, represented by the year at Hereford, in a trip to the East Indies. When Emma airily dispenses with the threatening overtones of her vision and justifies the dismissal with that lame saw "for the sake of the children," Drabble implies that the child Emma is protecting is Emma herself.—JOAN MANHEIMER, "Margaret Drabble and the Journey to the Self," *SLI*, Fall 1978, p. 131

Janet Bird in Margaret Drabble's *The Realms of Gold* (1975) can contemplate disaster with some satisfaction. Although she does not, in the course of the novel, leave her immature, domineering husband nor her baby, she frequently indulges in fantasies of disasters; she tries to imagine something that will improve her life, something like "a cataclysm, a volcano, a fire, an outbreak of war, anything to break the unremitting nothingness of her existence." Only a change on the order of a geological revolution will help her domestic doldrums, so radical is the change she perceives as necessary. Drabble's narrator ponders the rooted myth of sacrificial domesticity which limits Janet: "Society offers Pyrex dishes and silver teaspoons as bribes, as bargains, as anesthesia against self-sacrifice. Stuck about with silver forks and new carving knives, as in a form of acupuncture, the woman lays herself upon the altar, upon the couch, half numb." Janet's cousin, Dr. Frances Wingate, who is both a scientist and a mother, has quite evidently awakened from her numbness, and literally tossed away the trappings of bridal sacrifice by divorcing her husband. One evening she threw all of her coffee cups at his head, one by one, "and advised him to get out of the house forever. He had done as advised." Frances's comic understatement here expresses her easy strength and her confidence in her ability to meet a crisis, or even to perpetrate one. When a situation is intolerable, she can take action—and smile at the action later.

Janet cannot take action so easily; she tries to be content with fantasies of cataclysm. Late one evening she pours hot wax from a candle into an ashtray decorated with a zodiac design. She wonders if people, seeing her, might think her a witch. She sits, "pouring wax onto an ancient symbol, pointlessly. If disinterred as from the ruins of Pompeii, what little rite would it be assumed she had been enacting, what gods would she have been seen to propitiate?" Janet is truly an "underground" figure, playing at swamping the entire zodiac in hot wax from the "hollow green crater in the wide candle." She see herself as oppressed, buried, interred; naturally, she envisions a volcanic eruption.

She is also drawn to books about military eruptions; she reads novelistic accounts of war and concentration camps. In one novel dealing with these grim subjects, she reads about a Jewish woman who tosses her baby from the window of a train as it moves toward a concentration camp. Janet reflects on the episode:

> She had thrown the baby into the arms of a Polish peasant woman, who was hoeing the turnip field, and as the train moved on inexorably to extinction, the Polish woman and the Jewish woman had exchanged looks of profound significance, and the Polish woman had picked up the baby and had embraced and kissed it with a promise of devotion as the train moved out of sight.

Janet wonders if she likes such stories because of the "death and the destruction? Or the baby salvaged and harvested like a turnip from the field?" The unexpectedness, the inappropriateness almost, of comparing a baby to a turnip, and especially in circumstances so painful and desperate, indicate Janet's wry distance from her own despair. She feels that she would almost like to toss away her own baby, Hugh; she suspects that she is not the best mother for him, but she knows too that there is "no way of getting off this train." She will have to raise her turnip herself.

The imagery of two women and a baby assumes a symbolic aura during Janet's visit to her great aunt Constance Ollerenshaw's dilapidated house on the outskirts of Tockley. After struggling along a path overgrown with tangled foliage, Janet sees the partially boarded-up cottage where her aunt lives. Suddenly Aunt Connie's threatening face appears at a window. Aunt Connie angrily shakes a stick and raps on the window; a dog barks, and Janet fears that it will be let loose. She hastily places a box of Black Magic chocolates on the windowsill, and retreats, remembering that her aunt has the reputation of being a witch. And yet, Aunt Connie apparently wants to see the baby: "And Janet turned again, the last time, human, and she picked up her baby so that Great-Aunt Con could see him. Con stopped rapping, and stared. Hugh slept on, wrapped up in his baby blanket. A curious family group." It is a very ancient family group. This scene in a modern novel is almost an archetypal tableau of the Demeter and Persephone figures whose images recur in the prehistoric art of the Mediterranean area. Often the two female gods (mother and daughter, but essentially one god) were represented in sculpture with a baby between them, an infant passing from one to the other as though from life to death or from death to life. On some antique vases, a baby is portrayed sitting in a cornucopia which is held by Ge ("Earth," the mother of all the gods) as she rises from the ground; she extends the cornucopia and the baby toward Demeter. Interpreted symbolically, the scene between Janet and Aunt Connie, along with the scene from the novel Janet was reading, suggest a psychological regeneration, a passage from death to life. The baby represents not only itself, but Janet's rescuing of herself, we can assume, from psychological collapse or despair. The myth by which this regeneration is implied belongs to an antique female resurrection-fertility myth rather than to a male one.—JUDY LITTLE, "Feminist Comedy," *Comedy and the Woman Writer*, 1983, pp. 184–86

ESSAYS AND BELLES LETTRES

Arnold Bennett . . . is someone I have always felt warmly about; so too is Margaret Drabble, though I hadn't realized until now that perhaps the sources of these warm feelings were similar. Bennett was from Stoke-on-Trent, Drabble is from Sheffield, and while both eagerly left home and never wished to return, Bennett in his major novels and Drabble (in part by her reading of those novels) realized the hold these industrial midlands cities still had on them. There is a moment, in *The Summer Bird-Cage*, I think, when a Drabble heroine at a party or a fancy London pub finds herself thinking that the real London is not where she is but in the Long Acre, where the fruit and veg people work. Most of Bennett's life was like that; he wanted to be at the party, on the yacht, in the nightclub dancing, but real life, he knew, was elsewhere, in the Five Towns, in the Long Acre, or Sheffield. When Drabble discovered these qualities in herself, she knew how much Bennett had articulated them for her, and in this book she wants to pay homage to what he did for her and others like her. Given the special nature of Bennett's life—a hugely industrious (one almost wants to say industrialized) writer, immensely successful and quite wealthy, yet able to write at his best only about his grim home county—biography hardly seems the right form. The farther he got from the Five Towns, the more he enjoyed himself, the kinder he may have become, but the less there is to say about him. Drabble realizes this, says at the outset she will concentrate on "Bennett's background, his childhood and origins," which she does, but still, the great things here are all in the first part. After Bennett becomes a public success Drabble keeps at it, but it is work, for her and her reader. Until then, however, she does magnificently. It is like a Bennett novel, warm and detailed, rich in its sense of the past, unstinting in his exposure of meannesses and failings, yet fully assured that the truth will set free both subject and biographer.

The great mark of Drabble's assurance is her almost total lack of needless self-consciousness. She knows all her material is relevant somehow, and trusts it, so that the early chapters are filled with commentary on *The Old Wives' Tale* and the *Clayhanger* trilogy, used as illuminations of places, people, and feelings of Bennett's life; she knows, and so never needs to question, the way art is and isn't life, the way Bennett is and isn't Edwin Clayhanger, his father is and isn't Darius Clayhanger, his mother is and isn't Auntie Hamps. Likewise, she knows her own life is relevant here and brings it in easily and gracefully, again in perfect trust that she is right to do so.

. . . What Drabble wants to do, what she succeeds admirably in doing, is to tell the story of the life so that it recreates the sources and circumstances of the major novels, and so that, in turn, the novels can do the same for the life; and she does this by implicitly insisting that we ask ourselves all over again the terms by which we value writers we may value more highly than Bennett. The major explicit comparison she asks us to draw is with Virginia Woolf, for obvious reasons. It was Woolf who put Bennett down in her famous speech about Mrs. Brown, and when he is put down to this day it is usually in Woolf's terms; it was Woolf who represented, or at least seems to represent, a standard of social awareness and sensitivity whereby Bennett could be judged as a provincial stammerer; it is her novels whose air of the importance of private intensity seems designed to make Bennett's seem eternal and thingy; it is Woolf about whom Drabble herself wrote movingly a few years ago, as a sign that she had finally come to see the virtues of a writer whose social class and novelistic manner had hitherto seemed to her remote and overrated.

. . . Drabble's great virtue is her way of making Bennett a novelist, a man most alive in his fictions, without using biography simply as a coatrack for criticism, so that her plea for a kind of fiction is also her plea for a kind of human being. Bennett could be extremely artful, but he had no art, and only the most simple kind of professional guile; in addition, after he had found his métier in a few novels, he could not sustain it because the life of the Five Towns did not continue to interest him, even as memory. He was cut off from his past and never tried, as Aldous Huxley did, to break the mold of his life after it had once been formed, and he could not, as Trollope did, go on writing one big novel after another because of the terms his life established. So be.—Roger Sale, "Huxley and Bennett, Bedford and Drabble," *HdR*, Summer 1975, pp. 289–92

⟨*A Writer's Britain*⟩ is not a comprehensive study of all British writers who were affected by landscape, nor of all landscapes in Britain that affected writers. Nor does it purport to come to any decisive conclusions to which every writer and landscape cited is expected to make a dialectic contribution. It is, rather, a long ramble among writers whom Ms Drabble enjoys, with substantial quotations from their works bearing upon landscape, and her own comments on these and on the social conditions and attitudes which influenced them. It is thus hardly possible to 'review', except by rambling likewise in an equally subjective manner.

An example of her method (not random, but picked because I have recently been rereading *Bleak House*: and because not long ago I made my first trip to Lincolnshire and was surprised how like it was to what I had imagined from reading Tennyson):

Other writers describing Lincolnshire are full of Tennysonian echoes, inevitably. Dickens, the least enervating of writers, seems subdued by the scenery, and produces in *Bleak House* a dreariness that rivals the master's. . . .'The waters are out in Lincolnshire. The arch of the bridge in the park has been sapped and sopped away . . . etc.' An acquired taste, perhaps, this kind of atmosphere—but Tennyson acquired it early and passed it on to others. On leaving Somersby . . . he wrote to a friend, 'A known landskip is to me an old friend that continually talks to me of my youth and half forgotten things. . . .'

In short this is a book to dip into and browse about until you find a passage that meets your mood—a most unfashionable recommendation these days. The sterner student will no doubt mutter about self-indulgent nostalgia and ornaments for the 'coffee-table' of the leisured and loathsome monetarist. There is admittedly a great deal of nostalgia invoked, which is why I spoke of melancholy: though it is the nostalgia not of Ms Drabble (whose observations are often acid), but of the writers she quotes, nearly all of whom, from the earliest times have seen landscape as something they had known as children that is no longer what it was, or what they thought it was, or what a previous generation had hoped it to be. . . .

My emotion was purely derived from the mutability of familiar artefacts: and landscape in Britain is the biggest artefact of all, jungles and desert being outwith Ms Drabble's chosen boundaries. And yet, for some reason, throughout all of Jorge Lewinski's exquisite photographs that accompany her writing, there are hardly any people. It is not that the text ignores people. Ms Drabble herself, and those whom she quotes, are constantly discussing the human beings who inhabit the British landscape. But whatever they say, or whatever she says about them, is constantly undercut by these funereal images of strange empty fields, hills, woods, houses, gardens, streets, until—from the look of the book alone—one might think that our country was newly visited by the neutron bomb.

I don't understand this: some readers won't like it at all: others will enjoy it too much—people suggest politics *and we don't want to know*—(consider the violent response of certain right-wing art-critics recently to a colleague's mild suggestion that Constable's paintings were unpeopled because the artist had problems about his father being Boss of the Stour): but altogether it contributes to a very odd complex of emotions which goes far beyond the normal requirements of the Christmas-time fine-art market.—John Arden, "Inclosure like a Buonaparte," *NS*, Dec. 7, 1976, pp. 903–4

MARGARET DRABBLE
"A Woman Writer" (1973)
On Gender and Writing
ed. Michelene Wandor
1983, pp. 156–59

I have spent so long pondering the advantages and disadvantages of being a woman writer that on some issues I have thoroughly confused myself. I think I hold the position that as there is nothing wrong with being a woman (a bold enough statement in some ways) so there is nothing wrong with being a woman writer. One should object to being described as a lady novelist, but only on grounds of terminology. There is nothing pejorative about being described as a woman novelist, for women have always been as good at the job as men. I never thought of looking for an insult in the phrase, just as it never occurs to me that it is an insult to be described as an English writer, or a British writer, or even as a writer born in Yorkshire. It is a fact, that's all. And some women novelists are very different from men novelists. Some aren't. As a sexual adjective in this context can only be descriptive, and not discriminative, I don't see why one should object to it, as some do. But I haven't always thought this, and maybe I will change my mind yet again, when some new evidence of real discrimination and prejudice, from a reader or a reviewer, is brought my way. I simply discount people who say they don't read women novelists. They probably don't read men novelists either. Why should they? I don't particularly want everyone to read my books. I wouldn't mind being described as a woman doctor, or a woman pilot, if I were one, so long as it didn't imply that I was bad at the job. And I think women who feel that they object to being called women writers show a certain lack of confidence in their own work. But I may of course be wrong. I've no intention of being dogmatic about the issue.

It is true that in some areas one does meet a positive hostility towards the woman writer. Some men simply don't like women who do anything at all, out of unthinking traditional prejudice, or out of real fear. Some people, of both sexes, don't like what women have to say these days—Edna O'Brien has said so many unwelcome truths that she has been attacked in the most unreasonable terms by the most reasonable of people, and the issue here is surely sexual. And some men quite genuinely, and with some cause, resent the apparently superior freedom of the woman writer. This issue is bound up with so many others that it can hardly be distinguished, but it's something I'd like to discuss here, because I haven't seen it discussed often before. A few years ago I think I said to some interviewer that I thought some women found it easier to settle down to writing than men because they had husbands to support them, therefore they didn't have to (and in many cases, because of small children, couldn't) work: this was interpreted by another paper, which I think I would have tried to sue if I had read it in time, as my saying that all women novelists including myself lived off their husbands and wrote for amusement. That's not the point for the moment: the point is, is it true that women are at a positive advantage in the career of novelist, because they don't have to earn their livings? To some women, this is clearly an irrelevant issue, but what of those married women who write while their children are small, and succeed in establishing themselves? Would they have had the energy to do it, if they had had to work full time at something else? There have been plenty of writers in the last decade who have started work in precisely this way—one could say that the poor things wrote bitterly out of frustration, loneliness and misery, or one could say that they were lucky to be given the chance and the leisure to feel such productive emotions. (Several men I know, it must be admitted, have been propelled to write by exactly the same emotions—one, doing a very dull job packing exam papers, took a box of paper home in desperation and wrote his first successful work.) Men evidently do resent the feeling that women are leisurely part-time workers, free to dabble in non-remunerative pursuits: Auberon Waugh once reviewed a novel by Nina Bawden by commenting on the fact that it was all very well for lady writers to write when their husbands could support them by good jobs in the BBC. Doctors and lawyers have said to me that if they didn't have a job to do and a family to keep, they too could write. I usually reply by saying that many women have families to keep and do other jobs as well as writing novels, but I rarely quite have the nerve to take the next political step, which is to assert that rearing

small children is extremely arduous, and that anyone who has the energy to write novels at the same time is not a dilettante but a miracle of will power and perseverance, employing more energy a day than most men in most jobs I have observed.

There is, however, a real problem here. I met a friend the other day, a writer, who had just returned from a visit to the States, and she said that a pattern was developing there whereby the husband, who had a good well-paid job, would quite often take three days at home with the children, while his wife went off 'to try to be a writer'. I don't know what I feel about this. I ought to approve but I'm not sure if I do. The other thing that worries me slightly is that women seem at times to get positively preferential treatment, once they are established. Getting oneself established may be a sweat, but once a woman has made it—this is true in any sphere—how the press and television will love her, particularly if she is reasonably photogenic and smiles a lot in a suitable feminine manner. Out of a group of mixed writers, it is usually the woman who gets photographed, interviewed, asked to sit on committees. I am not quite sure what one's political response to this ought to be. How should one react to the role of being the statutory woman writer in a gathering? Demand equal representation? Refuse to serve? Graciously accept, as one might an offered seat in a tube, or a hand with one's luggage?

These might seem trivial issues, but they're not really, they are the stuff of daily life. And they do also point to the area in which I think women now may have the most profound and well-earned advantages: the area of subject matter. It is commonplace to deplore the dearth of large or heroic issues in Britain today—how much better to have Vietnam, how much finer to write of South Africa. The British novel will die without its causes. But women have causes still—plenty of them, as the growing interest in Women's Liberation demonstrates. And the novel is the ideal place to voice them, discuss them, try them out. The large amount of fiction written by women in the last decade, since the highly significant publication of Doris Lessing's *Golden Notebook*, bears witness that a lot of women started to worry about the same things at the same time, and turned to fiction to express their anxieties—not only because, traditionally, and despite the spread of education, they still had nowhere else to turn, but also because fiction is ideally suited to such themes. Many of the Women's Liberation proposals cannot be brought about through a change in the law (though some can and should)—they are matter of a shift in public opinion, a change in attitude of women to themselves, of men to women, of women to men. These shifts and changes cover every area of human life, from the most incidental to the most profound: they involve how we behave socially, at parties and after parties, how we spend our money, how we treat our employers and our employees, how we behave sexually and domestically. Many people read novels in order to find patterns or images for a possible future—to know how to behave, what to hope to be like. We do not want to resemble the women of the past, but where is our future? This is precisely the question that many novels written by women are trying to answer: some in comic terms, some in tragic, some in speculative. We live in an unchartered world, as far as manners and morals are concerned, we are having to make up our own morality as we go. Our subject matter is enormous, there are whole new patterns to create. There is no point in sneering at women writers for writing of problems of sexual behaviour, of maternity, of gynaecology—those who feel the need to do it are actively engaged in creating a new pattern, a new blueprint. This area of personal relationships verges constantly on the political: it is not a narrow backwater of introversion, it is the main current which is changing the daily quality of our lives. The truest advantage of being a woman writer now is that never before, perhaps, have women had so much to say, and so great a hope of speaking to some effect.

VIRGINIA K. BEARDS
From "Margaret Drabble: Novels of a Cautious Feminist"
Critique, Autumn 1973, pp. 35–46

Margaret Drabble's bleak pessimism regarding love, marriage, and the casual disasters besetting the female locked into heterosexuality and a less radical life style is the focus of her first five novels, written since 1964. Published and praised in England, she seems little read in the United States, a transatlantic reader's loss since the currency of her vision is remarkable.

Bungled and achieved female self-definition is her consistent theme; her women might set out to pay homage to patriarchy's dearest forms but en route their increasing awareness of the absurdity of their sexual, social, and economic positions results in their befuddlement and defeat within the system. Only occasionally and in a limited sense do her women manage to infiltrate intellectually or economically the masculine milieu. Drabble turns to the novel to explore the various options of women today; she evidently lacks the idealism that active feminist politics demands while her awareness of human inequities needs no heightening through consciousness raising sessions. The conversion of the sexual protest into novels is what makes her interesting. The choices of artist over activist and imitation over frontal attack allow a subtlety and sensitivity that politics frequently precludes.

Margaret Drabble leisurely inspects patterns of female development and the nuances of both male oppression and sexual liberation; unlike her political counterpart who is sustained by a vision of a new order, Drabble's outlook is grim. Her conclusions are often nihilistic and suggest sexual tyranny is here to stay, a component of a deterministic universe. Neither a missionary, an idealist, nor a prophet, Drabble offers the reader practical imitations of the real world. The novels incisively diagnose female complaints while avoiding talky and dubious prognoses and treatment programs; rhetoric and wish-fulfillment are, mercifully, out of bounds in her work. Because the English novel has traditionally contributed to social reform through its criticism of social inequities, the enduring gains in woman's rights may as well be made by cautious and introspective artists, such as Drabble, as by the movement's activists and political theoreticians.

The inevitable problems of the mid-twentieth-century woman provide the specific plot complications in all Drabble's novels; both female and male character is revealed and developed in relation to familiar feminist issues of education, sexuality, marriage, motherhood, and economic dependence. Take education. Three ideas from theorist Kate Millett are relevant to a reading of Drabble as an artist working with a common ideology. Millett argues that the equation of knowledge with power results in the "fairly systematic ignorance patriarchy imposes on women."[1] Expanding the idea she considers the education women receive when they slip by the sexual screening processes of higher learning or when they seek refuge in a woman's college. She notes that women often pursue studies that are anachronistic; males enter scientific and technological disciplines crucial to our age while women usually

genteelly commit themselves in their studies to the ideals of renaissance humanism. (What an irony, when one considers that the "liberal arts" originally referred to the studies available to a "free man"—one who was not a serf!) Millett concludes female education in the humanities "is hardly more than an extension of the 'accomplishments' they once cultivated in preparation for the marriage market."

In Drabble's first novel, *A Summer Bird-Cage* (1963), Sarah comes down from Oxford with "a lovely, shiny, useless new degree," goes to Paris to tutor French girls privately—a course that one cannot imagine a male "first" following—and after a few months is relieved when her sister's imminent wedding provides an excuse to return to England. School-marming it in Paris lacks both seriousness and future to a girl who had in happier days headily opened a college essay on Hobbes with: "In the *Leviathan* Hobbes demonstrates nothing adequately except the limitations of his own studybound conception of human nature." Her return to England somewhat heightens her awareness of sexual inequality yet she never frees herself enough from sexual conditioning to act on her own behalf. She becomes rather vaguely employed at the BBC "filing things" and rejects an academic career. Her explanation as to why she will not become a don indites everyone's absurd attitudes to the female out of the kitchen or bedroom:

> I used to fancy myself as one [a don]. But I'll tell you what's wrong with that. It's sex. You can't be a sexy don. It's all right for men being learned and attractive, but for a woman it's a mistake. It detracts from the essential seriousness of the business. . . . You'd soon find yourself having to play it down instead of up if you wanted to get to the top, and when you've only got one life that seems a pity.[2]

But the choice is not easy. She lunches with academic friends of her research scientist fiance who is currently working in America. They kindly invite her out in the spirit of "for old times' sake" yet the experience underlines for her the secondary status of the educated woman within patriarchy:

> It was a nice thought, and a nice lunch, but it made me feel curiously passe, and I felt the impulse to tell everyone that I had got a degree too, as good as any of theirs, which is always a danger signal. I resisted it. . . . I felt as though everyone else was leading a marvellous progressive life except me, and I had been subtly left behind.

The title of the novel comes from John Webster's lovely simile, "'Tis just like a summer bird cage in a garden/the birds that are without despair to get/in, and the birds that are within despair and are in a consumption for fear they shall never get out." It indicates Drabble's artistic preoccupation: the themes of sexual conflict and domestic entrapment are developed in relation to several other "birds" as well as Sarah. Her sister, Louise, splendidly drunk and in dirty underwear, puts on an elegant white bridesdress to marry a wealthy, irascible homosexual novelist as a way out of "the secretarial course-coffee bar degradation" that London offers her. Her bizarre alternative shows the enormity of the marriage value in her upper middle-class society and, its corollary, female laziness and non-aggression. Sarah's roommate, Gillian, has just flown the cage by walking out on her painter-husband who demanded her services as model, domestic, and sexual partner. Drabble's clear vision of the damaged female ego is never better than in the anecdote Gillian tells about her marriage. After bitterly complaining of her boredom to her husband—she said she felt like a "still life"—he cruelly pushed canvas, paints, and brushes at her and, anticipating his triumph, gamefully ordered her to paint him. Of course, she failed; her art work was, by her own admission, like a child's. The anecdote implies much that is apropos to the sexual battle as seen by both the novelist and women's liberation activists: the woman is conditioned to accept a role, but she is unhappy being treated as an incompetent child in some things and as a capable helpmate in others. Her latent abilities, talents, and any shreds of skill in the male realm are discouraged until she becomes, in fact, truly incapacitated. As this point the egocentric male mate can breathe a sigh of relief and carry on unharassed. To Gillian, a female of developing consciousness, her status in a marriage of this type is untenable and so, like Nora, she leaves.

Drabble's consideration of what often happens to intelligent but traditionally educated women in marriage is further developed in her later novels. *The Garrick Year* (1964) opens with a chilling scene in which Emma Evans, its central character, is literally being devoured by men. As she sits nursing her voracious infant son, she is verbally assaulted by her actor-husband who informs her that in the interest of his career they are going to move to a provincial town with a prestigious repertory theater. The move spells both physical and mental hardship. In addition to its logistics, she will have to turn down an offer in television—ironically, by a company which was going "to have another attempt at the equality of the sexes by allowing women to announce serious events as well as forthcoming programmes"—that would have got her out of her London nursery and back into life. Exhausted and aware that arguing will make her milk stop and thus her child will be badgering her all night, she sits passively listening in a classic double bind—damned if she responds to her husband and damned if she does not. A pathetic fear of loneliness, belief in family unity, plus a twisted commitment to the concept of marriage keeps Emma from wishing her husband farewell and sending him off to the provinces. Her devotion to the marriage is suspect since she has rejected him sexually and, in fact, practices sexual appeasement in finally agreeing to the provincial theater adventure. She says yes to the move in bed that night in return for his consent "to be understanding about having his hand pushed off my thighs, in view of Joseph [the baby] and my weariness." . . .

Clara Maugham in *Jerusalem the Golden* (1967) also shows female aimlessness caused by the pressure of cultural values. She drifts into graduate school in London because she cannot face the drabness of life in her provincial town, while her friend, Clelia, finds her marginal job in an art gallery has become a baby-sitting service for its owner. The nearly catatonic Jane Gray of *The Waterfall* (1969) is a minor poet who has ceased writing with the onset of marriage. She resumes writing only after turning her sexually chauvinistic husband out and finding an erotically perfect relation with another man. Drabble always keeps her women in the traditional sex role; they love men, not one another. Jane Gray's paradoxical embracing of the so-called male oppressor in order to gain freedom is not, however, presented as an ideal solution. She is emancipated through coitus itself; Drabble insists on emphasizing the void of intellectual, social, and artistic compatibility between the couple. The novel only concedes that better sex makes Jane slightly more functional and diminishes her withdrawal symptoms. The couple's inability to find anything beyond splendid orgasm in their relation heightens her sense of isolation. She considers herself in "sexual bondage" after meeting James.

Unmarried women who operate somewhat outside patriarchal values function better in Drabble's world. With *The Millstone* (1965) she moves away from the traditional woman who stays unhappily married. Here she considers life without marriage or male dominance. The novel suggests a growth in the author's feminist consciousness, a search for alternatives. Educated Rosamund Stacey finds herself pregnant but rejects both abortion and marriage. The knowledge that she is equipped to earn her living as a scholar allows her to remain independent and have the child. She follows an achievement pattern more prevalent with males—her career progresses not in spite of the offspring but because of it. Rosamund's reaction to her dependent is "male"—needing more income she accelerates her scholarly work and is acknowledged accordingly. Conversely, a common middle-class "female" reaction to motherhood is to use it as an excuse not to succeed outside of the home or, indeed, to go out of the home at all. Significantly, Rosamund successfully defines herself in relation to values other than the male-superiority/female-dependency ones of patriarchy.

While Drabble presents women who eventually free themselves from the strictures of marriage and female underachievement, sexual dis-ease is epidemic among them. In her earlier novels sexual intercourse has a variety of distressing attributes: the woman may feel physical pain or tedium, she may trade sex for real security or an imagined need, she may act rather than participate. We have much fake thrashing about and little real passion until *The Waterfall*. Because her women are ill at ease with their bodies in the novels, Drabble's use of the first-person narrative works beautifully. Properly brought up and repressed middle-class women tell their stories; their sexual reticences, silences, and strategies of avoidance result in full-drawn portraits of the class and culturally eroded female libido. For instance, the narrator of *A Summer Bird-Cage* evades describing sex altogether. Marriages fall apart, love affairs are begun, the absent fiance is sorely missed but rarely a word from anyone says what happened in bed. While the novel is surely about marriage and sexual politics as we understand the terms today, passion does not soil its sheets. The focus is on the shifting power relations between lovers and mates, but the narrator, Sarah, neither actively loving nor mating in the novel's present, is saved from having to face sex squarely. Her fiance is away for a year and she is writing both to pass the time and to examine female alternatives from which, presumably, she will eventually have to choose. Accordingly, we have analysis but no explicit presentation of sex. The narrator coolly observes her sister and roommate in and out of marriage, thinks closely about the caging of women in matrimony, and waits "to take up . . . life again" when her fiance returns.

In *The Garrick Year* Drabble wryly deploys on the most subversive sexual myths of our time and moves closer to sex which is, after all, even when not articulated, crucial in her novels. Somewhat surprisingly, the narrator is a twenty-eight-year-old female tease. Unlike *A Summer Bird-Cage* where other people's sexual relations are analyzed by a chaste narrator, the narrator's emotional life is here under scrutiny. Perhaps for the wrong reasons—revenge on an egotistical husband, a need to confirm her continued attractiveness, a desire to be gossiped about, and an urge to snap the dreariness of days spent with two small children and a dependent au pair— Emma Evans drifts into an affair which takes forever to be consummated and, alas, simultaneously finished. As a portrait of the frigid-seductive woman with a muddled concept of both male and female sexual rights, the novel is wise and complete. Emma's absurd relation with Wyndham Farrar, her actor-husband's director, involves covertly wheeling about the Cotswolds in a sportscar and dining in rustic inns. Her pathetic pleasures come from eating avocado pears by candlelight and from the knowledge that "people are talking." Excuses are offered to the lover (and the reader) for her withholding: she is tired from the babies, the doorbell rings. The problem is not temporal, which Emma herself senses when she admits:

> The reluctance was wholly on my side. . . . I simply could not bring myself to do it. Kissing I did not mind: in fact I soon discovered that anything above the waist, so to speak, I did not mind, but that anything below was out of the question. . . . It is quite clear, I suppose, to all, that this pace suited me far more than it suited Wyndham Farrar, men being what they are and women being what they are *said* to be.[3]

The inclusion of "said" presents what the liberation theorists have gone to chapters and even books to express. Here is the woman who has internalized the values of her culture yet who, unfortunately, still wanly questions them. The lingering nineteenth-century myth that women do not enjoy sex is operating here, and the passage anticipates Germaine Greer's theory of the female eunuch. Somewhere under her stunning secondary sex characteristics, Emma's libido stirs feebly although it has been culturally maimed to the extent that she lacks the ability to express it with any sort of elan. She is not supposed to enjoy sex but dimly suspects she could. . . .

The dilemma of the centrality yet inadequacy of heterosexual relations for females runs through all of Drabble's novels but is never as fully expressed until *The Waterfall*. The idea that human happiness is not allowed for in the universal program is ancient, but its clear working out in female terms with the mores of contemporary patriarchal society playing the Furies to the erotically hubris-ridden woman is Drabble's distinctive contribution. Being both a feminist and a compassionate pessimist who can relate isolation to causes deeper than the simply temporal and political, she has an interest also in man, society, and civilization. That she is currently working on a novel told from the masculine point of view comes as no surprise. Margaret Drabble will undoubtedly continue to explore questions that are finally human and impartial to sexual distinction.

Notes

1. Kate Millett, *Sexual Politics* (London, 1971), p. 42.
2. Margaret Drabble, *A Summer Bird-Cage* (London: Weidenfeld and Nicolson, 1963), p. 183–84.
3. Margaret Drabble, *The Garrick Year* (London: Weidenfeld and Nicolson, 1964), p. 128. (My italics.)

JANE CAMPBELL
From "Margaret Drabble and the Search for Analogy"
The Practical Vision
eds. Jane Campbell and James Doyle
1978, pp. 134–43

Even a casual reading reveals that there is a great deal about literature in her novels. As the characters and author search for illumination, other writers' works are used as touchstones or parallels, sometimes as warnings, and as true or false or ambiguous formulas against which the described and lived experiences of her novels are tested. The titles of six of the novels make some allusion to literary works or figures. The first, *A Summer Bird-Cage* (1963), echoes a passage by John Webster about varieties of human entrapment; in this book the young Sarah, with her eyes on her sister's mysteriously unattractive marriage, ponders her own future. *The Garrick Year*

(1964) is about a theatrical marriage and is named for the company of actors to which the husband, David, belongs, and which has taken the couple away from London, where the wife had hopes of a career; the company, of course, is named for the eighteenth-century actor and author. The title of *The Millstone* (1965) alludes to the Biblical warning against the destruction of innocence, and has, according to Margaret Drabble, a double reference, to a burden and to salvation.[1] Its subject is the birth of an illegitimate child and the awakening of maternal love. *Jerusalem the Golden* (1967) borrows from the hymn by J. M. Neale and ironically describes a young girl's escape from provincial life and her quest for love and glamour; the end of the novel, though open, suggests that she has found a false Jerusalem. *The Needle's Eye* (1972), which has been accurately summarized as being about "the difficulties of being good,"[2] refers to the Biblical statement of the incompatibility of riches and eternal life. Rose, its heroine, has chosen to interpret the text in its hardest sense, rejecting the lax modern explanation that the Needle's Eye was simply a narrow gate in Jerusalem. The most recent of the seven, *The Realms of Gold* (1975), derives its title from Keats's sonnet marking the discovery of riches; the most cheerful in outlook, it deals with the unexpected discovery of values in various places. Only *The Waterfall* (1969) lacks a literary title. It is named for its central symbol, which is both a card trick performed by the heroine's lover and a real waterfall in the Pennines. Like the other titles, this one reflects the ambiguities perceived by the author's imagination, since we must consider whether the gift of love and liberation which James gives to Jane is simply a skillful act or an experience of grace. This title thus continues the exploration of artifice and truth which the other titles suggest.

The novels often tell their stories by evoking other stories. Margaret Drabble has said that *Middlemarch* provided the basis for the relationship of the two sisters in *A Summer Bird-Cage* (in the book, Sarah notes that a reunion with Louise was "like something out of *Middlemarch* or even Jane Austen"[3]). The author has also admitted that a passage in *Jerusalem the Golden*, in which Clara reads about her dying mother's youthful hopes and vows to escape her mother's fate of entrapment in a narrow, unfulfilling environment, has analogies in Arnold Bennett (whose biography Drabble has written) and in Maupassant.[4] The knowledgeable reader will also see the implied parallel between Rosamund, the scholarly unwed mother in *The Millstone*, and the heroine of "The Complaint of Rosamund," a poem by Samuel Daniel and one of the subjects of her research.[5] Both Rosamunds must accept the results of lovemaking. Rosamund's flatmate Lydia is a novelist and so is Joe, one of the two men with whom Rosamund has been going out, pretending to each that she is sleeping with the other. The process of turning life into art is graphically demonstrated here, when Rosamund finds that she and her baby Octavia have become material for Lydia's latest novel; she is annoyed by the presentation of herself as an escapist, using her "luxury" research to evade realities, and feels that there is poetic justice in Octavia's destruction of the only copy of the manuscript. In *Jerusalem the Golden* Clara's Jerusalem is embodied in her friendship with the Denham family, with its aura of culture, tradition and love, and the mother of the family has written a novel called *Custom and Ceremony*, taking its title from Yeats's poem "A Prayer for My Daughter." That poem ends with these lines:

> How but in custom and in ceremony
> Are innocence and beauty born?
> Ceremony's a name for the rich horn,
> And custom for the spreading laurel tree.[6]

In the context of Clara's story, which includes an un-ceremonious mating with the married son of the family on the floor of his office, the resonance of these lines is ironic. Earlier, when Clara saw two of the sisters in the family together, she was reminded of Christina Rossetti's "Goblin Market" (p. 128): that story also, with its elements of threatening evil, eroticism and sacrificial love, provides interesting parallels with the main story.

Like their author, Drabble's characters are in the habit of using literature for "guidance or help or illumination."[7] Their lives are concerned with writing in various ways, and literary references come naturally to them. Sarah is a recent graduate of Oxford who as a student prided herself on her essays; her brother-in-law Stephen writes slick, successful novels, and Sarah observes the way in which the social behaviour of their friends becomes transformed into the situations in his books—not, she thinks, with total truthfulness. Besides her thesis, Rosamund writes reviews; she is used to making relationships between life and books, and as she views Octavia's destructive work on Lydia's manuscript she recalls the parallel case of Carlyle and John Stuart Mill. "My mind had always boggled at what Mill had said to Carlyle, at what Carlyle had said to Mill: well, now I had done it. Now I would find out" (pp. 171–72). Sometimes other works provide the basis for a shorthand character sketch, as when Sarah, pondering her sister's enig-matic nature and strangely mechanical marriage, remembers Louise's wedding flowers, a stiff bouquet of lilies, and applies to them a line from Shakespeare's Sonnet 94, "Lilies that fester smell far worse than weeds" (*Bird-Cage*, p. 72). The narrator explains Clara's enjoyment of the plays of Racine and Cor-neille:

> Their ways were hers. For one event, five acts of deliberation. But she played alone, because the other people would not play. And she thought . . . that if she ever could find the personages for the rest of her tragedy, then her happiness would be complete. (*Jerusalem*, p. 65)

What she finds is a clandestine affair with a disillusioned, sad man. The reader measures the gap between Clara's self-seeking dream and the reality. In *The Waterfall*, a much more com-plicated question is examined, and the concern of the reader is directed toward the proper evaluation of Jane's story-telling rather than to the events themselves. Jane's struggle to define the saving qualities of a relationship which is at the same time a routine, even sordid affair is put in terms of Charlotte Brontë's life and art:

> Reader, I loved him: as Charlotte Brontë said. Which was Charlotte Brontë's man, the one she cre-ated and wept for and longed for, or the poor curate that had her and killed her, her sexual measure, her sexual match? (*Waterfall*, p. 89)

Jane has to distinguish among three men (as, in a different way, Charlotte Brontë did): James the common adulterer, James the saviour and rescuer, and Malcolm, who at the end of the book is still her husband. Other fictitious heroines—Sue Bridehead, Maggie Tulliver—haunt her, and indicate the discrepancy and the similarity between two eras of woman's experience.

> But love is nothing new. Even women have suffered from it, in history. It is a classic malady, and com-monly it requires participants of both sexes. Perhaps I'll go mad with guilt, like Sue Bridehead, or drown myself in an effort to reclaim lost renunciations, like Maggie Tulliver. (p. 163)

She continues:

> Maggie Tulliver never slept with her man [who, like Jane's, was her cousin Lucy's husband]: she did all the damage there was to be done, to Lucy, to herself, to the two men who loved her, and then, like a woman of another age, she refrained. In this age, what is to be done? We drown in the first chapter. I worry about the sexual doom of womanhood, its sad inheritance. (p. 164)

In these examples the experience of literature is used as a help in dealing with the issues of life. The relationship of the literary parallel or echo is, I believe, living and creative. It does not seem to be, as Bernard Bergonzi implies in his provocative book *The Situation of the Novel*, a parasitical relationship be-traying the comatose state of modern British fiction. These references are not made for the sake of adding intellectual glamour to the characters or of providing a facile exercise for the well-read reader; rather, they involve the reader with the author in a reassessment of the value of fiction and offer a statement of faith both in the human importance of story-telling and in the continuity of all narrative efforts. Bergonzi finds in such echoes an indication that the form of fiction is "losing its total commitment to originality and the immediate unique response to individual experience."[8] Perhaps what Margaret Drabble is asking us to accept is that originality has never been possible, and that we may find this fact reassuring rather than depressing, since it argues for vitality quite as much as for impotence in the face of the perennial problems.

Certainly her characters find in literature a consolation as well as a challenge. Frances in *The Realms of Gold* recites to herself a speech from Shakespeare, sonnets from Keats (includ-ing, the reader speculates, the one from which the title comes) and from Milton, an ode from Horace and a piece of Virgil as a solace in toothache as she had earlier done in childbirth (p. 57). Later, at the burial of her nephew who, having inherited the family tendency to depression, has committed suicide and killed his baby, it is natural that Frances, as an archaeologist, should think of Keats's grave in Rome and the churchyard of Gray's "Elegy" (p. 341). The less mature heroines of some of the earlier novels (as Valerie Grosvenor Myer has pointed out)[9] reach through their experience an appreciation of the meaning of literature which is a measure of their growth in imaginative sympathy. Emma, renouncing romance and dreams of in-dependence to bow to the demands of domestic responsibility, now repentantly weeps "real wet tears" at the early poems of Wordsworth which she had laughed at as a schoolgirl. Now, after the suicide by drowning of Julian, the young man with whom she had imagined herself having an affair, and her res-cue of her small daughter from the same river, she sees that "they are as moving as air disasters, those poems, they have as high a content of uninflated truth" (*Garrick Year*, p. 222). Similarly, Rosamund learns to relate her feelings for Octavia to Ben Jonson's love for his son (*Millstone*, p. 147). Her grasp of her subject has been humanized, and she has, at the same time, painfully arrived at a deeper relationship with individual words. The language in which she reports on her feelings for the newborn child is a touching mixture of pedantic restraint and humble recognition: "Love, I suppose one might call it, and the first of my life" (p. 118). She has already noted the discoveries about life that she had made during her pregnancy: "I am sure that my discoveries were common discoveries; if they were not, they would not be worth recording" (p. 78). Some of them were the facts her idealistic socialist parents had taught her about "the blows of fate and circumstance" under which others suffered. She says, "I had always felt for others in theory . . . but now, myself no longer free, myself suffering, I may say that I felt it in my heart" (p. 79). From the beginning Margaret Drabble has seen that the imaginative apprehension of clichés can be an act of wisdom. Sarah, appealed to by her sister Louise for help when Louise's husband has discovered her with her lover, concludes that—contrary to what she had believed—blood is thicker than water (*Bird-Cage*, p. 192). When Louise has arrived to take refuge in Sarah's flat, the sisters consider the possibility that "all the fairy-story things" like wicked stepmothers, like the novelist's convention of marrying for money (as Louise has just admitted doing) may be true after all (p. 195). Truth and fiction coincide.

The shaping process by which facts of life are made into art is also an ongoing topic in the novels. In the first novel Sarah argues with Stephen about a novel which she admires: Stephen, the professional, says that the book would have been more effective if set in "a slightly lower social setting" and Sarah challenges this view: "He was writing about those people because those were the people he was writing about" (*Bird-Cage*, p. 59). She is upholding the autonomy of art, although she does so rather simplistically. Later, she uses Stephen's work as a guide to the steps involved in achieving a style and finding plots which will present things truthfully:

> Satire won't do. Worldliness won't do. But until you can do them both you can't do anything. Immaturity is no good, and they made me feel immature, all those people [at a party], even those I could see through: they caught undertones I couldn't, though they didn't even know they were doing it. The thing is that I couldn't start to feel them in my terms because I couldn't really feel them in theirs, and one needs the double background. Perhaps it can be learned by long apprenticeship and dedicated exploration: I hope so. Perhaps it's only me that takes refuge in things like chance, unchartered encounters, cars in the night, roads going anywhere so long as it's not somewhere that other people know better. (p. 128)

In this novel the problems of selection are handled with a fairly light touch; as her work progresses Margaret Drabble shows a much deeper awareness of the question of whether truth can ever be told, of the moral, aesthetic and psychological implications of the choice of what is to be told, and of the sense in which all literature is a form of lying. Rosamund neglects to tell her friends about her experience of holding another woman's child in the clinic she attends before her baby is born: "I realised that I had not taken it in, I had not got it into a state fit for anecdote. . . . I did not find out what it had meant to me until after the birth of my own child" (*Millstone*, p. 82). At the time all she sees is the fact of human interdependence. Earlier, she and Lydia had discussed Hardy's use of coincidence, relating this technique to the role of accident in life. Lydia, after being refused an abortion, has had a miscarriage after being hit by a bus; Rosamund, who has become pregnant as a result of her first sexual experience, has tried to induce an abortion and failed. They consider the question of whether Hardy's novels show a profound or merely a mechanical attitude to life. Despite the fact that the bus accident happened, Lydia says that she could not put that kind of thing into a book: "I am not convinced by it, it hadn't got the stamp of reality on it to me." Rosamund, on the other hand, finds Hardy truthful (p. 75). Other aspects of the relationship of art to life are explored when Rosamund is annoyed to find that Defoe's *Journal of the Plague Year* is fictional, not factual, and then is annoyed at her own annoyance "as I have always maintained that I hold an Aristotelian and not a Platonic view of fact and fiction" (p. 169).

Meanwhile, Octavia is ripping up Lydia's manuscript. The interconnections of life and literature in this novel are richer and more amusing than in the two books which precede it or in *Jerusalem the Golden* which follows it, and the power of literature is more deeply felt.

It is in *The Waterfall*, the fifth novel, however, that the difficulties of truth-telling are made the main subject of the novel. Among the seven, this stands out as the "novelist's novel," and I shall examine it at some length. The burden of the narration is shared between a first-person and a third-person narrator, but both are Jane, the central character, and she is sometimes the rhapsodic teller of a tale of rescue and redemption through love and sometimes the detached and even sceptical assessor struggling for insight into this affair, and making her lover James, as one reviewer remarked, "as dismissible as a character in fiction."[10] As the book begins, the third-person narrator speaks and introduces Jane, alone with her small son and newborn daughter after her husband has left her, and James, visiting her and caring for her and beginning to love her. Then Jane breaks in on her own story:

> It won't, of course, do: as an account, I mean, of what took place. I tried, I tried for so long to reconcile, to find a style that would express it, to find a system that would excuse me, to construct a new meaning, having kicked the old one out, but I couldn't do it, so here I am, resorting to the old broken medium. (p. 48)

We perceive now that she was telling the story from the start, share her recognition that her choices of style and form have moral connections, and participate in her attempt to tell the truth. She says:

> The ways of regarding an event, so different, don't add up to a whole; they are mutually exclusive: the social view, the sexual view, the circumstantial view, the moral view, these visions contradict each other; they do not supplement one another; they cancel one another, they destroy one another. (p. 49)

Here is an awareness of the other possible stories hovering about the boundaries of the told one, of the necessity of omissions which can become falsehoods, and of the dangerous power of the artist. To tell her love story, a story of "grace and miracles" (p. 52), she has had to leave out her feelings for the baby; she has been unable to give consideration to the points of view of Lucy or of Malcolm; she has made her story, symbolically if not literally, a dialogue, for "the only other parts are non-speaking parts" (p. 89). Although—particularly after the car crash which almost killed James and revealed the affair to Lucy—guilt keeps threatening to overcome her, Jane has chosen not to tell the story of guilt (p. 242). She continues to be troubled by the knowledge that lies are inevitable, especially in a love story: "Lies, lies, it's all lies. . . . Oh, I meant to deceive, I meant to draw analogies, but I've done worse than that, I've misrepresented"[11] (p. 89). She has tried to describe "a passion, a love, an unreal life, a life in limbo, without anxiety, guilt, corpses . . . , the pure flower of love itself, blossoming out of God knows what rottenness, out of decay, from dead men's lives, growing out of my dead body like a tulip" (p. 89). She has not been able to describe the conditions of her life with James, and instead has fallen back on language of enchantment. Yet, to the end she insists that the isolated story she has chosen to tell, "that sequence of discovery and recognition that I would call love" (p. 49), has validity. The story James has created for her is true. "When James looked at me, he saw me, myself. This is no fancy, no conceit. He redeemed me by knowing me, he corrupted me by sharing my knowledge," she says early in the novel (p. 54), and at the end "he changed me forever and I am now what he made" (p. 245). Whatever else may be said about the affair, it has released Jane from her state of neurotic fear, and she can now move freely in the outer, ordinary world.

As Jane is searching for ways of telling a true story, she, a poet, meditates on the truth of poetry. She was first attracted to Malcolm, a classical guitarist and singer, by his song:

> Then wilt thou speak of banqueting delights
> Of masks and revels which sweet youth did make.
> Of tourneys and great challenges of knights
> And all these triumphs for thy beauty's sake:
> When thou hast told these honours done to thee
> Then tell, O tell how thou didst murder me.

The song (by Thomas Campion) is about story-telling, and Jane comments, "it made its own conclusion of our lives: for I did in a sense murder him, and I murdered him in the true lyrical sense" (p. 93). Yet the poets are to be blamed, she thinks, for giving us love and death in images of pure beauty, for real murder is "hideously ugly"; "in vain do the poets try to disguise and excuse and purify these things" (p. 93). Still, the images of art retain their power over us: "Nevertheless, I prefer to think of Malcolm, innocent, passionate, singing of murder, than to think of him with his fingers and thumbs sunk into my shoulders, beating my head against the bedroom wall" (p. 93). In an early short story, "A Voyage to Cythera," Margaret Drabble evoked the images of the daydreaming fancy in the heroine's vision of "some possible other country of the passions" to be described "in terms of myth or allegory."[12] This world, it seems to her, cannot be satisfactorily related to the real world, "the poetry of inspiration being to a certain extent. . . the poetry of ignorance, and the connections between symbols a destructive folly to draw."[13] In *The Waterfall* Jane picks up this theme:

> Perhaps love can't survive a context: perhaps it dies if it admits the outside world or crumbles to dust at the breath of coarser air. But that air is the real air, I know it. I can't make the connections; I can't join it up. And yet love has a reality, a quotidian reality, it must have. . . . (pp. 89–90)

Despite her statement that she cannot make the connections, Jane has made some by the end of the book; yet the problem cannot be finally solved. After the car accident which cut short their planned trip to Norway, their imagined "other country," Jane, staying in a hotel to be near James in the hospital, hears a song on a television programme her children are watching. A serving girl implores her beloved knight as he sleeps:

> For seven long years I served for you,
> The bloody cloth I wrung for you,
> The glassy hill I climbed for you,
> Will you not wake and turn to me?
>   (p. 211)

Later, she tries to dismiss such artistic configurations, but finds that they cannot be dismissed. We need them:

> Why else had those stories been created, those tales of entranced lovers kept alive through the years by faith, those fables of sleepers and dreamers awoken finally by the intensity and endurance of desire? Will you not wake and turn to me? I must have been mad to think these thoughts. And yet madder still to abandon them. (p. 230)

Like Malcolm's song, this one is prophetic. James does wake and turn to her. Jane and the reader are left, however, with the open ontological question of the reality of art. On the one hand, James was real, says Jane, "I swear it" (p. 89); on the other, the story like all stories was a fabrication. The mountain scenery she and James go to see after his recovery is "real, unlike James and me, it exists" on the ordinary level of experience; yet it is also "an example of the sublime" (p. 251). The ending must be open. She could, she sees, have given her story a different ending, could have killed James in the car, as the "moral view" of the events might demand; would that be a "feminine ending"? Or she could have maimed him, as Charlotte Brontë maimed Rochester so that the other Jane could have him. But she loved him too much, and besides, "the truth is that he recovered" (p. 246). Meanwhile they are left with their supporting documents: the hospital's notes on James's case for the insurance company, and Jane's poems of grief for a lost love, written when she thought he was dying. "I had the experience without the loss; for free" (p. 249). Both sets of documents are, in fact, falsifications, since James's, from the hospital, identifies Jane as his wife. Yet both have their own truthfulness. The ending which Jane does provide, "as a finale," is their weekend trip to Yorkshire where they see the waterfall, the symbolic counterpart of James's card trick. It is "a lovely organic balance of shapes and curves, a wildness contained within a bodily limit" (p. 252). There is even a shepherd; it is a pastoral idyll. Yet—typically—this narrator cannot leave the matter there. She gives us another, less elevated image, a mouthful of Scotch mixed with talcum powder accidently swallowed by James that night, and, evoking the methods of more experimental writers, provides both another rejected ending—making James impotent—and the "true" one: after having a clot in her leg she has stopped taking birth control pills. "I prefer to suffer, I think" (p. 255). The ending is open, leaving room for further exploration of the "connections between symbols."[14]

Notes

1. Nancy S. Hardin, "An Interview with Margaret Drabble," *Contemporary Literature* 14/4 (Autumn 1973), 280.
2. Anthony Thwaite, Review of *The Needle's Eye*, p. 430.
3. *A Summer Bird-Cage* (Penguin, 1967), p. 171. Further references to this text will be made in parentheses. For *The Garrick Year, The Millstone, Jerusalem the Golden* and *The Waterfall*, the Weidenfeld and Nicolson editions have been used; for *The Needle's Eye*, the edition by Alfred A. Knopf (New York) and for *The Realms of Gold*, the Penguin edition (1977). All references to these texts will be made in parentheses.
4. Bernard Bergonzi, *The Situation of the Novel* (London: Macmillan, 1970), p. 22. He is citing a BBC recording, 1967.
5. Nancy S. Hardin, "Drabble's *The Millstone*: A Fable for Our Times," *Critique: Studies in Modern Fiction* 15/1 (1973), 22–34, points out the significance of the parallel.
6. "A Prayer for My Daughter," ll. 77–80, in *The Collected Poems of W. B. Yeats* (London: Macmillan, 1955). The epigraph to *The Needle's Eye* is a misquotation of the opening lines of Yeats's "The Fascination of What's Difficult." Margaret Drabble has said that she had in mind here not so much herself as her characters; see "Margaret Drabble Talks to Terry Coleman," *Manchester Guardian Daily*, April 1, 1972, p. 8.
7. Hardin, "An Interview with Margaret Drabble," 280.
8. Bergonzi, *Situation*, pp. 22–23.
9. *Margaret Drabble: Puritanism and Permissiveness* (New York: Barnes and Noble, 1974), pp. 128–29.
10. Maureen Howard, Review of *The Waterfall*, *New York Times Book Review*, November 23, 1969, p. 67.
11. See Ellen Cronan Rose, "Margaret Drabble: Surviving the Future," *Critique* 15/1 (1973), 5–20, for a thematic study of the first six novels. It is strange that in an otherwise perceptive examination Rose should say (p. 10) that the first-person narrative begins at this point (p. 89); it in fact begins much earlier (p. 48).
12. "A Voyage to Cythera," *Mademoiselle*, December 1967, p. 149.

13. Ibid., p. 150.

14. Critics have disagreed about whether the method used in *The Waterfall* succeeds. Maureen Howard in her review says that the "seemingly effortless design" of the card trick is missing in the novel; *The Times Literary Supplement* finds both the moral structure and the narrative method unsuccessful. On the other hand, Myer recognizes that *The Waterfall* is "a novel partly about the difficulties of writing a novel" (p. 123) and says that the "apparent shapelessness" is "transcended by an art which creates a coherent and beautiful pattern out of incoherence and contradiction" (p. 23). As I hope I have shown, I agree with Myer, although I would quibble with her statement of the question posed by the novel: "Which is more important, art, the product of the imagination, creating a second reality, or life itself?" (p. 143). It seems to me that the question concerns rather the discrepancy between two views of life.

COLIN BUTLER

"Margaret Drabble: *The Millstone* and *Wordsworth*"

English Studies, 1978, pp. 353–60

Even if the name of Wordsworth were not mentioned in *The Millstone* and even if the dates of publication of *The Millstone* and *Wordsworth* were less proximate it would remain clear that the work of fiction and the work of criticism were germane.[1] Both exhibit the same assumptions and values despite the fact that the novel was, by its nature, exempt from many of the pre-determining forces of its critical successor. What induced Miss Drabble to express her interest in Wordsworth in the form that she did or where, indeed, the initiatives lay is not yet a matter of public record. Nevertheless, it is significant that her chosen medium was a popularizing one, intended, according to the preface of the general editor, for 'the ordinary man who reads for pleasure'. As we shall see, ordinariness and its cognates are operative concepts in *Wordsworth* and *The Millstone*, and the question is then how this similarity has come about and what it signifies? A beginning may be made with *Wordsworth*.

Paraphrasing the Preface to the 1800 edition of the *Lyrical Ballads* Miss Drabble writes that 'there is nothing "special" about poetry . . . it [deals with] the permanent, enduring interests of the human heart'. And it is Wordsworth's 'matter-of-factness, his habit of giving unromantic[2] details of when, who, where and how' that is said to impart to his poems 'the ring of truth'. The association of this kind of specificity with truth is, of course, a post-Romantic and decidedly post-Wordsworthian tendency for it was the insistent assimilation of the immediate and commonplace apprehensions of the finite mind to what Coleridge called 'the eternal act of creation in the infinite I AM'[3] which distinguished the Romantics more than anything else from their realist successors. Miss Drabble's formulations—and similar examples are to be found everywhere in *Wordsworth*—imply that it is truth of a special kind that interests her, namely, such truth as is limited to life in its concrete and particular manifestations. A predictable result of this is that attention to 'real life' as the term is ordinarily understood becomes a virtue in itself. Gray, for example, is reprehended for his presentation of '"rustic folk"': '[he] is patronizing, and he writes as though he does not really know them', whereas Wordsworth is esteemed for his 'world of real people, living and suffering'. Again Pope, in a passage which makes one wonder just how Miss Drabble would have differentiated between Pope and Wordsworth had the occasion for extended consideration arisen, is singled out for his 'closeness to the facts of real life', whereas Goldsmith is taken to task, despite 'some real knowledge and observation', for a lack of precision in his

characterization—a thoroughly realist censure. In themselves, these assessments are not without justification. But the procrustean nature of the approach which gave rise to them necessarily emerges when Miss Drabble addresses herself to those aspects of Wordsworth which extend beyond the here and now.

Miss Drabble's position is in effect that such aspects don't really matter (the adverb is used advisedly). She writes: '[Wordsworth] very rarely thinks in the abstract, with his head only; all the most visionary and mystical passages in *The Prelude* are directly linked to some ordinary physical event. . . . He may go beyond everyday life, but he always starts from it'. And again, more explicitly, with reference to *Intimations of Immortality*: 'His philosophy has been compared to Plato's, but it is in fact less of an abstract system than a description of his own personal experience of life. . . .'

The connotations of 'abstract' as it is used here are ambiguous. Initially, taken in conjunction with 'with his head only', it presumably is intended to imply what Coleridge contemned as 'philosophy made up of notions and mere logical entities'[4]—in other words, a kind of Glass Bead Game *avant la lettre*. But this is not the end of the matter. Simply put, this kind of philosophizing was unacceptable to Coleridge not because of its remoteness from everyday life but because, ultimately, of its restrictive allegiance to it. To use Miss Drabble's term, but the opposite of her meaning, it was not abstract enough; or as Coleridge insists, with his own procedures in mind: 'If it be said that this is idealism, let it be remembered that it is only so far idealism as it is at the same time, *and on that very account*, the truest and most binding realism'.[5]

For present purposes Wordsworth's general position, whatever reservations may be made about his abilities as a philosopher,[6] is sufficiently close to Coleridge's to be encompassed by it. It is adequately stated in *Tintern Abbey* in a passage which Miss Drabble quotes but which, significantly, she adduces primarily to establish a case *per contra* for 'the simpler ballads':

> And I have felt
> A presence that disturbs me with the joy
> Of elevated thoughts; a sense sublime
> Of something far more deeply interfused,
> Whose dwelling is the light of setting suns,
> And the round ocean and the living air,
> And the blue sky, and in the mind of man:
> A motion and a spirit, that impels
> All thinking things, all objects of all thought,
> And rolls through all things . . . (93–102)

Platonic or not, this is something more than a description of '[Wordsworth's] own personal experience of life', it is a deliberate attempt to extend the significance of experience in a particular way such as to invert Miss Drabble's 'he may go beyond everyday life, but he always starts from it'; and it makes of poetry something special indeed as a consequence. Miss Drabble's elevation of 'closeness to the facts of real life' to the position of a critical absolute and her tendentious employment of 'abstract' clearly derive from the prepotent conviction that everyday life is the *only* reality; from which follows that the 'permanent, enduring interests of the human heart' are important not for their transcendental but for their immanent significance, the experiencing self being the ultimate point of reference. This brings us to *The Millstone*.

The Millstone constitutes a vernacular rendition of the here and now in fictional form as seen from the perspective of moral disavowal. Its conceptual as well as its physical boundaries are implied by its insistence on actual places—Broadcasting House, Oxford Circus, the British Museum and so forth—within which Rosamund Stacey's moral drama will be played out. *Her* world, presumed to be directly or indirectly familiar to the contemporary reader, is characterized by a pervasive inability to cater to more than the more superficial parts of human existence. The inheritor of a long and successful series of liberal reforms, it thrives on the assumption that society's requirements are minimal, as are the individual's requirements of himself, and fosters thereby a curious kind of self-regarding restlessness as life fails to meet the expectations of ready satisfaction that are placed upon it. Issues are raised there in a cursory sort of way but they are seldom adequately defined or taken to a point of decision. All of this makes Rosamund's history exceptional and, therefore, worth narrating in detail.

Such a world as she inhabits will inevitably bring a certain kind of person to the fore. There is Dick, for example, who 'earned his living by writing something or other for a television company' but who is 'not wholly committed to his work'; or Alex, deriving pleasure from prostituting his talents in advertising; or Lydia, persuaded that life is most appropriately seen in terms of literary plausibility; or Joe Hurt, avatar of the previous generation's Angry Young Man with his 'insolent ill-will', threatening to become the victim of his own creative facility; or Roger Henderson, well-heeled, glamorously boorish and idly fascinated with the *outré*. It is the 'raffish seedy literary milieu' that constitutes the source of Rosamund's appeal for him and his unabashed egotism that attracts him to her. Hurt and Henderson are attached by equally spurious considerations: 'each considered the other to have a kind of worldliness that was lacking in himself, and despised and revered the other accordingly'. For all their vague artiness none of them, unlike the Arnoldian Miss Drabble,[7] sees the work of art itself as referring to anything beyond himself. Nevertheless, for all their triviality, selfishness and enveigling irresponsibility they are indubitably 'there' with all the prepollence of an established ethos and as such they exact a reckoning.

The moral free-for-all (which in its way is no less conformist for all that) in which Rosamund, 'a child of the age', finds herself affords her the opportunity to construct a way of life that accommodates simultaneously her symbolic fear of sexual congress and her aversion to being left out of things. The price paid is emotional growth ('All I had to sacrifice was interest and love. I could do without these things'). Her achievement is an evasive as well as a diminished form of existence, a rationalized state of personal and social deception made possible by a coincidence of personal and social inadequacy. Thus it is apposite that Rosamund's salvation (there is much transmuted Protestantism in the novel) should be set in train by a correspondingly evasive and conformist encounter, the obliteration of the consequences of which would be socially rehabilitating but, it transpires, humanly self-defeating—apposite because consequences of this order were the one thing both the act and the attitude which gave rise to it were intended to preclude. The fruit of that act legitimizes Rosamund not by being illegitimate and therefore fashionably outrageous but by bringing about an unpredicted and, once experienced, irrevocable revision of values. As Rosamund's 'shock of discovery'[8] takes effect she becomes aware of herself from the point of view of a number of novel considerations, not all of which are pleasant. One of these is time.

A sense of time comes relatively late to Rosamund who, in her early days, treats it like so much else as something extrinsic to herself and therefore, in the interests of a fixed and manageable *modus vivendi*, banishable:

> In those days, at that age, such things seemed possible and permissible: and as I did them, I thought that

I was creating love in my own way and in my own time . . . In ignorance and innocence I built my own confines, and by the time I was old enough to know what I had done, there was no longer time to undo it.

The transition from 'my own time' to 'there was no longer time' marks a fundamental change of consciousness which, as with all major preoccupations of *The Millstone*, has its parallel in *Wordsworth*. The comment on *Intimations of Immortality* quoted above was for convenience's sake left incomplete. It concludes, in fact, with the words ' . . . his own personal life and the process of ageing', a conceptual linking that is urged throughout *The Millstone* by means of a narrative technique consisting largely in retrospective assessment from the ebbing present of advancing years. What the precise age of the narrator is supposed to be is unimportant. What we are told is that she is going grey, that is, is bearing the marks both of experience and of age as an outer sign of their integration into her consciousness. In short, what she has acquired is a lively awareness of what it means to exist, a sense of being in which the worthwhile and the problematical are no longer separable (the threat to Octavia's life brings a sense of death as well as of attachment that contrasts significantly with Rosamund's earlier blithe attempts at an abortion). And while it is true that the absence of a sustaining adult relationship—the distorting consequence of a distorted past—makes Rosamund something of a special case, it remains arguable that to the extent that ageing and death come to be discerned as ineluctable realities, her specialness is more one of degree than of kind.

Such discernment, more portentous and more mature than the modes of living proffered by Swinging London and therefore extra-ordinary in the only sense Miss Drabble pays consistent attention to, requires certain qualities to which she gives explicit statement in *Wordsworth*; and again a peculiar bias is evident. In her discussion of *Peele Castle* she writes:

> Once more, we hear the note of *determination*; Wordsworth is a man of willpower, and he will face the grimness of tragedy without dishonesty. Life is bad, but it must be borne, and if we are to bear it then we must look it in the face . . . There is no point in trying to evade reality. It is much better to strengthen ourselves by contemplating it with fortitude.

The emphasis on honesty, fortitude and clear-sightedness needs no special commentary save in this particular: that in Wordsworth these qualities subsist in a view of life that is much more complicated than Miss Drabble's. The death by drowning of John Wordsworth was not only a severe personal loss for his brother, it occasioned in addition a pressing need for religious affirmation which was now as difficult and urgent as it had been relatively straightforward 'beneath a sky of bliss'. By moving in her remarks too readily from the complexity of Wordsworth's profound tribulation to a depreciatory final paragraph on 'the comfort of Christianity' Miss Drabble minimizes this aspect of *Peele Castle* to the advantage of her, not Wordsworth's, flat statement that 'life is bad' and to the concentration on purely personal resources she sees as being necessarily entailed by that point of view. There is no 'hope' in the Wordsworthian sense in Miss Drabble. There is only the (consequent) resolve to confront its absence with integrity and with what advantages there are *in* life once they have been clearly recognized.[9]

In *The Millstone*, for which Miss Drabble's assessment of *Peele Castle* could well serve as a statement of theme, the baby is manifestly intended both to provoke and to justify just such a recognition. When its existence first becomes known it is regarded automatically as an object, not a person and, therefore, disposable.[10] Only when it has lodged itself in Rosamund's consciousness as well as in her body does it begin to promote a growing comprehension of its own significance as a living thing and of the increasingly multivalent nature of its mother-to-be. Its father, George, is a measure of the difference. His relationship with Rosamund is characterized initially as 'a convergence of frailties', 'a sense of touch without contact' and both participants are assessed as 'rivals in hypocrisy'. Like Rosamund, George has evolved a *modus vivendi* which restricts living to its least demanding aspects ('two fish, embalmed in the living frozen river'), and their appropriately mannered and tenuous relationship represents, for each in his own way, the damage wrought by the attempt to secure continuation without development. George stays put; but Rosamund matures into a fuller and therefore essentially ambiguous understanding of 'the common feelings and common destiny of human beings'.[11] The process is marked by a series of firsts:

> Love, I suppose one might call it, and the first of my life. But now for the first time I felt dread on another's behalf . . . Life would never be a simple question of self-denial again. I knew something now of the quality of life . . . based on fact and not on hope.

By having the baby Rosamund's life has been both enriched and darkened. It has been enriched by means of a vivid experience of 'the pleasure which there is in life itself'.[12] And it has been darkened inasmuch as, for the first time also, life has been seen as something painful and finite as well. To this extent it is 'bad'; and to this extent it is to be borne with fortitude, not hope.

The extrapolation of worthwhileness from the provisional opportunities of the here and now is the guiding light both of *The Millstone* and of *Wordsworth* and explains both their similarity, despite the ostensible disparity of their subject matter, and Miss Drabble's consistent tendency to make of Wordsworth much more of a realist than he actually was. But to suspend discussion there would be to overlook a further point of correspondence between the novel and *Wordsworth*, namely, the social extension of Rosamund's discoveries. *A propos* of Wordsworth's increasing conservatism Miss Drabble writes: 'A loss of faith in social progress and human equality is extremely common in middle age'; and although she cogently adduces 'the violent horrors of the French Revolution, and the worse terrors of Napoleon's conquests' as reasons for this change she also remarks, with no appearance of discrimination, that '[Wordsworth] was no longer a young man without responsibilities, but a middle-aged man with a family to keep' and that 'the change was, of course, partly due to the natural process of time'. It is difficult to see how these factors are supposed to relate to each other. The French Revolution and Napoleon may stand, of course: their dispiriting effects were in any case not confined to Wordsworth. But the assumption of marital status, while leading possibly to a loss of opportunity, does not necessarily issue in a loss of faith; and the notorious diminutions of middle age tend rather to result in a simple loss of interest.

The matter might nevertheless be allowed to rest as description of a given case were it not for the fact that the same perfunctoriness recurs elsewhere. For example: Beaupuis is rightly identified as a major influence on Wordsworth but in a way that raises as many questions as it answers. It is probably true that 'Wordsworth owes his social conscience more to Beaupuis than to any revolutionary Godwinian tract' and it is

also probably true that 'the man's character meant as much to him as any abstract theory'. But it is surely misleading to proceed from this to a generalized distinction between 'radical and theoretical' on the one hand and 'the warm and real' on the other, if only because no reason is given why the former should not profitably issue in the latter and not in 'impractical extremist notions' or 'rash' idealism; just as no reason is given why those who seek to alleviate obvious material hardship should be the least inclined to see 'all working men as saints in disguise'.[13]

The genealogy of Miss Drabble's position is to be found in *The Millstone*. Of Rosamund's parents we read:

> Such tact, such withdrawal, such avoidance. Such fear of causing pain, such willingness to receive and take pains. It is a morality, all right, a well-established, traditional, English morality, moreover it is my morality, whether I like it or not. But there are things in me that cannot take it . . .

It is clear from the context that Miss Drabble is interested less in what she calls a morality than in motivation; and that 'mentality' would probably have been the better word. The insinuation is that the altruism of Rosamund's parents, even— the psychology is Nietzsche and water—their 'willingness to receive and take pains' is an expression of their determination to avoid confronting the proposition that life is *essentially* painful. Thus, for example, when apprised of Rosamund's changed condition they do the decent thing and remove themselves even further but what Miss Drabble writes is: 'They did not wish to cause me *or themselves* pain . . . so they went to India instead' (my italics). Their disposition in turn influences Rosamund's early organisation of her own life in accordance with the principle of minimal exposure. Like Dr Sloper in *Washington Square* (this must be the point of an otherwise gratuitous reference) her parents have for questionable reasons endeavoured to secure their offspring from the risks of life ('nor could I feel that weight till my own arms had tested it'), with the consequence that her later attempts at readjustment are unnecessarily difficult and incomplete.

Rosamund has a different view of life that has been stifled but not eradicated by parental interference:

> Life is not fair . . . It is unfair on every score and every count and in every particular, and those who, like my parents, attempt to level it out are doomed to failure.

The unfairness of life is here not a matter of a given political or economic order but a *donnée* of human existence *tout court* and it is her overriding sense of this that lies behind Miss Drabble's antipathy to what she chooses to call 'rash' idealism just as it lies behind her indictment of socialism (which is, significantly, confined to placing cleaning ladies in positions of unnecessary temptation) and, more persuasively, her rejection of the mindless hedonism of Swinging London. The issue for her is one of honesty, of seeing life clearly from an appropriately pessimistic point of view and any mode of thought (or absence of thought) which conceals this is automatically open to censure. There is, of course, something to this. Nevertheless, one is, perhaps even more than ever, entitled to ask why human suffering should not be minimized even if it cannot be eliminated.

On this point Miss Drabble is less than adequate. Rosamund's *éducation sentimentale* inevitably leads to an awareness of suffering in others—'companions in endurance' they are half-ironically called, 'whose existence I had hardly noticed'. These people are intensely compassionated with ('As at the doctor's, I was reduced almost to tears by the variety of human misery that presented itself'), but at the crucial point the line of thought turns inward and contemplative: 'I felt nothing in common with these people . . . and yet I was one of them . . . trapped in a human limit'. Even when the bounds of Rosamund's own resolution and independence are acknowledged one misses the next logical step. Of Miss Drabble's own version of the leech-gatherer we read: 'She was going painfully slowly along the other side of the road. . . . There was a solemnity about her imperceptible progress that impressed me deeply: she stood there, patiently waiting, like a warning, like a portent, like a figure from another world . . . I saw that from now on I, like that woman, was going to have to ask for help, and from strangers too'. Yet apart from a request for a baby-minder when Rosamund has to fetch medicine from the chemist's no action is taken which would lead these encounters beyond an acknowledgment of 'sad necessity'. In part this is understandable, since Rosamund is meant to be seen as being handicapped from the outset ('I who could not even ask for love or friendship'). But when she says at the conclusion that 'there was one thing in the world that I knew about, and that one thing was Octavia' it is difficult to resist the thought that even in terms of the novel (which is, after all, under the novelist's control), too little is being said. The novel's major discriminations are well made and important but, like *Wordsworth*, it has no social dimension worth the name even if full weight is given to the implication that Octavia will bridge the gap between the inner and the outer world more successfully than her mother. Perhaps she will. But it would be nice to know how.

Notes

1. Margaret Drabble, *The Millstone* (London, 1965) and *Wordsworth* (*Literature in Perspective*) (London, 1966).
2. Cp. George Whalley, 'England: Romantic—Romanticism' in '*Romantic*' *and its Cognates: The European History of a Word*, ed.

Hans Eichner (Toronto, 1972), p. 253: 'Before the end of the [nineteenth] century the word ['romantic'] had quietly taken root as a referential term that cast iridescent colours, irritating for its vagueness yet scarcely arousing resolute definition'.
3. S. T. Coleridge, *Biographia Literaria*, ed. George Watson (London, 1971), p. 167.
4. Ibid., p. 149.
5. Ibid., p. 148. My italics.
6. Miss Drabble clearly subscribes to the view advanced in F. R. Leavis, *Revaluation: Tradition and Development in English Poetry* (London, 1936), chapter 5 (listed in her bibliography), although she may also have had J. S. Mill's opinion in mind.
7. Both in her eschewal of an explicit political programme and in her trust in the maieutic effects of literature—the epithet is perhaps doubly appropriate—to bring about '*general* perfection, developing all parts of our society' (*Culture and Anarchy*, ed. J. Dover Wilson [Cambridge, 1966], p. 11).
8. The phrase is from Miss Drabble's own preface to *Wordsworth*.
9. The point is driven home in *The Millstone*: 'A bad investment, I knew, this affection [for Octavia], and one that would leave me in the dark and the cold in years to come; but then what warmer passion ever lasted longer than six months?' and is reiterated in Miss Drabble's discussion of Wordsworth's decline ('It was a sad future, and a depressing one . . . ').
10. Referring to the Soldier's Tale in *The Prelude* Miss Drabble writes that '[Wordsworth] is aware, as he makes his offer, of things that had not even crossed Goldsmith's mind; to him the soldier is not an object but a person'.
11. The phrase is J. S. Mill's and is quoted with obvious approbation in *Wordsworth*: 'Wordsworth taught me a greatly increased interest in the common feelings and common destiny of human beings'. Miss Drabble adds: '[Wordsworth's poetry] taught him that life was still worth living; it taught him to feel for ordinary men'.
12. Wordsworth, *Michael* (not quoted by Miss Drabble).
13. The phrase is an echo of an earlier and similarly tendentious distinction: '[*The Idiot Boy*] is not an idealized portrait; it makes no attempt to portray Betty as a model mother, or a saint of womanhood. Instead it is true to life . . . '

LORD DUNSANY

1878–1957

Edward John Moreton Drax Plunkett was born July 24, 1878, in his family estate in County Meath, Ireland; he became the eighteenth Baron Dunsany upon the death of his father in 1899. He attended Eton and Sandhurst, and served in the Boer War. Afterwards he began writing short stories of exotic fantasy— *The Gods of Pegana* (1905), *Time and the Gods* (1906), and *A Dreamer's Tales* (1910)—and in 1909 was encouraged by W. B. Yeats to write plays for the Abbey Theatre. These plays became hugely popular both in England and in America; at one time Dunsany had five plays running simultaneously on Broadway. He was to serve in World War I, but was wounded in the Dublin riots of 1916; later he joined the Coldstream Guards in Flanders.

After the war he and his wife Beatrice settled down in Castle Dunsany, although they traveled widely. Dunsany made extensive lecture tours of the United States from 1919 to 1920, and in 1928, and also traveled to Africa, India, and elsewhere to pursue his ardent hobby of big-game hunting. Between the wars Dunsany was a much sought-after writer, and contributed extensively to the *Atlantic Monthly, Saturday Evening Post, Collier's*, and other periodicals. In 1941 he accepted the Byron Professorship of English Literature in Athens, but had to be evacuated when the Germans invaded. In 1943 he delivered the Donnellan lectures at Trinity College, Dublin, and in 1945 wrote a series of essays on the future of civilisation, *A Glimpse from a Watch Tower*, in which he wrote the following after hearing of the atomic bomb: "I think that a new era started yesterday . . . henceforth we are all people with a mission, a strange mission, not to destroy the world." Lord Dunsany died on October 25, 1957.

Dunsany always wrote with a quill pen. He wrote prolifically—stories, plays, novels, essays, letters—and with incredible rapidity: he wrote A *Night at an Inn* between tea and dinner one afternoon. Although associated with such Irish writers as Yeats, A.E., and J. M. Synge, he was never strictly a member of the "Irish Renaissance." Dunsany is perhaps the single most influential figure in modern fantasy fiction, and resonances of his work can be detected in the writings of E. R. Eddison, J. R. R. Tolkien, H. P. Lovecraft, and many others.

Personal

Every morning the *Los Angeles Times* was left in plain sight near the breakfast table. Without a glance he pushed it aside. He would not clutter his mind with reports of crime and political crises that were the usual grist of news. He knew that preoccupation with human relationships of the workaday world is apt to dull one's sense to the spiritual yearnings and imaginative flights of which the human soul is capable. But he had a shrewd idea of what was happening in the arena of world politics and sometimes, in conversation, he dropped a caustic comment that blasted the folly of dull diplomats and power-seeking radicals.

Among older people it began to be remembered that his plays had once been the rage in New York and his *Wonder Tales* the delight of those who love fantasy. The voices of strangers spoke to me over the telephone asking if they might come to meet him: authors, actors, poets, a dancer, a diplomat. One awestruck woman's voice asked if it were really true that he was in Palos Verdes. "Oh," she sighed, "to think I am breathing the same air with him." I invited her to come nearer and take a deep breath.

Invited and uninvited they came to morning coffee and afternoon tea. They sat and adored him. His impeccable dignity and natural charm were all that they could have desired. He enchanted them. . . .

Describing his flight over Arizona, he said, "The sun shone on the ramparts of uninhabited cities and there was a parliament of mountains sitting around their council tables." And of the period between the two great wars, "The dance of death paused only long enough to change partners." He described a river in Africa which he had seen from the air as, "A dark sluggish river, like an old cart horse, when suddenly stung by a whip, plunging forward, the river plunges over a precipice." To a man who was discussing the tremendous increase given our defensive power by the hydrogen bomb, Dunsany threw off this comparison: "It is as if, walking in a garden, two men watched snails crawling, and one man said, 'My snail will win,' and the other man replied, 'My horse will win the Derby.' We've increased our power to destroy a million times, but how much have we increased our wisdom?"— HAZEL LITTLE-FIELD, "Porridge and Pomegranates," *Lord Dunsany: King of Dreams*, 1959, pp. 47–48

General

Never, as in this time it seems to me, have we so much needed guidance from poets; for eighty years machinery has altered and increased, changing and changing again the face of England, changing our habits, our needs, our mode of life, our thoughts, our language, and our very selves. We are very proud of it, we boast of it, we are glad that we have changed quicker than others change; and what is it all for?—where are we going? I have not seen the answers in the Press; there is no clue to it in the Palace of Westminster; they do not know in either House of Parliament.

And the poets go on writing as of old. Sometimes they write of high ethereal things that are as far from us as the gates of the dawn, like that remote, unplaced, undated play, Yeats's *King's Threshold*; and sometimes they write about our daily affairs, as in Masefield's *Widow in Bye Street*. And in the one case I hear men and woman say, "Yes, I would read poetry if only poets would write about the things that interest us, the things of our own time." And in the other case they say, "It is too sordid; a poet should not write of such sordid things." Thus they speak when the poet's moth-winged fancy flits down to the very fields that they themselves, the people of this age, have slimed and made foul with gold. . . .

The soul is not soothed by a hundred miles an hour, the mind is not made easy in shops in Bond Street by four hundred and five hundred per cent profits, not yet may happiness be found for certain even by all the wickedness of honoured and wealthy vendors of patent drugs and adulterated food. With such men as these last, money will always remain; but more and more every year I hope we may find men turning away towards simplicity and beauty, realising that though money *may* buy happiness, yet it is only a medium, while the poets have on sale in exchange for nothing those ideals, fancies, and phantasies out of which happiness is made. For not a penny is earned, not a thing done but it was to help to carry out some man's ambition to make some little fancy a little easier; and men's ambitions and men's fancies are the poet's raw material, and it is only short-sighted, unpractical millionaires that think that the stamped gold coins which they give their days in exchange for are at all an end in themselves, or that fail to see that that very happiness that they hope their money may buy is often thrown away for the sake of making that money. O all ye business men, praise ye money, for I sometimes think it is all you ever get. It may be that before we grow simpler and sincerer we may grow even worse. A substitute is yet to be found for water, as there has been for beer and salt; it is yet to be widely advertised, sold, and drunk like many another wickedness, but people must some day turn from all these things and go one by one to the camp where the good men dwell—not the poets only, but all who do work for its own sake and do it well. There are two great divisions among them, the true and the sham; I judge them by their works. In one class are all the snobs, all the pretenders, the writers of advertisements, the keepers of shops (except such as are honest), the makers of antique furniture and the buyers of it, the manufacturers of all things that are meant to look what they are not, the lovers of ugliness, not all the sinners, but all that sin meanly for the sake of gain, however honoured their stations. And in the other class are the men with spades, men near to the fields and natural like the harvests, soldiers and sailors, patriots, not politicians, common labourers, not labour-leaders, policemen, kings, and all (though happily the list is too long) who do any work well for the sake of the work, and not so as to sell it at an unjust price to the first ignorant customer. In this class are the poets. And this whole class should hold fast together to resist the false that is spreading over the world—false knowledge, false work, false food. The rough seafaring man may be ignorant of the poet, but they have the bond between them of work well done, which sets them utterly apart from the mean makers of cough-cures, and Cabinet Ministers answering in the affirmative.

And of such a class the poets should be the leaders; for of all materials for labour, dreams are the hardest, and the artificer in ideas is the chief of workers, who out of nothing will make a piece of work that may stop a child from crying or lead nations to higher things. For what is it to be a poet? It is to see at a glance the glory of the world, to see beauty in all its forms and manifestations, to feel ugliness like a pain, to resent the wrongs of others as bitterly as one's own, to know mankind as others know single men, to know Nature as botanists know a flower, to be thought a fool, to hear at moments the clear voice of God.—LORD DUNSANY, "Nowadays" (1912), *The Ghosts of the Heaviside Layer and Other Fantasms*, 1980, pp. 131–38

As yet, Lord Dunsany is little known in America for his tales. Yet it is doubtful whether, in future, he will stand as high for his plays as for his intangible, slight, atmospheric stories of mortals braving the super-mortals who dwell in dim spaces and of their terror and crushing defeats—yes, even of men's piteous willingness to accept as gods the strange towering things of stone that bear chisel marks but that, because of long years of sacrificial offerings and belief, are none the less deities, mocking mere men. His stories are tales of terror, of atmosphere, of the eternal verities, set with gem-like, highly connotative phrases, full of deep poetic beauty, but concerned nowhere so much with men as with men's elder brethren the stars. . . .

In Dunsany's plays, as in his stories, there is one great dominant—an ironic juxtaposition—generally, a juxtaposition of impious mortals with the great Things that sit above—always a juxtaposition and one ironically put. In *The Tents of the Arabs*, there is a king who longs for the desert, set against an Arab who longs to be king; in *The Golden Doom*, the writing of two little children is the cause of an empire's fall; in *King Arginenes*, a slave overthrows a king and then hungers for bones, like a slave; in *The Gods of the Mountain* and *A Night at an Inn*, the immortal deities, though only stone idols, stalk out of the darkness to revenge horribly an impious deed done to them.

Dunsany has appeared as a prodigy in our unimaginative age, yet he has certain literary analogies that are interesting to trace. To Wedekind, he is allied in the use of strange, ironic symbolism; to Poe, in his power to create an atmosphere of terror; to Lafcadio Hearn in a delicate artistry of phrase and a fatalistic philosophy of sorrow; to Kipling, otherwise his very pole, in his orientalism, in his wandering in weird by-paths, in his love of high-lights in tale-telling; to Barrie, occasionally, in whimsey, as "The Loot of Bombarsharna"; to the less known Strindberg of *Advent* and *The Dream Play* in the spaciousness of his imagination and his challenging deities and sense of the sorrow of life; to James Stephens in his fantastic melange of poetry, irony, and philosophy; in the striding gods among the modern figures of his tales.

Dunsany's two greatest analogues, however, are perhaps Maeterlinck and William Blake—that strange, half-mad Blake who wandered in heaven and hell, writing prophetic books, picturing them marvellously; like Dunsany, creating new gods, naming them strange names.

So, too, to Maeterlinck, Dunsany is somewhat akin. As Maeterlinck has dramatized terror in *The Intruder* and *The Death of Tintagiles*, so Dunsany has made terror his dominant, in a whole range of stories and tales. Both writers take us to strange worlds—Maeterlinck to one remotely mediaeval: Dunsany, to one that suggests Assyria, Babylonia, and ancient Egypt. Both deal with the eternal verities—Maeterlinck with the eternal verity of love; Dunsany, with the great eternities of time and space and gods that watch the fall of cities and even the coming of man "from under eyebrows white with years." Both writers have that power of showing the things of the eternal under the thin guise of the transitory that we call sym-

bolism; both are thoroughly pagan, with an abode of spirits that still lean wistfully toward the warm, sunny earth.

In the literary influences traceable upon Dunsany, there is a surprising dearth of the Celtic legend that has so inspired the modern Irish movement; Dunsany scarcely borrows from this legacy; his is, rather, the spirit of the olden tale-tellers who made legends themselves, and whose legends we but dustily inherit.

The great influence upon Dunsany's work is not Celtic but Oriental. The cheat tale—a characteristic Oriental tale—is abundant; it is set in Oriental settings of a dim past; it is told with Oriental opulence of color and often with Oriental forms of speech.

The source of Dunsany's thoroughly pagan inspiration is, oddly enough, the Bible. Never were Biblical religious precepts more opposed than in these idol-filled tales of unknown gods and of doubt. Yet never was a Biblical inspiration more directly traceable. For these are tales of the eternals to whom man is but a small thing; strange tales full of heathen gods and heathen idols, but always told with a sense of the great wideness beyond man.

The Bible was, avowedly, Dunsany's model, and he shows its influence not only in his thought but in his style, as in the directness of his narration, its succinctness and graphic quality, the fine flavor of his old Saxon words, even the use of the typical Hebraic parallelism. . . .

Such is Lord Dunsany—strange soldier, poet, dreamer— now in Londonderry Barracks waiting a call that may send him, like the rest of the flower of Europe, to his doom.— EMMA GARRETT BOYD, "Lord Dunsany, Dreamer," *Forum*, April 1917, pp. 499–508

Dunsany has opened for us the great gates leading into that other world so near, and yet so distant from us all. Like all the little people his creatures have no souls, for if they had then Time might overtake them. For the only thing in all the whole wide world that is imperishable, the only thing that Time stands baffled before, is a dream, even a little one. And that is most of all what Dunsany has told us, that a too great intensity of interest with the things of everyday life, the transient things, is just so much ground given up to that great scourge of all the ages, Time. In our fight with him he hurls the years at us, and our houses crumble, our cities fall into ruin, and our civilization passes away. All our learning, all our wealth, all our accomplishment cannot turn him even so much as a minute from his path. And all we have with which to oppose him are dreams. Only against them is Time powerless.

The world is very tired of thinking, especially about itself, and we who are each a part of the world are all tired too. We have thought so much lately. There seems to be hardly a human problem left untouched, and uninvestigated, and there seems to be hardly a human problem solved. Perhaps we have thought too much and dreamed too little. We have passed from the drama of the boudoir to that of the laboratory and the dissecting room; it may well be that the time has come when these things shall leave us, when we shall pass from the drama of the moment to the drama of all time, and from the destruction of little things to the preservation of great things.

It seems to me that there must be no one who can see the plays of Lord Dunsany or read them without feeling an immense sense of relief as at the release of some intolerable burden. His plays and tales are told to us as very few could have told them for more than many years. He is one of the great figures in a great literary movement—in some ways he is the greatest figure—and whatever Time may do to blot from the memory of man that which has passed, I think that the work of Dunsany will remain for always. For he has dreamed, and dreams are imperishable. He has shown us beauty, which is truth, and truth is immortal. And so, while Lord Dunsany will in due course come to "pass away at his residence", it is quite as certain that he will never die.—EDWARD HALE BIERSTADT, *Dunsany the Dramatist*, 1919, pp. 156–58

Works

DRAMA

It is hard to define just what makes these plays what they are. But certain qualities are tangible. Their deep and rich symbolism is one. It is the kind of symbolism for which the advances of modern psychology has prepared us—the kind that is inseparable from life itself as we are only just beginning to understand it. Another quality is their capacity for suggesting at once the intimate unity and appalling vastness of life. In *The Golden Doom* the fate of an empire and a little boy's desire for a new plaything become linked as facts of equal importance in the web of fate. In *The Gods of the Mountain* we meet with an atmosphere of fatality comparable only to that found in the Greek dramas. The crime of *hybris*, which to the Greeks was the "unforgivable sin," is here made as real to us as it was to them.

But these remarks of mine about the inner significance of the plays should not tempt anybody into thinking them deficient in that element of formal perfection without which they could not be classed as works of art. They are, indeed, "things of beauty," and their beauty inheres in their design as well as in their style. Through all of them the greatest possible economy of means has been observed, so that not a word, not a tone, not a gesture is wasted in obtaining the effect aimed at. The dialogue of Maeterlinck is suggested, but not more than suggested. The words spoken by the characters of Maeterlinck are often so vague as to be practically meaningless. The characters of Lord Dunsany speak as simply as those of Maeterlinck, but always sharply to the point; there can be no mistaking of what they mean, and that meaning serves always to carry the action of the play forward. And each play of Lord Dunsany's is an exciting adventure, conveying to the reader an exhilarating sense of motion without ever descending to old-fashioned stage tricks for the production of that sense. This means that they combine to an extraordinary degree the qualities which make separately for theatrical or literary success.—EDWIN BJÖRKMAN, "Introduction" to *Five Plays*, 1916, pp. x–xii

Back at Dunsany I spent February shooting snipe, and in March I wrote several stories, in one of which I returned to Bethmoora to write more about the Emperor Thuba Mleen. I was also given two books to review by the editor of *The Saturday Review*. And on March 23rd I wrote a one-act play, which, little though I thought it at the time, was to open a new path along which my dreams were to wander. This is the way that I came to write it: I met Mr. W. B. Yeats for the first time, and he asked me to write a play for his Abbey Theatre. I said I couldn't write plays. He said that I might write a play about a picture that I had drawn and which Miss Eva Hamilton, the artist, had told him about: it was a picture of a burglar breaking into Paradise and being punished by the irony of finding emptiness and stars as he opens the golden gates. I still said that I was sure I could not write a play. There may be a certain laziness in such assumptions, as they settle definitely the question of whether or not one should work in a certain direction. Then Mr. Yeats said: "I think I must get somebody else to do it." That stung me to rise from that lethargy, for I did not want

somebody else to go off with my idea. This was in the early afternoon, and during that afternoon I wrote *The Glittering Gate*. When I showed it to Mr. Yeats he told me that some dialogue would be needed while the burglar was breaking open the gate; so I added a bit; but all the rest of the play was done at a sitting. Soon it was staged at the Abbey Theatre; and, while the drama was all new to me, I used sometimes to talk of the plots of plays that occurred to me, asking my elders whether my plots would be any use, and being discouraged. But before I learned not to talk about new plots for plays to anyone, there were one or two very great successes in London made from those very plots.—LORD DUNSANY, "In Zaccarath," *Patches of Sunlight*, 1938, pp. 154–55

FICTION

We are all fictionists nowadays: Lord Dunsany, however, is that rare creature in literature, the fabulist. He does not aim at imposing forms on what we call reality—graceful, impressive or significant forms; he aims at transporting us from this reality altogether. He is like the man who comes to the hunters' lodges and says "You wonder at the moon. I will tell you how the moon was made and why." And having told them about the moon he goes on to tell them about marvellous cities that are beyond the forest and about the jewel that is in the unicorn's horn. If such a one were rebuked for filling the folk with dreams and idle tales, he might (had he the philosophy) make reply: "I have kept alive their spirit of wonder, and wonder in man is holy." Lord Dunsany speaking for himself would say with Blake "Imagination is the man." He would, I think, go on to declare that the one thing worth doing for mankind is to make their imaginations more and more exalted. One can hardly detect a social idea in his work. There is one there, however. It is one of unrelenting hostility to everything that impoverishes man's imagination—to mean cities, to commercial interests, to a culture that arises out of material organization. He dwells forever upon things that arouse the imagination—upon swords and cities, upon temples and palaces, upon slaves in their revolt and kings in their unhappiness. He has the mind of a myth-maker, and he can give ships and cities and whirlpools vast and proper shapes.—PADRAIC COLUM, "Introduction" to *A Dreamer's Tales and Other Stories*, 1917, p. xvii

Neither Lord Dunsany nor James Stephens had carried on the tradition of any previous writer of Irish fiction. They cannot be associated with the other storytellers. James Stephens began by making a slight concession to the accepted convention of the novel, but before *The Charwoman's Daughter* had reached many chapters that convention was abandoned. Lord Dunsany, on the other hand, has conceded only so much in his short stories as to suggest their ancestry in the fairy tale.

In 1905 *The Gods of Pegana* passed almost unperceived amidst the more avowedly Celtic literature of the moment. Indeed, it is unlikely that many readers who then saw the name of Lord Dunsany for the first time would have associated the book with the Irish movement in which its author was so generously interested. Coming forward as the creator of a new mythology, he could not readily be identified with a literary tradition whose strength was rooted in the soil of Gaelic legend and antiquity. Lord Dunsany invented his own antiquity, whose history was found in *The Gods of Pegana*. With a strange power of imagination he set forth the hierarchy of Pegana's gods, the greater and minor deities. Marvellous Beings, who play with worlds and suns, with life and death, their mere nomenclature is full of weird suggestion. There is not an event in the cosmic evolution known to us which Lord Dunsany has failed to elaborate into some beautiful legend. But, whereas the first volume was essentially the record of a new theogony, *Time and the Gods* (1908) is a collection of myths, which naturally attach themselves to the phenomena witnessed by the men whom the Pegana deities created for their amusement. In allowing his fancy to interpret the great elemental mysteries of nature, the rising of the winds or the coming of light, the author shows the same delicate poetic imagination as assisted him in the creation of the mighty figures who peopled his original cosmos. Yet, with a true sense of the mythus, Lord Dunsany controls fantasy, so that he is never betrayed into any conflict with the natural laws, as understood by comtemporary science. His fable of the *South Wind*, for example, is as accurate in its representation of the facts as it is charming in its tender poetry.

The *Leitmotiv* of his work, whether the narrative be of gods or men, is the mysterious warfare between the phenomenal world and the forces of Time and Change. Even the "gods of Pegana" live beneath the shadow of this conflict which must one day result in their overthrow. Lord Dunsany's later work, *The Sword of Welleran* (1908), *A Dreamer's Tales* (1910) and *The Book of Wonder* (1912), is concerned more specifically with this aspect of existence. Here we learn of those wonderful cities, Perdondaris and Babbulkund, whose fabulous beauties are obliterated in a moment of Time, when something swift and terrible swallows them up, leaving only the whispering sands above them. The most beautiful prose the author has written is in these stories, beginning with *In the Land of Time* from *Time and the Gods*, which tell of the passing away of human achievement at the assault of nature aided by her relentless accomplices. Yet he has demonstrated his mastery of the grotesque and horrible in tales which recall those of Poe or Ambrose Bierce. His later work lacks glamour and spontaneity, and does not give the measure of his power, which is best seen in *The Sword of Welleran* and *A Dreamer's Tales*. There Lord Dunsany showed a wealth of bizarre and terrible fantasy of the same high quality as characterised his previous essays in mythological narrative. The latter, however, are his enduring share in the reawakening of the Celtic imagination of which the Literary Revival is the manifestation.—ERNEST BOYD, *Ireland's Literary Renaissance*, 1922, pp. 412–14

W. B. YEATS
From "Introduction" to
Selections from the Writings of Lord Dunsany
1912

Some of the writers of our school have intended, so far as any creative art can have deliberate intention, to make . . . a change having more meaning and implications than a few sentences can define. When I was first moved by Lord Dunsany's work I thought that he would more help this change if he could bring his imagination into the old Irish legendary world instead of those magic lands of his with their vague Eastern air; but even as I urged him I knew that he could not, without losing his rich beauty of careless suggestion, and the persons and images that for ancestry have all those romantic ideas that are somewhere in the background of all our minds. He could not have made Slieve-na-mon nor Slieve Fua incredible and phantastic enough, because that prolonged study of a past age, necessary before he could separate them from modern association, would have changed the spontaneity of his mood to something learned, premeditated, and scientific. . . .

His work which seems today so much on the outside, as it were, of life and daily interest, may yet seem to those students I have imagined rooted in both. Did not the Maeterlinck of *Pelleas and Melisande* seem to be outside life? and now he has so influenced other writers, he has been so much written about, he has been associated with so much celebrated music, he has been talked about by so many charming ladies, that he is less a vapour than that Dumas *fils* who wrote of such a living in Paris. And has not Edgar Allan Poe, having entered the imagination of Baudelaire, touched that of Europe? for there are seeds still carried upon a tree, and seeds so light they drift upon the wind and yet can prove that they, give them but time, carry a big tree. Had I read 'The Fall of Babbulkund' or 'Idle Days on the Yann' when a boy I had perhaps been changed for better or worse, and looked to that first reading as the creation of my world; for when we are young the less circumstantial, the further from common life a book is, the more does it touch our hearts and make us dream. We are idle, unhappy and exorbitant, and like the young Blake admit no city beautiful that is not paved with gold and silver. . . .

These plays and stories have for their continual theme the passing away of gods and men and cities before the mysterious power which is sometimes called by some great god's name but more often 'Time.' His travellers, who travel by so many rivers and deserts and listen to sounding names none heard before, come back with no tale that does not tell of vague rebellion against that power, and all the beautiful things they have seen get something of their charm from the pathos of fragility. This poet who has imagined colours, ceremonies and incredible processions that never passed before the eyes of Edgar Allan Poe or of De Quincey, and remembered as much fabulous beauty as Sir John Mandeville, has yet never wearied of the most universal of emotions and the one most constantly associated with the sense of beauty; and when we come to examine those astonishments that seemed so alien we find that he has but transfigured with beauty the common sights of the world. He describes the dance in the air of large butterflies as we have seen it in the sun-steeped air of noon. 'And they danced but danced idly, on the wings of the air, as some haughty queen of distant conquered lands might in her poverty and exile dance in some encampment of the gipsies for the mere bread to live by, but beyond this would never abate her pride to dance for one fragment more.' He can show us the movement of sand, as we have seen it where the sea shore meets the grass, but so changed that it becomes the deserts of the world: 'and all that night the desert said many things softly and in a whisper but I knew not what he said. Only the sand knew and arose and was troubled and lay down again and the wind knew. Then, as the hours of the night went by, these two discovered the foot-tracks wherewith we had disturbed the holy desert and they troubled over them and covered them up; and then the wind lay down and the sand rested.' Or he will invent some incredible sound that will yet call before us the strange sounds of the night, as when he says, 'sometimes some monster of the river coughed.' And how he can play upon our fears with that great gate of his carved from a single ivory tusk dropped by some terrible beast; or with his tribe of wanderers that pass about the city telling one another tales that we know to be terrible from the blanched faces of the listeners though they tell them in an unknown tongue; or with his stone gods of the mountain, for 'when we see rock walking it is terrible' 'rock should not walk in the evening.'

Yet say what I will, so strange is the pleasure that they give, so hard to analyse and describe, I do not know why these stories and plays delight me. Now they set me thinking of some old Irish jewel work, now of a sword covered with Indian Arabesques that hangs in a friend's hall, now of St. Mark's at Venice, now of cloud palaces at the sundown; but more often still of a strange country or state of the soul that once for a few weeks I entered in deep sleep and after lost and have ever mourned and desired.

H. P. LOVECRAFT
From "The Modern Masters" (1927)
Supernatural Horror in Literature
1973, pp. 98–100

Unexcelled in the sorcery of crystalline singing prose, and supreme in the creation of a gorgeous and languorous world of iridescently exotic vision, is Edward John Moreton Drax Plunkett, Eighteenth Baron Dunsany, whose tales and short plays form an almost unique element in our literature. Inventor of a new mythology and weaver of surprising folklore, Lord Dunsany stands dedicated to a strange world of fantastic beauty, and pledged to eternal warfare against the coarseness and ugliness of diurnal reality. His point of view is the most truly cosmic of any held in the literature of any period. As sensitive as Poe to dramatic values and the significance of isolated words and details, and far better equipped rhetorically through a simple lyric style based on the prose of the King James Bible, this author draws with tremendous effectiveness on nearly every body of myth and legend within the circle of European culture; producing a composite or eclectic cycle of phantasy in which Eastern colour, Hellenic form, Teutonic sombreness and Celtic wistfulness are so superbly blended that each sustains and supplements the rest without sacrifice of perfect congruity and homogeneity. In most cases Dunsany's lands are fabulous—"beyond the East," or "at the edge of the world." His system of original personal and place names, with roots drawn from classical, Oriental, and other sources, is a marvel of versatile inventiveness and poetic discrimination; as one may see from such specimens as "Argimenes," "Bethmoora," "Poltarness," "Camorak," "Illuriel," or "Sardathrion."

Beauty rather than terror is the keynote of Dunsany's work. He loves the vivid green of jade and of copper domes, and the delicate flush of sunset on the ivory minarets of impossible dream-cities. Humour and irony, too, are often present to impart a gentle cynicism and modify what might otherwise possess a naive intensity. Nevertheless, as is inevitable in a master of triumphant unreality, there are occasional touches of cosmic fright which come well within the authentic tradition. Dunsany loves to hint slyly and adroitly of monstrous things and incredible dooms, as one hints in a fairy tale. In *The Book of Wonder* we read of Hlo-Hlo, the gigantic spider-idol which does not always stay at home; of what the Sphinx feared in the forest; of Slith, the thief who jumps over the edge of the world after seeing a certain light lit and knowing *who* lit it; of the anthropophagous Gibbelins, who inhabit an evil tower and guard a treasure; of the Gnoles, who live in the forest and from whom it is not well to steal; of the City of Never, and the eyes that watch in the Under Pits; and of kindred things of darkness. A *Dreamer's Tales* tells of the mystery that sent forth all men from Bethmoora in the desert; of the vast gate of Perdondaris, that was carved from a *single piece* of ivory; and of the voyage of poor old Bill, whose captain cursed the crew and paid calls on nasty-looking isles new-risen from the sea, with low thatched cottages having evil, obscure windows.

Many of Dunsany's short plays are replete with spectral fear. In *The Gods of the Mountain* seven beggars impersonate the seven green idols on a distant hill, and enjoy ease and honour in a city of worshippers until they hear that *the real idols are missing from their wonted seats.* A very ungainly sight in the dusk is reported to them—"rock should not walk in the evening"—and at last, as they sit awaiting the arrival of a troop of dancers, they note that the approaching footsteps are heavier than those of good dancers ought to be. Then things ensue, and in the end the presumptuous blasphemers are turned to green jade statues by the very walking statues whose sanctity they outraged. But mere plot is the very least merit of this marvellously effective play. The incidents and developments are those of a supreme master, so that the whole forms one of the most important contributions of the present age not only to drama, but to literature in general. A *Night at an Inn* tells of four thieves who have stolen the emerald eye of Klesh, a monstrous Hindoo god. They lure to their room and succeed in slaying the three priestly avengers who are on their track, but in the night Klesh comes gropingly for his eye; and having gained it and departed, calls each of the despoilers out into the darkness for an unnamed punishment. In *The Laughter of the Gods* there is a doomed city at the jungle's edge, and a ghostly lutanist heard only by those about to die (cf. Alice's spectral harpsichord in Hawthorne's *House of the Seven Gables*); whilst *The Queen's Enemies* retells the anecdote of Herodotus in which a vengeful princess invites her foes to a subterranean banquet and lets in the Nile to drown them.

But no amount of mere description can convey more than a fraction of Lord Dunsany's pervasive charm. His prismatic cities and unheard-of rites are touched with a sureness which only mastery can engender, and we thrill with a sense of actual participation in his secret mysteries. To the truly imaginative he is a talisman and a key unlocking rich storehouses of dream and fragmentary memory; so that we may think of him not only as a poet, but as one who makes each reader a poet as well.

LAWRENCE DURRELL

1912–

Lawrence George Durrell was born on February 27, 1912, in Julundur, India to British colonial parents. After attending the College of St. George, Darjeeling, India, and St. Edmund's School in Canterbury, he deliberately failed his Oxford entrance exams and launched into a number of odd jobs: racing cars, playing jazz piano, selling real estate, running a photo studio, teaching, and many others. He traveled and wrote extensively, becoming a protege and lifelong friend of Henry Miller. Durrell's Milleresque semi-autobiographical novel *The Black Book*, published in Paris in 1936, won him notoriety, critical plaudits, and frequent censorship.

During World War II, Durrell worked as a press attaché in Athens, Cairo, and Alexandria, where he set his best-known work, *The Alexandria Quartet* (*Justine*, 1957; *Balthazar*, 1958; *Mountolive*, 1958; *Clea*, 1960). Durrell calls the *Quartet* "a four-decker novel whose form is based on the relativity proposition." Durrell went on to publish another series, *The Revolt of Aphrodite*; he is currently at work on *The Avignon Quincunx*.

In addition to his novels, Durrell has published poems, translations, critical essays, plays, and several travel books. Many critics regard his poetry, which has been overshadowed by his success as a novelist, as his best work, a view which Durrell himself shares.

Durrell lives with his fourth wife in Provence, France, and has two daughters. Zoologist and author Gerald Durrell offers a lovingly irreverent view of his brother "Larry" in *My Family and Other Animals* and *Birds, Beasts, and Relatives*.

Personal

My birth and unbringing? I was born in India. Went to school there—under the Himalayas. The most wonderful memories, a brief dream of Tibet until I was eleven. Then that mean, shabby little island up there wrung my guts out of me and tried to destroy anything singular and unique in me. My so-called upbringing was quite an uproar. I have always broken stable when I was unhappy. The list of schools I've been to would be a yard long. I failed every known civil service exam. I hymned and whored in London—playing jazz in a night-club, composing jazz songs, working in real estate. Never really starved, but I wonder whether thin rations are not another degree of starvation. I met Nancy in an equally precarious position and we struck up an incongruous partnership: a dream of broken bottles, sputum, tinned food, rancid meat, urinals, the smell of the lock hospitals. And so . . . well, we did a bit of drinking and dying. The second lesson according to St. Paul. Ran a photographic studio together. It crashed. Tried posters, short stories, journalism, everything short of selling our bottoms to a clergyman. I wrote a cheap novel. Sold it. Well, that altered things. Here was a stable profession for me to follow. Art for money's sake. I began. My second I finished when we reached here. After that, the deluge. All this epic *Iliad* of course took about three or four years. Feels like a million.

Well, there it is. My life is like a chopped worm. Until eleven marvellous memories. White white the Himalayas from the dormitory windows. The gentle black Jesuits praying to Our Lady and outside on the frontier roads the Chinese walking stiffly and Tibetans playing cards on the ground, the blue fissures in the hill—God, what a dream—the passes into Lhasa blue with ice and thawing softly towards the holy forbidden city. I think Tibet is for me what China is to you. I lived on the edge of it with a kind of nursery-rhyme happiness. I wanted to go one summer into the passes. They promised to take me. But I left without going—alamort—it is a kind of unreasoning disease when I think of it. I am illogical again like a child. I whimper. I pant. And so on.—LAWRENCE DURRELL, Letter to Henry Miller (January 1937), *Lawrence Durrell and Henry*

Miller: A Private Correspondence, ed. George Wickes, 1963, pp. 60–61

From the moment of his entry on the scene, the rhythm of events accelerated, as though all life had been switched into a higher gear. The days and nights grew gayer and brighter, as if lit up by the approach of a comet. The world was clearly racing towards another internecine slaughter while optimism and good cheer reached an all-time high in the Villa Seurat.

Larry's marvellously modulated voice rang through the chosen *quartier*, gave body to our hopes and laughter. Jupiter in the ascendant of his horoscope seemed to cast a beneficent glow upon our days. The minor keys were discarded, the ear-splitting prestissimo of the finale was about to begin.

I am not sufficiently naïve to believe that all that happened during that period was Larry's doing, but it is significant that he was there when it happened. And nothing happened that was not fortunate: I recall several extremely successful love affairs of mine that fall into that period, for which surely I can't give him any credit. My second book, *Le Quartuor en Ré-Majeur*, was coming out. We had begun to publish *The Booster*, the riotous magazine of which I have spoken at length elsewhere. There were even a few cheques in the post! And all the time Larry was there, was there like Kilroy, pulling his weight, helping things along, like a lusty midwife.

Evoking the impact of his sudden advent; looking back at the events with the recoil of the years, I cannot help but feel that his coming to Paris at that particular time was in a way pre-ordained by a sort of Olympian providence. Apart from his desire to meet Henry Miller, and perhaps also to get a taste of Paris, he had no good reason to leave his Ionian island. Yet he had to come. The moment was ripe as an abscess and would have to be lanced soon. No one knew how soon, and Larry couldn't have known it as he embarked for France, the princely figurehead despatched to us as an emissary of no one can tell what secret powers at work, for the express purpose of spreading the glad tidings at the brink of the abyss. His arrival was timed with split-second accuracy, prepared in every detail by a host of invisible stewards as it were. And as he landed in the Villa

Seurat out of the blue, like an omen that hadn't been predicted, his Jupiterian personality at once galvanised our minds
into new patterns, reaffirmed the stimulus of our *joie de vivre*,
instilled a new zest into our laughter. His presence coloured
the closing scene of the Paris period, as the scherzando of the
finale re-echoes the leitmotif of the andante. His mission was
to add the supreme touch of spice to the flavour of an epoch.

And how well Larry acquitted himself of that mission!
There was no let-up. The days passed like so many hours,
already numbered. The weather was superb, the barometer
steady. Everything was exciting, portentous, pleasurable. What
I remember best of this blessed tailend of our life in Paris, are
the laughter, the food, the marvellous talks we had together in
the cafés, the restaurants: the steaks seemed tenderer and more
à point than ever, and every wine had a vintage flavour, even
the vinegary *vin blanc* we used to guzzle in the *bistrots* around
the Parc Monsouris while playing billiards. The words flowed
from our typewriters with greater speed and vehemence and we
ran pleasantly amok in the pages of *The Booster*. In brief, we
led a charmed life and felt there was no risk attached to going
haywire. The situation was too good to last.

One morning Larry walked into my room in the Impasse
du Rouet and said without preamble: "Start packing. We're off
to London, Nancy and I, and you're coming along." Not another word. Never asking me if I cared for going to England,
just ordering me about in his turbulent Jupiter Junior fashion.
What could I do? I packed. A taxi downstairs, in which Nancy
was waiting for us, took us to the Gare du Nord. The boat train
was already under steam. No time to say good-bye to Paris,
which was just as well: we might never have left.

We arrived in London that same evening, and I am here
still. The date was December, 1938. A few months after
Munich; less than a year before the outbreak of war. Things
were going to be grim but we didn't know it yet.—ALFRED
PERLÈS, *My Friend Lawrence Durrell*, 1961, pp. 12–14

General

When Lawrence Durrell's *Justine* appeared in 1957, I wondered why, with the exception of Howard Nemerov, none of
our major critics had anything to say. Now, after the publication of *Balthazar* and *Mountolive*, two of the three projected
"sibling" novels to *Justine*, I can better understand the silence.
The temptation to say merely that Durrell sometimes writes
extremely well and sometimes not so well, and let it go at that,
is almost, but not quite, overwhelming. . . .

Durrell's faults are easily summarized. Most of them are a
backlash, a slopping over of energies: metaphors run out of
hand, needlessly multiplied analogies, repetitious descriptions.
His humor is occasionally too heavy and his *sententiae* too
obvious. With a few exceptions, he is weak at characterizing
his people by their speech, and he lacks, as a philosophical
novelist, Dostoevsky's genius for drama, for inventing situations where action and thought are indistinguishable. He works
in fragments and private encounters, rarely confronting more
than two or three characters at a time. The worst one can say of
Durrell, I think, is that he is a genuine enthusiast, but he is
blessed with an intelligence that overcomes most of the vices of
enthusiasm.

Any idea or cluster of ideas, no matter how tired it may
seem, will yield a complete version of the world if explored
thoroughly enough, even the ideas of moderation and non-
commitment so well exploited by Robert Frost. Durrell answers Frost's famous maxim by saying, in effect: I was not a
political fence-straddler in my youth for fear of being a political
fence-straddler in my old age. The overt "lesson" of Frost is

humane resignation; the covert, presented *matter* is the primitive wildness of things. Durrell, though as gentle a man as
Frost, reverses this equation. His overt material is one with his
philosophizing, exotic and extreme—all polyglot literary amor-
ism, bed-hopping voyeurism, and jolly perversity.

What renders this sane, and distinguishes him from Paul
Bowles and others of that sunburnt fraternity, is not only his
"beautiful intelligence" (in Nemerov's words) and highhearted,
delicate, athletic gusto, his range and keenness of experience,
but most of all, his historical imagination. On a modest scale,
he belongs in the line of Thackeray, Stendhal, and Turgenev
as one of the scientific chroniclers of power, one of the serious
political novelists for whom nothing is more interesting than
the exact equation at any time or place between imagination,
power, and mind. Like Stendhal, he is a connoisseur of
melodrama.—R. W. FLINT, "A Major Novelist," *Cmty*, April
1959, pp. 353–54

Here Mr. Durrell appears unequivocally in the light of a
romantic. Time-Truth, in view of the above quotation, seems
to correspond roughly with *élan vital*. It is axial, radiating from
and contained in ourselves and it is only through an understanding of ourselves in relation to the cosmos, of ourselves
living in Space-Time, that we can hope to perceive something
of the truth about life. If Sainte-Beuve's definition of
Romanticism as *l'exaltation du Moi* still holds good, we may
well be heading for a Romantic Revival in England.

This *Moi*, the raw material of Romanticism, has of course
undergone some violent changes since Sainte-Beuve's day.
Freud has come and gone since then; Chateaubriand's René
would hardly have recognized Leopold Bloom as his spiritual
brother and would have been even more bewildered by a Darley plunged in Relativity, though with his feet still stuck firmly
in the Freudian clay. Sex looms large in the new Romanticism, and for Mr. Durrell it has immense and mysterious
importance. I think we may deduce from his work that he
believes sex to be the depot of all human activity and that it is
through the study of man's sexual life that one can best understand the hidden truth about him, "the truth of Time." For
instance, he believes it is impossible to understand what Man
really is without admitting the essential bisexuality of all human beings. This fact, of course, was a mythological commonplace and it has been scientifically proved in our own time
that there is no such thing as a purely male or purely female
being, that sex is a matter of dosage. Mr. Durrell's Scobie—a
truly wonderful old homosexual scoundrel and to my mind one
of the best comic characters in modern Eng. Lit.—plunges us
straight back into myth. Poor old Scobie, seventy, rheumatic,
an ex-sailor ("I put to sea every night in my dreams, old man"),
and holding precariously onto a job in the Egyptian Police, has
what he described as Tendencies. Occasionally he is irresistibly
moved to dress in outlandish female clothes and prowl the
town. ("It's only when the Fleet's in. . . . Of course, if there
was any trouble, I'd say I was in disguise. I am a policeman
when you come to think of it. After all, even Lawrence of
Arabia wore a nightshirt, didn't he?") This conduct leads to his
undoing and he is bashed to death by drunken sailors down by
the docks, then treated to a grandiose official funeral. He
appears frequently, on and off, throughout the three "spatial"
volumes, then as we take a jump forward in Time, in *Clea*, we
find him surprisingly but significantly transformed into a Coptic saint, "El Skob," with a shrine, a feast-day, and a legendary
existence of miracle-working. (It is notably recounted of him
that he had the ability to change himself at will into a woman
and by sleeping with impotent men render them virile.) Scobie, in fact, seems to be a manifestation of Tiresias, and Tire-

sias is a manifestation of Man's "possibilities" and the intercalated realities of which he is composed. "Time carries us forward by the momentum of those feelings inside us of which we ourselves are least conscious," writes Clea to Darley, apropos of Justine. Scobie-Tiresias is simply acting out the hidden drama of which most people are unaware but which is necessary in the cosmic sense. The old reprobate, stirring his poisonous artificial whiskey in his bath tub, is a link-up with the essential myths, which seem to have known all that Freud and Einstein have revealed to us with such éclat. Perhaps this great forward leap which mankind has taken during the last half-century has merely landed it back in the lap of its beginnings?—CECILY MACKWORTH, "Durrell and the New Romanticism," *TC*, March 1960, pp. 209–11

Durrell's explicit theme is an examination of modern love in its various aspects, a theme that in itself generates curiosity when it derives from an Englishman. Clearly following D. H. Lawrence in his attempt to "free" the English novel, Durrell suggests that sexual love—almost the only kind that exists for him—is a form of knowledge, literally as well as etymologically. "'He knew her,' as the Bible says!" Clea then adds that sex "'is the joint or coupling which unites the male and female ends of knowledge merely—a cloud of unknowing! When a culture goes bad in its sex all knowledge is impeded.'" The sexual demand, she seems to suggest as Durrell's spokesman, is also the cultural demand; and the spirit of place, when it operates effectively, will in itself force a certain kind of sexuality, a particular kind of love.

Durrell will not divorce sex from love, and when his couples unite, they do so sexually, demonstrating that the relationship, at least then, is physically right. Alexandria provides the sensual background: the sense of place allows a naturalness of sexual expression that borders on the promiscuous, and at the same time it suggests a healthy freedom from puritanical repression. Consequently, Durrell both follows Lawrence's quest for sexual freedom and rejects Lawrence's horror of promiscuity. Often, what Durrell calls love is sexual passion, bodily expedience, a need for physical relief, a physiological moment when intercourse is possible—but rarely does love express the deepest feelings of which an individual is capable. His couples pair off too easily for real love to be at the root of their desire. Love, as Lawrence realized, affected the lover and caused changes in personality that stemmed directly from his feelings. A person in love was one possessed. Love, accordingly, allowed for little else and thwarted other activity. For Durrell, however, the feeling of love partakes too readily of the sensuality of Alexandria, and therefore without real love the novels lack adequate tension.

In the serious novel, love should of course create conflicts, whether they be conflicts within one's own feelings or with society. It is evident, from the dramatic effectiveness of the love scenes in his better novels, that Lawrence realized this. In the easy freedom of *his* lovers in their sexual relationships, however, Durrell is surely closer to Henry Miller than to Lawrence. Miller, perhaps even more than Lawrence, helped free the literary atmosphere, and Durrell's *Black Book* (1938), a shadowy source for the *Quartet*, shows Miller's influence. For both writers, Durrell and Miller, the sexual relationship is spontaneous, neither the cause of tensions nor the direct product of neurosis. Love frees rather than imprisons the individual. Love and sex are equated indivisibly, and the lover gives of himself as freely as he wishes to receive. In Miller's view, one holds nothing back, has no regrets, and asks no more than one is willing to offer. A novel based on such a philosophy

can be robust, humorous, and sympathetic, but it cannot be serious, tragic, or even dramatic.

Durrell at his best fluctuates between Miller's and Lawrence's views. Since the publication of *The Tropic of Cancer* in the thirties, the world's problems have multiplied, as Durrell realizes, and this attitude must carry over into the love relationship as well. The freedom for which Miller agitated, is now more complicated, especially after Lawrence himself imposed a sense of responsibility; accordingly, Durrell focuses his attention somewhere in between. He offers not so much a sense of responsibility in the relationship as a shearing away of the demand for happiness, so that the lover, even while loving, recognizes that he is at the mercy of an uncontrollable doom. Durrell, accordingly, seems more interested in the psychology of love than Miller, and here he once again approaches Lawrence's views. For Durrell, love can be spontaneous—between Darley and the sick dancer, Melissa, for example; but it can also be tortuous—between Nessim and Justine, Darley and Justine, Pursewarden and Justine, Pursewarden and his sister, Liza. The very ease with which these characters indulge in physical love bespeaks a certain sadness—that love has little significance when sensuality overwhelms.

Always in the background of these major affairs are the even more tortured and grotesque minor ones, involving the dissolute Capodistria, the sensual Amaril and Pombal, and various homosexuals and bisexuals. The result is a mosaic of happy and unhappy affairs, ever-expanding and contracting like the novel form itself. No one relationship ever stands still, for doubling affairs (while Justine is married to Nessim, she uses Darley to get closer to Pursewarden, whom, according to Balthazar, she really "loves"), paralleling situations, and involutions in time all keep the love affairs protean. If one compared the love element to a chameleon, he could see how the affairs are constantly assuming new colors, new formations, new positions to suit the moment. Never remaining fixed, each affair blends into its background and and becomes virtually indistinguishable from it.—FREDERICK R. KARL, "Lawrence Durrell: Physical and Metaphysical Love," *The Contemporary English Novel*, 1962, pp. 44–47

Works

THE ALEXANDRIA QUARTET

There is something in Durrell's work for almost every reader, for men and women of every creed and nationality. Since Durrell went to great pains to put it there ("I needed money desperately"), his huge success may be described as entirely deliberate. He has thrown into the *Quartet* every imaginable sort of character, every sort of situation, even every sort of tone, style and literary influence. The result is the closest thing to an all-purpose novel that has ever been attempted, and the flow of happy customers from all nations is a testimony to Durrell's determination to close no frontiers and impose no preferences. Anything goes—and everything has gone in.

The problem that arises with this sort of writing is one of form, *i.e.*, how to make one strong parcel out of so many differently shaped commodities, how to impose method on what would otherwise be madness. Durrell's solution—which many regard as the most revolutionary innovation in modern fiction—was not only to throw all his thoughts and characters into an invented city but to hitch space and time together under the yoke of Albert Einstein. "*The Quartet*," Durrell writes, "is a four-decker novel whose form is based on the relativity propostion. Three sides of space and one of time constitute the soup-mix recipe."

On hearing this a mathematician wrote Durrell a short, tart note: "Dear Boy, Poppycock! [This] is a mathematical concept and to try and make literature from such things is rubbish." Murmuring politely, "He may well be right," Durrell proceeded with his demonstration. In *Justine*, the first novel of the *Quartet*, he described all the events and characters through the eyes of one person, as is done in an ordinary novel. Naturally the reader thinks on laying down *Justine* that he has read the whole story—only to find on picking up the second novel, *Balthazar*, that the person who told the story in *Justine* misunderstood most of what was happening because he saw everything strictly from his own point of view, which was a "relative" one. So in *Balthazar* a character of that name corrects the mistakes of *Justine* and shows what "really" happened—except that in the third novel, *Mountolive*, the reader finds that Balthazar, too, was speaking "relatively" and that the characters had all kinds of motives and the events all kinds of causes which he never suspected. In the fourth novel, *Clea*, the reader is told what happens to the characters several years after the now untangled events of the first three books took place. This is where time joins up with what has happened in space—like three sides to the market square and a clock tower on the fourth.

So simplified a view of relativity may not be sound Einstein but it makes for a spectacular whodunit, a serial drama that, instead of steadily advancing, continuously folds in on itself. How it works for all the characters can be seen simply by taking one of them as an example. In the first book the beautiful Jewish heroine Justine is apparently betraying her Egyptian husband, Nessim, by having an affair with the Irishman who tells the story. But in the second book we learn that the affair was only a blind: Justine wanted her husband's jealousy to be focused on the Irishman so that she could have a serious, unsuspected affair with a certain important official. But the third book shows that this, too, is an incomplete version of the truth. Justine does not "betray" her husband in the way we think. On the contrary, the two of them are inseparably united as leaders of an underground movement, shipping arms to Palestine. Justine's "infidelity" is part of her political duties.

It is easy to imagine how intriguing this method is when applied to scores of characters. Moreover, even if the whole Einsteinian base of the *Quartet* is dismissed as poppycock, there is still the curious thrill—like that of the ground shifting under one's feet—that the experiment with time provides.

"All very well," says the man who hasn't read Durrell, "but what's the story about?" This is a question that much amuses Durrell, who has seen more than one critic sit down briskly to answer it and finish up with a ream of paper and his own head in the wastebasket. Not even Durrell can put down the exact nature of the *Quartet*, though he can provide it with half a dozen natures, all different and all contradictory. Durrell has called his four-decker simply "an investigation of modern love." He has said that it illustrates "the sexual act playing the part of our 'knowing' machine—much in the manner indicated in the King James Bible: 'And Cain knew his wife, and she conceived and bare Enoch.'"

But he has also suggested that there is nothing in a person *to* know, and that the *Quartet* shows that "human personality as such is an illusion." Off on still another tangent, he has declared that the *Quartet* is simply the work of "a poet who has stumbled into prose" and who uses the theory of relativity as an up-to-date floor "to do a poetic dance upon." Finally, he has declared that "the whole business of the four books, apart from other things, shows how an artist grows up."—Nigel Dennis, "New Four-Star King of Novelists," *Life*, November 21, 1960, pp. 98–100

In this work Durrell has set himself the unenviable task of working out what he says is a "morphological form one might appropriately call 'classical'—for our time." To him it is a self-evident proposition that Joyce and Proust were working with Bergsonian "Duration," whereas the definitive form for our age must be derived from the space-time continuum. He employs the metaphor of a prepared soup-mix in which three volumes will deal with space and one with time—obviously *Justine*, *Balthazar*, and *Mountolive* constitute the space volumes, and *Clea* adds the time element. He explains that the first three are to be considered "siblings," more or less contemporaneous recountings of the same complex of happenings from different points of view, whereas *Clea* is a true "sequel" since it occurs after the events treated in the preceding three volumes. In addition, he has handled point of view, which he calls the "subject-object relation," much as Faulkner did in *The Sound and the Fury*. In this case, Darley, an Irish schoolmaster, relates volume one, Balthazar is largely responsible for volume two, and volume three is objective narration, both in the sense of omniscient point of view and in the sense of seeing Darley as an "object" rather than as the viewing "subject." Volume four returns largely to Darley's point of view.

If Durrell is to support the contention that his achievement in this form is unique (and thus "classical" in T. S. Eliot's sense of exhausting the possibilities in the genre for his age) then he must have contributed a new element which did not appear in the work of his forbears or comtemporaries. He tries to prove just this in the prefatory "Note" to *Balthazar* in which he makes the remark about Proust and Joyce.

Actually, Durrell is not nearly as original as he maintains. One has only to think of Proust to be re-infused with the lovingly detailed treatments of Combray, Méséglise, Balbec, and Venice, or particular spots like the inner courtyard of the Guermantes Paris residence, Aunt Léonie's bedroom, and the like. Here, surely, is a sense of place and a commitment to the claims of space that has little to do with Bergson's *durée*. In particular scenes, too, such as the occasion on which Marcel receives a garbled telegram in Venice, seemingly proving Albertine's existence long after her death; or the incident of the Duchesse de Guermantes' red shoes; or in M. Swann's anguished pursuit of the elusive Odette before their marriage, one finds a rich consciousness of the complex interworkings of space and time—to say nothing of Marcel's astonished apostrophes on the miracle of the telephone and the airplane. Equally strongly in Joyce do we find a nearly monomaniac preoccupation with the surface of Dublin and with the spatial deployment of its inhabitants. In "Wandering Rocks" of *Ulysses*, for example, the interweaving of time and space is unimaginably complex, as the Viceregal procession blends in with Father Conmee's walk, the wanderings of Stephen's sisters, and the temporal-spatial juggling of countless other Dubliners. Indeed, the entire substance of this book is a demonstration of how far an artist can go in substituting a space-time continuum for standard chronological or causational plotting.

Lawrence Durrell's true originality is that he retains the suspense and pleasure associated with traditional plots though he writes using multiple points of view, stream of consciousness, and the other features of what had heretofore been called the "experimental" novel. With Proust and Joyce and Virginia Woolf, plot—in the sense of a temporally related series of events—was almost entirely banished from the novel. The centrality of finely spun contemplation *about* event necessarily pushed event into an already achieved past (as in *Mrs. Dalloway*) or out to the blank margins of the text (as in *Ulysses*), where one can only infer the action from the contemplation about it. Durrell, to be sure, is also dealing in the first three volumes with an already achieved set of events, but he vivifies the events by dribbling out in carefully spaced increments astoundingly different and conflicting interpretations of the same set of characters and events and motives. Thus the *Alexandria Quartet* is, in that sense, a truly relativistic treatment of reality. . . .

To be sure, no reader could, on having finished the *Quartet*, reconstruct the plot chronologically or causally in any detail—it *is* only an impression of traditional plotting that Durrell imparts. Once the reader is submerged in the milieu of the novels, he feels the author can lead him in any direction and still reveal fascinating new characters and situations or totally fresh views of events that have already happened. If there is a metaphor that adequately conveys the form of the novels, it would have to be that of standing at the hub of a wheel that projects spokes in all directions and dimensions; the reader feels the author is capable of following any spoke at will. In addition, no matter what spoke is explored, the reader also continuously feels that he is at the hub of countless fresh possibilities which are moving out in all directions. Thus one of the distinctive qualities of this form is that one never feels the book is finished, even though it has a structure that looks premeditated: volumes one and two end with letters to and from Clea, who seems to stand as a final authority, and when volume four turns directly to Clea herself, one feels that this is the direction in which one has already been traveling.

This sense of a lack of finality within a structural pattern may easily be Durrell's contribution to the form of the modern novel although at least one writer finds that Ford Madox Ford antedated Durrell in this technique. On finishing *Justine*, the reader feels that he has assimilated a certain delimited situation; in opening *Balthazar*, he finds that a large number of the assumptions he was led to accept in *Justine* are clearly false; as this process continues in *Mountolive* and *Clea*, the reader becomes wary—he refuses to accept any event as final or any interpretation as definitive. He develops a relativistic view which acknowledges the truth of appearances on the basis of what he knows at the moment, but he prepares himself for the possibility that any of these assumptions may be completely reversed later on. When Narouz murders Toto de Brunel at the close of *Balthazar*, the reader is not completely perplexed to learn that Narouz thought this was Justine; why Narouz should want to murder Justine is not entirely clear, but the reader feels the reason does not matter because there must be a motive, and even if it were given, it might be reversed later on—or else Toto might not be dead, just as Capodistria was not actually murdered, although the reader thought so at the end of *Justine*. If the reader objects to this lack of finality, Durrell might well reply that this is the same perplexity with which laymen greeted the first discoveries of modern physics.—FRANK BALDANZA, "Lawrence Durrell's 'Word Continuum,'" *Crt*, Spring–Summer 1961, pp. 4–11

The Alexandria Quartet seems to be built on the idea that one person can be different things to different observers, that a sequence of events can be interpreted in various ways and no way is any truer than another. The idea is neither novel nor true; or, if true, then true within such narrow limits that no tetralogy or 'quartet' or 'word-continuum' can safely be based on it. That Durell manages to make it seem true for a while is a credit to his poetic talent: his 'views of Alexandria' are so sharply focused as almost to persuade us that *anything* he tells us is true even if it contradicts something else. It is also a discredit to his 'characters', who lack precisely character. Does

Justine love Darley? Is she merely using him to conceal her love for Pursewarden? (And would this manoeuvre be as likely as Durrell assumes?) Or is it the Palestine conspiracy which claims her real love? Was she or wasn't she raped as a child? Has she a 'wicked fashionable face'? Or a 'black stern' one? Did her child die in a brothel? Did she have no child? Durrell doesn't want to know. When everything is true, nothing is true. Off come the glamorous veils one by one—they are still coming off when the series 'ends'. Life isn't like this: more to the point, there seems no reason why art should be. Perhaps it is in a desperate attempt to endow his creations with character that Durrell deprives them of limbs. Capodistria wears a black patch over his eye, Scobie has a glass eye, and Hamid, Abdul and (in the end) Nessim are all one-eyed. Liz is completely blind, so is her daughter. Panayotis has had his tongue cut out. Balthazar loses his teeth and almost his hands. Clea loses a hand, Nessim a finger along with the eye, and Leila her beauty. Semira, on the contrary, gains a nose. Casualties among the minor non-characters are equally high: heads are chopped off, bits of ears removed, faces mashed by a hippo-hide whip, foreskins tumble in a continuous shower and eunuchs abound. Moreover, practically every horror happens at least twice—for instance, the camel being chopped up alive—or is told twice. But all the violence at Durrell's command cannot create *character*. And alas the two promisingly solid human creations of the quartet are undone by Durrell's lack of trust in them.—D. J. EN-RIGHT, "Alexandrian Nights' Entertainments," *Conspirators and Poets*, 1966, pp. 112–13

OTHER NOVELS

The young Durrell of the 1940's was fired with the awareness of his own potential. He knew that the excitement Miller's work created in him indicated that he too would ultimately experiment and originate. He was self-conscious about the similarities between his *Cefalû* and Huxley's novels, and he certainly was aware that the formula he was using was trite. His detached attitude toward the work was a defense—and healthy and informed.

The particular satisfactions in the novel come from the Durrellian sensibilities superimposed on an old formula. The novel owes much to Aldous Huxley, but it also has a voice of its own. Addressed to those who care, it takes its issues seriously. A safe interval above the thrillers that it rather deliberately imitates, it instructs while it entertains; and it always distinguishes between the two values.

Durrell's careful attention to the past histories of his characters reveals his conscience. He could not let the formula take over completely. Yet these attempts to give depth and dimensions to the characters almost sabotage the whole business by adding irrelevant details. Most of the characters, however, carry the burden of allegory gracefully. They are stereotypes, of course, for the demands of the morality control that aspect of characterization. Miss Dombey, the missionary, *is a missionary*—not much else. And Campion is the average of all brilliant and cynical artists.

The writing is professionally smooth. Durrell has learned his trade. In *Cefalû* he is using a conventional form that he can handle. He must get a cast of characters to set sail together, must get a group of them into the labyrinth—and some of them out again. And he must make it all add up. The central metaphor, the labyrinth, takes the characters to Crete, and each of the seven major characters enters the labyrinth as part of his own search. The attitude of each toward the labyrinth and the degree of his anxiety shape the individual destinies.

Several characters, like the American reporter in the first scene, and Katina, the servant-wife, dangle; for they belong

only to the story-framework which includes a prelude called "The Argument" and an epilogue called "At Cefalû." But no major character is not accounted for fully in the end. Some of the surprises—such as the fact that the hoax was *fixed* (the statues were really genuine) and that Axelos is married to his servant—are manipulated and heavy. Yet the novel ends with an authentic sigh.—JOHN A. WEIGEL, *Lawrence Durrell*, 1965, pp. 49–50

The great spirit that broods over *The Black Book* is not, however, that of Henry Miller but that of T. S. Eliot. Essentially, *The Black Book* is a set of variations on *The Waste Land*. *The Waste Land* is a poem about sterility, about the late autumn or early winter (in the Spenglerian sense) of a culture. This sterility is poetically reflected in the sterility of the most potentially creative and potentially destructive of all human relationships, that of sexual love. Yet the drive of the poem is a desperate, perhaps impossible quest to get beyond sterility. Its setting is a phantasmagoric London, modulated in a dream-like fashion, though vividly physically present. There is a perpetual juxtaposition of that which is sordid, the carbuncular bank clerk, the girl opening tinned food and drying her combinations on the window sill, with all the echoes of ancientness and splendour in London's memory, Spenser's Thames, the pleasant whining of a mandoline in a Lower Thames Street pub, St. Magnus Martyr with its inexplicable splendour of Ionian white and gold. In the language, Elizabethan allusion or pastiche juxtaposes with cockney slang. The horror, the boredom, the disgust, which *The Waste Land* embodies so vividly, are pierced from above and below with sudden glory and compassion. A profound death-wish transforms itself into an agonizing pilgrimage towards the sources of life.

The Black Book is *Waste Land*-like in its setting, but I mean that in a moral, not in a topographical sense. I have in mind a much broader resemblance, the sense of a contrast between the magic of an older England, a past magic that comes alive to Lawrence Lucifer in the pastoral presence, nymph or shepherdess, of his *anima*-figure, suddenly alive in a world of rough stone cottages and apple blossom—the contrast between that lost pastoral world and the comic-macabre or comic-grotesque hell, the city detritus of a once organic culture, that Lawrence Lucifer is more often exploring. The rich past chokes him; he feels he is treading on corpses. He is caught, as Tarquin and Gregory are caught, between a rich cultural inheritance, which has gone dead, and a world of brute impulse. The inherited culture breeds a fastidiousness, which in the end is *fastidium*, disgust with life.

In characters like Clare, Lobo, and Perez (the names suggest *Gerontion*, the Sweeney poems, and *Sweeney Agonistes*) mere brute impulse reveals itself with a sterile disgustingness that might seem to justify a cultural disgust. A way out is suggested only indirectly, in the rebelliousness and disgust of the hero, and in Death Gregory's perpetual verging, in his relationship with his pitiable wife and mistress Grace (her name is not unsymptomatic), on 'the awful daring of a moment's surrender', which never in the end takes place. There is no way out, either, for any of the characters except Lawrence Lucifer, through art. Death Gregory's writing builds the walls of isolation closer round him, Eliot's 'prison', Dante's '*orribile torre*'. Lawrence Lucifer's own role, like his name, is ambiguous: is he a bearer of light into dark places, or a rebel angel, relishing the torment of all these damned souls? Or for all the energy of his protests, is he himself among them? 'Give, sympathize, control': the final impact of *The Black Book* is as ambiguous as the final impact of *The Waste Land*. We ought to give, sympathize, and control, but can we? What real seren-

ity and wisdom has Lawr⟨ ⟩
whole book not a project⟨ ⟩
lence? And has the *anim⟨ ⟩*
Lucifer: 'Your poetry is ⟨ ⟩
style. And I don't unders⟨ ⟩
the same woman at the ⟨ ⟩

This girl's voice expr⟨ ⟩
life and art, for the 'noth⟨ ⟩
natural to young women,⟨ ⟩
young men. Her words w⟨ ⟩
because of their cool ind⟨ ⟩
hatred', of Gothic suffer⟨ ⟩
subject-matter. And her a⟨ ⟩
his poems, sometimes, a⟨ ⟩
rence Durrell would ever⟨ ⟩
naked burning impact of⟨ ⟩
rocky bareness, sparse el⟨ ⟩
remain a Gothic spirit: F⟨ ⟩
stuffing, verbal copiousn⟨ ⟩
and whirling words'. *The⟨ ⟩*
tuousness, morbidity, bla⟨ ⟩
pity, and in its occasio⟨ ⟩
naturalism, records the ⟨ ⟩
anti-classical talent.—G. ⟨ ⟩
Book," Lawrence Durrell⟨ ⟩

Durrell's new book, *Tur⟨ ⟩*
thin, relaxed novel, whic⟨ ⟩
Quartet, no longer even ⟨ ⟩
by what he is writing abou⟨ ⟩
mon with the earlier fict⟨ ⟩
and Istanbul instead of Al⟨ ⟩
has been considerably m⟨ ⟩
predilection for very high⟨ ⟩
salon on the one hand, ⟨ ⟩

In a note at the end ⟨ ⟩
and there in the text atte⟨ ⟩
from *The Alexandria Qu⟨ ⟩*
this is intentional." A ph⟨ ⟩
understating, for what ⟨ ⟩
ashamed self-imitation. If⟨ ⟩
cism less flashy, many f⟨ ⟩
unchanged. Darley, the ⟨ ⟩
Felix Charlock, a recordi⟨ ⟩
the story in *Tunc*. Pursew⟨ ⟩
divided into two people: K⟨ ⟩
poet, and Caradoc, a scab⟨ ⟩
tite, Scobie, reappears in ⟨ ⟩
broken-down clown "with⟨ ⟩
much the same: the little ⟨ ⟩
Athens prostitute who en⟨ ⟩
acquiring a tragic dignity⟨ ⟩
book, Charlock is given a ⟨ ⟩
company called Merlin, a⟨ ⟩
he marries Benedicta, the⟨ ⟩
another version of Justine:⟨ ⟩
deal richer. (She also has s⟨ ⟩
somewhat more Gothic.)⟨ ⟩

In smaller ways, too,⟨ ⟩
his earlier writings. At on⟨ ⟩
lidded gaze of a French m⟨ ⟩
of the faces of the young?⟨ ⟩
the great tuck box of sex ⟨ ⟩
moldy." Compare this wi⟨ ⟩
"Alexandria," published in ⟨ ⟩
pantry for jars/Marked 'Pl⟨ ⟩

to the r⟨ ⟩
add, in ⟨ ⟩
pantry"⟨ ⟩
Durrell⟨ ⟩
tance to ⟨ ⟩
he a fri⟨ ⟩
GONZI,⟨ ⟩

Mr. Law⟨ ⟩
kind of tr⟨ ⟩
sensitive;⟨ ⟩
a quick ⟨ ⟩
of clothi⟨ ⟩
sion and ⟨ ⟩
with the ⟨ ⟩
islands.⟨ ⟩

The ⟨ ⟩
island of ⟨ ⟩
Press Off⟨ ⟩
time whe⟨ ⟩
was a pe⟨ ⟩
tively; bu⟨ ⟩
ministrat⟨ ⟩
absurd. ⟨ ⟩
people a⟨ ⟩
Not that ⟨ ⟩
to read. ⟨ ⟩
for they ⟨ ⟩
gaps and ⟨ ⟩
that is p⟨ ⟩
qualities ⟨ ⟩
pages ar⟨ ⟩
general's ⟨ ⟩
cents an⟨ ⟩
scattered⟨ ⟩
Mr. Dur⟨ ⟩
whole bo⟨ ⟩
is not n⟨ ⟩
municati⟨ ⟩
like a g⟨ ⟩
whether ⟨ ⟩
his eye i⟨ ⟩
that he s⟨ ⟩
past.⟨ ⟩

The ⟨ ⟩
framewo⟨ ⟩
leisurely ⟨ ⟩
troduced ⟨ ⟩
their app⟨ ⟩
the main ⟨ ⟩
of landsc⟨ ⟩
this pure⟨ ⟩
friendshi⟨ ⟩
why the ⟨ ⟩
characte⟨ ⟩

The ⟨ ⟩
becomes ⟨ ⟩
Johnson.⟨ ⟩
scenes h⟨ ⟩
Soroni, ⟨ ⟩
and endi⟨ ⟩
best piec⟨ ⟩
is full of ⟨ ⟩
many oth⟨ ⟩
dancing.⟨ ⟩

ition of the portentous word "great.") One might
ing, that the sensibility that can see sex as a "great
"great tuck-box" looks somewhat insensitive, but
long upheld a "pagan" and "Mediterranean" resis-
much fussiness in these matters. Not for nothing is
and admirer of Henry Miller.—BERNARD BER-
ile Incense," *NYRB*, July 11, 1968, p. 38

TRAVEL

ce Durrell is extremely well qualified to write the
book which we all enjoy. He is gay, vivacious and
enjoys sights and sounds, colours and tastes; he has
or the eccentric character and the unusual article
r furniture; his prose is often alight with the preci-
enthusiasm of poetry. And he has fallen in love
atest beauty in the world—Greece and the Greek

bject of ⟨*Reflections on a Marine Venus*⟩ is the
odes, where he was working as a Foreign Service
r in the period after the end of the war up till the
Rhodes was restored to the Greek Government. It
d of great interest both politically and administra-
Mr. Durrell scarcely touches upon politics or ad-
except in so far as they seem to him amusing or
at chiefly engages his attention is the landscape, the
perhaps less satisfactorily, the history of the island.
historical passages are in the least dull or difficult
erely doubt whether Frazer would have approved;
idiosyncratic and conversational; they are full of
guenesses; they proceed with an unsteady motion
ably good for the liver but which has none of the
the scholarly and relentless steamroller. Many
devoted to Demetrius Poliorcetes, but this great
me is never once, I think, correctly spelled. Ac-
reathings on Greek words are sometimes left un-
he great sieges of the Turks are just omitted because
d feels that "it would be cruel to devote less than a
to them." But, although this is not Frazer's way, it
ssarily a bad way. Mr. Durrell succeeds in com-
his own restless and abounding enthusiasm and,
d talker, scarcely allows one the time to wonder
judgments and his information are true or not. For
pon the present and it is to illuminate the present
ches at any light which may come to hand from the

book is skilfully contrived, being written in a
of friendship, of long walks and expeditions and
onversations in a delicious garden. We are in-
the author's friends thoroughly enough to enjoy
ances, but not so intimately as to distract us from
eme. For it is in the re-creation of atmosphere and
e that Mr. Durrell chiefly excels, in "memories of
unlight, these dancing summer days passed in idle
and humour by the maned Aegean." (I do not know
egean should be "maned," but I like the word; it is
ic of Mr. Durrell's manner.)
are a few, a very few, occasions when Mr. Durrell
ntentious, and at this he is not half so good as Dr.
But in describing large, complicated and animated
s excellent. The whole account of the "panagyri" at
ginning with a delightful altercation round a bus,
on a note of calm and human dignity, is one of the
of writing about the Mediterranean which I know. It
vit, sympathy and precision and contains, among
r fine passages, a most brilliant description of Greek

I think that in this book Mr. Durrell has done what he
meant to do. He has re-created for himself the moments of his
own happiness and he will have made his readers either wish
that they could go to Rhodes or believe that they have actually
been there.—REX WARNER, "Aegean Sky," *Spec*, Aug. 21,
1953, pp. 203–204

Durrell believes that the task of the travel writer is "to isolate
the germ in the people which is expressed by their landscape."
Travel becomes "a sort of science of intuitions," "the education
of the sensibility." To be educated, the traveler must first identify. "Ten minutes of this sort of quiet inner identification will
give you the notion of the Greek landscape which you could
not get in twenty years of studying ancient Greek texts."
Identification seems simple, "for all landscapes ask the same
question in the same whisper. 'I am watching you—are you
watching yourself in me?'" Durrell's approach is that of the
outsider and the romantic; places exist for his sake. They are—
as titles of his other works suggest—private countries, personal
landscapes. Living on private income and public relations jobs
with the British Government, Durrell identifies with the mythic elements and *status quo* of a place, and closes his eyes to
social and political problems. . . .

Inside Durrell's work is a quest for a self in union with the
universe, a self-created godlike Eastern being antithetical to
modern Western man. Durrell's writings are attempts to "deliver" this self. "Down the Styx," another surrealistic piece
included in the new collection, records a journey through the
rivers of death toward just such a rebirth. At the conclusion,
there is a womb, and "the body of a young boy, lying in a pool
of blood. . . . He is the firstborn." He is the same boy who, at
the conclusion of *The Black Book*, written twenty years earlier,
is reborn—without parents—out of the dead land, England,
into the landscape of his heart's desire, the Greek island.

As a catalyst for rebirth, Durrell seems to need union with
stony, sun-washed landscapes, landscapes like the Greek island
or Provence, or the place of his birth and childhood, India. His
repeated attempts to identify with landscapes like that of the
Greek island seem, in part, a result of his longing for the
childhood landscape. Uprooted from the foot of the Himalayas
at the age of 11 and transplanted to the gray sidewalks of England, Durrell remembers India as a dazzling and holy place.
Unhappy in England, he envisioned himself as a foreigner
whose "real" self England was murdering. Corfu, the Greek
island to which he went after "escaping" England, seems to
have been potentially a return to the lost self. Island scenes in
many of Durrell's works suggest that his longing for the island
masks a longing for the Eden of childhood. There may even be
an Oedipal aspect to that longing. In the conclusion of the
Quartet, for example, Darley (the main author-identification
figure) must cut Clea and himself away from a perfect but
sterile island retreat in order to grow up.

Like his own description of Miller, Durrell is "the type of
creative man who is *making use* of his art in order to grow by
it." Durrell uses landscape and landscape writing to create and
explore a self-image. His places are "spirited" by his compulsion to project himself as a mythic being enveloped by an
immortal landscape.—JOAN GOULIANOS, "Landscape of the
Heart," *Nation*, July 14, 1969, pp. 56–57

DRAMA

The quality of the verse plays contrasts sharply with that of the
poems and fiction; where the latter reveal a generally increasing
maturity and grasp of materials, the former manifest a regressive pattern. The more recent poetry and prose encompass a
firmness of image and a vastness of scale generally lacking in

the smaller, more tentative early attempts. The plays, however, diminish chronologically from the lush complexity of *Sappho*, to the fascinating but programmatic *Acté*, to the nearly sterile *Irish Faustus*.

The plays all hark back to Renaissance stagecraft in their use of dramatic verse, psychologically inevitable plotting, and contemporizing of history or legend. *Sappho* revitalizes and humanizes the long-vilified Greek poet; *Acté* portrays a beautiful slave princess who leads a doomed rebellion against Nero's misrule; *An Irish Faustus* gives a Durrellean twist to that hoary but inexhaustible fable. All have been performed, but with limited success. *Sappho*, for instance, ran for only twelve performances in Hamburg; *Acté*, for twenty-six. Yet *Sappho* was hailed as "the outstanding offering" at the Edinburgh Festival of 1961, as a play containing "ample evidence that novelist Durrell could become a major English dramatist" in the modern verse play form pioneered by Eliot, Auden, and Frye. . . .

At the play's heart is its title character; Sappho (not the sexual deviant of legend) reigns like an inspiriting Greek muse over the amorous, artistic, and spiritual life of Lesbos. Each of these three facets finds personification, directly or antithetically, in one of the play's major male figures. The antiamorous Kreon, Sappho's husband, is weak and indulgent, aging rapidly and greedy for the passing power money confers, a man "incapable of suffering from more than mild irritations." The even less attractive Pittakos, the military hero in the process of becoming tyrant, unconsciously parodies the aesthetic vision. A forerunner of *Acté's* Nero, he tells Sappho, appalled at the direction of his career, that he would be an artist of reality, a reality manifesting itself most truly in the form of war.

> A bad medium, you might say, a bad medium.
> Yet from an indifferent soldier I have risen
> To something like an artist in my work.

Swaggeringly self-confident, Pittakos learns too late of the bitterness inherent in the fulfillment of such desires as his. Glutted with victory, he returns to reclaim the Sappho who had been his mistress before his rise to power: "You famous—I victorious. It is all, all/As I imagined it. . ." But Sappho not only mocks his smug self-assurance and sense of embodying divine righteousness but also ridicules his soldier's standard ("Never to question? Always to act?") and ultimately leads the forces which overcome and destroy him.

The third of the triad is Phaon, Pittakos' antithetical twin brother, who alone offers Sappho not meaningless physical contact but real kindredship of spirit. Phaon is in fact the paradigm of Durrellean affirmation, the form against which his fictional protagonists may be measured. . . .

Acté exists on a lower level of intensity than *Sappho*. Its characters, complexities, colors, and poetry are less incandescent, less animate. Where *Sappho* approaches tragedy, *Acté* or *The Prisoners of Time*, as Durrell says in "An Author's Note" to his second play, is melodrama, with starcrossed lovers doomed when duty makes them enemies. Yet of greater interest than the basic love-hate relationship between Acté, the rebellious Scythian princess, and Fabius, Nero's loyal but impassioned and compassionate general, is the relationship of art and life. Even more than in *Sappho*, all the characters are dominated by a sense of style, an intimation that, regardless of consequences, life cannot be amorphous but must, like art, conform to rules of regularity. . . .

If *Acté* is a step or two below *Sappho*, then *An Irish Faustus* is a flight of stairs still still further down. The disappointments of the play are many: the painful unevenness of the language and the poetry; the awkward break in the middle as the magic ring shifts in function from mere object to a symbol

of Faustus' illusions; the ponderously heavy Gothic machinery; uncertainties of motivation and haphazardness of thematic development. In fact, the work fails so badly as drama that, according to *Time*, "Durrell himself was hooted from the stage at the end" of the Hamburg performance. . . .

It might be useful, as a final comment, to suggest a reason for Durrell's steady decline as a dramatist. His line of development in the plays is really a surprising, perhaps even alien, one, for it runs counter to that of the poems and the fiction. The poems and the fiction emphasize that the process of transformation (or maturation), enabling a character either to begin to create as an artist or to feel he no longer needs to, parallels or heralds his being freed of checks on his ability to love. But love, around which Durrell constructs his finest edifices, increasingly dissipates its power in the plays. In them, we take Phaon's achievement most seriously, largely because of his brief but successful affair with Sappho, even though he feels constrained to abandon her when societal pressures threaten to reimpose standards he had done well to move beyond. The problems of *Acté* are greater than those of *Sappho* because of the dual focus of the former: the love affair of Acté and Fabius has dramatic significance, but it goes nowhere; Petronius attains the heraldic universe, but he has nothing meaningful to say of love. And *Irish Faustus*, with its protagonist a middle-aged pedagogue and Margaret a silly schoolgirl, is hollow at the core because, instead of love, the most impassioned expression in Durrell's best work of man's aliveness, he substitutes, in the final scene, the pallid comradeship of a staid old English club. And since no passion ever rears its unruly head *there*, no vision can long evade the stodgy death, confining and trite, that invariably lies in wait in an atmosphere and setting of such unresponsive, even antihuman, design.

Concomitantly, the key to the failure lies in the landscape and Durrell's declining sense of place in the plays. *Sappho* employs landscape in a way that might be termed classical Durrell. Lesbos, though essentially vital in nature, is landscape too pervasive and willful, and which one must flee to achieve meaningful existence; in contrast, the peaceful beauty of "Noname" conforms exactly to the needs of the rejuvenated Phaon and serves as objective correlative for the validity of his new life. Landscape thus plays a fundamental role in *Sappho*, one inextricable from its themes, characters, and poetry.

In *Acté*, to parallel Durrell's less certain conrol of his materials (especially his love theme), landscape plays a less organically central role. Rome is *any* seat of power; Scythia, *any* outlying, rebellious colony; and, most vague, the last scene in Petronius' country villa occurs simply "far from Rome." Finally, in *Irish Faustus*—where the heraldic universe is highly abstract and love impossible—landscape is virtually nonexistent. The few passing references to rain-sodden Ireland and the snow-capped peaks at the end do not alter the fact the *Irish Faustus* takes place anywhere and nowhere, and that the characters are in touch not with a real place but with only a projection of themselves. And the rule in Durrell is that to inhabit a negative or a too dominant landscape may ultimately stifle life, but to inhabit none at all, as is the case with Faustus and those about him, not only precludes even the *possibility* of life but invariably devitalizes the work containing them.— ALAN WARREN FRIEDMAN, "The Evolving Lawrence Durrell," *Lawrence Durrell and* The Alexandria Quartet, 1970, pp. 25–44

CRITICISM

The book of literary criticism—that *Key to Modern British Poetry* which Durrell assembled from his Argentine lectures—

can be a helpful, though once in a while misleading, introduction to many of the most important themes he was later to develop, for in it he traces out the ideas that at the time of its 1952 publication seemed to him to be of dominant importance, not just to contemporary poetry but to contemporary man as well.

Durrell's image of reality as it is presented in his *Key* can be reduced, it seems to me, to two not altogether dissimilar landscapes—both of them founded on relativity principles—and to an implicit pattern behind both of them that may be a good deal more like an absolute.

The first of the two landscapes is, of course, the external one developed by Einstein and popularized by men like Eddington and Whitehead, landscape oddly like Baudelaire's symbolist forest, where people watch trees watching people. For one important aspect of the relativity theory, the Principle of Indeterminacy, effectively cuts the ground out from under the neat causality of nineteenth-century science. The new physics, Durrell points out, "is founded upon the theory that we cannot observe the course of nature without disturbing it." Perhaps the most significant consequence of this theory is that it altogether changes the nature of knowledge. For when we can never observe without to some extent corrupting the thing observed, we soon find we have to discard the notion of verifiable truth. Truth, if it is to be ascertained at all, becomes available only through a kind of intuition: we imagine what things might be like if we weren't around observing; we do our best to get rid of the observer's perspective! "Under the terms of the new idea a precise knowledge of the outer world becomes an impossibility. This is because we and the outer world (subject and object) constitute a whole." If we are part of a whole, Durrell insists, "we can no longer objectify it successfully." Try as we will, we'll never have the comfortable assurance that we see things as they are!

The literary consequence of this notion, Durrell realizes, is momentous; for the relativity theory involves a reorientation for the modern writer not only toward the materials of his art but also toward himself, his audience, his world. It shows up, Durrell contends, both in the places in which it might be expected to appear—the plots, say, of Joyce and Virginia Woolf, the characterization of Gide, the poetic structure of Eliot's "Gerontion"—and also in the places we are least likely to look for it: in symbol, in metaphor, in incidental imagery, even in sentence structure.

Durrell works through a good deal of modern literature to document his point. But for us the most obvious demonstration is in Durrell himself, who rather tentatively in *The Black Book*, and then with great assurance in *The Alexandria Quartet*, and finally in greatest intricacy in *Monsieur*, creates a dense arrangement of constantly discovering, constantly qualifying observers, each of whom distorts the scene he observes and is in turn distorted by it. There is really no single "true" view of any of the events offered. Only with total knowledge, Durrell darkly suggests, could we approach such a view. With such knowledge, of course, what we would see would be most spectacular for, seeing everything, we would be spectators of pure unadulterated process. Or so it would for a while seem to us, the characters dancing through a frantic interrelationship in much the same way that atoms in a balloonful of hot air bound and rebound against one another. But we would soon realize, if we were witty enough, that the patterns we saw those atoms creating were—because of our limited (and distorting) visions—patterns as much of our own construction as of the atoms themselves.

. . . ⟨I⟩t is ultimately the "continuum" of Einsteinian physics that is to act as a metaphor for the kind of art Durrell proposes for himself, the "word continuum" of *The Alexandria Quartet* and certain of the poems reflecting not just the way the characters of a work (its "particles") are affected by one another and by an observer, but more importantly how the events of a novel are deployed, not just in space and not just in the "time-saturated" chronologies of nineteenth-century fiction but in a new "space-time." For time, Durrell believes, is "the measure of our death-consciousness," and when our notions of time began to change, first under the impact of Darwin and then under the impact of Einstein, all of our ideas about life and death began to change too. Locating evidence of this change in such different works as Eliot's *Four Quartets*, Rilke's *Duinese Elegies*, and Joyce's *Ulysses*, Durrell decides that Einstein's treatment of time, not in serial fashion but rather as a pervasive aspect of the space-time continuum, forced onto our more perceptive writers a new view of life and a new form in which to express that view.—JOHN UNTERECKER, "Lawrence Durrell," *Six Contemporary British Novelists*, ed. George Stade, 1976, pp. 237–41

POETRY

Durrell is the Gauguin of modern poetry, a Gauguin whose Marquesas was an isle of Greece. The verb is in the past because those happy days are gone. Like other epicurean hermits of art, Durrell has discovered that our present history refuses to let the solitary alone. During the war he was ousted from his island, and Egypt became his abode. The period, then, of his Golden Age is over; his writing has entered an Alexandrian phase. What comes after this we have still to wait for; but I find it most unlikely to believe that even a return to the metropolitan landscape can silence a talent as powerful as his.

"My skill," writes Durrell, "is in words only"; a modesty that tells no more than half the truth. But before we examine his supra-verbal talent, it might be as well briefly to distinguish one or two types of this "skill in words" and decide which one is peculiarly his.

Working on the principle of elimination, we can begin by saying it is not a matter of virtuosity alone. There is more in the style of this poet than a deft manipulation of words—tightrope walking on consonants and vowels in the manner of de Banville's "Odes Funambulesques." Neither does this poetry consist mainly of rhetoric, where words and phrases mount on stilts and speak through the megaphone of persuasion. Of that kind of verbal skill, which is really verbal fluency—the ready effervescence of words that seems to form the chief attraction of such poets as Henry Treece—there is little in the verse of Durrell. It is true there is no verbal sparseness here: the fountains flow freely enough, and the words come roundly and rapidly to hand. But the readiness and richness of this poet is primarily an imaginative one, giving rise to a host of images; a full bloodstream of comparisons. It would, however, be clearly wrong to confuse this poetry with that type which issues from its author as a series of exclamations, one after another, as sensations overtake him. The other side to Durrell's teeming imagination is his power of organizing his impressions, of ordering his thoughts till each poem is the result of what Rossetti described as "fundamental brainwork."

Tentatively, then, one may define Mr. Durrell's "skill in words" as an architectural talent; the skill of one who, figuratively speaking, lays the bricks to his own blueprints; the skill of designer and executant combined; the art of the clairvoyant and the craft of the poet-mason. . . .

"Sight alone produces an instantaneous impulse," wrote Gauguin in his diary. Opposed to this, Durrell has the power to render abstract qualities visible, to present ideas in pictorial terms; as when he speaks of children as "These gruesome little artists of the impulse," "cast down like asterisks among their toys," of Fabre as "This pollen-hunter of exact observation," or "the ends of longings like unconnected nerves." This is not to say that the faculty of plastic description is not also his, as the following quotation shows:

> For look. The mauve street is swallowed
> And the bats have begun to stitch slowly

or when with record brevity, he flashes a picture of "the hard blue winterset" before us, or with subtle accuracy tells us how

> Day rings in the higher airs
> Pure with cicadas, and slowing
> Like a pulse to smoke from farms,
> Extinguished in the exhausted earth,
> Unclenching like a fist and going.

Sometimes this fine comparative sense produces the rare recherché image ("Now dense as clouded urine moves the lake," "restless as a wick afloat in water"), or that figure of speech which the Elizabethans called "the conceit" ("Fatherless as shoes walking over dead leaves"). Neither are these "surprise" similes invariably successful in their effect. The note of calculation is occasionally heard and the spontaneous essential tone is lost. So the poet writes of

> Ten summers, lazy as fishes . . .
> Ten winters, nude as thimbles

while in another poem he speaks of "The light running like fishes among the leaves." Both references are permissible, of course, but from neither do we get that burning revelation, that sense of rediscovery, which the finest metaphorical speech can produce.

. . . ⟨O⟩ne must insist that Durrell is more than the literary poet, more than a melodious conjuror of speech. He is, in fact, a "metaphysical" poet. This element of profound thoughtfulness in his verse has undoubtedly been much ignored; the more so because his first poems, *A Private County*, contained as many baits for the appreciative senses as for the critical and questioning mind. Certainly all the gambits of lyrical writing are to be found in this first book: the incisive pathos of the finale from the poem "In Arcadia":

> Something died out by this river; but it seems
> Less than a nightingale ago;

the haunting music of a nocturne in the lines:

> Here stars come soft to pasture
> And all doors lead to sleep;

the onomatopoeic control of vowels, as in

> Diminishing the foolish cool
> Haunting note of the dove;

or the concentrated conciseness of:

> nothing grows
> But the ocean expunges.

Perhaps the metaphysical note is first heard in the poem "Fangbrand" (subtitled "A Biography"), which tells how a man came to live by himself on a Greek island, how the island changed him, and how he died there. The actions of the character and his thoughts are subordinated to the slow spelling-out of the tale of a man in relation to a landscape. All one sees is the man's figure posed against the background of the island; and the man is felt to represent mankind as the island seems to stand for nature.

By the vividness of the imagery and the philosophical serenity of the poem the author evokes the immediacy of time—what Goethe once termed "the eternal present." On this island the problem of living, the meaning of his own personal existence, comes home to the man with the added force of silence:

> Measured in the heart's small flask
> The spirit's disturbance: the one voice
> Saying "Renounce," the other
> Answering "Be"; the division
> Of the darkness into faces
> Crying "Too late" "Too late."
>
> Truth's metaphor is the needle,
> The magnetic north of purpose
> Striving against the true north
> Of self: Fangbrand found it out,
> The final dualism in very self,
> An old man holding an asphodel.

His peace finally made with nature, the once difficult discipline of living becomes an easy spontaneous joy; and in due time knowledge is followed by death:

> Time's chemicals mock the hunter
> For crumbs of doctrine; Fangbrand
> Died with his art like a vase.
> The grave in the rock,
> Sweetened by saffron, bubbles water
> Like a smile, an animal truth.

In maturity of attitude, depth of insight, and roundness of diction "Fangbrand" has a good claim to be considered as one of the most satisfying poems published since 1940.—DEREK STANFORD, "Lawrence Durrell: An Early View of His Poetry" (1948), *The World of Lawrence Durrell*, ed. Harry T. Moore, 1962, pp. 38–45

One of the best, and certainly one of the most civilized writers in England today is Lawrence Durrell. Maybe that is why he is what is called inadequately known on this side. He has written a couple of superlative travel books, literary essays, miscellaneous *belles lettres*, four volumes of poetry, and two novels, different from each other and each quite unlike any other fictions of our day—at least until they produce imitators. Grove Press has gathered a selection of the poems. The only thing wrong with it is that it is much too short. I enjoy Durrell's poetry more than that of anybody else anywhere near his age—now writing in the British Isles. In fact, only MacDiarmid, Muir and Read appeal to me as much. It is a poetry of tone, the communication of the precise quality of a very precious kind of revery—animalism and skeptic faith recollected in tranquillity. Wallace Stevens wrote with the same emotional subject matter, but his poetry is cooked and strident in comparison with Durrell's easy relaxation. Again, he is gifted with a gentle, unself-conscious eroticism very rare in our nasty and Puritan world—never nastier than amongst our advanced *emancipés*.

The poet who has probably influenced him most is Georgis Kavafis, the only homosexual writer in history who was not ridden with guilt. Durrell's loves and adventures have been more normal and less random, so that he is saved from Kavafis' heart-rending nostalgia for vanished and vanishing fulfillment. No one writing verse today can better evoke a scene, a place, a room, a situation, the body of a woman, alive at just that fleeting moment that it lived, with all the meaning of its present, and all the pathos of its vanishing. Again, no one can better bow over unspeaking, resonant strings. Durrell's overtones and references would be destroyed by notes. It is just a haunting flavor of Gibbon's Theodora—lurking in the background with her rumors of bearpits and brothels—that counts in Durrell's poem to a modern intellectual tart of the same name. What glitters in the foreground is the gold fleck in the living girl's eye. And it is all done so simply, with never a mirror; the best kind of legerdemain, without a stick of apparatus. Durrell's ancestor is Horace. Someday, when the world has calmed down, we will again realize that Horace is the perfect artist he was known to be in less troubled times. Right now, Lawrence Durrell is the only person I know who has the guts to walk in his footsteps.—KENNETH REXROTH, "The Footsteps of Horace," *Nation*, May 18, 1951, p. 444

Readers who know Mr. Durrell's *Bitter Lemons* will have noticed that he has two styles—one for facts and one for fancies. The first is remarkable for its fair-mindedness, the second is the kind of thing that, with the Alexandria Quartet, has gathered a dangerously opulent self-assurance and draws from the reviewers terms like "hauntingly sensual" and testimonials as to Durrell's ability to create atmosphere "dazzlingly beautiful, and suffocatingly evil". In the teeth of common consent, one is prompted to wonder whether this famous style, which has a good deal in common with the poetry, hasn't been overrated and whether the facetal technique of the Quartet isn't nearer to Browning's *Ring and the Book* than to Proust, with a good deal of unwholesomeness superadded. The lengthy periods, the tuppence-coloured proliferation of adjectives, the sharp brittle skill are certainly far removed from Proust's Ruskinian particularity and his hold on both moral and sensuous detail. Durrell's novelist's prose and his poetry are of a piece. The clogged prose is a fit medium for the presence of dwarfs, incest, nefarious sexuality: it creates a world as morally unintelligible as John Webster's and as stylistically overdressed as Djuna Barnes' *Nightwood*. The poetry has a comparable fuzziness, an improviser's smart redundancies as he weaves a theme to no particular end and attempts to dazzle us with style. Style is not enough. Viewpoint succeeds viewpoint in the novels to create, not Proustian irony or anything analogous (the analogy has been made) to Picasso's multi-faceted awareness, but simply a world of moral relativity. Cadence succeeds liquid cadence in so many of the poems to produce an effect of atmospheric muddle. . . .

The all-over impression derived from Durrell's *Collected Poems* is one of slackness. His undeniable skill, his way with words, cannot disguise the fact that he has no moral discoveries to offer. The Mediterranean world on which so much of his poetry draws is not that of Pound's Tempio where "one thought cuts through another with clean edge". It is a world of malady and the style that Durrell brings to it flatters by inflating its weaknesses.—CHARLES TOMLINSON, "And the Eyelids Are a Little Weary," *Poetry*, April 1961, pp. 53–54

LIONEL TRILLING
From *"The Quartet*: Two Reviews" (1960)
The World of Lawrence Durrell
ed. Harry T. Moore
1962, pp. 56–65

When I wrote about Lawrence Durrell's *Justine* and *Balthazar* last summer, I said of the author that he was "the first contemporary novelist in a long time to captivate my imagination to the extent of leading me to believe that he is telling me something new, of convincing me that he is truly interested in what he is writing about." This was meant as high praise and I did not modify it much by what I said thereafter. But I did put up a signal to let it be known that I might want to

make some reservations at a later time—I said that I was aware of aspects of Mr. Durrell's work that I was not easy with and had not yet come to terms with. That statement was more definite than it should have been; actually I was not "aware" of any "aspects"; all I really meant was that there was something about Mr. Durrell's novels that troubled me, although I did not know what it was.

Now that I have read the third and fourth of what Mr. Durrell calls the *Alexandria Quartet*, *Mountolive* published earlier this year and the recent *Clea*, I think I know what disquieted me. It is that all the novels, and the *Quartet* as a whole, stand in a peculiar negative relation to the will.

Having identified the disturbing element, I must admit that I cannot put it forward as an aesthetic fault. Who would undertake to say that the faculty of the will should be manifest in any given novel to this or that extent, or that it must be judged to have one or another degree of importance in human life? Yet the history of the novel shows it to be the genre which is characterized by its preoccupation with the will, and we naturally respond with some surprise or uneasiness when the traditional tendency does not show itself, or is reversed. The great essential subject of the novel would seem to be the individual who is in some way disadvantaged by circumstance and who is determined to overcome his disadvantage and to achieve freedom or fulfilment. And then, apart from the behavior that seems to us to be the novel's natural concern, there is the temperament of the novelists themselves. Of all literary artists they are the most overt in their commitment to the will. They are the most ambitious personally; they seek most to impose themselves, and to demonstrate their power in the range of their production and in the authority of their moral judgment. A *Lives of the Novelists* which would begin with Richardson and end with Lawrence, Proust, Joyce, and Mann would give us a collection of the most imperious wills of modern times.

Perhaps it was the sense of this intensity of will and the intuition that it could grow no greater, that led people about a decade ago to talk about the novel as being "dead." In effect they were saying that they could not conceive how anyone could go beyond the modern masters in their determination to engage and surround and fascinate and dominate the souls of their readers. And if one could not, how was one to be a novelist at all, except in a way that didn't matter?

We can almost suppose that Mr. Durrell confronted this question explicitly, and hit upon the answer that the only possible way was by inverting the tendency of the novel, by chucking out the will. We can fancy that at this crucial point in his career he read *The Man Who Died* and found in Lawrence's story of resurrection a parable of the possible rebirth of the novel—the world to be thought of not as a field upon which the battle for salvation is fought but simply as the offer of life. Or we can imagine that he read Schopenhauer's *The World as Will and Representation* and said: "The World-as-Will is about played out—we are tired of the moral will and the social will and the disguised religious will; the novel is tired of all these wills. Let us now try the World-as-Representation, the world seen quietly, as an object, and if not without desire, then at least without fierce, ultimate, abstract desire. This German philosopher tells us that the purpose of art is not to arouse but to compose the soul. Perhaps he is right, let us try."

The will, of course, cannot be dismissed out of hand, and the artist cannot (alas?) do without it. At the end of Mr. Durrell's *Quartet* the novelist Darley, who clearly bears some close surrogate relation to the author, having long failed to write in a way that pleases himself or anybody, is at last able to know that he has achieved salvation, that he is at the great moment of "an artist coming of age"—as bold as that, quite as if we had reached the end of *Sons and Lovers* or *A Portrait of the Artist as a Young Man*, or any of the scores of lesser *Bildungsromane* of the 1920's. No, the will is not easily got rid of, neither in the novelist nor in his characters. One of the chief dramatic elements of the *Quartet*—it is fully disclosed in *Mountolive*—is the great Coptic political intrigue in which Nessim Hosnani is involved; in a remarkable love scene, Nessim, who has failed to win Justine in marriage, does at last overcome her resistance and draws her into a passionate involvement with him by telling her of the plot and making her party to it; she is captivated by his display of will.

Yet the very will itself becomes an element of the World-as-Representation. The actual political meaning of the plot has no great weight with Justine; for her the real value of the enterprise lies in its danger—the threat of death makes love and sexuality the more intense. And it may be said in general of the acts of the will in the *Quartet* that they are drained of their literalness, of their directness and force, that they are informed *as if* they were real, the actors being conscious of the *as if*. Ideals of loyalty and responsibility suffuse the *Quartet*, and have reference not only to persons but to nations—it is striking, indeed, how important the idea of the nation is in the novels, and how much feeling the characters direct to entities as large as Egypt, England, France, and Greece. Leila Hosnani, the mother of Nessim and Narouz, loves the young David Mountolive not only because he is charming, but because he is English, and he loves her because she is for him the soul of Egypt. Even the outrageous novelist, Ludwig Pursewarden, who has conducted a lifelong war against English culture, is committed to his nation, and even his friend, Pombal, of the French foreign service, falls in love with defeated France at the same moment, and in much the same way, that, after a career of sexual athleticism, he for the first time falls in love with a woman.

But even the idea of the nation is absorbed into the general *as if*, and succumbs to the prevailing unreality of the objects of the will—was any English ambassador ever so little concerned with the actualities of diplomacy, with the facts of power and intrigue, as Mountolive? As any reader of the *Quartet* is likely to conceive of the will, it is a peculiarly European faculty, which has found its modern expression in Protestantism, Romanticism, and the ideals of the middle class in its classic period—it is highly moralized, giving the greatest possible value to individuality as far as it can be thought of as one's own, seeing the world as the great stage which has been readied for the significant behavior of the hero: all our notions of tragedy depend upon our conception of the will. But the tragic European will simply cannot function in the *Quartet*, if only because the locality in which its action takes place does not submit to being made into the great stage of the world. Alexandria, so far from being a stage, is itself the protagonist of the action, a being far more complex and interesting than any of its inhabitants, having its own way and its own rights, its own life and its own secret will to which the life and the will of the individual are subordinate.

The intensity of the personal existence of the city derives in large part from its history, and history is a felt presence in the *Quartet*, conceived of as a tendency of happening in which human will may indeed assert itself, although to little avail. Mark Antony is virtually one of the dramatis personae of the novels; in *Clea*, Darley and Clea make love on the tiny island which Clea believes to be the one to which Antony fled after Cleopatra had brought about his ruin by her panic at Actium;

the music under the earth that was heard when the voice called "the gods desert Antony" still reverberates in the city, and not only because it is the subject of one of the most famous poems of Cavafy, the Alexandrian poet who is made to figure in the *Quartet* as the city's soul becomes articulate.

What we of Europe and America call the past is part of Alexandria's actual present—ancient ways and the ancient peoples are before our eyes, and scenes that would seem bizarre and perfervid in the pages of *The Golden Bough* are of common occurrence, such scenes, for example, as the days-long mourning for Narouz Hosnani with which *Mountolive* ends, or, earlier in the same novel, the cutting-up of the still-living camels for the feast, or the religious festivals with their circumcision and prostitution booths and their possessed holy men. The ancient modes of thought are still in force—the existence of occult powers is taken for granted; scrying, second sight, palmistry, necromancy are matters of received fact with people of cultivation as well as with the primitive masses; this is the "mysterious East" of Western legend, with its belief in Kismet, or in guessed-at wills before which the will of man is of small account. And death or disablement or disfigurement can strike suddenly either at the behest of an occult or of some more powerful or beforehanded human will than one's own.

In this ancient circumstance the nature of the human personality is different from what we of Europe and America expect it to be. It is not, as I have implied, that the human virtues that we know have no existence and no appeal. Loyalty, devotion, tenderness, concern for the welfare of others are, indeed, displayed in a notable way by all the characters of the *Quartet*. "Moral" is a word that would be beyond their powers of utterance, perhaps beyond Mr. Durrell's, yet their lives are touched by considerations of goodness at every point; what is lacking is the binding force of the will which keeps steady the objects of their desire, and creates the idea of permanence and intention. This accounts for the ease and grace of their existence, for their never being torn between two possible ways of behavior, for their never displaying the harshness of moral judgment of each other. Two things only are of undoubted value in the *Quartet* and both are beyond the reach of the moral will. They are love and art—love which must follow its own laws and is not to be constrained; art which submits to no rule or purpose, existing for itself. The love that is represented in the *Quartet* is never linked to moral sanctions of any kind. The art that is imagined is without that moral urgency which is the hallmark of modern art; perhaps its paradigm is the scene in which Justine, searching for her kidnapped little daughter in a brothel, holds enchanted the swarm of child-prostitutes with an ancient romance; and the four words which, we are told, "presage . . . the story of an artist coming of age" are "Once upon a time . . ."

And indeed the aesthetic of the *Quartet* can best be understood by reference to the author's desire to recapture in the novel whatever charm lies in those four words, all that they imply of pleasure rather than will. It is to this end, for example, that Darley has been created to serve as the narrator of all the novels except *Mountolive*. Darley is himself a character among others, and he is not held in especial esteem by his friends and lovers; he never knows everything that might be known and he is the victim of a most elaborate deception practiced upon him by Justine and Nessim. Yet he does what he can, he tells what he knows. The devices that Mr. Durrell permits him to use to gather information are transparent and not always credible—the novels of other men, diaries, letters of infinite length, monologuists who are nearly as untiring as Conrad's Marlow; there are even two friends who, when he wants to evoke the image of the transvestite police-officer Scobie, are such perfect mimics that they can "do" Scobie for pages on end. It is as if Mr. Durrell were telling us that he has no intention of setting up as the novelist, of sitting enthroned like the Logos itself, in the fashion of Proust or Joyce or Mann or Lawrence. I include Lawrence because of his novels which are in the control of strict, impenetrable, universal logic; but the Lawrence of many of the shorter stories was manifestly trying to shed the weight and solemnity of his role of Genius-novelist, to speak in the voice of human intercourse, not in the voice of Art; and for that reason perhaps, among others, he is one of the literary heroes of the *Quartet*. Lawrence had his own express quarrel with the will and he sought a prose in which the rhetoric of the will was not dominant.

And this, I take it, is the prose that Mr. Durrell is trying for. I am not always of a single mind about it, but I know that it is doing a very useful thing—it is helping to save the language of the novel from Joyce. For the fact is that after reading Joyce it is very hard to take the prose of most novelists: Joyce makes it seem slack, vulgar, over-familiar. Indeed, if one reads Joyce with admiration, one conspires with him in his feeling that the presence of a reader is an impertinence, that to use language for purposes of communication is disgusting, a practice of the lowborn. Thus far had the creative will gone in pride, and the only way a novelist might again find a language was to do what Mr. Durrell has done, to take the posture of the man who begins "Once upon a time . . ." to announce, that is, that he is going to tell a story—really *tell* it as against representing it—and that it is he who is telling it, and that he, or his simulacrum-surrogate, can only speak in his own way, as a person, sometimes high, sometimes low, sometimes business-like, sometimes moved by wonder.

That last is important. My impression of most contemporary novels that come my way is that they say to me, "Let me give you for your file yet another instance of what you know so well, thus reassuring you of your high degree of sympathy with human frustration at no cost whatever. I will also tell you what, of course, you quite understand, how very bad The Culture is, and how it is to blame for the way people are when it isn't their own fault." Mr. Durrell's novels are much more naïve; they say, "Let me tell you something interesting. Once upon a time. . . ." Some of the things he tells I listen to with one or another degree of incredulity. I don't believe in homunculi made in a bottle by Cabalists. The camels sitting quiet while they are dismembered I can scarcely credit, but why should Mr. Durrell lie about a thing like that? The prophecy and second sight and scrying are amusing to suspend disbelief in, and if I am truthful I have to confess that I was once set back on my heels by what someone read in my palm. The story of the physician Amaril and the beautiful girl with no nose (she is eventually provided with one) is implausible, but I like Isaak Dinesen. It is at least apparently true that the holy men do pierce and burn themselves without harm or pain. Maybe this is all storyteller's nonsense, the usual mystery of the East, but it consorts with my sense of the way people ought to be, in a novel at any rate—that is to say, objects of wonder. And it is in the element of wonder that Mr. Durrell's characters move, like Clea and Darley in one of their several underwater scenes, flaming with phosphorus. I find it possible to suppose that if they were to be taken "in themselves," as we say, that would not be so very interesting, but in their ambience of Alexandria and of wonder they exist with a quite splendid intensity of life. * I make an exception of the great Pursewarden at whose wit and wisdom and charm everyone marvels—I find him a self-conscious bore, and in nothing is he so disappointing as in

Darley's discovery that his bitterness is really tenderness. Mr. Durrell can do much better than that, and does, in the fierce, fluctuating passions of Nessim and Justine, in the Esau-like figure of Narouz, in the beautiful, brilliant, and ruined Leila, in the canonized clown Scobie, in the general, curious vivacity of the *Quartet*.

*Addendum: I was making phrases in a hurry when I said this. Neither of them exists in any such way. But the ambience in which they exist is nevertheless to be admired.—L. T.

BENJAMIN DE MOTT
From "Grading the Emanglons"
The Hudson Review, Autumn 1960, pp. 457–64

Henri Michaux, a barbarian who knows the road east better even than Lawrence Durrell, has some observations in one of his imaginary voyages that are worth twice the price of a NoDoz to readers just embarking on The *Alexandria Quartet*. Michaux's subject is a tribe of Great Garaban called the Emanglons which has a passion for remoteness in art. The effects of this passion are various but consistent, and evident in all quarters. Emanglon theaters are bare of greasy actors; the latter play their parts in separate buildings from which images are transmitted to the form-loving audience by mirror-play. "Some words, that come from the ceiling, are spoken in [the actors'] names." Emanglon concert halls hide the sweating musicians in the wings. As for the stuff performed: "Their music with its dying sounds always seems to be coming through a mattress. That's what [the Emanglons] like: tenuous sounds, coming from nobody knows where, fading out every second, tremblng and uncertain melodies which finish off, however, in great harmonic surfaces—wide layers suddenly outspread."

The use of this report is twofold to a man who aims to make his way uncomplainingly through *Justine* or *Balthazar*. Like every subtle definition of an enlightened audience, it raises the possibility that high art always is bewildering, and Durrell's reader needs to be reminded of this possibility if he is to keep the iron in himself from page to page. Beyond this the report, which (hostilely regarded) can stand as a characterization of a whole genre of literary confusion, offers serviceable terms for the description of Durrell's unique effects. The man's "sound," for example, is by abrupt terms tenuous and dying, sudden and voluminous; much of it issues from nobody knows where. His characters in *Justine* and *Balthazar* play to mirrors and prisms, like the Emanglon actors, and are difficult to see and hear; the words spoken in their names come down from the ceiling.[1] And, at first glance, *remote*, a key critical term in the Michaux country, seems likely to be an appropriate "positive" label for Durrell's world as well.

What but remoteness could be expected in a work set in Egypt? Readers of Olivia Manning or P. H. Newby will call this an ignorant question, but only Egyptians will deny that the country is far away. Mosques and muezzins do not figure in the daily experience of Everyman, and the same can be said of many other items in the opening volumes of this tetralogy—a silver Rolls with daffodil hubcaps, a Babylonian barber shop, copulations of boabs, an axe murder of a camel, a bazaar where male prostitutes are tattooed, a character who spends his life travelling on ocean liners with a perfect woman called Sabina who is made of rubber ("Sabina had a wonderful wardrobe. It was a sight to see them come into the dining room"), and a man who, when asked why he is carrying another man's head in his gamebag, replies with no humorous intention: "More troubles with Bedouin labour could have cost us a thousand trees next year. It was too much of a risk to take. Besides, he was going to poison me." But in art anything can be made familiar, and if the case were otherwise, the remoteness of *Justine* and *Balthazar* would still have to be regarded as a consequence less of matter than of manner.

The chief narrator of both books is an English writer named Darley who is situated on a Mediterranean island in the company of a person called "the child." In *Justine* Darley is setting down the truth about certain people and events known to him in years spent in Alexandria; in *Balthazar* he is reviewing *Justine* in light of "The Interlinear"—a body of suggested revisions put forward by the first reader of his manuscript, a pederast named Balthazar who knows the same people and events, and considers Darley to be wanting in perceptiveness about them. The impression given by both books is that a series of related happenings of the sort described by the word *story* no doubt exists in some *ur*-text—a work that would be as valuable to Durrell's audience as a reading knowledge of Russian is to a man who wishes to know Tolstoy in the original. But in the absence of this text, the focus seems Emanglonianly dim, and the order of significance of its objects is not easy to ascertain. (*Justine* is presumably "about" the fatal lady who bears that name, but before Justine's hour arrives another fatal lady named Melissa is given much space, a circumstance which has the effect not only of perplexing the curious reader, but of dulling his appetite for fatality.) Names turn up on the page, are sung at by the narrator, and shortly disappear—for no specified reason. Then in *Balthazar* the narrator is chided for offering a mistaken explanation of the disappearances—when, as well as can be remembered, no explanation whatever had been offered. The names themselves—Pombal, Narouz, Abu Kar, Capodistria—have great piquancy, and the words spoken to and for them are remarkably fluent. But few of the messages convey much hint of what is called the real, or of any other agent capable of disturbing the taut Garabanian air of non-existence.

Nor would it appear, to judge from the tone of the enterprise, and the dominant rhetoric, that the writer likes such disturbances. As indicated before, his stall is jammed with Gothic gimcracks: epigraphs from Sade, a stolen child, man-eating birds, poisonings, hat-pin murders, vampires, religious frenzies, houses of child prostitution, circumcision spectacles, visions, lepers, bullwhips—not to speak again of the extraordinary gallery of fatal women. (A. is consumptive and smokes hashish; B. has her fine face destroyed by the pox; C. is raped as a child; D. has an abortion and afterward a harpoon tears off her hand.) And like most barkers of this stock Durrell prefers to speak in the unreal idiom of romance. He is faithful not only to the cliché ("Truth will out," "They drifted apart") and the "short ironic" laugh and sob, but also to the breathless leading question ("And Clea, what of her?" "And Scobie, what of him?" "And Pursewarden?" "Ah, Pursewarden . . ."). And as often as not the leading questions lead only to passages of *sententiae* and *profundum* ("'Every man,' [Justine] writes elsewhere, and here I can hear the hoarse and sorrowful accents of her voice repeating the words as she writes them; 'Every man is made of clay and daimon, and no woman can nourish both'"), or to an Expressionist tableau:

I turned my head to look at Justine. She was holding up her wrists at me, her face carved into a grimace. She held them joined together as if by invisible manacles. She exhibited these imaginary handcuffs for a long moment before dropping her hands back into her lap, and then, abruptly, swift as a snake, she

crossed to the divan where I lay and sat down at my feet, uttering as she did so, in a voice vibrating with remorseful resentment, the words: "Why Darley? O why?"

. . .Evidence of manipulation is everywhere visible. In *Balthazar* a Coptic rich man marries a fatal Jewess; his reason for doing so, according to the reporting intelligence of the moment, is that he is passionately in love with the lady. In *Mountolive* his reason is differently described; according to the reporting intelligence of that book, his purpose in marrying is to strengthen his hand in anti-British negotiations with Palestine. (As a Coptic, a Christian, the man believes that he will lessen Palestinian suspicion if he takes a Jewish wife.) The motives are revealed during a telephone conversation—the same conversation in each volume. In *Balthazar* the words spoken are reported as follows:

Nessim [the rich man] took the lift up to his office, and sitting down at his desk wrote upon a card the following words: "My dearest Clea, Justine has agreed to marry me. I could never do this if I thought it would qualify or interfere in any way with either her love for you or mine . . ." Then, appalled by the thought that whatever he might write to Clea might sound mawkish, he tore the note up and folded his arms. After a long moment of thought he picked up the polished telephone and dialled Capodistria's number. "Da Capo" he said quietly. "You remember my plans for marrying Justine? All is well." He replaced the receiver slowly, as if it weighed a ton, and sat staring at his own reflection in the polished desk.

In *Mountolive* the conversaion is reported as follows:

It was some hours later, when he was sitting at his desk, that Nessim after a long moment of thought, picked up the polished telephone and dialled Capodistria's number. "Da Capo," he said quietly, "you remember my plans for marrying Justine? All is well. We have a new ally. I want you to be the first to announce it to the committee. I think now they will show no more reservation about my not being a Jew—since I am to be married to one. What do you say?"

This finagling with motives may not please traditionalists—but lowbrow Emanglons, schooled to scorn the notion that serious writers do not withhold information for cheap reasons, are likely to find it as much to their taste as the mysterious music of *Justine*. And this in itself confirms the original assertion, that the ostensibly "naturalistic" parts of The Alexandria Quartet are only a shade less attractive to (undemanding) admirers of remoteness than those that are ostensibly "experimental."

. . . ⟨A⟩dmirers of Durrell . . . claim that poetry has been absent from the novel for years—which, at a certain level, is true. And they argue that Durrell has brought poetry back to the form—which, at a certain level, is also true. But at what level? *Justine* and *Balthazar* have interest as an indication of what *Aureng-Zebe* would be like if it were rewritten by a post-Lawrentian, in the manner of Pater, to be played underwater—and to say this is to grant that both books possess unusual literary, or poetical qualities: but the qualities are not admirable. Durrell is chockablock with imagery, indeed the principle of his employment of images is that of the saturation air raid of other times—but the reader, though given opportunities to admire flames and explosions in other neighborhoods, ultimately is numbered among the maimed. The poetry that Durrell brings back, in short, is bad poetry—an item which despite its power to stimulate the opportunistic is of slight value. Again: it is claimed that Durrell has given fiction some of its old substance as an instrument of thought, that he fills his pages with intellection of a weight and passion unequaled by any recent novelist. The measure of truth in this contention is, as in the previous instance, not contemptible. Novelists rarely concern themselves directly nowadays with metaphysics or epistemology, and Durrell does concern himself with these subjects: he is, as it were, always thinking. Regrettably, though, he is not a first-rate thinker. The burden of intellection in his first volumes rests upon commonplace observations about the fictive nature of human life, and in *Mountolive* and *Clea*, where most of the thinking is done by the great writer, Pursewarden, the substance of the ideas, if any, is buried in Blakeian prophetics and Irish (or elves and fairies division) Lawrentianism. . . .

The painful truth thus suggested is that even the invocation of Emanglon standards, which celebrate (not condemn) confusion and monstrosities of the kind described above, fails to validate the large claims made for the author of The Quartets as a novelist, experimenter, seer, and baroque painter. Durrell's language has no taint of the nonfiction novelist's drabness, but its complications smell more of vulgar "poetical" pretentiousness than of ambitious effort to arrive at difficult, encompassing truths. His study of the illicit and the ugly is not pornographic, and is often informative, but what it lays open is a scab of local self-contempt rather than the heart of a universal corruption. The possibility that his work as a whole should be thought of as a long anti-novel, a purposeful or Dada-ist mingling of styles, indicates the range of its potential interest—but the possibility is undercut by the absence of the note of amused self-awareness that lends authority to such productions. At their best his ideas *are* ideas, but since they are available elsewhere and since in his preachment of them Durrell is frequently hysterical, he does not qualify as an original or subtle mind. His belief that the need is urgent for a new formula of psychic health is unexceptionable, but since his tone is sickly and his preoccupations mean, he himself seems little more than a symptom of the wretchedness he bemoans. He is remote—this bears repeating: but in failing to comprehend that the end of remoteness is, ideally, the defeat of vulgarity, pretension, and private agony, he links himself only with the commoners of the Emanglon tribe, whose preference for the far-out is cant.

To say this much is not to deny that *Mountolive* is a readable novel with a brilliant opening chapter, and that moments of power occur at intervals in all four books, and that in conception the whole work raises extraordinary hopes. (Though the English need for a successful imaginative novelist, an alternative to the flatness of C. P. Snow and to the weary rhythm and blues of the aging Angries, is particularly acute, whole continents share it.) Neither is it to pretend that readable novels can be brought to general attention at present unless accompanied by volumes of notes for other novels, theories, ramshackle intellection, and murmurings from Cyril Connolly about "the spirit of Alexandria, sensual and skeptical, self-torturing and passionate." (Reviewers unprovided with such suggestions of momentousness cannot invoke the mighty names and huge accomplishments of the past which alone rouse apathetic audiences.) But these concessions and allusions to sociology do little to support the enthusiast who sets Durrell in the company of Proust or Conrad, and not much more to justify the sympathetic critic who attempts to place him honorably among the Emanglons. The terms of the latter tribe probably are narrow, precious, insubstantial—"useless for Shakespeare." But the standard they raise, as even the most reluctant

and tentative testings of The Alexandria Quartet seem bound to suggest, is a good deal higher than lowbrow aesthetes and four-card tricks in the form of novels are ever likely to reach.

Notes

1. Durrell discourses at length in *Justine* and elsewhere about art, mirrors and prisms (see below), and it may as well be noted here that the preoccupation is monotonously apparent in his poetry. See "Eight Aspects of Melissa," "On Mirrors," "The Daily Mirror," "Je est un autre," "Nicosia," "Delos," "Channel," the first poem "At Alexandria," "Penelope," "Basil the Hermit," "Fangbrand," "Father Nicholas His Death," "In the Ionian," "To Ping-Kû, Asleep," "Letter to Seferis the Greek," the sixth "Letter in Darkness," etc.

GERALD JAY GOLDBERG
From "The Search for the Artist in Some Recent British Fiction"
The South Atlantic Quarterly, 1963, pp. 387–92

This search for the man through the art is characteristic of much contemporary British fiction which presents the artist as hero. Considering its scope, the Alexandria quartet of Lawrence Durrell is one of the most impressive recent treatments of this subject. Although Durrell's preface to *Balthazar* describes his theme as "an investigation of modern love," in an interview printed in the magazine *Encounter* he states, "When you read *Clea* I hope you will feel that Darley was necessarily as he was in *Justine* because the whole business of the four books, apart from other things, shows the way an artist grows up."[1] As an exploration of love, "bi-sexual Eros" or otherwise, the novels are jejune—as profound as a penny dreadful. But as an analysis of the writer in search of himself through his craft, these books yield something of value from a mixed bag. Durrell, in portraying the artist in quest of himself, has dramatized the myths which Harold Rosenberg finds characteristic of action painting:

> The tension of the private myth is the content of every painting of this vanguard. The act on the canvas springs from an attempt to resurrect the saving moment in his "story" when the painter first felt himself released from Value—myth of past self-recognition. Or it attempts to initiate a new moment in which the painter will realize his total personality—myth of future self-recognition.[2]

It is within the novelist's province since he works in time (even if this is not his subject), and it is Durrell's achievement, since his hero is, in fact, an artist seeking identity, to produce a work which reveals not only the moment of discovery, but the logbook of the journey as well.

By means of the written reconstruction of his Alexandrine experience, the Darley of *Justine* struggles to find meaning in the past, to determine the nature of self in the present. For this artist-*manqué* the path to self-discovery is writing, and he becomes a voluntary exile from Egypt, retreating with Melissa's child to an island in the Cyclades, in order, paradoxically, to assimilate and belong. The emphasis throughout *Justine* is on what experience means for Darley, and the structure of the novel reflects this focus. It is Darley's intent to record happenings not in chronological order, but in the order in which they first became significant for him. This is clearly the pattern which Durrell has followed. And Darley's description of how Arnauti, the author of *Moeurs*, "almost by mistake pierced the hard banausic shell of Alexandria and discovered himself" prefigures his own final development in *Clea*—the "artist coming of age."

Durrell holds that truth is manifold rather than absolute, and, as did Gide in *Les Faux-Monnayeurs* and Huxley in *Point Counter Point*, he has tried to express this idea through the form of his work:

> I suppose [writes Balthazar] that if you wished somehow to incorporate all I am telling you into your own Justine manuscript now, you would find yourself with a curious sort of book—the story would be told, so to speak, in layers. Unwittingly I may have supplied you with a form, something out of the way! Not unlike Pursewarden's idea of a series of novels with "sliding panels" as he called them. Or else, perhaps, like some medieval palimpsest where different sorts of truth are thrown down one upon the other, the one obliterating or perhaps supplementing another.

In *Balthazar*, however, one finds neither layers nor supplement; the information contained in the Interlinear functions solely by negating rather than augmenting Darley's construction of past events found in *Justine*. The nexus of truth is sacrificed to a new reality which patently labels the female "sibling" an impostor. It is not Darley's appraisal of the facts that is found wanting in Durrell's second novel, so much as Darley's facts. We learn, for example, that much of *Moeurs* was invented and does not exactly parallel Justine's past; that Cohen, Melissa's aged lover, traded not only in furs but information as well, working as a French agent in Syria; and that Narouz, the harelipped and harebrained younger brother of Nessim, has a mortal passion for Clea. But the crucial piece of information unknown to the Darley of *Justine* is that the heroine used him as a decoy to cloak her meetings with another, that Justine loved the writer Pursewarden and not the writer Darley. In the light of this information, *Balthazar* appears less a palimpsest than a palinode.

But the revelations made in *Balthazar* and *Mountolive* are meaningful in that they lead to the Darley of *Clea*, though they have little value as a depiction of the "whole truth" or the complexity of reality. The Interlinear is Darley's school and the beginning of his education as an artist. He starts to copy it in an attempt to feel more personally its separate existence and to understand its message. That he does endeavor to profit from Balthazar's report is significant, for this fact brings Durrell's second novel of the quartet into the thematic orbit of the developing artist's search for identity. "From the vantage-point of this island," Darley reflects,

> I can see it all in the doubleness, in the intercalation of fact and fancy, with new eyes; and re-reading, re-working reality in the light of all I now know, I am surprised to find that my feelings themselves have changed, have grown, have deepened even. Perhaps then the destruction of my private Alexandria was necessary . . . perhaps buried in all this there lies the germ and substance of a truth—time's usufruct—which, if I can accommodate it, will carry me a little further in what is really a search for my proper self.

"Destruction" is the key word here, for Darley must surrender, as the reader is obliged to, the earlier version if he is to entertain and mature through the new one; hence, what we have is not a double vision which tells us more about character but a different one which tells us more about events.

It is Pursewarden's contention that "The object of writing is to grow a personality which in the end enables man to transcend art." Considering the dominant thematic movement of the tetralogy, however, it would seem to be Durrell's belief that a "personality" must be grown before one can even begin to write. Perhaps this lack is what makes Darley such an unreal and unattractive fictional hero, surrounded as he is by the dynamic and beauteous Justine, the ironic and cynical Pursewarden, the volatile Narouz, and the flamboyant pederast, Scobie. One might speculate that if Darley is to write the novel that Durrell hoped to write, the novel that views life in cross-section and not from different points on the same plane, he must discover the sovereignty of others and the anima of self; this, in fact, is what the tetralogy is all about.

Although the third book of the series deals mainly with the relationship of Leila Hosnani, the mother of Nessim and Narouz, with David Mountolive, and Darley appears to be only a subordinate actor, there is a pattern of reference which has the latter as focus, and this serves as a vinculum with the other novels in Durrell's portrait of the developing artist. At one point, for example, Pursewarden describes Darley as a "vaguely amiable bespectacled creature" with a "nice round babyish back to the head which one sees in cultural types; slight stoop, fair hair, and the shyness that goes with Great Emotions imperfectly kept under control," and by his very presence reveals the schoolteacher as artist-*manqué*. Everything that Pursewarden is, Darley is not. Of Darley, Pursewarden writes:

> I like particularly the way he sits on his hands with excitement when he discusses art, which he insists on doing with Yours Truly—why? I answer as best I can and drink my *arak*. But this generalized sort of conversation puts me out of humor. For the artist, I think, as for the public, no such thing as art exists; it only exists for the critics and those who live in the forebrain. Artist and public simply register, like a seismograph, an electromagnetic charge which can't be rationalized. One only knows that a transmission of sorts goes on, true or false, successful or unsuccessful, according to chance. But to try to break down the elements and nose them over—one gets nowhere. (I suspect this approach to art is common to all those who cannot surrender themselves to it!)

It is this surrender which Darley finally seems to be capable of at the conclusion of *Clea*.

Clea, the last movement in the Alexandria quartet, once again has Darley as narrator, but this book is a sequel to the three other novels, and the setting is an Egypt transfigured by war. When Darley returns, he enters a different Alexandria, but the most telling change has occurred in the observer himself. Darley's transformation is marked outwardly and superficially by the fact that he no longer stoops and has given up spectacles. More importantly, he has profited from an awareness of failure. Darley observes that,

> if I had been enriched by the experience of this island interlude, it was perhaps because of this total failure to record the inner truth of the city. I had now come face to face with the nature of time, that ailment of the human psyche. I had been forced to admit defeat on paper. Yet curiously enough the act of writing had in itself brought me another sort of increase; by the very *failure* of words, which sink one by one into the measureless caverns of the imagination and gutter out. An expensive way to begin living, yes; but then we artists are driven towards personal lives nourished in these strange techniques of self-pursuit.

But Darley's evolution is far from complete. He is haunted by Pursewarden's words, "'There is no Other; there is only oneself facing forever the problem of one's self-discovery!'" and must still suffer the purgatory of exposure to Pursewarden's notebook. What he finds there is a blistering attack on his pusil-lanimity both as artist and man. His ability to take this es-sentially accurate, if somewhat "Parnassian," criticism without cringing or trying to dismiss it signals the growth of the artist. It is when he reads Pursewarden's letters, however, that some-thing like Epiphany occurs. Sitting in Clea's room alone and by candlelight—a setting worthy of Hugo—Darley pores over the letters and discovers not only the genius of Pursewarden but himself as well. In its objectivity and freedom from pettiness, Darley's decision to save the letters (although they are ul-timately destroyed by Pursewarden's sister, Liza) may be taken as an exemplar of his development.

Justine, Balthazar, Mountolive, and *Clea* embody Law-rence Durrell's effort to present different simultaneous versions of reality, and I have indicated why, considering both their substance and form, the novels fail to achieve his grand design. Nevertheless, tacit in the author's conception is the notion of the complexity of man in a multifarious society. Given this awareness, it is not strange that a major theme in these novels is the hero's search for identity. The birth of an artist is the subject of the Alexandria quartet, and his struggle to realize self is symbolic of that of all men. A truth borne home inescapably within the past sixty years is that the representative hero of our basically unheroic age is the artist himself, and when Pursewar-den writes, "Heed me, reader, for the artist is you, all of us— the statue must disengage itself from the dull block of marble which houses it and start to live," he expresses an idea upon which a large segment of twentieth-century fiction is predi-cated.

Notes

1. Kenneth Young, "A Dialogue with Durrell," XIII (December, 1959), 62.
2. *The Tradition of the New* (New York, 1959), p. 31.

LOUIS FRAIBERG
From "Durrell's Dissonant Quartet"
Contemporary British Novelists
ed. Charles Shapiro
1965, pp. 16–26

There are interesting characters in the *Alexandria Quartet*, but Justine in not one of them. Her beauty, intelligence, attractiveness, and what in another might have become her drama, are all negated by the engulfing emptiness which is to be found at her center. And this is appropriate since she is the prototype and symbol of the malaise which Lawrence Durrell depicts as the affliction of modern man. This dis-ease arises from the impossibility of attaining wholeness as a person, and the book is an account of some of the different ways in which wholeness, and therefore fulfillment, is sought by the Alexan-drians. Justine is the most outstandingly unsuccessful of them all.

The search is conducted by two classes of people, or-dinary—if we may call any of the characters in this novel ordinary—and gifted. The former seek their salvation through sex, the latter through art. Durrell himself says the book is an investigation of modern love, and this is true as far as it goes, for the physical act of sex is seen by his characters as the key to reality and therefore to the possibility of becoming whole by entering into a right relationship with the world as it is. It is my thesis that it fails them and that the ones who come closest to finding the real reality are those whose vocation provides them

with quite a different key: pain through mutilation and the knowledge of death. Durrell appears to lose sight of his original intention and, as the *Quartet* progresses, his focus shifts to the artist as seer. The mere lovers are left to discover for themselves how futile love is.

In Durrell's view the intelligible world has suffered a loss of the values which create selfhood and has precipitated us into a desperate attempt to replace them. His characters thus are existentialists trying to become transcendentalists in order that they may become existentialists once more. They are looking for a glimpse of the heraldic universe, the abode of truth, and their method is the compulsive immersion in a bath of experi-ence, the experience of art, of politics, of war, of love.

It is a bath rather than a crucible because the immersion is passive, a watching to see what will happen rather than a test-ing of the potentialities of the self when challenged. The trou-ble is that, by Durrell's definition, most of them have no self, and this lack is what frustrates if it does not precisely doom them. It makes them incapable of tragedy, incapable of feeling, and capable only of suffering pain. It sends them on a search for something strong enough to penetrate their defensive shells and make up for what is missing within, even at the cost of suffering. They hope this will prove to them that the world is real and that they do not merely exist but actually live in it.

A measure of how slim their chances are is the clumsiness which they display in the quest. They seem to try out nearly all the possible love relationships in a parody of the method of the social scientists. It is as though a great chart has been drawn up showing the various ways in which A and B and C can impinge upon each other and that then each of them sets out systemat-ically to test as many as lie within his power [perhaps capacity is a better word]. And the parody is developed still further by the relentless analysis to which each experimental coupling is sub-jected before, during, and after the act. These directly shared introspections are supplemented by related insights occurring in conversations with others, in letters, or, notably, in excerpts from Arnauti's novel *Moeurs*, and in Pursewarden's notebook. The great preoccupation is hardly ever out of their minds, and it furnishes an important part of the texture of the entire *Quar-tet*, so important that many readers take it for the essence of the book.

The gradual revelation of Justine as lover dominates this aspect of the *Quartet*, though it may not be immediately appar-ent on a first reading since there is such a bewildering succes-sion of other lovers and such kaleidoscopic shifts of place, focus, and tempo. But it is possible to see her character from outside the novel, as it were, by unifying along realistic lines some of the elements of Durrell's prismatic technique. What we get then is an impression which corresponds to the *gestalten* we receive through seeing people in a series of unrelated situa-tions. In both instances, though the mosaic is far from com-plete, there is enough of it to establish a coherent configura-tion. Justine is then revealed to us as a character of a more familiar kind than we were aware of while under the spell of Alexandria, though—or perhaps because—this process divests her of considerable exoticism and surprise.

Justine—that "tiresome old sexual turnstile through which presumably we must all pass," as Pursewarden resigned-ly calls her—is the key to the first level on which the *Quartet* may be read. Here are displayed the author's expressly stated intentions toward his creations. In the words of Pursewarden again:

> You see, Justine, I believe that Gods are men and
> men Gods; they intrude on each other's lives, trying
> to express themselves through each other. . . . And

then (listen) I think that very few people realize that sex is a psychic and not a physical act. The clumsy coupling of human beings is simply a biological paraphrase of this truth—a primitive method of introducing minds to each other, engaging them.

Its psychic quality is to him a reality which is accessible to scrutiny by the mind and not a mystique whose ultimate significance is derived from an experience that bypasses intellection altogether.

It is interesting to look at Justine from this point of view by reconstructing the narrative line and recapitulating her own passing through the turnstiles of other loves. Despite the "many others" who achieve only incidental mention as her early lovers and despite some uncertainty as to chronological sequence left by our threading the maze in this mirror-house of a *Quartet*, a more or less consistent pattern emerges. That is, if Justine were to appear as a character in another novel, one in which time were treated in the familiar way, we should immediately recognize her.

Her background is obscure. We learn that the most important event in her early life has been Capodistria's rape of her as a child; we are not told at what age. The resulting trauma has produced what she calls The Check, a massive inhibition which makes it impossible for her to love freely and which impels her to devote herself to a persistent search for a cure. This is not the sole explanation of her motives—Durrell is careful to reject such oversimplification—it is not even the genesis of them. She is obviously one of those whose disposition is not ardent, though she tries mightily to act with passion. When she succeeds, it is only temporarily and only in a specific constellation of circumstances that happens to appeal to certain sides of her nature. When the external situation changes, she subsides once more into her normally less intense state. Through innate passivity, through the unstated influences of her upbringing, and through the crystallizing effect of the childhood rape, she has been driven back upon herself, only to find there that she cannot feel. In flight from this emotional vacuum she reaches out toward the world of love in hope of finding in it a talisman that will stir her into life. Intuitively recognizing her lack of inner resources, she seeks rescue by some external agency. Justine's love-life which follows from this is the paradigm of the human condition as Durrell portrays it and as he causes it to be explained by Pursewarden.

It is not the "clumsy coupling" of bodies that is at the center of this book, even though its depiction and consequences occupy most of the space and even though Durrell himself advertises the *Quartet* as an investigation of modern love, which most readers take to mean physical sexual encounters. As Pursewarden's remark shows, the psychic significance of the act is the key. And throughout Justine's adventures—throughout the meaningful events in the lives of all the other characters—what matters most is the egocentric, isolated position of the individual and his amoral attempt to use the rest of the world for his own rescue. This is the way Durrell depicts love. Through seemingly countless demonstrations it is made clear that, in the *Quartet*, love is self-love and furthermore that it is a failure.

Justine proves this again and again in her curiously joyless loves. Her marriage to Arnauti fails in part because he does not recognize that her lack of affect is constitutional and that her attempts to acquire some are, to say the least, ambivalent. In his relentless amateur psychologizing he misses the point and so dooms his effort to cure Justine of The Check and win all her love for himself.

She has suffered a loss which Arnauti apparently ignores; it is nowhere indicated that he deals with it or even that he understands its meaning to her. This is the disappearance of her child, and she responds to it as though it were the loss of part of her body. When this is superimposed upon her natural gelidity—thus connecting the generalized shock with an object which, besides having a meaning of its own, also unconsciously represents the organs of loving—it is as though she has accepted defeat and will henceforth be governed by the need to defend herself against the danger of feeling once more. Arnauti's bungling attacks on her defenses against affect can serve only to alienate her from him, and this is what happens. He loses the case.

The "affair" with Clea also exhibits some of the aspects of narcissism. It is more or less passive on Justine's part; apparently it was Clea who initiated it and who finally broke it off. Justine appears to have accepted it temporarily because its inherent sterility was well suited to her temperament. Clea was using her for her own purposes—artistic ones, as it turned out—and both women gained something from the fact that the relationship was based on exhibitionism. For Clea, Justine was a model whose intriguing exterior promised the unraveling of a mystery. Only later did she discover that the beautiful mask concealed a blankness. For Justine, the display of her beauty, her visible body, was enough. There being little within, she obtained such pleasure as she could from her external appearance. Her deadened affective life and Clea's distraction by other interests combined to make the "affair" a pallid one. Justine seems to have accepted its termination with equanimity and to have retained her friendship with Clea.

She had much better luck with Pursewarden. His refusal to let her dominate him enabled her to nourish the comforting illusion that she could have experienced real love if only he had been willing to accept her on her terms. But he sensibly refused to let her take him seriously, and—this proved to be a touch of genius—"discovered to her the fact that she was ridiculous." It was his naturalness, forthrightness, and humor that brought this about, and these qualities, so irresistible to her, were paradoxically the very ones that made it impossible for her to capture him. His devotion to the physical realities of life and his conviction of their moral worth—again paradoxically, they seem to have been among the compelling reasons for his suicide—went far to help her overcome the worst effects of The Check.

Their first love-making came as a result of his conquest of her "by impudence," as Balthazar remarked. In the course of it she was induced to laugh at him and even at herself a little. But it was the fact that he was "utterly himself in a curious way" which aroused in her "an unfamiliar passionate curiosity," another instance of her inability to feel passion except in some way extraneous to love itself even while she was reaching out toward what was genuine in him.

At this point Pursewarden pulled his brilliant psychological coup. He attacked the image of Claudia in *Moeurs*, which Justine had adopted as part of a comforting defensive pattern of self-pity, making it unnecessary for her to face the psychic truth about herself. He simply refused to regard her as a case, as the misguided Arnauti had done, and told her bluntly that she had in all probability tacitly invited the rape by Capodistria and that moreover she had almost certainly enjoyed it, upon which the conquest by impudence became something much more valuable to her: therapy by insult. Pursewarden's heavyhandedness furnished enough of a shock at last to breach this particular defense, and it succeeded because she was sufficiently attached to him to accept it. His motives, too, were different from Arnauti's since he was not seeking personal gain. By keeping himself impregnable to her ardors he was thus able to administer the first check to The Check.

With the same heavyhandedness, again made possible by what may be called the therapeutic nature of their relationship, he conceived the idea of making her go back to the brothel where her child had died. She went willingly, outwardly cool and composed. She had been incapable of acknowledging the child's death and had tried to maintain the illusion that it had simply been lost so that she could continue to live for the sake of searching for it. Now, through Pursewarden's mediation, she entered the room, lay upon the old divan which had become for her the symbol of her loss, and stroked it "with a calm, voluptuous gesture" as though finally reconciling herself to the reality of death by a symbolic act of mothering. When soon afterward the child prostitutes swarmed into the room, she won them over with another motherly act, telling them a story—the story of the "great many petalled love" of Yuna and Aziz! Completely hers now that they had been treated as little children, "They said farewell in voices of heartbreaking sweetness," and she took her departure, emotionally exhausted.

Thereafter she appeared to be almost completely free of the effects of the rape and the death of her child, although her native lack of ardor still prevented her from attaining the full satisfaction of love. When she returned to Nessim and to the marriage which both acknowledged to be without love, she was able to bring passion to it only in response to his invitation to share the dangers of the Palestine plot in which he was one of the leaders. Its failure, resulting in Nessim's political impotence and physical wounding in an air raid—he lost a finger and an eye—destroyed the basis for their renewed intimacy and transformed their desperately contrived semblance of love into its opposite. When Darley visited Justine following these events, she had turned into a sullen, irascible virago who could only hate Nessim and whose conversation with him was limited almost entirely to insult, recrimination, and loathing.

Her renaissance at the end of the fourth book is reported by Clea to be connected with "something much bigger this time." She is apparently reconciled with Nessim on pretty much the old terms, evidently because he is essentially repeating his former role. And she is radiant, her eyes sparkling with delight at her ascendancy over the toad-like Memlik who had previously been such a menace to them both. This is Justine in her element. Clea writes Darley: "It was as if, like some powerful engine of destruction, she had suddenly switched on again. She has never looked happier or younger." The passion which is presumably once more possible for her is passion in the service of the externally induced political excitement, not love.

Justine is the model for the loves of all the other Alexandrians. It is a lack of centrality like hers which is central to their seeking, and what they seek is the contriving of an integument whose surface is sensitive to the stimuli of the real outer world. When they succeed—which they often do for a brief time—their involvement along the entire periphery occupies all of their attention and keeps them from noticing that none of the sensation is reaching the interior where, in any case, there is nothing that can meaningfully engage it. Beneath the sensitized skin the whole Alexandrian museum turns out to be a display of specimens of psychic taxidermy.

This is strikingly developed by Durrell's use of the symbolism of masks and mirrors. Not only are faces masked but whole bodies are concealed by shapeless dominoes. This makes possible such melodramatic events as the murder of Toto de Brunel and the love affair of Amaril and the virtuous Semira. But more fundamentally, the coverings serve to conceal as well as to reveal the essence of the individual as he conceives or wishes

it. They are, in fact, the chief means by which any part of the truth of a character can be expressed and communicated, for they afford the opportunity to take on an almost unlimited number of qualities which exist only in the wearer's fantasy or which come from outside and do not really belong to him.

Either way the purpose is served: a *gestalt* is assembled and attributed to the fantast, and this substitutes for a genuine personality. It is altogether fitting that the glimpses of these people which can be obtained in a mirror show only a flattened view from a single angle. Since the images have no depth, what the Alexandrians see there are facets, not faces. In a sense, the mirrors are masks, too, differing from the domino in that the fractional truths they convey are based on perceptions rather than concealments and therefore better suited to tell the viewer what the actor wants him to know. This is most especially true when one of the Alexandrians is looking at his own reflection.

The overt symbolism of masks and mirrors is accompanied by the conscious acting out of parts by the characters. Poor simple Darley is dismayed to discover, in Balthazar's *Interlinear*, how he has been cast in the role of decoy by Justine. His acting has been unwitting, but the others usually know what they are about. For Mountolive the role arises from his professional duties as a diplomat; the others have more private reasons. In essence they are seeking the inner truths about themselves, but this is not forthcoming because they too are hollow, and the only truth available to them is peripheral. There is no personal integrity or significance except as it may be inferred from the tangential contact, and the *Quartet* offers no novelistic proof that such an inference is valid. When Nessim tells Justine that he is weary of the eternal role-playing necessitated by his plot and says, "If only we did not have to keep on acting a part, Justine," she responds with, "Ah, Nessim! Then I should not know who I was."

By masking and mirroring the faces they put on to meet the faces that they meet, Justine and the other Alexandrian lovers are able to place before others, and keep before themselves, artificial constructions to stimulate and receive such love as they are capable of. That is, of course, the love of Narcissus for his reflection in the pool, and it shares with it the qualities of shallowness and of providing an idealized object for the affections, one which does not demand the giving up of total absorption in one's own fancied excellences. No attempt is made to look below the surface; there is nothing there, and anyway the surface is wholly satisfying—until somebody throws a pebble into the pool. The masks and the mirrors are symbols of the body itself as the beloved.

This being so, the investigation of modern love has led up the blind alley of narcissism. On this level, the *Quartet* has not kept its implied promise to show how salvation may be attained through love, since the love that it depicts is primitive, rudimentary, unrealized. The endless experimentation is neither free loving nor self-realizing but a compulsive search for the only true freedom, that which comes from voluntary commitment to another, not from acquisition but from identification. But Justine collects scalps, not hearts.

ALAN WARREN FRIEDMAN
From "Place and Durrell's Island Books"

Modern Fiction Studies, Autumn 1967, pp. 330–35

P*rospero's Cell*, in Lawrence Clark Powell's words, "is a Mediterranean prose-poem to rank with *Fountains in the Sand, Sea and Sardinia*, and *The Colossus of Maroussi*."[1] Like its successors, Durrell's first island book employs many of fiction's techniques. For, in ways typical of his novels, Durrell here creates characters indeterminate and variable, yet of imposing stature ("It is a sophism to imagine that there is any strict dividing line between the waking world and the world of dreams. N. and I, for example, are confused by the sense of several contemporaneous lives being lived inside us; the sensation of being mere points of reference for space and time," and, "We are lucky in our friends. Two of them seem of almost mythological quality . . ."), an aesthetic conflict concerning the various possibilities of interpreting and re-ordering reality ("here we are," says the Count, the character of greatest and freest imagination, "each of us collecting and arranging our common knowledge according to the form dictated to him by his temperament. In all cases it will not be the whole picture, though it will be the whole picture for you,")[2] a setting vast, pervasive, and alive ("Zarian gives a discourse on landscape as a form of metaphysics. 'The divine Plato said once that in Greece you see God with his compasses and dividers,'" and, "Nowhere else has there ever been a landscape so aware of itself, conforming so marvellously to the dimensions of a human existence"); and, perhaps most interestingly, an "Epilogue in Alexandria" (where, after all, the book was written), offering the same kind of perspective shifts as the Workpoints appended to the *Quartet* novels.

Durrell's intense awareness of place imposes a kind of unity on his otherwise disparate material—for he mixes his semi-literary journal with humorous anecdotes, aesthetic-philosophic discussions and meditations, more or less scholarly essays on selected aspects of the island, and the various apparatus already indicated. And the landscape and the atmosphere serve as touchstones, as controlling metaphors, for Durrell not only writes of them with often lyric intensity, but he raises them—in a manner anticipating the Alexandria of the *Quartet*—to mythopoeic significance. "Other countries," he writes early in the book, "may offer you discoveries in manners or love or landscape; Greece offers you something harder—the discovery of yourself." And because this has been true for Durrell, and because on Corfu the writing has gone well and life has been good, the "Epilogue in Alexandria" reads like the saddest of endings: the disillusionment following the loss of innocence. "In these summer twilights the city [Alexandria] lies in its jumble of pastel tones, faintly veined like an exhausted petal. . . . The last landmark on the edge of Africa. The battleships in their arrowed blackness turn slowly in the harbour. The loss of Greece has been an amputation. All Epictetus could not console one against it."

For with the coming of the war and the loss of Greece has followed the demise of love: "There is simply patience to be exercised. Patience and endurance and love. Some of us have vanished from the picture; some have had their love converted into black bile by the misery they have witnessed." And the final words of the book suggest the profundity of despair now gripping the world and its artists. "Seen through the transforming lens of memory," a deracinated Durrell writes, "the past seemed so enchanted that even thought would be unworthy of it. We never speak of it, having escaped: the house in ruins, the little black cutter smashed. I think only that the shrine with the three black cypresses and the tiny rockpool where we bathed must still be left. Visited by the lowland summer mists the trembling landscape must still lie throughout the long afternoons, glowing and altering like a Chinese water-colour where the light of the sky leaks in. But can all these hastily written pages ever recreate more than a fraction of it?"

The answer apparently is "no"—at least for Durrell the man, and his sense of inadequacy and hopeless frustration

manifests itself in the failure of his marriage in Egypt during the war. As for Durrell the artist, he has succeeded perhaps better than he believes, for *Prospero's Cell* is a richly evocative book, with its many well-portrayed incidents and characters serving as a check on the tendency towards vagueness and abstraction. The inaction of the book, though an accurate reflection of the langorousness of pre-war Greece, is something of a weakness—perhaps the main one of the book. But such self-indulgence, though Durrell still gives way to it at times, becomes rarer in his more mature writings. A pattern emerges in the island books: from casual, pre-war Corfu Durrell shifts to the post-war Rhodes—with its desperate need of immediate action—of *Reflections on a Marine Venus*,[3] and then to the incipient civil-war Cypriot atmosphere of the tense and compelling *Bitter Lemons*.[4]

If being cast out of Corfu represents a fall from innocence for Durrell and his Greek world, then the re-entry into Rhodes is an attempt at lifting the guilt that has descended. Or, to shift the metaphor to the one central to *Reflections on a Marine Venus* and to much of his other writings, Durrell seeks a cure for the spiritual diseases plaguing virtually all his characters—here made manifest by the war and its after-effects. The narrator of *Marine Venus* writes of a people and a world ravaged by sickness and death, and he returns to his beloved Greece with great trepidation, as if going to visit an old, ailing friend who, he fears, may already be dead by the time he arrives. As he prepares to leave Alexandria "that spring afternoon of 1945," he thinks: "Tomorrow I should see for myself whether the old Greek ambience had survived the war, whether it was still a reality based in the landscape and the people—or whether we had simply invented it for ourselves in the old days, living comfortably on foreign exchange, patronising reality with our fancies and making bad literature from them."

Durrell's own "disease" is "islomania," an ailment "as yet unclassified by medical science. . . . A rare but by no means unknown affliction of spirit," it causes its victims to "find islands somehow irresistible." And *Reflections on a Marine Venus*, Durrell adds, "is by intention a sort of anatomy of islomania"—that is, in effect, an examination of the complex interrelationship of stricken moth and compelling flame. For again Durrell does not offer simply a descriptive survey of his island, but rather a probing which is at once revelatory and exploratory, at once therapeutic and self-analytic, at once a finished work of art and one prematurely made public with the skeleton of its scaffolding still lying about.

The technique is one of planned formlessness, a deploying of the many pieces comprising the Rhodian mosaic, rather than a straightforward guide to the island or a continuous narrative of events occurring there. "If I have sacrificed form," Durrell writes in terms anticipating his technical concerns in the *Quartet*, "it is for something better, sifting into the material now some old notes from a forgotten scrapbook, now a letter: all the quotidian stuff which might give a common reader the feeling of life lived in a historic present." Like the Count in *Prospero's Cell*, Mills, an Englishman wholly a creature of Mediterranean Greece, tells Durrell the kind of portrait of the island he should write: "'Not history or myth—but landscape and atmosphere somehow. "A companion" is the sort of idea. You ought to try for the landscape—and even these queer months of transition from desolation to normality.'"

Mills himself aids greatly in this transition for, like Fonvisin in *Panic Spring*, an early Durrell novel, and Balthazar and Amaril in the *Quartet*, he is a doctor not only endowed with remarkable curative power, but one who actually personifies soundness of body and mind. "It would be difficult," Durrell remarks of Mills, "to think of anyone who seemed to be such a walking certificate for good health; it simply oozed from him, from his candid face, fresh complexion, sensitive finger." In fact, Mills, like most exceptionally healthy people, takes illness as something of an affront, a misdeed perpetrated by the patient simply, or at least primarily, to get attention.

In his Introduction to Georg Groddeck's *Book of the It*, Durrell notes that Groddeck conceived of a man's physical condition (that uneasy mean between the two abstract extremes of total health and total illness) as the outward manifestation of the internal man. Thus disease and illness are seen as expressions of a man's personal identity. To someone not totally committed to accepting his theory, Groddeck seems at times to carry it to absurd lengths—for instance, in asking an injured patient, "What was your idea in breaking your arm?"[5] Still, much of what Groddeck says can be accepted—we do, for example, tend to associate certain diseases with certain people, and see an appropriateness in *that* person's having *that* malady—especially with regard to the infirmities of literary characters. The blinding of Oedipus or of Gloucester, for instance, is clearly an objective correlative for spiritual blindness; the impotence of Jake Barnes or of Clifford Chatterley tells us something of the spiritual crippling caused by modern war and its aftermath, on the one hand, and by de-humanized technology on the other. Disease or injury strikes, at one time or another, virtually every important character in Durrell's *Quartet*, and it invariably symbolizes some major aspect of the personality it strikes.

This relationship of disease and personality has little place in Durrell's earliest writings, although there are hints of it in *The Black Book* and *The Dark Labyrinth*. In *Marine Venus*, however, Mills serves to focus Durrell's increasing interest in the subject; and he is written of in terms anticipating the subsequent involvement with Groddeck. "His diagnosis of disease," Durrell notes, "seemed somehow to be a criticism, not of the functioning of one specific organ, but of the whole man. Like all born healers he had realized, without formulating the idea, that disease has its roots in a faulty metaphysic, in a way of life. And the patient who took him a cyst to lance or a wheezing lung to think about, was always disturbed by the deliberate careful scrutiny of those clear blue eyes. One felt slightly ashamed of being ill in the presence of Mills. It was as if, staring at you as you stood there, he were waiting for you to justify your illness, to deliver yourself in some way of the hidden causes of it."

Durrell's own disease, islomania, though it is not fatal, remains nonetheless uncured. In the Epilogue to his second island book he associates it with the permanent "wound" (obviously a consequence of love) he has received from his "Marine Venus." Durrell not only rediscovers the ambience of pre-war Greece, but he helps to resuscitate it during his stay on

Rhodes—both in his work while on the island and in this book—for he correctly notes that, "by this writing," all his friends and all they have experienced on Rhodes are made forever a part "of this small green island" and of "the greater arc" which is all of Greece (*Venus*, pp. 183–184). But though Durrell in his work and in his art contributes to the rebuilding of a world and a way of life, he once again fails at love—and in the Epilogue he is once more alone with the child, with E. (Eve), his second wife, no longer "a familiar, a critic, a lover" (*Venus*, p. 16).

The poignancy of Eve's loss, however, is far less intense than that of Nancy in *Prospero's Cell*, since the former receives scant treatment as a character. *Marine Venus*, like its predecessor, is richly evocative, containing several fine characterizations (especially Mills) and much good talk; but it represents something of a falling off, for it lacks the subjective immediacy of the first island book. The art is present, but not so artlessly deployed, and we get only intermittent glimpses of the artist's attempting to come to grips with the virtually intractable materials of both the creative process and his life, of both art and love. As a consequence, where *Prospero's Cell* seems of the very essence of Corfu (and of Durrell's persistent attempt to understand that essence in terms of himself), *Marine Venus*, though like all of Durrell's prose it contains vivid description and fine insights, is not so much *of* Rhodes as simply *about* it.

The last of Durrell's island books is by far his best, for it has all the virtues of the earlier ones and none of their failings—plus the fortuitous advantage of a significant plot. *Bitter Lemons* (originally *Bitter Lemons of Cyprus*) not only captures an atmosphere and a tone, a way of life and a people, but it details and examines the destruction of the Cypriot peace that culminates in the disastrous outbreak of civil war. The sense of place, then, is brilliantly and appropriately subordinated to the sense of the moment.

Notes

1. Introductory Note to *A Landmark Gone*, p. i. This pamphlet, privately printed for Powell, is a kind of précis, often word for word, of *Prospero's Cell*.
2. On the same page, the Count is asked to describe the kind of book the narrator *will* write of Corfu. "'It is difficult to say,' says the Count. 'A portrait inexact in detail, containing bright splinters of landscape, written out roughly, as if to get rid of something which was troubling the optic nerves.'" A comment which could serve as an accurate blurb for *Prospero's Cell*—and much of Durrell's other writings as well.
3. Lawrence Durrell, *Reflections on a Marine Venus: A Companion to the Landscape of Rhodes* (New York, 1962). Hereafter cited in the text as *Venus*.
4. Lawrence Durrell, *Bitter Lemons* (New York, 1957). Hereafter cited in the text as *BL*.
5. Quoted by Durrell, Introduction to *The Book of the It* (New York, 1961), p. viii.

ADDITIONAL READING

MARGERY ALLINGHAM

Craig, Patricia, and Mary Cadogan. *The Lady Investigates*. London: Gollancz, 1981.

Haycraft, Howard. *Murder for Pleasure*. New York: Appleton-Century, 1941.

Pike, B. A. "Margery Allingham's Albert Campion: A Chronological Examination of the Novels in Which He Appears." *Armchair Detective* 9 (1975–76): 1–6, 95–101; 10 (1977): 25–29, 117–25, 244–48, 324–35; 11 (1978): 34–44.

A. ALVAREZ

Howe, Irving. "Books." *Harper's Magazine* 244 (June 1972): 102–5.

Kermode, Frank. "Interesting but Tough." *Spectator*, 3 March 1961, pp. 288–99.

Kostelanetz, Richard. "Into the Pressure Cooker." *Massachusetts Review* 9 (1968): 595–98.

Petrie, Paul. "Three Critics." *Poetry* 95 (1959): 125–26.

ERIC AMBLER

Ambrosetti, Ronald. "The World of Eric Ambler." In *Dimensions of Detective Fiction*, ed. Larry N. Landrum Bowling Green, OH: Bowling Green University Popular Press, 1976.

Byrne, E. B., and Otto M. Penzler, comps. *Attacks of Taste*. New York: Gotham Book Mart, 1971.

Haffmans, Gerd. *Über Eric Ambler*. Zurich: Diogenes Verlag, 1979.

Hopkins, Joel. "An Interview with Eric Ambler." *Journal of Popular Culture* 9 (1975): 285–93.

James, Clive. "Eric Ambler." *New Review* 1 (September 1974): 63–69.

Lambert, Gavin. *The Dangerous Edge*. London: Barrie & Jenkins, 1975.

KINGSLEY AMIS

Degnan, James P. *Hudson Review* 25 (1972): 330–37.

Gardner, Philip. *Kingsley Amis*. Boston: Twayne, 1981.

Gohn, Jack Benoit. "The Novels of Kinglsey Amis: A Reading." Ph.D. diss.: Johns Hopkins University, 1975.

Irwin, Michael. "The Unkindest Cut of All." *Times Literary Supplement*, 8 October 1976, p. 1269.

MacLeod, Norman. "This Familiar Regressive Series: Aspects of Style in the Novels of Kingsley Amis." In *Edinburgh Studies in English and Scots*, ed. A. J. Aitken et al. London: Longmans, 1971, pp. 121–143.

Orel, Harold. "The Decline and Fall of a Comic Novelist: Kingsley Amis." *Kansas Quarterly* 1 (1969): 17–22.

Salwak, Dale. *Kingsley Amis: A Reference Guide*. Boston: G. K. Hall, 1978.

Spacks, Patricia Meyer. "In the Dumps." *Yale Review* 64 (1976): 585–87.

Voorhees, Richard J. "Kingsley Amis: Three Hurrahs and a Reservation." *Queen's Quarterly* 79 (1973): 38–46.

JOHN ARDEN

Hunt, Albert. *Arden: A Study of His Plays*. London: Eyre Methuen, 1974.

King, Kimball. *Twenty Modern British Playwrights: A Bibliography, 1956 to 1976*. New York: Garland, 1977.

Leeming, Glenda. *John Arden*. London: Longmans, 1974.

Shrapnel, Susan. "John Arden and the Public Stage." *Cambridge Quarterly* 4 (1969): 225–36.

Trussler, Simon. *John Arden*. New York: Columbia University Press, 1973.

W. H. AUDEN

Bogan, Louise. *New Yorker*, 14 April 1945, pp. 78, 81.

Brophy, James D. *W. H. Auden*. New York: Columbia University Press, 1970.

Davie, Donald. *The Hawk's Eye*. New York: Oxford University Press, 1972.

Ehrenpreis, Irvin. "Inside Auden's Landscape." *New York Review of Books*, 3 February 1977, pp. 10–12.

Farnan, Dorothy J. *Auden in Love*. New York: Simon & Schuster, 1984.

Grigson, Geoffrey. *Saturday Review*, 30 July 1932, p. 31.

Kermode, Frank. "Faithing and Blithing." *Listener*, 26 October 1972, pp. 551–52.

Kermode, Frank. "The Poet in Praise of Limestone." *Atlantic Monthly* 225 (May 1970): 67–71.

Leavis, F. R. *Listener*, 22 June 1932, p. 100.

Roth, Robert. "The Sophistication of Auden: A Sketch in Longinian Method." *Modern Philology* 48 (1950–51): 193–204.

Wilson, Edmund. "W. H. Auden in America." In *Auden*. Englewood Cliffs, NJ: Prentice-Hall, 1964.

J. G. BALLARD

Aldiss, Brian. "The Wounded Land: J. G. Ballard." In *SF: The Other Side of Realism*, ed. Thomas D. Clareson. Bowling Green, OH: Bowling Green University Popular Press, 1971, pp. 116–29.

Ballard, J. G. *Empire of the Sun*. New York: Simon & Schuster, 1984.

Godard, James, and David Pringle, eds. *J. G. Ballard: The First Twenty Years*. Hayes, England: Bran's Head Books, 1976.

Pringle, David. *Earth is the Alien Planet: J. G. Ballard's Four-Dimensional Nightmare*. San Bernardino, CA: Borgo Press, 1979.

Re/Search Publications. *Re/Search 8/9* (special J. G. Ballard issue). San Francisco: Re/Search Publications, 1984.

GEORGE BARKER

Beecham, Audrey. "George Barker." *Life and Letters Today* 25 (1940): 273–81.

Daiches, David. "The Lyricism of George Barker." *Poetry* 69 (1947): 336–46.

Fodaski, Martha. "Three Memorial Sonnets." In *Master Poems of the English Language*, ed. Oscar Williams. New York: Trident Press, 1966.

Heath-Stubbs, John, and Martin Green, eds. *Homage to George Barker on His Sixtieth Birthday*. London: Martin Brian and O'Keeffe, 1973.

Scarfe, Francis. "George Barker: A Pure Poet." In *Auden and After*. London: Routledge, 1942.

J. M. BARRIE

Blake, George. *Barrie and the Kailyard School.* London: Arthur Barker, 1951.

Dale, A. "Peter Pan's Pater." *Cosmopolitan* 52 (1912): 793–96.

Garland, Herbert. A *Bibliography of the Writings of Sir James Matthew Barrie, Bart., O.M.* London: Bookman's Journal, 1928.

Green, Roger Lancelyn. *J. M. Barrie.* London: Bodley Head, 1960.

McGraw, William R. "James M. Barrie's Concept of Dramatic Action." *Modern Drama* 5 (1962): 133–41.

Mackail, Denis. *The Story of J. M. B.* London: Peter Davies, 1941.

Roy, James A. *James Matthew Barrie.* London: Jarrolds, 1937.

Stevenson, Lionel. "A Source for Barrie's *Peter Pan*." *Philological Quarterly* 7 (1929): 210–14.

SAMUEL BECKETT

Calder, John, ed. *Beckett at 60: A Festschrift.* London: Calder & Boyars, 1967.

Delye, Huguette. *Samuel Beckett; ou, La philosophie de l'absurde.* Aix-la-Provence: La Pensée universitaire, 1960.

Federman, Raymond. *Journey to Chaos: Samuel Beckett's Early Fiction.* Berkeley: University of California Press, 1965.

Federman, Raymond, and John Fletcher. *Samuel Beckett: His Works and His Critics: An Essay in Bibliography.* Berkeley: University of California Press, 1970.

Fletcher, John. *Samuel Beckett's Art.* New York: Barnes & Noble, 1967.

Hayman, Ronald. *Samuel Beckett.* London: Heinemann, 1968.

Kenner, Hugh. *Samuel Beckett: A Critical Study.* New York: Grove Press, 1961.

Simpson, Alan. *Beckett and Behan and a Theatre in Dublin.* London: Routledge & Kegan Paul, 1962.

MAX BEERBOHM

Behrman, S. N. *Portrait of Max.* New York: Random House, 1960.

Cecil, Lord David. *Max: A Biography.* Boston: Houghton Mifflin, 1965.

Felstiner, John. "Max Beerbohm and the Wings of Henry James." *Kenyon Review* 29 (1967): 449–71.

Gallatin, A. E., and L. M. Oliver. A *Bibliography of the Works of Max Beerbohm.* Cambridge, Mass.: Harvard University Press, 1952.

Hart-Davis, Rupert. A *Catalogue of the Caricatures of Max Beerbohm.* Cambridge, Mass.: Harvard University Press, 1972.

Macdonald, Dwight. *Parodies: An Anthology from Chaucer to Beerbohm—and After.* London: Faber & Faber, 1960.

Moers, Ellen. *The Dandy: Brummell to Beerbohm.* London: Secker & Warburg, 1960.

BRENDAN BEHAN

Arthurs, Peter. *With Brendan Behan.* New York: St. Martin's Press, 1981.

Behan, Dominic. *My Brother Brendan.* New York: Simon & Schuster, 1965.

De Burca, Seamus. *Brendan Behan: A Memoir.* Newark, DE: Proscenium Press, 1971.

Jeffs, Rae. *Brendan Behan: Man and Showman.* London: Hutchinson, 1966.

Kearney, Colbert. *The Writings of Brendan Behan.* New York: St. Martin's Press, 1977.

MacInnes, Colin. "The Writings of Brendan Behan." *London Magazine* NS 2 (August 1962): 53–61.

Mikhail, E. H., ed. *Brendan Behan: An Annotated Bibliography of Criticism.* New York: Barnes & Noble, 1980.

Mikhail, E. H., ed. *Brendan Behan: Interviews and Recollections.* Totowa, NJ: Barnes & Noble, 1982. 2 vols.

Taylor, John Russell. "Way Down East." In *Anger and After.* London: Methuen, 1962, pp. 123–30.

HILAIRE BELLOC

Hamilton, Robert. *Hilaire Belloc: An Introduction to His Spirit and Work.* London: Douglas Organ, 1945.

Jebb, Eleanor, and Reginald Jebb. *Testimony to Hilaire Belloc.* London: Methuen, 1956.

Lodge, David. "Chesterbelloc and the Jews." In *The Novelist at the Crossroads.* Ithaca, NY: Cornell University Press, 1971.

McCarthy, John P. *Hilaire Belloc: Edwardian Radical.* Indianapolis: Liberty Press, 1978.

Mandell, C. Creighton, and Edward Shanks. *Hilaire Belloc: The Man and His Work.* London: Methuen, 1916.

Morton, J. B. *Hilaire Belloc: A Memoir.* London: Hollis & Carter, 1955.

Speaight, Robert. *The Life of Hilaire Belloc.* London: Hollis & Carter, 1957.

ARNOLD BENNETT

Bennett, Marguerite. *Arnold Bennett.* London: A. M. Philpot, 1925.

Conacher, W. M. "Arnold Bennett and the French Realists." *Queen's Quarterly* 56 (1949): 400–417.

Darton, F. J. Harvey. *Arnold Bennett.* New York: Henry Holt, 1915.

Drabble, Margaret. *Arnold Bennett: A Biography.* London: Weidenfeld & Nicolson, 1974.

Hall, James. *Arnold Bennett: Primitivism and Taste.* Seattle: University of Washington Press, 1959.

Kreuz, Irving. "Mr. Bennett and Mrs. Woolf." *Modern Fiction Studies* 8 (1962): 103–15.

Pound, Reginald. *Arnold Bennett: A Biography.* New York: Harcourt, Brace, 1953.

Simons, J. B. *Arnold Bennett and His Novels.* Oxford: Basil Blackwell, 1936.

Wain, John. *Arnold Bennett.* New York: Columbia University Press, 1967.

E. F. BENSON

Benson, E. F. *Final Edition.* New York: Appleton-Century, 1940.

"E. F. Benson Dead; English Author, 72." *New York Times*, 1 March 1940, p. 21.

Roberts, R. Ellis. "Freddie Benson's Story." *Saturday Review*, 19 October 1940, pp. 18–20.

JOHN BERGER

Blumenfeld, Yorick. "The Critic as a Revolutionary." *Atlantic Monthly* 223 (May 1969): 99–101.

Pfeil, Fred. "*Pig Earth* and *About Looking*." *Minnesota Review*, Fall 1980, pp. 123–26.

Ryle, John. "Catching Up, Fiction: *Pig Earth*." *Times Literary Supplement*, 7 December 1979, p. 104.

Szanto, George. "Oppositional Way-Signs: Some Passages within John Berger's History-Making, History-Unravelling Experiment." *College English* 40 (1978): 364–78.

JOHN BETJEMAN

Brooke, Jocelyn. *Ronald Firbank and John Betjeman*. London: Longmans, 1966.

Clive, James. *At the Pillars of Hercules*. London: Jonathan Cape, 1979.

Lancaster, Osbert. *With an Eye to the Future*. London: Faber & Faber, 1965.

Richards, J. M. *Memoirs of an Unjust Fella*. London: Weidenfeld & Nicolson, 1980.

Wain, John. *Essays on Literature and Ideas*. New York: Macmillan, 1963.

EDMUND BLUNDEN

Hardie, Alec M. *Edmund Blunden*. London: Longmans, 1958.

Johnston, John H. *English Poetry of the First World War*. Princeton: Princeton University Press, 1964.

Kirkpatrick, B. J. A *Bibliography of Edmund Blunden*. Oxford: Clarendon Press, 1979.

Mallon, Thomas. *Edmund Blunden*. Boston: Twayne, 1983.

Squire, J. C. *Essays on Poetry*. London: Hodder & Stoughton, 1923.

EDWARD BOND

Barth, Adolf K. H. "The Aggressive 'Theatrum Mundi' of Edward Bond: *Narrow Road to the Deep North*." *Modern Drama* 18 (1975): 189–200.

Cohn, Ruby. *Modern Shakespeare Offshoots*. Princeton: Princeton University Press, 1976.

Coult, Tony. *The Plays of Edward Bond*. London: Eyre Methuen, 1978.

Hay, Malcolm, and Philip Roberts. *Bond: A Study of His Plays*. London: Eyre Methuen, 1980.

Hay, Malcolm, and Philip Roberts. *Edward Bond: A Companion to His Plays*. London: Theatre Quarterly, 1978.

Scharine, Richard. *The Plays of Edward Bond*. Lewisburg, PA: Bucknell University Press, 1976.

ELIZABETH BOWEN

Austin, Allan E. *Elizabeth Bowen*. New York: Twayne, 1971.

Dangerfield, George. "Narrowing Horizons." *Saturday Review of Literature*, 21 January 1939, p. 6.

Greene, Graham. *The Spectator*, 7 October 1938, p. 578.

Hall, James. *The Lunatic Giant in the Drawing Room*. Bloomington: Indiana University Press, 1968.

Kenney, Edwin. *Elizabeth Bowen*. Cranbury, NJ: Associated University Press, 1975.

Wilson, Angus. "Introduction" to *The Collected Stories of Elizabeth Bowen*. New York: Knopf, 1981.

JOHN BRAINE

Karl, Frederick R. A *Reader's Guide to the Contemporary English Novel*. New York: Farrar, Straus & Giroux, 1972.

Lee, James W. *John Braine*. New York: Twayne, 1968.

Mizener, Arthur. "Another Dubious Battle." *New York Times Book Review*, 20 March 1960, pp. 4, 22.

Salwak, Dale. *John Braine and John Wain: A Reference Guide*. Boston: G. K. Hall, 1980.

Waugh, Auberon. "Celebrating the Bourgeois World." *The Spectator*, 18 November 1972, p. 797.

ROBERT BRIDGES

Baker, J. Gordon. "Robert Bridges' Concept of Nature." *PMLA* 54 (1939): 1181–97.

Beaum, R. "Profundity Revisited: Bridges and His Critics." *Dalhousie Review* 44 (1965): 172–79.

Dumbleton, William A. "Bridges and the Hopkins MSS: 1889–1930." *Thought* 47 (1972): 428–46.

Kellog, George A. "Bridges' 'Milton's Prosody' and Renaissance Metrical Theory." *PMLA* 68 (1953): 268–85.

Kelshall, T. M. *Robert Bridges*. Folcroft, PA: Folcroft Editions, 1976.

McKay, George L. A *Bibliography of Robert Bridges*. New York: Columbia University Press, 1933.

Sparrow, John. *Robert Bridges*. London: Longmans, 1962.

Wright, Elizabeth Cox. *Metaphor, Sound, and Meaning in Bridges' "The Testament of Beauty."* Philadephia: University of Pennsylvania Press, 1951.

RUPERT BROOKE

Hassall, Christopher Vernon. *Rupert Brooke: A Biography*. New York: Harcourt, Brace & World, 1964.

James, Henry. "Preface" to *Letters from America* by Rupert Brooke. London: Sidgwick & Jackson, 1916.

Marsh, Sir Edward. *Rupert Brooke: A Memoir*. New York: John Lane, 1918.

Pearsall, Robert Brainard. *Rupert Brooke: The Man and Poet*. Amsterdam: Rodopi, 1974.

Rogers, Timothy. *Rupert Brooke*. London: Routledge & Kegan Paul, 1971.

JOHN BUCHAN

Hodge, David. "John Buchan." *The Living Age* 292 (1917): 171–75.

Smith, Janet Adam. *John Buchan: A Biography*. Boston: Little, Brown, 1965.

Smith, Janet Adam. *John Buchan and His World*. New York: Scribner's, 1979.

Turner, Arthur C. *Mr. Buchan, Writer*. London: SCM Press, 1949.

BASIL BUNTING

Connolly, Cyril. "Basil Bunting: 1." In *Evening Colonade*. New York: Harcourt, Brace & Jovanovich, 1973, pp. 365–68.

Porter, Peter. "Poetry." *London Magazine* NS 9 (1969): 76–80.

Terrell, Carroll F., ed. *Basil Bunting: Man and Poet*. Orono, ME: National Poetry Foundation, 1981.

Williams, Jonathan. *Descant on Rawthey's Madrigal: Conversations with Basil Bunting*. Lexington, KY: Gnomon Press, 1968.

ANTHONY BURGESS

Burgess, Anthony. "Genesis and Headache." In *Afterwords: Novelists on Their Novels*, ed. Thomas McCormack. New York: Harper & Row, 1969, pp. 28–47.

Coale, Samuel. *Anthony Burgess*. New York: Frederick Ungar, 1981.

Cullinan, John. "Anthony Burgess's A *Clockwork Orange*: Two Versions." *English Language Notes* 9 (1972): 287–92.

DeVitis, A. A. *Anthony Burgess*. New York: Twayne, 1972.

Dix, Carol M. *Anthony Burgess*. Harlow, Essex, England: Longmans, 1971.

Mathews, Richard. *The Clockwork Universe of Anthony Burgess*. San Bernardino, CA: Borgo Press, 1978.

ROY CAMPBELL

Abrahams, L. "Roy Campbell: Conquistador-Refugee." *Theoria* 8 (1956): 46–65.

Collins, H. "Roy Campbell: The Talking Bronco." *Boston University Studies in English* 4 (1960): 49–63.

Krige, Uys. "Introduction" to *Poems of Roy Campbell*. Cape Town: M. Miller, 1960.

Monroe, Harriet. "On a High Horse." *Poetry* 38 (1931): 95–100.

Paton, Alan. "Roy Campbell: Poet and Man." *Theoria* 9 (1957): 19–31.

Smith, R. "Campbell and His French Sources." *Journal of Comparative Literature* 22 (1970): 1–18.

Temple, F. J., and R. Lyle, eds. *Hommage a Roy Campbell*. Montpellier: La Licorne, 1958.

Weightman, J. C. "A Pedant Finds Fault." *Twentieth Century* 153 (1953): 135–41.

PAUL VINCENT CARROLL

Brown, John Mason. "*Cathleen ni Houlihan* and *Shadow and Substance*." In *Two on the Aisle*. New York: W. W. Norton, 1938.

Coleman, Anne. "Paul Vincent Carroll's View of Irish Life." *Catholic World* 192 (1960): 87–89.

Doyle, Paul A. *Paul Vincent Carroll*. Lewisburg, PA: Bucknell University Press, 1971.

Sitzmann, Marion. *Indomitable Irishery: Paul Vicnet Carroll*. Salzburg: Institut für Englische Sprache, 1975.

"The Substance of Paul Vincent Carroll." *New York Times Book Review*, 30 January 1938, p. 1.

JOYCE CARY

Adams, Hazard. *Joyce Cary's Trilogies*. Miami: Florida State University Press, 1983.

Allen, Walter Ernest. *Joyce Cary*. London: Longmans, 1963.

Cary, Joyce. "Introduction" to *First Trilogy*. New York: Harper & Row, 1958.

Cecil, Lord David. "Tendencies of the Heart." *London Times*, 4 April 1957, p. 14.

Mahood, M. M. *Joyce Cary's Africa*. London: Camelot Press, 1964.

Orwell, George. "Foreword" to *The Case for African Independence*. London: Secker & Warburg, 1941.

Schorer, Mark. "The Socially Extensive Novel." *Adam International Review* 18 (1950): 31–32.

Stewart, Douglas. "Joyce Cary—Protestantism." In *The Ark of God*. London: Carey Kingsdale Press, 1961.

G. K. CHESTERTON

Bogaerts, Anthony. *Chesterton and the Victorian Age*. New York: Haskell House, 1966.

Boyd, Ian. *The Novels of G. K. Chesterton: A Study in Art and Propaganda*. New York: Barnes & Noble, 1975.

Carol, Sister A. C. *G. K. Chesterton: The Dynamic Classicist*. Delhi: Motilal Banarsidass, 1971.

Dale, Alzina Stone. *The Outline of Sanity: A Biography of G. K. Chesterton*. Grand Rapids: Eerdmans, 1982.

Hollis, Christopher. *The Mind of Chesterton*. London: Hollis & Carter, 1970.

Sullivan, John. *G. K. Chesterton: A Bibliography*. New York: Barnes & Noble, 1958.

Ward, Maisie. *Gilbert Keith Chesterton*. New York: Sheed & Ward, 1943.

AGATHA CHRISTIE

Barnard, Robert. *A Talent to Deceive: An Appreciation of Agatha Christie*. New York: Dodd, Mead, 1980.

Cawelti, J. G. *Adventure, Mystery, Romance*. Chicago: University of Chicago Press, 1976.

Keating, H. R. F., ed. *Agatha Christie: First Lady of Crime*. New York: Holt, Rinehart & Winston, 1977.

Maida, Patricia D., and Nicholas B. Spornick. *Murder She Wrote: A Study of Agatha Christie's Detective Fiction*. Bowling Green, OH: Bowling Green State University Popular Press, 1982.

Osborne, Charles. *The Life and Crimes of Agatha Christie*. New York: Holt, Rinehart & Winston, 1982.

ARTHUR C. CLARKE

Menger, Lucy. "The Appeal of *Childhood's End*." In *Critical Encounters: Writers and Themes in Science Fiction*, ed. Dick Riley. New York: Frederick Ungar, 1978.

Moylan, Tom. "Ideological Contradiction in Clarke's *The City and the Stars*." *Science-Fiction Studies* 4 (July 1977): 150–57.

Otten, Terry. "The Fallen and Evolving Worlds of *2001*." *Mosaic* 13 (1980): 41–50.

Rabkin, Eric S. *Arthur C. Clarke*. Mercer Island, WA: Starmont House, 1980.

Slusser, George Edgar. *The Space Odysseys of Arthur C. Clarke*. San Bernardino, CA: Borgo Press, 1978.

AUSTIN CLARKE

Craig, Maurice. "The Poetry of Austin Clarke." *The Bell*, September 1942, pp. 413–19.

Donoghue, Denis. 'Five in the Great Vein.' *New Review*, August 1974, pp. 69–72.

Harmon, Maurice. *Irish Literature (Modern) 1800–1967: A Reader's Guide*. Dublin: Dolmen Press, 1969.

Martin, Augustine. "Rediscovery of Austin Clarke." *Studies*, Winter 1965, pp. 408–34.

Mercier, Vivian. "Austin Clarke—The Poet in the Theatre." *Chimera* 5 (1947): 25–36.

Montague, John, and Liam Miller, eds. *A Tribute to Austin Clarke on His 70th Birthday, 9 May 1966*. Dublin: Dolmen Press, 1966.

Sealy, Douglas. "Austin Clarke: A Survey of His Work." *Dubliner*, January–February 1963, pp. 7–34.

Strong, L. A. G. "Three Irish Poets." *Commonweal* 22 (1935): 433–37.

PADRAIC COLUM

Alexander, Calvert. *Catholic Literary Revival*. Milwaukee: Bruce Publishing Co., 1935.

Gwynn, Stephen. *Irish Literature and Drama in the English Language*. London: T. Nelson & Sons, 1936.

Howarth, Herbert. *The Irish Writers, 1890–1940*. London: Rockliff, 1958.

Ryan, John. *Remembering How We Stood: Bohemian Dublin at the Mid-Century*. New York: Taplinger, 1975.

Strong, L. A. G. *Personal Remarks*. London: Peter Nevill, 1953.

IVY COMPTON-BURNETT

Baldanza, Frank. *Ivy Compton-Burnett*. New York: Twayne, 1964.

Bradbury, Malcolm. "Unhappy Families Are All Alike." *Encounter* 41 (July 1973): 71–74.

"A Conversation between I. Compton-Burnett and M. Jourdain." In *Orion: A Miscellany*. Volume I. London: Nicolson & Watson, 1945.

Cottrell, Beekman Waldron. "Conversation Piece: Four Twentieth-Century English Novelists." Diss.: Columbia University, 1956.

"Interview with Miss Compton-Burnett." *Review of English Literature* 3 (1962): 96–112.

Kettle, Arnold. "Ivy Compton-Burnett." In *An Introduction to the English Novel: Volume II, Henry James to 1950*. London: Hutchinson, 1953 (2nd ed. 1967).

Nevius, Blake. *Ivy Compton-Burnett*. New York: Columbia University Press, 1970.

Spurling, Hilary. *Ivy: The Life of I. Compton-Burnett*. New York: Knopf, 1984.

JOSEPH CONRAD

Bendz, Ernst. *Jospeh Conrad: An Appreciation*. Gothenberg, Sweden: N. J. Gompert, 1923.

Bowen, Elizabeth. *Collected Impressions*. New York: Knopf, 1950.

Bradbrook, M. C. *Joseph Conrad: Poland's English Genius*. Cambridge: Cambridge University Press, 1941.

Crankshaw, Edward. *Joseph Conrad: Some Aspects of the Art of the Novel*. London: Bodley Head, 1936.

Evans, Robert O. "Conradiana: The Present State of the Art." *Sewanee Review* 91 (1983).

Follett, Wilson. *Joseph Conrad: A Study*. Garden City, NY: Doubleday, 1915.

Las Vergnas, Raymond. *Joseph Conrad*. Paris: H. Didier, 1938.

O'Flaherty, Liam. *Joseph Conrad*. London: E. Lahr, [1930].

Stauffer, Ruth M. *Joseph Conrad: His Romantic Realism*. Boston: Four Seas, 1922.

Vidam, Ivo. "New Approaches to Conrad." *Massachusetts Review*, 11 (1970): 545–63.

BARON CORVO

Bainbridge, H. C. "Corvo the Enigma." In *Twice Seven*. London: Routledge, 1934, pp. 76–139.

Glucker, John. "The Metrical Pattern in Rolfe." *Antigonish Review*, Spring 1970, pp. 46–51.

Greene, Graham. "A Spoiled Priest." In *Collected Essays*. New York: Viking, 1969, pp. 179–181.

Lawrence, D. H. "Baron Corvo." *Adelphi*, December 1925, pp. 502–6.

Woolf, Cecil. *A Bibliography of Frederick Baron Corvo*. London: Hart-Davis, 1957.

NOEL COWARD

Breit, Harvey. "Talk With Noel Coward." *New York Times Book Review*, 25 February 1951, p. 16.

Brown, John Mason. "English Laughter—Past and Present." *Saturday Review of Literature*, 23 November 1946, pp. 24–28.

Rogers, John G. "Noel Coward on Noel Coward." *New York Magazine*, 8 December 1963, p. 35.

Trewin, J. C. "Tap-Tap." In *Dramatists of Today*. London: Staples Press, 1953, pp. 151–61.

DONALD DAVIE

Bedient, Calvin. "On Donald Davie." *Iowa Review* 2 (1971): 66–88.

Dekker, George. "Donald Davie: New and Divergent Lines in English Poetry." *Agenda*, Summer 1976, pp. 45–56.

Dodsworth, Martin. "Donald Davie." *Agenda*, Summer 1976, pp. 15–32.

Morrison, Blake. "A Voice of Even Tenor." *Times Literary Supplement*, 6 January 1978, p. 15.

Schmidt, Michael. "'Time and Again': The Recent Poetry of Donald Davie." *Agenda*, Summer 1976, pp. 33–44.

Weiss, Theodore. "A Slave to His Art." *New York Times Book Review*, 7 October 1984, p. 15.

C. DAY LEWIS

Caudwell, Christopher. *Further Studies in a Dying Culture*. London: Bodley Head, 1949.

Deutsch, Babette. *This Modern Poetry*. New York: W. W. Norton, 1935.

Dyment, Clifford. *C. Day Lewis*. London: Longmans, 1955.

Henderson, Philip. *The Poet and Society*. London: Secker & Warburg, 1939.

Symons, Julian. *The Thirties, a Dream Revolved*. London: Cresset, 1960.

WALTER DE LA MARE

Atkins, John. *Walter de la Mare: An Exploration*. London: C. & J. Temple, 1947.

Cecil, Lord David. *The English Poets*. London: Collins, 1942.

Chesterton, G. K. "Walter de la Mare." *Fortnightly Review* 131 (1932): 47–53.

Church, Richard. "Walter de la Mare." *Fortnightly Review* 153 (1940): 304–11.

Duffin, Henry Charles. *Walter de la Mare: A Study of His Poetry*. London: Sidgwick & Jackson, 1949.

Jones, Llewellyn. "Walter de la Mare: Poet of Tishnar." In *First Impressions*. New York: Knopf, 1925.

Megroz, R. L. *Walter de la Mare: A Biographical and Critical Study*. London: Hodder & Stoughton, 1924.

Reid, Forrest. *Walter de la Mare: A Critical Study*. London: Faber & Faber, 1929.

NIGEL DENNIS

Bailey, Anthony. "Lost Personalities in a Modern Setting." *Commonweal* 63 (1955): 95–96.

Baker, Carlos. "Not Tracts, but Trots for Our Time." *New York Times Book Review*, 13 December 1964, p. 4.

Littler, Frank. "The Ordeal of X." *New York Times Book Review*, 30 October 1966, p. 73.

Rolo, Charles J. "Reader's Choice." *Atlantic Monthly* 196 (December 1955): 94–95.

DENIS DEVLIN

Mizener, Arthur. *Nation*, 10 August 1946, p. 160.

Rodman, Selden. *New Republic*, 29 July 1946, p. 106.

KEITH DOUGLAS

Glover, Jon. "Person and Politics: Commitment in the Forties." *Poetry Nation* 3 (1974): 69–80.

Graham, Desmond. *Keith Douglas 1920–1944: A Biography*. London: Oxford University Press, 1974.

O'Brien, S. P. "Keith Douglas's Poetry." M.A. thesis: University of Birmingham, 1976–77.

Smith, Rowland. Review of *Complete Poems. Dalhousie Review* 58 (1978–79): 763–72.

Wagner, Robert James. "The Poetry of Keith Douglas (1920–1944)." Ph.D. diss.: University of Pennsylvania, 1974.

ARTHUR CONAN DOYLE

Baring-Gould, W. S. *Sherlock Holmes of Baker Street*. New York: C. N. Potter, 1962.

Brown, Ivor. *Conan Doyle: A Biography of the Creator of Sherlock Holmes*. London: Hamilton, 1972.

Carr, John Dickson. *The Life of Sir Arthur Conan Doyle*. New York: Harper, 1949.

De Waal, Ronald. *The International Sherlock Holmes*. Hamden, CT.: Archon Books, 1980.

De Waal, Ronald. *The World Bibliography of Sherlock Holmes*. Boston: New York Graphic Society, 1974.

Edwards, Owen Dudley. *The Quest for Sherlock Holmes*. New York: Barnes & Noble, 1983.

Hall, Trevor H. *Sherlock Holmes: Ten Literary Studies*. New York: St. Martin's Press, 1969.

Klinefelter, Walter. *Sherlock Holmes in Portrait and Profile*. Syracuse: Syracuse University Press, 1963.

Starrett, Vincent. *The Private Life of Sherlock Holmes*. Chicago: University of Chicago Press, 1960.

MARGARET DRABBLE

Davis, Cynthia A. "Unfolding Form: Narrative Approach and Theme in *The Realms of Gold*." *Modern Language Quarterly* 40 (1980): 390–402.

Hardin, Nancy S. "An Interview with Margaret Drabble." *Contemporary Literature* 14 (1973): 273–95.

Myer, Valerie Grosvenor. *Margaret Drabble: Puritanism and Permissiveness*. New York: Barnes & Noble, 1974.

Rose, Ellen Cronan. "Drabble's *The Middle Ground*: 'Mid-Life' Narrative Strategies." *Critique* 23 (1982): 69–81.

Sadler, Lynn Veach. "'The Society We Have': The Search for Meaning in Drabble's *The Middle Ground*." *Critique* 23 (1982): 83–93.

Whittier, Gayle. "Mistresses and Madonnas in the Novels of Margaret Drabble." In *Gender and Literary Voice*, ed. Janet Todd. New York: Holmes & Meier, 1980.

LORD DUNSANY

Amory, Mark. *Biography of Lord Dunsany*. London: Collins, 1972.

Boyd, Ernest. "Lord Dunsany: Fantaisiste." In *Appreciations and Depreciations*. New York: John Lane, 1918.

Jeffares, A. Norman. *Anglo-Irish Literature*. New York: Schocken Books, 1982.

Lovecraft, H. P. "Lord Dunsany and His Work." In *Marginalia*. Sauk City, WI: Arkham House, 1944.

O'Conor, Norreys Jephson. "Lord Dunsany: Irishman." In *Changing Ireland*. Cambridge, MA: Harvard University Press, 1924.

LAWRENCE DURRELL

Arthos, John. "Lawrence Durrell's Gnosticism." *The Personalist* 43 (1962): 360–73.

Glicksberg, Charles I. "The Fictional World of Lawrence Durrell." *Bucknell Review* 11 (1963): 118–33.

Hawkins, Tiger Tim. *Eve: The Common Muse of Henry Miller and Lawrence Durrell*. San Francisco: Ahab Press, 1963.

Littlejohn, David. "The Permanence of Durrell." *Colorado Quarterly* 14 (1965): 63–71.

Morcos, Mona Louis. "Elements of the Autobiographical in *The Alexandria Quartet*." *Modern Fiction Studies* 13 (1967): 343–59.

Scholes, Robert. *The Fabulators*. New York: Oxford University Press, 1967.

Thomas, Alan G., and James A. Brigham. *Lawrence Durrell: An Illustrated Checklist*. Carbondale: Southern Illinois University Press, 1983.

Unterecker, John. *Lawrence Durrell*. New York: Columbia University Press, 1964.

ACKNOWLEDGMENTS

Advent Books. JAMES BLISH (as "William Atheling, Jr."), *More Issues at Hand*, copyright © 1970. Reprinted by permission.

America. PETER MATTHEWS, "The Giddy, the Grim and the Gay," Feb. 18, 1978, copyright © 1978. Reprinted by permission.

American Review. GEOFFREY STONE, "Roy Campbell: Romantic Paradox," Dec. 1936, copyright © 1936. ROBERT PENN WARREN, "Twelve Poets," May 1934, copyright © 1934. Reprinted by permission of *American Review*.

The American Scholar. HAROLD A. LARRABEE, "Robert Bridges and George Santayana," Jan. 1932; BONNIE MENES, "Sherlock Holmes and Sociology," Winter 1980/81. Reprinted by permission of the *American Scholar*.

Archon Books/The Shoe String Press, Inc. JEAN E. KENNARD, "Anthony Burgess: Double Vision," *Number and Nightmare: Forms of Fantasy in Contemporary Fiction*, copyright © 1975. Reprinted by permission.

The Atlantic Monthly. FERRIS GREENSLET, "John Buchan," Sept. 1943; EVELYN WAUGH, "Max Beerbohm: A Lesson in Manners," Sept. 1956. Reprinted by permission.

Barnes & Noble Books. HERMIONE LEE, "The Life Room," *Elizabeth Bowen*, copyright © 1981. LIONEL STEVENSON, "A Group of Able Dames," "Elegant Wits, Cynical Satirists," *The History of the English Novel, Volume XI*, copyright © 1967 by Lionel Stevenson. Reprinted by permission of Barnes & Noble Books.

The Beacon Press. HUGH KENNER, "Samuel Beckett: Comedian of the Impasse," *Flaubert, Joyce and Beckett: The Stoic Comedians*, copyright © 1962 by Hugh Kenner. Reprinted by permission.

Boston University Studies in English. EDWARD WAGENKNECHT, "Walter de la Mare, Book Reviewer," copyright © 1955, 1956 by the Trustees of Boston University. Reprinted by permission.

Bowes & Bowes Publishers Ltd. DOUGLAS HEWITT, "Conrad and the 'Few Simple Notions,'" *Conrad: A Reassessment*, copyright © 1952. Reprinted by permission of Bowes & Bowes Ltd.

Bowling Green University Popular Press. LEROY PANEK, "Margery Allingham," "Agatha Christie," *Watteau's Shepherds*, copyright © 1979. LEROY PANEK, "Erik Ambler," *The Special Branch*, copyright © 1981. Reprinted by permission of the Bowling Green University Popular Press.

Cambridge University Press. DONALD DAVIE, "Italophils," *These the Companions*, copyright © 1982. WILLIAM EMPSON, *Experiment*, Spring 1931. MAURICE EVANS, "Style and Argument," *G. K. Chesterton*, copyright © 1939. G. S. GORDON, *Robert Bridges*, copyright © 1946. Reprinted by permission of Cambridge University Press.

Jonathan Cape Ltd. EDMUND BLUNDEN, "The Ideal Laureate," *The Mind's Eye*, copyright © 1934. HUGH I'ANSON FAUSSET, "Edmund Blunden's Later Poetry," *Poets and Pundits*, copyright © 1947. C. DAY LEWIS, "Broken Images," *The Poetic Image*, copyright © 1947. T. E. LAWRENCE, "Letter to John Buchan, Dec. 26, 1928," *The Letters of T. E. Lawrence*, edited by David Garnett, copyright © 1938. ROBERT LIDDELL, "The Novels of I. Compton-Burnett," *A Treatise on the Novel*, copyright © 1947. Reprinted by permission of Jonathan Cape Ltd.

Cassell & Co. ARNOLD BENNETT, *The Journals of Arnold Bennett*, edited by Newman Flower, copyright © 1932. A. J. A. SYMONS, "Introduction" to *The Desire and Pursuit of the Whole*, copyright © 1934. Reprinted by permission.

Chatto & Windus. TERRY EAGLETON, "Joseph Conrad and 'Under Western Eyes,'" *Exiles and Emigres*, copyright © 1970. D. J. ENRIGHT, "Alexandrian Nights' Entertainments," *Conspirators and Poets*, copyright © 1966. JOHN FLETCHER, *The Novels of Samuel Beckett*, copyright © 1964. F. R. LEAVIS, *New Bearings in English Poetry*, copyright © 1950, 1954. ANDREW WRIGHT, "The World as Character," *Joyce Cary: A Preface to His Novels*, copyright © 1958. Reprinted by permission of Chatto & Windus.

Chillmark Press. EDMUND BLUNDEN, "Introduction" to *The Collected Poems of Keith Douglas*, copyright © 1966. TED HUGHES, "Biographical Notes and Introduction," *Selected Poems of Keith Douglas*, copyright © 1964. FRANK KERMODE, "Henry Miller and John Betjeman," *Puzzles and Epiphanies*, copyright © 1962. Reprinted by permission.

William Collins & Sons. H. DOUGLAS THOMSON, "The Orthodox Detective Story," *Masters of Mystery*, copyright © 1931. Reprinted by permission of William Collins & Sons.

The Colonial Press. LIONEL ABEL, "Beckett and Metatheatre," *Metatheatre*, copyright © 1963. Reprinted by permission.

Columbia University Press. WILLIAM VAN O'CONNOR, *Joyce Cary*, copyright © 1966. RAYMOND J. PORTER, *Brendan Behan*, copyright © 1973. JOHN UNTERECKER, "Lawrence Durrell," *Six Contemporary British Novelists*, edited by George Stade, copyright © 1976. Reprinted by permission of Columbia University Press.

Commonweal. MARK TAYLOR, "Auden's Vision of Eros," October 26, 1973. Reprinted by permission of *Commonweal*.

Constable & Co., Ltd. JOHN BAYLEY, "W. H. Auden," *The Romantic Survival: A Study in Poetic Evolution*, copyright © 1957. Reprinted by permission of Constable & Co., Ltd.

Cornell University Press. FREDERICK BUELL, "Idea and Voice," *Auden as a Social Poet*, copyright © 1973 by Cornell University. Reprinted by permission of Cornell University Press.

Critical Quarterly. BERNARD BERGONZI, "Chesterton and/or Belloc," Spring 1959, copyright © 1959. IAN WATT, "Story and Idea in Conrad's *The Shadow Line*," Summer 1960, copyright © 1960. Reprinted by permission of the authors.

Criticism. PAUL A. BOVÉ, "R. P. Blackmur and the Job of the Critic: Turning from the New Criticism," Fall 1983. FREDERICK R. KARL, "Conrad's Literary Theory," Fall 1960. Reprinted by permission of *Criticism*.

Critique. FRANK BALDANZA, "Lawrence Durrell's 'Word Continuum,'" Spring-Summer 1961, copyright © 1961. VIRGINIA K. BEARDS, 'Margaret Drabble: Novels of a Cautious Feminist," Autumn 1973, copyright © 1973. BERNARD MCCABE, "Ivy Compton-Burnett, an English Eccentric," Winter-Spring 1960, copyright © 1960. Reprinted by permission of *Critique*.

Daedalus. JOHN R. BOLY, "Auden and the Romantic Tradition in *The Age of Anxiety*," Summer 1982, copyright © by The American Academy of Arts and Sciences. Reprinted by permission of *Daedalus*.

J. M. Dent & Sons Ltd. M. L. RIDLEY, "A Misrated Author?" *Second Thoughts*, copyright © 1965. Reprinted by permission of J. M. Dent & Sons Ltd.

Andre Deutsch, Ltd. G. S. FRASER, "Indian Summer," "Looking Back and Forward in the 1940s," "The Novel in the 1950s," "The 1930s and the Second World War," *The Modern Writer and His World*, copyright © 1953, 1964 by G. S. Fraser. Reprinted by permission.

The Dolmen Press, Ltd. SUSAN HALPERN, *Austin Clarke, His Life and Works*, copyright © 1974. NIALL SHERIDAN, "Introduction" to *The Heavenly Foreigner*, edited by Brian Coffey, copyright © 1967. Reprinted by permission of The Dolmen Press, Ltd.

Doubleday & Company, Inc. JERRY ALLEN, "The Men," *The Sea Years of Joseph Conrad*, copyright © 1965. Reprinted by permission of Jerry Allen. W. H. AUDEN, "Introduction" to John Betjeman's *Slick But Not Streamlined*, copyright © 1947 by W. H. Auden.

Dover Publications, Inc. H. P. LOVECRAFT, "The Modern Masters" and "The Weird Tradition in America," *Supernatural Horror in Literature*, copyright © 1973. Reprinted by permission of Dover Publications, Inc.

Duckworth & Co. Ltd. JOHN BATCHELOR, "Conrad," *The Edwardian Novelists*, copyright © 1982. Reprinted by permission.

E. P. Dutton. LAWRENCE DURRELL, "Letter to Henry Miller, Jan. 1937," *Lawrence Durrell and Henry Miller: A Private Correspondence*, copyright © 1962, 1963. ROBERT PHILLIPS, "Preface" to *The Collected Stories of Noel Coward*, copyright © 1983. Reprinted by permission of E. P. Dutton.

Paul Elek Ltd. KINGSLEY AMIS, "Four Fluent Fellows," W. W. ROBSON, "Father Brown and Others," *G. K. Chesterton: A Centenary Appraisal*, edited by John Sullivan, copyright © 1974. Reprinted by permission.

Encounter. W. H. AUDEN, "Am I That I Am?" April 1955, copyright © 1955. BERNARD BERGONZI, "Auden and the Audenesque," Feb. 1975, copyright © 1975. GERTRUDE HIMMELFARB, "John Buchan: An Untimely Appreciation," Sept. 1960, copyright © 1960. GEOFFREY GRIGSON, "The Extremists of Al Alvarez," Aug. 1972, copyright © 1972. Reprinted by permission of *Encounter*.

Essays in Criticism. E. M. W. TILLYARD, "The Secret Agent Reconsidered," July 1961. Reprinted by permission of *Essays in Criticism*.

Estate of W. H. Auden. W. H. AUDEN, "Foreword" to *G. K. Chesterton: A Selection from His Non-Fictional Prose*, published by Faber & Faber, Ltd. Copyright © 1970 by W. H. Auden. Reprinted by permission of the Estate of W. H. Auden.

Estate of John Mason Brown. JOHN MASON BROWN, "Ireland and the White Steed," *Broadway in Review*, copyright © 1940 by W. W. Norton & Company. Reprinted by permission of the Estate of John Mason Brown.

Faber and Faber Ltd. KINGSLEY AMIS, "Introduction" to *G. K. Chesterton: Selected Stories*, copyright © 1972; W. H. AUDEN, "Foreword" to *G. K. Chesterton: A Selection from His Non-Fictional Prose*, copyright © 1970 by W. H. Auden; RUSSELL BRAIN, "The Little Nowhere," *Tea with Walter de la Mare*, copyright © 1957; ANTHONY BURGESS, "A Sort of Rebels," *The Novel Now: A Student's Guide to Contemporary Fiction*, copyright © 1967 by Anthony Burgess; WALTER DE LA MARE, "Maps Actual and Imaginary," "Rupert Brooke and the Intellectual Imagination," *Pleasures and Speculations*, copyright © 1940; reprinted by permission of The Society of Authors. LAWRENCE DURRELL, "Introduction" to *Alamein to Zem Zem*, copyright © 1966 by Lawrence Durrell; G. S. FRASER, "A Watershed: The Black Book," *Lawrence Durrell: A Study*, copyright © 1968 by G. S. Fraser; GRAHAM GREENE, "The Short Stories," *A Tribute to Walter de la Mare on His Seventy-Fifth Birthday*, copyright © 1948; LAWRENCE KITCHIN, "Arden," *Drama in the Sixties*, copyright © 1966 by Lawrence Kitchin; J. B. PRIESTLEY, "What Lovely Things," *A Tribute to Walter de la Mare on His Seventy-Fifth Birthday*, copyright © 1948; H. M. TOMLINSON, "War Books," *The Criterion*, April 1930. Reprinted by permission of Faber and Faber Ltd.

John Farquharson Ltd. COLIN WATSON, "The Little World of Mayhem Parva," *Snobbery with Violence*, copyright © 1971. Reprinted by permission of John Farquharson Ltd.

Farrar, Straus and Giroux. EDWARD BOND, "Author's Program Note on *The Sea*," *Bingo and The Sea*, copyright © 1975; FREDERICK R. KARL, "The Intimate World of Ivy Compton-Burnett," "Lawrence Durrell: Physical and Metaphysical Love," *The Contemporary English Novel*, copyright © 1962 by Frederick Karl; EDMUND WILSON, "A Miscellany of Max Beerbohm," *The Bit between My Teeth*, copyright © 1965 by Edmund Wilson. Reprinted by permission of the publishers.

Garnstone Press. CICELY GREIG, *Ivy Compton-Burnett: A Memoir*, copyright © 1972. Reprinted by permission.

Gaslight Publications. C. FREDERICK KITTLE, "Afterword" to *The Stark Munro Letters*, copyright © 1982 by Jack W. Tracy. Reprinted by permission.

The Georgia Review. WOLFGANG ISER, "The Pattern of Negativity in Beckett's Prose," Vol. 29, No. 3 (1975), copyright © 1975. Reprinted by permission of the *Georgia Review*.

Grove Press. MAURICE BLANCHOT, "Where Now: Who Now?" *On Contemporary Literature*, ed. Richard Kostelanetz, copyright © 1964. RICHARD N. COE, "Words and Numbers," *Samuel Beckett*, copyright © 1964 by Richard N. Coe. ALAIN ROBBE-GRILLET, "Samuel Beckett or Presence on the Stage," *For a New Novel*, copyright © 1965. Reprinted by permission of Grove Press.

G. K. Hall & Co.—Twayne Publishers. DORIS ROSS MCCROSSON, "A Final Estimate," *Walter de la Mare*, copyright © 1966. MICHAEL H. MARKEL., *Hilaire Belloc*, copyright © 1982. MALCOLM PAGE, *John Arden*, copyright © 1984. KENNETH T. REED, *S. N. Behrman*, copyright © 1975. Reprinted by permission of G. K. Hall & Co.

Harcourt, Brace, Jovanovich, Inc. NORMAN DOUGLAS, *Looking Back*, copyright © 1933 by Norman Douglas. E. M. FORSTER, "Joseph Conrad: A Note," *Abinger Harvest*, copyright © 1936, 1964 by E. M. Forster. MICHAEL HAMBURGER, "Town and Country:

Phenotypes and Archetypes," *The Truth of Poetry: Tensions in Modern Poetry from Baudelaire to the 1960's*, copyright © 1969 by Michael Hamburger. JOHN HOLLOW, *Against the Night, the Stars*, copyright © 1983. MARY MCCARTHY, "The Inventions of Ivy Compton-Burnett," *The Writing on the Wall and Other Literary Essays*, copyright © 1970 by Harcourt, Brace and World. ANTHONY WEST, "Ivy Compton-Burnett," *Principles and Persuasions*, copyright © 1957 by Anthony West. Reprinted by permission of Harcourt Brace Jovanovich, Inc.

Harvard University Press. DOUGLAS BUSH, "From the Nineties to the Present," *Mythology and the Romantic Tradition in English Poetry*, copyright © 1937, 1965 by Douglas Bush. ALBERT GUERARD, "On the Nigger of the Narcissus," *Conrad the Novelist*, copyright © 1958 by the President and Fellows of Harvard College; *Robert Bridges*, copyright © 1942 by the President and Fellows of Harvard College. Renewed 1970 by Albert Guerard. J. HILLIS MILLER, "Lord Jim: Repetition as Subversion of Organic Form," *Fiction and Repetition: Seven English Novels*, copyright © 1982 by J. Hillis Miller; THOMAS COLBORN MOSER, "The Exhaustion of Creative Energy," *Joseph Conrad: Achievement and Decline*, copyright © 1957 by the President and Fellows of Harvard College. Reprinted by permission of the publisher.

Hibernia. SEAMUS HEANEY, "Shorts for Auden," Oct. 8, 1976, copyright © 1976. Reprinted by permission.

Holt, Rinehart & Winston. BRIGID BROPHY, "I. Compton-Burnett," *Don't Never Forget*, copyright © 1966. JOHN GASSNER, "Beckett's *Endgame* and Symbolism," *Theatre at the Crosroads*, copyright © 1960. MURRAY KRIEGER, "Joseph Conrad: Action, Inaction, and Extremity," *The Tragic Vision*, copyright © 1960. Reprinted by permission of Holt, Rinehart & Winston.

The Hudson Review. ROGER SALE, "Huxley and Bennett, Bedford and Drabble," Summer 1975. BENJAMIN DE MOTT, "Grading the Emanglons," Autumn 1960. J. MITCHELL MORSE, "The Contemplative Life according to Samuel Beckett," Winter 1962–3. NORTHROP FRYE, "The Nightmare Life in Death," Autumn 1960. Reprinted by permission of the *Hudson Review*.

Hutchinson Educational Publishing Ltd. RICHARD HOGGART, "Introduction to Auden's Poetry," *W. H. Auden: A Selection*, copyright © 1961. Reprinted by permission.

Indiana University Press. JAMES G. HEPBURN, *The Art of Arnold Bennett*, copyright © 1963. Reprinted by permission of Indiana University Press.

Michael Joseph Ltd. JOYCE CARY, "Unfinished Novels," *Selected Essays*, edited by A. G. Bishop, copyright © 1976. GOLDEN L. LARSEN, "The Contemporaneity of Joyce Cary: A Comparison with Joseph Conrad," *The Dark Descent: Social Change and Moral Responsibility in the Novels of Joyce Cary*, copyright © 1965. DONALD WEEKS, "Introduction" to *Corvo*, copyright © 1971. Reprinted by permission of Michael Joseph Ltd.

Journal of Modern Literature. RUTH PERLMUTTER, "Beckett's *Film* and Beckett and Film," Vol. 6, No. 1, copyright © 1977. Reprinted by permission.

Alfred A. Knopf, Inc.—Random House, Inc. W. H. AUDEN, "One of the Family," "Walter de la Mare," *Forewards and Afterwards*, copyright © 1973 by W. H. Auden; "Making, Knowing and Judging," *The Dyer's Hand*, copyright © 1948, 1950, 1952, 1953, 1954, 1956, 1957, 1958, 1960, 1962 by W. H. Auden. Reprinted by permission of Random House, Inc. MAX BEERBOHM, "At the St. James's Theatre," *Around Theatres*, copyright © 1930 by Max Beerbohm; reprinted by permission of Alfred A. Knopf, Inc. JOHN FELSTINER, "Visual Metaphor," *The Lies of Art*, copyright © 1972 by John Felstiner; reprinted by permission of the author. HUGH KENNER, *A Colder Eye*, copyright © 1983 by Hugh Kenner; reprinted by permission of Alfred A. Knopf, Inc. ROBERT PENN WARREN, "The Great Mirage: Conrad and Nostromo," *Selected Essays*, copyright © 1941, 1958 by permisssion of Random House, Inc. VINCENT STARRETT, "From Poe to Poirot," *Books Alive: A Profane Chronicle of Literary Endeavor and Literary Misdemeanor*, copyright © 1940 by Vincent Starrett; reprinted by permission of Random House, Inc. IGOR STRAVINSKY, ROBERT CRAFT, "Interviews," *Themes and Episodes*, copyright © 1966; reprinted by permission of Alfred A. Knopf. EDWARD WAGEN-KNECHT, "Introduction" to *Collected Tales of Walter de la Mare*, copyright © 1950; reprinted by permission of Alfred A. Knopf. JOHN UPDIKE, "Auden Feat," *Picked-Up Pieces*, copyright © 1965; reprinted by permission of Alfred A. Knopf, Inc.

John Knox Press. LOIS AND STEPHEN ROSE, *The Shattered Ring*, copyright © 1970. Reprinted by permission.

Robert Krieger Publishing Co., Inc. ALVIN E. RODIN and JACK D. KEY, *Medical Casebook of Doctor Arthur Conan Coyle*, copyright © 1984. Reprinted by permission of Robert Krieger Publishing Co., Inc.

Wilfrid Laurier University Press. JANE CAMPBELL, "Margaret Drabble and the Search for Analogy," *The Practical Vision: Essays in English Literature in Honour of Flora Roy*, copyright © 1978. Reprinted by permission.

Life Magazine. NIGEL DENNIS, "New Four-Star King of Novelists," Nov. 21, 1960. Reprinted by permission of *Life*.

The Literary Review. WILLIAM TURNER LEVY, "Padraic Colum, Poet," Summer 1958. Reprinted by permission of *The Literary Review*.

The London Magazine. ANGUS WILSON, "Ivy Compton-Burnett," July 1955, copyright © 1955. Reprinted by permission.

Longman Group Ltd. ELIZABETH BOWEN, *Collected Impressions*, copyright © 1950. RENÉE HAYNES, *Hilaire Belloc*, copyright © 1953. D. W. JEFFERSON, "A Note on Ivy Compton-Burnett," *A Review of English Literature*, April 1960. Copyright © 1960. Reprinted by permission of Longman Group Ltd.

Louisiana State University Press. ALLAN WARREN FRIEDMAN, "Conrad's Picaresque Narrator," *Multivalence*, copyright © 1978. Reprinted by permission of Louisiana State University Press.

McGill-Queens University Press. ROWLAND SMITH, *Lyric and Polemic: The Literary Personality of Roy Campbell*, copyright © 1972. Reprinted by permission of McGill-Queens University Press.

Macmillan & Co. Ltd. BERNARD BERGONZI, "Between Nostalgia and Nightmare," *The Situation of the Novel*, copyright © 1970; "Graves, Blunden, Read," *Heroes' Twilight: A Study of the Literature of the Great War*, copyright © 1980. MICHAEL MACLIAMMOIR, "Problem Plays," *The Irish Theatre*, copyright © 1939. W. B. YEATS, "Mr. Robert Bridges," *The Correspondence of Robert Bridges and W. B. Yeats*, edited by Richard J. Finneran, copyright © 1977. Reprinted by permission of Macmillan & Co., London.

Macmillan Publishing Co. (New York). BERNARD BERGONZI, "Roy Campbell: Outsider on the Right," *The Turn of a Century*, copyright © 1973. PADRAIC COLUM, "Introduction" to *The Collected Poems of Austin Clarke*, copyright © 1936. CHARLES MORGAN, "Edmund Blunden's 'Thomasine,'" *Reflections in a Mirror*, copyright © 1947. H. G. WELLS, *Experiment in Autobiography*, copyright © 1934. Reprinted by permission.

The Magazine of Fantasy and Science Fiction. ALGIS BUDRYS, "Books," March 1983, copyright © 1983. Reprinted by permission.

Massachusetts Review. WILLIAM H. PRITCHARD, "The Novels of Anthony Burgess," Summer 1966, copyright © 1966. RICHARD WEBER, "Austin Clarke: The Arch Poet of Dublin," Spring 1970. Reprinted by permission of the *Massachusetts Review*.

Methuen & Co. JOHN RUSSELL TAYLOR, "Presented at Court," *Anger and After*, copyright © 1962; "Edward Bond," *The Second Wave: British Drama for the Seventies*, copyright © 1971. IAN WATT, "Conrad, James and Chance," *Imagined Worlds*, edited by Maynard Mack and Ian Gregor, copyright © 1968. Reprinted by permission.

Michigan State University Press. ANDRÉ GIDE, "Joseph Conrad," and VERNON YOUNG, "Trial by Water," *The Art of Joseph Conrad: A Critical Symposium*, edited by R. W. Stallman, copyright © 1960. Reprinted by permission of Michigan State University Press.

Modern Drama. ANTONY EASTHOPE, "Hamm, Clov, and Dramatic Method in *Endgame*," Feb. 1968. Reprinted by permission of Modern Drama.

Modern Fiction Studies. ALAN WARREN FRIEDMAN, "Place and Durrell's Island Books," Autumn 1967. GLORIA L. YOUNG, "Quest and Discovery," Winter 1982–3. Reprinted by permission of *Modern Fiction Studies*.

Mouton & Co. HARRIET BLODGETT, "Gain in Paradise Lost," *Patterns of Reality*, copyright © 1975. GILES MITCHELL, "Herself Sur-

prised," *The Art Theme in Joyce Cary's Trilogy*, copyright © 1971. Reprinted by permission.

The Nation. JOAN GOULIANOS, "Landscape of the Heart," July 14, 1969. RANDALL JARRELL, April 12, 1941. Reprinted by permission of the *Nation*.

New Directions Publishing Corporation. WILLIAM EMPSON, *Seven Types of Ambiguity*, copyright © 1930, 1953. KENNETH REXROTH, "Introduction," to *The New British Poets*, copyright © 1949. DYLAN THOMAS, "Walter de la Mare as a Prose Writer," *Quite Early One Morning*, copyright © 1948. Reprinted by permission of New Directions Publishing Corporation and David Higham Associates Ltd.

The New Republic. SAUL BELLOW, "A Personal Record," February 22, 1954. ERIC BENTLEY, "The Talent of Samuel Beckett," May 14, 1956. HILARY CORKE, "Getting to the Bottom of the Top," November 3, 1962. JOSEPH EPSTEIN, "The Beerbohm Revival," June 27, 1964. IAN WATT, "'Very Funny . . . Unbelievably Tough,'" August 29, 1960. EDMUND WILSON, "Edmund Wilson Regrets the Retrograde: The Oxford Boys Becalmed," February 24, 1937. Reprinted by permission of the *New Republic*.

The New Statesman and Nation. WALTER ALLEN, Jan. 30, 1954. A. ALVAREZ, "Braine at the Top," Oct. 5, 1962. CYRIL CONNOLLY, Jan. 19, 1929. TERRY EAGLETON, "A Sort of Fiction," Jan. 15, 1980. P. N. FURBANK, "Cool," March 22, 1968. RICHARD HOGGART, "Intelligence and Insight," April 12, 1958. M. M. MAHOOD, "Joyce Cary in Africa, 1913–20," Oct. 1, 1960. RAYMOND MORTIMER, Oct. 8, 1938. BENEDICT NIGHTINGALE, "The Bourgeois Bard," Nov. 23, 1973. V. S. PRITCHETT, "Walter de la Mare," June 30, 1956. "Books in General (The Weekend Review)," Oct. 27, 1951. "Miss Compton-Burnett," March 5, 1955. "From the Horse's Mouth," Nov. 15, 1958. S. K. RATCLIFFE, "Arthur Conan Doyle," July 12, 1930. CHRISTOPHER RICKS, "The Epicence," April 5, 1963. J. D. SCOTT, "New Novels," August 25, 1951. DESMOND SHAWE-TAYLOR, "Discrimination," Jan. 11, 1941. PAUL THEROUX, "Personal Products," May 3, 1974. Reprinted by permission.

The New Yorker. L. E. SISSMAN, "Kingsley Amis at Halfway House," April 26, 1969. Reprinted by permission of *The New Yorker*. GEORGE STEINER, "Scroll and Keys," April 13, 1981, copyright © 1981. EDMUND WILSON, "Is It Possible to Pat Kingsley Amis?" March 24, 1956. Reprinted by permission.

New York Review of Books. W. H. AUDEN, "Doing Oneself In," April 20, 1972, copyright © 1972. BERNARD BERGONZI, "Stale Incense," July 11, 1968, copyright © 1968. DENIS DONOGHUE, "Good Grief," July 19, 1973, copyright © 1973. G. S. FRASER, "Three British Poets," June 25, 1964, copyright © 1964. V. S. PRITCHETT, "Pleasures of Malice," June 23, 1977, copyright © 1977. STEPHEN SPENDER, "W. H. Auden (1907–1973)," Nov. 29, 1973, copyright © 1973. MICHAEL WOOD, "This is Not the End of the World," Jan. 25, 1979, copyright © 1979. Reprinted by permission of *The New York Review of Books*.

The New York Times Co., Inc. CARLOS BAKER, "A Poet Considers His Technique," Dec. 28, 1947. DONALD BARR, "A Definition of Love," July 19, 1953. ANTHONY BOUCHER, "Criminals at Large," April 10, 1955. MALCOLM BRADBURY, "Fly Away," Dec. 9, 1979. PAUL DELANY, "John Berger's Socialist Imagination," Jan. 11, 1976. WILLIAM GOYEN, "Small Talk on the Way to Damnation," Nov. 18, 1956. R. B. HEILMAN, "Some Milestones in the Poet's Growth," Aug. 5, 1945. JOSEPH WOOD KRUTCH, "Mr. Ambler's Spies," March 16, 1952. C. DAY LEWIS, "With a Flair for Creating Alarm," July 26, 1953. CHARLES POORE, "The Lambs and Their Smug Shepherd," June 20, 1948. EUDORA WELTY, "Victorian Half-Breed," Oct. 31, 1943; "As If She Had Been Invited Into This World," Jan. 5, 1975. MICHAEL WOOD, "A Love Song to What Would Be Lost," March 6, 1983. Reprinted by permission.

New York University Press. F. R. LEAVIS, "Joseph Conrad," *The Great Tradition*, copyright © 1968. Reprinted by permission.

Martinus Nijhoff. J. G. RIEWALD, "Max Beerbohm and Oscar Wilde," *Sir Max Beerbohm, Man and Writer*, copyright © 1953. Reprinted by permission.

Oxford University Press. ROBERT MARTIN ADAMS, *AfterJoyce: Studies in Fiction after Ulysses*, copyright © 1977. EDWARD CALLAN, "The Post-Romantic Hero," *Auden: A Carnival of the Intellect*, copyright © 1983. FREDERICK CREWS, "Conrad's Uneasiness—And Ours," *Out of My System*, copyright © 1975. DONALD DAVIE, "Lucky Jim and the Hobbits," "The Hawk's Eye," *Thomas Hardy and British Poetry*, copyright © 1972. DONALD DAVIE, "Note to 'With the Grain,'" *Collected Poems 1950–1970*, copyright © 1972. MARTIN ESSLIN, "Samuel Beckett," *The Novelist as Philosopher: Studies in French Fiction, 1935–1960*, copyright © 1962. DESMOND GRAHAM, "Preface," "Letter to J. C. Hall," in *The Complete Poems of Keith Douglas*, copyright © 1978. JEAN G. RITZ, "Two Poets Discuss Each Other's Verse," *Robert Bridges and Gerard Manley Hopkins, 1863–1889: A Literary Friendship*, copyright © 1960. NOWELL CHARLES SMITH, "Introduction" to *Notes on* The Testament of Beauty, copyright © 1940. EDWARD THOMPSON, *Robert Bridges 1844–1930*, copyright © 1944. CHARLES WILLIAMS, "Robert Bridges," "Walter de la Mare," "Gilbert Keith Chesterton," "Edmund Blunden," *Poetry at Present*, copyright © 1930.

Parnassus: Poetry in Review. THEODORE WEISS, "Between Two Worlds or On the Move," Fall/Winter 1974, copyright © 1974. Reprinted by permission of *Parnassus*.

Partisan Review. E. M. CIORAN, "Encounters with Beckett," translated by Raymond Federman and Jean A. Sommermeyer, copyright © 1976. ELIZABETH FOX-GENOVESE, "The Ambiguities of Female Identity: A Reading of the Novels of Margaret Drabble," copyright © 1979. ELIZABETH HARDWICK, "Elizabeth Bowen's Fiction," copyright © 1949. DANIEL F. HOWARD, "Leveling," Summer 1970 copyright © 1970. FRANK KERMODE, "Fiction Chronicle," copyright © 1960. DELMORE SCHWARTZ, Sept.–Oct. copyright © 1947. Reprinted by permission of the *Partisan Review*.

Poetry. HUGH KENNER, "A Resurrected Poet," September 1951, copyright © 1951 by The Modern Poetry Association. WILLIAM JAY SMITH, "Master of Silences, Walter de la Mare 1873–1956," first appeared in *Poetry*, Nov. 1957, copyright © 1957 by The Modern Poetry Association. Also appeared in *The Streaks of the Tulip: Selected Criticism*, Delacorte Press, 1972. Reprinted by permission of William Jay Smith.

Princeton University Press. LAWRENCE HARVEY, *Samuel Beckett, Poet and Critic, 1929–1949*, copyright © 1970 JOHN H. JOHNSTON, "The Early Poets," *English Poetry of the First World War*, copyright 1964. ELAINE SHOWALTER, "Beyond the Female Aesthetic: Contemporary Women Novelists," *A Literature of Their Own: British Women Novelists from Brontë to Lessing*, copyright © 1977. Excerpts reprinted with permission of Princeton University Press.

Purdue University Press. MAURICE HARMON, "The Later Poetry of Austin Clarke," *The Celtic Cross*, edited by Ray B. Browne, William John Roscelli and Richard Loftus, copyright © 1964. Reprinted by permission of Purdue Research Foundation.

Routledge & Kegan Paul Ltd. MARGARET DRABBLE, "A Woman Writer," *On Gender and Writing*, edited by Michelene Wandor, copyright © 1983. BRIAN FINNEY, "Beckett's Shorter Fiction," *Beckett: The Shape Changes*, edited by Katharine Worth, copyright © 1975. COLIN GREENLAND, "The Works of J. G. Ballard," *The Entropy Exhibition*, copyright © 1983. D. E. S. MAXWELL, "C. Day Lewis: Between Two Worlds," *Poets of the Thirties*, copyright © 1969. JOHN PILLING, "Writings on Literature and Art," *Samuel Beckett*, copyright © 1976. Reprinted by permission.

Rutgers University Press. RUBY COHN, "Endgame," *Samuel Beckett: The Comic Gamut*, copyright © 1962. Reprinted by permission of Rutgers University Press.

St. Martin's Press. DAVID I. GROSSVOGEL, "Death Deferred," *Art in Crime Writing*, edited by Bernard Bernstock, copyright © 1983. Reprinted by permission of St. Martin's Press, Inc. and Macmillan and Co. Ltd.

Science-Fiction Studies. CHARLES NICOL, "J. G. Ballard and the Limits of Mainstream Science Fiction," July 1976, copyright © 1976. Reprinted by permission.

Charles Scribner's Sons. ERNEST HEMINGWAY, "Conrad, Optimist and Moralist," *By-Line Ernest Hemingway*, copyright © 1967. EDWARD SACKVILLE-WEST, "Ladies Whose Bright Pens . . . ," *Inclinations*, copyright © 1949. Reprinted by permission.

Sewanee Review. BONAMY DOBRÉE, "No Man's Land," Spring 1957, copyright © 1957 by the University of the South. FRANK L. KERSNOWSKI, "The Fabulous Reality of Denis Devlin," Winter 1973, copyright © 1973 by the University of the South. Reprinted by permission of the *Sewanee Review*.

Sheed & Ward Ltd. HILAIRE BELLOC, *On the Place of Gilbert Keith Chesterton in English Letters*, copyright © 1940. G. K. CHESTERTON, "Sherlock Holmes," *A Handful of Authors*, copyright © 1953. HUGH KENNER, *Paradox in Chesterton*, copyright © 1947. Reprinted by permission.

Simon & Schuster. MAX BEERBOHM, "Why I Ought Not to Have Become a Dramatic Critic," *Around Theatres*, copyright © 1930. Reprinted by permission of Simon & Schuster.

South Atlantic Quarterly. GERALD JAY GOLDBERG, "The Search for the Artist in Some Recent British Fiction," copyright © 1963. HOMER E. WOODBRIDGE, "Noel Coward," July 1938, copyright © 1938. Reprinted by permission of the *South Atlantic Quarterly*.

Southern Illinois University Press. ZACK BOWEN, "Fiction, Biographies, Essays," *Padraic Colum: A Biographical-Critical Introduction*, copyright © 1970. LOUIS FRAIBERG, "Durrell's Dissonant Quartet," *Contemporary British Novelists*, edited by Charles Shapiro, copyright © 1965. MARY HURLEY MORAN, "Drabble's Dark Universe," *Margaret Drabble: Existing Within Structures*, copyright © 1983 by the Board of Trustees, Southern Illinois University. Reprinted by permission of the Southern Illinois University Press.

The Spectator. E. F. BENSON, "Max," Jan. 31, 1931, copyright © 1931. ANTHONY BURGESS, "Treasures and Fetters," Feb. 24, 1964, copyright © 1964. PHILIP LARKIN, "What's Become of Wystan?" July 15, 1960, copyright © 1960. ANTHONY POWELL, "Kingsley's Heroes," Nov. 29, 1963, copyright © 1963. MORDECAI RICHLER, "Tougher at the Bottom," Oct. 19, 1962, copyright © 1962. REX WARNER, "Aegean Sky," Aug. 21, 1953, copyright © 1953. Reprinted by permission of *The Spectator*, Ltd.

Taplinger Publishing Co., Inc. EUGENE TANZY, "Contrasting Views of Man and the Evolutionary Process: *Back to Methuselah* and *Childhood's End*," *Arthur C. Clarke*, edited by Joseph D. Olander and Martin Harry Greenberg, copyright © 1977. Reprinted by permission.

Times Literary Supplement. G. S. FRASER, "They Also Serve," Feb. 10, 1956, copyright © 1956. F. R. LEAVIS, March 19, 1931, copyright © 1931. Reprinted by permission of the *Times Literary Supplement*.

The Twentieth Century. KINGLSEY AMIS, "One World and Its Way," Aug. 1955, copyright © 1955. Reprinted by permission of the *Twentieth Century*.

Universe Books, Inc. PEGGY GUGGENHEIM, *Out of This Century: Confessions of an Art Addict*, copyright © 1946, 1960, 1979 by Peggy Guggenheim. Reprinted by permission of Universe Books, Inc.

University of Alabama Press. GEOFFREY AGGELER, *Anthony Burgess: The Artist as Novelist*, copyright © 1979. Reprinted by permission.

University of Chicago Press. HAROLD BLOOM, *The Ringers in the Tower*, copyright © 1971; GERMAINE BRÉE, "The Strange World of Beckett's 'grands articulés,'" *Samuel Beckett Now*, copyright © 1970; LIONEL STEVENSON, "Contemporary Poets," *Darwin Among the Poets*, copyright © 1932. Reprinted by permission of the University of Chicago Press.

University of Delaware Press. DONALD STANFORD, "Preface" to *In the Classic Mode: The Achievement of Robert Bridges*, copyright © 1978. Reprinted by permission of Associated University Presses.

University of Georgia Press. DOUGLAS MCMILLAN, "*Nostromo*: The Theology of Revolution," *The Classic British Novel*, edited by H. M. Harper and C. Edge, copyright © 1972. Reprinted by permission of the University of Georgia Press.

University of Minnesota Press. ROBERT HOGAN, "Paul Vincent Carroll: The Rebel as Prodigal Son," *After the Irish Renaissance*, copyright © 1967. Reprinted by permission of the University of Minnesota Press.

University of Nebraska Press. JUDY LITTLE, "Feminist Comedy," *Comedy and the Woman Writer*, copyright © 1983. WALTER F. WRIGHT, "Adventures Often Among Masterpieces," *Arnold Ben-*

nett: Romantic Realist, copyright © 1971. Reprinted by permission of the University of Nebraska Press.

University of North Carolina Press. CLEANTH BROOKS, "Frost, MacLeish, and Auden," *Modern Poetry and the Tradition*, copyright © 1939. Reprinted by permission of the University of North Carolina Press.

University of Oklahoma Press. ALAN WARREN FRIEDMAN, "The Evolving Lawrence Durrell," *Lawrence Durrell and the Alexandria Quartet: Art for Love's Sake*, copyright © 1970. Reprinted by permission of the University of Oklahoma Press.

University of Pennsylvania Press. ROBERT BLOOM, "The Uses of Irresolution: A Survey of the Fiction," "Not Honour More: The Morality of Exasperation and the Indeterminate Pinnacle," *The Indeterminate World*, copyright © 1962. Reprinted by permission of the University of Pennsylvania Press.

University of Pittsburgh Press. CHARLES G. HOFFMAN, "There's a War On," *Joyce Cary*, copyright © 1964. Reprinted by permission of the University of Pittsburgh Press.

University of Texas Press. JORGE LUIS BORGES, "On Chesterton," *Other Inquisitions, 1937–1952*, translated by Ruth L. C. Simms, copyright © 1964. Reprinted by permission of the University of Texas Press.

University of Wisconsin Press. BERNARD BERGONZI, "Davie, Larkin, and the State of England," *Contemporary Literature*, copyright © 1977. IHAB HASSAN, "Beckett: Imagination Ending," *The Dismemberment of Orpheus*, copyright © 1982. RICHARD LOFTUS,

"Austin Clarke, Ireland of the Black Church," "Padraic Colum: The Peasant Nation," *Nationalism in Modern Anglo-Irish Poetry*, copyright © 1964. Reprinted by permission of the University of Wisconsin Press.

Vanity Fair. JOSEPH BRODSKY, "To Please a Shadow," Oct. 1983, copyright © 1983. Reprinted by permission.

The Viking Press. GRAHAM GREENE, "The Last Buchan," *The Lost Childhood and Other Essays*, copyright © 1951; "Frederick Rolfe: Edwardian Inferno," *Collected Essays*, copyright © 1981. EDWARD MENDELSON, "The Watershed," *Early Auden*, copyright © 1981. MARIANNE MOORE, "W. H. Auden," *Predilections*, copyright © 1955. SIEGFRIED SASSOON, *The Weald of Youth*, copyright © 1942. Reprinted by permission.

The Woburn Press. A. ALVAREZ, "Introduction: Absurdity and the Absurd," *Beckett*, copyright © 1973. Reprinted by permission.

Yale French Studies. EDITH KERN, "Beckett's Knight of Infinite Indignation," 29 (Spring-Summer 1962), copyright © 1962. Reprinted by permission of *Yale French Studies*.

The Yale Review. ALFRED CORN, "An Anglo-Irish Novelist," Summer 1978, copyright © 1978. LAWRENCE LIEBERMAN, Winter 1973, copyright © 1973. Reprinted by permission of *The Yale Review*.

Yale University Press. JACQUES GUICHARNAUD, "Existence Onstage: Samuel Beckett," *Modern French Theatre from Giraudoux to Genet*, copyright © 1967. R. W. B. LEWIS, "The Current of Conrad's 'Victory,'" *Trials of the Word*, copyright © 1965. Reprinted by permission of Yale University Press.